Asian Handbook
for Theological Education and Ecumenism

Asian Handbook
for Theological Education and Ecumenism

Editors:
Hope Antone, Wati Longchar, Hyunju Bae, Huang Po Ho and Dietrich Werner

Forewords by
Ery Hutarabat Lebang, Olav Fykse Tveit and Kim Young Ju

Christian World Imprints

First published 2013 by Regnum Books International (Regnum is an imprint of the Oxford Centre for Mission Studies)

First Published in India, 2018 by

Christian World Imprints
Christian Publishing & Books from India
H-12 Bali Nagar, **New Delhi-110015**
info@christianworldimprints.com
www.ChristianWorldImprints.com
Phone: +91 11 25465925

ISBN: 978-93-5148-315-1

The publication of this book in India is made possible by permission of the Oxford Centre for Mission Studies

"For where two or three are gathered in my name,
I am there among them." (Jesus, Matth 18, 20)

"There is neither Jew nor Greek,
There is neither slave nor free person,
There is neither man nor woman,
For you are all one in Christ Jesus." (Apostle Paul; Gal 3,28)

Where the mind is without fear and the head is held high;
Where knowledge is free;
Where the world has not been broken up into fragments by narrow domestic walls;
Where words come out from the depth of truth;
Where tireless striving stretches its arms towards perfection:
Where the clear stream of reason has not lost its way into the dreary desert sand of dead habit;
Where the mind is lead forward by thee into ever-widening thought and action –
Into that heaven of freedom, my Father, let my country awake.

~ Rabindranath Tagore ~

Quoted from the liturgy of Week of Prayer for Christian Unity 2013, in that year prepared by the Student Christian Movement of India (SCMI), a 10,000 member organization which celebrated its 100th anniversary in 2012, in consultation with the National Council of Churches in India and the All India Catholic University Federation.
See prayer liturgy and prayers under:
http://www.oikoumene.org/en/programmes/unity-mission-evangelism-and-spirituality/spirituality-and-worship/week-of-prayer-for-christian-unity.html
http://www.ctbi.org.uk/CGLA/606

Explanation for cover picture: The painting from the Indian artist Sudhir Bairagi (1935-2000) "Blessing Christ in Kolkata with Howrah Bridge and Slums", is a visible expression of the inculturation of Christian faith in Asia. The artist was a member of the Church of North India (CNI), where one of his brothers served as a bishop. The combination of Christ and Indian cities including slums is a unique topic to him. Richard Taylor wrote in his book: Jesus in Indian painting (Madras 1975, p. 161): "I believe that Bairagi is the first Indian Christian painter to include such social concerns in his paintings of Christ – and I welcome it. This may be a more real Indigenization of Christian painting than either Yogi-Jesus or Rajasthani Madonnas."

Bairagis painting marks the presence of Christ in the midst of the contradictory and divergent realities of the Asian context, characterized by the simultaneity of several religious traditions, poverty in slums, ethnic plurality, pre-modern life styles as well as the achievements of modernity. The painting is presently located in the staircase of the CNI Bishop's house of Calcutta where a photo was taken by Charles Ringrow, Programme Coordinator, Diocese of Calcutta, for presenting it on the cover of the Asian Handbook on Theological Education and Ecumenism. The Bishop of Calcutta, The Rt. Revd. Ashoke Biswas has given kind permission to reproduce the photo. The idea for this was inspired by the rich publication from Anand Amaladass and Gudrun Löwner: Christian Themes in Indian Art, New Delhi 2012, where the painting from Bairagi is described on page 134.

The painting also reminds of the famous witness and passionate work of late Canon Subir Biswas at the Cathedral of Calcutta (seen left side of the painting), an outstanding Anglican priest who stressed the dignity of all those marginalized and intentionally related the work of the Cathedral towards the needs of the city. He was familiar with the Christian artist Baraigi who's Christian art was exhibited in the Cathedral on several occasions. Till today 25 paintings of Bairagi are on permanent display in the cathedral. Canon Subir Biswas died on 13th November 1977 at the age of only 43 years, but he has incorporated essential features of what contemporary ecumenism in Asian contexts is all about (see the publication: Lord, Let Me Share. Meditations. Life and Writings of Canon Subir Biswas, compiled by E.C. John, The Ecumenical Christian Academy. National Council of Churches, India. March 2012).

Contents

Foreword – Henriette Hutabarat Lebang

I was a student at Jakarta Theological Seminary, a leading ecumenical theological institution in Indonesia, from 1972 to 1977. One of the enriching moments in the classroom was when our professors in those days returned from conferences organized by the Christian Conference of Asia (CCA) or the Association for Theological Education in South East Asia (ATESEA) and immediately shared with us students the papers and discussions in the conferences they just attended. It has inspired many of us! Unlike many of the theological books that we found in the shelves of our library in those days, these papers introduced new insights as authentic theological reflections that had emerged from within Asian soil and spirituality. In 1970s a new curriculum was introduced in this theological school which focused on the so-called *theology in loco.* A theological consultation entitled "PergumulanRangkap" or "double wrestle" was organized by the National Council of Churches in Indonesia which had become the source of inspiration for the renewing process of theological education towards the development of Indonesian contextual theologies. This development, which I believe, had happened also in many Asian theological institutions was strongly affirmed by a leading Asian theologian, Shoki Coe as he said:

> …, if theological education is to move forward in renewal and reform, it must simultaneously be involved in a 'double wrestle' (these words, incidentally, were the theme of a Consultation on Theological Education, held in Indonesia a year or two ago). By them I mean wrestling with the Text from which all texts are derived and to which they point, in order to be faithful to it in the context; and wrestling with the context in which the reality of the Text is at work, in order to be relevant to it.[1]

Such endeavors of 'double wrestle' have continued in Asia up to now. The publication of this book "*Asian Handbook for Theological Education and Ecumenism: Being One in Christ – Learning to be the Church Together"* is a landmark in ecumenical life in Asia. It is a collection of articles that reflects the ongoing 'double wrestle' as the churches in Asia reflect theologically on what it means to be the churches in Asia in each particular period of time, especially in expressing their unity in Christ and in witnessing together the love of Christ amidst the realities and challenges posed by the changing and pluralistic context of Asian communities. There is no doubt that this handbook will contribute significantly to the ongoing theological reflections and discussions in the area of theological education, both in formal and informal modes. It is my sincere hope that teachers and students of theological institutions will be inspired and encouraged to continue the exercise of 'double wrestle', particularly in accompanying the churches in Asia to be partners of God in promoting life for all in very concrete ways.

This publication is timely, as it has been planned to be launched in the Assembly of the World Council of Churches in Busan, South Korea in 2013. Many of the articles in this book echo the ongoing cry of Asian people for life, peace and justice. Thus, this book is an expression of the contribution of Asian theological thinking to the theme of the Assembly: "God of Life, lead us to Justice and Peace."

---

[1]Shoki Coe, "Contextualization as the Way Toward Reform – The Aim and Purpose of Theological Education" in Recollection and Reflection (Taiwan: Formosan Christians for Self-Determination, 1993), p. 268.

On behalf of the Christian Conference of Asia let me join the editorial team to express my gratitude to the contributors of the articles in this book which present a wide spectrum of perspectives that can surely enrich the conversation and promote the inclusive spirit in theological discourses in Asia and around the world. A special appreciation to the editorial team who worked tirelessly in developing the outline of this book and in organizing all the work that had to be done to publish this book. A vote of thanks to the World Council of Churches, particularly the Program on Ecumenical Theological Education (ETE) for collaborating with CCA and other theological associations and institutions in Asia and the support provided to make this publication possible. May this publication become a blessing for many who are in the pursuit of knowledge and understanding, and in the path of learning to be the Church together.

Henriette Hutabarat Lebang
General Secretary, Christian Conference of Asia

Foreword – Olav Fykse Tveit

This impressive and comprehensive new Asian Handbook for Theological Education and Ecumenism, focussing on resources for teaching on Christian unity and common witness, is a timely and unique contribution for the 10th assembly of the World Council of Churches in Busan, South Korea. The theme for the assembly, "God of ife, lead us to peace with justice" sets the tone and theological horizon for a new formulation of Asian ecumenism which is at the heart of this volume:

- It is the promise of the God of life for all which is the inspiring motive and horizon for Asian ecumenism, a continent which throughout history has seen a lot of denial of life while at the same time being home to most of the world's living religions;
- It is the spirit of an open prayer which stretches out hands to all people of good will, which guides the witness and service of Christian churches in Asian contexts in the midst of multiple conflicts, poverty and distorted and fundamentalist forms of religious traditions and will be able to really nurture a new spirit of ecumenism and dialogue in the generations to come;
- It is the joint witness for justice, peace and integrity of ecological life for all creation which provides the context for political and social witness of Christian churches together in many Asian countries.

According to the United Nations Department of Economics and Social Affairs, as of 2010 Asia was home for 745 million young people (out of 1.2 billion in the world). That means "in 2010, 62 percent of all young people age 15 to 24 lived in Asia" (http://esa.un.org). Asian Christian communities replicate this reality with a large number of young persons needing leaders who can equip them with Christian faith and practices to be dynamic witnesses for the gospel of Jesus Christ. The dream of most of the young people and their families is to have a good education for better life. Education continues to be most revered asset in Asia. It is not only education for prosperity but the society expects from educated young people to be morally and ethically upright people. Therefore preserving the religious heritages (as historic religions are considered as custodians of moral and spiritual values) has significant priority in Asia. Religions are revered entities in Asia and have great influence on all aspects of life."[1]

Having in mind this tremendous relevance of both higher education and religious traditions in Asia the editorial group which was behind this ambitious research and publication project towards an Asian Handbook for Theological Education and Ecumenism under the leadership of the ETE program of WCC can only be congratulated for this huge task and for what it has achieved in fulfilling it. Theological Education in Asia needs to be inspired by a broad and holistic vision of unity, peace and justice for all. This is well captured in the title "Theological Education and Ecumenism" which for WCC is spelled out in its vision for 'ecumenism', i.e. its concern for Christian unity and common witness. Knowing that this term does not appeal for all Asian churches (also due to lack of proper information and the perpetuation of some distorted and outmoded images on ecumenism which for long have lost their relevance) WCC has invited all major Christian traditions, Christian movements and global and regional partner networks to take part in

---

[1] H.S. Wilson, Report of a Conference of Deans of Divinity schools in Southeast Asia, Taiwan, June 2012

the WCC assembly in Korea in 2013. It is our goal to build a common future together and to do this, firmly rooted in our Christian tradition and equally firmly rooted in the committment for the love of all neighbours, whatever religious tradition they represent.

I had stated on another occasion during the Oslo conference in June 2012 on the "The future of theology in the changing landscapes of universities in Europe and beyond":

> It is important for me that the tasks of doing theology and working in theological education in our beginning 21st century are properly related to both the current challenges and ecumenical horizons of World Christianity as well as to the needs and longings of the whole world for justice and peace. It is the key conviction of this paper that ecumenism is an imperative for doing theology today. Theological reflection today requires attitudes, a culture and structures of mutual accountability within the wider ecumenical context. We all need to be challenged by others. And we also need to be able to challenge others in an accountable way. Ecumenical sensitivity and competence in theology and theological education entails that we have to listen with the ears of the other in order to properly understand his/her theology and. Unless we widen the horizons of denominational theology for both the changing realities of World Christianity and the longing for justice and for reconciliation in this world we cannot properly serve the whole Gospel and strengthen the unity of the church and the integrity of its witness.[2]

We do hope that this book, both in its printed and a later digital version, will make its way into the hands of Asian theological educators, will inspire students and will be a standard reference volume to be consulted in any major Asian theological library, both in universities as well as in church-related seminaries.

> "Christian theology for our understanding always and in all continents has a double accountability: Christian theology relates to the church – and we emphasize – always to the whole church – by providing solid grounding and critical reflection for authentic Christian public witness, mission and social service of Christian churches in a context which is marked by massive changes in the landscape of World Christianity. And Christian theology relates to the world – and we emphasize to the whole world – as the Gospel of Jesus Christ irrevocably relates to the whole world and its reconciliation with God. The old and fundamental key vocation within the ecumenical movement, to relate the whole Gospel, the whole Church and the whole world properly to each other, therefore has a fundamental importance for what is going to be considered about the present and future of Christian theology and theological education."[3]

We congratulate those who have undertaken and contributed to this magnificent project and express our hope that this *Asian Handbook for Theological Education and Ecumenism* will serve this double accountability and service of Christian theology and theological education for Christianity in Asia for many years to come, for the glory of God and the presence of his Kingdom.

Olav Fykse Tveit
WCC General Secretary

---

[2] Olav Fykse Tveit, Theology and unity in the changing landscape of World Christianity, Keynote address to Oslo conference on the role and relevance of Christian theology in university contexts, June 2012

[3] Theology and unity in the changing landscape of World Christianity, Key-Note Adress Olav Fykse Tveit, General Secretary, WCC, during the Oslo consultation of WCC-ETE on the "The future of theology in the changing landscapes of universities in Europe and beyond", Oslo 6th of June 2012, page 2

Foreword – Kim Young-Ju

It is with great pleasure and pride to receive this timely and precious Asian Handbook for Theological Education and Ecumenism. Having in mind the 10th Assembly of the World Council of Churches being held in Busan, Korea in 2013, the timely release of this handbook truly marks a milestone in theological education.

While the delegates and guests rejoice in the assembly celebrating the unity of the churches worldwide, the assembly will also be able to assure the revitalization of the much beloved ecumenical movement through nurturing future generations of Christian leaders through various activities, but especially through ecumenical theological education and training. I am confident that we all share the same legacy of the ecumenical movement that embodies our most profound belief and wish for Christian unity and beyond. In the same time it is our historical task and call to give-forth what we have rejoiced in to future generations to let it flourish even more. For this, I firmly believe the Asian Handbook for Theological Education and Ecumenism will provide the necessary basic material with its selected invaluable resource material expressing voices of faith commitment and compassion from the Asian region.

The Asian region is a multi-faceted one, which makes it nearly an impossible mission to accommodate all the different aspects and demands. Hence, I cannot but deeply congratulate the editors and the leadership of the WCC-ETE program for having accomplished this huge task.

It is again with great pleasure and joy to receive this handbook, which signals an investment towards the future of the ecumenical movement in Asia. Being a region with limited available resources and extreme diversity, education and training is widely thought to be a significant way of opening a new future of common witness and sharing in various areas. The quest for education and training shall conclude in the self-realization and fulfillment of each individual being in a setting of mutual sharing and communal life in Asia.

The release of this tremendously rich resource book, right in time of the occasion of the 10th assembly of the World Council of Churches, will open new dimensions of exploring new ways of community life, common witness, mutual enrichment and guidance of Asian churches through the new era of ecumenism.

The National Council of Churches in Korea, along with all its member churches has been greatly gifted with the faithful accompaniment by other churches through the most difficult times of the Korean people. It is mainly through those experiences that the Korean churches have witnessed true ecumenical compassion. With the experience of hosting the 10th assembly of the WCC the Korean churches are looking towards a new future of ecumenism. It shows that the capacities of the Korean churches have reached a significant point of sharing even more resources for the betterment of the whole world community and for mutual enrichment.

Considering the multi-religious context of Korea and its surroundings, the resource material on teaching ecumenism in Asia through Asian eyes published in this volume will provide new ways of approaching and 'living' ecumenism in the 21st century. Based on the Asian history and tradition of 'living with other faiths' we can now refer to academically based grounds where we all can share different insights guided by this timely publication. The 'living approach' and the 'epistemological approach' to Asian ecumenism shall not be contradicting each other but rather complementing. Therefore, the "Asian Handbook for Theological Education and Ecumenism" from and for the Asian context is to be regarded as a significant milestone for all the complementary ways of nurturing future generations of Christian leaders, as well as reflecting on the current and past of the ecumenical movement in Asia.

On behalf of the National Council of Churches in Korea and its member churches, I warmly welcome this timely and most significant publication and shall remain in prayers as Jesus states,

> My prayer is not for them alone. I pray also for those who will believe in me through their message, that all of them may be one, Father, just as you are in me and I am in you. May they also be in us so that the world may believe that you have sent me. I have given them the glory that you gave me, that they may be one as we are one – I in them and you in me – so that they may be brought to complete unity. Then the world will know that you sent me and have loved them even as you have loved me. (John 17:20-23)

Kim Young-Ju
General Secretary, National Council of Churches in Korea

Editorial: Being One in Christ – Learning to be Church Together

The 10th assembly of WCC in Busan, South Korea, which takes place from 30th October to 9th November 2013, will highlight the vitality and growth of Asian Christianity and increase the need for proper knowledge and resources for learning about Asian Christianity. Both theological education and more information on the particular contexts and historical developments of Asian churches are crucial for the future of Asian Christianity in the 21st century. As Christianity is a minority tradition in the vast realities of multi-religious Asian contexts (8,5% of Asian populations in 2010) it can only take proper roots and continue its growth by proper education both on the centuries old different religious traditions of Asia as well as on the distinct histories of Christian churches and their common witness and service in Asian societies. Asian ecumenism, i.e. inter-church cooperation and joint service to the whole of society – are much older than western ecumenism of the 19th and 20th century. This Handbook answers the urgent need for having more solid historical and theological information for theological education on the different dimensions of Christian unity and common Christian witness in multi-faith contexts in Asia.

Behind this first-ever published *Asian Handbook for Theological Education and Ecumenism* is a four year process of intense editorial working, strategic network-building and conceptualization: The need for updated resources for learning and teaching on Christian unity and common witness in Asia (for many, referred to as "Asian ecumenism") had been expressed several times by many theological educators on various occasions – e.g. at the ATESEA Theological Teachers' Academy in Kota Kinabalo in 2008, at a meeting of the Regional Committee of the South Asia Solidarity Endowment Fund for Theological Education in Kathmandu in 2008 and at various meetings conducted by the Christian Conference of Asia-Faith Mission and Unity (CCA-FMU). No such book exists for the time being nor do we find a comprehensive Handbook until now, which would review past achievements, major learnings and current themes and challenges for Asian ecumenism in the 21st century. Neither is there a Handbook for students of theology who need an orientation on the situation of Christian churches and inter-denominational cooperation in their own neighboring countries in Asia. It was even stated by the Joint Consultation of the CCA General Committee, attended by members of the WCC Central Committee from Asia, the NCC General Secretaries and the Asia Regional Group in the Hope Centre, Dhaka, Bangladesh (31st of August to the 3rd of September 2008):

> We are also aware that in Asia there is a malaise in the ecumenical movement, requiring our serious and urgent attention. This is manifested in a number of ways, including: the declining interest and lack of significant number of young people coming into the ecumenical movement, lack of visionary leadership, the seeming loss of ecumenical memory, and the failure of Asia to determine and set its own agenda. We recognize that there is a strong desire for new paradigms and models of ecumenical work and engagement.[1]

---

[1] Joint communique from 3.9. 2008 on „Revitalizing the Ecumenical Movement in Asia", in: http://www.oikoumene.org/en/resources/documents/wcc-programmes/ecumenical-movement-in-the-21st-century/non-member-churches-ecumenical-organizations/revitalizing-the-ecumenical-movement-in-asia.html

It was during the WCC Workshop on the Future of Theological Education Networking in Asia, which took place from 2nd-5th July 2010 in Bangkok Institute of Theology (BIT), Thailand, that first plans were drawn up for an Asian Resource Book on Learning and Teaching Ecumenism, as the title would read. Following the WCC initiative and example to publish the global "Handbook of Theological Education in World Christianity"[2] at the occasion of the Edinburgh 2010 conference and building both on the achievements and earlier publications on Asian ecumenism which existed already[3] as well as research done on the state of affairs in Asian theological education[4], plans were made to prepare for a major Asian Handbook which would provide more than a mere repetition of the historical periods of the ecumenical movement in its forms related to the West. A lot of publications are available already on historical ecumenism as emerging after the First and Second World War in the 20th century, in the West. But this new Handbook was conceptualized to focus on the contemporary challenges and contextual demands for living the unity of Christian faith and shaping a common Christian witness together in present-day Asian contexts. As the first project outline from 2010 had stated:

> The resource book for teaching ecumenism will be from Asian perspectives and will include major contextual key articles, historical overviews, and bibliography for teaching ecumenism in seminaries and Bible schools of Asia. The objectives are
>
> a. To develop Asian perspectives on ecumenism, taking into consideration various regional and denominational perspectives.

---

[2] *The Handbook for Theological Education in World Christianity*, published by Regnum Publisher in June 2010 (800 pages) (eds. Dietrich Werner, David Esterline, Namsoon Kang, Joshua Raja) has some 16 contributions from the Asian continent, but at that stage could not do justice to the complexities and varieties of theological education processes in the vast regions of Asia.

[3] Hans Rudi Weber, *Asia and the Ecumenical Movement* (1966); Yap Kim Hao, *From Prapat to Colombo: History of Christian Conference of Asia* (1995); *Ninan Koshi, A History of the Ecumenical Movement in Asia, Two volumes 2004;* Toshimasa Yamamoto, *History of Asian Ecumenical Movement,* Tokyo, Japan, *Publisher* Shinkyou Shuppan-sha in 2007; Abraham, K. C. (ed.): *Ecumenism In Asia : Essays In Honour Of Feliciano Carino,* Bangalore : Association for Theological Education in South East Asia : Board of Theological Education-Senate of Serampore College, cop. 1999; Ariarajah, Wesley: The Ecumenical Movement in Asia in the Context of Asian Socio-political Realities. In: Kim, Sebastian (ed.): *Christian Theology in Asia*; Cambridge: Cambridge University Press, 2008. pp. 227-250; England, John C. [et al.] (eds.): *Asian Christian theologies : a research guide to authors, movements, sources.* Vols 1-3. Maryknoll: Orbis Books, 2002-2004; Hao, Yap Kim: *From Parapat to Colombo : History of the Christian Conference of Asia* (1957-1995). Hong Kong: Christian Conference of Asia, 1995 ; Koshy, Ninan (ed.): *A History Of The Ecumenical Movement In Asia*, Hong Kong: World Student Christian Federation, 2004 ; Victor, Vinod, Leslie Nathaniel, Leslie, Suryaprakash, P (eds.): *Ecumenism: Prospects And Challenges: Festschrift To The Rev. G. Dyvasirvadam,* Delhi: ISPCK, 2001; *Windows Into Ecumenism: Essays In Honour Of Ahn Jae Woong.* (Introduction by D. Preman Niles) Hong Kong: Christian Conference of Asia, 2005; Zachariah, Mathai (ed.): *Ecumenism In India : Essays In Honour Of The Rev. M. A. Thomas,* Delhi: ISPCK, 1980; Massey, James. *Ecumenism in India Today.* Bangalore: BTESSC/SATHRI, 2008; Paul, Rajaiah D. Paul, *Ecumenism in Action.* Madras: CLS, 1972; Philip, T.V. *Ecumenism in Asia.* Delhi: ISPCK & CSS, 1994; Zachariah, Mathai (ed), *Ecumenism in India: Essays in Honour of the Rev. M.A. Thomas.* Delhi: ISPCK, 1980; Niles, Preman, D. (ed) *Windows into Ecumenism – Essays in Honour of Ahn Jae Woong.* CCA: Hong Kong, 2005; Koshy, Ninan (ed), *A History of the Ecumenical Movement in Asia – Volume I & II.* Hong Kong: The World Student Christian Federation Asia-Pacific Region, Asia and Pacific Alliance of YMCAs and the Christian Conference of Asia, 2004; Antone, Hope. S. (ed), *Living in Oikoumene*: Hong Kong: CCA, 2003; Thiagarajah, Daniel & Wati Longchar, *Visioning New Life Together Among Asian Religions.* Hong Kong: CCA, 2002; Widyatmadja, Josef, Longchar, Wati, Joseph, M.P. (eds), *They Left by Another Road: Rerouting Mission and Ecumenism in Asia.* Chiangmai: CCA, 2007; Snaitang, O.L. *A History of Ecumenical Movement.* Bangalore: BTESSC/SATHRI, 2007 (reprint).

[4] Dietrich Werner (ed), Training to be Ministers in Asia. Contextualizing Theological Education in Multi-Faith Contexts. Historical, Contextual and Theological Perspectives from different Asian countries. PTCA Series. No 3, Kolkata, PTCA 2012

> b. To provide a resource book for theological educators in Asia for teaching ecumenism with Asian perspectives.
>
> The outline will be discussed with representatives of the theological associations. Asian writers known for their ecumenical perspectives and commitment will be invited to contribute to the resource book.... Theological institutions and churches in Asia will be the primary beneficiaries of this project. Teachers and students will have a resource book on ecumenism from Asian perspectives.[5]

At the initiative of ETE/WCC (Dr. Dietrich Werner) an editorial group was identified which brought together representatives from CCA, Faith, Unity and Mission (FMU) (Dr. Hope Antone, with CCA until 2011, now with United Board for Christian Higher Education in Hongkong), from Senate of Serampore, India (Dr. Wati Longchar), later joined by Dr. Bae Hyunju (Busan Presbyterian University and KAATS, Korea) and Dr. Huang Po Ho (PTCA).

An enriching and wide-spread process was thus started and the editors began to approach contributors and to ask for fresh perspectives on selected topics to be contributed to this volume. Meetings of the core editorial board took place alongside the newly emerging Asian Forum on Theological Education (AFTE) which met in June 2011 in Trinity Theological College (TTC) Singapore, during the Programme for Theology and Cultures in Asia (PTCA) Programme Committee Meeting and in Sabah Theological Seminary, in Kota Kinabalu on 15-16 January, 2012 and during the second Asian Forum on Theological Education (AFTE) conference which took place in Amanat Agung Theological Seminary in Jakarta, from August 29 to September August 1st 2012.

From the outset the proposed structure of the Handbook was identified as including at least seven major sections:

- Faces of Contemporary Asian Ecumenism
- Biblical and Theological Perspectives of Ecumenism
- Historical Introduction to Ecumenism in Asia
- Issues Related to Ecumenism in Asia
- Regional Surveys on Ecumenism in Asia
- Women in Asian Ecumenism

What unfolded however in the more sustained editorial working process for the Asian Handbook Project was an overwhelming panorama of rich and diverse perspectives on a new and broader concept of Asian commitment to Christian unity and common witness which can inspire and enrich ministerial formation and theological education in Asian countries in the years to come.

We have asked a large spectrum of contributors from different Christian traditions in Asia, including many of those who at present do not belong to WCC member churches, but have vital links with member churches, as we wanted to practise in the editorial process itself what we believe in terms of inclusivity and integration for the future of Asian ecumenism. We are aware as well, however, that there still are several shortcomings even in this huge volume as we could not cover all fields and themes which contribute to the deepening and development of theological education and ministerial formation on Christian unity and common witness in Asia. Also we could not accept all manuscripts which were sent to us due to limitations of space, limitations due to the clear focus of this Handbook as well as time constraints.

The process of editorial work, of encouraging colleagues to write and to contribute, of discovering relevant themes and new dimensions of what belongs to serving the unity of Christ's church and the unity of all Asian people has more than proved some of the *key motivations and convictions* which had accompanied this project from the very beginning, but have even grown in the course of its completion:

---

[5] Project Outline for Asian Resource Book on Ecumenism, Bangkok, 26 June 2010

1. Growing Christianity in Asia needs well informed and biblically sound theological education and formation on what contributes to the biblical foundations of Christian unity and common witness in Asia. While Christianity remains a minority religion in most of the Asian countries there has still been an overall increase of the Christian population in Asia between 1910 and today (2010) from 2.4% to 8.5 % which pushed the Asian Christian population to over 292 million today, with a particular increase of Christian populations in South East Asia (from 10.8% to 21.8%) (but also a sharp decrease in Western Asia from 22.9% to 5.7%).[6] The national surveys of the situation of Christianity and inter-church cooperation in Asian countries in part 5 of this Handbook ("Churches together in God's Mission – Mapping Asian ecumenism") which are brought together for the first time in this format, underline the need for more 'intercontextuality'[7] in Asian ecumenism and express the vitality, the breadth and depth of Christian witness in Asian countries at the beginning of the 21st century;[8]
2. We need to promote new models of wider and evangelical Asian ecumenism in which polarizations of the past are overcome and so-called 'Evangelicals' and so-called 'Ecumenicals' cannot be misunderstood anymore and projected as exclusive opposites because this simply does not match with emerging realities in the 21st century. The new kind of broader and evangelical ecumenism in Asia this Handbook is giving witness to takes the best from historical ecumenism (which to a large extent has grown with historical protestant mainline churches, including many evangelical Christians) and learns as well from evangelical renewal and charismatic churches. The broader and more inclusive ecumenism is bringing together essentials and characteristic marks from several renewal movements in Asian churches and holds them together in a fruitful tension and synthesis so as to strengthen Christian unity and common witness in Asia. Thus in this new broader evangelical ecumenism in Asia both firm rootedness in Scripture and church tradition, commitment to contextual mission and culturally sensitive evangelism as well as engagement for common witness for peace and justice and dialogue with all people of good will from other faith traditions belong together in an integrated understanding of the holistic nature of the Christian mission.
3. Theological education, Christian unity and common witness in Asia are vital not only for the future of Asian Christianity and for the profile of Asian church leaders but also for the social and political witness of Christian churches in Asian nations and informed political and prophetic witness in civil society. In Asia it is often Christian churches, which are the only or a major partner in civil society in Asian contexts. The promotion of Christian unity and common witness and the work for dialogue with other Christian faith traditions as well as people of other faiths in theological education are not issues which can be restricted to inner church affairs. Taking the fundamental concern for Christian

---

[6] See: Todd M. Johnson, Kenneth R. Ross (eds): Atlas of Global Christianity, Edinburgh 2010, page 136ff; see also: Global Christianity – A Report on the Size and Distribution of the World's Christian Population, Section on Asia-Pacific, in: The Pew Forum on Religion and Public Life 2011; http://www.pewforum.org/Christian/Global-Christianity-asia-pacific.aspx

[7] Dietrich Werner, Contextuality, Inter-Contextuality and Ecumenicity in Theological Education in: Dietrich Werner, Theological Education in World Christianity. Ecumenical Perspectives and Future Priorities, Kolkata 2011, p. 3-25, part. p. 19ff.

[8] The editors are aware of the fact that the country related survey articles under ‚Mapping Asian Ecumenism' are not covering the full range of the geographical region of Asia, but mainly those countries where churches have had some relations with CCA. It belongs to the limitations of this Asian Handbook, that it would have needed an additional effort also to cover those Asian countries with majority orthodox populations like Russia, Armenia and Georgia which relate more to the Conference of European Churches, as well as to cover the full range of majority Muslim countries in Asia which however have their distinct history of a smaller Christian presence and churches as well, like the Asian Republics of Azerbaijan, Kyrgyzstan, Tajikistan, Turkmenistan, Uzbekistan, Kazakhstan or Turkey, Afghanistan and the arab speaking countries of Asia like Bahrain, Irak, Kuweit, Oman, Quatar, Yemen.

unity and common witness seriously presents an overall concern with clear relevance also for social and political development in Asian societies and can be regarded as even a crucial factor for the future of higher education policies in Asia.

4. This Handbook conveys the conviction that the work for strengthening collaboration and quality standards for theological education and ministerial formation programmes in Asia needs to continue, mainly implemented through the network of regional theological associations of theological schools. It is important that churches enrich, assist and complement each other in their systems and programmes for theological education in Asia. Encouraging a new style and commitment to interdenominational cooperation in theological education and research and cross-border cooperation in ministerial formation is urgently needed and should be strengthened over against tendencies for each denominational tradition to seek its own advantage.[9] The work which has emerged during the past years in the formation of the Asian Forum on Theological Education (AFTE)[10] – facilitated and supported both by CCA and WCC and its program on ETE – has great potential and needs continued visual and written expression. Circulating and sharing this common Asian Handbook for Theological Education and Ecumenism in wider circles can greatly enhance this process;
5. This Handbook also confirms the conviction that despite some ongoing shortcomings in some churches as well as higher education institutions there is a unique role women have played in contributing to Asian theological wisdom, knowledge and expertise in theological research. This is true particularly in areas which are vital for the very survival of humanity in Asia, such as issues of HIV and AIDS, Gender issues and concerns for peace and overcoming violence as also issues of indigenous people. Only a good scholarly collaboration between men and women in Asian theological education on ecumenism can pave the way for a brighter future.

This Handbook will be presented as an Asian gift to the forthcoming 10th assembly of the World Council of Churches which is to take place in November 2013 in Busan, South Korea. The emphasis the editors have put on the future of Asian ecumenism, witness to justice peace and the integrity of life in this Handbook corresponds to the theme of the assembly in Asia "God of Life, lead us to justice and peace". This theme is also the prayer which accompanies this book on its journey through the churches and theological colleges and schools in Asia.

We are grateful for enormous support we have received in completing this project: our gratitude goes to each one in the group of the main editors, Hope Antone, Wati Longchar, Huang Po Ho, Bae Hyunju, Dietrich Werner. Sincere gratitude also needs to be expressed to the team which assisted in terms of language editing in English (Iris Devadason, Bangalore; Maria van Heemstra, Geneva). A special word of appreciation needs to be extended to the typesetting team around Tony Gray in Oxford. A major word of gratitude goes to our publishing houses, Wonsuk Ma from Regnum Publishing, Oxford for the Western edition and Huang Po Ho from Programme for Theology and Cultures in Asia and the Christian Literature Society of Korea (CLSK) for the North Asian edition.

We also have to give thanks for generous financial support and assistance to this project which has come from WCC/ETE Geneva and from EMW Germany Hamburg.

[9] See also: Dietrich Werner, *Training to be ministers in Asia. Contextualizing Theological Education in Multi-faith Contexts*, PTCA Series No. 3, Kolkata, 2012

[10] http://www.oikoumene.org/en/resources/documents/wcc-programmes/education-and-ecumenical-formation/ecumenical-theological-education-ete/the-future-of-theological-education-in-asia/asian-forum-on-theological-education-afte.html

The editors of the Asian Handbook for Theological Education and Ecumenism

January 2013
Hope Antone, Wati Longchar, Hyunju Bae, Huang Po Ho, Dietrich Werner

List of Contributors

David ANDRIANOFF: currently working on a project for the staff of World Vision Cambodia; worked for Christian organizations in Laos, Mongolia and Malaysia, including compilation of the history of the Protestant church in Vietnam and Laos. <dandrianoff@hotmail.com>

Hope S. ANTONE: Program Officer, United Board for Christian Higher Education in Asia; formerly Joint Executive Secretary, Christian Conference of Asia – Faith, Mission and Unity, then lecturer at Payap University in Chiang Mai, Thailand; member of the United Church of Christ in the Philippines. <hopeantone@gmail.com>

S. Wesley ARIARAJAH: Professor of Ecumenical Theology, Drew University School of Theology in New Jersey; formerly Director of Interfaith Dialogue Program and Deputy General Secretary, World Council of Churches; member Methodist Church in Sri Lanka. <wariaraj@drew.edu>

Siga ARLES: Founder-Director, Centre for Contemporary Christianity in Bangalore, Professor of Missiology; formerly Principal of South India Biblical Seminary and Vice-Principal of Serampore College; member Church of South India. <sigaarles@gmail.com>

Stephen ARULAMPALAM: Lecturer, Theological College of Lanka; Priest of the Anglican Church; formerly Secretary of Jaffna Christian Union consisting of Methodist, Anglican, Church of South India and Salvation Army; affiliated with the Church of Ceylon. <arulampalamstephen@gmail.com>

Connie AU: Director, Research Centre, Synergy Institute of Leadership in Hong Kong; adjunct faculty, Asia Pacific Theological Seminary; member of ECHOS (Youth Commission of the World Council of Churches), Unity and Church Relations Committee of Hong Kong Christian Council, and Theological Committee, Asia Pacific Theological Association. <conniehoyanau@googlemail.com>

Hyunju BAE: Professor of New Testament Studies at Busan Presbyterian University, Director of the Institute of Theology and Ministry for Life, Member of Presbyterian Church of Korea. <61baehj@hanmail.net>

J. B. BANAWIRATMA: Professor of Theology at Duta Wacana Christian University, Yogyakarta, Indonesia. <banawiratma@ukdw.ac.id; jbbana@yahoo.com>

Liberato C. BAUTISTA: Assistant General Secretary for United Nations and International Affairs Main Representative to the United Nations General Board of Church and Society of the United Methodist Church. <LBautista@umc-gbcs.org>

CAO Shengjie: Director, Advisory Committee of China Christian Council and The Three-Self Movement Committee of the Protestant Churches of China (CCC/TSPM); member of the Shanghai Research Institute of Culture and History of the People's Republic of China; formerly President of China Christian Council. <cccshengjie@163.com>

Edmund Kee-Fook CHIA: Malaysian Roman Catholic; Faculty Member of Australian Catholic University in Melbourne; formerly Secretary of Ecumenical and Interreligious Affairs, Federation of Asian Bishops' Conferences (FABC) and Associate Professor, Catholic Theological Union in Chicago. <Edmund.Chia@acu.edu.au>

CHIU Shu-pin: Member of Presbyterian Church in Taiwan; Dean of Academic Affairs, Yu-shan Theological College and Seminary; formerly Preacher in Ho-Pin-Tao Presbyterian Church. <chiushupin@gmail.com>

Mathews George CHUNAKARA: Director of International Affairs, World Council of Churches; formerly WCC Asia Secretary, Executive Secretary of Christian Conference of Asia, Liaison Secretary of WCC-CCA Indo-China program; member of Mar Thoma Syrian Church in India. <Mathews.George@wcc-coe.org>

CHUNG Sook Ja: Director, Namyangju Women's Center for Migrant Workers and Founding Pastor, Women Church in Seoul, Korea; Ordained Minister of the Presbyterian Church in the Republic of Korea. <chungsookja@daum.net>

David Anirudha DAS: General Secretary of the National Council of Churches in Bangladesh and Volunteer Pastor of Rajashon Baptist Church; formerly Senior Administrative Officer of PROSHIKA (Center for Human Development); member of the Bangladesh Baptist Church Sangha (BBCS). <daviddas1824@yahoo.com>

Somen DAS: Professor of Systematic Theology and Ethics at Serampore College in India, former Principal of Bishop's College

Albino DA COSTA: Local Pastor at Ekaristi Church in Dili; formerly the General Secretary of the Igreja Protestante Iha Timor Lorosa'e (IPTL) / The Protestant Church in East Timor. <osta23470@yahoo.com>

Caesar D'MELLO: Consultant in Development, Just Tourism, Peace and Conflict Solution; formerly Executive Director, Ecumenical Coalition on Tourism (ECOT), and Christian World Service Australia (CWS), NCC Australia. Member, Roman Catholic Church, residing in Australia <caesarmdm@gmail.com>

Kenneth DOBSON: Minister of Presbyterian Church (USA); formerly Pastor in the USA then Missionary in Thailand in Theological Education and Christian Higher Education; currently Advisor to the President of Payap University, Chiang Mai, Thailand. <kdobsonatpayap@gmail.com>

John Carol ENGLAND: formerly Chief Editor and Author of *Asian Christian Theologies* (3 vols. 2001-2004) and currently a Part-time Teacher and Writer, affiliated to the Presbyterian Church of Aotearoa New Zealand and its co-operative ventures and to the Hewitson Library, Knox College, Dunedin. <rmpe22@xtra.co.nz>

Leonard FERNANDO: Director of Postgraduate Studies, Vidyajyoti College of Theology, Professor of Church History and Theology, and Editor of *Vidyajyoti Journal of Theological Reflection*; formerly Principal, Vidyajyoti College of Theology; Jesuit Priest of the Roman Catholic Church of India. <leofern@gmail.com>

Roger GAIKWAD: General Secretary, National Council of Churches in India; formerly Principal, Aizawl Theological College, Aizawl, Mizoram, India; ordained Minister of the Presbyterian Church of India. <ncciroger@gmail.com>

Bayarjargal GARAMTSEREN: Bible translator and PhD candidate at the University of Cambridge, United Kingdom. Formerly Board member of Mongolian Evangelical Alliance, he now oversees the Mongolian Christian Fellowship in the United Kingdom.

K. M. GEORGE: Principal of the Orthodox Theological Seminary in Kottayam, Kerala, India; Priest of the Malankara Orthodox Syrian Church in India, formerly served as Moderator of the WCC Programme Committee, <frkmgeorge@hotmail.com>

Naw Eh Tar GAY: Lecturer in New Testament and Academic Dean of Myanmar Institute of Theology (MIT), Insein, Yangon; formerly Dean of Students at MIT; affiliated with the Baptist Church in Myanmar. <ehtargay@gmail.com>

David GILL: Minister of the Uniting Church in Australia; formerly General Secretary of the Uniting Church in Australia and the National Council of Churches in Australia. <seekdavid@gmail.com>

Aruna GNANADASON: Formerly Director of WCC Women's programme, Coordinator of the Justice, Peace and Creation Team, served in the leadership team of the World Council of Churches; member of the Church of South India; presently lives and works in Chennai as freelance writer, speaker and editor. <agnanadason@gmail.com>

Adonis Abelard O. GOROSPE: Associate Professor for Theology and Church History and currently serving as the Academic Dean of Asian Theological Seminary and a member of St. John United Methodist Church in the Philippines. <adonisgorospe@yahoo.com>

Richard HOWELL: General Secretary of Asia Evangelical Alliance and Evangelical Fellowship of India; member of Global Christian Forum committee; formerly Principal, Allahabad Bible Seminary and Vice-President, World Evangelical Alliance; presently a Visiting Faculty at Sam Higginbottom Institute of Agriculture Technology and Science (SHIATS) and Director, Global Leadership and Research Institute; ordained Minister of the Evangelical Church of India. <efi@swissmail.org>

Victor W. C. HSU: Director of International Aid and Education, and Adjunct Advisor on North Korea, School of Public Policy and Management, Korea Development Institute; formerly Former WCC Executive Secretary, Commission of the Churches on International Affairs (CCIA) <victorhsu62011@gmail.com>

HUANG Po Ho: Professor of Theology and Vice President of Chang Jung Christian University in Taiwan; formerly President, Tainan Theological College and Seminary; Dean of Programme for Theology and Cultures in Asia (PTCA), ordained Minister of the Presbyterian Church in Taiwan. <cjcupekho@gmail.com>

Ipe JOSEPH: General Secretary, All India Sunday School Association; formerly General Secretary of National Council of Churches in India; ordained Minister of the Mar Thoma Syrian Church. <ipejoseph@rediffmail.com>

M. P. JOSEPH: Professor of Theology at Chang Jung Christian University School of Theology, Taiwan; formerly Lecturer of Theology at United Theological College, Bangalore and at New College, Edinburgh; member of Church of South India. <josephlila@gmail.com>

Maqsood KAMIL: Professor of Systematic Theology & Homiletics of Gujranwala Theological Seminary, Pakistan; Pastor and Former Executive Secretary of the Presbyterian Church of Pakistan; PhD student at Oxford Centre for Mission Studies, Great Britain. <drmaqsoodkamil@gmail.com>

Carmencita KARAGDAG: Coordinator of People's Forum on Peace for Life; formerly Program Secretary for Ecumenical Education and Nurture of the National Council of Churches in the Philippines, and Youth Secretary, Christian Conference of Asia; affiliated with the Iglesia Filipina Independiente church of the Philippines. <cpk@peaceforlife.org>

Hugh P. KEMP: Academic Dean and Head of Mission Studies at Redcliffe College, Gloucester, United Kingdom. He holds a MTh is Mongolian Christian history (Australian College of Theology) and a PhD in Religious Studies (Victoria University of Wellington), author of "Steppe by Step – Mongolia's Christians" <hkemp@redcliffe.org>

KIM Yong Bock: Chancellor, Asia Pacific Center for Integral Study of Life; formerly President of Hanil University and Presbyterian Theological Seminary; ordained Minister of the Presbyterian Church of Korea. <oikozoe@kornet.net>

Illangasinghe KUMARA: Bishop Emeritus of Kurunagala Diocese, Sri Lanka from Church of Ceylon (Sri Lanka); former Principal of Lanka Theological College of Lanka, Pilimatalawa, Sri Lanka; presently serving on the Steering Committee for Theological Education in the Anglican Communion and also a Member of the Inter Anglican Standing Commission on Unity, Faith and Order; <bis.kumara61@gmail.com>

KYAW THAN: Lecturer, International Doctoral Program, College of Religious Studies, Mahidol University in Bangkok; formerly General Secretary of the Christian Conference of Asia. <k_than@hotmail.com>

Mohan LABEER: Executive Secretary of the Board for Theological Education at the Senate of Serampore College (BTESSC) in India; former Principal of Tamilnadu Theological Seminary, Madurai; <secretary@btessc.org>

Liza B. LAMIS: A Baptist Christian, formerly Coordinator of Women's Program, National Council of Churches in the Philippines; past National Coordinator, Association of Women in Theology (AWIT) in the Philippines, and Communications Consultant with the Christian Conference of Asia (CCA). <lizablamis@gmail.com >

LEE Hong Jung: General Secretary of Presbyterian Church of Korea; formerly Executive Secretary of Justice, International Affairs, Development and Service of Christian Conference of Asia, then President of Asia-Pacific Christian College and Seminary; ordained minister of the Presbyterian Church of Korea. <beyondhj@hanmail.net>

Moon-Sook LEE: Executive Secretary Asian Church Women Conference, Seoul, South Korea

Yeong Mee LEE: Professor of Old Testament Studies, Hanshin University Seoul Korea, Executive Secretary of Korean Association of Accredited Theological Schools, Presbyterian Church in the Republic of Korea (PROK) <ymlee@hs.ac.kr>

LO Lung-kwong: Director and Professor of the Divinity School of Chung Chi College, The Chinese University of Hong Kong and former President of The Methodist Church, Hong Kong. <lklohkg@yahoo.com>

Wati LONGCHAR: Professor of Christian Theology and Dean of Senate Centre for Extension and Pastoral Theological Research of the Senate of Serampore College (University); formerly Director of Tribal Study Centre of Eastern Theological College, Jorhat, Assam, and Asian consultant of Ecumenical Theological Education of WCC/CCA; member of Council of Baptist Churches in North East India. <wlongchar@gmail.com>

Samuel LONGKUMER: Associate Professor of Religion and Philosophy at Bishop's College, Kolkata; member of the Council of Baptist Churches in North East India. <slongkumer@hotmail.com>

Atola LONKUMER: Associate Professor in the Department of Religions at Leonard Theological College, Jabalpur, MP, INDIA; participant of CWME study process towards new mission statement of WCC; co-editor of *Putting Names with Faces. Women's Impact in Mission History*, Abingdon Press Nashville 2012; member of Baptist Church of Nagaland. <atolalongkumer2@hotmail.com>

Narayan MAHARJAN: Coordinator of the Christian Concern Group Nepal (CCGN) and United Christian Alliance of Nepal (UCAN) <mnpmaharjan@gmail.com>

Deenabandhu MANCHALA: WCC programme executive for Justice and Inclusive Communities, for Executive Secretary for peace Concerns at WCC; pastor in the Andhra Evangelical Lutheran Church; editor of the book, "Dalit Theology in the Twenty-First Century: Discordant Voices, Discerning Pathways"; <Deenabandhu. Manchala@wcc-coe.org>

Varghese MANIMALA: Director of Henry Martyn Institute, Hyderabad, India; <varghesemanimala46@gmail.com>

Monica Jyotsna MELANCHTHON: Member of the Andhra Evangelical Lutheran Church, Professor of Old Testament, former lecturer at Gurukul Lutheran Theological College, Chennai, India and now with the United Faculty of Theology, MCD University of Divinity, Melbourne, Australia. <monixm@gmail.com> or <monica.melanchthon@ctm.uca.edu.au>

MIN Young Jin: former Director of Korean Bible Society; formerly Professor of Old Testament Studies at Methodist Theological University. <yjmin@mail.bskorea.or.kr>

Zakaria J. NGELOW: Executive Director of OaseIntim, a Christian non-government organization; formerly Dean of a Theological School in Makassar; affiliated with the South Sulawesi Christian Church in Indonesia**.** <zngelow@yahoo.com>

Smith NGULH ZA THAWNG: Lecturer cum Chaplain, Tedim Christian College; formerly General Secretary, Myanmar Council of Churches; ordained Minister of the Myanmar Baptist Convention, Myanmar. <thawngphik@gmail.com>

PARK Kyung-seo: President, Korean Center for United Nations Human Rights Policy (KOCUN), formerly Asia Secretary of the World Council of Churches & Ambassador at large for Human Rights of the Republic of Korea; member of Presbyterian Church in the Republic of Korea. <pksoyo@hotmail.com>

PARK Seong-Won: Pastor of Presbyterian Church of Korea and currently serving as Professor of Theology at Young Nam Theological University and Seminary in Korea and Member of the Central Committee of the World Council of Churches, Executive Secretary of the National Hosting Committee of NCCK for the 10th assembly of the WCC. <parkswon@hotmail.com>

Joseph Deva Komar PETER: Faculty at Malaysia Theological Seminary; Director of the Institute of World Religions, and of the Tamil Theological Education by Extension; Pastor, Methodist Church in Malaysia. <joe8162915@yahoo.com>

Michael Nai-Chiu POON: Director and Asian Christianity Research Coordinator, Centre for the Study of Christianity in Asia (CSCA) of the Trinity Theological College (TTC) in Singapore; member of the Inter-Anglican Standing Commission for Unity, Faith and Order, and an Anglican member on the Anglican – Roman Catholic International Commission. Editor of the *CSCA Christianity in Southeast Asia Series*. Honorary Canon, Saint Andrew's Cathedral; member of Anglican Church. <mncpoon@ttc.edu.sg>

Joseph PRABHAKAR: Associate Professor, United Theological College, Bangalore, India; Pastor from Andhra Evangelical Lutheran Church, Andhra Pradesh, India; <jpdayam@gmail.com>

J. Paul RAJASHEKAR: the Luther D. Reed Professor of Systematic Theology and former Academic Dean of Lutheran Theological Seminary at Philadelphia; formerly served as a professor at the United Theological College, Bangalore, India, and as Executive Secretary for Theology at the Lutheran World Federation. <rajashekar@ltsp.edu>

Van Arun RASMEY: General Secretary of Kampuchea Christian Council; Project Officer of Christian Reformed World Relief Committee (CRWRC) Cambodia. <arunrasmey_van@yahoo.com >

Rex Resurreccion B. REYES, Jr.: General Secretary of the National Council of Churches in the Philippines, formerly Program Secretary for Christian Unity and Ecumenical Relations, NCCP; ordained priest of the Episcopal Church in the Philippines. <padirex@gmail.com>

K.B. ROKAYA: General Secretary of National Council of Churches in Nepal, Kathmandu. <drrokaya2000@yahoo.com>

Sebouh SARKISSIAN: Archbishop, Primate of the Armenian Diocese of Tehran, Armenian Orthodox Church in Iran; formerly Catholicosal Vicare in Kuwait and Gulf countries; member of the Armenian Orthodox and Apostolic Church, Holy See of Cilicia, Antelias-Lebanon. <sebouhss@hotmail.com>

Erlinda N. SENTURIAS: Chair of Medical Action Group, Inc., and Volunteer Physician at the Traditional Medicine and Integrative Medicine of the Philippine General Hospital, formerly Consultant on HIV & AIDS of the Christian Conference of Asia; member of the United Church of Christ in the Philippines. <erlinda.senturias@gmail.com >

Hermen SHASTRI: General Secretary of the Council of Churches of Malaysia, former Dean of Seminari Theoloji of Malaysia; member of the Faith and Order Commission of the World Council of Churches; ordained Minister of the Methodist Church of Malaysia. <ccmwwcom@tm.net.my>

Martin Lukito SINAGA: Lecturer at Jakarta Theological Seminary (STT-Jakarta), Pastor of the Batak-Simalungun Church of Indonesia, formerly served as Study Secretary for Theology and the Church at the Lutheran World Federation (2009-2012). <mlsinaga@yahoo.com>

Overland SNAITANG: Professor of History of Christianity at Aizawl Theological College, Mizoram, India; former President of Church History Association of India; affiliated with the Church of God in Shillong, India. <olsnaitangrevdr@yahoo.in>

David Kwang-sun SUH: Professor emeritus of Theology at Ewha Womans University, Honorary Professor at Chinese University of Hong Kong, formerly Vice President for Programs of the United

Board for Christian Higher Education in Asia (Hong Kong), and ordained Minister of the Presbyterian Church of Korea. <dkssuh@gmail.com>

Corazon TABING-REYES: Executive Secretary, International Committee of the Fellowship of the Least Coin, Union Theological Seminary, Dasmarinas City, Cavite, Philippines

Pradit TAKERNGRANGSARIT: ordained by the Church of Christ in Thailand, awarded the rank of Assistant Professor by the Royal Thai Ministry of Education, and the degree of Doctor of Theology in Old Testament by the University of Melbourne; retired in 2012 as President of Payap University in Chiang Mai, Thailand.

Ganesh TAMANG: Former Principal of Nepal Institute of Theology (NIT) in Kathmandu, currently serving as Pastor in Hope Church, Kathmandu, <ganeshtmg@yahoo.com >

TANG Sui Tung: Head Librarian of Lutheran Theological Seminary in Hong Kong and Executive Committee member of the Forum of Asian Theological Librarians (ForATL) <ltslib@hotmail.com>

THU En Yu: Principal, Sabah Theological Seminary; Secretary of Malaysian Association of Theological Schools; formerly Bishop of the Basel Christian Church of Malaysia, and President, Association for Theological Education in South East Asia (ATESEA); ordained Minister of the Basel Christian Church of Malaysia. <eythu@stssabah.org>

Tu Thien Van TRUONG: Vice President for Academic Affairs at Union University of California and Principal of Gospel Theological Institute (under establishment); member of Vietnam Christian Mission. <truongvanthientu@yahoo.com>

Michael WALLACE: Vicar of All Saints' Parish and Chaplain of Selwyn College, Dunedin and formerly General Secretary of the World Student Christian Federation (2004-2010); priest of the Anglican Church in Aotearoa New Zealand and Polynesia. <mwmwallace@hotmail.com>

Jiawei WANG: faculty member at *Nanjing* Union *Theological* Seminary, teaching courses in History of Christian Thought and Chinese Christian Spirituality, < wjwyiyi@yahoo.com.cn>

Lhatru WANGCHUK: Secretary General of National Christian Council of Bhutan, Principal of Himalayan Theological Seminary; PhD in Missiology candidate doing research on "Gross National Happiness from the Perspectives of Buddhism and Christianity"; senior Pastor of Bhutan Lutheran Church. <lwangchuk1966@gmail.com>

Dietrich WERNER: International Programme Coordinator for WCC Programme for Ecumenical Theological Education (ETE) in Geneva; lecturer in Missiology, Ecumenism and World Christianity; co-founder of the Global Digital Library for Theology and Ecumenism (GlobeTheoLib); main Editor of the Handbook for Theological Education in World Christianity; ordained Pastor from Evangelical Lutheran Church in Northelbia, Hamburg, Germany; <dietrich.werner@wcc-coe.org>

H.S. WILSON: Executive Director of The Foundation for Theological Education in South East Asia and guest Professor at Karnataka Theological College, Mangalore, India; formerly Professor of Mission and Cultures at Lutheran Theological Seminary at Philadelphia; a Presbyter of the Church of South India and Presbyterian Church, USA. <ftewilson@gmail.com>

WONG Wai Ching Angela: Associate Professor, Department of Cultural and Religious Studies and Head, Graduate Division of Gender Studies of The Chinese University of Hong Kong; formerly President of Christian Conference of Asia and Chairperson of World Student Christian Federation Institution; member of Hong Kong Anglican Church. <wcwong@arts.cuhk.edu.hk>

Toshimasa YAMAMOTO: Professor and Chaplain at Kwansei Gakuin University in Kobe, Japan; formerly General Secretary of the National Christian Council in Japan; ordained United Methodist clergy. <ToshiYamamoto@kwansei.ac.jp >

PART I

HISTORICAL AND CONTEXTUAL PERSPECTIVES ON ASIAN ECUMENISM

(1) Asian Ecumenism Before the Ecumenical Movement

John England

It is the intention of this article to shed some light on Inter-church co-operation and 'worldly' service of churches in Asia before the beginning of the ecumenical movement. Beginnings can be traced back to the 3rd century.

There can be few developments more significant in recent decades, for our understanding and knowledge of Christian History and theology, than the recovery for the whole church of 'the other half'' of our Christian story. This is the record and witness, the writings and thought, of Asian Christians and churches before the year 1500; before, that is, the wide-spread arrival of western traders, missionaries and colonizers.

The pre-colonial history of Christianity in the region is now much more widely known[1], although serious study of its present applications, for education, theology and mission, has barely begun. This 'other half' (or more) of the history of the world-wide church, and more than half the world's population, is still largely ignored – not least in its ecumenical dimensions – not only by western Church historians but by many of our colleagues in our own countries. That history however is now well established.

To be put most briefly, Christian presence in our region – of west, central, east, southeast and south Asia, dates from the 2nd century; was found in at least a dozen countries east of Persia by the 8th century, and throughout all Asian regions by the 16th century: from Afghanistan eastwards to Turkestan, Tibet, China, Mongolia, Korea and Japan; and southwards to India, Sri Lanka, Burma, Siam, Indochina and the East Indies[2]. There are whole libraries of its histories, literatures and archives which reveal not only the persistence of ancient, and often culture-confined traditions, but also of dynamic movements in mission and ecumenical action, of service and theology, from which we can learn, and live, much of our faith today.

It cannot be overstated that records for these people and places represent the wide spread of non-Western Christian traditions, which developed, as early as the late second century, in conscious distinction from Greek and Latin thought-forms and standards. In some areas of both the Roman and Persian Empires Nestorian and Jacobite Christianity fostered also, in the fifth and sixth centuries, the beginnings of Semitic 'nationalism'.

1. World-Oriented and Ecumenical Mission: The First Ten Centuries

In this period there were many features of church life which can be recognized as already 'ecumenical', that is, not just in limited inter-church relations, but *centered upon Christian concern with others, for the whole world and for the everyday life and faith of all people in their own place.* (This is despite the

---

[1] See for example, A.S.Atiya *A History of Eastern Christianity* (London: Methuen, 1968 & Kraus, 1991; S.H.Moffett *A History of Christianity in Asia* vol.1 (San Francisco: Harper Collins, 1992); J.C.England *Hidden History of Christianity in Asia* (Delhi: ISPCK, 1998; T.V.Philip *East of the Euphrates. Early Christianity in Asia* (Delhi: CSS & ISPCK, 1998; I.Gillman & H-J. Klimkeit *Christians in Asia before 1500* (Richmond: Curzon, 1999); Mattam, Mar Ab. *Forgotten East.* Satna: Ephrem's Pubns., 2000; Baum, W. & D.W. Winkler *The Church of the East.* London & New York: Routledge Curzon, 2003; C.Baumer *The Church of the East. An Illustrated History of Assyrian Christianity*. London' Tauris, 2006.

[2] The communions sometimes collectively termed 'Oriental Orthodox' include Syrian Orthodox/Jacobite/Monophysite, who with the 'Nestorian'/Church of the East/Tachin, rejected Chalcedon doctrines (and a Roman 'Pope'), in contrast to the Chalcedonian/Melkite communions.

protracted and often bitter debate by some 'theologians' on aspects of denominational belief or of church polity, which have often seemed to dominate some studies of church history).

Far more important for ongoing Christian (and worldly) mission was the courageous witness and missionary endeavor (often blocked or persecuted for being 'Christian', not as this or that sectarian) of the prophetic and monastic movements; along with long traditions of education, medical care and state service, by generations of Persians, Arabs, Turks, Syrians, Indians & Chinese. Included among them were merchants and camel-drivers, scholars and teachers, women and men religious, prophets, soldiers, physicians, chieftainesses, chiefs and khans, linguists, mothers, chancellors, preachers, and writers. The large majority of these were in 'secular' occupations, often carried out with little regard for either religious or denominational limitations[3]. In the earliest period, for which records from West, South and Central Asia are the most plentiful, there are therefore numberless examples of 'ecumenical' engagement, mission and writing, spread far beyond their own communion or nationality: a small selection of these follows.

In the 2nd century: *Tatian of Adiabene* (northern Iraq) produced the first *Harmony of the Gospels*, and vigorously advocated localized (non-western) witness and theology. His writing and witness became widely influential throughout West and Central Asia. In the same century, *Bardaisan* compiled his *Book of the Laws of the Lands* which chronicles the presence of Christians (of various communions) as far east as Afghanistan and as far south as India. In Bactria (Afghanistan) he writes of Christian women who showed in their daily lives the qualities of life that linked them with Christian communities throughout the region[4].

In South India, where there had been Christian churches since the 2nd century or earlier, it is clear from many sources that Christians were 'Indian in culture', 'Christian in religion', community-oriented and partners with Hindu neighbours, in many ways. They were often, for example, 'trustees of the temple' as Hindus were of the church. They included local religious festivals & observances in their liturgy; and often shared articles used in festivals, from drums to elephants![5] Hindu customs regarding bathing, lamp-lighting or sleeping were shared by Christians, although often given Christian interpretation[6]. So in many ways it can be said that the life of St Thomas Christians 'was strikingly similar', and in sympathy with, their Hindu neighbours; this was certainly a strong element of an ecumenical awareness.

Christian colleges in Persia, at Edessa (Urfa) and Nisibis, from the 2nd century on also, trained many who – lay people or religious – became merchants or interpreters, counsellors or administrators along any part of the 'silk routes', from Persia to Japan to the east or Java to the south. The medical school at Jundishapur (Beth Lapat) trained physicians who later, and ecumenically, served shahs and caliphs, khans and abbots across the region. Many cities, throughout Asia were therefore also centres for Christian worship and training, in some localities until as late as the 14th or 15th centuries. These could be found, for example, from Antioch in the west to Quilon in south India; from Samarqand to Chang An (Xian, China).

In the next few centuries Eastern theologians, such as *Theodore of Mopsuestia* (d.428) and *Nestorius* (d.452) – and later – *A-Lo-Pen* (early 7th century China), and *Timothy I* (Patriarch 780-823), taught and wrote on the similarity of Jesus Christ's life struggles' to ours, and of Christ's humanity to ours, so that we find him in our everyday world[7]. This is certainly a 'worldly' focus for theology and was also embodied in the lives of many of our Asian forebears of those centuries.

---

[3] A 'common religiosity' for many of these communions included stress on Christians being the 'new people' (replacing the Hebrew 'chosen people'; upon the humanity & the physical body of Jesus Christ; upon 'spiritual marriage', emphasising the Holy Spirit as 'Mother'; and on the Church as a pilgrim group on the way to the fulfilled 'kingdom'. (see Gillman & Klimkeit 1999, pp.61ff.)

[4] Ibid p.43.

[5] J.C.England 1998, p.60.

[6] For the extent of 'cultural exchange & assimilation see L.W.Brown *The Christians of St Thomas* (London, 1956) p.75, Gillman & Klimkeit 1999, 169 ff.

[7] Refer *Asian Christian Theologies. A Research Guide to Authors, Movements, Sources* 3 vols. ed. John C. England et al. Delhi: ISPCK, Maryknoll NY: Orbis; Manila: Claretian 2001-2004) vol.1 pp.8ff.

Then also there are many other records of the commitment of our Christian forebears to the concrete needs of surrounding communities. A neat summary of this appears at the end of the so-called 'Nestorian' or *'Sian-fu'* (China) Monument (c.780 C.E.), where "reverent service and proper worship" is defined as: "The hungry came and were fed. The cold came and they were clothed. The sick were healed and raised up. The dead were buried and laid to rest."

The same spread of occupations and life-styles for Christians, as noted earlier, can be seen in other lands to the east of Persia. Here too there were many other ethnic groups to be found now, including Syrian, Chinese, Indian, Malay, Tai, Tibeto-Burman, Korean, Japanese, Tribal and Mongol. This was a remarkable extension of Christian presence, mission and service across the whole Asian region – and along with the varying responses of state rulers or religious leaders was the setting for individual and group commitment to 'ecumenical mission'. Some examples follow:

Euphemia, the Christian prophetic widow of Kurdistan (6th century), adopted the simplest life-style which yet united both contemplation and social action. She befriended destitute families, regularly visited and helped the sick, homeless and disabled, and welcomed refugees. Euphemia also directly challenged rich citizens, at their gates (!), to provide food, shelter and justice for their poor, saying to them "What mighty thing are you going to do for Christ, he to whom all your wealth belongs?" [8]

Hunayn ibn-Ishaq (Arab Christian, 9th century), who is described as one of the greatest scholars and translators of the age – in Greek, Persian, Arabic (see below) – also became private physician to the Caliph *al-Mutawakkil*. Imprisoned by him for refusing rich rewards to concoct a poison for an enemy, *Hunayn* declared "My religion decrees that we should do good even to our enemies...and my profession is instituted for the benefit of humanity and limited to their relief and cure.." [9]

In the same period Syriac (Christian) culture was flourishing in Persia and this was the setting for many examples of co-operation between those of different communions, and even faiths. In Baghdad of the 8th to 10th centuries in particular, there was creative and intensive encounter between cultures, faiths, and languages. Muslim and Christian scholars such as *Hunayn*, co-operated in the shared endeavour of translating Greek and Syriac classics into Arabic. These were to be the chief sources through which 'European' scholars would later discover the world of Greek learning. Again, a major ecumenical undertaking.

At this time too, Christian and Buddhist scholars of central and east Asia, were co-operating in research and translation. An outstanding example is the collaboration between the Christian monk *Ching-ching* (Adam) from China and the Indian Buddhist monk *Prajna,* in translating the Buddhist *Satparamitra* Sutra into Chinese. Here were preludes to the ecumenical exchanges and mutual borrowing that is reflected in many Christian Sutras from the 9th-11th centuries, and that have been discovered in Central and East Asia.[10] (see below).

Then there were the series of amicable debates in those years (despite many others less amicable!), between Christian and Muslim leaders: for example between Patriarch *Timothy I* with the Caliph *Mahdi* (c.780). In the 10th century, there were debates between *Yahya ibn Adi* and *Theodore Abu Qurra* with Muslim guests of the (Christian?)Caliph *al Mamun*[11]. There are preludes here also, to the dialogues held much later at the courts of the Mongol Khans (see below). In these debates it was not an 'open-minded acceptance of truth wherever that may be found', but at their best there was at least willingness in these

---

[8] S. Brock & S.A.Harvey (eds.) *Holy Women of the Syrian Orient* (Berkeley: University of California Press, 1987) pp.126ff.

[9] P.K.Hitti *History of the Arabs. From the Earliest Times to the Present.* 10th edn. (New York: St Martin's Press, 1974) pp.312 ff.

[10] I.Gillman & H-J. Klimkeit 1999, p.182.

[11] D.Thomas (ed.) *Christians at the Heart of Islamic Rule. Church Life & Scholarship in 'Abbasid Iraq* (Leiden: Brill, 2003) especially chaps.5,7,8.

debates – urged or accepted by the Caliph or Khan of course – to listen to each other, to discuss together, and to recognize at least, the differing traditions within one's own communion.

It should be remembered here that from 325 to 869 CE, eight 'Ecumenical Councils' were held, some achieving less consensus and reconciliation (!) than others. Supposedly including Christians from the 'whole inhabited earth' (*oikumene*), they were also accepted, supposedly, by all churches in both the 'East' and the 'West', although only some Asian communions did so. Despite major and sometimes bitter controversies, the overall aim of each was however to establish, or restore, unity for the whole church, in order to both recognize and enlarge 'the mission of the church' in the world.

There is surprisingly contemporary ecumenical relevance also for many countries in, for example, the mobility and diversity of congregational life in the Churches of the East: in their passion for world-wide mission along with a close identification with local peoples; in the emphasis made by their theologians upon the human life of Jesus and the inter-connectedness of all in the created world; in the work of their scholars in humane letters, arts and sciences; in their blend of cultural and religious openness with a clear Christian identity; in the integration, in life and witness, of worship and secular life, of spirituality with education and medicine, agriculture and administration. [12] And this is despite the many weaknesses also discernible in much of the history of many Asian churches of that time.

2. World-Centered Mission and Ecumenical Encounter: The Tenth to Fifteenth Centuries

In this period ecumenical 'presence' and 'mission' take even more diverse forms. This can be seen first in the collections of the important Christian manuscripts discovered in East Turkestan – Turfan and Dunhuang especially – from the 9th-12th centuries. These are in more than a score of languages and of a dozen subjects; historical and scientific, medical and astrological, theological and liturgical. Manuscripts of important Christian teachings often retell lengthy sections from the Gospels, or re-shape earlier creeds and canticles, but using local language and idiom, image and metaphor.[13] Context is here taken most seriously as is the involvement in 'worldly' service.

During the centuries when the Church of the East was most widely present in the Asian region, and numbering more Christians than in the Latin and Greek communions combined (5th-11th centuries), these extant records show that Christian communities in many countries were open to, and also were nourished by, ecumenical experiences in their own context. Not only did they co-exist peacefully with those of other faiths, but they also happily exchanged, and grew in understanding of religious faith and life through this encounter.

The most significant writings we still have from them take the form of sutras (the Buddhist 'gospels'), and freely use e.g. Buddhist or Taoist terms and imagery to present New Testament teaching. Terms chosen for "salvation", "the holy Spirit", 'kingdom of God" are also vividly contextual, reflecting the landscape and life-condition of Christians widely scattered across deserts, mountains, steppes and coastlands.[14]

Judging from the paintings and manuscripts discovered at Dunhuang, the Christian community there, included by the 8th century, scholars, merchants, scribes, skilled artists and craftsmen. This was similar to

---

[12] J.C.England 1998, chap.2; S.H.Moffett 1992, pp.77f.

[13] See for example, P.Y.Saeki *The Nestorian Documents and Relics in China* (Tokyo: Maruzen, 1951); J.C.England pp.124.ff.; I.Gillman & H-J Klimkeit 1999, pp.275ff.; M.Palmer *The Jesus Sutras Rediscovering the Lost Scrolls of Taoist Christianity* (New York: Ballantyne Wellspring, 2001; R.Riegert & T.Moore *The Lost Sutras of Jesus. Unlocking the Ancient Wisdom of the Xian Monks* (London: Souvenir Press, 2004); C.Baumer, 2006 pp.187ff..

[14] J.Foster *The Church of the Tang Dynasty* (London: SPCK, 1939) pp.154ff. For example the Holy Spirit is the 'cool wind'; salvation is 'refreshing dew', 'a raft on a sea of flame', 'liberation from sorrow'; creation is the 'divine arrow' constantly held in flight by God, who remains the 'unseen archer', within & also beyond this world.

records found in the Turfan district and to those (recorded in large cemeteries) at Tokmak and Pishkek (Kyrgyzstan), where hundreds (!) of scholars and merchants, priests, soldiers and ecclesiatics – with their families – were buried: Chinese and Persian, Uighur (Turk) and Indian, Syrian and Mongol.[15] In a return exchange, scholars have found evidence of major Christian influence in such Mahayana teachings as those concerning the nature and work of *Bodhisattvas,* in Pure Land teachings and in some of the beliefs that developed for the *Prajnaparamita* (the Lady 'Wisdom beyond Wisdom').

But the wider dimensions of Ecumenism are also present here. From the earliest period, in Persia (pre-400 C.E.), until the later history of Mongol ascendancy (14th century), the role of Christians in key professions, and their commitment to all that promoted peoples' welfare, is widely recorded. In medical care and education in particular, they had founded both universities and medical schools by the 4th century, later to be spread in many countries east of Persia. And libraries, in their colleges, monasteries and churches included a wide range of medical and historical writings, in addition to Biblical, liturgical and ecclesiastical materials.

From at least the 8th century on also, significant numbers in the major Mongol clans (east, central and west Asia) were already Christian, as were members of many Khan families. Prominent among these were the mothers and wives of at least nine Khans. Most notable was *Sorghagtani Beki,* mother of *Khubilai Khan* (13th century). She ensured that her tribes stood out as being free of abuses of power; moderated *Khubilai Khan's* policies; and was widely lauded – by European missionaries, Persian historians and Syrian physicians alike – as "towering above all the women of the world".[16] Although her back-ground was Church of the East, her life and 'ministry' were clearly 'ecumenical'...

But most remarkable were the family dynasties of physicians, counselors and in particular, chief administrative officers, upon whom Shahs, Caliphs and Khans were dependent over many centuries. Names and in some cases, bio-data have survived for some of these. The roles of significant women are also to be found there.[17] The position of 'Chancellor' or 'Vizier' was sometimes hereditary in families such as that of the Christian *Ai Hsieh* from the 12th century. Pre-eminent amongst *Kublai Khan's* officials as Chancellor and Director of the Offices of Astronomy and Medicine, *Ai Hsieh* yet rejected all bribes and astrological speculations. He is also reported to have curbed a number of major injustices, even persuading Kublai Khan to forego planned oppressive military campaigns.[18] Here was not only inter-faith encounter, dialogue and social concern but also the exercise of appropriate power in vast polyglot, multi-cultural communities.

In 13th century Karakorum also, the Khan *Mangu* convened inter-faith debates between representatives of the Christian (jointly Nestorian and Roman Catholic), Muslim and 'Tuin' (i.e. Buddhist, Manichaean and Shamanist) communities. Later Il-khans such as *Hulagu* ('Persia'), were reported to be influenced towards moderating the use of armed conflict, by such inter-religious encounters, as they were by their Christian wives. The lives and aspirations of Mongol khans and their families are greatly more diverse than wide-spread myth would suggest.

3. The Sixteenth-Nineteenth Centuries

This period presents a very wide spectrum of ecumenical examples in the life of Christian communities. In the more limited sense of church and inter-faith ecumenical relations, these range from tentative recognition of diversity within one's own tradition, to Christian affirmation of pristine 'Hindu' beliefs; to

---

[15] J.Stewart *Nestorian Missionary Enterprise: the Story of a Church on Fire*. (Edinburgh: T.& T. Clark; Madras: Christian Literary Society, 1928) pp.206ff.

[16] M.Rossabi *Kubilai Khan His Life and Times* (Berkeley: University of California, 1988) pp.11ff.

[17] J.C.England 1998, pp.82ff.

[18] A.C.Moule *Christians in China before the Year 1550* (London, SPCK, 1930)pp.228ff.

presentation of the Gospel in Confucian terms; or to acceptance of some Buddhist or Shinto practices as means of preserving faith.[19] As well, a number of further inter-faith dialogues are recorded, often in detail, (e.g. in India, China, Vietnam and Japan). These are most interesting as early ecumenical endeavors even though the aims of each participant are often, at least in part, 'evangelistic', and sometimes political.

For the 'larger ecumenism' of ('inter-faith') commitment to the world and its people we have to look for movements apparently outside the 'mainstream' of Asian church history. These would include the struggles of persecuted Christian minorities to survive oppression and to continue caring for their immediate community (e.g. in Japan, Vietnam, and Ceylon); the work of scholars and others to present the implications of the Christian Gospel for cultural reform or policies of government (e.g. in Korea, China, the Philippines); and 'subversive' groups/movements which reshaped the style of Christian presence under colonial or totalitarian regimes (e.g. in Japan, Korea, India, the Philippines). The continuing role of liturgy, prayer and Biblical study (however interpreted) remain central for almost all these groups and movements, as does the often over-looked participation and leadership of women.

Looking more closely at such movements and individuals we discover many instances of wider inter-church or world-centered aims and endeavors. I will be able to include here only a few representative examples from the numerous cases available. Amongst these, are the inter-faith endeavors in early-17th century China, by a number of neo-Confucian literati, to restore and complete Confucianism as a path to national reform. This they found presented in a Christianity which was sensitively grounded also in ancient Chinese tradition. So Christian faith is here an amplification and intensification of neo-Confucian wisdom. But Christian teaching is also modified and enriched in this encounter, just as Confucian teachings are modified in the light of Christian faith.

Then from the early -17th century also we can trace the emergence in Vietnam of "The Three Fathers" (*Ba Cha*) theology – in which God is High Father, the king of one's country medium father and one's blood father is low father. This merging of Confucian and Christian insights was to form basis for much later contextual reflection and life. It appears first in *Alexandre de Rhodes'* book *Phep giang tam ngay* (Catechism explained in eight days) of 1651[20], and it would become a central tradition in later Catholic thought in Vietnam; often merged with strong nationalism, as in *Danh Duc Tuan* (d.1875), and much later, in scholars such as *Hoang Gia Khanh* (b.1955)

This can be seen also in the thought and labours of *Nguyen Truong To* (b.1827). A scholar of classical Chinese, he was also a teacher, architect and prolific Catholic writer. In 1861, he submitted a stream of memorandums to the Emperor, advocating extensive reforms in the administration of justice, taxation, the army and international affairs. This was to make possible equitable incomes, indigenous production and the elimination of corruption. "Urgent measures", in which he personally also worked, included the formation of co-operatives, of creches and hospices and the development of irrigation and land settlement schemes. [21]

In India, in the late 17th, and early 18th centuries, over thirty conferences had been held between Danish missionaries and *'Malabarian Brahmans'*. (The reports were edited by *Bartolomaeus Ziegenbalg* and published in London in 1719). Later in the 18th century Sanskrit scholars and French Jesuits, collaborate to present Sanskrit documents entitled Pristine Hinduism Vindicated: in which Christian meaning was discerned in the religious insights of the Hindu texts.[22] The authors clearly believed that the central truths

[19] See writings included in *Asian Christian Theologies 2001-2004*, vol.1 pp.27ff.

[20] Outlined in P.C.Phan *Mission & Catechesis Alexandre de Rhodes & Inculturation in Seventeenth Century Vietnam* (Maryknoll NY: Orbis, 1998) pp.220ff.

[21] Nguyen Truong To's writings have been collected in *Nguyen Trung To 1830-1871* ed. Ba Can Truong (Ho Chi Minh Ville: Institute of Research on Chinese & Vietnamese Culture, 1991. See also *Asian Christian Theologies* 2001-2004, vol. 2, pp.567ff.

[22] A. Amaladas & R.F.Young *The Indian Christiad. A Concise Anthology of Didactic & Devotional Literature. in Early Church Sanskrit* (Anand: Gujarat Sahitya Prakash, 1995)

of Hinduism were "wholly congruent with the Christian faith". It is thus an early example of contextualizing but more important than the content, for our purpose, is the ecumenical collaboration which produced it.

In 19th century India, amongst many who studied and integrated central insights of Hinduism into Christian faith – including *P.C. Moozoomdar* (1840-1905), *Keshub Chandra Sen* (1838-1884), *Krishna Mohan Banerjee* (1813-1885), and *Brahmabandhav Upadhyaya* (1861-1907) – was a remarkable woman, *Pandita Ramabai* (1858-1922). Her Brahmin father had against custom, taught his wife and daughters Sanskrit. In Calcutta the Senate of the University of Calcutta uniquely honoured her with the prestigious titles, *Pandita* and *Saraswathi* in acknowledgement of her learning. She joined the *Brahmo Samaj* (a reformist Hindu association) and in 1883 she deepened her knowledge of Christ and Christianity with *Nehemiah Goreh*, then receiving baptism in the Anglican Church. From 1886 to 1888 *Ramabai* lectured and studied social reform in America, also canvassing support for a House for Brahmin child-widows – the *Sharada Sadan*.

The *Pandita* also worked on Marathi Bible translation, but her main contribution is the pioneering work that she did for the liberation of Indian women, causing many Indians to rethink their attitudes to, and treatment of, women. In theology she sought a less dogmatic, less metaphysical Christianity, in tune with her Hindu ethos and with more direct experience of the Holy Spirit. She also denounced the denominational divisions within Christianity – only when Christians overcame divisions and established one united and indigenous Christian Church would they be worthy to preach Christ to the Indians. She then challenged believers to go out to serve society as she herself had done.[23]

In the Philippines, *Don Pedro Pelaez* (d. 1863) was the principal leader in the movement of Filipino clergy from 1849 on to rectify injustices within the church and to establish a church in which Filipino and Spaniard were equally regarded. He became lecturer in both philosophy and theology, secretary to the Archbishop and administrator of the Manila Diocese. But in his teaching and writings he was an eminent advocate for the Filipinization of the church, drawing on a wide knowledge of history, scientific discovery, canon law and theology. There he articulated a theology of national identity and Filipino Christianity in its social and political application and fostered wide Filipino participation in this.

His famous protégé, *José Apolonio Burgos*, was martyred in 1872 for his learned advocacy for an independent church and people. While remaining loyal to Rome, Burgos had strongly rejected the colonialist policies and abuses of the Friars and worked tirelessly for social justice, Filipino identity and a Filipino church. [24] Later, others such as *Isabelo de los Reyes* (d. 1938) would 'Filipinize' Christian faith through a merging of native folk-lore and religion with traditional Catholic beliefs.

And for Japan, there is *Takahashi Goro* (1856-1935), born into a Samurai family in Niigata. He became a talented linguist and co-operated in the translation of the Japanese Bible. His particular study however was widely in Buddhism. He became 'the leading Christian expert' on Buddhism in the 1880s, amongst other prominent Christians like *Ibuka Kajinosuke, Hiraiwa Yoshiyasu, Uemura Masahisa and Kozaki Hiromichi* who also showed a deep concern for the understanding of Buddhism.

Takahashi himself remained critical of many aspects of Buddhism in many articles of his that appeared in the journal *Rikugo Zasshi* and in four volumes he wrote on Japanese religion. But while these had an apologetic purpose, he nevertheless argued for an unbiased search for truth in all religious study. "Leave

---

[23] See for example, *Pandita Ramabai Through Her Own Words: Selected Works*. Comp. & ed. Meera Kosambi (New Delhi: Oxford University Press, 2000); P. Gupta *Pandita Ramabai Saraswati: Her Life and Work* (London: Asia Publishing House, 1970).

[24] Refer Schumacher, John N. *Revolutionary Clergy: The Filipino Clergy and the Nationalist Movement, 1850-1903*. (Quezon City: Ateneo de Manila University Press, 1981); *Father Jose Burgos: Priest and Nationalist*. (Quezon City: Ateneo de Manila University Press, 1972); *Father Jose Burgos A Documentary History. With Spanish Documents and their Translation*. (Ateneo de Manila University Press, 1999).

prejudice," he wrote in *Rikugo Zasshi*, "forget the conventional criticism; open your minds and empty your hearts and consider thoroughly what I have written about Buddhism... and make your own impartial judgement". Despite his rejection of many Buddhist doctrines his work is known as the start of serious and comprehensive inter-faith study in Japan.[25]

Ecumenical theology and action was to develop in many streams in the 19th and 20th centuries. Just to consider inter-denominational conferences of missionaries in the region: these were first held in India from 1825 (although they were first proposed by William Carey in 1806). They became regular events in India in that century and later occurred also in Japan (from 1872) and in China (from 1877). In India they came to include a growing number of nationals, and to consider not only the issues of 'comity' in mission but also the questions of Christian unity and the role of a national 'three-self' Church in each country. Missionary unions and associations were often formed, sometimes in association with local or national movements: in emergency relief, education and publication, social concern and inter-faith activities. But the pattern for future joint action in mission and theological formulation was largely set by movements of students within and outside the region, in YMCAs (from 1854) and YWCAs (from 1875), in SCMs, and in particular, in activities of the WSCF (from 1895).The participation and leadership of Asian Christians in these, as in subsequent ecumenical movements was, and is, extensive.

Conclusion

To recognize in the few examples given above in their very diverse contexts, an 'ecumenical spirit', or even an 'ecumenical purpose', is yet to ignore the central thrust of their histories. For that is the move from 'interest' or even 'intention' to the *enactment* of a common faith and vision – that of embodied love for neighbour, community and world. These are to be seen in the qualities of life-in-community; of sensibility, compassion and creativity that are revealed; in the restoration or fulfillment of distinctly human life being attempted or hoped for, whatever the details of rite or doctrine or ideology may have been. Here we see deep concern for the other as the driving force of the one faith, for one humanity: through collaboration in study, in translation or teaching, in joint Church actions, in advocacy for people's welfare, in movements for radical change, and in personal dedication for the everyday life and faith of all people in their own place. What qualities of life-in-community, of sensibility, compassion and creativity, are revealed – or can be validly inferred – in them? What kind of human life was being attempted or hoped for, whatever the details of rite or doctrine or ideology may have been?

For the periods outlined, a central conclusion could well be – as I have spoken of it before – that from a (renewed) experience of the concrete life-situations of our people, in for example, 'live-in' encounters, there could come a greater freedom to 'live on the fringe' and develop new forms of 'non-institutional' Christian presence. These could be authentically rooted both in particular secular worlds and in new patterns of Christian community life, study, and prayer. This too could be a mutually beneficial co-existence with neighbors of other faiths such as Hinduism, Buddhism and Islam; survival despite repression and persecution; creative biblical interpretation, theology and spirituality – all offering rich resources for the present life, thought and action of all Christians

And a final question we are left with: How can we therefore enlist 'church leaders'..., activists..., seminary staff... directly in such encounter, study and mutual commitment? Practical steps could well be taken to implement fuller ecumenical orientation towards our peoples where they are today, through action-oriented field-education in our seminaries; co-operation in training (including church history) programmes with our regional networks of study- and social-action centers (and seminaries); and live-in exposures arranged as the regular prelude to our ecumenical conferences and assemblies. In these and similar ways I

[25] Thelle, Notto R. Buddhism and Christianity in Japan: From Conflict to Dialogue 1854-1899 (Honolulu: University of Hawaii Press, 1987) pp.71.ff.

believe, we can carry forward the long heritage of people-oriented and ecumenical mission in our region, finding creatively new and prophetic forms for our commitment to the 'oikumene' in coming decades.

Bibliography

Asian Christian Theologies. A Research Guide to Authors, Movements, Sources 3 vols. ed. John C. England et al. Delhi: ISPCK, Maryknoll NY: Orbis; Manila: Claretian 2001-2004) vol.1

A.S.Atiya *A History of Eastern Christianity* (London: Methuen, 1968 & Kraus, 1991;

Baum, W. & D.W. Winkler *The Church of the East*. London & New York: Routledge Curzon, 2003;

C.Baumer *The Church of the East. An Illustrated History of Assyrian Christianity*. London' Tauris, 2006.

S. Brock & S.A.Harvey (eds.) *Holy Women of the Syrian Orient* (Berkeley: University of California Press, 1987)

L.W.Brown *The Christians of St Thomas* (London, 1956)

J.C.England *Hidden History of Christianity in Asia* (Delhi: ISPCK, 1998;

I.Gillman & H-J. Klimkeit *Christians in Asia before 1500* (Richmond: Curzon, 1999);

Mattam, Mar Ab. *Forgotten East*. Satna: Ephrem's Pubns., 2000;

S.H.Moffett *A History of Christianity in Asia* vol.1 (San Francisco: Harper Collins, 1992);

A.C.Moule *Christians in China before the Year 1550* (London, SPCK, 1930)

T.V.Philip *East of the Euphrates. Early Christianity in Asia* (Delhi: CSS & ISPCK, 1998;

J.Stewart *Nestorian Missionary Enterprise: the Story of a Church on Fire*. (Edinburgh: T.& T. Clark; Madras: Christian Literary Society, 1928)

D.Thomas (ed.) *Christians at the Heart of Islamic Rule. Church Life & Scholarship in 'Abbasid Iraq* (Leiden: Brill, 2003)

(2) EARLY BEGINNINGS OF THE ASIAN ECUMENICAL MOVEMENT

Kyaw Than

Early Beginnings in Asia

It is often those who do not give much attention to the very beginnings of the Church in Asia who usually identify Christianity as a religion brought to Asia by Western missionaries. For the sake of the younger generations it is useful to note that when we speak of the beginnings of the ecumenical movement in Asia we need to reach back to the days of the formation of the first student YMCA at Jaffna College in Ceylon in 1882, or the ecumenical student conference at Doshisha Christian College at Kyoto, Japan in early July 1889.

Even the historical origins of the Church itself will need to be understood in terms of the location of the earthly ministry of our Lord Jesus Christ who chose to be born in a manger in a lowly cattleshed in Bethlehem, a small city in the huge expanse of the continent of Asia stretching from the eastern shores of the Mediterranean Sea to the Pacific Ocean itself.[1] Hence, the earliest churches developed in Asia. In the canonical books of the scriptures, e.g. in Acts 11.26, we read: "And in Antioch the disciples were first time called Christians (Greek *Kristeenos*: follower of Christ), not Catholic or Protestant, liberal or orthodox. In that descriptive name we find the common basis of our unity. The community of followers grew in that part of Asia where our Lord went about during the years of His earthly ministry. After He went up to heaven the Holy Spirit, as He promised, descended on the community gathered in one place in Jerusalem. According to Luke's account, Jews from Media, Arabia and Parthia, then stretching as far as north India, were among the crowds that day. The disciples went forth from Asia to different regions of the then known world. Because of the vision Paul had[2], in which he saw a man from Macedonia standing and begging him to go over to help, Paul went from Asia to Europe to proclaim the good news of Jesus Christ. Churches grew in Europe and from Europe the good news of Jesus Christ spread to the Americas.[3]

Due to the witness of Philip to the Ethiopian eunuch who had great authority under Candace, the then queen of the Ethiopians, he became a follower of Jesus. Speaking of my own experience and contacts through the work of the World Council of Churches, I had the opportunity to visit Ethiopia and witnessed how the followers of Christ in that nation continue to form a substantial majority of the Ethiopian population. It was the State Church until the 1947 Marxist revolution. But from 1991 there has been unprecedented freedom of worship and witness.

Eusibias, known as the father of Church history (ref. his *Historica Ecclesiastica*) declared that Thaddaeus (i.e. Judas or Addai in Syriac), one of Christ's disciples, worked in Edessa, a town in Asia Minor (east Turkey) halfway between Damascus and Mt. Arafat. It is 25 miles from Haran where Abraham's father died. According to tradition Thaddaeus and Bartholomew were looked upon as the original evangelizers of Armenia. In 310 A.D. King Tiridates of Armenia declared Christianity as the faith of the nation. Remembering that Emperor Constantine's Edict of Toleration was given only in 313 A.D. we may note that during the time of Gregory, the chief bishop (or Catholicos), the city of Echmiadzin became the continuing center of the Armenian Church. (I had the privilege in December 1959 of visiting this ancient{but also current} Asian Christian city, and to be received by the church authorities, as a member of

---

[1] *Layman's Guide to Ecumenicity* by Grace D. Orr (Nebraska 1956)

[2] *The Common Evangelistic Task of the Churches in E. Asia* (Ed.) Kyaw Than (Rangoon 1957

[3] *Witnesses Together* (Ed.) Kyaw Than (Rangoon 1959)

the initial delegation led by Dr. Visser't Hooft, for ecumenical contacts with the Orthodox churches who were considering joining the World Council of Churches).

'The affirmation that Christianity has its manifestation originally in Asia is critically important to understand the history of the church and the ecumenical movement in Asia. Jerusalem, Bethlehem, Antioch, and Armenia are all in Asia geographically though for a time from 63 A.D. Judea came under Roman rule. Asia was the cradle of Christian culture, architecture, literature and art. And in the very early days of the church, its first centers were in Asia. Asia produced the first known church building, the first New Testament translation, perhaps the first Christian king, the first Christian poets, and even arguably the first Christian State. Asian Christians endured the greatest persecutions. They mounted global ventures in missionary expansion the West could not match until the thirteenth century." It is interesting to remember that these facts were observed and proclaimed by a western academic Samuel H. Moffett in his *A History of Christianity in Asia*.

I hope the points I have made and the quotations above will enable the readers to appreciate the facts and affirm as Asian Christians that Christianity is indigenous to Asia and that we should not read Asian church history, as beginning only when the later modern western missionary movement reached our shores.

We must also recognize that the church in the East enjoyed its unity in spite of the controversies the early ecumenical councils were called to deal with. To me the tragic moment was the Great Schism of 1054 when the church of the West and of the East went separate ways. We need also to recognize that though we, as Asians, are in the East, the traditions of most of the churches we belong to came out of the need for 'reformation' of the Western churches!

Christian Unity

What the Hongkong Consultation of 1966 had done was to formulate a statement which was descriptive, on the one hand, of the intrinsic life of the churches in Asia and the Christian communities within them – a life which is theirs in their calling in the Gospel. On the other hand, it was also descriptive of the actual life of these churches as it is lived by their members in the world of which they were a part. In this double situation of the churches and the issues presented by it, lie both the nature and content of the faith confessed and the scope and depth of the challenges which a confessing Church must face.

It is a route-map which has been plotted so that Hong Kong can represent a beginning. From it must flow a richer life together for the churches in Asia… From a common confession must follow also among the churches in Asia a greater commitment to the cause of mission, a greater dedication in the quest for unity and a greater willingness to be and become themselves renewed in faith and contemporary obedience. In doing this, the churches in Asia cannot stand alone. They will need to be sustained by the common life which their members share with all those among whom they live and by their fellowship within the whole household of faith.

> Therefore, my beloved brothers, stand firm and immoveable, and work for the Lord always, work without limit, since you know that in the Lord your labor cannot be lost (I Cor. 15.58).

Christian Encounter with People of Other Beliefs

The Christian encounter is, by its nature, a meeting of persons with persons. Christians meet with and are met by fellow persons in the normal converse of life. Growing urbanization makes this meeting inevitable and even irritating. Life in the villages, too, is no longer the life of a harmonious community; it involves a great deal of mutual questioning. It is from within this life together that Christians seek to transmit, interpret and give evidence of the good news of God's purpose for all people and for all the world as it has been made manifest in Jesus Christ. Christian encounter is an encounter with people as people, both in their religious life and in their non-religious life; both in what they hold to be sacred and in what they hold to be secular.

To present the gospel of God in Jesus Christ to people is to challenge them with God's searching judgment of all religions, including Christianity which is implicit in the gospel. No conversation concerning the gospel can have true seriousness unless those who take part in it, Christian or not, religious or not, recognize that the gospel is addressed to all precisely as they are, to each in one's condition of alienation from God, and that it comes to all with the invitation that they live by God's forgiving mercy as it is offered to all through Jesus Christ, the risen Lord who died for them. It is Jesus whom people must encounter. The concern of the Christian is not to confront men with Christianity but with the event and person of Christ.

In the first place, there is absolute necessity of studying and understanding the beliefs and practices of devotion of those with whom Christians would converse; not simply the classical formulations of their beliefs but the actual ways in which people hold their convictions and live their lives. In some parts of Asia the issues which divide people are primarily religious. In others, the issues are primarily cultural. Christians must learn to bear witness to the gospel in both circumstances.

In the second place, there is common ground in the questions to which people are seeking answers, just as much as there is a wide divergence in the answers themselves. Besides, there is the disturbing fact that when Christ is met, He raises new questions in addition to demanding that old questions be answered at deeper levels.

In the third place, there is the necessity that Christians so share with others a common secular life, that there is established with them a relation of friendship and mutuality. In particular, there are many services to the community as a whole in which people of all beliefs can act together in fruitful cooperation. There are also the many problems posed by a rapidly changing world and its technological developments which ought to be studied and solved together by people of all persuasions.

The encounter with people of other beliefs cannot be a pure question of verbal conversation. The disposition of God towards people in Jesus Christ cannot, in the last analysis, be communicated apart from a life which makes it credible. It must be demonstrated by those who bear His name.

The demonstration must go hand in hand with the work of interpretation. With what boldness did men like John and Paul press into the service of the gospel the terminology of Greek philosophy, the symbols of the mystery religions and the structures of thought of the Gnostics? The Christians of Asia must live more actually within the cultures of their own peoples. This may involve the abandoning of much that is familiar – a kind of self-emptying which will be both painful and dangerous. But it is only so that the Spirit will show how the faith may be restated in the idiom of the indigenous cultures, in forms of community life where the faith becomes luminous, and in actions relevant to the needs of contemporary society.

The dialogical situation within which the Christian encounter takes place is characterized, therefore, by the universality of the Gospel as it encompasses all people, the mutuality that is promised when the dialogue takes place in honest and loving openness, and the finality of Christ Himself who alone is Lord.

Modern Attempts for Reunion

Having traced the historical origins of the church and the growth of the gathered community of our Lord, we also need to recognize how in the modern times the communities of believers seek to recover the 'first love' they had lost. With the growth of denominations brought by the western missionaries, Asian Christians became dissatisfied with the labels they were given. It was important that they had acknowledged Jesus as their personal Lord and Saviour. As such the important issue was that they were

Christians. Their identity as Baptists, Episcopalians or Methodists was secondary or even unimportant. The lay ecumenical organizations such as the Student Christian Movement, the YMCA, and the YWCA, which developed in Asia in the late nineteenth century, also provided the needed inspiration and opportunity for Asian students and youth to express their desire for Christian unity.

Hans Reudi Weber, in his book, *Asia and the Ecumenical Movement*, stated: 'While for some Western countries an ecumenical history might perhaps be written without mentioning the work of the SCMs, YM/YWCAs this is quite impossible for Asia. In modern Asian ecumenical history it was these ecumenical youth movements which pioneered to set the pattern'.

The telegram signed by five hundred students attending the first national Christian Students conference of Japan at Kyoto in 1889 saying, 'Make Jesus King', led to the process of the formation of the World Student Christian Federation six years later. The theme of the Kyoto conference was: 'Christian Students United for World Conquest'.

At the 1938 World Missionary Conference held at Tambaram, near Madras in South India, the delegates from Asian churches and other so-called 'younger churches' urged for more than mere cooperation among churches. They affirmed that the need was for setting as a goal the visible and organic union of the divided churches.

Because of the theological homework that was carefully done, the formation of the Church of South India in 1947 was an exemplary development which actually started in 1908 with the union between Presbyterians and Congregationalists. The United Church of North India was formed in 1924, United Church of Christ in Japan in 1941, the Church of Christ in Thailand in 1947, and the United Church of Christ in the Philippines by 1948.

It is also important to note that the Council of Churches in Indonesia has now changed its name to the Communion of Churches in Indonesia with the intent that its members no more continue to have their business as usual but would press for that day when the churches can become constituent parts of a united Church.

The story of the attempts to develop structures of belonging together for the members of the Christian Conference of Asia are endless. At this stage we need to turn our attention to very significant and insightful perspectives arising out of the Consultation convened by the East Asia Christian Conference held at Hong Kong in 1966.

Confessing the Faith in Asia Today

"Confessing" denotes an enterprise in which the churches are engaged. It is a continuing enterprise of which it is not possible to say at any stage – the confession has been made; nor to claim that now a normative confession has been set up by which churches are bound in the future. There will be many confessions and many acts of confessing on the way.

However, this does not mean that there is no norm for the confessing life of the churches. The norm exists in the testimony of Holy Scripture and the continuing confessions of the Church universal. So it is legitimate to talk about "the Confession", "confessions", and "confessing". In the last analysis, every confession and every act of confessing is but a response to Christ's confession, who is Himself the true Confessor.

The task of translating the Gospel into contemporary Asian terms demands among other things, a serious re-appraisal of the historic confessions of the faith in the light of the present-day Asian scene.

At the E.A.C.C. Second Assembly held at Bangkok (1964), this task was looked at in its several aspects and the decision was taken to convene a special consultation to begin work on it. A fairly lengthy quotation from the statement, "Confessional Families and The Churches in Asia", adopted at Bangkok will indicate the main argument which laid down the terms of reference for that consultation:

> There are in the world, families of churches which share a common tradition and history and make their own distinctive witness to the Christian faith. Some do it by using a common confession, others by insisting on a particular relation between faith and order, others by establishing a relationship of full communion between themselves on the basis of a common understanding of the Church, and still others by maintaining within the total Christian position certain emphases as peculiarly their own. Churches that belong to the same denomination bear the same *Nomen*. They have a common name.
>
> In speaking of the churches in Asia attention is naturally drawn to what happens as the result of the Church's mission. The fruit of the Church's mission, which is the building up of the Body of Christ, necessarily implies the extension of the churches. At the same time this extension cannot be the mere growth of denominations. When the Holy Spirit calls a new people into the life of the Church, the life takes a new form in accordance with the specific experience of that people. Transplantation always involves transformation. From this point of view it is evident that even the use of the word "families" is not satisfactory.
>
> In this whole discussion the point of departure has to be that the Church exists to confess Christ in its immediate setting in the world and that, therefore, in speaking about the Church and the churches we must speak about Mission, Unity and Truth together and as ultimately inseparable.
>
> Our common Scriptures, our common confession of Jesus Christ as Lord, the life we have been given together in Him, our common mission for Him, and our common belonging to the *Una Sancta* – these things will not leave us alone. Thus arises, particularly in the lands of the Younger Churches, the overriding concern that Christians in every locality should be, in spite of their different "names", identified and identifiable as a people together. The identity of the denomination is, in relation to this, a secondary concern. The chief problem to be tackled here is the need to devise structures of belonging in which denominational boundaries are crossed. Ecumenical experience shows that whereas co-operation in action can take place at almost every point, it is at the point of structure, ecclesiastical and missionary, that dividing walls become insurmountable. The fact must be faced that, while in the West the churches drew up their historic confessions and adopted their various forms of Church order in the light of controversies that took place within the Church and within Christendom, the confessional need of the churches in Asia is primarily in relation to their mission to the world. The issues for them do not so much concern those things in which the churches differ from one another as those things which Christians together must confess before the world. Indeed, even in the lands where the historic confessions and confessional positions had their origin, the present missionary situation of the churches calls for a radical questioning of the adequacy of these confessions.

The Bangkok statement[4] also indicated the close connection which exists between this search for a common confession in which the churches must engage and the quest for Church unity. It said:

> It is a function of confessional churches to point uniting and united churches to the necessity of drawing up their own confessions in relation to the missionary situation in which they find themselves; not that it is enough for a church to draw up its confession once for all; its confession must be constantly related to the "now" at which it stands.

At Kandy at a special consultation convened by the E.A.C.C. (1965) on "Confessional Families and the Churches in Asia", two further emphases were made. The first was the importance of autonomy for the churches in Asia, and the relation between the issues of autonomy and of Church unity. To quote:

> When we speak of the Churches in Asia as exercising their autonomy, we mean specifically that a church must be able under God to make its own response to its Lord in the specific situation in which, along with the other churches in the same region, it has been called to mission. When a church exercises its autonomy, it is not simply seeking organizational independence which by itself can spell spiritual weakness. Rather, the issue is

[4] See: G. C. Jackson, Report from Bangkok, in: IRM 53, issue 211, pages 307-317, July 1946

> whether a church in a specific situation or region is free to make its own decisions in obedience to God in the fullness of the life of grace.
>
> A consideration of the issues concerning autonomy lead naturally to a consideration of the issues concerning Church Union. As autonomy is part of the nature of a church, so is unity; and the one subserves the other. In Asia today, the compulsion to give expression to this unity in organic Church Union rests on the common demands of the mission. In Asia there has been no Christendom. The differences which have seemed to justify division of the churches in the West are not necessarily acceptable justifications in Asia. Everywhere the central issues lie between the churches together and the world. The issues between the churches themselves must be taken up in this context.[5]

The second emphasis made in the report issued by the Kandy Consultation and contained in a section entitled "Confessing Christ in the Asian Contemporary Situation", was to distinguish between a confessional and a confessing theology. This distinction was described as follows:

> We have inherited the "Great Tradition" of the Gospel from those who brought the Gospel to Asia, but we believe that Christ has more of His truth to reveal to us, as we seek to understand His work among men in their several Asian cultures, their different religions and their involvement in the Asian revolution. In the past we have been too tied to inherited traditional conceptual forms of confession to make such ventures. Such formulations have been signposts and pointers to the truth, but we have often interpreted them, or had them interpreted for us as the final word of truth so that we have encamped around them, forgetting that even as people of other times and cultures made their own confession, we too must do the same in our time and culture. When we make absolute the written confessions of the churches of another culture or age, we become incapable of discovering the new depths of truth God can reveal to us in Christ amidst Asian life.
>
> A confessing theology, i.e. a theology which is the result of the wrestling of an Asian Church with its Asian environment, will naturally not be specifically confessional even though it may be indebted to many confessional traditions. A confessional type of theology, inherited by an Asian Church as part of its tradition, is usually a source of division; while a confessing theology will under-gird the movement toward unity and union in the churches of Asia.

The Kandy statement drew attention also to the necessity of a confessing Church being in dialogue with those of other faiths and beliefs. It said:

> A living theology must speak to the actual questions men in Asia are asking in the midst of their dilemmas; their hopes, aspirations and achievements; their doubts, despair and suffering. It must also speak in relation to the answers that are being given by Asian religions and philosophies, both in their classical form and in new forms created by the impact on them of western thought, secularism and science. Christian theology will fulfill its task in Asia only as the Asian churches, as servants of God's Word and revelation in Jesus Christ, speak to the Asian situation and from involvement in it.[6]

Conclusion

I hope the foregoing sections of this paper help us to get an idea about the way the churches developed in Asia, and also about the thought of the East Asia Christian Conference (now CCA) regarding the way Asian Christians understand their faith and life.

---

[5] See: Autonomy and Church Union in the Church of Asia, in: IRM, vol. 55, issue 218, pages 195-204, April 1966.
[6] See: Confessing the Faith in Asia today. A statement issued by the East Asia Christian Conference, held in Hongkong, October 26-November 3, 1966.

First, I hope some of us contemporary and potential servers in the ecumenical movement in our continent will take time to study the historical development of the church in the Patristic era. (*Patres Ecclesia* in Latin means 'Fathers of the church'). Study of this early period of church history will remind us that the church and Christianity began in Asia itself and are not imports from the west. The works of the theologians of that early period of the church, including Augustine, bishop of Hippo in North Africa, in the fourth century, helped shape Christian thought and doctrine for the churches in the generations that followed. I remember how the late Dr. Visser't Hoof in his time expressed his desire for Christian scholars to take up Patristic studies. I believe it is not too late for CCA to encourage and assist relevant Asian Christian leaders to devote their time and study to research and share their findings and reflections about the life and mission of the believing Asian communities of that era.

Second, I want to underline the thoughts arising out of the Hong Kong 1966 Consultation on "Confessing the Faith in Asia Today:" When I have had occasion to do so I have pointed out the importance of the insights arising out of that meeting. It was referred to by some of those days as a major Asian Faith and Order meeting. It was commented that the Asian churchmen reached quite promptly a genuine consensus and adopted such important statements without having to go through long drawn-out debates, unlike what could have been the case for churchpersons of the western world.

My purpose in quoting at length and reproducing the selections of these statements is to challenge the present generation of CCA members to launch focused and sustained efforts to follow up the work that was begun and to seek to embody concretely the insights of those earlier leaders, with the intention in each national situation in this continent to go beyond conciliar cooperation to manifestation of a gathered community, in the form of a church organically united in its fellowship, witness and service. As Hong Kong itself said it was a route-map which has been plotted so that Hong Kong can represent only a beginning. From it must flow a richer life together for the churches in Asia.

Third, EACC (CCA) was concerned from the beginning with the development of a strategic missionary approach to a whole continent. Instead of piecemeal initiatives planned according to the vision and resources of a given denomination, the intended approach would consider the place and role of the initiative concerned if it contributes to the realization of that larger strategy. The Christian community in a given country in joint action with those in the neighboring nations, or as a church with perspective of its witness and service for the whole continent may seek to demonstrate in word and deeds of love the wholeness of Christ's purpose for humankind. As I stated earlier regarding the reconfiguration of the ecumenical movement, some of the millennium development goals of the UN as adopted in September 2000 may be relevant as examples in terms of the kind of approach mentioned above. I refer here only to the first and seventh of the eight goals listed viz. eradication of extreme hunger and poverty and ensuring environmental sustainability.

In the pursuit of these efforts, may the Lord of the Church grant us, members of the churches in Asia, to recover that first love with which the early church was blessed to be the instrument and token of His salvation to the peoples among whom she was placed. May the believing communities in our continent be His gathered people bringing in our time the good news of Christ who gave His life for the redemption of the world.

Bibliography

EACC *Confessing the Faith in Asia Today,* (Redfern NSW 1967)
John.C. England, *The Hidden History of Christianity in Asia* by (ISPCK New Delhi 1996)
Ninan Koshy, *A History of the Ecumenical Movement in Asia*, Vol. I (Hong Kong 2004)
S.H. Moffett, *A History of Christianity in Asia*, Vol. I. by (New York 1992)
Rienzi Pereira, Is Ecumenism valid for our times?, digitally published in:
http://www.cca.org.hk/resource/ctc/ctc-xxv-1-2/1-10_rienzie_perera.pdf

Kyaw Than, *The Common Evangelistic Task of the Churches in E. Asia* (Ed.) (Rangoon 1957)
Kyaw Than, *Witnesses Together* (Ed.) (Rangoon 1959)
Hans Ruedi Weber, *Asia and the Ecumenical Movement*, (SCM London 1966)

(3) ASIAN ECUMENISM AFTER EDINBURGH 1910

O.L. Snaitang

Introduction

As the historic Edinburgh World Missionary Conference 1910[1] has had its numerous centennial celebrations worldwide and as the reflections even after 2010 are going on, it is apt that another bout of recollecting and rethinking on its impact is seen as important, necessary and relevant to lend credence to a re-examination on "Ecumenism After Edinburgh, 1910." Many scholarly documents, studies and presentations have come up during the centennial celebrations and as the ecumenical movement is a dynamic and forward movement, the intense appetite for further reflections from different sections in the Church and society has until today received materials that might lead to a certain level of academic satisfaction. The more those studies have been done on the subject the more the search for further contribution is on. That is the beauty of modern ecumenical movement studies especially in the Asian context. The aim of this essay is to trace the development of ecumenism after the Edinburgh World Missionary Conference, 1910. This study is done on the assumption that Edinburgh is not only the main source for the rise of the modern ecumenical movement globally but served as a participatory inspiration to the local or regional ecumenical aspirations.

World Missionary Conference, Edinburgh, 1910: Background

(a) Background of the WMC, 1910

The World Missionary Conference, Edinburgh 1910 had grown in the vicissitudes of the growing pietistic developments in Germany, the rise of evangelical spiritual student movements both in the U. S. and the U.K, revival movement, evangelical awakening, missionary movement and more importantly European imperialism in the 18th and 19th centuries. Leaders of most of these movements, like John R. Mott and other ecumenical statesmen have put up their strong united efforts for the creation of a unified missionary body. It was they who were instrumental in bringing together Western Christian missionaries, administrative leaders in home missionary boards, native Christians and leading Christian organizations to a common gathering in Edinburgh in 1910. Its primary intended ecumenical or interdenominational objective was that unity was for world evangelization. In other words, the initial commitment of the ecumenical leaders was their affirmation that the Gospel of Jesus Christ should reach to every creature. They saw it not just as a necessity but equally as an urgency. Therefore, the World Missionary Conference, Edinburgh 1910 was initially conceived as ecumenical in the womb of missionary vision and mission.

The World Missionary Conference that met on 14th – 23rd June 1910 was a widely represented Conference. Its significance was that the Conference was an officially recognized conference. Delegates did not attend it out of their own interests but were deputed officially by their respective missionary boards or churches. The Edinburgh, 1910 dwelt seriously on the programme of planning for successful evangelization of the world in this generation. Their togetherness and united struggles were well expressed

---

[1] For more information, see K. S. Latourette, "Ecumenical Bearings of the Missionary Movement and the International Missionary Council" in R. Rouse and S. C. Neil, eds, *A History of the Ecumenical Movement 1517 – 1948* (1954), pp. 355- 402. Cf. T.V. Philip, *Edinburgh to Salvador Twentieth Century Ecumenical Missiology: A Historical Study of the Ecumenical Discussions on Mission* (1994), pp. 26 – 29.

in daily worship services, group discussions in addition to their deliberations in business sessions. The main theme of their discussion was that the task of uniting is urgent for world evangelization – a task of fulfilling Christ's Great Commission. Given their serious concentration on the utmost importance of immediate evangelization of the non-Christian world, the conference appeared to have passed over certain theological issues that were implicit in several Protestant Churches. Their unanimous agreement on the supremacy of the Bible, salvation through Jesus Christ, the urgency of evangelization and commitment to reach the Gospel to the unreached and unevangelized world could have been the reasons that had generated consensual convergence on the feasibility of ecumenical cooperation and interdenominational operation even in the midst of theological divergences.

(b) Ecumenical enthusiasm

The importance of the Edinburgh 1910 was well evident in its policy of maintaining a consultative spirit with different missionary societies or boards in their united and common tasks for achieving the desired and intended missiological targets.[2] The main topics of the Conference were evangelistic, educational, theological Gospel to the non-Christian religions, preparation of missionary operation and unity. These ambitious and evangelical topics were practically appealing and served as attracting messages to the Western world.

The influence of the Conference was such that it subsequently led to the creation of a sense of global ecclesiastical oneness among churches of Protestant traditions, different nationalities and cultural systems. The Anglo-Catholic communion too which had never shown interest in ecumenical gatherings in the past had now changed its mind and took serious interest by being actively involved in the Conference. The Edinburgh ecumenical gathering received significant inspiration by their involvement and cooperation.

Ecumenical enthusiasm was also witnessed in the participation of delegates from the non-Western world and Asia in particular. There were seventeen of such representatives who attended the Conference officially. Rev. V. S. Azariah from India was an example of a delegate that represented the younger churches in India.[3] The openness of the conference was evident in giving him a chance to address the Conference in which he focused on areas relating to equality between the missionaries and native converts besides expressing his gratitude for the sacrifices of Western missionaries. The seriousness of the Conference was also evident in the setting up of the Continuation Committee. John R. Mott was appointed as its chairman and Joseph H. Oldham as Secretary. Their active role in the process provided the needed continuous leadership in the ecumenical building process and had the consequence of leading it in a stable manner.

The Conference appeared to have devoted its focus to mission and simply ignored serious discussion on doctrinal issues. It also did not give attention to the debate on concepts of mission. It might not be an exaggeration to say that the Edinburgh Conference, 1910 was a missionary conference of Western missions by majority of Western missionaries and for the Western interests with the support of most selected native delegates, of course! It was informed that following the Conference, the pioneer ecumenical statesman, John R. Mott made his personal visits to Asia, Africa and Europe with the objective of implementing the visions of the Edinburgh conference in areas of organizing national councils and promotion of cooperative ecumenism. His visits to countries in Asia took place from 1912 to 1913. The tour had produced positive results as national councils were formed in most countries in places that he had visited like India, China, Japan, Burma (Myanmar) and others in addition to countries in Africa, Europe and North America alike. The venture facilitated a closer international network of ecumenical co-operation. John R. Mott's

---

[2] Read W. R. Hogg, *Ecumenical Foundations: A History of the IMC and Its 19th Century Background* (1952).

[3] V. S. Azariah's Address to the World Missionary Conference, Edinburgh, 1910, see M. K. Kuriakose, ed., *History of Christianity in India: Source Materials* (1982), pp. 303-308.

colleague, Joseph H Oldham too joined in the strengthening of the movement by taking the lead in the publication of the **International Review of Mission** in 1912. Though these activities were no doubt encouraging their dynamic mission appeared to have carried certain elements of imperialistic implication.

A Continued Committee that was Emergent[4]

But for the role of the Continuation Committee and the Emergency Committee, the subsequent impact of the Edinburgh 1910 conference would have been slow and insignificant. The Continuation Committee kept the Edinburgh ecumenical tempo moving. The leaders' vision in promoting interdenominational contacts worldwide made the Churches and Mission Societies active in promoting ecumenical understanding and creating a sense of unity even in the midst of diversity. The contribution of its journal that had served as a mouth piece was also noteworthy.

The influential role of the forward movement was greatly disturbed and almost brought to a standstill by the explosion of World War I. German Protestant representatives could no longer attend the committee meetings of the Continuation Committee because of the War. The role of Joseph Oldham, John R. Mott, Soderblom and others during this critical period was well acknowledged because of their tenacity in keeping the ecumenical vision alive and active. This led to the formation of the Emergency Committee in 1918 – a Committee that implemented its ecumenical vision even without the representation of members from Germany.

It was also reported that through the help of the Emergency Committee, the deed that was known as the Versailles Treaty's Article 438 was concluded in which the German missions were protected for their being dispossessed. The Committee served as a reconciling agent in the midst of a fluid relationship between allies of warring countries in the West. Help was also extended to most German deserted mission fields in Africa, India and the Pacific islands. In this manner, the wounds of the War in the process received a healing touch and the almost perpetual disconnection was bridged.

Progresses and Challenges in the International Missionary Council[5]

(a) Formation of the Council and its progress

The continuous efforts of the Continuation and the Emergency Committees had in the end contributed to the successful creation of the International Missionary Council (IMC) at Lake Mohonk in the U. S. in 1921. This successful venture had the consequence of institutionalizing the movement. The formation of the Council also confirmed its ecumenical shift from a movement of mission societies to an organization of church leaders. Ever since its formation, the IMC held several meetings in Asia, Africa and in the Western world. In several ways, the IMC translated its vision in a progressive manner. It attended to most- asked missionary questions, inspired national missionary councils in different nations through consultations, meetings and in making these national councils responded to national issues that touched upon freedom of faith, missionary liberty and areas of seeking justice and equality. Its vision was also to reach the desired objective of raising indigenous churches in addition to fighting against racism and other social questions such as the use of opium.

The IMC held successful meetings at Jerusalem in 1928, Tambaram, India in 1938, Whitby in Canada in 1947, Willingen, Germany in 1952 and Accra in Ghana in 1957. Finally, the IMC merged with the World Council of Churches (WCC) in New Delhi Assembly in 1961. In all these conferences, the IMC has passed

---

[4] Cf. O. L. Snaitang, *A History of Ecumenical Movement: An Introduction* (2004), pp. 106f.

[5] For further information, Cf. W. R. Hogg, *Ecumenical Foundations: A History of the IMC and Its 19th Century Background* (1952), K. S. Latourette, *Op. Cit.*, pp. 355ff.

through changes that in the end proved itself true of its perfect humanity of changing, adapting and submerging even under undue pressures.

(b). Challenges from the Jerusalem Conference

The first challenge that had come from the Jerusalem IMC, 1928 was with regard to the distinction between the older and the younger churches. The issue appeared to have harped on the relationship between the western mission societies and the younger churches in the mission fields. Most representatives from the non-western world, like Cheng Ching-Yi of China desired equal partnership and sought a church-to-church connection or relationship.

Secondly, the missionary spirit that was espoused in Edinburgh.1910, tended to have received a jolt at the Jerusalem Conference following its re-evaluation of the situation in the western world. Its message was that religions should unite and stand together in fighting against a secular, materialistic and non-religious life style that had dominated the Western societies. The Conference no longer saw any problem in adopting what one might call a syncretistic form of mission. Closely related to this paradigm shift in Christian mission, was the emphasis that was given to the social aspects of Christian mission. Its eyes were now open towards the social problems that mostly became apparent in Western societies like the growing rise of the use of narcotics, problems of migrant workers, as well as forced and child labour in industrial sectors.

Though the Tambaram Conference, 1938 underscored the Barthian revealed theology it nevertheless laid emphasis on the centrality of the church rather than on mission. Both the West and the non-Western world required the Church's evangelistic mission. Besides that, there was a call for the indigenization of the Gospel and adoption of a positive approach and attitude towards other religious faiths.

In the context of missiological changes that had taken place in the previous Conferences, what had turned the Christian mission understanding upside down was the rediscovery and reinterpretation of *missio dei* at the Willingen Conference, 1952. The reinterpretation and rediscovery then paved the way for getting rid of the theological problem that pertains to mission. The explanation was that the mission of God or *Missio Dei* deals directly with the world and the Church does not deserve special claim of being the only channel of God's mission rather a privileged instrument of 'God's mission of redemption and the recreation of humanity and the cosmos.' While this reinterpretation has revolutionized the ancient Trinitarian theological position, it also brought the concept that mission and church cannot be separated. In other words, the church and mission are closely intertwined and united.

As a result of this reinterpretation and understanding, the IMC was merged and integrated with the WCC in New Delhi Assembly in 1961. This merger brought about another breakthrough in the history of the ecumenical movement. But from the perspective of the Lausanne Congress on World Evangelization (LCWE), 1974, this development resulted in giving birth to the Evangelical and the Ecumenical streams of the modern ecumenical movement. So, the IMC became one of the departments of the WCC known as the Division of World Mission and Evangelism. However,in the eyes of the evangelical Christians, the change from a World Mission to a department represented a 'demise in mission.'[6]

[6] R. E. Hedlund, *Roots of the Great Debate on Mission* (1993), p. 155.

Missionary Influence that Gave Birth to a World Church Body

(a) Life and Work Movement:[7]

The impact of the Edinburgh Conference was also evident in the rise of the Life and Work and Faith and Order Movements. Though a search for interdenominational Christian cooperation in order to help the poor and the needy had begun in Germany in the 19th century, it was the Edinburgh Conference that had direct influence on Bishop Nathan Soderblom of Sweden to seek ecumenical support for life and work. After much discussion and deliberation, the Life and Work Movement could hold its first conference in Stockholm in August 19 – 29, 1925. The movement received support from the Patriarchs of Alexandria and Jerusalem and members from the Orthodox Church. Bishop William Temple and several ecclesiastical leaders in Great Britain too extended their substantive support through their cooperation and participation in the movement. In their opinion, Churches have a greater responsibility in serving the poor, victims of war and the unfortunate in addition to promoting peace in a broken and divided world. Churches' positive response and cooperation in the movement was a fulfillment of the much oft quoted slogan: 'service unites, doctrine divides.'

The movement could devote to the task of Christian service. It was successful in finding out ways and means of promoting wider Christian unity for service that subsequently led to bringing together different churches to a common platform in the interest of rendering help and relief to unfortunate people because of the war. It also worked in the area of developing an international law that would curb the rise of world conflicts and war.

The second conference of the movement was held at Oxford on 12-16 July 1937 and discussed the said subjects in a serious manner but finally approved the proposal for integration along with the Faith and Order movement toward the formation of a world unified ecumenical body, the World Council of Churches. Following this decision, the movement's meeting at Utrecht on 13 May 1938 processed all official proceedings and transferred all duties and functions to the new Provisional Committee of the anticipated formation of the WCC.

(b) Faith and Order Movement:[8]

The World Missionary Conference, Edinburgh 1910 sent out its successful message to the world. Though it was able to take up mission issues in right earnest it however passed over discussion on the theological questions. Bishop Charles Brendt of the Protestant Episcopal Church in the United States who attended the Edinburgh Conference and admired its ecumenical success was however dissatisfied because the Conference could not take up the problem of theological differences in different churches.

The Protestant Episcopal Church in the United States extended support to Bishop Brendt's initiative. Under his leadership, a preliminary meeting for the World Conference was held in Geneva during 12th – 20th August 1920 in which representatives from as many as 70 churches from 40 nations had turned up. While the Orthodox Church responded positively to the faith and order movement, the Roman Catholic Church was not in a position to send a positive note. Following this meeting, the First World Conference on Faith and Order was held at Lausanne, Switzerland in August 1927 in which 385 delegates, mostly deputed officially, from 108 churches around the world participated in.

Most of the theological issues that were taken up at the Lausanne Conference included the call to Christian unity; the message of the church to the world; nature of the church; common confession of faith;

---

[7] See Nils Karlstrom, "Movements for International Friendship and Life and Work 1910-1925" in R. Ruth and S. C. Neil, *Op. Cit.*, pp. 509 -542.

[8] Cf. T. Tatlow, "The World Conference on Faith and Order" in R. Rouse and S. C. Neil, pp.405- 441. See also Alan Falconer, ed., *Faith and Order in Moshi* (1998).

ministry, the sacraments and above all Christian unity. Its success was such that despite theological differences that had torn the Christian world apart, church leaders could come together to discuss and dialogue even on issues of theological differences. Its duty was to serve as an agent of churches in the preparatory work of discussing areas that remained as obstacles to reunion. It also worked in clearing misunderstanding among churches on sensitive theological issues. As its objective was not to formulate guidelines and dictate terms to churches, the movement engaged in preparing reports out of its meetings to be sent to churches for consideration and further suggestion.

Though the Faith and Order Movement was mostly of Western Churches and Western representatives, there was however a slight and shadowy Asian presence in it. An Asian representative by the name Joseph S. Notoda attended the preliminary meeting that was held in Geneva in 1920 but his silence did not produce any significant impact. Others who have made it to the movement and were inducted as members of the Continuation Committee were P. L. Chang, Joseph K. Oohiai and S. K. Datta.

V. S. Azariah was one of four Asian representatives at Lausanne, 1927. His presence was greatly felt through his expression saying that ecclesiastical disunity especially in Asia is a sin in addition to its being a hurdle to mission and evangelization. In the Edinburgh Faith and Order Conference, 1937 there were 13 Asian representatives whose presence had contributed to its universal progress. Even in the midst of Western domination in the theological meeting, the decision that resulted in the inclusion of D. T. Niles in the Faith and Order Executive Committee in 1947 was no doubt a significant regional breakthrough. He was the first Asian representative at that level.

Asian representatives in this world body took active part in meetings through meaningful discussions and speeches. It was they who mostly expressed that Christian division was a visible sin in Christian mission. They also underscored the importance of Christian unity, equality between younger churches and older churches in the West and friendship in international Christian relations.

Like the World Missionary Conference and the Life and Work Movement, the Faith and Order Movement too had achieved in bringing churches together in committees, consultations and conferences. It contributed towards the breaking down of the state of isolation. Members from different confessions and traditions who existed almost completely apart from one another for a long period of time, could now meet, stay, worship and discuss together numerous theological issues. The movement had the effect of promoting a sense of unity and solidarity. Each discovered the value of the other's traditions and learnt to respect one another. It could draw to its movement, churches that were not members of the WCC, like the Roman Catholics and others.

(c) The World Council of Churches, 1948:[9]

Finally, when both the Life and Work and the Faith and Order Movements decided to merge together, that decision resulted in the initial formation of the World Council of Churches in 1938. This historic ecumenical venture was able to move on despite tremendous disruption of World War II. Following the war, the WCC was inaugurated at Amsterdam in August 22, 1948. This world church body was in due course further widened by the merger of the International Missionary council in 1961 and the World Council of Christian Education (WCCE) in 1971. Around 147 churches of Protestant traditions from 44 nations appeared to have taken part in it. Though at its formation the WCC could set up 12 departments, like the Faith and Order, Evangelism, Study, Laity, Youth, Women, Ecumenical Institute, International Affairs, Inter-church Aid/Refugees, Publications, Library and Finance it nevertheless designed itself in a flexible manner that the organizational structure of the WCC could be adapted, expanded and modified

[9] W.A Visser't Hooft, *The Genesis and Formation of the World Council of Churches* (1982). Cf. M. VanElderen, *Introducing the World Council of Churches* (1990) and also from an Asian information M. M. Thomas, *My Ecumenical Journey 1947 – 1975* (1990), pp. 301ff.

after a collective study and evaluation. Hence in less than seven years of its existence, the WCC reorganized its structure under four divisions like 1) Studies – Faith and Order; Church and Society; Evangelism and Missionary Studies, 2) Ecumenical Action – Youth; Laity; Men and Women in Church and Society; Ecumenical Institute, 3) Inter-church Aid/Refugees and International Affairs, and 4) Information. Its Programme Units viz., Faith and Witness; Justice and Service; and Education and Renewal featured prominently in its activities.

The office headquarters at Geneva provided a convenient occasion for member churches and other world bodies. Over and above its broad-based activities that affected not only the affairs of churches, the WCC could explore possibilities of reaching out to different religious traditions of the world, communities, ideologies and numerous other areas. The role of its Assembly was also noteworthy. It normally meets once in seven years. Members who attended the WCC Assembly could express one's vision and feelings and in a way its major contribution was in fostering international cooperation and making the WCC alive and active.

Evangelical Movement and Its Response to the WCC

The rise of the Modern Missionary Movement [10] might well have been attributed to the influence of the evangelical, revival and students' interdenominational movements. As we are aware, the World Missionary Conference, 1910 and the IMC had grown up in the vicissitudes of the Pietistic movement, Evangelical revival upsurge, inter-denominational movements, world missionary adventure and colonial expansion and domination. It was mostly with the objective of world evangelization that the ecumenical discussion at the historic World Missionary Conference, 1910, was shaped and influenced by.John R Mott and other ecumenical leaders were ecumenists with profound evangelical convictions. However, one should not pass over the colonial influence in the evangelical world mission enterprise at that time. Though a full description of this aspect is necessary, given the limited scope of this essay, it will be sufficient to understand the intensity of colonial laden implication as words like the "unevangelized," the "unreached," the "non-Christian world" or the "unfinished task" that appeared in most of the IMC discussions which were highly judgmental.

As a reiteration, the success that led to the formation of the WCC in 1948 was counted as the greatest breakthrough in the history of global Christianity. By contrast, however, the evangelicals who tended to contemplate that the WCC line of thinking could have turned out beyond the Biblical conviction appeared to have not been in agreement with it.[11] As a consequence, their move witnessed the creation of the World Evangelical Fellowship (WEF) in 1951.[12] Some of the main reasons why this body was formed was the fear lest the Word of God is no more accepted as supreme, inspired and infallible authority and that belief in universal salvation would lead to syncretism and the inclusion of people of other faiths in interfaith dialogue would be lowering down of the missionary spirit would endanger world evangelization and church growth.[13]

---

[10] Read J. Herbert Kane, *A Global View of Christian Missions* (1975); Stephen Neil, *A History of Christian Missions*; K. S. Latourette, *A History of Christianity: The Great Century* Vols. 4 & 5 (1971); David J. Bosh, *Transforming Mission: Paradigm Shift in Theology of Mission* (1991), S. B. Bevans, R. P. Schroeder, *Constants in Context: A Theology of Mission for Today* (2004).

[11] See Robert E. Webber, *The Church in the World: Opposition, Tension or Transformation? (*1986), pp. 169ff.

[12] A comprehensive history of the World Evangelical Fellowship may be referred to David M. Howard, *The Dream That Would Not Die: The Birth and Growth of the World Evangelical Fellowship 1846-1986* (1986). Cf. William W. Wells, *Ibid.*, pp. 239f.

[13] An evangelical position on the development may be found in Ralph D. Winter, ed., *The Evangelical Response to Bangkok* (1973).

What had further bolstered the evangelical movement was the accession (integration) of the IMC with the WCC at the New Delhi Assembly in 1961. Most evangelical leaders were disappointed by this development and regarded it as a setback to mission and evangelism. Some of them called this merger as the "demise" of evangelism.[14] In order to keep their movement alive, the evangelicals conducted international conferences in Wheaton Congress, 1966, Berlin in December 1966 and at Green Lake in 1971. Other international gatherings were also held in Lausanne, 1974; Pattaya, 1980; Edinburgh, 1980; Wheaton, 1983; Manila 1989 and in several other countries. These conferences made concerted efforts to maintain Scriptural supremacy, uniqueness of Jesus Christ, the importance of mission and evangelism and to garner inter-denominational support and co-operation.[15]

Though it is rather unfortunate that the Christian movement continues to produce divergent opinions and movements even in the context of ecumenical unity and solidarity this still reflects people's maturity in ecumenical thinking.

Union of Episcopal and non-Episcopal Communions

Another significant impact of the Edinburgh Conference was the development that led to the union of Episcopal and non-Episcopal churches in India.

Experiences in the mission fields have made the missionaries develop a sense of uneasiness on their differences. Inter-mission co-operation, union institutions and confessional union in south India had come up well before the creation of the South India United Church in 1908. The rise of union institutions like Madras Christian College (1887); the Christian Medical College and Hospital, Vellore; the United Theological College, Bangalore (1910) and many others had contributed to inter-denominational co-operation. It was in the midst of these developments that the impact of the Edinburgh Conference, 1910 resulted in the setting up of the National Missionary Council in India in 1914 and the NCCI later, which remains a historic ecumenical milestone.

Churches that belonged to Calvinistic, Episcopal and Revival traditions merged together and formed the Church of South India (CSI) in 1947. [16] These three traditions had their origins in the West. Their theological differences, independent administrations, ecclesiastical mudslinging in their own countries have successfully been transported to India. Now, following the influence and impact of the Edinburgh, 1910 the formation of the CSI was an ecumenical miracle in the history of world Christianity because of the victory in the union of episcopal and non-episcopal communions.

Another major ecumenical success was the development that finally led to the formation of the Church of North India (CNI) in 1970.[17] The search for union of churches in the North that had started much before the Edinburgh Conference, 1910 received a boost by the impact of the World Missionary Conference, 1910 and through the formation of the Church of South India. In North India too one witnessed the merger of both Episcopal and non-Episcopal communions.

---

[14] Cf. Harvey T. Hoekstra, *The World Council of Churches and the Demise of Evangelism* (1979), Chaps. 2 & 3. See also Roger E. Hedlund, *Roots of the Great Debate on Mission* (1993), p. 155.

[15] Donald McGavran, ed., *The Conciliar – Evangelical Debate: The Crucial Documents, 1964 – 1976* (1977).

[16] For detail information, see Benkt Sundkler, *Church of South India* (1964); K.M George, *Church of South India Life in Union 1947-1997* (1999).

[17] D. K. Sahu, *United & Uniting: A History of the Church North India* (2001)

The Joint Council and Communion of Churches in India [18]

The post-Edinburgh 1910, influence on the Indian ecumenical venture appeared to have infiltrated the inner circle of the mainline churches also. The negotiation that resulted in the formation of a joint theological commission by the CSI, the CNI and the Malankara Mar Thoma Syrian Church in 1973 was an ecumenical initiative on the right path. The reason why it called for such positive comment was because its objective was for bringing together these three divergent traditions to a common platform, co-operation and union. Subsequently, the initiative led to the creation of the Joint Council of the Church of North India, the Church of South India and the Malankara Mar Thoma Syrian Church in 1978. The stated Preamble which reads "The Joint Council of the CNI, CSI, MTC, has been constituted as the visible origin for common action by the three churches which recognize themselves as belonging to the one church of Jesus Christ in India, even while remaining as autonomous churches, each having its own identity of traditions and organization structure" is sufficient to unearth its inner urge and commitment.

The success of the Joint Council (JC) was well evident in their commitment to recognize and to accept each other as fellow members of the Body of Christ. This commitment facilitated all three to enter upon mutual fellowship and negotiation. It also enabled the publication of a common order of worship which included the liturgies of all the three traditions. In it the Heads of the churches are mentioned and prayed for in the worship services. More importantly, however, was the serious contemplation and proposal to forge a common name "the Bharat Christian Church" – a united name in diversity.

The plan for union was always there in the minds of the leaders of the JC. Though the goal to achieve the "Bharat Christian Church" had not been taken up in the JC's ecumenical agenda the official members of the CSI, the Mar Thoma Church and the CNI who met again in Kocin, Kerala in March 2004 moved ahead by pledging their commitment to unity and so formed the Communion of Churches in India (CCI).

The Eastern Churches and the Ecumenical Movement[19]

Churches of Eastern Traditions too which could have been a by-product of the Edinburgh Conference 1910, responded positively to the modern ecumenical movement and began to officially cooperate with it since 1920. The Ecumenical Patriarch, then the Metropolitan of Thyateria, Germanos, played an active role in the formation of the Faith and Order Movement in 1920. He deputed official delegates to the preliminary meeting on Faith and Order, which was held in Geneva in 1920. Although the Russian Orthodox Church and some others did not respond favourably to this ecumenical progressive, most of the Churches of the Eastern Traditions continued their involvement in the ecumenical meetings even after major changes following the merger of the Life and Work and the Faith and Order Movements.

Later, after years of the WCC's continued efforts and negotiation, the Russian Orthodox Church too changed its negative stand and cooperated with the modern ecumenical movement. The outcome from the meeting with the Russian Orthodox Church at Utrecht in 1958 was fruitful, constructive and creative in a way that led to the clearance of misunderstandings and doubts. Following the successful visit of the WCC officials to the Moscow Patriarchate in December 1959 the Russian Orthodox Church and other Eastern Churches, entered the WCC in 1961 as full members.

---

[18] Cf. *The Joint Council of CNI, CSI, Marthoma Church* (1981).

[19] V. T. Istavridis, "The Orthodox Churches in the Ecumenical Movement 1948 – 1968" in Harold E. Fey, *The Ecumenical Advance: A History of the Ecumenical Movement 1948 – 1968* Vol. II (1970), pp. 287ff.

Changing Catholic Attitude Towards the Ecumenical Movement

The Catholic attitude to churches of Protestant persuasions and the modern ecumenical movement before the second Vatican Council was at best very negative. It used to regard itself as the "only ark of salvation" and outside the Catholic Church there was no salvation. Protestants and other Christian groups were looked down upon as "strayed sheep", "backsliders", "schismatic" or "separated brethren". Based on this fixed perception, the Catholic Church regarded any initiative for Christian unity only on one condition and that was a return or surrender to its divine fold. It was with this preconceived understanding that the Church did not see any profit in attending the Edinburgh conference 1910. However, though their response to the invitation to the Edinburgh World Missionary Conference was not favourable the ecumenical spirit played its role to shape and change their once hardened hearts. Upon the election of Pope John XXIII in 1958 to the highest Papal office, the Catholic Church's negative attitude to the ecumenical movement and non-Catholic churches was changed into a positive environment. Non-Catholic Christians were henceforth regarded as partners or brethren that could enter into dialogue and collaboration.

Under his leadership, Pope John XXIII surprised the whole Christian world by making his announcement on 25th January, 1959 for convening the Second Ecumenical Vatican Council in 1961.[20] He established the Secretariat for Promoting Christian Unity in May 17th 1959. This newly established office played a constructive role in fostering and fulfilling ecumenical understanding. As a result of this venture, the Catholic Church sent two observers to the meeting of the Faith and Order Commission and of the WCC Central Committee meeting in 1960 and more importantly to the Third WCC Assembly in New Delhi in 1961. The promulgation of the Decree on Ecumenism made the Church to realize and accept that the triune God is working in churches and communities beyond its boundaries. Then, another positive ecumenical development was the creation of the Joint Working Group (JWG) in 1965 for the advancement of Christian unity and ecumenical cooperation. The JWG was composed of six official representatives from the Catholic Church and eight from the WCC. This closer cooperation and participation was further bolstered by the personal visit of Pope Paul VI to the WCC Office in Geneva in 1969. The positive result was seen not only in its relationship with the world ecumenical body but in its dialogue with different Protestant confessional bodies and national councils including continental Christian councils or conferences.

Modern Ecumenism Inspired Confessional Bodies[21]

The 16th century reformation could well be regarded as the mother of confessional identities. These denominational societies grew, expanded and spread to other areas in the world. The emergence of the ecumenical Christian body appeared to have immersed denominational churches but the fact remains that the more Christian leaders were ecumenical the more they become denominationally conscious. As of the recent past and even today, confessional bodies are more important than the world ecumenical body. For instance, the World Council of Churches is just a federal or conciliar body of churches. Because it does not have legislative, executive, administrative or judicial powers on the member churches, the confessional bodies have become more important in ecclesiastical affairs. That is the reason why if the Catholic Church wants to engage in any serious dialogue on ecclesiastical matters it does not go to the WCC, although it actively involves with it, but directly to the respective confessional body.

---

[20] Cf. Austin Flaunery, ed., *Vatican Council II : The Conciliar and the Post Conciliar Documents* (1991), pp. 412 – 509. Also read Lukas Visher, "The Ecumenical Movement and the Roman Catholic Church" in Harold E. Fey, ed., *The Ecumenical Advance* (1970), pp. 311ff.

[21] Cf. R. Rouse, "Other Aspects of the Ecumenical Movement 1910 – 1948" in R. Rouse and S. C. Neil, pp. 613ff. See O. L. Snaitang, *Op. Cit.*, pp. 176ff.

(a) The World Alliance of Reformed Churches (WARC)

Though the Reformed and the Congregationalists hailed from the same confessional family, in the 19th century they functioned independently. While the Alliance of Reformed Churches was formed in 1875, the International Congregational Council was organized in 1891. Following the significant impact of the modern ecumenical movement in the 20th century, these two independent bodies experienced losses than gains in the globalized ecumenical world. In my assessment, their participation and investment in the ecumenical movement had made them realize the importance of preserving their identity and role in other parts of the world. Their independent existence would help neither their traditions nor the ecumenical body. So, given the realization of their common heritage, they merged together and formed the World Alliance of Reformed Churches (WARC) in 1970 (today called "World Communion of Reformed Churches", WCRC). Ecumenism thus gave inspiration to a renewed confessionalism.

(b) The Baptist World Alliance

As a result of the rising impact of the Church's missionary movement worldwide, the Baptists saw the need of forming an international alliance. This vision gradually led to the formation of the Baptist World Alliance in London in 1905. One of the main objectives in its formation was mostly in strengthening its world's mission. Its activities were seen in international aid, evangelization, educational mission, communications and promotion of young people in different areas of involvement. It is six regional organizations that made up the BWA, viz., the All African Baptist Fellowship, Asian Baptist Federation, Caribbean Baptist Fellowship, European Baptist Federation, North American Baptist Fellowship and Union of Baptists of Latin America. Because of the influence of the missionary spirit, most Baptist leaders agreed to disagree in areas related to the modern ecumenical movement or the WCC.

The change in the second half of the 20th century made the Baptists see the necessity of engaging in inter-confessional dialogue with the WARC from 1973 onwards, with the Catholic Church from 1984 and with the Lutheran Church from 1986. It is the influence of the modern ecumenical spirit that contributed to a changed attitude among the conservative leaders.

(c) The World Methodist Council (WMC)

The influence of the 20th century modern ecumenical movement on the WMC is by no means insignificant. Though it was founded 1881 under the name the Ecumenical Methodist Conference, it was changed to the World Methodist Council in 1951. It was the growing rise of the ecumenical impact in world Christianity that contributed to the realization of a strong confessional body for significant survival and continued preservation of the Methodist heritage and identity. Its vision was to promote the Methodist distinctive, to facilitate churches of the same origin together in fellowship, co-operation and united service.

The WMC's attitude to the emergence of the modern ecumenical movement was positive. It also approved and pledged its loyalty to the formation of the WCC. Soon after strengthening its own position, the WMC began to have dialogue with the Catholic Church in 1967 and with the Orthodox Church, the Anglican and the confessional bodies like the World Alliance of Reformed Churches and the Lutheran World Federation.

(d) The Lutheran World Federation (LWF)

Formed in 1947, the Lutheran World Federation (LWF) is by far the largest confessional body. Though the Lutherans understood the importance of their distinctive identity and had attempted bringing their unity and solidarity in the nineteenth century that realization was mostly confined to a single country as in the US or in Germany. The sudden rise of the modern ecumenical influence in the 20th century witnessed the formation of the Lutheran World Convention in 1923. Its formation was also attributed to their response to the war victims due to the Second World War.

The Lutherans made a positive response to the rise and formation of the WCC. They also worked in close cooperation with and support of the WCC. The LWF has initiated conversations with the Catholic Church, the Orthodox, the Anglican Church, the Reformed, the Baptist and the Methodist also.

(e) The Disciples Ecumenical Consultative Council (DECC)

The impact of the modern ecumenical movement on the Disciples of Christ was such that although its confessional unity was started in the US in the 19th century it nevertheless gained significant momentum in the 20th century that resulted in the organization of the Disciples Ecumenical Consultative Council (DECC). It was reported that the Disciples of Christ took active part in most interdenominational ventures in the 20th century including the process that led to the formation of the WCC. The DECC encourages inter-denominational and ecumenical relationships and was involved in conversation, dialogue and discussion with the Catholic Church, the Russian Orthodox Church and the WARC.

(f) The Pentecostal World Conference (PWC)

The Churches of Pentecostal persuasion too could not remain isolated from the ecumenical movement. A realization that differences among themselves would neither help them nor serve others especially in the gradual influence of modern ecumenism, prompted their desire to form the Pentecostal World Conference (PWC) and they did so in Zurich, Switzerland in 1947.

Though the Pentecostal Churches did not believe in agreement on any issues related to the ecumenical movement the fact that they were able to form a collective body was a great achievement. While some leaders favored the movement on the WCC line, others looked at it as a symbol of apostasy. Pentecostal churches in Chile and Brazil have, however, become members of the WCC in 1961 and 1969 respectively. David Du Plessis, an important Pentecostal ecumenical figure, who was positive to the modern ecumenical movement, attended and participated in all the WCC Assemblies from Evanston to Vancouver. His ecumenical interests and involvement witnessed cross denominational dialogue and discussion with the Catholic Church and other churches in Finland, the Netherlands and in South Africa.

The rise of the modern ecumenical movement, therefore, had the consequence of inspiring and strengthening confessional fellowships.

Ecumenical Contribution to the Emergence of Continental Conferences

Regional Christian Conferences have a significant role to promote ecumenical awareness and understanding in different regions of the globe. The description here will be of three conferences, viz., Christian Conference of Asia, All Africa Christian Conference and Pacific Conference of Churches.

(a) Christian Conference of Asia (CCA)[22]

While T. V. Philip believed that ecumenism in Asia had its origin from Asian Christians in Asian soil, Hans Reudi Weber attributed it to the Chinese YMCA that convened the Far Eastern Olympic Games in Shanghai in 1921. Though there could have been elements of truth in their arguments history is also proof that progressive Asian Christian participation in the Edinburgh Conference in 1910 was well acknowledged. In other words, ecumenism in Asia grew out of the combination of Asian rejection of Western denominationalism, missionaries' initiatives and the World Missionary Conference, 1910. The influence of John R. Mott's visit to different Asian countries should under no circumstances be slighted.

---

[22] M.M Thomas, *My Ecumenical Journey*, pp. 198ff. cf. T.V. Philip, *Ecumenism in Asia* (1994), pp. 137 – 174. For more information about the ecumenical development in Asia, read N. Koshy, *A History of the Ecumenical Movement in Asia* Vols. I & ed., II (2004 & 2004).

Most national councils in the continent were organized after Mott's visit. The Tambaram IMC in 1938 was instrumental in making Asian leaders see the utmost need of the East Asia Conference. National leaders from China and Japan who had greater passion for a regional section of the IMC, and had even proposed the setting up of the IMC Far Eastern Office at Tambaram, India.

Asian ecumenical leaders' aspiration for a separate Asian Conference was never in vain. The East Asia Christian Conference (EACC) finally came into existence at Parapat in 1957 and was inaugurated in Kuala Lumpur, Malaysia in 1959. Seeing the need of covering the large Asian continent, the name EACC was in due course changed to the Christian Conference of Asia (CCA) in 1973. It is an international conference with an Asian regional outlook. The CCA took up Asian realities as its priorities. While making concerted efforts in promoting ecumenical awareness and understanding in Asia through interdenominational relations, seminars, publication and academic activities, the CCA also took serious note of the challenges of socio-economic, political, linguistic and religious problems. Its cooperation with the Federation of Asian Bishops Conference (FABC) translated its ecumenical vision into reality.

(b) All Africa Conference of Churches

The formation of the All Africa Conference of Churches (AACC) in Ibadan, Nigeria in 1958 was a historic milestone in Asian Christianity. Side by side with the growing emergence of African nationalism and nationhood, it was in most probability the impact of the IMC and the WCC that had generated ecumenical cooperation in Africa. Its office was located in Nairobi in 1965. The activities of the AACC involved both the spiritual and the material. Its spiritual affairs included the stress on the promotion of the African Sunday School Curriculum Project and the Ecumenical Programme for Emergency Action in Africa. It also addressed the socio-political problems in the continent. Its mission in reconciling the warring factions in Sudan in 1972 was well recognized and appreciated.

The AACC was also a constituent part of the World Council of Churches and worked in close cooperation with other ecumenical bodies. Its programmes became evident in rendering inter-Church Aid, helping the refugees and social development through education, employment and self-help programmes, and medical and health service.

(c) Pacific Conference of Churches (PCC)

The idea to form the regional Pacific Conference of Churches was first conceived at the Malua Conference in 1961. It was then formed at the Assembly that was held in Lifou Island in 1966. The setting up of a Pacific Theological College in Suva in 1966 was another development under this ecumenical initiative in addition to the formation of the ecumenical associations of theological schools, viz., the South Pacific Association of Theological Schools (SPATS) for institutions east of Papua New Guinea and the Melanesian Association of Theological Schools (MATS) for institutions in Papua New Guinea and the Solomon Islands. The incorporation of the promotion of the ecumenical Christian education in its jurisdiction was also noteworthy because of the preparation of a Christian educational curriculum based on indigenous experiences. The PCC office is situated at Suva, Fiji.

Cooperation with the Catholics began in full swing after Vatican II. The Catholic Church joined the PCC in 1976. Participation and sharing of resources in theological education had contributed to widening the ecumenical image of the PCC. Other activities included the promotion of women's leadership in church and society, rural development and reconstruction.

The Lima Text on Baptism, Eucharist and Ministry (BEM)[22]

Another important development after Edinburgh 1910, was the ecumenical proposal on baptism, eucharist and ministry (BEM) at Lima in 1982. The BEM or the Lima Text is a united declaration of the WCC Faith and Order Commission that was held at Lima, Peru in January 1982. The Text did not come in a hurried manner. Church leaders had started discussing these three sacramental subjects right from the Lausanne Faith and Order Conference in 1927. It was taken up again in Edinburgh 1937, Lund 1952, and Montreal 1963 and in plenary sessions from Chichester 1949 to Lima 1982. The Lima Text, therefore, was a declaration that had come out of many years of study, consultation and dialogue among the member churches of the WCC and also with substantive input from the Roman Catholic Church. The official representatives of the BEM steering committee were from the Orthodox, Lutheran, Reformed, Methodist, Roman Catholic and Baptist traditions.

Following these long years of reflection, suggestion and discussion the Lima Text comes out as an instrument of ecclesiastical harmony even in the midst of diverse ideologies and rituals. It is also a treasury of unity in diversity. Its importance is well evident in its being able to incorporate numerous diverse elements of member churches including that of the Catholic Church. In the context of a long history of differences, the Lima Text achieved a great amount of understanding, agreement and a peaceful move towards higher levels of organic unity. It sends a strong message to the twenty first century Christianity that theological differences can be sorted out if groups are willing to dialogue even on the thorniest issues of Baptism, Eucharist and Ministry.

Response to People of Other Faiths, Justice and Biodiversity

(a) WCC and People of Other Faiths and Ideologies

Following the reinterpretation of the concept of mission at the Jerusalem meeting in 1928, the subsequent years witnessed a changed attitude that made the WCC leaders now look to other faiths. This changed missiological position had the consequence of creating a sub-unit on Dialogue with People of Living Faiths and Ideologies in 1975. Dr. Stanley J. Samartha was appointed its first director. He led the sub-unit from 1975 to 1981. [23] This was one of the areas that had come from the Asian voices.[at least]omit?

(b) Justice, Peace and the Integrity of Creation (JPIC)[24]

The other areas that the world ecumenical body had identified and worked on have been social issues and biodiversity. Its concern was in respect of the dignity, freedom and general welfare of human beings and for a healthy environment. In order to achieve its objectives, the ecumenical movement came out clearly and openly fighting against powers that engage in violation of human rights and against dehumanization. Its social programmes that envisaged for a just, participatory and sustainable society had received sufficient attention in the WCC Assembly in Nairobi, 1975. Its aim was to make an appropriate response to the oppressive and dehumanized situations through in-depth study and to come out with a unified vision and action for the promotion of a sound and healthy human community.

As the world situation witnessed the increasing rise of poverty, social discrimination, oppression, alienation and injustices, the world ecumenical body took up the question of social justice as a major action plan and a priority. The task of securing justice, peace and development in the society is possible only

---

[22] For a matured response on the BEM Document, read J. Jayakiran Sebastian "Infant Versus Believers' Baptism: Search for Ecumenical Understanding" in Vinod Victor, et. al, eds., *Ecumenism*, (2001), pp. 125 – 131.

[23] Cf. S. J. Samartha, ed., *Living Faiths and the Ecumenical Movement* (1971).

[24] See O. L. Snaitang, pp. 218 – 222.

when there is provision for people's participation. At the same time, it is the people themselves who should get the benefits but not the structural powers.

It is not just human beings that need justice and development but the whole creation too. Given the danger of Mother earth and its environment following deforestation, pollution, depletion of non-renewable resources like oil and minerals and other consuming factors that led to the destruction of the entire ecological system, the WCC in its Bucharest meeting in 1974 dwelt greatly on the subject of sustainability. It is a challenge to the inhuman trends that put humankind and all life systems and their future at risk. While before the Vancouver Assembly, 1983 the WCC looked up to the member churches and national councils to respond and tackle the human made activities that threatened the earth's continued existence and sustainability in the Vancouver Assembly, the ecumenical body realized the need and cooperation of non-member churches and organizations, national and regional institutions also,m to explore ways and means of working together with people of other faiths and belief systems. The Assembly unleashed what was popularly known as justice, peace and the integrity of creation.

Ecumenism and the Victims of Injustices

(a) Women in the ecumenical movement

Though women's participation in the ecumenical movement was far unnoticed in its early period[25] it however received significant attention in subsequent years. Most of the delegates who represented at the first Assembly of the WCC in Amsterdam 1948 were men.[26] Kathleen Bliss, Sarah Chakko and others were outstanding ecumenical leaders who had made the difference in the movement. Bliss' address on *The Service and Status of Women in the Churches* in the first WCC Assembly in 1948 was well accepted as an important contribution and led to the setting up of a permanent commission on the life and work of women in the church. Sarah Chakko[27] too took part in the session of the Assembly and drew its attention by reading a report on the role and status of women from 58 countries in the church which had sent a strong message to the ecumenical bodies. The first half of the 20th century ecumenical history though did not draw attention to the contributing role of women.

The Evanston WCC Assembly in 1954 formed the department on the co-operation of men and women in church and society and appointed Madeleine Barot to head it in the capacity of the first executive secretary. A theological consultation that was held at Herrenalb in 1956 brought about major change in people's outlook in respect to women's equal role in the church and society and especially in the ecumenical body. The WCC Assembly deeply felt that the low representation of women in the church and the ecumenical departments was alarming. The term 'sexism' that was used in and after the Uppsala Assembly in the late 1960s was recognized as both a concept and a system that condoned discrimination of a person by sex and implied oppression.[28]

The UN declaration of 1975 as the International Year for Women had great influence on the ecumenical movement. As a preparation for this designated year, the WCC organized an All-Women's Consultation in

---

[25] Some textbooks on the history of the ecumenical movement, like Ruth Rouse & Stephen C. Neil, eds, *A History of the Ecumenical Movement 1517-1948* Vol. I (1954/1986) and Harold E. Fey, ed., *The Ecumenical Advance: A History of the Ecumenical Movement 1948-1968* Vol. II (1970) and others appeared to have passed over on the part of women in the ecumenical movement.

[26] G. A. Visser't Hooft, *The Genesis of the World Council of Churches* (1982). This book could be regarded as a firsthand account of the WCC,

[27] See M. Kurian, *Sarah Chakko: A Voice of Women in the Ecumenical Movement* (1998).

[28] Contemporary feminist theologians whose writings have shaken the traditional male-dominated theological paradigm appeared to have found representative following in Rosemary Reuther and Elizabeth Fiorenza.

Berlin in 1974 for churches' awareness and action in respect to the empowerment of women. The Berlin impact was seen at the WCC Assembly that was held at Nairobi in 1975 in which one whole plenary session was given to women's concerns. Their importance was also given sufficient reflection in the Assembly's official reports and recommendations. The launching of an ecumenical study programme on "The Community of Women and Men in the Church" under the joint supervision of the Faith and Order and the sub-unit on Women in Church and Society in 1978 and under the leadership of Constance Parvey as a full-time director was an indication of a positive and serious ecumenical response. Her active role had major impact worldwide and contributed to the preparation of the international conference that would be held in Sheffield, England in 1981.[29] The message from the Sheffield Conference to the world was so challenging that the traditional concept of male supremacy and superiority in church and society was questioned.

The Vancouver WCC Assembly in 1983 witnessed a significant participation of women in which 12 women took part as main speakers in major plenary sessions besides leading in worship services and debates as well during the sessions. The changed attitude that had come from both outside and inside the ecumenical body made the WCC declare the years 1988-1998 as the Ecumenical Decade of Churches in Solidarity with Women. [30] The Women's Ecumenical Decade made a fervent plea to member churches, women's associations and action groups, to women and men in general[31] to re-evaluate their attitude to women and to seek change. Churches too worked for equality and sharing of power. Eventually, the Decade was a decade of churches, ecumenical institutions and departments, NGOs, the WCC and all working together in support and solidarity with women. It also desired that the participation of women in church and society at large[32] throughout their history should be total.

The major emphases through the Ecumenical Decade focused on areas that led to women's empowerment: equality in leadership and in the decision-making process; women's issues given priority; ensuring that people's mindset and work places should be free from sexism, racism and classism and churches should make serious commitments and actions in the larger interests of women.

(b) Racism: Program to Combat Racism (PCR)

Following the Uppsala Assembly, 1969 the program to combat racism took off officially in 1969. Though the church did not entertain racism in a Christian community its presence in certain sections of human societies posed a serious threat to humanity. Racism is a concept, a system and a practice that alienates, marginalizes and oppresses human beings on the grounds of sex, colour, race or class. The post-Edinburgh 1910, saw the struggle of the ecumenical body in its fight against racism. J. H. Oldham came out openly condemning this social evil through his writings way back in 1924. The International Missionary Council, Jerusalem in 1928 took up this issue in stronger terms and the WCC Assembly, 1948 not only condemned racism in human society but made a strong plea to churches to fight and stamp it out from society.

The PCR conducted programmes that explained and promulgated the inhuman nature of racism. Its fight became evident in restoring justice, equality and liberty to the unfortunate victims of racial prejudice as it fought for the rights of the aborigines in Australia and against apartheid in South Africa. It also aired its views in favour and support of the minorities in Asia and South America.

---

[29] Constance F. Parvey, ed., *The Community of Men and Women in the Church: The Sheffield Report* (1983).

[30] Cf. Kim Vaiphei, ed., *Feminism: A North East Indian Perspective* (1995), pp. 1-3.

[31] Concerns of women may well be referred to books like by Mercy Oduyoye, *Who Will Role the Stone Away: The Ecumenical Decade of the Churches in Solidarity with Women* (1990) and an article by Priscilla Padolina, "Ecumenical Decade of Churches in Solidarity with Women" in *Dictionary of the Ecumenical Movement* (1991), pp. 339-340.

[32] Cf. Pauline Webb, "Women in the Church and Society" in *Dictionary of the Ecumenical Movement* (1991), pp. 1069 – 1072.

(c) Human rights

Human beings are more important than any well structured institution. The question of human rights comes out prominently in today's world because of certain developments that did not respect its value.

Given its fight against racism, sexism and classism, WCC had become a pioneer in areas of social reforms and liberation in world Christianity at least. Though there is validity in tackling this problem the world ecumenical body should become aware that there are still some people's groups in tribal India and in other parts in third world countries, who could well be called as 'humans without rights'. Groups like the Terao, Monsang, Bru and others in Northeast India, the Cholanayaks in the South and many others in Arunachal Pradesh are among the vulnerable who could well be identified as groups of the endangered level. Their populations, like the Terao in Manipur or the Cholanayak in Kerala have become alarmingly negligible.

The Jarwas of Andaman & Nicobar islands, who are the surviving humans of the ancient past, are now on the verge of extinction. Their population is about 200 in all. This group of people now appeared to have received the best material facilities in terms of food, medicines, clothing and other resources. Given the protection and the kind of service that had been given to the Jarwas, one may tend to remark that the investment is rather late to meet the Jarwas whose survival is mostly at stake today. It may not be wrong to name such people and their situation as 'rights without being human'- because they get sufficient and classified benefits only at a time when their survival and continued existence de facto is already almost bleak!

Admittedly, the WCC had played an integral role in the preparation of the UN draft that resulted in the promulgation of the Universal Declaration of Human Rights in 1940s. It had also seriously addressed this issue right at its inauguration in Amsterdam in 1948 and issued declarations and statements that enabled churches to carry out their commitments and duties against abuses of human rights in different areas and to see that there is respect for the value of human persons.

The WCC made a serious commitment to this agenda and invested greatly in its implementation. It called upon its member churches around the world not just to think and discuss but to act with immediate attention for the restoration of human dignity, legitimate rights and values of individual persons, communities and social groups. Regional and national ecumenical councils and conferences were also instructed to give adequate devotion to it and to take it up urgently by creating human rights commissions.

Concluding Remarks

A survey of the ecumenical development after the Edinburgh 1910, is a survey of the people's vision and concerted efforts in making the missionary council alive and active, the changing missiological understandings in the history of the International Missionary Council, the emergence of the life and work and the faith and order movements that led to the formation of the World Council of Churches, response of the evangelicals to modern ecumenism, contribution to the union of the episcopal and non-episcopal churches in India, positive responses from the Eastern Churches and the Catholic Church during and after the Vatican II, the inspiration that the confessional bodies had received from the modern ecumenical movement, the contribution that resulted in the rise of continental councils or conferences, the promulgation of the Lima Document on Baptism, Eucharist and Ministry, issues and activities that touched upon people of other faiths, justice, peace and the integrity of creation and the WCC's commitment to victims of injustices and human rights. Even if there are areas that this essay was not able to bring out it is sufficient to state how ecumenism after the Edinburgh 1910, has identified and worked in most sectors in the world. In other words, the areas that ecumenism had involved in had reference to both churches, mission societies, theological education, human beings and also non-human aspects in this period.

Bibliography

V. S. Azariah's Address to the World Missionary Conference, Edinburgh, 1910, see M. K. Kuriakose, ed., *History of Christianity in India: Source Materials* (1982), pp. 303-308

Harold E. Fey, *The Ecumenical Advance: A History of the Ecumenical Movement 1948 – 1968* Vol. II (1970)

R. E. Hedlund, *Roots of the Great Debate on Mission* (1993)

David M. Howard, *The Dream That Would Not Die: The Birth and Growth of the World Evangelical Fellowship 1846-1986* (1986).

W. R. Hogg, *Ecumenical Foundations: A History of the IMC and Its 19th Century Background* (1952)

K. S. Latourette, "Ecumenical Bearings of the Missionary Movement and the International Missionary Council" in R. Rouse and S. C. Neil, eds, *A History of the Ecumenical Movement 1517 – 1948* (1954), pp. 355- 402

R. Rouse and S. C. Neil, eds, *A History of the Ecumenical Movement 1517 – 1948* (1954)

D. K. Sahu, *United & Uniting: A History of the Church North India* (2001)

O. L. Snaitang, *A History of Ecumenical Movement: An Introduction* (2004)

M. M. Thomas, *My Ecumenical Journey 1947 – 1975* (1990)

Marlin VanElderen, *Introducing the World Council of Churches* (1990)

W.A Visser't Hooft, *The Genesis and Formation of the World Council of Churches* (1982).

(4) The Rise of Asian Pacific Christianity and Challenges for the Church Universal

Michael Nai-Chiu Poon

This essay assesses Asian Protestant contributions to ecumenism since the Pacific War in the mid 20th century. It identifies some of the structural problems in Protestant approaches, and suggests how these may be overcome. The Pacific Rim, in fact, reveals a fresh understanding of communal life. The essay ends by suggesting ways by which the Asian churches can conduct their life and witness better by connecting with the fundamental structure of life in the Pacific Rim.

Ecumenism amid the Asian Revolution

From the early 20th century, Asian churches have begun to find ways to connect with and learn from one another. Inter-visitations among Asian Christian leaders brought Asian Christians in touch with one another. Student movements, nationalism and war emergencies provided the occasion for Asian leaders to think, speak and act together. Local churches also began to explore ways to give institutional expression in their common faith and witness.[1] The World Missionary Conference held at Tambaram, India in 1938 was a high point. It discussed concrete actions for promoting co-operative Christian efforts in eastern Asia.

It is important to underline that these ecumenical explorations took place amid pressing political and social pressures in Asia. Churches therefore needed to respond to what Indian church leader Rajah Manikam described as "Asian Revolution" in new ways. He said:

> The multitudes which inhabit East Asia are today caught in the terrific maelstrom of a gigantic revolution…. A dynamic and militant communism challenges the Christian Church in most parts of East Asia. Contending crusading forces of revitalized old religions shout their slogans, and engage in violent conflict with Christianity. A great void, a moral vacuum, has been formed by bleak disappointment with life, and consequent despair which finds life empty of meaning…. However, all this darkness and the troubled conditions of life in East Asia offer an unprecedented opportunity to Christian forces. The situation calls for Christian light and Christian witness.

He made clear that the Asian Revolution referred not only to the revolt against western expansion and colonial domination, but also to the fundamental and far-reaching transformations brought about by industrialisation and secularisation in the post Pacific War years.[2]

Asia started to reorganise its societies immediately after the Pacific War in 1945. The Japanese military occupation had set off huge social and political upheavals, and raised the expectations for change among Asian churches and the wider society. Indonesia immediately asserted its independence unilaterally in 1945. Other Asian nations declared their independence soon after. The Bandung Conference in Indonesia in 1955 was a landmark gathering of 'non-aligned' nations against western interests. Asian churches were busy in reconnecting with one another amid a time of hope and uncertainty. The Eastern Asia Christian Conference "The Christian Prospect in Eastern Asia" held in Bangkok in 1949 – soon after the Communist victory in China – was the first occasion where national councils of churches in Asia met after the Pacific War to consider their Christian task on a continental scale. The Conference on 'Theological Education in Southeast Asia' in Bangkok in 1956 paved the way for the formation of the Association of Theological Schools in South East Asia. In March 1957, Protestant church leaders from eleven Asian countries founded

---

[1] Hans-Ruedi Weber, *Asia and the Ecumenical Movement, 1895-1961* (London: SCM Press, 1966), 277-281.

[2] Rajah B. Manikam, *Christianity and the Asian Revolution* (Madras: Diocesan Press, 1955), 3-12.

the East Asia Christian Conference (EACC) – renamed Christian Conference of Asia (CCA) in 1972 – in Prapat, Indonesia. Churches from Burma, Ceylon, India, Indonesia, Japan, Korea, Malaya and Singapore, Pakistan, the Philippines, Taiwan and Thailand participated in the conference. It was the first in a series of regional developments in the post- war global ecumenical movement.

The ecumenical movement was important for western churches and mission societies. It gave them a global forum to explore the manner of their continuing presence in former mission fields and colonies. Transition to local leadership was not merely an administrative matter. Mission agencies would continue to send aids and personnel to churches that had now passed to local hands. There was however a deeper intellectual challenge. Historic churches in the previous heartland of Christianity could no longer claim to be the guardian of universality. Christianity had moved beyond the European mind and experience. Churches worldwide therefore needed to rediscover ways to connect with one another and to express their unity in new ways. In Henry van Dusen's memorable words in 1947, a "world church" came about just in time "to an age destined to survive, or to expire, as one world."[3] The forming of the World Council of Churches, the creation of global confessional families, and the proposal for a *Missio Dei* missiology were largely responses to the new situations in the second half of the 20th century.

Asian churches made impressive intellectual contributions amid this re-ordering of church relationship. Rajah Manikam, D. T. Niles, Shoki Coe and Koyama Kosuke were among the towering Asian church leaders of the day. The results were impressive. The Association of Theological Schools in South East Asia (ATSSEA) – later renamed Association for Theological Education in South East Asia (ATESEA), the South East Asia Graduate School of Theology (SEAGST) consortium and the SEAGST Doctor of Theology programme provided exemplary models of theological education for churches outside the west. In 1963, Situation Conferences were held in Madras (India), Amagisanso (Japan) and Singapore to explore ways that geographically neighbouring churches could come together for "joint action in mission." The ATSSEA academic journal *The South East Asia Journal of Theology* became the main forum of creative theological reflection from the late 1950s to the early 1980s. Indeed, Shoki Coe's contextualising theology was borne out of Asia's ecumenical explorations from the 1950s to the 1970s. It is arguably Asia's lasting theological contribution to world Christianity.[4] In Coe's own words:

> Contextualizing theology takes the concrete local context seriously. It is rooted in a concrete, particular situation. Is there, then, a danger of losing the catholicity of the Gospel? … Catholicity is both a gift and a task. As a gift, we must see how it was given. This was in a very concrete way, by the Word which became flesh and dwelt among us at a particular time and place. I believe, in fact, that the incarnation is the divine form of contextualization, and if this is so, the way we receive this gift is also through our following His way. That is what I mean by contextualization. As the catholicity of the Gospel is given through the Word becoming flesh, so our task should be through our responsive contextualization, taking our own concrete, local contexts seriously…. The true catholicity is a gift which only becomes ours as we draw our basic power from the gospel of the Incarnate Word. True catholicity could not possibly be a colourless uniformity, but must be a rich fullness of truth and grace, which unfolds and manifests itself as we take the diversified contexts in time and space, where we are set, and respond faithfully as the Incarnate Word did on our behalf, once and for all…. Contextuality-contextualization, as our human response, are at most and at best a provisional and fragmentary witness of that divine contextualization of the incarnation. Ours can only be in following in His steps as an ongoing process of the pilgrim people. But in doing so we can accept our relativity with hope and even with joy, as we see in our

---

[3] Henry P. van Dusen, *World Christianity; Yesterday, Today, Tomorrow* (New York,: Abingdon-Cokesbury Press, 1947), 251.

[4] See Michael Poon, "Shoki Coe and the Rise of Asia Pacific Christianity," in Shoki Coe, *Christian Mission And the Test of Discipleship*, ed. Michael Poon (Singapore: Trinity Theological College, 2012); "The History and Development of Theological Education in South East Asia," in *Handbook of Theological Education in World Christianity*, ed. Dietrich Werner and others (Oxford: Regnum, 2010), 375-403.

faithful responses the sign of the divine contextualization unfolding its purpose for the liberation and salvation of mankind.[5]

EACC/CCA became especially an important forum for Asian churches to make a strong case for regional identity and to challenge the continuing dominance of the west in the reordering of world Christianity. For EACC, geographically neighbouring churches should foster closer coordination and joint action for mission and unity with one another, rather than devote their limited and stretched resources in international and denominational programmes. EACC especially devoted its 1961 Bangalore and 1964 Bangkok meetings to discuss this concern. It insisted that churches in every locality should, despite their different [denominational] "names," be identified and identifiable as a people together. They need to devise "structures of belonging in which denominational boundaries are crossed."

> The primary structure through which the churches in Asia found one another across denominational boundaries was that of the National Christian Council.... It is irresponsible to make the existence of confessional families a convenience for proliferating meetings which attach denominational labels where such labels are irrelevant. This is the specific problem of confessionalism – of making an 'ism' out of a legitimate confessional or denominational position. There is an increasing conviction in the Churches in Asia, that those churches which are in the same country or region should find one another and, in that place, live a common life.[6]

EACC also raised questions about centralising tendencies in the World Council of Churches that would continue to put Asian churches under western rule. EACC argued that ecumenical bodies in Asia were not meant to be a frontline "Asian desk," whose primary task was to interpret Asian situations to the international headquarters. The CCA General Secretariat Report in 1977 made this clear:

> [CCA has] a primary responsibility to build up Asian relationships and interpret Asian thinking to Asians.... One of the strengths of the CCA programme has been its relative smallness which gives some flexibility in operation. The fear is felt that if CCA begins to respond to the agendas of other groups outside Asia it will lose some of its indigenous character and consequent effectiveness.[7]

The re-ordering of west-east relationships are not the only concern. Asian churches were finding their feet in newly independent countries. Rightly, each church needed to attend to its particular national situation. They also needed to discover ways to connect to one another. The 1963 Situation Conferences underlined this. M. M. Thomas (EACC Secretary for Church and Society Concerns) made this clear in the 1964 Assembly: "Only national programmes of study can be real and relevant to the Churches at this time of nation-state, national integration and national development.... We should not only have inter-Asian regional conferences, but encourage 'national initiatives' in the study of religion and society."[8]

Clearly, a powerful undercurrent was at work. New Asian nations and churches emerging out of the ruins of the Pacific War were suspicious of any sign of empire building in Asia. After all, Japan justified its

---

[5] Shoki Coe, "In Search of Renewal in Theological Education," *Theological Education* 9, no. 4 (1973): 242-243..

[6] East Asia Christian Conference, "Confessional Families and the Churches in Asia," in *The Christian Community within the Human Community: Containing Statements from the Bangkok Assembly of the EACC Feb.-March 1964: minutes, part 2* (Bangalore: C. L. S. Press, 1964), 72-75. See also the Asian challenge to confessionalism in Weber, *Asia and Ecumenical Movement*, 291; Harold Edward Fey, "Confessional Families and the Ecumenical Movement" in *The Ecumenical Advance: A History of the Ecumenical Movement. Vol. 2 1948-1968*, ed. Harold Edward Fey (Geneva: World Council of Churches, 1986), 124-125.

[7] Ron O'Grady, *Singapore to Penang: The Christian Conference of Asia from 1973 to 1977* (Singapore: CCA, 1977), 16.

[8] East Asia Christian Conference, *Church's Witness in Relation to Religion and Society International Affairs, Religious Liberty; Programme for 1964-68* (Madras: Diocesan Press, 1964), 25.

military occupation of Asia under the banner of establishing the "Greater East Asia Co-Prosperity Sphere." This left a legacy of deep unease toward any form of pan-Asian unity. National sovereignty became an overriding concern. Indeed, Asia consists of new nation states not only of unequal socio-economic strengths and contrasting ethno-linguistic situations, but also with unresolved histories of hostility and competing stories of nation building. Nation building also gave rise to ethno-nationalist conflicts. The unrests in Kalimantan, Sulawesi, and Maluku in Indonesia; the Mindanao conflicts in the Philippines; the Malaysia-Indonesia conflict over Borneo; Myanmar's state policies towards ethnic minorities; and the Thailand-Malaysia disputes over southern Thailand are cases in point.

Ironically, therefore, former colonial powers and mission boards became an important source of identity for Asian churches. Churches with tiny minorities would use their foreign links to establish their credentials. There was a deep fear of being absorbed by powerful neighbours. Perhaps East Malaysian churches would see themselves different from their West Malaysian counterparts. In Myanmar, the Chins would hold onto their Baptist links, and the Karens their Anglican ties in a Burmese dominated nation. EACC avoided establishing a permanent headquarters in its early years. The dispersive character kept the regional offices modest and guarded against emerging centres of excellence from competing against one another. This continued until 1974 when Singapore became the headquarters of CCA, the newly renamed EACC.

Asian churches, therefore, faced a structural problem from the start. They needed to stand united to restructure relationship with international organisations and their former parent churches. At the same time, the need to define themselves from their Asian neighbours led them to go in separate ways.

However, even deeper undercurrents were at work. Post- war ecumenical developments were under the grips of a crisis mentality. The first was the looming Communist threat to the newly independent nations. The conflicts in Korea, Malaya and Indonesia were cases in point. Alongside this was the globalising of Christian conflicts that had their origins in the west, but had now spread to the younger churches in the southern continents. The fundamentalist-liberal dispute, and the split between the moderate evangelicals and their ultra-fundamentalist counterparts in the United States of America became globalised in the 1950s.The southern continents became, so to speak, a contested ground for influence, political and ecclesiastical. Clearly, the United States of America was a main driving force behind many crusades. Communist influence among the young in Southeast Asia was a key concern in the programmatic Anderson-Smith Report on theological education in Southeast Asia in 1952.[9] Carl McIntire set up the International Council of Christian Churches global network to counter the work of John MacKay and the World Council of Churches. To him, WCC was sympathetic to the Communist cause. This happened despite Carl McIntire and John Mackay being fellow Princetonians! Bangkok was the scene where McIntire and MacKay convened parallel conferences in December 1949.[10] In lesser degrees, evangelicals adopted similar tactics to counter what they saw to be liberal influences among Asian churches. The World Evangelical Fellowship, for instance, convened a 'Theological Assistance Program' Consultation in Singapore in 1970 when the ecumenical Theological Education Fund (TEF) Third Mandate was launched. It eventually set up the Asia Theological Association as an alternative to the ecumenical ATESEA body.[11]

---

[9] S. R. Anderson and C. Stanley Smith, *The Anderson-Smith Report on Theological Education in Southeast Asia: Especially as It Relates to the Training of Chinese for the Christian Ministry: The Report of a Survey Commission, 1951-1952* (New York: Board of Founders, Nanking Theological Seminary, 1952); Michael Poon, "The Association for Theological Education in South East Asia, 1959-2002: A Pilgrimage in Theological Education," in *Supporting Asian Christianity's Transition from Mission to Church: A History of the Foundation for Theological Education in South East Asia*, ed. Samuel Campbell Pearson (Grand Rapids: Eerdmans, 2010), 363-402, 417-431.

[10] Carl McIntire, *The Battle of Bangkok: Second Missionary Journey* (Collingwood: Christian Beacon Press, 1950).

[11] Michael Poon,"The History and Development of Theological Education in South East Asia," 378-279.

However well meaning these initiatives were, they distracted the fledging churches in Asia from the central tasks that EACC identified. They inculcated an outlook of what Henry van Dusen had identified as "the scandal of dependence." Most of the advances in theological education in the 1960s and 1970s depended on John Rockefeller's generous gift to the TEF,[12] and funding from the Foundation for Theological Education in South East Asia. As a result of this American dependence, the financially more capable national churches were reluctant to put money into pan-Asian projects. CCA's expulsion from Singapore by the authorities in 1987 under the Internal Security Act underscored how pan-Asian ecumenical involvement can become dispensable when national security and interest are at stake. Who then are left to fund the ecumenical projects? Region wide projects became largely grant driven from the mid 1970s. Shoki Coe (at that time director of the TEF) was concerned that contextualisation was at risk of becoming "merely a slogan or a fad" for grant application purposes. This was the main contention behind a sharp exchange between Shoki Coe and ATSSEA executive director Emerito Nacpil in 1977.[13] The series of ATESEA sponsored Theological Seminary-Workshops ended by mid- 1990s, near the time when FTESEA (Foundation for Theological Education in South East Asia) funding support could no longer be taken for granted.[14] The financial mismanagement that brought ATESEA to near collapse in 2008 underlined the huge challenge pan-Asian ecumenical projects faced, especially when they had become largely grant driven. After all, only foreign money was at stake.

1941 and the Rise of Pacific Rim Christianity

The above shows that Asian churches need to recover a fresh vision to place their relationships with one another and with the wider Body of Christ independent of western funding and interest. Post- colonial, post- missionary and post- denominational accounts may well be inadequate to describe the realities and challenges that Asian churches faced in their ecumenical journeys. Such models may in fact constrain Asian churches to continue to look to the west for blame and praise, and so excuse them from discharging their moral obligations to their geographically proximate neighbours. How can Asian churches rediscover new spiritual horizons for relationships? A time-space reorientation may well provide a fruitful way forward.

Briefly, the year 1941 is a significant reference point for Asian societies. The Japanese military invasion of Pearl Harbour in December 1941 and the conquest of Southeast Asia the following year drew attention to the social networks of the trans-Pacific and their growing importance in shaping global events. The Japanese military occupation of eastern Asia from 1942 to 1945 gave the area a regional unity that no Asian and western power had ever achieved. The Japanese, as a rising Asian nation, humiliated the Americans, French, Dutch and British and raised the hopes of local nationalist movements. This made it untenable for western powers to reassume their former status quo after the Pacific War. The Japanese occupation unleashed huge population movements, awoke nationalist sentiments, undermined the impression of omnipotence of European powers and paved the way for America's presence at the western seaboard of the Pacific Rim. It gave Southeast Asia a regional identity that it had never possessed. In this sense, 1941 is a very significant turning point for Asia than 1945. It set off fundamental processes of re-orientation and rediscovery among Asian churches. Asia hitherto had looked west across the deserts and continents to Europe. It now looks east across the Pacific Ocean to America and draws on the closer resources across the seas in the island world of Southeast Asia and of the Australasian world. The British

---

[12] Charles Ranson, "The Theological Education Fund." *IRM* 47, no. 188 (1958): 432-438.
[13] See Michael Poon, "The Association for Theological Education in South East Asia, 1959-2002: A Pilgrimage in Theological Education," 386-387.
[14] Ibid., 399.

military retreat from the east of Suez in 1971 symbolised the close of an era of European encounter with Asia.

To the present day, 1941 brings to surface many suppressed memories and unresolved tensions that Asians still are uncomfortable with to confront together. For example, to the present time, Singapore, Malaysia and Indonesia find it difficult to talk about their tri-nation relations; the violence that marked their history of nation building in the 1950s and 1960s are still too fresh for them to face up together. The glaring absence of any reference work on contemporary pan-Asian church history underscores this unease. History writing is a theological reading of memories; therefore, the historical void shows that Asian churches have not been able to see to connect their experiences to God's saving purposes. Ironically, Asian churches find it safer to continue with anti-colonial and anti-missionary rhetoric. It is easier to blame the west for present woes and failures; to confront what is real and current, however, is much more difficult. Therefore, 1941 highlights questions about moral duties and social obligations that Asian churches and their wider societies should no longer evade. These moral and social duties include questions about how Asian societies can share more equitably; how churches can support oppressed Christian groups in politically powerful nations; and how Christians can rise above their national interests in order to work together. D. T. Niles famously entitled his farewell report to the EACC: *Ideas and Service.*[15] Ideas and service could however only remain at the individual level, as "ideas and service" of like-minded persons who happen to be interested in ecumenism. The challenge today is whether the socio-politically and economically variegated Asian churches can discover a deeper foundation to situate their relationships, and to work together as collective bodies for the common good of their wider societies.

Social ties however are largely geologically and geographically dependent, even in this globalising era. Asia's geological configuration is different from that of the trans-Atlantic world. This is especially true for 'Southeast Asia.' It rests on two stable continental platforms, and two major arcs of volcanic instability that stretch from the Indonesian to the Philippines islands. The region consists of a series of geographical conversations between lands and seas, highlands and lowlands, rivers and mountains. The geological and geographical configuration of the Pacific Rim therefore contrasts sharply with that of the trans-Atlantic world. Christendom was about applying the principles of the Gospel and of canon laws to all areas of social life. The stable geological conditions in Western Europe and the east coasts of North and 'Latin' America made this construction of a common cultural and linguistic world possible. The cathedrals witness to a form of Christianity that rests on confessional statements, institutional uniformity and historical stability: one church, one bishop, one king, one realm. But vulnerability, volatility and fragility are the central features of social life in Asia. To the present day, migrant workers, refugees of war and stateless peoples testify to the fragile and fluid conditions in human life that are punctuated by the eruptions of wars, tsunamis and earthquakes. Makeshift tents replace cathedrals as carriers of Christianity at the start of the third millennium. Peoples are on the move; and so too faith is on the move. For many, life is apocalyptic. They live under the constant threat of an impending end. Such Pacific Rim experiences arguably epitomise this wider shift in present day human experience worldwide: from continental to maritime interchange. Peoples are launched out to the seas: to face uncertain times, embrace strange horizons, and at the same time, to make fresh starts in life. One can no longer approach life by rote.

It is therefore no accident that 'Southeast Asia' was the heartland of the Asian Revolution. Norton Ginsburg's magisterial treatise *The Pattern of Asia* arguably gives the best characterisation of this variegated region.[16] Historically, this southeast corner of the Asia continent, or to change the perspective, the southwest Asia Pacific Rim, was a passage rather than a focus of developmental concentration. It is a

---

[15] Niles, Daniel Thambyrajah. *Ideas and Services. A Report of the East Asia Christian Conference 1957-67.* Christchurch, New Zealand: National Council of Churches, 1968.

[16] Norton Ginsburg and John E. Brush. *The Pattern of Asia* (Englewood Cliffs, N.J.: Prentice-Hall, 1958), 290-320.

maritime passage between continents. Historically it has served as a funnel for migration of peoples under the pressure of political events in South Asia and China. Southeast Asia is therefore multiethnic, multilingual, multicultural and multi-religious: it is a gathering and dispersing place for peoples. Pope John Paul II's encyclical *Ecclesia in Asia* depicted Asia as "the cradle of the world's major religions – Judaism, Christianity, Islam and Hinduism. It is the birthplace of many other spiritual traditions such as Buddhism, Taoism, Confucianism, Zoroastrianism, Jainism, Sikhism and Shintoism. Millions also espouse traditional or tribal religions, with varying degrees of structured ritual and formal religious teaching.... This "being Asian" is best discovered and affirmed not in confrontation and opposition, but in the spirit of complementarity and harmony."[17] More so, southwest Asia Pacific Rim is the crucible in which these traditions interact with one another. Therefore, more than elsewhere, peoples who live there need to acquire the "capacity for accommodation and a natural openness to the mutual enrichment of peoples in the midst of a plurality of religions and cultures."[18]

In similar ways, there is no clear single reference point in the southwest Asia Pacific Rim. Jakarta, Singapore, Yangon, Bangkok, Hanoi and Manila each capitalise on their own historical ties and geographical locations to connect with Asia and the wider world in their unique ways. Within each country, there are sizeable minorities of different ethnic, linguistic and religious origins. Even the ethnic Chinese themselves cannot readily communicate with one another because they speak different Han-languages.

Such are the settings in which D. T. Niles, Shoki Coe, Koyama Kosuke and the first generation of post 1941 church leaders began their ecumenical journeys. The shift from trans-Atlantic to trans-Pacific represents a truer and more radical account of present-day Christianity. There is no short cut to the theological task of understanding the world and God's saving work afresh. Andrew Walls has famously drawn attention to a southward shift of Christian demography to the southern continents. This however cannot account for the deeper shifts that world Christianity finds itself at the beginning of the third millennium because a mere 'southward' demographic shift does not necessarily demand an intellectual re-orientation. The benchmarks of Christianity can remain unchanged; Christianity can still be understood in Christendom terms. Ecumenical experiences in the Pacific Rim, however highlight the geological and geographical foundation of world Christianity. The Pacific Rim however opens up spiritual horizons and awakes moral tasks that Christendom experiences cannot reveal. If there is a need for the church universal to rediscover a new theological grammar, syntax and semantics for today's world, the Pacific Rim may well be a fruitful arena for this theological work. In this sense, Shoki Coe's legacy of contextualising theology carries a wide and enduring significance for ecumenism. The struggle between text and context is a continuing missiological task, because human societies are thrown into uncertain and volatile situations. Christian discipleship demands fresh and innovative approaches to life.

Ecumenism and Christian Discipleship in the Pacific Rim

How then could Asian churches continue this contextualising journey together? In the first faith and order conference in Asia held in 1965, Shoki Coe and his contemporaries spearheaded the change of the conference theme. The original theme "The Confession of the Faith in Asia Today" became "Confessing the Faith in Asia Today." Shoki Coe explained:

> By and large, the churches in Asia are the fruits of the modern missionary movement; they have heard and received the Faith confessed to them, but they cannot stop there otherwise they would not really have heard and

[17] *Ecclesia in Asia*, 6 November 1999, 6.
[18] Ibid.

> received.... In confessing, the life and death of the churches in Asia are at stake.... In this matter of confessing lies the authentic selfhood in Christ of the churches in Asia.[19]

What then does the Pacific Rim reveal about the character of confessing the Mystery of Faith in Asia and in the wider world today? Briefly:

1. Asian churches need to connect the bewildering experiences of human dislocation and migration to God's journey in the Incarnation of the Word. "He came to that which was his own, but his own did not receive him. Yet to all who did receive him, to those who believed in his name, he gave the right to become children of God.... The Word became flesh and made his dwelling among us. We have seen his glory, the glory of the one and only Son, who came from the Father, full of grace and truth" (Jn.1:11-14). Salvation is effected through the God-initiated reversal of fortune (2 Cor. 8:9; Phil. 2: 6-11), in which the glory of God – truth and grace in full measure – is revealed amid dispossession. The 4th century church father Athanasius summed up his insight in the Incarnation of the Word with this phrase:

> For He was made man that we might be made God; and He manifested Himself by a body that we might receive the idea of the unseen Father; and He endured the insolence of men that we might inherit immortality (*incarn.* 54).

Theosis, therefore, is a life journey. Participation in divine life depends on our capacity to receive – to welcome to our roof – what seems alien. Hospitality, therefore, discloses grace and truth. It turns despair to hope, and darkness to glory. This vision speaks to peoples in the Pacific Rim in powerful ways. The Pacific Rim is built on histories of movements of people, under the pressure of political upheavals and economic opportunities. The 19th century bond slave movements from China to the eastern Pacific Rim, Australia, and Malaya are cases in point. The migration of Foochow Methodist communities to Sibu and Sitiawan at the turn of the 20th century is another. More recent, the movement of migrant workers from economically poorer to richer countries in Asia underlined the huge economic polarisation since the ending of the Pacific War. Instances of ethnic violence have also led to such dislocation of people. Cultural diversity in Asian societies is built on migration and dislocation. Offering hospitality is a continuing moral and practical demand. Hospitality goes beyond giving short-term aids. It poses the challenge to live alongside others of different cultural and linguistic background, as well as the need for them to build a common habitat together.

The character of Christian discipleship among Asian churches, therefore, can potentially hold out a social vision that western societies have lost. To adopt John Paul II's words: Being human "is best discovered and affirmed not in confrontation and opposition, but in the spirit of complementarity and harmony." The religious wars that western Christianity wage even today are often premised on a need to assert a distinct and separate public space for one's own understanding of the faith. Each group needs to demarcate and protect its own time and space boundaries. Rival carriers of the same denomination even wage war against one another, to the huge discredit of Christianity. The current fratricidal war among Anglican churches is a case in point.

2. The Pacific Rim embodies many presences and reference points. The emotional, political and spiritual connection that western Christianity attaches to Rome, Constantinople and Geneva is not replicated in the Pacific Rim. No single creed or ecclesiastical polity can apply to all the diverse situations. No one single solution can apply to all. "A time is coming when you will worship the Father neither on this mountain nor in Jerusalem. You Samaritans worship what you do not know; we worship what we do know, for salvation is from the Jews.... God is spirit, and his worshippers must worship in the Spirit and in truth" (Jn. 4: 21-24). Churches and societies across Asia do not connect with one another in hierarchical ways.

---

[19] C. H. Hwang, "*Confessing* the Faith in Asia Today," *South East Asia Journal of Theology* 8, no. 1-2 (1966): 65-66.

Powerful presences, like that of China, India and the United States of America, can in fact become overbearing and threatening to the variegated societies that are spread out in the hills, valleys, and islands in the Pacific Rim. Dominating presences can translate into imperialist projects that can mask instances of injustice to vulnerable societies in the name of nation building and societal advances. The Taiwanese struggle for self-determination in the face of the Kuomintang regime is a case in point. Shoki Coe's leadership in this struggle underscores the political responsibility that churches cannot evade. The more recent struggle between the Malaysian church and the national government on the issue of the name of God provides another example. Asian churches need to speak out for, and live up to a social horizon that transcends the political ambition of earthly powers. Governments can of course circumscribe the churches' social roles and public visibility. Occasionally, churches run the risk of becoming part of the state apparatus for their fragile situation makes it especially vulnerable to state manipulation. More so, churches across Asia need to support one another in confessing Christ in the public realm.

3. It follows that spiritual renewals come in the form of independent movements of the Holy Spirit as much as in church institutions. Independent lay initiatives play an increasingly more important role to Christian advances than clergy-sanctioned projects. The charismatic revivals in East Timor, Singapore, and Bario in the 1960s and the 1970s were important turning points in the churches in Indonesia, Singapore, and Malaysia. Earlier, the movements of peoples within the Pacific Rim have inspired several significant spiritual movements. The anti-Christian movements in China in the 1920s led to the birth of local-led revival movements. The social dislocations brought about by the Sino-Japanese War led to huge population movements, and with them, the transformation of spiritual traditions in Southeast Asia. In 1935, Andrew Gih and the Bethel Evangelistic Band launched out to North America at the same time when John Sung established a new base in Southeast Asia. Californian forms of Christianity – in the form of church growth strategy, charismatic renewal, and spiritual warfare practice – affected Christian practice on the other end of the Pacific. Korean forms of Christianity at the same time find new expressions in America. True ecumenism in the Pacific Rim, therefore, is no longer the preserve of historic Christianity. Bilateral ecumenical dialogues – for example, International Roman Catholic – Anglican or Orthodox – Roman Catholic conversations, as well may only have limited use in a Christian world that no longer follows the logic of historic Christianity. There is an urgent need to embrace independent movements in the wider ecumenical undertakings in Asia. At the same time, there is an equally pressing need for those in the independent movements to deepen the theological nature of their own spiritual journeys.[20]

Cardinal Joseph Ratzinger (before he became Pope Benedict XVI) in fact spearheaded this appeal. His address to the 1998 Congress "The Theological Locus of Ecclesial Movements" set the stage for putting new ecclesial movements on a solid theological and ecclesiastical footing.[21] First, he linked the new ecclesial movements to the church's central call of evangelisation. He called them the "irruptions of the Holy Spirit":[22] the response of the Holy Spirit to the challenges of secularisation in the present-day. Pope John Paul II underscored this message. For him, the movements contribute to the twofold task in evangelisation: "solid, in-depth Christian formation" on the one hand and "powerful proclamation" to the world on the other:

> In our world, often dominated by a secularized culture which encourages and promotes models of life without God … we see an urgent need for powerful proclamation and solid, in-depth Christian formation…. There is a

[20] Michael Poon, "The Theological Locus of Christian Movements in Southeast Asia," in *Christian Movements in Southeast Asia: A Theological Exploration* (Singapore: Trinity Theological College, 2010), ix-xxxv.
[21] Joseph Ratzinger, "The Theological Locus of Ecclesial Movements," *Communio* 25 (1998): 480-504.
[22] Ibid., 482.

> need for living Christian communities! And here are the movements and the new ecclesial communities; they are the response, given by the Holy Spirit, to this critical challenge at the end of the millennium.[23]

4. The geological instability in the Pacific Rim highlights the apocalyptic character of human societies. But the apocalypse is not mainly about dislocation and dispossession; it brings about a new eucharistic community, where peoples of all nations can find their hostilities reconciled at the Feast of the Lamb. Human history, on one level, is a story of stolen goods. In Oliver O'Donovan's words: "The monstrous inequity of generational succession is that all our possession becomes a kind of robbery, something we have taken from those who shared it with us but with whom we cannot share in return."[24] The reticence that often greets discussions on nation building experiences underscore the secret guilt which still infect every Asian nation regarding their immediate forebears. Nation making in Asia was accompanied by a history of ethnic riots, border disputes, religious violence and regional rivalry. It can lead to huge polarisation of material possession within the same society and across Asia.

It is remarkable how tsunami and earthquakes can unleash a spirit of generous sharing among Asian neighbours. Natural disasters often become occasions where peoples rediscover their communal bonds amid national hostilities and prejudices. There is of course a deeper truth in such spontaneous acts of synchronic sharing. Saint Paul put it this way: "The time is short. From now on… those who use the things of the world as if not engrossed in them. For this world in its present form is passing away" (1 Cor. 7: 29-31). The acts of sharing are signs to the final eucharistic feast, where goods and charism (a) ??are shared and enjoyed together across the table. The 'End' is therefore not about tradition and legacy; God's final purposes for creation is about communion instead: communion with God, with one another, and with the whole created order. Amid the self-absorbing exercises in nation building, a new movement of the Spirit is needed to spur Asian churches to labour for a shared world, in which all peoples live together in security.

Much is at stake for Asian churches and world Christianity at the beginning of the third millennium. Pacific Rim churches can assert their global influences in world Christianity through their increasingly material wealth. Such influence could become imperialist projects. Shoki Coe and his generation of Asian church leaders pointed us to the continuing need to interpret our faith and situations in the vision of the eternal city. The ecumenical movement, therefore, in the last analysis, would not become another instance of Christendom building. It is about an adventure in grace and in truth. To borrow Shoki Coe's words:

> [Ecumenical journeys] are at most and at best a provisional and fragmentary witness of that divine contextualization of the incarnation. Ours can only be in following in His steps as an ongoing process of the pilgrim people. But in doing so we can accept our relativity with hope and even with joy, as we see in our faithful responses the sign of the divine contextualization unfolding its purpose for the liberation and salvation of mankind.

Bibliography

Coe, Shoki. *Christian Mission and the Test of Discipleship*. Edited by Michael Poon. Singapore: Trinity Theological College, 2012.

———. "In Search of Renewal in Theological Education." *Theological Education* 9, no. 4 (1973): 233-243.

Ginsburg, Norton Sydney, and John E. Brush. *The Pattern of Asia*. Englewood Cliffs, N.J.: Prentice-Hall,

[23] John Paul II, *Speech of the Holy Father Pope John Paul II Meeting with Ecclesial Movements and New Communities* (30 May 1998), 7.

[24] Oliver O'Donovan, *The Desire of the Nations* (Cambridge: Cambridge UP, 1996), 187-188.

1958.
Manikam, Rajah Bhushanam. *Christianity and the Asian Revolution*. Madras: Published for Friendship Press, New York, 1955.
Niles, Daniel Thambyrajah. *Ideas and Services. A Report of the East Asia Christian Conference 1957-67*. Christchurch, New Zealand: National Council of Churches, 1968.
Poon, Michael. "The Association for Theological Education in South East Asia, 1959-2002: A Pilgrimage in Theological Education." In *Supporting Asian Christianity's Transition from Mission to Church: A History of the Foundation for Theological Education in South East Asia*, edited by Samuel Campbell Pearson, 363-402, 417-431. Grand Rapids: Eerdmans, 2010.
———. *Christian Movements in Southeast Asia: A Theological Exploration*. Singapore: Trinity Theological College, 2010.
———. *Church Partnerships in Asia: A Singapore Conversation*. Singapore: Trinity Theological College, 2011.

(5) China's Re-Entry into Asian and World Ecumenism and its Relations to Other Asian Churches

Jiawei Wang

1. A Historical Review of China's Re-entry into Asian and World Ecumenism

Although the history of the protestant church in China is short, some excellent church leaders from China contributed to serving the universal church in the twentieth century, which can be seen already as a vital contribution of the Chinese Church to world ecumenism: Among them were Cheng Ching-yi, vice-president of the International Missionary Council, T.C.Koo, who was working as a secretary of the federation, Professor T.C.Chao, who was a member of the first presidium/committee of the World Council of Churches and Miss Wu Yi-fang, who was an outstanding figure in the International Missionary Council.[1] Before the foundation of the Republic of China in 1949, there were four churches from China present at the first assembly of the World Council of Churches in Amsterdam 1948. Dr. T.C.Chao was elected as one of the presidents of the WCC. As Rev. Gao Ying has pointed out, the protestant churches in China at that time were among the few so-called younger churches active in the ecumenical movement in its formative stage. Dr. T.C. Chao was the only president from non-Euro-American churches.[2] During the period of the war breaking out on the Korean peninsula in 1950, Chao resigned from his position as he opposed the policy of the WCC on this war. After 1956, when K.H.Ting worked in the central committee of the WCC, the Chinese churches ceased the relationship with the WCC and quit from the ecumenical movement.[3]

Thus, there is a long historical gap of relationships between the Chinese church and other outside churches from the 1950s to the end of the 1970s when the Cultural Revolution ended. The estrangement between the churches of China and the WCC had lasted for forty years till 1991 after the end of the Cold War. With new developments in the political and economic realm, the Chinese Church started the process of rejoining the world ecumenical family. The first Chinese delegation of religious leaders attended the international meeting of the World Conference on Religion and Peace in the US in 1979.[4] This event was the key to reopen the door of the Church in China to the WCC and other Asian churches. Christian leaders and bodies worldwide had new chances to renew and to make contact with the Chinese Church leaders, including Bishop K.H.Ting. At that time,Yap Kim Hao, the general secretary of the Christian Conference of Asia appealed to the Asian ecumenical body to establish a more close relationship with the Chinese churches. He was the first Church leader from abroad and the leading representative of the Asian churches who was invited to visit China in October 1980. After Yap Kim Hao's visit, Chinese church leaders participated in a consultation held by the Christian Conference of Asia in Hong Kong in 1981. This was the first occasion and an important meeting for Chinese church leaders exchanging theological ideas and views with delegations of other Asian churches and national councils. Bishop K.H.Ting, Shen De-rong and Han

---

[1] Cf. Ninan Koshy, *A History of The Ecumenical Movement In Asia (Vol.I)*, WSCFAPR/APA of YMCAs,CCA,2004, p.84.

[2] See Gao Ying, *A Chinese Perspective on the Ecumenical Movement, in Chinese Theological Review:13*, Foundation for Theological Education in Southeast, 1999. p.78.

[3] Cf. Ninan Koshy, *A History of The Ecumenical Movement In Asia (Vol.I)*, WSCFAPR/APA of YMCAs,CCA,2004, p.210.

[4] Ibid, p.211.

Wen-chao, president, general secretary and associate general secretary represented respectively the China Christian Council and the Committee of Three-Self Patriotic Movement.[5]

After a preparation of one decade, the timing was ripe for the Chinese Church to return to the family of the WCC. In 1991, a delegation from The China Christian Council attended the assembly of WCC held in Canberra, Australia. This signified the Protestant Church of China rejoining the WCC again as a member church officially. As Philip L. Wickeri mentioned in his book *Reconstructing Christianity in China*, K.H.Ting regarded WCC membership as important for both China and the CCC. "It would give both China and the CCC a voice in the most important international Christian body, and also greater visibility on the world stage. Membership would also help broaden the CCC's outlook on theology, the church and the world." [6] Afterwards, interactions and visits between the Chinese Church and other national churches have become more frequent and regular. In the meantime, church leaders from China and other Asian countries and areas also entered the phase of establishing close relationships and contacts amongst themselves.. Chinese church leaders like Bishop Ting and Han Wen-chao played a prominent role in the course of making friendship with other Asian churches. Since then, they devoted themselves to develop partnership and friendship with the universal churches. This article focuses on the relationship between the church in China and other churches in Asia which demonstrate the development of the ecumenical movement among Asian churches from Chinese perspectives.

According to the statistics (however incomplete), between 1991 and 2011, the China Christian Council has invited several national church delegations and individuals to visit China. Chinese representatives also were sent to partner churches in Asia to attend big events, major conferences and other church activities etc. During these two decades, the Chinese church had introduced regular visiting among other Asian churches for promoting mutual understanding and cooperation, especially for demonstrating an active and dynamic image of the Church in China after the policy of opening and reformation which was carried out all over China. With all Asian churches and organizations, there was a system of regular contacts and visits established, like with the National Council of Churches in South Korea, the churches of different denominations in Hong Kong, Taiwan, Macau and so on. Besides these, due to the interest for enhancing friendship and removing misunderstanding, Chinese church leaders also warmly invited the leaders and delegations from the National Council of Churches in the Philippines, the Asian Church Women's Conference, the Communion of Churches in Indonesia and the Christian Conference of Asia during 1991-1992. These series of mutual visits fulfilled the purpose of exchanging ideas and learning from each other as well as making friends with other Asian churches. As Bishop Ting said in his address to the Union Theological Seminary in the Philippines in 1993, "We in China have a high evaluation of the witness of the Christians in the Philippines to Jesus Christ, calling people's attention to human worth as children of God and to democracy as the mandate of history in accordance to the will of God. We, the church in China, have much to learn from our fellow Christians in the Philippines. "[7]

During the second decade, more and more cooperation and visits were developed between churches in mainland China and churches in Hong Kong in the fields of mission, theological education, sacred music and charity works etc. After earlier years of hostility, relations between Taiwan and mainland China appear to be rapidly improving in recent years. Good relationships are also developing in the circle of the respected churches. There are more individual and group visits, folk or official exchanges and collaboration among churches, theological colleges and universities in Taiwan and mainland China.

---

[5] Ibid, p.212.

[6] Philip L. Wickeri, *Reconstructing Christianity in China*, Orbis Books, Maryknoll, New York, 2007. p.320.

[7] K.H. Ting, "*One Chinese Christian's View of God*" from his book *Love Never Ends*, Yilin Press, Nanjing,2000. p.429

2. Major Fields of Interaction between Chinese Christianity and Other Parts of Asia's Christianity

There are mainly two kinds of interaction between the Chinese churches and other Asian churches. The first major dimension of interaction consists of mutual visits and exchange between the churches; the second major dimension consists of communication and cooperation for theological education in Asia.

(a) Visits and exchange activities between church circles

After becoming an official member of WCC, the priority for China Christian Council was to establish friendship with Asian churches and especially to create good relations with the neighboring country churches like the churches in Japan, South Korea and Singapore etc.

The CCC established friendship with the Japanese Church in 1983 and afterwards some mutual but informal visits had taken place frequently between the two churches (1984, 1996, 1999, 2004, 2007). In 1996, a delegation of the National Christian Council in Japan (NCC) visited China officially and declared this as an important event. Although there was the historic problem of the Sino-Japanese War during 1936-1945 which had caused a big gap between the two countries and their churches, at that time it were the President Rev. Kentaro Takeuchi and the General Secretary Rev. Munetoshi Maejima who expressed their apology on behalf of the Japanese Christians towards all the aggressions of the Japanese army to Chinese people in modern history. They apologized for Japanese militarists' cruelty and their invading acts to China and its innocent people. They prayed to build up friendship between the Christians in the two countries based on peace and trust as China and Japan must shoulder the responsibility of becoming crucial peace-makes in Asia[8]. It was a key conviction that Christians have a crucial responsibility for peace-making. Chinese Christians were also later invited by the Japanese churches to visit and attend important events such as conferences and prayer meetings held in Japan. One of the more recent visits was a delegation of CCC which was warmly received by NCC in April 2007. Presbyter Ji Jianhong addressed over 50 Japanese member churches and organizations and talked about how to spread the message of reconciliation according to the Holy Scripture and being ambassadors of peace. The Chinese Church appreciates the Japanese Church for respecting the three-self principle[9] and the serious Chinese standpoint on the issue of Taiwan. For enhancing friendship with the Chinese Church in Asia, the Japanese Church plays an important role of reconciling the relations between the two countries. The Japanese Churches also have made a clear declaration about their standpoint on the Sino-Japanese War and the Japanese invasion of China and their support for the 'One China' policy.

In 1992, the People's Republic of China and the Republic of Korea established official diplomatic relations. Due to this good political situation, the China Christian Council also started to develop friendly relations with the National Council of Churches in Korea (NCCK) through mutual visits and consultations, held in Nanjing and Seoul respectively in 1993, 1995, 1997, 2006. Due to the effective approaches applied in these relations both of the churches and people in the two countries are now closely linked and live peacefully with each other. Furthermore, both of the churches have committed themselves to make contributions for constructing a "Harmonious Asia" and a "Harmonious World". Besides these activities during recent years CCC also has established a good relation with the Yoido Full Gospel Church[10] which is the largest Pentecostal Christian congregation in South Korea and in the world. There were some mutual visits with Yoido Full Gospel Church in 2011 and in 2012. All these church activities show that the Chinese Church has an open mind to interact with the churches from various backgrounds.

---

[8] *"Japanese Church Announcement on the visit in 1996"*, from *Tian Feng*, 1996, August, China Christian Council&Three-Self Patriotic Movement(CCC&TSPM) P.33.

[9] See: http://en.wikipedia.org/wiki/Three-Self_Patriotic_Movement

[10] The Full Gospel Church was founded and led by David Yonggi Cho since 1958.

Meanwhile, also a good friendship and partnership between the Chinese Church and the churches of Singapore has been established by the grace of God. There have been on more then 10 occasions official and mutual visits between two sides and also many unofficial visits happened frequently among Christians in the two countries related to the fields of church communication, Bible ministry[11], theological education as well as social service. Particularly the Anglican Church in Singapore has a close relation with CCC during two decades now which was facilitated by the efforts of Singaporean-Chinese church leaders like the former Archbishop John Chew who visited China many times and committed himself to the ministry of church exchange and theological training programs in China. The four big denominational churches in Singapore like the Anglican Church, the Methodist Church, the Presbyterian Church and the Baptist Church have major congregations which are Singaporean-Chinese and who can speak Chinese, which makes church exchange activities easier than with English-speaking churches. Trinity Theological College in Singapore (TTC) has trained many seminary teachers and pastors from mainland China through short-term courses and long-term study programs to pursue the master's degree or doctorate in theology. Most of the graduates are now serving devotedly in the churches and seminaries all over China.

(b) Communication and cooperation

Besides close interaction with other Asian churches, the Chinese Church has regular and frequent communication and cooperation particularly in the area of theological education. For instance, there was a Consultation held on Relationships and Cooperation in Mission between Chinese and Korean Churches at Nanjing Union Theological Seminary on Sept.7th-9th in 1993. This was actually the first consultation between the Chinese Church and the Korean Church. Twenty-nine representatives from both sides, China Christian Council/TSPM and the National Council of Churches in Korea attended this conference and discussed vital topics like fellowship and exchange among churches, social service and how to cope with heresies and so on. Bishop Ting, Luo Guanzong, Bishop Shen Yifan, Dr. Han Wen-chao and Rev. Wu Aien (a female Chinese-Korean pastor), Rev. Kwon Ho Kyung (General Secretary of NCCK) and other Korean church leaders attended this important meeting. Dr. Han Wen-chao as one of the speakers expressed his idea of "mutual respect and mutual cooperation" between two churches. He said, "The Chinese Church has got much help from churches overseas including the Korean Churches in the areas of spirituality, theological thinking, Bible study and pastoral work etc. especially in the field of training pastoral personnel."[12]

In 1999, the Korean version of Bishop Ting's work *Love Never Ends* was published in South Korea. Bishop Ting was invited to visit Seoul and attended the launching of the publishing of *Love Never Ends* on Oct.21, 1999. This was the first theological book written by a Chinese theologian which was introduced to the Korean Church since the People's Republic of China was founded in 1949. The publishing of Bishop Ting's book in Korea demonstrated the open mind of the universal church, especially the Asian churches, towards a common spiritual treasure in the world of Christianity. At the same time, it made Korean Christians understand theology in the Chinese context. The publication was not only an academic achievement, but also a substantial contribution to Asia's Christianity. The translator Dr. Kim Jong Koo, in the Foreword summarized Bishop Ting's opinion thus:

1. God's supreme attribute is love which strongly affected Christianity to take root in the soil of the Chinese context,
2. Christianity has an inclusive attitude to all that is good, kind, beautiful and true in human nature outside Christianity and this can justify the views of Christians and contribute to better understanding of Christians by non-Christians

---

[11] The office of United Bible Societies Asia and Pacific Area and China Partnership is set up in Singapore.

[12] Han Wenzao, "*Mutual Respect, Mutual Cooperation*", from *Tian Feng*, 1993 November, CCC & TSPM, Shanghai. P.26.

3. The positive effect of religions is emphasized by Chinese society. Bishop Ting ndeavours to correct the negative idea contained in the slogan "Religion is the opium of people" which was dominant for a long time but nobody would claim this statement anymore now. He had hoped that this book would prove to be a guide book for all people who have a commitment for evangelization to understand the Church and theology in China.[13]

Furthermore, the first theological seminar between the Chinese Church and Korean Churches was held in Nanjing in February 2001. Church pastors and theologians from both sides attended this seminar. Emeritus Vice-President Chen Zeming recalled the cooperation in the area of theology between the two Churches in his address, especially his friendship with Dr. Kim Yong Bock and Dr. Kim Jong Goo. He mentioned that he had set the course on "Minjung Theology" for the postgraduates in Nanjing Union Theological Seminary since 1994, which was welcomed and attracted the interest of students. Chen Zeming thought that Minjung Theology was closely related with Bishop Ting's theology and relatively complementary. There are a few similarities between these two theological ways of thinking, which could be mutually shared by them although the two countries had great differences in culture, society, and political systems. He expressed the hope of developing extensive cooperation with the field of ,Korean theology sharing common experiences and achievements as well as seeking to establish the theologies for Asia and the third world in the future.[14] "We two parts hope to renew and improve the understanding toward history and theology through this exchange, enhancing our collaboration for the mission ministry in Asia and the third world during the next century of economic globalization and regionalization." [15]

In addition, there were a few theological seminars on Biblical study which were held with Asian church organizations and seminaries during the past two decades in China as well. In March 1996, the international seminar entitled "Reading the Bible through Asian Eyes" was held by the Christian Conference of Asia (Youth) at Nanjing Union Theological Seminary. Chinese Christian scholars introduced the theology and development of church and freedom of religions in Chinese society to other Asian scholars. This seminar was a wonderful opportunity for sharing about the various contexts and opinions of churches and theological research.

(c) Women's ministry

In 1988， a delegation of the Asian Church Women's Conference (ACWC) visited China for the first time and established some friendship with our Chinese women in the church. In 1992, the president Monica Manna and executive secretary Eunice Kim visited China again and suggested more communication and visits to be established in the future. In 1994, the 7 delegates of ACWC visited China and exchanged ideas on rethinking the role of women to serve in the church, how to read the Bible from the perspective of Asian women and how to better serve in society etc. Rev. Cao Shengjie accompanied this delegation and some churches in cities like Hangzhou, Shanghai, Nanjing, Beijing and Xi'an were visited. They had a wonderful interaction and exchange with women Christians in China including women pastors, teachers, seminarians and lay people. Due to these exchanges and interactions, the Chinese Church started to pay more attention to women's ministry in China and set up a Committee of Church Women's Ministry at the China Christian Council in 1993. This committee appeals to all women Christians in the Chinese churches to improve qualities of faith, thinking and culture and to make better contributions to Church and society. Rev. Cao Shengjie suggested that the Chinese Church should emphasize the importance of women's ministry in the local churches at different levels and to learn from churches abroad about their working experiences which

---

[13] Kim Jong Goo, *"Foreword of Love Never Ends (Korean Version)"*, from *Tian Feng*, 1999 December, CCC&TSPM, Shanghai. P.12.

[14] See Chen Zeming, "*The Achievement of Church in China and Prospects of 21st Century*", in his book *Seeking and Witnessing,* 2007, CCC&TSPM, Shanghai. P.171.

[15] Ibid, p167.

was very encouraging and provided stimulating examples. She gave us three points to follow up in the women ministry.

1. To organize discussions on women's-related issues and to develop activities particularly addressed to women;
2. to broaden the view and outlook of women by helping them to love both church and society;
3. to train their talents for the church and to improve the ability of women.[16]

(d) Bible Printing and Distributing Ministry

During the past two decades, the Chinese Church has made a great progress with achievements in the ministry of printing and distributing Chinese Bibles, a process aiming to satisfy the growing need of Christians for reading the Bible all over China. Since the 1980s the Chinese Church was supported by the United Bible Societies (UBS) China Partnership for realizing a vision of printing and distributing Chinese Bibles nationally. This massive historical project became possible due to the coordinated fund-raising efforts of 37 member Bible Societies and two UBS Regional Centers. In 1988, the Amity Printing Company Ltd (APC) was formed through a joint venture agreement between Amity Foundation and the UBS Publishing Co Ltd. In its first year alone, APC has produced around half a million copies of the Bible. Besides Chinese domestic production, Amity is also a major exporter of quality Bibles for customers in over 70 countries. This figure includes Bibles destined for mainland Protestant and Catholic churches and Bibles exported in 80 different languages such as English, German, Spanish, and French, together with many African languages. Between 1988 and September 2011, more than 88.9 million copies of the Bible were printed, out of which 55.7 million were meant for distribution within China and 33.2 million was destined for export abroad. Amity Printing Company Ltd (APC) moved to a new factory in May 2008, having a capacity to print 18 million bibles a year.[17]

As Bishop Ting has stated, the Bible unites us. Over the last 26 years, UBS has helped to make Biblical resources affordable to the Chinese people by lowering the cost of production through Bible-paper subsidies. In recent years, UBS's partnership with the Chinese Church has also expanded to include Bible translations of minority languages, Bible literacy programs and the production of Scripture resources in Braille, audio, video and CD-ROM formats. UBS has also assisted in the provision of vans for Bible distribution.[18] The Bible Resource Centre was founded by UBS and established in Nanjing Union Theological Seminary in 2011. Besides this, the Old Testament Bible Seminar supported by UBS was held at Nanjing Union Theological Seminary in February 2012. It offered a unique opportunity for teachers of Old Testament from 17 seminaries and Bible schools in China to exchange teaching experiences and problems as well as learning from other OT experts from Malaysia and Singapore.

In the area of Bible translation revision work, for instance, the UBS in 1983 consulted with Hong Kong, Taiwan, Malaysia and Singapore Bible Societies about revising the Chinese Union Version (CUV) from 1919. Afterwards, some Biblical scholars from mainland China were invited to join together in this important work with other Chinese biblical scholars and translators from Hong Kong, Taiwan, Malaysia and Singapore. The CUV revision work was transferred to Hong Kong Bible Society (HKBS) after 2000. In 2006 the New Testament of CUV and in 2007 the New Testament with Psalms and Proverbs of CUV were published by HKBS. Finally, the complete Revised Chinese Union Version was published by the Hong Kong Bible Society in September 2010. This is a great effort to benefit and help more and more

---

[16] Cao Shengjie, "*Rethinking of the Women Ministry in the Church of China after accompanying the delegation of ACWC*" from *Tian Feng*, 1994,9 CCC&TSPM, Shanghai. P.21.

[17] The related information is recited from the official websites of UBS China Partnership (http://www.ubscp.org) and Amity Printing Co. Ltd (www.amityprinting.com)

[18] The related information is recited from the official websites of UBS China Partnership (http://www.ubscp.org)

Chinese people including Christians and non-Christians to understand the Word of God through the modern Chinese language.

To actively demonstrate the development of Bible ministry work in China, for the first time a Bible Ministry Exhibition was held in Hong Kong in 2005 and then in 2006, 2007 and 2011 it was successively shown in the United States (Los Angeles, Atlanta and New York), Germany and then for a second time in the United States (Washington D.C., Chicago, Dallas and Charlotte). This Chinese Bible Exhibition was a very good platform to open a window for Christians overseas to remove any misunderstanding with regard to the Church in China and enhance friendship and mutual understanding with others.

(e) Communication and collaborations with the churches of Hong Kong and Taiwan

The Church in China (CCC&TSPM) has very close communication and collaboration links with the churches in Hong Kong. Some cross-denominational church organizations like Hong Kong Christian Council (HKCC) and The Hong Kong Chinese Christian Churches Union (HKCCCU) as well as denominational church organizations like Hong Kong Council of the Church of Christ in China (HKCCC), Hong Kong Anglican Church, Lutheran Church, Baptist Church and Christian publishers and some charity foundations visited mainland China frequently and regularly. Their visits are very fruitful and helpful for launching more church work in the grassroots level. As Rev. Su Chengyi said all these activities are good opportunities for emotional exchange, ministry exchange and exchange of theological education.[19] Particularly, since July 1997 when Hong Kong was returned to China this has opened the door of communication and cooperation between Hong Kong and mainland China in the areas of Bible study, spiritual and pastoral training, medical assistance and reconstruction after disasters like floods, earthquakes etc. All churches are committed to develop good-neighborly and friendly relations on the basis of mutual respect for each other and the principles of non-subordination and non-interference in each other's internal affairs. As Rev. Zhou Yongjian pointed out in a Chinese Church Ministry Consultation in 1997, this principle complies with the idea of "One Country, Two Systems"[20] which is aiming to retain equality, mutual benefit and peaceful co-existence between both sides. All the ministry work should be based on "mutual respect" which means caring for each other, supporting each other and working together. The Hong Kong Church is playing the role of offering aid and support to the Church in China and making contribution to the Christians and non-Christians in mainland China.[21] The China Christian Council often invites Christian scholars and church leaders giving short-term lectures from Hong Kong and Taiwan such as Dr. Li Zhigang and Rev. Zhou Lianhua etc.

The ecumenical movement in Hong Kong is mainly promoted by Hong Kong Christian Council as HKCC is one of the members of WCC which keeps contact with other denominations and strives to facilitate mutual communication and fellowship. The ecumenical organization on the regional level is the Christian Conference of Asia which helps churches in Hong Kong to participate in the discussions and workshops on some issues of common concern for all the Asian churches.

---

[19] Su Chengyi, *"Emotional Exchange, Ministry Exchange and Exchange of Theological Education*", from *Tian Feng*, 1996, April, CCC&TSPM, Shanghai. P.33.

[20] "One Country, Two Systems"-A politic idea formally put forward by Deng Xiaoping, then leader of China, in the early 1980s to reunify the country. Deng suggested that there should only be one China, but the regions of Hong Kong, Macao and Taiwan, once reunified with the rest of the country, could retain their original economic and political systems while other parts keep pursuing socialism. This arrangement was observed when the country resumed sovereignty over Hong Kong and Macao in 1997 and 1999 respectively. The two cities are now the special administrative regions of the country with a high degree of autonomy.

[21] Zhou Yongjian, "*An Outlook On Relations and Cooperation between Churches in Hong Kong and Mainland China*", from *Tian Feng*, 1997 August, CCC&TSPM, Shanghai. P.22.

Politically, Taiwan is regarded as a part of China even now although it is still not governed by the central Chinese government. However, the relations between mainland China and Taiwan have become closer due to the open policy of direct links in post, transportation and trade between Chinese mainland and Taiwan since November 2008. In church circles, the development of cross-Strait relations has been stable during the past years. For instance, the famous pastor Rev. Zhou Lianhua from Taiwan has been to some seminaries in mainland China many times for visiting and lecturing on how to equip the workers of Christ etc. He strongly supports mutual visits, seminars and all kinds of cross- Strait communication. Although he is over 90, he is still participating in and guiding the translation and revision work of the Bible in the Chinese United Version. During recent years, the cross-Strait relations among churches and Christian organizations became closer and more constructive in terms of communication of sacred music, theological education, church ministry and social work.

In April of 2009, the first delegation from Chinese theological education from mainland China visited Taiwan and attended the "Forum of Development of Theological Education of Taiwan and Mainland" held in the Taiwan Baptist Theological Seminary. This was the first time for both sides for an official exchange at a theological seminary. The purpose was to deepen the interaction and understanding among seminaries in the area of theological education. After this visit, a few mutual visits and forums were held cross-Strait between the churches in 2010 and 2011. For pastors and church workers from Taiwan, they regarded these friendly visits as "travel of learning", "travel of touching" which changed their one-sided ideas toward the Church in Mainland China. Furthermore, all these exchanges enhanced the mutual-understanding, facilitated further collaboration and sharing of resources for better serving the Lord and people cross the Straits.

(f) Other church exchanges

Besides these, the China Christian Council is also the representative of Christianity in the China Conference on Religion and Peace (CCRP) and has attended the 6th Asia Conference on Religion and Peace (ACRP) in Indonesia in 2002 after suspending the membership of ACRP in 1996. In August 2010, the delegation of CCRP attended the IPCR[22] International Seminar held in Seoul, Korea. The title of this seminar was "Building an East Asian Peace Community and the Role of the International Society". The present president of the CCC, Rev. Gao Feng was one of speakers addressing the theme of "Taking History as A Mirror, Cherishing Peace and Creating The Future Together" in the seminar.[23] After one year, in November 2011, the delegation of the Korean Conference on Religion and Peace visited China and met the church leaders of CCC. Both sides are hoping to have continuous and beneficial contacts for making a valuable contribution to the peace of the world.

The 2nd global gathering of Global Christian Forum (GCF) was held at Manado, Indonesia, in October 2011. This gathering was co-organized by the World Council of Churches, the Pentecostal Churches Fellowship, the Fellowship of Evangelical Churches and Institutions and the Catholic Bishops' Conference. China Christian Council was for the first time invited to send representatives to attend this event. The committee of GCF attached importance to the participation of the Chinese Church. The Chinese Christian representatives were not only sharing faith experiences in the groups but also presented a good witness of the faith development of Chinese Christianity collectively in the plenary of the assembly which was a very precious chance of demonstrating the long history of the Chinese Church and the renewal of Christianity in China. It was necessary to express our clear conviction that the Chinese Church currently not only focuses on its own theological development and characteristic features, but also that it emphasizes

---

[22] See website of International Peaqce Corps of Religions (IPCR): http://ipcr.or.kr/sub/01_01.php. This is also related to China Committee Religion and Peace, see:
http://www.cppcc.gov.cn/ccrp/2012/05/10/ARTI1336631725478941.shtml

[23] See: http://www.ccctspm.org/english/enews/2010/919/1091977.html

its interest and open mind for embracing and relating to the global churches in World Christianity. The Chinese Church is regarded as the "Church Risen again in China" and is recognized and realized in its importance by more and more churches from various traditions, cultures and countries.[24]

It has become clear through all these developments, ministries and activities of the Chinese Church how Chinese Christianity in the past two decades has developed a stronger sense of being related to the ecumenical movement in various ways, how it is progressing in its relationships with other Asian churches and how it understands its own role as the Chinese Church within the Asian ecumenical family. It has grown up after a long silent period and is actively preaching the good news of the Lord to its people, and at the same time is a fruitful witness for the Lord in relating to the fellowship of universal churches.

3. Rethinking and Assessing the Development of Chinese Christianity in the 21st Century

The deceased bishop Shen Yifan once said that the problem of membership of the Chinese Church in the global ecumenical family had been solved in the WCC assembly of Canberra. It was on this occasion that the China Christian Council had been accepted again as one regular member church in the WCC after 40 years, which was a big issue in the church life of China. Since 1960s the WCC has been supporting the standpoint of the "One China" policy and it was one of the international organizations to propose at the earliest possible moment the People's Republic of China to join the United Nations. All these achievements were due to the 'Three-self policy' and the continuous efforts to walk on the road of solidarity and union of various churches in China.[25]

In the letter from Bishop Ting to the former secretary of WCC, Emilio Castro, it was stated that "joining in the WCC as a member church is an important step. We pray that God grant his grace to enhance the communications of our church to the churches worldwide, deepen our faith, love and hope as the disciples of Christ, to bear a better witness for Christ. "[26]

As the experienced church leader Han Wen-chao said in one interview, "we will be benefited from the universal churches for better spiritual nourishment by joining in the WCC. And our church run by the 'three-self' principle will be improved step by step through it as well. At the same time, our membership accepted in the WCC demonstrates that China Christianity and 'three-self' principlel is identified with Chinese Christians and supported by the churches worldwide which offer us an opportunity to show our attitude to socialistic China, the reason to practice the three-self principle and how we deal with the issue of denominations plus how we do better 'governing, supporting and propagating' the Church in China etc."[27]

Therefore, the Chinese Church insists on the principle of "running churches independently, self-governing, self-supporting and self-propagating" for the churches orderly growth in China. This is also the foundation for the Chinese Church and its capacity to playing an important role both globally and in terms of relations to other Asian churches and mission networks in the context of rapid economic growth and extensive international influence of China. However, there are still some problems restricting the Chinese Church to raise its voice and contribute to decisions in the big family of Asian Churches. One of the reasons is that the China Christian Council has not become a member of the Christian Conference of Asia (CCA) which is a regional ecumenical organization representing 17 National Councils and a 100 Churches in 21 countries.[28] The CCC has not established official relations with the CCA so far because one of the

---

[24] See http://www.ccctspm.org/news/de_re/2011/1017/111017921.html

[25] Cf. Shen Yifan, *"Memorable 15 days in Canberra"*, from *Tian Feng*, 1991 May, CCC&TSPM, Shanghai. p.6,8,9

[26] K.H.Ting, *"A Letter to WCC Secretary"*, from *Tian Feng* 1991 July, CCC&TSPM, Shanghai. P.13.

[27] Han Wen-chao, *"An Interview to Vice-President of CCC Han Wenzao"*, from *Tian Feng* 1991 July, CCC&TSPM, Shanghai. P.13.

[28] CCA member churches are from Aotearoa New Zealand, Australia, Bangladesh, Bhutan, Cambodia, Hong Kong SAR, India, Indonesia, Iran, Laos, Myanmar, Nepal, Japan, Korea, Malaysia, Pakistan, Philippines, Sri Lanka, Taiwan,

member churches, the Taiwan Presbyterian Church adheres to the standpoint of "Taiwan independence", which is a big obstacle hindering regular and official communication between the CCC and the CCA. Nevertheless, some friendly representatives from CCA have pursued closer contacts with the Chinese Church through church visits and communication in the recent years. The former General Secretary Prawate Khid-arn visited China with his delegation in February 2010, which was a good chance for understanding the current situation of developments of China's Christianity and conveying its achievements to the other member churches and organizations in Asia.

Thus, maintaining an adherence to the "One China" policy is the cornerstone for the Chinese Church developing good relations with various churches in different countries and backgrounds. When the former General Secretary of WCC, Samuel Kobia, visited China in November 2006, he identified with the "One China" policy and the "Three-self" principle as the secret of fast church growth and success in China's Christianity. Particularly, the "Three-self" principle had made the Chinese Church dynamic and integrated into society. It also supports the continuous development of Chinese theology and Christian participation in social services. Samuel Kobia appreciated the achievements of Chinese Christianity in the process of entering into the post-denominational period and running the church independently. He also anticipated that the Chinese Church would think of more responsibilities towards the universal churches and participate in the work of the WCC more devotedly, by making a significant contribution to the ecumenical movement in the 21st Century.[29] Therefore it must be the common dream of the Chinese Church and other Asian Churches to keep open good and effective channels of communication and cooperation in the future.

To conclude,I agree with two Asian scholars' opinion that "The changing ideological and political climate of international relations in Asia and in other parts of the world and the equally changing complexion of Chinese economic, social and political life have clearly begun to break down this wall of separation between China and the rest of Asia, and should, in the not too distant future, also erode more fully the barriers that have kept the Chinese churches from the mainstream of the ecumenical movement in Asia."[30] As a member of WCC and a representative of Asian churches, the Church in China currently is in a 'golden age' of growth and development in the Chinese society and ecumenical family. We Chinese Christians should undertake the due responsibility of building up the body of Christ in this plural world. We pray that the time of a fuller fellowship and wide exchange between Chinese churches and other churches in Asia will be realized in the process of the ecumenical movement by our joint effort and grace of God.

Bibliography

Ninan Koshy, *A History of The Ecumenical Movement In Asia (Vol.I)*, WSCFAPR/APA of YMCAs,CCA,2004

K.H. Ting, *Love Never Ends*, Yilin Press, Nanjing, 2000

Han Wenzao, "*Mutual Respect, Mutual Cooperation*", from *Tian Feng*, 1993 November, CCC&TSPM, Shanghai. P.26

Philip L. Wickeri, *Reconstructing Christianity in China*, Orbis Books, Maryknoll, New York, 2007

Gao Ying, *A Chinese Perspective on the Ecumenical Movement, in Chinese Theological Review:13*, Foundation for Theological Education in Southeast, 1999. p.78

Thailand and Timor Leste.

[29] Cf. Chen Meiling, *"Interview of Samuel Kobia General Secretary of WCC"*, from *Tian Feng* 2007 January, CCC&TSPM, Shanghai. P.30.

[30] Wang Peng (Ed.), *"Cosmic Christ and Ecumenical Fellowship"* by (Philippine) Feliciano and Theresa Carino from *Seeking Truth in Love,* China Religious Culture Publisher, Beijing. P.376.

Chen Zeming, "*The Achievement of Church in China and Prospects of 21st Century*", in his book *Seeking and Witnessing,* 2007, CCC&TSPM, Shanghai. p.171

(6) Orthodox Presence in the Asian Ecumenical Movement

K.M. George

Any historical reflection on the Orthodox participation in the Ecumenical Movement in Asia will have to critically deal with various elements including the following:

- Asia and Christianity
- Emergence of the Asian Ecumenical Movement
- Orthodox presence in Asia and its ecumenical significance

1. Asia and Christianity

The very word Asia originated in the Graeco-Roman imperial geography which spoke of *Asia Minor* and *Asia Major*. However, many regions of present day Asia were simply *terra incognita* for the Romans. It was given a concrete geo-political form during the Western colonial movement beginning with the arrival of the Portuguese navigator Vasco da Gama, who landed in an ancient port near Calicut on the Malabar cost in present-day Kerala, a south western state of India. The Portuguese colonial invasion of Asia was followed up by other Western powers.

The idea of *Asia* as one entity was created by the European mind during this colonial period. The Western explorers and colonial authorities recognized the immense cultural, ethnic and linguistic diversity existing among the countries in Asia. However to them the people of Pakistan and India and those of China and Japan were all 'Asian' with a broad spectrum of other nations and cultures in between. There is a certain common ground of Asian-ness linking all these diverse cultures and nations. The overall approach to Reality in Asia, despite rich internal diversity and sometimes substantial divergence, is very different from the general western approach developed especially during the second millennium of the Christian era. One may be puzzled by the apparently very different world views represented, for example, between the philosophy of Advaita Vedanta in India and the Confucian ethics in China yet one may discern a certain common Asian ethos running through all ancient Asian systems of philosophy, spirituality and ethics. Religious roots and the spread of Buddhism, for instance, are a connecting link that forged a certain cultural commonality in many of the Asian countries.

2. Eastern Christianity and Asia

In the first millennium of the Common Era there were two streams of the tradition of Christianity in Asia, one followed by the other chronologically, and the two merging subsequently in the 16th century, about the time of the arrival of the Portuguese Roman Catholics and colonial powers in Asia. The important point here is that both these streams were "oriental" in origin and character and reached Asia long before the continent came into contact with European Christianity. They are the following:

(a) The St. Thomas tradition

Thomas, one of the 12 Apostles of Jesus Christ, is traditionally believed to have arrived in India, precisely at the ancient port of Kodungalloor in present-day Kerala on the south west cost of India in AD 52. (Recent excavations have unearthed an ancient town called *Pattanam* not very far from Kodungalloor. It shows evidence of ancient trade and commerce between the Kerala coast *and* Romans, Greeks, Arabs and Jews before Christ, and in the early Christian period). The strong and living tradition of Indian Christians living in Kerala and in Diaspora has always faithfully attested to the arrival of Thomas as the foundational event of Christianity in Asia. Circumstantial evidences for this event are prolific. The Christian tradition that survived in India from then on had a distinctly Eastern flavor.

In the 4th century there were several waves of immigration of Christians from the Persian empire due to persecution and for trade to the Malabar cost (Kerala) where Christians were already present. These immigrants of old still retain, to some extent, their ethnic identity and generally practice endogamy though they live together with the other Kerala Christians in the same faith and practices.

Now divided between Oriental Orthodox, East Syrian, Roman Catholic and Protestant streams the St. Thomas Christians are a flourishing and influential community in Kerala. The efforts to overcome their division that occurred since the 16th century due to the aggressive missionary practices of the Portuguese Roman Catholic missionaries and then the rather soft mission of the British missionaries are as old as the division. Although the attribute 'ecumenical' for Church union efforts is of 20th century origin, some of the discerning and wise persons in the divided Indian Christian community always longed and worked for unity.

(b) East Syrian spiritual connections

The other stream consisted in the arrival of East Syrian Christian traders and missionaries from the Mesopotamian region to India, China and greater Asia. China still retains the 7th century steleand the inscription commemorating the arrival of East Syrian "Alopen" and the "Nestorian" missionaries.[1] In several countries in Asia from India to China, we have ancient stone crosses associated with East Syrian missionaries and traders. In India it is generally called "Persian Cross" or more recently as "St. Thomas' Cross". However, while the Indian Christian community in Kerala continued to retain the live memory of this heritage, there was no trace of any living Christian community in China claiming this heritage when the western colonial and missionary bodies arrived there.

3. Asian Ecumenical Movement and Orthodox Presence

The modern Ecumenical Movement has its origin in the early 20th century arising mainly from the missionary interests of Western Protestant Churches. In Asia, this was reflected naturally in the then young Churches founded by western missionary efforts. So it was, of course, confined to churches of the Reformation tradition.

The Orthodox presence in Asia, or rather Eastern Christianity was mainly confined to the historic Malankara Orthodox Syrian Church (sometime wrongly called Jacobite) which traces its origin to the preaching of the Gospel of Christ by Thomas the Apostle. In fact, there is a group of churches based in Kerala, India, belonging to the Roman Catholic, Orthodox and Protestant traditions, but jointly affirming the *St Thomas Tradition*. These Christians in general are locally called *Nazranis* (probably meaning 'the followers of the Nazarene'). Since the Portuguese colonial times a section of the Thomas Christians has been affiliated to the western tradition of the then Roman Catholic Church. Heavily Latinized by the work of the Jesuit and Carmelite missionaries under Roman juridical and canonical authority and almost losing the eastern ecclesiological heritage, this section of the *Nazranis*, generally called Syro-Malabar Catholics, are now making serious efforts to regain their lost Eastern heritage. In the 16th century the Indian church of St Thomas, bitterly persecuted by the Portuguese authorities, sought help from Oriental patriarchates including the Syrian and Coptic Churches, in order to counter the efforts of proselytisation and inquisitorial oppression from the Western Roman Catholic authorities in the 16th and 17th centuries. In AD 1665 the arrival of a bishop called Mor Gregorios Abdul Jalil from Jerusalem, in response to a request from India, started a new chapter in the history of the St Thomas Christians. Instead of the gradually introduced East

---

[1] See for instance: http://en.wikipedia.org/wiki/Nestorian_Stele

Syriac liturgy prevalent in the Indian church until then, the west Syrian or Antiochian liturgical tradition and practices were introduced. The present Orthodox Church in India now follows this liturgical heritage. It was welcomed by the people because it did not violate their original Eastern sense of the St. Thomas Tradition nor did it challenge the sense of autonomy of the Indian Church. The ascetical spirituality of the Oriental Christian monks and bishops who occasionally visited India blended very well with the Indian Hindu ethos of asceticism. However, towards the end of the 19th century Syrian patriarchal authority making jurisdictional claims over the Indian Church began to impose on the church in the spirit and style of the then prevailing colonial regimes. This provoked the Indian Orthodox Church, and led to a series of legal wrangling and conflicts that still haunt the Church. Since all this is not about any doctrine of faith, but essentially a question of jurisdictional claims on the side of the patriarchate of Antioch over the Indian church *versus* the deep sense of autonomy of the church of St Thomas which had enjoyed freedom and self rule since ancient times, there is hope among the faithful that this division would be healed and unity would be restored. In the 19th century with the arrival of the British missionaries and their missionary efforts, another section, though smaller, of the ancient community was attracted to the teachings of Reformation tradition. This eventually split the ancient church, and the separation between the Orthodox Church and the newly reformed *Marthoma* church on doctrinal grounds was the sad result of this division.

In modern times there are small Russian, Greek, Armenian, Coptic, Syrian and other Eastern traditions in different parts of Asia due to immigration and trade. There are small Asian Orthodox Churches like the Korean Orthodox Church of the Greek tradition. The Malankara Orthodox Church has a strong Diaspora in Malaysia, Singapore and Australia. These Diaspora communities including those newly converted from local communities largely follow the liturgical and spiritual traditions of their mother churches. There is hardly anything called an "Asianization" happening in these Diaspora communities except perhaps in such areas as liturgical language and iconography.

These Diaspora Orthodox communities are generally open to ecumenical initiatives, mainly because their parent bodies are all members of the WCC and are committed to ecumenical collaboration. The Malankara (Indian) Orthodox Church became a founding member of the WCC in 1948, in Amsterdam.

If we take the Christian Conference of Asia (CCA) as a major structural expression of Asian ecumenism, the Malankara Orthodox Church has been involved in it since the early 1970s. Metropolitan Mathews Mar Coorilos (later Catholicos Marthoma Mathews I), Fr Paul Verghese (later Metropolitan Paulos Mar Gregorios), Fr Philipose Thomas (later Metropolitan Mar Eusebios), to mention just a few, had been prominently involved in the ecumenical work of the CCA and promoted its connections with the Malankara Orthodox Church of India.

4. Theological Significance of the Orthodox Presence in Asia

Unlike the Western Churches, the Orthodox Eastern Churches have never been involved in any systematic proselytizing mission in Asia. Therefore, one does not find any significant Orthodox presence in Asia except in India where the historic Malankara Church existed since apostolic times. Therefore, as everywhere, it is not the quantitative but qualitative theological and spiritual presence of Orthodox Churches that is of any significance.

Let me mention three broad areas:

(a) Inter-faith experience and cooperation

While Christian churches in the West almost always lived in a rather mono-cultural European setting until about the second half of the 20th century Asian Christians have always been living in a pluralistic context with a broad spectrum of religions, cultures, ethnicities and worldviews. Asia, being the home of some major religions, has been hospitable to Christianity as well, just as it has always been open to a vast array of greatly divergent spiritual and philosophical systems.

The Malankara Orthodox Church has developed a certain *modus vivendi* with the majority of the Hindu population and others over the centuries. The implications of this long dialogue of life are important for the wider ecumenical concerns of global Christianity, especially since some prophets of doom foresee a clash of civilizations rooted in major religions of the world.

It is now generally perceived that the emergence of religious and cultural pluralism constitutes a major challenge for global Christianity, particularly for the classical mainline western churches which, with notable exceptions, continue to take their mono-cultural settings for granted. In this context the Asian experience of the Orthodox Church and its presence and mission on this continent acquire a paradigmatic character.

The first thing that strikes an outside observer is probably the minority status of the Christian Church in Asia. In India, for example, it is still less than 3% of the total population of more than 1.1 billion. In spite of the existence in India of a Christian community from the first century AD and the massive efforts of the Portuguese and the British missionaries since the 16th century to Christianize India, the Christian population has not registered any significant quantitative growth. It should also be noted that ancient Oriental Christianity in India has had no bitter memory of any persecution from local rulers or any aggressive opposition from other religions. (It may be a paradox that local Christians in Kerala suffered persecution not from non-Christian authorities or neighbors but from Christian brothers from the west during the Portuguese period). In fact, the centuries-old experience of St Thomas tradition of Christianity in the Southern state of Kerala has, more or less, been that of acceptance and respect in a heavily caste-ridden society.

It is noteworthy that the Orthodox church in Asia or anywhere else does not give priority to any mission of conversion of non-Christians or proselytisation of other Christians. The mission emphasis is rather on bearing witness (*martyria*) to Christ in other ways rather than quantitative and numerical growth of the church. There are certainly occasional voluntary conversions to the Orthodox Church due to several factors like marriage, personal conviction of those who seek the apostolic faith, predilection for spiritual practices like fasting and emphasis on liturgical experience, attraction to a monastic and acetic life and so on. However, the eastern Church attaches much importance to respecting other faiths and maintaining genuine friendliness to neighbors as forms of radiating Christ's love for the world. There is an obvious divergence in this respect between the Orthodox churches and the traditional western churches. The latter in general believe strongly in conversion as an integral part of preaching the Gospel of Christ and the mission of the Church.

Asia has the experience of two ancient missions much earlier than the western Christian mission. The Buddhist mission that started in India, some 2000 years before the west's European colonial Christian missions began coming to Asia. That mission of the Buddha, the Enlightened One, changed the face of Asia in a considerable way, and it has generally been perceived to be peaceful and nonviolent respecting local cultures and other faiths. Then Asia had the Christian mission of St Thomas and later the East Syrian ("Nestorian") mission in the first Christian millennium. This again was very peaceful though it lacked imperial might and the massive colonial outfit.

So the ecumenical question regarding Christian Mission and interfaith relations in Asia can be raised anew from this historical perspective. Christian Mission can be nothing but the dissemination of God's love for the world. The Gospel of Christ is the Gospel of Love. Whatever we think or do against this ultimate principle of love is against the Gospel. Any preaching of the gospel that undermines the Gospel message itself is not part of the Christian mission.

The Christian Church in Asia in its Eastern ethos has a lot of potential to enter deep into the spiritual genius of other Asian religions like Hinduism, Buddhism, Jainism and Taoism. Any common ground that appears to the genuine seekers in these religions need to be affirmed as our common human heritage endowed by the Creator to all humanity. Affirmation of commonality rather than the assertion of difference must be the rule in a genuine dialogue between different faiths.

The biblical question '*who is your neighbor'?* is still being raised in response to the ancient commandment ' *Love your neighbor as yourself'*. The answer always points to a *Samaritan*, the one who is doctrinally heretical, culturally outcaste and spiritually out of communion with you. It is this despised, unredeemed and cast- out stranger who becomes the true neighbor in a critical moment of your life. He has already shown supreme love to you in your pain and suffering, and is willing to do more for you. What would be your response?

When we consider the ultimate divine commandment to love one's neighbor in relation to interfaith dialogue and cooperation, the parable of Jesus enlightens us with a new revolutionary insight. It is the Other who apparently does not share your doctrine of faith or worships your God who becomes your neighbor. As Asian Christians in general can acknowledge, they sometimes get more solid human support, true friendship and love from their neighbors of other faiths than from their own fold. An important ecumenical aspect of the mission of the Church in pluralistic Asia is to create, cherish and foster this genuine neighborliness. This is one significant manner in which we bear witness to Christ, the Good Samaritan, who bore our sins and healed our wounds out of pure love and compassion.

(b) Ecclesiology

Orthodox Churches maintain an ecclesiology which they attribute to the spirit and structure of "the one undivided Church". "The local Church ecclesiology" of the Orthodox Churches rather than a "universal church ecclesiology" may go along more smoothly with the Asian spirit of plurality, harmony, hospitality and respect to the other. A *qualitative catholicity* is the Orthodox alternative to the claims of any *quantitative universality* of number or geographical extension. The Buddhist tradition, for instance, has created a new spirit in Asia of combining tolerance and compassion as well as diversity and unity across the Asian religious landscape.

The metaphor of the *Body of Christ* used by Apostle Paul is taken very seriously in the Orthodox tradition. There is a tendency in academic circles to minimize the importance of this Pauline image as merely a metaphor. However in the Patristic tradition of the Church it is a constitutive element of ecclesiology. The Church as the Body of Christ is One. The unity of the Church is affirmed by the Orthodox churches on the basis of the integral and holistic character of the Body of Christ. In the Ecumenical Movement, and its doctrinal arm of Faith and Order, the Orthodox Churches tirelessly stand for the undivided witness of the Church as one Body. It does not deny any true cultural, linguistic and liturgical diversity. In fact, the Local Church Ecclesiology of the Orthodox tradition has always promoted all genuine diversity and distinct identities in the unity and wholeness of the Body of Christ. The ineffable perception of the Triune nature of Godhead in which the distinct identity or *Hypostasis* of the Father, of the Son and of the Holy Spirit sharing the one *Ousia* or Essence underlines the unity and catholicity of the Church, the Body of Christ. This is to be newly interpreted and understood in Asia where the immense diversities can threaten its unity with fatal political and economic consequences. An ecclesiology for Asia requires the emphasis on the oneness of the body of humanity, the sacred character of that body, the inter dependence of the limbs of the body, justice and peace in the mutual sharing and assistance within the body and the sense of oneness with all creation as the larger Body of Christ. The emphasis is not on legalistic authority structures or a pyramidical hierarchy or a simple linear perception of history and progress, but on the organic and holistic life of the Body continually renewed and perfected by the dynamic indwelling of the Holy Spirit.

An Asian ecclesiology rooted in the Body of Christ and drawing lessons from the harmony of religions in Asia and from the Eastern Christian tradition will be of great value to the wider world. It will be a radically new way of bearing witness to Christ.

(c) Spirituality and ethics

Spirituality is an area of rich potential for the Orthodox presence in Asia. The Eastern Christian spiritual and ethical understanding of reality has a large common ground with Asian religious philosophies and spiritual mindset in general. The Orthodox understanding of *theosis* or divinization and the transfiguration of the created world rooted in a holistic, incarnational theology has openings to the Asian vision of unity, and diversity, transcendence, renunciation and compassion. The ascetic-monastic values in both Orthodox and Asian spiritual understanding have striking parallels.

The Asian ethical stand based on the integrity of the family and social bonds and values promoting justice, non-violence (*ahimsa*) and respect for creation can be further explored ecumenically by the Orthodox tradition and Asian religions together. There is great potential for a mutually enriching give and take here. Issues of poverty and injustice, marginalization and exploitation are to be addressed jointly by Eastern Christianity and Asian religions since there is a heavy emphasis in both on transcendence, ritual and meditative tranquility, sometimes at the expense of a prophetic commitment for the transformation of the economic, social and political structures aimed at the common good and a just socio-economic order. This broadens the ecumenical vocation of the Church in Asia as well as creates a domain of wider Asian Ecumenism that takes into account the profound Asian religious-spiritual heritage.

Bibliography

Koshy Ninan, *A History of the Ecumenical Movement in Asia*, Vol 1, WSCF, YMCA,CCA, Hong Kong,2004

Daniel David, *The Orthodox Church of India*, New Delhi, 1986

Cherian C.V., *A History of Christianity in India: A History of the Orthodox Church AD 52-2002*, Kottayam, Academic Publishers (2003)

George Kondothra, "Theological Education in the Oriental Orthodox Tradition," in Dietrich Werner et al, *Handbook of Theological Education in World Christianity: Theological Perspectives, Regional Surveys, Ecumenical trends,* Regnum Studies in Global Christianity (2010), p.623-628

George K.M., *Interfacing theology with culture,* Delhi (2010)

Thomas, Meladath Kurian, *The Indian Way of Christanity*, Saarbruecken, Germany, Lambart Acadamic Publications, 2012

(7) Asian Ecumenism from Roman Catholic Perspective

Edmund Kee-Fook Chia

The Context of Christian Division

Molly and Angeline became best friends. They had come from different parts of the country to begin college studies. Having found each other on day one they became almost inseparable, going everywhere together and doing everything together. The majority of the students in the college were Muslims and Buddhists whilst Molly and Angeline were Christians. They met at the Christian Fellowship Center and henceforth its activities became the focal point of their day-to-day life. Things went on smoothly until the semester break when they returned home. Angeline's parents were horrified that she was no longer attending a Roman Catholic mass on Sundays but was instead going for the Baptist service at Molly's church.

Such is the situation a number of Catholics in Asia find themselves confronted with. As Christians they are minorities in their nation but as Catholics they find themselves having to segregate even also from their own fellow Christians. This has as much to do with the centuries-old doctrinal differences as with the effects of colonialism in Asian lands. That the majority of Christians in the Philippines and Vietnam are Catholics and those in Indonesia are Protestants is testimony to the colonial legacy.[1] The Philippines was colonized by the Spaniards and Vietnam by the French (both predominantly Catholic countries), while the Dutch Protestants colonized Indonesia. At the local level the colonial practice was to encourage only one or two church tradition to establish itself in particular islands or cities or villages. Thus where there was already a Presbyterian church in town chances were the Lutherans were not invited to establish a mission there. Or, if the Roman Catholics had a school in a village in all probability the Methodists were asked to build elsewhere.

Of course, the division due to theological and denominational differences runs even more deeply in the Asian Christian's psyche. This can be traced back to the Reformation and to what Catholics call the Counter-Reformation, in particular the ecclesiastical reforms put in place by the Council of Trent (1543-1565).[2] Let us examine just three of these divisive differences. If Luther insisted on the doctrine of *sola scriptura* ("by scripture alone"), Trent emphasized the theology of the Church's Tradition. Hence, for the Catholic the teaching office of the Church became an indispensable source of Christian doctrine whilst for the Protestant the Bible is the only necessary source. Catholics therefore looked towards the Magisterium in interpreting God's will as revealed in scripture while Protestants believed that the Bible required no interpretation outside of itself. Furthermore, if Luther preached the doctrine of *sola fide* ("by faith alone"), Roman Catholicism maintained that good works are not so much necessary but remain significant for the justification of one's soul. Thus Protestants emphasized faith in Christ and the explicit acceptance of Jesus as Lord and savior, while Catholics accentuated the role of the seven sacraments and the theological virtue of good works. Finally, if Luther advanced the doctrine of *solo Christus* ("through Christ alone"), Roman Catholicism allowed for other ways of mediation between God and humanity. Aside from rejecting Marian devotions and intercessions of the saints, Protestants also generally believe in the priesthood of all believers while Catholics hold the priestly ordination of men by apostolic succession as essential to their

---

[1] See Peter C. Phan (ed.), *Christianities in Asia* (Malden, MA: Wiley-Blackwell, 2011).

[2] Though the division caused by the Great Schism between the Eastern and Western Church happened five centuries earlier a lot of the divisions in Asia are between the Roman Catholic Church and the Churches of the Reformation era since Orthodox Churches are few in numbers.

faith. This Tridentine theology which was passed down from generation to generation was as much instrumental for sustaining the Roman Catholic identity as it was for distinguishing them from the Christians of the other denominations.

Vatican II and Catholic Ecumenism

This was to go on for more than 400 years until the Second Vatican Council (1962-1965) which more than revolutionized the Roman Catholic Church. At the convocation of the Council, Pope John XXIII made it clear that unlike Trent which was called in response to the Protestant Reformation and Vatican I to the challenge of modernity, Vatican II was called to embark on what he called an *aggiornamento* or church updating and renewal. Of significance is that Vatican II ought to seek reconciliation with the world which the Church had marginalized itself from, including the world of modernity, the world of other religions, and the world of other Christian denominations.[3]

As if to put into practice the last objective, the pope had established the Secretariat for Promoting Christian Unity in 1960 to assist in preparing for the Council. The Secretariat then invited leading figures from the Protestant community and Orthodox Churches to attend the Council as observers. This was in itself another significant step as it meant the entire deliberation of the Council Fathers was done in full view of their "separated brethren." In fact, that label alone was already a vast improvement as, prior to that, Protestants were known more as heretics and schismatics. These steps were clear proofs that the Roman Catholic Church was taking seriously the task of healing the division which had been going on for more than four centuries.

In the third year of Vatican II, the Synod fathers issued in 1964 a document entitled *Unitatis Redintegratio* (UR), the decree on Ecumenism. The document began with this assertion: "The restoration of unity among all Christians is one of the principal concerns of the Second Vatican Council" (*UR*, 1).[4] It then went on to acknowledge that "the differences that exist in varying degrees between [the other Christian denominations] and the Catholic Church – whether in doctrine and sometimes in discipline, or concerning the structure of the Church – do indeed create many obstacles, sometimes serious ones, to full ecclesiastical communion" (*UR*, 2). The Council then went on to exhort "all the Catholic faithful to recognize the signs of the times and to take an active and intelligent part in the work of ecumenism" (*UR*, 4). It insisted that "Catholics, in their ecumenical work, must assuredly be concerned for their separated brethren, praying for them, keeping them informed about the Church, making the first approaches toward them" (*UR*, 4). The Council then unambiguously states that "the attainment of union is the concern of the whole Church, faithful and shepherds alike" (*UR*, 5).

One of the first tasks that the post-Vatican II Church took was the publication of an Ecumenical Directory to provide more specific guidelines for what the ministry of ecumenism actually entails.[5] It then began to actively seek out dialogue partners to further the vision of Christian unity. In the last 40 years the Roman Catholic Church has been engaged in numerous encounters, including bilateral international theological dialogues with the Orthodox Church, the Anglican Communion, the World Alliance of Reformed Churches, the World Methodist Council, the Baptist World Alliance, the Disciples of Christ

---

[3] See John W. O'Malley, *What Happened at Vatican II* (Cambridge, MA: Belknap Press of Harvard University Press, 2008).

[4] Second Vatican Council, *Unitatis Redintegratio: Decree on Ecumenism* (1964), http://www.vatican.va/archive/hist_councils/ii_vatican_council/documents/vat-ii_decree_19641121_unitatis-redintegratio_en.html.

[5] The Pontifical Council for Promoting Christian Unity, http://www.vatican.va/roman_curia/pontifical_councils/chrstuni/documents/rc_pc_chrstuni_pro_20051996_chrstuni_pro_en.html.

Church, and some Pentecostal groups. Topics which these ecumenical dialogues have dealt with include understanding and collaboration in the diffusion of the Bible as well as explorations of theological and doctrinal issues as diverse as Baptism, Eucharist, and Ministry as well as of the Church's Teaching Authority, the Apostolic Tradition, and Revelation and Faith. These activities continue and many difficult theological divergences have been addressed.

The Federation of Asian Bishops' Conferences

While the thrust towards ecumenical dialogues was taking place at the universal Church level, the Asian Catholic Church was also embarking on its own process, albeit from another direction. Represented by the Federation of Asian Bishops' Conferences (FABC), it has taken some significant strides in promoting Christian unity. The FABC actually has its roots in Vatican II as the Asian bishops got to know one another for the first time only during the 1960s when they were meeting in Rome. They maintained their relationship upon their return to Asia and subsequently toyed with the idea of setting up some sort of structure to help build upon the new spirit of communion established amongst themselves.

The papal visit of Pope Paul VI to Asia in 1970 provided the occasion for the Asian bishops to come together in Manila, the Philippines. During the gathering the idea of a Federation of Asian Bishops' Conferences (FABC) was conceived and conceptualized. Indian theologian Felix Wilfred had this to say about the Asian Bishops' Meeting (ABM) in Manila: "Never before had Asian bishops come together to exchange experiences and to deliberate jointly on common questions and problems facing the continent. The meeting marked the beginning of a new consciousness of the many traditional links that united the various peoples of this part of the globe."[6]

At the end of the meeting the bishops issued a message in which they acknowledged that as part of the "awakening, we see the face of an Asia at long last coming to birth as a true community of peoples. For barriers which have so long isolated our nations from one another are falling one by one, and the desire grows among us to know each other and to find each other as Asian, sister-nations among whom relationships of friendship and trust, of collaboration, sharing and genuine solidarity may be firmly lastingly wrought" (*ABM,* 12).

A fundamental aspect in the building of these relationships, the bishops realized, is with their Protestant brothers and sisters of Asia. Cognizant of the history and reality of the Catholic-Protestant division, which continues to pervade much of the churches in Asia, they saw this as a critical concern to be addressed. They therefore proclaimed that "[g]athered together, then, in Christ's presence, we turn to the other Christian churches and communities in Asia, seeking to collaborate with them in our efforts for the development of our peoples, for freedom, justice and peace" (*ABM,* 25)[7].

Ecumenism in the Asian Catholic Church

As can be seen from the last statement, for the Asian Church ecumenism is not so much about theological dialogues as it is about working together in the service of Asia's people and society. That is why for the FABC ecumenism has primarily taken the form of collaborative ventures with other Christian organizations and especially the Christian Conference of Asia (CCA). For example, in 1971 the FABC's Office of Human Development and the CCA's unit of Urban Rural Mission participated in establishing the Asian Committee for People's Organization and in 1982 to found the Ecumenical Coalition on Third

[6] Felix Wilfred, "The Federation of Asian Bishops' Conferences (FABC): Orientations, Challenges and Impact," in Gaudencio Rosales and C. G. Arévalo (ed.), *For All the People of Asia: Federation of Asian Bishops' Conferences,* Documents from 1970 to 1991, vol. 1 (Quezon City: Claretian, 1997), xxiii.

[7] "Asian Bishops' Meeting," in *Ibid.*, 3-8.

World Tourism and in 1987 the FABC and CCA hosted a conference in Singapore to reflect on the theme of "Living and Working Together with Sisters and Brothers of Other Faiths in Asia."[8] These collaborative actions can also be called ecumenism *ad extra*, i.e., the actions are in the service not of the *ad intra* concerns or needs of the respective churches but on behalf of the Asian societies and cultures as a whole.

It was not until the early 1990s that the FABC and the CCA finally decided that it was time to actively pursue the agenda of ecumenism *per se*. Together they established a task force which resulted in the formation of the Asian Ecumenical Committee (AEC). This is a high-powered committee of seven representatives from each side, tasked with exploring concrete means for the promotion of Christian unity in Asia. Amongst its first and most tangible fruits was a series of programs entitled Asian Movement for Christian Unity (AMCU). These AMCUs brought together equal number of representatives from both the CCA and FABC to study and deliberate together on issues of specific concern to the ecumenical agenda. It was here that ecclesiological and theological issues were raised, exploring how a common vision for Christian unity in Asia can be arrived at. Arising from these AMCUs were follow-up programs in the form of Joint Ecumenical Formation (JEF) courses and the Asian Conference of Theological Students (ACTS). The former is a program devised to discuss modules for the formation of grassroots leaders so as to encourage active involvement in ecumenism and the latter a forum which brings together students from seminaries and theological institutions to explore concerns peculiar to Asia with the hope that they will be the ecumenical leaders of the future. They have been highly successful endeavors.

Another project which has enhanced the CCA-FABC ecumenical relationship has been the joint staff meetings. These are meetings which bring together the staff members of the CCA and the executive secretaries of the various offices of the FABC. They are effective in that the staff members on both sides are then introduced not only to each other's counterpart working in the other organization but also to the programs and resources of the other. A consequence of these meetings is the active sharing of resources as well as greater collaboration between the two bodies when attending to similar social and cultural problems for the benefit of all the peoples of Asia. It is worth reiterating that the fundamental concern which undergirds all of these ecumenical collaborations is the betterment of Asian society. The Final Statement of the first AMCU expresses this well: "Without a sensitive awareness of and an involvement in our cultures and religions, especially as they relate to the struggles of women, indigenous people, and the marginalized and the oppressed for their justice and identity, we will not be able to realize fully [the visible unity of the Church] in Asia."[9]

Ecumenism of Table Fellowship

Aside from the documents which have been drafted and institutional partnerships which been built up there is also another more important dimension to ecumenism that has been fostered. I refer here to the informal relationships cultivated on account of the meetings between the representatives of both sides in what I will call the ecumenism of table fellowship. Yes, some of the most serious deliberations and cooperative ventures actually take place not so much in the conference rooms but in the dining halls. In dialogue we bring not only our ideas and traditions to the table but our whole selves and friendship as well. And because many conferences happen over several days at a retreat center or hotel the living-in experience is an especially privileged and grace occasion for the building up of special bonds and trust amongst the participants. The Final Statement of AMCU III said as much:

---

[8] See Virginia Fabella, "The Roman Catholic Church in the Asian Ecumenical Movement," in Ninan Koshy (ed.), *A History of the Ecumenical Movement in Asia, Volume II* (Hong Kong: WSCF Asia-Pacific, Asia and Pacific Alliance of YMCAs & Christian Conference of Asia, 2004), 115-138.

[9] Franz-Josef Eilers (ed.), *For All the Peoples of Asia: Federation of Asian Bishops' Conferences,* Documents from 1992 to 1996, vol. 2 (Quezon City: Claretian, 1997), 180.

> We, the participants of AMCU III, coming from the different churches in Asia and beyond, are grateful to God for this unique ecumenical experience of living together, praying together and reflecting together on our common mission in Asia. We were able to shed prejudices, discover valuable treasures in other churches and listen to the Spirit speaking through ourselves and others. We appeal to our own churches to commit themselves fully to this ecumenical vision and fellowship to which God calls us all that we may give a common witness and help build a new Asia transformed by the values of the Gospel.[10]

The same can be said about the ecumenism that is happening on a day-to-day basis in Asia. Many Catholics are engaged in informal ecumenical dialogues with their Protestant friends in the workplace, school, neighborhood, or marketplace. Many are in the same boat as Angeline and Molly. They meet in college and become best friends, with no thought whatsoever to their denominational differences. By the time they realize that their faith life is different, such as Protestants having different views of the sacraments or that Catholics understand the Bible differently, their relationship would have been so deep that these differences don't matter anymore. In other words, in view of the natural dialogue of life that has already been taking place there is really no need for the dialogue of theology to resolve the differences. Ecumenical dialogue, in such circumstances, makes little sense.

Formal ecumenism is important and makes sense mainly for those who grow up with constricted and exclusive views of faith. For the younger generation of Catholics this is probably not the case. In a sense they harbor little prejudice of their Christian friends of other denominations if for no other reason than because they themselves have little knowledge of their own faith! Unlike their parents' generation the Catholic young are more likely to be interacting across faith and denominational lines simply because they grow up in less segregated environments. Also, because of the higher rate of mobility where one travels across state lines or even national boundaries for study or work, the strength of tradition weakens. For instance, one is no longer able to attend the church of childhood years or participate in celebrations peculiar to one's family church. Thus, when traditional practices or belief systems begin to slip away, worshipping in other churches (especially those where your best friend worships) becomes commonplace.

Ecumenism for the Postmodern Youth

Besides, these younger Catholics have little knowledge of the specific theological differences across Christian denominations. They have not been catechized into reacting against the faith of their Christian friends. Even if they were, they would be more accepting of the differences anyway. This is in part because many of today's youth would have grown up in the virtual world of infinite possibilities and shaped by the postmodern ethos of relativity and openness. Postmodernism is not only inclusive of diversity but is also wary of exclusivity and claims to normativity and superiority.[11] Postmodernists thrive best on tentativeness and multiplicity and shun oneness, universality or even uniformity. Thus, for the postmodern young, religious denominational differences are by no means problematic; they are a given and should be appreciated as such. In a sense they may not even feel compelled to choose one over another and so may be considered post-denominational Christians. The more important element for choosing a Christian community or place of worship is that they feel safe and comfortable as well as a sense of acceptance and belonging. Theological and doctrinal differences mean little especially when weighed against these socio-relational traits.

In such circumstances ecumenism can even be regarded as redundant since the deep-seated divisions between Christian denominations may not have formed as yet. Moreover, the very idea and aim of

---

[10] Franz-Josef Eilers (ed.), *For All the Peoples of Asia: Federation of Asian Bishops' Conferences*, Document from 1997 to 2001, vol. 3 (Quezon City: Claretian, 2002), 154.

[11] Paul F. Knitter, *Theologies of Religions* (Maryknoll, NY: Orbis, 2002), 174-175.

ecumenism, which is the unity of all Christians, comes across not only as lofty and impossible but unnecessary as well. Thus, the prayer of Jesus in John 17: 21, *ut unum sint* ("that they may be one"), which is also the name of the latest encyclical on ecumenism issued by the Catholic Church, does not really ring a bell in the ears of the postmodern Catholic.[12] Perhaps, for them, the ecumenism of the marketplace has done more in bringing about the unity of Christians than the formal ecumenical dialogues that have been taking place. Perhaps this is the new face of ecumenism for the postmodern world, which might be tending towards being post-denominational and even post-religious. The experience of Molly and Angeline are by no means unique. In fact, they may constitute the norm of today's youth. While they pose challenges to the faith community, they also signal hope for a new vision of communion and unity of all Christians.

Bibliography

Eilers, Franz-Josef (ed.), *For All the Peoples of Asia: Federation of Asian Bishops' Conferences,* Documents from 1992 to 1996, vol. 2 (Quezon City: Claretian, 1997).

Eilers, Franz-Josef (ed.), *For All the Peoples of Asia: Federation of Asian Bishops' Conferences*, Document from 1997 to 2001, vol. 3 (Quezon City: Claretian, 2002).

John Paul II, *Ut Unum Sint: On Commitment to Ecumenism* (1995), 1995.05.25http://www.vatican.va/holy_father/john_paul_ii/encyclicals/documents/hf_jp-ii_enc_25051995_ut-unum-sint_en.html.

Knitter, Paul F., *Theologies of Religions* (Maryknoll, NY: Orbis, 2002).

Koshy, Ninan (ed.), *A History of the Ecumenical Movement in Asia, Volume II* (Hong Kong: WSCF Asia-Pacific, Asia and Pacific Alliance of YMCAs & Christian Conference of Asia, 2004).

O'Malley, John W., *What Happened at Vatican II* (Cambridge, MA: Belknap Press of Harvard University Press, 2008).

Phan, Peter C. (ed.), *Christianities in Asia* (Malden, MA: Wiley-Blackwell, 2011).

Pontifical Council for Promoting Christian Unity, http://www.vatican.va/roman_curia/pontifical_councils/chrstuni/documents/rc_pc_chrstuni_pro_20051996_chrstuni_pro_en.html.

Rosales, Gaudencio and Arévalo, C. G. (ed.), *For All the People of Asia: Federation of Asian Bishops' Conferences,* Documents from 1970 to 1991, vol. 1 (Quezon City: Claretian, 1997).

Second Vatican Council, *Unitatis Redintegratio: Decree on Ecumenism* (1964), http://www.vatican.va/archive/hist_councils/ii_vatican_council/documents/vat-ii_decree_19641121_unitatis-redintegratio_en.html.

[12] Pope John Paul II, *Ut Unum Sint: On Commitment to Ecumenism* (1995), 1995.05.25http://www.vatican.va/holy_father/john_paul_ii/encyclicals/documents/hf_jp-ii_enc_25051995_ut-unum-sint_en.html

(8) Giving Shape to a New Ecumenical Vision in Asia[1]

Feliciano V. Carino / Thomas Michael

The Asian Movement for Christian Unity (AMCU) was conceived in 1994 by the two largest Christian bodies in Asia – the Christian Conference of Asia (CCA) and the Federation of Asian Bishops' Conferences (FABC). Its goal is to promote unity at the local, national and continental levels among Christ's disciples in Asia.

Among other initiatives, the Asian Movement for Christian Unity has organized seminars involving church leaders, theologians and ecumenical officers. `The first (AMCU I) took place in Hong Kong, March 1996, with the theme, "Theology of Ecumenism." AMCU II was held in Bali, Indonesia, January 1998, on the theme, "Ecumenical Formation as Churches of Asia Move towards the Next Millennium."

The third seminar (AMCU III) brought some 50 participants – including senior representatives of the World Council of Churches and the Pontifical Council for Promoting Christian Unity – to Chiang Mai, Thailand, January 27 – February, 2001. Its theme, "Giving Shape to a New Ecumenical Vision in Asia," echoed the encouragement given by the CCA (at its two most recent assemblies), and by Pope John Paul II (in his 1999 Apostolic Exhortation *Ecclesia in Asia,* no. 30) that our churches should enter into a process of prayer and discussion to explore the possibilities of new ecumenical structures and associations for promoting Christian unity.

An Ecumenism of Communion

Communion is the heart of the ecclesial reality. To be a church means and demands that we enter into relationship with other churches. Koinonia exists, to some extent, between all Christian churches. Identifying, owning, nurturing and deepening this reality is the ecumenical task. Developing such relationships is all the more necessary in the Asian context. Christians have to bear a common witness and together engage in our common mission, in dialogue with our neighbours of all faiths, in the context of Asia's massive poverty and injustice. Our search for unity and our mission are inseparably united.

The driving force behind our ecumenical vision is the reconciling love of God in Jesus Christ, and his passionate prayer that all his disciples may be united (John 17:20-21). Christian unity is motivated by the Gospel, nothing less.

The theological foundation of our unity is our common baptism by which all Christians are really incorporated into the one body of Christ. "For we were all baptized by one Spirit into one Body" (1 Cor 12:13; Eph 4:4-6; also I Cor 11: 17-29). Affirmation of our common baptism beckons us to express our unity visibly in common witness (Matt 25:31-46). Our search for unity is a response to God's plan of gathering all the people of God (Jer 23:3, 31:10, Ez 37:21), and "to bring all things in heaven and earth

---

[1] This is a reprint from FABC/CCA Paper from AMCU Conference in Chiangmai, Thailand 2001: ASIAN MOVEMENT FOR CHRISTIAN UNITY (AMCU III). A Joint CCA – FABC Project. GIVING SHAPE TO A NEW ECUMENICAL VISION. Christian Conference of Asia and Federation of Asian Bishops' Conferences, Chiangmai, Thailand, January 27 – February 1, 2001, FABC Paper 99; see also: Our Pilgrimage in Hope: Proceedings of the First Three Seminars of the Asian Movement for Christian Unity (AMCU I, AMCU II, AMCU III). Christian Conference of Asia, Federation of Asian Bishops' Conferences. Office of Ecumenical and Interreligious Affairs, St. Pauls 2011, 299 pages; see also: Franz-Josef Eilers (ed.), *For All the Peoples of Asia: Federation of Asian Bishops' Conferences*, Documents from 1997 to 2001, vol. 3, (Quezon City: Claretian, 2002); see also on the website of FABC: http://www.fabc.org/fabc%20papers/fabc_paper_99.pdf; http://www.fabc.org/offices/oeia/history.html and: http://www.fabc.org/fabc%20papers/fabc_paper_92s.pdf

together under one head" (Eph 1:10). The church of Jesus Christ has to become truly "a sacrament and sign of unity of the whole humankind" *(Lumen Gentium 1, Unitatis Redintegratio 2)*

I. The Need for Conversion

To catch up with the vision of unity our churches and all Christians need a radical conversion, a conversion of heart. It requires a radical transformation in our way of thinking, acting and living, especially in relation to other churches. It challenges every kind of self-sufficiency and triumphalism, and invites us to see the positive values of other Christian traditions. This change of heart has to be reinforced by a life of common prayer and worship.

Formation of ecumenical associations in every Asian country is an integral part of our present ecumenical vision. However, it must be underlined that such councils or fellowships of churches are not super-churches or substitutes for our goal of full unity. Ecumenical structures are never ends in themselves. They exist to help our churches to pray together, think together, enter into a deeper understanding of the mystery of the Gospel together, share the treasures of faith together, and become part, together, of Asia's struggles for justice and peace.

Our common faith and baptism compels us to work together in a fellowship, though there still may be differences among the churches. After all, the ecumenical goal is not to create a uniform church, but a fellowship of churches that maintain their respective diversities and identities. Membership in a council of churches does not necessarily imply full recognition of other member churches (cf. the WCC's Toronto Statement on "The Church, the Churches, and the World Council of Churches" 1950). Such membership can enrich all the member churches by enabling their mutual sharing of gifts, and can help them move towards the visible unity which Christ wills for his people.

Toward Inclusive Ecumenical Associations

Inspired by this vision, driven by these convictions, participants in AMCU III urge the churches in Asia to find ways of giving clearer, visible expression to our common Christian calling. Different situations, of course, require different responses. No single structure will fit every national context; and already there are several models for closer cooperation that merit wider consideration.

What is important, as a matter of urgency, is that our churches – those that belong to national ecumenical bodies as well as those, including many bishops' conferences and synods, that at present do not – should respond positively, imaginatively, courageously to the invitation to enter into a process of prayer and reflection, aimed at finding a way of structuring their relationships that will more effectively serve the ecumenical movement in our time.

In each country, a joint working group might be set up by the churches to examine their existing relationships and bring forward proposals for improvements, and even for alternative ecumenical structures. While any church remains apart from the growing fellowship of Christ's people, that fellowship must be considered sadly incomplete. Fears and difficulties felt by particular churches should be discussed frankly, confident that Christ will not abandon his people to their divisions.

All ecumenical structures are to serve the churches' witness to the reconciling power of God in Jesus Christ. The test of their effectiveness, ultimately, is found in relations between Christian people in each place. National ecumenical structures are to assist and encourage, never to stifle, the initiatives of local churches in witness and service.

Similar questions need to be addressed in terms of continental ecumenical relationships. CCA and FABC, through their Asian Ecumenical Committee, will continue to seek ways for more effective cooperation – coordinating activities, for example, through regular staff meetings and joint ecumenical courses and programs. Some national bishops' conferences may wish to pursue the possibility of direct membership in CCA. The question of moving towards a new regional ecumenical body, in place of CCA, remains open for future consideration.

Echo Meetings in Asian Countries

What is the next step? As proposed above, churches in countries throughout Asia are urged to pursue this thinking in their own settings. An "echo" meeting, replicating nationally what AMCU III has tried to be regionally, might prove helpful. Responses to these considerations from the churches of each country are requested, indicating the actions being taken, forconsideration by the next meeting of the Asian Ecumenical Committee in 2002.

We, the participants of AMCU III, coming from the different churches in Asia and beyond, are grateful to God for this unique ecumenical experience of living together, praying together and reflecting together on our common mission in Asia. We were able to shed prejudices, discover valuable treasures in other churches and listen to the Spirit speaking through ourselves and others. We appeal to our own churches to commit themselves fully to this ecumenical vision and fellowship to which God calls us all, that we may give a common witness and help build a new Asia transformed by the values of the Gospel.

II. Giving Shape To A New Ecumenical Vision In Asia: Some Introductory Reflections (Feliciano Carino)

1. Introduction

Though coming from the world of business, it is worth noting what Reinhold Wurth says about "vision" as a way of avoiding the "trap" of either presenting "vision" as simply a "fantastic idea but is totally detached from reality;" or as a "simplistic suggestion or cheap recipe" that has no chance of coming into organizational reality. Wurth writes:

> Visions are spiritual high nights between past and future. Visions are more than dreams since they can be supported with arguments. Nevertheless they are less than strategic plans because visions go beyond the time-scale of the latter. Learning from the experiences of the past but at the same time detaching himself from them, the successful visionary attempts to anticipate the future in his thoughts as boldly and as realistically as he can. If he succeeds in formulating this future in a way which is to some extent valid, i.e., credible and viable for an (enterprise), a successful visionary can be a successful businessman.[2]

Talking about "giving shape to a new ecumenical vision" should be understood, as I see it, as a way of anticipating and formulating the ecumenical future in a valid, credible and viable way. There are ecumenical antecedents and experiences, common theological perspectives and historical conditions, that provide it its validity, credibility, and viability.

2. Some Ecumenical Antecedents

From the side of the Christian Conference of Asia (CCA), the ecumenical antecedents are clear and specific.

A. At the Asia Mission Conference (AMC) of the CCA, that was held in Cipanas, Indonesia in 1989, an encompassing and challenging resolution was passed for the future of the ecumenical movement in Asia. Noting the "yearning" for a "common witness" and for the Church's "unity and renewal," and recognizing that "ecumenical structures are provisional expressions of the ecumenical vision," the resolution urged the CCA and the Federation of Asian Bishops' Conferences (FABC) to set in motion a process by which "a

---

[2] Reinhold Worth, cited in Hans Kung, A *Global Ethics for Global Politics and Economics,* Oxford U.P.: 1998, p. xvi.

new ecumenical reality might emerge in Asia" that would include in its direct fellowship and structure the constituencies of the CCA and the FABC. There was FABC participation at the Cipanas Conference and in the working group that drafted and proposed the resolution. It is clear from the way the resolution was worded that, among many theological and ecclesiological questions that were considered, there was expressed the conviction and the hope that the shape of ecumenical life in Asia can and should respond to the challenge of a more inclusive and comprehensive ecumenical fellowship.

B. In Manila, Philippines, at the 9th General Assembly of the CCA, the Cipanas resolution was adopted with the affirmation of "willingness" on the part of the CCA to "rethink CCA's ethos, constitution, programs and ways of work in the quest for a more adequate expression of Asian ecumenism." In adopting this resolution, the Assembly invited the FABC to set up with the CCA a "task force" to "explore the possibility of Catholic membership in the CCA, or *of a successor Asian ecumenical structure*... "that could enable such a wider ecumenical fellowship.[3]

Over the past several years, the "task force" has been appointed and has undertaken its work. It is now the Asia Ecumenical Committee (AFC). The ABC has met several times over the past five years, and has set up the Asian Movement of Christian Unity (AMCU) as an organ of its work. As a result of these organizational bodies, and affirming "the unity that already exists among us," joint activity between the two bodies has intensified as initial expressions of giving shape to a new level of ecumenical life and relationships. A Joint Staff meeting has been held; more direct and constant communication among various desks of both bodies has followed; areas of possible common work and programs have began to be identified more clearly; and most important of all, mutual participation in each other's life and work has increased considerably.

The latter include the participation of the CCA in the Special Synod of Bishops for Asia that was held in the Vatican in 1998; the involvement of FABC faculty and participants in the Asian Ecumenical Course of the CCA; a joint Ecumenical Formation Course that was held for South Asia in Bangalore in 1999; CCA participation in the FABC Plenary in Bangkok in 1999; PARC participation in the CCA visit to the Middle East on the issue of "migrant workers"; and CCA participation in a number of FABC meetings on "Social Communication. "As I noted in my report to the 11th General Assembly of the CCA in Tomohon, as a result of all of these, we have become "friends" sharing life with each other, and not only participants trying to overcome the sense of strangeness that has kept us distant from each other.

3. Common Theological Perspectives and Historical Imperatives

Theological imperatives and convictions and the pressure of Christian witness in the new historical conditions of Asia give added validity, credibility and viability to the challenge of "giving shape to a new ecumenical vision in Asia."

The Biblical and theological imperatives and basis for Christian unity and the unity and renewal of the Church – so much of which have accumulated in ecumenical history, in recent Biblical, theological and ecclesiological pronouncements of Catholic, Orthodox and Protestant bodies, and the ongoing discussions of critical issues of doctrine and worship among various Christian Confessions – give validity to this effort. Jesus prayed "that they may all be one." In this prayer, Jesus indicates Divine will for the unity of the Church and of Christians. He also roots the imperative and the basis of this unity in the unity of the Godhead, and the credibility and prerequisite of the task of evangelization and of the Church's mission to the world. As the basis on which AMCU has been organized notes rightly, there is as a result of this a "unity that already exists among us" that we need to manifest and make more visible in ever more concrete and specific ways as an integral part of the life and mission of the Church in Asia. The recent Papal Exhortation, *Ecclesia in Asia,* underscores this point strongly in its assertion that "division is a counter-

[3] Christian Conference of Asia, *Christ Our Peace.' Building a Just Society,*p. 84.

witness to Jesus Christ," and therefore "a scandal" and hindrance to the work of evangelization. This means, on the practical level, a joining together by Christian Churches in a "process of prayer and consultation in order to explore the possibilities of new ecumenical structures and associations to promote Christian unity".[4] For the CCA, the vision of "life together" that manifests itself in a "one ecumenical fellowship" of Churches and Christian bodies on the national, regional and world levels has always been a part of its ecumenical hope. Indeed, it considers this a "special, specific and privileged" task of the ecumenical movement in Asia

The possibility and the coming into being of a "more comprehensive expression" of Christian unity and of the ecumenical fellowship in Asia should be seen as in itself a prophetic manifestation of the possibility embodied in Christian faith and life for unity in a deeply and painfully divided, fractious, and conflict-ridden world. In itself, it gives credibility and substance to Christian claims for unity and reconciliation and the power that can bring these into being. Philip Potter, a past General Secretary of the World Council of Churches, pointed this out not too long ago. "One of the greatest services that the Christian community can render to the world," writes Potter, "(is to) mobilize and awaken the dormant forces of the Christian community, and demonstrate in its own life that these are actually stronger than the barriers that separate nation from nation, class from class, race from race...Such conscious (community) implies a sense of solidarity, a willingness to suffer together, a determination not to let oneself be cut off from fellow Christians by any event, not even by war or revolution, and a burning desire to realize the visible unity of the Church." In the divided and conflict-ridden world in which we live, the wider and enlivened fellowship of Christians across confessional, geographic,cultural and other boundaries offers a message of hope.

Recent experiences in the life of conciliar expressions of the ecumenical movement have given a new and important basis to talk about what it means to give structural shape to the ecumenical vision. On the one hand, there has emerged a more critical understanding of the character, the possibilities and the limits of "ecumenical councils" as expressions of ecumenical life. There is as a result a greater sensitivity and realism concerning what they can do and cannot do, and what can and cannot be expected of them in regard to the life of the Church and of its witness in the world. There has emerged too a critical and serious effort to look at other possible structures by which ecumenical fellowship might be made visible. On the other hand, the experience of Catholic membership in various Councils of Churches nationally and regionally in Asia and in various parts of the world have provided valuable and critical lessons about what structural shape might be given to a more inclusive and comprehensive ecumenical fellowship. There is in other words historical and theological grounds on which the challenge of giving shape to a new ecumenical vision can be discussed viably and credibly.

As we are told constantly, we enter at the beginning of the 21st century the most dynamic and challenging period of Asian history. As *Asiaweek* has noted recently, Asia in the 21st century "has become a global force in every field." The explosion of the new world of communication of which Asia has been a part, the pace and volatility of Asian economic life and development, the unfinished tasks of nation-building that have erupted in many places, the continuing areas of war and the challenges of peace and reconciliation, the new world of religious activism and militancy, and the new challenges of international relations in a global world, among others, provide dynamism and volatility to Asian life, and the historical imperatives to the life and mission of the Church that requires ecumenical vision and commitment.

Finally, and in a most important way, the challenge of giving shape to a new ecumenical vision involves the multiplication and joining together of resources, experiences and insights for giving expression to the varied manifestations of Asian Christianity, of Asian spirituality, religious life and theology, and of Asian Churches' witness to Asian economic, social, political and cultural life. It also involves, in the most

[4] John Paul II, *Ecclesia in Asia,* para. 30.

practical level, the task of putting together and multiplying limited human, material and other resources for the undertaking of common work.

IV. Some Concluding Remarks

For the CCA, in short, in reaching the point of talking with the FABC about the task of "giving shape to a new ecumenical vision," we reach a new and a major point in ecumenical discussion and consultation in Asia. We realize that in engaging in these consultations, we are not making any specific commitments to any new structure of ecumenical life or relationships. We also realize, however, that in sharing life and thought together we enter into the realm of possibilities that the Holy Spirit might foist upon us. We must en-
gage in these consultations with a sense of openness to what the Holy Spirit might ask of us to do in order to manifest more fully the unity that has been given to us and that is a part of our life. Ecumenical life, after all, has never been the result of our work or our achievement but of our response to the fresh urgings of the Holy Spirit. I personally feel glad therefore that we have been able to have this meeting together, and hope very much that we will do what it takes to move further in our ecumenical journey together.

III. The Spirit's Gift to the Churches: New Ecumenical Visions and Associations (Father Thomas Michel)

When we look back on the century which has recently ended, we see a period of great turbulence for humankind. The rise and fall of totalitarian ideologies, devastating World Wars, the demise of colonialism, and the unprecedented advance of technology have all made the 2Oth Century a time of exceptional achievement, but also a time of widespread war and human suffering. What will historians of the future find to be of most lasting importance in the great events that affected human life, both for good and for bad, during this century?

When we turn our gaze to the history of the Christian people and their Churches during this same period, can we identify those key movements of God's grace that stand out as evidence of God's continuing care, of the Holy Spirit's constant activity in the ongoing pilgrimage on earth of Christ's disciples? In my opinion, future Church historians might well consider the growth of the Ecumenical Movement throughout this past century to be one of the most significant signs of God's accompanying and guiding the Church of Christ. These future historians might see the 2Oth Century as the time when the Spirit was actively motivating Christians and showing them the path to rebuild the unity that Christ has always desired for his disciples.

The Ecumenical Movement has certainly been a movement of great grace for Christians. It is an expression of *faith* in our profession of one baptism, one Lord, one God who is Father of all. Ecumenism is an affirmation that Jesus Christ desires his disciples to be united in faith so that together we bear witness to God's saving deeds in the life, death and resurrection of Christ, continually reenacted in history by the power of the Spirit. The Ecumenical Movement proceeds from a painful awareness that the unity which Christ established among his disciples is not yet visible to people, because of the multiplicity of churches and ecclesial bodies, and because of the frequent mutual suspicion and enmity and conflict that have characterized relations among Christian groups. Of all religions we appear to the conscientious observer to be the most divided. We might say that despite the unity of faith that we profess, what we all too often bear witness to is our disunity. I was once asked by a Muslim friend, "Why don't you Christians want to pray together? Every group of you insists on having your own church buildings, your own worship services, your own projects in society."

The Ecumenical Movement is also an expression of *hope.* It arises from the conviction among Christians that the divisions we have known and grown up with, that have kept us apart for so many centuries, and whose origins have been often forgotten except by scholarly researchers, need not go on forever. The conviction behind the Ecumenical Movement is that there is something that we can do, with God's guidance and in the power of grace, to move from disunity to greater visible unity. Throughout the course of the 2Oth century, the Ecumenical Movement has grown from the concern of a few to become a central force in the life of Christian Churches.

The Ecumenical Movement is also an expression of *love.* It is a realization among Christians that Christians of other Churches are not our enemies, to be excluded, condemned, struggled against, overcome, defeated. Rather, they are our brothers and sisters with whom we share the deepest bond possible on earth, a communion rooted in the powerful presence of our Master and Saviour Jesus Christ. Through ecumenism, we learn that we can live with other Christians, work with them, worship and praise God together with them, forgive them and seek their forgiveness, teach them and learn from them, all this to God's greater glory.

I believe that in this work of grace that we call Ecumenism, one of the most effective instruments that God has used to bring about the success of the movement are the new forms of ecumenical association that have arisen in the course of the past century. National and regional Councils of Churches and Christian Councils are one of the clear signs of the Spirit's activity in the ecumenical movement that account for its dynamism and growth.

In 1900, there were no Councils of Churches, the first appearing in France in 1905. Today, a century later, there are 103 national and regional Councils. In the Roman Catholic Church, the awareness of the value of Church Councils for promoting Christian unity, while belated, has moved even more quickly. At the time of the Second Vatican Council in the 19608, the Catholic Church was not a member of a Council of Churches anywhere in the world. Today, less than forty years later, the Catholic Church is a full member of 58 national or regional councils of Churches in over 70 countries.

Can we deny the work of the Spirit in a phenomenon that seems to parallel the course of the century – from zero in 1900 to 103 in 2000, Roman Catholic participation moving from zero in 1965 to 58 in 2000? Can we claim that this is only an accident of history? When we try to discern the "signs of the times," the ways in which the Spirit is at work in the Churches today, must we not acknowledge that the Holy Spirit has been instrumental in inspiring the formation of Church councils, and their guiding, fostering their maturation to become central elements of ecclesial life?

We have come to discover what Councils of Churches and similar ecumenical associations can be, and also what they are not. They are not a superchurch, where the member bodies lose their identity and power of independent decision. They are not an end in themselves, or the goal of Christian unity, but rather privileged instruments on the path to greater unity in Christ. They are not simply a consolidation of offices and coordination of activities.

Councils of Churches are, rather, an occasion of grace by which Christians of various communions can come to know each other, to appreciate those elements of the one Christian tradition which each confession has variously preserved and developed, to join together in addressing the social problems of the region, to be challenged by trying to see themselves as their fellow Christians see them, and to overcome the centuries of distrust and prejudices that centuries of isolation have allowed to occur. In short, they are schools where God can teach us how to love one another better. Isn't this what Christian life is all about? Isn't this, ultimately, how the world will know that we are Christ's disciples?

I believe that such an awareness of the value of Church councils for Christian renewal forms the background of Pope John Paul's recommendation to Christians in Asia in his 1999 exhortation, *Ecclesia in Asia.* There the Pope encourages us to enter into a process of prayer and discussion with Christians of other Churches, in order to explore the possibilities of new ecumenical structures and associations for promoting Christian unity.

The Pope makes it clear that the search for effective associations to promote unity is not something that each Church can do on its own. It is, he says, by embarking on the project together of praying about this, of studying the issues jointly, of reflecting with one another about the pros and cons, of facing the obstacles and difficulties and counter-arguments, that we allow the Holy Spirit to guide us where the Spirit wills.

If this seminar, AMCU III, is to be seen as a first effort on the part of Catholics to implement the recommendation of the Pope in *Ecclesia in Asia,* it must equally be recognized as an important step on the part of the member Churches and Synods of the Christian Conference of Asia to implement the decisions of their General Assemblies in Manila and Colombo which called on their members to meet with Roman Catholic leaders to pursue this same goal. My colleague, Dr. Carino, has well traced the antecedents of the Christian Conference of Asia commitment to work with the Catholic Church to find new and inclusive ecumenical structures and associations. Catholics, in their turn, must be grateful to their fellow Christians of the CCA for the leadership and inspiration they have given in this direction.

Where the Spirit will lead us in our deliberations we do not know, but we do know that in opening ourselves to the grace which will be offered on these days, we are asking God to show us the way, we are asking God to make us instruments of building unity with sisters and brothers who, like us, profess Jesus Christ as Lord and Savior.

I would like to conclude with a personal reflection. Last June, I took part as an observer in the CCA General Assembly held in Tomohon, Indonesia. I found it very moving to discover in the official CCA delegations from Taiwan and Australia Roman Catholic sisters and brothers. My overriding impression of their presence was one of feeling "how right this is"; that "this is where we belong"; "this is the shape of the future" already existing among us in seminal form. I felt exposed to new possibilities, to wondering about ongoing work of the Spirit. Will future historians look back someday on AMCU III as an event in the life of Christians in Asia, when together the Churches set themselves on a course leading to deeper union in faith, hope, and love?

(9) ASIAN ECUMENISM FROM EVANGELICAL PERSPECTIVE

Richard Howell

It's difficult to disagree with the statement that our human systematizations and schematizations of faith remain partial. Our belief that God has revealed Godself by God's works, words and in the person of Jesus Christ does not bestow us with omniscience. In the process of theologizing we should not attempt to place God in a box. God has revealed God's plan for creation and God graciously invites the Church to join God's own journey of redemption, sanctification and completion. Our journey with God is that of unequals. This is awesome, a humbling experience and an example for all to follow. We must never belittle others who may be at different stages of ecumenical journey with one another and God. The world Church with all its diversity must follow the promptings of the Holy Spirit; this will open up new vistas.

New Wine Skins for New Wine

Charismatic Christianity which is the driving engine of the contemporary awakening is also largely responsible for the dramatic shift of Christianity's centre of gravity from the Northern Hemisphere to Southern. Many influenced by the charismatic movement have joined mainline churches, both Protestant and Roman Catholic; while others have formed a distinct Pentecostal ecclesiastical bloc. Pentecostal/Charismatic were nearly 550 million in 2005 and the projections estimate that by 2025 the number will increase to 800 million. The Charismatic movement has brought a dramatic shift in Christian identities. How do we understand the identity of the person who believes in Lutheran understanding of grace, exercises the gift of speaking in unknown tongues and prophecies, advocates Wesleyan emphasis on Holiness and is a member of a Baptist or a Pentecostal church? Multiple Christian identity is a reality, particularly visible in Asia where denominational boundaries are often porous. This reality was forcefully witnessed early this year when in a meeting in Delhi called by the National United Christian Forum (NUCF) which comprises of the Catholic Bishops Conference of India, the National Council of Churches in India and the Evangelical Fellowship of India, about thirty young and old gathered to share their journeys of faith. The sharing started with two young participants, a female and a male, who shared their personal encounters with Jesus Christ, their calls to ministry, their experiences of the gift of speaking in unknown tongues. If they had not mentioned that they belonged to the catholic archdiocese of Delhi, it was easy to conclude they were Pentecostals. To understand this new work of God demands new wine skins. The sharing of personal faith journeys helps in discovering and discerning how the Holy Spirit is renewing God's people. This promotes unity as it helps overcome age-old prejudices and road blocks, and certainly can lead to joint witness and mission in the world. Spirituality strengthens and promotes ecumenism. We must create space for all followers of Jesus Christ for conversations. As D.K. Sahu writes: "The conversation should focus on creating space that would allow room for conversation, fellowship and movement oriented to strengthen, challenge and complement each other. To have a space does not mean to fight for space but rather to seek and discover what others are doing."[1]

---

[1] Sahu, D. K. "A Gathered Community of Witness and Service," in *Global Christian Forum Transforming Ecumenism,* Ed. Richard Howell, Evangelical Fellowship of India, 2007: 137.

Ecumenical Gatherings in Asia

The Global Christian Forum (GCF) from 2nd-4th May 2004 in Hong Kong hosted a regional consultation with participants from Asia and the Pacific. It was organised in cooperation with the Christian Conference of Asia (CCA), the Federation of Asian Bishops' Conference of Asia (FABC), and the Evangelical Fellowship of Asia (EFA) for the purpose of reflecting on our journey with Jesus Christ in Asia. The meeting brought 47 Asian participants, 27 coming from Evangelical and Pentecostal churches. The broad range of participants included the Anglican, Catholic, Evangelical, Mar Thoma, Orthodox, Pentecostal, Protestants and members of the Salvation Army. The strength of the GCF- initiated gathering is the sharing of faith journeys by all participants. In Hong Kong, the bulk ofthe first two days programmes was allocated to sharing.

The shared experience of faith helped discover a unity among participants that transcends all differences. Arising out of this sharing the participants developed a new awareness of one another's existence and spirituality and with it the importance of being the Church in Asia. A follow-up meeting under the banner GCF in Asia was organised in Bangkok 21st-23rd September 2006 with participants reflecting on the theme "Affirming our one Saviour in Common Witness."[2]. Following the gathering in Bangkok the Christian Conference of Asia (CCA), and Federation of Asian Bishops' Conferences (FABC), officially invited the Evangelical Fellowship of Asia (name changed to Asia Evangelical Alliance in 2008) to officially participate in the Asia Movement for Christian Unity (AMC) 1V held at Kuala Lumpur, Malaysia in 2007. The theme of the conference was "Our Common Witness in Contemporary Asia." AMCU V was held from December 2nd-4th, 2010 in Bangkok, Thailand, with the theme "One in the apostles' teaching, fellowship, breaking of bread and prayer" (cf. Acts 2:42), which also was the theme of the later 2011 Week of Prayer for Christian Unity This was an occasion for Christian leaders in Asia to meditate on the importance of our devotion to the teachings of the apostles and fellowship, to the breaking of bread, and the prayers – elements that unite us, though we are many, in the one Body of Christ.

Jesus Christ the Supreme Witness

That Jesus Christ is the supreme witness to the truth remains for evangelical and Pentecostal churches a foundational pillar in its ecumenical dialogue and partnership. The World Missionary Conference held in Jerusalem in 1928 placed a revisionist understanding of the mission of the Church, which held that claim about the uniqueness and finality of Christ was no longer tenable in view of the reality of other faiths. This position has radical theological implications for Christianity and for the Church, as was eventually demonstrated by the 1960 conference of the World Student Christian Federation at Strasbourg whose theme was "The Life and Mission of the Church." As Lamin Sanneh has pointed out, 'The Church was no longer considered the repository of unchanging truths but the axis of a new realism, that religious virtues like faith and hope were not charters for resignation and fatalism but the warrants for self-improvement; that the Last Judgment was not the end of the world but the summons to social justice; and everlasting life was not a blissful, deathless existence beyond time and space but a free, prosperous, and happy life here and now. The move was to "deontologize" the Church, which means, in effect, to shun primacy of doctrine and to commit instead to contextual engagement.'[3] As the report of the World Council of Churches put it, it is the world, not the church that now wrote God's agenda. Instead of the Church as a starting point for the action of mission that involves God and moves to the world, God is understood as the instigator of mission

---

[2] Sarah Rowland Jones "The Global Christian Forum A Narrative History," in *Global Christian Forum Transforming Ecumenism,* Ed. Richard Howell, Evangelical Fellowship of India, 2007: 12-13.

[3] Sanneh, Lamin. *Disciples of All Nations*. Oxford University Press, 2008:274

directly in the world. This theological position held by many ecumenical churches remains a bone of contention for ecumenical cooperation.

However ecumenical cooperation will gain momentum; this hope is strengthened since 28th June 2011 when history was made as the World Council of Churches, Pontifical Council for Interreligious Dialogue and World Evangelical Alliance, after years of dialogue, jointly issued a statement: "Christian Witness in a Multi-Religious World," Recommendations for Conduct, at the headquarters of the WCC in Geneva, Switzerland. Stating a basis for Christian witness, the statement affirms: "Jesus Christ is the supreme witness (cf. John 18:37). Christian witness is always a sharing in his witness, which takes the form of proclamation of the kingdom, service to neighbour and the total gift of self even if that act of giving leads to the cross. Just as the Father sent the Son in the power of the Holy Spirit, so believers are sent in mission to witness in word and action to the love of the triune God."

The good news of the gospel and ontological reality of the church are non-negotiable for evangelical and Pentecostal churches in any ecumenical endeavors.

While the number of mainline Protestant missionaries from the Western world is decreasing, the evangelical missionary numbers are increasing steadily, complemented by a rising tide of Asian missionaries. South Korea alone has plans for a hundred thousand missionaries. Lamin Sanneh comments, "It is likely that churches in South Korea, rather than churches in the West, will play a key role on the new Christian frontier about to open in China, which might well become a dominant axis of the religion, with hard-to-imagine implications for the rest of the world."[4] There is a growing **trend** of ecumenical partnership in doing mission and not to repeat the mistakes of Europe, where the gospel and European culture went hand in hand. The followers of Christ do not have to forego their culture to become loyal Christians and be responsible citizens of their nations.

Wonsuk Ma has sharply focused the issue of cooperation, as he states: "The extremely individualistic nature of 'evangelical' has spent much time and energy trying to figure out who is in and who is out. Anyone who is out should be 'evangelised,' be they Catholic or otherwise."[5] However, he also raises the issue: "It is noticeable that the ecumenical movement which has worked to bring various Christian churches together has created, ironically, an environment for some churches to find it simply impossible to approach the network. It has inadvertently formed a "game plan" to know which belongs to the "in church" and which are "outside" of the circle. How the Catholic Church has defined a genuine church and a second class church is a similar practice."[6]

Addressing Issues of Common Concern

However, in spite of theological differences, the Churches in Asia have come together in ecumenical cooperation to address issues of common concern. In many Asian countries, despotism and political authoritarianism and militarism continue to affect the lives of the people. For example, in China, liberal economy exists along with political centralization and autocracy. The situation is similar in North Korea, Myanmar and Vietnam, while in the Maldives, which is an Islamist country, there is no freedom of religion. In India, which guarantees religious freedom, cases of human rights violation is on the increase. The poor and the marginalized are defenseless before the tyranny of the free market. While there is growth of middle class consumerism and commercialization of every realm of society the gulf between the rich and the poor is on the increase. Protecting the environment is a major concern. Asia is a home of rich biodiversity. The mode of development accelerated by technology and market has created an

---

[4] Ibid., xxii

[5] Ma, Wonsuk, "Discerning What God is Doing Among His People," in *Revisioning Christian Unity: The Global Christian Forum*, Hubert van Beek, ed., Regnum Books International UK, 2009: 89

[6] Ibid.

environmental crisis in Asian countries. Gender inequality and exploitation of women is on the increase with trafficking of women. The issues of HIV and AIDS require our urgent attention in removing the stigma attached to them and promoting care.

Ecumenism must go beyond intellectual content-orientation dialogue to a more holistic praxis-orientation and united witness. Our journey together with Jesus Christ is a witness to the reality that every Church is catholic because the whole Christ is present in the church through the Holy Spirit, and at the same time every person who confesses Jesus as Lord is a catholic person because the whole Christ dwells in everyone through the Holy Spirit. To journey together for common witness is not an option but a theological imperative.

Evangelical and Pentecostals are committed to continue together our journey with Jesus Christ to strengthen our common witness. For this to become a structural reality new wine skins are needed.

Bibliography

Ma, Wonsuk, "Discerning What God is Doing Among His People," in *Revisioning Christian Unity: The Global Christian Forum*, Hubert van Beek, ed., Regnum Books International UK, 2009: 89

Sahu, D. K. "A Gathered Community of Witness and Service," in *Global Christian Forum Transforming Ecumenism,* Ed. Richard Howell, Evangelical Fellowship of India, 2007: 137

Sanneh, Lamin. *Disciples of All Nations*. Oxford University Press, 2008

(10) Asian Ecumenism from Pentecostal Perspective

Connie Ho Yan Au

Pentecostalism in Asia

Historically, Pentecostalism in Asia was spread both by native and western Pentecostals. The former group moulded Pentecostalism as indigenous Christianity in Asia. It was not only developed based on any denominational doctrines and institutions, but also by praxis derived from self-interpretation of the Bible according to its own Asian cultural and religious context and personal experience of the divine, such as the True Jesus Church and Jesus Family in China.[1] Western Pentecostal missionaries were either independent revivalists or members of a Pentecostal denomination, such as the Assemblies of God, Pentecostal Assemblies of Canada, Finnish Pentecostals, Pentecostal Holiness Church, Foursquare Church and Oneness Pentecostals. They were prompted by their revival experience and the urgency for mission before the second coming of Jesus. Their dedication in going to a particular country was proved by the 'missionary tongues', the spiritual gift of speaking in the language of that country based on Acts 2.[2] However, it was a common case that when they arrived there they could not speak the language. Despite their wrong expectation of the gift of the Spirit, their complete dependence on the power of the Spirit in mission distinguished them from the mainline Protestant and Roman Catholic missionaries. Besides building schools, hospitals, orphanages and other humanitarian institutions to preach the gospel, Pentecostals strongly believed in the power of the Holy Spirit in mission. Their use of healing, exorcism, prophecy and other gifts enlivens the gospel – not only to be heard, but also seen and felt. Their 'full gospel' not just proclaims the Jesus recorded in the Bible in the past, but the Lord who works in the present and future.[3]

As many Asian countries are stricken by poverty due to colonialism, capitalism, communism and injustice in social, commercial and governmental systems, this full gospel has drawn their attention and raised expectation. Healing demonstrates God's gracious care and power to the poor who cannot afford medical care. Spirit baptism ushers in self-confidence, which motivates them to seek upward social mobility. The charismata are believed to be freely distributed to all Christians, women and men, poor and rich, outcasts and elites, slaves and masters, laity and clergy, empowering the marginalised to serve in church and society. In China, Korea and Japan, where Confucianism is deeply rooted in the culture so that women have to surrender to men and the youth to the elderly; and in India where the caste system determines the fate of one's life according to their 'inborn' social status, charismata are not merely a matter

---

[1] Hwa Yung, 'Pentecostalism and the Asian Church', *Asian and Pentecostal: The Charismatic Face of Christianity in Asia*, Allan Anderson and Edmond Tang, eds. (Baguio City: Regnum, 2005), 49.

[2] S. C. Todd, the founder of Bible Missionary Society and a missionary in Macao, recorded that when T. J. McIntosh landed in Macao in 1908, he believed that he was endowed with the gift of speaking Chinese from the Holy Spirit. But it did not take long for him to realise that he could not utter a single Chinese word and had to rely on an interpreter to preach. S. C, Todd, "An Open Letter: Being a Calm Review of the Speaking in Tongues in South China", (possibly written in 1909).

[3] For the Pentecostals who adopt the Holiness tradition, such as the Pentecostal Holiness Church, the 'full gospel' consists of five elements: Jesus is the Saviour; Jesus is the sanctifier; Jesus is the baptiser in the Holy Spirit; Jesus is a healer; and Jesus is the soon-coming king. For the 'Finished Work' Pentecostals, such as the Assemblies of God and the Foursquare Church, it does not include 'Jesus is a sanctifier' as they believe that the work of sanctification is accomplished on the cross, so whoever admits Jesus as the Saviour, s/he is cleansed simultaneously.

of religious experience, but social liberation.[4] As folk religions, shamanism and witchcraft permeate every aspect of life in Asia, especially in tribal areas, yet it is not unusual for people to be attacked and possessed by demons even though they worship spirits with good intention. For those whose jobs are exposed to nature, such as in fishing and farming, worship to the spirits of the sea, mountain, rain and wind is a logical way to seek good harvest and protection from natural disasters and evil spirits. As far as Pentecostals are concerned, mission to these people is not so much the preaching *about* the words, but fighting *with* the words and the power of the Spirit in spiritual warfare to deliver those who are manipulated and humiliated by demons.[5]

Although Pentecostal missionaries came to Asia with alternative interpretation and spiritual expressions of the gospel, they shared one thing in common with other Protestant and Catholic missionaries – coming with the doctrines and ecclesiastical systems of their own denominations. Division and separatism among denominations were implanted from the West to Asia and this situation continued even after authority was handed over from missionaries to the locals. As some of them still hold the problematic eschatology, anti-ecumenism and anti-Catholicism taught by the headquarters in the United States and other western countries, they have unconsciously inherited the prejudice and hatred of their mother churches.[6] Consequently, ecumenism has not firmly taken root among Pentecostals in Asian soil; building up relationships with other Protestants and Catholics is often unimaginable. Nevertheless, a handful of Asian Classical Pentecostals have been involved in ecumenical dialogues and institutions. No matter how indifferent and unformed they are about ecumenism, they have unconsciously contributed to the ecumenical movement at the grassroots level when they are consciously holding large-scale revival and healing conventions.

Pentecostalism and Grassroots Unity

At both academic and ecclesial levels, there has not been consensus on by what theory Pentecostalism should be defined. Some people argue that it should be defined by doctrines, namely Spirit Baptism evidenced by speaking in tongues and the use of gifts, which has been safeguarded by Classical Pentecostal denominations. But this approach has been challenged as the so-called 'Pentecostal manifestations' do not happen only in Pentecostal denominational churches, but also among Protestant, Catholic and independent Christian communities. Hence, some scholars propose a more inclusive approach to defining Pentecostalism, and that is, by phenomena, such as Spirit baptism, speaking in tongues, prophecy, exorcism, healing, seeing visions and dreams.[7] It connotes a biblical and phenomenological fact that the

[4] Wonsuk and Julie Ma observe that the cell group model introduced by Yonggi Cho at the Yoido Full Gospel Church provides leadership opportunities for women, which is unimaginable in the Korean patriarchal society. Wonsuk and Julie Ma, "Jesus Christ in Asia: Our Journey with Him as Pentecostal Believers", *International Review of Mission*, 94/375 (October 2005), p. 496.

[5] In my interview with the elderly, mostly retired fishermen and life-long members of the Pentecostal Holiness Church Rousseau Memorial Assembly in Hong Kong (in July 2009), I gathered that when they were young they prayed to many kinds of spirit for protection; but still they were attacked by evil spirits and were sick for weeks. They were healed when the missionaries of the Pentecostal Holiness Church from the United States cast out demons and prayed for their healing. Thus, they decided to abandon their faith in spirits and believe in Jesus Christ.

[6] For example, the General Council of the Assemblies of God in the United States condemned the WCC as the scarlet whore and religious Babylon of Revelation in 1963. Allan Anderson, *Introduction to Pentecostalism,* p. 250. Catholics have also been accused by Pentecostals as the 'Whore of Babylon". For example, Frances Swaggart, wife of Pentecostal televangelist Jimmy Swaggart, wrote a book called *The Modern Babylon* (Baton Rouge, LA: World Evangelism Press, 2006.) See also John L. Allen, "If Demography is Destiny, Pentecostals are the Ecumenical Future", *National Catholic Reporter*, 28 January 2008. http://ncronline.org/node/11567 (accessed on 17 April).

[7] See Allan Anderson, *Spreading Fires: The Missionary Nature of Early Pentecostalism* (London: SCM Press, 2004);

Spirit and its work are not limited to Pentecostal churches, but they are given to all Christians who confess Jesus as their Lord and Saviour. It also suggests that Pentecostalism is a grassroots movement since its formation is not through developing doctrines by theologians or ecclesiastical officials, but through primal and spontaneous experiences of the Spirit among people of different races, gender and ages. Ministry is not only done by clergy, but also by laity who are endowed with the power of the Spirit, based on Joel 2:28-29. Worship can happen not because a priest is conducting the liturgy, but because the worshipping community desires to honour God. This grassroots nature of Pentecostalism attracts those who suffer from marginalisation simply because of their gender, race, age or social status, as they recognise that the grace and gifts of the Spirit are also available for them. This boundary-crossing feature of Pentecostalism vividly demonstrates its innate ecumenical nature – embracing all human beings in the same *oikoumene*. In this article, Pentecostalism includes classical denominational Pentecostalism, the charismatics who are members of mainline Protestant and Roman Catholic churches and have Pentecostal experiences, and the independent charismatics who are not affiliated to any denominations.

The charismatic renewal creates reconciliation and unity among Christians of various traditions at the grassroots level, especially between Protestants and Roman Catholics. It happens through spontaneous worship where people can express themselves freely to God and people with physical and emotional expressions. Serving each other with gifts and intercession is also a way to show God's care through fellow Christians. In contrast to ecumenical dialogue which is cerebral, cognitive and official, this grassroots unity is experiential, affective and local.[8] As religious experiences are generally the gateway for Asians to encounter a religion instead of the logicality of doctrines and rationality of the ecclesiastical system, ecumenism in Asian Pentecostalism is not so much about reaching theological and institutional consensus through dialogue, but (re-)building up a trusting relationship through common experiences in the Spirit, mutual acceptance, and forgiveness through sanctification of sin and the outpouring of love flowing from God, then to fellow Christians at the grassroots level. Since the Holy Spirit endows power and concrete experiences among Christians, a pneumatological approach to ecumenism creating a living *koinonia* would make more sense to Asians rather than solely a cognitive Christo-centric ecumenism.

In the Philippines, the El Shaddai DWXI Prayer Partners Fellowship International was given birth by a rich and 'born-again' Roman Catholic, Bro. Mariano ('Mike') Z. Velarde, in 1984. It is an organisation promoting the Catholic charismatic renewal in the Philippines and worldwide.[9] This movement 'envisions to bring about a revival of the true Christian spirit in the Catholic faith. It aims to raise up a community of faith-filled generous believers of our Lord Jesus Christ as recorded in Acts 2:42-47, which by Divine Guidance and Providence has now miraculously established these communities in many areas worldwide.'[10] It does not follow traditional Catholic liturgy, but a spontaneous worship style. Healing of serious diseases and broken relationships took place and the lame and paralytic stood up and walked. As these features are shared by Roman Catholics, Protestant charismatics and Pentecostals, they become springboards for them to build up relationship at the grassroots level. Since El Shaddai has spread to many regions, such as Hong Kong, Singapore, Japan, the United States, Canada, Italy, Greece and so on, its ecumenical influence has been immeasurable.[11]

The charismatic renewal has also been healing divisions between mainline churches and Pentecostal and charismatic churches. For decades, Pentecostals and charismatics have been accused of radicalism,

---

Michael Bergunder, The South Indian Movement in the Twentieth Century (Grand Rapids, Michigan: William B. Eerdmans Publishing Company, 2008).

[8] Connie Ho Yan Au, *Grassroots Unity in the Charismatic Renewal* (Eugene: Wipf & Stock, 2011), p. 2.

[9] http://www.freewebs.com/elshaddai-dwxippfi/outreachesprograms.htm

[10] *Ibid.*

[11] W. Ma, "Philippines", Stanley M. Burgess, Eduard M. van der Maas (eds) *International Dictionary of Pentecostal and Charismatic Movements*, p. 206.

emotionalism and irrationalism in their praxis and lack of theological reasoning. However, as they have seen significant numerical growth and mainline churches also find those experiences happening in their own congregations, reconciliation between the two groups has been brought into reality. In Taiwan, the Prayer Mountain Revival Movement has drawn Protestants together through renewal since 1982. It is neither a church nor a denominational organisation although the leader, Daniel Dai, is a Southern Baptist minister. Thousands of members of various churches, ranging from evangelical, charismatic to conciliar, pray together on mountains during weekends for the common purpose of spiritual renewal. The movement does not only unite Christians of different denominations, but also indigenous and Chinese Taiwanese as well as Taiwanese and Western Christians through the work of the co-founder, Allen Swanson.[12] This combined charismatic and ecumenical stream has continued to enhance the relationship between mainline Protestant and charismatic churches. Most of the Presbyterians and Baptists have accepted the work of the Spirit and collaborated with Pentecostals and charismatics for public revival and prayer conventions. One of the contributors is Peter Chu, the senior pastor of Truth Church, which was a charismatic church founded in Hong Kong and planted in Taiwan. At the Taiwan World Day of Prayer in 2006, he and another charismatic, Chu Tai Shen, the senior pastor of Taipei Glory Church and the founder of Taipei Association of Christian Churches, exhorted the congregation of over 30,000 in Taipei to kneel down and confess the sin of division between evangelical and charismatics. Christians from both sides embraced and blessed each other and hoped for unity. At the same event held in the southern city in Taiwan, Gaoxiong, more than 3,000 Christians from various churches and ethnic groups prayed for the outpouring of the Holy Spirit upon the whole island.[13] This charismatic and ecumenical stream is not only spread through occasional conventions, but through publications and multi-media devices. The Elim Bookstore, founded by Elder Andrew Chang in 1982, has made a contribution to sustaining this joint movement among Chinese-speaking Christians throughout Asia.[14]

In Singapore, the charismatic renewal began in 1935 when the Chinese revivalist, Song Shangjie (John Sung), held an evangelistic meeting and preached about holiness, infilling by the Spirit and the Word. More than two thousand people attended the meeting and several hundreds were converted. His use of spiritual gifts, especially healing, brought salvation to concrete reality. The renewal spread to Anglicans and Wesleyan Methodists in the 1970s. The Anglican Bishop, Chiu Ban It, was inspired by Dennis Bennett's *Nine O'Clock in the Morning* and desired the outpouring of the Holy Spirit in 1972.[15] Since then, the Anglican Church held 'Prayers for Healing Services', 'Praise and Prayer' meetings and Spiritual Renewal Seminar which brought renewal to Christians from other denominations. The Wesley Methodist Church held a special charismatic service alongside the traditional liturgy in response to the need of the charismatic Methodists.[16] Although Pentecostalism was able to grow in the Anglican Communion, it was strongly opposed by evangelicals. In 1995, Lawrence Khong, the pastor of Faith Community Baptist Church organised a movement called 'Vision 2001'. It was aimed to mend the divisions caused by conservative evangelical enmity against Pentecostalism and by younger pastors leaving their churches to found their own independent churches, so that Christians could serve the society together and destroy

[12] M. A. Rubinstein, "Taiwan", Stanley M. Burgess, Eduard M. van der Maas (eds) *International Dictionary of Pentecostal and Charismatic Movements* (Grand Rapids, Michigan: Zondervan, 2002), pp. 260-261.
[13] Choi Man Ching, "Churches Took Unity Seriously at Taiwan World Day of Prayer", *Kingdom Revival Times (HK)*, http://www.krt.com.hk/modules/news/article.php?storyid=3411 (accessed on 15 April 2012). The title is translated from Chinese into English by the author.
[14] http://www.hosanna-tod.com/front/bin/ptdetail.phtml?Part=hm-9912-07&Category=28958 (accessed on 14 April 2012).
[15] Dennis Bennett, *Nine O'clock in the Morning*. Gainesville, FL: Bridge-Logos Publishers, 1970.
[16] D. Tan, "Singapore", Stanley M. Burgess, Eduard M. van der Maas (eds) *International Dictionary of Pentecostal and Charismatic Movements*, p. 225; Connie Ho Yan Au, *Grassroots Unity in the Charismatic Renewal*, p. 105.

'Satan's perimeter' with the concept of spiritual warfare. It successfully mobilised Christians to participate in 'prayerwalk' in the city according to the planned routes designed with the idea of 'spiritual mapping'. By 2000, the movement evolved into a patriotic campaign called 'LoveSingapore', proclaiming God's love for Singapore and encouraging citizens not to migrate to foreign countries.[17] In 2008, the movement focused on global poverty and justice and gathered Christians from various traditions to pray and work for the poor.[18]

This ecumenical effect of the charismatic renewal also happens between some of the Three-Self and underground churches in China. The latter ones are stigmatised by the communist government as politically-provocative religious societies due to their practice of spiritual power. They were betrayed and severely oppressed by their fellow Christians belonging to Three-Self churches in the 1950s to 1970s. Hence, doctrinal issues are not major causes of division, but the political constitution violating freedom of religion. However, as the communist government launched a reform in its policy on religions in the 1980s, Christians from both sides have had more contact with and influence on each other. It has become more common for members of the Three-Self churches to experience healing, exorcism, speaking in tongues and prophecy. Some of their church leaders invite Pentecostals to explain the theological implications of these phenomena and to provide guidance on how to exercise spiritual power appropriately.[19] As spiritual experiences have been blurring the political boundary, it is hopeful that dialogue and reconciliation will happen among Chinese Christians in the near future.

Although grassroots unity has brought about an unprecedented ecumenical scenario, it is not the answer to all divisions. Sentimental unity through common experiences in the Spirit can create fellowship among laity, but it cannot solve the institutional and doctrinal issues that divide churches. The most obvious example is that Roman Catholic and Protestant charismatics cannot share the Lord's Supper together. Hence, grassroots unity and official dialogue need to complement each other. The former one can create a foundation of friendship preparing for honest and sincere conversations on some sensitive doctrinal issues. The latter one enhances mutual understandings and patience for each other, which is the criterion of any sustaining and mature relationship. The former one serves as a point of departure for an ecumenical journey; the latter one realises growth in agreements in the thorny pilgrimage. The former one brings about ecumenical enjoyment; the latter one requires and develops ecumenical commitment. Elements of both sides are important and more Pentecostals have committed to official ecumenical engagements besides unconsciously nurturing grassroots unity.

Official Ecumenical Involvements

For decades, Pentecostals and charismatics have been sceptical about ecumenical institutions. Some Classical Pentecostals who are influenced by fundamentalism condemn these institutions as the signs of the end times mentioned in the Book of Revelation. Their ecumenical bias is derived from their problematic

---

[17] Daniel P. S. Goh, "State and Social Christianity in Post-colonial Singapore", *SOJOURN: Journal of Social Issues in Southeast Asia*, 25/1 (2010), pp. 78-82. For details of the 'LoveSingapore' movement, please refer to Tan-Chow Mayling, *Pentecostal Theology for the Twenty-First Century: Engaging with Multi-faith Singapore* (Aldershot: Ashgate, 2007).

[18] Daniel P. S. Goh, "State and Social Christianity in Post-colonial Singapore", p. 85.

[19] Dennis Balcombe, senior pastor of the Revival Church in Hong Kong, had been secretly working for house churches since the 1970s until recently when he was officially invited by a Three-Self church in Wuhan. He observed that many official churches were full of young people. Baptism in the Holy Spirit, speaking in tongues, prophecy, dancing and healing happened every Sunday. (Dennis Balcombe, "New Wine in new Wineskins – Fires of Holy Ghost Revival Burning in China's Official and Registered Churches", website of the Revival Chinese Ministries International. http://rcmi.wordpress.com/ Accessed on 23 April 2012.)

eschatology consolidated with a subjective interpretation of certain apocalyptic symbolisms in the Bible.[20] Some of the churches in Asia, Africa and Latin America founded by missionaries from North America are pressurised by their mother church not to be involved in the ecumenical movement.[21] Some of them are willing to participate in the mainstream ecumenical movement, but it is difficult for them to accommodate themselves into the constitution, practice and worship style of these ecumenical institutions, which cater to the mainline Protestant churches. Some of them find sufficiency in their wealthy mega-churches and they focus on expanding the church everywhere in the world. Hence, they do not feel the need to collaborate with other churches. Some of them regard themselves as the true church and Christians of other churches as not saved. Similar to the pre-Vatican II Roman Catholic Church, they think that ecumenism is about getting others to become Pentecostal. Some of them cannot easily lay down the continuing memory of being persecuted and marginalised by mainline Protestant churches and the Roman Catholic Church since the movement started in the early twentieth century. In some instances, persecution against Pentecostals is a joint plot between the church and the totalitarian regime.[22] Despite all these negative factors, some independent Pentecostal ecumenists have actively engaged in ecumenical dialogues. They have engaged in official dialogues with the Roman Catholics since 1972, World Alliance of Reformed Churches in 1996-2000,[23] World Lutheran Federation in 2004-2010[24] and Baptist World Alliance in December 2011.[25] A Joint Consultative Group between the World Council of Churches (WCC) and some Pentecostals has held meetings every year since 2000. However, these events were predominantly initiated by North American independent Classical Pentecostals, who are not endorsed by their churches to be involved in those dialogues. European Pentecostals are invited occasionally, but Africans, Latin Americans and Asians, whose churches are spectacularly thriving, are hardly there.[26]

Nevertheless, some Asian Pentecostal churches actively participate in the ecumenical movement. The Assemblies of God of Korea Yoido General Council and Assemblies of God (Seodaemun) became members of the National Council of Churches of Korea (NCCK) in July 1996. Since Busan in Korea was chosen to be the venue for the WCC's tenth general assembly, the NCCK has been responsible for the preparation. Lee Young Hoon, the senior pastor of Yoido Full Gospel Church, expressed his full support for the preparation to WCC's General Secretary.[27] In Malaysia, due to religious oppression from the Muslim-dominated government, Pentecostal churches are in favour of joining ecumenical organisations. The Assemblies of God, Full Gospel Assembly, Full Gospel Tabernacle and the Sidang Injil Borneo Sabah, Sarawak and Semenanjung are members of the National Evangelical Christian Fellowship (NECF),

---

[20] C. M. Robeck, "Pentecostals and Christian Unity: Facing the Challenge", *Pneuma: The Journal of the Society for Pentecostal Studies*, 26/2 (Fall 2004), p. 323.

[21] Robeck notes that David Yonggi Cho, former senior pastor of the Yoido Full Gospel Church, had authorised his members to be involved in the meeting of the Joint Consultative Group between the World Council of Church and Classical Pentecostals in 2000, but he was under much pressure from the World Assemblies of God Fellowship that he withdrew his decision (C. M. Robeck, "Pentecostals and Christian Unity", p. 328, footnote 33).

[22] C. M. Robeck, "Pentecostals and Christian Unity", pp. 310-312.

[23] http://www.warc.ch/dt/erl1/20.html (accessed on 13 April 2012). Among the fourteen Pentecostal members, only two were Asians, Wonsuk and Julie Ma.

[24] *Lutherans and Pentecostals in Dialogue* (Strasbourg: Institute for Ecumenical Research, 2010), p. 2.

[25] Bob Allen, "Baptists, Pentecostals Seek Common Ground", *Christian Century*, 20 December 2011. http://www.christiancentury.org/article/2011-12/baptists-pentecostals-seek-common-ground (accessed on 16 April 2012).

[26] Jelle Creemers, 'Intertwined Problems of Representation and Reception in Pentecostal Ecumenical Involvement: A Case Study', *One in Christ* 45.1 (July, 2011), 143.

[27] "Korean Pentecostal Church Reaffirms Support for WCC 10th Assembly", 4 June 2010. http://www.oikoumene.org/en/news/news-management/eng/a/article/1634/korean-pentecostal-church.html?tx_ttnews%5Bswords%5D=Lee%20Young%20Hoon&cHash=cb10af730285a6589f48a82b25be073b (accessed on 16 April 2012).

working together with Baptists, Methodists, Presbyterians and the Salvation Army. NECF was founded in 1983 in the light of the prohibition of non-Christians possessing a Malay Bible in 1981 and the restricted availability of worship sites, which caused independent churches not being able to establish themselves.[28] The NECF is a member of the Christian Federation of Malaysia (CFM) which is a national Christian umbrella that also includes the Catholic Diocese of Malaysia, and the Council of Churches of Malaysia formed by the Anglican, Methodist and Lutheran churches. Through the CFM, Pentecostals can directly work with mainline Protestants and Roman Catholics.

Besides working with other churches, ecumenism, as far as Pentecostals are concerned, is also about resolving the accumulated internal schisms throughout the last century. The Pentecostal World Fellowship (PWF) is a widely-recognised ecumenical organisation by Pentecostals.[29] It was founded by David du Plessis, Leonard Steiner, J. Roswell Flower and Donald Gee in 1947, aiming to ‘unite and mobilize the global Spirit-filled family in completing the Great Commission of Jesus Christ’.[30] For decades, it was dominated by American and European Pentecostals, but in recent years, Asian Pentecostals have played a significant role. In January 2012, it accepted three new member churches and two of them were Asians.[31] The number of member churches has increased to 59. Of this number, 21 are from Asia Pacific, 14 from North America, 11 from Europe, 9 from Africa and 4 from South America.[32] Since 2010, the PWF has been chaired for the first time by an Asian, Prince Guneratnam, who is the senior pastor of Calvary Church, one of the largest Assemblies of God churches in Malaysia.[33] The secretary is Mathew K. Thomas from India, the president of the Central India Theological Seminary. The advisory committee involves leaders from Japan, India and Hong Kong. On Sek Leang, the General Superintendent of the Assemblies of God in Malaysia, is the host chairperson of the general triennial conference in August 2013 in Kuala Lumpur.[34] These leaders represent some of the fastest-growing churches in Asia and their collaboration conveys a significant message of unity to millions of Pentecostals.

More importantly, under Prince Guneratnam’s leadership, the PWF has become more open to other traditions. He supported Bishop James Leggett’s idea to invite the WCC General Secretary, Olav Fykse Tveit, to address over two thousand Pentecostals from seventy countries at the 22nd general conference of the PWF in Stockholm in August 2010. Fykse Tveit’s wife has Pentecostal relatives and he has been involved in processing the applications of some Pentecostal churches to become full members of the

[28] http://www.necf.org.my/index.cfm?&menuid=3 (accessed on 16 April 2012).

[29] It was formerly called Pentecostal World Conference.

[30] http://www.pentecostalworldfellowship.org/ (accessed on 13 April 2012).

[31] The three new members are Jireh Evangel Church Planting Philippines led by Chuck Chua and Robert Lim and the Assemblies of God of Korea Yoido General Council (including the Yoido Full Gospel Church and the member churches of the Council) led by Lee Young Hoon and one from South America, Federacion Confraternidad Evangelica Pentecostal led by Ruben Salomone. http://www.pentecostalworldfellowship.org/526 (accessed on 13 April 2012).

[32] http://www.pentecostalworldfellowship.org/526 (accessed on 13 April 2012).

[33] The leadership was shared by L. Steiner from Switzerland, Donald Gee from England, W. E. McAlister from Canada, H. P. Courtney and T. F. Zimmerman from the United States in the first two decades. Zimmerman, the former General Secretary of the Assemblies of God, was the chairperson from 1967 to 1989 (Percy S. Brewster took over the leadership in 1970 temporarily). He led the AG to be member of the National Association of Evangelicals and was strongly opposed to any ecumenical efforts with other mainline churches and the Roman Catholic Church. Under his leadership, the AG relinquished David du Plessis’ credential as the AG ordained minister in 1962 due to his ecumenical involvements with the Vatican and the WCC. They only recovered his credential in 1980. It was not surprising that PWC was also an anti-ecumenical Pentecostal fellowship. After Zimmerman, the PWC continued to be chaired by Americans, R. H. Hughes (1989-1998), T. L. Trask (1998-2005) and James D. Leggett (2005-2010). (C. M. Robeck, “Pentecostal World Conference”, Stanley M. Burgess, Eduard M. van der Maas (eds) *International Dictionary of Pentecostal and Charismatic Movements,* p. 973; Allan Anderson, *Introduction to Pentecostalism*, p. 53; 146-147; 249-250; http://www.pentecostalworldfellowship.org/history (accessed on 14 April 2012).

[34] http://www.pentecostalworldfellowship.org/526 (accessed on 13 April 2012).

Christian Council of Norway. He was positive about the shared witness of unity between the WCC and Pentecostals, saying, 'That you have welcomed me here today is one such sign of hope.'[35] Guneratnam is also a committee member of the Global Christian Forum (GCF) and met the Ecumenical Patriarch of Constantinople at the GCF's meeting in Istanbul in January 2011.[36] He signed a letter, on behalf of the PWF, to endorse Harold Hunter to be a leader in the Orthodox-Pentecostal dialogue, which is the first endorsement of the PWF for such an ecumenical venture.[37]

Relations with the Roman Catholic Church

Although the grassroots unity derived from charismatic experiences in the Spirit spread across all churches, including the Roman Catholic Church, there is still a huge gap in doctrinal and theological issues between Pentecostals and Roman Catholics. From the Catholic perspective, the rapid growth of Pentecostalism in Asia is a threat of proselytism and is alarming the Church to respond accordingly. The Pontifical Council for the Promotion of Christian Unity (PCPCU), presided by Cardinal Walter Kasper, held a seminar in July 2006 in South Korea and was attended by representatives from ten Asian Episcopal Conferences.[38] One of the discussions was about the 'pastoral challenges posed by the growth of Pentecostals on the Continent of Asia'. Juan Usma Gómez, a Vatican official responsible for Catholic/Pentecostal relations, highlighted that the biggest challenges to the Catholics was not the numerical growth of the Pentecostals, but their denial of Catholics as 'true Christians', manifested from their 'illegitimate actions of evangelisation', 'acts of proselytism' and 'the lack of respect for Catholics and aggressive behaviours towards them.' As a result, it was impossible to build up 'neighbourly relations and exchanges' with them. To face this problem positively, Gómez recommended to the PCPCU to study the 'forms, expressions, influence and presence in the local context' of Pentecostalism. He also proposed that the Roman Catholic Church could take this situation as an opportunity to renew the church rather than as a threat to it. He listed some elements which the Catholics could learn from the Pentecostals regarding pastoral ministry, including 'the immediacy and accessibility to Pentecostal teaching and doctrine; the effectiveness of their preaching, which can inspire emotion and sentiment in those it addresses; and their constant presence and closeness to people, which makes it possible to establish daily bonds of communion and brotherhood.'[39] A similar conference, entitled 'The Search for Christian Unity: Where We Stand Today", was held in the following year in Manila. Apart from mentioning the strengths and weaknesses of Pentecostalism, the Catholic leaders urged for a '"necessary" environment to retain members' through creating a 'warmer atmosphere in church, a more joyful worship service, and greater openness to the contributions of laity'. They also suggested launching weekly Bible studies as an arena for lay people to share testimonies and retreat.[40]

---

[35] Olav Fykse Tveit, "Greetings to the 22nd Pentecostal World Conference, 24-27 August 2010 in Stockholm, Sweden", http://www.oikoumene.org/en/resources/documents/general-secretary/speeches/greetings-to-the-22nd-pentecostal-world-conference.html (accessed on 13 April 2012).
[36] http://www.pentecostalworldfellowship.org/52 (accessed on 13 April 2012).
[37] Email from Harold Hunter, 10 April 2012.
[38] They were from Korea, Indonesia, Macao, Myanmar, the Philippines, Thailand, Vietnam, the Federation of Asian Bishops' Conferences, Bangladesh and Hong Kong. Juan Usma Gómez, "Marking Christian Unity Worldwide: Asian Pentecostalism, Methodist 'Justification'", a report to the Pontifical Council for the Promotion of Christian Unity, http://www.vatican.va/roman_curia/pontifical_councils/chrstuni/eccl-comm-docs/rc_pc_chrstuni_doc_20070110_pentecostals_en.html (accessed on 13 March 2012).
[39] *Ibid.*
[40] Michelle A. Vu, "Pentecostal Growth in Asia Challenges Catholic Church", *Christian Post* (14 February 2007), http://www.christianpost.com/news/pentecostal-growth-in-asia-challenges-catholic-church-25817/ (accessed on 10 April 2012)

Although Roman Catholics and Pentecostals see themselves very different from each other doctrinally, liturgically and pastorally, scholars have observed that in fact, Pentecostals share more commonalities with Catholics than mainline Protestants and evangelicals.[41] Some people even names Pentecostalism as 'Catholicism without priests.'[42] Instead of solely relying on the Bible, they both emphasise spiritual revelation and discernment in God's presence in prayers and devotion. They both believe in salvation through faith and deeds, which was especially obvious among Classical Pentecostals in the early twentieth century who taught about restitution as a concrete way to show one's determination of repentance, which can be found in medieval Catholic teaching on indulgence. Another commonality is the practice of healing although Roman Catholics regard it as a sacrament and Pentecostals as a charism. Jeff Gros suggests that healing can be a key to reconciliation between Catholics and Pentecostals as it can be used mutually not only for the restoration of the wholeness of physical bodies, but also the Body of Christ.[43] If 'demography is destiny', as Augustus Comte claims, then Catholics and Pentecostals who represent the two largest Christian populations in the world would probably determine the ecumenical future. Since Asia is one of the continents seeing rapid growth of Pentecostalism, Asian Pentecostals are potentially able to contribute to grassroots and official ecumenism in the twenty-first century.

Conclusion

In 1959, the first General Secretary of the WCC, Willem Visser t'Hooft, prophetically identified Asian ecumenism as liberation from division, from western Christian manipulation and from historians' wrong predictions of the decline of Asian mission and Christianity, based on their observation of what had happened to their western mother churches. He exhorted Asian churches to prove themselves by their 'spiritual independence', 'true rootedness in Asia' and their 'evangelistic passion'. He acknowledged Asians' acquaintance with the spiritual world and declared, "It is their calling to provide a great surprise to the worldly-wise who count without the work of the Holy Spirit." He also encouraged Asian churches to voice out when they noticed that the World Council of Churches was moving towards a 'Western council of churches'.[44] I am not sure if Visser t'Hooft's prediction has come true for all Asian churches, but certainly it can be applied to Asian Pentecostalism. By the power of the Holy Spirit, Asian Pentecostal churches have developed their 'spiritual independence', 'true rootedness in Asia' and 'evangelistic passion'. The examples of the Philippines, Taiwan, Singapore, China, Korea and Malaysia listed in this article reveal that what they have achieved is not only their own spiritual and numerical growth, but also a deeper commitment to mutual acknowledgement and collaboration as one Body of Christ. Since Asia has been a hot pot of religious conflicts, terrorism, poverty, injustice of global trade, sexism, racism, dictatorship, pollution and nuclear power, Pentecostal and other churches need to lend strength and share discernments with each other to face these complicated issues and be a witness to the world.

Bibliography

Allen, John L. "If Demography is Destiny, Pentecostals are the Ecumenical Future", *National Catholic Reporter*, 28 January 2008. http://ncronline.org/node/11567 (accessed on 17 April).

[41] Walter Hollenweger, *Origins and Development Worldwide* (Baker Academic, 2006), pp. 144-180.
[42] Quoted in Harvey Cox, *Fire from Heaven: The Rise of Pentecostal Spirituality and the Reshaping of Religion in the Twenty-first Century* (New York: Addison-Wesley Publishing Company, 1995), p. 178.
[43] Jeff Gros, "It Seems Good to the Holy Spirit and to Us: The Ecclesial Vocation of the Pentecostal Scholar", paper presented at the annual conference of the Society for Pentecostal Studies, 29 February-3 March 2012.
[44] W. A. Visser t' Hooft, "The Significance of the Asian Churches in the Ecumenical Movement", *The Ecumenical Review*, XI/4 (July 1959), pp. 375-376.

Anderson, Allan. *Spreading Fires: The Missionary Nature of Early Pentecostalism.* London: SCM Press, 2004.

Anderson, Allan and Edmond Tang, eds. *Asian and Pentecostal: The Charismatic Face of Christianity in Asia*. Baguio City: Regnum, 2005.

Au, Connie Ho Yan. *Grassroots Unity in the Charismatic Renewal.* Eugene: Wipf & Stock, 201

Bergunder, Michael. *The South Indian Movement in the Twentieth Century.* Grand Rapids, Michigan: William B. Eerdmans Publishing Company, 2008.

Burgess, Stanley M. and Eduard M. van der Maas, eds. *International Dictionary of Pentecostal and Charismatic Movements*. Grand Rapids, Michigan: Zondervan, 2002.

Cox, Harvey. *Fire from Heaven: The Rise of Pentecostal Spirituality and the Reshaping of Religion in the Twenty-first Century.* New York: Addison-Wesley Publishing Company, 1995.

Gros, Jeff. "It Seems Good to the Holy Spirit and to Us: The Ecclesial Vocation of the Pentecostal Scholar", a paper presented at the annual conference of the Society for Pentecostal Studies, 29 February-3 March 2012.

Hollenweger, Walter. *Origins and Development Worldwide*. Baker Academic, 2006.

Ma, Wonsuk and Julie. "Jesus Christ in Asia: Our Journey with Him as Pentecostal Believers", in *International Review of Mission*, 94/375 (October 2005).

Robeck, C. M. "Pentecostals and Christian Unity: Facing the Challenge", in *Pneuma: The Journal of the Society for Pentecostal Studies*, 26/2 (Fall 2004).

Visser t' Hooft, W. A. "The Significance of the Asian Churches in the Ecumenical Movement", *The Ecumenical Review*, XI/4 (July 1959).

Vu, Michelle A. "Pentecostal Growth in Asia Challenges Catholic Church", *Christian Post* (14 February 2007), http://www.christianpost.com/news/pentecostal-growth-in-asia-challenges-catholic-church-25817/ (accessed on 10 April 2012).

(11) Relations Between Ecumenicals and Evangelicals in Asia

Siga Arles

1. Some Factors Which Motivate 'Anti-Ecumenism'

Historically a sense of distrust has been implanted in the minds of the 'evangelicals' about the 'ecumenicals' – as not rooted in the authority of the Bible, – as not committed to evangelism and church growth and – as not promoting conversion. This suspicion led to a relationship of enmity. At times this was promoted by the international links and monetary investments from the global structures. The place of money serves as a major reason for the parallel and polarizing journey. Theological differences often are held out as the reason for the parallel course but I am convinced that while there may be some differences that exist, there is enough common ground in terms of faith affirmations and missional commitments which could hold both evangelicals and ecumenicals together in unity and partnership. As far as the majority of the world is concerned, the funding from the First World is at the root of the unfortunate process of dividing and preserving the dividedness, often posing / portraying the differences disproportionately.

A major issue in building bridges between the camps is the fact that members of each camp are in closer touch with their own global counterparts, than with their native Christians from the other camp. The meetings with each other are rare and insufficient to develop meaningful relationships. They remain secure in their separation as funds are at their disposal to carry on separatist agendas. They do not take time to meet each other as they are busy in their own corners with their own programs. As the statement goes 'out of sight – out of mind', and the separation and distance keep each unaware of the other at the local level. There may be some awareness of global developments in the other camp, but much ignorance of local developments. This is a serious matter for us to address if we wish to see the unity of the Body of Christ in meaningful ways.

The un-evangelical as well as the un-ecumenical attitudes should be curbed from both camps. What I note is that there is apathy over relating across camps on the part of many. Among the leadership there is either a sense of angst and fear about the other or a sense of arrogance that the other does not matter. This chronic situation of illness could only be corrected if we bring the two camps together into commitment on common goals, common purposes and common activities relating to the mission of the church.

2. 'Ecumenicals' – As an Identity

The technical usage of the word 'ecumenical' as an identifier of a group of people, perhaps, was a twentieth century phenomenon. Though John Wesley and William Carey are described as ecumenical in their times, the naming is by later perspectives. When the Missionary movement was globally organized under the International Missionary Council and the two study commissions – 'Faith and Order' and 'Life and Work' – emphasized the need for the unity of the body of Christ, in the process of the birthing of the World Council of Churches, this concept was conceived and the word was coined. To embrace the whole inhabited earth – oikumene – led to 'ecumenism' as the process. Those who committed themselves to such thought and action were identified as the ecumenicals. The Missionary Movement gave birth to the Ecumenical Movement with the formation of WCC. Increasingly the people of the member churches of WCC became known as ecumenical Christians. But the sad tale is that the term was only known and used by the theologically trained clergy and the literate laity; the vast majority of the membership remained theologically and biblically illiterate and did not know the term or its meaning. To a vast majority of the members of the Church of South India (to which I belong – and which church is praised as a heroic example of ecumenism), this term and its significance is largely unknown and ill comprehended. Such a statement is not far from the reality that exists.

3. 'Evangelicals' – As an Identity

The technical usage of the word 'evangelicals' as an identifier of a group of people, perhaps, was a much older phenomenon in the history of the Christian church. Even at the period of Reformation, we hear of the protesting groups referred to as evangelicals. This practice continued in Latin America, where Christians were either a majority of Roman Catholics or the much divided Protestants, who were invariably known as the evangelicals. Within the Church of England the distinction of the High Church as the Anglo-Catholic and the Low Church as the Evangelical prevailed. The Society for the Propagation of the Gospel in Foreign Parts and the Church Missionary Society were the missionary arms of the respective sections of the Anglican Church. William Pitt and William Wilberforce were known as the 'evangelical politicians' during the time when William Carey and his contemporaries approached the British parliament for 'anti-sati' legislation. Within the Church of Scotland one talked in those days of the liberals, the moderates and the evangelicals. Thus within the Western church the identity of certain groups as evangelicals was common. When the missionary expansion of the church happened during the 18th and the 19th centuries in the Eastern parts and the Southern hemisphere, the church not only spread with its denominational divisions but also with its division as the evangelical and liberal churches, later the ecumenical churches. The church around the world has inherited the dividedness and has not overcome the ill effects of it.

Whereas the distinction of the ecumenical and evangelical identities continued to intensify in the formation of the two global structures such as the World Council of Churches (formed in 1948) and World Evangelical Fellowship (formed in 1951), both with a large initiative of the Western theologians and Western church leaders, there was an inclusion of the Asian leaders and voices in the formation and functional mode. The spirit of ecumenism in India led to the formation of the Church of South India already on 27 September 1947, even before the formation of the WCC at Easter 1948. The spirit of evangelical faith commitment in India led to the formation of the Evangelical Fellowship of India even ahead of the formation of WEF in the same year 1951.

4. The Asian Church and the Polarization of the Evangelicals and the Ecumenicals

The global developments of this polarized Christianity was a largely western phenomenon but it had its roots and developments in the Asian soil, particularly in India. Certainly for the ecumenical thought and structure formation, some of the key personalities who were to influence global developments were based at and worked their thought and theology in the mission field in India: Stephen Neill, Charles Ranson and Lesslie Newbigin who were tall figures during the period between 1940s to 1980s. They worked in the Tamil country in South India based at Tinnevelly, Kanjeepuram-Chenglepet-Madras and Madurai.[1]

Not only did the western persons based in India influence the global developments of ecumenical thought and practice, it was also shaped by a certain number of Indians who were articulate and active as architects of ecumenicalism. This could be attested from what Philip Potter spoke in 1982 at the Silver Jubilee celebrations of the Christian Institute for the Study of Religion and Society at Bangalore. He said

---

[1] One of the best sources of information on the history of the development of the missionary and ecumenical movements from the nineteenth century is the thesis of William Richey Hogg, *Ecumenical Foundations, A History of the International Missionary Council and Its Nineteenth Century Background,* New York: Harper and Brothers, 1952.

(in what appears a light hearted comment with depth of meaning) that the World Council of Churches at Geneva was being run by an Indian mafia set in CISRS in Bangalore!

> Indeed it has often been enviously remarked that the World Council was run by an Indian "mafia", and that "mafia" was centred around the Christian Institute (CISRS)... Indians have been the first Third World people to enter into critical dialogue with the First World and to do so with freedom and panache. The CISRS is the most conspicuous example of this..., I can think of no other institute of this kind anywhere in the world which has been so influential and so productive.[2]

Thinkers from the CISRS group such as PD Devanandan, Russell Chandran, MM Thomas (WCC Central Committee chairman), Stanley Samartha (the first to lead the WCC Sub-unit on Dialogue), Samuel Amirtham (Director for Program on Theological Education), MA Thomas (Director of Ecumenical Christian Centre), TK Thomas, Samuel Parmar, EV Mathew, CT Kurien, Saral Chatterji and a host of others impacted the various strategic avenues of thought and practice in the decades after the birth of the ecumenical movement.[3]

Similarly, even in the evangelical movement around the world we could locate both the western missionaries who worked in India as well as Indian leaders who helped shape the global evangelical movement. Significant names could be Eli Stanley Jones, Donald McGavran, Jack Dain, Wesley Duewel and such along with Ben Wati and Theodore Williams who were presidents of World Evangelical Fellowship, Saphir Athyal who was on the Planning Committee of the Lausanne Committee for World Evangelization, John Richard of the AD 2000 Movement, Vinay Samuel of INFEMIT, Ken Gnanakan of WEF Theological Commission and a host of others who played significant roles in the shaping of an evangelical movement.

5. Relationships – Some Global Developments

The relationship between the ecumenicals and evangelicals globally remained unhealthy and competitive, polarized and divisive. Later in this essay we shall consider the motivating factors which promoted and perpetuated this divide. During the sixties and seventies this divide was acute and rigid. The Uppsala Assembly (1968), the Bangkok conference (1973) and the Nairobi Assembly (1975) were blamed by the evangelicals who rallied their strength at Berlin (1966) and Lausanne (1974). In the eighties, there was an attempt to overcome the divide and to try to relate with one another. For instance, Raymond Fung, the evangelism secretary of WCC, a Baptist pastor from Hong Kong, participated in some evangelical events and related with the Partnership in Mission Asia conference at London in 1986. With his help, the Latin American Theological Fraternity, the African Theological Fraternity and the Partnership in Mission Asia – which all together later formed the International Fellowship of Evangelical Mission Theologians (INFEMIT)- met in 1987 at Stuttgart, along with the Commission on Mission and Evangelism of the WCC and explored possibilities of mutual relationships.[4] As a result of such efforts during the 1990s and after, the relationship was steadily healed and it has improved through the decades. Let us trace the history of this unsteady relationship by highlighting certain salient features, particularly from the Asian context.

---

[2] See Philip Potter, "Jubilee Convention Address" in *Religion and Society,* XXX:3&4, September to December, 1983, p2.

[3] See Chapter Five: "The Contribution of the Christian Institute for the Study of Religion and Society" in Siga Arles, *Missiological Education: An Indian Exploration,* Bangalore: Centre for Contemporary Christianity, 2006, pp99-127, especially pp120ff.

[4] See the report of this gathering: Albrecht Hauser & Vinay Samuel (eds.), *Integral Evangelism,* Paternoster: Regnum Publications, 1988.

6. Relationships in India: The EFI and its relation to NCCI

When the EFI was formed, some of the members of the North American church denominations which claimed to be evangelical churches – such as the Wesleyan, Free Methodist, Christian and Missionary Alliance, Nazarene and similar others felt that they alone qualified to be members of the evangelical movement. They would not consider those evangelicals who were members of the historic mainline / mainstream larger churches which were members of the NCCI / WCC as worthy to be included in the evangelical movement. With Everett Cattell, the first General Secretary of EFI, the group had much discussion and finally it was resolved to include within the movement both groups of evangelicals – those from the mainstream churches connected with NCCI as well as the strictly evangelical denominations. Robert McMahon who wrote the history of EFI[5] commented:

> There was a move to exclude from membership of EFI any whose missions or churches were linked to the National Christian Council or other 'ecumenical' bodies. Cattell and others pleaded that "EFI be kept open to all convinced evangelicals whatever their affiliations". Hence EFI "adopted a position of neutrality towards the ecumenical movement".[6]

EFI was not anti-NCCI or a competitor with NCCI in its original purpose. It minded the area of evangelism and mission and recognized NCCI as tending to the churches.

Though for a period the EFI had many secretaries drawn from mainline churches such as the Methodist, CSI, CNI and the Baptist, in the later period slowly it drifted into the hands of people from the so called purely evangelical churches, such as the St. Thomas Evangelical, Christian and Missionary Alliance, Evangelical Church of India, etc.,

The first time I attended an EFI conference was in 1970 when I found there was a sharp disagreement within the fellowship. Members from the smaller evangelical churches did not feel comfortable with EFI which remained a 'fellowship structure' but did not represent their concerns in the nation. Whereas NCCI was representing the churches, this group distrusted NCCI and judged EFI as inadequate, and hence proposed the formation of a new structure to fend for them. As a result the Federation of Evangelical Churches of India (FECI) was formed in 1974. It was a sort of parallel structure to NCCI.

Later at the turn of the century, there arose the Hindu militancy under the Rashtriya Swayam Sevak Sangh, Bharatiya Janata Party and the Hindutva brigade which unleashed attacks on the churches in various parts of the country. Often the independent churches were attacked. They felt that the NCCI was not representing their plight. They also felt that the FECI was broad and did not address specific issues within the Hindutva setting. Hence, in order for voicing the concerns of the persecuted to the government, some pastors and groups rallied the independent churches and formed the All India Christian Council (AICC). Thus, there grew multiple structures with duplication.

What developed thus in India was similar to the developments in the continental mega structures such as the Evangelical Fellowship of Asia (EFA) and the Christian Council of Asia (CCA). With parallel and polarizing developments, there always remained a subtle and obvious tug-of-war situation within relationships. Each camp held its own programs, consultations and conferences with no reference to the other. The parallel journey only meant duplication of efforts and expenses, which proved wasteful and redundant, with no cumulative impact on the society around.

---

[5] Robert McMahon, *To God Be the Glory: An Account of the EFI's First Twenty Years, 1951-1970,* Delhi: MSS, 1970.

[6] Quoted by Siga Arles, "Evangelical Movement in India – An Evaluation" in Siga Arles & I. Ben Wati (eds.), *Pilgrimage 2100: A Self Reflection on Indian Evangelicalism,* Bangalore: Centre for Contemporary Christianity, 1995, p32.

7. The Formation and Significance of the Lausanne Movement

Further to the WEF, the evangelical movement grew stronger with the formation of the Lausanne Committee for World Evangelization (LCWE). The worldward journey of the ecumenical movement [through its conferences on Church and Society at Geneva (1966), Fourth Assembly of WCC at Uppsala in 1968, Commission on World Mission and Evangelism consultation at Bangkok in 1973] aroused a systematic and consistent reaction among the evangelicals under the leadership of Billy Graham, John RW Stott, Jack Dain and others. The Berlin Congress in 1966 and Lausanne Conference in 1974 paved the way for a global movement to promote the evangelical cause and cohesiveness. This in a way intensified the division and polarization within the body. The Asian Leadership Congress on Evangelism (ALCOE) formed a structure for Asian evangelical momentum.

8. Theological Education and the Inner Divide in Asia – BTESSC / ATESEA & ATA

In South Asia, particularly for India, the Senate of Serampore College was the source of theological and ministerial formation. Equally the Association for Theological Education in South East Asia (ATESEA) and its counterpart for North East Asia, provided similar standardization and accreditation. Much of the ecumenical formation was under their influence. The Theological Education Fund (TEF formed in 1958 at IMC Ghana) shaped the process of contextualization in theological education in line with the worldward journey of the ecumenical movement. Theology in context took the socio-economic, religious and political realities seriously and attempted what later was recognized as the wholistic gospel and ministry. Ecumenical Theological Education shaped the ministry and mission of the churches of Asia.

To begin with the evangelical movement distrusted this sort of development and felt that evangelism was crowded out of the agenda of the ecumenical structures and their theological education. Hence, by 1970 there arose an effort from the WEF Theological Commission to form an equivalent to TEF, namely Theological Assistance Program (TAP), to assist theological colleges to develop a clear evangelical ministry formation.[7] It led later to the formation of the International Council for Evangelical Theological Education (ICETE) with its 8 international branches[8], of which the Asian branch is the Asia Theological Association (ATA) as an accrediting agency for evangelical theological education all across Asia. In the past 40 years it has grown to accredit well over 250 institutions in every nation in Asia, from Japan to Jordan.[9] I had the privilege of participating in the ICETE triennial conferences at Chiang Mai in Thailand (2006) and Sopron in Hungary (2009) and meeting with the leaders from all the eight branch structures.

In as much as the World Council of Churches has developed its TEF into the Program for Theological Education (PTE) and later into the Ecumenical Theological Education (ETE) and is catering for the explorations into various curricular revisions, contextualization and viability of relevant theological education around the world, ICETE does the same within the evangelical orbit. The 2009 ICETE conference dealt with workshops on topics such as:

---

[7] Bruce Nicholls of New Zealand records the history of formation and activities of TAP as the first architect of the TAP along with Saphir Athyal. Their efforts led to the formation of ATA. Nicholls edited TAP News and systematically helped to grow the movement.

[8] The 8 branches of ICETE are: 1) Accrediting Council for Theological Education in Africa (ACTEA), 2) Asia Theological Association (ATA), 3) Caribbean Evangelical Theological Association (CETA), 4) European Evangelical Accrediting Association (EEAA), 5) Euro-Asian Accrediting Association (E-AAA), 6) Association for Evangelical Theological Education in Latin America (AETAL), 7) Association for Biblical Higher Education (ABHE) and 8) South Pacific Association of Bible Colleges (SPABC).

[9] See the special 40th anniversary volume of ATA released at the Hong Kong Assembly: Bong Rin Ro, Ken Gnanakan, Joseph Shao, Bruce Nicholls, Theresa Roco Lua and Julie Belding (eds.), *New Era New Vision; Celebrating 40 Years of the Asia Theological Association,* Manila: ATA, 2010.

- Biblical and theological foundations for curriculum development
- The challenge of character formation in TE
- Doing TE in community
- Mission beyond evangelism
- Integral mission and TE
- Practicing relational intelligence in TE
- Shaping global TE locally
- Technological solutions for TE in the network generation
- Is information technology taking over TE?[10]

The quest for contextualization that TEF floated could be seen echoing in the efforts of ICETE and the ATA as well. Some of the concerns as found in the articles in the ATA journal are indicative of the similarity in the search for relevance in theological education in both camps. During 2002 to 2009, when I served as the Editor of the *Journal of Asian Evangelical Theology* of ATA, the following editorials and articles expressed the concerns that were shared with the constituency at national and regional consultations:

- "A Call for Doing Theology in 21st Century Asia"[11],
- "Transform World: A Call of our Times"[12],
- "Theological Education: The 'Story' of Impacting Asian Pluralist Contexts"[13],
- "Theological Education in Asia: A Health Check"[14],
- "Each Congregation a Seminary: The Need for Team Ministry"[15],
- "Prophetic Voice of the Gospel in Contemporary Asia"[16],
- "Mission Challenge – Bigger than ever in Asia!"[17],
- "Theological Curriculum Change for the Local 21st Century Context"[18],
- "New Horizons for Theological Education in Today's Changing World"[19],
- "Theological Education for Missionary Formation"[20],
- "Missiological Education in India: Journey to Become Academically Authentic and Contextually Relevant"[21],
- "Theological Education Towards 2020" & "A Response"[22],
- "Governance of Theological Education: Patterns and Prospects"[23],
- "Theological Education & Global Tertiary Education: Risks and Opportunities"[24],
- "Shifting Paradigms in Theological Education – An Asian Perspective"[25],
- "The Use of Technology to Promote Learning in Asian Theological Institutions"[26]

---

[10] Taken from the Conference Handbook of *ICETE Consultation 2009, Sopron, Hungary,* 5-9 October 2009.
[11] *Journal of Asian Evangelical Theology,* 11:1 & 2, June & December 2003, pp1-2.
[12] *Journal of Asian Evangelical Theology,* 13:1, June 2005, pp1-3.
[13] *Journal of Asian Evangelical Theology,* 14:1, June 2006, pp1-5.
[14] *Journal of Asian Evangelical Theology,* 14:2, December 2006, pp3-7.
[15] *Journal of Asian Evangelical Theology,* 15:1, June 2007, pp3-6.
[16] *Journal of Asian Evangelical Theology,* 15:2, December 2007, pp3-7.
[17] *Journal of Asian Evangelical Theology,* 16:1 & 2, June & December 2008, pp3-6.
[18] Lee Wanak, *Journal of Asian Evangelical Theology,* 10:1&2, 2002, pp63-77.
[19] Bruce Nicholls, *Journal of Asian Evangelical Theology,* 11:1&2, 2003, pp61-68.
[20] Dasan Jeyaraj, *Journal of Asian Evangelical Theology,* 12:1&2, 2004, pp139-172.
[21] Fanai Hrangkhuma, *Journal of Asian Evangelical Theology,* 13:1, June 2005, pp103-120.
[22] Ivan Satyavrata & Allan Harkness, *Journal of Asian Evangelical Theology,* 13:2, Dec.2005, pp71-91.
[23] Siga Arles, *Journal of Asian Evangelical Theology,* 14:1, June 2006, pp53-69.
[24] Alister McGrath, *Journal of Asian Evangelical Theology,* 14:2, Dec.2006, pp12-28.
[25] Vinay K. Samuel, *Journal of Asian Evangelical Theology,* 15:1&2, 2007, pp8-14.

- "Learning Expectations of Students and Faculty in Theological Education: A South East Asian Theological College Survey"[27]

At the 40th anniversary of ATA a collection of essays were released titled *Tending the Seedbeds: Educational Perspectives on Theological Education in Asia*[28] in which the explorations by many Asian authors from the evangelical camp parallel the efforts as seen in the ecumenical theological education.

Rather than dividedness, there is need for developing a cohesiveness in TE and thus in the total church and ministry around the world. Healing energies ought to be let loose in the global churches and in the local setting.

9. The Drawing Closer of the NCCI, EFI and CBCI

In the Indian setting, the recent two decades have seen a sincere effort on the part of the National Council of Churches in India, Evangelical Fellowship of India and the Catholic Bishops Conference of India. The very fact of the fanaticism of the Hindutva brigade and their attacks on the church has paved the way for the minority Christian community of 3% to come together in ecumenical togetherness for the sake of survival. After Vatican II the Roman Catholics have become open to relate with the Protestants. The Orthodox have come into fellowship with WCC and NCCI. Several pastors from both South and North are keen to present a united front to withstand the attacks of the Hindutva brigade. Beside the AICC, a large gathering of Christian workers and pastors in Bangalore founded a Federation of Christian Churches and Organizations (FCCO) to develop a united front. It has become a very common phenomenon nowadays to find much mutual recognition and desire to work together. An example is the formation of the Bangalore Inter Theologate Seminar (BITS) to bring the Roman Catholic and Protestant professors and students from the seminaries in and around Bangalore to interact and learn together.[29]

Many new efforts are pulling us together, such as when the Karnataka State government led by the BJP imposed a ban on beef eating, we Christians of all denominations met together with Hindus and Muslims to raise our voice of protest. Thus, the inner divide in the church is often challenged by external pressures. On Saturday, 14 July 2012, the Hindus, Sikhs, Buddhists and Christians came together and formed the United Minority Front in Bangalore to challenge the BJP government and its communal politics. Wider ecumenism is floated and promoted by Christian participation.

10. The Un-Ecumenical Approach of the Party Ecumenicals

I had often been disillusioned by the way persons working for ecumenical structures show an attitude of aloofness and dislike towards people who do not belong within their camp. While attending an international ecumenical mission conference, I was talking with a key leader of the ecumenical movement from an Asian country. When I referred to the names of some of the evangelicals in his particular country, his disapproval of them was shocking! I expected him to warmly relate to those names and talk lovingly about them and their significance in the church in his country. But no! He was simply negative. This hurt me as this person was an employee in the ecumenical structure. He seemed to lack the ecumenical spirit of acceptance.. I feel that there are too many un-ecumenical persons who are talking on ecumenism as paid agents.

---

[26] Calvin Chong, *Journal of Asian Evangelical Theology*, 15:1&2, 2007, pp113-118.

[27] Allan G. Harkenss, *Journal of Asian Evangelical Theology*, 16:1&2, 2008, pp124-143.

[28] See Allan Harkness (ed.), Manila: Asia Theological Association, 2010.

[29] BITS was a program launched from the Ecumenical Christian Centre during the time of Dr. Mani Chacko and I served as one of its Presidents. The annual meeting of representatives from all theological colleges in the faculty colloquium and BITS seminar provide the opportunity to enhance ecumenical relationships.

Ecumenism has gone through various stages of development and deterioration. In an article on "Ecumenical Relations"[30] for the 2007 conference of the Fellowship of Indian Missiologists at Kashmir, I recounted and identified different trends of ecumenism that I observe, such as: *positive ecumenism* (WCC & NCC), *stunted ecumenism* (Joint Council of CSI, CNI, MTC), *fake ecumenism* (many experiments, committees and consultations which prolong endlessly without resolutions), *forced ecumenism* (such as in totalitarian settings) and *genuine ecumenism* (formation of CSI and CNI).

While teaching a course on the History of Ecumenical Movement at Serampore College, along with my students I was interacting on the process of wider union that was initiated in India by the Church of South India and Church of North India along with the Malankara Mar Thoma Syrian Church. They first set up a theological commission in 1973 "for the purpose of bringing together all these three bodies to a common fellowship, cooperation and unity"[31] and later formed a Joint Council in 1978.

> The Joint Council of the CNI, CSI, MTC, has been constituted as the visible origin for common action by the three churches which recognize themselves as belonging to the one Church of Jesus Christ in India, even while remaining as autonomous churches, each having its own identity or traditions and organizational structure.[32]

The Joint Council failed to lead to the formation of the Bharat Christian Church and in 2004 still explored "to pursue their discussion on the ways towards unity and pledged their commitment to the formation of the Communion of Churches in India (CCI)".[33] It appeared to me that CSI and CNI were open for such union whereas the Syrian Orthodox doctrine and ethos were too precious for the Mar Thoma Church to give up for the sake of unity.. Yet, they keep active in ecumenical talks, consultations and conferences, taking leadership roles in the ecumenical movement – which movement may never really achieve its goals. A paradox! The ecumenical dialogue between CSI and the Lutheran and the American Methodists had failed in the very first two decades after the birth of the CSI. Today, sadly, the failure continues.

It disheartens me to notice how people who talk much about ecumenism and participate in great conferences and committees of ecumenical movement, fail to actualize by simple acts of communion together in their own places. A CSI leader reflected of his experience while studying for his Master degree at the Orthodox Seminary in Kottayam, which was one part of the Federated Faculty under the Senate of Serampore College. When attending worship with eucharist, he was included in the peace sharing, but excluded from the elements of the body and blood – it was not given to him. His fellow post graduate students and teachers from the Orthodox church shared in the holy communion and would not include him in it, since he was from the Church of South India. My experience was similar: while attending a national consultation organized by the Ishvani Kendra at Pune, a Roman Catholic missiology professor who stood next to me, found it hard to pass the elements to me, a Protestant Missiologist! But he was interacting with me in conferences on great missiological themes, justice questions and the need for ecumenism! Such is the reality which we have to counter and correct with a sense of urgency.

---

[30] See Siga Arles, "Ecumenical Relations" in Joseph Mattam & Joseph Valiamangalam (eds.), *Building Solidarity: Challenges to Christian Mission,* FOIM XII, Delhi: ISPCK for FOIM, 2008, pp223-231.
[31] See O.L. Snaitang, *A History of Ecumenical Movemetn: An Introduction,* Bangalore: BTESSC / SATHRI, 2004, 2006, 2007, p123.
[32] *Ibid.,* p124.
[33] *Ibid.,*

11. The Un-Evangelical Approach of the Party Evangelicals

A fellow doctoral student at the University of Aberdeen, Kwame Bediako, a Ghanaian Presbyterian, retorted with high emotion about the 'party evangelicals' who were no real evangelicals! They have created an evangelical party and are promoting membership into that party. Rather than truly promoting and living the implications of the evangelical spirit, they are concerned about being in and developing the party! This promotes among them a tendency to count the party more important than the individuals. Hence, one does not mind to backstab and disown and throw out people for even minor differences. Instead of being 'good news' to each other, such party members turn out to be terrible 'bad news' to those within the camp with whom they develop disagreements. It is revealing to hear what Everett Cattell said about the evangelicals, at the early stage of steering the new born EFI as its secretary:

> No one knows better than those of us who have laboured for evangelical co-operation and unity how grave are the weaknesses and how deep are the sins that are covered by this label.[34]

The failure of evangelical unity is a historic reality. There is a level of unity but that is never deep enough or large enough. Hence, there is the repeating tendency to form numerous structures and duplicating efforts. Indian evangelicalism has seen EFI, FECI, AICC and also the floating of National Fellowship of Evangelicals with their Consultation on National Strategy. Even the formation of India Missions Association to bring the indigenous mission societies of India together at times appeared as though it was a competitive development which had to be sorted out amicably.

While unity and relationship within and among evangelicals is a tough issue, to develop unity and relationship with those who are non-evangelical, non-Protestant and non-christian – definitely presents a tougher option.

12. An Exciting Proposal – "Evangelicals are True Ecumenicals"

J.J. Harris was final year BD student at Serampore College when I joined the faculty to teach Missiology and to develop Mission Studies at Post Graduate level. He wrote his BD thesis comparing and contrasting the major indigenous mission societies in India. Later he did his M.Th at SAIACS where I taught two modules to the Missiology students. In my class, Harris was drawn to the history of the way the church movement developed in its ecumenical and evangelical dividedness and found the need to study it in depth. Hence, for his D.Miss. research he chose this as his topic and worked hard to argue the point of his conclusion that *Evangelicals are True Ecumenicals*[35]. He saw 'the Futility of Polarization' and studied the contrast between the two camps in the church. Harris states:

> ...being evangelical or ecumenical is not as singular as it may at first seem. It is very difficult to make a clear division between the two. Separating evangelical and ecumenical Christians is a misleading classification since an increasing number of Christians belong[s] in the overlap....the compartmentalization has been done not on the basis of people or denominations but only on the basis of ideologies.[36]

Tracing the history Harris came to realize that only the truly evangelical persons who were touched by the good news of Jesus Christ in its fullness could qualify to embrace the whole wide world with the love

---

[34] Everett Cattell, "The EFI and the Ecumenical Movement" *National Christian Council Review,* January 1965, p11. Quoted in Siga Arles, "Evangelical Movement in India..." *op.cit.*, p29.

[35] J.J. Harris, *Evangelicals are True Ecumenicals: The Theological Pilgrimage of the Indian Church: A Study of Contrast – The Futility of Polarisation,* Madras: Mission Educational Books, 2008.

[36] *Ibid.,* p14.

of God and become ecumenical in practice. Other than that, those who remain within the church as nominal members without an experience of new birth, may never understand God's heart for the world – the love and plan of God in mission.

The 1991 Canberra Assembly of the World Council of Churches affirmed:

> A reconciled and renewed creation is the goal of church's mission. The vision of God uniting all things in Christ is the driving force of its life sharing. Sharing also means that we work to overcome economic disparities and social antagonisms between classes, castes, races, sexes, and cultures.[37]

The problem in ecumenism is identified by Bishop Coorilos as the tendency towards 'monistic unity' of the church in terms of its ecclesiastical structures; and he proposes the possibility of a 'pluriform ecumenism' as the solution.[38] The basic rationale for unity and ecumenism, he further proposes, is placed firstly in the nature of godhead as triune and secondly in the missional purpose of the church.[39]

> The basic motivation for ecumenism… comes from our understanding of the Trinity, as the integral economy (*oikonomia*) of Godhead known to consist in the community of persons (Father, Son and Holy Spirit) existing in unity… we understand our call and responsibility to wider ecumenism as "from our faith in the Trinitarian mystery, God's life of communion and interchange.[40]

> We appeal that our efforts towards unity need to be for the sake of mission and in that extent ensure that our efforts towards visible forms of oneness are not smacked by institutional and communal interests. Therefore, we call upon the churches in India to explore new and credible forms of Christian unity that would enhance the cause of the Gospel.[41]

Thus the rootedness in biblical basis and the faithfulness to the mission of the church are the hallmarks which should characterize our journey into the future as the one united faith community, united in the one God and in His mission to the universe.

Each little congregation in every locality has to align with this God and His mission and thus express the oneness of the body, as the household of God. A CSI clergyman lamented on the character and the desecration suffered by the denominational church in the past:

> Where is the household of God in India? They are in the remote villages, worshipping the Lord in small places of worship. They do not know much of the Bible or the doctrines of the church, but they know Christ. They take pride in saying 'I am CSI', 'I am a Roman Catholic'…. They are so fanatic about their church… cannot find anything good in another denomination. Few years back, if a boy or girl got married outside the Catholic church, the parents lost membership of the church and to get back the membership, they had to make open confession of the mistake in the congregation and pay a fine. The church hierarchy nursed this spirit of hatred… obsessed with

---

[37] Quoted in George Mathew Nalunnakkal, "Mission and Unity in the Context of Contemporary Challenges" in George Mathew Nalunnakkal and Abraham P Athyal (eds.), *Quest for Justice: Perspectives for Mission and Unity,* Delhi: NCCI, Gurukul & ISPCK, 2000, p72.

[38] G.M. Nalunnakkal, "Ecumenism: Challenges Ahead" in Vinod Victor, Leslie Nathaniel & P Suryaprakash (eds.), *Ecumenism: Prospects and Challenges,* Delhi: ISPCK for CSI Synod Youth & Pastoral Aid Departments, 2001, pp115-123.

[39] Nalunnakkal, "Ecumenism: Challenges Ahead", *op.cit.,* pp120f.

[40] *Ibid.,* Quoted from Anand Spenser, "Towards Wider Ecumenism: A Motivation from Biblical Insights" in *National Council of Churches Review,* Vol.CXX, No.7, August 2000, p683.

[41] G.M. Nalunnakkal & A.P. Athyal (eds.), *Quest for Justice: Perspectives on Mission and Unity, op.cit.,* p134.

denominational fanaticism. Reaching the grass root communities with the message of the household of God gives success to ecumenical thinking.[42]

Dr. Chandran Devanesan of Madras Christian College recollected his childhood experiences and his friends hurling childish hatred at each other with slogans such as: "Catholic, catholic, go to hell" and a reciprocal "Protestant, protestant, go to hell".[43] Thirty years later when I went to a Roman Catholic High School in my hometown, the clerk at the school office did not count me a Christian since I was a Protestant! The old style animosities have to be eradicated. Ecumenism must become complete. Post-Vatican II developments have certainly opened out large scale ecumenical relationship within the old church. There are signs for a better future as we have grown through the decades of the twentieth century.

As we traced the history of developments and identified positive trends in the recent decades, there is much hope for the Church of our Lord Jesus Christ to pull together and to serve the human community with the good news of our Lord and to cause the necessary transformation of life both for here and into eternity. The evangelical, the ecumenical, the orthodox, the catholic and all factions should live together in Jesus the integrating power of God for the reconciliation of the vertical and the horizontal dimensions in the universe wherein we humans are the crown of God's creation.

13. The Role of Theological Education – Future Prospects

The responsibility to alter the situation squarely lies in the seminary! The teachers have to set an example of balance – of truly evangelical and truly ecumenical thought and lifestyle. Hence, within the citadels of learning, to initiate a process of renewed thinking among teachers is urgent. The Ecumenical Theological Education program of the World Council of Churches has initiated several avenues of exploration for bridging the divide.

Section 7 "Overcoming the legacy of the ecumenical / evangelical divide in theological education in Asia" of the Memorandum on the Future of Theological Education in Asia is an important initiative in our times. Dietrich Werner has promoted similar efforts as part of his work in ETE. The observation made is correct:

> The ongoing evangelical/ecumenical divide in the area of theological education which in some Asian contexts is more visible and influential than in others today is absorbing more energies and creates more distortions than is adequate and necessary for facing the common missionary tasks of Asian Christianity in the 21st century.[44]

And the proposal made is also very appropriate:

> The urgent need to spell out a clear profile for a biblically sound, contextually relevant and spiritually nurturing theological education for Asian churches can be answered only if all committed Christian traditions are working together rather than losing money and energies in unfruitful debates of the past and maintaining polarized profiles in order just to please different background donors.[45]

The other major reference paper was the Global Study Report on Theological Education for the Edinburgh 2010 conference which had an explicit section on this issue. Here again, in similar vein the section 20 interprets the specific situation within India. In the section titled "Structural divides and

---

[42] G. Devakadasham, "Ecumenism: Prospects and Possibilities – Begin at the Base" in Vinod Victor, et.al., *Ecumenism: Prospects and Challenges, op.cit.,* pp323f.

[4343] See Chandran Devanesan, *Thoughts on Christian Education: Christ and Student Unrest,* Madras: CLS, 1982.

[44] See Dietrich Werner, *et.al.,* Memorandum on the Future of Theological Education in Asia – Draft January 2012. p7.

[45] *Ibid.,*

potentials for cooperation in different networks of theological education – a case study on the interrelation between Serampore and ATA – related colleges in India", the situation study aptly denotes the need and way forward.[46]

Dietrich Werner makes mention that "Kirsteen Kim put together the final volume from the Edinburgh 2010 conference which would certainly deserve its own evaluation in this context. It would be exciting to discuss this in more detail together".[47] He exhorts saying:

> There will [be] no major progress in ecumenical orientation and contextualization of theological education in Asia unless… deliberate attempts are made for *bridging the institutional divide between Asian ecumenical networks in theological education and global and regional evangelical and Pentecostal networks of theological education in Asia.*[48]

> What needs to be justified for the future of Asian Christianity in the 21st century is not whether and why these distinct identities historically have emerged, but whether it still makes sense and is responsible to continue with mutual isolation between different Christian networks for theological education instead of joining forces in common mission and for strengthening the unity of the Christian church in Asia.[49]

The plans to develop cooperative momentum in theological education for all of Asia by bringing closer affinity and work relationships amongst existing structures of theological education and accreditation with a concerted initiative to march towards 2050 is a very welcome effort of the ETE/WCC. We should await with hope to see the fruits of such efforts and initiatives and give complete cooperation and loyalty from our own quarters with a sense of the largeness and oneness of the body of Christ and the mission of God.

Bibliography

Anderson, S.R. and C. Stanley Smith, *The Anderson-Smith Report on Theological Education in Southeast Asia: Especially as It Relates to the Training of Chinese for the Christian Ministry: The Report of a Survey Commission, 1951-1952,* New York: Board of Founders, Nanking Theological Seminary, 1952.

Arles, Siga, *Missiological Education: An Indian Exploration,* Bangalore: Centre for Contemporary Christianity, 2006.

Arles, Siga, *Theological Education for the Mission of the Church in India: 1947-1987,* Frankfurt: Verlag Peter Lang Studies in the Intercultural History of Christianity, 1991.

Arles, Siga "Evangelical Movement in India – An Evaluation" in Siga Arles & I. Ben Wati (eds.), *Pilgrimage 2100: A Self Reflection on Indian Evangelicalism,* Bangalore: Centre for Contemporary Christianity, 1995.

Arles, Siga, "Ecumenical Relations" in Joseph Mattam & Joseph Valiamangalam (eds.), *Building Solidarity: Challenges to Christian Mission,* FOIM XII, Delhi: ISPCK for FOIM, 2008, pp223-231.

Cattell, Everett, "The EFI and the Ecumenical Movement" *National Christian Council Review,* January 1965, p11.

Harris, J.J., *Evangelicals are True Ecumenicals: The Theological Pilgrimage of the Indian Church: A Study of Contrast – The Futility of Polarisation,* Madras: Mission Educational Books, 2008.

---

[46] See the reports from ETE/WCC: Dietrich Werner, et.al., *Theological Education in World Christianity – Joint Information Service of ETE/WCC & WOCATI: World Report on the Future of Theological Education in the 21st Century,* November 2009: *Challenges and Opportunities in Theological Education in 21st Century: Pointers for a New International Debate on Theological Education,* Edinburgh 2010 – International Study Group, Theological Education World Study Report 2009, October 2009. Section 20, pp78f.

[47] Email of Dietrich Werner to Siga Arles, dated 16 May 2012

[48] Dietrich Werner, *et.al.,* Memorandum… *Op.Cit.,* p8.

[49] *Ibid.,*

Hauser, Albrecht & Vinay Samuel (eds.), *Integral Evangelism,* Paternoster: Regnum Publications, 1988.

Hogg, William Richey, *Ecumenical Foundations, A History of the International Missionary Council and Its Nineteenth Century Background,* New York: Harper and Brothers, 1952.

McMahon, Robert, *To God Be the Glory: An Account of the EFI's First Twenty Years, 1951-1970,* Delhi: MSS, 1970.

Nalunnakkal, George Mathew and Abraham P Athyal (eds.), *Quest for Justice: Perspectives for Mission and Unity,* Delhi: NCCI, Gurukul & ISPCK, 2000.

Poon, Michael, "The Association for Theological Education in South East Asia, 1959-2002: A Pilgrimage in Theological Education," in Samuel Campbell Pearson (ed.), *Supporting Asian Christianity's Transition from Mission to Church: A History of the Foundation for Theological Education in South East Asia*, Grand Rapids: Eerdmans, 2010, 363-402, 417-431.

Potter, Philip, "Jubilee Convention Address" in *Religion and Society,* XXX: 3&4, September to December, 1983, p2.

Ro, Bong Rin, Ken Gnanakan, Joseph Shao, Bruce Nicholls, Theresa Roco Lua and Julie Belding (eds.), *New Era New Vision; Celebrating 40 Years of the Asia Theological Association,* Manila: ATA, 2010.

Snaitang, O.L., *A History of Ecumenical Movemetn: An Introduction,* Bangalore: BTESSC / SATHRI, 2004, 2006, 2007, p123.

Spenser, Anand, "Towards Wider Ecumenism: A Motivation from Biblical Insights" in *National Council of Churches Review,* Vol.CXX, No.7, August 2000, p683.

Victor, Vinod, Leslie Nathaniel & P Suryaprakash (eds.), *Ecumenism: Prospects and Challenges,* Delhi: ISPCK for CSI Synod Youth & Pastoral Aid Departments, 2001.

(12) Contributions of Sunday School Movements to Ecumenism in Asia

Ipe Joseph

Introduction

The largest continent, Asia, spreads from the Atlantic to the Pacific and its countries are generally classified as West, Central, North East, South East and South Asia. From the beginning of Christianity Asian countries experienced ecumenical expressions of a varied nature. Though Sunday School movements did not exist in the early periods, there had been effective instruments of Christian nurture even from early times. In the introductory part of this essay we re-look at the early periods and divide the historical periods in the life of the Asian Church into three:

1. The first thirteen centuries
2. The colonial period.
3. The present period of sixty to seventy years.

The usual practice is to call the present period "the post colonial era". Though it is chronologically correct to call it this, it is not sentimentally expedient because we do not want to define our history in terms of colonialism any more. It is true that neo-colonial powers are prowling in all Asian countries even now. Yet, we are now empowered to decide our own destiny.

The transfer of faith from one generation to another was always considered to be the duty of the faithful. Even in the Old Testament times this duty was well communicated. "Children are a gift from the Lord; they are a real blessing" (Ps. 27.3) They are like talents entrusted to the stewards by the Master. "Never forget these commands that I am giving you today. Teach them to your children. Repeat them when you are at home and when you are away, when you are resting and when you are working. Tie them on your arm and wear them on your foreheads as reminders. Write them on the door post of your houses and your gates" (De.6:6-9)

Nurture in faith was a compulsory mandate given to every family. Paul says to Timothy, "I am reminded of your sincere faith, a faith that dwelt first in your grandmother Lois and your mother Eunice and now, I am sure, dwells in you as well." (2Tim.1.5). Home was the *Sunday School* at that time. Paul continues, "You then, my child, be strengthened by the grace that is in Christ Jesus, and what you have heard from me in the presence of many witnesses entrust faithful men who will be able to teach others also." (2Tim. 2.5).

It is good to remember that *teaching, preaching and healing* which are the components of the three-fold ministry of Jesus are practised by the Church without fail. Jesus as a teacher also was a great story teller. Don't we see the primordial form of the *Sunday School* when we look at the picture of Jesus blessing the children!

The First Period of Asian Christianity

The Gospel came to Asia soon after the ascension of our Lord. While Paul and other missionaries were spreading the gospel among the Greeks, Romans and the barbarian tribes in the West, there was an equally great movement in Edessa, Persia, Arabia, Central Asia, China and India. St. Thomas visited the sub-continent of India in 52 A.D. and spread Christianity. The great traveler Cosmas Indicapleustes observed that there were Christians in south-west and central India, Sri Lanka, Burma South and North Vietnam Areas and Siam.

Before the end of the 5th century Persian missionaries were making converts among the Huns and Turks in central Asia. Timothy, a Nestorian patriarch, wrote that a King of the Turks had become Christian along with his people. He mentions ordaining Metropolitans for the Turks and for Tibet. There was also reference about the death of a Metropolitan in China. Nestorian missionaries were already at work in China in about A.D. 635, in Japan in 736 and in Indonesia as early as 7th Century B.C. It is to be believed that for the first thirteen centuries of Christianity, the Christian Church was flourishing in all parts of Asia. It was able to hold together all these countries beyond the limitations of their borders.

However, there was clearly no organized Sunday School at that time as we have today. Faith transmission was done mainly through liturgy and catechism. The Bible was not translated to the vernaculars and the liturgy was mostly in Syriac. Monasteries were the centers of learning. The learning process was through an oral tradition and the faithful were expected to learn the essentials of faith by heart. It is this faith that held the churches in Asia together.

The Roman Catholic Church had their own missionaries and Episcopal structures wherever they went. Attendance in Catechism was compulsory. This channel kept the Roman Catholic Church intact under Papal supremacy all over the world. Martin Luther initiated the Reformation and made the *Small Catechism* as a counter teaching to keep the reformed communities together. In both cases it was such Christian nurture which was the life-stream of the Church

The Second Period of Asian Christianity

This period is usually called the *colonial period* since most of the Asian countries were by now under colonial rule for varying lengths of time. The Portuguese were the first to arrive in many countries. With them they brought Roman Catholic missionaries. The papal supremacy started overshadowing the already existing Nestorian and Syrian Churches. The Portuguese were followed by the Dutch, Spanish and British colonial powers. Francis Xavier, William Carey Barthalomeo Ziegenbalg and Hudson Taylor are some of the great missionaries of this era. The colonial powers did not give much value to the local cultures of the Asian countries. They looked at their colonies as merely a source for making economic gains. The missionaries regarded the people of the colonies as heathens and sinful pagans who needed to be converted to their faith and culture. They gave no value to the spirituality of the great religions already existing in Asia.

It is during the colonial period that the modern Sunday School movement originated. Robert Raikes who lived in Gloucester, 1735-1811 is considered to be the father of the modern Sunday School movement. He was very concerned about the children of poor parents who mostly worked in mines and lived in very dirty conditions. The adolescent children were indulging in all kinds of anti-social activities, For such children he started the first Sunday school in the home of Mrs. Meredit. The Sunday School movement grew up very fast in UK and spread to all the colonial areas too. Missionaries who were working in the homeland and colonies together formed the International Missionary Council in 1921. It was primarily formed for comity- to build understanding as to where each missionary organization should work. The IMC developed its various departments of mission and started implementing them through different regions. Christian Nurture and Christian education were among their priorities. The nurture of the new converts was the main focus.

Side by side the World Council of Christian Education also came into being which gave importance to Sunday schools, their curricula and training of teachers. It is to be recognized that the ministry of Christian nurture was a strong instrument which held together the Christendom of the colonial years. Even the regular school system often reflected the nature of Sunday school because the teachers were evangelists and the curriculum had much Bible and religious teachings in it. The missionary compounds always had three things in them: a Church, a School and a Hospital reminding the ministry of preaching, teaching and healing. The Schools turned out to be Sunday Schools on weekends. It is these missionary compounds which were also teaching centers that brought together believers and seekers.

It is to be gratefully recognized that the colonial period made positive contributions also in the ecumenical areas especially related to Christian nurture. A Gospel-centered curriculum, training of teachers as in secular schools and motivation towards a missionary attitude are among the their contributions. It may be good to look at a case study to understand the impact of Sunday School movement on the life of the church even in the colonial days.

The Serampore Trio Carey, Marshman and Ward started the first Sunday school in South Asia in 1800. The first Sunday School Convention met in Allahabad in 1896. The meeting resolved, "We take the action in forming the India Sunday School Union (ISSU) believing that the present state of our Sunday School work in India demands it and such a step will result in the union and harmony among Christians in India and in the glory of God." ISSU received support from World Sunday School Convention, the British National Sunday School union and the International Bible reading Association (IBRA). In 1890 Dr. J.L Philip from USA was appointed as the General Secretary of ISSU. He traveled all over the subcontinent covering areas now belonging to India, Pakistan, Bangladesh and Sri Lanka.

There was a strong co-operation among denominational churches in the Sunday school ministry. The India Sunday School Union (ISSU) produced teaching notes for all these denominations. These notes were published in the ISSU journal. In 1895 Rev. Richard Burgess became the General Secretary. In addition to South Asia, he traveled to China and even went across to Egypt. The ISSU had its Centre in Coonoor, South India. By 1925 they started the annual Teacher Training Institute and in 1926 the Annual Summer Institute which served many denominations. By 1959, the ISSU had two curriculum projects which were translated into 18 languages. In 1968 moral Instruction lessons were prepared with the help of Orient Longman. For about 8 decades the Sunday School Union held the churches together. However, by 1977 the ISSU had to travel downhill and its work stopped for many years. Now it is being revived and given a new life

The Third Period of Asian Christianity

Now we come to the second part of the essay where we will take a more close look at the third phase of Christianity in Asian Countries namely that of the modern era of freedom. This covers a period of the last 60-70 years. Most of the Asian countries became free from colonial powers. South Asian Countries became free from the British rule. North eastern countries had to go through the painful Pacific war and the Japanese occupation before they got independence. The demise of the Soviet Union resulted in the emergence of new Central Asian Independent countries like Kazhakhstan, Uzbekistan Tajikistan, Kyrguzstan, Turkmenistan and Siberia.

In 1999 East Timor emerged as the newest Asian Country after 400 years of Portuguese and almost 15 years of Indonesian occupation. The Korean war ended in the division of Korea into North and South.

In the ecumenical area also many new things happened. The World Council of Churches was formed in 1948. It became a confluence of several ecumenical streams. The Christian Conference of Asia (EACC and later CCA) took birth in 1959 as the exciting symbol of Asian ecumenism. In most of the Asian countries National Christian Councils took shape and they were seen as the emerging expression of national ecumenism.

The World Council of Christian Education (WCCE) of which the Sunday School was an integral part merged with WCC in 1971. It is observed that with the merger the emphasis on Sunday school for the children dropped out from the priority agenda. However, until two decades ago WCC used to run regular ecumenical learning workshops in Asia and elsewhere. The workshop on methodology of Sunday Schools held in Hyderabad, India and the workshop on Christian education in a pluralistic society held in New

Delhi are cases in point. They brought together almost all Indian churches for joint action. However, at present the Sunday school does not directly appear anywhere in the programs of the World Council of Churches (or NCCs).

The Sunday School is perhaps the only instrument of Christian nurture now along with the VBS/ Summer School.The following are some of the observations which emerge from the author's exposure and experience in the area of Sunday School Movements for the past four decades.

1. Due to industrialization, a market-oriented life, competitiveness, materialism and migration parents have discarded their responsibility of Christian nurture of their children.
2. In the life of the believer and the Church there are certain themes which can be best operated through ecumenical channels. They in turn enrich ecumenism. Sunday School is such an activity with high ecumenical potential. Some others are programs of gender justice, ecological justice Dalit concerns and peace concerns. These can take the faithful beyond the barriers of denominations and even religions.
3. There are denominational Sunday schools, Ecumenical Sunday school movements and newly emerging Sunday school systems. Along with the new and independent churches new Sunday schools also are emerging. Some of them specifically focus on new converts. In the mainline churches Sunday school has taken a back seat. In the budget of many of the churches the category of the Sunday School gets the least or nil. Pastors are not well trained to handle Sunday School. In the theological Seminaries of the mainline churches training in Sunday school is one among the many subjects in a full credit course. It is time to show the red flag!
4. Systematic training of teachers and a well-balanced curriculum are two main factors which Asian Sunday schools lack. To teach in a school the teacher should be a qualified person. In the Sunday School, anybody can teach! There is a great dearth of qualified and committed Sunday school teachers.
5. In Asia there is a struggle between *the ecumenicals* and *the evangelicals* concerning the purpose, methodology and training in Sunday school. It is commonly believed that the evangelicals are Bible centered and the ecumenical are society centered. Now a third group has emerged namely the "power gospel people" who are selling the gospel commercially with slogans and seemingly propagating a gospel where the crown is available without the cross!
6. At the all- Asian level we do not have a Sunday School union or net-work. What is available now is the channel of National Councils. Many of the National Councils of Asian churches have programmes of youth, women, theological education and education for peace and justice. Going through all the websites one can hardly see any specific allocation for Sunday schools in the programs of churches.

The All India Sunday School Association (AISSA) is a Related Agency of the NCC India. A related agency usually means that it is an instrument floated by the Council for a specific service purpose. NCCI has seven such related Agencies. They are AISSA, Christian Institute for the Study of Religion and Society, Christian Literature Society, Christian Medical association, Church's Auxiliary for Social Action, Ecumenical Church Loan Fund, Henry Martyn Institute: International Centre for Research, Interfaith Relation and Reconciliation. Their names are self explanatory of their functions. AISSA is for Christian Education and specifically the Sunday school arm of the Council.

Soon after the ISSU which was catering to the Sunday School area from colonial times became defunct the NCCI organized the Christian Education Council of India as its national program. AISSA later on became its successor.

In 1982 the All India Sunday School and Christian Education Conference was held in Secunderabad, India. Representatives from World Council of Churches, Christian Conference of Asia, Christian Education Movement in UK and over 60 delegates from member churches of NCCI attended the conference. In response to the need expressed by the churches in India through these delegates, a national level ecumenical body for Christian education namely AISSA was born. AISSA celebrated its silver jubilee in 2007.

The main Activities of AISSA are:

- National Sunday School Teacher Trainers' Certificate Course
- Ecumenical Regional 10-day Certificate Course
- Denomination- based 10-day Cadre Building Course
- Regional 2-day and 1-day Training
- Village Sunday School Teachers' Training
- Curriculum building for all age groups – Graded and un-graded
- Peace Education
- Networking of Sunday Schools

Publications of AISSA are:

- Graded curriculum: *Being God's People in God's World*
- Ungraded curriculum: *Masihi* Baalak (Hindi)
- Sunday School Teacher's Handbook in Hindi, English, Tamil, Telugu, Kannada, Marathi, Oriya and Malayalam
- Christian Educators' Training Manual
- IBRA Notes every year: *Words for Today, Light for Our Path*

The Ecumenical contributions of AISSA may be briefly summed up as follows:

1. It is able to bring together 30 member Churches of NCCI which belong to the Protestant, Orthodox and bridge churches like Mar Thoma for the common cause of Christian nurture. When at a time the denominational churches are losing their focus on Sunday School ministry such a venture only can help in the formation of faith among the younger generation.
2. AISSA through its Trainers' training and regular teachers training is able to build up teaching teams in all denominations and linguistic groups.
3. AISSA's Curriculum "Being God's People in God's World" is a well-balanced curriculum, a perfect blend of personal commitment and social action.. All denominations can use this. The un-graded curriculum "Masihi Baalak" (Children of the Lord) is useful for one-teacher and village Sunday Schools.
4. AISSA in partnership with IBRA has reached all the member churches with daily Bible reading notes. It helps and encourages the faithful to make the Word of God the centre of their lives.
5. The curriculum is due for revision now. In Nov. 2010 AISSA organized a Christian Educators Round table in partnership with NCCI. The main purpose was to articulate, as well as formulate within lesson plans, values of inclusiveness and gender justice, eco- justice, water management, poverty concerns, peace issues and religious plurality. These will be integrated in the new Curriculum which will be available for use in July 2012. The young generation will become aware of these emerging issues and be equipped to respond to them using Christian ethical principles.
6. Exchange visits between Sunday schools of different churches has been a very powerful force in enhancing ecumenism. The first experiment was the Mizo Sunday school from far North-East India visiting the Mar Thoma Sunday School in South India five years ago. Thereafter every year an exchange visit continues.

In addition AISSA organises the celebration of World Sunday School Day in the first Sunday of November every year.

Other National Councils also have similar encouraging stories. However, an organized National Sunday school system is yet to be formed in many Asian countries.

Some suggestions may be placed before the Asian ecumenical community for strengthening the ministry though Sunday Schools:

1. Asian countries which have a strong Sunday School network need to help in the capacity building of other nations in this respect through sharing resources and exchange programs.
2. Ultimately at ground level, the responsibility of the Sunday school rests with the local congregations. Capacity building at denominational level also is necessary. The National Councils can give leadership in this area.
3. Sunday School unions need to emerge in the sub-regions of Asia – North East, South East, West and Central and South.
4. In the regional ecumenical organization Sunday school ministry needs to find a deserving place along with its programs of theological education, Asia Ecumenical Courses for women and youth.

If we do not build up the young generation there will not be any Church in future. To keep the churches strong and united Sunday school is perhaps the most effective channel.

It has a double duty: to build a *counter culture* of Christian values to confront the market values of our present day and to promote the purpose of our Lord, "that they all may be one". We are being challenged to respond to this demand.

Bibliography

Batumalai, S: *An Introduction to Asian theology*, New Delhi ISPCK Publication, 1991

Evers, George: *The Churches in Asia*, New Delhi, ISPCK Publication 2005

Kessler, Diane & Kinnamon, Michael: *Councils of Churches and the Ecumenical Vision* Geneva. WCC Publications 2000

WCC Handbook: *A Practical Guide to Ecumenical Learning*, WCC Publication 1989

CCA, *Chiang Mai to Kuala Lumpur*, CCA publications 2009

Philip T.V: *Reflections on Christian Mission in Asia,* ISPCK Publication 2000

Websites of National Councils in Asia

Websites of ISSU & AISSA:

http://issuho.org/default.aspx

http://aissa.in/

PART II

BIBLICAL AND THEOLOGICAL PERSPECTIVES ON ASIAN ECUMENISM

(13) Biblical Foundations of Ecumenism Through Asian Eyes

Somen Das

Introduction

We should not read the Bible carelessly. We have to read it carefully and critically. The Bible is vast and complex in scope and character. Its vocabulary and content are rich and differentiated. It contains history, mythology, prophecy, poetry, apocalyptic literature and apocryphal documents. Therefore, very often its language is symbolic, metaphorical and parabolic. We cannot read the Bible literally and mechanically. It is not a *mantra*. It is an ancient document, bearing witness to the faith of the pioneers of Christianity. Its depth and dimensions are still being explored in the twenty-first century. In spite of the ambiguities and contradictions in the Bible, it remains relevant and important.

We can approach the Bible in two basic ways: deductive and inductive, while looking at it as a whole and selecting specific narratives for our purpose. We can look at it telescopically as well as through a microscope. Let us begin our exploration with some Old Testament Perspectives.

1. Wider Ecumenism in the Old Testament

The Bible begins with a vision of wider ecumenism – the context and the content of the whole inhabited earth as recorded in the first two chapters of the Book of Genesis. Obviously, the account of creation is not a scientific statement, but a faith-affirmation. It is very significant to note that although the second chapter contains the Yahwehist tradition, written around 800 B. C. E., it is placed second by the ancient biblical editors. There is a definitive theological significance to this chronology. The first chapter contains materials from a priestly source that is about four hundred years later, i.e., 450 B. C. E. Why this prioritization? The priestly tradition is clearly theocentric and cosmos-oriented. The Yahwehist tradition is more anthropocentric. Thus the priority is established: God is the creator of plants and animals, fish in the water, and birds of the air. God is the source and origin of life and the living. The context, the ambience, is engendered. This creation-creative process takes six long days. According to the Biblical calculation, "For a thousand years in your sight are like yesterday when it is past, or like a watch in the night" (Ps 90:4). This means that basically, the creation narratives are not contradicting the theory of evolution. But the main point is that *anthropos* is situated in the cosmos from the perspective of *theos*. Or to put it in another way, the *ochlos* is located within the wider *oikos*. The whole inhabited earth is the household of God. In Bengal today a new nexus is being forged – *MA* (mother) – *MATI* (earth, land, soil)- *MANUSH* (humanity). This is the wider ecumenism we need to nurture. This is our point of departure for our study of the Bible.

The creator-God is the fundamental thrust of the Old Testament. This is quite pervasive and powerful. Genesis 1:1 is the refrain which recalls directly and indirectly important ancient faith statements on God the creator of the universe (Ps 8; Isa 40: 28; 45: 12; 54:5). This means that the God of the Old Testament is inclusive in character from the beginning. The source of the creation narrative is a Babylonian myth, which is non-Jewish. This means that the ancient Jews were willing to learn, modify and incorporate stories and ideas from their immediate neighboring religions and cultures. This becomes obvious during their long sojourn in Egypt as slaves and in Babylon as captives. Such defining moments in their arduous history inculcated among the Jews an open mind and a sensitive heart. It was painful but enriching. Moses, their reluctant leader, was nourished and nurtured in the palace of Pharaoh. He married the daughter of Jethro, a Midianite priest (Ex 3:1; 18: 1-12). Later, he was married to a Cushite woman. When Aaron and Miriam, his brother and sister respectively, criticized Moses for the inter-racial, inter-religious marriage, God had affirmed, "Of all my household he alone is faithful". Miriam is struck with leprosy (Num 12: 1-15). Similarly, the story of Ruth, a Moabite woman, is very revealing. She is portrayed as becoming even an ancestor of David. In her own words, "Where you go, I will go, where you lodge, I will lodge: Your people shall be my people, and your God, my God. Where you die, I will die" (Ruth 1: 16-17). Such is the nature of identification in this household of God. Earlier, the ancient Jews suffered from tribalism, communalism, and parochialism, leading to the language of "My God" and "Your God." At one time, they thought of themselves as a "chosen people", "a treasured possession" and "holy to the Lord." But gradually over the millenniums, they made a paradigm shift from tribalism to universalism. Such is the nature of change and transition.

2. God's Universalism

God is the maker of the heaven and the earth. God has made the humans in God's image and likeness (Gen 1:26-27). We carry "the breath of life" gifted by God (Gen 2:7). There is an affirmative, an intrinsic relationship between God and all of humanity as between humanity and the earth. This inseparable intimacy is demonstrated in the name ADAM which derives from *adama*: a Hebrew noun of feminine gender, meaning earth, topsoil or ground. Eve is from *hawa*, meaning the living. She is the mother of all living (Gen 3:20). Therefore, Adam and Eve signify soil and the living. Thus there is no discrimination and prejudice over against nature and other living creatures in God. God's universalism is reflected in many of the narratives of the Old Testament.

The Book of Jonah is one episode that testifies to God's universalism. God tells the prophet Jonah to go to Nineveh but he refused. He wanted to escape the call of God but failed miserably. He reluctantly responded after a second summons, hoping that God would destroy the people of Nineveh. But God did not oblige the narrow-mined Jewish Jonah and the latter was angry,

> But this was very displeasing to Jonah, and he became angry… I knew that you are a gracious God and merciful, slow to anger, and abounding in steadfast love, and ready to relent from punishing (Jon 4: 1-3).

This means that Jonah knew God's objective character of steadfast love, *hesed*, but he was eager to project God in his own, more narrow image which led him to deny God's objectivity and universal love God however cannot be one's own subjective projection. The rest of the chapter is a direct challenge to Jonah. God interrogates him twice, "is it right for you to be angry?" (4: 4b and 9a). Jonah persists in his indignation, "Yes, angry enough to die." Finally, God exposes him thoroughly and shows his mistake. The Jewish people took a long time to learn God's universal love and justice. They had tried to privatize and monopolize God. They sometimes perceived of God as their private property or possession. We cannot own a copyright on God. We belong to God but God does not belong to us in an exclusive sense. God belongs to all. The Jewish people were chosen for a purpose. It was a summons to responsibility, to be an instrument of God's universal love and justice. The global God becomes local.

The Jews of ancient Israel did not have a homogeneous culture and monolithic religion. They were made up of twelve different tribes. They freely borrowed the rites and rituals, customs and practices, feasts and festivals from their neighboring communities, including the Assyrians, Acadians, Ammonites, Canaanites, Edomites, Hittites, Phoenicians and others (mentioned in Genesis, 2 Kings, 2 Chronicles, Judges and Isaiah). Earlier, I had mentioned the Egyptian influence. The creation narratives are borrowed from the Babylonian myth. The story of the great flood is mentioned in many ancient civilizations and cultures. The Persian King, Cyrus, is referred to as God's anointed, the shepherd, who will carry out God's purpose (Isa 44:28; 45:1). Thus the subsequent affirmation, "Your gates shall always be open, day and night they shall not be shut, so that nations shall bring you their wealth "(Isa 60:11). Therefore, wider ecumenism has to be conceived in terms of God's universal love, his universal reign and his universal will for justice.

3. God's Righteousness and Justice

The God of the Old Testament is not perceived as being a neutral or impassionate, passive being. God is not suffering from *ataraxia* (insensitivity) or *apatheia* (apathy) like in Greek tradition. God cannot be dehistoricized. God intervenes and identifies with those who are poor in body, mind, and spirit. Thus his/her ecumenism is not vague and abstract. Fundamentally, religion was not perceived in terms of rites and rituals but in terms of its relevance and significance for righteousness and justice. We cannot miss this theological thrust of the Hebrew people. The following Biblical text makes it explicit:

> I hate, I despise your festivals, and I take no delight in your solemn assemblies ... Take away from me the noise of your songs; I will not listen to the melody of your harps. But let justice roll down like waters, and righteousness like an ever-flowing stream (Am 5: 21-24).

Similarly, prophet Micah asserts as follows:

> With what shall I come before the Lord, and bow myself before God on high? ... Will the Lord be pleased with thousands of rams? ... He has told you, O mortal, what is good; and what does the Lord require of you but to do justice, and to love kindness, and to walk humbly with your God? (Mic 6: 6-8).

Proto-Isaiah or Isaiah of Jerusalem makes a similar affirmation:

> What to me is the multitude of your sacrifices? Says the Lord; I have had enough of burnt offerings of rams and the fat of fed beasts... Wash yourselves; make yourselves clean; remove the evil of your doings from before my eyes; cease to do evil, learn to do good; seek justice, rescue the oppressed, defend the orphan, plead for the widow (Isa 1: 11-17).

There are several other texts that clarify this divine priority and perspective (I Sam 15: 22-23; Ps. 40:6; 51: 16-17). This means God's righteousness and justice cannot be confined to the prophetic literature of the Old Testament. It is found in the Pentateuch (first five Books), the historical books like I and II Kings and I and II Chronicles, the poetic books like Psalms, Job, Proverbs, the apocalyptic literature like Daniel, the apocryphal or the Deuterocanonical, and wisdom literature. But it is true that the ancient Jewish prophets were quite forthright about this divine direction. Their prophetic parallelism, mentioned earlier, and prophetic symbolism like the plumb line (Am 7: 7-8), testify to God's universalism in terms of righteousness and justice. Righteousness, *tsedech*, is directly correlated with justice, *mispat.* God's righteousness is the criterion for human justice. Thus the ancient writers were not satisfied with the reciprocal, punitive, vindictive justice. In the name of God, they pleaded for a liberating and life-giving justice. It has a creative and transformative quality. At this stage in their long history, they not only believed in one universal God but definitively in moral monotheism. Consequently, they were indignant at the people's religion which at that stage promoted immorality and religious indifference. They believed in corporate personality and social solidarity. The human being is a psycho-somatic unity and therefore religion must embrace *all* and the whole of reality. This is the wider ecumenism we need to practice and promote particularly in Asia. Poverty and plurality is our reality.

The Old Testament writers were sensitive to and concerned about oppression and exploitation. They did not spare either the kings or the commoners regarding this principle although the latter were the victims. Thus the Hebrew words like, *rash (without social standing and resources)*, *ebyon (in want, needy, poor)*, *dal (the weak, the poor, the reduced ones)*, and *anawim* (the poor or the 'little ones'; those who are afflicted by oppression)are frequently used to describe the human predicament. It is good to remember that *rash* is used twenty-one times, especially in the Book of Proverbs; *ebyon* is used sixty-one times, especially in the Book of Psalms and the prophets; *dal* is used forty-eight times, especially in the Prophetical literature, in the Book of Job and Proverbs; *ani* is used eighty times and *anaw* is used 25 times, especially in the Psalms and the Prophets. These words are picturesque and potent. They demonstrate vividly the righteous indignation of the prophets against mass, massive and pervasive poverty in ancient Israel. This means *oikoumene, the ecumenical concern,* must include *oikonomos, the right and just ordering of economy.*

Conclusion

In this brief reflection, I have attempted to look at the issue of wider ecumenism from an Old Testament perspective. In this endeavor, I have established the idea that wider ecumenism is not empty and meaningless. In the Old Testament it has to be an external-physical realm characterized by God's universality, righteousness and justice. It has to do with the *oikos*, *oikoumene*, and *oikonomos*. In Asia we are confronted with the issue of intra-religious and inter-religious relationships. Asia has given birth to some of the major ancient religions which are living and relevant. It is imperative for us to promote pluralism and remove poverty in Asia in the name of Jesus.

4. Wider Ecumenism in New Testament Perspectives

While in this earlier part, I have examined wider ecumenism in terms of *oikos*, *oikoumene*, and *oikonomos* this nexus is also promoted and practiced, supported and strengthened in the New Testament tradition on which we will shed some light in this second part. Thus there is a fundamental unity and cohesion in the Bible with few exceptions. Much of Christianity in Asia continues to be individualistic, other-worldly and in-ward-looking. It is not authentically ecumenical in character and content. Ecumenism is not just a denominational issue. In fact, it is much more. It has to do with the *whole* and *all* of reality on earth. Physically, we are on earth. But the Bible beacons us to become an earth-community theologically as well as ethically. We have created our own disjunction. Asia is a continent of numerous religions, ancient and modern. To be ecumenical also means to become conscious of the multi-religious dimensions of our contexts and our commitment to interfaith dialogue in Asia. Let us examine the New Testament to discover the divine demands with regard to wider ecumenism.

(a) Jesus as wider ecumenism incarnate

Incarnation of God in Jesus the Christ is an ecumenical event. God does not remain remote and abstract. God becomes tangible and visible in Jesus. He is made up of flesh and blood, rooted in and related to the heat and dust, the rough and tumble of the earth. Thus the Johannine affirmation: "God so loved the *world*" (Jn. 3:16) and "the word became *flesh*" (Jn 1:14). These are the defining characteristics of the incarnation. This gives him his identity and thereby he is able to identify with full humanity. Jesus is not an appearance, a docetic figure or a gnostic being. He is of the sinful flesh, *sarx*, belonging to the *cosmos*, the world. He is not a disembodied, fleshless reality.

In his life and work Jesus was involved in and identified with the grassroots, ground reality. He did not belong to the elite, rich class. He was *with*, *for* and *from* the people. People's problems and predicament were his concerns. He did not understand his spirituality in terms of separation but in terms of identification. The Pharisees and the Scribes were always grumbling about his association with the "tax collectors and sinners" and even eating and drinking with them (Mk 2: 15-17; Lk 15:1-2; 5:27-32; Mt 9:9-

13). Such people were considered 'outcast'. In another context Jesus is more categorical: "I tell you, tax collectors and the prostitutes are going into the kingdom of God ahead of you" (Mt 21:31b). This clearly indicates his priority and perspective. There is a reversal of values or trans-valuation of values. His morality and ethics is not legalistic and traditional. He was not self-righteous and hypocritical about his relationships.

The salvific action of Jesus cannot be privatized and de-historicized. It is well embedded in history, among the people and in the whole of creation. This is demonstrated in the synoptic tradition. It points to Jesus' relationships and references. He was in complete harmony with the world of animals and vegetation. He talked freely about the birds of the air, the lilies of the field, and the foxes in their holes (Mt 6:26-30). Jesus reaffirms in speech and action the Lordship or the sovereignty of God over history and the whole of creation. Indeed, Christology is related to anthropology in the context of cosmology. The Nativity story is told in detail with animals, shepherds, stable and a manger. The host of angles announces the good news: "Glory to God in the highest heaven, and peace on earth for all those pleasing him" (Lk 2:14). Jesus came to promote fullness of life designated as shalom in Hebrew thinking. Consequently, we cannot indulge in reductionism about the Gospel of God in Jesus the Christ and make it non-relational and even anti-natural.

The apostolic tradition, developed by the pioneer Paul, Peter and the others, was aware of and acquainted with the universal or the cosmic significance of the disclosure of the divine. They proclaimed that nature has the potential within it which needs to be recovered and liberated. Thus the Pauline proclamation is loud and clear,

> For the *creation* waits with eager longing for the re-vealing of the children of God; for the *creation* was subjected to futility … that the *creation* itself will be set free from its bondage to decay and will obtain the freedom of the glory of the children of God. We know that the whole *creation* has been groaning in labor pains until now; and not only the *creation*, but we ourselves, who have the first fruits of the Spirit … (Rom 8: 18-23a).

It is notable that within six verses, the Greek word, *ktisis*, is used five times.

The liberation of the whole of creation is the direction and goal of the Gospel. In the purpose of God, the creation must be a cosmos and not a chaos, a uni-verse and not a multi-verse. Thus unity and harmony are intrinsic to the origin and goal. This is being restored and recovered. Therefore, a radical transition is made from alienation to reconciliation. Paul persists from this holistic perspective and affirms that "If anyone is in Christ, there is a new creation; everything old has passed away; see, everything has become new" (II Cor. 5:17). This theological-ethical thrust is endorsed and encouraged in another Letter of Paul,

> He [Jesus] is the image of the invisible God, the first-born of all creation, for in him all things in heaven and on earth were created … For in him all the fullness of God was pleased to dwell, and through him God was pleased to reconcile to himself all things, whether on earth or in heaven, by making peace through the blood of the cross (read Col 1: 15-20).

In short, Jesus' ecumenism included the whole of creation.

(b) Jesus' universalism

Jesus in his mission and ministry embodied God's universal grace, love and forgiveness. He came to break human-made barriers and build bridges of understanding and action. He was willing to learn from non-Jewish sources and people like the Syrophoenician or the Canaanite woman who came to Jesus in faith (Mk 7: 24-30; repeated in Mt 15: 21-28). Initially Jesus was reluctant, but he was moved by her faith and healed her daughter. Similar is Jesus' encounter with a Roman centurion (Mt 8: 5-13; repeated in Lk 7: 7-10). In this context Jesus is compelled to comment:

> Truly I tell you, in no one in Israel have I found such faith. I tell you, many will come from east and west and will eat with Abraham and Isaac and Jacob in the kingdom of heaven. While the heirs of the kingdom will be thrown into the outer darkness ... (Mt 8: 10-12).

Jesus' long conversation with a *Samaritan woman* of dubious character is very revealing and provokes his disciples (Jn 4: 7-26). The Jews and the Samaritans were at enmity with each other. Therefore, it is not surprising that his disciples on their return, when they discovered Jesus being in conversation with a Samaritan woman, were rather offended by the way Jesus acted. They were 'astonished' (Jn 4: 27), in fact, they must have been really irritated or even angry with Jesus!

The ancient apostles took a long time to come out of their religio-cultural captivity. Consequently, Christianity was considered a Jewish sect in the first century Palestine. People like Peter and Paul struggled with their engrained, Jewish prejudice. They judged other people from this narrow, exclusive perspective. Slowly but surely, they learnt to transcend boundaries. They began to sort it out in an open debate in the first council in Jerusalem in about 50 C. E., recorded in Acts 15: 1-21. They together unanimously resolved to remove the barrier of circumcision and began to reach out to the non-Jewish world. Acts of the Apostles also records the struggle of Peter as a Jew. This culture and religion had shaped his idea of purity and pollution, of what is clean and unclean. After his prolonged confrontation with God and himself, he was compelled to confess that "God has shown me that I should not call anyone profane or unclean" (Acts 10: 28b; read the whole narrative from verses 1 to 35, repeated in Acts 11: 1-18).

After this roof-top experience, Peter made a theological-ethical affirmation that "I truly understand that God shows no partiality, but in every nation anyone who fears him and does what is right is acceptable to him" (Acts 10: 34-35). Similarly, Paul, in one of his missionary journeys, had a learning experience in the intellectual capital of the Graeco-Roman world. During his short sojourn in Athens, he went to the public market every day and held debates and dialogue with the Epicurean and Stoic philosophers and the devout people (Acts 17: 17-18). Only after such a mutual exchange of ideas, Paul decided to address the Athenians at Areopagus. In his address, he appreciated the people for their religiosity, noting their inscription, "To an unknown god" (17:23), and then went on to assert, "What therefore you worship as unknown, this I proclaim to you. The God who made the world and everything in it, he who is Lord of heaven and earth..." (17:24). He quoted from the Athenian poets, endorsing this theological thrust. Paul categorically suggests that God is ecumenical and universal. He is definitively theocentric.

Consequently, the pioneers of the Christian faith were willing to identify and express full solidarity with the non-Jewish people (See I Cor 9:19-23).

(c) Jesus' commitment to righteousness and justice

Jesus did not indulge in false universalism and vague ecumenism. To believe in the universal and ecumenical God must mean righteousness and justice. His *metanoic* ministry was based on *agape*. This love is not vague and sentimental. Essentially, this love is governed by the will or will-power longing for and leading to righteousness and justice. So he said, "For I tell you, unless your righteousness exceeds that of the scribes and the Pharisees, you will never enter the kingdom of heaven" (Mt 5:20). We are called to promote God's righteousness and not self-righteousness. That is the fundamental difference between Jesus' spirituality and Pharisaic spirituality.

Like the ancient prophets, Jesus commitment to righteousness is integral to justice. For a long time, the Christian Church has been busy with diaconal ministry. We have neglected or ignored justice-oriented action. In the name of God and Jesus we must make a drastic shift from *diakonia* to *dikaiosune*. Jesus made this categorically clear in his proclamation:

> Woe to you, scribes and Pharisees, hypocrites! For you tithe mint, dill, and cumin, and have neglected the weightier matters of the law: justice and mercy and faith. It is these you ought to have practiced without neglecting the others! (Mt 23: 23; the whole chapter is relevant).

Jesus' focus on justice is made crystal clear in his sharp distinction between the rich and the poor. There are several references to this as when he uttered, "It is easier for a camel to go through the eye of a needle than for a rich person to enter the kingdom of God" (Mk 10: 23; repeated in Mt 19:24; Lk 18:25; read also Lk 6:20b-21a, 24-25a). The parable of the Rich man and Lazarus (Lk 16: 19-25) illustrates the huge gap between the rich and the poor and the consequences of it. He gives an identity and dignity by naming the poor person but the rich man remains unnamed. Once he challenged a Rich Young Ruler (Mk 10: 17-25) but the latter did not respond positively. This indictment of the rich is expressed vehemently in the Book of James in particular when the writer affirms,

> You rich people, weep and wail for the miseries that are coming to you. Your riches have rotted, and your clothes are moth-eaten. Your gold and silver has rusted, and their rust will be evidence against you and it will eat your flesh like fire. Listen, the wages of the labourers who mowed your fields, which you kept back by fraud, cry out and the cries of the harvesters have reached the ears of the Lord (Jas 5: 1-4; read up to verse six).

There is one Biblical text that is puzzling and contrary to the idea expressed above – *for you always have the poor with you* (Mk 14: 7a; repeated in Mt 26: 11a; Jn. 12:6a). Such a text makes us acutely aware of the fact that the ancient text was conceived within its own religio-cultural context. The Lukan narrative (7: 37-50) gives the detail. A Pharisee named Simon had invited Jesus to a dinner party and the latter obliged. But the host was shocked by the intrusion of a woman, who was living an immoral life (7:37). Immediately, there was confusion, consternation and finally a confrontation with Jesus for her presence. The oil was worth "three hundred denarii", which is equivalent to nearly a whole year's wages for a worker. Even his own disciples asked, "Why this waste? It could have been sold for a large sum and the money given to the poor" (Mt 26: 8-9). The host was not interested in the price of the oil or the poor. His anger was against the woman in particular. At this juncture, Jesus realizes the motivation of those who were complaining. He realized that very often, the poor are objects of charity. They become means to gain God's favor. Consequently, Jesus knew that such a sum could not do justice. At the same time, Jesus comprehended the sincerity and honesty of the woman. The oil symbolized her sweat, tears and blood as well as her longing for authentic love and forgiveness. Jesus forgives the woman and in the process locates poverty within the larger theological-ethical framework. Therefore, this text cannot be used as an excuse for not doing justice for the vulnerable. The text cannot be put outside its context or be universalized as an argument against charity.

Firstly, for Jesus justice basically means structural-systemic transformation. As such Jesus very often challenged the *Pharisees* as a group on several issues. Secondly, he was concerned about the *sabbath system*, which was in operation during his time. Thirdly, he was concerned about the Jewish *legal system*, which was dehumanizing and destroying human relationships. Fourthly, Jesus was *gender*-sensitive and therefore worked for gender-justice in his own way. Fifthly, Jesus openly challenged the *temple system* in Jerusalem. It was detrimental to the development of a just, equitable society. Sixthly, Jesus' understanding and practice of *power* was radically different from the exercise of power by Pharaohs, Caesars, kings and other non-religious and religious leaders of the time. His own disciples were quite accommodating to the ways of the world about power (read Mk 10: 35-45; repeated in Mt 20: 20-28). These are explicit examples of Jesus' larger concern and a wider vision. This was his Messianic ministry. He came to introduce and invite us to such a *kingdom* of God.

Conclusion

In these biblical reflections, I have attempted to suggest that wider ecumenism must include economic and environmental concerns. They are integrally related to each other in the Old and New Testament. That is the testimony of the early Church. These concerns are constitutive of Christian spirituality. It is for us to hold on to such a holistic, wholesome Gospel. Such a Gospel should motivate and move us to justice-oriented action in the world. We are suffering from resignation, fatalism and defeatism in the modern world. We must HOPE and hope is "a bird at dawn, already singing in the dark."[1] St. Augustine had affirmed, "Hope has two lovely daughters – - Anger and Courage. Anger, so that what must not be, shall not be; Courage so that what must be, shall be." We must continue to have faith in God and hope for a new future.

[1] Faith is the bird that feels the light and sings when the dawn is still dark.", from Rabindranath Tagore quotes (Indian Poet, Playwright and Essayist, Won the Nobel Prize for Literature in 1913, 1861-1941)

(14) Old Testament Perspectives on Ecumenism

Monica Jyotsna Melanchthon

What does the Old Testament say about Ecumenism? In order to answer this question, we first need to define what ecumenism is. Ecumenism is commonly understood to be the unity of the churches built on a common faith in the Triune God and on common Christian values. The fellowship of churches which comprise and steer the ecumenical movement confess the Lord Jesus Christ as savior according to the Scriptures. These churches seek to fulfill together their common calling to the glory of the one God, Creator, Son and Holy Spirit; a calling that is rooted in the search for Christian unity, uniting the churches in witness, mission, service and renewal, and committing them to the path of obedience to Christ and to his prayer "that they all may be one…so that the world may believe (John 17: 21).

According to O. Cullmann, this unity has to be built through diversity. Unity, he maintains should not be just a desire for closeness, or a model for coexistence which means that we simply tolerate one another out of historical and political necessity without really loving one another, in that we continue to present ourselves as separated brothers and sisters.[1] This is not a matter of levelling out the differences, or of harmonizing despite the differences, nor is it a question of aligning the churches alongside one another without any interaction, in a kind of static unity imposed by history or by the State. The Ecumenical movement is a prophetic movement of sister churches compelled by the power of the Holy Spirit to try and live and work together.

Building unity among churches therefore means promoting "communion in complimentarity," that is not seeking convergence but allowing the divergences to subsist and recognizing the richness they have to offer. Accepting these differences will make it possible to reaffirm the dignity of each church, because every local church in its own setting and with its own realities represents the body of Christ in a particular form, given that there is a recognizable nucleus of truth preserved in each confession. The unity of God's church/people is therefore at the heart of the Ecumenical movement and of the Christian faith. It is God's will for God's people to be one and together – to be united and diverse at the same time.

Christians need to strive to be one not because it is expedient or efficient but because God has called into existence one people. This is the affirmation with which the Old Testament begins its story of God's people, Israel. The Creation narrative with its emphasis on the two attributes of 'the breath of life' and 'the image of God' (Genesis 1) given to all human beings irrespective of caste, color, creed, ethnicity or language, guarantee human beings a privileged place among living things and affirm our common humanity. They provide grounds for respect for life and justice and the right for *all* human beings to claim them. This means the right of equality of access to basic life needs as well as political, economic, spiritual and cultural goods for all people. It confers on all people a worth or dignity that no person or system – whether political, economic, or social – can take away. This calling extends to all of humanity. This generous conferring of dignity and calling has its origin and basis in the free and unmerited love of God, which is at the root of all creative activity.[2] This view of creation wrought by a gracious God, with its emphasis on the sociality of human nature, provides the basis on which to formulate relationships and unity between human persons.[3]

---

[1] O. Cullmann, *Unity through Diversity: Its Foundations and a Contribution to the Discussion Concerning its Actualization, (*Philadelphia: Fortress Press, 1988).
[2] John Macquarrie, *The Faith of the People of God* (London: SCM, 1972), 49.
[3] Lois Gehr Livezey, "A Christian Vision for Sexual Justice: Theological and Ethical Reflections on Violence against Women," *In God's Image*, Vol. 10 (1991): 27.

But this 'unity' (an ambiguous term, to say the least!) that arises out of a common origin should not be seen as 'uniformity', (another problematic term!). The genealogies which comprise a discernible part of the book of Genesis make this effectively clear. They are significant for they say something about the origins and early history of the human race, and more particularly the people of Israel. The Table of Nations in Genesis 10 is important for it pretends to embrace the entire pre-Israelite world and its population. This genealogy is a good example of a text that reveals the unity and diversity that exists within a human community. It emphasizes the notion that all humankind known to Israel, diverse as it is, nationally and geographically, urban or nomadic, is descended from a single stock.[4] It is another expression of the profound consciousness of the unity of humankind, and it offers an "unparalleled ecumenical vision of human reality".[5] It presents the human race as a family[6]. The phrases "sons of" and "fathered" express the idea that all humankind known to Israel is descended from a single stock. All people are sons of (*sic*) Noah as well as sons of (*sic)* Adam.[7] The text therefore stresses the network of interrelationships among all peoples.[8] This relationship and unity is already given to humankind as a gift. The text affirms that all nations derive their historical existence from the life giving power of God and are called to be responsive to God. No nation or people are given ground or reason for being other than this one God who has formed all creatures.

Despite this emphasis on the one and single origin of humanity in the prologue to the Hebrew Bible, the unity of the human race exists in a tension with diversity. The 'Tower of Babel' incident in Genesis 11 is understood as an example of what a homogenous community (one language and one speech) might attempt to do. It might in its seemingly united state destroy the diversity exemplified in the Table of Nations for the purpose of gaining power and recognition. God intervenes to ensure stratification and diversity, for multiplication and populating the earth, against this human effort to maintain homogeneity and concentration in one place symbolized by the tower.[9] The narrative's placement at the end of the primeval history (Genesis 1-11) is an appropriate final comment on the state of humanity pointing back to problems – for human reality involves dissonance, difference, lack of community between people and a separation from God[10]. Yet, this dissonance is something that the human community needs to overcome and strive towards oneness. Diversity, difference and variation are an indication of the richness of the human community, to be seen as a potential, and not a problem.

The Old Testament therefore describes a people, namely Israel, as being both diverse and united, a people who are to be God's instrument to witness to the nations. The ancestral story begins with the calling of Abraham by God (Genesis 12) which includes the blessing of land and the promise to make Abraham a great nation and through him all the nations of the earth will be blessed (Genesis 15:18). The descendants of Abraham will be unique, but all the nations will refer to Abraham as the father of that people. The Moabites, and the Ammonites (through the daughters of Lot – Genesis 19), the Edomites (through Ishmael

---

[4] John Skinner, *A Critical and Exegetical Commentary on Genesis,* Second ed., (Edinburgh: T & T Clark, 1930) 188. Cf. Also B. Oded, "The Table of Nations (Genesis 10) – A Socio-cultural Approach," *ZAW* 98 (1986).

[5] Walter Brueggemann, *Genesis*, Interpretation (Atlanta: John Knox, 1982) 94.

[6] John J. Scullion, *Genesis: A Commentary for Students, Teachers, and Preachers*, OTS (Collegeville, Minnesota: The Liturgical Press, 1992) 89.

[7] Gordon J. Wenham, *Genesis 1-15*, 215.

[8] Only names are in fact listed. No clue at all is given to determine the territory further nor is there any indication of the relationship to each other of the peoples named.

[9] Cf. Nahum M. Sarna *Understanding Genesis: The World of the Bible in the Light of History.* New York: Schocken, 1966; U. Cassuto, *A Commentary on the Book of Genesis, Part II: From Noah to Abraham, A Commentary on Genesis VI: 9-XI: 32*, trans. Israel Abraham. Jerusalem: Magnes, Hebrew University, 1964.

[10] Susan Niditch, *Chaos to Cosmo: Studies in Biblical patterns of Creation* (Chico, California: Scholars, 1985), 63.

– Genesis 36) are all descendants of Abraham. Here, then, is the unity of a people who will be united in Abraham whom God has called.

This combination of unity and diversity is maintained in the narratives about the twelve tribes who descend from Abraham and Sarah, Isaac and Rebecca and Jacob, Rachel and Leah. A pattern emerges as these patriarchs and their wives provide the origin of the tribes (Genesis 49). The twelve tribes of the one people, Israel, become a characteristic feature that God uses for God's plan of salvation. In the Old Testament the twelve tribes of Israel express a unity of people (an imperfect unity no doubt) but twelve tribes equally elected to form this chosen people by God. The tribal confederation signifies both the gathering into unity of one people and a diversity in that each tribe has its own continued existence and autonomy.

But there was more than common ancestry that was needed to hold and keep the tribes together; to counteract and ease the tensions between the unity and the diversity of the tribes, challenged also by competition and struggle for land and leadership. A mechanism or structuring idea that would aid them in their life together as 'one' people, to enforce unity was essential. In this context, the immutability of the covenant is at least theoretically assumed. Derived from an early idea of mutual agreement between two or more parties comprised of human beings, the covenant within the Old Testament is a religious obligation, more of a command, imposed by God upon the differing tribes of Israel. The set of commands were to regulate the relationship between the tribes and God and between the members of the tribes (cf. the Decalogue in Exodus 20 and the Book of the Covenant in Exodus 20-23). God makes certain promises with these commands, and all the tribes agree to keep the commands. The promises are conditioned on their obedience. In general, the covenant of God with the Israelite tribes is a divine ordinance, with signs and pledges on God's part, and with promises for their obedience and penalties for disobedience; an alliance of friendship between God and the tribes, which is accepted by the tribes. But this alliance has consequences and effects for relationships between members. The obligation to obey is expected of all tribes and all tribes were equally responsible for the consequences of disobedience. This acceptance of Yahweh as God and the obligation to the dictates of the covenants made (religious and ethical) provides for both unity and uniformity among the tribes.

The same dialectic can be observed even in the times following the reign of Solomon and the split between the tribes (1 Kings 12). The Northern kingdom of Israel and that of Judah in the South formed one people of God. A division had taken place, but the obligations to the covenant remained, and this bound them to each other and to the same God. Israel and Judah though divided, to some extent still addressed themselves to the central shrine which functioned as a center of worship and communion at Jerusalem. They were two nations, but the allegiance to one another as people of a single covenant gathered in worship, kept the unity willed by God and remembered by the prophets.

But it was a precarious and fragile unity most of the time, or perhaps all the time. God had chosen these people to work out God's purpose in the world and in such a nation raised up prophets to direct God's chosen and frequently unfaithful people back to their calling and vocation of unity. The context of the prophet's work was primarily one of a nation that had broken its covenant with God; was often oblivious to the consequences of the choices it had made. The prophetic literature is replete with expressions of prophetic impatience and frustration with the religious cult of the nation in the guise that it was, devoid of the qualities of justice and righteousness and the seemingly lack of sensitivity on the part of the nation's leadership (king and priest) to the prevalent structural imbalances in the society; the havoc and suffering that was being caused on the less privileged in society, the poor, the women, the orphan, and the stranger in their midst. The lives and acts of the people revealed that they had forgotten the covenant of Yahweh and its demands that enshrined the very character of God. The prophetic task was to critique this forgetting, to remind and lead the tribes back to the religious and ethical demands of the covenant and reinstate unity among tribes. Second Isaiah chapter 60 is one good example of the prophetic attempt to restore the scattered unity of Israel so that it may be a light to the nations and extend God's salvation throughout the world (cf. also Ezekiel 20:34; 34:12-13 and Hosea 14).

God judges and punishes God's unfaithful people but the same God also offers to them the promise of forgiveness, reconciliation and healing. After the fall of the two nations and the devastation of Jerusalem, the notion of a 'remnant' becomes significant. This small group of united faithful is introduced as those who will witness to God's love to the nations.

If Ecumenism is about unity despite our differences, then the Old Testament is unambiguous in its message. The human race shares one origin, namely God and it is in this common origin that we find humanity's nobility and inherent value and oneness; that all peoples are interlocked by give and take, by inter-relatedness, that they constitute one family, one world civilization; that the one and the same God, creates the united and diverse people to be God's witness to the nations. Even in the face of escalating and repetitious sin, God intends and hopes by means of this one and diverse people to live out God's love for the entire human race. In the course of the Israelite story given to us there is an obvious lack of 'uniformity' within this one people, the twelve tribes of Israel and full agreement is rare. Unanimity or consensus among the people seems to have existed only during the making of the covenant and this did not last long. The unity of the people is not a uniformity among the people; rather, it reveals itself as a unity in the living out and acting upon the dictates of the covenant and in the knowledge and recognition of the one God of these diverse tribes as they gather as a single people in the acknowledgement and worship of the one God.

Bibliography

Walter Brueggemann, *Genesis*, Interpretation (Atlanta: John Knox, 1982) 94

U. Cassuto, *A Commentary on the Book of Genesis, Part II: From Noah to Abraham, A Commentary on Genesis VI: 9-XI: 32*, trans. Israel Abraham. Jerusalem: Magnes, Hebrew University, 1964

O. Cullmann, *Unity through Diversity: Its Foundations and a Contribution to the Discussion Concerning its Actualization,* (Philadelphia: Fortress Press, 1988)

Lois Gehr Livezey, "A Christian Vision for Sexual Justice: Theological and Ethical Reflections on Violence against Women," *In God's Image*, Vol. 10 (1991): 27

John Macquarrie, *The Faith of the People of God* (London: SCM, 1972)

Susan Niditch, *Chaos to Cosmo: Studies in Biblical patterns of Creation* (Chico, California: Scholars, 1985)

Nahum M. Sarna *Understanding Genesis: The World of the Bible in the Light of History.*
New York: Schocken, 1966

John J. Scullion, *Genesis: A Commentary for Students, Teachers, and Preachers*, OTS (Collegeville, Minnesota: The Liturgical Press, 1992)

John Skinner, *A Critical and Exegetical Commentary on Genesis,* Second ed., (Edinburgh: T & T Clark, 1930

(15) New Testament Perspectives on Ecumenism

Hyunju Bae

Ecumenism[1] in Asia deals with Asian reality. Poverty, illness, cultural-religious diversity, colonial experiences, political oppression, military confrontation, social strife and discrimination, ecological degradation, and patriarchal domination are some prominent conditions among its multi-layered problems. Christians' ecumenical response to the Asian reality is a daunting task, as the challenges are immense. In Asian Christians' ecumenical journey the Bible plays a crucial role in providing a fertile ground on which we are summoned, repent, and take a courageous leap to imagine a better world and act for it. Particularly, we Asian Christians embarking on the journey of faith in the midst of an empire[2] are eager to explore the New Testament, each and every document of which was written in the time of the Roman Empire, in order to find the fruitful inspirations that enable us to dream the alternatives that would not conform to the rule of empire. If "the problem with empire has to do with forms of top-down control … that do not allow those within its reach to pursue alternative purposes,"[3] then our free enterprise to intersect the New Testament and ecumenism in search for the counter-visions already amounts to the one of the first steps to challenge the rule of empire.

Among a variety of themes in the New Testament which are relevant for the understanding of ecumenism, this article attempts to zoom in on the Kingdom of God that Jesus proclaimed and lived out, as both the Kingdom of God and ecumenism resonate in their search for an alternative reality. Above all, this article will highlight the alternative economy and society envisioned in the Kingdom of God. Jesus spent most of his life in the countryside of Galilee. Being a colony of the Roman Empire, Palestine was witness of an ever-deteriorating economic situation. As a carpenter by trade and thus as a member of village community, Jesus was familiar with the economic exploitation which caused the suffering of peasants and the problem of the disintegration of the rural community life. It is natural to expect to find distinct economic values and concerns in the Kingdom of God that Jesus proclaimed. The kind of alternative economy that Jesus advocated for can operate only in an alternative society that is aware of the interdependence of people and prioritizes the quality of human relationships.[4] Secondly, the alternative

---

[1] Etymologically, "ecumenism" derives from the term *oikoumenē* in Greek. It goes back to a verb, "*oikeō*" (inhabit). In the Greco-Hellenistic era, the *oikoumenē* connoted first the geographical meaning of "the inhabited world" in distinction from unhabited land, and then, the cultural meaning of "the world of culture." During the Roman imperial period, the expansion of the territory effected a more political concept of *oikoumenē*, which signified "the known world," as it was continuously expanded in proportion to the Roman invasion and world conquest. In Philo, one can find a cosmological application of the *oikoumenē*. In the New Testament, the term appears 15 times. It is used above all geographically, referring to the inhabited world, "all nations and the whole earth"(Mt 24:14; Lk 4:5, 21:26; Acts 11:28; 17:31; 19:27; Rom 10:18; Heb 1:6; 2:5; Rev 3:10; 12:9; 16:14). While Luke likes this term, Paul does not employ the word except in the quotation from Psalm 19:4 in Rom 10:18. In Lk 2:1 the term seems to be associated with the political claim to register and tax all world under Roman imperial hegemony. Gerhard Kittel and Gerhard Friedrich, ed., "*he oikoumenē*," *Theological Dictionary of the New Testament*, vol. 5, trans. Geoffrey W. Bromiley (Grand Rapids: WM. B. Eerdmans Publishing Company, 1967), 157-159.

[2] "Empire, in sum, has to do with massive concentration of power that permeate all aspects of life and that cannot be controlled by any one actor alone…. Empire seeks to extend its control as far as possible; not only geographically, politically, and economically – these factors are commonly recognized – but also intellectually, emotionally, psychologically, spiritually, culturally, and religiously. Joerg Rieger, *Christ and Empire: From Paul to Postcolonial Times* (Minneapolis: Fortress Press, 2007), 2-3.

[3] *Ibid.*, 3.

[4] Much of the depiction of the alternative economy and society in the kingdom of God in this section relies on the following article: Hyunju Bae, "The Economy of the Roman Empire and the Alternative Economy of Jesus," *Madang:*

culture in the Kingdom of God, which sustains the alternative economy and the alternative society, will be explored. The alternative culture most fundamentally addresses the way of life, which reflects a value system and a set of political, spiritual, and mental postures and practices that befit the citizens of the Kingdom of God, both individually and communally. In this article, the alternative culture is characterized, among others, by healing and freedom, a reorientation of power and leadership, and a transformation of the self. Thirdly, we will consider the significance of the Kingdom of God for Asian ecumenism. In conclusion, the challenge of the Kingdom of God for the institutionalized church in Asia will be highlighted.

1. The Alternative Economy and the Alternative Society in the Kingdom of God

According to Mark, the historical Jesus launched his brief but intense and powerful ministry by proclaiming that "the Kingdom of God has come near" (Mk 1:15). The Kingdom of God, or the Reign of God, was an overarching metaphor by which Jesus named the new reality that came into being in his own activities. Luke paraphrases this "tensive symbol,"[5] that is, the Kingdom of God, in the parlance of Isaiah (Isa 61:1-2): "The Spirit of the Lord is upon me, because he has anointed me to bring good news to the poor. He has sent me to proclaim release to the captives and recovery of sight to the blind, to let the oppressed go free, to proclaim the year of the Lord's favor" (Lk 4:18-19). It is noteworthy that the Kingdom of God, in this Lukan pneumatological version, brings together the economic good news along with a personal therapeutic healing and a social and political liberation. With this integral portrayal in mind, we will here focus on the economic message of the Kingdom of God.

The Kingdom of God promised good news and granted blessings to the poor (Lk 4:18; 6:20; 7:22);[6] it pronounced judgment against the earthly rulers who brought bad news to the poor and inflicted a curse on them. Jesus' criticism against the economically oppressive status quo had two targets. One was the economic system of the Roman Empire, a glimpse of which is given in the episode of the conversation about taxation: when some Pharisees and Herodians asked Jesus whether it was lawful to pay taxes to the emperor or not, Jesus penetrated their hypocrisy and ulterior motives to trap him in his response and offered the challenging reply that "Give to the emperor the things that are the emperor's and to God the things that are God's" (Mk 12:13-17). One thing clear about this much-debated remark is that Jesus pronounced something that disrupted and disturbed the political and economic conformism of the questioners, even though he did not espouse the armed resistance against taxation. Jesus' answer was "not the solution of a problem but the indication of problem."[7] If Jesus had assigned the rule of God to the spiritual realm that has nothing to do with the political realm of the Caesar and thus had clearly supported and legitimated Roman taxation, the accusation that he forbade people to pay taxes to the emperor would not have arisen (Lk 23:2).[8]

International Journal of Contextual Theology in East Asia 9 (2008), 7-27. For a recent biblical contribution to this issue, see Richard A. Horsley, *Covenant Economics: A Biblical Vision of Justice for All* (Louisville: Westminster John Knox Press, 2009).

[5] A "tensive symbol" refers to a symbol which has "a set of meanings that can neither be exhausted nor adequately expressed by any one referent." Norman Perrin, *Jesus and the Language of the Kingdom* (London: SCM Press, 1976), 30.

[6] Klaus Wengst, *Pax Romana and the Peace of Jesus Christ* (London: SCM Press, 1986), 65.

[7] *Ibid*., 60.

[8] "They began to accuse him, saying, 'We found this man perverting our nation, forbidding us to pay taxes to the emperor, and saying that he himself is the Messiah, a king.'"(Lk 23:2). Jesus didn't distinguish between the internal spiritual realm of God and the external political sphere of Caesar in accordance of the so-called two-kingdom theory. Jesus embarrassed the questioners, who took the imperial tax system for granted, to remind them of their assumed identity as the people of God. "If they themselves belong to God and are indebted to him [*sic*] first and in all things,

The other is the Jewish religious establishment which did not lessen but doubled the economic exploitation of the people. Jesus cleansed the Temple, the symbolic center of the religious legitimation of the status quo, by driving out "those who were selling and those were buying in the temple," and overturning "the tables of the money changers and the seats of those who sold doves" (Mk 11:15-17). His head-on collision with the Temple, his naming of it as "a den of robbers" (Mk 11:17) and his prophecy regarding the destruction of the Temple (Mk 13:1-2) led to the chief priests' and scribes' conspiracy to kill him (Mk 11:18; Mk 14:1-2). It is conceivable that Jesus challenged not only the religious corruption, but also the economic structure of the temple-state sanctioned by the priestly aristocracy. In sum, standing in the age-old covenantal and prophetic traditional commands which defend the rights of the poor,[9] Jesus criticized the dual structure of the economic exploitation created by the collusion of the Roman Empire and its client Jewish rulers. Jesus denounced a society in which "to those who have, more will be given; and from those who have nothing, even what they have will be taken away" (Mk 4:25).

The alternative economy of the Kingdom of God builds on what is known as "the moral economy of the peasant"[10] and then modifies it. The moral economy of the peasant is a subsistence-oriented ethic of peasants which came into being because of the peasants' need for a reliable subsistence. It revolves around a kind of peasant politics that put into practice various forms of collaboration and mutuality within the village. The Kingdom of God has much resonance with "the horizontal support network," on which the moral economy of the peasant draws. However, the moral economy of the peasant fell short of challenging the patronage system itself, which was the social backbone of hierarchical centralization of the Roman Empire. In such a situation, Jesus presented God as the ultimate sole patron of people. The centralizing patronage system feeds on greed, and Mammon plays the role of an idol. By teaching iconoclastically that "you cannot serve God and Mammon (Lk 16:13; Mt 6:24), Jesus dethrones Mammon and opens up a new horizon in which one can imagine an alternative economy that serves and pleases God. In such an economy, God's preferential option for the poor and the divine will for the redistribution of the resources should be respected (Lk 1:51-53; 6:20-26; cf. 4:18-19; 19:1-10). The subversiveness of the divine economy is well attested to in its demand for the cancellation of debts, as the centralized economy of the Roman Empire relied on the accumulation of debt (Mt 18:12-35; Lk 7:41-43; 11:4b; 16:1-13).[11] The petitions in the prayer for the kingdom entail the request of subsistence bread and the abolition of debt (Mt 6:10-12; Lk 11:2-4). The cancellation of debts and the release of debt slaves were "key mechanisms in the moral economy of the Israelite peasantry"(Deut 15:1-6; Ex 21:1-7; Lev 25).[12]

The Kingdom of God advocated the spirit of "unconditional hospitality" or "radical generosity," which "includes the sick, the impure, the sinners, and the tax collectors, that is, the outsiders excluded from the

---

what about the fact that they use Caesar's money and also pay taxes?" *Ibid.*, 59-60. The entrapment question boomeranged on to the questioners, as it questioned their integrity. It is you, the Pharisees and the Herodians, who should decide whether to engage in Caesar's system or to belong to God's order with taking yourselves whole. By the way, "Jesus and his followers may not have been subject to taxes: a carpenter (Mk 6:3) who is not engaged in his craft, fisherman who have left their fishing gear by the lake (Mark 1.16-20), a publican who has left his post (Mk 2:14) have no income and therefore cannot be taxed by their ruler – nor could they be taxed by the Roman authorities. In fact they had escaped taxation long since at the price of a very uncertain existence." *Ibid.*, 59. Yet the point of Jesus' question is not to criticize those who paid the tax, because many collaborating members in Jesus' movement, who did not adopt the itinerant life style, must have paid the tax. Jesus' concern was to unmask the ulterior motive of the opponents.

[9] Ex 20:22-23:19, Jer 34:8-22, Isa 61:1-2 and passim.

[10] James C. Scott, *The Moral Economy of the Peasant: Rebellion and Subsistence in Southeast Asia* (New Haven and London: Yale University Press, 1976).

[11] Bae, "The Economy of the Roman Empire," 7-27.

[12] Richard A. Horsley, *Jesus and Empire: The Kingdom of God and the New World Disorder* (Minneapolis: Fortress Press, 2003), 115.

village economy (Lk 4:18-19; 7:22; 14:13, 21; 16:20-21)."[13] The divine economy in which Jesus wanted to eliminate discrimination against the marginalized in the village community was a challenge to the peasants who had taken for granted the exclusion of the unclean and the sinners on the basis of purity law. While the moral economy of the peasant operated in the mentality of what the anthropologists call "the limited good society" which led to a defensive strategy towards outsiders,[14] the alternative economy in the Kingdom of God invited people to open the door to outsiders. At the same time, Jesus' teaching to give alms (Lk 11:41; 12:33; cf. 18:22), lend "expecting nothing in return" (Lk 6:35) and invite those who cannot repay (Lk 14:-12-13) also discloses the spirit of radical generosity. Furthermore, life with Jesus made room for the unexpected experience of abundance, which mutual sharing and solidarity would enable. The memory of the feeding of the five thousand with five loaves and two fish conveyed the sense of amazement in which people experienced full life through practicing mutual sharing and solidarity when they were together with Jesus (Mk 6:30-44; Mt 14:13-21; Lk 9:10-17; Jn 6:1-14).

The bedrock in the divine economy is God's boundary-breaking compassion. When Jesus instructed to love one's enemies, it could have reminded people of "the context of covenant renewal," in which love refers "to concrete economic practices in village community, such as canceling debts and generous mutual sharing of resources."[15] Such an economic practice is predicated on the theological insight that God is boundlessly merciful (Mt 5:43-48; Lk 6:27-36). This theological guideline illuminates the fundamental value in the alternative society which is the matrix where the alternative economy in the Kingdom of God is enacted. There divine compassion restores human relationship. "The exploitative economic system has brought curse on human relationship. 'It was not so much the curse on the ground that needed lifting; it was the curse on human relationships.'"[16] In contrast, in the alternative society a sober sensibility for human interdependence and mutual relationship, broken by a "closed ideal of self-sufficiency and insensitive ego-centrism that the well-to-do pursue"[17](Lk 12:16-20; 16:19-31), is to be restored in a way that the right for the subsistence of the least is greatly respected.

Indeed, for Jesus' disciples, to taste the Kingdom of God was to enter an alternative society where they experienced a new community and a new network of human relationships as a new family. "Truly I tell you, there is no one who has left house or brothers or sisters or mother or father or children or fields, for my sake and for the sake of the good news, who will not receive a hundredfold now in this age – houses, brothers and sisters, mothers, and children, and fields with persecutions – and in the age to come eternal life" (Mk 10:29-30). In the alternative society that the Kingdom of God ushers in "God's abundant reward is experienced not so much in the allocation of property to individuals or individual families as in a creation of a human support network and new human relations."[18] It is noteworthy that according to Mark the emergence of this new society cannot but undergo "persecutions" (Mk 10:30), which amount to the birth pangs of a creative movement. Interestingly, a father is not given in the new family, and it could be taken as an explicit criticism of patriarchy, which perpetuates hierarchical authoritarianism or paternalism in every unit of social communities.

---

[13] Bae, "The Economy of the Roman Empire," 21.

[14] Bruce J. Malina, *The New Testament World: Insights from Cultural Anthropology*, revised edition (Louisville: Westminster/John Knox Press, 1993), 90-116.

[15] Horsley, *Jesus and Empire*, 127

[16] Bae, "The Economy of the Roman Empire," 23. The quotation is originally from C. C. McCown, *The Genesis of the Social Gospel* (New York: Knopf, 1929), 207.

[17] *Ibid.*, 21.

[18] Douglas E. Oakman, *Jesus and the Economic Question of His Day*, Studies in the Bible and Early Christianity, vol. 9 (Lewiston/Queenston: Edwin Mellen Press, 1986), 143. Quoted in *Ibid.*, 22.

2. The Alternative Culture in the Kingdom of God

New economic and social fabric would be sustained by a new consciousness and new practice, that is, new culture, which is no less than "the way of life, which reflects a value system and a set of political, spiritual, and mental postures and practices that befit the citizens of the Kingdom of God both individually and communally," as indicated above. It is by now clear that the alternative economy and the alternative society in the Kingdom of God can only operate on the basis of the fundamental value system which gives stress on the Mammon-nullifying sovereignty and boundless compassion of God vertically speaking, and human interdependence, mutuality, and unconditional hospitality, horizontally speaking. Jesus' proclamation and practice confirms that the kingdom of God is fraught with numerous further clues for the alternative culture. Three points deserve our attention in this vein.

(a) Healing and freedom

Jesus made the Kingdom of God palpable to the people by his ministry of healing and exorcism. Healing was also exercised by the contemporary miracle performers and magicians, and the distinctiveness of Jesus lay in the fact that he associated it with the enactment of the Kingdom of God. "But if it is by the finger of God that I cast out the demons, then the kingdom of God has come to you" (Lk 11:20; Mt 12:28; Mk 3:20-30). One of the effects of the Roman imperial regime was people's illnesses and different forms of demonic possession. The stories in Mark 5 demonstrate that Jesus countered the devastating effects of the empire and brought life back to his suffering people through his ministry of exorcism and healing. According to Mark 5, Jesus drove out the unclean spirit named 'legion,' i.e. the Roman army, from a violent demoniac (Mk 5:1-20). Subsequently Jesus healed a woman who had been suffering from hemorrhages for twelve years, and restored Jairus' twelve-year-old daughter, who has been considered dead, to life (Mk 5:21-43). Given that the number "twelve" symbolizes the twelve tribes of Israel, i.e. the people of God, it is noteworthy that in this passage the people of God is represented by a hemorrhaging woman and a dead girl, both of whom the Jewish society marginalized.

Physical malady and mental disorder caused not only somatic pain, but also disruption in interpersonal communication and exclusion from social interaction. Jesus' ministry of healing and exorcism liberated people from the grip of individualized pain, most of which resulted from the structural injustice, and at the same time restored the wholeness and the capacity for social communication. "When the demon had gone out, the one who had been mute spoke" (Lk 11:14; Mt 9:32; 12:22). The Kingdom of God reinstated the voice to the voiceless, thus enabling social interaction. After the exorcism, the ex-demoniac, who had had the legion, was sitting with Jesus, "clothed and in his right mind" (Mk 5:15). The Gerasene demoniac overcame the alienation from the social self and came back to his social life. Against the imperial culture which routinely produced the demoniacs, the psycho-somatically sick, and the alienated selves, the alternative culture in the Kingdom of God unleashed the energy of counteracting the effects of imperial domination through healing. People were reborn as healthy social agents.

Healing is part of the sign that the Kingdom of God frees people from the Satanic domination, which has driven people into physical illness, economic misery and social alienation. In this divine delivery, healing and the good tidings to the poor are inseparable. "Go and tell John what you have seen and heard: the blind receive their sight, the lame walk, the lepers are cleansed, the deaf hear, the dead are raised, the poor have good news brought to them" (Lk 7:22). The Kingdom of God is permeated and accompanied by with charismatic/therapeutic *and* prophetic events, which are the dynamic twin movements of the Holy Spirit. It is noteworthy that Jesus wanted his disciples to continuously practice the healing ministry in order to clarify that the Kingdom of God signifies the divine intervention which breaks the shackles of multi-dimensional oppression (Mk 6:7-13; Mt 10:5-15; Lk 9:1-6; 10:1-12).

Healing in the Kingdom of God is not the goal itself, but an invitation to a relationship with God. The ultimate hope in a hopeless situation is God, whose sovereign initiative is free from the rule of Satan (Mk

3:20-30). Healing is a taste of this divine freedom, which is oriented towards the redemption of the people and creation. The acknowledgement of the redemptive divine freedom engenders the epistemological freedom on the human side, which helps one to overcome pessimism and despair and awaken to a recognition that "one's life does not consist in the abundance of possessions" (Lk 12:15). While Jesus taught the disciples to pray for the daily bread, he posed a question of fundamental priority, asking if life is not "more than food, and the body more than clothing" (Mt 6:25). Such freedom or wisdom, arising from the trust in the redemptive freedom of God, signifies a creative seed of the "already" in the world of the "not yet," and ushers in the alternative culture in the Kingdom of God. There the appropriate human responses to the initiative of God, such as repentance (Mk 1:15), rebirth (Jn 3:3-4), and keeping awake (Mk 13:32-37; Mt 24:40-42), also find their niches. The spirituality of vulnerability comes to the fore as well, as it runs counter to the idolatry in which one attempts to acquire a guaranteed security by means of something that is not God, e.g. the accumulation of wealth and power (Lk 12:20; 13:34). Finally, a sense of wonder and amazement is also an important element of the alternative culture in the Kingdom of God. It is revealed in the parable of the seed growing of itself, in which the kingdom of God freely comes into existence apart from human calculation and control (Mk 4:26-29).

(b) Reconfiguration of power and leadership

The Kingdom of God requires a radical reconfiguration of power. When Jesus said that the rulers, either the conquerors or their minions, "lord it over" the people, and that "their great ones are tyrants over them" (Mk 10:42), He might have evoked people's century-old first-hand experiences of the imperial power exercised by the Egyptians, Assyrians, Babylonians, Persians, Greeks and then Romans. The power implemented by imperial hegemony was characterized by the monopoly of material resources, oppressive top-down authoritarianism, and unilateral hierarchy. It exploited and debilitated the subjugated and made them invisible and voiceless. Jesus denounced the political, economic, and social violence embedded in such a structural power.

The power that Jesus put into operation was of a different order. It is noteworthy that Jesus' alternatives revealed their initial contour in his concrete daily interaction with people, that is, his spirituality and leadership. Prompting the 'servanthood' as a quality of true leadership or facilitation, Jesus proposed and embodied a different kind of power. The locus of power was transferred from a hierarchical hegemony to a relational and reciprocal horizon. For instance, in his healing ministry, he decentralized the power by acknowledging the participatory contribution that the patient made in enacting the event of healing, and thus discarding a superior posture as the healer. After healing the woman who suffered from hemorrhaging for twelve years, Jesus said, "your faith has made you well" (Mk 5:34). The distinction between a powerful and superior healer and a powerless and inferior patient, or the cleavage between an active giver and a passive receiver, disappeared. Healing happened in an in-between space of encounter, charged with the hope of the patient to become wholesome and the sympathy of Jesus to help. Healing was not just the one-sided manifestation of the ability of an individual charismatic leader. Jesus proposed mutuality, cooperation and a relational horizon as the very platform for the manifestation of power and channeled people's attention to it.

Another episode in which we find Jesus decentralizing power and transferring it into a relational horizon is the story of His encounter with a Syro-Phoenician woman (Mk 7:24-30). According to Mark, after his interaction with the woman, Jesus changed his original rigid stance of rejection and consented to an exorcism of her possessed child at distance. The basis of his change of attitude was not to test her faith, as many commentators interpret. Jesus revoked his original position *because of her words* (Mk 7:29: "for saying that, you may go-the demon has left your daughter"). Like the stubborn widow who dauntlessly stays the course in front of rejection (Lk 18:1-8), this Syro-Phoenician mother never withdrew and challenged the logic of Jesus' original position of rejection. Jesus allowed himself to be persuaded by the strange other in this encounter. Jesus' authority did not lie in a non-communicating unilateral authoritarianism, but in his acceptance of the other and openness to negotiation. By acknowledging the power of the women's active agency, maternity and intelligence, Jesus showed that the miracle of healing took place as the outcome of the dynamic interaction of the two agents. In the alternative culture in the Kingdom of God the power could flow bottom-up and a participatory relationality replaced the monopoly of power.

Jesus in these stories demonstrated what positive masculinities are like.[19] The image of Jesus, who decentralized his own power as the superior charismatic healer and acknowledged the active contribution of women, is far from being dominant, hegemonic, controlling or paternalistic. Full of compassion, sensitive receptivity and respect, Jesus showed that his spirituality and leadership operated in partnership with people. He was inclusive of a gentile woman, doubly marginalized, allowing himself to be persuaded by her. Jesus' familiarity with the so-called feminine within himself is revealed in the account that he was able to weep over the death of a friend (Jn 11:35). These images of Jesus are a wonderful model that serves the Christians who "work towards re-defining, re-ordering, re-orienting and thus transforming dominant masculinity."[20] It turns out to be an antidote for the traditional portrayal of Jesus as an authoritarian monopolist of power. At the same time, such an understanding of Jesus could offer fertile ground for constructing a new Christology in which reciprocal interdependence and the process of mutual transformation are valued.

(c) Transformation of the self

It is stated above that Jesus advocated the unconditional hospitality in the alternative economy. Its boundary-crossing message was a radical challenge to the "limited-good" mentality of peasant, as it asked the one to step out of the comfort zone both in epistemology and in social relationship. The usual self relies on the conventional wisdom, which offers the basic common-sense help for survival. A certain set of the notions of boundary, identity, and security matter here. In contrast Jesus did not promote "'clean identities, living at safe distances from one another."[21] Jesus went beyond the conventional wisdom. Against the purity law (Mk 7:15-16; Mt 23:25-26; Lk 11:37-41), one of the representative conventional wisdoms of that time, Jesus made himself vulnerable by allowing himself to be polluted through contact with the unclean people, that is, people with all kinds of disease, sinners and prostitutes. He became notorious for his table fellowship with sinners and tax collectors (Mk 2:15-17) and was rebuked for being "a glutton and a drunkard, a friend of tax collectors and sinners" (Mt 11:19; Lk 7:34).

The most challenging instruction that goes against the grain of the boundary-drawing conventional wisdom is Jesus' teaching to love one's enemies (Lk 7:27, 35; Mt 5:44), and to do good and lend, "expecting nothing in return" (Lk 6:35). Such an extreme boundary-transcending act and unconditional hospitality automatically neither guaranteed success nor a corresponding response in kind from the recipient. Instead, what is surely promised is an intimate relationship with God: the practitioners of all-embracing radicalism will become "children of the Most High" (Lk 6:35). The ultimate ground for the boundary-breaking inclusion and embrace is God, who is kind even "to the ungrateful and the wicked" (Lk 6:35). The courage to break up with the conventional wisdom springs from the faith in God who is boundlessly compassionate (Lk 6:36). The intercessory prayer for "those who abuse and persecute you" (Lk 6:28; Mt 5:44) can be pronounced not so much by those paralyzed by fear, hatred and passivity as by

---

[19] Patricia Sheerattan-Bisnauth and Philip Vinod Peacock, ed., *Created in God's Image: From Hegemony To Hegemony*, A Church Manual on Men as Partners: Promoting Positive Masculinites (Geneva: WCC and WCRC, 2010).
[20] *Ibid*., 3.
[21] Miroslav Volf, *Exclusion and Embrace: A Theological Exploration of Identity, Otherness, and Reconciliation* (Nashville: Abingdon Press, 1996), 126.

those who, being full of compassion, actively take initiative in seeking "an end of enmity, but not the end of the enemy."[22]

Jesus' radical politics of inclusion, vulnerability, and compassion runs counter to the politics of holiness driven by the observance of purity law and resulting in exclusion, separation and discrimination.[23] Jesus taught that there should be space for the other, and created a community of disciples to practice such a non-exclusionary identity.[24] His disciples consisted not so much of homogeneous people as of heterogeneous folks such as fishermen, tax collectors, Zealots, women and so on. In this community of varied disciples, already besieged by the hostile environment, Jesus did not envisage an idealized conflict-free zone. Practicing negotiation with the other should begin from within the community and apply to the relationships beyond the community. It seems that Jesus would like his disciples to form a Christian identity that is inclusive and dialogic, and learn forgiveness, patience and tolerance such that the presence of boundlessly compassionate God among them is palpable inside and outside the community. A formation of a Christian identity involves a profound transformation of the usual self.

3. The Significance of the Kingdom of God for Asian Ecumenism

An ecumenical understanding of the New Testament does not purport a value-neutral, objective and detached reading of the text. Informed by the historical and theological insights offered by critical scholarship, it is contextually motivated by a desire to make sense of the text for the sake of the economic, political, social and spiritual emancipation of all the peoples in Asia and the world. For this very purpose the significance of the theme of the Kingdom of God is immense. Above all, the Kingdom of God can serve as a litmus test for meaningful Christologies, which would speak to peoples' concrete struggle for survival and human dignity in Asia. Palestine, the land of Jesus' birth, can be considered to be part of, or very adjacent to, West Asia. Yet when Jesus was introduced to Asia by missionaries in the fifteenth century, he had been heavily formatted by Western dogmatic and cultural grammar. The result was that the historical Jesus came to be too often eclipsed by the abstract, imperialistic, and individualistic Christological formulations. Unfortunately, these Christological portrayals tended to alienate people in Asia from encountering Jesus in a meaningful way. In reality Jesus of Nazareth lived his life in and around the dusty villages in a Roman colony, showed interest in the concrete subsistence issues of the bread, clothing and debts of the grassroots peasants as their friend, and triggered a people's movement called the Kingdom of God. Jesus "raises up the helpless and lives out with them an alternative to the existing order."[25] Therefore, if any Christological construction attempts at faithfully expressing the meaning of the historical Jesus who lived up to his vision as a person-in-the-community in first-century Palestine, it should do justice to the horizon of the Kingdom of God in a down-to-earth, anti-imperialistic, and relational way. In this regard, to bring to the fore the Kingdom of God is a preliminary indispensable step for the enterprise to "re-Asianize and refashion Jesus on Asian terms to meet the contextual needs of Asian peoples."[26]

There are further benefits to emphasizing the Kingdom of God in the Asian ecumenical reading of the New Testament. With the Kingdom of God as its framework, Jesus' suffering and crucifixion gains its appropriate interpretative context. Jesus the liberator lived a full life igniting the renewal movement of his people, which aimed at the realization of their abundant life, and his resistance against the impregnable status quo resulted in his death. Often the doctrine of the salvific effect of his suffering has falsely indulged

---

[22] Wengst, *Pax Romana,* 69.
[23] Marcus J. Borg, *Jesus a New Vision: Spirit, Culture, and the Life of Discipleship* (New York: HarperSan Francisco, 1987), 86-93, 131-40, 157-63, 183-84, 196-97.
[24] Volf, *Exclusion and Embrace*, 64.
[25] Wengst, *Pax Romana*, 68.
[26] R. S. Sugirtharajah, ed., *Asian Faces of Jesus* (Maryknoll: Orbis Books, 1993), "Prologue and Perspectives."

in legitimizing, muting and beautifying the suffering of the victims. Many Asian Christian women are no strangers to such a bad theology which endorses a vicious cycle of sado-masochism and religiously covers up the suffering of the marginalized. Jesus' passion and crucifixion took place neither due to his passive resignation nor because of his submission to the injustice of structural violence. Overwhelmed with a compassionate passion for his people, Jesus embraced suffering and even death which the struggle against the earthly powers inevitably involved. The *zoephilia* (love of life), not *necrophilia* (love of death), was the motive for Jesus' sacrifice (Jn 12:24). This is one of the very reasons why his cross, not only his resurrection, came to be ultimately interpreted as a sign of victory, not a sign of defeat. Christological reflection reasons that it was through the cross that God identified with humanity. Therefore the movement of the Kingdom of God brings to the fore the good news of the divine love that is stronger than death in its fervent hope for the flourishing of all people. It sustains the dignity and secret joy of the disciples of Jesus Christ in Asia, who experience affliction and suffering in their struggle for justice and peace because of their participation in that divine love.

Besides, to construct a transformative Christian identity which is inclusive and dialogic at both personal and communal levels,[27] as indicated above, concerns the Christians in Asia, who find themselves living in a multi-religious and conflict-ridden milieu. The formation of the ecumenical personality and community, which is mature enough to embrace the other and foster the ability to work with both intramural and extramural neighbors, is a critical task. For only then we will be equipped with the effective resources to deal with the rise of fundamentalism, which aggravates conflicts and tension and ruins peace by molding personalities and communities that are exclusionary and non-dialogic. A transformation of the self ushered in by the Kingdom of God matters for ecumenism in Asia.

This leads to a challenge proposed by Jesus to Asian culture. According to Matthew 10:34-36 (Lk 12:49-53), Jesus did not come to bring peace to the earth, but a sword to "the 'household', the smallest, firmest and most basic unit in society, with a patriarchal and hierarchical structure… in whom the existing order was most markedly manifest."[28] While the head of the household was usually oppressed by the social power structure in the village community, he often uncritically reproduced the patriarchal and hierarchical structure within the family. The Kingdom of God is concerned with the most immediate area of human life. The man and woman are to live in a mutually respectful partnership. Children's respect of for their parents is an important commandment but parents should respect their children also. Unlike Micah, who indicted family division, that is, a son against his father, a daughter against her mother, and a daughter-in-law against her mother-in-law, as the sign for the corruption of people (Mic 7:6), Jesus "does not lament over this division from below; that is precisely what he wants."[29] Whether this strange statement derives from the "experiences of the community that confessing Jesus led to grievous divisions in the most intimate spheres,"[30] or traces back to Jesus' denial of family control (Mk 3:31-34), what comes to the fore is the respect of the individual and the significance of full individuation. A human being is created in God's image, is to be respected as such, and is not to be forced to sacrifice himself or herself for the sake of the community. In contrast to the Western context often plagued by extreme individualism, the community-oriented Asian culture has a danger of eclipsing the voice of the individual, especially young and/or female, within the community. The traditional hierarchy on the basis of age and gender often do not invigorate a democratic process and egalitarian relationship. A viable community does not reduce a person-in-the-community[31] to a means to an end, but values the diverse individual voices from below, in order to

---

[27] S. Wesley Ariarajah, *Not Without My Neighbour: Issues in Interfaith Relations* (Geneva: WCC Publications, 1999).
[28] Wengst, Pax Romana, 61-62.
[29] *Ibid.*, 62.
[30] *Ibid.*, 198.
[31] This term is quoted from Herman E. Daly and John B. Cobb, Jr. *For the Common Good: Redirecting the Economy toward Community, the Environment, and a Sustainable Future, second edition* (Boston: Beacon Press, 1994), 159-

prevent a culture of silence, blind obedience, and paternalism (Isa 42:3). Family and faith community are called to work as a rich matrix which inspires and sustains each and every individual member, created in God's image, to incessantly grow to become "imitators of God" (Eph 5:1). In the globalized contemporary world, an effective faith community should be "a combination of both the Eastern emphasis on communality and the Western emphasis on individuality."[32] To create a culture which inherits the Asian traditional communal quality and simultaneously transforms its precious relational sensitivity towards giving respectful heed to the individual voice is one of the struggles in which Asian feminist theologies engage.[33]

Finally, the simple fact that the original setting for Jesus' movement for the Kingdom of God was the villages in rural areas might have some connotation for ecumenism in Asia. Although the capital cities of Asia seek to emulate Western cosmopolitan centrism, it is undeniable that in Asia life of the majority of the population revolves in and around villages, where people maintain their traditional and indigenous culture. Asian ecumenism needs to beware of an ancient cultural usage of Hellenistic *oikoumenē* which idealized cosmopolitanism in the Greco-Hellenistic civilization on the basis of contempt for the countryside as well as everything non-Greek, which was despised as barbarian. Although the term "ecumenism" derived from the Greek *oikoumenē*, Asian ecumenism needs to keep a critical distance from the Western, now Asian, infatuation with cosmopolitanism, taking its root in the millennium-old Greco-Roman ideal of cultural *oikoumenē*. In the contemporary age when the Earth groans and too many village communities in the South suffer from ecological degradation and the centralizing and funneling cosmopolitan entity is to be reviewed based on the concept of ecological debt,[34] Asian ecumenism is called to imagine a new civilization that values a decentralized and viable network of a community of communities, not only urban but also rural, flourishing in a just peace and abundant life for all.

4. Conclusion

As space does not allow us to explore other ecumenical terrains in the New Testament,[35] this article focused on the kingdom of God in the Gospels as a locus where, through its rich meaning, one can have a

175.

[32] Jung Young Lee, *The Trinity in Asian Perspective* (Nashville: Abingdon Press, 1996), 194. Lee uses this phrase in expounding "trinitarian family life," but the "trinitarian living" in a constant negotiation of unity and plurality, and of time and eternity, is to be practiced in church life and community life. 180-211.

[33] "The home-and-family tends to be a forgotten place even though it is a basic institution of education within the larger society. However, it is a place where patriarchal attitudes, ideas, and values are reinforced daily in all aspects of family life.... The need for creating a new form and patterns of a relationship between man and woman, husband and wife must be approached on a more personal level.... By working through this at the personal level, half the job is already done when men and women enter consciously into an equal and mutual partnership in the total life and mission of the church." Yong Ting Jin, "New Ways of Being Church: A Protestant Perspective," in *We Dare To Dream: Doing Theology as Asian Women*, ed. Virginia Fabella M. M. and Sun Ai Lee Park (Maryknoll: Orbis Books, 1989), 50-51.

[34] Athena K. Peralta, ed., *Ecological Debt: The Peoples of the South Are the Creditors: Cases from Ecuador, Mozambique, Brazil and indi*a, Programme on Ecological Debt, WCC (Quezon City, Philippines: Troika Press).

[35] In particular, Paul attempted to internationalize, what Jesus practiced locally and nationally. The historical Paul seldom used the term, "the kingdom of God," but Paul's faith in the crucified and risen Lord and his gospel was far from an otherworldly individualistic message. The apostle for the Gentiles sought to revive the nations through the formation of the alternative societies of the citizens whose citizenship belonged to the reign of God (Phil 3:20). His counter-imperial apocalyptic vision, the creation of the solidarity network of sharing material resources beyond national boundaries, for which he risked his own life, and the respectful friendship with women partners such as Phoebe and Prisca are not understandable unless we consider his ardent urge to form the alternative communities throughout the Roman Empire according to the will of God revealed in Jesus Christ. Richard A. Horsley, ed., *Paul and Politics: Essays in Honor of Krister Stendahl* (Harrisburg: Trinity Press International, 2000); idem, ed., *Paul and*

biblical understanding of the multiple challenges for ecumenism in Asia. The portrayal of the Kingdom of God in light of an alternative economy, society, and culture allows us neither to domesticate its message nor to be content with its depoliticizing spiritualization. The eschatological nature of the Kingdom of God does not countervail the importance of the enactment of qualitatively different economic, social, and cultural life on earth.[36] Although Jesus did not wage armed warfare against the powerful authorities, the Kingdom of God engaged in a thorough criticism of their oppressive structural power. Jesus criticized the greedy hegemony of the rulers and their insatiable egocentric practices, while encouraging the horizontal support network of the survival-oriented grassroots village people. At the same time, he invited and challenged the village peasants to move beyond the boundary-drawing exclusionary policy towards the other and become inclusive. What was at stake for Jesus' disciples as regards the Kingdom of God was to open up their inner eyes (Mt 6:23; Lk 11:34-35) wide so as to discern God's gracious initiative to create a new reality in freedom, and to make their decision for the obedience to faithfully follow it. The faith and wisdom with which the disciples awakened to the new divine reality enabled and motivated them to live full life with a fundamentally transformed self and create a new power basis for communal and social life. Spiritual and epistemological revolution is the cornerstone of envisioning a political and social transformation implied in the Kingdom of God.[37]

The Kingdom of God is a constant reminder to the institutionalized church of what its essential vocation amounts to in this world. If the church hopes to remain faithful to its vocation, the therapeutic, prophetic and sapiential vision of the Kingdom of God should come to its center stage, working as its constant corrective.[38] If the church wants to be guided by the vision of the Kingdom of God and serve the world as the covenantal community of faith, hope, love, healing, solidarity and prophetic imagination, it should not compartmentalize what the Kingdom of God does not: the charismatic, prophetic, and sapiential horizons in the Christian faith. In that respect an unproductive split or an entrenched erosive division among the so-called evangelical, ecumenical/prophetic, and Pentecostal camps in the contemporary church in Asia should be overcome. Overall the Bible holds a comprehensive, truly ecumenical scope, and the church needs to try to live up to it. For instance, evangelical and Pentecostal Christianities need an ecumenical community and network, if they want to go beyond the individual and parochial appropriation of Christian faith and the Holy Spirit and to seriously engage in the public battle against structural evil in the world.[39] Without prophetic anchorage and ecumenical network, evangelism and Pentecostalism risk being metamorphosed into an individualistic prosperity Gospel and turning an ecstatic Spirit experience into a pseudo-mysticism without the discipleship of cross-bearing. In contrast, without an incessant personal renewal on the basis of the Word and spiritual transformation, ecumenical faith which engages in public resistance runs a risk of falling into activism and sometimes into dispirited moralism of the weary who carry heavy burden, never tasting the true rest coming from Jesus Christ who said "my yoke is easy, and my burden is light" (Mt 11:30). The contemporary church in Asia should know better than the evangelical-Pentecostal-ecumenical tripartite divide which wastes Christian resources and energy. What matters is not so much a partial understanding of the Bible as its integral, comprehensive and truly ecumenical construal, which would help Christians to confront in solidarity the unprecedented multi-dimensional global crisis.

The Kingdom of God Jesus proclaimed and lived out is a paradigmatic peak in the history of the Bible, which was written in the shadow of many empires, and from which one can retrieve "a history of faithful

---

Empire: Religion and Power in Roman Imperial Society (Harrisburg, Trinity Press International, 1997).

[36] Wengst, *Pax Romana*, 64

[37] Horsley, *Jesus and Empire*, 103; Richard A. Horsley and Neil Asher Silberman, *The Message and the Kingdom: How Jesus and Paul Ignited a Revolution and Transformed the Ancient World* (Minneapolis: Fortress Press, 1997).

[38] For the reading of the Lukan narrative on the birth of the first church in light of a prophetic pentacostalism, see Hyunju Bae, "Engaging Prophetic Ministry in Asia," *CTC Bulletin* 25/3(2009), 17-24.

[39] Volf, *Exclusion and Embrace*, 51-53.

resistance."[40] To that extent, it is the food for the soul of the Christians in Asia, who strive for the fullness of life for all in a faithful resistance against the contemporary empire.

Bibliography

Hyunju Bae, "The Economy of the Roman Empire and the Alternative Economy of Jesus," *Madang: International Journal of Contextual Theology in East Asia* 9 (2008), 7-27

Herman E. Daly and John B. Cobb, Jr. *For the Common Good: Redirecting the Economy toward Community, the Environment, and a Sustainable Future, second edition* (Boston: Beacon Press, 1994)

Richard A. Horsley, *Jesus and Empire: The Kingdom of God and the New World Disorder* (Minneapolis: Fortress Press, 2003)

Richard A. Horsley, *Covenant Economics: A Biblical Vision of Justice for All* (Louisville: Westminster John Knox Press, 2009)

Richard A. Horsley and Neil Asher Silberman, *The Message and the Kingdom: How Jesus and Paul Ignited a Revolution and Transformed the Ancient World* (Minneapolis: Fortress Press, 1997)

Douglas E. Oakman, *Jesus and the Economic Question of His Day*, Studies in the Bible and Early Christianity, vol. 9 (Lewiston/Queenston: Edwin Mellen Press, 1986)

Joerg Rieger, *Christ and Empire: From Paul to Postcolonial Times* (Minneapolis: Fortress Press, 2007)

James C. Scott, *The Moral Economy of the Peasant: Rebellion and Subsistence in Southeast Asia* (New Haven and London: Yale University Press, 1976)

Jung Young Lee, *The Trinity in Asian Perspective* (Nashville: Abingdon Press, 1996)

R. S. Sugirtharajah, ed., *Asian Faces of Jesus* (Maryknoll: Orbis Books, 1993)

Miroslav Volf, *Exclusion and Embrace: A Theological Exploration of Identity, Otherness, and Reconciliation* (Nashville: Abingdon Press, 1996)

We Dare To Dream: Doing Theology as Asian Women, ed. Virginia Fabella M. M. and Sun Ai Lee Park (Maryknoll: Orbis Books, 1989)

Klaus Wengst, *Pax Romana and the Peace of Jesus Christ* (London: SCM Press, 1986)

---

[40] Richard A. Horsley, ed., *In the Shadow of Empire: Reclaiming the Bible as a History of faithful Resistance* (Louisville · London: Westminster John Knox Press, 2008).

(16) Contextual Biblical Hermeneutics in the Context of Asia – A Korean Perspective

Yeong Mee Lee

1. Introduction

Globalization and global markets are driving the people against life and have them live in despair. Traditional tensions and conflicts between classes, races and gender, have not only been intensified but have become complicated and violent. Changes are rapid and unpredictable. Job security is being threatened. People live in fear of insecurity for their future. The national social welfare and security systems are being dismantled in the process of the global marketization, and by being integrated into the worldwide market. Facing this global change liberation movements that have been struggling for social justice in the past are now struggling for peace and security for life.

The search for the meaning of life becomes the central focus of theology in the era of globalization. The vision of the good and full life, the transformation of the conditions of life, and the steps towards enjoyment of life together are major concerns for us in Korea. The task of biblical interpretation is to find references, not only in the Bible, but in the people's lives, for articulating a vision for life, analyzing the conditions of life and developing a praxis for a sustainable and decent life. The objective is to liberate life from the forces of death and the destruction of life in the context of globalization.

Asian theology, in particular, involves the vision and imagination of life in Asia. It speaks to the actual questions that men and women in Asia are asking in the midst of their dilemmas, hopes, aspirations and achievements, as well as their doubts, despair and suffering. It must also speak in relation to the answers that are being given by Asian religions and philosophies, both in their classical form and in forms created by the impact on them of Western thought, secularism and science.

2. Contextual Biblical Hermeneutics in Asia

All biblical hermeneutics is contextual. Although there has been a belief that the historical critical study of the Bible, anchored in Western scholarship, especially that of Germany, is objective, and that the contextual study of the Bible is confessional and subjective, it is important to note that the former is also a way to approach the Bible in the context of European history, in the wake of modernity since the Renaissance movement. Biblical studies in Asia, in which Christianity was later implanted and where cultural and religious traditions are abundant, require different biblical hermeneutics that attempt to better understand the Scripture in the particular life context of Asia's cultural and religious traditions.

Asian biblical hermeneutics takes the texts of the Bible as a contextual interpretation of the divine revelation dating from and rooted in the context of biblical times. Articulating the meaning of the text is articulating what was assumed when those ancient believers interpreted the divine revelation within their contexts.[1] This approach is different from traditional exegetical interpretations of the Bible, which delve into the meaning of the Bible first and then apply its significance to the present situation. Contextual biblical hermeneutics is a spontaneous act of interpretation that analyzes biblical writer's interpretation of the divine revelation of biblical times in parallel interaction with modern interpretations of the divine revelation in present time. Analogy is made between the hermeneutical points of view found in the Bible

---

[1] Daniel Patte et al eds., *Global Bible Commentary* (Nashville: Abingdon Press, 2004), xxii.

and those in the present reality. The weight and role of the Bible and current reality is equal in hermeneutical perspective as both present attempts and references to examine the meaning of life from their respective realities. Both the ancient Bible and the present life and contexts of readers are the objects of interpretation. The Bible as canon functions as the archetype of a theologically committed reading of the present reality for Christians.

Asian people's lives and realities are as important as the texts of the Bible for this contextual biblical hermeneutics. Critically engaged in issues of church and society, and committed to working for change in church and society, such interpretations analyze the religiously and culturally pluralistic contexts of Asia in which we find ourselves. Asian contextual biblical hermeneutics pays particular attention to the voices of women, minorities and the marginalized. Asian contextual biblical hermeneutics has been developed by Suh Nam Dong and Ahn Byung Boo in Korea, C.S. Song in Taiwan, Archie C.C. Lee in Hong Kong, Monica Melanchthon in India, and R. S. Sugirtharajah in Singapore. All emphasize the importance of reading the Bible within their own cultural and religious traditions. Suh Nam Dong, a Korean Minjung theologian, suggests the merging and interrelation of two stories, the biblical stories and the stories of Asian people, the Asian folklores.[2] C.S. Song developed a special hermeneutics and method of story related theology.[3] Archie Lee proposes a cross-textual reading in biblical studies.[4] R.S. Sugirtharajah suggests to include a contrapunctal reading of Biblical tradition, which demands that students have been effectively introduced to texts, related critical tools and contextual hermeneutical issues.[5] This approach establishes connections and creates bonds between texts of different contexts as a method of engaging equal partners in a dialogical hermeneutical task. It avoids the denunciation of texts from different contexts just from the perspective of one's own context. This contrapunctal reading according to this author has to be applied both within and across theological disciplines.

Asia is a vast and diverse continent and hard to be defined in a single image or voice. This essay intends to focus on an example of contextual biblical hermeneutics presented from Korean Minjung theological perspective. It will introduce a brief history of Minjung theology in the Korean context and will suggest a justice oriented and life affirming biblical hermeneutics as one form of Asian contextual biblical hermeneutics in the time of globalization.

2. Minjung Theology and the Bible

(a) An historical overview on Minjung theology

Minjung theology is a type of Asian contextual theology that was born in response to the suffering of the Minjung under the Park regime in the 60s and70s. It was further developed in 1980s through the struggle for democracy under the regime of Jeon who became President of Korea and suppressed a Minjung demonstration for democracy which took place in the city of Kwangju. While the Minjung theology during the 1960s and 70s focused on the economic and cultural conditions of the Minjung, Minjung theology during the 1980s dealt with political and social concerns that had been evoked by the Minjung movement for democracy. Minjung theology addresses political issues related to democracy and develops a revolutionary approach to theology focusing on the material and social conditions of life of the Minjung.[6]

---

[2] Suh Name-dong, "Historical References for a Theology of Minjung," in ed, by CCA, *Minjung Theology: People as the Subject of History,* 155-182.

[3] C.S. Song, In the Beginning were Stories, not Texts (Eugene, Oregon: CASCADE Books, 2011)

[4] Archie Lee, "Biblical Interpretation in Asian Perspective," *Asian Journal of Theology* 7(1993), 35-39.

[5] R.S. Sugirtharajah, "Postcolonial Criticism and Asian Biblical Studies," in D. Preman Niles ed., *Critical Engagement in the Asian Context: Implications for Theological Education and Christian Studies*, 73-84.

[6] Choi, Hyung Mook, *Korean Social-revolutionary Movement and Christian Theology* (Nadan, 1992).

The Korean political environment has rapidly changed during the past decade. Korean society is suffering from new phenomena of economic, social and cultural crises, since the financial crisis and the International Monetary Fund (IMF) intervention in 1997-98. The pressure of IMF on the Korean government for structural reform in the financial and corporate sectors caused President Kim Dae-jung's structural reform and increased the unemployment rate. As a result of structural reform many people, including both blue and white color workers, lost their jobs and are still unemployed or have had to survive with part-time jobs.[7]. Korea indeed jumped into the global market without much preparation. Globalization is experienced as a process of global integration all peoples and nations into one global market, driven by the global capital.[8] In the process of globalization that dominates all aspects of life,[9] the traditional concept of Minjung is no longer evident, despite the fact that the majority of jobless and seasonal or migrant laborers can be certainly considered as the "Minjung" of the globalized world.

(b) Minjung as a hermeneutical point of view

The term "Minjung" was first used in 1975 in an academic discourse by two scholars to refer to those who are marginalized from the dominant society through multifaceted discrimination visible in economic, cultural, social and gender dimensions. Minjung theology explores the social reality of the Minjung as the starting point for the formulation of Christian theology. The reality does not refer to an individualistic existential framework for what describes human existence. It is a sociopolitical or socioeconomic framework. This is because the reality of oppressive and miserable social existence has a certain primacy over other dimensions and necessitates a deliberate act of theological reflection. Therefore the collective experience of the Minjung, i.e. the "social biography of the Minjung," serves as hermeneutical basis of the Minjung theology for interpreting the Bible, the tradition, and history. The term today does not to refer a certain social class. Rather, it is a hermeneutical term that stands for the right of the oppressed and marginalized in society.

(c) The Bible as a reference of theology in parallel with the life of Minjung

As mentioned earlier, Minjung theological biblical hermeneutics does not start from doctrines or the Bible itself but from the very life of the Minjung, who share their struggles, pains, sufferings, aspirations, successes and failures and visions for hope for new heavens and earth. Seeking the meaning of their suffering and joy of life, one examines the Bible to see how it interactes with the suffering and joy of life on similar hermeneutical issues. In this reading, the sources of Minjung theology are not limited to the Bible or to the Church doctrine. The Minjung's life stories, traditions and history are also included. Minjung theologians consider God as a term and reality which is closely interrelated with history. Suh Nam Dong states that God is actualized in and through the historical process. For him, "God works through history … History itself is God."[10] and history is not limited to Christian history but includes all human history. For this reason, Minjung theology develops an appreciation for the presence of God and the knowledge of God within Korean history even before Christianity was introduced to Korea.

---

[7] Currently, in Korea, Non-standard, temporary, or part-time workers occupy 55% of the whole work force. In Korea, the flexibility of labor is so high that most of the population is exposed to the threat of unemployment and poverty. Re-cited from Kwon, Jin-Kwan, "Contextual Theology and Theological Education: Korea," David Kwang-sun Suh et. Al. eds. *Charting the Future of Theology and Theological Education in Asian Contexts* (ISPCK, 2004), 87

[8] Kim Yong Bock, "Globalization: Challenge to the People's Movement." http://www.oikozoe.or.kr

[9] Kim Yong Bock, "An Asian Proposal for the Future Directions of Theological Curricula in the Context of Globalization, David Kwang-sun Suh et. Al. eds. *Charting the Future of Theology and Theological Education in Asian Contexts* (ISPCK, 2004), 249.

[10] Suh Nam Dong, *In Search of Minjung Theology* (Seoul:Hangilsa, 1983), 171

(d) Minjung biblical hermeneutics: a justice oriented and life-affirming reading

Minjung theology envisions justice and peace for the oppressed and marginalized. In the era of despair, it stands with the marginalized and empowers them in their struggle for hope. To advocate a just and peaceful life, a Minjung theological reading of the Bible finds two parallel motives in the Bible and people's lives: the divine work of liberation of the oppressed and the prophetic vision empower the marginalized. It suggests a life affirming visualization of the God of liberation through the metaphor of a child-birth. God liberates as a child is liberated and thrown into life in the process of a birth, not like a conqueror or military ruler – rejecting some of the militant metaphors which are also around in biblical tradition, but a mother gives birth to a new life.

3. Exodus and the Korean Minjung Movement as the Divine Work of Liberation

If *hapiru*, the oppressed slaves in Egypt, are a biblical parallel image of the Minjung in modern Korea, the Exodus is a biblical paradigm of the Minjung liberation movement. Minjung theology highlights the socio-political and economic dimensions of the Exodus narrative, rather than idealizing its understanding in an abstract spiritual or just personal dimension. Biblical stories according to this perspective unfold their full meaning when they are re-actualized in and through Minjung's praxis of sociopolitical liberation today. The Minjung themselves become the bridge that connects the hermeneutical gap between the liberating events of the Bible and the experiences and struggles of liberation today. The context or the nature of today's social reality of the Minjung is quite different. Yet the belief of the Minjung in God who is understood as delivering the oppressed from social and political bondage relates the Korean Minjung closely to the the heart of the biblical tradition.

The confession of God who is perceived to stand on the side of the Hebrew slaves as standing on the side of the oppressed Minjung today provides the hermeneutical bridge between the Bible and the life of present Minjung. The past experience of the Exodus in biblical history provides hope for the present situation of the Minjung today.

4. Prophetic Power of Han and Lament (Lamentations 3:1-66)

Life is full of joys and sorrows. The book of lamentations deals with the agony during the time of extreme suffering. It was the time when a mother even was forced to eat the flesh of her own child. Nothing can describe the degree of the suffering more vividly than this statement. In facing an extreme suffering, people's reaction are diverse. The biblical reaction to intense suffering as expressed in Lamentations 3 provides a meaningful analogy to the Korean theological reflection on the reality of *han*, which is a common motive in Minjung theology

Lamentation 3 introduces three voices of 'I,' 'He(*gebel*),' and 'We,' each of which show their reaction to the suffering. In the relevant chapter, 'I' referred to people of the disaster (vv. 1-24) and explains the special suffering of 'He/gebel' who suffers because of the sin of the community (vv. 25-39). 'He' is a member of the community. But he is separated from others as the one who is faithful to God and is waiting for salvation. He bears the agony of the community upon him. 'I' then calls the people to return to God immediately. 'We' responds to him with the confession of their sins (vv. 40-47). The responses of these three bodies illustrate the importance of a common confession of sin and collective acts of responsibility to overcome the suffering and eventually to bring salvation.

In an analogy between the biblical text and the Korean context today, the biblical narrator and contemporary Minjung theologians, represented as "I" in Lamentation 3, play an interrelated role to explore the situation of the suffering and the agony of the one, "He," who takes up the sufferings of the community upon him. "I" evokes the confession of the people, "We" their commitment to participate in the struggle as the suffering of Minjung is not just an individual matter but a reality of politically oppressive and miserable social existence. Therefore, in Minjung theology, the collective experience of Minjung, i.e. the "social biography of the Minjung," serves as hermeneutical basis of theology.

Minjung theologians have reflected on the collective experience of suffering by deepening the theological reflection on the Korean concept of *han*. Han is a Korean term for an underlying feeling of being oppressed and downtrodden, declared without hope and any promise of life. It is an accumulation of feelings of being suppressed and marginalized. It refers to a reality which is very deeply rooted in Korean history and culture. The country's entire way of life has been profoundly shaped by experiences of han, of bitterness and oppression. Koreans have suffered innumerous invasions by powerful surrounding nations so that the very existence of the Korean nation has come to be understood as an experience of *han*. Under Confucianism's strict imposition of laws and customs discriminating against women, the existence of women was experienced as a condensation of *han* itself. Han is experienced as moral evil, the suppression of any human dignity enforced by imperialistic, feudalistic, and ideological powers, and also by gender discrimination.

In the stage of *han*, in a situation of hopelessness and despair, Christian faith communities cannot remain silent but need to share the suffering of Minjung and to be 'priests of *han*.' The responsibility of the community, of the church is to share the agony with Minjung and resolve its suffering. Thus the church ought to be the comforter and to cut the vicious circle of violence and to change it into a progressive movement. For this purpose, churches ought to be a sanctuary for those who are progressing out of the dark for deliverance.

4. Life-Affirming and Empowering Imaginations of the God of Liberation

The emphasis on the liberating power of God who delivers the oppressed from trouble is a powerful and dynamic image inspired by deep biblical traditions. Yet this image and the underlying experiences of deep suffering can also turn into destructive and violent perceptions and energies. Therefore we need a life affirming and empowering imagination of God which is rooted in the biblical motif of the creation narrative itself. The biblical tradition of creation should not be seen as an ancillary to redemption anymore. It is a motif in its own right as exhibited particularly by Second Isaiah and the Priestly Writer.[11]

It is the creation motif in the tradition of the Second Isaiah which has introduced the child-birth imagery. The figure of a travailing woman is used to describe the divine creative action for redemption in the book of Isaiah. In Isaiah 45:9-10, for example, the image of a travailing woman is used, together with the images of a potter and a begetting father, in order to illustrate the creative action and energy of God. Also Deuteronomy 32:18 employs the image of a travailing woman to refer to the first formation of Israel as the people of God:

> You were unmindful of the Rock that bore you
> You forgot the God who gave you childbirth

In each line, the words of childbirth, *yld* and *hyl*, describes the divine action of creation or salvation as providing a new childbirth to Israel. God's action here in the parallel line is perceived exclusively in maternal terms, because the verb *hyl* elsewhere in the Bible takes only a feminine subject.[12] As the child-birth imagery here refers to the first formation of Israel as the people of God, the same imagery is used to describe the restoration of the people of God in Isaiah 66:7-9. In Isaiah 66:7-9 an even more radical image is used than in the previous presentation of the first childbirth of Israel, because here it is not God but Zion

[11] Preman Niles, "Introduction," in *Minjung Theology*, 4.
[12] Phyllis Trible, *God and the Rhetoric of Sexuality* (OBT; Philadelphia: Fortress Press, 1978), 63.

who gives childbirth to the people if Israel and God plays the role of a midwife. At the same time, the text clarifies that it is God who ultimately makes the childbirth possible.

The description of creation through the child-birth metaphor is insightful and relevant for the reflections of Minjung theology. The creator God is presented like a woman in labor. He does not appear as a removed, omniscient, all controlling super power, but as a creative source of all life. God endures labor pains in order to bring forth a new people[13] rather than supervising the life of people from above. Here, God is seen as an imminent creative energy in the life of Minjung, a creative power. Secondly, the understanding of creation through the child-birth metaphor is related to salvation, the labor for the creation of a new life. The divine dynamic process of creation which is "like a woman in labor" indicates neither panic nor fear, but rather God's powerful activity and its awesome effects. God endures the pangs in order to bring forth new hope and life. Thirdly, the understanding of creation through the child-birth metaphor prevents us from perceiving the suffering of the Minjung as totally miserable or hopeless, the suffering of the Minjung on the contrary connotes hope and has a creative energy and potential dynamic for new life within it. The suffering will eventually transform into joy, because God who suffers with the Minjung is the God of new creation. Fourthly, the understanding of creation through the child-birth metaphor depicts salvation and creation not as a one-time event but as a continuos process towards creating a new heaven and earth in the present reality. As a mother continues to nurture her just-born baby until she grows up and knows how to share love with others, God and human beings continue to take care of the new creation until the wholeness and mutuality in this world are restored.

5. Conclusion

This essay has tried to outline the approach of Minjung theological reading of the Bible in searching for a just and peaceful life and envisioning new hope for the oppressed and marginalized in times of despair and ambiguity. The central focus of Minjung biblical hermeneutics is to articulate the meaning of liberation process in which God acts as the liberator with the power of people's solidarity. This approach emphasizes the subjectivity of Minjung in the history of liberation, being not the passive receptors of the divine grace of salvation, but subjects of salvation history in partnership with God the liberator.

Minjung theological hermeneutics of the Bible places the social biography of the life of the Minjung in parallel interaction with the biblical texts. Minjung theological hermeneutics of the Bible pays attention to the prophetic power of lament or outcry as exposed in the biblical book of Lamentation and experienced historically in the reality of *han*. The lament of people provokes the divine action of salvation and empowers others for solidarity in the common process of liberation.

Bibliography

Kim Yong Bock, "An Asian Proposal for the Future Directions of Theological Curricula in the Context of Globalization, David Kwang-sun Suh et. Al. eds. *Charting the Future of Theology and Theological Education in Asian Contexts* (ISPCK, 2004)

Choi, Hyung Mook, *Korean Social-revolutionary Movement and Christian Theology* (Nadan, 1992).

Archie Lee, "Biblical Interpretation in Asian Perspective," *Asian Journal of Theology* 7(1993), 35-39.

Suh Name-dong, "Historical References for a Theology of Minjung," in ed, by CCA, *Minjung Theology: People as the Subject of History,* 155-182

Daniel Patte et al eds., *Global Bible Commentary* (Nashville: Abingdon Press, 2004)

C.S. Song, In the Beginning were Stories, not Texts (Eugene, Oregon: CASCADE Books, 2011

[13] L.L. Bronner, "Gynomorphic Imagery in Exilic Isaiah (40-66)," *Dor le Dor* 12 (1983-84): 77.

R.S. Sugirtharajah, "Postcolonial Criticism and Asian Biblical Studies," in D. Preman Niles ed., *Critical Engagement in the Asian Context: Implications for Theological Education and Christian Studies*, 73-84

(17) Contributions of Bible Translation for Ecumenism in Asia

Min Young Jin

1. How many countries are there in the Asia Pacific?

For the Korean Bible Society,[1] which has been carrying out Bible work as a member of the United Bible Societies[2], the Middle East is a far away region whereas the Pacific Islands are much closer. As regards to Bible translation work around the world, The United Bible Societies have been classifying the regions of the world for the past century into four areas, namely Africa, the Americas, Europe and Middle East, and the Asia Pacific as it pursued its biblical translation work. There are two definitions for the Asia Pacific region:[3] that of the APEC (Asia-PacificEconomic Cooperation) and the other of the United Bible Societies (UBS). The UBS's definition excludes Russia and countries of North and South America despite these regions beingare located along the Pacific Coast but includes the various countries in the South Pacific and Indian Oceans.

The UBS Asia-Pacific area is comprised of Australia, Afghanistan, Bangladesh, Cambodia, China, East Timor, Hong Kong, India (and Bhutan), Indonesia, Iran, Japan, Laos, Malaysia, Micronesia, Mongolia, Myanmar, Nepal, New Zealand, Pakistan, Papua New Guinea, Philippines, Singapore (and Brunei), South Korea (North Korea), South Pacific (consisting of New Caledonia, Fiji, Vanuatu, Solomon Islands, Cook Islands, Niue, Tonga, American Samoa, Western Samoa, Wallis, Kiribati and Nauru), Sri Lanka (and Maldives), Taiwan, Thailand and Vietnam. Among these Bible work is being carried out in about 40 countries where either a Bible Society or Bible Society ministry is being undertaken in some way.[4]

The world population today according to the United States Census Bureau (USCB), is estimated at 7.01 billion. The USCB estimates that it exceeded 7 billion on March 12, 2012.[5] It is said that about 4.2 billion people, which is about 60% of the global population, live in the Asia Pacific region. Among them, 310 million, i.e. 8.5% are Christians.[6] Globally there are 1 billion Catholics and 0.9 billion Protestants, meaning that there are 1.9 billion Christians around the world. This covers 33% of the overall population on earth.

2. How many languages are there in Asia Pacific Region?

Although the exact number of languages may never be determined, it is estimated that roughly 6,800 languages are spoken on this planet. Among them 96% are spoken by a mere 4% of the world's population.

---

[1] The Korean Bible Society was founded in 1895

[2] "The United Bible Societies (UBS) is a worldwide association of Bible Societies. In 1946 delegates from 13 countries formed the UBS, as an effort to coordinate the activities of the bible societies. The United Bible Societies is made up of 146 national Bible Societies operating in over 200 countries and territories. Together, they are the biggest translator, publisher and distributor of the Bible in the world. They are also active in areas such as literacy training, HIV and AIDS prevention and disaster relief. Bible Societies work with all Christian Churches and many international non-governmental organisations." (http://www.unitedbiblesocieties.org).

[3] APEC currently has 21 members, including most countries with a coastline on the Pacific Ocean. Australia, Brunei, Canada, Chile, People's Republic of China, Hong Kong, Indonesia, Japan, Republic of Korea, Malaysia, Mexico, New Zealand, Papua New Guinea, Peru, Philippines, Russia, Singapore, Republic of China, Thailand, United States, Vietnam. (from Wikipedia).

[4] http://intranet2.biblesocieties.org/intranet/publish/intranet/UBSSO/asia-pacific/asia_pacific.php

[5] http://en.wikipedia.org/wiki/World_population

[6] http://www.infoplease.com/ipa/A0904108.html

Ethnologue, an encyclopedic reference work produced by the Summer Institute of Linguistics cataloging all of the world's 6,909 known living languages, estimates that 2,322 are spoken in Asia, 2,110 in Africa, 1,250 in the Pacific, 993 in the Americas and 234 in Europe."[7]

This means that there are about 3,500 languages in use in the Asia Pacific region.

As of December 31, 2010 full Bibles are available in 469 languages around the world. The New Testament has been translated into 1,231 languages, and portions of the Scripture into 827 languages. When we add up these figures, altogether 2,527 languages will have translations of the Bible or portions by the end of 2010. In the Asia Pacific region alone, the entire Bible text has been translated in 185 languages, the New Testament in 530 languages, and Scripture portions in 348 languages, which means that a total of 1,063 languages have either the full Bible, New Testament, or Scripture portions translated into their own language.[8]

In summary, there are 6,800 languages currently in use by the 7 billion people living on earth. Among them, 2,527 languages have portions or full translation of the Bible, and Bible translation is currently underway in about 2,000 additional languages. Now the Bible is waiting to be translated into 2,273 languages used by 353 million people. It is expected that, by the end of this century, all living languages used around the world, that is all surviving languages, will have translations.[9]

3. Bible Translation by the Korean Bible Society and Ecumenism

It was 1885 when Methodist missionary, Appenzeller, and Presbyterian missionary, Underwood, came to Korea, although the work of translating the Bible into the Korean language had begun in China and Japan before the arrival of Protestant missionaries in Korea. In China, Ross and MacIntyre's translation team translated and published the *Gospel of Luke* (1882) and the *Gospel of John* (1882), while in Japan Soo Jeong Lee, with the support of the American Bible Society, translated the Gospel of Mark (1885). In the previous year Lee added Korean endings to the Chinese translations of the four Gospels and the book of Acts for Korean readers, and edited and published in Japan the Kuntan-Corean Scriptures so that Koreans could also read the Scriptures.

Bible translation work that was undertaken outside of the country immediately led to distribution of the Scriptures. From China, Koreans who worked with Ross to translate the Bible brought the Scriptures into Korea and distributed them. Chinese colporteurs came along with them and took part in Scripture distribution. From Japan, Japanese Christians established Bible depots in cities like Pusan, Wonsan and there were many Japanese residents, and started distributing Scriptures translated into the Korean language. By the time the missionaries came in 1885, there were people who had already read the Korean Scriptures and awaiting the missionaries to become Christians.[10]

In 1895, the Bible Society was established in Korea, and through the collaboration of the National Bible Society of Scotland (NBSS, now the Scottish Bible Society), the British and Foreign Bible Society (BFBS), and the American Bible Society, the *Korean New Testament* was published in 1900, and the entire Bible translated into the *Korean Bible* in 1911. What is significant is that these Bible translations were not the work of an individual or church. Rather missionaries from different churches and Korean co-workers came together and accomplished this official translation with support from Bible Societies like the NBSS, BFBS and ABS. It is noteworthy that the United Bible Societies (established in 1946) and the World

---

[7] http://www.ethnologue.com/ethno_docs/distribution.asp?by=area
[8] http://www.bskorea.or.kr/
[9] http://intranet2.biblesocieties.org
[10] Oak, Sung Deuk & Mahn Yol Yi, *The History of Korean Bible Society*, Vol. 1(Korean), (Korean Bible Society, 1993), 23-119

Council of Churches (established in 1948) had begun at around the same time in history an ecumenical endeavors envisioning unity among churches.

For more than 100 years Korean churches have accepted and used this Bible for their church worship. For the past century this Korean Bible has undergone three revisions – the first in 1938, the second in 1961 and the latest in 1998. It is still this *Holy Bible Hangul and Revised* that is officially used and preached from the 60,000 pulpits of the Korean Protestant churches, which are divided into more than 150 church denominations.[11]

The Korean Bible Society published the Korean New Testament New Translation in 1967. This translation was the first attempt by Korean scholars to translate the Bible directly from the original Greek text. It was initially planned to translate also the Old Testament, but as the UBS and the Vatican agreed to cooperate inter-confessionally for Bible translations, KBS quickly substituted the plan to carry out the Old Testament translation with the project to undertake an inter-confessional Bible translation. As a result KBS published the *Common Translation of the New Testament in 1970* and the *Common Translation of the Holy Bible* in 1977. The Common Translation was published as two editions – the Protestant Edition which included only the 66 proto-canonical books, and the Catholic Edition which also included the deutero-canonical books.

Until the Roman Catholic Church in Korea announced the plan to replace the *Common Translation Bible* and use their newly translated *Seonggyeong* (Holy Bible) in 2005, the *Common Translation Bible* was the official church translation used for more than 30 years at church services. In case of Protestant churches, only a few denominations and individual churches accepted the *Common Translation Bible* because it was a translation based on dynamic-equivalence principles, not formal-equivalence and because vocabulary selected was too heavily influenced by the Catholic terms.

In 1993 KBS published the *New Korean Standard Version* (*Pyojunsaebunyeok*), which was translated by scholars commissioned to work on the translation project by each Protestant denomination. Compared to the English translations, it is similar to the English translation of the *New Revised Standard Version*, which takes a middle path between the dynamic-equivalence and formal-equivalence translations. As the translation was revised, it was renamed *Saebunyeok* (transliteration of *Revised New Korean Standard Version)* from its previous name of *Pyojunsaebunyeok* (transliteration of *New Korean Standard Version*).

Compared to the Revised Korean version (*Holy Bible Hangul and Revised*), the *Revised New Korean Standard Version (RNKSV)* is in the contemporary Korean language, which has both the Old and New Testaments translated from critical editions like the BHS and NTG 27th edition. Reflected in the RNKSV is textual criticism, and discriminative words have been removed from the text. This translation is read among the youth but is still used in a very limited number of churches in Korea.

Korea is the only nation where North and South are divided by ideological differences. For the past 60 years people have been restricted from visiting each other and each have had different government systems in place.

Although people of North and South use the same Korean language, the grammar is changing between the two. There is also considerable number of words that have come to acquire different meanings. In the midst of such changes North Korea's Korean Christian Federation revised the South Korean Common Translation Bible in the early 1980s by adapting its grammar, vocabulary, expressions to the North Korean standards. This version is thus called the "Pyong Yang Recension of the Korean Bible Society's Common Translation". The translation itself remains the same with amendments in the vocabulary and grammatical elements.

[11] Since 2000, a small number of churches and church denominations have begun using their own Bible translations for church worship services, but the exact figures are unavailable.

From the perspective of mission and ecumenical spirit, it is profoundly meaningful that the North Korean Protestant churches took the Common Translation Bible, which was not accepted by the South Korean Protestant churches, and revised and accepted the translation.

4. Korean Equivalents for Deity

During the period from the time the Bible Society was established till the publication of the first Korean Bible, Korean churches were able to reach an agreement on the selection and decision on the Korean equivalents corresponding to the Hebrew *Elohim* and the Greek *Theos*. Based on their own experiences in Bible translation, BFBS, NBSS and ABS, which were helping translators and the translation process, approached the issue of translating names of deities very carefully. Translating the names of deities had been an issue since the early stages of Bible translation. In short, there was mixed use of native Korean words like "하느님(*ha-neu-nim*)", "하□님 (*ha-na-nim*)", "하나님(*ha-na-nim*)", while attempts were made to adopt Chinese words such as "천주(天主 *chon-ju*, 'the Lord of Heaven')", "상제(上帝 *sang-je*, 'the Supreme Lord')", "신(神 *sin*, 'god')". Words like "하느님(*ha-neu-nim*)", "하□님 (*ha-na-nim*)", "하나님(*ha-na-nim*)" were all developed from "하□님(*ha-nal-nim*)", of which the morpheme is "하늘(*ha-neul*, 'heaven')". In other words, it is a word formed by adding the honorific suffix of "-님(*-nim*)" to "하늘(*ha-neul*, 'heaven')".

Among native Korean terms, the Protestant Church accepted "하나님(*ha-na-nim*)" and the Roman Catholic Church "하느님(*ha-neu-nim*)". The Catholics are also using the Chinese term, "천주(天主 *chon-ju*, 'the Lord of Heaven')" alongside the native Korean term "하느님 (*ha-neu-nim*)". Among the Protestant churches, "하나님(*ha-na-nim*)" is in general use, but "신(神 *sin*)", which originated from Chinese, is also used in theological statements. The term "상제(上帝 *sang-je*, 'the Supreme Lord')" is no longer used.

The tetragrammaton, YHWH, has traditionally been translated as "Jehowah" in accordance with the American Standard Version, but in the *Common Translation Bible* (1977) translated it into "Yahweh", and in the *New Korean Standard Version (1993)* "*ju*(主; LORD)". The Hebrew YHWH has been translated into "Jehovah", "Yahweh", and "Lord" in major translations of the Bible used in Korean churches.

Such issues are commonly found in some areas of the Asia Pacific. Translating the names of deities or selecting the receptor language equivalents continues to be carefully discussed in Korea, China, Japan, Mongolia and several countries of the Indochina region because they go beyond the issue of lexicography, linguistics or translation studies and have a direct influence on mission and the naturalization of Christianity. They should not be regarded as something a certain church denomination has to take care of. Rather, churches should come together and seek to resolve them in unity.

5. Nestorian Experiment in Tang Dynasty China

The problem of hermeneutics is related to the fact that when the Scriptures of a religion enter into an alien country and are translated into the language of that land, the translation cannot avoid borrowing terms from other religions. It is also related to the fact that, when a new concept is introduced, a similar concept of the native religion or culture is used. As the result of cultural intercourse between the two religions, the original concept of the new religion experiences a creative reduction or expansion of its meaning. Buddhism in China is known to us as a hermeneutical Buddhism. For this reason some scholars try to find the oriental "hermeneutics" of Nestorianism in China as a hermeneutical Christianity. The concept of "hermeneutics" and the reason for referring to both Buddhism and Nestorianism in China as hermeneutical religions, are well summarized in the following quotation:

"The historical encounter of Christianity with the Orient started when Christianity spread into India and China through Central Asia. In the process, Christianity discovered a new identity which was not realized in the West. The Gospel of Christianity experienced the formation of its own Asian identity that was different from that of the West. Nestorian Christianity in China is a typical model of oriental Christianity. Through Nestorianism, one can find the characteristics of "hermeneutics" of every foreign religion."

"Hermeneutics" refers to the universal phenomenon that the system of a religion or a culture, transferred from one region to another, can take root deeply in new ground only by putting on clothes of the culture in which the new religion will unfold. A typical example of such a phenomenon can be found in the spread of Buddhism from India into China. When Buddhism was brought into China from India in the 4th century A.D., Chinese people preferred to understand it from the perspective of similar Chinese thoughts and relate the new concept to familiar Chinese concepts. Accepting Buddhism, Chinese people understood the new religion in connection with their traditional terms and their own way of thinking. This phenomenon is in accord with the hermeneutical awareness that understanding is impossible without a concrete horizon of understanding or *Vorverständnis*. Such Buddhism is called "hermeneutical Buddhism".[12]

By the second century Christianity had spread throughout the East – from Arabia, through Turkey and Iraq, to Persia. In the third century Christianity also spread to the Indian Ocean. In the first half of the fifth century the Church of the East was rocked by a theological controversy so serious that it resulted in schism. This was the so-called Nestorian controversy. Nestorius taught that Jesus Christ had two distinct natures: divine and human. Nestorius was condemned at the Council of Ephesus in 431, but his teaching spread, and by 451 the Nestorians were almost completely cut off from the rest of the patriarchate of Antioch.[13]

The Acts of Thomas, a very ancient tradition given in the third century, makes Thomas the Apostle to India, and, consequently, Indian Christians are commonly referred to as Christians of St. Thomas. China received Christianity from Persia in the seventh century. According to the Chinese Nestorian Inscriptions (大秦景教流行中國碑) erected in 781, it was in 635 that the Nestorian missionaries, including Alopen (or Abraham, 阿羅本), came to Chang'an (長安, present day Xian), the capital city of the T'ang dynasty, and in 638 they built the Daqin Temple (大秦寺). At that time, there were 21 monks in the temple.[14]

The Nestorian Church generally prospered until the fall of Baghdad to the Mongols in 1258, when the widespread disruption in the Middle East drained its vitality. The most detrimental effect of the Muslim conquest on the Nestorian Church in the countries lying between Persia and China was that its missionary activity, begun among the Mongols, Turks, and Chinese, was cut off. Eventually the early blossoming of Christianity in China died.[15]

Under the Mongols, the conditions of the Nestorians were generally peaceful. Hulagu Kahan, who took Baghdad in 1268, and most of his successors favored the Nestorians. Kessler points out that Mongol khans favored Nestorians not only because they were opposed to the Mohammedans, the political foes of the Mongols, but also on account of the superficial similarity between Nestorian Christianity and the Mongol type of Buddhism; and Nestorianism influenced some of the *khans* through their Christian wives. Certain Mongol rulers are known to have become converts to Christianity, particularly in the district of the Keraites, south of Lake Baikal.[16]

The following text is quoted from the Nestorian *Jesus' Teaching on Almsgiving* (世尊布施論):

---

[12] Seng-Chul Kim, *Land and Wind – An Attempt at Molding Oriental Theology*, Seoul: Dasan Gelbang, 1994, p. 193 (Korean).

[13] Information from Matti Moosa, "Nestorian Church", in *The Encyclopedia of Religion*, Vol. 10, ed., by Mircea Eliade (New York: Macmillian Publishing Company, 1987), pp. 369-372, esp. p.369-370.

[14] Kwang-Soo Kim, "Nestorianism" in *The Christian Encyclopedia,* Vol. 1, ed., by Ki-Moon Lee, Seoul: Christian Literature Press, 1980, pp. 597-601, esp. p. 594 (Korean).

[15] Matti Moosa, p. 370.

[16] K. Kessler, "Nestorians" in *The New Schaff-Herzog Encyclopedia of Religious Knowledge*, Vol. III, ed., Samuel Macauley Jackson, New York and London: Funk and Wagnalls Company, 1910, p.121.

> *Lokajyestha* (世尊, World's most venerable: The Lord, Jesus) said, "Whenever you give alms, do not let the people know what you are doing. Whenever you give alms, your almsgiving may be known only by *Lokajyestha* (世尊, World's most venerable: The Lord, God). When you give alms, do not let your right hand know what your left hand is doing." (*Jesus' Teaching on Almsgiving*)

The above text is a summary of Matthew 6:2-4. We can pay attention to the terms which the Nestorian text borrowed from Buddhism. The Lord Jesus is translated as *Lokajyestha* (世尊, World's most venerable), one of the highest titles of Buddha, literally meaning "world's most venerable, lord of worlds". God is also translated as *Lokajyestha*(世尊). Both Jesus and God have the same Chinese equivalent, *Lokajyestha* (世尊). This may be a reflection of the theological view that both God and God's Son Jesus are one and the same person.[17]

In the book *Jesus the Messiah* (序聽 迷詩所經), God is translated as "Buddha (佛 陀)", and sometimes as "天尊", a title of Buddha, i.e. the highest of of divine beings. The word "Buddha (佛)" is derived from "Buddh", which means "to be aware of, conceive, observe, wake". Buddha means "completely conscious, enlightened", and came to mean the enlightener. The Chinese translation is 覺 meaning to perceive, be aware, awake; and 智 meaning *gnosis*, knowledge. There is an Eternal Buddha, and multitudes of Buddhas, but the personality of a Supreme Buddha, an Adi Buddha, is not defined.[18] 天尊 means the most honoured among devas, a title of Buddha, i.e. the highest of divine beings. This title was given by the Taoists to their divinities as a counterpart to the Buddhist 世尊."[19]

The Nestorian name of Simon Peter is *Sangha*(僧伽), a Buddhist term which means

1. an assembly, collection, company, society,
2. the corporate assembly of at least three (formerly four) monks under a chairman, empowered to hear confession, grant absolution, and to ordain, and
3. the church or monastic order.

The term *Sang* (僧) used alone has come to mean a monk, or monks in general.[20] The Nestorian name of Simon Peter associates him with a Buddhist monk.

The tetragrammaton יהוה(YHWH) is translated as 阿羅訶. "a(阿)", the first letter in 阿羅訶 is the first letter of the Sanskrit Siddham alphabet. From it are supposed to be born all the other letters, and it is the first sound uttered by the human mouth. It has, therefore, numerous mystical indications. It also indicates Amitabha Buddha (阿彌陀佛), the Buddha of infinite qualities, known as "boundless light (無量光)" and "boundless age (無量數)". This name indicates an idealization rather than a historic personality, the idea of eternal light and life.[21]

6. Mongolian Equivalents for Deity

One of the controversial problems in the Mongolian Bible translation is related to the Mongolian equivalent for deity. On the one hand, the Mongolian Bible Translation Committee composed of foreign missionaries in Mongolia, maintains that the Hebrew *Elohim* and the Greek *Theos* should be translated into the Mongolian *Burkhan* (佛汗), not only because the term was used in early Mongolian versions[22] and

---

[17] Kami, Naomichi, *Introduction to Nestorianism,* Tokyo: Kyobunkan, 1981, pp.98-99 (Japanese).
[18] A Dictionary of Chines Buddhist Terms(Motilal Banarsidass Pub, 2000), p.225.
[19] DCBT, p. 145.
[20] DCBT, p.420.
[21] DCBT, p.287.
[22] For example, *Mongolian Old Testament,* translated by Isaac Jacob Schmidt(1779-1847), and published at Sanktpeterburg in 1840. The Hebrew *Elohim* is translated into Mongolian *Burkhan.*

because the Mongolian people have historically understood the term to refer to deity, but also because there is no guarantee that the newly coined word for God will take a deep hold on the popular mind.

On the other hand, the John Gibbens translationteam used to insist that Christianity cannot use the Buddhist term *Burkhan,* not only because it is the title of Buddha, but also because it is necessary for Mongolian Christians to have a Mongolian equivalent for deity which can fully convey the biblical concept of God. The Gibben's team made a new Mongolian expression for God *Eurngtngchin Ezeng* ЕРТӨНЦИЙН ЭЗЭН, which means "Lord of the Universe".

It is necessary to refer to the experiences of neighbouring countries such as China, Korea and Japan. In any country and at any time one of the most important decisions in every translation of the Bible is the proper equivalent of deity because it is not easy for translators to find a word which has the same meaning in the receptor language.

In summary, the term 'burhan', and even the shamanist term 'tenger', are specific terms for specific deities. Neither has been proven to be a generic term as are *elohim* and *theos.* It is also clear that both 'burhan' and 'tenger' are living and current names of deities in Mongolian consciousness. The question then is whether Mongolians can accept the proper noun of Buddha for the generic *elohim* and *theos* of the Bible, which then has to take on the specific meanings of those terms in the person of YHWH of the Bible. The history of Chinggis Khan and many after him has been to avoid doing just that.

From the experiences of Bible translation in China and Mongolia, we learned the necessity of the following positive appropriation:

1. The biblical message cannot be conveyed without the hermeneutical process.
2. In Bible translation borrowing words is inescapable.
3. Sometimes it is better to borrow terms from the Indigenous religions to express the biblical message than to coin new words.
4. The biblical message expressed with borrowed terms sometimes leads to the formation of a new identity that is different from that of other cultures.
5. In case of the Mongolian Bible translation, both *Burkhan* and *Eurngtngchin*
6. *Ezeng* are likely to be used as the Mongolian equivalents for deity for the time being
7. in the different Bible translation teams.
8. After such examination the Mongolian Christians should decide which symbol can convey the biblical idea more effectively. Both *Burkhan* and *Erngtngchin Ezeng* are symbols of ideas.
9. They may choose one or both symbols.

7. The Encounter of "Logos" and "Tao(道)"

In the beginning was the Word,
and the Word was with God,
and the Word was God; (Joh 1:1 YLT)[23]

When we look at the history of Chinese Bible translations, the Greek *Logos* of John 1:1 has always been translated into *Tao* whenever a new Bible translation project is initiated.

In the beginning was the *Tao*(道)
and the *Tao*(道) was with God,
and the *Tao*(道) was God;

[23] Young's Literal Translation of the Holy Bible 1862/1887/1898, by J. N. Young.

Tao (Chinese: 道) literally means the "way", but can also be interpreted as road, channel, path, doctrine or line. In Taoism it refers to "the One, which is natural, spontaneous, eternal, nameless and indescribable. It is at once the beginning of all things and the way in which all things pursue their course". "It has variously been denoted as the 'flow of the universe', a 'conceptually necessary ontological ground', or a demonstration of nature. The *Tao* also is something that individuals can find immanent in themselves."[24]

The statement about Tao (道 Way) and Ming (名 Name) in Chapter one of the Tao Te Ching provides a crucial insight to understanding the Bible afresh, especially the Hebrew text of ´e|hyè ´ášer ´e|hyè in Exodus 3:14. This Hebrew text has traditionally been translated as "I Am Who I AM" or "I Will Be What I Will Be".

> God said to Moshe,
> "*Ehyeh Asher Ehyeh* [I am/will be what I am/will be],"
> and added, "Here is what to say to the people of Isra'el:
> '*Ehyeh* [I Am *or* I Will Be] has sent me to you.'"
> (Exo 3:14 CJB)

When we interpret the text with YHWH and *Tao*, referring to the text, "道可道, 非 常道" (The Way that can be described is not the true Way) in Chapter 1 of the *Tao Te Ching*, it leads us to realize the limitations of theism, i.e. the theological definition of God cannot be a permanent definition of God.

YHWH is an ineffable name. We can give it a temporary name and use it but it cannot be permanent. The insight needed to acknowledge that God cannot be named can be obtained from the statement "名可名，非常名" (The name that can be named is not the constant Name) in Chapter 1 of the *Tao Te Ching.*

In Japanese Bible translations the *Logos* has been translated as *Kotoba* (言葉 こと ば meaning the Word). In Korea the tradition has been to adopt them both. Earlier Korean translations translated the Greek *Logos* as *Tao*, followingthe traditions of Chinese Bible translations. The fact that *Logos,* which refers to Jesus and ultimately God, was translated as *Tao* in early Korean translations is extremely important from the missiological perspective. The learned class of Korea during those times were familiar with the Taoism of the Orient and, among the various reasons that explain how they could easily embrace Christianity, is that they were familiar with the Taoistic concept of "道成人身"(*Tao* became human being); this has greatly contributed to the spread of Christianity in Korea. Even when the *Korean Bible* was published in 1911, *Tao*(도, 道*)* was used and transcribed alongside *Word* (말씀 *mal-sseum*) within the text.

In the *Revised Korean Version* published in 1938, *Word* (말씀 *mal-sseum*) alone was kept in the text, while *Tao* (道*)* was moved to footnotes, and this arrangement continues to the present.

> In the beginning was the *Tao*(道)/Word(*mal-sseum* 말씀)
> and the *Tao*(道)/Word(*mal-sseum* 말씀) was with God,
> and the *Tao*(道)/Word(*mal-sseum* 말씀) was God;

There is, however, an opinion from etymologists that is not well known among the public. It holds that in the Korean shamanistic tradition the term *Word* (말씀 *mal-sseum*) itself was the origin of "하나님 *ha-na-nim*)" and "*sin* (신, 神)".

The Korean etymological dictionary informs that "말씀 (*mal-sseum*)" was originally "언신 (言神, *un-sin,* 'Word God')" in shamanism.[25]

---

[24] See article "Tao" in Wikipedia

[25] The word "*mal-ssam*"(말□) [or "*mal-sseum*"(말씀)] appears in *Yongbi eocheonga*(龍飛御天歌)(1447). "the honorific expression *mal-sseum*(말씀) was originally Word God(言神) in Korean Shamanism.". For *Yongbi*

In any case the statement that "In the beginning, the *Tao* (道)/Word (말씀 *mal-sseum*) was with God, and the *Tao* (道) was God" became the critical contact point for the spread of Christianity not only in the sinosphere but especially in Korea.

---

eocheonga see "*Yongbi eocheonga*" in Wikipedia. 말□≪용비어천가(1447)≫ "존대 말은 샤마니즘 신의 어원이다. [말;言]+[슴;神]->....." http://kin.naver.com/openkr/detail.nhn?docId=85089

(18) Building the Household of God Together in Asia – Theological Perspectives on Ecumenism

Huang Po Ho

Introduction

The concept of ecumenism is derived from the ancient Greek word *oikos*, which is equivalent to the concept of household or family. The Greek word "*οικουμένη*" (oikoumene) means "the whole inhabited world", which once referred specifically to the Roman Empire and was adopted by the early church to describe the visible unity of the Church (Eph 4:3) and the "whole inhabited earth" (Mt 24.14). The meaning of ecumenism, put in the Christian context, thus received its new meaning in reference to the worldwide church, its universal body or authority, such as an "ecumenical council" or also in a term like "ecumenical patriarch".

The contemporary implication of the term has shifted its connotation from the traditional perception to the current efforts to bring unity to the people of God and the churches. The ecumenical movement now signifies a commitment to build the household of God. The traditional understanding of the house of God referred to initiatives aimed at greater Christian unity or church cooperation in responding to the particular concerns of the Christian denominational divisions in its history. It is, however, the expansion of the meaning of ecumenism, which has taken place under the current challenges recognizing the various divisive elements, that has led to splits within the churches and within societies at different stages of human history.

Contemporary Ecumenical Movement and Its Challenges

The ecumenical councils, which were considered the global conferences of ecclesiastical dignitaries and theological experts convened to discuss and settle matters of church doctrine and practice, were questioned with regard to their all-inclusive ecumenical nature. But critical questions were raised on this all-inclusive character from different perspectives and different cultural and philosophical mindsets already after the second gathering of an ecumenical council.[1] Past church divisions have created not only a schism in Christianity but also hostilities between denominational churches. This situation was especially true after the Reformation that took place in the 16th century. Therefore, the founding of the World Council of Churches in 1948 marked a significant milestone for the contemporary ecumenical movement. Formed through a merger of the "Life and Work Movement" and the "Faith and Order Movement" in 1948, the World Council of Churches (WCC) today is a worldwide fellowship of 349 global, regional and sub-regional, national and local churches, seeking unity, common witness and common Christian service.

Along with the development and growth of the WCC, the concept and understanding of ecumenism has been challenged and expanded. The WCC was founded as a worldwide Christian fellowship for church

---

[1] The acceptance of the early councils of the Ancient Church varies between different branches of Christian denominations. The Christological disputes have led some churches to withdraw their recognition of the council of Chalcedon as being truly ecumenical: for instance, the Church of the East, being accused as Nestorian, accepts only the first two councils as ecumenical; the Oriental Orthodox Churches accepts the first three; and the Eastern Orthodox Church and most of the Protestant churches recognized only seven councils as ecumenical, which were held from the 4th to the 9th century before the East-West Schism. The Roman Catholic Church, however, continues to hold general councils and reckons them also as ecumenical.

denominations. Its member churches include the Orthodox churches, the numerous denominations of the Protestant churches, including the Anglican, Baptist, Lutheran, Methodist, Reformed, some United and a number of independent churches. Individual Pentecostal and some Old Catholic churches have also joined as members. Today this ecumenical organization represents some 560 million Christians from 349 churches in more than 110 countries all over the world.

The rapid expansion of membership has brought to the Council a rich fellowship and exchange among its member churches, and has also deepened the Christian witness of unity. It is, however, the significant contribution of the young churches from the third world countries which – based on their cultural specificities and mission experiences – have challenged the traditional ecclesio-centric understanding of ecumenism, which focused on the ecumenical ministry only in terms of the unity of churches. Generally speaking, third world people and churches experienced divisions not so much caused by the doctrinal debates among the Christians, as was being experienced by the Western churches, rather people and churches in the global South were divided by factors relating to political, economic, and social conditions, as well as ideological differences. Many churches in the so-called 'mission lands' came to be divided simply because of the Western missionary activities that were organized denominationally. The traditional concept of ecumenism that has concentrated on disputes of denominational theologies, which were caused or reinforced a fragmentation of the landscape of the different denominational churches, is no longer sufficient and valid to deal with the new social, political and interfaith issues being raised by younger churches from the third world.

Widening the Concept of Ecumenism

With the entry, or rather eruption, of third world churches onto the map of WCC membership, the concept of ecumenism was challenged to widen its scope. The household of God (*oikos*) has been reinterpreted as expanding from its original concern for the unity of Church to an interest in strengthening the unity of all people. Nowadays it is moving toward a proper inclusion of perspectives for the "integrity of God's whole creation".

As mentioned in the previous section, the division of churches that occurred in the so-called "mission lands" was not caused primarily by the disputes of doctrinal understandings, but often by 'non-theological factors'. The forces that prevent people from being truly united are forces of economic exploitation, political oppression, social domination and cultural discrimination. The emergence of the third world churches in the chart of WCC membership, contributed not only to enlarging its scope of fellowship in terms of the participating numbers and church denominations. It has also brought more tensions and conflicts to this ecumenical family as it was pushed to seek new ways to overcome divisions and attain true unity for both the churches and peoples.

A new form of ecumenical theological reflection thus emerged to elaborate the contextual issues and propose common Christian convictions for overcoming these social, political and ideological forces of division. Different contextual theologies were articulated and suggested. Among them were Feminist Theologies, Liberation Theologies, Marginalized (black and aborigines) Theologies and Theologies of Religions (Cultures), which have made a tremendous impact and far-reaching contributions to the new course of the ecumenical movement from the 1960s towards the end of the last century. The recent issues related to globalization and post-modern/post-colonial discourses were also at the core of the new theological and ecumenical debates.

Another topic that has influenced the new ecumenical theological discourse is the issue of ecology. The results of the global warming that causes extreme weather have not only threatened the survival of lives in the whole inhabited world, but also posed a fundamental challenge to the legitimacy of some of the traditional understandings of human relations with their partner creatures. This challenge to the traditional conceptualization of the role of the human species as being masters over the rest of creation and creatures has implied a critique also of the nature of Christian theology, which was developed along the line of an andro-anthropocentric pattern of theological thinking. A new paradigm of theology that derives from the perspective of ecological justice is desirable and necessary for the ecumenical movement to accommodate the wider concept of ecumenism that includes the whole creation as the frame of reference and understands it as the one household of God.[2]

Distinctive Asian Contributions to the Ecumenical Movement

The Asian world in general was categorized as part of the 'third world' before the era of globalization. It is a continent with religious plenitude and plurality, which possesses profound cultures and age old histories. However, most of the people in Asia have experienced political colonization and dictatorial oppressions, economic poverty and exploitation, cultural and religious diversity and discrimination, patriarchal domination, and also environmental degradation, not to mention the threats from the super power empires as well as the military confrontations taking place within. Therefore ecumenism has to deal with these current Asian realities.

With the emergence of a liberating nationalism against Western imperialism and colonization, Asian countries have rediscovered the wider concept of ecumenism, i.e. the unity of the whole people. Stanley J. Samartha, for instance, has proposed a new style of ecumenism in the following argument:

> ...with a broadening awareness of the world perspective of religious pluralism today and with several world organizations seeking a greater measure of corporation the time has come to search for a new style of ecumenism encompassing the whole of humanity, but which recognizes within itself the creative particularities of pluralism.[3]

In other words, while the traditional ecumenical movement, which began in the Western countries, has focused on the unity of churches, Asian ecumenism has been directed to a wider scope of *oikos,* i.e. people's ecumenism. As the division of churches in the Asian context involved not only the disputes *within* the Christian family, but also the power issues in society related to socio-political, economical, and even cultural/religious interests, the pursuit for real unity amongst Christian Churches cannot be attained without a simultaneous struggle for the unity of the people in society. Thus a traditional concept of an ecclesial ecumenism had to be expanded to a people's ecumenism.

In the contexts of Asia, where most of the world religions have settled, Christian churches are challenged to live together with the peoples of various living faiths. Interfaith relations have proven to be a decisive factor in people's divisions or for uniting processes. Interfaith relations were traditionally categorized as an issue in the area of "inter-religious dialogue," instead of being presented as an organic part of "ecumenism". But "ecumenism" which in former periods was understood to refer exclusively to the relation between Christians and churches cannot be confined just to inner Christian issues. This clear-cut distinction cannot be sustained any longer in Asia. As the Christians are an absolute minority in most of the countries in this continent, a restriction of the target of ecumenism to a perspective that only focuses on Christians or the mutual relationship of church communities will not only miss important causes of the

---

[2] Po Ho Huang, "A Paradigm Shift of Theology and the Holistic Redemption to God's Creation," an unpublished paper. addressed to "Inter-regional Doctoral Students Colloquium," held in Kolkata, India, Dec. 7-11, 2010.
[3] Stanley J. Samartha, *Courage for Dialogue, Ecumenical Issues in Inter-religious Relationships*, (Geneva: WCC, 1981), 343.

church division and unity[4], but also distort the true meaning of *Oikomene*, the prospect of peace and reconciliation for the whole inhabited world. New Asian theologies of cultures and religions are therefore developing in the region in order to widen the theological scope of orientation and properly accommodate the experiences of life-and-death struggles that Christian mission takes up in the midst of the Asian plural religious context.

Building the Household of God in Asia Together

Taking root in its missionary history, Asian ecumenism has articulated a challenge to break away from Christian attitudes of superiority and domination introduced by Western colonialism and a traditional missionary concept of Christendom. A new and radical shift in approach for the Christian mission in Asia is urgently needed as a starting point for the new phase of the ecumenical journey. This new orientation will inevitably lead to the transformation of many aspects of Christian activities relating to the building of the household of God in Asia:

(a) Reconstructing Asian Ecumenical Theology

The traditional missionary Christianity has constructed a theology with assumptions to justify Western superiority and colonization based on the theological justification of a perception of religious conversion that considers the Gospel superior over non-Christian cultures. Third world contextual theologies which have developed since the 1970s, under the encouragement of the third mandate of The Theological Education Fund (TEF) of the World Council of Churches, attempted to correct this. Asian contextual theologies of cultures and religions thereby remain a critical counter force to certain traditional missionary concepts even today.

Doing contextual theologies in Asia inevitably implies dealing with common issues facing most of the third world, which are related to the daily struggles of people. These issues include: gender discrimination, poverty and exploitation, colonization, militarization, minority and marginalization, as well suffering caused by diseases, natural disasters and globalization. Beyond these are distinctive elements that mark the Asian world, which can be taken up for theological reflection in order to enrich the humble Christian witness towards peace and harmony, i.e. Christian theologies of inter-religious relations and theologies of ecology.

As mentioned, Asia is a religiously plural and diverse continent: almost all world religions have found their home in this continent. This colorful cultural-religious panorama can bring to the inhabitants of the Asian region either enrichment and profound wisdom or major division and deep hostility. A relevant Asian theology of religions that helps Christians and their neighbors to live together harmoniously with mutual respect is urgent. Furthermore, in order to develop a faithful response to the call to serve the unity of the whole inhabited world created by God, Asian Christian theology can no longer neglect the issue of ecology that requires a radical repentance from the traditional theological presupposition of a dominating relationship of the human species over nature and the rest of creatures. These two areas of theological endeavors will definitely widen our scope of ecumenism to accommodate challenges facing us in the new era.

(b) Promoting Asian Solidarity

Asian ecumenism was initiated against the background of two Asian experiences which are in tension with each other, though also correlated: Asia was confronted with Western colonization and invasive missionary

---

[4] In Asia many churches were divided in the cause of ethnic and cultural differences, and these elements have their impacts across religious boundary. Therefore, unless the unity of people is attained, there will not be unity that can be reached for Christians or churches.

activities on the one hand, and the fragmentation of the continent and division of churches on the other. Asia is the world's largest and most populous continent: it hosts nearly the 60% of the world human population. These populations are spread all over the countries in the region surrounded by the Pacific and Indian oceans. In addition to being segregated within the Asian people commonly faced threats from Western colonial countries. The ecumenical movement in Asia thus has to develop its strength dialectically relating both to the enhancement of solidarity on the one hand and resistance against imperialist colonialism and exploitation on the other.

Asian ecumenism without any doubt has also to stretch out beyond geographical Asia. However, as far as the specific emphasis of regional ecumenism is concerned, the causes of the tensions, divisions and challenges within the region inevitably have to come to the forefront of the ecumenical discourse. Asian ecumenism has to work for Asian common tasks that reflect a deep feeling and desire for the unity of Asian people, while at the same time pursuing a healthy and just relationship with people from other parts of the world. It is therefore important to uphold the fundamental Christian value of Justice, Peace and the Integrity of Creation, as a guiding principle for the future of the Asian ecumenical movement.

(c) Reclaiming People's Ecumenism

The Asian ecumenical movement also has to face the common problem of the contemporary ecumenical movement which has become institutionalized and has lost some of its character as a dynamic movement. The emphasis on church unity within the contemporary ecumenical movement has sometimes led to ecumenism being reduced to a consortium of institutional churches. If ecumenism is being reduced to an inter-ecclesial movement, its gatherings will be represented only by clerical leaders of hierarchical churches and Christian institutions, while the grassroots laity and powerless members are marginalized, if not excluded, from the scenario. The fellowships created by ecumenism then become gatherings of church hierarchies instead of gatherings also involving local congregational members or ordinary people.

If the ecumenical movement becomes narrowed down and exclusively institutionally oriented it runs the risk of not properly addressing and eliminating the divisions among grassroots Christians and facing the real challenges created by invasive missionary activities, not to speak of a possible failure to address in a wider sense the causes of the segregation that continue to plague Asians of different faiths or the relationships between Christians and people from non religious backgrounds. As ecumenism is meant to unite the whole inhabited world, it should be a movement primarily of people, not institutions.

Doing People's Ecumenism According to Jesus' Movement

A genuine people's ecumenism should be geared towards reviving the "Jesus' movement" which is about following Jesus with the expectation to experience and to give witness to signs of the Kingdom of God. If we take the ecumenical movement as a means for churches to proclaim the coming of the Kingdom of God, we will be convinced that the most authentic paradigm of ecumenical movement is the Jesus' movement itself. By revisiting the witnesses of the evangelists concerning Jesus' ministries, teachings, healing works, and His life and death from the perspective of ecumenism, we will be enlightened about characteristic marks of a true ecumenism:

1. The Jesus' movement is a movement for the Reign of God; therefore witness to the Reign of God should be taken as the ultimate intention of the ecumenical movement. To proclaim and actualize the Reign of God in this world is the foundation of the Christian ecumenical movement and a solid base for wider unity; it is therefore the essence of ecumenism. To be truly ecumenical thus means to participate in the movement for the Reign of God.

2. The Jesus' movement is by nature a movement of incarnation and identification. It was a movement set off by the recognition and confession of the messianic identity of Jesus by his followers. Therefore the

very nature and dynamics of the movement is the transforming power of incarnation, a power that makes the Divine becoming human in order to transform the human being into a saint. This incarnational character of the movement was not only sustained by the way the person of Jesus Christ had come into being, but also derives from the teaching and life witness of Jesus in his leadership of the movement, as Paul has interpreted this to the Philippines in his letter:

> "Have this mind among yourselves, which is yours in Christ Jesus, who, though he was in the form of God, did not count equality with God a thing to be grasped, but emptied himself, taking the form of a servant, being born in the likeness of men. And being found in human form he humbled himself and became obedient unto death, even death on a cross." (Philippines 2.5-8)

The Jesus' movement was a movement directed to the ordinary, the downtrodden, and the marginalized with a self-humbling identification of sacrificial love. The ecumenical movement thus has an essential mission to transform society with a love that identifies with the victims, the poor, and the suffering.

3. The Jesus' movement is a cross-boundary movement. Even though there are scholars questioning about the intention of Jesus to bring the Gospel outside the Jewish community, the Christian religion, which was formed out of the Jesus' movement, is by nature a religion that transcends the boundaries of Jewish tradition in order to reach peoples of different nations and ethnic groups. It now has to go even further to cross the human boundary to create a harmonious relation with all creatures. It has grown to a religion with universal perspectives and often even cosmic orientation. A true ecumenical movement must become a movement that possesses this dynamic, and which is bold enough to cross boundaries to give witness to the coming of the Divine new creation.

4. Last but not least, the Jesus' movement is a movement of healing. The inhabited world is God's creation, and an ecumenical movement that tries to hold together this inhabited world can attain its mission only if it demonstrates the healing power which mends wounds and empowers broken lives. The task of the ecumenical movement is therefore to become a living witness to the healing and liberating presence of God.

Conclusion

Ecumenism in its essence is a movement of witness to God's Kingdom which is holistic, worldwide, and cosmological. Although Asian ecumenism concentrates on the particular experiences and issues concerning people in Asia, it should not confine its perspectives and reflections to the Asian region alone. Instead it should emphasize the contributions which the Asian perspective can make to enhance the well-being of all the people on earth and just relations between all creatures in Asia and beyond.

Bibliography

Stanley J. Samartha, Courage for Dialogue, Ecumenical Issues in Inter-religious Relationships, (Geneva: WCC, 1981)

Windows into Ecumenism: essays in honour of Ahn Jae Woong, Hong Kong, CCA, 2005

Towards the Sovereignty of the People, edited by CTC-CCA (Hong Kong: CCA, 1983).

Koshy, Ninan (ed.). A History of the Ecumenical Movement in Asia. (Hong kong: WSCFAP,APAY,CCA, 2004).

Thiagarajah, Daniel S and Longchar, A. Wati (eds.), Visioning New Life together among Asian Religions – The Third Congress of Asian Theologians (Hong Kong: CCA, 2002)

Manila to Colombo, The Christian Conference of Asia from 1990-1995 (Hong Kong: CCA, 1995)

PHILIP T.V Ecumenism in Asia, India: ISPCK & CSS, 1998

(19) Widening Christian Unity as a Challenge for Ecumenism in Asia

Hermen Shastri

The Enduring Ecumenical Task

The Ecumenical Movement has been an important force of church renewal because it has been guided by a vision of the unity of all God's people for the sake of the renewal of the human community.

Drawing inspiration from the words of Jesus during his farewell discourse to his disciples, he interceded; *"... That they may become completely one, so that the world may know that you have sent me...", (John 17:22-23 NRSV).* Those called to share in the vision of Christ see the call to unity not just as an option but as a gospel imperative, integral to what it means to be God's people in the world together.

Since the 20th century the ecumenical movement has gained momentum and given shape to church relations and mission in the world. The movement has been defined as a developing process in and among churches "by which Christian churches that have been separated by doctrinal, social, ethnic, political and institutional factors move toward cooperation and unity, by mutual understanding and respect through dialogue; by cooperation or common witness to whatever divine gifts and gospel values they already share and experience; and by a common search for that unity which the Lord wills for his one and only church". [1]

From an ecumenical perspective Christ's call to unity is animated and directed by the double thrust of what it means to be a church.

On the one hand the vision of unity has an enduring inter-ecclesial thrust. It calls the church to a constant review of its inner spiritual life to ensure that, in everything, it teaches, promotes and preserves the unity that Christ wills for his Church, which is the one holy Catholic and apostolic church. In this sense unity is to be celebrated as a "gift" endowed on the church by Christ and sustained by the work of the Holy Spirit. To that end the ecumenical movement has been a major factor in transforming the inherited self-understanding of the churches and their denominational and institutional identity in relation to the comprehensive ministry of the whole people of God in its multiple forms.

On the other, it has a dynamic missional outward thrust. It calls the church to critical reflection of its witness in the world. A divided church would have little to offer to a broken and fragmented world in urgent need of healing, reconciliation and peace. Indeed, the church can only be a sign and foretaste of God's redemptive and restorative intention for all humankind if it remains a relevant sign of God's uniting purpose in and for the world.[2]

Each Christian community lives among and for the sake of a wider human community. Bearing the ecumenical vision, churches seek to become viable communities of hope and healing, inclusive communities of sharing in solidarity, and peaceful communities which build and sustain relationships of reconciliation and mutual empowerment.

Ecumenism in Asia has always held this double thrust of unity as the church sought to be faithful in its witness, mission and service in a region richly endowed by great civilizations, living faiths and great cultural diversities.

From the time of its inception and later growth, the East Asia Christian Conference (EACC – 1957) and later the Christian Conference of Asia (CCA- 1973) realized that ecumenism in the region cannot be restricted to overcoming inter-confessional issues within the framework denominational divisions inherited

---

[1] Thomas F. Stransky, "*The Ecumencial Movement" in The HarperCollins Encyclopedia of Catholicism*, ed by Richard P. McBrien, New York, Harper Collins Publishers 1995, p 456

[2] Ibid. p. 457

from the West. It had to find ways to be relevant and faithful to the diverse contexts of Asia and rethink the relationships of unity and diversity as well as the interaction of the global and local in expressing the ecumenical vision.

What Constitutes the Wider Unity of Asian Ecumenism?

The term wider unity, or wider ecumenism, has been used by many to describe a larger constellation of actors on the ecumenical scene who may or may not be part of formal ecumenical structures and who view their contributions as transcending traditional notions ecclesial organic unity. As has been observed:

> Since the rapid decolonization of the world after the Second World War, the traditional Christian heartland, which in 1948 had embraced the local churches of the North Atlantic, Eastern Europe and Mediterranean areas, is fading in its dominant influence over the Southern Hemisphere. The local churches in Africa, Asia, the Caribbean, Latin America, and Oceania are becoming their own subjects of theological articulations, personal and social ethical stances, spiritualities, church disciplines, and interchurch cooperation in common witness. These new centers do not accept without question the ecumenical priorities of renewal, mission, and unity that are based on the historical experience of church divisions: East and West, and later in the West, The Roman Catholic Church and the churches that issue from the Reformations[2]

The unfolding wider unity that has been part of ecumenical discourse in Asia from the beginning continues to mirror the interplay of different forces that are affecting both converging and diverging understandings of ecumenism.

"The People of God Among all God's Peoples: Frontiers in Christian Mission" was the theme of a significant theological roundtable discussion that was organized by the CCA and the Council of World Mission in 1999. The theme reflects in very clear terms the double thrust of the search of Christian unity that characterizes the Asian journey.

The final report makes bold assertions: "*Despite all that still divides us, we dare to speak of our "common witness"* a witness in unity and solidarity with all humankind. Aware of our individual and institutional weaknesses and of the many compromises of our mission that we have made and accepted in the past, but conscious also of the power of God, 'who is strong when we are weak,' we as Orthodox, Protestant and Catholic Christians – reaffirm our commitment to move beyond confessional differences and the social barriers of our own making, as we accept with joy the mission of active faith which Jesus Christ bequeathed to his disciples. In this way, we can understand ourselves to be the people of God among all God's peoples." [3]

As was succinctly put by early pioneers in Asian ecumenism:

> the fact must be faced that while in the west the churches drew up their historic confessions and adopted their various forms of church order in the light of the controversies that took place within the church and within Christendom, the confessional need of the churches in Asia is primarily in relation to their mission to the world. Issues for them do not so much concern those things in which the churches differ from one another as those things which Christians together must confess before the world.[4]

---

[3] Philip L. Wickeri (ed), Report from a Theological Roundatable sponsored by Christian Conference of Asia and the Council of World Mission, November 11-17, 1999 Hong Kong: Christian Conference of Asia 2000 p. 53

[4] U Kyaw Tha, "Some features of the Asian Ecumenical Movement", in CTC Bulletin Vol XXVII, No 1, June 2011, Chiang Mai, Christian Conference of Asia p.6

The assertion made here reflects in substance what has been said and well-documented by the early Asian ecumenical visionaries, CCA assemblies and the various conferences and consultations held over the years.[5]

One significant historical station in articulating the wider unity the churches in Asia came from the EACC Faith and Order Consultation in Hong Kong in 1966. It took up precisely the meaning of *"Confessing the Faith in Asia today."* It said,

> The purpose and power of God need to be discerned as well within as outside the church; as well in those movements of the Holy Spirit that are working for the unity and richness of the Church, as in those developments within the life of the nations through which the Holy Spirit is seeking to build a life of unity and abundance for the world. That is why Christians need to listen to those outside the churches as they speak about the life, its meaning and its possibilities, so that out of such listening may come a greater understanding of faith itself. To confess Christ is to point to Him wherever He is at work and follow Him in whatever He is doing.[6]

In the course of Asian ecumenical history churches discovered that where Christ is at work is precisely among the poor and the oppressed. Unless a strong solidarity exists with the struggles of the least, the last, and the powerless people of Asia, the Gospel message will not touch the people at the deepest level of transformative action. Expressing ecumenical solidarity with the suffering peoples of Asia became a defining feature of Asian ecumenism.[7]

Essential characteristics of *"costly unity"* in solidarity with the poor and oppressed include a common basis of faith in the way of the cross; a full commitment to bearing one another's burdens, a commitment to justice; the responsible use of earth's resources; sharing resources for the common good; and the pursuit of peace-building by a commitment to non-violence.

It is, therefore, no surprise to note that the many programmes organized by the EACC/CCA sought to bring to the table reflections and discourses from representatives of a wide variety of churches and movements to address the urgent and pressing issues of social injustice in many parts of Asia.

The oft quoted vision of the ecumenical movement articulated by the renowned former General Secretary of the EACC is a case in point. When enquired about the relationship of churches to the wider movements working for the renewal of society, D.T. Niles had this to say:

> The heart of the solution to this problem lies in building up within the life of each country a group of men and women, both older and younger, who are willing to probe the frontiers of the Christian enterprise. The Churches as institutions are geared more to conserving the gains of the past than attempting the tasks of the future. The necessity, therefore, is for the churches to have frontiersmen who are willing, as it were, to venture into unchartered territory, whether of thought or action or organization, and to risk the mistakes that kind of adventure demands. To give to these frontiersmen a sense of solidarity encouragement and sharpened insight is a prime concerns for such an organization as the EACC.[8]

---

[5] Refer to discussions of the meaning of wider ecumenism in Ninan Koshy, A History of the Ecumenical Movement in Asia, Vol.1, Hong Kong, WSCFAPR/APAYMCA/CCA, 2004: pg 348ff

[6] As cited in M.M.Thomas, *Christian Action in Asian Struggles*, EACC 5th Assembly Addresses, Singapore: Christian Conference of Asia 1973. P5

[7] For a fuller treatment of such issues see, Feliciano V. Carino and Marina True (ed), *Faith and Life in Contemporary Asian Realities*, Report of the Asia Conference on Church and Society of the CCA. Darwin Sept. 23-30, 1999, Hong Kong: Christian Conference of Asia 2000

[8] D.T. Niles, *Ideas and Services, A report of the East Asia Christian Conference 1957-1967*, Christchurch: New Zealand National Council of Churches, 2968, p7

There is no better definition of the wider unity of Asian ecumenism than this prophetic stance of promoting solidarity on the broadest level for the genuine transformation of human society inspired and driven by the vision of the Kingdom of God.

CCA – A *"Conferencing"* Instrument in Service of the Wider Unity

It is significant to note that renaming the EACC as the CCA took place at an Assembly that met in Singapore under the theme: "*Christian Action in the Asian struggle.*"

The delegates voted overwhelmingly for the word "*Conference",* implying an openness and a lesser insistence on bureaucratic ecclesial structures. No strategies for common witness and mission that did not embrace the total people of God, and especially the powerless and marginalized of Asian societies, can contribute to an authentic unity that will speak relevantly to the Asian people. [9]

It should be noted that the Constitution of the CCA states its purpose as follows: "Believing that the purpose of God for the church in Asia is life together in a common obedience to Him for the doing of His Will in the World, the Christian Conference of Asia (formerly the East Asia Christian Conference) exists as an organ of continuing co-operation among the churches and national Christian bodies in Asia within the framework of the wider ecumenical movement." The use of the term "wider ecumenical movement" implied that CCA would not set itself up as a "super church" but rather as a body that would give expression to a variety of voices from all over Asia with as agenda the social transformation of societies on the basis of justice, peace and the integrity of God's creation. In that sense CCA would be a "movement among movements" for social change.

It is significant to note that Asia is able to pride itself in having a number of "united churches" which came about through "Faith and Order" negotiations and organic restructuring. Some of these churches claim the historic episcopate, namely, the Church of South India, the Church of North India, the Church of Pakistan and the Church of Bangladesh, while others, such as the Philippine Independent Church, Church of Christ, Thailand, Kyodan of Japan and the China Christian Council, have come about as a result of other factors.[10]

Seeking Unity Within the Framework of the Wider Ecumenical Movement

The following are a sampling of "*some*" of the ecumenical partnerships that the "*conferencing*" body of CCA has forged over the years to enrich and vitalize the work of CCA.

(a) Drawing insights from national ecumenical forums

Unlike the WCC the CCA includes as part of its constituent members the various National Councils of Churches that exist in the region.

---

[9] Refer to the speech of Goh Keng Swee, the Deputy Prime Minister of Singapore to the Assembly who cited justice for the poor as a central concern in Asia, as cited by Yap Kim Hao, "from Parapat to Colombo, History of the Christian Conference Of Asia (1957-1995) Hong Kong Christian Conference of Asia, 1995 p.62ff

[10] For an interesting reflections of the viability if united churches see, S. B Joshua – "The Future of the Ecumenical Movement L from the Perspective of a member of a United Church", in Thomas Best & Gunther Gassmann (ed) "On the way to fuller Koinonia, official report of the fifth World Conference on Faith and Order", Geneva: WCC publications 1994: p 146ff

Most of the National Councils (NCC) found their impetus and inspiration from the call to unity that ensued from the 1910 Edinburgh Missionary Conference. Asian church leaders soon realized that unity should be a national project first, before it could become a global one.[11]

The NCC became an experiment in searching for "wider unity" as it managed to incorporate churches and Christian organizations that were not formal members of the World Council of Churches, or, for theological reasons, wished to maintain some distance so as to be identified with the global ecumenical movement.

Furthermore, the Councils were driven by contextual considerations as they committed themselves to a national fellowship in order to manifest unity in the respective countries, where Christians often found themselves to be a minority community.

The NCCs participation in the CCA provided the Asian ecumenical movement with a rich reservoir of talent and expertise to foster collaborative ventures. It also provided an ecumenical network that connected CCA to church leaders from a broad spectrum of churches and organizations. They also served to infuse justice issues in ecumenical discourse, many arising from national struggles dealing with a host of human rights issues. [12]

(b) CCA-Roman Catholic ecumenical collaboration

Although great strides in ecumenical openness and commitment of the Roman Catholic Church took place after the Second Vatican Council, relations with the various Protestant confessional families were only robust within the formal structures of Faith and Order of the WCC and the bilateral confessions initiated by the Vatican.

In many parts of Asia, there was an apparent lack of ecumenical collaboration both nationally and regionally.

Things began to change from the early 1990s. The CCA leadership deliberated on finding ways to initiate conversations which led to closer ecumenical ties with its Catholic regional counterpart of the Federation of Bishops' Conferences of Asia (FABC)

In 1993 the first formal gathering of church leaders and theologians was held in Hua Hin, Thailand, receiving a warm reception. By the second gathering in 1996 on Cheung Chau Island, Hong Kong, the 42 participants representing both the CCA and FABC were bold enough to initiate an Asian Movement for Christian Unity (AMCU).

The basis of the ecumenical fellowship between CCA and FABC was meant to be "contextual with a pastoral thrust", meaning fostering collaboration on common causes of concern to the Asian people. It was not meant to be a formal Faith and Order structure in Asia. Ecumenical conversations to deal with doctrinal divisions were left to the Pontifical Council for the promotion of Christian Unity, housed at the Vatican.

The Asian Movement for Christian Unity held the vision that collaboration was greatly needed in three areas, namely;

> a) Asian churches need new ways of theologizing which should be inspired by the specific context and needs of Asia, common workshops should be organized for theologizing in Asia.
>
> b) Collaboration among the seminaries theological colleges, faculties and institutes is absolutely necessary for the ecumenical education of future pastors and priests. Joint programmes, exchange of teachers and resources

[11] In Asia we have 16 NCCs: from earliest to the latest they are: (India (1914), Myanmar (1914/1949), Sri Lanka (1914), Pakistan (1914/1948), Bangladesh 1914/1949), Korea (1924), the Philippines (1929/1949,1963), Malaysia (1947), Singapore (1948/1961, 1974),Indonesia 91950), Australia (1948/1960/1994), Taiwan (1966/1991), Japan (1948), Hong Kong (1954), Cambodia 91998), Nepal (1999)

[12] For an interesting evaluation of the role of NCCs within the wider ecumenism see, the Ecumenical review, Vol. 4.5, Number 3, July 1993, Geneva: World Council of Churches

have to be encouraged. In teaching theological subjects, their ecumenical aspects and implications must be highlighted.

c) A course on Ecumenism should be compulsory in seminaries and theological faculties. It should cover the history and traditions of all churches, the history of the ecumenical movement, contemporary ecumenical discussions, and the emerging doctrinal convergence among churches. The BEM document must be an essential part of the curriculum.[13]

As succeeding AMCU gatherings were held, many of the envisioned collaboration took shape with such activities as the CCA FABC Asia Ecumenical Committee, Congresses of Asian Theologians, Asia Ecumenical Courses and the ecumenical gathering of Seminary students.

Such ecumenical encounters have inspired some Catholic Bishops to participate more fully in NCCs or initiate the creation of new national ecumenical forums that widened the ecumenical fellowships.

(c) Contacts with the Asian Evangelical Fellowship

Evangelicals are made up of Protestant church traditions and individual Christians in mainstream Protestant denominations who see themselves as championing less formal ecumenical structures in order that the central truths of the Christian faith are not clouded by accommodations that dissipate the evangelization thrust of the churches.

They associate the ecumenical movement with the implicit goal of a "super-church" and the broadening of the ecumenical agenda, giving birth to theologies displacing the urgency of the propagations of the faith with other social causes calling for greater social justice in societies.

Yet the common use of "evangelical" and "ecumenical" as mutually exclusive does not apply in many parts of Asia. As pointed our earlier there are many churches and evangelical-based organizations, which relate to NCCs and other national forums, who see no need to formalize relations with the WCC.

CCA has sought to relate with the Evangelical Fellowship of Asia (EFA) in a less formal way of working "*towards exploration, mutual understanding and the appreciation of differences.*"[14]

To this end, evangelical leaders are also invited to participate in the conferences organized at the CCA-FABC level.

It is significant to note that, with the advent of the Global Forum (GFC) from 1998 onwards, a new platform that broadens the ecumenical fellowship to embrace Catholics, Orthodox, Protestants, Evangelicals, Pentecostals and Charismatic churches was initiated.

With periodical regional and global gatherings taking place from 2002 onwards, it became clear to those participating and representing such a diverse gamut of Christianity that the "fellowship" (as opposed to a formal institution like WCC) was mutually enriching as it fostered a new breath of ecumenical encounters. Till this day, the GCF remains independent from any and all formal ecumenical structures and only exists to nurture an *"inclusive network of relationships"*.[15]

The WCC and the CCA have participated in this "*wider unity*" endeavour and see in it the potential to bridge ecumenical gaps with churches and groups who remain hostile to institutional structures of ecumenism globally or regionally.

---

[13] Confer, *Our Pilgrimage in Hope, Proceedings of the first there seminars of the Asian Movement for Christian Unity*, Hong Kong: The Christian Conference of Asia, 2001

[14] See General Committee of the CCA Minutes 13-16 May 2002 (Taiwan), Hong Kong: Christian Conference of Asia, pg 59

[15] For more details of the history of the Global Christian Forum see Richard Howell (ed), *Global Christian Forum-transforming Ecumenism*, New Delhi: Evangelical Fellowship of India 2007

(d) Contacts with inter-faith movements in Asia

It has often been argued that Christian unity has to do with overcoming suspicions and doctrinal differences among churches. Asian Christians involved in ecumenism in Asia, however, are ready to point out that "*human solidarity*" encompasses other faith communities that share their life space together and in many ways challenge churches to relate meaningfully to other truth claims and spiritualities predating Christianity.

Furthermore, Asian Christianity is often viewed by other faith traditions as translated on to Asian soil via the colonial and neo-colonial influence and history of invasions of Western powers. In an attempt to "*de-Westernize*" Christianity, Churches in Asia seek to nurture an ecumenical spiritual tradition that does not antagonize or denigrate other faith traditions.

In building peace within the framework of the peaceful co-existence of various faith traditions, Asian ecumenism has insisted that "*wider unity*" also involves mutual respect and dialogue with interfaith movements in Asia.[16]

The CCA has been involved in various interfaith organizations so as to foster such relations and seek collaboration to address some of the pressing social issues in Asia such as poverty eradication, discrimination of marginalized communities, gender justice, and people living with HIV/AIDS among others.

Realizing that all the great living faith traditions are present in Asia, the specific contribution that Asian churches can bring to global ecumenism is its interfaith theologies that are informed by centuries of co-existence, interaction, and shared wisdom among the different faith communities.

The Task Ahead – Finding the Way Together

In his final report to the General Committee of CCA, Dr. Feliciano V. Carino, a veteran Asian ecumenist and former General Secretary of the CCA, put forward some concerns he felt would shape ecumenical endeavours in the future.[17]

He emphasized the need for ecumenical life and leadership to develop the capacity *"to receive and give creative sense of this wider theological and ecclesiological range"* as to what it means to be a church in Asia. This is because in Asia being a church involves a multiplicity of diverse manifestations of theological and ecclesiological traditions and confessional positions.

To work towards a cohesive ecumenical vision would involve a constant appraisal of the quality of the fellowship of churches. The concept of "Koinonia" as participating, sharing and manifesting the pattern of communion as in the relational unity of the divine Trinity seems to provide a relevant theological basis for the goal of unity in Asia.

Second, he pointed out that "a greater multiplicity and plurality of religious claims towards the remaking and reordering of the social order that could lead to a proliferation of already numerous religious and ethnic conflict, or the greater appreciation of the meaning of plurality," would remain an indelible task in peace making in Asia. How do we appropriate shared wisdom and share universal values from other faiths in such a way that does not dilute our own faith distinctions. The global ethic espousal by the Parliament of World religion (Do to others as you would have others do to you) has great support among Asian religious leaders. The way of ecumenical unity in this sense can be understood as a commitment to

---

[16] For example, CCA co-organised an Asian Religious Leaders Conference under the theme: *"Be Peacemakers in Asia Today"* 12-16 November 2007 in Chiangmai, Thailand. One of the crucial recommendations was the setting-up of an Asian Interfaith Network for Justice and Peace. CCA continues to participate in collaborative meetings with other interfaith partners throughout the different parts of Asia.

[17] Confer, Report of the General Secretary in Minutes of the Executive Committee of the CCA, Hong Kong SAR, China, 30th Nov-1st Dec, 2000, p 23ff

human solidarity and social liberation; just peace and reconciliation constitute primary ingredients of the human aspirations of our time.

Third, he pleaded for "*an earnest desire for ecumenical formation.*" In order to raise a new generation of church leaders who would tackle unity and renewal as a primary challenge and vocation worthy of their fullest devotion would very much depend on finding creative ways to promote and sustain ecumenism.

Would ecumenism survive without a structure that had been in place for so long and is shunned by a new generation of leaders who view institutional ecumenism as debilitating and outdated? Do we really believe what we say about ecumenical structures being provisional, destined to be transformed for the sake of the unity movement it seeks to advance?

It is here that impulses from "*wider ecumenism and unity*" call for a formation to take place beyond traditional ecumenical structures.

In the final analysis ecumenism is not a matter of programmes, structures or activities; it is primarily a way of being Church. It is that set of perspectives on faith, that quality of relationships with other Christians, that openness to others, within which we are called to wrestle with the fundamental question of obedience and seek together the vision needed to put our respective churches, communities and world in order.

It is this gospel of God's outreaching love that should nurture our churches and inspire them to reach out so as to overcome what still divides them.

The unity of God's people among the peoples of God is the creative work of the Holy Spirit in all times and in all places. Are we ready to embrace the new challenges of the wider ecumenism?

Bibliography

Antone, Hope S. (ed.) *Life Together: Memories and dreams*, Chiang Mai: Christian Conference of Asia 2010

Chunkara, Matthew George, "A Survey of the Ecumenical Scenario in Asia: Prospects and Challenges", CTC Bulletin, Vol XXII, No.2, August 2006, Chiangmai, CCA

Koshy, Ninan, *A History of the Ecumenical Movement in Asia, Vol I*, Hong Kong: WSCFAP,APAY,CCA, 2004

Philip, T.V., *Ecumenism in Asia*, India: ISPCK & CSS, 1998

(20) Widening Christian Unity: An Evangelical and Pentecostal Perspective

Adonis Abelard O. Gorospe

Introduction

In 1985 to 1987, a young American Methodist layperson by the name of John R. Mott went on a world tour that included the countries of Ceylon, India, China, and Japan and brought to Asia an ecumenical movement that is centered on Jesus Christ.[1] This ecumenical movement took root in Asian soil fostered by the struggle of Asian nations for political independence,[2] pioneered by Asian students associated with the World Student Christian Federation,[3] and aided by the efforts of Mott.[4] The Asian contribution to the growth of the ecumenical movement in Asia lies in the pioneering work of Christ's Asian ambassadors from Japan, China, India, and Ceylon,[5] and the cooperative effort of Asian ecumenical leaders through the East Asia Christian Conference,[6] a body constituted by churches, national councils of churches and Christian councils at Prapat, Indonesia in 1957. Today, under the name, Christian Conference of Asia (CCA), this body, together with the Federation of Asian Bishops' Conferences of the Roman Catholic Church (FABC), forms the Asian Ecumenical Committee that founded the Asian Movement for Christian Unity and monitors activities and programmes in the field of ecumenical formation.[7]

Recent Positive Perspectives for Asian Ecumenism

In recent years, the outlook for the growth of the ecumenical movement in Asia is hopeful given current positive developments. These include the growth of ecumenical awareness in the Roman Catholic Church leading to a less polemic stance,[8] the unprecedented hosting of the Third Global Christian Forum by a Pentecostal Church, the Yoido Full Gospel Church, at Seoul, South Korea in November 2010,[9] and the inclusion of the Evangelical Fellowship of Asia in the Asian Movement for Christian Unity in 2007.[10]

Challenges from other Churches to Evangelicals and Pentecostals

The continuing growth of Asian ecumenical awareness, however, is not without its challenges. For one, the Pontifical Council for Promoting Christian Unity mentions prevailing negative attitudes that are exhibited by the Roman Catholics themselves towards Evangelicals which include persistent fear, suspicion and

---

[1] Hans-Ruedi Weber, *Asia and the Ecumenical Movement 1895-1961* (Bloomsbury Street, London: SCM Press, 1966), 16-17.
[2] Ibid., 30.
[3] Ibid., 54-55. See also pp. 69-90.
[4] Ibid., 68.
[5] Ibid., 251-276.
[6] Ibid., 27-292.
[7] http://oukoumene.org/memeber-churches/regions/asia/cca.html.
[8] See "Ecumenism Today: The Situation in the Catholic Church," A document of the Pontifical Council for Promoting Christian Unity, Presented by Bishop Brian Farrell, in http://www.vatican.va/roman_curia/pontifical_councils/chrstuni/documents/rc_pc_chrstuni_doc_20041121_farrell-ecumenismo_en.html.
[9] http://www.worldevangelicals.org/news/article.htm?id=3282&cat=main.
[10] http://oukoumene.org/memeber-churches/regions/asia/cca.html.

mistrust because of the use of media and public campaigns to criticize Catholic doctrines and bring up negative situations to attack the Church. The memory of past negative historical events, both recent and remote, in fact poses a crucial challenge to ecumenical relations. Some believe that ecumenism weakens the evangelizing mission and the faith of the Church. Finally, newer Evangelical and Pentecostal communities are considered sects and not true Ecclesial Communities.[11]

Not all the negative attitudes are on the Catholic side. The Pontifical Council for Christian Unity also points to "a non-recognition of the Christian character of Catholics by some Evangelical and Pentecostal groups" as one of the perceived hindrances to Christian unity, especially in Latin America.[12] In this author's own experience, this holds true for Asia as well, especially in areas, like the Philippines, for example, where Roman Catholics on one hand, and both Evangelicals and Pentecostals on the other, have had a long history of polemics and proselytism.

Because many Pentecostals are also part of the Evangelical movement, both Evangelicals and Pentecostals tend to share many Evangelical traditions. This includes similar positions toward ecumenism. In this study, then, I would not be treating the challenges posed by both Evangelicals and Pentecostals to the growth of ecumenical awareness separately. I would also reflect on how such challenges maybe surmounted by fostering a more inclusive attitude among Evangelicals and Pentecostals toward those who do not share a similar tradition with them.

Evangelical and Pentecostal Challenges to Ecumenism

Protestantism was a reform movement whose concern was the church and not the world. Consequently, Protestantism did not originally foster a missionary concern. Several people's movements within the church engendered and shaped its missionary zeal. Pietism, the spiritual movement within the German Lutheran State Church, sparked the formation of mission-minded societies in England and Denmark.[13] One particularly mission-oriented group of Pietism, the Moravian Brethren, encountered John Wesley when he travelled to North America and this eventually led to the Evangelical Awakening in England.[14] The Evangelical Awakening in Wesley's time prepared the way for William Carey and the modern missionary movement.[15] The missionary impetus begun by Carey fostered cooperation between missionaries and gave rise to the world missionary movement, the broadly attended missionary conferences in many regions of the world, and the world student movement.[16] "It is not surprising that the ecumenical movement evolved from the world missionary movement."[17] Pietism, the Protestant missionary movement, movements of cooperation, and the student movement all shared one undying concern – the mandate to pursue the unfinished missionary obligation. The missionary and ecumenical movements originate from these common roots.[18]

One of the distinctives of Evangelicalism is its emphasis on the urgency of the church's missionary task. Thus, it can be said that Evangelicalism shares something in common with the ecumenical movement. Despite the Evangelical antecedents of the modern ecumenical movement, however, Evangelicalism continues to be wary of the growth of ecumenism.

---

[11] See "Ecumenism Today" in footnote 9.
[12] Ibid.
[13] "Evangelical and Ecumenical Antecedents," http://www.ichenetwork.net/P1_P4.pdf, 1-2.
[14] Ibid., 3.
[15] Ibid.
[16] Ibid., 7-12.
[17] Ibid., 8.
[18] "Evangelical and Ecumenical Antecedents," 12.

In a book published in 1957, the same year that the East Asia Christian Conference was founded, J. Marcellus Kik has already expressed the apprehensions that Evangelicals have concerning the ecumenical movement. The first of these apprehensions has to do with the way ecumenism is defined. There are two nuances that the proponents of the ecumenical movement have given to the Greek word *oikoumene.* The first refers to the "fostering of good relations among existing Christian churches, manifesting their fundamental agreement, and stressing their spiritual unity" while retaining each of their distinctive "polity, worship, and creed."[19] The second nuance refers to the bringing of the Church of Christ "into an empirical existence," i.e., the embodiment of the un-embodied Church of Christ, making it visible as a "comprehensive organization under" the "control of a hierarchy or council."[20] In opposition to these two nuances, Evangelicals affirm the New Testament understanding of unity as the "unity of faith and of the knowledge of the Son of God unto the measure of the stature of the fullness of Christ." Though Evangelicals do not discount the need for organization and the effort to work together for the common good without losing one's distinct confession, they do believe that unity does not come from federal union nor from one visible organization but from the mystical union with Christ.[21]

Another apprehension of Evangelicals regarding ecumenism is the latter's alleged tendency to present Christ as less than what the Scriptures present him to be. In place of the ecumenist's formula, "our Lord Jesus Christ as God and Saviour," Evangelicals demand a more explicit statement of Christ as "the second person of the Trinity, God-incarnate, Son of the living God, virgin born, Head of the Church, and Lord of the nations."[22]

Evangelicals are also disconcerted by what they perceive to be the efforts of ecumenists to depreciate theology in order to achieve unity, harmony, and peace through the development of a common church structure. For Evangelicals, only the development of distinctive theological doctrines based on the truth revealed in the Scriptures serve to unify rather than separate large numbers of people.[23]

Other misgivings by Evangelicals concerning the ecumenical movement include the ecumenists' perceived tendency to seek union by tolerating a wide variety of beliefs, some of which the Evangelicals consider to be unwarranted by Scripture,[24] the emphasis on the church as one visible institution versus the church as one company of believers forming the invisible Body of Christ, and the fear of the extension of clerical control as a result of a centrally controlled ecclesiastical organization.[25]

In a more recent publication, Esther Byle Bruland relates the testimony of Richard Mouw concerning his involvement in ecumenical relations. Mouw expresses some of the concerns articulated by Kik. These include the concern for Biblical teaching and the concern over the way the ecumenical movement reformulates theology for the sake of organizational unity. Mouw finds that involvement as an individual in ecumenical dialogue is far more comfortable for him than working for organizational unity.[26]

In a related story, Bruland narrates the story of a Pentecostal who aired the same misgiving as Kik regarding the ecumenical emphasis on the visibility of the church versus the Pentecostal teaching of the invisible church as well as the concern over the compromise of doctrinal distinctions.[27]

---

[19] J. Marcellus Kik, *Ecumenism and the Evangelical* (Philadelphia, Pennsylvania: The Presbyterian and Reformed Publishing Company, 1957), 3.
[20] Ibid.
[21] Ibid., 4 and 9.
[22] Ibid., 11.
[23] *Ecumenism and the Evangelical*, 13.
[24] Ibid., 14-15.
[25] Ibid., 16-17.
[26] Esther Byle Bruland, *Regathering: The Church from "They" to "We"* (Grand Rapids, Michigan: William B. Eerdmans Publishing Company, 1995), 44-45.
[27] Ibid., 45-46.

Two Evangelicals reiterated the emphasis on Scripture as the foundation for unity among Christians.[28]

Not all the objections, however, revolve around the key doctrines of the Scripture, the church and the basis of Christian unity.

Bishop Cesar Vicente P. Punzalan III, a bishop of the Baptist General Conference serving in the Philippines, believes that Evangelicals in the Philippines focus everything on the work of savings souls, thinking this to be the most important task of all. This narrow focus is often based on the belief that the Lord is coming soon.[29] Because of this focus, Evangelicals are not as interested in forming ecumenical partnerships with non-Evangelicals.

Dick O. Eugenio, a theologian of the Nazarene Church teaching at the Asia-Pacific Nazarene Theological Seminary, also in the Philippines, says, "The term *partnership* is probably what's putting others off. Partnership entails the ascription of equal status between parties, and some Evangelicals might think that they have more to offer to non-Evangelicals, i.e. the latter is just a recipient, not a conversation partner that can offer something valuable to the former."[30]

In this author's experience, most Evangelicals and Pentecostals tend to look at Catholics as people needing salvation. Hence, for them, evangelism, not ecumenism, is the preferred approach in dealing with Catholics.

Fostering Ecumenical Awareness in Asia

Bishop Punzalan thinks that the spiritual and moral transformation of a nation is beyond the scope and capacity of Evangelicals alone. Engaging in dialogue and participation in ecumenical endeavours will contribute to the transformation of a community and a nation. Most ecumenical endeavours focus on the issue of the lack of social peace, the lack of public justice, the lack of righteousness among national leaders and the lack of economic sufficiency for the masses which often result in religious extremism. There are so many issues that Christians of different traditions can work on together, for example, spiritual transformation in the public square and in the marketplace, and the advocacy for better ecological stewardship. Evangelicals do not have a monopoly on the best answers to these questions. Often, Evangelical spirituality is very much uninvolved and private. It is high time for Evangelicals to stop turning their backs and engage.[31]

Nazarene Church theologian Dick Eugenio believes that "the church is One, and dialogue with our brothers and sisters in the One Catholic church should be considered as an essential aspect of our Christian faith and life."[32]

How could ecumenical unity be widened further?

The Pontifical Council for Promoting Christian Unity suggests several avenues by which the goal for Christian unity may be pursued. First, the impact of increasing globalization forces Christians in all Churches to pay more attention to "spiritual ecumenism – conversion of mind and heart to Christ, joint prayer for unity." Second, the work of ecumenism needs to be pursued in three areas: the development of "organic pastoral programs" on the local level, the "ecumenical education" of church members and leaders,

---

[28] Ibid., 50, 59.

[29] In response to the emailed survey question, "What are some of the objections Evangelicals have against forming ecumenical partnerships with non-Evangelicals?", dated April 19, 2012, 6:27 P.M.

[30] In response to the emailed survey question, "What are some of the objections Evangelicals have against forming ecumenical partnerships with non-Evangelicals?", dated April 24, 2012, 10:27 A.M.

[31] In response to the emailed survey question, "Should Evangelicals partner with non-Evangelicals in ecumenical endeavors?", dated April 19, 2012, 6:27 P.M.

[32] In response to the emailed survey question, "Should Evangelicals partner with non-Evangelicals in ecumenical endeavors?", dated April 24, 2012, 10:27 A.M.

and the response to the problem of proselytizing. Third, "ecumenism can only be promoted on a solid doctrinal basis, on serious dialogue between divided Christians." Lastly, "the work of unity can flourish only within a deep and convincing spirituality, a spirituality of Christian hope and courage."[33]

The Pentecostal emphasis on the work of the Spirit seems to prepare the way for the development of a greater experience of Christian unity.[34]

Seeing oneself as the obstacle to Christian communion and acknowledging it before God tends to diminish the suspicions that Evangelicals have toward ecumenism.[35]

Margaret O'Gara, a Roman Catholic ecumenical scholar, suggests that the development of deep friendship between ecumenical scholars and colleagues help the development of ecumenism in three ways. First, it sets the context for ecumenism by revealing and sustaining collaboration in ecumenical work. Second, it enables the improved understanding of one another's positions. Last, it fosters the necessary perseverance leading to the success of the ecumenical work.[36]

Amos Yong proposes three ways for Pentecostals to be more ecumenically aware. First, they need to educate themselves. Second, they need to be more intentional about meeting with other Christians. Third, they need to plan inter-congregational activities centred around worship, prayer, and the reading and exploration of Scripture. Yong exhorts:

> As Pentecostals, we need to ask ourselves what the Holy Spirit is doing in the world (Rev. 2-3, passim). As people led by the Spirit, how can we discern what God is doing in the Church and how that work affects the Church's witness to the world? The world has seen enough denominational strife, abstract theological speculation, futile doctrinal disputes, and Christian polemics. What the world needs is the love of God. Pentecostals, more than others, should know what it means to have been touched by the love of God in ways that while not marginalizing theology and doctrine, certainly do not exalt its place either. And, far beyond intellectual activity, Pentecostals emphasize the empowerment of the Holy Spirit for mission. ... So, the question that remains is this: what is the Holy Spirit doing to break down the barriers between Christians, and how can we as Pentecostals be involved in this essential task of taking the love of God to the world?[37]

In response to the question, "Would there be possible ways that will allow Evangelicals to partner with non-Evangelicals in ecumenical endeavours?", Bishop Punzalan says,

> Evangelicals need to realize that we cannot live out our spirituality in isolation. We often claim we are the salt and light of the world but we often like to engage our saltiness and our light according to the narrow confines of our ecclesiological engagements. Our existence is often hijacked by the evangelism agenda, and it often lead us to embrace a hierarchical view of ecclesiology, that is, whatever is about saving souls is very much important than facing the structural evil of the lack of justice, the lack of social peace, the lack of national righteousness and the lack of economic sufficiency for most of our brethren.
>
> Ecumenical endeavours are not the magic pill for the social and spiritual ills of the land. But it is often the most strategic and right direction to go as a faith community in seeking the Shalom of our cities. When the drug menace strikes like crack or shabu at our communities (thanks to our porous borders, the war in Afghanistan that obliterated 80% of the supply of cocaine, and the abundance of the narcotic plant, epihedrine in China and Southeast Asia and the relatively easy manufacturing process) we ALL suffer and are greatly affected. The 26-30

---

[33] See "Ecumenism Today."
[34] *Regathering*, 71.
[35] Ibid., 75.
[36] Margaret O'Gara, "The Theological Significance of Friendship in the Ecumenical Movement," in That The World May Believe: Essays on Mission and Unity in Honour of George Vandervelde, Edited by Micahel W. Goheen and Margaret O'Gara (Lanham/Boulder/New York/Toronto/Oxford: University Press of America, 2006), 124, 127, 129.
[37] Amos Yong, "Pentecostalism and Ecumenism: Past, Present and Future," Pneuma Review (Winter 2002).

typhoons that hit the Philippines annually make no distinction of our religious colour, and come to think of it, ecumenism often does the heavy lifting in the relief, rehab and development ministry for those badly hit by these typhoons.

We will be wise to get into the bus of ecumenical endeavours.[38]

Dick Eugenio suggests dialogue as a way of widening ecumenical participation. He says that

> Evangelicals need to realize that we are not the only true Christians on earth. Even in the academia, theologians are realizing more and more that the Eastern Orthodox church has a lot of offer to our theology, as correctives and illumination. The beauty of a dialogue is that all participants gain something from each other. Everyone is both a speaker and a recipient.[39]

Corrie De Boer, a former faculty of Asian Theological Seminary and current regent of Bakke Graduate University, who has developed multiple ecumenical networking relationships with individuals and organizations in her work among the urban poor in the Philippines, suggests that

> More than just dialogues, there can be significant creative collaboration in ministering among the poor, bringing about peace and justice, caring for the earth, socio-economic and political transformation, leadership development, and other fields promoting the welfare of our society.[40]

Christian unity does not develop overnight nor does it come automatically. We need to work at it. Despite the legitimate objections of many Evangelicals and Pentecostals against forming ecumenical relationships, there are nevertheless persuasive grounds for us to do so. It is this author's hope that this brief study will help in some way to bring these ecumenical relationships into reality.

Bibliography

Esther Byle Bruland, *Regathering: The Church from "They" to "We"* (Grand Rapids, Michigan: William B. Eerdmans Publishing Company, 1995)

J. Marcellus Kik, *Ecumenism and the Evangelical* (Philadelphia, Pennsylvania: The Presbyterian and Reformed Publishing Company, 1957)

Margaret O'Gara, "The Theological Significance of Friendship in the Ecumenical Movement," in That The World May Believe: Essays on Mission and Unity in Honour of George Vandervelde, Edited by Micahel W. Goheen and Margaret O'Gara (Lanham/Boulder/New York/Toronto/Oxford: University Press of America, 2006), 124-129

Hans-Ruedi Weber, *Asia and the Ecumenical Movement 1895-1961* (Bloomsbury Street, London: SCM Press, 1966)

Amos Yong, "Pentecostalism and Ecumenism: Past, Present and Future," Pneuma Review (Winter 2002).

---

[38] Email response, April 19, 2012, 6:27 P.M.

[39] Email response, april 24, 2012, 10:27 A,M.

[40] Email response, april 19, 2012, 8:06 P.M.

(21) INTERROGATING ASIAN ECCLESIOLOGIES FOR A PURPOSEFUL THEOLOGICAL ENGAGEMENT FOR ASIAN ECUMENISM

Deenabandhu Manchala

A rich variety of themes have featured Asian theological reflection during the past several decades. Interfaith dialogue, inculturation, mission as struggles for justice, human rights, peace, and reconciliation, and against dictatorships, colonisation, and neo-colonisation; re-reading the bible through Asian eyes, and theologies in dialogue with the religious and cultural traditions, and peoples' struggles, such as Minjung theology, Dalit theology and feminist theology, tribal theology, etc., are a few to mention. In fact, many of these reflections have also inspired or contributed to theological reflections elsewhere.

However, one rarely gets to discern the consciousness of the reality of Asian churches in these theological articulations. To put it differently, theological reflection is often done without the church being its point of reference. This alienation between our theologians and seminaries on one hand and our churches on the other has allowed both to remain as they are without mutually challenging and changing. Although the scope of any creative theology is and ought to be the whole world, it is first addressed to the community of believers in order that the community becomes the sign and instrument of the vision that any theology upholds. This raises a fundamental question: Are our churches responding to the demands of contexts in which they are placed or they still engaged in outworn theological debates while uncritically imitating models of church life that have been worked out elsewhere?

This necessitates the need to take seriously the diverse and complex Asian ecclesial reality. Except for some churches in Kerala, India, the rest have their roots in European Christianity. Likewise, except in South Korea and the Philippines, Christians are small in number and are known by different western identities and forms of ecclesial life. Most of these are also composed of socially and economically disempowered sections, with very little or no public space at all, as fragmented minority communities, often in hostile contexts. While some churches are vibrant and flourishing, others are dwindling or existing as threatened communities hardly with any voice or visibility. While some have found their niche and identity in their own contexts, others are still rooted in their western ecclesiastical traditions. The phenomenon of an increasing number of post denominational ecclesial formations and the expansionist theologies that drive them, must also be taken into account.

Furthermore, we are also confronted with an enormous task of having to deal with a variety of notions, models and expressions of being church, emerging from different confessional traditions and geo-political situations. These may be summarized with the help of some imagery. 'For some, the church is like the Noah's ark with all the chosen on board while the rest are destined to the deluge. For others, the church is like a transit lounge with passengers waiting to be transported to another world. For those with higher degrees of Christian enthusiasm, the church is the foundation of the kingdom of God and hence, they take upon themselves the task of its expansion rather aggressively, often hurting the sentiments of those who belong to other faith traditions. For some, the church is like an asylum – a place or an event providing solace to those who are emotionally disturbed and are not otherwise confident of being morally responsible in their social behaviour or are assured of miraculous interventions. These notions are nurtured constantly through hymns and lyrics, liturgy, preaching, teaching, prayers, sacraments, forms of mission, evangelism and diakonia'.[1] The visible forms of the church too are complex. Those non-traditional churches tend to exist as exclusive religious communities, pre-occupied with the agenda of increasing their numbers and

---

[1] Deenabandhu Manchala, "Re-Visioning Ecclesia in the light of the Dalit Experience", a D. Th dissertation, Bangalore, SATHRI, 2001, p.2.

catering to the purely spiritual needs of their members, while the traditional churches assert their identities through liturgies, and operate as institutions with bureaucratic structures, mind-boggling constitutional procedures, and often, unfortunately, are driven by unchristian power dynamics. These are mostly managed by a privileged few – the urban, middle class, dominant caste, males whose value orientations shape an agenda, which is, by and large, confined to purely spiritual and ecclesiastical concerns, expansion, charity, and service.[2] In a social ethos where the priorities, values and norms of the dominant determine what is worthy and acceptable, these churches seem to deliberately ignore the fact that they are largely composed of the urban and rural poor, or exist in contexts of mass poverty.

On issues of justice, human rights, and public morality, most of these churches maintain neutral positions. While claiming to be open communities of faith, in many cases, these exist like narrow communities in terms of their social relationships.[3] Cultures of domination and discrimination, such as caste hierarchy, patriarchy, classism, rich-poor and urban-rural divide, and of consumerism and power-mongering seem to flourish in many churches. The implications of this ecclesiological ambiguity of Asian churches are embarrassing. In the words of Mar Osthathios, who quips after a survey of the structures of the Indian churches: "None of these has the marks of the kingdom of God, no implementation of the Nazareth manifesto, no *kenosis* of the incarnation, but caste-structures, class distinctions, authoritarianism, parochialism, self-centredness and denominational pride"[4].

These varied and complex expressions of the church in Asia not only make the identification of any one form as an adequate expression of the Christian faith difficult but also make the task of ecclesiological reformulation both complex and necessary. Searching for relevance is a sign of life, an indication of the urge to set things right in order to make sense to the people within and outside. The Church consists always of people in concrete situations of life. Therefore, there is a need to continuously search for authenticity and credibility and for constant reformulation and reformation. Hence, the adage: *ecclesia semper reformanda*. The church, therefore, though a theological idea, is essentially a social reality. As a social institution with concrete historical beings as its members, the empirical church is influenced by its context which includes cultural and ideological moorings, experiences of the community, identities of the people and their social and economic locations. Much of what we have as theologies of the church in Asia are influenced by theologies that made sense to a distinct people in a different context of time and space. A conference organized by the Christian Conference of Asia on "Tradition and Innovation: A search for a relevant ecclesiology in Asia" in Kandy, Sri Lanka in 1982 said, "The basic problem with many of the inherited ecclesiologies from the west is their lack of wholeness. For instance, they were hierarchy-oriented and bourgeois in values, and heavily weighted with Christian triumphalism. A basic concern for the poor and the need was usually absent. Absent too was the kenotic or self-emptying lifestyle which Jesus Christ typified. The inherited ecclesiologies that exhibit these shortcomings were labeled as partial ecclesiologies as opposed to a holistic ecclesiology which would not only carry the "right" emphases but would be undergirded by a holistic theology that is both historical and eschatological, vertical and horizontal, personal and social, spiritual and political, and in solidarity with the poor."[5] Therefore, the sociological categories of context, people and their collective experiences need to be the lens and instruments for any theological or ecclesiological exploration seeking to be relevant. No one would deny the extent of contextualisation that has already taken place. But what needs to be investigated is the nature and extent of

---

[2] Cf. Felix Wilfred talks about the aberrations in the Indian Church life, though from a Roman catholic view point. "Temptations of the Church in India Today", *Vidyajyothi*, Vol.XLVII:7, pp. 320-333.

[3] Ninan Koshy, *Caste in Kerala Churches*, Bangalore, CISRS, 1968, p.84.

[4] Geevarghese Mar Osthathios, "A Critical Evaluation of Our Inherited Ecclesiologies and Present Practices", *Heritage and Mission, New Frontiers of the Church in Kerala: Ecclesiological Study Project,* ed. by P.T. Thomas, et al., *Manganam, Kerala*, Kerala Council of Churches, 1989, p.71.

[5] *Tradition and Innovation: A search for a relevant ecclesiology in Asia*, ed.by, CTC-CCA, Singapore, 1983, p.14.

the processes of contextualisation, to whom have these forms of contextualization been relevant, and in what significant ways have they enriched the meaning of the life of the Church.

Dr. Ambedkar, one of the greatest social reformers of India, once said that the social vision of any religion is its most validating principle. Ernst Troeltsch too in his *Social Teachings of the Christian Churches* wrote: 'The key to understanding Christian faith lay in understanding its practical social expressions'[6]. Perhaps it may be difficult to hold any empirical church as a fully adequate expression of the Christian faith. There are two connected but distinct features of the church that need to be recognised in ecclesiological discourse. One is that as a sociological entity the church depends on and interacts with the values, trends and systems that govern the civil society. The second one is, that as a visible expression of a theological idea, the church is expected to be different from the rest of the social units. During the course of history, these two natures of the Church have `acted and reacted upon each other in such a complex way that it is often impossible to discern which is cause and which is effect, or to perceive whether the facts are expressing doctrine or the doctrine is merely a reflection of the facts'.[7] The contextual realities and the tradition of the Church as handed down and adapted, both as external factors exert a decisive influence on the concretisation of a theological idea – Church in each context of time and space. Ecclesiological formulations that we have inherited were attempted to be formulated within the background of the originating community's structural, functional expressions[8] and options and therefore, not automatically relevant to the people elsewhere, particularly to the people of Asia whose context and experience are significantly different. In other words, alien contextual and experiential bases hamper the church from re-imagining itself in ways that are relevant and faithful.

This necessitates the need to look at Asia with all its complexity and richness as an opportunity and a resource for discerning possibilities for a relevant and meaningful ecclesial presence. Asian cultural and spiritual resources are ancient, diverse, complex, and strongly intertwined with religious, ethnic and linguistic traditions. These have been the sites and sources of wisdom and worldviews that shaped the history and civilisation of the Asian people in many distinct ways. These are not only ancient but dynamic and have also been going through rapid processes of change, as much as or more than they could affect changes. Sweeping tides of secularism as well as fundamentalism, technological advancements and economic growth have been affecting several changes, more importantly on human self-understanding and structures of human relationships. In spite of its rich, timeless and complex history of cultures and spiritualities, Asia has also been a home for the largest number of the poor in the world, for military dictatorships, for terrorism, for fundamentalism and bigotry, for gross human rights' violations and human abuse, for the obnoxious caste system, for abuse of women and children and for striking contrasts between the rich and the poor. Many of these have also been and continue to be instruments of the hegemonic powers. I believe that it is necessary to explore to what extent Asia's cultures and spiritual traditions have been responsible for these realities. Even as we want to dive into the vast sea of some of Asia's dominant spiritual traditions, let us also be aware that these have been and continue to be either sources of the continued institutionalization of injustice and legitimization of human abuse or have remained helpless and powerless to counter these ugly realities. Otherwise, we may be romanticizing them more than they deserve, and fail to take note of new and progressive sites and sources.

---

[6] Ernst Troeltsch, The Social Teachings of the Christian Church Vol I and II, Westminster, John Knox Press, Reprint 1992

[7] Maurice Goguel, *The Primitive Church,* New York, Macmillan Co, 1964, p.22.

[8] John Munsey Turner, "Church and State" in *The Dictionary of the Ecumenical Movement,* Geneva, WCC, & Grand Rapids, William Eerdmans Co., 1991, pp.167-169.

Signposts towards relevant Asian ecclesiologies

Just as much as it is useful, it may not be possible to do a detailed examination of the vast and diverse reality of Asian wisdom and culture on one hand and its geo-politics on the other, to identify the way ahead. As said earlier, Asia is vast, diverse with all its distinctness and specificities in each context. Any broad categorization or generalizations are not only incongruous but also impossible. Therefore, I do not attempt an Asian ecclesiology relevant for all contexts and people but only identify a few signposts towards relevant Asian ecclesiologies. I would like to deviate from the familiar trails, and instead explore what are perhaps unconventional but living cultural traditions of those on the margins of Asian societies. Almost all Asian societies have been the sites of intense struggles for political freedom, economic justice, human rights and human dignity, and against fundamentalism, bigotry, caste system, patriarchal abuse, environmental destruction, foreign occupation, neo-colonization, and the list is long. Several movements and initiatives are bringing together millions of people across religious, ethnic and other boundaries in each of these contexts to struggle for justice, peace and life for all. People are getting together not because of any religious motivation or ideological orientations but because of their belief in and commitment to certain values as mentioned above. I would like us to focus on these aspirations of the people on the margins for our purpose of discerning the way ahead. As Samuel Ryan puts it aptly, "...in all such struggles and movements for dignity and food for the masses, a spirituality is implied. And this spirituality is liberational.... If we believe in God as the ultimate and ineluctable imperative of justice, love, freedom, and peace, we must hold that at the basis of every struggle and every move for liberation and life and dignity and rice for the riceless, there is a divine force, there is the Holy Spirit, there is a profound spirituality that, once made explicit, can add clarity, strength, and a sense of direction to life and to struggle for life".[9] These point towards a spirituality aside from any religious or religio-cultural trappings but is grounded in the human capacity to be good and just and inspired by the vision of a society that is just and inclusive, an aspiration that is deeply embedded, though over powered by dominant interests, in all religious traditions and communities. Chandra Muzaffar, another Asian Muslim intellectual, writes, "the unity of humankind transcends our particular religious identities but it does not negate them, by celebrating our religious identity we realize our common humanity – a humanity that embraces our natural environment and indeed the whole of cosmos."[10] It is spirituality of resistance and active hope, inspiring courageous and creative action in several contexts in Asia. Let me, therefore, on the basis of this premise – the emerging common Asian spirituality, identify the signposts for our ecclesiological exploration.

1. Church as faithful people in context

Any empirical church consists of faithful people in a given context, and their identities and experiences influence their being the church and their Christian witness. Because of the influence of the inherited theologies and ecclesiologies, these expressions too have been very institutional and *status quo oriented.* Although the church is constantly referred to as people but in reality it exists as an institution, organisation or community. For instance, most Asian Churches have pioneered in the areas of education and health and their contribution have always been lauded. But today these have been taken over the industry. The changed and changing Asian realities point towards the need to re-imagine ecclesial presence and practice in response to these yearnings of people struggling for justice, and life with dignity. Furthermore, in a world where most religious traditions have often been the high priests of the powerful, legitimizing and justifying all the excesses of the state and powers, the Asian churches need to rediscover themselves on the

---

[9] Samuel Rayan, "The Search for an Asian Spirituality of Liberation", ed. by Virginia Fabella et al, *Asian Christian Spirituality*, Maryknoll, New York, 1992, p. 17.

[10] Chandra Muzaffar, "Religion in the Asia pacific Region: the challenge without and the change within", in Joseph A. Camilleri, ed, *Religion and Culture in Asia Pacific: Violence or Healing*, Vista Publications, Melbourne 2001, p.38.

side of the victims of power and seek to be the moral voice or the conscience keepers of the society rather than existing or operating either as mere religious communities or as social service organizations. [11]

Perhaps ecumenical theology can help us to re-imagine the church as the people of faith, people with a purpose and calling in each given context. The ecumenical movement is essentially a spirituality movement. It is about building relationships based on the values of justice, compassion and freedom. The word "ecumenical" is derived from the Greek word "*oikoumene*", meaning the whole inhabited world as one household. It assumes that we live and relate with one another as one people within the earthly home given to us by God. The ecumenical movement, as an instrument of Christian unity, has time and again, upheld that its purpose is not to serve its own interests or those of the institutional structures of the churches, but to serve the causes of justice and peace, and to transform the world through critical and creative engagement. In other words, being ecumenical is a way of participating in the shaping of the world, a way of being the salt of the earth and the light of the world and of bringing about the kingdom of God in each context of time and space. To that extent, *oikoumene* is a movement for the affirmation of life – a movement to uphold the sanctity, integrity and dignity of life of all people. It is an alternative vision of the world, guided by the values of justice and peace, a way of churches being change agents, conscience keepers and instruments of God's mission in the world. As such it is a movement of resistance and hope. In a world dominated by hegemonic powers, *Oikoumene* is and has to be a movement of nurturers of dissenting conscience.

The marginalized communities in Asia are on a similar movement towards a radical spiritual transformation. Swami Agnivesh, a well-known Hindu social reformer, writes, "Spirituality comprises the deeper core of religions. Justice is the essence of spirituality. In a legal sense, justice is mostly a matter of redressing individual and, at times, collective grievances. Spiritually, justice calls for the creation of wholesome conditions of the life and the affirmation of basic values whereby human beings are helped to attain fullness and find fulfilment in life. Spiritually, justice has a social foundation; for we are social creatures. Spirituality is not a matter of some formulae or dogmas. It is a dynamic phenomenon that expresses itself through an ongoing engagement with the human predicament". [12] He continues, "The worth of a religious and social system is best demonstrated by the way it treats its least fortunate members and by the integrity and honesty of its elite....Corruption manifests itself when philosophers, seers, intellectuals and religious authorities have not done their homework....All major human advancements and improvements whether it the abolition of slavery, women's rights, freedom of conscience, children's rights., the Human Rights declaration, the secular state, and environmental awareness have come from sources outside of the religious establishment".[13] These initiatives of people have been the change-makers. This contextual awareness can help the Asian churches to be a part of this stream of change-makers. "The demand here is not so much to maintain what may be called "the universal characteristics of the church" but rather to be authentic manifestations of the church in a particular context. The move is away from the universal to the particular and from uniformity to plurality", asserts another Asian theologian, Michael Amaladoss.[14]

---

[11] Mathai Zachariah in his searing analysis of the Indian churches writes, "Most Christians in India see the Church as a communal body, one community among other communities, as a *quam* or as a *Samudayam*, serving itself and fighting for its rights at different levels." (*Inside the Indian Church,* Delhi, ISPCK, 1994, p.4.)

[12] Swami Agnivesh, *Applied Spirituality for Justice Unlimited*, New Delhi, Dharma Pratisthan, 2005.p. 35.

[13] Swami Agnivesh, "Striving for a truly spiritual culture", in Joseph A. Camilleri, ed., *Religion and Culture in Asia Pacific: Violence or Healing*, Vista Publications, Melbourne 2001, p.137.

[14] Michael Amaladoss, *Life in Freedom: Liberation Theologies from Asia*, Maryknoll, New York, Orbis Books, 1997, p.15.

2. The church as a network of partners in mission

'Community' is the most commonly used image to describe the church. However, as said earlier, communities are not always and necessarily guided by the values of equality, justice and mutual interdependence. Most often, communities are narrow and inward looking in composition and goals. Even as we hold the church as a community, it must be asserted that the church is called into being for the purpose of being the sign and symbol of the coming reign of God. In other words, we do not belong to the church for our own interests but in order to be a part of God's plan to make God's reign to happen in every here and now through their presence and witness.

This implies that the institutional presence of the church, theologies that glorify power and maintain neutral positions on justice, and those expressions of discipleship pre-occupied with the salvation of souls for another world, do not fit into this criteria. Many organised and organisational expressions of Christian presence are led and driven by these value orientations. The theologies which many Asian churches have inherited and cherish are those which are steeped in the legacies of western anthropocentrism, colonization, racial superiority, Just war theories and temporal-spiritual dichotomies. As Chakkariah, a famous Indian theologian in 20th century, exposes this unhelpful reality of the Indian churches: "The Indian David cannot fight in the armour, and with the sword, of Saul."[15]

Likewise, today, there is a growing number of ecumenically committed Christian groups throughout Asia that are on the frontiers, struggling for the rights of the people, engaged in inter-religious dialogue and co-operation and searching for a human community in an alienated world. Their stand goes beyond the ecclesiological understandings of the traditional churches to those deeper human realities of sin, suffering and alienation. On the other hand, many churches and ecumenical organizations are still led by the traditional north – south relationship patterns, with management policies formulated as per the terms of those who have the resources, and driven more and more by the analysis and priorities of the development agencies in the North. There are also those churches – with long histories and ecclesiastical power who exercise themselves, their perspectives and interests in shaping the character and content of ecumenical institutions.

Michael Amaladoss succinctly describes this tension: "The church is divided between those who want to struggle with the poor and those who see such struggle either as political activity in which the church should not be involved or as leading to a compromise with Marxist movements.... The struggling Christians therefore are looking for a church of the people, a prophetic and serving presence in the community, open to other Christians, believers and all people of good will who are also struggling for the reign of God in solidarity with groups of people everywhere who share the same dream and visions".[16]

If the church is for the world, and not for its self-perpetuation, then Asian churches must open themselves to the realities around – the challenges as well as possibilities for its witness, and rediscover themselves where God is present with the people in their struggle for life, justice and dignity. Churches need to be prophetic, change-oriented and transformative in their presence and practice, and in order to do this, they must rid themselves of what has been given to them and find new reasons for their existence and action. The new Faith and Order Statement on Church has a pointed remark to make: "Jesus said that he came so that human beings may have life in abundance (cf. John 10:10); his followers acknowledge their responsibility to defend human life and dignity. These are obligations on churches as much as on individual believers. Each context will provide its own clues to discern what is the appropriate Christian response within any particular set of circumstances. Even now, divided Christian communities can and do carry out such discernment together and have acted jointly to bring relief to suffering human beings and to help create a society that fosters human dignity. Christians will seek to promote the values of the kingdom of

---

[15] As quoted by T.V. Philip, "Search for an Ecclesiology in Asia", in *Tradition and Innovation*, *op.cit.*, p.120

[16] Michael Amaladoss, *Ibid.*, p.19.

God by working together with adherents of other religions and even with those of no religious belief".[17] The necessity of genuine partnership and of the internalisation of the values of what we profess is yet another resource that these living spiritual traditions of the poor offer.

3. The church as a just and inclusive community

Asian cultures are often praised for their communitarian values, for their strong institutions of family and sense of community. But these are also known for their oppressive hold, for their overtones of feudalism, patriarchy, caste, ethnocentrism, narrow parochial religious interests, linguistic chauvinism, etc. the privileged and powerful within these are the ones who benefit most from it. The poor in Asia are interrogating and resisting these conceptions and formations. True Christian unity therefore has a radical and subversive dimension of breaking all false formations of unity and to set people free to unite at much deeper levels with respect, compassion and justice.

The traditions and aspirations of Asia's marginalized point towards new rallying points for human togetherness, namely, the values that make and keep life on earth worthwhile and vibrant. It is no more identities nor ideologies but visions of better world, and values that bring people together. Ecumenism in Asia has always been driven by this notion of dialogue and action for life, beyond the confines of Christian self-interests. P. D. Devananadan wrote in 1948: "To us the younger Churches it is the international nature of our faith that strikes the imagination; to you of the older churches it is the interdenominational character of ecumenical Christianity that compels admiration. To us it is vital that ecumenical Christianity be both international and missionary".[18]In other words, it has not been orthodoxy but orthopraxy that has been the mark of Asian ecumenical witness. Ecumenism is not unity but inclusivity.

Furthermore, in an increasingly post-denominational ecclesial scenario, where the hold or influence of denominational theologies is very tenuous, continued work on seeking doctrinal convergence may not help as a remedy against the root causes of church divisions, though not unnecessary, to make some advance on the theological level. We need to recognise that there are many other factors that divide the community and even the church, such as national and ethnic identities, issues of social justice and human rights, etc. Many of the theological convergence attempts so far have not focused on the sins and scandals of discrimination and exclusion of many within the church – the indigenous peoples, Dalits, and other oppressed groups, those who are oppressed by racism, people living with disabilities, the migrants and refugees, etc. Any pursuit of unity without attempting for an advance in inclusivity and justice internally in the church can turn out to be mere charade. "Any church which attempts to seek partnership and to be in communion with others while not being just and inclusive within, and while not doing anything about the same, is not only deceptive but also an embarrassment to the faith that it claims to affirm and live out in the world. Inclusivity within is necessary for the credibility of the church's pursuits and propagations of unity."[19]

The pursuit of Christian unity is rooted in the biblical mandate of witness. Unity is for mission and that mission is the realisation of God's reign of justice and peace. If these are not ultimate goals of Christian unity and mission, both have no relevance and purpose. These would only turn out to be instruments of power and of Christian self interest. Unity is a dynamic process, there is nothing final about the form or composition of any united church. It is an act of a pilgrim people who know themselves to be on the move

---

[17] The Church Towards a Common Vision Faith & Order Commission, 2012, World Council of Churches, Geneva, §64 & 66.

[18] Ninan Koshy, ed. ,*A History of the Ecumenical Movement in Asia,* Volume I, WSCF, YMCA and CCA, Hong Kong, 2004, p. 30.

[19] Deenabandhu Manchala, "Expanding the Ambit: Dalit Theological Contribution to Ecumenical Social Thought", ed.by., Sathianathan Clarke, Deenabandhu Manchala and Philip Vinod Peacock, Dalit *Theology in the Twenty-first Century: Discordant Voices, Discerning Pathways*, New Delhi, OUP, 2010, pp.44-45.

towards an unknown future. But such open-endedness is possible only when it is centered on Christ and on what it means to be part of his church. Liberation from the false security of denominational labels and customs requires a common rediscovery of those shared convictions that are central to the faith and life of the church. As a joint consultation of Christian Conference of Asia and Federation of Asian Bishops' Conference on "New Asian Ecumenism" in Chiang Mai, Thailand in 2001, said: "The possibility and the coming into being of a "more comprehensive expression" of Christian unity and of the ecumenical fellowship of Asia should be seen as in itself a prophetic manifestation of the possibility embodied in Christian faith and life for unity in a deeply and painfully divided, fractious, and conflict-ridden world. In itself, it gives credibility and substance to Christian claims for unity and reconciliation and the power that can bring these into being".[20] This reiterates another assertion on Asian ecclesiology in 1987: "The experience of Christian unity, therefore, seems to seek an open-ended ecclesiology where the major issues of church life, worship and witness are not necessarily solved beforehand but are worked out in the process of becoming a church in a context. Such an experience of union is also people-oriented, rather than doctrine-centred, so that the uniting experience seems to heighten the people centredness of its ecclesiology.... If our ecclesiology is indeed to be people-oriented and Christ-centred, then we need to re-examine our ecclesiology from the point of view of those who, for one reason or another, seem to be excluded from or have limited participation in the total life of the church to do so is to work towards an ecclesiology that will neither fence some people out nor fence some others in. Indeed, it is to work towards an inclusive ecclesiology."[21]

4. The church as a community celebrating diversity

Asia is perhaps the most diverse continent in the world, with diversity at every level. In fact, our new world of 21st century too is increasingly becoming diverse. A vast array of religions, languages, ethnicities, cultures, histories, living habits etc., describe the diverse reality of Asia. In spite of the tensions and conflicts, most Asian communities have the capacity to overcome differences and negotiate spaces for self-expression as well as possibilities for interdependence. In a way, they do not view diversity as a problem but as strength and asset. On the other hand, they celebrate their diversity and affirm and respect one another's identity and distinctness".[22] Almost every society in all parts of the world is touched by the phenomenon of plurality of languages, religions and ethnicity. This is also leading to several tensions, discrimination and exclusion and the consequent violence against the vulnerable sections. However, while some Asian communities have been too narrow and parochial, the movements and traditions of the poor have been able to transcend boundaries. Despite the tensions and problem that diversity sometimes creates, Asians have the extraordinary ability to celebrate it. In a context of diversity and in a cultural ethos which views diversity not as a problem but as a source of celebration and joy, we need to re-imagine unity not in terms of overcoming differences but in affirming and respecting differences and diversity.

Christian conciliar ecumenism that lays at the foundation of the 20th century ecumenical movement is influenced by western cultural attitudes towards diversity and plurality. Although theologically well grounded, much of these had its roots in western culture and history that gave birth to organizational structures that sought to hold power, resources and opinions together for cohesive institutional presence. On the other hand, Hindus, Muslims, Buddhists, Jains, Sikhism, etc., do not have rigid organizational structures and are also not pre-occupied with organized expressions of unity. Yet they are flourishing religious persuasions, drawing and involving millions around the world. The Asian churches find their space within this ethos of religious pluralism which is not predominantly Christian, not institutional, but of natural, philosophical, theistic and atheistic religious traditions which have existed for centuries without

---

[20] http://www.fabc.org/fabc%20papers/fabc_paper_99.pdf, p.9.
[21] *Tradition and Innovation*, p. 17.
[22] *Tradition and Innovation*, p. 16.

organisational structures and rules and norms. Reflecting on the shape and content of ecumenism in Asia in the new century, the participants of a joint consultation of Christian Conference of Asia and Federation of Asian Bishops' Conference in Chiang Mai, Thailand in 2001, said: "All ecumenical structures are to serve the churches' witness to the reconciling power of God in Jesus Christ. The test of their effectiveness, ultimately, is found in relations between Christian people in each place. National ecumenical structures are to assist and encourage, never to stifle, the initiatives of local churches in witness and service".[23]

The idea of structured unity, though theologically sound, must, therefore, not result in unity at the level of organisations only. Furthermore, in a predominantly pluralistic world, and Asia in particular, where other religious communities do not have organized institutional expressions like churches and their councils, and where attempts towards unity among these are virtually non-existent, the Christian agenda of seeking unity can even be a dangerous pursuit, one that can evoke fear and hostility. The realities of intense power dynamics and struggle, and of the presence and practice of classism, sexism, casteism, racism, ableism (in reference to people with disabilities) and ageism right within churches is an evidence of the shallowness and futility of pursuing this form of unity. In fact these bear negative witness to the unity that we seek in Christ. Most Asian churches are known by western names, with triumphalistic disdain for other religions. There is hardly any spirit of partnership with other communities of faith. Some current western concepts of or approaches towards *oikoumene* seem narrow and church-based, accenting a great deal on visible organisational expressions of unity. However, visible unity does not necessarily mean overcoming denominational identities but embracing differences for the sake of a common goal and calling. As the new Faith and Order Statement on Church says:

> Legitimate diversity in the life of communion is a gift from the Lord. The Holy Spirit bestows a variety of complementary gifts on the faithful for the common good (cf. 1 Cor. 12:4-7). The disciples are called to be fully united (cf. Acts 2:44-47; 4:32-37), while respectful of and enriched by their diversities (1 Cor. 12:14-26). Cultural and historical factors contribute to the rich diversity within the Church. The Gospel needs to be proclaimed in languages, symbols and images that are relevant to particular times and contexts so as to be lived authentically in each time and place. Legitimate diversity is compromised whenever Christians consider their own cultural expressions of the gospel as the only authentic ones, to be imposed upon Christians of other cultures.[24]

A broader and inclusive moral agenda and larger social vision and openness to new realities are necessary in the pursuits of Christian unity. Values such as the aspirations for justice, equality and dignity for all bring many marginalized people together and they seek to align themselves with all who are committed to a progressive and inclusive social vision. Such an understanding would imply seeking non-institutional forms of unity and being open to people of other faiths and no-faiths for the sake of life and its integrity in today's world.... Thus ecumenism itself assumes a new character and purpose, proposing radical changes to church's self-understanding and its understanding of unity itself.[25] A common identity and political economy is not the answer but an ethics of respect, dignity and justice is what makes the world worthwhile.

Ecumenism is not about overcoming diversity and difference but celebrating diversity, and being able to live with differences guided by the values of justice and inclusivity. Diversity is a self expression of God – God's generosity, creativity and wisdom. Appreciation of diversity, in fact, tests and enhances our capacity to love, forgive, to be compassionate, considerate and just, in other words to be human. Any theological

---

[23] http://www.fabc.org/fabc%20papers/fabc_paper_99.pdf, p.5.

[24] The Church Towards a Common Vision, Faith & Order Commission, World Council of Churches, Geneva 2012, §28.

[25] Deenabandhu Manchala, *Op.Cit.* p.45.

formulation that attempts to directly or tacitly undermine diversity or views it as a problem to overcome or thinks it is possible only to do good things and to be involved in mission, when we submit ourselves to a centralized authority needs to be seriously questioned. Much of the problems of violence, aggression, abuse, and irresponsible use of power are rooted in this reluctance to cope with the challenge of diversity which is from God. Asia is pluralistic to the core and there are several layers of plurality within each broad category. Asia's diversity and richness of religious expressions also point towards a spirituality that is beyond the confines of any religious identity. Many Asian theological streams have recognized this element of common spirit in all the religious traditions. In such a context, Christo-centric and even theo-centric accents have to be carefully nuanced. How do we affirm our faith in God in Jesus Christ in ways that do not offend or undermine those who are already at God's work? We may, therefore, grapple for expressions of Christian faith that can enable greater expressions of human solidarity.

5. Churches in dialogue with theologies of life

This also points us in the direction of theologies arising out of the struggle for life. If we believe that the church is for the whole wide world, then our continued dependence on western theologies is not helpful to reach the goal. The preoccupation of some of these archaic traditional ones has been the church and its place in the world, and hence may not be helpful for discerning new expressions that need to be broad and inclusive in an increasingly complex and pluralistic world. They have neither helped Christianity to remain rooted in the western soil nor have they been able to inspire revolutionary changes or challenge the powers that be. Broadly categorized as contextual theologies, many Asian theologies – Minjung, Dalit, Tribal, Asian women's, and many other specific creative expressions, on the other hand, have arisen out of their engagement with the life-world of the poor and the marginalized of the Asian societies. As Craig Nessan writes, "Theology emerging from the new continent of post Christendom… is a theology that is engaged in social and political praxis in solidarity with the *minjung* of the earth. It is a theology that is in the process of recovering, honouring and intentionally thematising its Jewish identity, it is a theology that is by nature inter-religious, conversant and creatively transformed by the reality of Buddhist, Confucian, Taoist and indigenous religious traditions…. It is a theology in which the Christendom distinction between theology and ethics no longer holds. It is a theology that is already leading the Christian church toward a new world order". [26]

The future of the Asian churches depends on their ability to re-anchor themselves in these contextual theologies everywhere, especially those arising out of multi-religious contexts, to find a meaningful and purposeful existence. With their interaction with the movements for justice and life, the Asian churches would be able to articulate alternative visions, and a new paradigm for a purposeful ecclesial existence. As Felix Wilfred writes, "It is in the context of the struggles of the subject to make faith as an integral part of their spiritual quest theology becomes more creative and responding to the issues of life. This process underlying all genuine Asian theologies could be termed as "appropriation of faith".[27] Perhaps, it may be worthwhile to mention two such attempts. One is an attempt "Toward an Asian ecclesiology based on the Asian Liberation Theology and Minjung Theology", a Ph.D dissertation by Do Woong Park who identifies issues and elements that contribute to the development of an appropriate ecclesiology in the Asian context by drawing from two Christian theologies that rose from the Asian context of poverty, oppression, and multifaceted religiousness. These are, the Asian Theology of Liberation and Minjung Theology. [28] The other is a D.Th dissertation, "Re-visioning Ecclesia: An attempt towards an Indian ecclesiology with the

---

[26] Craig L. Nessan, in Paul S. Chung, et al, ed., *Asian Contextual Theology for the Third Millennium: Theology of Minjung in Fourth-Eye Formation,* Eugene, Oregon, Pickwick Publications, 2007, p.353.
[27] Felix Wilfred, Margins : Site of Asian Theologies, New Delhi, ISPCK, 2008, p.137.
[28] http://udini.proquest.com/view/toward-an-asian-ecclesiology-based-goid:304638518/

experience of the Dalits in India as a point of engagement" by Deenabandhu Manchala.[29] The study only holds that the Church is not merely a community that gives a sense of belonging but one that motivates constructive action, and presents itself as an alternative community. In response to their experience of community which is exclusive and hierarchical, the Dalits want the Church to be a community-progressive, inclusive and different from the wider community. The study infers that the Indian churches cannot exist as communities, a one among many communities, but as communities that work together as a moral ferment to rebuild greater expressions of community that are beyond caste, religious, regional and linguistic boundaries giving one another a sense of warmth, fellowship and solidarity. This is the alternative that the *oikos* of God (the household of God) can offer to the caste-ridden and now presently market driven individualistic social culture in India.

Through its own being and doing, the church is called to witness that it is possible for all God's people to be one, for the sake of life and for the world that God has created. One of the distinct ways in which the churches have made positive differences in history is when they understood themselves as movements of people and when they were with the people in the way our Lord was. It was their ability to read the signs of the times, and to understand the purpose of their being in those contexts, that made them creative, life-affirming forces. The Asian churches, need to be constantly on the move, open to change, discerning change, in order that we may not only stay relevant but also play a creative part in shaping the world, in ways that make sense to the least and the last.

Bibliography

The Church Towards a Common Vision, Faith & Order Commission, 2012, World Council of Churches, Geneva,

Tradition and Innovation: A search for a relevant ecclesiology in Asia, ed. by CTC-CCA, Singapore, 1983

Ninan Koshy, *Caste in Kerala Churches*, Bangalore, CISRS, 1968

Deenabandhu Manchala, Re-Visioning Ecclesia: An attempt towards an Indian ecclesiology with the experience of the Malas and Madigas in Dommeru and Jonnada in Andhra Pradesh as a point of engagement", Bangalore, SATHRI, 2001.

Geevarghese Mar Osthathios, "A Critical Evaluation of Our Inherited Ecclesiologies and Present Practices", *Heritage and Mission, New Frontiers of the Church in Kerala: Ecclesiological Study Project,* ed. by P.T. Thomas, et al., *Manganam, Kerala*, Kerala Council of Churches, 1989,

Samuel Rayan, "The Search for an Asian Spirituality of Liberation", ed. by Virginia Fabella et al, *Asian Christian Spirituality*, Mary knoll, New York, 1992

Mathai Zachariah, *Inside the Indian Church,* Delhi, ISPCK, 1994

[29] "Re-visioning Ecclesia: An attempt towards an Indian ecclesiology with the experience of the Malas and Madigas in Dommeru and Jonnada in Andhra Pradesh as a point of engagement", Bangalore, SATHRI, 2001. See p.219.

(22) "TOGETHER TOWARDS LIFE": THE NEW MISSION STATEMENT 2012 OF CWME/WCC AND ITS RELEVANCE TO ASIAN ECUMENISM AND MISSION

Atola Longkumer

"The crucified Christ who is the centre is always in motion towards the periphery; he challenges the power of religious and political idolatry."[1] Kosuke Koyama

Introduction

The term 'Asian Century'[2] is often used in the media accompanied by a confident description of economic growth of Asian countries affording unprecedented wealth to some. Indeed, there is a palpable confidence of an emerging Asia as best exemplified by the title of a book *The New Asian Hemisphere: The Irresistible Shift of Global Power to the Eas*t, authored by Kishore Mahbubani, a former Singaporean diplomat. The term "Asian Century" apparently encapsulates the massive globalisation and impact of market forces along with the growing middle-class phenomenon, a consumerist class in several Asian contexts. Indeed, there is undeniable growth and changes sweeping across the continent of Asia. The formation of BRIC (Brazil, Russia, India, China) and ASEAN (Association of South East Asian Nations) provides added confidence both economically and politically. To be sure, among the BRIC nations, Brazil and Russia do not belong to the Asian continent, yet, it surely illustrates the powerful circle of cooperation Asian nations are capable of forming in the global level for the benefit of their respective nations' economic well-being and political power.

The term 'Asian Century' is imaginable given the growing presence and importance of some of its nations, yet, it would be myopic and akin to the syndrome of the ostrich head in sand, if the notion of 'Asian Century' is limited to the apparent economic growth, while ignoring the more pressing needs of peace, justice and equity in the continent. This essay is written shortly after powerful incidents and events took place in Asian nations that attracted intense global attention: South Korea elected its first female president, Park Guen-hye, a conservative and the daughter of Korea's powerful former dictator; the brutal gang-rape of a medical student and her death in India; the ethnic clashes at the borderlands of Myanmar, Bangladesh with the Rohinyas; the protest against nuclear energy in India; the resurgence of religious fundamentalism; the many natural calamities-floods, draughts, forest fires, landslides- and the regular reports of corruptions endemic to almost all the Asian nations. The challenges for societies and government and churches are not limited to these mentioned issues.

The description and usage of the term Asian itself needs a clarification, for there is hardly any cultural or political essence in the term Asian, except that it is a term used by the Ancient Greece and popularised by European travellers, explorers, missionaries, and imperialists.[3] Any discussion, therefore pertaining to Asia today need to be undergirded by the fact that Asia cannot be described in monolithic terms. The

---

[1] Kosuke Koyama, "The Crucified Christ Challenge Human Power" address delivered at the WCC Conference on Mission and Evangelism, Melbourne, 1980 in Michael Kinnamon and Brian E. Cope, eds., *The Ecumenical Movement: An Anthology of Key Texts and Voices* (Grand Rapids: Wm.B. Eerdmans Publishing Co, 1997), 368-371.

[2] A phrase apparently that emerged during a meeting of Chinese Premier Deng Xiaoping and Indian Prime Minister Rajiv Gandhi and formally employed by the Foreign Affairs of USA see, http://en.wikipedia.org/wiki/Asian_Century accessed 31.1 2013

[3] See Philip Bowring, "What is Asia?" in http://afe.easia.columbia.edu/geography/geo_whatis.html accessed 31.1.2013. See also Peter C. Phan ed., *Christianities in Asia* (Oxford: Blackwell, 2011), 2-8.

cultures, religions, historical developments, political systems and languages are as varied and diverse as the geographical diversity the continent presents. Asia comprises, in general terms, China to Jordan, Myanmar to Kyrgyzstan. Kenneth Ross and Todd R. Johnson[4] have divided Asia into four larger regions in the following way: Eastern Asia comprising of China, Japan, South Korea, North Korea, Taiwan, and Mongolia; South-eastern Asia, comprising of Vietnam, Indonesia, the Philippines, Thailand, Cambodia, Burma, Singapore, Malaysia, Laos, and Timor; South-central Asia, includes India, Nepal, Bhutan, Pakistan, Bangladesh, Sri Lanka, Afghanistan, Tajikistan, Kyrgyzstan, Kazakhstan, Uzbekistan and Western Asia, consisting of Turkey, Georgia, Armenia, Lebanon, Syria, Cyprus, Iraq, Palestine, Israel, UAE, Saudi Arabia, Jordan, Yemen, and Oman. These regional categories are helpful in a general way, but they do not encapsulate the spectrum of diversity and plurality each country presents, even within nation states of Asia.

Ancient civilizations, such as the Vedic/Indic and Confucianism that pre-date western civilization are in Asia. Major religions of the world, viz., Buddhism, Christianity, Confucianism, Hinduism, Islam, Jainism, Judaism, Sikhism, Zoroastrianism and a myriad of indigenous religiosities have their roots in Asia. A crucial feature to be noted in relation to religions in Asia is the degree of relative tolerance towards other religions. Without ignoring the contestations and conflicts at certain historical periods, it would not be farfetched to underline the relative receptiveness of another religion in the region. Historical illustrations abound but suffice here a few: the Islamic King Akbar and the Jesuit missionaries in sixteenth century; Buddhism and its growth outside the land of its origin; the cross-fertilization between Islamic mystics Sufi and Bhakti of Hinduism.[5]

These preliminary remarks provide direction to the task of the present essay, which is to provide a reflection on the CWME New Mission Statement (NMS) from an Asian ecumenism perspective. Such an engagement is undergirded by the following facts:

- Asia is heterogeneous in every aspect of society,
- Asia is ancient yet emerging in modern times,
- Asia is witnessing an explosion of growth in Christianity observed both in China and India, the two most populous nations in the world.

A word of clarity upon the usage of the term Asian Ecumenism is necessary. In ecumenical parlance, the term is often employed to describe the regions of Eastern Asia, South Eastern Asia, South Asia to use the divisions as demarcated by Ross and Johnson. The present essay continues this usage in discussing the significance of the New Mission Statement (NMS)[6] of the World Council of Churches from an Asian contextual perspective. Again, 'Asian contextual perspective' is used in a general geographical sense since there is no essential Asian context but rather a poly-context. Furthermore, as a text written in post-post-modernity, wherein subjectivity is acknowledged, the following reflection is conditioned by the lens of an indigenous woman belonging to the global south Christianity, a context which in general terms shares characteristics of being missionized by Western missionaries under colonial rule and having been initiated into the modern world for affording both good and ill outcomes in equal measure.

---

[4] Todd M. Johnson, Kenneth R. Ross eds., *Atlas of Global Christianity 1910-2010* (Edinburgh: Edinburgh University Press, 2009).

[5] For a detailed yet macro history of Christianity in Asia that includes the larger socio-religious background see, Samuel Hugh Moffet, *A History of Christianity in Asia* 2 Volumes (Maryknoll: Orbis Books, 1998)

[6]http://www.oikoumene.org/en/resources/documents/wcc-commissions/mission-and-evangelism/together-towards-life-mission-and-evangelism-in-changing-landscapes.html accessed 31.1.2013

Together Towards Life: CWME/WCC New Mission Document 2012

The Commission on World Mission and Evangelism (CWME) of the World Council of Churches (WCC) has prepared a new document on mission, to be presented at the 10th Assembly of WCC, at Busan, South Korea in October 2013. Jooseop Keum, the Secretary of the CWME and Geevarghese Mor Coorilos (George Mathew Nalunnakkal), the Moderator of the CWME have steered the process of the writing the New Mission Statement (NMS). The title of the NMS is *Together towards Life: Mission and Evangelism in a Changing Landscape.*[7] The NMS is significant for many reasons: it is the first official mission statement since the 1982. Furthermore, it has been prepared in consultation with the community of mission scholars from different parts of the world, relatively representational in denominational, gender, and regional perspectives. It is commendable for the ecumenical participation in its preparation: Evangelical, Orthodox, Protestant and Roman Catholic mission articulations can be seen in the new document.

The new document comes as a result of a prolonged, deep engagement and study of various dimensions of mission in the light of the shifts and changes taking place in the global scenario. A long study process on mission was initiated just after the WCC Assembly at Porto Alegro, Brazil in 2006. The draft of the statement was presented and discussed in a global consultation during the CWME pre-assembly meeting held in Manila in March 2012. In this pre-Assembly global consultation more than 200 mission theologians and practitioners and church leaders representing the different Church traditions had intense deliberations following the Filipino cultural practice of local consultation called *Talakayan.* Many participants gave comments on the draft document, which are reflected in the final document as presented to the WCC Central Committee in Crete, 8 August to 5 September 2012, for approval.

Together towards Life, is indeed a significant mission document which provides vision and direction for the church in her mission and evangelism articulation and practice. Jooseop Keum, the secretary of the CWME summed up the importance of the new mission document in the following statement, "the statement aims to bring new issues and convictions to the upcoming WCC Assembly, since the concepts of mission and evangelism have changed significantly during the last three decades."[8] Kirsteen Kim succinctly provides the missional dimension that "the overall goal of this mission is understood to be "that they may have life…in all its fullness" (John 10:10), and thus has linked it to the theme of the Busan Assembly: God of life, lead us to justice and peace.[9]

Some points are worth noting: in true reflection of the shift of the epicentre of Christianity, it is significant that the leadership in preparing the document has come from Asia, one of whom is the Metropolitan Bishop of the Syrian Orthodox Church in India. It must also be highlighted that the leadership includes a woman from Europe, Kirsteen Kim, the vice-moderator of the CWME, who is one of the leading women professors of Mission and World Christianity.

Salient Features of the New Mission Document 2012

The NMS is titled *Together towards Life: Mission and Evangelism in a Changing Landscape* and presented in accessible language and structure with numbered paragraphs in 112 points. The NMS is presented in four main sections:

- Spirit of Mission: Breathe of Life
- Spirit of Liberation: Mission from the Margins
- Spirit of Community: Church on the Move

[7] See: http://www.oikoumene.org/en/resources/documents/wcc-commissions/mission-and-evangelism.html
[8] www.oikoumene.org Accessed 31.1.13.
[9] Kirsteen Kim, "Introducing the New Statement on Mission and Evangelism", in *International Review of Mission*, Vol 101, No.2 November 2012, pages 316-321

- Spirit of Pentecost: Good News for All

These four sections are further divided into sub-sections and titled in the following ways: Mission of the spirit; Mission and Flourishing of Creation; Spiritual gifts and Discernment; Transformation spirituality; Why margins and Marginalisation? Mission as struggle and resistance; Mission seeking justice and inclusivity; Mission as healing and wholeness; God's mission and the life of the church; God's mission and the church's unity; God empowers the church in mission; Local congregation: new initiatives; The call to evangelize; Evangelism in Christ's way; Evangelism, inter-faith dialogue and Christian presence; Evangelism and cultures. The concluding remark is aptly titled **Feast of Life** and presents 10 affirmations.

The 10 affirmations of the NMS are listed here below, for the sole reason to illustrate the deep commitment and desire of the CWME to provide guidance to the global Christian community to participate in God's mission which is fullness of life to all, expressed and experienced by all in peace and inclusive justice, with equity for all. The affirmations are:

1. We affirm that the purpose of God's mission is fullness of life (John 10:10) and this is the criterion for discernment in mission.
2. We affirm that mission begins with God's act of creation and continues in re-creation, by the enlivening power of the Holy Spirit.
3. We affirm that spirituality is the source of energy for mission and that mission in the spirit is transformative.
4. We affirm that the mission of God's Spirit is to renew the whole creation.
5. We affirm that today mission movements are emerging from the global South and East, which are multi-directional and many-faceted.
6. We affirm that marginalized people are agents of mission and exercise a prophetic role which emphasizes that fullness of life is for all.
7. We affirm that the economy of God is based on values of love and justice for all and that transformative mission resists idolatry in the free market economy.
8. We affirm that the Gospel of Jesus Christ is good news in all ages and places and should be proclaimed in the Spirit of love and humility.
9. We affirm that dialogue and cooperation for life are integral to mission and evangelism.
10. We affirm that God moves and empowers the church in mission. (102-111)

I have listed the above affirmations to demonstrate the flavour and the range of missional issues discussed coupled with comprehensive yet succinct commentary on each section indicating the intense labour and commitment that has accompanied the preparation and the final statement of the NMS of the CWME. The NMS rightly emphasizes the "changing landscapes" of the contemporary world. Undoubtedly, the world has witnessed immense changes in the last three decades since 1982 when the last CWME Mission Statement[10] was prepared. The following list describes some of the changed landscapes: The Cold War has ended; China has become the second largest economy of the world; the Berlin Wall has fallen; there is dramatic increase in global migration; the epicentre of Christianity has shifted from its traditional centre; economic instability is constant, there is an explosion of information technology; the ideology that purports a "clash of civilizations" seems to have taken grip of thinkers and citizens alike; there is a growing rise in fear of foreigners while multiculturalism is declared a failure and environmental destruction has reached unprecedented levels. Asia is part of these changing landscapes, both as a powerful influence to the changing global trajectories as well as witnessing the impact of the changing global scenario in specific Asian contexts.

---

[10] For the full text of the 1982 Mission Statement, see, "Mission and Evangelism: And Ecumenical Affirmation" in *International Review of Mission* vol.71. No. 284, 1982, pp. 432-447.

The overall scenario is one of a general 'angst': victimization and vulnerability of those who are excluded either from the ruling class or the economic class continues; militarisation of nations is on the rise; growing nationalist, right wing politics are getting more common in more nations. It is within such painfully divided changing landscapes that the NMS declares with visionary commitment *Together towards Life* and life in its fullness to all. The Statement declares boldly, "[t]he church is a gift of God to the world for its transformation towards the kingdom of God. Its mission is to bring new life and announce the loving presence of God in our world. We must participate in God's mission in unity, overcoming the divisions and tensions that exist among us, so that the world may believe and all may be one (John 17:21). The church, as the communion of Christ's disciples, must become an inclusive community and exists to bring healing and reconciliation to the world."[11]

The section on the **Spirit of Liberation: Mission from the Margins** makes this NMS powerfully significant. While there was an emphasis on the victims and the vulnerables of powerful structures already in the 1982 Mission Statement, a paternalist attitude is betrayed by the title of the section in the 1982 statement itself, which reads, "Good news to the poor." In contrast, both in language and content the section of the New Mission Statement 2012 is more radical and explicitly denounces the powers that exploit and sustain margins, and the NMS declares unequivocally the margins as the agents of mission. Margins are the vulnerables who are excluded from justice and dignity, living in constant threat to their survival because of different powerful structures which define the centre. Mission from the margins, therefore is an alternative missional movement that recognizes, names and asserts those excluded by the powerful, and the conventional centre (36-54). This aspect is a radical feature of the NMS, it is corrective of the earlier mission understanding wherein the *locus* of mission was the margins, hence, mission *to* the margins, making the margins recipients rather than active agents. Mission expressed in this way has been complicit with the system of privileges and life denying structures, continuing oppressive cultures that sustain marginalisation.(41)

Implications for Asian Ecumenism

In the preceding section of the 2012 mission statement the context of Asia is described, which is itself multi-faceted, diverse and pluralistic and undoubtedly presents many challenges and opportunity for the church in Asia. A word needs to be mentioned with regard to the 'church in Asia', as it is sufficiently understood that the history of the church in Asia is as diverse as the larger socio-economic context of the continent. Hence, 'the church in Asia' is employed for the general Christian community in the region that is comprised of many denominations, historical periods, and distinct liturgies. Within such times as today, as some would refer to it as 'Asian Century', it is important to revisit the concept of Asian Ecumenism and its implication in the light of the NMS of the CWME. What roles might the church in Asia assume to translate the vision of the NMS in lived Christian spirituality? Who are the margins in Asia that need to be identified, embraced, named, empowered, included, and listened to as active agents? What strategic and prophetic steps must the church take to empower the congregations so that *Together towards Life: fullness for all* can become a reality and not remain a mere inspiring rhetoric?

In the following section six areas of ecumenical proactive *koinonia* are proposed, to ensure the translation of the NMS into lived spirituality among Asian Christians:

- Pentecostal/Charismatic Christianity
- Peace-building
- Indigenous peoples
- Gender

[11] See No 10 of the New Mission Statement, henceforth only the number will be referenced.

- Inter-religious engagement
- Theological education

To be sure, the possibilities of Asian ecumenical *koinonia* are not limited to these six areas, neither are these areas new in ecumenical cooperation. Rather these concerns are but re-iterated, demonstrating their continual importance and highlighting the need to weave into them the thread of Margins[12] by making conscious interventions on behalf of the Margins.

Pentecostal/Charismatic Christianity

The NMS recognizes the growing presence and significance of Pentecostal/Charismatic Christianity as a global phenomenon, expressed in different "localities as one of the most noteworthy characteristics of world Christianity" (5). Along with the crucial recognition and commentary on the role of the Holy Spirit as source and enabler of mission, drawn from the Bible, there is also the prophetic assertion made in the NMS, that the Christian community in Asia should take cognizance of the mission of the Triune God to flourish in Asia, which is fullness of life for all.

Pentecostal/Charismatic Christianity provides both an opportunity and challenge to Christians in Asia, while it has a "minority appeal" in the contexts of dominant world religions. It also has the potential for an Asian indigenisation of Christianity, wherein native cultural elements find expression.[13]Yet the reality can be something quite different, "the highly competitive market value has influenced Christian missions, some wants to be winners over others, this can lead to (an) aggressive mode of persuading Christians who already belong to a church to change denominational allegiance. Seeking numerical growth at all costs is incompatible with the respect for others required of Christian disciples."(62)

It is important that Christian mission reflects the self-emptying act of God, against the perils of self-agenda and numerical growth goals. In the light of the guidance of the NMS, Asian churches would do well to continue to explore ways of mutual enrichments: what can be learned from the phenomenon of growing attraction to the Pentecostal/Charismatic Christianity? By the same token, how do churches incorporate into their mission the dimension of Christian spirituality which calls for seeking justice and the common good of society?

Peace building

As noted earlier, the confidence of a growing prominence of the Asian continent is marred by a list of conflicts and tensions: there is the apparent territorial expansionist attitude; increasing militarisation of many Asian nations (ironically, the countries having the highest percentage of its populations living below the Poverty Line, have drastically increased their defence budget); skirmishes along international borders; ethnic clashes such as with the Rohingyas; tribal tensions in the Northeast India; the re-unification of the Koreas; inter-caste/religions conflicts seen in many Asian countries; the tensions in relation to the South China Sea; human rights abuse by the state, etc. These conflicts and tension are threatening life and its fullness for the citizens of Asia. If Asia is the most populous continent in the world with a high concentration of young people, yet highly diverse, it is also home to ancient civilizations and religious traditions which are peaceful and tolerant. For instance, India, is described as having an "eclectic pluralist"

[12] The capital 'M' is used advisedly to indicate that the margins are no longer by the periphery, serving as objectives in mission, but rather, named as with a proper noun, a distinct identity, an empowerment and given active agency.

[13] David Martin, "Issues Affecting The Study of Pentecostalism in Asia" in Allan Anderson and Edmond Tang, eds., *Asian and Pentecostal: The Charismatic Face of Christianity in Asia* (Oxford: Regnum Books International, 2005), 27-36

ancient culture, which provided peaceful accommodation and tolerance to diverse religiosities.[14] One of the features that would ensure fullness of life would be when there is peace coupled with justice and equity. The Christian community in Asia is called upon to engage deliberately, prophetically amidst conflicts and tensions. One such prophetic engagement in Asia is provided by the Bishop Alberto Ramento Human Rights Centre of the *Iglesia Filipina Independiente* (Philippine Independent Church). The Human Rights Centre was named after the assassinated bishop, Bishop Alberto Ramento y Baldovino, who was murdered in 2006.[15] The concept and practice of Sanctuary is about providing shelter and protection to human rights activist and engagement in advocacy for human rights in the context of Philippines. Another example is the effort of Christian theologians in South Korea working for a peaceful reunification of the divided Korea.[16] These organic activists and Christian intellectuals have much to contribute to the much needed area of peace-building in Asia.

Indigenous Peoples

Asia is home to a myriad of groups of people categorised as Indigenous people, from the Ainu of Japan to the Nagas and the Mundas, Oraons of India, from the Ilongots of Philippines to the Karen, Chin of Myanmar to name a few. While the term "indigenous" is contested and consensus remains to be achieved,[17] a broad description of the indigenous peoples and cultures can be offered by identifying some features shared in common. These features would be: experience of invasion and subjugation by dominant group; proximity of life and nature; oral based knowledge *vis-a-vis* written knowledge; a spirituality that is not institutionalised nor possesses canonised sacred texts; a social structure based on clan and kinship and hence a community-centric society.

In the last decades the economic and political powers amassed by many Asian nations means victimization of the most vulnerables of these nations: the indigenous communities. A growing chasm between the dominant and the minorities exists; inequalities and dominations are vivid to any keen observer. Indigenous peoples, along with other margins of Asian societies continue to be victims in the profit oriented globalisation that do not consider any of the human costs and human rights. Conflicts, environmental degradation, human trafficking, depletion of natural resources, commercialized tourism are some of the larger challenges faced by indigenous communities in Asia. Indigenous peoples struggle with issues pertaining to human rights, self-determination, sustainable development, forest and biodiversity conservation, amidst greedy globalisation, assertion of dominant powers, profit and consumerist oriented market, land-grabbing by multinational corporates. Indigenous people's concern is "to ensure that indigenous people's rights are given due attention and respect in order to prevent further marginalisation or outright destruction of indigenous livelihoods, cultures and societies."[18]

A caveat is needed that indigenous communities are not without its own flaws.[19] Therefore it is vital to be guarded against any romanticization, reification, and glorification of any culture, without abrogating the history of victimisation and subjugation.[20]

---

[14] See, Wendy Doniger, *The Hindus: An Alternative History* (New York: Penguin Group, 2009).

[15] http://www.oikoumene.org/es/documentacion/documents/comisiones-del-cmi/asuntos-internacionales/regional-concerns/asia/message-of-condolences-on-the-death-of-bishop-alberto-ramento.html accessed 31 February, 2013

[16] http://madangjournal.com/bbs/view.php?id=issues&page=1&sn1=&divpage=1&sn=off&ss=on&sc=on&select_arrange=headnum&desc=asc&no=93 accessed 7 February 2013.

[17] For a comprehensive discussion on the term indigenous see, Christian Erni, ed., *The Concept of Indigenous Peoples in Asia: A Resource Book* (Copenhagen, Denmark: International Work Group for Indigenous Affairs, 2008).

[18] Ibid., 13.

[19] For a comprehensive discussion on the value of cultures in relation to the liberative dimension of the gospel of Jesus Christ that also enables the need to be open for diversity, see, Steve B. Bevans, *Models of Contextual Theology*

Asian Ecumenism in the light of the NMS, which explicitly states the preference for the Margins and their well-being(43) cannot afford either to be ignorant or arrogant to the plight and the issues of justice for the indigenous communities in Asia.[21]

Gender

While the NMS does not name explicitly the social structure of patriarchy as a powerful and resistant source of oppression and negation of members of society, the whole document is undergirded by the principle of inclusion and emancipation of all, which surely include women and the third gender. The NMS calls to "confront" those structures that continue to oppress, marginalise and exclude (40) and ensure dignity and worth of all people (42).

Undoubtedly, women today are relatively more emancipated[22] and participate in the society and churches, yet there still remain some deliberate and radical policies to be made and implemented both in the church and the larger society in order to truly proclaim that all are equally accepted and respected.[23] The World Council of Churches has initiated programmes towards building more inclusive communities, such as the **An Ecumenical Decade of Churches in Solidarity with Women, 1988-1998.** Still there is more tokenism at best and continual resistance to women and the third gender as equal members at worst. Asia continues to be one of the most perilous regions for women: human trafficking, female foeticide, forced prostitution, rape, discrimination, sexual harassment, violence, exclusion from decision making, honour killing, domestic violence are pressing social challenges in many Asian societies.

There are resources and network among Asian churches, such as the Asian Network of Women Resource Centre,[24] which provide theological reflections, personal struggles and achievements as narratives for the enlightenment and empowerment of Christians. The questions to be posed: Are justice and inclusion issues limited to some consultations and some journals, only to be entertained once but then forgotten? How much deliberate effort do churches and its leadership put in to ensure the removal of rigid patriarchy that favours male and negates women? In true spirit of regional ecumenism, Asian Christians would do well to put in effort, resources and proactive action to ensure an inclusive society, reflecting truly the spirituality of Jesus Christ, which the NMS has articulated clearly. (97-100)

Inter-religious engagement

Asia is the continent that has faithful adherents of almost all religions-ranging from the so-called world religions characterised by possession of sacred texts to myriad of indigenous religions, based on oral traditions. Asia also provided the context for the most productive and vibrant engagement of Christian mission, thus resulting in Asia having a high percentage of the global Christian population on one hand,

---

(Maryknoll: Orbis, 1992, 2004); Kathryn Tanner, *Theories of Culture: A New Agenda for Theology* (Minneapolis: Augsburg Fortress, 1997).

[20] There is need for internal critique of any culture or society, I have argued for this perspective elsewhere, see, Atola Longkumer, "Not all is well in my ancestor's house: An Indigenous Theology of Internal Critique" in *The Ecumenical Review* vol 62, No. 4 December 2010, pp. 399-410

[21] The whole issue of The Ecumenical Review December 2010 published theological reflection from the location of indigenous communities. The Indigenous Theological Declaration was prepared under the leadership of late Maria Chavez Quispe, the then Program Secretary of the Indigenous People's concerns, WCC.

[22] From among many, an excellent, comprehensive reference see, Kwok Pui Lan, ed., *Christianity and Women*, 4 Volumes (New York: Routledge, 2009).

[23] Namsoon Kang, "The Centrality of Gender Justice in Prophetic Christianity and the Mission of the Church Reconsidered", in *International Review of Mission*, vol. 94/373, April 2005, pp. 279-289.

[24] See, http://www.awrc4ct.org/ accessed 9.2.13

and on the other hand and at the same time Asia continuing to provide a fecund region for religious encounters and dialogue among different religions. By the same token, Asia also witnesses increasing tensions and violence between religions. Incidentally, Asia has produced individuals who are renowned globally for their endorsement of non-violence and tolerance among religions: M.K. Gandhi and the Dalai Lama. The point to be noted is, that Asia has potential for religious encounters (for both ill and good) and simultaneously Asia also has the resources from historical repositories and lived contemporary spirituality for religious harmony. The NMS has re-iterated the crucial importance of Christian evangelism and its inter-relatedness with dialogue and respect of other religions (93-100), to stress its paramount importance, NMS lists the affirmations provided in the WCC document "*Christian Witness in a Multi-Religious World: Recommendations for Conduct.*"[25] Drawing from the Asian theological resources, such as C. S. Song, Kagawa Toyohiko, Stanley Samartha, Chung Hyun Kyong, Wesley Ariarajah, Kosuke Koyama, etc, continuous engagement and critical reflection is required from Asian Christians to ensure peaceful religious encounters.

Theological Education

In his foreword to the global theological education book, Archbishop Desmond Tutu stated the "crucial importance of theological education for the renewal of church's mission and service."[26] This statement can be applied to Asian ecumenical vision and practice too. Theological education remains crucial bridge for fellowship, cooperation, witness and translation of the NMS into Asian contexts. As the WCC Programme Secretary for Ecumenical Theological Education (ETE), Dietrich Werner has listed "core goals for ecumenical theological education" for Asian theological education from the perspective of ecumenical collaboration:

The following are the goals:

1. Beyond denominational self-centredness and fragmentation-Revitalizing ecumenical collaboration in theological education
2. Beyond the copy and paste mentality in theological education-a forward leap in Asian contextualization of theological education
3. Beyond elitist theological education-Theological education for the whole people of God in Asia
4. Beyond self-isolation of Christian churches in multi-faith contexts-Interfaith dialogue in theological education
5. Beyond miscommunication with living churches and their ministries – Spiritual formation in theological education
6. Beyond theological education as mere accumulation of knowledge – ecumenical formation as informed participation in the ecumenical movement.[27]

Anna May Say Pa (Myanmar), Afrie Songco Joye (USA/Philippines), H.S. Wilson (India/USA), Michael Poon (Singapore), Dietrich Werner (ETE-WCC/Geneva) among others are some contemporary theological educators, administrators engaged in active mentoring, cross-cultural resource sharing, ensuring theological networking and resources to reach the farthest corners of Asia. It is vital that the efforts of theological education receive adequate support from Asian church leadership and congregations.

---

[25] http://www.oikoumene.org/en/resources/documents/wcc-programmes/interreligious-dialogue-and-cooperation/christian-identity-in-pluralistic-societies/christian-witness-in-a-multi-religious-world.htm accessed 9.2.13

[26] Dietrich Werner, David Esterline, Namsoon Kang, Joshua Raja (eds), Handbook of Theological Education in World Christianity, Regnum Oxford, 2010

[27] Dietrich Werner, *Theological Education in World Christianity: Ecumenical Perspectives and Future Priorities* (Tainan: Programme for Theology and Cultures in Asia, 2011), 117.

Theological education contributes to the ministerial formation of the future church leaders and the theologians who will articulate the theological vision of the NMS for and from Asian contexts.

Conclusion

It is indeed the crucified Christ, whose life and work Christians witness, who has demonstrated preference for the periphery/Margins (Koyama). In fact to be and to come from Nazareth was in itself a statement of being identified with the Margins (Leonardo Boff). The NMS has resoundingly reiterated this vision of the gospel, wherein fullness of life to all is proclaimed. Writing on the history of the World Missionary Conference 1910, Brian Stanley quotes Robert E. Speer, the Presbyterian mission strategist to emphasise the need of Asian interpretations of Christianity,[28] which surely has come to fruition as the vibrant Christian community in today's Asia illustrate. In the light of the NMS the Asian Christian community is called to continue to participate in the mission of Christ, which is characterised by mutuality, reciprocity and inter-dependence in the common commitment to the salvation of all that ensures justice, dignity, and life for all as God in the event of Incarnation manifested.(29, 45, 86-92).

Bibliography

Michael Poon, ed, *Confessing the Faith in Asia Today: Shoki Coe and the Rise of the Asia Pacific Rim Christianity (*TTC, Singapore, 2012)

Christine Linemann-Perrin, Atola Longkumer, Afrie Songco Joye, eds., *Putting Names with Faces: Women's Impact in Mission History* (Abingdon, 2012)

Peter C. Phan, ed., *Christianities in Asia* (Blackwell, 2011)

Dietrich Werner, David Esterline, Namsoon Kang, Joshva Raja eds, *Handbook of Theological Education in World Christianity: Theological Perspectives, Ecumenical Trends, Regional Surveys* (Regnum, 2010)

Sebastian Kim C.H. ed, *Christian Theology in Asia* (Cambridge, 2008)

Wati Longchar, *A Theological Resource Book on Disability* (ATESEA 2007)

Allan Anderson and Edmond Tang eds, *Asian and Pentecostal: The Charismatic Face of Christianity in Asia* (Regnum Books, 2005)

Peter C. Phan, *Being Religious Interreligiously: Asian Perspectives on Interfaith Dialogue* (Orbis, 2004)

Kwok Pui Lan, *Introducing Asian Feminist Theology* (Sheffield, 2000)

R.S. Sugirtharajah, ed., *Asian Faces of Jesus* (Orbis, 1995)

K.C. Abraham, ed., *Third World Theologies: Commonalities and Divergences* (Orbis, 1990)

---

[28] Brian Stanley, *The World Missionary Conference, Edinburgh 1910* (Grand Rapids: Wm. Eerdmans Publishing Company, 2009), 130-131.

(23) THEOLOGICAL PERSPECTIVES ON RESPONSIBLE AND CONTEXTUAL EVANGELISM IN THE PLURALISTIC CONTEXT OF INDIA

Mohan Larbeer

When India was facing the problem of 'Religious Conversion' in Gujarat, Vajpayee was the Prime Minister and during his visit to the affected places he invited a national debate on conversion. This raised reactions from different quarters. All Christian leaders were disturbed about the open accusation of *conversion* by force or fraud. Persons like Arun Shourie even accused the Christian churches that Christians had only one agenda, that is 'conversion.' However, Archbishop Alan de Lastic welcomed the request of the Prime Minister and announced that Christian Leaders should face the debate with open mindedness.

In this controversy, Christian leaders defended their right to *conversion* from their Biblical and Theological bias by citing the fundamental right, Article 25 of the Constitution, which says that "All persons are equally entitled to freedom of conscience and the right freely to profess, practice and propagate religion." Even though the word conversion is missing in this article Christians interpreted that 'in spirit' includes "the freedom of Conversion." This interpretation of Christians however, was not accepted by the supreme court in its verdict on Article 25.

Plurality of religions, cultures, languages, customs and practices is the basic historical character of India. In a pluralist society, therefore, inter-religious relationships become an encounter of commitments. To ask a people to give up their commitment amounts to asking them to commit spiritual suicide. For one to ask a religious community to seek its own extension through the extinction of other communities is to diminish rather than to enhance the total life of the larger community.

Further, the Christian mission mandate needs to be reflected upon more deeply in the context of today's technological culture and in the context of religious fundamentalism. The politicisation of religion and the communalization of politics are threats to religious values in the present world. The uniqueness of Christ is to be presented in his suffering and vicarious death but not in terms of a conquering power. We cannot propagate any other way of liberation than of Jesus Christ but at the same time we cannot set limits to the saving power of God.

'Christ may be seen as one in whom humankind has been truly expressed. To look beyond the bounds of Christian history the Church is to be regarded as "fellowship of all seekers after truth" which finds its highest form of expression in the reign of God. God's call to build a "fraternal community" is not simply for the judgement of people but for the healing and wholeness of all.

Unfortunately, there is a widespread feeling of insecurity among some faith minorities, as they experience domination by the majority community and unjustifiable treatment at the hands of the state machinery. Sometimes the fear and anxiety created by this minority status forces this faith minority to organise 'campaigns' and 'crusades' and project statistical reports of 'one billion or two billion' to be reached which are really alien to the spiritual ethos of our country. This has led to some enmity between the different faith communities.

The word 'minority' is a very significant word reflected in different forms in the Bible. Israel was always a minority nation and prophets were also a minority. The disciples including Paul did not give statistics about the churches they founded and did not give any report about the numerical expansion of the churches as an argument to prove their commitment to Christ. The images used by Jesus are images of insignificant quantities – images of salt, leaven, light and mustard seed. The purpose of these minority images are meant to play a catalytical role rather than to nurture a mentality according to which everything needs to be transformed to one's own form and substance. Salt is used to increase the taste but not making the entire food salty.

Unfortunately in India there are different understandings of the 'Great Mandate', the Commission to Mission, on 'Evangelism' and on 'Conversion.' In order to create a movement towards some better and more common understanding on these core dimensions of Christian witness, the Board of Theological Education of the Senate of Serampore College (BTESSC) in 2012 developed an innovative initiative: BTESSC in collaboration with National Council of Churches in India, the Evangelical Fellowship of India, Interfaith Coalition for Peace organized the National Level Church Leaders consultation from 29th February to 2nd March, 2012 at ECC, Bangalore to develop an Indian document on the basis of the global document on *Christian Witness in a Multi-Religious World: Recommendations for Conduct* released by World Council of Churches, World Evangelical Alliance and Pontifical Council of Inter-religious Dialogue (Roman Catholic Church).[1]

The consultation was well attended by almost all denominations in India and representative groups from Evangelical fellowship. Church Leaders, Bishops from different denominations, Pastors, Theologians, Christian Activists, Missionaries from the field and representatives from the evangelical background attended the consultation which took place in Bangalore and is part of a longer history of debate in India on evangelism and inculturation.[2] In reflecting on the combined statement of WCC, WEA and the Vatican entitled, "*Christian Witness in a Multi-Religious World: Recommendations for Conduct*", the purpose was to produce recommendations for the conduct of relevant Christian witness and evangelism in India. Towards the end, an Indian document was released which is reproduced on the following pages:

Christian Witness in the Pluralistic Context of India: Recommendations for Conduct

During the last 65 years since Independence there have been countless acts of violence and attacks against these minorities. Such outbreaks of violence are planned, widespread, prolonged resulting in the loss of lives, injuries, psychological trauma and damage, destruction of properties, homes ,institutions, religious places and displacement on a large scale. Sadly these continue to take place even in the present times.

Targeted attacks take place against religious minorities because there is no respect for their religious identity and for their religious liberty. Why should conversion per se be a controversial matter? The right to adopt a religion of one's own choice is natural and fundamental. Why should anybody object if a man wishes to change his religion?

It would submit that those who would object to and obstruct conversion to a religion of a person's choice, are the ones who are creating disturbances and dividing society. Justice requires that people's right to religious liberty should be respected.

We are totally against any conversion by force, fraud and enticement. We do not admit unwilling candidates to Christianity and we regard such conversions as invalid. Strangely it is the others who raise the bogey of conversions by force, fraud and enticement. Let the converts themselves say that they were forced or cheated or baited.

Besides, the minorities will always be at a physical, psychological social, political, economic and cultural disadvantage in the midst of a vast majority. This is true particularly of Indian religious minorities which are altogether less than 20% among which are some very tiny communities. Their vulnerability is intensified because of the rise of fundamentalism, extremism and terrorism and politicization of religion with leaders surreptitiously appealing to the religious sentiments of the majority community. However it

---

[1] See: http://www.oikoumene.org/resources/documents/wcc-programmes/interreligious-dialogue-and-cooperation/christian-identity-in-pluralistic-societies/christian-witness-in-a-multi-religious-world.html.

[2] See the earlier consultation of FABC on evangelization and inculturation in 2000: http://www.fabc.org/offices/oe/docs/doc3.pdf

should also be noted that most of the majority community would be tolerant towards minorities. It is only a few elements and leaders who are fomenting fundamentalism in the country and vitiating the climate of religious harmony.

The authenticity of India's secularism will finally be judged by the kind of treatment meted out to its minorities in the country, a country, in which the ideal of secular democracy is translated into reality by the degree to which minorities feel safe and secure to live their lives in society with dignity, honour and equality.

Preamble

Mission belongs to the very being of the church. Proclaiming the word of God and witnessing to the world is essential for every Christian. At the same time, it is necessary to do so according to gospel principles, with full respect and love for all human beings and all creation.

Aware of the tensions between people and communities of different religious convictions and the urgent task of Christian witness, a consultation was held at the Ecumenical Christian Centre, Bangalore from 29 February to 02 March, 2012. It was organized by the National Council of Churches of India, the Evangelical Fellowship of India, Interfaith Coalition for Peace, and the Board of Theological Education of the Senate of Serampore College. The participants included delegations from the Catholic, Orthodox, and Protestant Churches of India. Having as our basis the text *Christian Witness in a Multi-Religious World: Recommendations for Conduct*,[3] we met to reflect and produce this new document. It is to serve as a set of recommendations for conduct in Christian witness in India. Here we address practical issues associated with Christian witness in the multi-religious, multi-cultural, multi-ethnic and ideological contexts of India. Ours is a country of rich diversity and a deep historical heritage, yet we acknowledge growing violence, poverty, fundamentalism, communalism, and marginalization of the Dalits, Tribals/Adivasis, OBCs, women, children, and other minorities.

The purpose of this document is to encourage all Christians, churches, church councils, mission bodies, and theological institutions to reflect on their current practices of Christian life and witness. We offer these recommendations to serve as guidelines for witness and mission among those of different religions and among those who do not profess any particular religion. It is hoped that Christians throughout India will study and apply this document in the light of their own experience in witnessing to their faith in Christ, both by word and deed.

Basis for Christian witness

1. For Christians it is a privilege and joy to give an account for the hope that is within us and to do so with gentleness and respect (cf. 1 Peter 3:15).
2. Jesus Christ is the supreme witness (cf. John 18:37). Christian witness is always a sharing in Christ's witness, which takes the form of proclamation of the gospel, service to neighbour, care for creation and the total gift of self even if that act of giving leads to the cross (Genesis 1:28, Leviticus 19:18). Just as the Father sent the Son in the power of the Holy Spirit, so believers are sent in mission to witness in word and action to the love of the Triune God.
3. The example and teaching of Jesus Christ and of the early church must be the guides for Christian mission. Christians have sought to follow Christ's way by proclaiming and sharing the good news of God's reign (cf. Luke 4:16-20).

---

[3] A document jointly produced by the World Council of Churches, the World Evangelical Alliance, and the Pontifical Council for Inter-religious Dialogue of the Vatican. It was launched on 28 June 2011. The full text is available at: http://www.oikoumene.org/resources/documents/wcc-programmes/interreligious-dialogue-and-cooperation/christian-identity-in-pluralistic-societies/christian-witness-in-a-multi-religious-world.html.

4. Christian witness in pluralistic India includes engaging in dialogue for life with people of different religions, cultures and ideologies (cf. Acts 17:22-28).
5. In some contexts, living and proclaiming the gospel is difficult, hindered or even prohibited, yet Christians are commissioned by Christ to continue faithfully in solidarity with one another in their witness to him (cf. Matthew 28:19-20; Mark 16:14-18; Luke 24:44-48; John 20:21; Acts 1:8).
6. Christian witness must reflect the fullness of life that Jesus came to offer. We oppose any inappropriate methods of exercising mission, such as resorting to deception and coercive means, which betray the gospel and may cause suffering to others. Such departures call for repentance and remind us of our need for God's continuing grace (cf. Romans 3:23).
7. We affirm that while it is our responsibility to witness to Christ, conversion is ultimately the work of the Holy Spirit (cf. John 16:7-9; Acts 10:44-47). We recognize that the Spirit blows where the Spirit wills in ways over which no human being has control (cf. John 3:8).
8. As the high priestly prayer of Jesus indicates, mission and unity belong together – "That they all may be one… so that the world may believe" (John 17:21). Christian witness is made more credible by our unity.

Guiding principles

Christians are called to honour the following principles as they seek to fulfil Christ's commission in an appropriate manner within the plurality of Indian contexts.

1. *Acting in God's love.* Christians believe that God is the source of all love and, accordingly, in our witness we are called to love our neighbour as ourselves (cf. Matthew 22:34-40; John 14:15).
2. *Imitating Jesus Christ.* In all aspects of life, and especially in their witness, Christians are called to follow the example and teachings of Jesus Christ (cf. John 20:21-23).
3. *The witness of families.* The family plays a central role in Christian witness. Just as Jesus was sent to reveal God's love through the medium of the human family, so also are families meant to reveal the love within the Holy Trinity. Children themselves can be very powerful witnesses, and Christians are called to model the wholesome and liberating power of the gospel in the family, particularly in contexts where families have not experienced God's love or are under different threats.
4. *Gospel values.* Christians are called to conduct themselves with integrity, love, compassion, and to overcome all arrogance, condescension and disparagement (cf. Galatians 5:22). Power and authority in our Churches and institutions needs to be exercised in the spirit of humility and service (cf. Philippians 2:3).
5. *Hospitality.* Table fellowship was an important feature of the prophetic hospitality that Jesus offered. Therefore, we are called to extend and receive hospitality to and from all, irrespective of class, caste, creed and gender.
6. *Acts of service.* We are called to serve (Mark 10:45). Acts of service, such as providing education, health care, relief services and upholding the integrity of creation are an integral part of witnessing to the gospel.
7. *Acts of justice.* We are called to act justly, to love tenderly and to recognize Christ in the least of our sisters and brothers (cf. Micah 6:8, Matt 25:45). These include the poor, women, children, Dalits, Tribals/Adivasis, OBCs, and others who struggle for dignity of life, identity, land, etc. Discrimination and the exploitation of situations of poverty and need have no place in Christian witness.
8. *Acts of healing.* Praying for and visiting the sick is an integral part of Christian witness. Many Christians are involved in acts of healing, including faith healing and reconciliation work. All are called to exercise discernment as we carry out these ministries, fully respecting human dignity and

ensuring that the vulnerability of people and their need for healing are not exploited. Care must be taken to avoid the commercialization of these ministries and the growth of personality cults.

9. *Promoting peace and rejecting violence.* We are called to be peacemakers and this demands that we reject all forms of violence – physical, psychological and social, including terrorism, ethnic, sexual and caste related violence. We also denounce repression by any religious or State authority, including the violation or destruction of places of worship, sacred symbols or texts.
10. *Freedom of religion and belief.* Religious freedom flows from the very dignity of the human person, which is grounded in the creation of all human beings in the image and likeness of God and the freedom of conscience (cf. Genesis 1:26). The right to publicly profess, practice, propagate and change one's religion is also guaranteed in the Indian Constitution (articles 25 and 26). All human beings have equal rights and responsibilities. Where any religion is instrumentalized for political ends, or where religious persecution occurs, Christians are called to engage in a prophetic witness denouncing such actions.
11. *Building inter-religious relationships.* We are called to commit ourselves to work with all people in mutual respect and solidarity. Christians should continue to build relationships of respect and trust with people of different religions so as to facilitate deeper understanding, reconciliation and cooperation for justice, peace and the common good.
12. *Respect for all people.* The liberating message of the gospel both challenges and enriches culture. Even when the gospel challenges certain aspects of culture, we are called to respect all people. We are also called to discern elements in our own culture, such as the caste system, that are challenged by the gospel (cf. Galatians 3:28).
13. *Bearing witness to the truth.* It is vital in our testimony that we are transparent, accountable and honest. Christians are to speak sincerely and respectfully; we are to listen in order to learn about and understand others' beliefs and practices, and are encouraged to acknowledge and appreciate what is true and good in them. Any comment or critical approach should be made in a spirit of mutual respect, making sure not to bear false witness concerning other religions.
14. *Ensuring personal discernment.* Christians are to acknowledge that changing one's religion is a decisive step that must be accompanied by sufficient time for reflection and preparation, through a process ensuring full personal freedom.
15. *Fullness of life.* Jesus came to give life and life in all its fullness (John 10:10). The gospel is life-affirming and so should Christians be. Therefore, we must challenge life-negating structures, such as the caste system, patriarchy (male domination) and ecological violence. The only adequate response to the liberating gospel is repentance for such sins (cf. Matthew 3:8).
16. *Sharing the Word.* Jesus, the Word incarnate, spent time preaching and proclaiming that the reign of God was near. Proclamation has a central place in Christian witness, as does sharing the faith in word and deed with neighbours near and far. Inviting them to follow Christ remains the priority in Christian mission (Romans 10:14-15).

Recommendations

We the participants of the Bangalore consultation offer these recommendations for consideration and action by all Christians in India.

1. *apply* the guidelines set out in this document in light of the needs and concerns of your own context and in the same ecumenical spirit of this document. Always *be aware* of the need for self-reflection and analysis of your witness and your lives.
2. *build* relationships of respect and trust with people of all religions, in particular at institutional levels between churches and other religious communities, engaging in on-going inter-religious dialogue as part of their Christian commitment. In certain contexts, where years of tension and

conflict have created deep suspicions and breaches of trust between and among communities, inter-religious dialogue can provide new opportunities for resolving conflicts, restoring justice, healing of memories, reconciliation and peace-building.

3. *encourage* Christians to *strengthen* their own Christian identity and faith commitment to Jesus while *deepening* their knowledge and understanding of different religions, and to do so taking into account the perspectives of the adherents of those religions. Christians should avoid misrepresenting the beliefs and practices of people of different religions.
4. *cooperate* with other faith communities and *participate in* civil society movements that engage in advocacy towards justice and the common good and, wherever possible, *stand together* in solidarity with all minority groups, especially religious minorities, and all who are in situations of conflict.
5. *call* on governments to ensure that freedom of religion is properly and comprehensively respected, recognizing that in many states religious institutions and persons are inhibited from exercising their mission.
6. *pray* for their neighbours and their well-being, recognizing that prayer is integral to who we are and what we do, as well as to Christ's mission.

Conclusion

This document was well received by the different churches, missionary movements and theological circles as a guideline for their conduct and also for their understanding of evangelism. This helps us to make positive affirmations about our neighbours. When *we* witness to our neighbours we should be open to their witness to us. Otherwise it cannot be a *mutual* witness. Christian witness demands co-operation and mutual understanding of all our neighbours who are also struggling against the forces of death. In India, we live among neighbours of other faiths whose lives are illumined by their religious values and truths. Through a number of centuries of conflict, struggle and immense human suffering, a certain delicate relationship between different religions has been established and maintained in our country. In our pluralistic society we need to overcome the secular indifference to religions which leaves no room for religious bias in public life. We also need to overcome the shallow religious tolerance which merely allows religions to co-exist without any creative interaction between them. We need a commitment that requires a sharing of faith with others and tolerance that makes mutual enrichment possible.

(24) Rewriting the History of Christianity in Asia from an Ecumenical Perspective

Leonard Fernando, SJ[1]

The word history is derived from the Greek word *historia* which means enquiry, or knowledge gained from enquiry. In the field of research, history uses narrative forms to present the data available. Thus we can say history is the discovery, organization and presentation of the sequence of events, knowledge of which is gained through patient and critical enquiry. The Germans use the noun *Geschichte* for history from the verb *geschehen* which means "to happen". Hindus use terms like *itihasa* (tradition: literally meaning "verily thus it happened") and *purana* (ancient story).[2]

Oral History and Written History

There is oral history and written history. Oral histories are passed on by word of mouth. When these oral memorials are put into written documentation we have written histories. The Greeks said that "alphabets were invented to preserve the memory of things." The Sanskrit word for letter or syllable is *akshara*, "imperishable". Whether in oral or written history, it is difficult to be objective in history because of the difficulty in determining the truth about the past. It is difficult because what happened is viewed and remembered differently, depending on the perspective in which that event is seen by each person or group. I am not speaking here about interpretation of the event or a distortion of history but of the problem of choosing whose perspectives are worth remembering and which events worth narrating. The choice made of persons who narrate events has its bearing on the history of a group.

Hermeneutics of Suspicion

I would like to apply the hermeneutics of suspicion to the histories of Christianity in Asia written so far by posing the questions: "Who writes whose history for whom?" "What are the sources they depend upon in writing the history?" "Are they mission and missionary centred or people centred?" "Are they ecumenical or denominational?" "Are they elite history or subaltern history?

In this paper I discuss principally the issue of writing the history of Christianity in India both in the past and in the present. I highlight the double shift adopted in the historiography of Christianity in India, especially in the multi-volume project of *History of Christianity in India* adopted and put into practice by the Church History Association of India: (1) ecumenical perspective, and (2) writing in the historical context of Indian communities. The shifts in the writing of the history of Christianity in India are presented in this paper as a case study. A similar research can be done for the history of Christianity in the different countries in Asia. The multi-volume Project and the bi-annual journal of the above mentioned Association, *Indian Church History Review*, can serve as a source and model.

---

[1] Fr. Dr. Leonard Fernando, S.J., is Professor of Church History at Vidyajyoti College of Theology, Delhi, and editor of the monthly journal *Vidyajyoti Journal of Theological Reflection*. From 1999 to 2008 he was editor of the bi-annual journal *Indian Church History Review* and now he is the General Editor of the CHAI six volume project of the History of Christianity in India.

[2] Ernst Breisach, "Historiography: An Overview," in *Encyclopedia of Religion*, vol. 6, edited by Lindsay Jones, Detroit: Thomson Gale, 2005, 4024.

As Felix Wilfred rightly observes, "The mainstream history of Indian Christianity is a story of how faith was transmitted, with missionaries playing the leading role."[3] There is a heavy dependence on the reports of the missionaries in writing the history. The small number of missionaries without the help of local agents could not have achieved any significant success in their ministries. Yet, the local agents are hardly mentioned in the missionary reports and when mentioned it is usually only by a fleeting reference to them and their activities. It should be also pointed out that even among the missionaries only the male missionaries get the pride of place in the missionary reports, the women missionaries and their activities being undervalued.

Though there are other groups of people who are not given their due place in missionary reports and eventually in the Indian Church history books, in this paper I shall restrict my focus to the two above mentioned issues – the local agents and women missionaries.[4] I would like to cite two examples from the history of Christianity in India – one Catholic and the other Protestant – to highlight the corrective measures that need to be taken up so that the history writings "bring into focus events and persons who have hitherto received no attention or only marginal reference."[5]

Local Agents

In the chapter on "The Christian Communities of the Coastal Regions of Tamil Nadu (1542-1700)" Fr Joseph Thekkedath narrates: "He [Francis Xavier] spent the next four months [in 1542-43, after baptizing the children born after the mass baptisms of 1536 and 1537 in the coastal Christian villages] in Tuticorin. The first three were employed in translating into Tamil the most essential parts of the small catechism. He did this with the help of the three local seminarians who had accompanied him from Goa, assisted also by other persons, who like his three seminarians had some knowledge of Portuguese in addition to their own native Tamil."[6] For this information Fr Thekkedath relies on George Schurhammer's books.[7] These seminarians from Goa were Xavier's interpreters and helpers in the imparting of Catholic religious instruction. But we do not have many details about them and their activities except that which has been made possible thanks to the comparative study of the Letters of Francis Xavier by Fr Joseph Costelloe. From these letters he shows that among the three seminarians who accompanied Francis Xavier in 1542 from Goa to Tamilnadu one was a minor seminarian and the other two were deacons, Gaspar and Manuel. All the three came from Tuticorin. Gaspar and Manuel were ordained priests in 1544.[8] Thekkedath mentions along with Gaspar and Manuel one more local priest Francis Coelho whom Francis Xavier left behind to carry on the work started by him.[9] Their role in the formation of the Christian community must

---

[3] Felix Wilfred, "Historiography of Indian Christianity: Some Reflections," *Vidyajyoti Journal of Theological Reflection* 73 (2009) 740.

[4] I am highlighting the issues in the missionary-centred church reports and history – not histories written based on the people whom missionaries address. I shall take that up for discussion when I discuss the multi-volume project of the Church History Association of India.

[5] Ibid.

[6] Joseph Thekkedath, *History of Christianity in India*. Vol. 2, Bangalore: Church History Association of India, 1988, 156.

[7] George Schurhammer, *Francis Xavier, His Life, His Times*, vol. 2. India 1541-1545, Rome: The Jesuit Historical Institute, 1977; George Schurhammer and Joseph Wicki, *Epistolae S. Francisci Xaverii aliaque eius Scripta*, 2 vols., Rome: Monumenta Historica Societatis Iesu, 1944-45.

[8] *The Letters and Instructions of Francis Xavier*, Translated and Introduced by M. Joseph Costelloe,S.J., Anand: Gujarat Sahitya Prakash, 1993. See the footnotes in pp. 50 and 60.

[9] Joseph Thekkedath, *History of Christianity in India*. Vol. 2, Bangalore: Church History Association of India, 1988, 162.

have been significant both as sub-deacons, deacons and as priests. But their activities and contribution are not recorded.

Besides them, the other local agents of the evangelization were catechists or headman (*kannakkapillai*) in each village. Francis Xavier appointed them and paid them from the 4000 *fanams* the King of Portugal had assigned to his work. The catechist conducted common prayers for the people each Sunday, baptized people when necessary and shared with the missionary the important village happenings. This structure proved successful and was followed in mission work elsewhere,[10] not only among the Catholics but also among the Protestants. Though their contribution to the building up of Christian community was great, their names and who worked where and with what success is not mentioned in the missionary sources.

Even about the local people who bore testimony to Christian faith with martyrdom very little information is available from the missionary sources. I give two examples. In 1544 many persons in the Mannar Island[11] embraced Christianity. Since they rejected the Raja's order[12] to return to their ancestral faith, the Raja sent his soldiers and six hundred of them were massacred. The rest fled to their relatives in Vedalai on the Indian mainland. These 600 Tamils may well have been the first Indian martyrs to die for the Christian faith. Francis Xavier wrote about this in his letter to his companions in Rome (January 27, 1545): "The king of the land acted with great cruelty and slew many of them because they had become Christians. May God our Lord be thanked that martyrs are not lacking in our days."[13] In this letter Francis Xavier narrates the actions taken by the Portuguese Governor of India to protect the Christians from the raja of Jaffna. But no information is available to us about the reaction of the local people who had to face persecution and martyrdom. For the people who had recently embraced Christianity this event must have been a shattering experience. Since this was the first event in India where a large number of Catholics died a martyr's death we would like to have more information on the people who faced martyrdom: who and what gave them courage. How did they cope with losing so many of them suddenly? But the missionary reports have nothing to say on these pertinent questions.

In 1549 in Vedalai, where the people from Mannar had sought refuge, there was once again martyrdom. Antony Criminali, an Italian Jesuit held in high esteem by the people, was killed. Along with him, a local Christian was martyred. But the missionary records have not cared to preserve his name or details about him.

These Brothers of Ours

On the other hand Henry Henriques, who succeeded Criminali as superior in the Fishery Coast, has left behind details about a group of local persons who were his collaborators in mission. He called them "these brothers of ours" and wrote highly in praise of them in two of his letters. On January 12, 1551, he wrote from Kochi to his companion Simon Rodrigues in Portugal:

> They [Christians in the Fishery Coast] show a great desire to serve God and they do this every time in a better way. They are quite ready to obey the Fathers, as if they lived under obedience, and they are quite ready to die for the love of Christ Our Lord. You may believe that one of the great consolations which we, Fathers and Brothers, have here is to see these men, or better *these brothers of ours,* because we consider them as such for their great virtue and for the deep *friendship* they have with us. And it is certain that in some of them we notice such virtues that we would be very grateful to God our Lord if he would grant them to us. *Such men edify the people very much by their good life*, free from all self-seeking. And so, after they are placed in the various

---

[10] Leonard Fernando & G. Gispert-Sauch, *Christianity in India*, New Delhi: Penguin, 2004, 91.
[11] Mannar island is off the south-eastern coast of Tamil Nadu, India and off the north-western coast of Sri Lanka.
[12] Raja of Jaffna, Sri Lanka.
[13] *The Letters and Instructions of Francis Xavier*, 118.

villages, by the goodness of God a very different fruit is produced in those places compared with the earlier times [when only foreign missionaries worked there].[14]

In 1552 Henriques wrote about this group of committed Christians to Ignatius Loyola in Rome:

These people live in the various villages teaching the Christian doctrine and helping us... We, the Fathers here, are very consoled and have a holy envy of them, as we see that we lack some of the virtues that shine so splendidly in them. We feel that in this way Christians will profit much from them as we see that in fact they do. We have a great confidence in God that in this way and other ways we have here with this people, if Our Lord for our sins would permit that in these parts of India there would be no Portuguese, *these Christians would among themselves carry on the Christian movement*, a thing that we think in few places of India could be carried on. [15]

The Visitor of the Jesuit Missions, Alessandro Valignano, in his report about the Indian Province of 1579-80, said that the children of the Fishery Coast knew the catechism of the Christian faith better than children in Europe! I would like to situate this report against the background of the state of affairs forty years earlier. When Francis Xavier landed in 1542 in the Fishery Coast, the Christians had only a Christian name and no knowledge of the Christian belief system. But within less than forty years the children in that area knew the catechism better than those in Europe! A handful of missionaries would not have been able to achieve such a great success without the help of the local agents – priests, catechists and collaborators. Henriques praises and gives information about the success story of his collaborators whom he calls "these brothers of ours". Unfortunately most mission reports do not give adequate information about the contributions of the local people for the spread of Christian faith. But "these native assistants were irreplaceable. It is high time that the Indian Christians tell their stories freed from the Eurocentric perspectives inherent in most missionary sources,"[16] observes Felix Wilfred. Fortunately in the recent years some attempts have been made in that direction by publication of Family Histories books giving more information on the contributions made by the catechists and other local people. We would like to mention two path-breaking books: *Puthiathore Samudayam* (A New Society) edited by David and Sarojini Packiamuthu and *Upateeciyar Cavarirayapillai* (1801-1874) (catechist Cavarirayapillai) edited by A. Sivasubramanian.[17]

Women Neglected

Not only the local agents but also the women among the missionaries have been neglected in the missionary reports and consequently also in the writing of the history of Christianity in India. This is highlighted by Ms Bharati in her article "Women's Predicament as they Encountered Christianity: A Case Study of C.M.S. Telugu Mission in Andhra."[18] Through a case study of a hundred years of Church

---

[14] J. Wicki, ed., *Documenta Indica* II (1550-1553), Rome: Monumenta Historica Societatis Jesu, 1950, 155. Italics is added.

[15] Wicki, *Documenta Indica* II, 301. Italics is added.

[16] Wilfred, "Historiography of Indian Christianity," 742.

[17] David and Sarojini Packiamuthu, eds., *Puthiathore Samudayam*, (in Tamil) Tirunelveli: Valarnthu Peruhuha Veliyidu, 2001. This book has appeared in English version: David and Sarojini Packiamuthu, eds. and trans., *Tirunelveli's Evangelical Christians: Two Centuries of Family amsavazhi Traditions*, gen. eds. Robert E. Frykenberg and Chris Barrigar, Bangalore: SAIACS Press, 2003; A. Sivasubramanian, ed., *Upateeciyar Cavarirayapillai* (1801-1874), (in Tamil) Nagercoil: Kalachuvadu Pathippagam, 2006.

[18] Bharati, "Women's Predicament as they Encountered Christianity: A Case Study of C.M.S. Telugu Mission in Andhra" *Indian Church History Review* 35/2 (December 2001) 147-167.

Missionary Society (C.M.S.) Telugu Mission in Andhra (1847-1947) she points out how women and their ministries were not adequately narrated in the writing of history.

In 1841 C.M.S. Telugu Mission was started in Masulipatam, and in course of time it spread to other areas of Andhra Pradesh. In the beginning C.M.S. was reluctant to send single women missionaries. So the wives of the missionaries became the pioneers of Christian women ministry in Andhra. Though they were the main source of contact with local families their work among the people was taken for granted. They were neither paid separately nor were they considered as missionaries. Bharati points out:

> In the missionary reports, records and mission journals usually the missionary gave report of his wife's ministry. She did not have anything to report on her own of the work she was doing. For example Mrs Sharkey, wife of one of the first missionaries in Machilipatnam, was given full-fledged missionary status after the death of her husband. However, we do not find her reporting separately about her work. The local missionary-in-charge became her spokesperson. In case anything was written by women there would be a prefix stating 'my wife [or Mrs ....] writes'. Even in women's magazines, for example in *Indian Female Evangelist* [January 9, 1872], it is men who wrote about the mission work. Men were the office bearers of female missions. For example, Rev Peachy was the secretary of Madras Church of England Zenana Missionary Society.[19]

Thus we see women missionaries and their activities were not given importance in the missionary reports. In such a situation it is not surprising that reports of local women as agents of transformation are hardly mentioned in the missionary reports. A similar situation exists in the Catholic Church regarding the apostolic activities of religious nuns. In most reports their activities are not reported. When mentioned it is often as a group (or congregation) participating in mission/education/social work, hardly ever names of individual sisters. In recent years the focus on Mother Teresa is of course an exception.

As we have seen, the women missionaries were made invisible and their voices were not heard although their contribution to the spread of Christianity and to the welfare of both Christians and non-Christians was immense. And when it comes to missionaries and local agents the latter had been given a minimal space. Moreover, the focus was on how the missionaries shared Christian faith with others and not how the local people assimilated it and made it their own and gave expressions to their new found faith. The early written histories of Christianity in India were denominational and they tended to be apologetic and even controversial, at times against a particular Christian community.[20]

It is against this background of denominational and mission-centred approach to the writing of history of Christianity in India that one should situate the giant step forward taken by the Church History Association of India (CHAI) to publish a multi-volume History of Christianity in India guided by a new perspective, and the shifts it took. I shall first narrate in a gist form the emergence of the Association and then explain in detail the multi-volume project and the new perspective it adopted. As one of the members of the first editorial board of this multi-volume Project, Dr John C.B. Webster, succinctly puts it:

> It emphatically rejected the mission history and the more institutional 'Church History' approach, and was in favour of a socio-cultural history of the Christian people in India. This was to have three other components as well: an ecumenical rather than a denominational approach; the region as the basic working unit of study; and the national, which emphasized comparisons and linkages between regions and developments that were more national than regional.[21]

---

[19] Bharati, "Women's Predicament as they Encountered Christianity" 148-149.

[20] See for a detailed discussion on this issue John C.B. Webster, *Historiography of Christianity in India*, New Delhi: Oxford University Press, 2012, 14-63.

[21] John C.B. Webster, *Historiography of Christianity in India*, New Delhi: Oxford University Press, 2012, 6.

Church History Association of India, Burma and Ceylon

A Church History Deputation to the Orient visited India in 1932.[22] This visit occasioned the formation of the Church History Association of India, Burma and Ceylon. During the visit of the Deputation, the National Christian Council convened a conference at Serampore on January 28, 1932, to discuss plans to stimulate the study of Church History and to collect and preserve valuable records of the history of Christianity in India. During the conference a proposal was made to form a Church History Association for India. Though nothing came out of this proposal at that time, two years later the Senate of Serampore took up this issue for discussion in its meeting on December 7, 1934 and proposed that steps be taken for the formation of a Church History Association for India, Burma and Ceylon.[23] Accordingly on February 1, 1935 Rev Dr G.H.C. Angus, the President of Senate of Serampore, Rev Dr Pakenham-Walsh, the Principal of Bishop's College, Calcutta and Rev Dr C.E. Abraham, the Registrar of the Senate of Serampore jointly called for a meeting at Calcutta of some leading Christians in that city to consider the proposal to form the Association. In that meeting the Church History Association of India, Burma and Ceylon was formed on the basis of some provisional rules, and Most Rev Foss Westcott, the Metropolitan Bishop of Calcutta and Rev Dr C.E. Abraham were elected Chairman and Secretary respectively. Recalling the events that led to the formation of the Church History Association the founder-member Rev Dr G.H.C. Angus recalled in his speech to the West Bengal members of the Association:

> There was the tendency among Western missionaries and their converts to put undue emphasis on European Christian traditions, history and theology at the expense of the Eastern churches; conversely some Indian Christians tended to ignore the experience of the rest of Christendom as irrelevant to India.... Above all there was the mutual ignorance about each other's work that prevailed among the different Churches and missions – a serious handicap to the growth of ecumenical consciousness.[24]

Bulletin of the Church History Association of India

While the meeting at Calcutta saw the importance of having representatives from Churches in India, Burma and Ceylon as members of the Executive committee, it decided that for the time being the members of the Executive Committee should be people living in and around Calcutta so that regular meetings can be held to discuss the plan of action. The first meeting of the Executive Committee was held on February 19, 1935. It is interesting to note that already in its first meeting one of the proposals made was to write a History of the Christian Church in India. To make that possible attempt was also made by the Association to establish a small library of source materials. It was also decided to publish an Annual Bulletin every year giving information about the activities of the Association. The Annual Bulletin appeared in 1936, 1937, 1938, and 1941. The war and its after-effects affected the functioning of the Association. Moreover, the President of the Association, the Most Rev Foss Westcott, died and many active members of the Association either retired or left the country. Yet the Secretary Rev Dr Abraham kept the Association going along with Rt.

---

[22] The two distinguished historians from USA were Prof S.J. Case, the Head of the Department of Church History at the Divinity School of the University of Chicago and Prof W.D. Schemerhorn, the Head of the Department of Church History at Garrett Biblical Institute at Evanston. A third member from England, Rev R. Morgan, Warden of the College of the Ascension, Selly Oak, Birmingham, who had visited China and Japan as part of the Deputation was not able to be part of the deputation. See H. Packenham-Walsh, "A Church History Association, The N.C.C. Review, 4 (1932) 198-200 as cited in F.S. Downs, "The Church History Association of India," *Indian Church History Review*, 23.2 (1989) 156.

[23] During the British rule it was customary to have organizations for the three nations India, Burma and Ceylon together.

[24] Cited in M.A. Laird, "Editorial," *Bulletin of the Church History Association of India* 1 (1961) 3.

Rev Noel Hall of Chotanagpur, the new President of the Association. During the first six years of its existence (1935-40),

1. Information regarding the availability of source material was gathered;
2. The active co-operation of Missions and Correspondents was enlisted;
3. Plans for the writing of a History of Christianity in India were set afoot and invitations to write sections of it were given to eminent writers like Bishop Stephen Neill;
4. Corresponding members were appointed in various places;
5. Interest in the work of the Association was created in different places;
6. Regional Church History Associations were formed, as in Dornakal, Andhra.[25]

The National Christian Council showed great interest in the works of the Association. The letter written by Rev J.Z. Hodge, the Secretary of the National Christian Council to the Secretary of the Church History Association testifies to that:

> Interest in your Association is extending. The Andhra Christian Council for example have taken the matter up and are organizing a branch there. I expect you are in touch with them. We hear also of interest developing in Bombay and I think your Executive might now well consider the desirability of giving the Association an all-India basis. We shall be very happy indeed to co-operate with you should you decide to do this by putting the matter before the various Provincial Christian Councils. We remember that the Association emerged as a result of the Church History Conference held at Serampore and convened by the N.C.C.[26]

In 1940 the Executive Committee was reorganized and included representatives of Missions and Churches outside of Bengal including Dr C.E. Chaney from Rangoon, Burma.

The Association published the following booklets:

1. *Pioneers and Leaders of the Church in India* (1938).
2. *A Calendar of the Church in India, Burma and Ceylon* (1940) and
3. *The South Indian Apostolate of St Thomas* by Mr K.N. Daniel (1952) to mark the 1900th anniversary of St Thomas' arrival in India.[27]

Greatly encouraged by the positive and encouraging responses it received for its letters from the Board of Theological Education of the National Christian Council and the leaders of the Churches and Principals of the Theological Colleges, the new Executive Committee decided to put into action the aims and objectives of the Association. The Aims and Objectives stipulated in the Provisional Rules[28] of the Church History Association of India were:

1. To interest itself in the collection and preservation of source-materials for the history of Christianity in India, by arranging for central depositories, preparing catalogues of documents available with different churches and missions, etc;
2. To stimulate research in Church History, especially in the history of the churches in India;
3. To perpetuate the memory of pioneers and leaders of the Church in India;
4. To form groups in various centres for discussion and study of problems connected with the life and history of the Church, ancient and modern, and to get into touch with existing groups having similar objects;
5. To promote instruction in Church History in English and in the vernaculars in India.[29]

---

[25] D.A. Christadoss, "The Church History Association of India," *Indian Journal of Theology* 9 (1960) 167.

[26] *Bulletin* 2, p. 5 as cited in D.A. Christadoss, "The Church History Association of India," *Indian Journal of Theology* 9 (1960) 168.

[27] See D.A. Christadoss, "The Church History Association of India," *Indian Journal of Theology* 9 (1960) 168.

[28] These Provisional Rules were adopted at the general meeting on February 1 and confirmed by the Executive Committee on February 19, 1935.

[29] "Church History Association of India. Provisional Rules," *Bulletin of the Church History Association of India* 1

Church History Association of India

In 1959 the Executive Committee had to be reconstituted. Except the Treasurer of the Association the services of others were not available, because they had either departed or retired. In its first meeting[30] the new Executive Committee decided to have the name of the Association changed into "The Church History Association of India" so as to limit the sphere of its work to the Indian Union.[31]

Ecumenical Organization

A major change happened in 1960s. Downs points out that "Until the 1960s the leadership of the Association came from the Calcutta region. The headquarters was in Serampore. The Association was Protestant, with the majority of its officers coming from the Anglican tradition."[32] Through a meeting held at Serampore in 1961 the association became "ecumenical" in so far as members from the Catholic Church – the largest Church in India – also became members if the Association. The Roman Catholic historians Fr. A.M. Mundadan, C.M.I. and Fr E.R. Hambye, S.J. became not only members but "quickly established themselves as among the most durable bulwarks of the Association."[33] In course of time members from the Orthodox and other Christian communities became members. These developments "made the Church History Association of India not only the most active of the "theological" professional organizations in the country, but also among the most ecumenical."[34]

Indian Church History Review

With the arrival of the new generation of historians from different Churches the goal to have a new way of writing the whole history of Christianity in India in an ecumenical way became clearer and its demand louder. Instead of the *Bulletin of the Church History Association of India* which the Association had published earlier and discontinued in 1941, it was decided to bring out a scholarly journal with the name *Indian Church History Review* (*ICHR*) from 1967. "It will to some extent continue the small Bulletin issued so far, but it will at the same time mean a fresh effort in which both Roman Catholic, Protestant and Orthodox scholars will participate."[35] The first issue of *ICHR* which appeared in 1967 enunciated the goals of *ICHR*. The main purposes were: (1) To publish articles and source materials to help in the writing of a standard work on the history of Christianity in India; and (2) to pioneer a new approach to the historical study of Christianity in India wherein Indian Christians will find their due place and a history of Christianity will be written in the context of the political and social history of India.

(1961) 19.

[30] It is not clear from the text available to us whether the new name was adopted in 1959 or 1960. See D.A. Christadoss, "Church History Association of India," *Bulletin of the Church History Association of India* 1 (1961) 4.

[31] D.A. Christadoss, "Church History Association of India," *Bulletin of the Church History Association of India* 1 (1961) 4.

[32] F.S. Downs, "The Church History Association of India," *Indian Church History Review*, 23.2 (1989) 157-58. Downs mentions that the Secretary of the Association, Mar Thomite C.E. Abraham, was a significant exception in this group of Anglicans.

[33] F.S. Downs, "Old Wine in New Skins?" Editorial, *Indian Church History Review*, 8.1 (1974) 1.

[34] F.S. Downs, "The Church History Association of India," *Indian Church History Review*, 23.2 (1989) 160.

[35] "The Mandate," *Indian Church History Review*, 8.1 (1974) 6.

International Commission of Comparative Church History

On February 1965 at the meeting of the Executive Committee it was decided to affiliate CHAI with the International Commission of Comparative Church History (ICCCH) (of the Congress of Historical Sciences) as its Indian Section. A vast majority of the members of the Association had already voted in favour of such a decision. The ICCCH in its Vienna Conference in September 1965 admitted the Indian Association by a unanimous vote.

Multi-Volume Project

The next major development happened in 1973. During the Second General Conference of CHAI held at Dharmaram College, Bangalore in October 1973 an editorial board was appointed to oversee the writing of a comprehensive history of the Church in India. "The members [of the editorial board] were chosen in view of their scholarship and ability, representing different Christian denominations – this being an ecumenical undertaking," writes Mundadan,[36] who was member of the editorial board from its inception and its General Editor till his death recently in August 2012. The members of the first editorial board were as follows: Rev. Dr D.V. Singh (General Editor), Dr T.V. Philip, Dr E.R. Hambye, S.J., Dr H. Grafe, Dr A.M. Mundadan, C.M.I., and Dr J.C.B. Webster.[37] The editors came from Roman Catholic, Lutheran, Mar Thoma, Presbyterian and Methodist traditions. [38]

The six-member Editorial Board at a meeting held in Secunderabad, Andhra Pradesh in February 1974 spelt out the approach to be taken in the writing of the proposed six-volume History of Christianity. It decided to part ways with the hitherto followed method of treating the history of Christianity in India "as an eastward extension of western ecclesiastical history."[39] It decided to write the history of Christianity in India "in the context of Indian history."[40] The socio-cultural aspect of India was insisted upon.

> The history of Christianity in India is viewed as an integral part of the socio-cultural history of the Indian people rather than as separate from it. The history will therefore focus attention upon the Christian *people* in India; upon who they were and how they understood themselves; [upon their social, religious, cultural and political encounters;] upon the changes which these encounters produced in them and in their appropriation of the Christian gospel as well as in the Indian culture and society of which they themselves were a part. These elements constitute the history of Christianity in India, and are not to be merely chapters tacked on to the end of an institutional study. This history should, therefore, provide an insight into the changing identity of the Christian people in India through the centuries.[41]

Ecumenical perspective was another ingredient element in the writing of the history of Christianity in India.

---

[36] A.M. Mundadan, "Six-volume Project of the Church History Association of India," *Indian Church History Review*, 19.1 (1985) 6.

[37] M.R. Westall, "Report on the General Conference of the Church History Association of India," *Indian Church History Review*, 7.2 (1973) 72.

[38] Despite the changes in the editorial board down the years care has been taken that the editorial board remains always an ecumenical group of historians.

[39] "A Scheme for a Comprehensive History of Christianity in India," *Indian Church History Review*, 8.2 (1974) 89.

[40] "A Scheme for a Comprehensive History of Christianity in India," *Indian Church History Review*, 8.2 (1974) 89.

[41] "A Scheme for a Comprehensive History of Christianity in India," *Indian Church History Review*, 8.2 (1974) 89. The words [upon their social, religious, cultural and political encounters;] are missing from this text. But they are found in F.S. Downs, "Old Wine in New Skins?" Editorial, *Indian Church History Review*, 8.1 (1974) 2.

> Christianity rather than any one section of the Christian Church will form the other basic framework for study. Denominational diversities will not be ignored or played down; here too both common features of different denominational experiences in each period and region will be explored, and the growth of the ecumenical movement in India described so that these basic unities may be seen along with the diversities.[42]

The Editorial board had high expectation from the volumes it was planning to publish.

> It is expected that this history will become the standard work in the field; that it will make an important contribution to the current understanding of the histories of India and of Christianity; that this will be the most up to date reference work for scholars interested in this field.[43]

So far six books from the multi-volume Project have been published. The second volume *History of Christianity in India from the Middle of the Sixteenth to the end of the Seventeenth Century* (1542-1700) by Dr Joseph Thekkedath, S.D.B., was released on October 1982 at Chennai by Dr M Santappa, Vice-Chancellor, Madras University. The first volume *History of Christianity in India up till the Middle of the Sixteenth Century* by Dr A. Mathias Mundadan, C.M.I. was released on February 1985 in Mumbai. The third volume *History of Christianity in India during the Eighteenth Century* by Dr E.R. Hambye, S.J. was published in 1997. The fourth and fifth volumes deal with History of Christianity in South India and North India in the nineteenth and twentieth centuries. They are in the process of being written as different parts of their volumes. That was due to the decision taken by the editorial board in 1987 to publish different parts of Volumes IV and V separately because there is so much to be written about the history of Christianity in India in these centuries. *History of Christianity in India, Volume IV, Part 2, Tamilnadu in the Nineteenth and Twentieth Centuries* by Dr Hugald Grafe was published on November 16, 1990. *History of Christianity in India, Volume V Part 5, North-East India in the Nineteenth and Twentieth Centuries* by Dr Frederick S. Downs was published on March 21, 1992. *History of Christianity in India, Volume V, Part 2, Northwest India in the Nineteenth and Twentieth Centuries* by Dr John C. B. Webster was released on October 30, 2012 by Prof. Basudev Chatterji, Chairman, Indian Council of Historical Research, Government of India. Other sections of these two volumes have been entrusted to different writers and are in various stages of writing.

In his presidential address given during the Sixth Triennial Conference of the Church History Association of India on October 18, 1985 in Ernakulam, Kerala, Cardinal Joseph Parecattil said:

> It is a matter of great satisfaction that an objective and open approach to history, a serious attempt at a deeper study of the history of Christianity in India has brought together the various Christian denominations. This coming together of scholars from the different Churches in India cannot but help create a better understanding of one another. It has been said that historical reasons have divided the Church of Christ. But the study of history must now bring them back to the path of unity. The meetings, discussions and various other activities of the Church History Association of India, especially the daring project of writing a multi-volume ecumenical history of the Indian Christians, will go a long way to promote the ecumenical cause.[44]

What Fr Mundadan mentioned in one of this reports as General Editor of the multi-volume project is worth recording: "The working of the Editorial Board for more than fifteen years has been and continues to be an enriching experience of sincere and cordial ecumenical co-operation."[45] CHAI continues to promote ecumenical cause. It is interesting to note that not only the members of the editorial board, consultants and

---

[42] "A Scheme for a Comprehensive History of Christianity in India," *Indian Church History Review*, 8.2 (1974) 90.
[43] "A Scheme for a Comprehensive History of Christianity in India," *Indian Church History Review*, 8.2 (1974) 90.
[44] Joseph Cardinal Parecattil, "Objective History: The Best Teacher," *Indian Church History Review*, 19.2 (1985) 98.
[45] As cited in F.S. Downs, "The Church History Association of India," *Indian Church History Review*, 23.2 (1989) 162.

writers of the multi-volume Project and contributors to *Indian Church History Review* but also the sponsors of the project are ecumenical. In the recently published volume the people who are thanked for their financial contribution makes that clear:

> We are thankful to the friends who have continued to encourage and support the project. We would not have been able to proceed with our work were it not for the generous grants made by Missio, Aachen (Germany), the National Council of Churches in India, the Catholic Bishops Conference of India, Leonard Theological College (Jabalpur), Dharmaram Vidya Kshetram (Bangalore), Simon Cardinal Pimenta (Archbishop of Bombay), the Theological Education Fund/Programme on Theological Education (an affiliate of the World Council of Churches), the Pontifical Society for the Propagation of Faith (Rome), the Congregation for the Oriental Churches (Rome), the Gesellschaft für Missionswissenschaft (Germany), and, for Volume IV, Part 2, the Evangelical Lutheran Mission (Leipzig Mission), Hildesheim (Germany) and the Evangelical Lutheran Church of Brunswick (Germany).[46]

Conclusion

Today CHAI is one of the most active ecumenical organisations in India having its regional meetings and Triennial national conferences and publishing a bi-annual journal and a multi-volume on *History of Christianity in India*. The bold, creative and timely step taken by CHAI to write the History not as a history of an institution but as history of a people with an ecumenical perspective has further promoted ecumenical spirit.

Other countries in Asia can profit from the attempts made by the multi-volume project of CHAI to rewrite their history with an ecumenical perspective. It is high time we make a conscious shift in the writing of history of Christianity in Asia. I envisage a historiography of Asian Christianity which will give focus on those who have so far received only marginal references and in the process those who were pushed to the periphery in the writing of history will come now to occupy the central place. We need to know what indigenous stories they created, to see what images they used to express their faith, what local miracles they recounted from generation to generation, what songs, hymns, dances, poems they created, what festivals they celebrated and how, including what they adopted and changed from traditions of other religions around them, etc. Perhaps this can be done not by trying a pure objectivity in writing (which never exists) but in consciously acknowledging our specific standpoint and pre-judgements, and by listening to the accounts of the "other". This is how "comparative theology" wants to proceed. This can be attempted also in historiography. For to listen to the accounts of the "other" we have to go beyond the missionary writings to the folk songs, diaries of catechists and other sources.[47] Webster in his concluding remarks in the book *Local Dalit Christian History* discusses the different sources available to write histories of Christian communities.[48] A history written by listening to the accounts available among the people will make Church history a people's history.

---

[46] See John C. B. Webster, *History of Christianity in India, Volume V, Part 2, Northwest India in the Nineteenth and Twentieth Centuries*, Bangalore: Church History Association of India, 2012, ix-x.

[47] Robert Frykenberg, mentions in his introduction to the book *Christians and Missionaries in India: Cross-Cultural Communication since 1500*, edited by Robert Eric Frykenberg, Grand Rapids, Michigan: Eerdmans, 2003, 25, about the forthcoming 3 volume diary of a catechist: *Diary of Savariraya Pillai: Tamil Village Schoolteacher*: 1834-1876, translated by David and Sarojini Packiamuthu, edited by R.E. Frykenberg, London: Grand Rapids. But we could not find any reference to this book in the recent book of Frykenberg (2010). May be it is still in the preparatory stage.

[48] Webster discusses the diverse source materials – mission sources, archeological sources, local stories and interviews – used by the different authors. See John. C.B. Webster, "Writing Local Dalit Christian History," *Local Dalit Christian History*, edited by George Oommen and John. C.B. Webster, Delhi: ISPCK, 2002, 130-146. John C.B. Webster in his

Bibliography

"A Scheme for a Comprehensive History of Christianity in India," *Indian Church History Review*, 8.2 (1974) 89-90.

Bharati, "Women's Predicament as they Encountered Christianity: A Case Study of C.M.S. Telugu Mission in Andhra" *Indian Church History Review* 35/2 (December 2001) 147-67.

Christadoss, D.A., "The Church History Association of India," *Indian Journal of Theology* 9 (1960) 166-68.

Christadoss, D.A., "Church History Association of India," *Bulletin of the Church History Association of India* 1 (1961) 3-5.

Downs, F.S., "Old Wine in New Skins?" Editorial, *Indian Church History Review*, 8.1 (1974) 1-4.

Downs, F.S., "The Church History Association of India," *Indian Church History Review*, 23.2 (1989) 156-63.

Downs, F.S., *History of Christianity in India, Volume V Part 5, North-East India in the Nineteenth and Twentieth Centuries*, Bangalore: Church History Association of India, 1992.

Fernando, Leonard & Gispert-Sauch, G., *Christianity in India*, New Delhi: Penguin, 2004.

Grafe, Hugald, *History of Christianity in India, Volume IV, Part 2, Tamilnadu in the Nineteenth and Twentieth Centuries*, Bangalore: Church History Association of India, 1990.

Hambye, E.R., *History of Christianity in India, Vol III, Eighteenth Century*, Bangalore: Church History Association of India, 1997.

Mundadan, A.M., "Six-volume Project of the Church History Association of India," *Indian Church History Review*, 19.1 (1985) 5-7.

Mundadan, A.M., *History of Christianity in India up till the Middle of the Sixteenth Century*, Bangalore: Church History Association of India, 1984.

Oommen, George and Webster, John. C.B., (ed.), *Local Dalit Christian History*, Delhi: ISPCK, 2002.

Packiamuthu, David and Sarojini, eds. and trans., *Tirunelveli's Evangelical Christians: Two Centuries of Family amsavazhi Traditions*, gen. eds. Robert E. Frykenberg and Chris Barrigar, Bangalore: SAIACS Press, 2003.

Parecattil, Joseph Cardinal, "Objective History: The Best Teacher," *Indian Church History Review*, 19.2 (1985) 95-98.

Thekkedath, Joseph, *History of Christianity in India*. Vol. II, *From the Middle of the Sixteenth to the End of the Sevententh Century (1542-1700)*, Bangalore: Church History Association of India, 1988.

Webster, John C. B., *A Social History of Christianity*, New Delhi: Oxford University Press, 2007

Webster, John C. B., *History of Christianity in India, Volume V, Part 2, Northwest India in the Nineteenth and Twentieth Centuries*, Bangalore: Church History Association of India, 2012.

Webster, John C. B., *Historiography of Christianity in India*, New Delhi: Oxford University Press, 2012.

Wilfred, Felix, "Historiography of Indian Christianity: Some Reflections," *Vidyajyoti Journal of Theological Reflection* 73 (2009) 737-51.

---

recent book *A Social History of Christianity* (New Delhi: Oxford University Press, 2007) has as its focus the history of the community and not the missionary.

PART III

LIFE, JUSTICE AND PEACE IN ASIAN ECUMENISM

(25) TOWARDS LIFE ENHANCING CIVILIZATION

Seong Won Park

The aspects of global crisis we are currently facing are serious. The situation is deeper and more fundamental. Is the current civilization sustainable and life-enhancing or destructive and life-destroying? There seems to be a general agreement that the current civilization is not sustainable.

We may be faced with a numerous agenda to deal with like the issues of eradication of poverty, social justice, peace and security, gender justice, community building and spiritual revitalization etc. However, I am convinced that one of the most serious challenges we have in this century in the world today is how to build a life-enhancing eco-community. This essay is to provoke a prophetic imagination on life-enhancing civilization, as one of the entry points to ecumenism from Asian perspective, not only from Asian philosophical wisdom, but also from experiences which some Asian pioneers attempted or are attempting in actual practices. I am sharing this in the hope that Asian churches and theologies, together with others in the global South, could make possible an ecumenical contribution to building a Life-enhancing civilization beyond the current human civilization which is becoming more and more destructive.

Situation of Global Society Today

What kind of a global society are we living in today? The world in which we are living today is full of crises, that is, multiple crises concerted by economic crisis, ecological crisis, geo-political crisis and many more crises including spiritual crisis.

Economic justice is at stake

The economy of life has been replaced by that of profit maximization for a select few at the cost and sacrifice of the life of many. The so-called Champaign glass economy allows only the top 20% of the world population to possess 83% of the world's wealth, while 80% of the world population shares the rest. This unjust economic system is excluding the majority of the world population from participation in the economy of life, facilitating speedy erosion of the earth, and wiping out any sense of common goods from people's mind.

There has been a warning on this system since the last decade. At the World Economic Forum in Davos in January 2008, George Soros, one of the world's top class speculators, gave a very significant warning by saying "the current crisis is not only the bust that follows the housing boom," and "it's basically the end of a 60-year period of continuing credit expansion." He went on to say, "A recession in the developed world is now more or less inevitable." And it is, he concluded, the "end of an era."

As Soros warned, the worldwide financial and economic crisis has continued and deepened as proven by what happened in the U.S., Dubai, Greece, Spain and probably many more in the future. Economists keep warning that there could be a Chinese economic crisis of which consequences would be about one thousand times bigger than that of the Dubai crisis.

Despite the clear symptoms and continued warnings, however, the governments of the G8 group of countries, international financial and trade institutions and neo-liberal corporatists have never paid any attention to the warning as well as the struggles and cries of suffering people. The recent financial crisis is like the beginning of a tremor signaling the "collapse" of the current dominant global economic system.

Economic justice today is at stake. The global South as well as the global North has no future for a Life-giving economy unless they adopt a paradigm different from that of the current economic model.

Ecological integrity is at stake

As we are experiencing in our daily lives, global warming and climate change have become one of the most serious life-threatening global problems that the whole creation is facing today.

According to the data of Prof. John van Klinken from Groningen University in the Netherlands,

- between 1850 and 1950 one animal species vanished every year;
- in the 1980s one animal species vanished per day;
- today, one animal species vanishes per hour
- and within 50 years, 25% of the animal and plant species will have vanished due to global warming.

The polar ice cap is 40% thinner than 40 years ago. In her interview with a Korean paper on 3 March 2008, Dr Clara Deser, senior scientist at the National Centre for Atmospheric Research said that the portion of the glacier in the Polar Regions that had melted down during the year of 2007 was what is expected to happen 10 or 20 years later. The global warming process is advancing 10 or 20 years faster than expected. There may be at least 200 million climate refugees by 2050.

Alan Durning pointed out that in the half century from 1950-2000, the global consumer classes produced and consumed as many goods and services as throughout the entire period of history prior to that date. As mammon keeps tempting us to BUY more, the time has come to say (good) BYE to consumerism.

Lawrence Livermore Caldeira said, "If we continue down the path we are going now, we will produce changes greater than any experienced in the past 300 million years." The ecological destruction is a fundamental violation of God's creation by humans. Today, the life of all living beings on earth is at stake.

The logic and beauty of God-created cosmos are at stake

In the symbiotic integration of the economy, political life and culture, the modern regime of science and technology is an organic mechanism used to manipulate, destroy and conquer the order of micro- and macro-cosmic life. The modern science and technology cause the aesthetic, ethical and spiritual disintegration of the living subjects of life. Although it espouses a "messianic claim" to free humanity from hunger and disease, it constitutes an arrogant form of power that desires to conquer the whole universe for human supremacy and greed.

In Korea today, the God-created beautiful rivers are being devastated and polluted in the name of "Four Main Rivers Development" project. God transformed chaos into cosmos through the creation process, but human beings transformed the cosmos into chaos in the name of so-called "progress", "development" or "civilization."

Peace and security of all nations are at stake

In the geo-political level under the rule of global empire, wars have been radically transformed in nature, into a permanent and limitless war in time and space. In the name of peace and security, the global empire is exercising the "omnipotent" power of military weapons systems of mass destruction, and intensive and total war.

The world spends 12 times more on military expenditures than on aid to developing countries. While military expenditure increases by 600 billion dollars per year, or 1 million dollars every minute, the world is reluctant to find the necessary funds to feed 15 million people who are dying from malnutrition.

Today, life and the fate of not only people on the globe but also all living beings are largely determined by the policy of the Empire and its allies, and therefore their peace and security are at stake.

Striving for Life-Giving Civilization

At this time of history, I believe that what we need today is to demythologize the current developmentalism based human civilization which is destructive on life and promote a Life-enhancing civilization. There is an urgent need for transforming the current life-stealing, life-killing and life-destroying civilization into a Life-giving civilization.

Neo-liberals argue that there is no alternative (TINA). In fact, however, there are many alternatives (TIMA). The search for forms of alternative spiritualities and theological thinking is not totally new. In fact, there have been a number of creative theological thinkers, in both East as well as the West. Hildegard of Bingen and St. Francis of Assisi come to mind. Their thinking was along the lines of *Ubuntu* and *Sangsaeng*. In a sense, their thinking had often been suppressed by the church because it deviated from the dominant theology of their time. Today we find ambitious efforts. For instance, Diarmuid O'Murchu, the Irish-born Roman Catholic priest and social psychologist, argues in favour of a paradigm shift in the fields of theology and spirituality. He suggests Quantum Theology in order to get away from established dichotomist or dualist patterns of thought. Scott Nearing and his wife have tried to live in nature, rejecting the capitalist, industrial, urban and modern life-style. There must be many more of this type of people around the world.

The *Hanmaum* (한마음, one mind) Community near Kwangju, Korea is one of a number of communities which are promoting this type of cosmic view and life-style. This is a community born out of the movement of farmers' struggle for social justice and democracy in Korea. Later, the community geared its focus of the struggle to ecological justice and earth democracy. It has been promoting natural artistic farming, healthy food production, ecological clothing, and traditional and ecological mud-house architecture that also can afford modern conveniences. The community also organized a producer-consumer direct-trade system based on the covenant concept. The community is a typical example of *Ubuntu* and *Sangsaeng*, as it seeks to be connected with nature and with other members of society in creative and life-affirming ways. Modeling an alternative way of living, the community is seeking to sustain life through a commitment to organic principles, expressed not only in its agriculture and industry, but in every aspect of its life, recognizing that these principles are predicted on a life-death cycle which is ever regenerating. This contrasts with the neo-liberal economic model which is being fixated on continuous growth, which is death-dealing, because of its emphasis on excessive consumption, unsustainable production and inequitable distribution.

Let me now pick out a couple of stories as a practical approach to Life-enhancing civilization. The first one is an ecumenical vision of Life-giving agriculture and the others are examples of individual commitment and practice.

Life-Giving Agriculture

One of the visions of ecumenical responses to neo-liberal economic globalization was not merely to reject neo-liberal paradigm of global economy. It also encouraged member churches to search for alternatives to globalization so that economy could be in service of life of people and the earth.

One of the attempts that were made is Life-giving Agriculture Global Forum which was held in 2005 in Wonju, Korea. The forum was organized by the Ecumenical Coalition for Alternatives to Globalization (ECAG), which was consisted of Geneva-based international ecumenical organizations, namely, World Alliance of Reformed Churches / WCRC, World Council of Churches, Lutheran World Federation, World Alliance of YMCAs, World YWCA, World Student Christian Federation, Mission Frontier in Mission and Pax Romana.

One of the main visions of ECAG was to search for alternatives to globalization, and the forum was held in search for such alternatives. Agriculture was chosen as their entry point, because it is the very foundation for life. Over 70 participants in 20 countries in Africa, Asia, Latin America, the Pacific, Europe and North America attended the forum and farmers practicing organic farming in their contexts as well as people who are involved in the organic farming were the main participants.

The forum had identified life-killing elements in current economic globalization, with international and corporate forces requiring farmers to conform to farming practices that are damaging the nature and local communities. The present dominant development model of agriculture is corporate and market-driven. The report of the Forum said that it is capital intensive, export-oriented, mono-cultural with profit as its motive. It compels farmers to use GMO seeds, pesticides, chemical fertilizers and automation. This leads to soil degradation, loss of indigenous seeds, bio-diversity, bio-piracy and concentration of lands in the hands of few. It restricts diversity of agriculture based on the food patterns that are dictated by fast-food companies, increases occupational losses, displacement, drought and migration.

The onslaught of dominant agriculture has impacted the survival of indigenous communities around the world. Agribusiness applies the same mechanisms and methods as in conventional farming to organic farming and continues to control and dominate the world food market. Governments in the name of growth-centred development are forced to follow the destructive model of agriculture benefiting the corporations, the developed countries and the rich in the developing countries.

Decades of these unsustainable agricultural practices have led to erosion of cultures, traditional knowledge and sustainable agricultural systems. Conventional agriculture defies all the values behind communitarian living. Therefore, this trend needs to be reversed and the life-killing agriculture should be altered into Life-giving agriculture.

At issue is sustainable life on planet earth. Faith in God, whose ultimate goal is fullness of life for all, is enabling people in different parts of the world to resist the pressures and go for life-supporting options in farming.

The most significant lessons that were obtained from the Forum can be highlighted in the following points:

Live-giving agriculture is possible!

The Forum began with field visits to six places over Korea where Life-giving agriculture is being practiced. The participants were impressed by the struggles and stories of those engaged in organic farming in Korea. There was a struggle to restore agricultural practice from the present life-threatening ways to an activity that is life-sustaining and life-nurturing. Contrary to the argument that there is no alternative to the highly industrialized approach, with continuous fertilizers, chemical and fuel input, the participants witnessed a number of alternatives already being practiced.

In the past, the Korean government had suppressed any attempts of organic farming. Over last fifteen years or more, some Christians as well as nature-loving farmers have devoted themselves to promote organic farming against conventional farming, resisting oppression of the government. After 15 years' struggle, the products of the organic agriculture began to be welcomed by the consumers who are looking for healthy food. Under this pressure from people, today, the Korean government has set up their agriculture policy to be environment-friendly agriculture. The demand of organic agricultural products are being increased globally and the future of organic farming is bright if we are successful in controlling multi-corporations' manipulation of organic agribusiness as they do in agricultural market. In Japan and Korea, there is a further development that maybe organic farming could be replaced with natural farming which is much closer to the original farming methodology as God has programmed in the beginning.

The household of producer and the consumer is not two, but one

"We take care of the customers' life and they take care of our life." This is what one of the farmers practicing organic farming in Wonju said to visitors. The organic farming communities in Korea developed a significant covenantal relationship between the producers and the consumers. Normally, the household of producers and consumers are understood as two different households; a producer's household and a consumer's one. But the farmer the participant met in Wonju said that the households of producers and the consumers are not two, but *one household* (한살림, *Hansallim* in Korean), because the producers are responsible for feeding the consumers with healthy food and the life of producers are dependent on consumers' solidarity. This is the very concept of convivial life style or covenanted life. For this reason, the organic agriculture movements have their names such as *Hansallim* (one household) or *Hanmaum* (one mind) etc.

Agriculture with a philosophy for reaffirming the basis of life

Agriculture is a philosophy for reaffirming the basis of life in fullness and moreover, is a driving forces and practice for foundational change of civilization. The modern development of civilization has been carried out as a process of industrialization, urbanization and modernization. People followed this process in the hope that their life will be flourishing as the development continues. However, people in the modern society today are tired of industrialized, urbanized and modernized life style. In Korea today, many families and children spend their weekend in the countryside where they could experience farming or any rural activities. The rise of industrial civilization has subjugated the rural to the urban and industrial way of life. But today, people are looking forward to more nature-friendly life style. Therefore, the Life-giving agriculture could become a driving force for transforming neo-liberal life style into less competitive, less speedy, less greedy, less selfish and egoistic life-style and promote more relaxed, harmonious with others and nature, and meditative life style than the urban life-rhythm. The Life-giving agriculture would remind people today of what it would mean to be a people of spirituality or faith in this time of history. It could be a driving force for transforming the stressful modern life into more relaxed ecological life.

Total transformation of agriculture into organic even natural farming is possible

When the US embargo was tightened after demise of socialist block, securing chemical fertilizers as well as energy was extremely difficult in Cuba. In September 1991, therefore, Cuban government set up a policy to transform the conventional agriculture into organic one in order to overcome the crisis. A research team of Stanford University described the attempt of Cuba as the most challenging experiment in human history. After all, Cuban experience turned out to be successful and today all agriculture in Cuba is basically organic. It was a human success through cooperation and solidarity among committed farmers, people, social workers, government officials, NGOs, and research teams. For the first two years, the productivity of agricultural products went down. From 1994, however, it began to catch up the level of conventional farming. The city of Havana was transformed into ecological city and food culture was transformed into vegetarian one. The health of people was improved and city atmosphere became enjoyable. The Cuban experience has demonstrated that adoption of agro-ecological methods and resources through plant-animal combinations and the alternative pest management technologies could bring about better productive and economic benefits in a socially equitable manner.

Abstracting the Cuban experience, the elements of the alternative paradigm are; 1) agro-ecological technology instead of chemicals, 2) redistribution of land to small farmers, 3) fair prices and markets for farmers, 4) greater emphasis on locality of production, and 5) re-inventing the new technologies and materials by grafting the modern science with the traditional management techniques and resources. Besides of the scientific achievement, the Cuban experience proves that resistance against empire is possible when all members of the community are united in search for alternatives.

Locally based economy and global solidarity are of importance

The forum gave us a clear lesson that economy is the best when it is organized locally. This is true particularly in relation to food resources. The Life-giving agriculture movement could give a certain assurance that local based economy is important and possible. What we need to continue to read the signs of the times is that the multi corporations are attempting at high jacking the organic agriculture by turning it into agribusiness. We need to watch over this attempt very carefully and resist any temptation the corporations are attempting at. For resisting this temptation, a strong solidarity among producers and consumers are necessary at the local level. A strong networking and solidarity is also needed globally so that organic farming community and consumers are not victimized again by the corporations.

Ghandi and Akinori

The two individuals that I want to introduce are the ones who rejected empire agenda and promoted alternative through their own commitment to alternatives. The first one is Mahatma Gandhi (1869-1948), a well-known Indian liberation movement leader and Kimura Akinori (1949 – present), a simple Japanese farmer. Mahatma Gandhi started the "*Swaraj*" movement as a means of resistance against the British Empire and the industrialization they brought to India. His self-supporting and self-governing village movement became an alternative to industrialization that destroyed not only the political, social and economic systems in India, but also people's culture and spirituality.

Wouldn't all the values, which he not only reflected but also practiced such as non-violence (*ahimsa*), truth, simplicity, spiritual and practical purity (*Brahmacharya*), faith (*satya*) and vegetarianism, be the sort of values that need to be promoted today in the context of consumerist society?

Some people say Gandhi's story is an old story. However, I think that we still can get a relevant inspiration from Gandhi for a Life-giving alternative vision like the "*Swaraj*" movement in today's context.

The other Asian I want to introduce does not have the stature of Mahatma Gandhi. He is a simple farmer by the name of Kimura Akinori who produces one of the world's best and most delicious apples through natural farming. The apple he produces does not spoil even after it is cut. The taste is fantastic and one cannot find such tasty apple in any other part of the world.

In his farm, no agricultural chemicals and no fertilizers are used. Human intervention is minimized. The whole farming process except minimal human assistance is left to nature. He allows the weeds to grow, because they are cooperating with the apple tress for inputting all recourses in the air into the roots of the tree. A cosmic orchestration of Life-giving process into the tree is being made throughout the year. His agricultural farming method is called "Artistic Natural Farming" meaning that the process is entirely left to artistic orchestration of the nature's Life-giving process.

His ten years' long struggle was not easy struggle. His struggle was a life and death struggle. His story goes this way. Having graduated from high school, Akinori started his apple farming in 1978. He was given a big apple farm by his own father, and after his marriage, three more apple farms were inherited from his parent-in-law. In the beginning, he followed the conventional way in his farming work. However, his wife was considerably sensitive to agricultural chemicals and therefore, he tried to find alternative ways of farming.

He, then, read a book written by Mr. Fukuoka Masanobu who had put together his experiences of natural farming. Akinori was so impressed by this agricultural methodology that he decided to apply this in his farming work.

Unfortunately, however, after applying the natural farming method, his apple farms began to be ruined. Nearly all apple trees were about to be blighted up due to vermin and weeds. He tried to exterminate vermin in a manual way without using any chemicals to save the trees. Unfortunately, however, it did not work well.

His livelihood was endangered and he became so poor that he had to survive by doing manual work in the city. No matter what difficulties he faced, he could not give up his attempt, saying, "If I gave up, it would mean that the world gives up." He regarded his failure as the failure of the whole world in experimenting natural farming.

However, the situation was getting worse and worse. After four years since he started, he could no longer continue his way, because it would end in the destruction of all his apple trees and the survival of his family would be at stake. One evening, he prepared a long rope and climbed up a high mountain with the intention of killing himself. Upon reaching the top he found a tree that was big enough to hang himself on. He threw the rope over one of the branches, but, fortunately or unfortunately, he did not succeed and instead the rope fell on the ground. As he went to pick it up, his attention was caught by what he thought was an extremely well grown apple tree deep in the mountain. Actually, it was not an apple tree, but an acorn tree. However, it appeared to Akinori as an apple tree. The issue is not his confusion about what kind of tree it was, but rather by what he realized: that the tree was producing a lot of lovely fruits, even though no one was taking care of it. It grew up deep in the mountain without any human intervention and produced perfect fruits.

He dug out some earth near the roots of the tree and was astonished to discover that the earth was so soft, while the earth in his apple farm was stony. He also discovered that all weeds around the tree played an important role in transporting nitrogen from the air into the earth. This method was mysterious and natural. In fact all trees in the mountain regions grow without human intervention.

He applied this method in his farming work, putting fresh earth into his apple farms, leaving all other process to be in tune with the rhythm of nature, permitting all sorts of weeds to grow. He had only two things to do; and the one was physical and the other, spiritual. The physical job was to take away some major harmful insects in a manual way until the trees became strong enough to cope with the attacks of the harmful insects. The spiritual work he did was to have a chat with the trees in order to encourage and be in solidarity with the trees, for instance, saying "Please try to survive for just one or two years, and then we will succeed."

After eight years long struggle, seven flowers came out and two of them bore lovely fruits. One year later all trees in all four farms blossomed flowers and bore the fruits. Finally all his apple trees began to produce a miraculous variety of apples that one could never find in any other part of the world. What struck me in this story was Akinori's perception that his failure could be the world's failure. In the conclusion of his book, the story of Noah is mentioned. When Noah built a ship high on the mountain, nobody understood his intention. However, it is this ark by which the world was saved. Noah did not follow the logic of this world, but followed God's logic. To me, there is no other way than going into radical alternatives if we intend to transform the current life-killing civilization into a Life-giving civilization.

My Personal Journey Toward Life-Giving Civilization

Let me now share my personal story which I am experiencing at the moment. From 1995 to 2004, almost a decade, I had worked in the WARC / WCRC with the responsibility of coordinating the *processus confessionis* programme. During this time, together with other ecumenical communities like the WCC, I had committed to work on ecumenical responses to neo-liberal economic globalization.

In September 2004, at the invitation of the Young Nam Theological Seminary located near a rural village in the Southern part of Korea, I returned to Korea for teaching theology at the seminary. As soon as I came back to Korea, I have tried to become involved in concrete work for alternatives, because one of the wishes while I had worked in Geneva was to implement what I had struggled for in the ecumenical movement.

As part of my efforts, I have set up courses at the seminary focusing on 'life' issue rather than dogmatic or speculative theology. I offered courses like "Theology of Life and Transformation of Society", "Theology and Spirituality in Tea Art", "Political Economy of God", "Cosmic Ministry", and "Ecumenical Theology and Mission." In particular, I opened a course on "Life-giving Agriculture and Cosmic Ministry" for transforming the students' orientation to church ministry. Usually when they are installed to be a minister, they tend to think that their ministry is focused on people. If we put ministry in the framework of "Creation Theology" or "Theology of Life", it makes no longer sense for it to be concerned with human beings only. In "Creation Theology", not only human beings, but also the whole of creation is in the care of God. Therefore, the perception that pastors are installed only for people must be changed. They are installed for the whole creation, and, therefore, their ministry should be cosmic rather than anthropocentric.

As a practical approach to the training, I have secured a small piece of land in the Seminary campus and, involved the students and other seminary family members in the effort of initiating organic farming. On every Wednesday afternoon, we have a lunch together and work in the plot. Apart from this, I have initiated a modest movement called "Waves of Life in Beauty" in order to systematically develop this type of cosmic theology, cosmic ministry and concrete witness to life-enhancing theology.

For my personal life, what could I do for alternatives? We have got a small house in the rural area and started to grow vegetables by ourselves. It was not easy for me to start farming as a person who has no experience at all. Therefore, we had to find an experienced farmer. We met an old, but highly experienced farmer nearby my place. A learning process has begun and after almost four years, our farming skills have progressed considerably. However, we are still at the level of producing only a limited variety of vegetables. Due to the limited plot and skills, we may have to remain at this level for the time being.

Contacts with farmers led us to develop a covenantal trade-system among the people. The farmer whom we contacted first was producing some grains, vegetables and fruits. So we have made a covenant that we buy what we need from them directly. If they do not produce what we need, they introduce us to their neighbors who are producing what we need. In such a way a network of a Life-giving trade-system came into being and, with it, a small covenant community was established. This small covenant community was not merely for trading of goods. When we meet together we mutually share a lot of wisdom for life. We share our professional knowledge. We share mutual concerns for life. We share pains and joys. We struggle for good life together and celebrate life in fullness together. In such a way, we have become a life-sharing community.

Since we are now able to be self-reliant on the food, we don't need to go to a corporation-run mammoth market or shopping malls, unless we need something which can be obtained only from there. If we have to go to the market, we try to go to a traditional or people's market.

In such a way, our economic life began to be transformed. We were able to resist consumerism and get our own economy organized according to our philosophy. We should not be subject to market logic or colonization of our consciousness by media propaganda on consumerism. Since the productions of vegetables we grow are more than we need, we share a lot of them with other families or friends. They share with us what they have and do not need. In such a way, an exchange of goods is being made that does not necessarily involve a currency. The menu on our food table was also changed. Meat consumption was minimized and vegetables, maximized. Gradually we have become practically vegetarian.

Traditional or people's markets are under serious threat by the corporation-run mammoth markets. Therefore we have started an advocating campaign for the traditional people's market. The traditional people's market is beneficial in many ways. First, the local economy can be re-established. One of the alternative ways to overcome neo-liberal economic globalization would be to promote the local economy as much as possible. Secondly, the traditional market can provide possibilities for the small farmers and small businesses to survive. Thirdly, human relationships in the traditional market are more than simply commercial. In the mammoth shopping mall, one can hardly find any humanity in commercial activities. The traditional/people's market is different. The traditional or people's market is a market with a human face. In Kenya, there is a social system called *Sokoni*, which is the market place. *Sokoni*, "in the market" in Swahili, is the place where people gather together around a fireplace to share life stories and information. This type of life-shared market needs to be promoted and strengthened.

One of the notable changes I have experienced while being engaged in this ecological life-style is a dramatic change in my spirituality. There is God's creation-code with which the whole eco-system works. In the name of industrialization, urbanization, modernization, developmentalism, science and modern technology, we have disturbed God's rhythm of life in the cosmos. This disturbance has resulted in the ecological catastrophe we face today. If too much intervention is made by human beings in God's cosmos, it would result in destroying the interconnectedness of all living beings. The harmony and rhythm of life that God codified in the cosmos could be disharmonized. Nowadays, I am re-learning Daoist teachings as my spiritual orientation. According to Daoism, less human intervention is closer to the Way (도, 道, *Dao*). The more human manipulation is being made, the more you are away from the Way of God. "Learning to unlearn his/her learning" is what Daoism keeps teaching for becoming a person to be closer to the Way. This unlearning process might be needed in order for too much technologically sophiscated human knowledge to be normalized. When I work in the plot, I feel that I have come back to God's rhythm of life, God's science in nature and God's wisdom of life. Diarmuid O'Murchu called this 'spiritual homecoming.' This is what I am experiencing these days.

A Concluding Remark

The Chinese concept of economy (경제제민, 經世濟民, *Jingshi ji min*) is almost identical with the biblical vision of economy. '*Jing*' means 'to manage.' '*Shi*' means 'the world.' '*Ji*' literally means 'to save,' maybe 'to make life possible and sustainable. And '*Min*' means 'people.' The literal meaning of the Chinese character for "economy" is "to save people by managing the world." If it is expressed in a Western way, it would mean "to make people's life possible and sustainable by managing the world." The focus here is to make the life of people possible and sustainable. Enabling the life of people is the main purpose of the Asian concept of economy. This is not only for economy, but also for all aspects of life of all living beings in God's *oikos*.

(26) Towards a Theology of Life for Justice and Peace in Asia

Kim Yong Bock

The Wisdom of the Whole of Life (Zoesophia: 생명학:生命學) is a new and fresh perspective for ecumenical movement, an alternative foundation for ecumenical pedagogy, that can revitalize faith and action in Asia and the world. We are in urgent need of a theological foundation from which to discern and reflect on the signs of the time. This perspective has three dimensions: 1) it recognizes that the life of all living beings is under the threat of omnicide; 2) it observes that life is being reduced into objects and fragments for control and manipulation, threatening its whole and holy nature; and 3) it remembers that in Asia and in the Bible (an Asian book) there are abundant wisdom and resources to enrich life, including the cosmic vision of life.

Here we take the theme of Christ as the Omega point of the universe of life. M.M. Thomas argues that Christ should be the centre of our Christian reflection; and K. H. Ting's theological affirmation on the "Cosmic Love of Christ"[1] is also a visionary indication of the importance of our proposal.

Some of my Asian friends are reluctant to do theological reflections from a Christological angle. They have some legitimate, understandable reasons. During the period of Western encroachment, the cross and Christ were symbols of conquest, representing a kind of "religious-political messianism" by the Western colonial powers. Nowadays the messianic language has often sent people into an orbit of discourse based on a totally otherworldly, apocalyptic eschatology. For some, the Christological "constriction" is too narrow and exclusive in the Asian context of many religions. In spite of these ambiguities, we need to rehabilitate Jesus talk, Christ talk and indeed the messianic discourse in our Asian theological reflection.

From the outset we want to make a bold Christological statement in the Asian context: Jesus Christ is the Wisdom of Life, and the Life of the World. Jesus the Messiah is the harbinger of the New Heaven and New Earth and therefore the new order of life of all living beings in the universe. We will concentrate on the latter affirmation in this essay. "Jesus Christ – the Life of the World (Cosmos)" is taken up as a Christological response to the signs of our times, when the dynamics of destruction and death are becoming ever more dominant. The Biblical theme of Jesus of Galilee against Pax Romana is a key axis of the ecumenical foundation.

---

[1] Cosmic Love of Christ: Ting makes a most creative theological statement about Christ. His theme is that Christ governs the whole universe with love and care, and that the essence of Christ's governance is love. He reminds us that the classical Chinese philosophical traditions and teachings teach the cosmic reality of harmony and that they have compassionate love as the ultimate reality of the cosmos. Ting brings out the historical experiences of the Chinese Nestorians, the Chinese Jesuits and the work of James Legge to show the Chinese classics have been important for theological developments for early Christian communities in China. He brings this theme, however, into the context of new China, liberated by the social revolution for which many revolutionaries are practicing love of the people and service to the people. For Ting these Chinese revolutionary leaders are those with highest moral standing, like the classical saints of traditional China. There can never be any segregation of non-Christians outside the church. Ting sees the agency of God working in the whole universe, and this means it works among the peoples and among political regimes outside the church as well as in the church. This conviction has led him to be in solidarity with communist revolutionaries in China, who liberated the Chinese people from the shackles of colonialism and feudalistic oppressive powers. Atheism by itself among the communists was not the final criteria of judgment to distinguish people and persons.

From Ecumenical Theology of Life to the Integral Study of Life

Today theological language is separated from the discourse of the world including Asia, especially the language of globalization, and does not engage the forces of the world. We propose that our theological foundation should find expression in a multi-disciplinary mode of discourse so that theological reflection can engage in the discourses of globalization.

Without much theoretical discussion, it is our proposal that all resources of life and reflections on it, be integrated under the whole notion of the Wisdom of Life (Zoesophia: 생명학 生命學). That is, a paradigm of holistic integration for reflections on life should be manifest in any community of spirituality, art, wisdom, philosophy or science. This notion of life should be differentiated from the "life sciences" within modern science, which operate to reduce and fragment, harming the integral discourse of life. Integral discourse refers to the manifold convergence of different discourses on the life of all living beings: the wisdom of life, East and West, traditional and modern, philosophical and scientific, religious and secular.

Let us begin with some historical precedents that treat the issue of life as a matter of wisdom. First is the Christological statement: Jesus Christ is the Wisdom (Sophia:智慧) of Life. The discourse of wisdom is holistic and integral, embracing all traditional and modern historical wisdom in both the East and the West. In Asian communities of Wisdom, religious and otherwise, the search for wisdom of life has been a central part of the history of peoples and nations. We can find a variety of religious, philosophical and cultural languages of wisdom in Asia. This heritage makes the ecumenical discourse on life in Asia especially rich.

This initiative can be introduced from the point of every global situation, transforming and overcoming the destructive domination of human wisdom and knowledge by the modern system. This should not be understood as an anachronistic return to the past, nor as romanticism fixed on the pre-modern local community. It should be regarded as a new, whole and creative effort to break through into the future by means of an infrastructure for study and reflection on life in a holistic way. We also need to inter-connect and cross-fertilize the local, national, regional and global initiatives inside and outside of existing institutions, provided that their perspectives are mutually convergent across various traditional boundaries. This process will constitute a multiple convergence of discourses.

Underlying this convergence, Christ the Wisdom of Life provides a creative, powerful fermentation of life and its wisdom. The Biblical discourse is the very wisdom of life. The people of God and their community of covenant, judges, prophets, and priests was a main part of the community of wisdom of life in Asia. At the time of Jesus, it was the community of disciples and apostles. As an Asian ecumenical community, we need to reflect upon life in Asia and search for Wisdom of life to overcome the powers of death and destruction, which now threaten the life of all beings and the cosmic garden.

From a Geo-Politics for Destruction and Death to a Vision of New Life in the Messianic Cosmos of Peace

Now we need to discern the reality of globalization. The recent globalization process has radically broken open all the geo-political boundaries. The global market regime has penetrated every corner of Asia and the whole world, causing injustice, impoverishment of peoples and destruction of earth life. Contrary to the globalization process, which reduces everything to one global dimension, the world should be understood multi-contextually and cross-contextually on all levels. This means that globalization in Asia must be understood locally as the base, and the divergent local experiences and reflections must form a convergent integration as a story of life (Zoegraphy). In all our deliberations, we need to scrutinize the complex matrix of global reality which brings suffering, destruction and death to the living beings in Asia. Therefore we need to forge a new "geo-politics" of life in contrast to the global regime of the world market and imperial domination.

The End of the Times? We are to discern the signs of times; and now we may be forced to discern the end of times on earth. Here we propose to diagnose and grasp the story of the whole life of all living beings, human and otherwise, through a Zoegraphy (story of life).

Earth is the abode of life for all beings together; thus "Oikonomia" of earth for the life of all living beings in the cosmos is the crux of our concern.

The story of life is not merely that of individual living beings. The global (whole) life (全生命=Ohn Saengmyong [Korean]) includes individual living entities (個體生命), life together of living beings, (SangSaeing-相生), UBUNTU in Africa, Convivencia in Latin America, and Conviviality in the West. The Greek phrase may be Koinonia of Zoe. It is the life of living beings in local villages, tribal/ethnic communities, national communities, continental regions, (Asia, Africa, Pacific, America and Europe) in planet earth, and in cosmic oikos. These are various loci of the "Oikonomia" of life. Living beings organize their abodes in bio-history and Zoe-history, in the history of civilizations. This may be called their "ZOEGRAPHY".

What is the Situation of the Earth, the Abode of Living Beings?

Cosmic Oikos of life under threat

This question opens the way for us to discern some signs of the times. The oikonomia (political economy) of life of all living beings on earth is under the threat of omnicide (total destruction of life). What are the root causes of this reality? Discourse on this question includes 1) the modern technocracy, 2) the global market 3) the geo-political hegemony and 4) the intoxication of cultural, religious and spiritual life.

This reality is a symbiosis of the scientific-technocratic conquest of epistemology, the pursuit of infinite growth for limitless profiteering, and the expansion of the global military regime for total war against life on earth. The religious ideologies and their ethical sophistries have served to justify the prevailing discourse on the problem, preaching optimism about the ingenuity of technological and engineering solutions, about the "sustainability" ethics of modified global capitalism (economic greed system), and about the "pax imperium" façade of global military hegemony.

Under this reality of power the whole of life in the lands of Asia is victimized is suffering. Besides the traditional forms of poverty and injustice, Asian peoples now face major distress under the dynamics of the neo-liberal global market regime, which is re-structuring and re-aligning the life of every person and every part of life. What is the Asian story of this reality? To answer this question, we must reflect from a Christological perspective, on the impact of the global market regime, the imperial hegemony, and the technocratic conquest of Asia. The whole process of history and the present reality is a convergent story of suffering and destruction of life of all living beings. It may be called "Thanatography (Story of Death 殺生學). It includes religious, ethnic, cultural, gender, political, socio-economic (poverty and hunger), and geo-political (wars) genocide of various kinds, as well as biocide and ecocide. Thanatography includes death and destruction due to disease and "natural disasters" that are not purely natural but are caused by human civilization. Under these conditions, the earth cannot be a blessed habitat for all living beings.

Theologically speaking, when the greed of the global economic regime serves only Mammon, when the hubris of power becomes demonic, when the global military hegemony of empire turns omnicidal, when human knowledge transgresses all limits to overturn Divine wisdom, and when the powers-that-be emerge with absolute truth claims, humanity faces a serious crisis. When the powers claim omnipotence and omniscience, and parade the "messianic" arrogance of triumphalism, this reality becomes the utterly serious issue of theology and faith.

The demand now is for a new movement of ecumenical theology of life, through a Trinitarian convergence of "Creation Theology as Resistance against Chaos," "Christology Against the Salvation

Claims of Empire" and "Pneumatology for the Spirit of Convivial Subjects and Against Demonic Intoxication of the Spirit."

Global integration of Asia, or globalization, is the newest manifestation of Western colonial and neo-colonial expansion. The geopolitical reality is being shaped by the global market regime of transnational production, transnational distribution and transnational financial transactions, together with the development of Western technocracy, the regime of technology and science, and technetronic cybernetics. The World Trade Organization is forcefully integrating the Asian nations into the global market, which unsurprisingly is dominated by global capital.

Oikonomia of life

The reality of suffering by the peoples in Asia is due partly to the objective conditions of their life in the context of globalization, but is aggravated by the absence of a renewal of faith as the subjective condition for life. At present, this reality is discussed in the context of optimism about the global capitalist market, the failure of socialist political economies, and the new global situation of massive suffering without hope. How is it possible for the suffering peoples to struggle for their tomorrow? In the background of this discussion are the futurology of the liberal social sciences and the progress philosophy of the Western utopia based upon modern technocracy[2] – a regime of science and technology.

The Kairotic geo-politics of the Messianic Reign is determined not by the limitations of space and time, whether these be natural, modern or cyber-technetronic, but by the imminent presence of the Spirit. It is neither in chronological order, which is determined by the sequence of past, present and future, nor is it determined by geographical space, arbitrary or natural. The Messianic geo-politics is determined by new and eternal life in the new cosmos.

In Asia there is a tradition of cosmic peace (太平盛代=Age of Great Peace and Prosperity), which integrates socio-economic prosperity and cosmic peace. In Asia, global military hegemony is closely integrated with the global market. As globalization pulls all national economies into the market, the issues of peace and security become more closely related to the issues of justice, and the poor and powerless are increasingly victimized.

From its earth-base, the "oikonomia of life" in local communities is being destroyed through violent onslaughts by the global and transnational capitalist regime, and the national economies of Asian nations have been integrated into the global regime. This is the structure of socio-economic violence that threatens the life of people, communities, and all living beings in Asian lands.

The issues of hunger, poverty and disease – abiding issues in Asian history – have taken on new forms as globalization wields its (neo-liberal) ideology of deregulation, especially in the nations of the South. National barriers are broken down, and decision-making on economic development matters has been shifted in large part from national governments in the developing world to the Western industrial states and international institutions such as the International Monetary Fund, World Bank and World Trade Organization, behind which are the transnational corporations of Western capital. National governments in the developing world are substantially weakened as they try to meet the challenges from global economic powers, and people's sovereignty is eroded. Transnational corporate powers have decisive influence, encroaching on people's economic life and eroding their national socio-economic sovereignty. Poverty and hunger today in Asia, Africa and other parts of the south are more and more the result of transnational dynamics. This new global system of poverty and hunger leaves the people without defense through

[2] Technocracy is a social regime in which the scientific and technological elite powers control the center or whole of the social system. The Western corporate institutions such as transnational corporations are key agents in the technocracy, which is closely related to the government and military academic research power centers.

democratic means. This global neo-liberal regime directly intensifies the poverty and hunger of the people as well as deepening the gap between poor and rich in international and national settings.

The unjust situation is aggravated by the absolute domination of speculative financial capital, which controls almost 98% of all global financial transactions, in contrast to the 2% occupied by trade payments. Furthermore, it is the transnational financial banks and funds that dominate this process, which caused the financial crises in Asia. Asian peoples and nations are deeply in debt due to global financial control by transnational capital. This is an important element in the increasing concentration and monopolization of economic power in the hands of the transnational corporations, which presently dominate the global economy and directly infringe the sovereignty of Asian peoples, their economic well-being and their self-reliance.

The neo-liberal market ideology subjugates all of life to the ideology of survival. It says that to overcome hunger and to eradicate poverty it is necessary to conquer the micro-world of life and to engineer and manipulate genes to increase food production. Ironically, this may be the final frontier of life as it is degraded and destroyed. The use of chemicals to increase food production has poisoned land, water and agricultural products. Genetic modification to increase food production has equally endangered the biosphere with a chain of unpredictable biological reactions.

The survival ideology also says that the production of chemical drugs and genetic modification are necessary to cure disease, to improve health, and even improve the very constitution of the human body by overcoming human deformation. Biotechnology has opened a Pandora's box. In fact, the for-profit market, under the guise of the survival ideology, is dictating biotech research, production of chemicals and genetic modification. Transnational corporations, which control pharmaceutical production and the biotechnology of genetic modification and production, are increasing their control over the global food and global health systems. It is ironic that more people are dying of hunger and malnutrition in the midst of such development and "improvement" in food production. It is also a mystery that more people suffer disease such as HIV/AIDS in the midst of the "miraculous" development of medical and pharmaceutical technology and production. The market plunges its uncontrollable, "demonic" hand into the very core of life on earth, not only destroying ecology but also degrading the inner core and nucleus of life itself.

The Asian ecumenical movement is to build the Oikos of God among the Okonomia of life of human and all other living beings in Asian lands. The people are the subjects of their own life. All living beings are resilient and resourceful subjects of life. The heart of their Oikonomia is justice and conviviality. They can restore their economic sovereignty and self-reliance from the base of their local communities, linking with national and international networks for alternative economic life. We need the vision and wisdom of all the people, rooted and inherited in history. We need to learn and share with each other for vision, wisdom and action – locally, nationally and internationally. Our ecumenical vision for the Oikonomia of the people should be a life-enhancing, life-fulfilling economy in the garden of life. The people in Asia need to have a vision of life full of justice, wholeness, and conviviality.

Eirene Christi (politics of peace for life) versus pax imperium under peril

In close interconnection with the global market, the process of emergence of Global Empire is breaking open the boundaries of nation states, and integrating them vertically into the dominant global power through inter-locking military alliances and cooperation. One of the emerging issues is peace under the global mono-polar military hegemony of the United States. In the late 20th century, it was expected that the dismantling of the Cold War global bi-polar military order would bring world peace, in a new geo-political situation freed from the possibility of a World War III that would destroy the whole inhabited world. The mono-polarization of global geo-politics eliminated the logic of balance of powers as the basic structure to prevent large-scale wars. The mono-polar hegemony of the U.S. and its development of a global military regime of weapons of mass destruction is one of the chief processes endangering global peace. Asian nations are being subjected to such development; and African, Latin American and European nations are deeply concerned about this issue of global peace.

Global geo-politics is very much dictated by the military and communication satellite systems under the command of U.S. power. Nuclear and bio-chemical weapons are being prepared for launch across regional and national boundaries. Cybernetic war-games are intensifying the virtual war strategy.

Some have pointed out the omnicidal aspect of recent regional wars, such as the one in Kosovo, due to the different, highly technological character of the present world military order. Such regional conflicts may occur in the Asian region. In Western Asia the Gulf War and the wars in Iraq and Afghanistan have been waged by the global empire. The process of the so-called Arab Spring, the intervention in Syria, and the tension with Iran are precisely the hegemonic politics of the global empire. One new area of geo-political tension is in the Asia-Pacific area, focusing on North East Asia around the Korean peninsula; another is in the India-Pakistan area. Most recently, the U.S. has declared its military strategy of Asian Pivot of US security, and its project to build a National Missile Defense system. This is directed ostensibly against North Korea, but is obviously also aimed at any potential military power coming from Asia, especially China. This strategy is triggering a chain of missile and arms races among India, Pakistan, China and Japan, in the area surrounding of the Korean peninsula.

The main point to recognize about recent wars is that they are occurring under a situation of worldwide mono-polar military hegemony. With the former Soviet bloc dismantled, U.S. military power seeks to consolidate its global dominance. This means that U.S. military intervention is taking place in all or most of the ongoing regional military conflicts. This will turn any regional war into a globally connected war; and any regional war will have the consequence of consolidating the global hegemony of mono-polar power. The global empire is acting for a "global peace" that is for nothing but its own security.

Wars are justified in the name of national security, which is based upon the ideology of survival of life, not fullness of life for all. The survivalist philosophy accents the powerful and strong against the weak and powerless; it upholds the exclusive minority, not the inclusive all. It also advocates a methodological anarchy using all means of violence to survive. This cannot be the goal of fullness of life for all. This kind of mono-polar geo-political situation poses a grave threat to life as a whole, not just to the life of peoples in Asia. We must find ways to achieve true peace, over against the unjust global hegemonic military order. We can understand more of this reality from stories of victimized life (*zoegraphy*) in the midst of the wars under the present military order.

The key ecumenical agenda in Asia is peace and security for life in its fullness. We should be reminded that the ideology of national (state) security does not mean security for people and life, and that peace for the powerful, hegemonic military powers does not mean peace for the weak and the powerless on earth. Various forms of military and political conflicts among the people and nations in Asia should be understood in the context of the global hegemonic concerns of the mono-polar power, which makes them more intense and fierce. The global empire's war strategy may be described as Crusade 2.0 plus Cold War 2.0 plus Permanent War on Terror in the most technocratic military regime to date.

In sharp contrast, the Biblical vision of peace and security for people and life is based upon God's justice, which is manifested among the people on earth and throughout the universe. Peace and security for life and for people are not based upon the ideology of survival of the fittest in a cosmic jungle – the philosophy of new social Darwinism. Such an ideology triggers a syndrome of collective survivalist behavior among nations and groups of nations, leading to a vicious cycle of violence and war. Security that protects life and people is based in a garden of life filled with love, justice and shalom.

Politics of peace

The people are peace makers on earth. Justice is the fruit of the people's struggle and the energy of all living beings in the cosmic order; it does not come from the work of the powers that be. The peoples of

Asia have achieved their sovereignty through national independence movements from colonialism and by overcoming their traditional despotic political shackles. But that national sovereignty is being seriously eroded in the process of globalization and global integration of the hegemonic politics of global empire. This is due partly to the erosion of state power in economic decision-making, partly to the opening of countries by developments in hi-tech communication and transportation, and partly to the mono-polar world military hegemony. The encroachment of transnational corporations and international institutions into national life is a major factor eroding the sovereignty of the people.

From the beginning, the building of political life in the model of the modern nation state has limited genuine democratic development for the authentic sovereignty of the people of Asia. In the process of so-called nation building, traditional authoritarian elements have not been completely transformed; and the arbitrary imposition of a territorial framework along with the "modern" political system has suppressed the rights of "sub-national" political, religious and ethnic communities, blocking their full, democratic participation in national political life.

In the context of globalization and the global market, in which national democratic participation and people's sovereignty are eroded and suppressed, it is necessary to redefine the rights of the people beyond the framework of nation-state. Peoples' rights – human, religious-cultural (ethnic and national), political and socio-economic – are not merely national but have become universal rights in the global context. Therefore peoples' movements for their rights are taking place at the local, national and global levels. National democratic political institutions exist to secure these rights, but under globalization they often betray them instead.

There is no alternative to democratic participation and participatory negotiation to resolve political conflicts within the nation. More and more, direct participation on the local, national and global levels is demanded to cope with new political situation of violent conflicts caused by globalization. These days we see on the Asian horizon the rapid emergence of new citizens' movements – civil society – for people's direct participation to realize their sovereignty in a holistic sense in the context of globalization. What is needed is the radicalization of democracy: participation and solidarity in global networks as well as local and national situations must be radically strengthened, as must nation-states.

Jesus proclaimed the good news of the Reign of God, and demonstrated the nature of politics: Serve the people and life so that they may become true participants in the Reign of God. This is His messianic politics. The principalities and powers must be made to serve God and the people. The Reign of God means the direct participation of the people in God's Sovereignty for the whole of Life. All the mediating institutions such as kings and priests must serve this process of direct participation. We may call this the politics of God. In the Reign of God all creation (all living things and people) participates directly in the fullness of life in justice, shalom, conviviality.

Justice, the foundation of life

Globalization causes the breakdown of the social order due to erosion of traditional social relations and fierce competition driven by the global market. Globalization's political and economic doctrine, neo-liberalism, is further expressed in the logic of new social Darwinism: limitless competition, survival of the fittest, and strong over weak.

Thus the weak and powerless, the poor and alienated, the old and differently able persons and living beings in nature are being placed in stronger chains of social bondage and cycles of violence. The people's social security is threatened and social justice is drastically eroded. The fulfillment of community life in the garden of earth is denied.

Traditional social conflicts and contradictions, such as class, caste, ethnic, cultural, religious, gender and racial conflicts, already form a web-work of injustice and violence. But more brutal violence is being created by neo-liberal politics, limitless market competition and mono-polar geopolitics in the social processes of the peoples in Asia: in families, villages, local and regional communities, and national societies. This new matrix of social conflicts and contradictions accelerates the intensity of violent confrontations on all levels. There is an urgent need for human and social security as an integral part of security for life (Zoe-security) based on justice and shalom.

Social peace (Shalom=well-being) is the aspiration of the people, who are suppressed unjustly and arbitrarily by traditional despotic powers, modernized national states, global market forces or a combination of these. Ethnic conflicts, prompted initially by the imposition of nation-states according to the Western model, are now caused by social and political upheavals provoked by the global market, and accelerate into vicious cycles of violent conflict under globalized military, political and economic power.

In all aspects of social relations and conflicts in Asia, the people – workers, peasants, urban poor, ethnic people, poor women, Dalits, Minjung and so on – are seeking justice for fullness of life. A special mention has to be made that justice cannot be realized only in socio-economic categories. Justice should be the foundational framework of all oppressed peoples. The Dalit people and those who live under discrimination on religious, social, cultural-ethnic or economic and political grounds, must be liberated for full and common life together on earth.

The ecumenical agenda in Asia is justice and Shalom, based on the Biblical foundation for justice and reconciliation through just resolution of conflicts. It is the ecumenical conviction that justice and Shalom are the foundation of life on earth; and this is the content and structure of God's Covenant with all living things.

Security and prosperity of life (fullness of life) is the vision of God's Creation, and of the Messianic Feast of Life and the prophetic movement of the Spirit of Life. The utopian Maitreiya Messianic vision of Western Paradise, the Confucian vision of T'aiping (Great Peace), and the Sunist vision of the Garden of Messianic Being (神仙圖) all converge in the Messianic vision of Life based on Justice and Shalom.

The spirit of life

The spirit of life is being crushed, demonized and intoxicated in the vortex of the global empire. Globalization has caused the so-called civilizational clash. The encroachment of the West into non-Western civilization is manifested in many forms, the most prominent of which is the cultural form of science and technology accompanied by industrial expansion. This form has easily crossed the lines of values and morals of non-Western civilizations and is having an extremely corrosive impact. For example, mass multi-media communication, driven by the market forces, erodes the cultural identities of Asian peoples, dismantles their values, and distorts their perceptions.

Especially information and media as a cultural commodity is controlled by the powerful in the market. The concentration of cultural power in the hands of the Western information and communication giants create a situation of cultural hegemony over peoples on a global scale. In the virtual world of cybernetics and in the world of communication media, the people are helpless to keep their own identity and life. People's participation in those worlds of cybernetics and communication is not merely a matter of technicalities. It is the question of struggle against cultural domination. It is claimed that informatics and hi-tech communication media will dominate the people's life in the 21st century. This is not a simply a continuation of the past, but it is a new stage of cultural domination and hegemony over the peoples in Asia.

In the past, Western colonialism brought in Western political and social, cultural and religious values that suppressed the traditional values of Asian civilizations and dismissed them as pre-modern. Western industrial expansion in Asia introduced the capitalist value system, which has significantly dismantled the economic and social values of the Asian peoples. Asian peoples urgently need to restore their cultural and ethnic identities, cultural values and cultural sensibilities in the new global context.

Globalization not only expands the Western market of cultural commodities but also accelerates the commoditization of Asian cultures. Music, arts and media products are subject to the dictates of the global market. The penetration and expansion of the cybernetic virtual world, dictated by the global market, is integrating Asian societies and thereby the life of the Asian peoples. The hi-tech multi-media are colonizing people's consciousness overall, through news, commercials, movies, video-audio products and other artistic and cultural products.

The global market has subjugated the people and lands in Asia to the insatiable culture of consumerism and hedonistic pleasure. This culture dominates the perceptions and sensibilities of the people, especially children and youth, driving young people into a desolate emotional wasteland. Commercial advertisements in the mass media create distorted perceptions. Hi-tech communication media and cultural commodities deeply penetrate and dominate the emotional world of perceptions and senses.

We should remember that people's life cannot be thought of without their distinct cultural heritages and expressions. God has blessed all nations (cultures and religions), promising a new identity for every nation and people. The Messianic feast of life embraces all nations and their cultures as integral parts of the new, full life. But Western Christianity, tied closely to Western civilization, has discriminated against Asian cultures and religions as "pagan" and "gentile." This is the fundamental error of Western Christian mission, which constitutes a serious historic and present problem for Asian Christian identity. Especially when nationalist forces, secular or religious, challenge Asian Christianity, the Asian Christian community should seek an authentic Asian identity for the sake of the Gospel. The forms of Christian life in Asia are still not Asian enough, which makes Asian people more likely to reject the message of the Christian churches and communities. An authentic Asian Christian identity will be the foundation upon which mission work in the cultural life of Asian peoples can be carried out.

Globalization of the modern Western culture creates market fetishes through the process of Western homogenization of all cultures, wiping out their unique and distinct contributions. On the other hand, diversity among national cultures mutually enhances every culture in the world. Meetings among diverse cultures should not only overcome cultural conflicts, but also should create a common garden of different cultural flowers. This will restore and nurture the culture of life.

The spirit of peace

The Spirit is the inner energy of peace for life, permeating the body of life – individual, family, village, community, nation, earth and cosmos – and fermenting the leaven of peace throughout. Traditionally Asian religions shape the reality of the Asian people. But globalization and its consequent social and political upheavals have brought about religious reactions and conflicts, including the rise of religious fundamentalism, in and outside the Christian community. Some Asian religions operate under such fundamentalist influences, as are some Christian groups, especially from the West. Asian religions are being seriously challenged by globalization, not merely by Western religious proselytism, but by the global cultural situation. Religious fundamentalism and globalization have close linkages, and Asian religions are reacting against globalization, sometimes creating very serious religious conflicts.

Asian religions, however, are reservoirs of wisdom for the life of people and all living beings, and we should approach Asian issues from a new multi-religious perspective and framework. Just as the Christian ecumenical movement is seeking renewal of Christian communities, Asian religions also seek transformative revitalization in their religious communities. Multi-religious renewal and reform may be the wellspring of wisdom with which we can meet the challenges of globalization and protect people and life. The perspective, vision and inspiration for the renewal and reformation of Asian religions come from the womb of the sufferings of the victimized. For Asian religions, too, have been forces of oppression and destruction of people and life in past history.

Religions in Asia are the backbone of life and people. They are the foundation of Asian civilizations. They provide a spiritual foundation for life. They make the Asian people and their communities rich, spiritually and culturally. They provide the moral fiber of the community. They are the basis of values for life and humanity. In order to overcome the forces of death and destruction, we believe that issues of peace, economic prosperity, sovereignty of the people, social justice and well-being, cultural identity and life as a whole should be approached from the perspective of multi-religious, multi-cultural and multi-philosophical ecumenism.

Kairotic reading of the history of multi-faith ecumenism: examples from the history of Christian communities in Korea and Asia

Christian connections with Messianic Buddhism have been made throughout the history of Asian Christianity. The first evidence is found in T'ang Nestorian Christianity (635-). In Nestorian Christian development, the Christian Messianic language is closely connected with the Buddhist messianic language of Maitraiya Buddha (Messiah=彌施阿). In the monument of T'ang Nestorianism, Christianity is presented in the Chinese Buddhist language. Moreover, the language of the Maitreya Buddha, which is a messianic Buddha, is used.[3] T'aiping Christianity is closely related to the White Lotus Buddhist sect, which is also messianic. A clear example is the Korean inter-religious ecumenism that was manifest in the March 1st Independence Movement in 1919, in which the Korean Christian Movement joined with the Buddhist messianic movement in the struggle of the Korean people against Japanese colonialism.

The Christian connection with Shilhak (Realist School of Confucianism) is another clear example. Roman Catholicism gave hope to the Korean people in 17th and 19th century Korea. The inter-religious synthesis of Roman Catholicism and the Realist School of Chosun Confucianism became the language and praxis in the movement for social transformation in Chosun society. The T'aiping Christian Movement in China also used the Confucian language is its movement to transform Chinese society in the middle of the 19th century. Confucianism is often regarded as a kind of utopian romanticism from the past Yao Sun age, the primeval golden age. But Chung Yak Yong, a scholar of the Realist School of Korean Confucianism, used the language of the Golden Age as a messianic language of hope and social transformation.

Just as the T'aiping Christian Movement connected itself with Chinese religious traditions, Korean Christianity practiced multi-religious ecumenism by joining with the Messianic religious tradition of Ch'ondokyo (the Heavenly Way), which is influenced by Christianity, in the March 1st Independence Movement, the political manifestation of the Messianic movement of hope among the Korean people. Ch'ondokyo is an indigenous Korean religion that contains the Shinson folk utopian tradition, the folk apocalyptic tradition of Chungkamnok, and Messianic Buddhism as well as the Messianic Christian language.

We can find many Christian connections with Asian religious traditions such as Islam, Hinduism, and other indigenous religions. This position is not merely for inter-religious dialogue. It is not merely for inter-religious cooperation without touching religious practices. When we refer to inter-religious ecumenism, we mean the deepest connections among Asian religious traditions for the praxis of the messianic movement. Christian messianic wisdom is inclusive of all energies and resources of the struggle for new life that rises in the history and life of the peoples in Asia. The Biblical praxis of new life will be strengthened, and it will catalyze the dynamics of new life among the Asian peoples.

The Christian connection with progressive social thought in modern times cannot be treated lightly. Although Western secular thought was accompanied by the colonial and imperial baggage, it made connections with the aspirations and struggles of the peoples in Asia, and gave a dynamic energy of hope to Asian peoples. Asian national struggles have drawn their resources from Western progressive thought.

[3] *The Christian Encyclopedia*, Vol. 1, pp. 592 ff.

Insofar as such thought provides energy and wisdom in the struggle for new life by Asian peoples, the Christian community needs to connect with it positively.

The peace of Jesus the Galilean against Pax Romana can be a cosmic pivot around which a multiple spiritual convergence of Asian religions may be catalyzed for cosmic peace, which in East Asia is called T'aiping (Great Peace=太平).

Cosmic gardens of life

Asian lands are gardens of life, full of resources and wisdom. The life of Asian peoples is also very much affected by ecological destruction, bio-chemical contamination of the food system and the consequent erosion of the basic grounds for health of the life of all living beings. There is an urgent need to restore the life environment in nature as well as in the political economy of the people.

From our ecumenical perspective, we can speak of the political economy of life against the forces of destruction of life. While natural death is an integral part of life, we cannot accept the forces that cause death and destruction of life against nature, and any arbitrary destruction of life and people would be against the will of God. As we have indicated above, the destruction of life is caused by war and disaster, hunger and poverty, illness and disease, political oppression and injustice, social violence and suppression, cultural desertification, religious bigotry and so on. These causes are all inter-connected. This process of destruction of life is being intensified by globalization.

However, in the globalization process we find a deep tendency toward the destruction of natural life, due to the essential contradiction between the industrial economy and the natural world. Besides exhausting natural resources, industry pollutes the air, the water and the soil; and thereby the natural environment is destroyed and thrown out of balance. Life on Planet Earth is no longer sustainable. This is an ecological degradation and destruction.

Under globalization there are two especially alarming trends to which our ecumenical movement should pay attention. One is the control and manipulation of the global food system by the transnational food industry. With the ostensible ideology of food production for the hungry and food for health, the TNCs are carrying out genetic modifications and chemical treatments of food that threaten natural life at its core. Also, with the ideology of curing illness and enhancing health, more and more scientists in many countries are undertaking the genetic manipulation of natural life forms, threatening all of life at its microcosmic core. One of the fundamental problems is that the whole process of genetic manipulation, as well as medical and pharmaceutical, scientific and technological operations, is basically market driven, its first priority being the maximization of profit. Chemical production of fertilizers, pesticides and herbicides is justified in the name of increased food production, and genetic engineering and modification are justified in similar ways. An ideology of eugenics and health is operating powerfully in the genetic manipulation of modern medicine and food production. Bio-chemical weapons – like nuclear bombs – are also anathema to life, people and environment.

Another problem is that the whole process is based upon a reductionist and fragmentary view of life. This is the built-in tendency of modern science and technology. Life is not viewed holistically and therefore cannot be viewed in an interconnected way. This narrow view prevents issues of justice, peace and happiness from being dealt with in an integral way. The whole process is dictated by the community of technocrats, and dominated by transnational corporate powers. Asian religions as well as Christian faith, on the contrary, view life from a holistic perspective.

Our ecumenical theology of life rejects the scientific and technological manipulation of life, which is based on a reductionist view of life and on the market ideology. God has blessed life on earth and made a covenant with all living things for their fulfillment. Our ecumenical agenda is to seek this security and fulfillment of life on earth in an integral and holistic way. Thus our understanding of life should be

Biblically and theologically based; and must be practiced in an integral way, overcoming the forces of death and destruction.

We would like to advance a notion of conviviality in which people and other living beings express a common life together in fullness. This accords with the Biblical teaching that God is in covenant with all living things and blesses them for prosperity (fullness of life). In the light of this ecumenical mandate, we believe that the integral study of life in Asia is an important task for the movement of life among the Asian peoples.

Zoesophia for vision of life

Is there emerging a new horizon for conviviality on earth? All living beings on earth are searching for such a vision, for they are the Juche (主體=Subject) of life. Juche means the Spirit that is embodied in the form of individual body, communal body and cosmic body. The Spirit groans with all living beings in their plight on earth.

The life of all living beings, though they suffer unto death, resurrects into a new embodiment, individual, communal and cosmic, on the Messianic journey. God is sovereign over the power of death and destruction of earth, for the sake of sovereignty of all living beings in God's embrace. Thus God is the partner of all living beings in their "subject" form. All creatures are SangSaeng (相生) subjects, just as God is a partner of life among all living beings. God is in covenant with all living beings and with the earth (Gen 9).

How about our radical openness to the wisdom of religions, cultures and philosophies outside of Christian theology? Care for creation is a promising theme for inter-religious dialogue." Like the Bhuddhist Compassion for All Living Beings and the Confucian 惻隱之心 (Heart of Jen in the Universe), etc., the pursuit of Wisdom of Life (Zoesophia) means a catalyzing dynamics toward a global convergence. This is called Ubuntu in Africa, SangSaeng in Asia, Convivencia in Latin America, and Conviviality in the West.

The following are some inter-linked dimensions of New Life in Wholeness

- Life of Peace: Against War and Destruction of Life
- Just and Healthy Life: Against Starvation, Hunger and Poverty
- Life of Direct and Common Participation in Solidarity Network: Against Oppression
- Life of Shalom (Secure Wellbeing with Justice): Against Social Conflict and Violence
- Life of Rich Meaningfulness and Fine Beauty: Against Desertifcation of Cultural Life
- Life of Vitality in the Macro- and Micro-Cosmos: Against the Destruction of Life
- Spirit of Life in the New Life Movement of All Living Beings
- Life of Bliss in Celebration Against a Life of Curse and Tragedy

Holy spiritual struggle for life in justice and peace

The Spirit of God is already working in God's Creation. It is the central dynamic moving to establish justice and shalom for life, as is demonstrated in the Exodus, the Jubilee, the Prophetic movements and the Apocalyptic movement for the new age (eschaton) for life.

The Spirit is the agency that establishes the subjectivity and the dynamics of life – new and eternal life. The Spirit is present over the universe; it is present in the depths of all life. The Spirit has no limitations due to geo-politics, nor is it determined by nature or the human community.

The Spirit gives hope and imagination to the life movement in the universe. "And in his (Christ's) name the Gentiles will hope (Matthew 12:21)." "To them God chose to make known how great among the Gentiles are the riches of the glory of this mystery, which is Christ in you, the hope of glory (Colossians 1:27)." The messianic hope is cosmic in scope and inner dynamics, determined by Christ's resurrection overcoming the power of death. The messianic hope invokes the messianic spirit among the people for their movement to overcome the power of evil and death in the world. All the nations (the oppressed) are invited to the messianic feast of life in the new Oikos under the new heaven and in the new earth. The Holy Spirit is the pervasive "Power" of life and hope among all the suffering people and in the groaning cosmos.

The geo-politics of the Egyptian, Babylonian, Assyrian, Greek and Roman imperial powers was subverted by the Kairotic geo-politics of the Messianic Reign of the new heaven and new earth, in which new and eternal life is celebrated in the new city (new Jerusalem) and the New Garden (Rev. 21 & 22). The creation of the cosmos and therein life in the Garden is the original Kairotic act of God to overcome the forces and powers of darkness and chaos that cause destruction of the order of creation, that is, the order of life. Christ is the decisive power of new, eternal life. Christ has overcome the power of death to realize the Resurrection of life. This is the Messianic Kairos. The Spirit is the ever-present power of life that renews life and gives the power for new life in the universe and in all dimensions. The Messianic geo-politics of cosmic Oikos, where new and eternal (full) life in the New City under the New Heaven and New Earth is celebrated, is a paradigm to overcome the existing geo-politics, providing the power and basis to overcome the powers of death present in the globalization process.

The Spirit is the power and energy of imagination, which worked dynamically in the life and koinonia of the early church, which suffered various persecutions of the "cross," just as Jesus suffered. The community had hope in the resurrection of the Messiah, whose Spirit energized the community for struggle. The Messianic praxis of Jesus was manifested in the spiritual movement of the early Christian community.

Once again the Spirit of the Messiah is the central dynamic of the movement for new life in the universe in the context of the Messianic Reign, to which all the peoples and nations are invited for the feast of eternal life in the new cosmos (new geo-politics.)

Recovery and Renewal of the Spirit of the Life in Asian Lands

Renewing and revitalizing the communities of faith in Asia is the first step towards the recovery of the spirit of life. Concern for spirituality in the Asian ecumenical movement has been spirituality for "combat," a militant spirituality for justice, freedom, peace, love and life. It is neither mystical intoxication nor other-worldly meditation alone. Neither is it a primitive, naïve spiritism, which we can find in people's communities. It is the source of hope and imagination; the source of vitality and life; and the source of people's struggle for justice, liberation, peace and celebration of life. This is particularly apparent in the liturgical experiences of people's communities. Christian community should be restored as a spiritual community par excellence. Spirituality should be expressed in liturgical action and celebration of life. This demands creative and radical liturgical renewal among the Christian communities in Asia, which are still in captivity to a rigid, traditionalist mode, not open to the whole life of the people. This liturgical renewal must be open to the finest traditions of the Asian religious and spiritual wisdoms as well, as it recaptures the biblical spiritual vitality. Veni Creator Spiritus!

Reading of the Bible in Asian Christian communities is one of the primary spiritual disciplines, leading people to the authentic grasp of the Gospel of Jesus Christ. The Western dogmatic and modernistic reading of the Biblical texts has hampered their holistic understanding. Bible reading has to be done in a Kairotic way through "Asian Eyes" in the midst of the suffering of the people and victimization of life in Asian lands. It also needs to be done concurrently with the reading of the Asian texts of wisdom in the religious, philosophical and cultural areas. It is bound to be a cross-textual reading of the Bible and many other scriptures, which will strengthen and enrich the spiritual power of the reading. This requires an open attitude for learning and sharing of the people's religious and spiritual traditions.

A Step into the Future: Reviving the Spirit of Life

Reviving the Spirit of Life means building a foundation of justice, participation, peace and conviviality (Integrity of Creation). Spiritual vitality must be manifested in the political economy of life, the participatory structure of political service, the process of overcoming hostilities and enmity, and the celebration of life. Cultural creativity and cultural action (education) is an integral part of spiritual exercise in the community of faith(s). The spirit of prophetic witness, sacrificial acts for peace, giving life to liberate life, and so on, should be manifest in the midst of life of the Asian peoples.

It is necessary for the Asian ecumenical movement to equip itself with an Asian theology of life. Though we cannot completely abandon our theological traditions, our theology should be radically involved in the life struggles of the people in Asian lands. We can no longer confine our theological reflection and studies within the traditional boundaries and divisions. A radical creativity that rises out of the midst of suffering by the people and victimization of life, will enable us to read the Bible with Kairotic sensitivity.

Due to space and my lack of competency we are not able to treat here the important issue of convergence of the Abrahamic faiths: the Judaic, Islamic and Christian faiths, but this is particularly important in the current geopolitical situation, for the following reasons: 1) The hegemony of the global empire is established in the Christian civilization. 2) It clashes with the peoples and nations of Islamic religions. 3) Though there is a strong establishment of Islam in Africa, at the same time West Asia, South Asia and South East Asia hold the majority of Islamic people in the world. 4) Christian faith and Islamic faith are cousins to each other in religious terms.

(27) CONFLICTS IN ASIA IN THE CONTEXT OF GLOBAL EMPIRE – A CHALLENGE TO ASIAN ECUMENISM

Carmencita Karagdag

I wish to start by citing the late Clement John's succinct but compelling depiction of global realities and the challenges facing the ecumenical movement. I do this not only to dramatize the imperative of peace, security and reconciliation in the midst of contemporary global empire, but also to honor one of the outstanding Asian figures in ecumenical peace advocacy whose untimely demise four years ago can only beggar an already vitiated and weakened ecumenical movement.

"We live in a world where international law is under threat, where one religious community is being demonized, where the powerful and dominant nations are trying to resolve the issue of terrorism through military action without bothering to address the root causes, where enemy images are evoked to curtail the fundamental rights of people, where pre-emptive war is cited as legitimate right of self-defense, where the nation-state is under threat both from within and outside resulting in the erosion of power and authority of the state to protect the interest of its people, where economic globalization is taking a heavy toll destroying traditional life-styles of the people and marginalizing the majority from its benefits. These are the challenges facing the world ecumenical movement in the 21st century."[1]

These were words spoken eight years ago at a meeting of National Council of Churches general secretaries in Asia. Yet they ring with contemporary resonance as, tragically, little has changed and the geopolitical landscape has, if anything, turned for the worse.

Particularly ominous and disquieting to peace advocates in Asia is the recent US President Obama's foreign policy pronouncement pivoting US geopolitical strategy to the Asia-Pacific region, already dubbed an "American lake" and, as declared in a statement issued by Asian participants at the WCC Pre-assembly gathering in Indonesia in 2005, "a principal battleground for geopolitical and geo-economic hegemonic domination". This current geopolitical shift from military alliance-building in Europe and military engagement in the Middle East – where the US remains mired in oil-driven wars of occupation – underlines the US's bid to counter and encircle China, now the second largest economy in the world, surpassing Japan, and perceived by the hegemonic power as its major contender and strategic rival for global suzerainty.

Only recently in Asia, tensions have escalated anew around the issue of North Korea acquiring nuclear weaponry. The Democratic Republic of Korea has also been quick to accuse South Korea, with the collusion of the US, of adventurous war maneuvers against its Northern rival. Contributing to widespread insecurity in Asia are the sprawling US bases stationed in Japan and South Korea or are in the process of being constructed despite local resistance, as in Okinawa's Henoku and South Korea's Jeju Island. Moreover, by having sent troops to Afghanistan and Iraq, Japan is now being increasingly integrated into the US's security architecture at the expense of its much-vaunted peace constitution. Not to be missed is heightened US military presence in the Philippines despite the dismantling in the 1990s of the US's largest overseas military bases in its former colony, through regular rotation of foreign troops under what is euphemistically called joint military exercises. The current standoff between the Philippines, presumably backed by its long-standing sponsor, and a more assertive China over a contested island in the South China Sea can only lead to further escalation of tensions in the region.

Neither has the nuclear rivalry between India and Pakistan as well as the conflicts around the Kashmir issue shown much sign of abating. Still reeling from a spate of suicide bombings and terrorist attacks,

[1] An excerpt in the minutes of one of the meetings of National Council of Churches general secretaries.

Pakistan has been besieged by US military incursions, including lethal drone attacks, presumably to flush out Al Qaeda elements from their mountain hideouts near the Afghanistan border. The gruesome killing of Osama Bin Laden by US forces last year in Pakistan constituted a serious breach and infringement of Pakistani sovereignty, underscoring anew that the global empire is never averse to employing military might unilaterally in the assertion of its 'global sovereignty' and 'global freedom of action'.

A region singularly blessed with a rich variety of ethnic groups, age-old cultural traditions and ancient religions – unmatched by any other region in the world – Asia has been convulsed by internal conflicts along ethnic, communal, and religious lines, many traceable to centuries of Western invasion and colonization. Ironically this rich diversity has been more of a bane than a boon for the people of Asia whose often persecuted ethnic, cultural and religious minorities are, along with the vast impoverished population of the region, also hapless victims of economic exploitation, social or cultural marginalization and political repression.

It is ironic that long-running internecine conflicts have become endemic in a region that prides itself as home to some of the greatest and most ancient civilizations and from whose womb the world's oldest philosophical and religious traditions, including Islam and Christianity, had been incubated. All sanctimoniously preach the imperatives of peace, ethical behavior and the values of love and compassion. Yet these same religions have been deeply implicated in many of the most virulent and destructive strifes.

These conflicts have, in the past decades, reached an unprecedented level of magnitude and barbarity. Untrammeled free-market globalization, the US war on terror in the aftermath of September 11, the unmitigated drive for control and plunder of increasingly scarce energy and highly coveted natural resources, the resurgence of religious fundamentalism and rise of religion as a political force – all related to the immoral project of empire-building – have radically altered the Asian geopolitical landscape, resulting in even more pernicious and intractable conflicts. Sadly those engaged in resistance against the life-denying forces of neo-liberal economics and hegemonic rule as well as in the task of peace-building and search for life-giving alternatives invariably face, along with the victims of wars, brutal militarization and more blatant political repression.

Deconstructing the Concepts of Peace, Security and Reconciliation

Peace and reconciliation have been at the heart of the ecumenical movement's vision and common striving for unity since its inception. After all what we now recognize as the ecumenical movement cannot but have been given impulse by the overwhelming challenges of peace-making and reconciliation in the wake of catastrophic divisions and violence wrought by the First and Second World Wars.

Yet the discourse on peace, security and reconciliation has been marked by conceptual ambiguities, making it incumbent on genuine peace-builders to deconstruct these high-sounding words. After all, it was in the name of peace that wars and empires like the Pax Romana and now Pax Americana have been justified. Peace advocates today face enormously daunting obstacles. For one thing, wars are profitable. And in this age of idolatry of the market and capital, everything is sacrificed at the altar of profit. Though wars result in large-scale destruction, enormous profits are made from lucrative defense contracts for reconstruction, for refurbishing the army, for further research to build sophisticated weaponry and nuclear technology. It is said that today war has become the leading profit-making and employment-generating industry. Nowhere is this more patent than in the heart of the empire where so-called democratic rule has been increasingly compromised by the powerful military industrial complex supported by neoconservative ideologues and Zionists, along with the American Religious Right and Christian fundamentalists. Former US President Bush's swaggering, if vacuous, claim that weapon makers are peace makers is instructive.

The challenge of peace-making has to be seen in the current context of increasingly rapacious and militarized globalization. It is this nexus of economic globalization and militarization that now constitutes ruthless empire building. For if the imperial project of globalization – now drawing wide resistance from its victims the world over – is to succeed, imperial security needs to be guaranteed, by force if necessary. In this light, the US-led global empire – more homogenizing, totalizing and encompassing than its predecessors – is arguably the main scourge of our times and the single most formidable force that stands in the way of our legitimate quest for genuine peace, security and reconciliation. As renowned scholar Dr. Chandra Muzaffar posited, "The greatest threat to world peace today is Washington's imperial power. It is a power that is embodied in the 800 odd military bases scattered in some 60 countries around the globe. Washington's annual military budget...encompasses programs that stretch from the depths of the ocean to the outer reaches of space."[2]

Ignored in the conventional usage of peace, which focuses on cessation of hostilities, are the root causes of conflicts and violence: massive hunger and abject poverty amidst scandalous wealth monopolized by a few, wholesale dispossession and displacement of subjugated peoples, plunder of oil and other prized or increasingly scarce resources, demise of nascent local industries due to influx of foreign capital, wanton ecological despoliation, grave cultural dislocation and loss of identity, the threat of western cultural homogenization – all largely attributable to capitalist globalization.

Peace, if it is to be authentic, has to be based on justice. Yet the concept of justice, as Ninan Koshy has underlined in his historical account of the ecumenical movement in Asia, is alien to globalization. "There is no 'scope' or 'space' for justice in globalization."[3] A system based on greed and whose principal motive is amassing profit at the expense of the impoverished can only breed conflicts and violence. Indeed, war and globalization go hand in hand. According to progressive writer Michel Dussodovsky, "Ultimately the purpose of "America's New War' is to transform sovereign nations into open territories (or 'free trade areas'), both through military means as well as through the imposition of deadly 'free market' reforms."[4]

The ecumenical movement has long challenged the conventional understanding of peace as absence of war, adhering instead to a vision of peace captured by the Hebrew word "shalom" understood as a profound sense of wholeness, of harmony, of genuine community which happens only when the brokenness of relations with God, fellow humans and the rest of creation has been forsaken and fully overcome. That is, when the root causes of war and enmities are decisively addressed. When entrenched structures of injustice that breed conflicts and violence are dismantled and transformed. Theologian Dr. MJ Joseph pointed out, "As the biblical religion is structured around the concept of the righteousness of God, the concept of justice is integral to peace."[5]

In the context of peace based on justice, progressive ecumenical discourse specially in Asia has contraposed the idea of people's security to national security and, given today's context of global empire, to imperial security. This draws some support from the UN itself which, in its Development Report of 1994, has enshrined the concept of "human security", defined as including "safety from chronic threats such as hunger, disease and repression as well as protection from sudden and harmful disruptions in the pattern of life". Though the understanding of human security would later be expanded to include economic, health and environmental concerns, the concept remains associated less with social than individual human rights.

The state-centric paradigm of national security in fact precludes people's security. The people's needs and rights are made subordinate to the narrow preoccupations of the state, particularly its self-serving interests in political and territorial self-preservation. In these times of war on terror and empire-building, notwithstanding US President Obama's sophisticated and more subtle rhetoric, it is in the name not only of

---

[2] Chandra Muzaffar, *Global Ethic or Global Hegemony?* (UK: ASEAN Academic Press LTD, 2005).
[3] Ninan Koshy (ed.), *A History of the Ecumenical Movement in Asia,* (Hongkong: Christian Conference of Asia, 2004) 334.
[4] Michel Dussodovsky, *America's War on Terrorism* (Philippines: Ibon Books, 2005).
[5] MJ Joseph, *One in Many, Many in One* (India: Christava Sahitya Samithi Trihuvalla, 2005).

national security, but of global or more precisely imperial security, that violence and aggression are wantonly unleashed, devoid of any moral and legal restraints. Playing on people's fears and manipulating the widespread paranoia engendered by the September 11 tragedy, the US has been able to build what is now viewed by many as a global police state.

Meanwhile, armed with new, draconian anti-terrorist laws patterned after the US Patriot Act, client regimes have engaged in massive curtailment of human rights and suppression of political dissenters, indiscriminately labeled terrorists or, in the case of the Philippines where church leaders have been among the victims of extrajudicial killings, "enemies of the state". Illegal arrests, torture, forced disappearances, secret prison camps, assassinations, political slayings, criminalization of migrants and specially the much-stereotyped and demonized Muslims, have become the order of the day. International humanitarian law and laws of civilized warfare are routinely waived for overriding national-security considerations.

Moreover so-called humanitarian intervention or "responsibility to protect" – which has seen a recrudescence in recent times as in the case of US-NATO bombing and dismemberment of Yugoslavia in 1999 and more recently, the blatant NATO takeover of Libya and the increasing threat of a similar intervention in beleaguered Syria – have been routinely used as moral justification for the use of force and convenient pretext for wars of plunder. Respected scholar Dr. Hans Koechler, who was appointed by the UN as special observer in the Lockerbie trial in the Netherlands, has this to say, "The revival of the just war concept in the new imperial environment rehabilitates war as a means of foreign policy. The taboo placed on the non-use of force has quickly vanished under the pressures of humanitarian realpolitik (i.e. realpolitik in humanitarian clothes)."[6]

Similarly, reconciliation is a theme that has dominated much of the ecumenical and faith-based discourse on peace, drawing a particularly strong justification from religious texts. Religious actors, exemplified by Archbishop Desmond Tutu, have played a key role in making reconciliation a fixture in today's global political discourse. However, like peace and security, reconciliation has lent itself open to much abuse and distortion. In light of amnesties not too infrequently offered for instance to former Latin American dictators prosecuted for some of the worst political crimes, the question has been asked, "when does reconciliation become a coddling of evil?" Often religious communities have felt duty-bound to preach reconciliation even in the face of blatant wrongs and injustice committed by one nation, ethnic group, race, gender or class against another. Yet to insist prematurely upon forgiveness and reconciliation can only contribute to the perpetuation of injustice and violence.

For instance, the Truth and Reconciliation Commission in South Africa has been invariably held as a model for non-violence and reconciliation. But often ignored is the fact that reconciliation became a realistic prospect only after the systemic and economic violence of the white apartheid regime had unraveled under the weight of a national liberation struggle that enjoyed wide international as well as ecumenical support. In Nepal prospects for national reconciliation have brightened following decades of internal strife. For the once religiously sanctified and repressive monarchical rule had been overthrown through a combination of non-violent protests and armed struggle led by local Maoists who are now a major force in a coalition government mandated to draft a new constitution.. What is clear from the above examples is that reconciliation can only ensue after a liberatory act from a confining, repressive and exploitative reality. This likewise involves undertaking significant redress of grievances and concrete restitution that pave the way for more thoroughgoing social transformation towards redistributive, restorative and, given the widespread environmental degradation and desperate state of our life-support system today, ecological justice.

In the progressive ecumenical tradition, reconciliation is thus understood as a restoration of union among alienated, divided and conflicting groups or individuals. In true religious fashion, it invariably

---

[6] Hans Köchler, *Global Justice or Global Revenge?,* (Austria: Springer-Verlag Wien, 2003) 304.

involves something deeper and more far-reaching: confession and genuine repentance by perpetrators on which basis alone forgiveness on the part of victims and hence authentic, life-giving reconciliation can be possible. Reconciliation cannot but be grounded on justice, calling to mind the eschatological vision of a new reconciled world. In Isaiah's powerful imagery, "The wolf shall live with the lamb, the leopard shall lie down with the kid…the cow and the bear shall graze, and their young shall lie down together; and the lion shall eat straw like an ox." (Isa. 11:6-8). Micah shares the same prophetic insight. "He shall judge between many peoples, and arbitrate between strong nations far away; they shall beat their swords into ploughshares, and their spears into pruning hooks; nation shall not lift up sword against nation, and neither shall they learn war any more. (Micah 4:3).

From our perspective as ecumenical leaders and activists, the three values of peace, security and reconciliation are inextricably intertwined. They are inseparable and indivisible. All revolve as if in an "axis of peace", to use the title of a book by Dr. Wesley Ariarajah, around the pivotal issue of justice.

Peace based on justice should not however be equated with the notion of "just peace" which, according to Dr. Ninan Koshy and Dr. Kim Yong-bock, has become a mantra of the World Council of Churches for its understanding of peace and justice. The two distinguished ecumenical thinkers issued a critical response to the Ecumenical Call for Just Peace, adopted at the WCC-convened International Ecumenical Peace Convocation in Jamaica in 2011. In their well-argued response sent to the Central Committee and general secretary of the WCC, Dr. Koshy and Dr. Kim dismissed "just peace" as a problematic term since its pacifist connotation and its appropriation by the global empire as moral justification for the use of force combine to "legitimize the peace that is being claimed by powers and principalities". They also underscored that with "just peace" now also a term in imperial lexicon – given that both US Presidents Bush and Obama had linked just peace to weapons, military alliance and war – the use of the concept in effect endorses what is more appropriately called "imperial peace."[7]

Towards A Revitalized Ecumenical Movement

Of special saliency to us, ecumenical workers and leaders in Asia, is the fact that religion has been inextricably embroiled and deeply implicated in today's conflicts. Sadly, religion has been co-opted by the war-mongers of our day. Empires since time immemorial have always thrived on religious sanctification and grandiose claims to cultural superiority for its project of domination. Like ancient Rome which filled its colonies with imperial images celebrating peace, fertility and prosperity to disguise its not-so-noble project of siphoning resources from colonies and accumulating power,[8] the US invokes freedom, democracy and economic development (along with peace and security) to justify the hegemonic drive.

In the current context of religious revivalism, these universalistic and monopolistic claims are framed in moral absolutes and garbed in the religious language of good versus evil. To quote from the declaration adopted in a 2006 consultation organized by the World Alliance of Reformed Churches and hosted by the People's Forum on Peace for Life in Manila, "The Christian religion of empire treats others as 'gentiles to be conquered, as the 'evil empire' to be destroyed or as the 'axis of evil' to be eradicated from the earth. The empire claims that the 'goodness' of the empire must overcome these 'evils'. Its false messianic spirit is imbued with the demonic."[9]

---

[7] Ninan Koshy and Yong-Bok Kim, Some Comments on the International Ecumenical Peace Convocation (IEPC) Message and "The Ecumenical Call for Justice", posted at http://www.peaceforlife.org/resources/faithresist/2011/11-0712-kimkoshy-iepccomments.html, July 12, 2011.

[8] Brian J. Walsh and Sylvia C. Keesmat, *Colossians Remixed: Subverting the Empire* (InterVarsity Press, 2004).

[9] "An Ecumenical Faith Stance against Global Empire for a Liberated Earth Community," *Reformed World, Vol. 56* (December 2006), 433-450.

The worldwide ecumenical movement has a long and powerful history of social and political engagement, taking clear faith-based positions on justice and peace. Its finest hour came when, despite threats to church unity, it boldly confronted dictatorial and military-led regimes that were then entrenched in Latin America and Asian countries like South Korea, the Philippines and Indonesia during the 60s and 70s, and threw its support to African liberation movements against Apartheid during the tumultuous seventies and eighties. In efforts to empower the disempowered and marginalized, it supported local projects like community organizing in urban poor communities as well as rural development among landless peasants.

And yet ironically, on two of the most critical issues of the day – namely, neo-liberal globalization and empire – ecumenical churches remain largely divided, mainly along South-North fault lines. The WCC document on Alternative Globalisation Addressing People and Earth (AGAPE), which highlights the violence and injustices as well as ecological despoliation wrought by militarized globalization and empire continues to provoke controversies and has been dismissed by some European ecumenical leaders and specialized agencies as too "naïve", "simplistic", "ideological" and hence analytically flawed. However to the credit of progressive Asian ecumenical leaders, along with their African and Latin American counterparts, this lopsided view has not been left unchallenged. Indeed there is no value-free or neutral reading of the Bible and biblical texts can only be apprehended from one's location in the prevailing social hierarchy.

At no time therefore in history is the religious community and the ecumenical movement faced with so huge and formidable a challenge. Unfortunately at no time is the ecumenical movement also so deeply divided and poorly equipped to tackle the critical challenges of the times.

Let me thus close, by going back to Clement John who made a similar assessment of the current sad state of ecumenical engagement. He lamented that "the principles of witness and sharing for common vision that were painstakingly developed by the pioneers of the ecumenical movement" are being totally ignored and that increasingly there has been erosion of commitment to the social justice agenda of the churches of the South. He pointed to the loss of ecumenical memory, lack of accountability on the part of some Northern partners, and the arrogance and power of money. He was particularly disturbed that these same Northern partners have developed, if not imposed, their own particular perspectives and framework for analysis of global issues and trends. He was also distressed that churches in the North tended to focus on the benefits of globalization, rather than on its shortcomings, giving way to social compromises instead of promoting resistance and alternatives. He thus challenged churches in Asia to reclaim leadership and exercise the right to set the ecumenical agenda.

Nonetheless it is to his lasting credit that Clement insisted to the end that ways of re-engaging, or to use the language of our present discourse, reconciling with partner churches in the North must be found. For indeed, if I may add, only a reconciled, united ecumenical family can face up to the monumental task of mobilizing a counter-imperial faith that promotes transnational alliances with other progressive faith communities and people's movements that may yet usher in a world without empire. Only then can the ecumenical movement become a powerful force for peace based on justice, people's security and genuine reconciliation.

Bibliography

Ariarajah, Wesley. *Axis of Peace: Christian Faith in Times of Violence and War.* Geneva: World Council of Churches, 2004.

Bendana, Alejandro. "What Kind of Peace is Being Built? Critical Assessments from the South," *International South Group Network.* Manila, 2003.

Dussodovsky, Michel. *America's War on Terrorism.* Philippines: Ibon Books, 2005.

Joseph, MJ. *One in Many, Many in One*. India: Christava Sahitya Samithi Trihuvalla, 2005.
Keesmat, Sylvia and Walsh, Brian. *Colossians Remixed: Subverting the Empire.* InterVarsity Press, 2004.
Köchler, Hans. *Global Justice or Global Revenge?* Austria: Springer-Verlag Wien, 2003.
Koshy, Ninan (ed.). *A History of the Ecumenical Movement in Asia.* Hongkong: Christian Conference of Asia, 2004.
Koshy, Ninan. *The Empire and Terrorism*. Mumbai: Vikas Adhyayan Kendra, 2006.
Muzaffar, Chandra. *Global Ethic or Global Hegemony?* UK: ASEAN Academic Press LTD, 2005.
"An Ecumenical Faith Stance against Global Empire for a Liberated Earth Community," *Reformed World, Vol. 56*. Philippines: August 17, 2006.
Make Peace: Do Justice. Hong Kong: Christian Conference of Asia, 1991.

(28) Ecumenism in Asia as Interfaith Dialogue – A Historical Survey

Wesley Ariarajah

Introduction

Much of the expansion of early Christianity was linked with colonial power. The Christianization of Europe was facilitated by the conversion of Roman emperor, Constantine, and the eventual adoption of Christianity as the official religion of the empire by those who followed him. Similarly, most of South and Central America became Roman Catholic based on the prevalent practice where the Pope automatically becoming the spiritual head of the territories ruled and conquered by the Spanish and Portuguese emperors. The British Empire, however, was more interested in trade and the collection of taxes from its colonies than in enforcing Christianity on them. Rather, it facilitated the work of missionary societies by subsidizing their work in education, health care and other forms of social services. This has meant that Christianity remained a minority religion in all Asian countries, with the exception of the Philippines which came under Spanish rule.

Christianity not only remained a minority religion in Asia but it also had to encounter religions that have had longer spiritual histories, with well developed theological and philosophical schools of thought, scriptures of profound depth and beauty, and a string of saints and sages. These religious traditions were also the cultural expressions of the Asian peoples, fortified by rituals, ceremonies, religious and social practices, and elaborate feasts and festivals that held the communities together. In other words, in Asia, Christianity encountered peoples who followed religious traditions that have for centuries been deeply embedded in their personal lives, social relations, and cultural expressions; religion had seeped into people's daily life and relationships.

In countries where Christianity had been, or continues to be the predominant religion, ecumenical movement has been concerned primarily with drawing the churches together in unity, mission and service so that they also discover the unity they have in Christ. Generally speaking, ecumenism in Asia also seeks to deal with these confessional and denominational divisions that had been transplanted into Asia. However, there had been some uneasiness in Asia in understanding ecumenism only in terms of Christian unity. If the ecumenism is about the "whole inhabited earth" and its unity, is it adequate to think of ecumenism in Asia only in terms of Christian unity? This uneasiness has led some to speak of the need for a "wider ecumenism" or an "ecumenism of religious traditions". Even though the idea has not yet struck deep roots, it is important to look upon the growth of interfaith dialogue and cooperation among religions as a dimension of ecumenical life of the churches and peoples of Asia. What I hope to do here is to give an outline of the development and growth of interfaith relations in Asia as part of our study of ecumenism in Asia. The first part deals with the role Asian missionaries and theologians played in the development of the concept of dialogue. The second section deals with Asian involvement in dialogue and I end with an evaluation of the current situation. Much of the material in this essay is taken from my contribution on this subject to the second volume of the *History of the Ecumenical Movement in Asia*, edited by Ninan Koshy.

Asian Role in the Development of the Concept of Dialogue

What has been the history of interfaith relations and dialogue in the Asian context, and how has it impacted ecumenism in Asia? This is a difficult question to deal with because of the complex nature of Asia. Each of the Asian countries has had its own history and different stories about the encounter of the Gospel with the religious traditions of the respective countries. Further Christianity was carried into Asia by different groups of people with a great variety of approaches to the extant religious traditions. The reception it has had also varied from county to country.

It is common too to readily associate Christianity in Asia predominantly with the Western colonial expansion into the region. In reality, there has been a long and fascinating relationship between Christianity and Asian religions from the very early stages of Christian history. No one exactly knows the very first contacts between the early Christians and the Asian religious traditions. One can, however, be certain that already at the time of Jesus there had been trade links between the Middle East and several countries in Asia, by sea to the Indian sub-continent and beyond, and by land, leading all the way to the provinces of China through what was eventually recognized as the 'Silk Route.' Such trade relations resulted in Arab, Jewish, Persian, and Armenian settlements in different parts of Asia.

It is in this context that we have the tradition of the arrival of Apostle Thomas himself to the South Western coast of India, which is the present Indian state of Kerala. Even though the historical veracity of St. Thomas' life and ministry in India between 52 – 72 C.E. remain contested, there is ample evidence to show that there had been a well-established and continuous Christian community of Syrian origins in India at least from around 200 C.E.[1]

What is of interest is that the early 'St. Thomas Christians' had very good relationship with the Hindu community around them. In fact, evidence suggests that they were accepted into the caste structure of India as the second in line, next only to the Brahmins. Christians incorporated many of the Hindu customs and practices into their religious observances and maintained close social relation with the Hindu neighbours. At the same time, they maintained ecclesiastical contact with the Patriarch in Syria and celebrated the liturgy handed down by tradition. So much so, the Christian relations to the Hindus at that time was said to be 'symbiotic', where they were able to be "Hindu in culture, Christian in religion and Oriental in worship."[2]

In a comprehensive study of Christianity in Asia before 1500 C.E., under the title *The Hidden History of Christianity in Asia*, John C. England lays out convincing evidence of wide spread presence of Eastern Christianity (under a variety of names as Syrian, Armenian, Nestorian etc.) in several countries including China, India, Tibet, Sri Lanka (then known as Taprobane, and later as Ceylon), Burma (Myanmar), Java, and perhaps in Korea and Japan (via China). It appears that Christians, as a religious community, lived in reasonable harmony with the religious traditions of the peoples and had modest successes in convincing others to follow its "Way."

All this was to change with the arrival of Western Christianity, first with explorers and trading Companies, and later with organized colonial rules based in Portugal, Spain, Holland, France, and Britain. A new era of Christian relations to peoples of other religious traditions opened in Asia, and with it, the nascent beginnings of ecumenical involvement.

Impact of Colonialism on Inter-Faith Relations

As indicated earlier trade was the initial Western interest in Asia. But soon the Western powers realized that political control of the Asian region would be the best way to facilitate trade. The Portuguese and the Spaniards brought in Roman Catholicism and the Dutch and British, the Protestant denominations. Initially

[1] See: Cheriyan, C. V, *A History of Christianity in Kerala – From the Mission of St. Thomas to the Arrival of Dasco da Gama: A.D.52 – 1498* (Kottayam: Kerala Historical Society, 1973).

[2] Menon, K. P. K., "Medieval Christianity in India – Part I, The Eastern Church" p.7 in: Perumalil, A.C. and Hambye, E.R. (eds.), *Christianity in India – A History in Ecumenical Perapective* (Allepey: Prakasam Publications, 1972) quoted in: England, John C., *The Hidden History of Christianity in India- The Churches of the East before 1500* (Delhi: ISPCK, 1996) p.66.

the intension of the colonizers in bringing clergy from their homelands was to provide religious services to those Western communities that had settled in Asian countries to promote trade and the political ambitions of the European rulers. But some, like Francis Xavier (1506 – 1552) of the Jesuit Order, saw the enormous potential it opened for the propagation of the Gospel. Other Roman Catholic Orders and Protestant missions followed his initiative.

What is of interest is to note that Colonization, Westernization, and Evangelization of the Asian continent were seen to be in a continuum. They enabled each other, and fed each other. The unholy alliance between the three was to reinforce the triumphalism and intolerance that had become one of the main traits of Western Christian theology and Christian approach to other religions ever since Christianity became the official religion of the Roman Empire.

The overall mission history in Asia, however, had been a mixed blessing. On the one hand, there were missionary activities that brought much humanization of Asian societies. Several missionary personnel lived sacrificial lives in the service of the people they met and did much to bring healing and wholeness into individual and social life. Much was done to bring modern education, medicine, technology etc., and to liberate women and children from oppression and servitude.

On the other hand, there was suppression of the religions and cultures of the peoples of Asia. Incentives, coercion, and even force were used to make Christians of others. At the theological level, many tended to treat the Asian religions, which they never quite understood, as mere 'paganism' or 'superstition' and, at best, misguided attempts to grasp the Divine. On the whole, mission theology looked at people of other religious traditions to be in 'error' and in need of the Gospel message and membership in the Christian community for their own salvation.

From the very beginning there were also dissenters. For instance when Robert de Nobili (born in Rome in 1577), another Jesuit, reached Goa, India, in 1605, he was quite shocked at the equation being made between evangelization and westernization in the Portuguese missionary effort. De Nobili studied Sanskrit and the Hindu religious literature, and on that basis defended the compatibility between Christian faith and many of the customs and practices of Hinduism. De Nobili's adoption of Hindu practices were deeply controversial within the Roman Catholic church, but it is also important to recognize that his adoption of Hinduism and its practices were still apologetic, for through them he was attempting to reach the upper classes in the caste structure within Hinduism with the Gospel message.[3]

De Nobili was not the first one to adopt this 'positive' approach to Asian religions. Already in China his compatriot Matteo Ricci (1552 – 1610), with his scientific knowledge, sympathetic approach to Chinese religion and culture, and ability to speak Chinese, was winning the favour of the governor of Kwangtung. But again, Ricci was interested in the proclamation of the Gospel, and his very first Chinese convert became the cause for suspicion and resentment among the people about his motives.

A study of the history of Christianity in China would show that the main concern of those who dissented with the main missionary enterprise was not so much religious but cultural, even though it is almost impossible to separate Chinese culture from its Confucian and Taoist moorings. The key word was 'sinicization', an attempt to make Christianity truly a Chinese religion. Many thinkers like. T. C. Chao, L.C. Wu and Y.T. Wu, among many other notable figures, spared no energy in thinking and acting to 'sinicize' Christianity, which laid the foundations for the eventual development of the patriotic 'Three-Self Movement' of self-support, self-governance, and self- propagation. These, however, did not constitute a radical re-thinking of Christian relationship to other religious traditions.

In India too those who were in dissent with the prevalent missiology of the missionary endeavour turned out to be pioneers in Indian Christian Theology rather than ones who explored new avenues to understand

[3] Mookenthottam, Antony, *Indian Theological Tendencies – Approaches and Problems for Further Research as Seen in the Works of Some Leading Indian Theologians* (Berne: Peter Lang, 1978) p. 26-29.

Christian relation to other religious traditions. Raja Rammohan Roy (1772-1833), Keshab Chander Sen (1838 – 1884), Brahmabandhab Upadhyaya (1861 – 1907), Nehemiah Goreh (1825 – 1895) and others showed greater interest in interpreting the Christian faith in the Hindu context, or of reforming Hinduism in the Christian context, than in asking searching questions on the reality of Hinduism itself. Similarly, a long list of others Christians in the 20th Century, like Jules Monchanin (1895-1957), Henri le Saux, re-named Swami Abhishiktananda (1910 – 1973), and Bede Griffiths were primarily interested in integrating the Hindu spirituality into their Christian vocation.

The real struggles over Christian understanding and approach to other religious traditions, in their own integrity as religious traditions, were to emerge mainly within the struggles of the ecumenical movement, especially in its expression as the Missionary Movement.

Beginnings of the Debate Within the Ecumenical Movement

It is difficult to pin down the date of the beginning of the modern ecumenical movement. A movement, by nature, is a process and it is recognized as a 'movement' only as it begins to gather momentum and attract the attention of a wide range of people. It would appear that the 'ecumenical movement', i.e., the movement that began to draw Christians across their confessional and denominational barriers in witness and service, began primarily among students. The isolated ecumenical groups of students, who were to eventually become the Student Christian Movement, were structured into the World Student Christian Federation (WSCF) in 1895 at Vadstena, Sweden. John R. Mott, then a leader in the Young Men's Christian Association in the United States, brought them together.

Mott himself was deeply invested in the missionary calling. Inspired by two significant events, the South India Missionary Conference at Madras, India (1900) and the follow up Missionary Conference four months later in New York, Mott decided to work towards a truly ecumenical World Mission Conference that would draw participants from all missionary societies and agencies. His vision was realized in 1910 at Edinburgh, Scotland, where some 1200 delegates came together with a sense of urgency of mission. Mott himself characterized the moment as "the decisive hour of Christian mission." His vision for the conference agenda was "the evangelization of the world in this generation", by which he meant that missionary societies should coordinate their personnel, resources, and strategies so that everyone in the world who lived at that time would have the opportunity to hear the challenge of the Gospel. The Theology of Religions that accompanied such a vision is obvious- other religions had no salvific value of their own and, therefore, it is the responsibility of the Christians to bring the saving knowledge to them all.

Asian Voices at Edinburgh

Even though the Edinburgh meeting was called to develop a global strategy for mission, thanks to the ecumenical voices from Asia, it became one of first global ecumenical events in which the question of Christian relationship to Asian religions was discussed with much intensity. The 'Asian' ecumenical voices at this conference, however, were not quite Asian, because there were, in fact, very few persons from the 'third world' at the Conference. Only 17 persons were from Asia. Among them were the youngest of the delegates, Cheng Ching-yi from China, and A. Z. Azariah, who had been the secretary of the YMCA and the leader of the Indian SCM, who made bold and notable contribution on the nature of mission and mission relations in Asia.[4] The voices on Christian relations to people of other religious traditions,

[4] See discussion in: Potter, Philip and Wieser, Thomas, *Seeking and Serving the Truth – First Hundred Years of the World Student Christian Federation* (Geneva: WCC Publications, 1997) p.31-33.

however, were to come from Western missionaries in the Asian mission fields who also represented the Asian concerns at the conference.

The Conference worked in 'Commissions' to deal with different aspects of mission in the 'non-Christian lands'. Commission I, on 'Carrying the Gospel to All the Non-Christian World', for instance, had the task of surveying "the unoccupied sections of the world, with the view to the speedy and complete occupation of these areas ..."[5] But there was also a Commission IV with the mandate to examine the 'Missionary Message in Relation to Non-Christian Religions'.

In preparation for this Commission a questionnaire had been sent to missionaries in the field on their experience of preaching the Gospel to peoples of other faith traditions. More than two hundred sets of answers, some of considerable length, were received. The responses that came from the Asian missionaries provide quite a fascinating reading.[6] Many of the well-known missionaries from the Indian sub-continent, like J. N. Farquhar, G. S. Eddy, A. G. Hogg, Bernard Lucas, Nicol Macnicol, C. F. Andrews etc. wrote of their positive experience of meeting with Hindus. They, like many other missionaries from other parts of Asia that responded to the questionnaire, were at odds with the predominant missionary approach of seeing other religions as in 'error' or as 'heathens'. Many spoke of their experience of people of other faiths as sincere, ethical, and devout persons in some sort of communion with God. The over all emphasis was on finding 'points of contact' between the religious life of the people of Asia and the Gospel message. J. N. Farquhar summarized the position in these words: "Christ's own attitude to Judaism ought to be our attitude to other faiths even if the gap is far greater and the historical connection absent." [7]

Even though the Commission IV report, drafted by D. S. Cairns of Aberdeen, Scotland, was characterized as a "lucid and glowing" statement "pulsating with life" and was, in fact, the highlight of the Conference, the overall thrust of the Conference was 'world outreach'. The other Commissions that dealt with missionary strategies and methods had the day. Following the Edinburgh meeting Mott himself went around the world, strengthening the YMCAs, facilitating the creation of National Christian Councils (NCCs) and more SCM units to give an ecumenical basis for the life and mission of the Christian community. In China, India, Korea, and Japan, Mott was able to lay strong foundations for strengthening the SCMs, again with major emphasis on bringing the non-Christian world under the 'Lordship of Christ.'

Call for Collaboration: The Jerusalem Conference

Despite this interest, a turning of the tide on Christian approach to other religious traditions began at the second World Mission Conference, called by the newly constituted International Missionary Council, held over Easter of 1928 at the Mount of Olives, Jerusalem. Several factors were responsible for the changing attitude towards other religious traditions within the ecumenical discussions. In the West, the rise of secularism was experienced as a major threat, and in the United States W. E. Hocking was leading a school of thought that the universal spread of secularism "required a new alignment of religious forces" and that this new alignment was possible because, despite the different names and systems, all religions "merged in the universal human faith in the Divine Being." [8] Hocking's 'liberal' views and his call for some kind of

---

[5] *World Mission Conference 1910, Report of Commission I: Carrying the Gospel to All the Non-Christian World* (Edinburgh/London: Oliphant, Anderson, and Ferrier, 1910) p.279.

[6] These responses, in typed and bound form, are available under the title, *Commission on Missionary Message*, at the Library of the Ecumenical Center, Geneva, along with the other papers and reports from the 1910 Conference.

[7] Farquhar, well known for his volume, *The Crown of Hinduism*, wrote a 43-page response to the questionnaire dealing with different aspects of Hindu-Christian relations.

[8] See the report on E. W. Hocking's contribution, *Report of the Jerusalem Meeting of the International Missionary Council- I* (London: Oxford University Press, 1928) p.369 f.

'World Religion' was resisted firmly by the European delegation, but the rise of secularism was recognized as a real problem.

From the East, the challenge came from another angle. J. N. Farquhar's concept of Christianity as the 'crown' or 'fulfillment' of other religions was gaining grounds, and the insistence of Asian Christians, especially those from China, on the need to indigenize the Christian faith required new approaches to other religions and the cultures rooted in them.

Moreover, there has also been a major change in the constituency of the Mission Conference. Where as in Edinburgh (1910) there were only 17 persons from the 'third world' in a gathering of 1200, in Jerusalem over one third of the about 1000 participants were from Asia, Africa, and Latin America. The Asian pressure on the ecumenical movement was gaining ground. In fact, of the seven Commissions of the meeting, the very first one was on 'The Christian Life and Message in Relation to Non-Christian Thought and Life.'

The Scottish missionary from Madras, Nicol Macnicol, made the Asian case for a new approach to Asian religious traditions within the ecumenical family. Speaking about Hinduism, he said that there was, of course, as Stanley Jones had suggested in Edinburgh, superstitious and oppressive dimensions of Hinduism that have to go. But that was not the only Hinduism we confront in 1928, he said. What we confront today is a religion that, "because of its long recorded history, because of the profundity of the speculation of its ancient sages, and because of the power that these ideas still exercise over the lives of multitudes in this land, demands to be treated with complete respect and is not afraid at times to claim to be possessed of a higher truth than any of its rivals ... it is this Hinduism that we wish to survey from without, as she stands among her rivals, proud, self-assertive, not any longer apologetic."[9]

Macnicol insisted that the religious traditions in Asia were themselves undergoing reformation and renewal, and that there is no more room for the egoism or aggression on the part of Christians, but respect and love: "As we draw near to the souls of our brethren (sic) with our message we must put off our shoes from our feet for the ground is holy."[10]

Macnicol's message was difficult for many of the Continental European delegates who were already disturbed by the developments in the United States. During the debate, K. T. Paul, the General Secretary of the YMCA in India, Burma and Ceylon, and P. Chenchiah, later to become one of the outstanding lay theologians of India, defended Macnicol's position, Chenchiah arguing that the non-Christian religions are no longer in opposition to Christianity "but like secular sciences have become the competitors of Christianity."

Francis Wei and T. C. Chao from China drew parallels between what Macnicol had to say about Hinduism and their own experience with Confucianism. They insisted that they saw the relationship of Christianity to China as one that "fulfills" the best in Confucian culture.[11]

'The Message' from Jerusalem is an eloquent witness on the Asian ecumenical impact on the wider ecumenical movement. While still maintaining the missionary emphasis, Jerusalem Report had many positive things to say about peoples of other religious traditions. First, it rejected the Christian imperial attitude to other religions: "...on our part we would repudiate any symptoms of a religious imperialism that would desire to impose beliefs and practices on others in order to manage their souls in their supposed interest. We obey God who respects our wills and we desire to respect those of others." Putting the emphasis on "sharing" the Christian message with "humility, penitence and love," it argued that Christians have not "sufficiently sought out the good and noble elements in the non-Christian beliefs."

It went even further to identify the 'noble elements' in religious traditions:

---

[9] Ibid, p.5

[10] Ibid. p. 17.

[11] Ibid. p. 358-59

> We recognize as part of the one Truth that sense of the majesty of God and the consequent reverence in worship which are conspicuous in Islam; the deep sympathy for the world's sorrow and unselfish search for the way of escape, which are at the heart of Buddhism; the desire for contact with Ultimate Reality conceived as spiritual, which is prominent in Hinduism; the belief in the moral order of the universe and consequent insistence on moral conduct, which are inculcated by Confucianism; the disinterested pursuit of truth and of human welfare which is often found in those who stand for secular civilization but do not accept Christ as their Lord and Saviour.

Despite the considerable hesitations on the part of the Continental European delegates, especially from Germany, the Jerusalem Message was able to fully accommodate the Asian concerns, mainly because of the diplomatic and drafting skills of Archbishop William Temple, who chaired the Message Committee.

Did the Jerusalem Message over reach itself? Did it too easily give in to the Asian pressure and derailed the missionary imperative? Many Europeans thought so. Once the participants had come down from the Mount of Olives, and the goodwill of the Easter tide that permeated the Jerusalem meeting had past, the issue of Christian relationship to people of other religious traditions would become a full-blown controversy. Many within the leadership of the missionary movement felt that mission was under threat. "The stage was being set for the need for a clear, concise, and considered position in relation to people of other faiths, for the Jerusalem and post-Jerusalem debates were to show an increasing and, some would say, chaotic diversity within the church on this issue. The Jerusalem meeting not only necessitated Tambaram 1938, but almost pre-determined its outcome."[12]

Asia and the 'Tambaram Controversy'

The third World Mission Conference was held in Tambaram, Madras. It was to have been held in China, but the upheavals in China required that it moved to Tambaram, to the newly built facilities of the Madras Christian College. This was the first World Mission Conference to be held in Asia and, after the Jerusalem experience, the leaders of the missionary movement decided to take on the issue of Christian approach to people of other faiths head on, so that a considered theological position might be developed.

In order to facilitate a good discussion, the leaders invited Hendrik Kraemer, a well-known Dutch missiologist, who had worked among Muslims in Egypt and in Indonesia and had been an important participant at Jerusalem, to write a volume that would make the case for mission. Kreamer's preparatory volume, *The Christian Message in a Non-Christian World*, became the centerpiece of the Tambaram meeting. His presentation, and the conclusions drawn from it, also animated the most diverse, intense, and spirited discussion ever on Christian relationship to people of other religious traditions within the Asian ecumenical scene.

It is beyond the scope of this essay to discuss Kraemer's contribution in detail. Using the concept of 'Biblical Realism' on the human condition, and Karl Barth's sharp distinction between Gospel as unique Divine Revelation, and all religions and cultures (including Christianity as a 'religion') as part of human sinfulness and rebellion against God, Kraemer developed at Tambaram the concept of "discontinuity". This argued that the Gospel can neither be the 'fulfillment' of any religion nor could be built on the 'noble values' found in other religious expressions. Rather, it challenges all adherents of religions to respond in faith to the unique revelation in Jesus Christ.

No doubt, both Asian participants and many missionaries working in Asia were up in arms against Kraemer, and Tambaram saw one of the most divisive and controversial debates on this issue within the ecumenical movement. T.C. Chao from China, D. G. Moses and P. Chenchiah from India, Karl L. Reichet from Hong Kong, A.G. Hogg from Madras, H.H. Farmer from England etc. made impassioned

[12] Ariarajah, S. Wesley, *Hindus and Christians – A Century of Protestant Ecumenical Thought* (Amsterdam: Editions Rodopi, and Grand Rapids: William Eearmans Publishing Company, 1991) p.50-51.

interventions challenging Kraemer's position. Other significant Asian participants included Toyohiko Kagawa of Japan, V. Azariah and Ralla Ram from India, D. T. Niles and Sabapathy Kulandran from Sri Lanka, C. Y. Cheng from China, and Leimena from Indonesia.

Visser't Hooft, who also attended the conference, was deeply impressed with the quality of interventions from those from the 'third world', especially from Asia. Speaking of his experience at Tambaram he said, "The real significance of the conference was that from now on it would be impossible to think of the missionary and indeed the total ecumenical task without taking the voice of the churches of Asia, Africa and Latin America seriously." [13]

The Asian participants carried the 'Tambaram Controversy' into all parts of Asia. In India the controversy attracted the attention of the "Rethinking Christianity in India" group. Well-known Indian theologians like A. J. Appasamy, V. Chakkarai, P. Chenchiah, P. D. Devanandan, M. M. Thomas and others began a process of delineating Asian ecumenical lines of thinking on Christian approach to people of other religious traditions. Unfortunately, the churches in the North Asia – China, Japan, Korea and Taiwan – were deeply embroiled in the political, social, and military upheavals in the region at this time. Yet, people like T. C. Chao, L. C. Wu, Y. T. Wu and others in China, and K. L. Reichelt, out of Tao Fong Shan in Hong Kong, kept the pressure up on rethinking Christianity and inter-religious relationships in the context of Confucianism and Buddhism. D. T. Niles of Sri Lanka began to pioneer a process of 'rethinking mission' in the context of the religious plurality in Asia. The Asian ecumenical scene became alive with post-Tambaram debates.

In Europe, however, the outbreak of the Second World War smothered post-Tambaram discussions. Instead, the urgency of Christians coming together to serve the war-torn world became the priority, resulting in the precipitation of the discussions that led to the formation of the World Council of Churches at its inaugural assembly in Amsterdam, 1948.

A New Beginning

The end of the Second World War (1939-1945) brought dramatic changes into the Asian ecumenical scene, the most important being the de-colonization of the Asian nations. However, the North Asian region was in utter turmoil with the collapse of Japan, the success of the Communist Revolution in China, consequent developments in Taiwan, the Korean War etc. Responding to the national situations, nation building, and formulating appropriate Christian responses to the political and social realities on the ground became the priorities for Asian churches and Christian leaders.

However, Asians got involved again in the ecumenical discussions on interfaith relations when the World Council of Churches and the International Missionary Council (which had not yet become part of the WCC) decided to jointly follow up the Tambaram discussions in a new study "The Word of God and the Living Faiths of Men" (sic.), launched in 1955. It was decided that this study would be done locally through the Christian Study Centers around the world, and the Asian Study Centers, like the ones in Bangalore and Hong Kong, were asked to study in some depth the nature of Christian relations to the faith of others. In India, P. D. Devanandan, who headed the Christian Institute for the Study and Religion and Society in Bangalore, followed an innovative idea of calling persons of other religious traditions to participate in these discussions, thus bringing in the concept of 'Dialogue' to the forefront. And at the third assembly of the WCC in New Delhi (1961) he spoke passionately against the idea of mission that intends to replace other religious traditions and argued for 'dialogue' as the way forward.[14]

---

[13] Memoirs, p.59.

[14] "Called to Witness," address to the Third Assembly of The World Council of Churches, New Delhi, 1961, revised and reprinted in: P. D. Devanandan, *Preparation for Dialogue*, (Bangalore: The Christian Institute for the Study of Religion and Society, 1964) p. 189 – 193.

In the meantime the Second Vatican Council, also meeting in the 60s, facilitated considerable advances within the Roman Catholic Church on Christian approach to other religious traditions.[15] Here too the Asian Roman Catholic theologians played a significant role in the formulations related to other religious traditions in important documents of the Vatican Council such as *Nostra Aetate* ("Declaration on the Relationship of the Church to Non-Christian Religions") and *Lumen Gentum* ("Dogmatic Constitution of the Church"). Following Vatican II, Asian Roman Catholic theologians began to make considerable advances both in re-thinking Christianity for plurality and in rebuilding Christian relations to others. New theological explorations in the context of religious plurality, inculturation of the liturgy, interfaith dialogue etc. were being pioneered within the Asian scene by leading Asian Roman Catholic thinkers.

The result of these developments was a fascinating ecumenical meeting in Kandy, Sri Lanka in 1967, which, for the first time, brought together Protestant, Orthodox, and Roman Catholic theologians to consider the Christian approach to people of other religious traditions. Kandy report rejected the Barth-Kraemer approach to people of other traditions. It argued that God's love and purpose of salvation extends to all peoples of every century, country and creed, that it is both individual and corporate, and embraces all aspects of human existence.[16]

The Kandy consultation had considerable influence on the WCC Uppsala Assembly (1968) discussions on Christian relations to people of other religious traditions, resulting in the acceptance of the concept of 'dialogue,' and leading eventually to the formation of the WCC Sub-Unit on Dialogue with People of Living Religions and Ideologies in 1971. After heated debates over the meaning and practice of Dialogue at the next assembly in Nairobi (1975), 'Guidelines on Dialogue' were drawn up at a major consultation in Chiang Mai, Thailand (1977) with the participation of many Asian theologians. This helped in establishing dialogue as a permanent program within the WCC.

It must be noted that almost all the major meetings that influenced the process were held in Asia, and all the main actors, including the WCC's Dialogue programme's first Director, Stanley J. Samartha, came from the Asian region. In other words, Asian ecumenism was at the heart of the global discussions that turn the tide on the global thinking on Christian relations to people of other religious traditions.

Asian Ecumenical Instrument

In the meantime the first meeting of the church leaders from all over East Asia had been called in 1949 under the able leadership of Rajah B. Manikam of India and S. C. Leung of China. This meeting, which gave an opportunity to consider the common issues, faced by the churches in Asia, led first to the formation of a secretariat to work among the churches and Christian Councils in Asia, and eventually to the creation of an Asian ecumenical instrument, the East Asia Christian Conference (EACC, later to become CCA).

From the very first Assembly in Kuala Lumpur, Malaysia, the EACC took on the issue of making the church in Asia truly Asian through creative responses to the religions and cultures of its peoples. Many of the subsequent assemblies, conferences, and General Committee meetings have emphasized the need for a positive and sympathetic approach to Asian religions and its followers.

At Kuala Lumpur, M. M. Thomas interpreted this positive and sympathetic approach primarily in terms of participating with people of other religious traditions and of secular ideologies in the 'humanization' of society. Conceiving salvation as humanization, Thomas argued that humanization provided the most

[15] See the papal encyclical *Ecclesium Suam*, and the Vatican II documents, "Declaration on the Relationship of the Church to Non-Christian Religions" (*Nostra Aetate*) and the "Dogmatic Constitution of the Church" (*Lumen Gentum*).
[16] For details see: Report of the Kandy Consultation, *Study Encounter* III, No. 2 (1967).

relevant point of entry to our dialogue with other religious traditions and ideologies at spiritual and theological depth.[17]

As the first General Secretary of the EACC at the founding assembly in Kula Lumpur, D. T. Niles agreed with Thomas, and the sentiment got reflected in the report of the assembly, which said that Christians should go into "every part of the life of our peoples, into politics, into social and national service, into the world of art and culture, to work in real partnership with non-Christians."[18]

It is important, however, to note that there was a substantial difference in approach between the WCC and the EACC (CCA) in the way this new approach bore fruit. In the WCC the interfaith relations work took the form of promoting actual dialogue events between peoples of different religious communities. Thus many bilateral and multi-lateral dialogues were organized at different levels. In fact, the newly created WCC Sub-Unit on Dialogue, under the leadership of Stanley A. Samartha, organized several interfaith dialogue events between Christians and Hindus, Christians and Buddhist etc. in Asia as well. Similarly the Asian YMCA also took interfaith relations as a key issue and facilitated several discussions and encounters across religious lines. It is of interest that the EACC then and its successor CCA now, did not have a separate program desk that was entirely devoted to the issue of Christian relationship to people of other religious traditions. Most of the time the interfaith relations issue was tagged onto either the Mission or Theology desks.

However, the new approach resulted in the proliferation of Asian Theological Thinking that took the religions and cultures of Asia seriously. Moe recently, theologians like Kosuke Koyama, C. S. Song, S. Yagi, Lynn A. de Silva, Aloysius Pieris, Raymond Panikkar, M. M. Thomas- to name only a few among many others, both within the Protestant and Roman Catholic traditions- developed quite a fascinating array of Christian theological thought in dialogue with the religions and cultures of Asia. All of them are built on a respectful and appreciative approach to other religious traditions. They call for an in-depth dialogue with the Asian religious and cultural reality. But most of them have little to say about building actual relationship with peoples of other religious traditions.

It is to this reality we now need to turn in the evaluative and concluding section of this essay.

An Evaluation

The story of the Asian Christian ecumenical relations to people of other religious traditions is very much tied up with the vicissitudes of history. As seen earlier, there was an active presence of Christianity in Asia before the colonial era, but almost all the Christian communities from that period, with the exception of the early traditions that survived in the South Western coast of India, had become extinct. Therefore, most of the churches in Asia are the product of the Western missions that came during the colonial period. This meant two things. First, most Christians were drawn out of other Asian religious communities, and the Christian missions completely separated them from an ongoing religion-based relations with their neighbours. Further, because of their negative evaluation of other religious traditions and the cultures that emanated from them, the early missions took steps to cut the Christian converts off from the cultures from which they had come. Thus the mainline missionary movement drove a wedge between the Christian community and the larger community.

This resulted in a psychological alienation between the Christian community and the larger community. Almost until after the end of the colonial era Christians in most Asian countries did not see themselves as part and parcel of the national communities of Asia Attempts at reconciling Christianity with the Chinese

[17] Thomas, M. M., *Salvation and Humanization: Some Crucial Issues of the Theology of Mission in Contemporary India* (Bangalore: CISRS, 1971) p. 20.

[18] *Witness Together*, The Official Report of the Inaugural assembly of the EACC, held at Kuala Lumpur, Malaya (Malaysia), 14 -24, 1959.

culture, therefore, had been an up-hill task for the enlightened Christian leaders in China. Even in post-colonial India, Indian Christian nationalist leaders like P. D. Devanandan and M. M. Thomas had to struggle to make a case for Christian participation in nation building with a church that was not ready and at times even suspicious of such an exercise.

Second, during the colonial period much of the Asian church leadership was in the hands of the missionaries; they also laid out the missiology and theology for the Asian churches. Thus, the Asian Christians were 'brought up' in a theological tradition that saw other religious traditions to be 'pagan', or at least in 'darkness and error', in need of the light of the Gospel. Asian churches' primary relationship to the surrounding community was defined in terms of mission, as understood by the missionary movement of that time. The interpretation of the Bible was also in the hands of the missionaries, who made it into book that carried, above all, the missionary imperative.

In this context, it was fortunate that several Western missionaries in Asia were themselves convinced of the fallacy of the traditional missiology that alienated Christians from other religious traditions and its peoples. They had the faith and courage, at times at much cost to themselves, to challenge the missionary movement from the inside. The Asian churches, however, ignored or marginalized all new thinking on relationship to other religions, whether it came from the missionaries or their own people.

Bishop S. Kulandran of Jaffna, Sri Lanka, recounts an interesting story of Kraemer's visit to him in Jaffna sometime after the Tambaram meeting. Kraemer, despite his theological position in Tambaram, had been maintaining very good relations and dialogue with the Muslims in Egypt and Indonesia. Kulandran says that having seen the church situation in Jaffna, Kraemer complained that the church seemed "withdrawn into a shell" and not leaning towards relationship with its non-Christian neighbours. "Dr. Kraemer's complaint and observation were quite correct" wrote Kulandran, "I was sorry to have to tell him that what had produced that attitude had been his own book. Dr. Kraemer might have been surprised, but it must be confessed that the book 'Christian Message in a Non-Christian World' had the effect of making the church to a large extent break off conversation with the non-Christian religionists." [19]

In other words, what Tambaram did was to re-enforce all the theologically negative attitudes towards other religious traditions. The hard-core Barth-Kraemer mission theology of Tambaram 1938 has a strangle hold on Asian churches to this day. In spite of the depth, vision, theological strength, and world-wide acclaim, Asian Theologies that look favourably on other religious traditions are still looked upon with suspicion, and have still not become part of the churches' life and thought in Asia.

Again, having imported the denominational divisions of Europe into Asia, the missionary movement, while promoting ecumenism among students and youth, did little to promote ecumenism within the churches in Asian region. Despite the emergence of the Church of South India and other church unity movements, an Asian ecumenical instrument itself was not established until 1959. Therefore the main ecumenical avenue that was open to Asian ecumenical leaders for a long time was only at the global level. This was a necessary evil, because the only way to bring about changes in Christian approach to peoples of other religious traditions at that time was to challenge the missiology of the missionary movement. All this meant that interfaith issues remained marginal to the immediate life of the Asian churches, and remains so to this day.

There is, however, a far more serious reason why inter-religious relationship as such has not been at center stage within Asian ecumenism. Asian ecumenical movement came into prominence at a time when Asian region was in social and political turmoil. On the one hand, many of the Asian countries were struggling, first to attain their independence from colonial rule, and then to find an adequate basis for

[19] S. Kulandran, "The Renaissance of Non-Christian Religions and a Definition of Approach to Non-Christians," mimeographed paper presented to the Study on the Word of God and Men of Other Faiths," (WCC Archives) Box 26.32.10, p.25.

nation building. On the other, the emergence of Communism in China as a major force to reckon with, the impact of the Cold War on the Korean peninsular, the aftermath of the fall of Japan etc. brought in common issues that affected the Asian communities across all religious barriers.

Therefore, a close scrutiny of the subjects and issues that pre-occupied the EACC and its successor, CCA, would show that the emphasis has been on the "people" of Asia. These were certainly not about the 'Christian people', but *all* the people of Asia and the problems they faced. Asian religious traditions were treated as one of the elements that contributed, negatively and positively, to the 'peoplehood' of the peoples of Asia. Faith, ideology, culture, and political vision etc. were seen as one complex whole that contributed to the "Asian reality," a much-used phrase within Asian ecumenism.

A good illustration of this approach is seen in the way religious traditions were treated in the CCA consultation on "Towards the Sovereignty of the People" called by the Commission on Theological Concerns, following the Bangalore assembly. The topics included: 'Faith and Political Visioning' (Harvey Perkins), 'Role of Ideology' (K. C. Abraham), 'The Process of Islamisation in Pakistan' (Clement John), 'Buddhist Political Visioning in Sri Lanka' (Aloysius Pieris), 'The Role of Confucianism, Taoism and Folk Religions in Shaping Perspectives of Chinese Political Vision' (Wang Hsien-chih), 'Political Vision and Cultural Traditions: The Case of Korea' (Kim Yong-bock) etc. All the religious traditions of Asia are here, and their role in the life of the peoples of Asia is taken seriously. And yet, Christian relationship to people of other religious traditions, as such, is not the focus.[20] In other words, what the Asian ecumenism appears to be concerned with is 'solidarity' with the 'people' across the religious lines, religions and cultures being treated as elements of the 'Asian reality'.

This approach is also seen in the Mission agenda of the Asian ecumenical movement. For instance, the Asia Mission Conference of 1989 had the following topics for which main address: 'The Mission of God in the Context of Suffering and Struggling Peoples of Asia,' 'Discovering Christ's Work among the People.' And the over all theme of the Conference reads: "Peoples of Asia, People of God.'[21] Here is a clear affirmation of all the peoples of Asia, in their religious and cultural diversity, as 'People of God.' And yet, there is little reflection on what it might mean for the relationship between peoples as belonging to specific religious traditions.

The legitimate concern of the Asian ecumenical movement with the 'peoples' of Asia, their sufferings, their immediate social, economic, and political priorities etc. also comes from the realization of the oppressive role that dimensions religion play in Asian societies. It has muted the concern to promote 'interfaith dialogue' as such, except in the context of participation in socio-political issues across religious lines. It is not surprising that while the WCC had a Sub-Unit (now an 'Office on Interreligious Relations and Dialogue') to promote interfaith relations and dialogues as such, the CCA, situated in the midst of such great diversity of religious traditions, had no such structural expression. This does not mean that the CCA did not take the religions and cultures seriously. Rather, they are treated as the ethos of the Asian theological task, and the context of the struggles to make Asian societies more just and humane. Much of the more direct interfaith dialogue work in Asia are delegated to Study Centers around Asia, and most of them work on an ecumenical basis. Consequently, while most of the Western churches today have 'interfaith ministries' at the local and national levels, they are rarely found in Asian churches.

One of the main reasons for this may also have to do with the reality that Christianity is a minority religion in most Asian countries. It is far easier for the churches in the West, being powerful majorities, (at least culturally), to initiate and promote interfaith relations and dialogue. Minority communities are more concerned with preserving their identities; they fear absorption and assimilation; and they can hardly lay down the terms of the dialogue. Historically Christian minorities in Asia have developed identities either in

---

[20] See: *Towards the Sovereignty of the People*, edited by CTC-CCA (Hong Kong: CCA, 1983).

[21] *Peoples of Asia, People of God – A Report of the Asia Mission Conference 1989* (Hong Kong: CCA, 1990).

opposition or in isolation from other religious traditions, because these religions are the ones that they, or their forbearers, had 'rejected' to espouse the Christian faith.

Looking to the Future

The Asian YMCA, however, recognizes the growing importance of interfaith relations for Asia and has been promoting interreligious dialogue as part of its program of activities. In October 1986, for instance, the Asian Alliance of the YMCAs called a conference on "Witness in a Multi-Religious Context" in which, in addition to Christian thinkers on interfaith dialogue, persons from other major religious traditions were called to reflect on the meaning of witness in pluralist situations.[22] Again, a regional consultation of the Asian YMCA, held in New Delhi, India, in October 96 had "Search for Meaning and Community" as the theme to explore issues of "Culture, Religion, and Spirituality" in the Asian context. The statement from this consultation said: "In solidarity with people of other faiths, we must mutually dialogue in respect and share, enrich, and correct each other as co-workers for the God of love."[23] These are only examples of the continuing interest in interfaith relations that the Asian YMCAs have introduced into the Asian scene.

Even though the Asian branch of the World Student Christian Federation, like the CCA, was more involved in justice issues, it facilitated the discussion of interfaith relations among churches and students by commissioning in 1985, in conjunction with the WCC, a popular volume on "The Bible and the People of Other faiths," which was translated, among others, into Asian languages as Japanese, Korean, Indonesian, Thai, and Malayalam. In so doing the WSCF sought to bring out the biblical basis for a new relationship with people of other religious traditions.[24]

The greater institutional involvement of the Roman Catholic Church into the Asian ecumenical scene has also brought important changes. The Roman Catholic Church too, particularly in Asia, has a long tradition of participating in the struggles of the people. At the same time, it has also learnt the art of treating the Asian religious traditions, despite of their ambiguities, as 'spiritual paths' that must be taken seriously. Aloysius Pieris of Sri Lanka, for instance, has pointed out that there are two realities of Asia that must be taken with equal seriousness in Christian theology and practice, namely, its crushing poverty, and its rich spirituality. If religiosity is one of the abiding characteristics of the Asian peoples, the Asian ecumenical movement can ill afford to ignore its specificity.

Significant changes have begun to take place. CCA's Asian Mission Conference in 1994 on "Called to Witness Together Amidst Asian Plurality" in Seoul, Korea, had speakers from the Hindu, Buddhist, Confucian, and Muslim traditions.[25] The recent sessions of the Congress of Asian Theologians, which brings together both the CCA constituency and the constituency of the Federation of Asian Bishops Conference (FABC), indicate a new interest in dealing with the reality of religious traditions in their specificity. It's Third Congress (August 2001) had as its theme, "Visioning New Life Together among Asian Religions," and had several persons of other religious tradition among the plenary speakers.[26] Asian Feminist theologians have begun to explore women's issues that cut across religious traditions and to engage women of other religious traditions in exploring gender issues. The elaborate network of women

---

[22] See proceedings in: *Witness in a Multi-Religious context: Report of the YMCA Seminar on Christian Witness in a Multi-Religious Context*, (Hong Kong: Asian Alliance of YMCAs, 1987.

[23] "Search for Meaning and Community: Statement from the Regional Consultation on Culture, Religion and Spirituality," *Asia YMCA*, Vol.XXIII, No. 2, December 1996, p.8.

[24] A joint publication by the WCC and the WSCF written by S. Wesley Ariarajah.

[25] See: *Turn Around: Called to Witness Together Amidst Asian Plurality, Asia Mission Conference, 1994, Seoul, Korea*, (Hong Kong: CCA, 1995) p.131-148.

[26] See: Thiagarajah, Daniel S and Longchar, A. Wati (eds.), *Visioning New Life together among Asian Religions – The Third Congress of Asian Theologians* (Hong Kong: CCA, 2002)

across the Asian nations include women n many religious traditions. It is also of interest that "Interfaith Encounters" is listed as one of the 'special concerns' of the CCA Youth program in the report to the Colombo assembly of the CCA, 1995.[27]

The new interest in Christian relationship to people of other religious traditions has also been necessitated by actual situations on the ground. The deterioration of relationship between sections of Hindu community and Christians in India, the new self-assertion of Islam in places like Pakistan and Indonesia, the role Buddhist self-understanding plays in the conflict in Sri Lanka, continuing conflict between Christians and Muslims in the Philippines etc., despite the socio-political and economic dimensions of these situations, also demand the need to build dialogue and relationship between Christians and peoples of other religious traditions.

In the long run, what Asia needs is a 'wider ecumenism' or an 'ecumenism of religious traditions' that transcend and run parallel to Christian ecumenism; the destiny of the Christian peoples of Asia is no doubt tied up with the destiny of all its peoples. Building actual relationships across religious communities, which are recognized for who they are, is a necessary process on the road to a wider ecumenism.

Bibliography

Cheriyan, C. V, *A History of Christianity in Kerala – From the Mission of St. Thomas to the Arrival of Dasco da Gama: A.D.52 – 1498* (Kottayam: Kerala Historical Society, 1973).

Menon, K. P. K., "Medieval Christianity in India – Part I, The Eastern Church" p.7 in: Perumalil, A.C. and Hambye, E.R. (eds.), *Christianity in India – A History in Ecumenical Perapective* (Allepey: Prakasam Publications, 1972) quoted in: England, John C., *The Hidden History of Christianity in India- The Churches of the East before 1500* (Delhi: ISPCK, 1996)

Potter, Philip and Wieser, Thomas, *Seeking and Serving the Truth – First Hundred Years of the World Student Christian Federation* (Geneva: WCC Publications, 1997)

E. W. Hocking's contribution, *Report of the Jerusalem Meeting of the International Missionary Council- I* (London: Oxford University Press, 1928)

Ariarajah, S. Wesley, *Hindus and Christians – A Century of Protestant Ecumenical Thought* (Amsterdam: Editions Rodopi, and Grand Rapids: William Eearmans Publishing Company, 1991)

Thomas, M. M., *Salvation and Humanization: Some Crucial Issues of the Theology of Mission in Contemporary India* (Bangalore: CISRS, 1971)

S. Kulandran, "The Renaissance of Non-Christian Religions and a Definition of Approach to Non-Christians," mimeographed paper presented to the Study on the Word of God and Men of Other Faiths," (WCC Archives)

[27] *Manila to Colombo, The Christian Conference of Asia from 1990-1995* (Hong Kong: CCA, 1995) p.114.

(29) INTERFAITH DIALOGUE AND COOPERATION AS ECUMENICAL MOVEMENT

J.B. Banawiratma

The ecumenical endeavor, *to be one in Christ's life*, is not a matter of activities. Ecumenism is a way of being Christian, a way of being Church. Ecumenism aims to develop the oneness in Christ, *to follow the Way*, and the Truth and the Life (Jn 14:6). Surely that "Interfaith Dialogue and Cooperation" is "Common Challenges to Ecumenism in Asia". Ecumenism in Asia should move in "Interfaith Dialogue and Cooperation". Today interfaith dialogue and cooperation becomes important part of Ecumenical Movement in Asia. This is contextual ecumenism, not more and not less. It means that today being Christian and being Church find its movement in interfaith dialogue and cooperation. I don't want to reduce ecumenism into relations to only non-Christian sisters and brothers. The relation among Christians will find its own place in the whole process of dialogue. Relations to sisters and brothers of other faith are part of my Christian identity. The following ideas about interfaith dialogue are not all new. They appeared already in other occasions. Nevertheless this paper will focus on the proposal of "interfaith dialogue and cooperation as ecumenical movement". Some examples I will take from Indonesia that I know better.

The interfaith movement 'from below' can be described with seven levels of interfaith dialogue. Those levels can also become seven moments of interfaith dialogue. We can begin anywhere, since we do not start from zero point. We will go through these 7 moments of dialogue and find what kind of ecumenism happens there.

1. Dialogue of life
2. Dialogue in social analysis and contextual ethics
3. Dialogue with my own resources in my community: Re-opening my traditions
4. Dialogue in sharing of faith experience within interfaith community
5. Dialogue in doing interfaith theology
6. Dialogue of action
7. Intrareligious dialogue

Where is interfaith cooperation? It can happen in all levels of dialogue. The community is already cooperative by willingly joining in dialogue. However in the framework of this article, cooperation has it special shape in the dialogue of action (level 6) for the transformation of societal life.

1. Dialogue of Life

Dialogue of life happens in small group who knows each other. In the dialogue of life people of different faiths share their daily lives as a *human community* with common human concerns. In the *dialogue of life* people strive to live in an open, neighbourly spirit, sharing their joys and sorrows, their human problems and preoccupations. Together they experience a common situation with its ups and downs, hopes and anxieties, and thus *common concerns emerge*. They are concerned about the need for clean water, good housing, adequate education, employment, et cetera. They share common stories and common dreams.

In the context of religious pluralism we have to prevent our ecumenical movement from becoming alienated "Christian tribes". A new way of being contextual Church should be the Church in dialogue and social transformation: "Let Christians, while witnessing to their own faith and way of life, acknowledge, preserve and encourage the spiritual and moral truths found among non-Christians, also their social life and cultures" (Vatican II 1965, NA, 2). As a human and limited reality, the Church can only exercise her mission and become a dynamic community of faith if she becomes a communion of communities of dialogue and transformation. By so living, the Church can more and more live out the community of Christ's disciples who are "not of this world", but "in this world", becoming sign and means of salvation.

We need a critical dialogue between cultural religious experiences and the symbols in the Christian traditions. Our goal is to uncover both the transformative and enslaving elements in all traditions, in order to cultivate the former and to eliminate the latter. Our unity in the life and mission of Christ takes place in our concrete contexts. Our ecumenical movement should proceed with a contextual approach, rather than from that of full unity. Based on the already existing unity, it should grow as far as achievable through the conciliar process. Our contextual ecumenism in Asia demands the building of Basic Human (and Inter-faith or inter-religious) Communities which empower the poor and oppressed towards integral liberation with the perspective of gender justice and caring for the environment. They witness and move in common (ecumenical) prophetic proclamation and liberative struggle.

Together with brothers and sisters of other faiths, the *Basic Inter-ecclesial Communities* should open towards *Basic Human Communities*[1]. A Basic Human Community can be described as a small community involved in social activities to eliminate suffering, to struggle for a just society, and to sustain the development of people and the environment. Primarily, they are poor people empowering themselves. Secondarily, they can be the facilitators struggling for and with them. They are crossing the boundaries of religions and beliefs; they are united in a life situation and a life concern. From the Christian perspective the concern of Basic Human Communities is fundamentally one related to Christian orthopraxis. In our Christian language it is a struggle for God's Reign. Hence, the Basic Human Community is a community of God's Reign. Basic Human Community is a response to the demand of Christian faith in our multi-cultural and multireligious context.

2. Dialogue in Social Analysis and Contextual Ethics

This level of dialogue tries to explain the condition of life and offer a responsible orientation to common well-being. Social analysis *is not value-free*, so it is important to be aware of the values endorsed by the group. Here value premises include *a preferential option for the poor* and *justice, peace and the integrity of creation*. In this level people of different faiths try to understand the reality of life socially and ethically.

Interreligious relationship is not limited to individual and private events only but is a communal encounter that happens in the public domain. It seems to be helpful to approach the interreligious relationship by considering the problem of the *public domain* and *the powers* that play their role in it. In 2004, the Indonesian Bishops' Conference wrote a Pastoral Note entitled "Public Civility: Towards a New Habitus of the Nation; Social Justice for All: A Socio-cultural Approach" (KWI 2004). The main concern of the bishops is the corruption within the *public civility*. Public civility should become, individually or collectively, the *habitus* of the nation, which shapes the way to feel, to think, to see, to understand, the way to approach, to act, and the way of a person or a group to relate to others in all activities.

Public civility is developed in the *public domain*, in which three axes of power play their role, namely, *State*, *market* and *community*. The balancing power of the State, the market and the community give shape to the public domain. The problem is that there is no balance and no control among these three axes of power. On the contrary, instead of balancing and controlling each other there is collusion between public agencies of the State and the business sector. The communities and people in general become victims of this degradation. The disciples of Christ as communities of hope should develop creative thoughts and actions as well as an alternative culture affecting the three axes of power in the public domain.

---

[1] A. Pieris, Contemporary Ecumenism and Asia's Search for Christ, in: Pedro A. de Achutegui (ed.), Towards A "Dialogue of Life": Ecumenism in the Asian Context. Manila (Ateneo University Publications: 1976) 154-174. And his another book on "An Asian Theology of Liberation. (NY: Maryknoll Orbis Books, 1988) pp. 57-58,121

Daniel Drache defines the public domain as the collective assets and goods.[2] People share these assets, which are open and accessible, in common and use them in common. The scope of the public domain is broad. It includes public spaces and places, public services like health, education and workplace. Its focus is on communal sharing of cultural, social and political interests as well as on the welfare of the community, the politics of Nation and State. All these elements are incorporated in the notion of public domain. The collective assets and goods belong to the public and cannot be sold. Another definition describes the public domain as an area of social life. "Central to it is the value of citizenship, equity and service and the notion of a public interest, distinct from private interests"[3]. Both Drache's and Marquand's definitions indicate the consciousness of living together, of shared life with sensibility to rights and interests of others with regard to public facilities. The public domain has something to do with the living "we".

As stated earlier, there are three axes of power in the public domain, namely, community, market and State[4]. The term "community" refers to the spontaneous relationship and to activities among people without any transactional and administrative character. The adhesiveness of the members will condition the living community. The community might be established by common history, territory, ethnicity, race, religion, and language. The term "market" denotes economic transactions between vendor and purchaser which are voluntarily and concern goods and services. Profit and loss as well as economic efficiency is the motives of the market. The term "State" refers concretely to public agencies. The State acts through them. For the sake of common welfare, they are in charge of the order of public life. They have the power to regulate the social order.

In every axis there are main agents like – in case of the State – a regent and a governor. Investors, entrepreneurs and industrialists belong to the axis of the market. A group of peasants developing organic agriculture belong to the axis of the community. However, everybody is involved in these axes. When we buy food or clothes we are in the arena of the market. We are, however, entering the public agency of the State when we need an identity card or a passport. And when we spontaneously plant more floras or have worship together or clean the whole village before certain celebration, we are engaged in the community. The relationships of these three axes and powers influence common life. The following diagram could be helpful.[5]

Every axis of power has the potential to defend and to promote the public domain, the sharing of life and, at the same time, to promote the interreligious relationship. But every axis could also do harm to the public domain and to interreligious relationship. Of course this diagram gives simple portrait of the national situation, but it can easily be enlarged to international and global relations.

There is intra-religious intolerance *among communities of the same religion*, namely, when there is no openness to other interpretations within the same religion. In other cases, interreligious intolerance *among communities of different religions* is a real problem. The power of the community can thus become also the source of damaging interreligious relationships. One community could violently force another community to follow their will without respecting the aims of the public agency. They do not respect the right of the other communities to have access to religious facilities in the public domain.

---

[2] D. Drache, Introduction: The Fundamentals of Our Time, Values and Goals that Are Inescapably Public" in: D. Drache (ed), *The Market or the Public Domain: Global Governance and the Asymmetry of Power.* London (Routledge) 2001, pp.1-34.

[3] David Marquand, Reinventing Gladstone? The public conscience and the public domain. In: Daniel Drache (Ed.). *The Market or the Public Domain. Global Governance & the Asymmetry of Power*. London (Routledge) 2001, p.74

[4] B. Herry-Priyono, Tiga Poros Indonesia", in: *Kompas* Jan 9, 2004a

[5] B. Herry-Priyono Ranah Publik. Dari Mulut Pemerintah ke Rahang Pasar". Manuscript, 2004.

The *State could be also part of the problem* rather than a *power of solution.* The law and regulation issued by the State could promote a solution and advancing interreligious relationship. In other cases the public agencies of the State are sources of the problems.

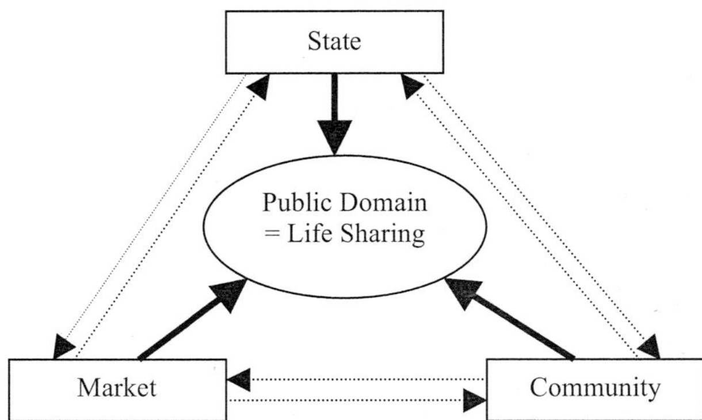

What about the power of the *market*? The problem arises when there is a collusion of powers, namely between the State and the market. A mining enterprise, for instance, could collude with the public agency of the State. If it shows neglect of the culture and the welfare of the community, then the people are exploited and the nature is destructed. In June 2005, Indonesia has been struck by the news that in some parts of Indonesia children are suffering from malnutrition, even to the point of starvation. The situation in the year 2011 is not better. One of the reasons is the commercialization of food in such a way that it has misled people's understanding of health. Through advertisements at television, children are fascinated by the packing of food. Poor people consume unhealthy food and have no access to public health services. Families and other institutions are too weak to face the power of media technology. Healthy food has been defeated by commercial food.[6] Here we have a clear example of how powerful the axis of the market is working through television. Supported by the policy of the State and by media technology, the market has spread disease and death. The fact of starvation in some parts of world raised our consciousness that poor people have no access to the public domain: education, health, opportunity for employment, environment, etc. They have no access to what is actually belonging to the public. The public domain has become a commercial domain whereas it should become the platform of building up public civility. There is no justice, no sharing of life and no sensibility to people's need.[7]

The public domain is intruded by the global power of the market. Globalization has become a source of marginalization and victimization. The problem of the public domain is therefore not merely a local or a national concern, it is interdependently international. It usually occurs through the collusion of business people with the public agencies of the State. The result is that the communities and the individuals become marginalized and victimized. It is therefore quite true that "the policy challenge is to erect strong barriers against the market intrusiveness into the public domain".[8] The interreligious relationship should go against the aggressive, exploitative performance of the market and stand on the side of the victims.

By over viewing the powers of the public domain, we understand that the progress of interreligious relationship depends on many factors:

1. The community of religion has to respect the dignity and the rights of other communities.

[6] Tan Shot Yen, Gizi Generasi Televisi. In: *Kompas* 15 June 2005, p.4.
[7] B. Herry-Priyono, Ranah Publik. Dari Mulut Pemerintah ke Rahang Pasar, ibid.,
[8] D. Drache, The Return of the Public Domain after the Triumph of Markets, ibid., p. 66.

2. The State with its public agencies has to defend and promote the public domain with public facilities accessible to all, with preference to the poor and the weak. "Power is called to be accountable; power is challenged to share, to care, to cherish and, above all, to give up its monopoly of interference and domination".[9]
3. The market should know its limits and may not aggressively push poor people into an inhuman condition. Civil society needs to be developed as a critical movement within all axes of powers.

3. Dialogue with My Own Resources in My Community: Re-Opening My Traditions

People of different faiths need to know their own religious traditions in order to understand reality from their faith perspective. New concern in a new context might challenge them to reinterpret certain traditions. In this level, human concern becomes faith concern. "I see the reality of life through the eyes of faith."

There will be no progress in ecumenical unity without an ecclesial transformation in which our churches will not be hindered by traditions and vested interests, so that they will be willing and able to cross the walls, carry the risks, endure wounds with patience, and undergo emotional, intellectual and moral conversion. Ecclesial transformation is no more and no less than the demands of placing the Gospel at the core of ecumenical unity (UUS, 20).

> As the gospel emerges more powerfully in the forms of Church life, we often discover, painfully sometimes, that the demands of God go against what at one time we had thought to be essentially related to the Church but which, in the light of the gospel, we discover to be part of our tradition by external custom rather than by inner necessity. Then we must accept the transformation even on the ecclesiastical level.[10]

We need to re-read our rich traditions with integrity and openness from the perspective of the primacy of evangelium-praxis. Certain Christian traditions reinterpreted from the concern for *orthopraxis* can bring themselves closer to and be united with other Christian traditions.

The reflection of John W. de Gruchy from the experience of crisis in South Africa, for example, comes to the conclusion that the Christian tradition under the influence of John Calvin (Reformed theology): "is best understood as a liberating theology that is catholic in its substance, evangelical in principle, and socially engaged and prophetic in its witness''.[11] From the Catholic tradition people can ask themselves whether Catholic theology is also best understood as a liberating theology, that is, contextually reformed, evangelical in principle, socially engaged and prophetically witness? Christian theologies should become part of the contextual struggle for and with the people for liberation to achieve full humanity. Then theology is not only "God-talk" business, but "God-act" oriented.

We cannot deny the facts of our own traditions. The unity of different traditions does not mean to dissolve one or the other. It would impoverish our Christian life were we to pretend to have no differences. In the Paschal celebration, people sing the Easter Proclamation, the *Exultet*, which proclaims: "O happy fault, o necessary sin of Adam, which gained for us so great a Redeemer". We can also sing "O happy fault, o necessary sin of Church division, which has gained for us such rich traditions communicating the life of Christ". We are called to accept the new life in Christ and the richness of our traditions communicating it. The crux of the matter is not to abolish traditions, but to *desacralize our own traditions*

---

[9] Diarmuid O'Murchu, *Our World in Transition. Making Sense of a Changing World.* (Sussex: The Book Guild Ltd 1997), p.155

[10] G. Baum, "Introduction" to Roger Schutz's understanding of ecumenism, in R. Schutz, *Unity: Man's Tomorrow*, (New York: Herder and Herder, 1963), p. 6

[11] John W. De Gruchy, *Liberating Reformed Theology. A South African Contribution to an Ecumenical Debate*, (Michigan: William B. Eerdmans Publishing Company, Cape Town: David Philip Publishers 1991), p. xii

in order to cross-fertilize each other. Hence, our ecumenical unity and mission must be done in humility, self-criticism and critical dialogue. Ecumenical unity is not to be achieved by mode of expansion of one over another, but by a mode of accepting our limits and extending our openness. The problem is how to distinguish between "Yes" to the decisiveness and relational distinctiveness of Jesus Christ and "No" to an exclusive Church tradition, for the sake of being a faithful Church, of being in Christ's life and mission. In this way our ecumenical journey goes through an approach of contextual unity rather than of full unity. It is a journeying together in the Spirit of Christ. This is in fact the core of our conciliar process.

Ecclesial transformation from below will raise a question of authority in our traditions. Here also we can learn from the feminist liberation perspective, since both ecumenism and feminism touch the problem of authority.[12] We have to confess that within our Churches there is gender injustice. How far can all within the Churches recognize and accept each other as sisters and brothers, unless we are willing to tackle the problem of authority?.[13]

The problem of authority arises also through an awareness of plurality in all aspects of life, which characterizes our societies today. In the area of religious experience, this plurality has been expanded through the shift of the experience of God, from extrinsic to intrinsic, from Outsider-God to Insider-God, from God outside the world to God inside the world. Accordingly, there is also a shift from the experience of religious authority (Bible, traditions, magisterium) to the authority of religious experience. The radical plurality in all aspects of our life has brought on a crisis of authority in religious life. The authority of the Churches is subject to criticism. Nevertheless, it can function to create Basic Christian Communities, Basic Interecclesial Community, which open themselves out to Basic Human Communities and thereby articulate and mediate the praxis of the liberating communities. Pieris puts it:

> The magisterial role in the Asian church has to be earned by the Master's competence to mediate liberation. Authority makes no external claims. Authority is competence to communicate freedom.[14]

The leadership of the communities can be analogically understood as "collegial" in as much as their leaders are together reading the signs of the times, discerning the call of God's Reign and mediating the Gospel praxis. Then, we have visible forms of unity in the communion of communities and communion of leadership. Through the contextual approach to ecumenical unity, all Christians could be grateful for the unity achieved on all levels. These above considerations affirm our commitment towards an approach *of reopening our traditions* and *transforming our Churches from below*.

4. Dialogue in Sharing of Faith at the Level of Experience Within Interfaith Community

Based on their respective traditions people share their religious experience and spiritual riches and enrich one another through *dialogue on religious experience*. Believers know where they stand and open themselves up to other religious traditions. They share their religious experience, prayer and contemplation, their ways of searching and following God or the Ultimate Mystery of life. Perhaps they could

---

[12] See: Margaret O'Garra, Ecumenism and Feminism in Dialogue on Authority, in: Melanie A. May (ed.), *Women and Church, The Challenge of Ecumenical Solidarity in an Age of Alienation*. (Grand Rapids: W.B. Eerdmans, and New York : Friendship Press, 1991), p.118-137; Kathleen S. Hurty, Ecumenical Leadership: Power and Women's Voices, in: Melanie A. May (ed.): *Women and Church, The Challenge of Ecumenical Solidarity in an Age of Alienation*. (Grang Rapids:W.B. Eerdmans, and New York: Friendship Press,1991), p.88-100; Nancy L. Cocks, Ecumenical Social Thought: A Christian Feminist Voice, in: *The Ecumenical Review*, 1991, pp. 43:341-348.

[13] Sun Ai Lee Park, A New Phase in the Ecumenical Movement: One Woman's Perspetive on Asian Activities, in: Melanie A. May (ed.): *Women and Church, The Challenge of Ecumenical Solidarity in an Age of Alienation*. (Grand Rapids: W.B. Eerdmans, New York:Friendship Press,1991) p.162

[14] A. Pieris, *An Asian Theology of Liberation*. Maryknoll, (N.Y.: Orbis Books 1988), p.86

come to pray together. In this level religious people try to avoid an aggressive and manipulative manner motivated by individual or communal egoism.

From May 20 to 22, 2005, more than 110 young people took part in a programme of an "interfaith live-in" (Kompas Yogyakarta 2005). This programme was compiled by the "Interfaith Forum for Peace in Asia" (IFPA) under the heading "Through spiritual exchange we promote the spirit of solidarity". Every participant lived in a community of another faith. Many religious communities of different faiths were involved in this programme, such as *Pondok Pesantren Nurul Ummahat*, *Pondok Pesantren Sunan Pandanaran* (Islam communities), *Vihara Mendut* and *Vihara Vidayasena* (Buddhist communities), *Asram GandhiYogyakarta* and *Pura Jagat Nata Banguntapan* (Hindu communities), *Wisma Nazareth* and *Novitiate of Sisters Carolus Borromeus* (Roman Catholic communities), *Yakkum Bethesda* and *Gereja Kristen Ambarukma* (Christian Protestant communities), and *Sanggar Candi Sapto Renggo Surokarsan* (Community of Javanese Belief *"Sapta Dharma"*). During the time of living within another religious community, the participants had opportunities of interfaith sharing.

Afterwards all participants took part in the sessions of evaluation through sharing and reflection. This kind of activities has also taken place in some other regions in Indonesia. Similar to the "interfaith live-in" is the interfaith camping. After such activities the participants usually express their experience of a new understanding of other faiths and other religions. They know the others better and, therefore, open up more easily to others and become willing to know more. The experiences of personal conversation and of a deep sharing of faith have changed their previous perceptions of other faiths and religions.

5. Dialogue in Doing Interfaith Theology

Theologians or specialists can conduct a *dialogue of theological exchange* on the scientific level, seeking to deepen their understanding of their respective religious heritages and to appreciate others' spiritual values. Mutual enrichment at a theological level can lead to reinterpretation and reorientation. Theological exchange should take the historical development of every religion into account. Inquiry is open and even suspicions can be discussed. For example, people can discuss issues of Christianisation, Islamisation and voice different opinions and interpretations of existing social situations. The way of contextual theology is the way of critical dialogue and communication. By sharing and witnessing we become more conscious that our interpretation is limited and that we need to engage in a continuous process of dialogue and reinterpretation. In so doing contextual theologies are able to come closer to the core of faith and its responsible manifestation here and now.

It is interresting to see the development of the study of religion. It has gone through the experiences of 1) comparative studies of religion, to 2) religious studies i.e. phenomenology and history of religion, and then 3) inter-religious studies. Like the process of evolution interreligious study as the latest development bring within itself the good elements from the previous. The process leaves the exclusive claim and exclusive objectivity. There is no value free in dealing with study. Religious studies built up from communication of various subjects involved with their experience, interpretation, and undertanding. Interreligious studies face at the problem of essentialism and objectivism, as well as relativism and subjectivism with narrative and contextual style. Moreover there is no value free analysis. Analysis happens in commitment and openness. So is in theology. The exclusive claim and the claim of objectivity are challenged. Many things that we might claim as Christian are actually belonging also to other faiths. There is a kind of overlapping values.

Open interreligious relations need to be supported by an open theology. Interreligious praxis and open theology should nourish each other. In an open theology people of different religions will not think only textually but also contextually. This entails expressing the revealed message of texts in dialogue with concrete day-to-day life, and to find the revealed message in day-to-day life in dialogue with texts.

6. Dialogue of Action

In his encyclical *Centesimus Annus*1991, Pope John Paul II mentioned the importance of actions related to the social message of the Church. In fact this is also true for the Church's proclamation in general.

> Today more than ever, the Church is aware that her social message will gain credibility more immediately from the witness of actions than as a result of its internal logic and consistency. This awareness is also a source of her preferential option for the poor, which is never exclusive or discriminatory toward other groups (CA. 57).

Ut Unum Sint (UUS, 43) describes solidarity as one of the fruits of dialogue. Nevertheless, in our interecclesial or even trans-ecclesial ecumenism we can also perceive a movement from the opposite direction.

> The church-to-church ecumenism could also be the spontaneous outcome of a common endeavor to discover the Asian face of Christ, that is to say, inter-ecclesial ecumenism here in Asia ought to be a by-product of the new praxis which is trans-ecclesial, Christ-centered and world-oriented.[15].

Interreligious dialogue and cooperation should work out *social problems with the aim of involving society*. Religious people cannot deny that they are part of society and politics. Interreligious harmony without common concern for political contexts would promote a false and unjust harmony. Through dialogue of action adherents of different faiths can work together to empower people with the perspective of social and gender justice, human rights, and ecological concern.

To be able to be one in Christ and to glorify God, the contextual face of Christ in the poor should be the focus of ecumenical unity. As we have already heard from Irenaeus, the glory of God is reflected in humanity restored to full life: "*Gloria Dei vivens homo*". Furthermore, there will be no fully restored humanity unless the oppression of the poor is overcome, in the words of Oscar Romero: "*Gloria Dei vivens pauper*"[16]. Our salvation is in following Jesus where He is, in restoring humanity to full life, in overcoming oppression, in glorifying God.

Many examples proof that common solidarity of different people of faith become strongest message of ecumenism as a way of life. Many churches have done much to take part in caring for the survivors of the natural disaster such earthquake and volcano's eruption. However our Churches need to learn more to be responsive to social disaster which is always there around us today. International link like World Social Forum is really a sign that solidarity not only in micro level, but in macro level can be struggled for.

Faced with the ambivalence of cultural, political and economical realities, a contextual response means discernment and either *affirmation* or *confrontation* with a view to the *transformation of societal life*. Interreligious people can thus form a serving, *dialogical and transformative community*.

7. Intra-Religious Dialogue

After engaging in interfaith dialogue everybody comes back to his or her personal faith. At this moment all believers go through self-criticism, moving towards a living faith that is enriched and renewed or transformed. Religious people become better persons of faith, individually and communally. After passing over to other religions, one comes back to his or her religion in a deeper level.[17]

---

[15] A. Pieris, "Contemporary Ecumenism and Asia's Search for Christ", in: Pedro A. de Achutegui (ed.), *Towards A "Dialogue of Life": Ecumenism in the Asian Context.* (Manila: Ateneo University Publications, 1976), p. 162

[16] John W, De Gruchy, *Liberating Reformed Theology- A South African Contribution to an Ecumenical Debate* (Michigan: William B. Eerdmans Publishing Company, Cape Town: David Philip Publishers, 1991), p.137

[17] John Dunne, *The Way of All the Earth: Experiments in Truth and Religion.* New York: Macmillan, 1972

In commenting "Intrareligious dialogue according to Ramon Llul" (*Libre del gentil e los tres avis*) Raimon Panikkar wrote:

> All these traits can be summarized in one: the passage from interreligious dialogue to intrareligious dialogue; from exteriority to interiority, from the condemnation of others to the examination of one's own conscience, from the problem of political power to personal issues, from dogma to mysticism, if you prefer. Until humanity's religious problem is seen and understood as an intimate, personal problem, until religion is fathomed and discovered as a dimension of the human being – and therefore something affecting all of us, until there is despair and lamenting over the human destiny we all form part of, until then we shall not be able to distinguish doctrinal disputes, political rivalries, and personal ambition from the true religious act that is common search for Man's very purpose and cooperation and accomplishment of the very destiny of the universe. Religion is far more a constitutive dimension of human than an institution.[18]

The various levels of honest dialogue 'from below' will highlight important elements of living together, which are *conversion* and *forgiveness*. To be converted means to be aware of the sins and faults that one has committed and, at the same time, to believe in the mercy of God's unlimited forgiveness. Conversion brings *new hope*, because one is not imprisoned by the past but is facing an open future. Willingness to forgive is a sign that one is ready to receive God's forgiveness. Conversely, unwillingness to forgive others is a sign that one is not yet ready to receive God's mercy and pardon.

The context of plurality and intense communication through all kinds of media today bring individuals and groups into new consciousness that identity cannot be separated from relations. Christian identity is defined in relations with others. The relation with brothers and sisters of other faith belong to the conception of Christian identity. Christians that relates to no others means make themselves isolated and marginalized. Today *to be religious is to be interreligious*. This truth can goes into such deep experience as Paul Knitter shares:

> In my case, the more I have discovered what really means to be 'in Christ Jesus' the more I have felt the need and the ability to listen to and learn from the Buddha, and do to discover my Buddha nature. [19]

Bibliography

De Gruchy, John W., *Liberating Reformed Theology. A South African Contribution to an Ecumenical Debate*. Michigan: William B. Eerdmans Publishing Company, Cape Town: David Philip Publishers 1991

Dunne, John, *The Way of All the Earth: Experiments in Truth and Religion*. New York: Macmillan 1972.

John Paul II, *Centesimus Annus* (CA), Encyclical on the 100th Anniversary of 'Rerum Novarum' 1991

John Paul II, *Ut Unum Sint* (= UUS), Encyclical Letter on Commitment to Ecumenism. Roma: Libreria Editrice Vaticana 1995

Knitter, Paul F, *Without Buddha I could not be a Christian*. Oxford: Oneworld 2009

O'Murchu, Diarmuid, *Our World in Transition. Making Sense of a Changing World*. Sussex: The Book Guild Ltd. 1997

Panikkar, Raimon, *The Intrareligious Dialogue*. (Revised Edition) New York: Paulist Press 1999

Pieris, A., *An Asian Theology of Liberation*. Maryknoll, N.Y.: Orbis Books. 1988

Vatican II, Council, "Nostra Aetate". Declaration on the relation of the Church to Non-Christian Religions. 1975

---

[18] Raimon Panikkar, (Revised Edition), *The Intrareligious Dialogue* (New York: Paulist Press,1999) p.114

[19] Paul F. Knitter, *Without Buddha I could not be a Christian(*Oxford: Oneworld,2009) p.216

(30) Christian-Muslim Dialogue in Asia – Indonesian Perspectives

Martin Lukito Sinaga

The history of interfaith dialogue in Asia should mainly be read as the story of amateurs: of those who love to engage their neighbours. As we know, the word "amateur" has a Latin source, *amator,* which means "lover, devoted friend, enthusiastic pursuer". Those who pursue enthusiastically dialogue in multi-religious Asia, then, are theologians who feel the need to go beyond what the missionaries have professionally taught them. They want to have a better way to approach their neighbours who have different religions. With little guidance from the missionary agencies on dealing with Islam, they must scratch deep into their Christian faith and use their own local wisdom, with the great love of an amateur, to relate dialogically with their Muslim neighbours.

From the Mission Field, and Kraemer's Legacy

In most Asian missionary fields, the church's relation with Islam was marked by acute tension. The study of the biggest Protestant church in Asia, the Batak Church of Indonesia[1], and its relation to Islam provides evidence of that tension and the uneasy relations.

During the colonial time in the 1820s, war was launched in the neighbourhood of the Batak people in Minangkabau area by the Dutch soldiers against the Padri front, who themselves had got from the Wahhabi-islamic ideology a revolutionary zeal of religious purity as well as an anti-colonial cry. Part of the zeal was to purify the Bataks from their infidelity; it has been reported by a Rhenish missionary (Schreiber) that there were around 200.000 civilians casualties among the Bataks who resisted the Padri.

The work of the Rhenish mission could not be separated from this strong Islam incursion into Batak land. Nommensen, who arrived in 1864, realized that the tide of Islam would move to the Batak inland and felt a call to Christianize the people before it was too late. Christianity and Islam then got into a race. When Nommensen worked in the southern part of the Batak land, while also surprised by some friendly Muslim towns, continued to believe that Islam was a political religion to control and dominate the Batak people.

Nommensen and The Rhenish mission agency, who worked through modern education, published documents to warn the Bataks not to follow Islam. A book written by a famous Rhenish missionary, J. Warneck, entitled "Church History" (published in 1901, in Batak`s language) clearly stated in one section that Islam would lead Christians along a false path. Another book, entitled "Do Not Go Wrong" (published in 1919, also in the Batak language) created public uproar in Batak. It was like a mission manual and strategy toward Islam as well as also about Christianity's continuous struggle against Islam and how to bring the Muslims to Christ. The Muslim-Bataks then collected 36.000 signatures to ban the publication.

Hendrik Kraemer also visited the Batak land, and understood that this uproar was a disadvantage for the mission itself. In his travel report (1930) he regretted this conflict and predicted a difficult future for the church in the midst of Islamic Indonesians.

However, Kraemer could not suggest a better way to relate to Islam. He himself produced a book similar to what the Rhenish society published, and received the same uproar from the Indonesian Muslim theologians. Kraemer's book, *The Religion of Islam* (published in 1928, and then translated to bahasa Indonesian) was intended to be an instructional manual for church leaders to do evangelism. In this book Kraemer wrote the feature of Islam as a unifying religion where politics and faith coalesce. To add to the

---

[1] See, Jansen Pardede, *Die Batakchristen auf Nordsumatra und ihr Verhältnis zu den Muslimen*, Johanes Gutenberg-Universität, Mainz: 1975

injury, Kraemer mentioned a heated issue called "satanic verses". Once, Kraemer noted in his book, the Prophet Muhammad recited (Quranic verses) before the people of Makkah; his recitation was a voice in the Quran where he acknowledged three gods among the deities of the Makkan people: Allat, Uzza and Manat. But not long afterwards Muhammad repented of his action. He also recounted that his acknowledgement of those three gods was not a revelation from the Lord God, but evil thoughts from *Iblis* (Satan).

To counter these ideas, a Muslim scholar from Indonesia, A.D. Haanie wrote a book, *Islam Menentang Kraemer*[2]. According to Haanie, Islam has no Pope in which religion and politics are united; rather Islam organizes politics through religious law. Haanie clarified Kraemer`s sweeping ideas, and instead emphasizes that in Islam government stands above religion, yet any government should have it`s religious foundation. Islamic government and its laws have a unique function, which is to guard the religion, life, property, honour, and independence of the people. And in rebuttal of the "satanic verses", Haanie replied that it was the writing of the "zindik" people, i.e. pagans, who pretended to be Muslim. This story was intended to deride the Prophet and has no validity in Islamic tradition.

Here, Kraemer, with his understanding of Islam and mission strategy, could not help the Indonesians (or Asians) to relate to their Muslim neighbours. In his special study on Kraemer missiology *vis a vis* Islam in Java (Indonesia), Th Sumartana concluded that Kraemer's theology does not take into account the present need for cooperation among religions in finding a solution for the Indonesian (as of the mostly Asian) problem, i.e. colonialism[3].

It is often mentioned that William Carey is the father of modern evangelism which left its marks in Asia. Although coming from a pietistic tradition, he realized that mission needs structures to relate to the native people; thus we see the so called social ministries in all Asian mission agencies. For Kraemer this is also true as he proposed the strategy of mission in the Muslim context. Health and educational institutions were introduced to the mission field, and the Javanese Christians only became the employees of this patron-client system of schools and hospitals. Here we found another serious reality from the mission field: the indigenous people and church did not obtain social and economic independence (which weakens their capacity to initiate their own structure of cooperation with their Muslim neighbours).

The arrival of Kraemer in Indonesia (1922) was part of the construction of the mission strategy, but again what was proposed was a non-dialogical approach to Islam. Parallel to this, local independent structures as means to pave any possible new approaches to the Muslims was also hampered by the missionary social ministries. All these experiences brought Kraemer into the Tambaram mission conference (1938), which gave evidence of the non-dialogical approach of Kraemer, the mission agencies and the younger Asian churches to Islam.

It was a pity that the suggestion of Jerobeam Mattheus[4], a local Christian figure and an amateur in church's enterprise, was not listened to in this matter. In the 1920s a Committee was formed to reflect on the social and religious situation of the Javanese-Indonesian Church and Kraemer was also part of it.

Jerobeam suggested that the Christians should catch up on the progress made by some Muslims regarding the nationalist movement for Indonesian independence, and one of the ways to do so was to allow the local Javanese leadership in all missionary enterprises. His proposal on power equality is based on the idea of Christian faith. He disliked the fact that God`s grace created a second class of church members, i.e. the local indigenous Christians.

In the light of this idea, Jerobeam suggested theological grounds and a breakthrough to relate to the Muslims, who themselves were active in the nationalist movement. He proposed the idea, rooted in his local wisdom, called "siwering kawilujengan" (sphere or the radiation of grace or salvation). Jerobeam

---

[2] Translated: *Islam Opposes Kraemer*, Yogyakarta, 1929

[3] See, Th. Sumartana, *Mission at the Crossroads; Indigenous Churches, European Missionaries, Islamic Associations and Socio-religious Change in Java* 1812-1936, Jakarta: BPK Gunung-Mulia, 1993).

[4] *Ibid.*, p. 149-150

believed that there was a sphere of salvation given by God to this world which encompasses all religions and all nations. God's mercy shelters all people. This should create solidarity among peoples who struggle for dignity and freedom. Therefore Jerobeam was convinced that the best way to be Christian was to independently join the social movement for national liberation and relate in an open theological perspective to one's Muslim brothers and sisters.

Step for Dialogue

For the indigenous Indonesian Christians the Second World War constituted a break from the missionary structure, but no reflection on the Christian-Muslim encounter took place, although during the time of independence Christians and Muslims worked hand in hand to oust their colonial masters. As early as 1930 a lay Christian, Amir Syarifuddin, already raised a prophetic voice toward the missionaries and Islam, "There is a time (for the missionaries) to come and a time to go. However, Christians must remain side by side with Muslims and other nationalists in their political aspirations". This is supported by T.B. Simatupang, himself an independent fighter, when he predicted that cooperation would be the future step for Indonesia Christians living in the context of Islam majority society:

> The result of the modernizing process in Indonesia will not necessarily be similar to the presently developed societies of the West in all aspects. The emerging modern culture will certainly embody many characteristics of Islam, Hinduism, and various other ethnic religio-cultural outlooks[5].

Here, some bases for dialogue were nailed down, then in 1960 dialogue started to get its fruit: together with the Indonesian Student Christian Movement and the National Council of Churches, clear statements were made and steps taken to develop cooperation with Islam. However, for Indonesian Christians, a confrontation against Islam would no longer be their mode of work and witness, the only choice was to work together dialogically[6].

Dialogue, Harmony and Development Program

Interreligious dialogue was not without problems; the legacy of mission and a left-over of Islamic political power remained. During the authoritarian regime of Suharto (1965-1998) dialogue was always overshadowed by "Kerukunan Beragama" (Religious Harmony). This religious harmony was part of a process of de-politicization imposed by the regime on society. The logic of the regime was that only after de-politicization could society be modernized and developed. This Harmony was also partly the government's way to solve the tensions between Christian and Muslim when laws on marriage (1974), religious courts (1989) and "ethics" in mission and "dakwah" (1967) were endorsed publicly. Disagreement on these three issues rose to a level which might have cause chaos in the newly independent state of Indonesia.

At this historical junction, the role of the ecumenical movement (in Indonesia through the body called, DGI/PGI – Persekutuan Gereja-gereja di Indonesia) was instrumental in bringing dialogue as the churches' mode of presence and witness. The ecumenical formula was then introduced, "constructive, creative,

---

[5] See Simatupang`s article, "Dynamic for Creative Maturity", in Gerald Anderson (ed.), *Asian Voices in Christian Theology*, Orbis Book, Maryknoll:1976.

[6] See Olaf Schumann, "Suatu Pengamatan tentang Hubungan Antar-Umat Beragama di Indonesia, Dilihat dari Sudut Pandang PGI", in *Gerakan Oikoumene, Tegar Mekar di Bumi Pancasila* -Ecumenical Movement: Stand and Grow in Pancasila Society-, BPK Gunung Mulia: Jakarta, 1990.

realistic and critical" as to how the Church engages with government, Islam and the society at large[7]. Thanks also to national "Weltanschauung" called *Pancasila*, through which relations with Islam is having it`s ground. *Pancasila* is a common worldview of the Indonesians, pointing to the value of inclusion and non-discrimination as the basis of Indonesian culture and society. And in the light of *Pancasila*, issues such as religious freedom could be proposed publicly. The ecumenical movement thusbecame a hub for Islamic studies, initiated by the Institute of Research and Development (under the leadership of Olaf Schumann) of the PGI, and sometimes work in tandem with an interfaith NGOs, such as DIAN/Interfidei (initiated by the late Th. Sumartana).

Sumarthana believed that dialogue between Christians and Muslims should be part of a democratic process and that only through dialogue could inter-communal relationships be built. Only if communities were able to put aside their unnecessary rivalry could democracy be consolidated. They called on people of religion to join hands in building an open democratic society by developing a dialogical attitude toward members of other religions. The result of their vision brought about a new interfaith movement, *Dian-Interfidei*, which has lead to a breakthrough in religious dialogue in Indonesia.

Dian-Interfidei can be seen as a promising genre in interfaith dialogue, particularly in the context of Islamic society. The urgent need for promoting an open and democratic society had to face both social issues and interreligious dialogue. This approach recognizes the religious dynamics in dialogue, but also found it in the context of social transformation. Only on this basis society and religion can be criticized and renewed. The centrality of people is recognized as agents of change inside society and religion.

A parallel breakthrough came from a late Muslim intellectual, Mukti Ali, who after graduating from McGill University, Montreal, Canada in 1957 introduced a limited series of studies in Yogyakarta. He also introduced the Comparative Study of Religion as a new subject in the Islamic State University of Yogyakarta in 1961. He recognized that the study of religion was a way to revitalize religions, because, in his view, a new appreciation of religions was needed when religions need to free themselves from a literal interpretation. The new approach created a huge interest in a scientific study of religious doctrine.

Mukti Ali discovered that only after students had had an intellectual understanding of different religions could dialogue proceed in a creative manner. He felt that they were able to meet adherents of other religions more freely and engage in meaningful dialogue. Other institutions developed similar programs in the same vein.

Neighbourology

It is worth noting the experience of Indonesian`s neighbours, i.e. Malaysia, especially as a model for better relations with Islam. Sadayandy Batumalai, a Malay Christian, introduced the so-called "theology of neighborology[8].". What he proposes is a plea for the Malaysian churches (also Indonesian and Filipino churches, who are also of Malay cultures) to be with their neighbor and realize that every Christian's destiny is bound up with that of the whole Malay community. Thus, the experiences and the expressions of being a faithful Christian should be connected with the cultural life and experiences of their Malay Muslim neighbors.

This theology begins by seeing that Christian communities' cultural context is the medium for Christians to relate to "others." Theology should be a reflection on a living faith with practical implications in the cultural arena, an arena in which Muslim neighbors also express their faith. Christians are called to share their faith-based *Muhibbah* (Arabic, "goodwill or affection") with their neighbor, so that a mutual

---

[7] See, Alle Hoekema and John Prior, "Theological Thinking by Indonesian Christians", in Karel Steenbrink and Jan Aritonang, *A History of Christianity in Indonesia*, Brill, Leiden:2008.

[8] see, Goeran Wiking, *Breaking the Pot: Contextual Responses to Survival Issues in Malaysian Churches*, Studia Missionalia Svecana XCVI, Lund:2004), p.119-145.

Muhibbah will be celebrated in their cultural life. The church can be rooted in that common culture through its engagement with Muslim neighbors.

Here, theology mainly is the discernment of God's transforming action among the peoples of different faiths. This theology sees Christ as a friend of others, who explains and shares his care with the neighbour. In following Him, Christians are called to be with the neighbors and to share Christ's care with them. Despite an Islamic resurgence, also politically, in some Southeast Asian societies, this "neighborology" must persistently express how the loving that comes from faith in Christ will transform political walls in this region. Thus, this theology is prophetic; the Word of truth should be the very practice of the churches. Although churches are in the minority in Asia, they need to be prophetic in insisting on this, since it is quite tempting for churches to compromise this Word for the sake of their own survival.

According to Batumalai, what follows is the ministry of intercession. Being a church always means a living community that cares for and shares the burdens of society. After engaging in the lives of its neighbors, the church should bring the cries of the people into its own spiritual life. Praying for our neighbors is a theological necessity in the life of the churches.

Neighborology reflects a possible way for what Indonesian/Asian Christians should develop theologically. The shared culture of Indonesia/Asia becomes the platform for churches engaging with their neighbors. According to the progressive Indonesia Islamic intellectual, Nurcholish Madjid, the notion of *kemaslahatan* (Indonesian: well-being of the people) is often mentioned as the common denominator for every religious action in society.

Ecumenical Learning and Christian-Muslim Dialogue in Asia

What we could learn from the succinct history of the Christian-Muslim dialogue in Asia/Indonesia-Malaysia above is the multi-layer relations that both religions had: from tension and being neighbours to social engagement for common dignity. In the light of this the church in Asia needs to take several steps if in the future dialogue with Muslims is expected to bring fruitful meaning and transformation.

Indeed, the Asian church needs to continue to criticize and overcome the limitations and legacy of the missionary theology and adopt strategies to deal with Islam. The so called "Kraemer and Tambaram" should be seriously investigated and overcome so that Asians will have a more open and dialogical theology of religious pluralism. Earlier I mentioned in this paper that in 1920 a local Javanese Christian proposed an inclusive theology of religions, but he was not listened toheard, power/knowledge dynamics should then always be the way of doing theology for the future of Asian independent theology.

To add to this stance, interfaith relations and dialogue in Asia should be carried out side by side with the call to transform society for a more democratic structure. In history, Christians and Muslims in Asia related to each other mainly so as to have their freedom and dignity against the oppressive colonial rulers. Common good and economic justice has become the very part of interfaith dialogue in Asia. Therefore both faiths need to develop their independent position to keep their prophetic voices heard.

In the light of this, the Asian perspective of ecumenism will always be meant as a celebration of God`s abundant grace to the one and whole humanity, in which the voices of the Muslims should be heard as to what that gracious act meant for them. Ecumenism that excludes people of other faiths excludes that very act of grace, therefore we should add here that ecumenism cannot be solely the business of Christian families. It is the work and hope of all the children of God on earth.

Therefore, common voices of Muslim and Christian about that grace and how to work it out for dignity and freedom are the very essence of Asian ecumenism. The so called "wider ecumenism[9]" should be also

[9] See, S. Wesley Ariarajah, "Wider Ecumenism: a Threat or a Promise", in *Ecumenical Review*, vol. 50, 1998.

appreciated and elaborated, since it is based on the belief that the destiny of the Christian in Asia is tied with the fate of its wider neighbours, i.e. all its people.

Bibliography

S. Wesley Ariarajah, "Wider Ecumenism: a Threat or a Promise", in *Ecumenical Review*, vol. 50, 1998.

Asghar Ali Engineer, *Islam and Liberation theology: Essays on Liberative Elements in Islam*, Sterling Publishers, New Delhi:1990

Alle Hoekema and John Prior, "Theological Thinking by Indonesian Christians", in Karel Steenbrink and Jan Aritonang, *A History of Christianity in Indonesia*, Brill, Leiden:2008

Jansen Pardede, *Die Batakchristen auf Nordsumatra und ihr Verhältnis zu den Muslimen*, Johanes Gutenberg-Universität, Mainz: 1975.

Paul Rajashekar and H.S. Wilson, *Islam in Asia: Perspective fro Christian-Muslim Encounter,* LWF-WARC, Geneva:1991.

Olaf Schumann, "Christian-Muslim Encounter in Indonesia" in Yvonne Yasbeck Haddad,. *Christian-Muslim Encounters*. Jacksonville: University Press of Florida, 1995,

T.B. Simatupang,"Dynamic for Creative Maturity", in Gerald Anderson (ed.), *Asian Voices in Christian Theology*, Orbis Book, Maryknoll:1976.

Th. Sumartana, *Mission at the Crossroads; Indigenous Churches, European Missionaries, Islamic Associations and Socio-religious Change in Java* 1812-1936, Jakarta: BPK Gunung-Mulia, 1993.

see, Goeran Wiking, *Breaking the Pot: Contextual Responses to Survival Issues in Malaysian Churches*, Studia Missionalia Svecana XCVI, Lund:2004.

(31) THE DIALOGICAL IMPERATIVE FOR RELIGIONS: A SEARCH INTO CHRISTIAN-MUSLIM RELATIONSHIPS IN ASIA

Varghese Manimala

As all of us know that although most of the people recognize the need for interreligious dialogue, and better cooperation among religions, still it is a compelling fact to be acknowledged that such a dialogue has taken a back seat in most of the countries. And as a result fundamentalism both overt and covert is on the increase, however vociferously we may protest. Hence, there needs to be a reassertion of the urgency of dialogue as well as cooperation among various religions in bringing about peace and harmony in the nations. Here what we aim to look at is the Christian-Muslim relationship in some parts of Asia particularly in India, Pakistan, Bangladesh, etc. There is no gain staying to the fact that in all these countries the religious minorities are meeting with unprecedented discrimination and oppression, and some of them flee to the neighbouring countries for refuge and protection. Their lives and properties are at risk, and in order to remain in their own country the demand of the fundamentalists is the changeover of their faith through conversion, and in this regard even girls are kidnapped, raped and forced into marriage. Thus a volatile situation exists, and we need to look at it sensitively and also objectively, and suggest methods to overcome the almost perilous situation. Hence in this paper our aim will be to look at interreligious dialogue in its authentic sense looking at the basic conditions for dialogue to succeed, and also how we cautiously yet determinedly need to proceed so that a great mission may not be lost sight of and we will be found guilty by the later generations. We can solve the conflicts only through dialogue and not through acrimony and accusations and counter-accusations. What is required from the parties in dialogue is to accept the fact that we are all partners in the dialogue of life, which will shape the future of the nations; and also the fact that all the religions have failed and no religion can make a claim to total authenticity. With this in mind let us look at some basic pre-suppositions and conditions for success in dialogue.

1. Basic Presuppositions

We need to look at some of the philosophical and theological presuppositions that underline the interreligious encounter:

1. No religion however advanced or great can claim to have monopoly of religion. Religion is the birthright of every human person and it is built into his/her being. Every religion or ideology is finite and historical in nature, and serves a historical need.
2. No religion or ideology can claim to know truth in its entirety or in other words the absolute truth. We are all truth-seekers and not truth-possessors. Hence a certain 'de-absolutization' of truth is needed.
3. As a result, cooperation and availability are required from the part of adherents of various religions and ideologies for the attainment of truth.
4. We must be ready to learn from our past history – most of the wars had a religious background and warmongers made use of religion for their own advantage[1].

---

[1] George Bush is said to have received a message from 'god' asking him to declare war on Iraq. We can imagine how one can make use of this kind of 'revelation' for destroying the enemy and furthering one's own advantage. He even seems to have telephoned to Jacques Chirac, the French President, urging France to join the invasion of Iraq because the world had arrived at the era prefigured by Gog and Magog, signifying the arrival of a great war in which all God's enemies would be destroyed and the Last Days of Divine Judgment arrive. Mr. Bush seemed convinced that his war on Iraq was this prophesied war, and tried to so convince Chirac. The French President was sufficiently disturbed by

5. Money and power have entered into religions and ideologies and distorted them. A concerted effort to isolate these evils is required.
6. Militancy and proselytism should be avoided by all religions and ideologies; they need to work for human liberation and development.
7. We are living in a world which earnestly seeks for liberation – *moksha* from all *dukkha*. All forms of suffering are to be conquered. There are various forms of suffering like (i) physical suffering, (ii) socio-economic suffering, (iii) nuclear arms race and war, (iv) ecological suffering, etc.
8. Religions and ideologies are imperfect and stand in need of mutual fecundation and fulfillment.

(a) Ground rules for dialogue

We can identify the following ground rules for dialogue which have proved to be essential and helpful for our work:

1. Partners in dialogue need to be identified with a religious or ideological community.
2. We need readiness to be *attentive* – genuine listening to what the dialogue partner is saying.
3. We must be *intelligent and reasonable* – a sincere effort is needed to understand what we have experienced and heard. Be responsible and als also ready for change if we are required to!
4. Interreligious and inter-ideological *dialogue are a two-sided project* – which calls for *intra-religious, intra-ideological, inter-religious* and *inter-ideological dialogue.*
5. There should be *complete honesty and sincerity* from the part of partners in dialogue.
6. The primary purpose of dialogue is *to learn for all sides involved.*
7. There should not be *any hard and fast assumptions as to points of disagreement.* We need to have *openness and sympathy* to the other partner.
8. *Dialogue can take place only between equals* – no superiority feeling will help.
9. Dialogue should be based on *mutual trust.*
10. Dialogue calls for *maturity* – dialogue partners must be at least *minimally self-critical of both themselves and their own religious or ideological tradition.*
11. Each participant must attempt to *experience the partner's religion or ideology "from within".*

(b) Goals of dialogue

Very often questions are asked about the goals of dialogue. Here I may put in very few words what are goals of dialogue; strictly speaking there is no goal beyond dialogue itself. But a few purposes of dialogue may be hinted at:

- The main goal of dialogue should be better understanding and promotion of human freedom and liberation.
- Dialogue should promote good relationships between human beings and communities – avoidance of domination.
- Common enterprises can be a meaningful result of dialogue.
- Promotion of human solidarity is an important goal of dialogue.
- Praxis oriented dialogue is a must.

Bush's state of mind to consult a theologian at the University of Lausanne in Switzerland for his opinion. The theologian told him that Gog is a mysterious figure from the land of Magog, of controversial Biblical significance, mentioned in the book of Genesis and again in Ezekiel and Revelation, taken by some to represent the nations of the world who are enemies of Israel at the end-time. The French President decided to keep the nature of these telephone conversations to himself so long as he (and, as it happened, Mr. Bush) remained in office. (Cf. *Frontline* Vol. 29, No. 24). See what harm can be done when religious fundamentalism coupled with madness and urge for domination assert themselves, and those persons affected by these attitudes at times masquerade and proclaim as protectors of democracy.

- Readiness to fight religious fanaticism and fundamentalism is essential.
- Dialogue aims at the promotion of respect for the human person, and readiness to fight discrimination in any form, even if it is religiously motivated.
- Dialogue involves the readiness to fight corruption in every form.
- Dialogue leads to a greater understanding about the partner's religion.

Thus we can think of various secular goals of dialogue; we need to acknowledge that as true dialogue of life proceeds it may take on a religious colouring as participants become interested in the life and activities of one another. A desire to learn about the religious activities of the other gives a momentum to study in a deeper measure about the participants' religions. Thus dialogue may enter upon different vistas and the participants should be open to this possibility.

2. The Necessity of Dialogue

Perhaps one important reality that the church has come to realize is that the splendid isolation in which she glorified herself is no longer tenable. Such isolation is an encapsulation which gnaws at the very root of the life of the church and society. If one does not come out of such imprisonment there is no future that is worth hoping for. In this context we can think of a few stages of life through which Christianity passed through and developed its own self-understanding. Prof. Raimon Panikkar calls them epochs of Christian history, and he divides them into five.[2] (1) The primary Christian understanding of the first centuries was that of *witness*. Early Christians did not consider themselves followers of a new religion, but they testified to the living words uttered at the banks of the Jordan and confirmed by the resurrection. As witnesses they testified to something that had transformed their lives, and remained a kind of suprahistorical event to them. They lived not merely in history; eschatology was an ever present factor. They were ready to die as martyrs giving testimony to the faith they professed. (2) The next period may be described by the word *conversion*. Although the world officially became "Christian," still the atmosphere was "pagan." Gradually Christians established themselves as a social and political entity; yet they were still aware that Constantine's declaration of Christianity as the state religion had its pitfalls. Christians were called to follow a different life-style from that of the world. The authentic Christian may be called to play a political role or may be attracted by the social force of Christianity, but the true criterion is the life-style, the purity of the heart. Being a Christian means to be converted to Christ, and although in the world they should live as if not of the world. Yet, conversion gradually attained a political connotation. (3) Perhaps, the word *crusade* characterizes the Christian self-understanding of this new epoch. Crusades continued from 8th to almost till the 16th century; and Christendom by then firmly established. The threat of Islam was always hanging as a Damocles' sword on Christianity, and it became a collective obsession. The Christian empire had to assert itself; the danger was sensed everywhere. Everybody was called to be a "soldier" for Christ. Reformation further strengthened this attitude. Christianity was a challenging undertaking, and it required courage, faith and decision. One had to become a Christian knight, a hero; one's sacred duty was to conquer the outside world for Christ or to win it back to Christ. In this epoch Christianity slowly developed the idea of being the only true religion (*vera religio*), and all other religions were viewed as false. *Vera religio* emerged as the sacred phrase, and gradually it came to mean: "the only true and salvation-bestowing institutionalized religion." This notion persisted for several centuries, and later with the discovery of America the scene changed; and as a result Christendom as a world order collapsed and Christianity as a religion evolved. (4) During this period ***mission*** became the main characteristic of the Christian religion even down to this day; the zeal to conquer was irresistible. Amerindians could not be regarded as a threat, such as the Muslims, nor did the former accuse the Christians of anything. The only

---

[2] Cf. Raimon Panikkar, *A Dwelling Place for Wisdom* (Westminster: John Knox Press, 1993), pp. 114-118.

justification for the *conquista* was the sole motive that America had to be Christianized. The ideology prevailed that Christians were obliged – or better had the *mission* – to proclaim the Gospel, and save all who stood in need of salvation; thus a true Christian was seen as a *missionary*. The theology of mission became the most accepted one. Still there were missionaries and theologians, who realized in their contact with other peoples of the world that these newly discovered religions, contained a treasure of spiritual goods. But this was not approved in the church and political circles because of the political expansion of the European states. In short, Christians had a mission duty toward the whole world, and up to today they are praying and paying for mission societies. But as we know today many Christians realize the fact that the mission can no longer be performed as in the past, and with this we reach the present age. (5) Today the new catchword is *dialogue*. Through interaction with other religions and cultures Christians in general have come to realize that they can no more conquer, nor even to convert; hence they wish to serve and to learn. Many of them are willing to offer themselves as serious partners in open dialogue – though not without understandable distrust on the part of other religions. There is a realization dawning upon many sincere Christians that dialogue is not another strategy but an open process for mutual enrichment and for getting better acquainted with each other.[3]

Any dialogue means a sustained conversation between parties who are not saying the same thing and who recognize and respect the differences, the contradictions and the mutual exclusions between their various ways of thinking. The object of dialogue is understanding and appreciation leading to further reflection upon the implication for one's own position of the convictions and sensitivities of the other traditions. Every human being finds it difficult to sustain contradictions and live with them. Instinctively we either try to destroy what is opposed to our understanding of truth or we pretend that the antithesis is unreal. We look for simple unity but in fact we are a structure of contradictions. It takes a high degree of maturity to let the opposites co-exist without pretending that they can be made compatible. We need to dispassionately see the opposition with its challenges, deal with them without surrendering any of one's own integrity or diminishing the content of one's examined convictions. Such a basic love has to precede before any reconciliation of ideas and beliefs. The loving that is expressed through the attempt to listen and understand and honour through the frank recognition and appreciation of the convictions that deny one's own through the opening of one's imagination to the real otherness of the other is the function of interreligious dialogue. Religions and ideologies have kept themselves off in hundreds of years of isolation and suspicion. Such a blissful isolation steeped in ignorance is no longer possible, and aggression as in the past is no more useful strategy either. There are various suspicions lingering in the hearts of many and they should not be shelved aside as irrelevant. Since every religion is a historically determined tradition of the response to what the Spirit of God has forever been setting before human beings' eyes, we must overcome the situation to find that each religion has become a self-consistent and almost closed system of culture and language. Communication between one such system and another is fraught with difficulty which must not be underestimated. Accompanying all these there will the problem of hermeneutics, as well as the different horizons of understanding developed by different cultures; and with hope we need to move forward.[4] In such an attitude we can look for a partial convergence of the horizons of understanding on the two sides. As a result there may arise a new common horizon for the partners in dialogue, even emergence of a new world with new possibilities and understanding, and thus the disclosure of new theological dimensions.

---

[3] As is evident this classification of Panikkar is quite illuminating and helpful to understand Christian history. Today what we need is an open mind and heart to approach other religions with an attitude of mutual search.

[4] Cf. Cf. Andreas D'Souza (ed.), *From Converting the Pagan to Dialogue with our Parnters: HMI's Fifty Years of Work of Evangelism and Interfaith Relations* (Delhi, ISPCK, 2009). The article by John B. Taylor, "The Theological Basis of Interfaith Dialogue," pp. 263-267.

3. Christian-Muslim Dialogue in General

As we live in a pluralistic world we have become very much aware of the various types of pluralism we are confronted with, and the question we are bound to ask is how can we live together in such a situation, not only merely practicing tolerance and a passive co-existence, but also how we can trust and be loyal to each other, and thus bring about an active pro-existence. Such a context calls for dialogue among people of various religions and ideologies. A dialogue is a dynamic contact between life and life, not only between one rational view against the other, which is directed towards living together, acting together, building the world anew together. A dialogue is a humanitarian activity in which intellectual, moral, social and practical dimensions are involved. In the manner of living and expressions human beings are different, and also there are a lot of differences that exist between different cultures and traditions. But it is important that all nations and groups ought to endeavour to come to an agreement on various fundamental problems. It is necessary that religions and ideologies should strive to abolish the social imbalances. We should realize that rooted in our own religions and ideologies, we should try to do maximum good to others who belong to different religions, cultures, etc. We as good believers are bound to build a world community, a pluralistic world community of justice, prosperity, based on mutual respect, love and trust.[5]

Before we go to look at in some detail into the situation of dialogue between these religions in some of the representative countries it may be good to look at the basic nature and problems that may come along in the dialogue between Christians and Muslims. As we know these religions are known as Abrahamic faiths, and there is a lot of commonality between these religions. At the same time a lot of differences exist about certain aspects of faith and practices. Hence, while entering into dialogue both parties need to exercise a good bit of caution. But for world peace and harmony this sort of dialogue has become very urgent as a new situation has developed due to the various wars that are being waged in the gulf countries, and these wars are seen by many as a confrontation between Christianity and Islam. It is the duty of Christianity especially to dissociate from the war mongers, and both religions should see their goal as building up of peace and harmony and conflict transformation. For this a good bit of de-politicizing of religion needs to take place. Also the goals of dialogue and forms of dialogue need to be understood at a greater depth. We can think of dialogue being both doctrinal and practical. Doctrinal or theological dialogue may be termed as confessional dialogue, and sometimes the parties engaged in dialogue may be so convinced of their faith that the religion of the dialogue partners may be looked at as false. There can be an attempt to convert the other in this kind of dialogue, and this can undermine dialogue itself. Another kind of dialogue may be called as 'truth-seeking dialogue.' The partners of such a dialogue need to admit that the axiom: truth, the whole truth, nothing but the truth is not possible to be upheld, and that truth has many facets and what we are able to reach are only certain aspects of the truth. As mentioned above the human being is not in a position to know the absolute or whole truth; also God (Truth) is greater than any human conception of Him. Hence what is needed is a radical re-consideration of our theological positions. All of us need to accept that we are all in history and in evolution and very much conditioned by these; hence all religious positions also take on a relative nature. This will call for a new theology with its basic consideration of the whole mankind as one community, which, as we know, is quite in conformity with the universalistic teaching inherent in all religions. Without a new theological approach to include all the world religions as the religious heritage of mankind and to find a respectable place for all religions in one's religious consciousness, the dream of interreligious harmony will ever remain unrealized.[6]

---

[5] Cf. Andreas, ibid. See the article by H. A. Mukti Ali, "Religions, Nations and the Search for a World Community," p. 232.

[6] Cf. Andreas, ibid. The article by Sam Bhajjan, "Muslims and Christians in an Indian Context: The Question of Dialogue," pp. 252-253. Also Ziaull Hasan Faruqi, "Ways and Means of Inter-Religious Harmony and Reconciliation," p. 185.

Perhaps, what is needed from the part of Christianity and Islam is that search for commonalities as well as the shared beliefs of both the religions be highlighted. Islam accepts Jesus as a great prophet and even considers him as a specially chosen one so as to be born of a virgin and even sinless. But as we know Muslims cannot accept the position of the Christians to the claim of Jesus' divinity or second person of the Holy Trinity. He is a prophet par excellence, but he did not die on the cross but was taken up to heaven. Even Muslims have no difficulty in accepting the second coming of Christ. To go to counteract the positions held by Muslims regarding Christ will be futile, and it can block even further dialogue. What is most important is that we should have the openness and courage to expose our experience to one another's questioning. If interfaith dialogue is to become sincere and deep we have to expose to one another the ways in which, within our separate households of faith, we wrestle with the questions that other religions put to us. We must be ready to lower our defenses and be ready to be confronted with the questions and be willing to be exposed. This will help us personally to grow and get rooted in our faith, for faith unless it is challenged is not true faith, it can be very much superstition and even bordering on fanaticism. We need to radically realize the fact that God is not a God of a tribe or a nation, but a universal God, the father and protector of all, and no religion or group can claim an exclusive knowledge of Him/Her, and even the little bit that we may pretend to know is only a small ray of truth for which we need to humble ourselves before such a simple and humble God and offer thanks for his continued revelation to humankind. There is no exclusive revelation to anybody, and consequently nobody or no religion is in a privileged position. The only privilege is to serve one another, and thus prove ourselves to be the children of such a benevolent God who makes the sun rise over the just and unjust, and make showers come down over the good and bad.

It is a fact that every religion has certain central truths and convictions, which they don't want to be debated upon. Christianity makes a claim to the absolute centrality of Jesus Christ, but at the same time it is good to remember that Jesus is not the sole possession of Christianity, rather Christ transcends Christianity. Christ can stand as the central figure in Christianity but as a religion it cannot make exclusive claim of Christ, for Christ is a universal person, a prophet; and it is good to remember that He did not come to establish a religion but initiated a movement of love. And he chose to stand by the poor, the abandoned, the despised, the sinners, women, and in one word the outcast. He made a preferential option for them and dared to stand by them for which he had to risk his life and die an ignominious death on the cross. He resisted the proud and could not tolerate the self-righteous, and even challenged the mighty. Such a Jesus is wanted by all people irrespective of religions or ideologies. Even Qur'ân speaks so highly about this prophet, although it cannot accept the position that he is Son of God because of the exclusive form of monotheism and understanding of the Trinity. What we need to do is that we acknowledge our limitations and try to understand others' positions so that we can widen the knowledge of our faith and commitment.

We need to be aware of the fact that every religion has its own "jealousies". By jealousies we refer to those points in every religion concerning which the believers are inwardly compelled to claim as a universal significance and finality. To quote a few examples: the Muslim conviction that the Holy Qur'ân is not just another revelation but is God's last word; the Jewish conviction that Israel's covenant and her attachment to the Holy land has a central significance in the determinate purpose of God; the Christian conviction that in the life and death and resurrection of Jesus God acted decisively for all mankind. Every profoundly convincing encounter with God is with a jealous God, which simply means that having experienced God in that way, no other God will do; and it is not helpful to condemn such positions as arrogant. Despite all these irreconcilable positions we should have the courage to expose our experience to one another's questioning, realizing that we do not possess the absolute truth or even understand the absolute truth. Besides letting one another know the absolutes in their own faith that may not be surrendered, the partners in the dialogue must also give serious reflection to the critique, which each inevitably bring to bear upon the convictions of the others, however painful and disturbing this may be. But this should not make us oblivious of the things that we have in common. We believe that the Ultimate

Reality upon which the faith of all believers is focused in every religion is the same, though our interpretations of its essential nature are still at variance. The new interchange and openness between men/women of different faiths has established the fact that all religions express an awareness of human alienation, enslavement, and need for healing and deliverance, and in all religions people experience an inward liberation, a sense of being accepted and made new. Though rituals of communities and individual prayer differ widely, yet the sense of oneness and communication with the gracious Divinity is common to them all, as is the hunger of the heart for such communion. To begin with this much common ground is a giant leap, and what we need is patient persistence.[7]

Another important point to be borne in mind is the fact if there is no intra-religious dialogue or intra-ideological dialogue, there cannot be an inter-religious or inter-ideological dialogue. If there is no basic openness among the practitioners of religions or ideologies it is almost impossible to enter into dialogue with partners from other religions and ideologies. Quite often this has not been insisted upon, but Raimon Panikkar has emphasized strongly that the former is a condition for the latter. Intra-religious or intra-ideological dialogue gives the disposition for inter-religious or inter-ideological dialogue. Very often we find that a fundamentalist community or church is not in a position to enter into true dialogue because the partners have no disposition for dialogue, since they see dialogue as a threat to their position, or even their very existence. Besides this, perhaps, another distinction which Panikkar, the apostle of interreligious dialogue, makes will be helpful. He distinguishes between ***dialectical dialogue*** and ***dialogical dialogue***. The dialectical dialogue refers to the subject matter of dialogue, it is about something, while dialogical dialogue indicates more the personal dimensions of dialogue; it is about those who are engaged in dialogue. While dialectical dialogue is a necessity, if dialogue ends on that level without proceeding to the dialogical level the results will not be lasting. Dialectics has an irreplaceable mediating function at the human level, and it cannot be brushed away in any truly human exchange. In dialogical dialogue persons do not want dialogue about something, but about themselves; the partner is not an object or a subject putting forth some objective thoughts to be discussed, but a thou, and not an it, a source of understanding. In such a dialogue one cannot predict or fathom the dynamism of being since it is guided not by mere evolution but also creativity.[8]

4. Christian-Muslim Dialogue in Asia:

After having discussed the generic notions about dialogue we should launch into the topic with which we are immediately concerned. But in dealing with this subject I must confess that the available data is very scanty. Although there may be books written on theology of dialogue and understanding of dialogue in the religions concerned on the praxis level how much is being practiced or effectively followed remains obscure. The dialogue of life takes place very much on the routine level, and one cannot get along without it. However, let me try to delineate, with all the limitations, the efforts of dialogue at various levels.

(a) Christian-Muslim relationship in India

It is a known fact there have been no serious conflicts between Christian and Muslims in India, and in fact some areas there have been cooperation between these communities especially during the recent attacks on

---

[7] Cf. Taylor, "Basis of Interfaith Dialogue," Andreas, pp. 268-276.

[8] For a rather detailed study on this topic one could very usefully consult Panikkar's book, *The Intra-Religious Dialogue* (New York: Paulist Press, 1999), and also an article by him in the book, *The World's Religious Traditions: Current Perspectives in Religious Studies*, edited by Frank Whaling (Edinburgh: T. & T. Clark Ltd. 1984), the article, "The Dialogical Dialogue." Also one can consult my book: *Toward Mutual Fecundation and Fulfilment of Religions: An Invitation to Transcendence and Dialogue with a Cosmotheandric Vision* (Delhi: ISPCK & Media House, 2009), Chapter 3.

Christians and Christian institutions by fundamentalist Hindus. They even came forward to protect the persons and properties of the Christians. Also there is cooperation between these communities especially for demanding the rights of the minorities from the government. There has been a concerted effort to bring up the education and living standards of the downtrodden in these communities. Although the wars in Iraq and Afghanistan did affect the Christian-Muslim relationship in various nations, India was spared of any violent actions. It is true there were a lot of subdued discussions but the religious leaders were sensible enough not to fan the flames of fundamentalism and bring about conflicts. There is a greater realization among the Christian and Muslim communities in India that they need each other. Since both communities are religious minorities there is a felt need to stand together. Hence on the practical level especially the political one there seems to be unproclaimed mutual support. Although Christians are a smaller minority the influence in the field of education and health care is quite high, and even can stand up to the majority community. Muslims numerically constitute a big minority (13% of the population) and exert an influence by vote bank but are economically and socially very poor. In many states where Christian influence is pronounced Muslims seem to follow the example set by their Christian brothers and sisters.

Henry Martyn Institute's Vision and Mission

A good many are aware of the nature and contribution of Henry Martyn Institute (HMI) in Hyderabad. It is a pioneering institute in the field of Christian-Muslim relationship. It was founded more than 80 years back in Lahore (Pakistan) for training missionaries to work among the Muslims; hence it called for a deeper study of Islam. Gradually the institute made a physical journey shifting from place to place and finally settling in Hyderabad, the capital of Andhra Pradesh, in South India. In this physical journey the institute also made an intellectual and attitudinal change that was thrust upon the institute because of the various vicissitudes. There began to come about a paradigm shift especially from the notion of conversion to a stress on interfaith relations. And today the institute stresses very much on a changed theology of pluralism and interreligious dialogue. We see pluralism as a blessing and not as a curse, and that every religion may flourish and give glory to God until its fire has gone out. We believe that religions mutually fecund and fulfill themselves; it cannot happen in isolation or a 'blessed' encapsulation. It is in mutual exchange and sharing that religions can grow and reach their destination. Every religion is historical and fulfils a historical need, and also no religion is fully perfect; human as it is deficiency accompanies it. With this in mind HMI with its multi-religious staff tries best to keep up multi-religious nature although it is a Christian institution. We try for promoting interreligious dialogue and activities as and when possibilities offer themselves, but at least a few times a year we have common celebrations, which bring together people of various religious backgrounds and ideologies. Also seminars are conducted for various groups taking into account the need of the times. We also collaborate with other NGOs in planning and reducing religious tensions and conflicts; and also work with them for rendering helps when conflicts occur. Although we may not be having very many theoretical discussions on dogmas and scriptures, we make it a point to do some activities which will be of help to further the dialogue of action, and in this context recently we held an international interreligious conference on Mysticism in which some Muslim brethren also took part and it was well appreciated so much so there is a lot of demand for follow-up action. We need a lot of creativity to carry on the mission of dialogue; there cannot be a prescribed form of dialogue. We need to adopt different modes and methods in accordance with the need of the occasion; and in this there will be variations from place to place even in the same country. The openness of the people will vary in accordance with the level of education, and the levels of spirituality, and the power for self-criticism. HMI's role in interreligious dialogue and conflict transformation and peace-building is very much appreciated internationally. This does not mean there is space for complacency, rather there should be the constant search that should go on regarding the mode of dialogue that should be practiced, and for this we need openness and the ability to renew and reform ourselves, as well as updating of our theology and philosophy.

(b) Christian-Muslim relationship in Pakistan

Although my knowledge of the situation is very much limited, still I would like to hint at what goes on in our neighbouring country.[9] As we are aware the religious and minority rights are not held sacred in Pakistan, and minorities especially the Christians and the Hindus live in fear because of the forced conversion, and the application of Shariah law etc. Ms. Romana Bashir whom I interviewed loves Pakistan very much and would like to continue her mission of interfaith encounter, and at the same time would like to work very much for the liberation of women, and raise the consciousness of the minorities. She finds that the only way to fight against the violation of human rights is to raise the level of education and self-reliance. On the whole Christians have the good will to be educated, and the church is playing a big role in this. The persecution of the Christians continues rather unabated, and even the only Christian minister in the government was shot dead at point blank. Women are raped and forced to marry the rapist by converting themselves to Islam. Laws are subverted to help the Muslims; the so-called blasphemy law is invoked without any evidence especially by the fundamentalist mullahs who usurp the power into their own hands. In addition to this there is political instability created by the corrupt system, and terrorism unleashed by the Taliban is very much active and the government looks helpless. The system of democracy is very brittle, and the army can call the shot at any moment. Politically Pakistan is a stooge of America and because of the uncertainty prevailing in that country US takes full advantage of the situation. The Christian Study Centre wants to promote dialogue between the Muslims and Christians and they make every effort, but success is not that forthcoming. Still they feel that the hope should not be lost, and there is no other way but to come to certain recognition of other religions, and thus to effect dialogue and cooperative social action. For this Christians may have to take the lead and promote education for all especially women, to work for the abolition of child labour, for respect for women, insistence on holding on to the original constitution as there is a plan to subvert it, and amendments are brought to suit only the majority religion. Stress on equal rights for all religions in government jobs including that of the president and prime minister should be seen as a priority. There should be a great struggle to keep up the pressure for dialogue as this is the only way to come to resolution of conflicts and peaceful co-existence. The hope should not be lost, and even in situations of persecution trusting in the risen Lord, efforts should be made to keep the process of dialogue to go on; one important step for this is formation of groups of people who think in this manner, and continue to highlight the good things that take place.

(c) Christian-Muslim dialogue in Bangladesh

Bangladesh is another Muslim country in the neigbhourhood of India, and in fact it was India which helped this nation to come into existence; from the name East Pakistan it got christened as Bangladesh. This nation has much in common with the people of West Bengal as before partition this was a contiguous area. A few years after its independence[10] it declared itself to be a Muslim nation, making Islam the official

[9] Here much what I will be saying is based on a recent interview I conducted with Ms. Romana Bashir, Executive Director of Peace and Development Foundation for Promotion of Inter-faith Dialogue and Social Harmony. This interview was held recently (Nov. 28, 2012) in Vienna, at Hilton Hotel during the inauguration of the King Abdulla International Centre for Interreligious and Intercultural Dialogue (KAICIID). She has been recently appointed on the committee of the Pontifical Commission for Dialogue.

[10] This author had the good opportunity to work on the borders of East Pakistan (later Bangladesh) during the liberation struggle, and soon after the war I went into Bangladesh and witnessed the horrors of the war. This is not the occasion to go into those matters. But I consider myself fortunate to have served the unfortunate refugees numbering many millions. Also I feel proud that my nation served the refugees the best way possible.

religion of the country. There have been some conflicts between Christians and Muslims in that country, but I think the understanding between these religions is much better than what we find in Pakistan. Christians are much better off also, it appears. Poverty plagues this country although very rich in resources; natural calamities like floods constantly ravage this beautiful nation. In general a relation of peaceful coexistence is seen between the Christians and Muslims. There may be small groups of Christians and Muslims entering into dialogue, but dialogue on an official level is not much heard of. Of course, the dialogue of life carries on.

(d) Christian-Muslim relations in other nations

Perhaps in a few sentences I would like to refer to Christian-Muslims relations in some other countries. In *Sri Lanka*, which fought a civil war for almost 30 years is in the process of recovering but without adequately addressing the grievances and problems of the affected people. There has been violation of human rights as reports tell us. Also perhaps, that is the only country in which Buddhists blatantly supported an oppressive regime and all the killing that went on. Also there were religious conflicts between Buddhists and Muslims in that tiny nation, but there weren't very serious conflicts between Christians and Muslims. Yet we do not hear very much active engagement in dialogue, or even dialogue in action. Perhaps, what is being done in certain areas goes unnoticed. Christians are a minority but seem to be rather influential and want to help the war affected people in the Northern part of the country. When the Portuguese invaded Sri Lanka they had clash with the Arabs and the local Muslims; they were using brute force and were harassing and taxing the Muslims. Portuguese were determined to convert the Muslims as well as Buddhists to Catholicism. Later when the Dutch occupied the country they were much more tolerant and were not that serious about conversion, as their main aim was trade; they were more interested in converting the local Catholics to their own protestant Dutch reformed church, than in converting Muslims, Buddhists and Hindus. As on date, and for a long time, there has been no conflict between the Muslims and Christians in Sri Lanka. Although there are generally accusations of conversions of Buddhists by fundamentalist sects of Christians there are no such allegations leveled on Christians by Muslims.[11]

Indonesia has the highest Muslim population, and also there is a significant Christian presence in that country. Indonesia is not a Muslim or secular state but *Pancaśīla* state. This is an adapted form of the *Pancaśīla* of the non-aligned nations, the initiative for which was taken by Nehru, Nasser and others. The five principles are: Belief in One God, Just and civilized humanity, Indonesian unity, Democracy under the wise guidance of representative consultations, and Social Justice for all the peoples of Indonesia. In addition we find that Sufism from the beginning exerted a great influence on the religious development of the nation. The acceptance of the *Pancaśīla* has forced the Muslims to adjust their interpretation of it to the life of the other communities. More than religious development national development is given priority. The religious denominations are expected to play an active role in creating a spiritual and ethical foundation for this development. All religions should recognize the living reality, namely the existence of a multi-religious community. They must find the best way to live together in harmony and to share in developing the community. This type of attitude prevents religious conflicts, and in general there is a good relationship between Christians and Muslims in Indonesia.[12]

I would like to refer to two more countries in Asia, namely Malaysia and the Philippines. In *Malaysia* Muslims constitute a majority about 55% of the population, the rest of the people belong to various religions like Buddhism, Christianity, Confucianism, Taoism, and indigenous beliefs. Islam plays a great

---

[11] Through a short interview and email I could get some information about Sri Lanka from Frances Bulathsinghala. She is the Director of South Asia Peacebuilding & Development Institute in Sri Lanka.

[12] Cf. *Islam In Asia: Perspectives for Encounter* (Geneva, 1992), Report of the Consultation sponsored by the Lutheran World Federation and the World Alliance of Reformed Church, paper by Einar M. Sitompul and M. S. Widdwissoeli, "Islam in Indonesia," pp. 84-96.

role in country's politics. Although the constitution guarantees religious freedom, Islam is rather intolerant towards other religions. Islam has become the uniting factor in Malaysia. Since Muslims have become more self-contained, the non-Muslims place more emphasis on their identity and religion; hence dangerous polarization along religious lines is occurring. Misunderstandings about other religions abound. The church need to take initiative to clear up the misunderstandings between the communities; and also should promote civic consciousness among its members. Although Christian churches have lost their educational and other institutions they should take it as a blessing and serve the nation with a spirit of commitment, and believing that this is the occasion to act as prophets. There are good Muslim leaders who are in favour of social justice; efforts must be made to join hands with them. Christians and Muslims should try to understand each other's struggles, fears, ambitions and joys; this is the only hope for eliminating mutual distrust and suspicion, and to enhance peace and harmony.[13]

Philippines: Muslims got settled in this country quite early, and until the arrival of the Spanish they progressed rapidly. More than 300 years wars were fought between the Muslims and Spanish-Philippino Christians. Although they wanted to convert the Muslims they were not very successful; for the Spanish these wars were considered as continuation of the crusades. Later when Americans occupied the country they too fought bitterly against the Muslims; thus Christian-Muslim relations became very strained. During the Second World War Philippino Christians and Muslims united to fight a guerrilla war against the Japanese troops, but this solidarity did not last long; it was a fight against a common enemy. After Independence during the Marcos period Muslim rebellion was ruthlessly put down making use of the martial law. During the Aquino administration an effort was made to patch up the relationship, and an area called Mindanao was reserved for the Muslim population, and made into an autonomous region. But with all these efforts Muslim-Christian dialogue continues on a decreasing scale, and much needs to be done to promote Muslim-Christian understanding and fellowship. Since Muslims are rather a small minority (5-6%) Christians need to show extra consideration and make the Muslims feel secure in the country.[14]

5. Conclusion

We have tried to delineate briefly the notion of interreligious dialogue, and also Christian-Muslim relationship in a few countries of Asia. Although the effort is limited yet we have pointed to some important areas of dialogue between Christians and Muslims in Asia. What we need is generosity and openness of heart to follow the path of dialogue without giving way to despondency. Through globalization we have come closer to each other, and international travel and communication have become a boon. But still the bane of ideological separation remains very much active on many levels of existence, and today we need to overcome the barrier of theological isolation. There is an ideology of competition very active both on the religious level as well as the political and economic levels. Belief that a particular religion is the sole possessor of the truth has lead to various conflicts. Hence, what we need today is not a theology of competition but of partnership, as especially John Hick has pointed out. In such a theology we will be able to come out of our exclusivism and inclusivism, and will recognize the pluralism that is at work, and will be able to see that we all have a universal God as our Father/Mother, and that we as human beings are brothers and sisters. Hence, we all stand in need of conversion (*metanoia*), change of heart. Then we will

---

[13] Cf. Ibid. See the paper in the book Islam in Asia, Ng Kiok Nam, "Islam in Malaysia," pp. 97-104. This author was again lucky to meet the Arch-bishop of Kaulalampur, Most Rev. Murphy Packiam, and talk about the Christian-Muslim relationship. Being an open minded person he was very positive, and he felt that the Christians especially the priests are not sufficiently open to other religious communities. He felt very much the need for strengthening interreligious dialogue.

[14] Cf. *Islam in Asia*, paper by Robert Day McAmis, "Contact and Conflict: A Historical Survey of Muslim-Christian Relations in the Philippines," pp. 110-117.

be able to move from isolation to negotiation, and when we think about it from a religious perspective it points to dialogue. The primary purpose of dialogue is understanding. Doctrines, spirituality, etc., are secondary although helpful. Once we achieve this we come to stage of integration. Dialogue needs to be understood as holding the promise rather than a threat to faith; it is a process of strengthening the faith. Dialogue has to become an activity, which leads to furthering of relationship on various levels. Dialogue needs to take on a cosmic dimension; it is a fundamental relationship with the world to which we are called. [15] We need the prophetic courage to stand for the cosmic and human dimension of dialogue. For practice of dialogue in the Asian context many things are to be taken into account; and a fruitful dialogue between Christians and Muslims can ensue if both groups are open to self-criticism and acceptance of others as sharers in faith. The mankind stands in need of what Panikkar calls 'contemplative love,'[16] which can transcend all barriers. We can only hope and pray for better disposition and initiatives from people of good will.

Bibliography

Ch. Srinivasa Rao (ed.). *Interfaith Dialogue and World Community*. Madras: C.L.S. 1991.

Kuttianimattathil, Jose. *Practice and Theoglogy of Interreligious Dialogue*. Bangalore. Kristu Jyoti Publications. 1998.

Lochhead, David. *The Theological Imperative: A Christian Reflection on Interfaith Encounter*. New York. Orbis Books. 1988.

Lutheran World Federation. *Islam in Asia: Perspectives for Christian-Muslim Encounter*. Geneva. 1992.

Manimala, Varghese. *Toward Mutual Fecundation and Fulfilment of Religions: An Invitation to Transcendence and Dialogue with a Cosmotheandric Vision*. Delhi: ISPCK & Media House. 2009

Neill, Stephen. *Christian Faith and Other Faiths*: The Christian Dialogue with Other Religions. London: Oxford University Press1965.

Riddell, Peter G. *Christians and Muslims: Pressures and Potential in a Post-9/11 World*. London: Inter-Varsity Press. 2004.

Panikkar, Raimon. *Dwellinging Place for Wisdom*. Westminster. John Knox Press. 1993.

_______. *Invisible Harmony: Essays on Contemplation & Responsibility*.

_______. *The Intra-Religious Dialogue*. New York: Paulist Press. 1999.

[15] One could fruitfully consult the book by David Lochhead, *The Dialogical Imperative: A Christian Reflection on Interfaith Encounter* (New York: Orbis Books, Maryknoll, 1988).

[16] Cf. Panikkar, *Dwelling Place for Wisdom*, p. 99.

(32) Reconciliation and Healing of Memories as a Need in Asian Ecumenism

Kumara Illangasinghe

Background

Plurality and diversity of the Asian context is positively considered as a gift from God and we make every effort to celebrate this diversity, rather than being frightened of it. As much as there are opportunities and the blessings, this plurality and the diversity also bring many challenges that can and already have led to destruction of communities in Asia. Many of the nations in Asia are either going through a civil war, are in post-conflict realities such as in Sri Lanka, Bhutan and Nepal or are at present embroiled in fatal conflicts as in the Philippines, East Timor, Afghanistan, Pakistan, India, Bangladesh, Maldives, Korea and Indonesia, either within or outside their nations.

Religious Ecumenism

The diversity of the Asian scene has to be used as a multipronged approach, while preserving individual identity and the cultural diversity. Ecumenism in the Asian context is not just limited to the Christian tradition and for all the Christian denominations, but is expected to go beyond. In the Asian setting we are called to widen our understanding to 'religious ecumenism', rather than limiting it to 'denominational ecumenism'. The word ecumenism derives from the word 'Oikoumene", which is widely understood as the 'whole inhabited earth'. The whole inhabited earth does not include only those of us who call ourselves Christians and follow Jesus Christ, who came amidst us in reconciling people who have drifted away, back to God. But this 'Oikoumene' is formed of all God's creation, all human beings irrespective of which language they speak or to which religious tradition they belong and the rest of God's creation that fosters and nurtures the supreme creation of God, the humans. Thus our understanding is of the wider ecumenism in our world and this is very significant for us who live and witness in a truly diverse and a pluralistic setting in Asia.

However, 'religious ecumenism' too does not limit us to the scope of 'wider ecumenism'. It further expects the ecumenists to harness all resources from the variety of faith and cultural traditions in Asia, for peace and coexistence, going beyond our individual and corporate identities. Often it is taken for granted by Christians mistakenly that words like reconciliation, repentance, counseling, resurrection etc are widely used by all communities and are acceptable to all. They are commonly in Christian usage and not among others. This gives us a further challenge to look for more commonly used words and phrases acceptable to all, in addition to the resources from the teachings. One of the greatest gifts that we need to value in this diverse context, is the importance of recognizing the needs of others, that will facilitate enormously and provide for the opportunity to coexist, in spite of the differences and the diversity.

Understanding of History

This is the process of healing that we need of our histories, both of the Church and that of the world. John Lucal said, "We have to learn how to heal our history. Not forget it, but heal it in full knowledge and acceptance of what has gone before. We have to learn how to accept responsibility, without admitting personal guilt, for what our ancestors have done to others".[1]

Even within the Christian communities this has become a certain necessity. Having gone through the conflicts in the past, the denominations too have moved on and evolved over centuries. Often they have continued the ministry of sharing the Gospel and evangelization in many diverse situation and cultures. The outcome may have further taken them away from each other. It is necessary to recognize that reality of evolution of the different denominations. They have also learnt to be independent of each other for their own survival, in almost all aspects of their lives and ministry. But what is lacking is the desire to come together in their witness. 'How can a divided Church sets the example or preach to a divided world?' is the question that is often asked and it continues to remain a challenge. It will certainly be too much to ask at this stage for the organic union of the Church, even though we need to keep that as our ultimate aim. What is necessary today is to coexist side by side and witness, respecting each other and the respective histories. That will assist enormously in the supreme task of presenting the Gospel and its values to a world embroiled in conflicts and divisions. This is exactly why we need reconciliation and the healing of our histories and memories, in order to ensure sustainable peace with justice within the Church and among the denominations and thereby for ecumenism in Asia.

Post War Reconciliation

A Sioux Indian Proverb goes like this. *"Everything we do affects the next seven generations".* [2] It is also important to note that many of the countries also have not been able to deal with post conflict situations in more creative and people friendly ways using all resources available. John Paul Lederach says, *"In conflict more than in any other experience, we see ourselves and others in new and profound ways and we seek to restore truth and love in ourselves. If we take care to look beyond the words and issues, we see God.... Conflict offers a path, a holy path towards revelation and reconciliation"* [3]. This very rare but positive aspect is generally ignored. The regimes that have given leadership for military approaches for resolving conflicts, have failed to use the post-war environment to build communities, by restoring and rebuilding relationships. There is a need to dispel suspicions and wield all communities into and within the fabric of one nation. Instead they have opted to follow the same methods of military operation for nation building. Ultimately such approaches have ended up in repression of people, the reason being the absence of negotiated, just and sustainable solutions. Such regimes continue to invest large sums of funding on weaponry and armed forces, thereby bringing unbearable hardships on ordinary, poor and voiceless people. This suppression by the forces has become necessary for the regimes to control the masses, when they rise up against such repressive regimes, when the economic and financial burdens become unbearable for them. This will certainly not lead to any reconciliation or healing of memories, but will continue to aggravate the suffering and the hopelessness. Even the *LLRC* [4] *report states that, "... despite the lapse of two years since the ending of the conflict, the violence, the suspicion and sense of discrimination are still prevalent in social and political life. Delay in the implementation of a clearly focused post conflict peace building agenda may have contributed to this situation".* [5]

Thus we see how difficult it is to facilitate reconciliation and commit ourselves in our ecumenical settings to ensure lasting peace. But our options as those involved in religious ecumenism are limited. We are compelled by the Gospel and are ready to commit ourselves to the journey towards reconciliation and

---

[1] John Lucal, 'The Berlin Wall, 1992 and beyond', The Way 31/1, January 1991, p 56

[2] Sioux Indian Proverb, Russ Parker, Healing Wounded History, Darton, Longman and Todd, London, 2001 P 122

[3] John Paul Lederach, The Journey Toward Reconciliation, Herald Press, Ontario, Canada, 1999, P 14

[4] LLRC is the Lessons Learnt and Reconciliation Commission appointed by the President of Sri Lanka.

[5] LLRC Report, Nov 2011, Sri Lanka, C R de Silva – President

peace, because it is correct according to our religious teachings. The end of our journey may not be assured or sure, but there are no short cuts for this in our understanding of Ecumenism especially in Asia, because of its nature of diversity and plurality.

It is significant for all to know that peace is not just the absence of war. Sustainable peace can be ensured only through negotiations and just and equitable resolutions on behalf of people. Peace is never made but it is always in the making. Such justice and equality is necessary for all ethnic, religious, regional, social and political sectors within communities.[6]

Peace is a spiritual, a theological as well as a juridical concept. It may look impossible, but we have a calling to change the sense of possibility in creating the space for peace, however slowly it may be but gathering momentum towards reconciliation by transforming relationships. Negotiated agreements alone will not make peace but people do. That is why relationships are valuable and for this purpose, it will be necessary for us to understand how conflicts emerge. They are not created by God. One of the most common ways which leads to conflicts in the Asian context is by the unconcerned and forceful domination of one group over the other for their own gains. By such action generally there will be the curtailing of opportunities and freedom of the weaker group.

In the following sections let us try to understand, some of the causes that can lead to conflicts that end up in wars and the respective remedies or ways to manage such conflicts, seen ecumenically in the widest sense of the word.

Management of Conflicts

Denying of an identity of any community by consecutive harmful steps will tend to make communities into non-entities. Depravation and continued suppression will lead to aggravated conflicts. Every such conflict has specific causes that have led to such reality, which generally tends to end up in civil wars. More and more attention has to be given to the preservation and the nurturing of identities of people and communities. All communities will have to learn to respect and care for identities, as they are God given and are unique for each person or the community. Therefore Ecumenism should foster a sense of belonging to all peoples and communities irrespective of language ,[7] and transcending ethnicity, race or religion.

There often is also unequal distribution of resources to some of the regions in many countries. Invariably such regions are those with minority or weaker communities, who do not possess the bargaining power for getting a bigger share. In many cases this is not limited only to financial and other social resources but ends up in the unequal delegation of power to the regions, depriving them of the opportunity of decision making for themselves. Instead regions or ethnic groups in minority situations then are compelled to depend on the mercy and the generosity if any of decision makers in the centre, and thereby the fundamental right of the community is denied or suppressed, as can be seen in many of the countries in the Asia, if not in all.

Such unequal distribution will lead to even more lack of resources in the periphery for the use of every one. It was St Chrysostom who once said that God has provided sufficiently for the sharing of all in God's creation but God has not provided sufficiently to satisfy the greed of a small section of the creation. It is a basic responsibility of any regime to protect, nurture and provide for all under its care. It is in that process

---

[6] The urgent need is to foster a sense of belonging to all peoples and communities irrespective of language, ethnicity, race or religion. The goal should be the harmony and reconciliation for sustainable peace and prosperity through improved intercommunal relationships based on trust, equality, confidence and mutual benefit.

[7] Identity is also linked up with the language they speak, read, write and communicate with and the geographical area to which people belong. Very often in the Asian context we have observed some attempts to uproot people and to demolish, change and disregard identities by conscious changing of the demography of the respective geographical areas, as we see in the post war context in the North and the East of Sri Lanka.

that we can often see that once there is no fully equal sharing of the limited resources available this is leading to harsh but reasonable reactions from the victims. It has never been easy to control such sentiments and emotions among people and their mobilization against such injustice. This has also led to the emergence of leaders who may have exhausted all means of peaceful actions to achieve their due share. It has always been in such situations that violence and forceful means have overtaken. We have observed many times where people have opted for non-violent action to invite attention of the regimes to their immediate problems, as it had taken place with the 'Satyagrahas' in the initial stages in Sri Lanka. Frustration has crept into the minds of the polity when there was the continued experience of their respective politicians, letting them down in all instances and using them through false promises and hopes, for their personal gains, thereby betraying the people's trust. Thus we see that the conflictual situations have become unavoidable for the deprived people, but the deprived people themselves are never the only cause, even though the ultimate results of their conflicts for such people often have been disastrous.

Disastrous situations which emerge over the years due to conflicts and wars have been characterized by separation, bitterness, hatred, lack of trust and confidence in each other, frustration, broken relationships and drifting away from each other and eventual hopelessness. Accompanying this there has been the added burden of the physical destruction of infrastructure, property and livelihoods leading to displacement, separation of families, disappearances. Thus the whole fabric of the society has been destroyed as it was the case in Afghanistan and Sri Lanka. The whole community will be engulfed in fear and this fear psychosis will spread to all aspects of life in any nation. With all such negative results, no person can expect to see any signs of the original causes any more that led to the conflict or the war in order to be properly dealt with. Such causes will continue to remain unattended as the survival games for the respective regimes have taken precedence. Regimes will probably claim victory in a conflict, but it will be a valuable lesson for all concerned to learn, that in the end there will not be any clear victors in any conflict, as shown in many occasions in the history. On the contrary all parties will be losers if violent solutions have prevailed. For example in the Sri Lankan context it is commonly stated nowadays that, 'the government and the armed forces may have claimed the land by a military procedure but they have certainly lost the people'. According to them the war may have ended, but certainly the conflict as such has not yet ended. That is not what people would really expect from a post-conflict situation which should be real reconciliation and better balancing of power and chances for life. Any lasting resolution of any conflict needs a win-win situation for all parties of the conflict in order to provide the basis for a lasting peace.

Reconciliation and Healing

It is in this context that we need reconciliation. Hannah Arendt commented, "Human societies could not exist without forgiveness and the public acts of contrition and confession that make reconciliation possible". [8] It will not be a 'once and for all' event but a continuing journey and a movement. It will be a process, a way of living and working. That will take time depending on the reality of the respective specific situations.[9]

It is important for us to understand the teaching on reconciliation in different religious traditions, as the Asian context is a manifestation of the plurality of religiosity. The scope of this paper will not permit to explore at least the basic understanding on reconciliation in all religions. Our attempt should be to establish the position taken by each tradition and if such concepts are not available in any of the religions, to explore the closest to reconciliation that we can identify, for the common purpose of creating trust and confidence

[8] Hannah Arendt, The Human Condition, The University of Chicago Press, 1958, p 236f

[9] The process will be a long and a hazardous one, with many challenges on the way. In a sense it will be a return to the original peaceful situation, if there was any, but the only difficulty will be to create the political will that is necessary to achieve such invaluable reality on the part of those who wield power and make decisions.

by rebuilding relationships. If there are differences of understanding, it will be necessary to explore such differences and look for common grounds. There is no doubt that we will be able to identify many resources for building trust and creating peace in all religions for this purpose. In this long journey one useful aspect will be to ensure mutual accountability of all to each other.

Accountability

This has been the most difficult part in all the attempts in the past. This does not mean that establishing accountability should be used as an opportunity to point fingers at or blame each other as this will not be of use or benefit to any of the parties to the conflict. However there are other creative ways of establishing accountability in or after conflict situations. Many people together with their families continue to suffer because they do not know and receive any information of their loved ones who have suffered as victims. Lack of information on the life of friends and relatives and the constant wrestling with the questions whether the dear ones are still alive is one of the most painful experiences. The fact that some of them have not been able to give the final religious rights to the loved ones themselves is a reason for their lingering and painful memory. Such victims need to have the chance to begin anew. It is a dire necessity to provide opportunities for them to cry out and forget the bitter experiences, which in itself can become a healing factor. If not they are bound to hang on to such feelings and emotions, for a long period of time.

Such healing is necessary for any community to resurrect after a conflict or a war. An important dimension that will facilitate such healing process is to create space for the victims to relate their stories to others. Many compassionate and sympathetic listening ears are essential for this process. Dietrich Bonhoeffer once said: the beginning of love for the brethren is learning to listen to them. A way of collecting these stories will help in formulating the authentic history of the people and the nation. It is difficult for us to believe that history can be erased or can be misrepresented. It was Milan Kundera who said, *"I remember, therefore I am. .... The first step in liquidating a people is to erase it's memory".* [10] That is not what we need in any of our situations. [11]

It is the desire of any human person to look for the truth or to unravel the truth. However the experience has been that those in authority will make every effort to suppress the truth, if that is not in their favor. We have seen this happening over many decades and centuries, and the truth has always been the casualty. Therefore the revelation of the truth is an integral part of any reconciliation and healing process.

Confession and Forgiveness

We are all conscious that healing and reconciliation in the Christian understanding demands repentance, apology and forgiveness. The creative response to such approach will be to offer compensation both materially and otherwise. If our concern is for Religious Ecumenism at this stage, it will be necessary to understand the concepts of forgiveness in all religious traditions. If such concepts are not available, we need to look for what is available that will suit the purpose. The understandings and the emphases may differ from each other. That difference of the concepts of forgiveness itself will be an opportunity as there will be more options, ways and methods to deal with the complex and diverse realities of the community, in order to reach the ultimate aim.

One of the main concerns and the final aims of this process will be to ensure that such conflicts will not be repeated again. As much as we need to build good will, understanding and harmony among and within

[10] Milan Kundera, The Book of Laughter and Forgetting, trans. M.Heim, Harmondsworth, Penguin, 1983, p 159

[11] It is a fact that most written histories are those of the dominant groups written according to them, to fulfill their needs and plans. However it remains the responsibility of the contemporary community to ensure that the truth is not allowed to be erased, suppressed or warped.

the communities, we also need to provide the necessary facilities to nurture such an environment. This task is very much in the hands of the majority community. While the majority community stretches the Olive branch first, the responsibility for changing unjust systems and social structures and creating new and more favorable and harmonious systems and structures for the future too will be in their hands. That will enhance the trust and confidence in each other and contributes enormously to the healing process. We should also work hard to create governance, administrative and social structures that create and foster interdependence among the different communities. The official policy on reconciliation in Sri Lanka emphasizes this aspect.[12] It has to further emphasize the quality of good governance, including much care and concern for the victims of the conflict which will be the only way to establish permanent, if not lasting and sustainable peace and love of each other again.

Ecumenical Learning to Become Agents for Reconciliation and Healing

The thirteenth general assembly of the Christian Conference of Asia in Kuala Lumpur 2010 was on the theme, "Called to Prophesy, Reconcile and Heal" and the assembly study material, bible studies, key presentations and the worship provided a wide range of insights that are relevant for this process in Asia. CCA had chosen this theme because "deep-seated differences over political and economic systems, ethnicity, gender, religion, beliefs and cultural traditions have prevented [Asian] countries from seeking and working towards a shared destiny," as former CCA general secretary Dr Prawate Khid-arn has said.

Planned as a two-week intensive course the Asian Ecumenical Course (AEC) was one of the highlights, if not a turning point in every participant's faith journey during the CCA conference. Participants shared life stories, social realities where each one grew up, and the big role the church had played in their formation. The Church, they learned, has an important role to play in the societies in ensuring peaceful co-existence and equity of resources. The unity of the Church is a powerful witness of the message of love.

Participants were challenged to be active partners and agents in the ecumenical movement as it is an evangelical imperative to bring people to Christ. They were reminded of Jesus' prayer for unity and to focus on the Church's efforts on things that unite. People of other faiths are not objects of conversion but people whose religious beliefs must be respected. At the AEC they were taught also to uphold the Asia-ness of the Christian practice in making use of their own songs and instruments in worship and in contextualizing the Bible in Asian realities. They were helped to celebrate the gift of their diversity and affirm their Asian spirituality.

The CCA assembly encouraged Christians in Asia to be prophets, reconcilers and healers and thus dare to speak against repression of the people in Asia and dare speak against disunity that crippled the Church to action, losing its powerful witness. Christian churches in Asia were called to dare speak against globalization that promotes consumerism and dehumanizes Asian communities and destroys the environment. They are called to speak love to communities of other faiths and to speak peace based on justice to abound in Asia as was never known before.

Metropolitan Coorilos said at this occasion: "In the midst of old and new forms of division that perpetuate enmity, discrimination, domination and exploitation, we are called to prophesy, to reconcile and to heal." It was the death on a Cross that brought Christians together, he said. The Cross of Christ alone has dismantled all walls of hostility and discrimination. Reconciliation in the modern globalised context therefore is more than mere conciliation. It is more than reconciling with the status quo; it is not about reconciling with the normative and dominant in an unjust society. But reconciliation is a trinitarian state of

---

[12] Policy on Reconciliation in Sri Lanka, states as part of the strategy, *"This will help create the feeling in each of the communities that their progress or downfall is inextricably linked with the process or downfall of the other communities and thus help to inculcate a strong sense of nationhood"*

being, consisting of a perfect or harmonious relationship between God, humanity and nature. "It is about restoring and reinstating just values and relationships. It is about reclaiming justice, peace and integrity of creation."

Discussions in the forum on a culture of violence and impunity touched on how attempts at reconciliation without justice resulted in impunity and the perpetuation of violent cultures. For instance, Timorese who fought with the Indonesians and no easy answer: reconciliation requires justice committed offences in the struggle for independence had been freed. That might have appeased Indonesia, but it did not build reconciliation among the Timorese. Justice was not seen to happen. The healing of memories forum said healing involved forgiveness, acceptance, repentance, and a safe space to share of pain and suffering. There were two aspects of memories, it said: collective and individual memories of healing. It said there was no healing without forgiveness from the oppressed and repentance for oppressor. "Healing is restoration of justice. It is a process of liberation and transformation between the oppressed and oppressors."

Different Asian Contexts for Reconciliation and Healing of Memories

It is important at this stage to understand how healing of memories is needed and done in some of the other affected countries in Asia. I intend to look at the experiences of Cambodia, Vietnam and the Philippines:

Cambodia

The horrific dimensions of the Cambodian genocide of 1975-1979, in which approximately 1.7 million people lost their lives (21% of the country's population), and which was one of the worst human tragedies of the last century, is widely known in Asia.[13] Within the peace agreements that were part of the reconciliation process in Cambodia the extent of the tragedy was formally recognized and respect for human rights was enshrined. In detail however, the agreements made focused mainly on political issues related to the cessation of hostilities, the provision for national elections and the rehabilitation and reconstruction of Cambodia.

It seems that the understanding of "reconciliation" was reduced and considered synonymous with the involvement of the four factions in Cambodia in a free and fair election. For the Cambodian people at that time, however, reconciliation was largely equated with the cessation of hostilities and the return of refugees. More complex questions of justice and reintegration were yet to become apparent. The defectors were allowed to resettle in and around the semi-autonomous zone of Pailin, a gem- and timber-rich area near the Thai border.

Currently, the main focus of reconciliation efforts in the Cambodian context is the ongoing issue of the creation of an Extraordinary Chamber of the Criminal Courts of Cambodia. The UN-Cambodian Khmer Rouge Tribunal, as it is more popularly known, would seek to try surviving key high-ranking members of the Democratic Kampuchea regime. For this a number of political deals were struck between the government and the former Khmer Rouge. Most notably, an amnesty was granted to Leng Sary for a death sentence imposed under a widely discredited Vietnamese-convened war crimes tribunal held in August 1979. At these forums, all sides, including the former Khmer Rouge, stated the need for truth, justice, healing and national reconciliation.

Each party has its own version of what happened: there is a particular truth according to the Khmer Rouge, the government, the international community and ordinary Cambodians. If a reconciliation process is to move forward and be seen to be trustworthy, each of these truths had to be accommodated to the satisfaction of all parties. From the discussions it was also clear that a tribunal is only one part of a

---

[13] See further information for instance on: http://www.yale.edu/cgp/

comprehensive process of reconciliation. In addition, there were almost no calls for reparation. It seemed that this was too abstract a concept of reconciliation to consider in a situation when the truth was not yet even known. Most people simply wished to be free of their suffering and return to the family life that was so cruelly interrupted through the refugee experience and policies of forced displacement. For them, real reconciliation would only be found when trust returns between individuals: when "they can smile at and trust each other again".

One potential path for finding this reconciliation is that of the national religion, Buddhism, to which at least 90 per cent of Cambodians are said to subscribe and which has a powerful influence in daily life. Buddhism has at its heart messages of compassion and reconciliation. Many Westerners perceive Buddhism as a doctrine of acceptance, which effectively hampers social change. A noted Khmer Buddhist monk, Yos Hut Khemacaro, explains that Khmer Buddhism in particular, arising as it does from an agrarian society that places high value on patron-client relationships and harmony, has provided "a strong disincentive among monks and the wider population to challenge the social order". Yet, despite these cultural constraints, he goes on to argue that the practice of the Dhamma (teachings of the Buddha) can lead to positive social action.

One practical example of this is the Dhammayietra, or annual "Pilgrimage of Truth" marches, which began in 1992. The first of these "Pilgrimage of Truth" marches saw hundreds of refugees who had been living in camps along the Thai-Cambodian border return to their homeland as they marched for four weeks from Battambang in the north-west to Phnom Penh. The spiritual leader of the pilgrimages, Maha Ghosananda, nominated three times for the Nobel Peace Prize, also made explicit the idea that the adoption of a Buddhist process does not mean that justice will not be served. He argues that reconciliation "does not mean that we surrender our rights and conditions" but instead that "we use love" to address these questions.

If Buddhism is to prove a useful tool in the process of national reconciliation, we must therefore ensure that it does not become as politicized as other aspects of reconciliation have. To avoid politicization Yos Hut Khemacaro advocates following the "Middle Path", the traditional metaphor for the Buddhist way – neither joining the fight nor hiding from it. The Middle Path of non-violence and compassion provides a model for solving undoubtedly political problems outside the adversarial framework implicit in partisanship. As these ideas arise from traditional Khmer concepts, they can help the Cambodian people to find their own peace instead of feeling that their problems can only be solved by outsiders.

Most closely linked to the question of the Khmer Rouge trial is the project of the Documentation Center of Cambodia.[14] Originating in an academic programme of Yale University, USA, this now independent Cambodian-run centre serves as a permanent resource for providing information about the Khmer Rouge, both in order to support potential litigants and to prevent such a tragedy happening in the future again. Its mission is perhaps best summed up in the title of its regular publication "Searching for the Truth". By stressing the importance of the truth above all else this project has chosen the non-partisan Middle Path in dealing with these extremely sensitive issues.

Until now, ordinary people have relied on their understanding of the law of karma and their instinct for survival as their means of healing, but many of these problems have undoubtedly been made worse by the lack of adequate treatment services or facilities. This problem has been acknowledged, and Cambodians are learning to deal with the question of mental illness in more constructive and healing ways. The work being done by some health sector organizations and emerging psychiatric facilities is another important step forward in facing up to the past.

Cambodians need to overcome the deep-seated mistrust of, and animosity towards each other that arose as the consequence of the Khmer Rouge and their aftermath. Open discussion, improvement in social

---

[14] See: http://www.dccam.org/

justice and human rights, education and health care for all – these are all fundamental to a step-by-step process of building mutual trust and understanding.

The work of the tribunal in Cambodia[15] is very important as it will uncover the truth and thus educate people about the past, provide justice for the victims, and promote the return of the rule of law to Cambodia. There must also be a role for ordinary people to play in reaching reconciliation at the level of everyday life, where old wounds are still deeply felt. The forums were a step, as are the other grass-roots programmes described here. Above all, these steps should be taken along the Middle Path, in full consultation with the Cambodian people.[16]

Vietnam

With the experiences in Cambodia in the background we can see the reality in Vietnam which has had some specific areas of emphasis in relation to the given historic conditions of the Vietnamese context. It is in the Vietnamese context that for reconciliation processes we can learn that research on narratives of woundedness and healing is more than simply listening to (more or less) nice stories. There are stories that are *hidden* between the lines; these need to be noticed and retrieved. There are stories that can be *toxic* to be exposed to; these need to be coped with and conceived. But there may be also certain stories that have a truly *healing* quality, stories that can contribute to peace and reconciliation. These three possible qualities of narratives are the focus of the following paragraphs.

A Vietnamese film that was vying for an Oscar, offered a glimpse into how Vietnam and the United States were healing decades-old war wounds, as well as how that war still generates emotional debate today. 'Don't Burn' is based on the wartime diary of 27-year-old Viet Cong physician Dang Thuy Tram, who was shot dead by U.S. soldiers in the early sixties as U.S. military involvement escalated in the country.[17] "Last night I dreamed of peace. I came back and saw everybody. Oh, the dream of peace and independence has burned in the hearts of 30 million people for so long," read part of Tram's diary. Her dream of peace became the core of the movie, whose script was written by Dang Nhat Minh, who also directed it.

There is a highly interesting Swedish research project employing an intergenerational perspective highlighting the different ways in which memories about the war between Vietnam and the USA are engraved in the social and individual body in a northern Vietnamese rural community. The research report from Helle Rydstrøm[18] makes a clear distinction between the war and the post-war generations in Vietnam in relation to their attempts to remember and/or forget brutality, sorrow and anger and to come to terms with what in Vietnam is referred to as the American War:

> "The war between the USA and Vietnam was experienced by the adult generations, who have embodied their war memories as a kind of poisonous knowledge that cannot easily be erased. Adults carry with them the memories and pains. To 'forget the past and look toward the future', therefore, remains an emotionally laden process of contradiction and ambivalence. Older generations remember how the war brutally and dramatically disrupted their lives. By narrating selected war memories to the younger generations, parents and grandparents can reconstruct themselves in relation to a certain period of life when they felt deeply disempowered." In looking to younger generations of North Vietnamese people however the research project realized that "Younger generations are not burdened by embodied war memories, because they did not experience the war themselves.

---

15 See: http://www.cambodiatribunal.org/

16 Reconciliation in Cambodia: Politics, Culture and Religion, Reconciliation AfterViolent Conflict – Handbook Series, International Institute for Democracy and Electoral Assistance 2003, Pg 49-53, Sweden.

17 See: http://www.imdb.com/title/tt1495738/

18 See: Helle Rydstrøm, Proximity and Distance: Vietnamese Memories of the War with the USA, in: Anthropological Forum Vol. 17, No. 1, March 2007, 21-39, see: http://www.lucram.lu.se/upload/LUPDF/Genusvetenskap/Helle_Proximity.pdf

> Therefore, it may be possible to 'not remember the past of war'. For most young Thinh Tri people, the past belongs to the past and can be addressed with less ambivalence and ambiguity than is possible for those inhabitants who survived the war. Young inhabitants attempt to capture and express the gap between the brutal war memories of their parents and grandparents on the one hand, and their own experiences of being engaged in a national process of seeking reconciliation with the USA, on the other. Hence, while the generations of parents and grandparents embody the American War, young people, rather, embody reconciliation. Young postwar Thinh Tri inhabitants face a double-sided process of reconciliation in which they have to reconcile themselves not only to the American War and the violence, pain and bitterness it caused but also to the gap between themselves and their parents and grandparents with regard to the extent to which they can 'forget the past and look toward the future'."[19]

The research thus sheds a light on the inter-generational differences in the needs for reconciliation and for listening to the memories of people in different generations. The process of healing of memories and reconciliation in the Vietnamese context is far from being finalized or completed.

Philippines

The context for healing of memories and reconciliation in the Philippines again is rather different.[20] One very interesting case study can be shared: The all-out-war in 2000 which displaced over a million civilians in Mindanao[21] brought the church in Pikit into a painful process of transformation. The parish, which was very exclusive at that time, was divided on whether or not to extend humanitarian assistance to Muslim evacuees who were mainly families of rebels and whom the Christians considered as their enemies. In war even the civilians take sides – the Christians with the military and the Muslims with the rebels. And so, even after the war was over in the battlefields, the silent war went on in the hearts of the people of Mindanao.

It was with the symposium 'Between War and Peace'[22] that the parish decided to break the walls of apathy and mediocrity arguing that helping the poor is not a matter of choice, but a duty and binding social responsibility. The parish organized the Disaster Response Team (DRT) composed mainly of young Muslim and Christian volunteers. Whether under the scorching heat of the sun or the pouring rain and amidst gunfire, these young volunteers distributed food to thousands of starving evacuees in various evacuation centers, effectively demolishing the myth that the war in Mindanao was religious in nature. They would eat together at the same table, pray together and even cry together when we heard that another baby had died in the evacuation center. In order to imagine and concretize that new vision of breaking the walls of apathy, the church initiated a series of consultations in the Basic Ecclesial Communities or BECs for the purpose of changing the vision-mission of the parish. The result was a new and inclusive vision that integrated two very important elements based in the context of the changing realities in Mindanao and in the world. One element was inter-religious dialogue and the other was peace-building. The parish has since created a special ministry with 12 full-time staff composed of Muslims and Christians who implement dialogue and peace-building activities at diocesan, parish and grassroots levels.[23]

---

[19] Helle Rydstrøm, Proximity and Distance: Vietnamese Memories of the War with the USA, in: Anthropological Forum Vol. 17, No. 1, March 2007, page 36

[20] For a detailed study on the historical context of Christian Muslim relations in Mindanao see:
Amado L. Picardal, Christian-Muslim Dialogue in Mindanao, Asian Christian Review vol.2 no.2&3 (Summer/Winter 2008), page 54ff

[21] See for details: http://www.gmanetwork.com/news/story/186572/opinion/blogs/all-out-war-in-mindanao; http://en.wikipedia.org/wiki/Presidency_of_Joseph_Estrada#War_against_the_MILF

[22] See: http://www.heks.ch/fileadmin/user_upload/domain1/1_news_and_service/pdf/Materialien/HEKS_Reader_Between_War_And_Peace.pdf

[23] See also: http://www.cdainc.com/cdawww/pdf/casestudy/steps_philippines_case_study_Pdf.pdf

Building bridges rather than walls was a necessity in that type of situation. Since then, the parish has been conducting seminars on the Cultures of Peace and Dialogue. These seminars, which normally last for three days, were attended by Muslims, Christians and Indigenous people. Included in the training module were topics on the history of Mindanao, conflict analysis, mediation and negotiation skills, cultural appreciation, inter-religious dialogue, and healing of biases and prejudices. The main objective of the seminar was basically to restore the broken relationship of people and to let the participants realize that it is possible for Christians, Muslims and indigenous tribes to work together for peace and reconciliation, even if a lot of people in Mindanao believe otherwise. They also conducted this seminar for members of the military and para-military troops and former Muslim rebels.

Creating public spaces for community building and reconciliation was another step. The parish has organized several villages inhabited by Muslims, Christians and indigenous people as part of a program for rebuilding the communities affected by war. Representatives of the parish along with local Muslim peace advocates negotiated with the military and MILF rebels not to make these villages a battleground for their forces. It was a long process that ended up with the commitment of both. Then, several socio-economic projects and peace-building activities were implemented in these villages with the aid of several funding agencies including HEKS and IRENE foundation. These communities are now called, 'Space for Peace and Children as Zones of Peace' communities where the local inhabitants are trying to live together in harmony.[24]

Hans Kung said, "There is no peace in the world as long as there is no peace among religions. And there is no peace among religions as long as there is no genuine dialogue among believers". The case study of Pikit can show how churches are transformed as soon as they are oriented not so much to build their own kingdom but to build the kingdom of God and to be instruments of God's goodness to every human being. In Pikit, Christians dared to plant the seed of goodness not even knowing if and when it is going to grow.

It is important to recognize that a peace process in Mindanao has not been merely a question of negotiations between the government and the MILF. Churches underlined that in addition to these high-level talks there must be discussions and processes of healing of memories and reconciliation amongst ordinary people in the communities equally involving the Muslim and Christian populations of contexts like that one of Mindanao. The objective of various current efforts in Mindanao has been to weave a «carpet of peace» at local level and only this broad-based process is able to help overcome the hatred, prejudices and suspicions that many people still harbor and to make way for reconciliation as a basis for a sustainable peace. The Mindanao Peace Weavers has become the largest coalition of a total of eight peace networks.[25] It is a consortium of churches, non-governmental organizations, academic circles, human rights groups and grassroots organizations, all working towards a peaceful resolution to the conflict in Mindanao. The coalition seeks to engage the government and the rebels in formal peace talks, implements civilian-led ceasefire monitoring and attempts to expand the peace zones. One of the eight peace networks is the Mindanao People's Caucus (MPC). Mindanao People's Caucus (MPC) – a Consortium of NGOs MPC is composed of twelve non-governmental organizations working in the areas where the major camps of the MILF are located.[26]

It was very successful to establish peace zones – villages of peace, where Muslims and Christians coexist. With the support of the Peace Weavers and NGOs the people in the most affected villages declared

---

[24] See again: http://www.cdainc.com/cdawww/pdf/casestudy/steps_philippines_case_study_Pdf.pdf; see also: Special Zone for Peace and Development Social Fund for Mindanao, in: http://www.chanrobles.com/legal3szopad.html#.UOtU56xrTYg

[25] See: http://www.c-r.org/organisation-profile/mindanao-peace-weavers and: http://mindanaopeaceweavers.org/salikami/

[26] Balay, a local partner organization of HEKS, is part of this network and implements livelihood projects in the peace zone of Pikit. The main objective of the MPC is to negotiate between the government, the military and the MILF.

their villages «peace villages». After long and difficult negotiations, the military and the rebels agreed to respect the «peace declaration» of the people living in these zones. These zones are now called «Space for Peace and Children as Zones of Peace» in which the villagers, Muslim, Christian and indigenous, pledge to live together in harmony and often celebrate religious festivities such as Christmas or Ramadan together – one convincing example of successful processes of healing of memories and reconstruction of harmonious relationships.

Resources, Steps and Tools for Reconciliation and Healing of Memories

What we can learn from these different Asian contexts: In the modern world challenges of conflictual situations in many regions call for a journey of healing of memories which includes conflict transformation. In this process a deliberate redeeming of the past is important. For example the history of Fr Michael Lapsley in South Africa who has been transformed from being a freedom fighter to a healer is significant for all other churches in this regard.[27] Deeper knowledge of conflicts and peace is a useful tool for creative peace-making. In this task the truth and reconciliation commissions and similar programmes and projects will enhance the capacity to reach the envisaged task. Information about ministries of reconciliation in different parts of the world, such as the Community of the Cross of Nails in Coventry and the work of the Cross of Nails centres[28] across the world are helpful in setting the path for this valuable ministry. It is incumbent upon us to look for the already existing models for conflict transformation and healing in the world, together with the resources available as functional tools.

For those engaged in education it is very valuable to reaffirm theological education as a tool for embedding a peace, justice and healing consciousness in the lives of the individuals as well as in the church. This will have to develop to a just, participatory and a sustainable society, with new dimensions for the contemporary challenges.

Key dimensions to be reflected and considered in any national or regional process of education and learning for reconciliation and healing of memories can be summarized as follows:

(a) Legislative reform

The process of recommending specific services to deal with the particular and extensive effects of trauma and grief requires secured legislative backing through the setting up of the National Healing and Reconciliation Commissions.

(b) Political will

Raking past atrocities and human rights abuses is an excruciating exercise. If badly managed, the exercise could backfire, and further widen the chasm in an already politically-fractured community. Indeed, this fear often deters the introduction of 'just' reconciliation processes where victims feel a genuine sense of satisfaction over the claimed entitlements. Hence, the political will to promote genuine reconciliation is paramount.

(c) Transformative and restorative justice

This is based on the understanding that healing and the transformation of harm is essential for the wholeness of people's lives. Emphasis here is on repairing harm caused or revealed by criminal behavior and is best achieved through cooperative processes that includes all stakeholders. The fundamental principles are that justice requires that different categories of people work together to restore those who

[27] See: http://www.healing-memories.org/

[28] See: http://www.crossofnails.org/about-us/

have been injured and that those most directly involved and affected should have the opportunity to participate fully in the response programme

(d) Civil society engagement

A successful national healing and reconciliation process requires meaningful engagement of civil society and the public at large. This is because a process aimed at responding to people's needs must necessarily involve the people affected by the conflict, especially at grassroots level. In this context, civil society organizations can play a vital role in monitoring the implementation of the reconciliation and healing processes. In this way, their work can give greater legitimacy to the healing process, thereby reinforcing the principle of bottom-up approaches which guarantee sustainable and transformative peace.

(e) Consensus building

It is essential to achieve widespread agreement on all aspects of national reconciliation. The process must be devoid of partisanship with those favoring and opposing a formal reconciliation process exhibiting political tolerance. Consensus and legitimacy of the outcome of the national reconciliation exercise will be enhanced where the government, human rights organizations and other interest groups work together to develop the framework and other key aspects of the national healing and reconciliation project.

(f) Truth-telling

True reconciliation cannot occur when the truths about past wrongs are not told. Truth-telling encourages the verification of past repressive actions and incidents by individuals and government. The process may also challenge stories widely, but inaccurately, circulated in the public domain as rumor. Knowledge of the truth helps to set the record straight and creates an environment where forgiveness may occur.

(g) Education for national healing and reconciliation

There is a need to educate the general community about the experiences of trauma and grief as well as their extent and effect on women, men, children, the elderly and the disabled. There is also a need for re-education on how communities that have experienced violent conflicts can coexist in peace and harmony. Educational programmes should be linked to processes of trauma-healing and reconciliation and should be acknowledged by the wider community, as affirmation of a public commitment to the broader healing process agenda.

(h) Research on trauma and grief

The centrality of the experiences of trauma and grief for the victimized people mean that these aspects should be informed by participatory research aimed at assessing the level of distress and disorder among the people. Issues of grief and bereavement as a result of violence and how these impact on people's wellbeing would be central to a holistic healing process.

(i) Counseling of trauma and grief

The availability of counseling services to help people deal with their experiences of trauma and grief as well as specific counseling to do with particular situations is important. Examples of such situations include those that are consequent upon abduction and disappearances, deaths in custody as well as forced separation of children from parents and guardians. Counseling formats would need to be specifically developed in holistic and culturally appropriate ways to deal with longstanding, past or profound traumatic experiences. Other useful indigenous initiatives include narrative therapy and family therapy in which affected people tell their stories about the violence and its consequences on themselves and family members which will help the younger generation understand what their parents and grandparents lived through as well as assist in the rebuilding of fractured societal relationships.

(j) Special healing places and community intervention programmes

There could be value in the development of special places of healing such as trauma healing centres and special nature parks where people can visit as part of the relaxation and therapeutic process, where people could visit and stay at such recreational places as part of the healing process. Such promotional projects would strengthen sustainable peace by furthering social investment and the unification of the social fabric of society. Thus, peace through community reconciliation, engagement and empowerment can yield powerful results.

(k) Memorialisation and ritualization

Taking cognizance of the cultural context and the memorialisation of the past is important. This would require physical reminders in the form of monuments, ceremonies, memorials or other ritual occasions aimed at contributing to the acknowledgement.

(l) Funding

One factor that often hinders the progress and success of reconciliation and national healing projects is funding. Reconciliation exercises are not only expensive, but time-consuming, emotional ventures that demand patience and resilience. Furthermore, apart from the operational budget, reconciliation must also have a human face. Words must be accompanied by actions such as restitution and compensation, but failure in most national healing and reconciliation projects has been attributed to lack of resources.

The Teaching of Ecumenism as Part of the Healing of Memories

Teaching of Ecumenism in a conflictual or a post conflictual situation has many challenges in addition to the above understanding of conflicts and their subsequent management. The teaching of ecumenism has both a historical and a contextual dimension, involving both a historical awareness of the root causes of a social or ethnic conflict and historic unfolding of identities which has contributed to it as well as a contextual understanding of the longing for identity in different social and political settings. Knowing about the past of ethnic, religious or denominational identities is a pre-condition for what types of identity building are transmitted into the future and whether these types of identity will reinforce or repeat past conflicts again or whether they can contribute to a lasting peace and reconciliation. It has been said on another occasion: 'The more an individual understand his or her past, the greater the possibility that he or she will be able to control what is passed on to the next generation.' (David Carder) The notion of democracy dictates that a balance must be achieved for this interaction of different ethnic, religious and cultural identities within a given region in a manner that is not at the expense of any community. Therefore teaching of ecumenism needs to contribute to more understanding and look beyond limited identity concepts. It needs to stress t*he* common need for integration in the society as a whole, not just for one part. In the case and history of Sri Lanka one can learn how to overcome the root causes of the conflict which is a result of failed aspirations and expectations and needs solutions which are satisfactory to all the communities and peoples of Sri Lanka. Ecumenical teaching and orientations for future generations have a profound responsibility to dispel widespread mutual suspicions and wield all communities into and within the fabric of one nation. The LLRC report of November 2011 had stated that, '... despite the lapse of two years since the ending of the conflict, the violence, the suspicion and sense of discrimination are still prevalent in social and political life. Delay in the implementation of a clearly focused post conflict peace building agenda may have contributed to this situation.' There is a huge task therefore for proper education and awareness building which would build up and reconstruct both individual identities and cultural diversity in a post-war situation and foster a sense of belonging to all peoples and communities irrespective of language, ethnicity, race or religion. The overarching goal of ecumenical education for peace and reconciliation should be the harmony in society and reconciliation for sustainable peace and prosperity through improved inter-communal relationships based on trust, equality, confidence and mutual benefit. The LLRC had stated that people from all corners of the country which came before the commission gave an almost palpable impression that this is Sri Lanka's moment of opportunity for Sri Lankans to chart a vision for a harmonious future for our nation and a wholesome Sri Lanka's identity. The process of education for reconciliation and healing of memories should also be accompanied by hard work to create governance, administrative and social structures that create and foster interdependence among themselves. This will help to create and enhance the feeling in each of the communities that their progress or downfall is inextricably linked with the process or downfall of the other communities and thus help to inculcate a strong sense of nationhood among Sri Lankans. It thus can only be underlined that reconciliation and healing of memories is one of the most crucial issues for many Asian societies and not the least Sri Lanka itself, as it is obvious that the addressing and resolution of political issues affecting the minorities is the most important part of a strategy to achieve national reconciliation which is the only way leading to proper and harmonious nation building in longer perspectives.

Bibliography

Achebe, Chinua. Things Fall Apart, Oxford, Heinemann International Publishing, 1988.

Hannah Arendt, The Human Condition, The University of Chicago Press, 1958

Chandler, David. Brother Number One: A Political Biography of Pol Pot, Boulder, Colo, Westview Press, 1992.

Gandhi, Mahathma. An Autobiography, The Story of My Experiments with Truth, Ahmedabad, India; The Navajivan Press, 1976.

George K M, The Silent Roots. Geneva: WCC Publications.

The Holy Bible, NRSV, Mowbray, London, 1989

Milan Kundera, The Book of Laughter and Forgetting, trans. M.Heim, Harmondsworth, Penguin, 1983

John Paul Lederach, The Journey Toward Reconciliation, Herald Press, Ontario, Canada, 1999

LLRC Report, Nov 2011, Sri Lanka, C R de Silva – President

Anne Long, Listening, 1990, Darton, Longman and Todd, London.

John Lucal, 'The Berlin Wall, 1992 and beyond', The Way 31/1, January 1991

Russ Parker, Healing Wounded History, Darton, Longman and Todd, London, 2001

Russ Parker, Forgiveness is Healing, London, DLT, 1993

Russ Parker, The Wild Spirit, London, Triangle, 1997

Reconciliation in Cambodia: Politics, Culture and Religion, Reconciliation After Violent Conflict – Handbook Series, International Institute for Democracy and Electoral Assistance 2003

Rajiva Wijesinha and Salma Yusuf, Sri Lankan Reconciliation, National Policy on Reconciliation: Working Document – Draft One, March 10, 2012, Youth Forum

Sharp, Gene. From Dictatorship to Democracy, The Albert Einstein Institution, East Boston, Massachusetts, 2003

Sharp, Gene. Politics of Non Violent Action, The Albert Einstein Institution, East Boston, Massachusetts, 1973.

Wink, Walter, Engaging the Powers, Discernment and Resistance in a World of Domination, 1992, Augsburg Fortress, USA.

Wink, Walter. When the Powers fall, Philadelphia, Fortress Press, 1998

(33) ECO-JUSTICE AND GLOBAL CLIMATE CHANGE AS AN ISSUE IN ASIAN ECUMENISM

Lee Hong Jung

1. Anthropogenic Global Climate Change

Global Climate Change (GCC) as the result of accumulating greenhouse gas emissions in the atmosphere has been one of the most pressing social and environmental issues of our time: it is the matter of life, and therefore of faith.

GCC is a long-term change in the statistical distribution of weather patterns or the statistical properties of the climate system over periods ranging from decades to millions of years, regardless of cause,which may be limited to a specific region or may occur across the whole Earth.[1] GCC reflects a change in the energy balance of the climate system, i.e. "a change in the relative balance between incoming solar radiation and outgoing infrared radiation from Earth": when this balance changes it is called "radiative forcing," and the processes that cause such changes are called "forcing mechanisms."[2] Forcing mechanisms can be either internal or external: internal forcing mechanisms are natural processes within the climate system itself, and external forcing mechanisms can be either natural or anthropogenic.[3]

GCC is used to refer specifically to climate change caused not by Earths' natural processes but by human activities. The United Nations Framework Convention on Climate Change (UNFCCC) defines climate change as "a change of climate which is attributed directly or indirectly to human activity that alters the composition of the global atmosphere and which is in addition to natural climate variability observed over comparable time periods." In this sense, used especially in the context of environmental policy, GCC is "synonymous with anthropogenic Global Warming."[4]

GCC as anthropogenic Global Warming is the current rise in the average temperature of Earth's oceans and atmosphere and its projected continuation. The scientific consensus is that GCC is largely caused by anthropogenic causes like fossil fuel-intensive energy consumption rather than celestial causes like solar radiation. GCC is occurring and was initiated by human activities: it "is largely irreversible."[5] Of most concern in the anthropogenic factors is the increase in CO2 levels due to emissions from fossil fuel combustion, followed by aerosols (particulate matter in the atmosphere) and cement manufacture. Other factors, including land use, ozone depletion, animal agriculture and deforestation, are also of concern in the roles they play in affecting climate, microclimate, and measures of climate variables.

GCC is human-induced, caused especially by the agro-industrial-economic complex and culture of the global North, which is characterized by the consumerist lifestyles of the elites of the developed and developing worlds: it views that development is commensurate with exploitation of the earth's natural

---

[1] See at http://en.wikipedia.org/wiki/Climate_change

[2] Ibid.

[3] For natural, e.g., changes in solar output, and for anthropogenic, e.g., increased emissions of greenhouse gases.

[4] Ibid., The National Academy of Sciences first used global warming in a 1979 paper called the Charney Report, it said: "if carbon dioxide continues to increase, [we find] no reason to doubt that climate changes will result and no reason to believe that these changes will be negligible." Global warming became more widely popular after 1988 when NASA climate scientist James Hansen used the term in a testimony to Congress. He said: "global warming has reached a level such that we can ascribe with a high degree of confidence a cause and effect relationship between the greenhouse effect and the observed warming."

[5] Cf. Susan Solomon, Gian-Kasper Plattner, Reto Knutti, and Pierre Friedlingstein, *Irreversible Climate Change Due to Carbon Dioxide Emission*, PNAS (Proceedings of the National Academy of Sciences of the United States of America) January 2009, at http://www.pnas.org/content/early/2009/01/28/0812721106.full.pdf+html.

resources. The Northern agro-industrial-economic complex makes CO2 foot-pints on the *oikoumene* in the course of over-production, over-consumption, and over-disuse, labelling all of creation as natural resources and making them as commodities.[6] This view of the Northern agro-industrial-economic complex has been fully reflected in a 500-year western history of human conquest of the whole earth life community.

2. Eco-Injustice: A History of Human Conquest of Life from Colonialism to Globalization

In the history of Columbus and post-Columbus, the western initiatives of 'openness' did not always mean mutual acceptance but more often forceful, uninvited invasions, i.e. conquests of 'otherness'. The 'West' hard heartedly took over the sustainable space and time of various first nations, 'cleansed' them of their diverse ethnicity, and broke down the diverse web of life. This was just a starting point of the history of Western colonialism, which has been a history of eco-genocide and eco-injustice against the whole of the 'earth household' through "the rape of nature"[7]

After Columbus, there have been more than 500 years of conquest and dominance by all means: economic and ecological oppression, patriarchy, racism etc.Throughout the history of the South in particular, the suffering and victimization of life in all creation under the decades of colonial, neo-colonial, and Cold War subjugation has been factual realities. After the Cold War Era, the world order has been directed towards globalization, and in this process the bipolar political economic ideologies have become a unipolar neo-liberal global market ideology. The global free market has become the complex venue where all living beings in the web of life have been turned into commodities.

Globalization is the accelerated integration of capital, production, and markets globally; it is a process driven by the logic of corporate profitability. With its main strategies of liberating the market through privatization, deregulation, and trade liberalization, it requires the unleashing of market forces and the removing or eroding of constraints imposed upon transnational corporations by labor, the society and state.In a real sense, globalization becomes a code name for the transnational 'corporatization' of the world.[8]

Under globalization, the myth that development naturally leads to unlimited growth is definitely exposed in terms of the ever-growing number of people living below the poverty line, in spite of substantial economic growth. The so-called development projects ensure big profits for big business but bring massive displacement for indigenous and aboriginal peoples, and ecological destruction of their lands. As a result, villages and traditional societies are either physically uprooted, or become economically and ecologically impossible to sustain. People are forced off their lands and into the huge slums surrounding major cities, and often witness their children choosing between starvation and crime, or prostitution.

In the South the local economy was rooted in its own soil; producers and consumers were closely linked in a community-based economy integrated with the local ecology. Today, local people are dependent on food and energy from thousands of miles away. The end result of all this long-distance transport of subsidized goods is that the sustainability of local economies is being drastically dismantled, and with it local communities that were once tied together by bonds of interdependence between economy and ecology are destroyed.[9]

---

[6]See WCC, *Statement on Eco-Justice and Ecological Debt* at http://www.oikoumene.org/en/resources/documents/central-committee/geneva-2009/reports-and-documents/report-on-public-issues/statement-on-eco-justice-and-ecological-debt.html

[7] Ernst Ulrich von Weizsacker, *Earth Politics* (London: Zed Books, 1994), p. 8

[8] See John Page, "Globalization Explained" in the Online Articles of the International Society for Ecology and Culture at http://www.isec.org.uk/articles.html

[9] See Helena Norberg-Hodge, "Reclaiming Our Food", and "Bringing the Food Economy Home", in the Online

Globalization is simply incompatible with ecological environmental sustainability. More trade means more transport and more pollution. Although GCC is a genuine and serious threat today, and a drastic reduction in greenhouse gases is needed to halt and reverse it, globalization demands the use of ever-larger quantities of fossil fuels by promoting the culture of over-production, over-consumption and over-disuse. In the South, foreign aid and investment promote infrastructures based on oil, gas and coal, despite the fact that the majority of the South could provide all its energy from renewable sources for a fraction ofthe ecological, cultural and economic cost of fossil fuels.

Globalization consequently also affects the health and food sectors. The continuing rise of poverty-related diseases in the South and the spread of HIV/AIDS, Mad Cow Disease, SARS, Bird Flu, etc. show clear evidence of the critical disorder and disintegration between the earth's ecosystem and human health system. Worst of all, we can no longer trust the food we eat. More public money is put into chemical, energy-intensive agriculture, and research into biotechnology, with the aim of allowing food to be transported even greater distances, survive even greater doses of pesticides, and ultimately to be produced without the troublesome need for farmers.

In short, globalization is a process of separation and disintegration between economy and ecology, health and ecology, history and nature, human and nature, and lifestyle and spirituality, i.e. a path towards a total breakdown of the deep sustainability of the web of life in the 'earth household'.[10]

3. Global Climate Change and Nuclear Renaissance: Human's On-going Death-Dealing Nuclear Foot-Prints

The nuclear possessed state governments and their technocrats – a hegemonic map of the nuclear 'Empire' – have constantly made their nuclear footprints on the *oikoumene* without having any regret. Since the bombings of Hiroshima and Nagasaki, from 1945 to 1998, nuclear weapons have been detonated on 2,053 occasions for testing purposes and demonstrations. An index of nuclear-power accidents documented 956 incidents from 1942 to 2007; and yet another documented more than 30,000 mishaps at US nuclear-power plants alone, many with the potential to have caused serious meltdowns, between the 1979 accident at Three Mile Island in Pennsylvania and 2009.

At the moment 440 nuclear power plants are operating in the world, and if sum up the planned nuclear power plants it will be over 700. In Korea, Japan, and China, respectively 21, 19, 55 nuclear power plants are operating, and near future will exceed total about 200 nuclear power plants. Along with nuclear weapons in North Korea, the North East Asia region will be soon the world most concentrated nuclear zone, and Korea become a nuclear besieged land. Globally more than 10,000 nuclear strategic weapons have been deployed.

When compared to other energy sources, nuclear power ranks higher than oil, coal, and natural gas systems in terms of fatalities, second only to hydro electric dams. Nuclear Fallout called "an ash of death" is nuclear radioactive waste which are in fact an almost inextinguishable fire which contaminate the layer of the earth and living organisms by radiating energy in the forms of radiation and heat. The nuclear detonations release CO2 and other greenhouse gases from burning, followed by more released from decay of dead organic matter. The detonations also insert oxides of nitrogen into the stratosphere that deplete the ozone layer around the Earth. This layer screens out UV-B radiation from the Sun, which causes genetic damage to life forms on the surface. The immediate effects of acute exposure in radiation led to excessive

---

Articles of the International Society for Ecology and Culture at http://www.isec.org.uk/articles.html

[10] According to the British Hadley Centre for Climate Change, billions of acres of South American rainforest will have turned intodesert by 2050. By the same year, another 30 million people will go hungry and an extra170 million will suffer from extreme water shortages. The number of people affected by coastal flooding will rise from fivemillion to 200 million by 2080.

burns and increase of carcinogenic diseases. The ecological impact of nuclear weapons and powers generates environmental side effects that are far more devastating than even the disastrous consequences of the initial blast. After all, the nuclear energy contributes towards health problems, displacement, pollution and invisible contamination passed on to future generations with incurable pain and suffering.

Given the current discourse surrounding GCC, the developed countries, making an effort to mitigate green gases, have considered less fossil fuel-intensive energy sources including nuclear energy. In this context, since about 2001 the term nuclear renaissance has been used to refer to a possible nuclear power industry revival with a new pro-nuclear rhetoric which incorporates carbon free and energy independent policies. Nuclear energy has been advertized that nuclear power plants emit substantially less CO2 during normal operations than do fossil fuel-fired plants. This has been increasingly touted and marketed by the global nuclear corporations as a green solution to GCC and a green alternative to fossil fuels.

In the case of USA, for the first time since the 1979 Three Mile Island and 1986 Chernobyl accidents, the construction of new nuclear power plants and billions of dollars in taxpayer-based federal nuclear energy subsidies have emerged in 2010.[11] With this new energy policy USA aims at least the following targets: substantial funding for nuclear energy and its technology development, export of nuclear technology, creating clean energy jobs, energy independence through developing nuclear energy as a domestic source of energy, green gas emission, global corporatization of nuclear energy business, etc.

What has been proved during the last 60 years is that nuclear power poses many threats to people and the environment, and these threats include the problems of processing, transport and storage of radioactive nuclear waste, the risk of nuclear weapons proliferation and terrorism, as well as health risks and environmental damage from uranium mining. In addition, reactors themselves are enormously complex machines where many things can and do go wrong, and there have been serious nuclear accidents, and the risks of using nuclear fission as a power source cannot be offset through the development of new technology. Also when all the energy-intensive stages of the nuclear fuel chain are considered, from uranium mining to nuclear decommissioning, nuclear power is not a low-carbon electricity source at all.

The nuclear victims of Hiroshima and Nagasaki, particularly the colonized Korean *minjung* victims, even after sixty five years, are suffering from the aftereffects of the first ever use of nuclear bombs. The children of Chernobyl are still suffering from the fear of cancer and other nuclear aftereffects. People in Fukushima will take an endless journey to overcome the memories of nuclear disasters which will contaminate the ever coming generations of the area. The human journey from Hiroshima to Fukushima has been a journey of cognitive dissonance which has dissolved the memories of nuclear disaster into the nuclear armament competition during the cold war period and the nuclear renaissance in the world of neo-liberal economic market globalization and GCC, instead of sublimating them into the world without nuclear weapons and power and green gases.

4. Eco-Justice and Ecological Debt

In order to overcome the crisis of eco-injustice and GCC, we should have a deep moral obligation to promote ecological justice by addressing the issue of ecological debt to peoples most affected by ecological destruction and to the earth household itself. Ecological debt refers to damage caused over time to ecosystems, places and peoples through production, consumption and disuse patterns, and the exploitation of ecosystems at the expense of the equitable rights of other countries, communities or individuals.

---

[11] The U.S. Senate is currently working to develop its version of the energy bill currently titled: "A Bill to Create Clean Energy Jobs, Promote Energy Independence, Reduce Global Warming Pollution, and Transition to a Clean Energy Economy."

Ecological debt lenses reveal that it is the global South who is the principal ecological creditor while the global North is the principal ecological debtor.It is primarily the debt owed by industrialized countries in the North to countries of the South on account of historical and current resource plundering, environmental degradation and the disproportionate appropriation of ecological space to dump greenhouse gases, toxic and nuclear wastes. It is the debt owed by economically and politically powerful national elites to marginalized citizens; the debt owed by current generations of humanity to future generations; and the debt owed by humankind to other life forms and the planet. It includes social damages such as the disintegration of indigenous and other local communities.[12]

GCC heightens the relationship of North-South inequity even further: industrialized countries are mainly responsible for greenhouse gas emissions causing GCC, and yet, the South will bear a bigger burden of the adverse effects of GCC including the displacement of people living in low-lying coastal areas and small island states and the loss of sources of livelihood, food insecurity, the reduced access to water and forced migration.Northern governments, institutions and corporations should take initiatives to drastically reduce their greenhouse gas emissions within and beyond UNFCCC, which stipulates the principles of historical responsibility and "common, but differentiated responsibilities" (CDR).[13]

In order to end the ecological indebtedness and to restore right relationships between peoples and between people and the earth, it is needed to re-order economic paradigms from consumerist, exploitive models to models that are respectful of localized economies, indigenous cultures and spiritualities, the earth's reproductive limits, as well as the right of other life forms to blossom. And all this begins with the recognition of the necessity of the paradigm shift in the world view.

5. The Issue on Ecological Justice as Seen in the Conciliar Ecumenical Movement

Christian faith in creation was constructively integrated into Justice, Peace, and Integrity of Creation (JPIC), an important ecumenical conciliar process of the WCC, originally intended as a program priority for the WCC by its Vancouver Assembly in 1983. In issuing this covenant process, WCC was responding to a situation of total self-destruction crisis of the humanity and the earth caused by systems of injustice. The JPIC process emphasized Christian faith of Christ as the life of the world and Christian resistance to the powers of death in economic exploitation, militarism, violations of human rights, racism, sexism, caste oppression, and the misuse of science and technology. In particular, the term "integrity of creation" helped clarify the biblical vision of peace with justice by re-affirming the doctrine of creation and of Trinitarian faith, beginning with God as Creator and therefore also Liberator and Sustainer.[14]

In 1990, the world convocation of JPIC was held in Seoul with its purpose to make theological affirmations on justice, peace and the integrity of creation, and to identify the major threats to life and their interconnectedness, proposing the acts of mutual commitment of the churches.[15]

At its Canberra Assembly (1991) the WCC gave prominence to JPIC, and the theme was re-affirmed in the Harare Assembly (1998) program guidelines committee report. In seeking a renewed basis for ecumenical social thought and action, a theology of life focuses on the life of all creation.[16]

---

[12] Moreover, industrialized Northern countries make disproportionate use of ecological space without adequate compensation, reparation or restitution. Northern countries' ecological footprint presently averages 6.4 ha/person: this is more than six times heavier than that of Southern countries at an average of 0.8 ha/person.

[13] See WCC, *Statement on Eco-Justice and Ecological Debt*, op.cit.

[14] See Preman Niles, Ecumenical Dictionary, "Article of the Month" Series, November 2003: "Justice, Peace, andthe Integrity of Creation" at http://www.wcc-coe.org/wcc/who/dictionary-article11.html

[15] Ibid.

[16] Ibid.

Alternative Globalization Addressing People and Earth (AGAPE) was an ecumenical process on economic globalization from Harare in 1998 to Porto Alegre 2006, which was prepared by the commission for Justice, Peace and Creation of WCC. The final document of the AGAPE process reported at the WCC 9th Porto Alegre Assembly captures the results of a seven-year global study process of the churches' responses to economic globalization particularly with contributions from the 2003 Assembly of the Lutheran World Federation (LWF) and the 2004 General Council of the World Alliance of Reformed Churches (WARC).[17]

The AGAPE process has examined the project of economic globalization, and the participants in the AGAPE process shared their concerns about the growing inequality, the concentration of wealth and power in the hands of a few and the destruction of the earth – all aggravating the scandal of poverty in the South and increasingly in the North. It confesses God as Creator endowing God's creation with integrity and human beings with dignity, God as Redeemer and Liberator freeing us from slavery and death, and God as Holy Spirit transforming and energizing us. Along with the main thematic issues of poverty, trade, finance, public goods and services, decent jobs, emancipated work and people's livelihoods, and churches and the power of empire, the AGAPE document deals with ecological issues on sustainable use of land and natural resources, and life-giving agriculture.[18]

Alongside the AGAPE process, the AGAPE study on Poverty, Wealth and Ecology (PWE), is exploring the interconnections between economic and ecological inequities, and proposing alternatives to neo-liberal economic globalization which link economy and ecology in ways that promote economic justice for all.[19]

Accompanying with PWE, the Oikotree Movement as a progressive people-centered form of ecumenical movement is advocating living faithfully through engaging in the struggle for justice in the economy and the earth; a spirituality of resistance and transformation; the formation of life-sustaining, justice-affirming communities, which embrace creation and humanity; advocacy of economic and ecological justice, and support for alternatives to an ecologically destructive economy; resistance to neo-liberal corporate globalization, patriarchy and empire; accompaniment with people and communities struggling to overcome economic and ecological injustice; solidarity in the struggle to change the systems that are destroying humanity and the earth; and inclusivity, diversity, openness and transparency.[20]

The Ecumenical Water Network (EWN) as an international network of churches and Christian organizations aims to promote the preservation, responsible management and the equitable distribution of water for all, based on the understanding that water is a gift of God and a fundamental human right. It advocates that water is to be preserved and shared for the benefit of all creatures and the wider creation. WCC Statement on Water for Life proposed by EWN was adopted by the WCC Porto Alegre Assembly in 2006.[21]

The coming WCC 10th Busan Assembly in 2013 with the integrated theme "God of Life, lead us Justice and Peace" will more emphasize ecological justice in a post-Fukushima context.

---

[17] See the WCC document *Alternative Globalization Addressing People and Earth* at http://www.oikoumene.org/en/resources/documents/assembly/porto-alegre-2006/3-preparatory-and-background-documents/alternative-globalization-addressing-people-and-earth-agape.html

[18] Ibid.

[19] See the WCC program Poverty, Wealth, and Ecology athttp://www.oikoumene.org/en/programmes/justice-diakonia-and-responsibility-for-creation/eco-justice/poverty-wealth-and-ecology.html

[20] See Oikotree Movement at http://www.oikotree.org

[21] See the WCC program at http://www.oikoumene.org/en/activities/ewn-home.html

6. Shifting a Paradigm of the World View from Cartesian-Newtonian to Life-Centric Systemic

As the new century moves with apocalyptic uncertainty down the path of globalization, we are faced with a whole series of global-local ecological crisis that are harming both the biosphere and human life in alarming ways. The principles of the existential and ecological interdependence of the earth household, which are on the basis of the spirituality of *kenosis* (self-emptying) and mutual caring for the fullness of life for all, has been denied in the name of progress and growth. An end result of modern science of nature based on the anthropocentric view of the world seems to be a green gas-filled, genetically modified, nuclear-fissured, and nuclear radiation-contaminated New World: what a world!

The underlying perceptual psychological distortion that afflicts modern humanity derives from the fact that most human societies subscribe to the concepts of an anthropocentric worldview – a dualistic view of humanity and nature. It allows the driving forces of globalization to shred the existential and ecological fabric matrix out of which humans are woven. It has provided the conceptual legitimacy of a view of life in society that sees the world as a jungle, and life within it as a continual struggle for survival. This way of Mammon's economy of life believes that unlimited material progress is to be achieved through economic and technological growth at the expense of nature and people that are the core of the Life Capital of the earth household.

In the life-centric view, the world is seen not as a pyramid with humans on top but as a web; humans are but one strand in that web, and as we destroy other strands, we destroy ourselves. In this interdependent living system, every organism is an integrated whole: it is a living system in its own right, and all systems nest, in a mutually kenotic and serving way, within other systems. Humans belong to the earth household, human psyche is earth-born, and humans contain eco-historical memories of continuous evolution in God's economy of Life. Humans are all embedded in and ultimately dependent on the spiral cyclical processes of the earth household. Human personality exists at the intersection of the ecological cycles of air, water and soil, and without these, there is no human self. However, through continuous anthropocentric conditioning, humans have inherited shallow, fictitious selves, and have created an incredibly pervasive illusion of separation from the earth.[22]

All micro and macro members of the earth household are now crying for a 'deep' healing and reconciliation, a peace with justice for the economy of Life, in order to ensure the sustainability of the whole interconnected and interdependent living system. The apocalyptic reality of the earth household today is an inevitable consequence of a history of anthropocentric conditioning, and it requires a radical shift in human perceptions, thinking, and values from the Cartesian-Newtonian mechanistic worldview to a holistic, ecological worldview, in which Life is at its cognitive centre. The life-centric systemic thinking requires integration between history and nature, and economy and ecology, and it can provide the in-depth foundational perception, strategy, and praxis for a 'deep' healing and reconciliation of the wounded and broken web of Life – the way to enhance the Life Capital of the earth household.[23]

God of Life give a critical warning and challenge to the arrogant humans, whom modify God's creation by genetic fabrication as if it is a machine, whom produce greenhouse gases due to over-production, over-consumption, over-disuse, and whom steal 'the fire of heaven' by nuclear fission. God interrogate them as seen in Job 38: 33, "Do you know the laws of the heavens? Can you set up God's dominion over the earth?" In Deuteronomy 30: 15 and 19, calling the heavens and the earth as witnesses against us, God set before us life and prosperity, death and destruction, life and death, blessings and curses, and command,

---

[22] See Lee Hong-Jung, "Healing and reconciliation as the basis for the sustainability of life: an ecological plea for a 'deep' healing and reconciliation", International Review of Mission, Vol. 94, No. 572, Geneva: WCC publication, January 2005.

[23] Ibid.

"Now choose life, so that you and your children may live and that you may love the Lord your God," because God is our Life!

Bibliography

Charles Birch, William Eakin, and Jay B. McDaniel, eds., Liberating Life, Maryknoll: Orbis Books, 1990
Leonardo Boff, Ecology & Liberation: A New Paradigm, Maryknoll: Orbis Books, 1995
David G. Hallman, Spiritual Values for Earth Community, Geneva: WCC Risk Book Series, 2000
Mary Heather MacKinnon and Moni McIntyre, eds., Readings in Ecology and Feminist Theology, Kansas City: Sheed & Ward, 1995
Lee Hong-Jung, "Healing and reconciliation as the basis for the sustainability of life: an ecological plea for a 'deep' healing and reconciliation", *International Review of Mission*, Vol. 94, No. 572, Geneva: WCC publication, January 2005
Ernst Ulrich von Weizsäcker, *Earth Politics*, London: Zed Books, 1994
http://en.wikipedia.org/wiki/Climate_change
http://www.oikotree.org
http://www.oikoumene.org/en/activities/ewn-home.html
http://www.oikoumene.org/en/resources/documents/assembly/porto-alegre-2006/3-preparatory-and-background-documents/alternative-globalization-addressing-people-and-earth-agape.html

(34) LEARNING FROM ASIAN RELIGIOUS TRADITIONS FOR ECO-JUSTICE

Samuel Longkumer

Humanity is confronted with a serious ecological crisis whose intensity and complexity is of paramount significance. It is an alarming fact that we are entering into an age of mass ecological suicide. Ecological degradation caused by massive pollution of earth, water, air, energy, space etc., is severely threatening and is affecting the very web of life. Humanity is well aware that we are losing the battle; we are beginning to lose our precarious grip upon planet earth. And in such a given context, the more one considers the whole question of ecological crisis, the more deeply is one led to the view that one need to look into the depths of ancient traditions in order to recapture the essence of and reverence for nature that they have expressed. Therefore, one needs to dive deep down into the religious resources and see whether it will help the modern humanity to co-exist harmoniously. Hence, in this paper we shall try to identify the meanings regarding *Pañcabhūtas* from select Asian religious traditions in order to see whether they function as a spiritual resource to work for an ecological balance today.

1. *Pañcamahābhūtas*[1] in Hinduism

The meaning of *Pañcabhūtas*, (five elements – namely, earth, water, fire, air, and ether) though in a loosely connected manner, can be found in a collection of poetry, mythology, rituals, sacrifices, *mantras*, metaphysics, *darśanas*, ancient science etc. If in the *Vedic Samhitās* the five elements are mainly pictured as natural phenomena personified as deities, in the *Upanisads* and the *Vedānta* we see them explained mainly as the five gross elements who are presided over by their deities, but the deities receiving their power by the energy of *Brahman* alone. *Īśvara* is the controller of the deities and the elements. Also, the meaning of the *pañcabhūtas* evolves in this later period to establish the integral relation between humans and the rest of the creation, in terms of the interpretation that both are the outcome of the combination of the five elements.

In the *Rg Veda* V.84; VII.49; X.168 etc. and also in some other *Samhitās*, the elements like earth, water and air/wind are referred in the sense of deities. Earth is known to all civilizations and cultures as the great Mother Goddess. In the *Atharva Veda* occurs a prayer to the earth, which draws attention to ecological balance. The earth is regarded as the upholder of the moral order (*AV.* XII.1).[2] The *Vedic* attitude toward the earth springs from humankind's primordial experience of being on the one hand a guest and on the other an offspring, of earth. The earth is undoubtedly mother, the foundation, the basis out of which emerges all that exists and on which everything rests.[3] She is praised in several *Rg Vedic* hymns.[4]

---

[1] The original *Sanskrit* term for *Pañca Mahābhūtas* is *Mahābhūtani* also called as *Mahātattvas* (*Pañca* – five, *Mahā* – great or basic, *Bhūtas* – elements) meaning the 'Five basic elements' namely, *Prthivī* – earth, *Āpah* – water, *Agni* (*tejas*) – fire, *Vāyu* – air, and *Dyaus* (*Ākāśa*) – ether/space. Generally they are regarded as the elements out of which all the material things in the world are created and to which they can be reduced. One regards them as prime substance of nature or *Prakrti* and being the sheath of nature they are regarded as the source of all beings both biotic and abiotic. All the visible elements are believed to be endowed with invisible energy (*Sakti*) and creative powers. Cf. T.N. Dharmadhikari, "*Bhūtas* in *Vedic* Rituals and Literature" in *Prakrti: Integral Vision,* Vol. II, edited by Sampat Narayanan (New Delhi: IGNCA., 1995), 7.

[2] Kapila Vatsyayan, *Ecology and Indian Myth* (New Delhi: AIACHE., 1986), 14.

[3] Raimundo Panikkar, *The Vedic Experience: Mantramañjarī* (London: Darton, Longman & Todd, 1977), 120.

[4] RV. V.84; SB. XIV.1.2.10; RV. III.51.5; SB. XI.5.6.3; RV. I.185; RV. I.160; RV. X.18.10-13; RV. I.24.1.

The waters are primeval element; everything rests on them.[5] In *Rg Veda* X.137.6,7; *Atharva Veda* V. II.3.6; VI.91.3; *Satapatha Brahmanas* III.6.1.7 etc. the waters are described as possessing an integral reality, and thus having healing power. Water is the great cleanser, second only to *Agni* (fire), the Great Purifier. In contemporary terminology, one would say that water cleanses and fire disinfects or sterilizes.[6] Again, *Rg Veda* VII.49; X.9, speaks of the divine waters and the waters of life. This reminds us of the fact that water is a substance that has the greatest dissolving power. Water is also considered as primordial element. In *RV*. X.45.1,3; I; VIII.43.9; X.121:7; *SB* VI.8.2.4, *Agni* is mentioned as the son of the Waters. At the sight of waters we find prayer welling within us and in prayer we become aware of the marvelous harmony of this universe. "In the waters, O Lord, is your seat!"[7]

In *RV*. X.2.3; X.2.4-5; X.51.8; X.31.10-11, *Agni* is described as "who knows and who fixes rites and seasons". *Agni* is the energy (*RV*. III.22), that recycles everything; ecologically speaking it represents the creation of life, its death and decomposition and re-creation of living matter through the all pervading energy of lord *Agni*. Clouds are thus called the "son of fire" (*RV*. X.31.10,11) because of the heat that causes the evaporation of water, that after condensation into clouds pours down rain. It is fire and heat or warmth that "pervades the whole universe and being manifested as lofty *Visnu* preserves life" (*RV*. X.1.3). *Agni* is present at all *Vedic* rites and that he is the giver of force, power and strength (*AV*.II.17.1-3; *AV*. V.30.14; *AV*. I.32.1,2; *AV*. V.24.2; *AV*.X.4; *AV*. XVI.6.9; *AV*.X.5).[8] In the *AV*. V.29.1 *Agni* is eulogized as physician and maker of remedies. *Agni* who "protect our children and descendents, and guard with ever-watchful care of our bodies".[9] Fire is associated to earth where plant grow, to water and air that are needed for the preparation of extracts by boiling, by distillation, by fumigation and by mixing with cooked food. It is *Agni* who puts everything right with energy as the great purifier. Out of the five ecological elements, *mahābhūta*, fire is thus the link between the material and the immaterial, between earth and water on one side and air and void on the other.[10]

Vāyu – Air is an essential part of our natural environment. We are all connected through air. Without Air – *Vāyu* no living beings can exist. Therefore, in *Rg Veda* X.151.4, Air – *Vāyu* is recognized as the breath of life, *prāna*, of all living beings. In *RV*. X.137.3; *RV*. X.186; *RV*. I.134, etc., Air – *Vāyu* is described as beneficial as it brings rain,[11] blessings in the form of medicine and healing, and holding the gift of eternal life etc. *Vāyu* is also considered as the Messenger of the gods, the bestower of the life-principle, and the seed of life.[12]

Ākāśa – Ether/Space is the generic term for space, the subtlest and most pervasive of the five basic elements. It is the visible as well as invisible forces, waves or vibrations that fill the air and the void or vacuum (*RV*. IX.18.1; IX.20.3; VIII.25.9). It is a perception that goes beyond the understanding of life and is the recognition of the much that we do not know about the processes of the universe.[13]

Vedic people thus lavish high praises upon various natural forces as divinities worthy of worship. The rivers and the earth are regarded to be goddesses, while the winds/air and fire is invoked as male deities. In the *Vedas*, earth and water are celebrated, asking for protection and glorifying the root constituents of the natural world. Fire as the energy, the force of evolution, the pulsating Life-Force. Air as the breath of life. And ether/space as invisible forces, waves or vibration that fill the air and the void. More than these, from

---

[5] Ibid., p. 116.
[6] M. Vannucci, *Ecological Readings in the Veda* (New Delhi: D.K. Printworld, 1994), 102.
[7] Raimundo Panikkar, op. cit., 117.
[8] M. Vannucci, op. cit., 102-105.
[9] Ralph T.H. Griffith, *The Hymns of the Rg Veda,* Vol. II (Varanasi: CSSO., 1971), 386.
[10] M. Vannucci, op. cit., 105,106.
[11] Ibid., 116,117.
[12] Raimundo Panikkar, op. cit., 131.
[13] M. Vannucci, op. cit., 117.

the earliest hymns an image of the human person arises that sees continuity between the individual and nature in the creation of the cosmos. Such an intimate relationship between nature and human order is established through various personifications of the earth, water, thunderstorms, and so forth.[14] And in the *Vedic* rituals, many of which are still performed today, invoke elemental forces.[15]

But when it comes to the *Upanisadic* speculations, deification of natural elements is replaced by the quest for the supreme, *Brahman-Ātman. Upanisads* perhaps takes more of an inward journey and ascension of consciousness, rather than the existing *Vedic* ceremonialism, worship and caste duties.[16] It is taught that *Brahman* desired to be many, created three elements viz. Fire, Water and Earth in their subtle forms and entered into them, and by their combination all other things have been formed (*Chāndogyopanisad* VI.2.3,4). Later on, five elements are mentioned namely, ether, air, fire, water, and earth (*Taittirīyopanisad* II.1.1).[17] It also describes that from the Imperishable all kinds of beings are issued, like sparks from a fire. It is from him, as he became personalized in creation, were born breath, and all organs of sense, ether, air, light, water, earth. Hence, as cosmic elements the five are understood to be clearly inter-linked and dependent to each other, each causing and affecting the other for the evolution and function of the universe. Behind all this mechanism is the acknowledgement of the *Brahman* as the ultimate source of the world (*Taittirīyopanisad* II.1.1).[18]

In the philosophical schools such as *Vedānta*, the cosmotheandric aspect of God, human person and nature becomes more prominent. According to Śankara,[19] it is the Supreme Lord *Ātman-Brahman* who first produces *Ākāśa* (ether) and from *Ākāśa* is produced the subtle element *Vāyu* (gaseous matter); from *Vāyu* comes off *Tejas* (fire); from *Tejas* comes off *Āp* (water); and *Āp* gives off *Prthivī* (earth). From these subtle elements (*suksma bhūtas*) appear gross elements (*mahā bhūtas*).[20] And it is in these elements that the Supreme Self abides and subsequently, these elements have activity only when they are presided over by someone else and it is the Supreme Lord who presides over them as their Self.[21]

It is further explained in *Vedānta* that all these elements are inseparably related to humans. The material world as well as the material body is constituted by the same five elements. Each element possesses both material (gross) and spiritual (subtle) qualities, and each sense organ is composed of the same element, the quality of which is sensed by it.[22] Thus, human person is integrally related to nature on the one hand and God on the other, according to the teaching of *Vedānta*.[23]

It was God who desired to create and he created everything that exists on earth, in water and sky. One must assume that it is God/*Brahman* who is the Inner-most Reality in the elements. Consequently, in all elements, *Brahman* is the inner guide and overseer, and as such, brings about their motions. The Self is

---

[14] *Tait.Samhita* IV.3.11.2; *YV*.3.35.36.3; *RV*.I.159.2; X.111.4; *AV*.I.11.2; XII.1; *RV*.VII.49.2; VI.50.7; VII.5.4; *AV*.II.28.3; *RV*. X.168; *AV*.I.33.3.

[15] Christopher Key Chapple, "Hindu Environmentalism: Traditional and Contemporary Resources" in *Worldviews and Ecology*, edited by Mary Evelyn & John A. Grim (New York: Orbis Books, 1994), 114-116.

[16] S. Radhakrishnan and Charles A. Moore (eds.), *A Source Book in Indian Philosophy* (Princeton: Princeton University Press, 1957), 38.

[17] Swami Ghanananda, "The Dawn of Indian Philosophy" in *The Cultural Heritage of India*, vol. I (Calcutta: RMIC., 1970), 343,344.

[18] R. D. Ranade, *A Constructive Survey of Upanishadic Philosophy* (Bombay: BVB., 1968), 55-70.

[19] *Aitareyopanisad Bhāsya* 1.1.3, *Mundakopanisad Bhāsya* 2.1.3, *Brhadāranyakopanisad Bhāsya* 3.6.1-8.

[20] D. P. Chattopadhyaya, "Lifeworld, Science and Technology: An Indian Perspective" in *Essays in Indian Philosophy*, edited by Sukharanjan Saha (Calcutta: Allied Publishers, 1997), 570.

[21] K. P. Aleaz, *The Relevance of Relation in Śankara's Advaita Vedānta* (Delhi: Kant Publications, 1996), 176.

[22] K.P. Aleaz, *Dimensions of Indian Religion: Study, Experience and Interaction* (Calcutta: Punthi Pustak, 1995), 118. *See* Kapila Vatsyayan, *Ecology and Indian Myth* (New Delhi: AIACHE., 1986), 5,6.

[23] Śankara *C.U.B*.5.1.15; *Br.U.B*.5.5.2; *B.S.B*. 2.4.14. cf. *B.S.B*. 2.4.20; *C.U*. 6.3.4; 6.4.7; *B.S.B*. 2.4.15-16.

within all and beyond all. The Supreme Lord abides in the elements of earth, water, fire, air and space as their Self and creates everything through profound meditation.[24]

2. *Pañcabhūtas* as Found in Other Religious Traditions

It is understood in the *Vedas* and *Vedānta* that the 'elements' are the primeval principles of creation, responsible in creating the world and all the material things in it including human person. Such concept is not exclusive to the Hindu tradition alone but it is evident in other religious traditions as well. Some of the traditional visions perceive human-nature as constituted of four or five elements and ascribe them as possessing both gross and subtle qualities.[25] Though such understanding may differ in meaning and content some may refer to the elements metaphorically and to some the names of the elements are symbolic.

(a) Chinese cosmogony

There are rich resources within the East Asian philosophical traditions for understanding how nature is viewed and the role of the human in nature. From the early integration of the human into the great triad with heaven and earth to the more complex metaphysical discussions of the relationship of principle (*li*) and material force (*ch'i*), the traditional Chinese worldview provides a wealth of suggestive resources for rethinking our contemporary situation.[26] The term *ch'i* has been translated by Wing-tsit Chan as "material force"; namely, something that consists of both matter and energy. It referred to the "psychophysiological power associated with blood and breath". He also suggests that the terms "matter" or "ether" are not adequate translations for *ch'i* because they only convey one aspect of the term.[27]

This *ch'i* has its manifestations in the seasons and in natural growth, as well as in moral relations in human life. *Ch'i* operates throughout the universe in a process of continual disintegration and integration, like the waxing and waning of *yin* and *yang*. In its disintegrated states, *ch'i* is scattered and diffused. Through integration, it forms matter, thereby giving rise to the manifold diversity of human beings and things.[28] *Ch'i* moves and flows in all directions and in all manners. Its two elements (*yin* and *yang*) unite and give rise to the concrete. Thus the multiplicity of things and human beings is produced. In their ceaseless successions of two elements of *yin* and *yang* constitute the great principles of the universe.[29] It is as Chou Tun-i states, "by the transformation of *yang* and its union with *yin*, the Five Agents of Water, Fire, Wood, Metal, and Earth arise" and since "the Five Agents constitute a system of *yin* and *yang*", they can be conceived as specific forms of *ch'i*.[30]

The theories of *yin* and *yang* and the five elements are a part of the ancient Chinese cosmogony. *Shangsu* (Book of Documents) contains the earliest textual reference of *wuxing* (five elements). "First we have the five elements water, fire, wood, metal and earth. Water moistens downward. Fire heats upward. Wood is both crooked and straight. Metal can be changed into various shapes. Earth is for planting crops. Moistening downwards makes the salty taste. Heating upwards makes the bitter taste. Crookedness and

---

[24] *Br.U.* III.7.3-23. Cf. Paul Deussen, *The System of the Vedānta* (Delhi: Oriental Publishers, 1972), 236.

[25] Baidyanath Saraswati, "Primal Elements: The Oral Traditions" in *Prakrti: The Integral Vision*, vol. 1, ed. by Kapila Vatsyayan (New Delhi: IGNCA., 1995), 10.

[26] Mary Evelyn Tucker, "An Ecological Cosmology" in *Ecological Prospects*, ed. by Christopher Key Chapple (Delhi: Indian Books Centre, 1995), 105.

[27] Ibid., 112.

[28] Ibid.

[29] Tu Wei-Ming, "The Continuity of Being: Chinese Visions of Nature" in *Nature in Asian Traditions of Thought: Essays in Environmental Philosophy*, ed. by J. Baird Callicott & Roger T. Ames (Delhi: Indian Books Centre, 1991), 73.

[30] Ibid., 75.

straightness make the sour taste. Changing into shapes makes the pungent taste. Crops make the sweet taste".[31]

Jin Chungfeng, a modern Chinese scholar, thinks that earth was the centre of the agricultural economic activities in ancient times, hence being placed in the centre (while wood, metal, fire, water are placed in the east, west, south, north respectively). The ancient Chinese linked space with time. East was linked with spring, south with summer, west with autumn, and north with winter. Earth controlled the four seasons and was the identification of human beings.[32] Human person is (the product of) the attributes of Heaven and Earth, (by) the interaction of the dual forces of nature, the union of the animal and intelligent (souls), and the finest subtle matter of the five elements.[33]

Lushi Chungiu associates the five elements with five colours, and also with the development of ancient Chinese history. During the time of Huangdi the spirit of earth prevailed and its colour was yellow, hence the yellow earth and Yellow emperor. During the time of *Yu* (the first king of the Xia dynasty), there was an exuberant vegetation in all the seasons which presented the colour of wood, i.e., green. During the time of Tang (the first king of Shang dynasty), the spirit of metal prevailed, presenting white colour. During king Wen of Zhou, the spirit of fire prevailed, presenting red colour. Fire would be replaced by water, which would present black colour. Water would then, be absorbed by earth, and the rotation of the five elements would continue endlessly till eternity.[34] The representative colours of the various seasons are the visual representations of the ecological environment. It makes sense to associate spring with green and wood as it is the season of growth of vegetation. Summer is associated with red and fire, as it is the hottest season with maximum sunshine. Associating autumn with white and metal needs a little more imagination. This probably had something to do with the withering of vegetation and transformation of a rich colourful world into whitish grey. Similarly the association of winter with water and black may be explained by the cold which forced people into hiding, thus bringing darkness. Besides this, black or other dark colours are used more often in winters.[35]

According to Chou Tun-i "it is human alone who receives (the Five Agents) in their highest excellence, and therefore s/he is most intelligent. His/her physical form appears, and his/her spirit develops consciousness. The five moral principles of his/her nature (humanity, rightness, propriety, wisdom, and faithfulness) are aroused by, and react to, the external world and engage in activity; good and evil are distinguished; and human affairs take place".[36] The major approach of ancient Chinese thinking was to synthesize human activities with their natural environment. The Chinese approach has been holistic. Although people did observe natural phenomena, they established too early an organic linkage between human and nature. One aspect of this human-nature synthesis was to humanize nature, attributing a human character to natural changes.[37] Human existence therefore, is based on five elements present in the environment and in the human body and thus earth, water, fire, wood and metal and all have to be balanced equally in order to experience healthy and congenial environment.

---

[31] Tang Chung, "Chinese Cosmogony: Man-Nature Synthesis" in *Prakrti: The Integral Vision*, vol. 1, ed. by Kapila Vatsyayan (New Delhi: IGNCA, 1995), 15.
[32] Ibid., 16.
[33] Book VII. III. 1, F. Max Muller ed., *The Sacred Books of China: The Texts of Confucianism*, vol. xxvii, part – III (Delhi: Low Price Publications, 1996), 380,381.
[34] Tang Chung, "Chinese Cosmogony: Man-Nature Synthesis", op. cit., 16,17.
[35] Ibid.
[36] Cited in Tu Wei-Ming, op. cit., 75.
[37] Tang Chung, op. cit., 19,20.

(b) Elements in the Tibetan Bön tradition

The five elements namely, earth, water, fire, air and space are considered in Tibetan culture to be the substance of all things and processes. The names of the elements are symbolic. They use the natural elements as fundamental metaphors to describe forces both internal and external. For example, physical properties are assigned to the elements: earth is solidity; water is cohesion; fire is temperature; air is motion; and space is the spatial dimension that accommodates the other four active elements. In addition, the elements are correlated to different emotions, temperaments, directions, colors, tastes, body types, illnesses, thinking styles, and character. And from these five elements arise the five senses and the five fields of sensual experience; the five negative emotions and the five wisdom; and the five extensions of the body. They are the five primary *prānas* or vital energies. They are the constituents of every physical, sensual, mental, and spiritual phenomenon.[38]

Five elements may seem too few to account for all the diversity in things and beings, but the five elements are five discriminations that continually branch into more subtle divisions. For instance, there are five major appendages to the torso: two legs, two arms, and a head. Each of these then branches into a further five: the arms and legs into five fingers and five toes each, the head into the five sense organs.[39] Further, flesh is described as earth; the blood and other bodily fluids as water; the electrical and chemical energies and metabolic heat as fire; the breath, oxygen and other gases as air; and the space the body occupies and the spaces in the body, as well as the consciousness, as the space element. Each of these five could be further analyzed in terms of the elements: in the flesh alone can be found solidity (earth), cohesion (water), temperature (fire), motility (air), and awareness (space). Thus the interactions of the five elements give rise not only to parts of the system, to individual bodies and planets, but also to all realms of existence in every dimension. The dynamism of the five elements lies under the complexities of all that exists.[40]

(c) Elements in tribal religion (earth, water, fire)

For the tribals the earth is considered as Mother from whom all sustenance comes to human beings and non-humans. The cosmos is a reservoir of sacred forces. From a religious perspective, the earth is the clearest epiphany of an ensemble of sacred apparitions: soil, stones, trees, vegetation,[41] animals, birds, water, air, sun shine and the like including human beings, and they are all bound to one another in an integral manner. The tribals have been holding such views from time immemorial and they have also understood human beings as an integral part of this macro-organism.[42] For them the earth is the foundation, the generative source, of every expression of existence. The land and forest, water and air and all nature's bounty are gifts of God. And they have been using these gifts as stewards and not as owners. Even to be the custodian of these gifts of God, it is the community and not the individuals who are primarily responsible for this stewardship of the earth.[43] One can find the tribes of *Santal* and *Kondh* in celebration of the earth seeking human welfare: "Let the earth be green with our crops. Let there be no hindrance to our movements. Let there prevail among us the spirit of mutual love and goodwill".[44]

---

[38] Tenzin Wangyal Rinpoche, *Healing with Form, Energy and Light: The Five Elements in Tibetan Shamanism, Tantra, and Dzogchen* (New Delhi: New Age Books, 2003), 1.
[39] Ibid., 2.
[40] Ibid., 2,3.
[41] Mircea Eliade & Lawrence E. Sullivan, "Earth", *The Encyclopedia of Religion*, vol. 4 (New York: Macmillan Publishing Co., 1987), 534.
[42] Nirmal Minz, "The *Adivasi* Perspectives on Ecology" in *Ecology: A Theological Response*, ed. by Andreas Nehring (Madras: Gurukul, 1994), 67-72.
[43] Ibid.
[44] Christopher Key Chapple, "Toward an Indigenous Indian Environmentalism" in *Purifying the Earthly Body of God: Religion and Ecology in Hindu India*, ed. by Lance E. Nelson (New Delhi: D.K. Printworld, 2000), 23.

In the primitive cultures, worship of the Mother Earth is almost a universal phenomenon. They consider earth as mother goddess and take special care to see that the *bhu-Mata* (Mother-Earth) is not hurt or offended in any way. In some cases, they even restrain from tilling the ground, fearing that it might wound the body of their mother, the earth.[45] Such is found in the case of *Ao Nagas*. During *Lijaba mong* (*Lijaba* – the creator of the earth and *mong* meaning ceremony), which is observed yearly in his honor,[46] everybody stays indoors,[47] and the days are strictly observed. No one may even husk rice or fetch firewood from the stakes outside the village;[48] also, cutting or digging of the earth/ground, going out and coming into the village, and manual labor are prohibited. It is believed that during these days *Lijaba* enters the earth just as a vital seed which gets buried beneath the soil and germinates as the life of plants.[49] One can also find extreme cases like Smohalla, an Indian prophet of the Umatilla tribe, who forbade his followers to dig the earth. According to him, it is a sin to wound or cut, tear or scratch our common mother by the labors of farming. He defended his anti-agricultural attitude by saying: "You ask me to plough the ground? Shall I take a knife and tear my mother's bosom? Then when I die she will not take me to her bosom to rest. You ask me to dig for stone? Shall I dig under her skin for her bones? You ask me to cut grass and make hay and sell it, and be rich like white person! But how dare I cut off my mother's hair?"[50]

Water is a source of nourishment to all the humanity and its importance is no exception to the tribals. They worship water and offer offerings to the water deity.[51] Such water worship is also found in *Ao Naga* tribe. In every *Ao* village there is a separate clan who used to worship the water. When drought strikes the land, when the water in the well or pond dries up due to drought, people hold a worship day to pray for rain. The elders of the village will take one *tzüshi* (Water vessel) and a cock and go to a place where they will pray and worship a big stone. After which, they will pour out the water from *tzüshi* (water vessel) pronouncing the name of god, *Anungtsüngba* (god of sky) to send showers of rain.[52] *Lothas* also call rain by beating the earth with sticks, calling to it to come and soak the earth well, and when done, while going away they sing "*O, dapotsisi, dapotsisi*". Which is a song sung by children when dancing in the wet. It represents the fall of the rain wetting their heads and trickling down their bodies, "Rain, rain, soak me".[53] Thus by worshipping and offering prayers and sacrifices, they strongly believed that they would receive abundant water and rain.

Fire is also given considerable importance in a tribal community. Fire with its warmth and light, fulfils a vital requirement of human life. Yet the same element can also wreak destruction. Both positive and negative functions are united in fire's role as an instrument of melting, refining, and purifying. In a religious context, fire has come to play a very large role in cult, myth, and symbolic speech. Some elements of fire worship and the use of fire in ritual and in symbolism are rooted in and developed out of practical experience of human beings.[54] In the Naga traditional religion fire plays a prominent role. For example when a site is selected for building a new house, the man goes and places two flat stones on the

---

[45] V.J. John, *The Ecological Vision of Jesus* (Thiruvalla: CSS., 2002), 78.
[46] I.T. Apok Aier, *The Religion of the Ao Nagas* (Mokokchung: Bendanganshi, 1990), 13.
[47] L. Imti Aier, *Ao Naga Social and Customary Genealogy* (Mokokchung: L. Imti Aier, 2nd ed., 1969), 31.
[48] J.P. Mills, *The Ao Naga* (Bombay: Oxford University Press, 1973), 221.
[49] A. Wati Longchar, "*Lijaba* – The Earth Entering Supreme Being: The Ao Naga Concept of God and Ecology" in *The Tribal Worldview and Ecology*, no. 2, ed. by A. Wati Longchar & Yangkahao Vashum (Jorhat: Tribal Study Centre, 1998), 29.
[50] Mircea Eliade, *Patterns in Comparative Religion* (London: Sheed & Ward, 1971), 246.
[51] E.W. Clark, *Ao Naga Dictionary* (Jorhat: BMP., 1911), 363.
[52] L. Imti Aier, *Aor Sobaliba aser Temzüng Ozüng* (Mokokchung: Imti Aier, 1981), 30.
[53] Jonathan H. Thumra, "The Primal Religious Tradition" in *Religious Traditions of India*, ed. by P.S. Daniel, *et al.*, (Delhi: ISPCK., 2001), 64.
[54] Vibha Joshi, "The Angami Fire and Water" in *Prakrti: The Integral Vision*, vol. I, ed. by Kapila Vatsyayan (New Delhi: IGNCA., 1995), 134.

site. That night he dreams, and if the dreams have been favourable, the next day he and his wife, taking fire, fuel, a fowl and other food, goes to the site and builds a fireplace with three stones and makes a fire. When the house is finished fire must be brought from the house of a *kika kepfüma*, i.e., a man who has performed the *lesü – genna* (taboo) and has horns on his house.[55] Wood only is burned in the fireplace, and if possible it is not allowed to go out. It is regarded as *genna* (taboo), or at least as a serious offence, to put out one's fire, though there seem to be no definite reason for this except that it is contrary to custom and unlucky for both parties.[56] Even omen is observed while lighting a fire, for instance, each person after killing his/her cock makes a fire, which he/she must light from a fire-stick and nothing else; matches or burning brands must not be used to light this fire, and in the lighting of the fire if the spark is first produced to the right of the stick the year will be good one for men, if to the left for women.[57]

3. *Pañcamahābhūtas*: A Link Between the Divine, Human and Nature

All physical objects, even the most subtle, are built up by the combination of these five elements. Our sense experience depends on them. What is decisive about everything is the principle of interconnection and interrelation of matter, as a result of which all its five forms go to the making of everything. Human person is, but a harmonious combination of all the elements. In his/her embodied existence, s/he is composed of matter, life, senses and mind and consciousness and self. And in the centre of human person, in his/her innermost self, resides God as his/her inner Controller (*antaryamin*). The structure of human person, the microcosm, corresponds exactly to the structure of the cosmos, the macrocosm. The ancient thinkers went further and said that each part and each member of human body has corresponding entities or realities in the cosmos. Thus the breath of human corresponds to the element wind; the flesh, bone and marrow of human corresponds to the element earth; the blood corresponds to the element water; the eyes to sun and moon; the ears to the ether; the blood vessels to rivers; the hairs on the body to herbs and tress, etc.[58]

These elements are not individual and a separated constituent of a whole but, rather, vectors or forces pervading the entire reality. They stand for the underlying unity behind the manifold appearances of all that they symbolize.[59] Hymns and myth of such intensity could not have been created by those who feared the elements, they were created by those who were intuitively aware of the necessity to keep the environment pure and clean within human beings.[60] Thus, *bhūtas* could be perceived though, just as simple 'matters', however, this matter or grossness is directed towards a 'subtle' inward spirituality. Here in the process of the unfoldment of the spirit the 'subtle' penetrates and actualizes the grosser ones. Of course they are not the objective counter parts of nature, but the subjective or spiritualized representation of the same.

These elements which comprise the microcosm of the biological human is also the macrocosm of the universe. It must be remembered that no single element is autonomous. It is in their ecological interaction that they assume significance.[61] We move and have being only through the energies and forces of the elements in our environment. Since the material world, body and the organs are of the same elements, it can be said that both human and nature are integrally related and are inter-dependent. And it is through

---

55 J.H. Hutton, *The Angami Nagas* (London: Oxford University Press, 1969), 52.
56 Ibid., 56.
57 Ibid., 204.
58 Augustine Thottakara, "A *Vedāntic* Perspective of Ecology," *Journal of Dharma*, vol. XXVI, No. 1 (January-March, 2001): 17.
59 Raimundo Panikkar, *The Vedic Experience: Mantramañjarī*, op. cit., 115.
60 Kapila Vatsyayan, *Ecology and Indian Myth*, op. cit., 22.
61 Ibid., 6.

human and nature that the creator is being manifested and on Him/Her they are ultimately dependent for their existence.[62]

The material world as well as the material body is constituted by the same five elements and each *indriya* (sense-organs) is composed of the same element whose quality is sensed by it, thus forming a living world where all the parts are dependent upon each other. This clearly indicates an unbroken continuum between living beings and the external World.[63] Therefore, the question of superiority does not arise, but only of mutual co-existence. It is in this context, we may point to the fact that if a disturbance is made in one part of this web its balance will be upset. Such disturbance may not just be in the outside world but also in the internal body and senses, which will ultimately disturb our relationship with the creator, since, every human and the objects of the universe derive their sustenance from the Absolute.[64]

4. *Pañcabhūtas* as a Spiritual Resource

Nature and human beings are constituted by the five great elements. This gives a clear picture that Nature is not alien to human beings but an inter-related part of them that is continually being made and nurtured by God. Every element has its own life, form, and location, but is all inter-connected and interdependent. In *Vedic* and *Vedāntic* thought, Nature is a progressive movement. The idea that everything, which we see in Nature and which the people conceive as 'gods', in reality is only expression of the One. Therefore, the simple mathematical equation is that if human persons protect, nourish and promote Nature, Nature will ultimately do the same for human persons; but if they disregard, demolish and destroy Nature, Nature may pay back in the same coin.[65] Moreover, it is God in nature, who supports, sustains and nourishes every life. Such ecological insights of the Indian cultural traditions have their own specific contributions toward spirituality of ecological harmony. Peaceful pro-existence and tolerance of the opposites in a given situation and calmness are spiritual values that are nurtured in an environment of ecological harmony.

Spirituality is about what human person can potentially become. It is also a process of infusion of divinity into the world. Eco-spirituality is living out the inner Goddess or God and embracing the whole creation in terms of the five elements. By revering life at large and celebrating the Cosmos a person manifests his/her inner divinity.[66] Eco-Spirituality therefore is about "All my relations". "It's all alive, it's all connected, it's all intelligent, and it's all relatives".[67] The present ecological crisis, which is global in character, is but a result of lost spirituality, which consequently led to breaking down of the great chain that connects human beings, all sentient beings and nature. Human person needs to learn to see the common elemental thread, which unites all humanity and nature. And such *bhūtanic* spirituality which, is eco-spirituality would certainly make humanity kinder and more co-operative not only with one another but with the whole of nature. An in-depth understanding of ancient religious traditions on the concept of nature is of respect and reverence for the earth and for all there in. Such an attitude of respect and reverence needs to be developed by the modern humanity because everyone and everything is in the web of connectedness.

---

[62] Cf. K.L. Seshagiri Rao, "The Five Great Elements (*Pañcamahābhūtas*): An Ecological Perspective" in *Hinduism and Ecology: The Intersection of Earth, Sky, and Water*, edited by Christopher Key Chapple & Mary Evelyn Tucker (New Delhi: Oxford University Press, 2001), 26.

[63] K.P. Aleaz, *Dimensions of Indian Religion,* op. cit., 118.

[64] Ranchor Prime, *Hinduism and Ecology Seeds of Truth* (Delhi: Motilal Banarsidass, 1996), 25.

[65] Augustine Thottakara, "A *Vedāntic* Perspective of Ecology", op. cit., 23,24.

[66] M.L. Dewan & B.D. Joshi (eds.), *Vedic Philosophy for Himalayan Eco-System Development* (New Delhi: Concept Publishing Co., 1993), 43,44.

[67] L.C. Jain, *Eco-Spirituality for Communal Harmony or Philosophy of Being* (Bangalore: Ecumenical Christian Centre, 2003), 6.

5. *Bhūtanic* Spirituality's Role in Overcoming the present Ecological Problems

The great elements – *bhūtas* have a great deal of spiritual essence stored for humanity to learn and incorporate into our systems. One needs to learn from great Mother Earth who is always giving and selfless. She is the basis of all life; all things rest on the earth as on a stage. The earth is the foundation, the basis out of which emerges all that exists and on which everything rests. Human person is of the earth and earthly, but earth is not simply nature, is not merely geographical or material; it is part of human person himself/herself, so that human person can no more live without the earth than s/he can live without a body.[68] Above all the earth is the Great Mother not only of human person but the Mother of plants and animals. All comes from the earth Mother and returns to her when its term is done. [69]

Water is a symbol of life. Water is a great purifier, a cleanser and is having healing power as *Rg Veda* clearly says "O Waters, stored with healing balm through which my body safe will be… Whatever sin is found in me, whatever wrong I may have done, if I have lied or falsely sworn, Waters, remove it far from me".[70] It brings life, it conveys divine energy, just as in modern parlance blood is the conveyor of human life.[71] Water symbolizes the primal substance from which all forms come and to which they will return. Every contact with water implies regeneration. In initiation rituals water confers a "new birth", in magic ritual it heals and funeral rites it assures rebirth after death.[72] Wherever, water appears, life appears or begins again. Water is the bearer of rejuvenation, of a new start, of redemption as well as creation.[73]

Fire can burn things and transform them into subtle form of energy. In the spiritual realm, this burning of fire can be interpreted as a process of transference of what is gross to subtler and higher realms of the reality. Fire carries the human offering to the divine world. In a more profound sense, this passage from gross to the subtle signifies the transmutation and refinement of the lower self of human person. In other words, it is an act of sublimating or channeling the lower instincts of worldly attachments toward the higher region of immortality.[74] Fire burns at the meeting-point of creation and destruction. All life is burning. It is moving, changing and turning in transformation. Within all life abides a flame of love and creation that goes beyond all the boundaries of what thought can define.[75]

Air holds the gift of eternal; it is the bestower of life-principle, the seed of life. It wanders free, is heard but not seen, is invisible, can only be felt, experienced, sensed, without being comprehended or understood. Air has the medicinal value, in it carries healing, a balm for all.[76] For it is said in *Rg Veda* "Breath of the Gods, and life germ of the universe, freely he wanders. We bring him our homage, whose voice may be heard but whose form is not seen".[77] The wind is fleeting, carefree and gay, that is why it has been said that God's spirit dwells in it. In the soft wind, reaching down invisibly from the wide spaces is God's loving touch, which fondles human person. The wind blows coolness to the feverish person and fills his/her heart with gladness.[78]

---

[68] Raimundo Panikkar, *The Vedic Experience Mantramañjarī*, op. cit., 120.
[69] Langdon Gilkey, *Nature, Reality, and the Sacred: The Nexus of Science and Religion* (Minneapolis: Fortress Press, 1993), 105.
[70] *RV.* X.9.7,8.
[71] Raimundo Panikkar, *The Vedic Experience Mantramañjarī*, op. cit., 116.
[72] K.P. Aleaz, "Waters in Vedic-Post Vedic Traditions", *Bangalore Theological Forum*, Vol. XXXVI, No. 1 (June 2004): 122-34.
[73] Langdon Gilkey, *Nature, Reality, and the Sacred: The Nexus of Science and Religion*, op. cit., 105.
[74] V. Sujatha, "The Philosophical Implications of *Yajña* and Sacrificial Fire: A Critique", *Journal of Dharma*, Vol. xxvi, No. 1 (January-March, 2001): 30.
[75] David Frawley, *Wisdom of the Ancient Seers: Mantras of the Rig Veda* (Delhi: Motilal Banarsidass, 1994), 74.
[76] Raimundo Panikkar, *Vedic Experience Mantramañjarī*, op. cit., 131.
[77] *RV.* X.168.4.
[78] Martin Kämpchen, *The Holy Waters* (Bangalore: Asian Trading Corporation, 1995), 36.

The One vibrated, moved. Through movement came about energy, heat – the primal energy of creation. This energy was the fervor of love, which desired to create, which desired to unfold itself from the One to the Many. And in this love-desire for creation everything has been created. God filled the whole wide emptiness and loneliness with the rhythm of sounds, filled emptiness and loneliness with the vibrations, the vigor.[79] And it is *Ākāśa*, which imparts its value to humanity with its vibrating energy, which enables humanity to communicate with one another.

The understanding of the *Bhūtas*, particularly in *Vedic* and *Vedāntic* tradition, explicitly describes how each element was created and how they are all related, one to another. Therefore, the life of our world depends upon the purity and balance of the five elements that surround us. *Bhūtas* clearly elucidates the relationship that human beings have with the world and with God. It is the principle that makes alive and preserves the life, always purifying, redeeming, what has been destroyed and tarnished. It has the power even to overcome death with new life.[80] Thus these elements – *Bhūtas* are a source of life, peace, immortality and spiritual bliss.

This is why, in such a context of ecological death or suicide, the *bhūtanic* spirituality becomes important. Over against the present society's disintegration of values and decadent moral order, the *bhūtanic* vision needs to be rekindled in each person to start journey from inward to touch the sacredness of the God as the ground of our being and then outward to a union of love with our neighbors and towards all of creation. Such reverence and spiritual essence that draws from the *bhūtas* would certainly oblige people to move against the present irreverence and disregard that one has towards nature. One needs to realize that harmony between humanity and nature is the key to a long-term survival of human species.

Today we need to cherish the values that various religious traditions have continued to profess over centuries. Our ancient scriptures have stressed that human and nature needs to live in close harmony. Humanity have been warned that when air, water and other elements of nature are polluted, seasons start working against their routines or cycles and vegetation gradually begins to ruin; this is most dangerous for all human beings. What modern humanity needs to do is to draw from the spiritual aspects embedded in the writings and admonitions of ancient sayings.[81] There is, no doubt, an immediate need to reinstate harmony with the nature. And this can be done only if one recognizes and reaffirms the association of the divinity in the nature together with the realization that we are part and parcel with the nature. And it is in such a context that *pañcabhūtas* become relevant and significant.

Spirit is around us and in us. All life is infused with spirit. And we are all part of that web of life that is infused with spirit. There is constant communication, knowledge and wisdom that are available to us through nature, if only we are willing to be open to it.[82] And eco-spirituality means that our experience of the divine comes through the natural world. We should always remember that the *Bhūtas* are God's creation. And therefore they are sacred, which means one should not destroy, pollute or inflict damage. It simply means that its rejection would endanger not only human life but also all of God's creation. Hence, mutual recognition and relationship is required. Each human person should make an effort to understand and uphold the spirituality that *bhūtas* advocates i.e., of oneness with God, human and nature, which would in turn, certainly help humanity in improving its chances of survival from the present ecological destruction.

Modern humanity must thus remember that we are constituted by great five elements; our surroundings are but these five elements and thus survival depends in relation to these elements. They are neither outside human person nor alien or hostile to humanity but matter of fact they are an inseparable part of our

---

[79] Ibid., 2,3.

[80] K.L. Seshagiri Rao, "The Five Great Elements (*Pañcamahābhūtas*): An Ecological Perspective", op. cit., 27.

[81] O.P. Dwivedi & B.N. Tiwari, *Environmental Crisis and Hindu Religion* (New Delhi: Gitanjali Publishing House, 1987), 99.

[82] L.C. Jain, op. cit., 6.

existence. What we need today is to join with Francis of Assisi in praising God on high for all His/Her creative works: The sun for the light by which we see, the wind for the air we breathe, the water for its usefulness, the fire for illuminating the night, the earth for giving us food and fodder.[83]

Bhūtas are God's creation. And therefore they are sacred, which means one should not destroy, pollute or inflict damage. It simply means that their rejection would endanger not only human life but also all of God's creation. Hence, mutual recognition and relationship is required. Because, one is also well aware that God, human and nature are within this world, and which continuously interact with one another. But such an interaction gets out of balance when proper reciprocity is not observed. This is why the spiritual dimensions of the *bhūtas* are to remind us to correct the imbalance that is caused by humanity by preserving and sustaining strong relationship. Unless and until humanity understands and upholds the spirituality that *bhūtas* advocates i.e., of oneness with God, human and nature, the chances of survival from the present ecological chaos stands slim. Perhaps the first step towards making a giant leap would be to realize that human person is constituted by the same elements as the nature and therefore we are one with the nature and that polluting them or destroying them is nothing but leading to a self-destruction.

Conclusion

Nature is not alien to human beings but an inter-related part and parcel of a world that is continually being made and nurtured by God. Every element has its own life, form, and location, but is all inter-connected and interdependent. They are the conditions and blessings of our individual and collective life. This brings us to the understanding that Nature and the environment is not something outside humanity but are an inseparable part of human existence.

The present ecological crisis, which is global in character, is a result of lost spirituality, which consequently led to breaking down of the great chain that connects human beings, all sentient things and nature. Human person needs to learn to see the common elemental thread, which unites all humanity and nature. And such *bhūtanic* spirituality would certainly make humanity kinder and more co-operative not only with one another but embracing the whole of nature. What is required of us today is to infuse divinity into the world, or to live out the inner Goddess or God that is within us and this can be termed as Eco-spirituality. Such is ecological spirituality, having intrinsic value and valuable in itself. True spirituality means, obeying the natural law, looking within not only oneself, but the whole of nature – to understand the internal reality of nature.

Bibliography

Aier, I.T. Apok. *The Religion of the Ao Nagas.* Mokokchung: Bendanganshi, 1990.

Callicott, J. Baird &

Ames, Roger T. *Nature in Asian Traditions of Thought: Essays in Environmental Philosophy.* Delhi: Indian Books Centre, 199.

Chapple, Christopher Key &

Mary Evelyn Tucker, ed. *Hinduism and Ecology: The Intersection of Earth, Sky, and Water.* Cambridge Massachusetts: Harvard University Press, 2000.

Chapple, Christopher

Key, ed. *Ecological Prospect.* Delhi: Sri Satyam Publications, 1995.

Dewan, M.L & Joshi, B.D. eds. *Vedic Philosophy for Himalayan Eco-System.* New Delhi: Concept Publishing Co., 1993.

[83] H. Paul Santmire, *The Travail of Nature: The Ambiguous Ecological Promise of Christian Theology* (Philadelphia: Fortress Press, 1985), 107.

Dwivedi, O.P. & Tiwari, B.N. *Environmental Crisis and Hindu Religion*. New Delhi: Gitanjali Publishing House, 1987.

Frawley, David. *Wisdom of the Ancient Seers: Mantras of the Rig Veda*. Delhi: Motilal Banarsidass, 1994.

Gilkey, Langdon. *Nature, Reality, and the Sacred: The Nexus of Science and Religion*. Minneapolis: Fortress Press, 1993.

Griffith, Ralph T.H. *The Hymns of the Rig Veda,* vol. II. Varanasi: CSSO., 1971.

Hutton, J.H.*The Angami Nagas*. London: Oxford University Press, 1969.

Jain, L.C. *Eco-Spirituality for Communal Harmony or Philosophy of Being*. Bangalore: Ecumenical Christian Centre, 2003.

Kämpchen, Martin. *The Holy Waters*. Bangalore: Asian Trading Corporation, 1995.

Müller, F. Max, ed.*The Sacred Books of the East,* vol. I-L. Oxford: Clarendon Press, 1910; Delhi: Low Price Publications, 1995.

Nelson, Lance E. *Purifying the Earthly Body of God: Religion and Ecology in Hindu India*. New Delhi: D.K. Printworld, 2000.

Panikkar, Raimundo. *The Vedic Experience Mantramañjarī*. London: Darton, Longman & Todd, 1977.

Prime, Ranchor. *Hinduism and Ecology: Seeds of Truth*. Delhi: Motilal Banarsidars, 1996.

Radhakrishnan, S & Charles A. Moore, ed. *A Source Book in Indian Philosophy*. New Jersey: Princeton University Press, 1957.

Ranade, R.D. *A Constructive Survey of Upanishadic Philosophy*. Bombay: Bharatiya Vidya Bhavan, 1968.

Rinpoche, Tenzin Wangyal. *Healing with Form, Energy and Light: The Five Elements in Tibetan Shamanism, Tantra, and Dzogchen*. New Delhi: New Age Books, 2003.

Santmire, H. Paul. *The Travail of Nature: The Ambiguous Ecological Promise of Christian Theology*. Philadelphia: Fortress Press, 1985.

Saraswati, Baidyanath, ed. *Prakriti: The Integral Vision*, vol. 5. New Delhi: IGNCA, 1995.

Tucker, Mary Evelyn &

Grim,John A. *Worldviews and Ecology*. New York: Orbis Books, 1994.

Vannucci, M. *Ecological Readings in the Veda: Matter-Energy-Life*. New Delhi: D.K. Printworld, 1994.

Vatsyayan, Kapila. *Ecology and Indian Myth*. New Delhi: All India Association for Christian Higher Education, 1986.

Vatsyayan, Kapila, ed. *Prakriti: The Integral Vision*, vol. I. New Delhi: IGNCA, 1995.

(35) POVERTY AND ECONOMIC JUSTICE IN ASIA – PERSPECTIVES FOR ECUMENICAL SOLIDARITY

M.P. Joseph

> We live in a world of unprecedented opulence of a kind that would have been hard even to imagine a century or two ago…And yet we also live in a world with remarkable deprivation, destitution and oppression. There are many new problems as well as old ones, including persistence of poverty and unfulfilled elementary needs, occurrence of famines and widespread hunger, violation of elementary political freedoms as well as of basic liberties, extensive neglect of the interests and agency of women and worsening threats to our environment and to the sustainability of our economic and social lives. Many of these deprivations can be observed, in one form or another, in rich countries as well as poor ones.
>
> Amarthya Sen, in *Development as Freedom*

Discourse on poverty has been important in the religious and political space for the past several decades. The growth of deplorable levels of deprivation among a large section of the populace in the world amid massive economic growth has invited moral indignation and thus prompted impassioned engagement. The World Food Programme of the United Nations constantly reminds us that "a child dies of hunger every five seconds even though the planet has more than enough food for all". There seems to be no reprieve to the massive increase in deprivation.

The unfortunate fact is that growth of deprivation cohabits with the rapid growth of the conditions to accumulate wealth. In recent years India showed its strength as an economic power house. Several Indians secured a covetous niche in the Forbes list of the wealthiest people in the world. Amid the iniquitous exhibition of its prowess in the global market space, India gained the scoffing status of having the highest number of undernourished people in the World. One in every three malnourished children in the world lives in India. Malnutrition accounts for 50 per cent of its child deaths, while 47 per cent of Indian children under the age of five are severely underweight with at least 16 per cent wasted. Among the Dalits and the tribal population, the percentage of malnourished children ranges from 70 to 73. In one of the most prosperous states, Maharashtra, 77 children die of hunger every day.

Deepening deprivation amidst affluence is a moral scandal. For the Church, this type of death is an expression of the negation of the Divine from the collective realm of people, since life is the greatest gift of God. Negation of life amounts to the negation of God.

Embedding of poverty and richness is not a story of India alone.[1] Affluence produces poverty around the world.

Economic variables offer a partial picture of the reality of deprivation. Loss of human dignity reifies human suffering. Various organizational norms informed by culture and traditions, including gender, race, ethnicity, and caste regulate one's relations to the prevailing modes of production. Dehumanization of people who are left in the margins of power relations is not merely the consequence of political and economic oppression and injustice, but that of a perverted concept of humanity presented by the dominant cultures and traditions. The long periods of caste oppression, patriarchal domination, colonialism, slavery and racism have constructed universal norms to understand the concept of a person. Sorely these

---

[1] Paul Krugman noted in November 2011 that all American redistribution of income away from the bottom 80% has gone to the highest-income 1% – and that a report looking only through 2005 found that almost two-thirds of the rising share of top 1% income went to the top 0.1% (the richest one-thousandth), who saw their income rise more than 400% from 1979 to 2005. "Americas Rich get Richer", http://hope.journ.wwu.edu/tpilgrim/j190/richgetricher.html

ideological constructions have refused the values of the people and monopolised the norms of the oppressor regarding human as a universal norm; oppressor, the slave holder, is the perfect norm of a human.

The struggle against poverty above all is a struggle to re-conquer the dignity as a human person and to sit at the "proper place within the circle of the human family."[2] Poverty discourse in its essence is a mode of combat where the poor demonstrate their determination to emerge from the abyss of non-existence to the summit of our historical existence to reinforce the presence of the non-being in the helm of history. These interventions of the poor are "the only true struggle for life within the whole history of humankind – the struggle between culture and uncultured, between civilization and barbarism, between freedom and slavery, between liberation and oppression, between life and death."[3]

Discourse on Poverty to Reconstruct Domination

However, the inhabitation of the poverty discourse in political and economic conversation claiming a dominant position is not always informed by a concern towards those who have been identified as poor. Rather, it has been informed by a realisation that the debate on poverty could be used as a tool for political and economic engineering around the world. As the term poverty and the people it represents invoke a feeling of empathy in the minds of the public, political and social engineers discovered that its use offers an enormous potential to regulate and legislate a specific economic and political model. The ecumenical discourse on poverty and justice is not always free from this political tarp of converting a moral consciousness based on the inherent goodness of people to construct a social system that ensures the presence of impoverished masses.

Conversion of public morality into a political theory was achieved by constructing a form of public consciousness that makes people believe that poverty is the single most serious moral and economic problem confronting the world. Poverty, according to this view, threatens the security and peace of the world, and thus needs strategic political attention.[4] This view is a fictitious political construct. In the recent past, it was the World Bank and its cohorts who proposed this idea and identified the people living in Asia, Africa, Latin and Central America, the Caribbean and the Pacific nations as poor.[5]

The World Bank theory was provoked by the observation made by President Harry Truman of the United States while delivering the inaugural speech in 1949. The President convincingly described the

---

[2] Engelbert Mveng, "African Theology: A Methodological Approach" in *Voices from the Third World*, Vol. XVIII, No. 1, June 1995, p. 108.

[3] Ibid. p. 108

[4] This view assumes that the prevailing economic political system ensures the security of human life. It is a total lie. As the World Food Program reports indicate, 18000 children die of hunger every day. It is an equivalent of six World Trade Centre type of disaster (September 11, 2001) visiting human community every day.

[5] Africa has "40 percent of the world's potential hydroelectric power supply; the bulk of the world's diamonds and chromium; 30 percent of the uranium in the non-communist world; 50 percent of the world's gold; 90 percent of its cobalt; 50 percent of its phosphates; 40 percent of its platinum; 7.5 percent of its coal; 8 percent of its known petroleum reserves; 12 percent of its natural gas; 3 per cent of its iron ore; and millions upon millions of acres of untilled farmland. There is not another continent blessed with such abundance and diversity" (Lamb, 1983, 20).
Angola, for example, "contains an estimated 11 percent of the world's known reserves of diamonds. Its diamonds are stunning: at an average price of about $140 a carat, with some reaching $350, they are second in quality only to Namibia's, and more than 12 times more valuable than Australia's" (The Economist, 14 September 1996, 68).
In addition, Africa has 64 percent of the world's manganese, 13 percent of its copper, and vast bauxite, nickel, and lead resources. It also accounts for 70 percent of cocoa, 60 percent of coffee, 50 percent of palm oil, and 20 percent of the total petroleum traded in the world market, excluding the United States and Russia.
Yet, Africa is classified as poor in the dominant discourse.

conditions of the poorer nations as appalling, defining them as underdeveloped areas. The importance of Truman's doctrine of poverty lies in the fact that while elevating poverty as the single most important issue that warrants attention from the world community, he also offered a diagnosis of why poverty exists in the world. This famous verdict, "poverty equals underdevelopment" was the whistle for the inauguration of the neo-colonial structures for global governance informed by the ideology of neo-liberalism disguised as development and modernisation.

The myth of underdevelopment presumed first that exploitation of the real producers is not a reason for the prevailing deprivation among the large populace. Instead it is their non-participation or truncated participation that has caused them to be poor. This is a lie fabricated to hide the "sin of the murder of the living labour". The reality is that those who toil with their body are the ones made as poor. The poor are not those who have no productive capabilities or participation in the relations of production; on the contrary they alone produce for the reproduction of life, yet, the fruits of their production have been appropriated by those who control the modes of production. "The poor are those who, in the relationship of domination, are the dominated, the instrumentalized, the alienated."[6] Therefore the poor are the correlative of sin[7]. In their person, they reify the fruits of sin, which is domination. Since the living labour objectifies their life in the product that they make, exploitation is an act of murder. To take the life of the poor is to kill – "and the death suffered by the poor as the fruit of the sin of the sinner, the rich."[8] Wealth according to this view is the objectified life of the poor and its accumulation is to shed blood.[9] Reiterating the latter Gustavo Gutierrez writes: "The poor are a by-product of the system in which we live and for which we are responsible. They are marginalized by our social and cultural world. They are oppressed, exploited proletariat, robbed of their labour and despoiled of their humanity."[10] Being a Christian and rich at the same time is a scandal for Christian faith.[11]

The Sin of Colonialism

The second ideological function behind the construction of the myth of underdevelopment was to hide the historical reasons that lead certain countries to deprivation and poverty. Critical social theories have suggested that it was colonial accumulation has decided the present dispensation in which certain countries are known as rich and a huge majority as poor. It is often observed that the pre-colonial phase of colonialism had three primary objectives which made decisive changes in the economic geography of the globe.

The first objective was the direct plunder of resources from the colonised land with a profound impact on the nations concerned. In a letter written in February 2002 to the heads of the European States, the Nicaraguan indigenous leader Guaicaipuro Cuauhtemoc reminded them that "the indigenous peoples gave a "loan" of 185,000 kilos of gold and 16 million tons of silver to the Europeans from 1503-1660"[12]. This was only one of such calculations. Such plunder continued from all the three major regions colonised by the Europeans. According British writer William Digby, between 1757 and 1815 – a period of crucial importance for the development of British capitalism – a sum of around 1,000,000,000 British pounds

---

6 Enrique Dussel, *Ethics and Community*, (New York: Orbis Books, 1986), p. 22
7 Dussel, *Ethics and Community, p. 22*
8 Dussel, *Ethics and Community, p. 24;*
9 Sirach 34:22b
10 Gustavo Gutierrez, *The Power of the Poor in History*, (London: SCM Press, 1983), p. 44-45
11 Mark 10: 21. To follow Christ, one should sell the accumulated wealth, which in reality is the blood of the poor.
12 Birgitte Feiring "Indigenous Peoples and Poverty: The Cases of Bolivia, Guatemala, Honduras and Nicaragua" (London: Minority Rights Group International, February 2003) p. 11

worth of treasure was taken by Britain from India.[13] The enormity of this amount is visualised when compared with the fact that even in the beginning of 19th century, the aggregate capital of all British companies operating in India amounted to 36,000,000 British pounds.[14]

The second colonial means of depriving the colonies of their right to life was by forcing upon them an international division of labour. English businessman and colonialist Cecil Rhodes's declaration explains the character of this new arrangement. He declared: "...we must find new lands from which we can easily obtain raw materials and at the same time exploit the cheap slave labour that is available from the natives of the colonies. The colonies would also provide a dumping ground for the surplus goods produced in our factories."[15]

While creating conditions of total dependency of the colonies on the European economic system, this division was arranged in such a manner that the value of a product was added only in the industrial sector. As a result, capital accumulation in the European countries swelled while, for the primary producers in the colonial nations, it led to total deprivation.

The third irony suffered by the colonies was the creation of the market space alluded to by Rhodes leading colonies into a hasty deindustrialisation process. Studies on ancient economic systems have often observed that, up to the 18th century, the economic conditions of China and India were relatively advanced, manufacturing and exporting the finest silk, muslin and other luxurious fabrics and articles at a time when the British were living in substantially poorer conditions.[16] However, the deindustrialisation of India was necessary to create a market for British textiles. Hamza Alavi observed that there were two detrimental policies to Indian industries. On the one hand, there was high level of protectionism in Britain to protect the infant British manufacturing industries against Indian textiles through the imposition of high tariffs, and on the other, de-industrialisation was organised on Indian soil. This includes legal measures to force Indian artisans to work in British factories and the prohibition of village weavers from engaging in production. The barbaric acts of cutting away the thumbs of the weavers in India by the British authorities were recalled in this context. The direct intervention had its impact. Between 1815 and 1832, cotton export from India fell thirteen times while British import to India rose 16 times.[17] These three processes had a profound impact on the economies of the colonies; they were deprived of their wealth, production relationship and the right to produce for their needs. The alienation and control over production led them to severe famine. It should be recalled that the first recorded famine in India was towards the end of the colonial period.

Equating poverty with underdevelopment is to reject the sin of colonialism. The underdevelopment doctrine created by the World Bank and the former colonial masters suggests that there are two primary reasons for the prevalence of poverty: non-participation in the market and cultural deficiency.

---

[13] William Digby, *Prosperous British India: A Revelation from Official records,* London: Unwin 1901), p. 534

[14] Romesh Dutt who was an officer in the British administration provides figures for Bengal, Bombay, and Madras provinces in India. According to his calculation, an average of 44 million sterling pounds is flown out of India annually. *The Economic History of India under Early British Rule: From the Rise of the British Power in 1757 to the Accession of Queen Victoria in 1837.* (London: Kegan Paul, Trench, Trubner & Co. Ltd., 1901), p. xiii

[15] Quoted by Edward Goldsmith "Development as Colonialism" in *The Case Against the Global Economy and for a Turn towards the Local,* eds. Jerry Mander and Edward Goldsmith (San Francisco: Sierra Club Books, 1996) p. 254. Goldsmith noted that Lord Lugard, the English governor of Nigeria and the former French president Jules ferry also expressed the same argument.

[16] Vera Anstey *The Economic Development of India* (London, 1929), p.5

[17] Hamza Alavi et.al. *Capitalism and Colonial Production.* (London: Croom Helm, 1982). Ha- Joon Chang convincingly describes this colonial economic scenario in his books *Kicking Away the Ladder,* (London: Anthem Press, 2003)

1. Poverty: A Result of Non-Participation in the Market

Neo-liberal capitalism can be defined as a religious phenomenon where the beingof a person is determined by one's countable and exchangeable possessions. Lack of exchangeable possessions is thus indicative of being poor. Exchangeability through the mediation of the market converts undifferentiated non-beings into identifiable persons. It therefore implies that participation in the market alone offers the right for a person to claim their personhood. This is based on the reconstruction of Cyprian's soteriological principle, "outside market, no salvation". It is the responsibility of the individual thus to gain exchangeability, exchangeable skills, exchangeable commodities, and exchangeable capital.

With the proposal to construct exchangeability as a normative principle for participation in the economic space, neo-liberalism has promoted commoditisation as a moral value to follow. Every aspect of life has been turned into commodities for exchange.

(a) An economy of owners

The proposal to assume exchangeability has three ramifications. Exchange presupposes an "economy of owners" because exchange is an activity among owners[18]. Right of entry into the market space is restricted to those who have exchangeable capital, commodities, or skills. Neo-liberalism, in essence, is an "owners-only club"[19]. Labour assumes value when it achieves exchangeability, which was determined by the dynamics of the changing market conditions. For example, if an artisan makes beautiful cane chairs and the market only favours plastic and steel chairs, the skills of the artisan, though aesthetically gifted, have no value, because cane chairs have lost theit exchangeability and the artisan was not capable of making plastic chairs. Meaning that the skills of the artisan are not exchangeable and thus he or she has no entry in the economic space. But on the other hand, young girls and boys who are willing to expose their nudity in front of a camera are considered as persons, because their body appearance has exchangeability in the advertisement market, though it is an inverted form of valuation.

The owners-only club has made billions of people in the world expendable, since they have no 'commoditable' skills or capital. Moreover, ownership in practice is the power to exclude the "other". As ownership rights increase, exclusion of people from the resources and market intensifies.

Market entry and participation has radically changed after the advent of "casino economy". The casino economy has captured and turned the market space for speculative capital trade and that process has further accelerated the marginalisation of people from the market. Textbook economics suggests that the role of stocks and shares is to pool the savings for more productive investments. Very seldom is this a reality. Capital circulated in the financial market has very little to do with production or trade. Hardly two per cent of transferable liquid capital exchanged in the global financial market accounts for production, distribution, and services.[20] Capital in speculative forms travels from one place to another in a matter of seconds to gather the already created surplus in respective countries. It avoids people and products yet takes away the surplus that people generate through hard labour. For the transfer of wealth from the casino economy requires only few seconds, thanks to the development of information technology. Casino capital has forced all activities in the market into the speculative realm. As a result agriculture, land, labour and the industrial relations of production have also assumed a speculative character.

Wealth is now created in the speculative market alone. And massive volumes of wealth is formed within a short span of time in the fluid space of the speculative market. Those who fail to participate in the speculative capital remain marginalised from the world of wealth. Moreover, the market of speculative capital has defeated all the given economic theories. It was traditionally considered that value was created

[18] C. T. Kurien, *The Economy: An Interpretative Introduction,* (New Delhi: Sage Publications, 1992) p. 117

[19] Kurien, *The Economy,* p. 117

[20] Kavaljit Singh *Globalization of Finance* (Delhi: Madhyam Books, 1998)

through a complex interaction between varied forms of raw material, capital and labour. Invalidating this traditional view, transnational capital claims to create value from nothing, from the void. Living labour has lost its capacity to create value, only money does. In casino capitalism, the worth of a person is not determined by her/his productive capability, but by their volatile appeal in the speculative space. Thus people, those who have capacity to produce have become redundant, expendable.

(b) Meritocracy

An economy based on exchangeability assumes that an individual is responsible for her or his economic success or failure. The market or the historical process including colonialism and slavery, caste and gender dominations should not be blamed for the growth of poverty. Individual merit and ambition are the normative values of the neo-liberal economy, "which signifies poor persons as irresponsible and undeserving, lacking ambition and merit."[21] As a result social values that sustained social relationships and offered dignity and created space for mutual respect have been replaced by market values such as "rabid individualism, and crass materialism, thereby turning social relationships into mere commercial ones."[22] It dehumanises social relationships making profit motivation the primary goal of human life.

The myth of meritocracy has percolated into the public consciousness as the only explanation for the why of poverty. Competition to prove one's merit has replaced values of cooperation and responsibility towards the other. Responsibility is viewed as an economic vice. Celebrated guru of neo-liberal economic policy, Friedrich Hayek opined that "love thy neighbor as thyself" is a tribal and primitive ethic which is unfit for and unworkable in the modern economic system.[23] To him social justice is incompatible with individual liberty; "the notion of social justice is simply a mirage, superstition, a cult, a quasi-religious belief, and the gravest threat to a free civilization."[24]

(c) Creative destruction

The market is based on the principles of creative destruction, a process in which an economic structure from within incessantly destroys the old one in order to increase the volume of exchange in the market space.[25] Branding the existing ones as obsolete encourages consumers to abandon the old to make space for new, even though its value has not diminished,. In the rat-race to control the market space, genocide of the "other" will become a spiritual blessing for the growth of the self. Only those who are vigilant enough to make innovations of the other obsolete in the shorter span of time succeed in the race.[26]

Creative destruction is not restricted to the field of commodities. Since labour has been largely de-personalised and converted to a commodity that is part of the economic exchange, creative destruction is a process of mutual annihilation. The myth of meritocracy and success has legitimised mutual annihilation. Ironically, with the control on the production of culture, the neo-liberal pundits were triumphant in making meritocracy common sense, and have reorganised critical social institutions, including education and religion, the primary arena for its demonstration. And as a logic of creative destruction a large section needs to be branded as obsolete, and every day the number of obsolete swells.

---

[21] Keri Day, "Global Economics and US Public Policy: Human Liberation for the Global Poor" *Black Theology: An International Journal*, Vol. 9, No 1 (2011), 13

[22] Day, "Global Economics and US Public Policy, p. 13

[23] Yoon-Jae Chang, "Economic Globalization and the Neo-liberalism of F. A. Hayek: A Theological Critique", *Quest*, Vol. 2, No. 2 (November 2003), p. 24

[24] Chang, "Economic Globalization", p. 24

[25] "Creative destruction" is a term coined by Joseph Schumpeter in his work entitled "Capitalism, Socialism and Democracy" (1942)

[26] See Thomas L. Friedman, *The Lexus and the Olive Tree: Understanding Globalization,* (New York: Farrar Straus Giroux, 1999) p. 11-12

2. Poverty: An Expression of Cultural Deficiency

The thesis on underdevelopment contended that poverty is to a large extent the result of cultural deficiencies of communities or individuals. The cultural deficiency argument, which itself is a myopic view on poverty, proposes that poor people share deviant cultural characteristics. The poor uphold certain normatives that refuse to accept the values of individual freedom, the achievement motivation, the ability to take risk, economic success, and a consumer culture, which are the foundations of the modern world system. Their allegiance to traditional norms helps to perpetuate their life of poverty. In the absence of a critical appropriation of modern economic values, this view holds that "it is impossible to liberate the economy from traditional restrictions to rational dynamism". According to the culture of poverty thesis, "there is a strong implication embedded in the culture of poverty that defects in the lifestyle of the poor [cultural deprivation] perpetuate poverty. Such defects are passed from one generation to the next. Under these circumstances it is extremely difficult for people, once trapped by the culture of poverty, to escape poverty."[27] As a legitimising theory for the domination of the dominant group over the other, this dubious argument proposes that cultural deficiencies typify a variety of racial, ethnic and gender groups. The political function of this theory is to suggest that economic differences among historically oppressed communities, such as the Dalits, women, Indigenous people, racial minorities, around the world are not due to the repressive experiences but due to the cultural differences in behaviour.[28] Rejecting the cultural deficiency argument, which suggests that normative commitments to modern economic values are imperative, Keri Day observed that "these normative commitments dismiss or underestimate the ways in which inequitable structures and practices impede impoverished persons and communities from experiencing flourishing and thriving. This normative focus on individual success to the exclusion of oppressive structures and institutional practices obscures a vision of moral action that could be an appropriate response to the inequities of advanced capitalist global political economy."[29]

Poverty Discourse in Asian Ecumenical Movements

The development of the concept of poverty among the Asian ecumenical movements has taken place in dialogue with the prevailing discussions found in the broader culture of the time. These concepts reflected a wide range of perspectives informed by specific social locations and political and theological persuasions, as well as the nature of the growth of these movements.

In the initial years, the ecumenical movement was a community of believers committed to the demands of the gospel. Its growth as a faith accompaniment to the challenges of the Bandung Conference inspired the pioneers to acknowledge that the gospel of redemption of the whole human race and the whole created world is the primary motif that lead to the creation of an organised structure of Asian ecumenism, in short its "solidarity of discipleship." This solidarity is not a strategic alliance of churches and Christian movements to negotiate and ensure a privileged place for Christianity in the religiously pluralistic society of Asia, but an alliance for searching in humility to locate a pertinent and virtuous way of being in discipleship to the living presence of the Divine, that seeks to transform life-negating systems and structures to life-giving forces.

These assertions were informed by the empirical realities of Asian nations in the fifties. Poverty was one of the defining realities in the majority of the post independent Asian countries. Memories of the famine of the mid forties created a scar in the minds of the national leaders. It was widely believed that famine in Bengal, which killed around 3.5 million people, was the result of the political decision of the British

[27] Eitzen, D. Stanley and Maxine Baca-Zinn, *Social Problem,* (Boston: Allyn and Bacon, 1994), p. 173
[28] Day, "Global Economics and US Public Policy, p. 18
[29] Day, "Global Economics and US Public Policy, p. 20

Empire. There was no overall grain shortage. Wheat was still being exported from India to support the war economy of the empire.[30]

These realities made the struggle against poverty to dwell in as a mediating principle for various national and regional ecumenical formations. To reassert the new-found determination, Asian ecumenical movement at its initial assembly declared that the struggles of the churches are not to be for the people, but with the people, where the people have the subject rights to define the goals of their encounter.

Two different positions were taking root in the ecumenical debates during that time as a means to address issues of poverty, marginalisation and deprivation. The victory of peasants in China against an exploitative system has ignited the imagination of Asia's poor in several regions. A language that verily harmonises with values of equality gained passionate listeners among the political movements, academy and the church. This group was convinced that social change is not just a teleological proposition, but was an empirical possibility, through which they appropriated the signs of their times. K. H. Ting of China offered a theological explanation to seek beyond the given systems of Asia in order to become a radical witness to the liberating spirit of Jesus. He observed that "Christians are challenged to seek a political and economic system that has the ability to limit the power of sin. Sin can only be healed by forgiveness, and grace. But our choices on economics and politics can limit and check sin. Therefore, making political choice is a faith question." His suggestion was to opt for a limited authoritarianism as an interterm political dispensation to ensure the germination of the conditions of equality that may irradiate poverty and will lead to greater democracy and participation.

The second position was informed by secular humanism; a consolidation of what Charles West termed as "technical humanist" and "revolutionary humanist". In the aftermath of Stalinist invasion of Czechoslovakia, humanist position started to take deeper roots as a means to address issues related to poverty and deprivation. The humanist leadership, except a few, started to distance themselves, or become radically critiques of the limited authoritarianism that socialist regimes promoted for organising state power. They looked towards liberal democracy as the appropriate model.

Appreciation for liberal democracy was based on the assumption that the urge for unity will assist to neutralise the contradictory traditions that Asia has. Moreover, modernity informed by liberal democracy creates a critical space for creative interaction between liberal education, economic development, technological growth, renewed of ideological ethos and radically new social power-structures.

In Asian debates, this position alluded to three priorities:

(a) The accentuation of the primacy of persons in politics and economics. D. T. Niles formulated this principle to construct a theology of self-hood.

(b*)* The inescapable need for creating economic structures that ensure the welfare for people. The inaugural meeting of the EACC states: "It should be affirmed strongly that economic welfare is a necessary means for good life." Since the totality of economic and social life is included in the cosmic purpose of God, the struggle for economic development is viewed as an expression of people's response to the challenges of God to give meaning to their life. Moreover, in the context of extreme poverty in Asia, the search for material security and economic justice is a sign of abundant life that Christ has promised. Thus through the participation in these efforts, churches assume the role of fellow workers of Christ.

Nevertheless, the term welfare is interchangeably used within the ecumenical debate with growth, and prosperity; meaning that economic prosperity equals good life. Citing faith in development as a "fundamentally rational process" to guarantee welfare, it assumes that development "implies a global

---

[30] A vivid and passionate account of the famine was given by Clive Branson, a British soldier stationed in India. Clive Branson, *British Soldier in India, the Letters of Clive Branson*, (New York: International Publishers, 1945)

process of change which will reach its ultimate goal of universal welfare and affluence, which is rational and can be understood, which can been (sic) steered and mastered"[31].

(c) The search for moral laws to regulate social and political life: This view presupposes that notwithstanding the exploitative structures of competitive market, and election obsessed liberal democracy, the establishment of a moral order is possible. The search for a moral order leads to the reassertion of the role of State, and thus called upon Asian Churches to offer critical, but creative support to the respective states.

Instead of offering a healthy conversation between these two positions, viz., liberal humanism and socialist democracy, the ecumenical movement weighted more towards the former one, but with an emphasis on the organisation of the poor and the marginalised for achieving the goals of liberalism. The modernity discourse in Asia, unlike the Western debate, rejected the place of technocracy that robs people of their subjectivity to shape their history, and argued that the "struggle against poverty and for economic development cannot be understood apart from the awakening of the people to a new sense of human dignity."[32] This new definition of modernity under-girded the primacy of the poor and the underprivileged to initiate changes in the oppressive conditions that perpetuate poverty and deprivation, but also suggests that it is a theological movement "and can be appreciated as an historical extension of the struggle of biblical faith against idolatry – religious or otherwise – and against magic and superstition."[33]

Not Charity, but Loving Relations

The ecumenical discourse on poverty alludes to two positions. (a) Nothing short of a reconstruction of the economic, political and social structures and values will have worth in addressing the empirical reality of poverty and marginalization.

Economics is viewed primarily as the art of relationship[34]: The Greek root of *oikos* denotes that economics is about the priorities and practices employed in the functioning of the household. The most fundamental aspect of the household is a loving, caring relationship between its members. Charity has no place in the household. Charity helps to reproduce hierarchical domination and power. Poverty cannot be irradiated by charity. Neither the technological fixes that development and modernisation theories suggests have any potential to irradiate poverty. Since the appropriation of profit is the locus of these theories, it again reproduces poverty and misery.

The splendour of the household lies in the innermost feeling of everyone about the well-being of the "other", the seeking the life and happiness of the other members of the household being the primary objective. Life is a reason for celebration in the household. Any forms of domination, gender, race, caste, class or age deprive the ability to experience the harmonious reality of what a household means. Through using the metaphor of the household to delineate the relationship between God and the created world, Jesus universalised the concept of relationship, exposing the tendency to reduce care among a nucleus group. This concept of universality reiterates that there is no space to entertain a category of a "stranger" in a household, and thus no space for the concept of otherness. Economics in essence is the relationship of

---

[31] Statement of Van Leeuwen, quoted by C.T. Kurien, *Poverty and Development,* (Madras: CLS, 1974), p. 199-200

[32] M.M. Thomas, "Modernization of Traditional Societies and the Struggle for a new Cultural Ethos" in *The Asian Meaning of Modernization,* Ed. Saral K. Chatterji, (Delhi: EACC, 1972), p. 20

[33] Emerito P. Nacpil, "Mission and Modernization" in *The Asian Meaning of Modernization,* Ed. Saral K. Chatterji, (Delhi: EACC, 1972), p. 128.

[34] C.T. Kurien offers a concise definition of economics "An economy is a structure of relationships among a group of people in terms of the manner in which they exercise control over resources, use resources and labour in the production of goods and services, and define and settle the claims of the members over what is produced." C.T. Kurien, *The Economy: An Interpretative Introduction,* (New Delhi: Sage Publications, 1992), p. 20

inclusiveness, the spiritual structure that enables everyone to care for the other person, for the collectivity of the whole, to treat every other person with respect and love and gain the courage to suffer for the well-being of the other.

However, neo-liberalism reinforced the idea that the "other" is only an object for the satisfaction of the "subject". This view regulates the mode of our inter-personal as well as human-nature relationship. It was the European slavery that offered an empirical lesson regarding the benefits of converting realities as "other". Social and political systems learned from this experience of slavery and accepted this value as a universal normative. As a result, the practice of 'mastery over' the other gained logical status as a line of wisdom to gain success in collective life. When the concept of civilisation emerged, the values of the slave masters were constructed as universal normatives and were defined as civilised values. Objectification of the 'other' thus appeared as an imperative to be counted as civilised. People, nature and even the concept of the Divine were re-constructed as objects. The ability and speed of the conversation of social realities into commodities for consumption determined the victory in market led societies. Logics of development and modernity only reiterated the wisdom of the slave masters; however, these concepts intensified this process of objectification of all social realities.

(b) The irruption of the poor will mark the dawn of society free of poverty and deprivation: This is because the poor alone are the social agency to change the situation of exploitation and marginalisation. The dawn marks the presence of those who were absent as persons in the history; when they occupy their proper place as respectable partners. The task of the rich with regards to irradiation of poverty is to stop exploiting others, to bring an end to the discriminative structures and cultures that lead to the dispossession of majority of the people. It is to reconstruct the economic political systems that depend upon the appropriation of the fruits of the labour of the 'other' by converting the "other" as a "thing". It means to secure a place in the world of the exploited social class, with its values, its cultural categories.

The Gospel of Mathew refuses to treat poverty as an economic problem; to this evangelist, poverty is a Christological statement issue. Mathew 25: 35 confirms that God in Christ is the poor. There is no room for identification with the poor or for an option for the poor that non-poor may make. The person who is hungry, or has no shelter, or is persecuted is God. If the poor are culturally deficient beings, it is God who is culturally perverted. If poverty is the outcome that the other is converted as an object for the satisfaction of the meritocratic society, it is God who has been objectified for exploitation. The promise of God for the consummation of history is the promise of the Poor.

Bibliography

Alavi, Hamza and Doug McEachem. *Capitalism and Colonial Production*. London: Croom Helm, 1983.

Chang, Ha- Joon. *Kicking Away the Ladder: Development Strategy in Historical Perspective.* London: Anthem Press, 2003.

Day, Keri. "Global Economics and US Public Policy: Human Liberation for the Global Poor" *Black Theology: An International Journal*, Vol 9, No 1 (2011): 9-33.

Dussel, Enrique. "The Sociohistorical Meaning of Liberation Theology (Reflection of its Origin and World Context)." In *Religion/Globalization: Theories and cases,* edited by Dwight Hopkins, Lois Ann Lorentzen, Eduardo Mendieta, and David Batstone, 33-45. Durham: Duke University Press, 2001.

Galeano, Eduardo. *Open Veins of Latin America: Five Centuries of the Pillage of a Continent.* New York: Monthly Review Press, 1973.

Gutierrez, Gustavo. *The Power of the Poor in History*. London: SCM Press, 1983.

Kurien, C. T. *Poverty and Development.* Madras: C. L. S., 1974.

Millwood, David. *The Poverty Makers.* Geneva: W.C.C., 1977.

Reinert, Erik S. Reinert. *How Rich Countries Got Rich and Why Poor Countries Stay Poor.* New York: Public Affairs, 2007.

Sachs, Jeffrey D. *The End of Poverty: How We can make It Happen in Our Lifetime.* London: Penguin, 2005.

Sen, Amartya. *Development as Freedom*. Oxford; Oxford University Press, 1999.

(36) ALTERNATIVE TOURISM AS AN ECUMENICAL CHALLENGE FOR JUSTICE IN ASIA

Caesar de Mello

Tourism: An Ethico-Theological Issue

Should Tourism be an ecumenical and theological concern?

The answer is 'Yes' because its negative impact is felt around the world, especially by communities in the global South. Tourism is one of the four largest industries in the world, and is a significant feature of most Asian countries ranging from India and Sri Lanka to the Philippines and South Korea. As an industry, it involves massive financial resources and economic power in the hands of a relative few. A structural analysis of mass commercial tourism in light of Christian social teachings and exegesis makes it a very relevant theological focus for churches in the Asian region called to pray, witness, and serve.

However, tourism escapes attention as a crucial justice and peace concern, unlike others, in theological discourse and ecumenical response. This is because the majority of people in church and society remain brainwashed into believing the notion widely propagated that tourism liberates the poor being 'smokeless', costless, clean, green, and non-polluting. Other benefits claimed without nuancing include the bringing in of income, foreign exchange, and employment, and the fostering of so-called understanding between peoples.[1] Such unexamined assertions have created a major gap in church and ecumenical thinking, and suggest a flawed understanding of how tourism operates and impinges, as will be elaborated later. Significantly, they gloss over the question of who benefits from tourism. While not denying some useful outcomes from tourism, overall a superficial and unquestioned construct persists that does not correspond with the reality of community, social, environmental, and economic damage. Such ignorance plays into the hands of the tourism industry, governments, and vested interests, who are resistant to shining a spotlight on the other side of tourism.

Impelled by the Gospel which enjoins that we act for our neighbour and social justice, we cannot rest with an outlook on tourism provided by those who profit from it, some of the powers and principalities of the day. Given the *diakonia* call, it is incumbent on us that we assess and critique tourism from the perspective of the victims of tourism development that remains grounded in the economic and political structures of today – women, children, indigenous peoples, those dispossessed of their land, the vulnerable, and others affected, who pay the human cost of tourism, and who are close to the heart of a compassionate God.

Churches in the 70s and 80s had already identified tourism emerging as a considerable challenge to the local people in the global South. As far back as 1980, ecumenically, and with the support of the WCC and the (Catholic) Federation of Asian Bishops' Conferences (FABC), they organized in Manila a landmark international Consultation of churches and civil society. Its participants noted:

> The one most glaring thing that surfaced from the deliberations of the Workshop was that tourism wreaked more havoc than brought benefits to recipient Third World countries.
>
> From an historical perspective, Third World countries have discovered time and again how their economies, cultures and social structures have been disrupted by the long-term effects of tourism.[2]

---

[1] Sachs, Jeffrey. Keynote Speech, UNWTO Global Forum, March 6 – 7, 2011. Andorra la Vella, Andorra.

[2] CCA/FABC. Conference Statement of the International Workshop on Tourism, sponsored by Christian Conference of

The Impact of Tourism

Today, the global tourism industry is much bigger than in the 80s. It is one of the four largest industries in the world alongside oil and fuels, arms and armaments, and pharmaceuticals. Tourism outlays according to some calculations amount to some 10 % of the global GDP, while employing globally around 300 million, or about 10 % of the global workforce. With rising incomes, the number of leisure travellers is steadily on the rise, with a billion tourism arrivals in a year globally now, and trending towards 1.6 billion by 2020, according to the estimates of the United Nations World Organisation (UNWTO).[3]

Asia, home for around 65 % of the world's population, and teeming with innumerable tourism destinations, is a magnet for tourists. To entice more of the world's tourists, catchy marketing slogans are used such as Incredible India, Amazing Thailand, Malaysia Truly Asia, Remarkable Indonesia, Beauty has an address: Oman, The Heart of Asia: Taiwan, Cambodia: The Kingdom of Wonder, Marvellous Melbourne, Infinitely Yours: Seoul, and others.

Despite what its advocates may claim, the kind of tourism seen in Asia and the wider global South indicates that, in its own way, it plays a role in impoverishing communities, alongside factors such as poverty, war, ethnic conflict, lack of infrastructure, lack of educational opportunities, corruption, inequitable distribution of wealth and resources, and trade injustice, among others. However, the negatives associated with tourism are not rendered as obvious as those linked with the other factors, thanks to the slick tourism advertising, the superficial assumptions regarding the 'benefits' of tourism, and the innate human desire to travel.

While it is not possible to go into much detail in this article, some of the multiple impact on communities in Asia can be analyzed and summarized as follows:

- **The diversion of essential people's resources** such as land, water, electricity, other infrastructure for the construction and maintenance of hotels, resorts, golf courses, amusement parks, airports, etc to cater to tourists. Generally these resources are in short supply but tourism operations and tourists have a prior claim on these over the local people whose poverty is in sharp contrast to the affluence enjoyed by a few. Observant travellers would have realized how hungry tourism is for land, water, energy, and other resources.
- **The social costs through abuse** of women and children, and their trafficking. Due to the informal and underground dimensions of this 'industry', it is difficult to arrive at exact figures of those involved. However, estimates of women and children caught up in sex tourism, both worldwide and in Asia, are placed at consistently high levels. This is unsurprising given that the push factor is very strong as a result of the growing poverty in communities.
- **The costs entailed in the commercialisation,** commodification and denigration of indigenous and local culture, and the threat to cultural identity that ensues. Local and indigenous customs, rituals, sacred shrines and places of worship, sacred music, ceremonial dress, traditions, and handiwork become just objects for many tourists without appreciation for their underlying meaning and heritage.
- **The loss to host countries** as a result of financial and related advantages gained by foreign and domestic business interests through tax concessions and holidays, subsidised land and other costs, import advantages, reduced wages and working conditions, tourism-friendly regulations, and other packages. For instance, it has been shown that the devastation by the Tsunami in 2004 could have been reduced had mangroves been retained s a protective buffer at some of the beaches. However, they were removed at the insistence of the tourism industry. Such practices still continue.

Asia and the Federation of Asian Bishops' Conferences, September 12 – 25, 1980, Manila

[3] UNWTO. *Tourism 2020 Vision*. 2001, Madrid

- **The social and economic consequences** of displacement caused by tourism development. For instance, many of the locations where tourism hotels and resorts are built and planned were agricultural fields of local farmers who are subsequently displaced for tourism development.
- **Ecological damage and loss** incurred in Asian countries in the course of sustaining inappropriate tourism enterprises and practices. Loss of bio-diversity worsens as, under the myth of 'eco-tourism', ecologically fragile sites and eco-systems are overexposed to tourists, who however keep on searching for other 'unspoilt' locations when one is destroyed. Effluents and other discharges imperil both water and land. We confront a tourism that is unresponsive to calls to limit to tourism numbers and destinations.
- **Climate change implications** through aviation and shipping, and heavy reliance on fossil fuels-based energy for lavish hotels, air-conditioning for ecologically unsound buildings, substantial consumption of electricity, etc. Expansion of airports in major cities, and the building of new ones in secondary and tertiary cities, will only intensify carbon emissions. Any discussion of climate change and its effects without reference to tourism is incomplete.
- **The cost to host communities through health hazards**, such as HIV/AIDS, drugs and narcotics, among others. Hotels, governments, and other related actors are loathe to take any or partial responsibility for these, fearing loss of tourists and income.
- **Human rights violations** and the damaging political exploitation that occur within tourism. For instance, the almost complete domination of Palestinian tourism and other related sectors by Israel is a case in point.[4]

It is argued by some proponents of growth economics that tourism's varied impact is a 'small' price to pay for achieving development. However, vulnerable communities bear the brunt of such 'progress' with its record of economic deprivation, anti-social behavior, and cultural and ecological damage, making people's suffering a focus for theology.

Tourism, Development, and the Myth of Poverty Alleviation

Developing economies in South, South East, and North East Asia look to tourism as a means to assist the poor. The UNWTO, the tourism industry, and governments posit that tourism is 'a motor for development', that it contributes to poverty alleviation in developing countries.[5]

The macro-economic data might suggest good returns for investors from tourism, but how do the poor benefit?

Modern tourism is accompanied by a serious level of 'leakage' of income and profits out of developing countries to overseas-based tourism businesses, airlines, cruise companies, hotel chains, food and drink exporters, and other interests.[6] And even though the poor are claimed to be beneficiaries of tourism policies, the major portion of what income remains in the country goes to the owners and investors. Furthermore, as the market laws of supply and demand come into play, tourists and others capable of paying higher prices for limited vital resources inflate costs beyond the reach of the local population, impoverishing them even further.

Little evidence exists to justify tourism as beneficial for vulnerable communities. While economic information is available on tourist arrivals, revenue earned and related statistics, often little or no social indicators on tourism's impact are generally kept. The employment generated in the local community is

[4] Kassis, Rami. *Introduction,* 'Combating Dispossession'. Alternative Tourism Group, Palestine, 2008

[5] Cabrini, Luigi. *'Tourism, Climate Change and the Millennium Development Goals'*, in 'Disaster Prevention in Tourism: Perspectives on Climate Justice'. Caesar D'Mello, Jonathan McKeown, and Sabine Minninger, Eds., ECOT, Chiang Mai, Thailand, 2009

[6] IFC, World Bank, MIGA. *Tourism and Global Development.* 2000

predominantly limited to the few lucky enough to be selected for low paying jobs such as guards, gardeners, cooks, cleaners, chamber maids, receptionists, lifeguards on beaches, and for other low grade or skilled tasks.[7] On the other hand, believing that tourists will come, a false security is created within the community, and those unemployed wait for their opportunity. In the meantime, productive work including farming and fishing is abandoned, and valuable skills lost to the community. As well, in different parts of Asia today tourism operations cause community, social, political, and even physical violence. Several places come to mind, including Goa, Kanyakumari, Kerala in India, north-eastern Sri Lanka, the Maldives, Bali in Indonesia, Boracay in the Phillipines, and parts of Thailand. It is often stated that due to the injection of resources through tourism into developing economies, the South owes a debt to the North. In fact, the reverse is true. The South subsidizes the tourism enterprise through costs borne by communities in various ways as discussed earlier. Eventually these far outweigh whatever gains are made from tourism. It is the Global North that owes a debt to the South.

Tourism is not a stand-alone reality. It is multi-faceted in that it relates to a mix of inter-related dimensions of culture, community, politics, economics, commerce, trade, locale, biodiversity, ecology, gender issues, and other aspects. Within this framework, tourism reflects a host of *a priori* positions and assumptions based on a neo-liberal economic philosophy based on the primacy of growth and the market, and incorporating the structural injustices inherent within such an ideology, making it futile to seek to 'reform' tourism.

Community Tourism

There is of course a better kind of tourism – Community Based Tourism – that is fair, sustainable, and respectful of the environment through conserving resources and using energy carefully. Such tourism is owned, managed, and assessed by the community with the purpose of enabling visitors to increase their awareness and learn about the community.[8] This ensures interaction between tourists and the local people, and helps the visitor to discover local habitats and wildlife, and celebrate and respect traditional cultures, rituals and wisdom. This form of tourism creates greater economic benefits for the local communities, enhances their quality of living, and builds local capacity as they engage in collaborative decision making. But it is not what mass commercial tourism would be interested in promoting.

Some Foci for Theological Exploration on Tourism

Contemporary tourism constitutes a human concern through its marginalizing of vulnerable communities, and hence is a theological concern. Insights and the methodology of Contextual Theology can assist in developing a new faith-based understanding of and response to the tourism challenge. It would be remiss for theological institutions and associations to stay dis-engaged from what has emerged as a major human issue. Their students need to be encouraged to research, study and advance appropriate responses to tourism's impact. Ethics, structural and social analysis, women's studies, 'green' studies, contextual theology and missiology, among others, provide sound and appropriate parameters for this exercise.

Twenty seven years ago, looking at tourism through the lens of theology, the Rev Harvey Perkins wrote:

> To talk of a theology of tourism is to seek a contextual theology in the midst of our historical involvement with the issues of Third World tourism, which will establish the human in the midst of the inhuman, the just in the

---

[7] O'Grady, Ron. *'The Threat of Tourism. Challenge to the Church'*, pp 63-64. Risk Book, WCC Publications, Geneva, 2006

[8] ECOT, *'Sustainable Tourism and CBT'*. Contours Vol 21, No 2, July 2011

> midst of the unjust, the participating in the midst of dominating, the delivering in the midst of captivity. It must reveal how our faith in God opens up to the possibilities of human freedom, and points to a better human society for which we must work. It should renew our actions as Christians, changing our emphasis, our directions and our processes.[9]

The above comment is still relevant for our times.

Given its multi-sided nature, tourism can be explored theologically in various directions. Two examples are provided below that in turn open the discussion to other related dimensions.

Tourism and objectification

Mass commercial tourism by its nature objectifies the other for personal satisfaction.[10] Women and children are reduced as objects for sensual pleasure. Local people serve tourists for a pittance with little work guarantee or satisfaction, but much alienation. To satisfy the tourists' gaze, nature is reduced as scenic objects. Culture is recycled and presented as something to watch without its deeper meaning.

Tourism promotes the wrong assumption that people can be enabled to gain fulfillment through interaction with objects, that a subject gains subjecthood by relating with an object. Almost all tourism advertising focuses on the enjoyment for the tourist without much reference to the local people. Interaction with objectified people or nature leads to the erosion of 'peopleness'. In the absence of a subject to subject relationship, people are deprived of their human dignity. All forms of objectification are anathema to God in whose image we are created.

The exploitative and objectifying nature of tourism in Asia springs from structures operating nationally and internationally. The rich and powerful of the world exercise their power over poor nations, and the economic and political elite within poor countries exploit the powerless in their own societies.

Tourism and the integrity of creation

There is an essential theological dimension to the investigation and reflection on tourism in the context of the integrity of creation. It points to God's creative nature whose outpouring is seen so dramatically in Genesis, with the declaration that 'God saw that it was good'.

Tourism is a profits-driven industry that exploits what it does not own. It thrives by marketing nature – the sun, sea, mountains, rivers, landscapes – icons from Genesis. What the industry serves, however, in Asia and the rest of the world, is an offering in large measure of what is described as 'sun, sand and sex' tourism, which is an affront to God's creation.

God's gifts have to be enjoyed with care and responsibility. We have to acknowledge that God's creation has been violated, and is in need of 'mending' due to the root cause of human greed and our captivity to the power of Mammon. The poor are at the mercy of an economic and political thinking that justifies the inequitable distribution of power, resources, rights, and the gifts of nature in an unwholesome reflection on God. The *oikoumene* whose fragile social and ecological balance has been upset by irresponsible human action challenges us to be an incarnational presence reflecting Christ's mind, love, and even ire.

Tourism, a dominant industry, needs to be prophetically challenged to understand that the earth belongs to all, not just to the financiers of the industry, the tourists, the world's affluent, or those who promote a kind of 'development' that does not benefit the poor. As Christians, we have the duty and the task to provide leadership through our ideas and practice.

---

[9] Perkins, Harvey. Theological Reflection on Tourism, Biblical Reflection on New Consciousness and a New Structure for Third World Tourism. ECTWT (ECOT), Thailand, 1985

[10] ECOT/NCCI. Chennai Statement on the Theology of Tourism. March 19 – 21, Chennai

Some Suggestions for Incorporating Tourism Within the Theological Curriculum

By its close nexus with the community and the wider society in different ways, tourism can point the theological student in the direction of several lines of theological exploration towards developing an alternative, responsible, ethical, pro-poor, and just tourism. Theological institutions can lead by putting together a well designed course and syllabus from a justice and pastoral perspective for theological and ministerial students.

Applying scriptural and Gospel values undergirding the *preferential option for the poor*, and using a contextual theology approach, areas for study, analysis, and reflection include:

1. Analyze and critique the unjust tourism structure and practices prevailing in specific parts of Asia in conflict with the call of the Kingdom.
2. Critique tourism from the point of view of the sub-altern and subsistence communities, indigenous people, women and children, the displaced, and others on the margin, applying the Kingdom values of equality and equity.
3. Study the potential of tourism as 'pilgrimage as alternative tourism' to stimulate an ethical engagement for mutuality, solidarity, and a real discovery of human community.
4. Analyze and challenge the content of media messages and tourism advertising.
5. Using specific examples and experience, question whether tourism truly alleviates poverty.
6. Within the context of integrity of creation and stewardship, study the link between tourism and climate justice.
7. Do a case study of the displacement of local people for tourism, and the after effects of this.
8. Study tourism's nexus with globalization and a neo-liberal form of capitalism.
9. Develop ways of empowering and sensitizing the church to advocate just tourism and lead the faithful accordingly.
10. Does contemporary experience suggest that tourism, leisure, and money, be contextualised within a 'structure of sin'?
11. Look at responding to tourism issues in an inter-faith context.
12. How acceptable is the model of Corporate Social Responsibility (CSR) used by the tourism industry to create a benign image of itself?
13. Investigate the reality and hype behind the claims often made that 'eco-tourism assists with bio-diversity'within the framework of stewardship of creation.

An international Asian workshop was a recent attempt at considering tourism in a theological light.[11] Some of its recommendations regarding tourism and the theological syllabus include:

1. Urge regional theological institutions such as the Senate of Serampore (University), the Association of Theological Schools in South East Asia, Asian Theological Association and other theological schools and bodies in Asia to develop a curriculum for ministerial candidates. Colleges and seminaries must be encouraged to offer it as a credited course, or as an interdisciplinary course.
2. Integrate tourism in other disciplines such as Christian Ethics, Social Analysis, Women's Studies, Tribal/Dalit theologies and Christian Ministry.
3. Start a scholarship program that will encourage research scholars to pursue the issue of tourism.
4. Conduct exposure programs for theological students under the supervision of appropriate alternative tourism organisations.
5. Offer training for theological teachers in order to lead courses and help with the evolving of methodological tools for analysing the negative impact of commercial tourism from a theological perspective.

---

[11] *Ibid.*

6. Request the National Council of Churches in India and similar peak bodies in Asia to integrate the issue of tourism in all its commissions.
7. Critique churches and their institutions collaborating with the tourism industry in light of its negative impact. Christian publications, the liturgy, and the pulpit can draw attention to these.

Conclusion

To sum up, churches and theological colleges have generally not addressed tourism in a serious way, despite its substantial impact on Asian society. Mass tourism has its roots in profit making, pleasure and hedonism, making it oblivious to life, culture and the environment, all of which it sees merely from an utilitarian viewpoint, thus denying their integrity and wholeness. The high energy, land and other demands of mass tourism as well as the infrastructure provided are threatening local livelihoods, displacing local people, endangering ecosystems, stretching drinking water resources, and having a negative social impact. Tourism also raises challenges regarding climate change, trafficking and sexual exploitation of women and children, and HIV AIDS. It breeds injustice, denies the right to live in dignity especially to the poor and the marginalised people, and brings destruction to God's creation. The present paradigm of tourism is indefensible, and needs to be replaced by a more just one.

The chain of exploitation and injustice resulting from contemporary tourism contradicts the testimonies of the Bible, and challenges the will of God who calls humankind to freedom and life in all its fullness. The degrading of human persons and communities insults God. This makes tourism an ethical, theological and missiological concern. The God who intervenes when the poor are affected will not turn a deaf ear to the victims of today's tourism industry – the vulnerable and marginalized. The suffering endured by communities should beckon us to resolute commitment and involvement in the work of liberating. In this we are inspired by the example of Jesus who by His words and action denounces injustice and announces the reign of God.

Bibliography

'Combating Dispossession. Towards a Code of Ethics for Tourism in Palestine'. Ranjan Solomon, Ed. Alternative Tourism Group, Palestine, 2008

'Disaster Prevention in Tourism: Perspectives on Climate Justice'. Caesar D'Mello, Jonathan McKeown, and Sabine Minninger, Eds., ECOT, Chiang Mai, Thailand, 2009.

Ecumenical Coalition On Tourism (ECOT)/Ecumenical Coalition On Third World Tourism (ECTWT). Contours Magazine Vol 1 – 21.

'Mission Perspective in Tourism'. Tan Chi Kiong (Ed.). ECOT/ECTWT, Hong Kong, 2001.

O'Grady, Ron. *'The Threat of Tourism. Challenge to the Church'*. Risk Book, WCC Publications, Geneva, 2006.

O'Grady, Ron. *'Third World Stopover'*. Risk Book Series, WCC Publications, Geneva. 1981.

Perkins, Harvey. *'Theological Reflection on Tourism. Biblical Reflection on New Consciousness and a New Structure for Third World Tourism'*. ECTWT (ECOT), Thailand, 1985.

'Third World Tourism', Ron O'Grady, Ed. CCA/ECTWT, Singapore, 1980

'Transforming Re-Forming Tourism'. Caesar D'Mello, Ed. ECOT, Chiang Mai, Thailand, 2007.

UNWTO. *Tourism 2020 Vision*. 2001, Madrid.

Urry, John. *'The Tourist Gaze. Leisure and Travel in Contemporary Societies'*. Sage Publications, London/New Delhi. 1990

PART IV

WOMEN AND MARGINAL COMMUNITIES IN ASIAN ECUMENISM

(37) Asian Women's Role in the Ecumenical Movement

Wong Wai Ching

Women's contribution has been an essential part of the success of the ecumenical movement. Women were the first evangelists, charged by the resurrected Christ to tell the good news to the people (Mark 16: 9-11). They were at the forefront of the Jesus movement as companions, supporters and resource providers (Matthew 27: 55-56). In the mission fields, starting from the sixteenth century, women were the preferred recipients of the gospel because they were more responsive to the Christian message of love and forgiveness. In turn, they often found in Christianity an exit from their oppressive cultures and marginal societal positions. However, despite their selfless and devoted contribution, and unlike their male counterparts, women evangelists and missionary co-workers have been rarely remembered as leaders in the early stage of the ecumenical movement.[1] Their voluntary services were counted only as extensions of their housewifely duties in support of their husbands and colleagues, and were therefore considered peripheral. Apparently, when the Asian ecumenical movement was formally launched in 1957 under the leadership of the East Asia Christian Conference (EACC), which was later renamed Christian Conference of Asia (CCA), there were women who accompanied their husbands or took part in the work as individual volunteers to provide whatever was needed in its formative phase. Unfortunately, their names were not passed down to us for our remembrance, unlike those of the pioneer male leaders and officers. The first official record of a woman worker had to wait until Ruth K. Cadwallader, the first CCA staff for Information, came on board between 1968 and 1972. Given her designated countries of affiliation, which were Thailand and the United States, Ms. Cadwallader was likely to be a missionary. But like all the other women in the early period of the Asian ecumenical movement, there was not much information about her.

Despite the sketchy records, women must have been there and contributed to the evolution and continuous development of the ecumenical mission. Like their male colleagues, they must have been convinced of the need to ground Christianity in the soil of Asian cultures and societies, and they must have dedicated a great deal of efforts in the building of hopes and visions for a future Asia of peace and justice. Unlike their male colleagues, these women began to draw their particular convictions and visions from the specific predicament and aspirations of women in Asia as time went by. More information surfaced in the latter years, beginning in the seventies and eighties. In this paper, I shall characterize women's roles in the ecumenical movement in Asia in three stages: (a) the founding days: as ground breaker; (b) the period of growth: as bridge builder; and (c) the recent time: as co-liberator.

1. The Founding Days: As Ground Breaker

Asian Christians protested at the 1910 World Missionary Conference in Edinburgh against European domination in mission work and its imperialistic approach to the "young churches" in Asia, and which assumed that all Asians shared the same destiny regardless of whether they were men or women. Although no woman's name was mentioned in the early defense of Asian indigenous Christianity, women were quick to deepen the focus from Asia in general to Asian women in particular. Some organized themselves and established the first Asian Christian Women's Conference in 1958. Some went into the Committee on Cooperation of Men and Women in Home, Church and Society at the EACC Inaugural Assembly in 1959. They started to organize the women's forum prior to the CCA Assembly in 1977, and successfully

[1] See the recent publication: Christine Lienemann-Perrin, Atola Longkumer, Afrie Songco Joye (eds.): Putting Names with Faces. Women's Impact in Mission History. Abingdon Press, Nashville, 2012.

established the CCA women's desk in 1981. These have all been important venues for women to gather as Asians, where they discovered that they were not only marginalized by Western theology as Asian Christians, but also by their fellow Asian Christian brothers as Asian women. They fought and negotiated for additional space for women to meet and reflect on the commonness and difference of their predicaments across the various countries; they learnt from one another's stories of struggle and resistance; and they were empowered to theologize their experiences afresh. Keen members of these gatherings participated in the establishment of the Women's Commission of the Ecumenical Association of Third World Theologians in 1983, and went on to organize the Asian Women's Resource Centre for Culture and Theology in 1988. Together with the women's committee of the World Student Christian Federation, which was constituted in 1984, they formed a solid network of ecumenical women in Asia as they began a series of programmes and publication thereafter.

With very minimal support, these various women's organizations began their mission and vision from scratch. While they had to fill the gap of the agenda dominated by their male Asian ecumenical colleagues, they were also challenged to differentiate themselves from the Western feminists so as to align with the movement of contextual Christianity. Their first task therefore was to identify the issues that Asian women in general were facing. In regional conferences and workshops conducted for women in Asia, participants from local churches and congregations engaged for the very first time in conducting social, economic, cultural and ideological analyses of their countries, Asia and the world. They were dedicated to seek nothing less than a transformation of the social order, beginning with the church. Since their early meetings, they have dealt with issues of women workers, women farmers, prostitution connected to tourism, victims of militarization, atomic bombs, and comfort women, or those who were identified as the most oppressed class and caste in the newly independent countries of Asia. Both gender and class analyses have been brought to use for conscientization as well as for programme planning. There has been a strong sense of solidarity built among women for the liberation of the sisters at the bottom rung of the society and for a mission and theology that could address the experience of women on the ground.

As soon as the CCA Assembly in 1977 in Penang identified the focus of Asian mission as "The Search for Full Humanity," Asian Christian women were quick to respond. Sun Ai Lee Park, one of the pioneer feminist theologians in Asia, contended that Asian women have been engaged in the mission of God from the beginning in their responses to people's cries, sufferings, aspirations and demands.[2] They have been called to take up their responsibility in the history of their lands and to be active agents in society in which the Kingdom of God must come. For Asian Christian women, ecumenical mission is to immerse in the needs they saw and to respond to the call they heard. As Asian women, they have been deeply involved in social service and action, witnessing and raising awareness among the poor, and doing justice, serving and living among the needy. Many have been members of national liberation movements, labor movements, anti-nuclear movements, as in the Korean unification movement, for example. They were keen to engage in the rebuilding of an alternative vision of a new world order, which is both life-centered and creation-centered, and which is based on a violence-free and just world. As such, Asian women have fully participated in the ecumenical beginning to take the context of Asia seriously, to respond by their immersion in mission with the poor and the needy of their respective countries, and to start reflecting on it theologically and seriously.

2. The Period of Growth: As Bridge Builder

Without official positions or titles, many women simply responded to the call to witness through immersion in the struggles and aspirations of the people. Women in Korea, for example, were encouraged

[2] Park, Sun Ai Lee, "Asian Women in Mission," *International Review of Mission*, 81 (1992): 280.

to work with the churches in the industrial worker's living areas and with farmers in some rural areas. They formed the core of the Minjung (people) church movement. Through their identification with the struggles of women of the grassroot communities – e.g. peasants, laborers, prostitutes, and the Minjung – women felt the connection between the various movements and the struggle for human rights and democratization. Through their work in the Minjung churches, they saw also the link between God's mission and the battle against feminization of poverty, human rights violations, racial and caste discrimination, ecological crisis and the struggles for building new societies in Asia. Their focus on women has actually led them to the concerns of the larger whole.

For these Asian women, doing the mission of God means challenging the many boundaries drawn by different religious institutions to keep women under multiple forms of oppression. Everyone must reflect on each others' limitations and lack of response to the Divine they revere. It is a mission seen in a prophetic role, promoting and defending common human and spiritual values. With respect to women's interests, all religions need to be liberated from their respective "sinful conditioning" – especially patriarchal conditioning – in order to become "true leaven in society."[3] All religions and local cultures need to be carefully analyzed in order to determine which aspects are life-giving and liberating and which are domesticating and alienating. This is a consensus built up among women from all major religions who met in Colombo in a conference on Inter-faith Dialogue in 1991.

As a result, these women sought a radical re-definition of the relationship of Christianity to non-Christian religions and subsequently also to non-religious worldviews and ideologies. Since then inter-religious dialogue has occupied a prominent place in Asian women's theological activities and thinking. Indeed, rather than engaging in discussion about meeting with peoples of other faiths, women have been sharing resources, going to market, living as neighbors with one another, be they Muslims, Hindus, Buddhists or followers of other folk religions. For women, inter-religious dialogue devoted to mutual understanding and removal of prejudice is just a normal way of life. Subsequently many women's workshops and conferences became venues for exploration of the common ground for women of different faiths to unite for the caring and fighting for women's basic living necessities, and rights to survival and protection. The most outstanding advocate of a life-centred syncretic approach to women's faith is Chung Hyun Kyung.[4]

In a way, women are natural "transgressors" of boundaries and, as such, they are also challenged to be bridge builders. As women have been living on the margins of various social and cultural divisions, they are able to cut across these divisions through their daily involvement in matters pertaining to family and children. Their marginal position in the religious and social institutions allows them to see the priority of the ecumenical agenda in personal commitment and relationships, in the building up of communities, in shared lives together, in face-to-face meetings, in relationships of love, trust, and Christian faithfulness. If mission means everything in the promotion of justice and participation in social transformation in response to the needs of people and societies, then building a world of reconciled relationships and bringing new values for upholding and sustaining life in a life-negating world must be placed at the core of it.

3. The Recent Time: As Co-Liberator

Since most women have assumed social and familial roles, ecumenical mission to them is never a one-way process but is participatory. Women's ecumenism is therefore always a story of mutual engagement in empowering themselves via struggles to meet their sisters' basic needs. It often involves healing

[3] Marlene Perera, "Toward the Twenty-first Century: An Asian Woman's Emerging Perceptions on Mission," *International Review of Mission*, 81 (1992): 234.
[4] Chung Hyun Kyung, *Struggle to Be the Sun Again: Introducing Asian Women's Theology* (Maryknoll, NY: Orbis, 1990), 113.

themselves as well as others with whom they come into contact. Prakai Nontawasee, a member of the CCA presidium from 1990-1995, called for the building of mission in mutual solidarity. Anyone who takes part in it should have compassion for one another so that there will be a meeting of different souls and persons.[5] It is a co-mission of humans and God in seeking and communicating divine truth and in a shared responsibility of being witnesses to the work for justice and peace. Ecumenism is therefore the building of partnership in mission.

Nevertheless, partnership between women and men has not been taken seriously for the most part in the life of the ecumenical movement. Issues of women were taken first as manifestation of the oppression of people in Asia and then later as a token concern by the male ecumenical colleagues. While women students had already been a part of the general committees and conferences of the World Student Christian Federation in 1913, equal participation of women in the various levels of the ecumenical bodies in Asia continues to be an ongoing battle even today. Since the seventies, women's pre-meetings and women's caucuses in between meetings began to raise a concerted demand for stronger women's participation in various committees and for proper representation on the official level. For the first time in the history of CCA, a woman, Jurgette Honculada from the Philippines, was elected with three other men to the presidium for the term from 1973 to 1977. Not until the next term, from 1977 to 1981, did two women get appointed as staff – i.e. Soewawi Gadroen from Indonesia as secretary for youth, and Elizabeth Tapia from the Philippines for women's concerns. Despite these symbolic gestures of improvement, most regional leadership and functional committees in the regional and national ecumenical bodies continue to be dominated by men and male clergy. Women's voices have remained nominal and marginal within the main organizational structures and decision-making bodies.

This gap between theory and practice has become one major point of contention between men and women in the ecumenical movement in Asia. Only with the later growth of a number of more enlightened men was it possible to launch a more constructive agenda for men and women partnership in the Asian ecumenical mission in the nineties. The first step was initiated by the SCM/WSCF Women's Programme which concluded that men are no longer seen as supporters to women's movement only but also as in need of liberation from patriarchy in order that a new humanity in God's image could emerge. This meant the realization of women's problems as men's problems, and that women's struggle for liberation is also men's struggle for liberation. In Yong Ting Jin's reflection, it is a call for "a covenant between women and men to search and find out the true and meaningful partnership in their personal/individual lives and their collective life."[6] In 1995, Esther Byu, then executive secretary for women's concerns of CCA, edited a volume titled *Affirming Difference, Celebrating Wholeness: A Partnership of Equals* giving testimony to the same. In 2000, a subregional consultation held in Colombo on the theme, "Partnership of Women and Men in Inclusive Community," called once again for the Church in Asia to "restore inclusiveness, equality, and harmony." So the first steps have been taken. Yet, true partnership between men and women remains to be seen or realized. It is a process of co-liberation from structures of domination toward grounding ecumenism not only in sound theological propositions but in concrete practices on the ground.

Bibliography

Chung, Hyun Kyung. *Struggle to Be the Sun Again: Introducing Asian Women's Theology*. Maryknoll, NY: Orbis, 1990.

Nontawasee, Prakai. "Mission in Mutual Solidarity." *In God's Image* (June 1989): 33-34.

---

[5] Prakai Nontawasee, "Mission in Mutual Solidarity," *In God's Image* (June 1989): 33-34.

[6] Yong Ting Jin, "Women's Journey with and within the SCMs and WSCF: A Perspective from the Asia-Pacific Region," in *Towards a Women's History in the World Student Christian Federation*, ed. Clarissa Balan-Sycip (Geneva: World Student Christian Federation, 1994), 62.

Park, Sun Ai Lee. "Asian Women in Mission," *International Review of Mission*, 81 (1992): 280.
Perera, Marlene. "Towards the Twenty-first Century: An Asian Woman's Emerging Perceptions on Mission." *International Review of Mission*, 81 (1992): 227-236.
Yong, Ting Jin. "Women's Journey with and within the SCMs and WSCF: A Perspective from the Asia-Pacific Region," in *Towards a Women's History in the World Student Christian Federation*. Clarissa Balan-Sycip, ed. Geneva: World Student Christian Federation, 1994.

(38) *The Fellowship of the Least Coin* as an Ecumenical Movement of Prayer for Peace, Justice and Reconciliation

Corazon Tabing-Reyes

What is the Fellowship of the Least Coin?

The Fellowship of the Least Coin[1] is a world-wide ecumenical movement of prayer for peace, justice and reconciliation. Through this movement Christian women around the world seek fellowship with each other and are reminded to live a reconciled and forgiving life with others. The emphasis is on the word **"least"**, because it is not a fund-raising project, but a movement of prayer for justice, peace and reconciliation. Anyone who wishes to join this movement makes a commitment to spend time in prayer whenever she has a strained relationship with another person, and to uphold in prayer others who are victims of jealousy, hatred, violence and injustice in the family, the community, the nation, and the world. Every time she prays for justice, peace and reconciliation, she sets aside a "least coin" of her currency as a tangible token of her prayer. She brings her least coins to a group in prayer. The amount collected by each country annually is sent to the FLC Fund c/o World Council of Churches in Geneva for reaching out in love through supporting projects among the least in different parts of the world. Each country's contribution is never publicized; only the total sum collected each year is announced.

How and When it Began

The idea for the Fellowship of the Least Coin emerged as a vision from God to Mrs. Shanti Solomon of India. She was part of the Pacific Mission Team of seven women from different countries that traveled in Asian countries after the World War II, in September 1956. It was organized by Dr. Margaret Shannon on behalf of the women of the Presbyterian Church of the United States. Shanti Solomon, who was refused a visa to Korea, went to Manila, Philippines while other members of the team proceeded to Korea. She reflected on the experiences of their travel in the war-torn countries of Asia and was inspired to promote reconciliation, justice and peace.

On the return of the team, she suggested that prayer could transcend every national boundary. She challenged the Christian women of Asia and the women from the Presbyterian Church of the United States to combine their efforts and resources and launch a project of justice, peace and reconciliation on an international basis. It was to be a project of Christian prayer and positive action in which every Christian woman could participate, no matter what her economic position was. Every time a woman prayed she was to set aside a **"least coin"** of her currency. It was an encouragement to the women of the team to demonstrate their unity in Christian faith, regardless of their country or economic circumstances. They all accepted it as their sincere desire to express their solidarity with suffering humanity and with women of every nation. In 1958, at the first Assembly of the Asian Church Women's Conference (ACWC) held in Hong Kong, the ACWC agreed to launch the Fellowship of the Least Coin. At the second Assembly in Thailand in 1962, the Assembly voted to make the promotion of the FLC a basic outreach programme of the ACWC. The East Asia Christian Conference (EACC), now known as the Christian Conference of Asia (CCA) administered the FLC fund from 1958-1970. In 1970 Mrs. Shanti Solomon, the founder, was named

[1] The International Committee of the Fellowship of the Least Coin (*ICFLC*) has its Office currently in the Philippines: c/o Union Theological Seminary, Dasmarinas City, Cavite, Philippines 4114, Email: icflcph@gmail.com, website: www.flc.net.ph. The current ICFLC Executive Secretary is Corazon Tabing-Reyes.

the Executive Secretary of the FLC and of the ACWC. The ACWC then took the responsibility to administer the FLC Fund until 1979 when the International Committee for the Fellowship of the Least Coin was organized.

FLC Logo

The idea for the FLC logo came from the late Mrs. Rayann Ma from Hong Kong, the first Chairperson of the first Assembly of the ACWC. The actual design was the gift of her brother-in-law, James Ma, a commercial artist.

It is folded hands in prayer, encircling a small plum flower, and which form a lotus flower. Lotus plant grows in the muddy pond but its flower rises above the murky water and opens beautifully and without blemish, fit as offering in the altar.

The printed logo in color is praying hands of women of different races.

Circle of Prayer

Feeling the need to reaffirm prayer as the vital element of the FLC, the ACWC asked the women of Hong Kong to prepare a booklet of prayer: "Circle of Prayer" to be used as prayer is offered and the least coin is set aside. Since then, the "Circle of Prayer" has become an important part of the FLC. Twenty-four meditations and prayers were written by women around the world and published by the International Committee for the FLC every two years.

It's Growth

The idea of the FLC quickly gained acceptance not only among the women of Asia to whom it was first presented, but among women of all the continents in the world. In 1966 when the FLC celebrated its tenth anniversary, women from 24 countries participated in the movement. By 1980, at the time of its Silver Jubilee, women from 75 countries had already joined the FLC. In 1986, women from over 80 countries around the world celebrated the fortieth anniversary of the FLC. The 50th anniversary in 2006 was fifty years of journeying in prayers and in partnership with the theme "Celebrating the Legacy, Visioning the Future and Living the Jubilee" and looking forward to another fifty years of dream shared and dream realized.

The International Committee for the FLC (ICFLC)

Because the FLC prayer movement became truly world-wide and the grants were made to the programmes and projects all over the world, an International Committee for the FLC (ICFLC) was formed in 1979 to administer the promotion, the interpretation of the movement and the allocation of the FLC grants. The International Committee comprises representatives of world-wide ecumenical women's organization and of regional ecumenical Conferences or Councils of the Churches. The ICFLC decides what programmes and projects are to be funded each year. Year after year the ICFLC learns to trust God more and more and to work in faith. The Committee meets every year to share the miraculous works of the FLC around the world and to decide on FLC grants for the following year. Application forms for project grants are received four months prior to the meeting. The members of the Committee study the application forms, pray about them, and discuss and decide on each project without knowing how much FLC funding will be available for the grants they wish to allocate for each year. The least coins from around the world come in with prayers, quietly and gradually, to meet the needs for each year. Our gentle, loving and compassionate God never fails us. God does great works through the humble, the least, the marginalized and the poor. That's the strength, the promise, the beauty, and the surprise upholding the FLC prayer movement.

Every year ICFLC is invited by different regions to hold its meeting in their country. An FLC workshop and exposure or visitation programme are added to the regular business meeting in order for the representatives to know more about the region and to be aware of the issues and the concerns of the people there. The ICFLC considers linking its meeting every fourth year with the Quadrennial Assembly of the ACWC.

FLC Grants

Each year about 35 to 50 projects are given grants. Regional Women's Desk of Ecumenical Conferences or Councils, the Women's Desk of the World Council of Churches and the World Day of Prayer International Committee are given block grants to enhance their work and to strengthen ecumenical solidarity. Emergency grants for disaster relief and rehabilitation are also given. Starting 2010, there is a Fellowship of the Least Coin Scholarship Award for Young Women.

The Uniqueness of the FLC

The FLC Prayer Movement is simple, yet significant and unique.

1. It brings Christian women together in a fellowship of prayer without any discrimination of race, nationality, culture or denomination. The Christian women of the world have solidarity with each other through their common concern and love for humankind and creation. Women throughout the world are bound together in both giving and receiving.
2. The offering is unique because all, whether rich or poor, educated or illiterate, urban or rural women, give only the smallest coin of their currency. All are within the same discipline and share the common concerns of women around the world.
3. It is stewardship, both of the idea as well as of the Fund. These least coins, when put together, become a large amount in the same way individual prayers offered by many members throughout the world become a strong force in bringing about reconciliation, peace and justice.

The uniqueness of the Fellowship in prayer, which binds us together in both giving and receiving, teaches us to appreciate differences; to understand and forgive one another; to live and work together inter-dependently as equal partners.

The Least Coin teaches us to be humble, to value the least and to trust that nothing is impossible for God who can do great things from out of the least and the unexpected.

Our concern and yearning for peace in the wounded and broken world, which moves us to spontaneously pray and give, becomes a powerful healing source for our own pain as well as for the pain of those whose lives have been touched by our prayers and gifts.

The inclusiveness of the Fellowship, which embraces us in a simple, yet profound act of prayer accompanied by a gift of love- "least coin"- encourages wider participation and provides resources for making peace and restoring broken relationships.

The God who promises to be with us always provides for our needs and never fails to love, to guide and protect us.

(39) ASIAN CHURCH WOMEN CONFERENCE – A SHORT SURVEY

Moon-Sook Lee

History of ACWC[1]

In 1956, the Presbyterian Church Women of the USA invited churchwomen from Asia, Africa, Latin America and Europe to their Assembly at Purdue University. At this meeting in Stony Point, many Asian church women leaders met for the first time, and they realized how little they knew about their own Asian situations. Miss Felicia Sunderal from India challenged other Asian women delegates to have as big a meeting as the one at Purdue.

With this discovery of a new Asian selfhood, there was an urge for ecumenical fellowship among the Asian Church Women. It was their prayerful wishes and beautiful dreams to have a fellowship gathering in Asia arranged by Asian sisters. God listened and heard their prayers and made it possible to have a conference in Hong Kong on November 12, 1958.

Since then, ACWC has continued to meet every four years. These women have been bound or sheltered too long by tradition and culture and have taken the role of the second-class citizens at home, in church and in society. Currently, in some countries, the women still struggle with the above plight. The ACWC has been a supportive fellowship in Christ. These women can reach out and share what is most dear in their hearts with their sisters in faith.

Vision of ACWC

The Asian Church Women's Conference envisions itself as a full partner with individuals and organizations that are dedicated to the enabling of women and the whole of humankind in the struggle towards the creation of a society where there is more meaningful peace, justice and love.

As an organization, ACWC envisions Asian women in unity become more capable of discovering themselves, and realizing their gifts and potentials, they contribute more forceful and sustained efforts towards the development of a stronger family and community, rooted in faith and sustained by the Holy Spirit so the Shalom may finally be attained.

As an advocate of women's rights and welfare, ACWC sees itself working beyond the boundaries of culture and creed, color and race so that stronger regional networks of women leaders and organizations may emerge that together and in unity recognize in action their role and responsibility in the family, the society and the church.

ACWC Day and Liturgy

Every third Sunday in November ACWC is calling for a day of common prayer within the ACWC for which a special ACWC liturgy is developed and shared between all related Asian churches.[2] As one example for the testimonies of committed Asian Christian women we might cite the witness which was part of the ACWC 2007 liturgy, relating to the anti-nuclear struggle and witness for peace and justice in Japan:

---

[1] See also: http://acwc.blogspot.ch/search/label/history

[2] http://acwc.blogspot.ch/search/label/ACWC%20day%20Liturgy

The Testimony of Suzuko Numata – Suzuko Numata is a Hiroshima storyteller. Let us listen to her testimony.

I was 21 at that time and full of joy, because my fiancé was back home on leave from the war, and in 2-3 days we were to celebrate our wedding.

August 6, 1945. Just as I was about to go downstairs after finishing the usual morning cleaning where I worked, a beautiful light – blue, red, green, yellow, orange – all these colors spread out in front of my eyes. It was the flash of the atomic bomb. The violent wind blew me about like a leaf in a gust of wind. In the midst of this raging torrent of desks and chairs, I was crushed under the rubble.

When I regained consciousness, I was told that only 3 cm of skin remained where my left foot had been severed at the ankle and that I was bleeding from the wound. Like many other injured people, my foot was left untreated, and as a result, two days later became gangrenous up to the knee joint. When the doctor announced that my leg would have to be amputated from the thigh, I cried defiantly, realizing that I would never again be able to work or get married. However, the people around me encouraged me to have the surgery by reminding me of the importance of the life that had been saved. For a long while, the leg that had been amputated hurt as if it were still there and caused me great suffering.

Moreover, at the end of the war I received the news that my fiancé had been killed in the war. The war took everything from me. If it had not been for the war, I would not have lost my leg, and my fiancé would not have died. Because of that despair and sadness, for two years I was unable to recover on my own.

Then one day my mother reproached me, and her words were the push I needed to begin living again and to learn to walk with a 4-kg artificial leg. I had already given up the idea of getting married, but making the best use of the dexterity left in my hands, I obtained a teaching certificate in home economics and was assigned to teach high school girls.

However, for 28 years I didn't speak a word about my wartime experiences. I didn't want to expose my scars in front of everyone. Then appearing in an American documentary pushed me into giving my testimony and becoming active in the peace movement. I was given this chance to regain my life through someone who had become a storyteller before me. For 20 years now in front of student groups who come to Hiroshima I have continued to testify to the importance of peace, to the horrors of the atomic bomb, and to the misery caused by war.

Furthermore, making a peace pilgrimage to Okinawa on crutches gave me the chance to come face to face with the problem of the wrongs Japan had committed during the war. It made me think about the fact that there were tragedies no one had told me about and tragedies I didn't know anything about that had led to the war. Through meeting and listening to the testimony of people there, I heard the cry for life itself. I encountered Korea through Korean atomic bomb survivors. I encountered China with its history of invasion and massacre, and Malaysia where civilians were also massacred. Through these journeys, I became aware of myself as one of the Japanese perpetrators of the war, and as a result of this unbearable feeling I apologized to them and have been able to continue this kind of exchange ever since.

One sister from China had survived 37 sword wounds all over her body, which had resulted in a miscarriage. While stroking each other's scars, we talked about how we wanted to let as many people as possible know how we got those scars.

By looking hard at both the wrongs done and the damage inflicted and through our experiences of telling the truth about history to succeeding generations, we must educate a generation to believe "we can't allow this mistake ever to happen again."

For humanity to continue to live happily, as my small personal campaign I am appealing to everyone to oppose war, nuclear weapons, discrimination, environmental pollution and the destruction of nature. My testimony is only one small seed of peace. I am planting many seeds, so please water them well. For this beautiful earth and for a wonderful future, let us all join to cultivate those seeds so that they will become big and strong.[3]

Last ACWC Assembly in Indonesia 2010

The last assembly of ACWC took place in Bogor, Indonesia in October 2010 and was attended by 59 delegates and 185 oberservers. The following Statement of the 14th Quadrennial Assembly indicates some of the major issues which were on the agenda:

> We the 59 delegates and 185 observers and guests from 26 countries, came together to deliberate on the theme of the Assembly "Asian Women Moving Forward: Non-Violent World, New Earth, Life in its Fulleness", 15-20 October, 2010 at Kinasih conference, Bogor, Indonesia.
>
> **We Acknowledge**
>
> - We rejoice in the Lord that Asian Women inspite of their various restricting circumstances are determined to move forward.
> - We understand that ACWC is committed to bring fullness of life for women and all creation.
>
> **The Present Scenario**
>
> - Asian countries are burdened with poverty, illiteracy, unhygienic living conditions, the ugly prong of HIV & AIDS and aggressive consumption of natural resources affect women and children.
> - Asian countries bear the result of environmental pollution, ecological imbalance.
> - Family violence is inherent in the Asian socio-cultural tradition.
> - Social evils like human trafficking and dowry system prevent women from enjoying the fullness of life, denying them basic human rights.
>
> **We dedicate ourselves**
>
> - As co-workers in God's creation and with prayerful spirit, we shall take initiatives and moves to improve the value of women in church, society and family.
> - God's word is the source of our strength, so we shall urge member churches of ACWC to re-read the Bible from women's perspective for its liberating power and way to fullness of life.
> - We value the strength and future leadership of young women so ACWC & FLC should motivate, mentor and induct them as ambassadors.
> - As we live in a pluralistic society we the church women should stand together side by side and hand in hand in love and peace.
> - We will be good caretakers of God's blessings, and fulfill God's purposes of transforming women's lives for a better world.
> - ACWC has the prophetic vision to bring about change in the lives of people so that they may have a fullness of life that God promises.
>
> Being Christian women of Asia, we pledge to carry out this prophetic tasks for the realization of a non-violent world, a new earth and life in its fullness.

2012 Asian Young Women's Forum

From 16-19 May 2012 a workshop of Asian Christian women leaders took place in Bangkok Christian Guest House under the title "Towards A Life-giving Community Based on JustPeace", hosted by the The

---

[3] *Extracted from Chikahiro Hiroiwa, Aogiri no shita de (Beneath the Chinese Parasol Tree), Akashi Shoten, 1993*

Women's Committee of the Church of Christ in Thailand. 30 Asian church women came together. The background of the Asian Young Women's Forum is the following:

Women have always been under prejudices and discriminations in many ways both inside and outside churches. The World Council of Churches (WCC) had declared 1988-1998 as the Decade of Churches in Solidarity with Women (the Decade) and proposed that the churches make policies to enable women to equally participate with men in decision-making bodies in church and society and to take measures to eradicate any kind of sexual abuses against women. The Decade challenged the patriarchal churches to be transformed into inclusive communities on the basis of gender-justice.

During the decade many issues were discussed and different actions followed. However, reflecting on the activities done in the name of the Decade, we found that the Decade was not of the 'churches' but of 'women' in solidarity with women. This means that churches have little changed for those 10 years in terms of gender justice. In fact, since the end of the Decade we have not even been able to see as much discussions of and movement for gender justice as during the Decade. Also, the world economic situation has made women's life condition even worse and it has also become more difficult for women to find spaces to speak out about their human rights.

As the WCC's 10th Assembly will be held in Pusan, Korea, in October/November 2013 this is an opportunity again to move towards a life-giving community based on just peace. Women may bring their voices to the table and raise issues within the church and society. In preparation for the assembly women were invited to share their experiences with one another and form a collective agenda with a common vision in order to stimulate the process of the movement towards gender justice. The Asian Church Women's Conference (ACWC) and the Christian Conference in Asia therefore planned the Asian Young Women's Forum to develop young women's leadership envisioning the future of the church and the world and to prepare for Asian women's positive participation in the WCC Assembly and form a new stream of the women's movement to transform our churches into life-giving communities after the Assembly.

The following personal account from an Australian young women representative sheds some light on the impact this meeting has had on all those who could join:

> As a young Christian women living in Australia it is often all too easy to focus inwardly, focus on what is happening in my network, my world and my community. Whilst this is valid for part of the time, I believe Christ has called us to so much more. The Young Women's Forum (YWF) held in Bangkok, 16-19 May 2012, was an opportunity to provide just that, an experience and encounter with passionate young Christian women who through their passion, faith and experiences were able to provide an insight into their life and culture that truly widened my focus and stretched me to consider my faith in so many different dimensions.
>
> The YWF, was an event put together with the objective to create and inspire life giving communities based on justice and peace. The three days of the conference led by Rev. Moon Sook, saw women from across Asia join together to share their personal stories, their culture and their faith. Throughout the conference a large emphasis was placed on allowing time for open sharing, dialogue and networking within smaller regional groups. Here each delegate was encouraged to speak about their culture and heritage with particular reference to the role of women in the church and society.
>
> As we sat in a our small groups and shared and listened to each others' experiences I reflected back to my thoughts before arriving in Bangkok. I remember sitting nervously on the plane not really sure what to expect when I arrived and pondering how well, we as women from so many different countries could truly connect. Now thinking back I realise how far from the mark I was, instead of seeing difference God created wholeness and an overwhelming sense of unity. This sense of togetherness was cemented in the story telling, a time where we as women came together uninhibited and transparent ready to talk about the issues we felt so critical and worthy of attention for women in our countries.

> As we continued to share in small groups we were asked to reflect on issues for women specifically with respect to economic vulnerability, violence and natural disasters. Key to our discussion was recognising the impact such vulnerability had on the women of our countries, churches and communities. As Christian women we acknowledged the inequality and the enormity of such issues as violence against women, its prevalence and sadly often its silence. For myself as a young women I was truly moved by the overwhelming acknowledgement of the vulnerability of women in all these areas, and none more so than the on-going issue of violence against women. Sadly each and every delegate reflected on stories that demonstrated the prevalence of violence against women in their country, as we shared the reality was striking where for some countries violence against women was as high as 1 in 4 women.

It is becomining evident in the work of ACWC again and again: Our societies are torn by discriminations, violence and injustices not only in sex but also in class, race and religion. But after the workshop in Bangakok 2012, one thing came across particulalrly in my mind: It is that Asia and other continents – in relation to what the Heavenly God wants us to make for the establishment of the Kingdom of justice and peace in this world, presently divided with borders and devastated by violence – may not have the same map in future as we have now in hand. The world we are asked to build may rather be one designed differently from what we see on the map today with all its national borders. We need opportunities all again to imagine an alternative world like human communities with no boundaries between all beings and no separation walls and powers to divide those who essentially belong together by the will of God.

(40) Contributions of Asian Women and Positive Masculinity in the Ecumenical Movement

Aruna Gnanadason

We met together, discussed together, argued from our different points of view, laughed together, danced and celebrated together and worshipped together. No questions were asked about our denominational or doctrinal differences, it really did not matter to this group of women drawn from churches across Asia. We were drawn from Protestant, Roman Catholic and Orthodox Churches, and there were with us women from other faiths and of no faith at all. The context was a meeting on Violence Against Women organized by the Christian Conference of Asia (CCA) with the World Council of Churches (WCC) and the Asian Women's Human Rights Council (AWHRC) in Bali, Indonesia in 1993. The discussions at this meeting were difficult and painful – women from all the countries in Asia shared their stories, their analysis of the various forms of violence they experience. It was sometimes personal stories but more often they were stories of women who were not there with us. Dalit and Indigenous/Tribal women spoke of the violence women experience in urban poor settlements of our cities (working in sweatshops or as vendors, workers in construction sites, as domestic workers, as prostitutes or as fisher folk); or from rural agriculture based contexts most often as landless agriculturists or bonded labourers.

Based on all this we said together:

> The family, along with the state today, has sought to control women through rigid definitions of sexuality and appropriate for itself reproductive rights and control over her body; violence and subjugation have been woven into institutionalized forms of religion whose patriarchal tenets have marginalized and domesticated the female and the feminine, shackling her and legitimizing violence against her. Social and legal codes of justice have either been blind to crimes against women like wife battering and prostitution that have in fact received tacit social approval; or have seen violations like sexual assault and rape as acts of individual aberration and deviance and has even rendered some totally invisible, as in the case of homophobia.[1]

To speak of the violence we experience as women is not easy but Asian women have recognized this as a theological challenge to transcend our victimization and transform our pain into political power and action. It is true that it is the very personal faith, a childlike spirituality, that has sustained Asian women who live in contexts of violence … but we so easily see the inseparable link between our faith and our obedient action in the world and demand a violence-free and safe world. This is just one example of the many times we have met together as women – ecumenically and very often with women of other faiths.

Women in Asia are convinced that they have something radically new to offer – a new way of understanding society, of human relationships and of being church. The courageous work that women do in all parts of Asia to deconstruct basic theological assumptions and reconstruct more inclusive and life affirming principles has been significant and the ecumenical movement has made important contributions to this surge among women.

---

[1] Quoted from "The Bali Declaration", in *Together with Courage: Women and Men Living without Violence against Women* (Geneva: World Council of Churches, 1998), p. 11. The Declaration came out of an Asian regional meeting on Violence Against Women organized by the CCA, the WCC and the AWHRC in which 50 women representing these organisations came together in Bali, Indonesia on August 1-6, 1993. The publication was put out by the WCC Women's Programme during the Ecumenical Decade of Churches in Solidarity with Women.

Women in the History of the Ecumenical Movement in Asia

It is women who have made the effort to write themselves into the history of the ecumenical movement. Most often "official" history books of Asian ecumenism or of the churches in Asia will be centered on the contributions of eminent male leaders and would sometimes devote a chapter to women almost as an add-on. It is time that a history of women in the ecumenical movement in Asia was written gathering together the remarkable lives of women acting and speaking collectively and ecumenically but also of individual women such as Sun Ai Lee Park, Virginia Fabella, Mary John Mananzan, Shanthi Solomon, Marianne Katoppo, Margaretha Hendricks, Hisako Kinukawa, Aiko Carter, Esther Byu, Shirin Samuel, Corazon Tabing Reyes, Elizabeth Tapia, Yong Tin Jin, Chung Hyun Kyung, Kwok Pui Lan, Leonie Liveris, Jenny Plane Te Paa, Jean Skuse, Gao Ying, Prasanna Kumari, Ruth Kao, Annathaie Abayasekara, Ruth Manorama, Agustina Lumentut, Henriette Hutabarat Lebang, Wong Wai Ching, Chung Sook Ja, and Priscilla Padolina, to name a very few. These names are just some among the thousands of women who have made and continue to make a mark in their churches and in the ecumenical movement at local, national and international levels and deserve honour – this list includes women of the Roman Catholic and Orthodox churches.

However, as has been rightly observed,

> Today, an increasing number of historians believe that the activities and contributions of women in most cultures and societies are least found in institutional records. Rather, alternative sources such as oral histories, private journals and diaries and autobiographies are given a much more important role in recovering the past, especially for women and the socially dis-privileged. Until these "unofficial" histories are explored, a writing of the history of women in the Asian ecumenical movement and their contribution to theological thinking will be far from complete.[2]

Additionally, the vastness of this continent, with almost two-thirds of the world's population with a diversity of peoples, cultures, religions and languages, makes any overview difficult. The writing of a new history of women in the Asian ecumenical movement could try to right this wrong. This article will only draw major strokes across this continent.

Some Historical Moments

It was the World Student Christian Federation that first challenged Christians to work ecumenically, when it made inroads into Asia in the 1880s and the first Asian Student Christian Conference was held in 1927. Local units of the Student Christian Movement emerged over the next decades and came together to form the Asia Pacific Regional body related to the World Student Christian Federation. About the same time, the Young Men's Christian Association (YMCA) and some years later the Young Women's Christian Association (YWCA) also emerged in Asia both at the national and regional levels, strengthening ecumenical cooperation. From the 1970s they have all included a special focus on Christian women's education and theological contributions, and leadership training for active engagement in their societies.

However, the earliest recorded committee on women's work among church women in Asia was the East Asia Home and Family Life Committee, renamed and reinstituted as the committee on "The Cooperation of Men and Women in Home Church and Society" during the inaugural assembly of the East Asia Christian Conference (EACC) in 1959. The EACC later became the Christian Conference of Asia (CCA). Initially, the focus of the work was on cooperation between women and men; there was no reference to the

---

[2] Wong Wai Ching Angela, "Women Doing Theology with the Asian Ecumenical Movement," in *A History of the Ecumenical Movement in Asia*, Vol. II, Ed. Ninan Koshy (Hong Kong: WSCF Asia Pacific Region, Asia and Pacific Alliance of YMCAs and the CCA, 2004), p. 86.

status of women in society or of the sexism in the church. At the Penang Assembly of the CCA in 1977, as the women got more organized, serious discussions on the role of women in church and society were initiated. This paved the way for the decisions taken in 1981, at the Bangalore Assembly of the CCA, when a Committee on Women's Concerns was set up with a full time staff person, Elizabeth Tapia, a Methodist from the Philippines. The programme has since then drawn women together from all over Asia and has covered a wide range of issues, including various manifestations of patriarchal violence, globalization, militarization, the church and its role in the life of women, reproductive technologies, sexuality and inter-faith dialogue, development of the leadership of women, to name some.

The three ecumenical organisations – the CCA, the Asia Pacific WSCF and the YMCA and YWCA – have worked together to lift up the concerns and voices of women over the decades.[3]

Women Forging Bonds of Solidarity

Among the many constructive ways in which women in Asia have been organized ecumenically, two significant ecumenical ventures deserve special mention. The Women's Commission of the Ecumenical Association of Third World Theologians called on women in each region to develop their own contextual feminist theologies. In response, in 1985, Asian women gathered in Manila, Philippines for a consultation on the theme, "Total Liberation from the Perspective of Women." This was preceded by national level ecumenical meetings in several Asian countries. In this process Roman Catholic women have played a key role and as equal partners with women from all church traditions. Thus began a wave of feminist theologizing by women in all parts of Asia who started to "reread" the Bible and "do theology" from a liberationist perspective, based on their own life experiences. Indonesian theologian Marianne Katoppo had published a path-breaking theological book entitled *Compassionate and Free* even earlier in 1979 – an encouraging incentive for Asian women to think and write theologically.

Korean feminist theologian Sun Ai Lee Park, with the encouragement of a few other women, launched *In God's Image*, a journal of Asian women in 1982. In 1988 she helped in creating the Asian Women's Resource Centre (AWRC). Both *IGI* and AWRC have provided an important platform and space for the development of Asian women's theologies. Through these instruments women of all church traditions, even those without formal theological training, have been able to express themselves theologically and contribute to the unique theological voice of Asian women.

Some Major Areas of Engagement of Asian Women

The complex context of Asia has played a pivotal role in framing the contributions of women to the ecumenical movement. The way patriarchy manifests itself in Asia is different from other contexts, being enmeshed with poverty and wealth; with the multi-religious and multi-cultural context of Asia and with socially constructed forms of discrimination and violence such as the caste system in South Asia or the context of Indigenous/Tribal women in all parts of Asia. The ecumenical movement in Asia has played a key role in helping define feminism, feminist theory and feminist theology for this continent as a contribution to national level initiatives in each Asian country and to world Christianity. The ecumenical initiatives mentioned above have provided a safe and inspiring space for women to come together and share their experiences to ask new questions and develop their own socio-political analysis and theological responses as well as to forge new forms of Asian solidarity.

[3] For this section, I have drawn from Wong Wai Ching Angela, "Women Doing Theology with the Asian Ecumenical Movement", *Ibid.* and from Priscilla Padolina, "All Sleeping Women Now Awake", in *With Love and With Passion*, ed. Elisabeth Raiser and Barbara Robra (Geneva: WCC Publications, 2001).

The renewal of the church and transformation of the society have been twin objectives of the Asian ecumenical women's movement which has always worked within the frame of the community of women and men. Over the past 40 years or so, women in Asia have faced challenges to their lives and integrity, but have emerged ever stronger with clear theological voices. This article highlights just three issues on which Asian women make unique contributions.

An eco-feminist theological contribution

There is a growing awareness that women and the poor are the primary victims of the deleterious impact of environmental degradation all over Asia. Asian women's understanding of the Earth and our relationship to it and to God is shaped by an Asian cosmology, which affirms the interdependence of all forms of life, the dialectical harmony between humanity and the divine; between human beings and the earth and between the male and female principles. Therefore, our reflections include our concern for humanity but also a caring concern for the earth which has been referred to as "the new poor". Asian women write of the indwelling of the divine in life and creation – God's immanence is stressed – both in the beauty of creation and in creation's sometimes fury in the form of earthquakes, floods, cyclones and even tsunamis.

The drying up of wells and village ponds and rivers, or the deliberate take-over of water sources and forests by the governments and private corporate investors for habitation, industrialization and profit-oriented extractive ventures are placing untold burdens on rural populations, particularly on women. This leads to mass migration to cities pushing more and more people into over-crowded urban poor settlements with poor sanitation and inadequate drinking water. Here they eke out a living – women and children also being susceptible to sexual violence and trafficking. This is the context that has influenced an eco-feminist theology in Asia – it is not an esoteric or romantic concept of the protection of the earth – but an affirmation that ecological, economic, political and social justice are interlinked concerns.

The good news is that women (particularly Indigenous women and poor women) have, in most parts of Asia, been the bearers of traditions of prudent care of the earth. This has strengthened a deeply spiritual bond between women and the earth, and has challenged feminist theology and given birth to a freshness in theology.[4]

The dialectic harmony between the male and female principles – seeking for positive masculinities

In the context of a deeply patriarchal society in Asia, in a context of the daily violence women (and children) live with, in a context where subordination has been drilled into the psyche of women by religion and the economic, political and cultural context of Asia, there is a slowly growing awareness and movement of men who realize that they too have lost out in a patriarchal world order. At the heart of most Asian cultures is this awareness of the essential harmony between men and women, but this has been lost over the ages as power and privilege that some men have enjoyed not only over women and children, but over other men has become the reigning order of the day.

As Philip Vinod Peacock, one such man who teaches Christian ethics at Bishop's College, in Kolkata, India describes it: "For too long now heteronormative[5] gender discrimination has served to subjugate women, lesser men and those that fall outside of our preconceived notions of gender roles and gender codes. To end this reign of patriarchy means we have to work hard to stop the literal and metaphorical slaughter of women, young girls and lesser men[6] on the altar of patriarchy." To "smash patriarchy" is his

---

[4] For further information see Kwok Pui Lan, *Introducing Asian Feminist Theology* (Sheffield: Sheffield Academic Press, 2000). Also see Aruna Gnanadason, *Listen to the Women, Listen to the Earth* (Geneva: WCC Publications, 2005).

[5] Philip Peacock coins this word to refer to how patriarchy has, through instruments of language, behaviour and societal ordering, made males the norm.

[6] Philip Peacock refers to the graded systems of subjugation based on caste, social and economic status, even among

call and so he continues, "It means that we radically commit ourselves to the ideals of feminist theology that seeks to dismantle all power and hierarchy and empower the oppressed. That, like Jesus, we seek to destabilize traditional power for the liberation of the oppressed."[7]

Forging bonds of unity with other women

Finally, ecumenical women in each nation of Asia have linked with secular women's efforts and with women of other faiths to bring transformation in the lives of women, to challenge violence in all its manifestations and to demand justice and dignity for all women and men – this too has had a deep impact on theology. One such important initiative is in Indonesia where a small but strong network of Christian and Muslim feminists are growing with the understanding that women of all faiths need to unravel the patriarchal moorings of their own religions so that the liberation potential of all religions can be unearthed.

Thus the understanding of ecumenism has been expanded by the experiences of Asian women who have realised that their voices ought to embrace the visions and perspectives of women of all faiths and no faith at all, if they have to respond to the call of Christ, "that they may all be one."

Bibliography

Gnanadason, Aruna. *Listen to the Women, Listen to the Earth.* Geneva: WCC Publications, 2005.

Kwok, Pui Lan. *Introducing Asian Feminist Theology.* Sheffield: Sheffield Academic Press, 2000.

Padolina, Priscilla. "All Sleeping Women Now Awake", in *With Love and With Passion.* Elisabeth Raiser and Barbara Robra, eds. Geneva: WCC Publications, 2001.

Peacock, Philip Vinod. "Jephtha's Daughter", an unpublished sermon preached at the Chapel of the Bishop's College, Kolkata, India on 8 July 2012.

"The Bali Declaration", in *Together with Courage: Women and Men Living without Violence against Women.* Geneva: World Council of Churches, 1998.

Wong, Wai Ching Angela. "Women Doing Theology with the Asian Ecumenical Movement," in *A History of the Ecumenical Movement in Asia*, Vol. II. Ninan Koshy, ed. Hong Kong: WSCF Asia Pacific Region, Asia and Pacific Alliance of YMCAs and the CCA, 2004.

---

the community of men rendering some men to be deemed "lesser" than other men.

[7] Quoted from a sermon preached by Philip Vinod Peacock, "Jephtha's Daughter", at the Chapel of the Bishop's College, Kolkata, India on 8 July 2012.

(41) Gender Justice and the Discourse on Sexual Minorities in Asian Ecumenism

Liza Lamis

Introduction

As an avowed feminist and having worked with sexually abused women in the churches in my ecumenical ministry, I am very particular about hearing and lending voice to the primary stakeholders of ecumenism, the marginalized and most vulnerable sectors. These marginalized communities are the women, gays, lesbians, bisexuals and the transgendered among us. I have taught gender and women's issues to various groups of women and men around Asia, trying to inculcate the importance of understanding and consequently changing reality from the specific perspective of women together with the other marginalized groups. Thus I always introduce myself as one who is passionate about gender justice and transformative ecumenical formation.

Gender justice shall be defined here as the ending of and, if necessary, the restitution for inequalities and injustices resulting in the marginalization, subordination, exploitation and abuse of women, gays, lesbians, bisexuals and transgendered people whom I shall refer to as the gender marginals. In other words, it is rendering justice to those who are oppressed on account of their being different in gender from what we normally know as the 'straights'. I will identify some justice issues concerning these marginalized communities mentioned, as well as possible ways in confronting them. Some doable recommendations in mainstreaming gender justice will also be offered. To do justice, especially with the least, the most vulnerable and the victimized among us, is crucial in achieving a more inclusive and wider ecumenism in Asia.

Gender Issues are Life-and-Death Issues

"Can gays go to heaven?" This question sometimes surfaces during ecumenical courses offered by the Christian Conference of Asia. The question assumes an exclusionary stance in registering doubt about the humanity of homosexual people based on the assumption that they are not 'normal' human beings as they are neither male nor female.

A dominant cultural reality in a male-centered and male-dominated world like Asia is that women are considered secondary human beings, and are not of equal worth with the men. Women's biological difference from men, for example, is cited as a basis to confine them at home to take care of children, kitchen and pigs, thereby limiting their potentials. Keeping the men from sharing the task of rearing the young denies them the opportunity to harness their human capacity to nurture and care. Typecasting on the basis of biology or sexual orientation is an extremely reductive practice that stifles human creativity. It also oversimplifies and hinders our understanding of the complexities of the oppression of marginalized groups.

Asia lives with a human reality of gender differences in matters of sexual orientation and preference, roles and biology. These differences are turned into justifications and bases for marginalizing, dominating, demonizing and inflicting violence on those who are different. The exclusion, oppression, exploitation and violence against marginalized and vulnerable people destroy not just their humanity, but all of humanity. How many lives have been claimed by violence against women? How many gay men have been killed because they are hated and 'sent to hell' even before their time? Gender issues are life-and-death concerns for many. Consequently, these are justice issues that all of humanity should be concerned about, and are deemed crucial in building a wider ecumenism in Asia.

Promoting a Wider Ecumenism

Worshipping a welcoming and an all-embracing God

Our God, the Creative One, created of 'a riot of difference' in creation. God intended not to eliminate difference but to make possible for us to accept each other, uphold each other in our differences, and to be able to communicate across our differences (Gen. 11.1-9; Acts 2.1-12). With God, difference is a gift to be celebrated, and not a reason to dominate, marginalize or harm. We are different yet equally created by the same God who loves differences. Additionally, to confront the misuse of difference is to give integrity to our God-talk and to God who created, welcomes and loves straight, lesbian, gay, bisexual and transgendered people.

God's truth is that we are all human beings and we share a common humanity. Embracing and celebrating difference, radically welcoming those who are different, is honoring God. Until we see others as full members of humanity with moral, spiritual and political agency, our actions and social structures will remain exclusionary, therefore unjust. To be inclusive in our theological anthropology means to imagine the divine and human in creative expressions, thus enabling us to see God in the face of other genders. God is even beyond gender expressions, yet unfinished in revealing the God-self in creation.

Promoting fullness of life for all

Since we all share a common humanity endowed by the Creator, however we conceive this Creator to be, we all share a common birthright which is life lived in its fullness (John 10.10). Jesus promised and showed us the path to realizing life in its fullness; that is, the path of justice. Therefore, the core business of the Christian faith is to do justice. And, this is what God requires of us (Micah 6.8).

To embrace and promote life in its fullness for all of creation, including nature, is thus to embrace and promote a wider ecumenism. It is to be inclusive and welcoming of everybody especially to those who are marginalized and disempowered, the sexual marginals among us. For Christians the question on judgment day is, 'What did you do to the least of Jesus' brothers and sisters?' and not 'Are you straight or gay?'

Practicing justice right in our own households

Our ecumenical witness would only have integrity when right in our own households we practice justice. How do we do justice to those among us who are the gender marginals?

Socially locating the marginals

A highly educated pastor once asked: "Does the discrimination of women still exist? Women are now in leadership positions." It is correct that some women are now in church leadership positions. But what are these women leaders doing? Under what circumstances did they assume leadership positions and how do they represent the sentiments of women on the ground? How about the rest of the church women? To generalize church women's (and others') realities is to trivialize gender fairness by ruling out genuine representation and meaningful participation in church decision-making bodies.

Asia is very plural and vast. Women, gays, lesbians, bisexuals and transgendered people experience marginalization and oppression differently on account of their particular contexts and specific locations. Their experiences and realities cannot be generalized. Accurate information from various perspectives, therefore, is essential in understanding reality towards changing our world. Only from the very specific contexts of oppression and exploitation can marginalized groups define justice and fullness of life for themselves.

Understanding power and oppression

The issue of power and oppression is central to achieving gender justice. It is a common reality on the ground that those who are marginalized and oppressed are the disempowered and who are logically found at the bottom of the heap. For this reason, they are always the potential victims of violence. To be able to change the status quo, a clear understanding of how power, especially that which is rooted in religious doctrines, and oppression work in gender relations is thus very important.

Hearing the voices from the margins

Voices of the marginalized and the victimized in a patriarchal world are muted. I learned from the women survivors and victims of sexual abuse in the church that they are not only silent about their abuses. They are also being silenced and eventually ostracized or expelled from church. This silence about their abuse the victims say is, in itself, violent.

My perennial wish and prayer for the churches is to have the will and the courage to hear and discern the challenge of marginal voices – that is, to transform the church and the world. In the story of the haemorrhaging woman in Mark 5.24-34, Jesus listened to the woman and accepted her challenge to authority and healed her. Jesus knew his power and authority, and what they were for. He opened himself up to the woman's challenge to put his power and authority in the service of the needy and the afflicted.

Marginal voices and life stories tell of a vital theological challenge and an urgent call to do justice. When these voices and stories are heard and affirmed, justice will begin to be realized. Instead of patronizing or ignoring the marginal voices, especially those of the victimized, ecumenical communities and movements must have the will and the courage to discern the call of justice.

Imagining the possible

Imagining an integrated humanity beyond our gender-shaped boxes is freeing ourselves from our rigid heterosexism. Human relationship is constitutive of our being human or struggling to be human. This relationship needs to be shaped by justice, mutuality and harmony. Seeking to be just, mutual and harmonious in our being human regardless of gender is to honor not only God's image in all of creation, but also to respect the limitless creativity of God.

Being inclusive in our language

Gender marginals need to be 'linguistically visible', too. Language gives shape and color to our imagination and names our reality. Likewise, our reality and creative imagination is capable of creating a new language. Using inclusive language is a way to help us imagine and create a new reality where everybody is welcome, acknowledged and honored.

To be gender-just is to recognize the gender marginals not just as a presence but as expected, capable and active participants in all human endeavors. To be gender-just is to empower the gender marginals towards becoming agents of their own quest for life lived in its fullness.

Building a Wider Ecumenism

When we accept gender justice issues as human issues and deal with these creatively and in community, we can contribute to the task of building a wider ecumenism in Asia. It is then that we would be able to effect the change we want.

The following are doable recommendations:

Reorient church formation programs. Ministers, priests, formators and leaders are influential nurturers of an ecumenical faith and consciousness. They are key in building an ecumenical orientation that is just and inclusive which is crucial in promoting a wider ecumenism in Asia. Gender justice issues, therefore, need to be integrated in all church formation programs particularly in theological, Sunday School and auxiliary organization formation programs and trainings.

Create and provide spaces for gender marginals in the church's liturgical life. In the Philippines, March is observed as Women's Month among the members of the National Council of Churches in the Philippines (NCCP). This is one way of highlighting women's issues in church life. This practice could be broadened by including all the gender marginals. After all, women share the same space of marginalization and oppression with the gays, lesbians and transgendered people.

Give special focus on the younger ones in cultivating gender-fair relationships. The young are constantly shaping gender identities, images and relationships. The next ecumenical leaders need nurturing in building gender relations founded on justice and not trapped in unjust valuation of different genders.

Encourage gender-sensitive men to lead gender sensitivity activities for men. The Institute of Women's Studies in Manila has already initiated the training of men to help others understand and overcome heterosexism, confront a socially conditioned masculinity and define a life-affirming one. An interesting model to explore is Jesus. What does it mean to be a man according to the life experiences of Jesus?

Hear them out. The gender marginals have spoken, they need to be seriously heard and the more life-giving potential of their voices considered. This must be the most important of all – to let them speak, participate and act for themselves. To let persons flourish into fullness also means to protect, uphold and promote their rights as human beings. This task is central to engendering gender justice towards a wider ecumenism in Asia.

In conclusion, achieving gender justice requires a lot of courage, creativity and will to stay radically open to the leading of our most creative God. It means being just, mutual and harmonious in our relationships with each other because we recognize our common heritage of life in its fullness as God's promise. Mainstreaming gender justice in the ecumenical movement surely will help ensure that a wider ecumenism in Asia is possible, and is done in the name of an All-embracing and Just God.

Bibliography

Bieringer, Reimund and Ma. Marilou Ibita. "Justice as Participation: Toward a Theology of Justice." *Himig Ugnayan* VIII, no. SY 2006-2007 (2007): 18-55.

Fernandez, Eleazar. *Reimagining the Human: Theological Anthropology in Response to Systemic Evil*. St. Louis, Missouri: Chalice Press, 2004.

Kang, Nam Soon. "The Centrality of Gender Justice in Prophetic Christianity and the Mission of the Church Reconsidered." *International Review of Mission* 94, no. 373 (April 2005): 278-290.

Keshgegian, Flora. "Power to Wound, Power to Mend: Toward a Non-Abusing Theology." *Journal of Religion and Abuse* 1, no. 1 (1999): 37-65.

Kinukawa, Hisako. *Women and Jesus in Mark: A Japanese Feminist Perspective*. Maryknoll, NY: Orbis Books, 1994.

Orevillo-Montenegro, Muriel. "Finding Our Voice and Subjectivity." *In God's Image* 24, no. 1 (2005): 9-17.

_________. "Rethinking Incarnation: An Asian Woman's Perspective." *Silliman Journal* 47, no. 1 (January to June 2006): 18-34.

Poling, James Newton. *The Abuse of Power: A Theological Problem.* Nashville: Abingdon Press, 1991.

Russell, Letty M. *Just Hospitality: God's Welcome in a World of Difference*. J. Shannon Clarkson and Kate M. Ott, eds. Louisville: Westminster John Knox Press, 2009.

____________ and Phyllis Trible, eds. *Hagar, Sarah and Their Children: Jewish, Christian and Muslim*

Perspectives. Louisville, Kentucky: Westminster John Knox Press, 2006.

Song, C. S. "Story is the Matrix of Theology." In *Theologies and Cultures* 5, no. 1 (June 2008): 28-48.

Tolbert, Mary Ann. "Mark." *In Women's Bible Commentary*, ed. Carol Newsom and Sharon Ringe, 350-362. Louisville: Westminster John Knox Press, 1998.

Wren, Brian. *What Language Shall I Borrow?* New York: Crossroad Publications, 1983.

(42) TRIBAL WOMEN IN ASIAN CHURCHES

Naw Eh Tar Gay

Asia is the world's largest continent with fifty-two countries inhabited by peoples with rich, ancient histories, diverse religions and cultures. Each nation is populated by multiple ethnic groups with one or some groups being the majority and others the minority. In China, for example, Han comprises the majority ethnic group while the rest are minorities, e.g. Dai, Hui, Miao, Lisu, Kachin and Wa. It is usually the minority groups, often identified as tribal, ethnic minority or indigenous, which are marginalized. Historically, they have been looked down upon, persecuted, and called 'barbarians' and 'idlers' due to their under-developed situation. Tribal people have suffered under colonial powers and governments which often denied them their human rights and displaced them from their lands and cultures.

Who are tribal people?

The terms "tribal" and "indigenous" have several meanings. In one sense, they are used to identify the original or earliest inhabitants of the land and their present descendants. They simply mean ethnic minorities or nationalities. In another sense, they mean marginalized groups living far from the centres of power. The term "tribal" sometimes has negative connotations. For example, the word is used to mean people who live a relatively isolated life, are economically and technologically backward, not fully assimilated in mainstream society, are socially alienated and discriminated in their own land. But some tribals have successfully integrated into the mainstream society. Nowadays, the tribals themselves have reclaimed the term and invested it with positive meanings for their own empowerment. By and large, tribal groups are also known as hill people, islanders, ethnic minorities, and aboriginal people.

Most tribal societies are patriarchal, though a few tribes like Khasis and Garos in India and Bangladesh and Menangkabaws in Indonesia are matrilineal societies. In male-dominated tribal societies, women are subordinate members who cannot inherit landed property, are undernourished due to poverty, and suffer from various forms of violence inflicted by persons as well as structures.

This paper focuses on tribal women in select Asian countries, their role in bringing together people across denominations, religions, ethnic and ideological divides, and their ways of theologizing, hermeneutics, alternative leadership, etc. which contribute to wider ecumenism in Asia.

Role of Tribal Women in the Ecumenical Movement

The ecumenical movement is a call for solidarity and unity based on common interests and concerns, and leads to a deeper understanding of oneself and others. The World Council of Churches (WCC) calls for churches to come together in unity, common witness, fellowship and struggle on issues of social justice. In Asia, the ecumenical movement is expressed by the Christian Conference of Asia (CCA) and the National Councils of Churches or National Christian Councils (NCC).

Church women's groups and denominational women's associations were active long before the regional organizations came to being. Ecumenical women's organizations were later organized to bring together denominational church women in fellowship, worship and social action. In countries with NCCs, usually there would be a women's desk or department that co-ordinates work among women of different denominations. Two regional organizations that have prioritized women's work are the Christian Conference of Asia and the World Student Christian Federation Asia-Pacific Region. Asian tribal women have also been active in the Young Women's Christian Association (YWCA), Women's Temperance

Movement, Asian Church Women's Conference (ACWC), International Fellowship of the Least Coin (IFLC), and Asian Women's Resource Centre for Culture and Theology (AWRC).

Contributions of tribal feminists' theological reflections have been made available through the Women's Commission of the Ecumenical Association of Third World Theologians (EATWOT), *In God's Image*, the journal of AWRC, the Program for Theology and Cultures in Asia (PTCA), and the Congress of Asian Theologians (CATS).

One of the objectives of the ecumenical movement has been gender equity, expressed through equal participation of men and women. The Community of Men and Women, a program lodged in the WCC Commission on Faith and Order, which culminated at an international consultation in 1982, led to changes in theological thinking and more equitable participation and relationship of men and women in church and society. To build on this momentum, WCC called for an *Ecumenical Decade of Churches in Solidarity with Women* (1988-1998), challenging churches to evaluate their teachings, structures and practices related to women. The decade aimed at full and equal participation of women in the church, an end to violence against women, promotion of women's empowerment and leadership, and recognition of women's diverse ministries and gifts. Despite mixed reviews about the results of the Ecumenical Decade by Asian women, it did make the churches aware that women would no longer be silent and submissive.

Asian Tribal Women and Their Ecumenical Involvement

In response to the WCC Decade campaign, the Uniting Church in *Australia* formed the Commission on Women and Men (CWM) with the vision of "The Church Made Whole." Recognizing sexism and racism are the main hindrance to the wholeness of the church, CWM focussed on gender-related issues of justice to challenge patriarchal structures of the church. Linking with women's networks including Aboriginal women, Islander women and women from non-English speaking backgrounds, CWM aims to break the silence in the church about violence against women, involving sexual, emotional, physical and psychological abuse, and promote women's full participation, including in leadership. A group of strong Aboriginal women got organised, including people with strong Christian background and those who were not involved in formal religion but were interested in community action. Out of a sense of identification with tribal ancestors and traditions, they studied women's spiritual and religious life, roles and lifestyles, and discovered Aboriginal women's role in religious life, such as performing their own sacred ceremonies. This promoted spiritual healing and renewal of sacred sites for women and helped to restore their tribal life that was destroyed by white colonists.[1] The Ngarrindjeri women's movement came about to protest the building of a bridge over a women's sacred site where "secret women's business" was done.[2] Aboriginal feminist theologian Anne Pattel-Gray has publicized the plight of Aboriginal people such as displacement from tribal lands and sacred sites, forced foster care for Aboriginal children and the subsequent loss of identity and culture and the discrimination in several aspects of life.[3] Lee Miena Skye explores in her study of Aboriginal women's Christology how the image of Jesus Christ changed, became one with creation, when inculturated into Indigenous spiritualities.

In *Bangladesh*, the Bengalis make up the majority of the population. The tribals, such Biharis, Chakmas, Garos, Khasis and Santals, constitute a minority and a most marginalized section of the population. Women's ecumenical activities are carried out by the Women's Desk of the National Council of Churches

---

[1] Anne Thomas, "Aboriginal Women in Australia: Their Role and Their Spirituality," *In God's Image* (December 1988): 30-33.

[2] Lee Miena Skye, "Yiminga (Spirit) Calling A Study of Australian Aboriginal Women's Contribution to Creation Theology- The Transformation of Christian Religion," *In God's Image,* Vol. 20, No. 4 (December 2001): 40-42.

[3] Anne Pattel-Gray, "For Our Children: Mapping Our Consciousness, Writing Our Voices," *In God's Image,* Vol. 13, No.2 (Summer 1994): 76-79.

of Bangladesh (NCCB). Together with Roman Catholic women, the NCCB Women's desk started *Netritto Proshikkhon Kendro* (Women's Ecumenical Leadership Training Centre) whose aim is to promote women's leadership, develop solidarity among women and sharpen their skills in re-reading the Bible from women's perspective. Some tribal women from Bangladesh attended the Indigenous Women's Alternative Leadership (IWALT), a three-year project of CCA (2005-2008) in partnership with WCC and the Sisters Network. Deacon Rakhi Drong from the Garo tribe was a participant who later organized two training programs in villages in partnership with Indigenous Women's Development Society in Bangladesh.

The Khmers make up 90% of the population of *Cambodia* (Kampuchea) while the indigenous tribal groups found in the northwest mountains form a minority. Aside from having been colonized by France, Cambodia fell under the control of the Khmer Rouge (1975-1979), which terrorized the country, killing many, separating families, and forcing people to work in labour camps. For many years, Christianity in Cambodia remained an underground movement until 1991 when the government opened its doors and since then many Christian denominations have worked freely in Cambodia. The Cambodia Christian Women's Association (CCWA) and Kampuchea Christian Council (KCC) Women's Desk organised leadership training programs for women, raising awareness and honing skills for their full participation in church and community. Women are empowered to participate in nation rebuilding and to upgrade their living standards. Skills training include literacy program, sewing, weaving, credit cooperative, reading the Bible with women's eyes, and leadership development. Different ecumenical women's groups have worked with KCC women, including CCA Women's Desk, ETE-WCC/CCA, AWRC and ACWC to promote women's leadership in Cambodia. AWRC's Women's Alternative Leadership for Transformation (WALT) was developed precisely to address the needs of the Cambodian women. Through CCA's Women's Accompanier for Vision and Empowerment (WEAVE), Dominica Lagat-Faurillo, was sent by NCC Philippines as an Ecumenical Accompanier working with Cambodian women. A new way of doing women's leadership capacity development and sharing of resources, WEAVE is striving to become a channel to heal, help, uplift and reach out to the suffering women.

Tribal people live in almost all the states in *India*. They are called "tribal" or "adivasi." In North East India, several indigenous peoples' independence movements are thriving despite the military's attempt at quelling them. Many tribal communities have embraced the Christian faith, seeking new identities and justice. Mizo women formed an ecumenical group called *Women Wing,* through which they do their fund raising ("a handful of rice" collection), charitable ministry for orphans and persons with disabilities. Through the *Women Wing* fellowship, they have their own worship services. But in some places, men are still in charge even in women's organizations or fellowships. The Evangelical and Baptist churches allow women to be ordained as church elders, but not as pastors. In Tripura, women are still not ordained, not allowed to participate in worship services or take part in Holy Communion during their menstrual period, and should cover their heads during worship. The Tripura Baptist Women's Society (TBWS) has its own women's fellowship on Saturdays and Thursdays and conducts ecumenical meetings and leadership training. A group of Sumi Naga women have formed the 'Sulimi Hoho' which comes under the umbrella of Naga Mothers' Association (NMA). The Sulimi Hoho not only works for the uplift of women but of society as well, serving as agent of peace and harmony between conflicting groups.[4] The adivasis are concerned about the destruction and despoliation of their lands by multi-national companies.

Indian tribal women have been theologizing and publishing their feminist tribal theology. One such publication was No More Tears in God's Garden of Justice: Tribal Women Doing Theology, and Side by Side: Naga Women Doing Theology in Search of Justice and Partnership edited by Limatula Longkumer. Tribal women have also been prominent in the struggle for eco-justice. In 1974, village women of the Reni forests in Uttar Pradesh joined hands and encircled the trees that were to be cut down. The women told the

[4] Zakali Shohe, "Women and the Dragon: Sumi Naga Women's Role towards Peace and Harmony," *In God's Image*, Vol. 23, No. 3 (September 2004), 50.

cutters they would have to first cut off their heads. The contractors withdrew and the forest was saved. The Chipko ('Chipko' means to hug) movement spread and generated pressure for a natural resource policy that is more sensitive to people's needs and ecological requirements.[5] The Deomali Mahila Society of Indigenous Women in Koraput, Orissa, and the Narmada Bachao Andolan (Save the Narmada Movement) are two protest movements which grew out of women's concerns for the lives of their communities and for the environment. The women challenge the breaking down of their traditional ways of life and culture and the injustices they experience in the name of "development."[6]

The archipelago of *Indonesia* comprises around 13,000 islands, inhabited by about 300 ethnic groups who speak approximately 250 dialects. One issue for Indonesian tribal women is land inheritance. For the Bataks, people get respect from society because of their ownership of lands, not because of their education or political position. So women are looked down because they do not own the land. Women are also pressured to get married and bear many children, especially sons. However, in churches, women church workers are encouraged to remain celibate to retain their holiness and to faithfully serve God. Indonesia has produced prominent women theologians, e.g. Marianne Katoppo whose book, *Compassionate and Free: An Asian Women's Theology*, opened the way for Asian women to theologize contextually and do feminist biblical hermeneutics. Others are El. Anna Marsiana, present Coordinator of AWRC; Septemmy Lakawa, faculty member of Jakarta Theological Seminary and past General Secretary of the Association of Theologically Educated Women in Indonesia and chief editor of SOPHIA, the first Indonesian women's theological journal; Henriette Hutabarat Lebang, present General Secretary of CCA; and Margaretha Hendriks-Ririmase, Vice-Moderator of WCC. They demonstrate the strong involvement of Indonesian women in the ecumenical movement.

Tribal women became involved in peacemaking and reconciliation in their own ways. During the struggle for independence, Aceh women gathered together, calling themselves women of peace and campaigning for peace.[7] In the time of conflict, Ambon was divided into Christian and Islamic communities. The Christians had surplus of industrial products while the Muslims had surplus of agricultural products. The border was closely watched by the military, making the exchange of goods difficult. Women from both communities started the border markets in order to exchange goods between them for their survival.[8] Thus, ethnic women in Indonesia have understood the importance of religious and ethnic tolerance, the need for different norms, cultures and values to be respected, and that participation in social and political organizations should lead to solidarity, justice and peace.[9]

In *Japan*, tribal groups are small in number, with no guarantee of basic human rights. In school, those who do not have Japanese names are bullied, looked down upon because of their culture. This often leads to self-hate and loss of identity. In this kind of situation, women are the double victims, left with scars on their bodies and minds with subordination in their homes and exploitation in society. The Buraku, a minority group of about 3,000,000 people, occupies the lowest social and economic level in Japan. The Buraku Liberation Movement (Buraku Kaiho Undo) strives to end discrimination and establish human rights for the Buraku people. Although some Buraku people joined the churches, they still experience some incidents of discrimination in the churches as well as in society.[10] The Ainu, numbering about 50,000, are

---

[5] Annabel Rodda, *Women and the Environment* (London and New Jersey: Zed Books, 1994), 110.

[6] Aruna Gnanadason, *Listen to the Women! Listen to the Earth* (Geneva: WCC Publications, 2005), 10-11.

[7] El. Anna Marsiana, "We Dare to Live, We Dare to Die," *In God's Image*, Vol. 22, No.3 (September 2003), 25.

[8] Ibid., 24.

[9] Wendy Kakerissa, Reflections and Contributions from Youth Workshop Participants (Indonesia, Sri Lanka), *Building a Culture of Peace, Religious and Ethnic Plurality in South and South East Asia* (Hong Kong: Christian Conference of Asia, 2004), 28-33.

[10] Kudo Eiichi, "Buraku Liberation Movement, Japan," *A Dictionary of Asian Christianity*, ed., Scott W. Sunquist (Grand Rapids, Michigan: William B. Eerdmans Co., 2001), 105-106.

people of Hokkaido. They were forcibly colonized, assimilated, relocated to areas where they had to change their lifestyle and livelihood. Their lands were expropriated for dam building project. The Cultural Protection Law is aimed at "reviving the Ainu culture," but it makes no mention of indigenous rights, including the right to lay claim to land.[11] Okinawans or Islanders live on several small islands in the southernmost part of Japan. Their land area holds 75% of the American military bases. Okinawans have suffered exploitation from both American and Japanese authorities. They were prohibited from using their Okinawan dialect. They were used as "sacrifice" during the Second World War. Their land was expropriated for military bases. A drama group made up of women from the Okinawa parish premiered a play, *Cry More, Fish*, which dramatically portrayed the depressed lives of Okinawans.[12] At the news that the military base would move to No, 15 women of No formed a new group, *Kamadu-gua no Tsudoi* and produced "Koe, koe, KOE" (literally "Voice, Voice, VOICE), a collection of writings revealing the distress of people living near military bases. The Nago movement produced a network of women's groups whose commitment was: No New Military Base on Our Island. Women carried out a walking demonstration in Nago, and later in Tokyo to deliver Okinawans' message to the whole of Japan. Women took part in fighting for peace and fighting against the Emperor system, which means fighting against control and discrimination.

Malaysia is made up of Malay, Chinese, Indian and indigenous groups such as the Orang Asli (original people) of Peninsular Malaysia, and the indigenous peoples of Sabah and Sarawak in East Malaysia, such as the Ibans, Dusuns, and Bajaus. The indigenous people have suffered abuse such as slavery, confinement, exploitation, displacement, and dispossession. Robbed of their lands, rivers, and forests, they have been resettled in other places, forced to work as farm or factory workers and other odd jobs. Thus, 80% of Orang Aslis are under the poverty line. Whenever they try to claim back their lands they are accused of being primitive, uncooperative, anti-development or disturbers of the peace. While they have entered into the mainstream of Malaysian life, many of the women and children suffer from the consequences. Women lost their traditional leadership roles and authority. In the past, women participated in decision making. Most of them practice their indigenous faith until quite recently. The Indigenous People's Network of Malaysia was formed to fight for their rights. Tijah Chopil, a Semai leader, recognized the importance of education for the indigenous people of Malaysia and started teaching in her home after her day's work. She organized the *Sinui Pai Nanek Sengik* (New Life, One Heart) aiming to unite and awaken the community to their problems. Networking with other Orang Asli tribes and indigenous communities in Malaysia, this group has also organized programs on biodiversity and Indigenous peoples' knowledge.

In the struggle for women's rights, women of all faiths work together in the *Women's Agenda for Change*. They have lobbied for women's participation in political leadership and in decision making at all levels. Malaysian women have struggled successfully for the Domestic Violence Act which was passed in 1997.[13] The aims of *Malaysian Women in Ministry and Theology* (MWMT) are to reread the bible from a women's perspective, to examine the structure of the church for equal participation of women, and to promote dialogue with women of other faiths for social transformation. They have challenged the Malaysian church to change its patriarchal attitudes and encouraged women to be trained theologically and participate in church ministry. They have held workshops to examine the status of women in society and the churches' structures, doctrines, theologies and biblical interpretation which have negative impact on women. They also have ecumenical services using inclusive language and imagery and expressing Asian

---

[11] Nobue Kuroda, "Being Connected with the Indigenous People, the Ainu, in their Struggle," *In God's Image*, Vol. 18, No. 4 (1999), 15-16.
[12] Kyoko Matayoshi, "From Okinawa: Living with U.S. Military Bases, and Okinawan Solidarity," *In God's Image*, Vol. 18, No. 4 (1999), 18-19.
[13] Dulcie Abraham, "Faith Made Tangible, *In God's Image*, Vo. 21, No. 3 (September 2002), 8.

women's identity and concerns. This ecumenical group works closely with the Asian Women's Resource Centre for Culture and Theology (AWRC).

Myanmar has many tribal groups speaking over 135 languages and dialects while its majority ethnic group is the Bama. Indigenous peoples were devotees of nature and ancestor spirits. Of the 6% Christian population, the tribals form the majority as the missionaries were more successful in reaching out to them than to the Buddhists. Myanmar tribal groups are actively involved in the ecumenical movement through their churches. The Myanmar Council of Churches (MCC) Women's Department relates with the women's departments of its member churches. Its tasks include educating women on current issues, promoting them in evangelism and mission work as well as leadership, consciousness-raising on their rights and roles. During the Ecumenical Decade, MCC women encouraged both men and women to make necessary changes in their attitudes towards each other and resist mutual discrimination, while also evaluating the structures, polity and teachings of the churches. MCC Women's Department also networks with AWRC, ACWC and IFLC.

Churches in Myanmar are still patriarchal. A few women pastors have been ordained in certain churches over the last few years. Most churches are still hesitant to ordain women or appoint women pastors. Yet, women students outnumber men attending theological schools and women actively participate in mission work outside and inside the churches. Through the work of the Association for Theological Education in Myanmar (ATEM), the teaching of Feminist Theology is now mandatory for its member schools. Women faculty from several seminaries, such as Anna May Say Pa, Htoo Htoo, Lwin Thida Oo, L. Fanang Lum and Khin Swe Oo, pooled their resources together to publish a feminist theology textbook, *Rice Table Salad: Myanmar Women Doing Theology Together*. ATEM also promotes gender equality in faculty development.

Myanmar tribal people continue to struggle for peace in the midst of conflicts that have led to loss of lives, internal displacement of people, or forced ethnic fleeing to refugee camps in neighbouring countries. Many tribal people suffer from land mines, forced labour, or use as human mine sweepers. Tribal women often bear the brunt of suffering when they are raped or forced to become objects of sex gratification of soldiers. Not considered as part of the peace process in the past, now, women want their voices for peace to be heard. During the peace talks between the Karen National Union (KNU) and the central government, for the first time, the KNU delegation was led by Zipporah Sein, its General Secretary, together with other Karen women. Women from the Karen Women Action Network led by Susanna Hla Hla Soe, together with women from other women NGOs led a signature campaign and sent out a call for peace in the Kachin State to the President, U Thein Sein. Ja Nan and Seng Raw from Nyein (Shalom) Foundation have organized Women for Peace workshops. May Sabai Phyu of the Gender Equality Network, together with other peace activists, organized peace marches in Naypyidaw and Yangon on the International Day for Peace (September 21, 2012) to call for peace in the Kachin and Rakhine States. The winds of change are blowing through the land of Myanmar. Aung San Suu Kyi, who for many years was held under house arrest, now sits in Parliament and has called tribal women to participate in transforming the nation and changing the lives of women so they might take up their proper place in society.

New Zealand, called Aotearoa or "land of the long white clouds" by the Maori indigenous people, was colonized by the British and other Europeans in the 18th century. Today, the Pakeha (white) population is in the majority and Maori remains as a minority tribal group. The Maoris have a rich and diverse culture and oral tradition of legends, poems, history and sage. They have a heritage of arts such as painting, sculpture, weaving, woodwork and architecture. The policy of assimilation carried out by the government led to the loss of culture including language among the younger generation. At present, there is a renaissance of arts and culture among younger Maoris and Maori is now taught to Maori children in the lower grades. Maori art is displayed in several museums but specifically in the Te Papa Tongarewa Museum in Wellington. Maori writers have contributed to making Maori context known worldwide. Patricia Grace's book

Mutuwhenua (1971) addressed difficult questions of biculturalism and the survival of the Maori community and culture. Keri Hulme's book *The Bone People* was awarded the prestigious Booker Prize in 1985. Kiri Te Kanawa is a world famous opera singer.

For Maori women, life continues to be a struggle for education, health and employment. In theological education and in the church, women continue to be marginalized more so than Maori men. Jenny Te Paa was the first Maori with a Doctor of Philosophy and among the first ordained Maori women in the Anglican Church in Aotearoa New Zealand and Polynesia. She was appointed as Dean of Te Rau Kahikatea, an indigenous constituent of the College of St. John the Evangelist. She was a member of the Commission on Ecumenical Theological Education and Ministerial Formation programme of the World Council of Churches. She also actively participates in her own tribal community development work. As a tribal woman, she enjoys the richness of ecumenical diversity and the privileged learning and teaching opportunities that diversity provides. Maori women have been struggling for ordination and trying to gain full access to higher theological education.[14]

Christian women in *Pakistan* are rarely in leadership or decision-making positions at any level. They mainly serve by working in hospitals, schools, hostels and colleges. Only a few Pakistani women are teachers at Bible schools. Churches do not encourage women to become ministers. However, there is a Synodical Women's Fellowship, a branch of the Church of Pakistan, which is a union of Anglican, Methodist, Scottish Presbyterian and Lutheran denominations. It attempts to raise awareness on women's rights at all levels and holds programs on Women's World Day of Prayer and Asian Women's Day to show solidarity with the other Christian women in the world. For Pakistani Christian women, the Ecumenical Decade was an opportunity to alert the churches to the need to include women in church ministries and to open up leadership positions for women. Shirin Samuel said the Decade was a time to recognise that there are other women in the world who are having similar concerns and that God intervenes in oppressive situations and the truth is revealed that men and women are equal in the sight of God.[15] One of their concerns was to reread the Bible, which led to the formation of a group named *Women in Reflection and Action.* The group also includes younger women, in order to train and motivate them to be leaders.[16]

The indigenous or tribal people in the *Philippines* number around 6.5 million. Despite the long history of colonization and neo-colonization (i.e. globalization) of the country, indigenous people have retained aspects of their ways of living that reflect environmental adaptation, sustainability, coexistence, common consensus, collective effort and communal ownership.[17] The National Council of Churches in the Philippines has had a desk focusing on the concerns of Indigenous people – which include solidarity and advocacy with them in their struggle against the expropriation of ancestral lands by government, foreign and local big businesses for commercial logging, plantations, dam projects and mining concessions. Such struggles are often met with persecution and violence. Meanwhile the indigenous women of the Philippines have also participated in and hosted the Indigenous Women's Alternative Leadership for Transformation organized by the Christian Conference of Asia to equip women to do theologizing by themselves as well as practice collective, transformative feminist leadership.

---

[14] Jenny Te Paa, "Being Church: A Maori Woman's Voice and Vision," *In God's Image*, Vol. 23, No. 2 (June 2004): 35-41.

[15] Shirin Samuel, "Pakistani Women's Experience of the Ecumenical Decade," *In God's Image,* Vol.17, No. 4 (1998): 44-47.

[16] *Ibid.*

[17] Melinda Grace B. Aoanan, "Churches and Seminaries: Appraising our Ecumenical Vision in Today's World", a paper for a consultation of the same title organized by the Christian Conference of Asia in cooperation with the National Council of Churches in the Philippines on 24-29 November 2008.

The issue of racism, particularly against aboriginal, indigenous, trial or racially and religiously marginalized groups has been a focus in Asia and particularly in *Taiwan*, which hosted a joint CCA-WCC conference to overcome racism and discrimination in 2000. The workshop on the theme, "Church Women's Role in Overcoming Racial/Ethnic/Minority/Religious Discrimination in Asia" was appropriately hosted by the Presbyterian Church in Taiwan at the Hsinchu College in Hsinchu City. Taiwan has about 30 indigenous or aboriginal tribes who have lived there for over a thousand years.

In *Thailand*, some of the tribal groups are Karen, Akha, Lahu, Lisu, Kayah among others. These tribal groups form their own denominational organizations with their women's departments. For example, the Karens formed the Thailand Karen Baptist Convention which is part of the ecumenical body Church of Christ in Thailand (CCT). As part of the women's network of CCT, the women join together in various activities such as Bible study groups, training programs, and skills and income generation groups. The Christian Conference of Asia Women's Desk has organized Women's Alternative Leadership for Transformation (WALT) for indigenous Thai women and indigenous women from neighbouring countries such as Myanmar, Laos and Cambodia. This training empowered the women to challenge male models of leadership and practise the feminist transformational leadership model. Through participatory sessions led by indigenous women leader the Bible was reinterpreted through women's eyes and women issues discussed. Due to the economic situation in Thailand some of the tribal girls are trafficked or lured into working in the sex tourism industry. Various non-government organizations are trying to help them change their lives by providing them education and skills training. Some of these women have become peer counsellors for various tribal groups especially on HIV/AIDS education. Tribal women theologians like Esther Danpongpee work on myths and legends of the Karen people to formulate a tribal creation theology for women's empowerment. An ecumenical partnership between CCT and Myanmar Council of Churches women's desks studied the problem of sex trafficking of tribal women from Myanmar into Thailand. A positive result was the establishment of the Myitta Women's Center in Kengtung, Shan State, where trafficked women are returned home or if they wished, given skills for income generation.

Conclusion

Tribal women have been involved in various ecumenical movements. They participate in dialogue with women of different denominations and religions and at the same time they claim their own rights and raise their voices. Their main concern is to bring solidarity among church members, denominations and religions. They are striving for "the creation of a church and society free from sexism, tokenism, classism, casteism, racism, clericalism and all forms of violence against women and other marginalised groups."[18] Tribal women are building communities of different ethnic, denominational and religious groups through common concerns such as education for all girls and women, reproductive health, liberation from gender-based violence, women's rights and leadership, and ecological justice. Tribal women take initiative in peace building processes through networking with other peace groups, organizing demonstrations and signature campaign for peace and being involved in peace negotiations and working for political and economic security of the conflict areas. Although tribal women have done what they can, still there is a need for solidarity between churches and tribal women in terms of struggling for women's rights and dignity. Uplifting tribal women's status and position as it is now continues to be a challenge.

---

[18] Pauline Chakkalakal, "Towards More Participatory Structures in the Church," *In God's Image,* Vol. 23, No. 2 (June 2004): 42-49.

Bibliography

Abraham, Dulcie. "Faith Made Tangible," *In God's Image*, Vol. 21, No. 3 (September 2002).

Chakkalakal, Pauline. "Towards More Participatory Structures in the Church," *In God's Image,* Vol. 23, No. 2 (June 2004): 42-49

Eiichi, Kudo. "Buraku Liberation Movement, Japan," *A Dictionary of Asian Christianity*, ed., Scott W. Sunquist. Grand Rapids, Michigan: William B. Eerdmans Co., 2001.

Gnanadason, Aruna. *Listen to the Women! Listen to the Earth.* Geneva: WCC Publications, 2005.

Kakerissa, Wendy. "Reflections and Contributions from Youth Workshop Participants." *Building a Culture of Peace, Religious and Ethnic Plurality in South and South East Asia*. Hong Kong: Christian Conference of Asia, 2004.

Kuroda, Nobue. "Being Connected with the Indigenous People, The Ainu in their Struggle." *In God's Image.* Vol. 18, No. 4 (1999): 15-16.

Marsiana, El. Anna. "We Dare to Live, We Dare to Die," *In God's Image*, Vol. 22, No. 3 (September 2003).

Matayoshi, Kyoko. "From Okinawa: Living with U.S. Military Bases, and Okinawan Solidarity," *In God's Image*. Vol. 18, No. 4 (1999).

Paa, Jenny Te. "Being Church: A Maori Woman's Voice and Vision." *In God's Image*. Vol. 23, No. 2 (June 2004): 35-41.

Pattel-Gray, Anne. "For Our Children: Mapping Our Consciousness, Writing Our Voices," *In God's Image,* Vol. 13, No. 2 (Summer 1994).

Rodda, Annabel. *Women and the Environment* (London and New Jersey: Zed Books, 1994), 110.

Samuel, Shirin. "Pakistani Women's Experience of the Ecumenical Decade." *In God's Image* Vol.17, No. 4 (1998): 44-47.

Shohe, Zakali. "Women and the Dragon: Sumi Naga Women's Role towards Peace and Harmony," *In God's Image*, Vol. 23, No. 3 (September 2004), 50.

Skye, Lee Miena. "Yiminga (Spirit) Calling A Study of Australian Aboriginal Women's Contribution to Creation Theology – The Transformation of Christian Religion," *In God's Image,* Vol. 20, No. 4 (December 2001).

Thomas, Anne. "Aboriginal Women in Australia: Their Role and Their Spirituality." *In God's Image* (December 1988): 30-33.

(43) Indigenous People's Response to Eco-Justice in Asia

Wati Longchar

Introduction

The impact on the earth of the greenhouse effect through gas emission, rising sea levels, global warming, the alarming pollution of air, water and other essentials is due to the life style of the rich people and rich countries.[1] Can the life-style of the rich be changed to save the earth? Eco-justice has to do with the dominant model of market economy and liberal capitalism; it is the root cause of social inequality and ecological injustice. Thus, eco-justice and social injustice are interconnected. Relating the two is a great challenge before humanity. The Christian theology of creation also bears to a certain degree the responsibility for bringing about today's ecological destruction. Our uncritical and partial interpretations of the Bible have supported the modern domination of nature. We need a theology that promotes respect and a caring attitude for all of God's creation. Recognizing this interrelated issue, this paper attempts to discuss the ecumenical responses to ecological issues from the experience of indigenous people.

Looking into the Roots of Ecological Crisis

Many thinkers point to two major factors that have contributed to the present ecological crisis. They are:

(a) Non-theological factors

1. The one-sided industrialization of economic development is the root cause of this ecological crisis. Every country wants to improve the living standards of its population by massive build up of industrialization. This puts tremendous pressures on non-renewable resources.
2. Consumerism and industrialization go hand in hand. Production for sale and expansion of market are the key factors to sustain the capitalist system. Industrialization can be sustained through the creation of a consumeristic society, a class of owners and a class of non-owners, endless accumulation, reinvestment for profit, manipulation of mass-media, political machinery, competition, exploitation, militarism and colonization of the poor, and exploitation of land and its resources. K.C. Abraham says that the present ecological crisis is the direct product of modern industrial and technological growth, and modern life-style. He writes that,

> A paradigm of development, the western industrial growth model, is almost universally accepted. It is a process whereby we use enormous capital and exploit natural resources, particularly the non-renewable ones. Ruthless exploitation of nature and fellow-beings is the inevitable consequence of this pattern of development. Decisions about the kind of goods to be produced and the type of technology to be used are influenced by the demand of consumerist economy where the controlling logic of growth is greed and not need. It creates imbalances between different sectors and allows massive exploitation of the rural and natural environment for the benefit of the dominant classes.[2]

---

[1] For example, the USA which has only 4% of world's population, emits 30% of all greenhouse gas emissions.

[2] K.C. Abraham, *Eco-justice: A New Agenda of Church's Mission* (Bombay: BUILD, no year), pp. 4-5.

3. Against the capitalist ideology of privatization of capital and competition, the socialist model of economy emerged as a substitute, but failed. Socialism could not provide an alternative, conducive environment for upholding the ecological balance and could not liberate the poor from the yoke of exploitation. Karl Marx upheld that, nature is a reservoir of raw materials, and nothing more, which are to be transformed through the building up of an industrialized society.[3] A basic difference between industrial capitalism and socialistic model of economy lies only in the means of ownership. Marx assumed that the exploitation of humans would be eliminated once the private ownership of the means of production is controlled by the producers themselves.
4. The problem lies in the perception of nature. Many scientists view nature as a machine. It has no inherent rights of its own, and we need not hesitate to manipulate, exploit and use it. With the scientific and technological revolution, the whole cosmos is perceived in a mechanical way. Humans are the centre of the world, and the point of reference. The value of other segments of God's creation is determined on the basis of their usefulness to humans.
5. Scientific and technological revolutions have in a way destroyed the sanctity of nature. The scientific method of reductionism thus took away the mystery out of creation. People began to believe that there is nothing amazing about the cosmos. By detaching God from nature and regarding it as secular, humanity has changed the relationship between humans and nature. Instead of perceiving nature as a subject to which we are inseparably related, nature is seen as objects from which we are totally detached and separated. Nature is something "out there" apart from us and apart from God. This detachment leads to an objective study of all, and then it leads to manipulation and domination. Without any religious restraints, it was presumed that this external material of creation can be exploited and abused.

(b) Theological Factors

Theology does not contribute directly to ecological crisis, but it influences and shapes the attitude of humans towards nature, and our relationship with other segments of God's creation. The confluence of four streams of thought has created a forceful current in dominant Christian traditions that set aside the truth of the communion of human beings with God's creation. It is important to see how they have influenced the attitude of humans and contributed to exploitation and abuse of Mother Earth.

MECHANICAL VIEW AND SECULARIZATION OF CREATION

This stream of thought is rooted in Western Enlightenment tradition which makes a sharp contrast between nature and history. The advancement of the knowledge of science and secularization of nature is interconnected. The advancement of knowledge in the field of science and technology in the sixteenth and seventeenth centuries brought industrial capitalism, market economy, mass production, democracy and rationalism. The whole created order began to be viewed objectively. Using the tools of mathematical calculations and experimental data, humans began to claim that one could understand the specific nature of the physical matter constituting the Earth, and the changes within it. Thus, Nature was seen purely from utilitarian perspective and lost its mystery and sacredness for the western worldview. People began to perceive that there is nothing amazing and sacred about the world; it is merely a sum-total of many material components and energies. Humans are capable of understanding, predicting, and controlling everything related to the world; we are separated from, and masters of, the earth. Natural resources are given only in so far as they are useful for the development of science and technology. Hence, this materialistic attitude of humans today is greatly shaped by such ideologies. Many people visualize human civilization in term of a highly mechanized and industrialized society. The booming of economic progress,

[3] George Mathew, *Dignity for All: Essays in Socialism and Democracy* (Delhi: Ajanta Publication, 1991), p. 5 ff.

high-tech mechanized life-style is perceived as attainment of higher quality of life. 'Growth' is seen as the only principle for liberation. The growth driven and consumerist economic system and one-sided development pursuits have led to colonization of others and laid ideological justification for subjugation and exploitation of non-renewable earth's resources on a massive scale. The concepts of 'care for one another', 'just economy' and '(*sabbath*) rest for creation' are considered as non-productive and the root of all human problems from poverty to sickness to political instability. Any attempt to slow down economic growth is labeled as immorality. Right to have dominion over God's creation is a biblical mandate and exploitation is seen as exercising human's creativity bestowed on them in the image of God (Gen 1:27, 28). This Enlightenment paradigm of euro-centric modernity rooted in the conquest of nature is the major cause of today's world crisis. Christian theologies have played their role in justifying this exploitation of Mother earth.

HIERARCHICAL STRUCTURE OF CREATION

In the Hebrew thought, man is the helm of the hierarchy, ruling over the family, the women, the slaves, etc. Several Christian theologians have explained God's creation within such a hierarchical structure. According to Thomas Aquinas, God, the Creator, in the beginning, simultaneously created a hierarchy of creatures, ordered according to their degree of perfection. In this hierarchical order, angels are at the highest peak. Angels are created, but purely spiritual beings and they are above human beings. Humans are the highest among the created material beings having ultimate right over the other creatures. This hierarchal order is divine design because "the imperfect beings are for the use of the perfect."[4] Imperfect beings are created to serve the need of more noble beings, for instance, plants draw their nutrients from the earth, animals feed on plants and these in turn serve human use. Therefore, lifeless beings exist for the sake of living beings, plants for animals and animals for humans. Having affirmed that, Aquinas went one step further and said that material creatures were created that they "might be assimilated to the divine goodness."[5] For him, those creatures lower than the rational human creature in the hierarchy simply assimilate divine goodness by fulfilling the needs of the human creatures. The whole material nature exists for humans because humanity alone possesses rationality. Human beings are above all creatures. The other non-human creatures are protected, preserved, sustained by God to serve human needs. This theology gives justification for manipulation and exploitation of other segments of God's creation.

ANTHROPOCENTRIC VIEW OF CREATION

Hierarchical and anthropocentric views of life are interrelated and they assume a similar theological position on creation. They view humanity as the point of reference for everything. Creation has meaning and values by serving the interests of humankind. According to Robert Borrong this view of life underlines nine assumptions:

1. Humans are separated from nature;
2. Prioritizing the rights of human beings over nature, but not emphasizing the responsibility of human beings;
3. Prioritizing the feelings of humans as centre of their apprehensiveness;
4. Policy and management of natural resources in the interests of human beings;
5. Solution to the ecological crisis through population control, especially in the poor countries;
6. Adherence to the philosophy of economic growth;
7. The main norm is profit vs. mloss;

---

[4] Thomas Aquinas, *Summa Theologia,* ed. by the English Dominican Fathers (Burns, Pates, Washbourne, Ltd., 1922), Part I, QQ LXXV-CII, p. 237.
[5] *Ibid.* p. 59.

8. Prioritizing short-term planning; and
9. Adjusting oneself to the prevailing political and economic system.[6]

This view has become the basis for greedy exploitation and depletion of nature's resources.

Protestant theologies added a theological justification to this view of life. Luther saw the whole creation of God as something which exists for the benefit of humans. He recognized nature simply as an existential springboard for grace. The ultimate purpose of creation is for the service and benefit of humans. Karl Barth also advocated a similar theology. For him, God is the "wholly other", the transcendent Lord, who can be known only when He chooses to reveal himself, as He did preeminently in Jesus Christ. Barth said that the Word is not the foremost principle of creation which gives all things; rather the Word is the first and foremost of God's address to humanity in Jesus Christ. God is not known through His creation, but only through Christ. Barth is very explicit that salvation history begins from the incarnation of Jesus Christ, but not from the creation. Barth further argued that this great history of salvation cannot be actualized if there is no place or space for it to occur. It needs a "showplace" or a "theatre" outside of God and humans.[7] This is the reason why God brought the created world into existence. It is very clear that Barth conceives creation simply as a showplace/theatre for the saving works of God. Everything is created solely for the sake of the realization of God's covenant with humanity in Jesus Christ. For the sake of election, nature is sustained, protected and upheld. Creation is merely a stage. It has no history, is not to be redeemed, but merely used. Bultmann also held a similar position. God is not to be perceived in the phenomena of nature but known and experienced in the `cave of the heart', in the inner personal experience.[8] This theology places creation in the secondary position.

DUALISTIC VIEW OF CREATION

This stream of thought is of Greek origin with its dualism of body and soul. The soul finds its true destiny by escaping from nature, creation and the world. Marcion taught that the visible world as the creation of the God of Israel, and a creation out of matter, was an evil work destined for destruction. The world is evil because a lesser god created it. This view stressed that God is absolutely different and distinct from His created nature. The world was understood to be the creation of demonic powers from the chaos of the darkness. The created world is purely material and fleshly, a full expression of evil. Origen held that God created the world because of a spiritual rebellion in heaven. The creation of the world was related to the fall into sin. The fallen spirits were put into the material world that had been created for them. Thus, the material world was created to become a place of purification where fallen humankind could be educated through suffering to regain the state of pure spiritual realm.[9] Origen valued the soul over the material world. The influence of dualism is evident among the Reformers. Nature and other material objects do not take part in the salvation and redemption of Christ. According to Luther, nature is not a witness to the glory of God. Nature is only a supplementary item which is the background to the salvation drama of human beings. This dualistic view of life led humans to believe that humankind are called upon to control nature and that the nature and the function of religion is to aid human beings in the execution of their task. This view contradicts biblical testimony. God's creation is redeemed when human beings respect the rhythm of nature and its dynamic.

---

[6] Robert Patannang Borrong, *Environmental Ethics and Ecological Theology: Ethics as Integral Part of Ecosphere from an Indonesian Perspective* (Geboren te Sandana, Indonesia, 2005), pp. 73-74.

[7] Karl Barth, *Church Dogmatic* (Edinburgh: T & T Clark, 1936-1961), 3.1. p. 97.

[8] W.S. Ariarajah, "World Religions and the Wholeness of Creation" in *Ecumenical Movement Tomorrow: Suggestion for Approaches and Alternatives.* Eds. Mark Reuver, Friedhelm Solms, Gerrit Huzer (Geneva: WCC Publications, 1993), p. 163.

[9] Robert P. Borrong, *op.cit.,* p. 98.

Most of the nineteenth century Evangelicals[10] took this dualistic position. The Evangelicals also recognized God's revelation only in the Word of God, but not in total creation of God. One can know God only through the Word but not through creation. The teaching of heaven and hell further reinforced undermining of God's creation. The world is coming to an end, all materials will be destroyed, but only souls will be saved and live eternally in heaven – other materials will perish. This doctrine made people to think that "This world is not our home. We are just a passenger". If this world is not our home, why should we take care of it?

The aim of this discussion is not to argue that theologians in the mainline Christian traditions have a negative attitude to creation. What we are trying to say is that because of their great interest in the uniqueness of God's action in history for human redemption, they were indifferent to God's creation. It is understandable that serious attention was not given to creation theology as they did not face the ecological crisis we face today. Moreover, one should not assume that Christianity does not have a creation theology. Paul Santmire in his book, *The Travail of Nature*[11], has shown convincingly that it is not fair to blame Christianity and its tradition like Lynn White,[12] to be `ecologically bankrupt'. Santmire's book shows a long historical study in which he has demonstrated ecological promises in Christian theology. He has shown immense ecological insights in the theology of Irenaeus, Augustine and especially of Francis of Assisi. But the fact is that these voices have never become part of the dominant Christian traditions. Their voices are still unheard and have not been integrated as part of Christian praxis and ethos.

However, it is clear that the dominant Christian theology have been too anthropocentric, hierarchical, mechanistic and dualistic in its approach and content. We need to acknowledge that

> The Judeo-Christian tradition bears to a certain degree responsibility for today's ecological destruction. ... But there can be no doubt that Christians have for too long neglected the theme of Creation in their theological reflection and teaching and have accepted values and perspectives which are foreign to the Biblical tradition. They have uncritically supported modern domination of nature.[13]

The dominant Judeo-Christian perceptions of life continue to promote greedy exploitation and depletion of nature's resources. Today we realize that such theologies of creation are destructive to life. The mindless destruction of earth's resources, and marginalization and subjugation of the indigenous people through war, cultural genocide, alienation, denial and suppression are deeply rooted in such a view of life. It has contributed in reducing the indigenous people and nature as mere commodities. Such theologies are not adequate to respond to the present ecological crisis. We need a theology that promotes respect and a caring attitude to all of God's creation. In this search, the indigenous spirituality may provide a new theological perspective.

---

[10] Most of the Asian churches are products of Evangelical movements in the West and we have inherited a very strong dualistic theology.

[11] *The Travail of Nature: The Ambiguous Ecological Promise of Christian Theology* (Philadelphia: Fortress Press, 1985).

[12] Lynn White accuses western Christianity as the most anthropocentric religion and arrogant towards nature that Christianity bears a huge burden of guilt for the ecological crisis. Critics of White argued that his thesis does not account for reckless attitudes towards nature evident in various non-Christian cultures, and that he ignored the ways in which the forces of industrialization, urbanization, and the capitalistic drive to increase wealth have caused a large measure of the world's ecological crisis. They see the problem as political and economic, rather than religious. White's response is that the `roots' of the crisis can be traced to Western Christendom's blessing of the methods and tools that have unlocked the modern world's conquest of nature. See Lynn White, Jr., "The Historical Roots of our Ecological Crisis" in *Western Man and Environmental Ethics,* ed. Ian Barbour (reading, Mass.: Addison-Wesley, 1973), pp. 55-65.

[13] *Listening to Creation Groaning,* John Knox Series 16 (Geneva: Centre International Reform John Knox), 2004, p.11.

Ecumenical Responses

There is an enormous variety of communiqués, reports and policies on climate justice, water, forest, land, etc. There is no single ecumenical response on eco-justice. Theologians however, who upheld the ecumenical vision of life, have made serious attempts to correct the dualistic, anthropocentric, androcentric and hierarchical view of life by affirming creation as an organic, inter-dependent, coherent and comprehensive whole. As it is not possible to highlight these various strands of thought, only a few individual perspectives are underlined here:

1. *Non-dualistic view of life* – Eco-feminist theologians identify that dualism rooted in patriarchy is the major cause of injustice which leads to war, militarism and the rape of the earth. Speaking on the inter-relationship between patriarchy and modern science, Vandana Shiva criticizes that,

> Modern science was a consciously gendered, patriarchal activity. As nature came to be seen more like a woman to be raped, gender too was recreated. Science as a male venture, based on the subjugation of female nature and female sex provided support for the polarization of gender. Patriarchy as the new scientific and technological power was a political need of emerging industrial capitalism. While on the one hand, the ideology of science sanctioned the denudation of nature; on the other, it legitimized the dependency of women and the authority of man. Science and masculinity were associated in domination over nature and femininity, and the ideologies of science and gender reinforced each other.[14]

Just as women are seen as being appropriately dominated by men, so also the earth is seen as an object to be conquered and dominated to fulfill the greed of humans. The earth is seen merely as a usable object, to be treated in an exploitative manner. This concept of domination, of reason (male) ruling over creation (earth, female) is carried to the extreme under capitalism with the development of technologies that are capable not only of dominating the earth, but also of destroying all living organisms and the plant itself.[15] Therefore, eco-feminists argued that the oppression of women and the oppression of creation are inter-connected. Then, how do the eco-feminist theologians respond to the eco-crisis?

They 'reimage' the concept of God. For example, Sallie McFague, an eco-feminist theologian, contends that the Judeo-Christian traditions which project God as King, ruler, lord, master, governor, and the concepts which accompany them, such as God is absolute, transcendent and omnipotent are patriarchal concepts. It permits no sense of mutuality, shared responsibility, reciprocity and love in terms of relationship between God and the world. Such a theology developed in the patriarchal language creates an attitude that God is far away from the world. He relates only to humans and controls the world through domination.[16] Thus, the whole Judeo-Christian traditions that project God with patriarchal, imperialistic and triumphalistic metaphors need to be reimaged in a more holistic and relational mode. Sallie McFague in her book, *The Body of God: An Ecological Theology,*[17] attempts to develop an organic model of theology. She calls for a radical change in human's attitude towards other creatures. Humans should not act as name-givers of and the rulers over creation, but rather act as gardeners, caretakers, parents, stewards, trustees, lovers, priests, co-creators and friends of the world. For instance, the image of God as the lover of the world gives a different relationship. Being in love does not mean sex, lust and desire. But the crux of love has to do with value. It is finding someone valuable and being found valuable.[18] God as lover is a moving power in the universe. God's love is the desire for union with that which is valuable. God as lover needs

---

[14] Vandana Shiva, *Staying Alive: Women, Ecology and Survival in India* (New Delhi: Call For Women, 1988), pp 17-18.
[15] Rosemary Ruether, *Sexism and God-Talk: Towards a Feminist Theology* (London: SCM Press, 1983), pp. 44 ff.
[16] Sallie McFague, *Models of God: Theology for an Ecological Nuclear Age* (Philadelphia: Fortress Press, 1989), p. 69.
[17] Sallie McFague, *The Body of God: An Ecological Theology* (Minneapolis: Augsburg Fortress, 1993).
[18] *Ibid.*, pp. 162-190.

the world as the lover needs each other. God as lover is interested in saving the entire cosmos that has become estranged and fragmented, sickened by unhealthy practices and threatened by death and extinction. Similarly, reimaging God as parent and friend of the world gives a feeling of friendship, care and love in a work that is sustained by a common vision.[19] McFague feels that this model would offer new possibilities of revisioning the God-world-human relationship. If we reflect on the characteristics of the lover shown by parents, lovers and friends, the word that come to our mind include `fidelity,' `nurture,' `attraction,' `self-sacrifice,' `passion,' `care,' `affection,' `responsibility,' `respect,' and `mutuality.'[20] These words suggest a power which is quite different from that associated with the models of lord, king and patriarch. It calls for a new way of interpreting Christian faith. This way of looking at the world is to find new meanings that God loves bodies. God suffers and that this world is a sacrament.[21]

2. *Inter-connected view of life*. Some of the contemporary theologians are involved in developing a pattern of Christian thought that builds upon a more connected view of the relationship between God, humanity and creation using the categories of process philosophy. Taking the process of philosophical framework, thinkers like John Cobb, Charles Birch, and others have adopted a unified perspective in which God does not live in a "second world" above history, but on the contrary, he lives and inter-acts as humans do in the historical realm. It is through inter-action that the world becomes the body of God. Each organism touches and changes the organism that influences it. Likewise, we act on God and God receives things from us.[22] It is an attempt made in the West to change the dualistic, anthropocentric and hierarchical view of creation and history, creation and redemption. Unless we build upon a more connected view of relationship between God, humanity and creation, we cannot make our cosmos sustainable.

3. *Sacramental view of creation and priestly function of humanity*. This view is rooted in the Orthodox tradition. It affirms that in the beginning, the Holy Trinity created the world `out of nothing', not out of pre-existent matter. Humanity, creation and the visible world, including angels and powers, are equally dependent on the power of God, both for their coming into being and for their continued existence.[23] The whole cosmic order, in the Orthodox tradition, is created not out of compulsion, but out of God's free will, goodness, wisdom, love and omnipotence. Since creation is the work of God, Orthodoxy sees the world as a created order having its own integrity. It is thus a positive reality and sacred.[24] It is the good work of the good God. Everything that God had made was very good because "first He conceived and His conception was the work carried out by His Word, and perfected by His Spirit."[25] As such, the world is a revelation of God (Cf. Rom. 1:19-20).

In the Orthodox view, humanity occupies the central place in creation. It is held that the creative energy of God took a gradually ascending path with humanity emerging as the last stage. The emergence of Adam as body-soul was a terminal event in the evolution of the universe. Because of body and soul in the human person, he/she is a citizen of two worlds; the human person becomes an active participant in both the intelligible and the sensible worlds. In other words, humans are members of both families – God and matter; they are made to enjoy both the divine and the terrestrial worlds. This means that humans are part of the material world and without the material world, humans cannot survive. God has created the humans in such a way that they exist only with the help of material world. This is the reason why "Christ became man and assumed a material body." Therefore, humanity stands on the boundary between the material and

---

[19] *Ibid.,* pp. 171-172.
[20] *Ibid.,* p. 176.
[21] Sallie McFague, *Models of God,* pp. 68 ff.
[22] E.H. Cousin, ed. *Process Theology: Basic Writings (New York: Newman Press, 1971), p. 123.*
[23] Gennadios Limouris, ed. *Justice, Peace and Integrity of Creation: Insights from Orthodox* (Geneva: WCC, 1987). Hereafter "Insights from Orthodox", p. 1.
[24] *Ibid.,* p. 2.
[25] *Ibid.,* p. 3.

spiritual worlds as a connecting link. Human beings are directly related to the earthly aspects of created existence as well as the uncreated existence of the Creator.[26]

Creation has neither the adequate consciousness nor the necessary freedom to respond to the sanctifying grace of redemption and salvation. It is only the human person who freely responds to the saving work of Christ. It is in this context that humans assume the role as priests over the material creation. Humanity, through the priestly function, leads creation to its completion and fulfillment in God.

Since God enters into total communion with all creation through Christ and the Holy Spirit, we celebrate Eucharist for the salvation of the whole world, and thus the Eucharistic bread and wine symbolize the universe, the whole created order. Creation is also called to share in the life and glory of the Creator. In the form of bread and wine, as elements coming from creation molded into new form by human hands and offered to God with the acknowledgement that all of creation is God's and that we are returning to God what belongs to God. When believers partake of the body and blood of Christ, God meets us in the very being of our biological existence.[27] Therefore, for the Orthodox, the call to participate in the Eucharist is extended to the whole of creation through human beings. As all creation suffered from the human fall, so the return and restoration of creation are also through human liberation and participating in God's life.

4. *Justice, Peace and Integrity of Creation – a call for unity beyond the boundary of churches and humanity*. The WCC programme on Justice, Peace and Integrity of Creation (JPIC)[28] attempts to show that justice, peace and the integrity of creation is one whole. The call has a threefold purpose: the first concern was to show that justice, peace and integrity of creation are essentially one whole; they are inseparable and indivisible. The second concern was to articulate theologically our understanding of the human predicament and spell out our specific Christian responsibility. And the third concern was to respond to the central question of the modern ecumenical movement, that is, the unity of the church. Theologically, it was a radical shift from the earlier assumption. The theological emphasis is now on the unity of the whole world, not only the church and humanity. Jesus Christ is seen as the centre of the whole cosmos. The Christ-event is viewed from the Trinitarian perspective. Instead of Christ `from above' who is above all, oriented towards a belief in the divinity of Jesus Christ as the second person of the Trinity, a Christology `from below' is taken seriously. With this change in emphasis, Jesus of Nazareth is perceived as the one who paid his life for the liberation of the poor, the oppressed and the whole cosmos. The whole earth is seen as a habitable home because God has established his covenant with the whole creation, and it is guided by the hope that God himself will dwell with humankind, with God's people. Thus the ecumenical movement is seen as a movement that attempts not only to bring the churches together but also "the whole

---

[26] Paulos Gregorios, *The Human Presence: An Orthodox View of Nature* (Geneva: WCC, 1979), p. 4.

[27] "Insights from Orthodox," p. 4.

[28] Between 1969 and 1983, thinkers like Paulos Mar Greogorios, Roger Shinn, Charles Birch, and others have helped the WCC to organize a major enquiry on the issue of scientific and technological revolution of our time. The WCC conference on "Science and Technology for Human development" (Bucharest 1974), and on "Faith, Science and the Future" (Boston 1979) have raised many of the assumptions of growth, resources and the use of technological power, suggesting the need for a "sustainable society" in the ecumenical forums provided for new perspectives: from `development' to `liberation'; from `modernization and economic growth' to the defence to `right to life' for all; from `overcoming crises' to `struggle against unjust structures'; from dialogue with experts and appeal to those in positions of responsibility to the `promotion of independence and empowerment of the marginalized majority of humankind'. When the WCC made the call to its member churches `to engage in a conciliar process of mutual commitment to justice, peace and integrity of creation,' the world of that time was facing one of the worst crises events in history. There were reports of wars and rumors of wars, causing untold suffering and misery to millions of people who were displaced and turned into refugees. Militarization of the world had reached alarming proportions and the threat of nuclear war and destruction loomed large. Moreover, with the ideology of an every-growing consumerism, urbanization and industrialization, the disintegration of creation was going on at an alarming rate. It was in this context that the Vancouver Assembly of WCC called its member churches to engage in a conciliar process of mutual commitment (covenant) to justice, peace and integrity of creation.

inhabited earth." It is a movement wherever Christians and others one way or the other seek to work for the unity of humankind and of the whole world.

Being-in-relationship becomes the core of the theological paradigm. *Oikoumene* is the order of relationships within this household. What is decisive is `habitability,' the sustainability or capacity for the survival of the inhabited earth. In other words, *oikoumene* is understood as the one household of life created and preserved by God, and thus it extends beyond the world of humankind, of one human race, to creation as a whole. This new paradigm `the household' supersedes the narrow vision that sees human history as the central category of interpretation. It reminds us that human history is bound up with the history of all living things and that the human household is incapable of survival without being related to other households, that is, the natural environment.

`Integrity of Creation' – the concept of `creation' or `integrity of creation' is a theological term that provides a fresh way of approaching the issues of justice and peace. `Creation' is a theological term that relates justice and peace. Preman Niles points out a two-fold theological significance of the term:

Firstly, by giving prominence to the doctrine of creation, we begin with the totality of all that God has created, and continues to create and sustain. An important thrust that has emerged from this shift is that, "we view creation theologically not simply as the initial divine act which set creation and history on the course," but rather as "a response to a continuous divine activity within which the struggle for justice, peace and the preservation of creation are located and within which they have meaning."[29] Thus it is to be seen as a theological term that helps us to recover the meaning of creation in our time, not simply as an ecological issue. To confess God as the Creator is therefore to affirm the truth that God created, and continues to maintain creation and thus the whole of creation belongs to God. This perspective on creation provides a new vision of eschatological metaphors of the `new heaven and earth' and the Kingdom of God."[30] They are not seen merely as temporal metaphors that impinge upon history, but as those signifying the space for justice and peace in creation now.[31] In short, it is a powerful symbol of hope.

Secondly, it implies that in maintaining the ecological balance, it provides a certain moral value or worth the Creator has bestowed on the whole of creation.[32] It thus draws our attention "to the relationships that have to be maintained not only between human communities, but also between humans and the earth and things of the earth."[33] It further emphasizes the inter-dependence within creation and the need to maintain it. The violation of this moral order or integrity leads to injustice and exploitation. The concept of `creation,' therefore, is another way of affirming about the need for "maintaining the justice of God in creation."[34] It is an affirmation of the goodness of God's creation and the intrinsic worth of all beings.

This understanding of creation enables us to reject the anthropocentric, hierarchical and patriarchal understandings of creation and all the forces that lead to the alienation of humans from each other; from creation, and also from God, the Creator. It calls us to move towards an eco-centred theology of creation which emphasizes the presence of God's Spirit in creation (cf. Gen 1;2, Ps. 104), and humans as the integral part of creation. Instead of dominating creation, men and women have the responsibility to preserve, cultivate the earth and to work with God for the sustainability of the planet. Moreover, it brings us to the realization that without a just and equitable distribution of resources and the liberation of people

---

[29] Preman D. Niles, *Resisting the Threat of Life: Covenanting for Justice, Peace and the Integrity of Creation* (Geneva: WCC Publication, 1989), p. 59.

[30] *Ibid.*, p. 59.

[31] *Ibid.*, p. 60.

[32] *Ibid.*, p. 61.

[33] *Ibid.*, p. 61.

[34] *Ibid.*, p. 61.

from all forms of bondage, humans cannot celebrate together the gracious love of the Creator and the goodness of creation.[35]

This paradigm shift in the theological emphasis of JPIC (Justice, Peace and Integrity of Creation) calls the churches to re-examine our earlier theological assumptions:

1. It challenges us to redefine our understanding of unity of church and mission. *Oikoumene* embraces the whole inhabited earth. It goes beyond unity of churches and human community; it extends beyond the world of humankind, of one human race, and to creation as a whole. Moreover, the mission of God is no longer limited to conversion and planting of churches. Mission is inclusive. It involves calling persons to commitment to the kingdom of God, justice and peace, and ecological health of the land.
2. It challenges us to affirm creation in a new way. Creation is not just things to be exploited. Every living creature possesses intrinsic value and right. Therefore, preserving the integrity of the whole inhabited earth and promoting an ecologically responsible development are a matter of faith and also a survival issue for the whole world.
3. This new way of approach to creation raises the issue of justice. Justice is not an abstract reality to be realized within human community alone, but it is how we live in the web of life in reciprocity with people, other creatures and the earth, recognizing that they are part of us and we are part of them.
4. The JPIC programme challenges us to search for a new ethical principle. Human communities must bear the responsibility towards the earth and its wholeness. The earth, with its diverse life forms is functioning as one coherent whole. The whole earth is God's creation and we need to respect its inherent value and rights. A lifestyle of high material consumption is unethical. Learning to live in a new way, not based on exploitation and injustice, would allow all to flourish in health and wholeness. In short, it demands a reciprocal life-style valuing all lives.

A Response from the Indigenous Peoples' Perspective

The indigenous peoples all over the world see a close affinity with all the ecumenical theological responses because of their emphasis on the right relationship with the whole of creation. The indigenous peoples throughout their history have been affirming the goodness and worth of creation as created and valued by God: its inter-dependence and inter-relatedness among humans, other creatures and the rest of creation. The following theological affirmations enrich the indigenous peoples' search for a new relationship with God's creation:

1. The eco-feminist theology reinforces not only a new perception of God's involvement in the world, but it also discovers that the oppression of the poor, women and the oppression of creation are inseparably related. The threat to creation and injustice against the poor, women and their dependent children are closely inter-related. The two are one issue. Thus they challenge us to re-examine the relationship between human beings and the non-human world, between humans and God and among human beings.
2. Through affirmation of the inter-relatedness of all creation, the Orthodox tradition enables us to discover the whole creation as an organic whole, a totality of reality in an integrated, coherent and comprehensive manner. Both the spiritual and materials worlds are not opposed to each other. They have a common origin, a common God, and therefore have a common destiny. They form one total reality of creation. In other words, the created world, including humanity is in perfect unity, in the same way as the human body is perfectly harmonized. This further leads us to view creation in its

[35] *Ibid.*, pp. 61-62.

integrity as a positive reality, the good works of God. It has got its own intrinsic right and worth. It is through the *energia* of God that creation continues to be sustained, upheld and perfected. Second, the affirmation of the central and unique role of humanity in the whole creation of God is imperative. Being created in God's own image, humanity transcends the material world because the human person participates in God both spiritually and physically unlike other segments of God's creation. Creation finds its completeness and fulfillment in God, the Creator and Sustainer of all living being. This idea helps us to reflect on human's ecological responsibility. Third, the 'dominion' of the human over creation is not only a right, but also a mission. The relationship between humanity and environment cannot be reduced to mere need and use alone. It demands a harmonious relationship. It includes the responsibility of care, love and respect. This theological affirmation needs to be integrated in our faith practice, if we want to make our cosmos sustainable.

3. Process theology brings the inter-connectedness of the whole human family within the totality of the whole network of the biological system which supports all forms of life. Creation is seen as an open system having its climax in Christ. The whole universe is caught up in the manifestation of God's acts in history.
4. The JPIC programme of the World Council of Churches helps us to affirm that justice, peace and creation are a whole. `Creation' as a theological concept relates all realities. At the heart of these affirmations of the universe, we see three theological insights: (i) the redemption of humanity is an integral part of the redemption of the whole creation, (ii) the Christ-event transcends the human realm, and all of creation is reconciled with Him as one, and (iii) the Holy Spirit is inseparably related to the whole cosmic order by creating, redeeming and by finally fulfilling it in the last great consummation.

Similarly, the indigenous people also affirm the following cosmic vision:

1. The land is the basis of all realities – human selfhood and identity. It perceives all realities from the creation perspectives.
2. There is no clear cut distinction between the sacred and the secular, religion and non-religion, etc., nor is there a dualism. It is holistic thinking.
3. With no creed or written scripture, the sacred truth is contained in their folklore, myths, dances, songs etc.
4. The Self of the Supreme Being is seen in creation and an inseparable relationship is maintained. The Sacred Power comes out from the soil. One cannot perceive the Supreme Being apart from creation. God is in creation.
5. No historical person enjoys the central part of their religion. The earth is the focal point of reference and all religious activities are centered on the soil.
6. The spirit is present and active in all life including trees, rocks, rivers, and not just in the individual heart.
7. It is not time-oriented, but event and person-oriented.
8. The land is sacred. It is our mother.
9. It is highly group/community oriented.
10. The whole world is the temple of God.

It is not surprising to note that there is a basic difference in the perception of reality between the indigenous people's worldview and ecumenical responses. One will note that in all ecumenical responses, humanity is the central point of reference and norm. But it is the other way round in the indigenous peoples' tradition. Creation is the key and the central point of reference and norm. The whole reality, including humanity, the Supreme Being and the Spirit or spirits is approached from the perspective of creation. In short, while the doctrine of creation is the subordinate category in the mainline Christian traditions, `creation' is the central category for understanding all realities in the indigenous peoples' cosmology. In other words, the affirmation that "the Supreme Being created heaven and earth and it belongs to him/her," is the starting point of their faith. This affirmation of the centrality of creation makes the indigenous people's cosmology different from others.

Therefore, for the indigenous peoples, a theology of creation is not merely a justice issue to be set alongside other justice concerns. It is the foundational theology of self-understanding out of which justice, and then peace will flow naturally and necessarily.[36] This is the reason why George Tinker, a native American theologian, argues that the WCC programme of JPIC should be reversed as Creation, Justice and Peace (CJP). He writes:

> I consistently argue in the WCC `Justice, Peace and the Integrity of Creation" process that it should have been titled, `Creation, Justice and Peace'. Such a theological prioritizing of creation on my part is far more than a prioritizing of environmental concerns. Rather it functions to provide a spiritual and theological foundation for justice. Respect for creation must necessarily result in justice, just as genuine justice necessarily in the achievement of peace.[37]

It is therefore true to affirm that, the indigenous peoples' culture, religion and spirituality cannot be conceived without creation/land. Humans always understand themselves as an integral part of creation and not apart from it. That harmony with creation is the starting point of the indigenous people's spirituality. For the indigenous peoples, commitment and dedication to the harmony of creation springs forth in love, nurture, care and acceptance. When there is justice in the land, the fields and forest and every living thing will dance and sing for joy (Ps. 96:11-12). An awareness of being one with the whole of creation is the spiritual foundation of the indigenous peoples.[38] Such an acknowledgement of sacredness and inter-relatedness of all creation are reinforced through the observance of taboo, totem, divination, festivals, and ceremonies. Such practices help them to connect spiritually with the earth and the surrounding environment. Hence, a theology of creation must begin with a self-understanding of the individuals and communities as part of creation.

All the ecumenical responses – the Orthodox, the process, the eco-feminist and JPIC – seem to view reality mainly from the anthropocentric perspective, but not from the perspective of creation itself. That is why, for them, the integrity of creation is one item of the agenda along with the other justice concerns. Humanity and their liberation is the central focus. Liberation of creation follows when humanity attains liberation. For example, the Orthodox tradition affirms that creation participates in God only through human beings. In other words, creation attains liberation and perfection in God only through human beings; creation is imperfect without humans.[39] Similarly, the eco-feminists though they see the oppression of women and eco-justice as one whole, their main thrust is liberation of women. The JPIC process also approaches the issue of creation in the same way. Human liberation is the focus of all concerns.

In all the ecumenical responses, the indigenous peoples' view of creation is not adequately integrated in spite of their closeness to creation/land. For example, the Seoul documents *Now is the Time*, has no reference to the creation spirituality of indigenous peoples except for this statement:

---

[36] Cf. George Tinker, "The Integrity of Creation: Restoring Trinitarian Balance," in *the Ecumenical Review,* vol. 41, No. 4, October, 1989), p. 535. Hereafter "Integrity of Creation."

[37] George Tinker, "Spirituality and Nature of American Personhood: Sovereignty and Solidarity", *Spirituality of the Third World,* ed. By K.C. Abraham & Bernadetta Mbuy-Beya (Maryknoll: New York: Orbis Books, 1994), pp. 127-128.

[38] George Tinker, "Integrity of Creation," p. 536.

[39] Cf. K.M. George, "Towards a Eucharist Ecology", in *Orthodox Perspective on Baptism, Eucharist and Ministry,* eds. By Gennadios Limouris and Nomilos Mecheal Vaporis (Brookline, Massachusetts: Holy Cross Orthodox Press, 1985), p. 51.

> We commit ourselves to join in solidarity with indigenous communities' struggle for the culture, spirituality and rights to land and sea ...[40]

Likewise in several documents and policies of the ecumenical movement, the insights from the indigenous people's spirituality are not integrated. Such an insensitive attitude towards the rich creation-centered spirituality of the indigenous peoples within the ecumenical family gives an impression that all Christian theologies of creation are approached from the perspective of the western progressive and linear interpretation of history and philosophy. Thus, the theologies of creation developed within the ecumenical family may not be directly relevant to respond to the aspirations and the problems of the indigenous people.

Seeking liberation from the anthropocentric framework will continue to marginalize the indigenous peoples who work and live close to the soil; they will still be looked down upon as objects of liberation. They will always be treated as inferior, uncivilized and primitive. Liberation therefore has to be found from the `creation' perspective. Justice concerns of creation should not be made as one of the justice concerns, but it should be made as the foundation of all justice concerns.

Conclusion

It is clear that the traditional Christian theologies have been too anthropocentric, patriarchal, hierarchical, mechanistic and dualistic in their approach and contents. The dominant Judeo-Christian perceptions of life continue to shape people's view of creation and promote a greedy exploitation and depletion of nature's resources. Today, we realize that such theologies of creation are destructive of life. The mindless destruction of earth's resources, and marginalization and subjugation of the indigenous people through war, cultural genocide, alienation, denial and suppression are deeply rooted in such a view of life. It has contributed in reducing the indigenous people and nature as mere commodities. Such theologies are not adequate to respond to the present ecological crisis. A new theological orientation that cares for and protects God's creation is imperative. In this search, the indigenous people's spirituality provides a new theological paradigm by affirming the centrality of creation.

Bibliography

K.C. Abraham, *Eco-justice: A New Agenda of Church's Mission* (Bombay: BUILD, no year)

Robert Patannang Borrong, *Environmental Ethics and Ecological Theology: Ethics as Integral Part of Ecosphere from an Indonesian Perspective* (Geboren te Sandana, Indonesie, 2005)

Sallie McFague, *Models of God: Theology for an Ecological Nuclear Age* (Philadelphia: Fortress Press, 1989)

Preman D. Niles, *Resisting the Threat of Life: Covenanting for Justice, Peace and the Integrity of Creation* (Geneva: WCC Publication, 1989)

Vandana Shiva, *Staying Alive: Women, Ecology and Survival in India* (New Delhi: Call For Women, 1988)

[40] Final Documents of World Convocation on JPIC, Seoul, 1990 (Geneva: WCC Publication, 1990), p. 19.

(44) Engaging the Powers and Public Theology from the Perspective of Indigenous Peoples as a Key Mandate in Asian Ecumenism

Liberato Bautista

Hold a moment longer! Not quite yet, gentlemen! Before you go I would like to say just a word about the Philippine business. I have been criticized a good deal about the Philippines, but don't deserve it. The truth is I didn't want the Philippines, and when they came to us, as a gift from the gods, I did not know what to do with them. When the Spanish War broke out Dewey was at Hongkong, and I ordered him to go to Manila and to capture or destroy the Spanish fleet, and he had to; because, if defeated, he had no place to refit on that side of the globe, and if the Dons were victorious they would likely cross the Pacific and ravage our Oregon and California coasts. And so he had to destroy the Spanish fleet, and did it! But that was as far as I thought then.

When I next realized that the Philippines had dropped into our laps I confess I did not know what to do with them. I sought counsel from all sides – Democrats as well as Republicans – but got little help. I thought first we would take only Manila; then Luzon; then other islands perhaps also. I walked the floor of the White House night after night until midnight; and I am not ashamed to tell you, gentlemen, that I went down on my knees and prayed Almighty God for light and guidance more than one night. And one night late it came to me this way – I don't know how it was, but it came: (1) That we could not give them back to Spain – that would be cowardly and dishonorable; (2) that we could not turn them over to France and Germany – our commercial rivals in the Orient – that would be bad business and discreditable; (3) that we could not leave them to themselves – they were unfit for self-government – and they would soon have anarchy and misrule over there worse than Spain's was; and (4) that there was nothing left for us to do but to take them all, and to educate the Filipinos, and uplift and civilize and Christianize them, and by God's grace do the very best we could by them, as our fellow-men for whom Christ also died. And then I went to bed, and went to sleep, and slept soundly, and the next morning I sent for the chief engineer of the War Department (our map-maker), and I told him to put the Philippines on the map of the United States (pointing to a large map on the wall of his office), and there they are, and there they will stay while I am President![1]

Public Theology: Confronting the Powers

If there is one area of public theology that truly engages the powers – in church and in society – it is that of indigenous peoples. Rooted in its traditional ways of being, knowing and doing, indigenous peoples confront powers in church and society that are equally tradition-bound. Asian societies have the most vibrant communities of indigenous peoples.

Religions, over time, have dealt with indigenous peoples in so many different ways, including both suppressing and cultivating their traditional cultures. Christian religion, in particular, having been co-terminus in introduction to Asia with colonizing projects of the West, have left indelible impact in the way indigenous peoples have been and are treated in Asian countries.

---

[1] General James Rusling, "Interview with President William McKinley," *The Christian Advocate*, 22 January 1903, p. 17. The interview recounts a meeting on November 21, 1899 between US President William McKinley and a delegation of five clergymen from the General Missionary Committee of the [Northern] Methodist Episcopal Church. Copy of this document is available at the United Methodist Archives at Drew University, in Madison, New Jersey, USA. See also Daniel Boone Schirmer and Stephen Rosskam Shalom, editors, *The Philippines Reader: A History of Colonialism, Neocolonialism, Dictatorship and Resistance* (Boston: Shalom End Press, 1987).

Asian churches, through the Christian Conference of Asia (CCA) and its members, have dealt, over the many years of its existence, and in the many places where its member churches are located, with issues arising out of the cries of indigenous peoples to be recognized as members of the body politic, with inherent human dignity no other than that same dignity that Christians assert as the gift of the divine image in every person. But alas, here lies the confrontation with both church and society.

Embedded in the colonial project of expansion and occupation was the handy and devastating use of papal bulls known as the Bulls of Donation from where are now deduced the so-called "Doctrine of Discovery" that ceded indigenous peoples' ancestral domains to the conquering colonial power on the proviso that such lands being ceded are not already Christian territories, and that they are not already inhabited by Christians. This resulted in the establishment by the conquering colonial power of political sovereignty over the lands and their inhabitants.[2]

Reports by the colonizing forces that eventually were filed in the colonial capitals (also the ecclesiastical capitals) were that the indigenous inhabitants at the point of contact – discovery is the word – were savages who did not exhibit the biological attributes (less than human was the assertion) and the demeanor of civilized (Western is the word) peoples. What proceeded from such a doctrine were the colonial project of plunder and pillage of indigenous resources and the genocidal decimation of indigenous inhabitants.

The conversion of the indigenous inhabitant took a political form, with the indigenous inhabitant having now become a subject at the disposal of the colonial occupiers, as well as ecclesiastical form, with the indigenous person having now become subject to the Roman ecclesiastical authorities, including conversion to Christianity. The most compelling account of atrocities brought about by colonial forces in their so-called "New World" [colonized territories] were reported back to the colonial capitals via the writings of the Spanish historian and Dominican friar, Bartolomé de las Casas.[3]

All through the centuries, both church and state reinforced each other's role with respect to indigenous peoples: for the state to assimilate them into the mainstream and for church to wean them from their 'animistic", "pagan", and "uncivilized ways". At first point of contact, the colonial project enforced through sword, rifle and cross aimed at civilizing indigenous peoples, including Christianizing them so that they too become worthy of the divine image. Increasingly, religious bodies are disavowing and repudiating the doctrine of discovery and instead finding ways to seek repentance from their historical complicity with such a doctrine and then finding ways to repair the damage.[4]

---

[2] Papal bulls are cited as the original source of the doctrine of discovery. They are also called Bulls of Donation. For example, Pope Nicholas V's papal bull in 1455 called *Romanus Pontifex* allowed Portugal to claim and conquer lands in West Africa. Pope Alexander VI's papal bull of 1493 called *Inter Caetera* extended to Spain the right to conquer newly-found lands. The Treaty of Tordesillas settled disputes between Portugal and Spain by declaring that only non-Christian lands could be taken and laying the formula that drew the line of demarcation when allocating the discoveries by the Spanish and Portuguese Crowns. See http://en.wikipedia.org/wiki/Discovery_doctrine and http://en.wikipedia.org/wiki/Treaty_of_tordesillas accessed on 6 January 2013.

[3] See http://en.wikipedia.org/wiki/Bartolom%C3%A9_de_las_Casas, accessed on 6 January 2013. A good background to Bartolomé de las Casas is Gustavo Gutierrez's *Las Casas: In Search of the Poor of Jesus Christ* (Maryknoll, New York: Orbis Books, 1993), translated into English from the Spanish original by Robert R. Barr.

[4] Some of the religious bodies that have repudiated the Doctrine of Discovery include the Anglican Church of Canada (see http://www.gc2009.org/ViewLegislation/view_leg_detail.aspx?id=983&type=Final, accessed on 6 January 2013), The Episcopal Church (see http://www.episcopalchurch.org/notice/episcopal-presiding-bishop-katharine-jefferts-schori-issues-pastoral-letter-doctrine-discover, accessed on 6 January 2013), the World Council of Churches (see http://www.oikoumene.org/en/resources/documents/executive-committee/bossey-february-2012/statement-on-the-doctrine-of-discovery-and-its-enduring-impact-on-indigenous-peoples.html, accessed on 6 January 2013). Churches in Australia and New Zealand have grappled with the issue of its aboriginal (Australia) and Maori peoples as have the churches in the Asia Pacific region. See for example http://www.oikoumene.org/en/resources/documents/wcc-programmes/public-witness-addressing-power-affirming-peace/poverty-wealth-and-ecology/neoliberal-paradigm/asia-

The latest major Christian denomination to repudiate the doctrine of discovery is The United Methodist Church. In 1992, with increasing awareness about the role of "Christian churches, including The United Methodist Church and its predecessors,...in the destruction of Native American people, culture and religious practices...and have not sufficiently confessed their complicity in this evil" then took the step which said "confession of our guilt is a first step toward the wholeness that the churches seek through the ecumenical movement." In 1992, it was resolved "[T]hat The United Methodist General Conference confesses that The United Methodist Church (and its predecessor bodies) has sinned and continues to sin against its Native American brothers and sisters and offers this formal apology for its participation, intended and unintended, in the violent colonization of their land."

Between 1992 and 2012, twenty years altogether, The United Methodist Church has revisited its position about Native Americans, with the latest statement in May of 2012 that clearly states that "all levels of The United Methodist Church are called to condemn the Doctrine of Discovery as a legal document and basis for the seizing of native lands and abuses of human rights of indigenous peoples." It further resolved, in this same document, "that The United Methodist Church will work toward eliminating the Doctrine of Discovery as a means to subjugate indigenous peoples of property and land."[5]

An action by the Geneva-based World Council of Churches, two months before the United Methodist resolution, tackled the moral, legal and ecclesiastical bearings of the Doctrine of Discovery. The ecumenical body denounced the doctrine and said that it is "fundamentally opposed to the gospel of Jesus Christ and...a violation of the inherent human rights that all individuals and peoples have received from God." In making its case, it described the doctrine saying that "The patterns of domination and oppression that continue to afflict Indigenous Peoples today throughout the world are found in numerous historical documents such as Papal Bulls, Royal Charters and court rulings. For example, the church documents *Dum Diversas* (1452) and *Romanus Pontifex* (1455) called for non-Christian peoples to be invaded, captured, vanquished, subdued, reduced to perpetual slavery and to have their possessions and property seized by Christian monarchs. Collectively, these and other concepts form a paradigm or pattern of domination that is still being used against Indigenous Peoples."[6]

And so today, as indigenous peoples organize to assert their inherent dignity and their hard-won human rights, quite necessarily they are confronting the powers bound with church and state. As indigenous peoples increasingly reclaim their indigenous identities and traditional knowledge, they are confronted with traditional understanding of church and state that are quite alien, if not detrimental to the preservation of traditional indigenous culture. A project led by the Pacific Asian American Center for Theology and Strategies based in Berkeley, California, proposed the unfaithing of colonialism. To it I add the decolonizing of faith.[7]

Indigenous peoples have not always been opposed to modernity even as it has always been uneasy with it. The modern nation state is a creature of modernity. But indigenous peoples have engaged nation states at the level of the United Nations, by having the UN's standard and norm setting mechanisms codify the

---

pacific-indigenous-peoples-hearing-on-poverty-wealth-and-ecology.html, accessed on 6 January 2013, and http://cca.org.hk/clusters/programmes.htm, accessed on 6 January 2013, where the Christian Conference of Asia, currently based in Chiang main, Thailand, included indigenous peoples as one of its concerns in a cluster of four groups of programmatic concerns.

[5] See pages 417 to 438 of *The Book of Resolutions of The United Methodist Church 2012* (Nashville, TN: The United Methodist Publishing House, 2012) for the relevant resolutions dealing with Native Americans and indigenous peoples.

[6] See Statement on the doctrine of discovery and its enduring impact on Indigenous Peoples, WCC Executive Committee, 14-17 February 2012, Bossey, Switzerland, in http://www.oikoumene.org/en/resources/documents/executive-committee/bossey-february-2012/statement-on-the-doctrine-of-discovery-and-its-enduring-impact-on-indigenous-peoples.html, accessed on 6 January 2013.

[7] Deborah Lee and Antonio Salas, *UnFaithing U.S. Colonialism* (Berkeley, California: PACTS and Dharma Cloud Publishers, 1999).

rights of indigenous peoples. [8]Having found cause with the UN, indigenous peoples have marked some success in crafting the Universal Declaration of the Rights of Indigenous Peoples and the setting up of the UN Permanent Forum on Indigenous Issues. This Permanent Forum was the venue in May 2012 of a hearing on the Doctrine of Discovery, this time with the participation of UN member-states, including the Holy See, and indigenous peoples' organizations and civil society. An official press release by the UN stated that this event "rang with strong calls on former colonial Governments to reassess their constitutional arrangements and restore the "first nation" status of native peoples, and on the Catholic Church to openly denounce the centuries-old "Doctrine of Discovery", which many civil society representatives said was the "shameful" root of the humiliation and marginalization indigenous people still suffered today."[9]

One of the major papers presented at this hearing by the Permanent Forum, and sponsored by a large group of peoples and organizations, was presented by Robert J. Miller of the Lewis and Clark Law School. The assertion was clear: that the Doctrine of Discovery forms the basis for the international law of colonialism.[10] Miller's paper, and his book that bears the same title, is an important contribution to a growing body of literature exposing the Doctrine of Discovery. Miller sufficiently expounded on what he called the ten elements of the Doctrine, namely: First discovery, actual occupancy and possession, preemption/European title, indigenous/native title, limited indigenous sovereign and commercial rights, contiguity, terra nullius, Christianity, civilization and conquest.[11]

Confronting the powers necessitated the assertion that indigenous peoples are members of the body politic and that they too are stakeholders in the crafting of not just their communities but of society at large. That assertion includes a claim at the table where decisions are made. If decisions are made about them, indigenous peoples claim that they must have "free, prior and informed consent" and not coerced into making decisions that are detrimental to their identities, culture and economy. That claim at the table includes religious tables where token representation in decision making must necessarily increase.

In my time as staff with the National Council of Churches in the Philippines (NCCP), around the same time that I was involved in the life and work of the CCA, the struggles and aspirations of indigenous peoples were concerns that pressed for attention.[12] They remain so today. CCA, together with NCCP, published the report "Minoritized and Dehumanized", dramatizing the fate of indigenous peoples and why church and state discourse, policies really, were intertwined with the cries for human dignity and participation in public life of indigenous peoples. In his Foreword to the report, George Ninan, then the Executive Secretary for Urban Rural Mission of CCA, asserted that "structures that dominate the socio-political life of the [Philippines] have in a systematic manner marginalized the tribal and Moro peoples. Stories that tell of heroic exploits of tribes and Moros against colonial powers have turned into tales of horror and cries of anguish."[13]

---

[8] For an example of how indigenous peoples have engaged UN human rights mechanisms, see Victoria Tauli-Corpuz and Erlyn Ruth Alcantara, Engaging the U.N. Special Rapporteur on Indigenous People: Opportunities and Challenges [The Philippine Mission of the UN Special Rapporteur on the Situation of Human rights and Fundamental Freedoms of Indigenous People] (Baguio City, Philippines: Tebtebba and Danish Development Agency, 2004).

[9] See http://www.un.org/News/Press/docs/2012/hr5089.doc.htm, accessed on 6 January 2013.

[10] Robert J. Miller wrote the book *Native America, Discovered and Conquered: Thomas Jefferson, Lewis & Clark, and Manifest Destiny* (Lincoln, Nebraska: University of Nebraska Press, 2008) *in which he made the link between the Doctrine of Discovery in the 1400s and the Manifest Destiny in 1848.*

[11] *Ibid.* See also http://lawlib.lclark.edu/blog/native_america/?p=5420 accessed on 6 January 2013.

[12] The public statements of the National Council of Churches in the Philippines (NCCP) are contained in three volumes called A Public Faith, A Social Witness: Statements and Resolutions of the National council of Churches in the Philippines. Volumes I and II, 1995. Volume III (Quezon City, Philippines: National Council of Churches in the Philippines).

[13] CCA and NCCP. *Minoritized and Dehumanized: Report and Reflections on the Condition of Tribal and Moro*

Many years later, now working as a representative at the United Nations for the General Board of Church and Society of The United Methodist Church, not only is my understanding of the struggles of indigenous peoples more intense, it has in fact become personal. Public discourse has joined with personal discourse. In the following pages I insert myself at the nexus of public and private discourse, for I, too, am indigenous.

Rootage and Anchor

I started writing about my indigenous roots as a matter of claiming self and identity that was submerged for years. My claim to my indigenous roots was an act of anchoring myself in both the land of my birth, the Philippines, and the many lands in which I have been privileged to meet many other peoples and cultures. This includes the United States where I currently reside.

My encounters of peoples and cultures different from mine made me appreciate their own claims of self and identity. These encounters, for the most part, enriched my knowledge of other peoples and cultures even as it led me to both question and challenge mine. And all for the better, I must say.

I found security in the knowledge that others know and appreciated me because I too appreciated them. Over the years I have proven that there is no greater security than that which is secured by mutual respect. Respect secured by subjugation is tenuous; it thrives on the back of exploitation. This is why the "discovery" and colonization of indigenous peoples is a matter to be taken seriously. In its wake, colonialism, and attendant slavery, exploited and oppressed peoples; plundered, pillaged and ravaged their territories and resources; and subjugated and corrupted indigenous cultures.

The manner in which Western religions were introduced – sword and the cross for 15th century colonial powers like Spain and Portugal, and rifle and the Bible for 19th century colonial power like the United States – smacks of the love that Jesus Christ offered so freely, and how freely one can receive that gracious love. [14]

(Re)Covering Self and Identity

As far as I am concerned, my father was a storyteller par excellence. He was known in our town as someone who could enliven public gatherings with the wit and wisdom that came with the stories and anecdotes he told and retold. He had a public persona that I eventually took on. After all, I was his adoring son who went around the social and public gatherings to learn and eventually partake of his gift of storytelling, only to lose it as I went on perfecting my facility with the English language and learning more of Western culture.

My father earned the respect of other people by nurturing honest dealings and loving and transparent relationships. He was born poor and remained one until he died at age 86. But his poverty was characterized with integrity. He may have been impoverished of earthly goods but had an abundance of goodwill and integrity. He was the epitome of perseverance. Learning his discipline augured well for me in the years of my youth on to adulthood especially as I crafted my own person, found my indigenous rootage, and anchored myself with the values of the land of my birth.

My father was a public man even as my mother was the opposite. She was very reserved publicly but very amiable and sociable among family and friends. She and my father were equally loved for the stories they told us. Storytelling was the vehicle through which their experience led to traditioning. They could read and write but the oral transmission of knowledge – through stories and anecdotes that were full of

---

Peoples in the Philippines (Hong Kong: Christian Conference of Asia – Urban Rural Mission and Quezon City, Philippines: National Council of Churches in the Philippines – Peoples' Action for Cultural Ties, 1984).

[14] Rusling, *op. cit.*

gems – are the ones that helped shape and mold my character. Who I am today – the core of my ethic and moral bearing – are rooted in the stories, myths, fables and all.

Indigenous knowledge depends on a great deal of storytelling. It is one method that is now equally paradoxically challenged – at risk of being eroded as a method by new media and digital technologies, which by the same media can also be preserved for posterity. Storytelling among indigenous peoples is of course mainly through oral recitation. Indigenous values are thus passed on from one generation to the next through storytelling. When I get the chance, I look forward to reading from cover to cover a new resource about Philippine oral traditions written by Filipino artist, scholar and cultural worker Grace Nono. Her preface to the book already fills my own longing: "to contribute to the restoration of the Filipino's ancestral dignity, the respect for the marginalized cultural experts such as oralists, a deeper understanding of the practice of Philippine oral traditions, and guidance for the new generations who wish to ground themselves in the values and lifeways of their foremothers and forefathers. "[15]

It was not until my adult life that I discovered a layer of self and identity that must indeed be constitutive of my being, knowing and doing, albeit I have not until adulthood acknowledged and claimed it publicly and openly. My mother comes from a family of Ibanag heritage. Ibanag is one of several ethnolinguistic and indigenous groups in the Philippines.

When I was a school kid and in high school, was I ashamed of my indigenous heritage? Not really. Partly because I never really cared about it. But more so because I did not know the significance of that part of my identity until I became an adult. In fact, even my mother was not as keen as I am now in claiming a stake of that heritage.

(Re)Naming the Powers

From hindsight, I now know that survival is a key driver in asserting self and identity. Over the centuries, up until today, indigenous peoples are struggling to assert their identity as human beings and their right to self-determination as collectivities. That struggle has become a subversion of efforts to marginalize, minoritize and even cut off indigenous peoples from the umbilical cord that connects them to *kapwa* (self/selves) and to Mother Earth.[16]

My father was Ilocano, a linguistic grouping in the Philippines that assimilated far more quickly into the colonial moorings of the Spanish conquistadores. Close to 400 years of Spanish colonialism and a hundred years of US imperial conquest in the Philippines resulted in the pervasive subjugation of a people whose indigenous ways of governance were eventually supplanted by something foreign to their imagination and practice. The legal jurisprudence in the Philippines even today is largely Spanish and American, requiring every student of Philippine law to be equally conversant of foreign legal regimes.

Nationhood and nation-building remains a continuing challenge for Philippines and to Filipinos, not the least Philippine indigenous peoples. And until my country's own indigenous roots are allowed to sprout to lend knowledge to indigenous governance and development, such nation-building, especially its economy

---

[15] Grace Nono, *The Shared Voice: Chanted and Spoken Narratives from the Philippines* (Pasig City: Anvil Publishing and Fundacion Santiago, 2008) p. 11.

[16] A voluminous book written by Katrin de Guia, *Kapwa: The Self in the Other: Worldviews and Lifestyles of Filipino Culture-Bearers* (Pasig City: Anvil Publishing, 2005) is, in the Foreword of Randolf S. David, "an actual attempt to piece together a fading narrative imagination from the traces that a vanishing breed of "culture-bearers" register in their works and embody in their lifestyles." The result, he said, "is a kind of archaeological psychology that is both affirming and provocative." A representative collection of resource dealing with kapwa and indigenous research is Teresita Obusan and Angelina R. Enriquez, editors, *Pamamaraan: Indigenous Knowledge and Evolving Research Paradigms* (Quezon City: Asian Center – University of the Philippines, 1994).

and culture, may yet continue to be molded in an alien culture, or at the least, a culture whose trappings as much as substance are not constitutive of the native Filipino *loob at kaluluwa* – of soul and spirit.

Through the might of Western sword and cross, and the suasion of mystifying Latin rites and rituals, the indigenous ways of knowing and doing that have existed for many centuries prior to colonization were rendered and judged backward and hence bound for subjugation, if not elimination, of memory if not body and territory. Through rifle and Bible, imperial conquest has introduced a violent rather than a loving and a forgiving God – a God whose creative act continues must surely include an ongoing process of reconstituting human communities so that none is alienated from another.

Public theology must take seriously an act of repentance where power wielders in public, and that includes religious institutions and institutions of the state, are to fully acknowledge this forced loss of indigenous memories. Public discourse on the minoritization and marginalization of indigenous peoples must include the matter of re-inscribing what has been expunged of historical records: that in winning their souls for Christ, many indigenous nations have lost their ancestral domains and traditional cultures at proportions not unreasonable to say genocidal. Religion and culture are tightly intertwined in both the marginalization as well as the emancipation of indigenous peoples.[17]

Any act and all acts of healing that recover the wholeness and humanity of indigenous peoples must address the ruptures in history that have violently submerged memories and remembrances, lives and livelihoods, truths and assertions, that constitutes indigenous identity and collectivity. The recovery of that truth is itself a matter of contestation – a political struggle with deep spiritual implications.[18]

Repentance, forgiveness and healing must necessarily restore the right relationships that will reinstate both indigenous and non-indigenous peoples as equal members of the body politic, sharing truths that implicate each other in each other's life, and sharing joys because a *clearing* – intellectual, moral, political space – has opened up so that both the indigenous and the non-indigenous, in the words of political ethicist Lester Edwin Ruiz can then look forward to the emergence of the "fundamentally new and better."

(Re)Covering Sacred Ground and Space

To (re)tell my story in first person, and dare juxtapose it in the crucible of other struggles and assertions of selves and identities – especially of sister and brother indigenous peoples – is an exercise in recovering memory. And it is humbling.

To claim wholeness for myself is to also lay claim to the wholeness of every indigenous person, including my mother and her Ibanag family. This claim, I pray, will heal at least for me, the fissures in my historical and biological memory. Indigenous peoples, as all peoples, are connected to a web of relationships that tangle and mingle us with the rest of the cosmological order. We are each related to the entirety of God's creation. We are brothers and sisters in Christ. That makes us sacred beings and the ground on which we stand and the horizon that gives us the vista of God's spacious creation equally sacred. There is no true spirituality that severs one divine creation from another. Every strand supports the creative web.

To claim my identity, and that of my mother's, is a claim on self-discovery. I and who I am is not discovered by others. I claim my wholeness as intended by my Creator. That claim allows me to have

---

[17] See the work of Sathianathan Clarke, *Dalits and Christianity: Subaltern Religion and Liberation Theology in India* (New Delhi: Oxford University Press, 1998). On page 46, writing about Dalits in India, Clarke asserted that "Thorough emancipation for Dalits cannot be achieved without a direct encounter and reconciliation with their history, which is inclusive of religion and culture."

[18] See Lester Edwin J. Ruiz, "Towards Communities of Resistance and Solidarity: Some Political and Philosophical Notes" in *TUGON: An Ecumenical Journal of Discussion and Opinion*, Vol. VII, No. 3 (Quezon City: National Council of Churches in the Philippines, 1987), pp. 13-14.

others dictate what I am and who I can be. By claiming my indigenous identity, I also claim my existence, even my dreams, which are equally inhabited by indigenous signs and symbols that also have claims on my spirituality.

This claim is my own way of refuting a long-standing and centuries-old doctrine that discovered, or so it claimed, the indigenous peoples – their identities, territories, resources and all. This so-called "doctrine of discovery" has launched and resulted in the pillage and plunder of indigenous cultures. It meant the subjugation of a people whose resources were then claimed on behalf of the crown heads of the Western hemispheric colonizing nations.

(Re)Location and Claiming Space

Many thousands of miles away, in the Philippines, where my mother's family is settled, learning about the Ibanags is even more challenging now that I reside in the United States. My consolation is that I work in a setting where I could learn of the plight of indigenous peoples around the world and give focus to promoting indigenous people's human rights to their identity as peoples and to their stake in determining the path of their development, including the preservation and propagation of their indigenous knowledge base and resources.

I write in the first person as my way of recovering the submerged indigenous person in me. It is to claim space and equity for my being and spirituality among God's children, not in spite of my being indigenous, but because I am indigenous. Even as I remain fluent in Ilocano, a dominant ethnolinguistic Philippine group that easily assimilated into the dominant culture and religion of the Spanish colonizers, such fluency is stymied by my inability to use my native language, including that of Ibanag, as mediums of formal speech and as well as research. This is not being helped by the fact that English has been so pervasively used and developed in the Philippines that indigenous grammar, syntax, even science, are underutilized and marginalized.

Up until my adult life, I introduced myself only as an Ilocano and have submerged the identity owed from my mother. I speak fluent Ilocano but only know a spattering of Ibanag, save two songs that my mother taught me in full. I went to school from elementary all the way to college perfecting yet another colonial language, English that was brought by Americans to the Philippines. I learned both written and spoken English the hard way. For every word in the Ilocano language that I used, I was fined five cents. This all happened at Thoburn Memorial Academy, the United Methodist high school which I attended. The fine was a disincentive to speak my mother tongue and an incentive to learn the colonial language, which was the official language of instruction, commerce and trade.

With English as medium of instruction came English literature with grammar and syntax, and culturally-bent idioms and metaphors, which did not translate easily. They needed deconstruction, not easing into but trying hard to find meaning in words and expressions that were culturally alien to one's life and existence.

It was clear to me I am a Filipino who spoke Tagalog, Ilocano and a very little Ibanag. As I learned and mastered the craft of writing in English, I also felt I was bartering away both the spontaneous and formal facility I had with my mother tongues of Ilocano and Filipino. My indigenous vocabulary remains rich even as I find difficulty in using them in formal writing and composition.

It was not my dilemma alone, but because the local languages were suppressed, these languages did not evolve the necessary idioms and metaphors that are dense in the so-called scientific and technical fields. I can neither deliver a decent speech or lecture nor write a coherent article using Ilocano. I did learn enough English to make me feel I had an edge in life and living compared to those who did not take English seriously for reasons I am sure are as valid as my own intentions. As my use of the English language increased, I felt the power of the colonial construct grip my thinking and imagination.

Even so, my student activism in my college years brought to the fore the paradox that came with one's ease and facility with the colonial, now international and commercial lingua franca and one's difficulty of using in the same manner one's own native tongue. Side by side Filipino and Ilocano, the Philippine national language, the colonial construct inhabited my body and soul. It became a force and power all its own. And it has gripped how I think, how I expound my thoughts. Even my dreams and nightmares, sometimes are in English.

Today though, I am increasingly thinking and analyzing in ways and forms that respect my indigenous roots. While I find it difficult, I am intentionally learning to sensitize my analytical work with the challenges brought about by ongoing scholarly research on and by indigenous peoples. I am intentionally attending events led by indigenous peoples so that I can learn more of who we are as peoples. Linda Tuhiwai-Smith's book, *Colonizing Methodologies: Research and Indigenous Peoples* (London: Zed Books, 1999), is an important work in this direction. She expounds on a method that raises important questions about the traditional Western scientific and philosophical tradition, specially its use of the detached third person in formal discourse and scholarly research.

In my journey to discover myself and my ancestral bearings, I want to make sure that I have a healthy dose of the intellectual and rational as well as the symbolic and narrational. While scientific research is showing us the way to a better understanding of indigenous peoples and their marginalization throughout history, the narratives and symbolic representations of indigenous peoples by themselves must be paramount. It is important for indigenous peoples to claim not only a knowledge of themselves, but to appropriate that knowledge to illumine their context, both past and present, and forge a claim upon their future. On this matter, an old publication by the Christian Theological Concerns of the Christian Conference of Asia that dealt with the triad of relationships that entwine and tangle church, state and people in the Philippines is seminal. The paper by social ethicist and ecumenist Feliciano V. Carino, included in the book, gives a powerful reminder about how the Christian or Biblical story have been turned into idioms of change in colonial Philippines so that in their appropriation by the people, the story "gave form and reshaped [the people's] own ideas of change and provided the idiom through which they conveyed themselves and for themselves their story of suffering and oppression as well as their hope for social redemption." [19]

The Intersections of Indigenous Peoples Perspectives and Struggles

The first person narrative is important in the metaphor of indigenous peoples. It is made more important in their continuing struggles for self-determination, which means control of their indigenous domains and territories, indigenous knowledge and cosmologies, indigenous governance and diplomacy, and their indigenous languages and spiritualities.

The increased contact among indigenous peoples around the world makes me hopeful. Such contacts allow for the sharing of experiences, even good practices that prosper indigenous human rights. It also allows indigenous peoples to find ways to intersect their struggles with other indigenous peoples, and others. In so doing they are subverting their marginalization by joining in the common project to better the world for peace and security, for human rights and sustainable development, and for inclusion and diversity.

The right to self-determination, which includes the right of peoples to fashion the development they need and is appropriate to them and the capacity of their resources, has long been frustrated by racism and

---

[19] See Feliciano V. Carino, "The Philippine Dialogue: An Interpretative Report", in Feliciano V. Carino, ed., *Church, State and People: The Philippines in the '80s [Report and Papers of a National Theological Dialogue, Manila, Philippines, November 10-13, 1980]* (Singapore: Christian Conference of Asia – The Commission on theological Concerns, 1981), p. 73.

colonialism. Today's globalization endangers such right even more. Victoria Tauli-Corpuz, an Igorot (of the Cordillera peoples of Northern Philippines) and a former chair of the United Nations Permanent Forum on Indigenous Issues, summarized both the historical past and the contemporary struggle of indigenous peoples in this manner: "The current wave of globalization presents a grave threat to our continuing existence as Indigenous Peoples. Our ancestor's struggles, which we have inherited, centered on seeking the rights taken away from us through the process of colonization, racism, discrimination, and marginalization. We achieved significant gains in these struggles but at the expense of tremendous sacrifices. There are Indigenous Peoples which have already disappeared from the face of this world because of continuing ethnocide, genocide and development aggression....any of our sacred lands and burial grounds are ravaged beyond rehabilitation by mining exploitation....(T)he new form of prospecting, called bioprospecting, now invades and colonizes the sacred spaces not only of our plants and animals but our own bodies."[20]

The nexus between racism and colonialism is quite clear but not easily acknowledged. Deeply ingrained in the humanities and sciences that formal education put us through are the products of racialized and colonized epistemologies. Anthropology, for example, has been described as the handmaiden of colonialism; the colonial condition having had a large impact on the formation of anthropological theories. Here, theologian Eleazar Fernandez (2004) contends that "Racism undergirds a certain way of construing and constructing the human....In this regard, racism is a question of anthropology, of who we are in relation to others." He asserted that "racism involves our deepest beliefs about the human....In spite of the claim that certain attributes are inherently human, the inherently human we often refer to is actually the result of a long process of social and cultural evolution."[21]

An Act of Repentance Requires Forgiveness; Forgiveness Requires Confession

For indigenous peoples who have been colonized, minoritized and marginalized, there is the necessary exercise of (re)covering memory and imagination. It is memory and the remembrance of submerged histories and imagination for the construction of sacred spaces and reconstruction of identities that have been wantonly dismembered by centuries of colonization and imperial domination. This exercise in memory and imagination is a subversive exercise.

The exercise is sometimes a very active act, which makes it subversive. This reminds me of the courageous act of indigenous Bontoc women of Mainit in the Mountain province of northern Luzon in the Philippines who confronted the mining giant, Benguet Corporation, which was digging tunnels in the Mainit mountains, by baring their breasts. For Bontoc women, baring their breasts was an act that "signified that they had no respect for the men intruding [into] their village."[22]

It is subversive because it is a memory of colonization and empire that has fragmented indigenous peoples from their indigenous identities as peoples and as nations who, as historical records show, have traded and entered into treaties as sovereign entities until the colonizers abrogated them unilaterally. It is subversive because it is a claim on one's identity as God's children, created in God's image, not as the world giveth, if you will, but as Jesus Christ hath freely given.[23]

---

[20] From a presentation by Victoria Tauli-Corpuz at the International Forum on Globalization held at George Washington University in Washington, D.C. in May 1996.

[21] Eleazar S. Fernandez, *Reimagining the Human: Theological Anthropology in Response to Systemic Evil* (St. Louis, Missouri: Chalice Press, 2004), p. 141.

[22] See Geraldine L. Fiag-oy, "Indigenous Women Struggle for Human Rights in the Cordilleras", in Liberato C. Bautista and Elizabeth Rifareal, editors, And *She Said No!: Human Rights, Women's Identities and Struggles* (Quezon City: National Council of Churches in the Philippines – Program Unit on Human Rights, 1990), p. 163.

[23] Interestingly, the most recent publication of the National council of Churches in the Philippines, focused on human

One aspect of fragmentation that is often glossed over beyond the usual peoples and nations categories is the fragment that is represented by being woman, and indigenous woman. Perhaps this is why my mother did not insist or give meaning to her being an Ibanag in ways that I would have wanted so that I can better understand myself as her son, an indigenous offspring of hers. Along this line, a collection of essays by women edited by post-colonial theorist Leny Mendoza-Strobel is so powerfully invigorating in the way they help us look at the process of decolonization and its connection to the Filipino indigenous Babaylan [priestess, especially one with a gift for healing] tradition.[24]

One good example of treaties that have been unilaterally disregarded is the Treaty of Waitangi, which was entered into between the *Maori* (indigenous populations of Aotearoa/New Zealand) and the *pakeha* (the non-indigenous settler/colonizers). Maoris, including Maori Christians, have been over the years reasserting the articles of this treaty. Imagination will now involve a project of decolonization and deconstruction of colonized self and selves so that they, once more, embody their indigenous identities and freely partake of the beautiful creature that they truly are in God's sight.

Any act of Christian repentance from complicity in the submersion of indigenous identities and cultures will perforce become parabolically subversive. Drawing upon the gospel narratives of empowerment and justice, such act of repentance will necessarily become a remembrance of minoritization that has systematically assigned indigenous peoples a minority status based, not on their number, but on their relation to the dominant culture.

Jesus' parables of the mustard seed did not extol the small so as to belittle what was big. What is often missed is that the parable extolled the need to recognize the small as constitutive of the entire big sum that comes from growth. What is exciting today is that indigenous peoples, scattered in many parts of the world, in their small and big numbers, reconnecting to realize what force and power they can muster when joined together in networks and coalitions. In doing so they are asserting their stake on decision making at every level – grassroots to global and back.

The Cordillera peoples of northern Philippines are certainly more in population than the lowlander Pampangos (from where my wife comes). The Cordilleras, for resisting Spanish colonialism are minoritized, while the few Pampangos, for easily assimilating to Spanish culture, especially the Roman Catholic religion, are but part of the majority.

Minoritization happens as a result of genocide, destruction, and the latter-day phenomenon of "development aggression" which is the systematic dislocation and dispersal of indigenous populations mostly in favor of corporate farming and development projects that do not benefit indigenous peoples.

---

rights, does not have an article singularly focused on the rights of indigenous peoples about which this Council has a very strong programmatic emphasis on. The Foreword was written by Fr. Rex R.B. Reyes, an Igorot [indigenous] Episcopalian priest, and in it he said: Christian response to the violation of human rights in the Philippines gives credence for the crying need of the people for a share of resources, opportunities and power in this country. It is a cry for social justice and a demand for those who wield power to be accountable primarily to the people. National Council of Churches in the Philippines. *In the Image of God...we Are Created: Reflections and Perspectives on Human Rights* (Quezon City, Philippines: National Council of Churches in the Philippines and European Union, 2012).

[24] Much like my reflections about the Christian faith I inherited from my parents, Mendoza-Strobel's own set of questions and reflections are illustrative of how dichotomies and compartments brought about by inherited idioms, including religious idioms, can reinforce colonization rather than emancipate and decolonize. She says: "If we recognize God and the different names that people around the planet have given to their mystical experiences, it is easier to accept our religious pluralism and will be able to honor and celebrate our diversity. Religion, after all, is the human attempt to create a story out of our various experiences of the sacred. God that is present in matter and in all species, and in the cosmos. How do we live out this faith that doesn't project the sacred into solely an anthropomorphic image of God? Or if we continue to keep our inherited faith, is there room for inclusion and expansion of meaning outside of its theological formation?" in Leny Mendoza-Strobel, editor, *Babaylan: Filipinos and the Call of the Indigenous* (Davao City: Ateneo de Davao University – Research and Publication Office, 2010), p. 28.

Imagining a world where we have come to terms with our confession of complicity, acts of repentance, and search for forgiveness, involves a project of reconstituting indigenous self and selves so that they, once more, become constitutive of the body politic, acting and determining freely, in relation to other ethnicities, large and small.

To seek forgiveness in our act of repentance seems to necessitate confessing our complicity in the marginalization and minoritization of indigenous peoples, rendering them alienated from their own culture, of other cultures, and of other living beings and things in the universe. Alienation and marginalization sap positive energies and corrupt the spirituality that ensues – for both the alienator and alienated. Native American human rights defender Thom White Wolf Fassett speaks of spirituality as the highest form of political consciousness. "Our oral histories and stories teach us lessons poignantly valuable today as we attempt to understand ourselves in the twenty-first century. We were told in the creator's original instructions that we have been provided with all the things necessary for life....Because we honor all life, living things below to our spiritual universe....The spiritual universe, then, embraces the creation that produces and sustains life."[25]

Marginalization and minoritization consigns indigenous peoples to inferiority and prevents them from meaningful interaction in almost every human endeavor, including political and economic which are activities that have defined so much their lives but has excluded them from participation. To illustrate, marginalization has pushed indigenous peoples from places where the dominant culture inhabited, mostly into the mountains. Imagination will now involve the recovery of lost territory as well as the assertion of peoplehood so that indigenous peoples interact with society as people of dignity and pride.

I write freely about who I am as a way to denote my own *presence* and to inscribe the *presence* of indigenous peoples – their hopes and dreams, their struggles and aspirations, for a peaceful and plural world. This is what indigenous peoples said in a conference in Chiang Mai, Thailand in October 2010: "We are Indigenous Peoples grouped – together and in Diaspora – into nations and communities around the world with a memory of colonialism and a continuing experience of plunder, assimilation and discrimination, domination and marginalization, of oppression and exploitation. The different countries from where we come are nation-states whose controlling paradigm of governance is national sovereignty. Our indigenous nations continue to exist in the margins of the nation-state. Our marginalization deprives us of creative and effective participation in the national decision-making processes."[26]

What Repentance Requires and Forgiveness Demands

Indigenous peoples see themselves from the very beginning in the totality of the cosmos in which they are but one critical component. It is in this light that they too have participated in standards setting, in the context of the United Nations and other international and multilateral venues. One aspect of engagement is in the area of sustainable development, especially with respect to the environment, more particularly climate change.[27]

Indigenous peoples participate in standard-setting perhaps as an anticipatory act. Through participation, there is anticipation of a better, more friendly, and more peaceful, more just, more sustainable world. And one that is hospitable to original peoples, native peoples, first peoples, and indigenous peoples. Indigenous

---

[25] Thom White Wolf Fassett, *Giving Our Hearts Away: Native American Survival* (New York City: Women's Division, General Board of Global Ministries – The United Methodist Church, 2008), pp. 27-28.

[26] Statement of participants in a conference convened by the World Council of Churches in October 1-6, 2000 in Chiang Mai, Thailand focused on indigenous peoples. See http://wcc-coe.org/wcc/what/interreligious/cd36-11.html accessed on 6 January 2013.

[27] An excellent guide on climate change and indigenous peoples is Victoria Tauli-Corpuz and others, editors, *Guide on Climate Change and Indigenous Peoples, Second Edition* (Baguio City, Philippines: Tebtebba, 2009).

peoples have realized that if they do not participate, the standard setting process will go on. If this process goes on without them, the worst for them could continue. And so they join, knowing that their aspirations can be frustrated by the temptations of assimilation and co-optation, even downright exclusion in fashioning their lives and future.

Now a classic, the book *Moving Heaven and Earth* (1982), described this dilemma of tribal Filipinos this way: "At the core of the tribal Filipinos' opposition to development projects by public and private enterprises is the desire to be treated as human beings capable of good judgment." A Lumad [indigenous] leader in Agusan del Sur, southern Philippines, lamented, "Why must others decide for us? Are we not capable of governing ourselves and carrying on relationships with our fellowmen? The problem is not that we are not capable, the problem is that we were not given the chance."[28]

Through almost a century of representation, and at least three decades of negotiation, the Universal Declaration of the Rights of Indigenous Peoples is a reality today. But one that is born out of struggle and not from a silver platter.[29]

The presence of indigenous peoples in the halls of multilateral negotiation remains low. Even then, their presence in decision making – in what happens in their territories and domains and at various local, national, regional and international settings – is increasingly acknowledged as crucial. The historic approval in 2000, by the United Nations Economic and Social Council, of the Permanent Forum on Indigenous Issues is a signal example of this crucial role.[30]

Among indigenous peoples, it is quite known that as early as 1923, Chief Deskaheh of the Haudenosaunee Nation travelled to Geneva, Switzerland to present to the League of Nations a defense of the rights of his people to live under their own laws, in their own land, and under their own faith. He returned home in 1925, not having been allowed to speak. His vision inspired many generations of indigenous peoples after him.[31]

A similar journey was done by Maori religious leader T.W. Ratana. He travelled first to London seeking an audience with King George to protest the breaking of the Treaty of Waitangi concluded between his people, the Maori, and New Zealand (Aotearoa). The treaty gave the Maoris ownership of their lands. Not granted access to King George, Ratana sent part of his delegation to Geneva at the League of Nations. He joined them there in 1925, but still, denied access.[32]

An honest to goodness act of repentance allows for indigenous peoples to name and articulate the harm done to them. It is truth-telling from their perspective. It includes naming the historic injustices that have hurt and marginalized a people. Writing one's narrative is itself a painful act for indigenous peoples.

Indigenous Peoples' Spirituality: What Apology and Confession Exacts

Spirituality pervades the entire being, knowing and doing of indigenous peoples. Their spirituality is in their struggles, and in their struggles is spirituality. When they assert their stewardship of land, indigenous peoples are also asserting their spirituality. Rev. Gelung Gondarra, an Australian Aborigine, expressed it best this way: "Our people are called nature farmers. We get and give back to the land. We know that the

[28] WCC and PEWG, *Moving Heaven and Earth: An Account of Filipinos Struggling to Change Their Lives and Society* (Manila, Philippines: Commission on the Churches' participation in Development – World Council of Churches and the Philippine Ecumenical Writing Group, 1982), p. 117.
[29] For the full text of the UN Declaration on the Rights of Indigenous Peoples, see http://www.un.org/esa/socdev/unpfii/documents/DRIPS_en.pdf accessed on 6 January 2013.
[30] For the portal to the UN Permanent Forum on Indigenous Issues, see http://social.un.org/index/IndigenousPeoples.aspx accessed on 6 January 2013.
[31] See http://haudenosauneeconfederacy.com/deskaheh.html, accessed on 6 January 2013.
[32] See http://social.un.org/index/IndigenousPeoples/AboutUsMembers/History.aspx, accessed on 6 January 2013.

land becomes like our mother. The Mother Earth produces life for the people to enjoy, and provides shelter and protection, and holds the values for our people's survival. The land gives us identity of who we are. It gives us knowledge to build strong relationships, which bind us together into a solid bond, which nobody can destroy."[33]

Indigenous people's reverence for the entire cosmos – the Mother Earth, the Pacha Mama – and their struggles to ensure and exact this reverence, is spirituality of an order that have far too long been denied, ignored, denigrated, even demolished and dismantled by many dominant religions, especially those that have been instrumental in their colonization. An act of repentance must proceed from a prior act – a statement of complicity and responsibility in the marginalization and subjugation of indigenous peoples. Repentance without confession would be hollow, much like cheap grace.

Under the Doctrine of Discovery, indigenous peoples were not human beings. In US President William McKinley's claim on the Philippine Islands, the Christian claim to not just politically claim the Philippines but to also claim it for Christ is so telling in what he said: "there was nothing left for us to do but to take them all, and to educate the Filipinos, and uplift and civilize and Christianize them, and by God's grace do the very best we could by them, as our fellow-men for whom Christ also died."[34]

Apology and confession is constitutive of a genuine and honest act of repentance. Beyond acknowledgement of responsibility and complicity, such acts must name the historic and contemporary forms of harm done on both indigenous peoples and non-indigenous. Historic slavery and colonialism, and its ongoing manifestations, including unbridled globalization, spell human rights violation on indigenous peoples. The continuing disregard for the principle of "free, prior and informed consent" is one such egregious violation on the self-determination that indigenous peoples assert.[35]

What Forgiveness Demands and Rectification Implies

Indeed, as in many other struggles indigenous peoples assert presence. Presence provides the possibility of bettering the situation of indigenous peoples. To be absent in the public arenas that affect indigenous peoples' lives and livelihoods could prosper destructive agendas against the Mother Earth. This would be detrimental to indigenous peoples as would be to the entire cosmos.

Indigenous peoples increasingly realize that conscientiously struggling for their own rights is as imperative as building and strengthening solidarity with all peoples. Indigenous peoples are aware that standard-setting venues are not the only arenas of struggle. It is not even the primary arena, even as it is an important arena.[36] The more creative imagination and anticipation are happening in indigenous communities reclaiming land and making them sustainable; reclaiming identity and making them dignified; reclaiming sacred space and giving home to their spirituality. The reverence for Mother Earth is happening among indigenous peoples in places where their spiritualities have taken roots and branches.

Indigenous peoples like myself who have accepted Jesus Christ as Lord and Savior claim not only the image of the divine in them, but also realize their share in transforming the world upon the claims of love

---

[33] WCC conference in Chiang Mai, Thailand, *op. cit.*

[34] Rusling, *op. cit.*

[35] For a substantive treatment on indigenous peoples issues, including the principle of "free, prior and informed consent", sustainable development and self-determination, see Victoria Tauli-Corpuz, Leah Enkwise-Abayao and Raymond de Chavez, editors, *Indigenous People's Self-Determined Development: Towards and Alternative Development Paradigm* (Baguio City, Philippines: Tebtebba, 2010).

[36] For examples of many arenas of struggle and engagement by indigenous peoples, see Jerry Mander and Victoria Tauli-Corpuz, editors, *Paradigm Wars: Indigenous Peoples' Resistance to Economic Globalization [A Special Report of the International Forum on Globalization – Committee on Indigenous Peoples]* (San Francisco, California: International Forum on Globalization, 2006).

and justice, grace and mercy, indeed salvation, that Christ freely offers. The transitional justice that results from confession to repentance is an arduous one. What is clear is the indigenous peoples are God's people too and that they are truly co-creators with God in the building of God's kindom.

The accession recently by the US government to the UN Declaration on the Rights of Indigenous Peoples is encouraging. About this Declaration, Pres. Obama said: "The aspirations it affirms – including respect for the institutions and rich cultures of native peoples – are one we must always seek to fulfill. But I want to be clear: What matters far more than words – what matters far more than resolution or declaration – are actions to match these words."[37]

The Universal Declaration of the Rights of Indigenous Peoples is quite instructive in what might constitute transitional justice. Article 26 of the declaration states: "(I)ndigenous peoples have the right to the lands, territories and resources which they have traditionally owned, occupied or otherwise used or acquired." Article 28 provides language about redress and restitution. It states that indigenous peoples have the "right to redress", including "restitution" or "just, fair and equitable compensation" for lands and resources they have traditionally owned or occupied, but which have been "confiscated, taken or occupied" without their consent.[38]

The complicity of religion with conflict, including the most intractable ones, has ample documentation. A transitional justice framework (a term popularized by Russell Daye), it seems to me, would necessitate the unfaithing of colonialism and the decolonization of faith so that God's unmerited grace and boundless love are freely received and freely given, minus the adulteration of any political, economic, social and cultural system that in any case falls short of the Kingdom of God.[39]

The Pursuit of Wholeness: Finding Ways to Heal

As religious bodies continue to seek ways to find ways of healing relationships with indigenous peoples, confessing their complicity to their colonization and oppression, which is what the 2012 General Conference of The United Methodist Church (April 23-May 4, 2012, Tampa, Florida, USA) did through what it called an "Act of Repentance," it is wise to ask ourselves, individually and collectively, "Repentance from what and forgiveness by whom?"

It is worth repeating here what is often said but almost always hard to follow: "No reconciliation without forgiveness; no forgiveness without repentance; and no repentance without restitution." How indeed do we move from confession to repentance so that our act is credible and acceptable? What forms of redress and restitution will truly express repentance that might move into reconciliation and forgiveness?

It seems to me that reconciliation is attitudinal ("I will not steal your land anymore.") while rectification is behavioral ("I will return the land that I stole.") Among indigenous peoples attitude and behavior must join up so that the search for wholeness is truly holistic – for indigenous peoples and everyone, including the diversity and plurality of the cosmos that is God's creation. The joining up can be expressed in respecting and following the principle of "free, prior and informed consent."

This principle gives to a community and its peoples the right to give or withhold its consent to proposed projects that may affect the lands they customarily own, occupy or otherwise use. This principle is crucial, for example, in the struggle of indigenous peoples to prohibit unsustainable mining practices in their

---

[37] See http://abcnews.go.com/blogs/politics/2010/12/obama-supports-un-on-indigenous-peoples-rights-we-can-move-forward/ accessed on 6 January 2013.

[38] The full text of the UN Declaration on the Rights of Indigenous Peoples can be found at http://www.un.org/esa/socdev/unpfii/documents/DRIPS_en.pdf, accessed on 6 January 2013.

[39] See Russell Daye, *Political Forgiveness: Lessons from South Africa.* (Maryknoll, N.Y.: Orbis Books, 2004).

ancestral domains and territories. The principle is equally crucial in dispute and conflict resolution involving traditional and indigenous communities.[40]

The Act of Repentance and the Anticipation of Forgiveness

It took and is taking centuries to move from truth telling to apology and confession, and then on to an act of repentance. It may also take that long for the repentance to be received and move into forgiveness by the peoples and communities that were hurt.

We must be realistic about the possibilities that an act of repentance offers even as we must joyfully anticipate what forgiveness might open up for the embrace of peoples once hurt by another. This is no less than that same search for peace and pursuing it so that the peace of Christ that passes no understanding pervades each and all relationships.

To anticipate forgiveness is to imagine reconciliation, reconstruction and reconstitution in ways we may not have seen and experienced before. An act of repentance must not be stymied by the imagination such act conjures. It must move with the vision of what God might yet surprise God's people to cause us to sing "in awesome wonder."

Reality Check: Challenges and Opportunities

I started with a description of international standard setting and a characterization of how and where it is happening. I indicated the fact that standard-setting is an act of inscribing rights and exacting obligations. Such rights and the corresponding obligations generated reflect the state of recognition that the international community is able to yield under economic, political and cultural conditions brought to the fore by contending but interested parties.

Restorative justice gives some clues about the possibilities of forgiveness. Repentance and forgiveness necessitates laying on the table all our resources – sources of power and dominion – to be reconstituted personally, politically and collectively so that personal relations, relations in the body politic, and our relations with the rest of the created order, once more truly reflect harmony in a redeemed creation.

Some Matters of Concern and Consideration

A. The venue in which most standard-setting happens is the *United Nations*. The United Nations is a grouping of nation-states. These nation-states affirm sovereignty in their affairs and relations with other nation-states. Indigenous nations are not members of the current organizational configuration of the United Nations. A new paradigm of international relations appears to be urgent to bring the United Nations closer to its preambular statement of "We the peoples of the United Nations." It seems to me that this statement provides the possibility of reconfiguring the United Nations to include Indigenous Peoples and their nations.[41]

B. The controlling paradigm that guides current international relations, and hence governs and delimits the conduct of international affairs at the United Nations, is *national sovereignty*. While standard-setting is aimed at the "universalization" of values, as in human rights, the obligations evolved for these values are

---

[40] See Chandra K. Roy, Victoria Tauli-Corpuz and Amanda Romero-Medina, editors, *Beyond the Silencing of the Guns* (Baguio City: Philippines: Tebtebba, 2004).

[41] This book is a clear, substantive yet concise introduction to the place and role of indigenous people in international law: S. James Anaya, *Indigenous Peoples in International Law* (New York and Oxford: Oxford University Press, 1996). For the Preamble of the United Nations Charter, see http://www.un.org/en/documents/charter/preamble.shtml, accessed on 6 January 2013.

delimited by what national sovereignty is able to concede in the international front. When obligations cannot be reached and agreed upon, the standards simply say, "these are our highest aspirations."

Nevertheless, the available international standards are regarded as checks against this sovereignty. It seems to me that a paradox remains. Sovereignty is what undergirds the struggle of Indigenous Peoples for self-determination. But sovereignty is what has entrenched the modern state in what it is today – unyielding to aspirations for self-determination from among what it considers part of its sovereign domain. Short of a reformation in international affairs, what seems needed, at the very least, and it is a gargantuan task, is what Falk, Ruiz and Walker suggest in "reframing the international,"[42] one perhaps, that now includes all hitherto marginalized peoples and voices, including indigenous nations.

C. The agent of national sovereignty remains to be the *nation-state*. This nation-state construct continues to prosper the discourse of national security over and above peoples' security. In this conception, indigenous peoples may be nations but they do not have the status of states. This nation-state construct of the modern era continues to frustrate self-determination struggles of indigenous peoples. Even then, the nation-state as a paradigm is becoming inadequate in explaining and containing the rapid developments in the economic sphere.

Globalization, propelled by global capital, is crossing hitherto sovereign borders. The unreachable mountains and the far hills, the rugged terrains and impassable river tributaries, the margins and edges in which many Indigenous Peoples have been pushed into, have all become the cyberlanes of globalized communications. Even a wireless cell phone and a laptop computer can be launched from the boondocks of the Sierra Madre. The movement of capital is far more nuanced in the globalized scheme, but not for labor. Workers are not as free to move as capital. If they do move, they are called migrant workers rather than transborder labor which they really are. Globalization disdains sovereignty. With sovereignty the possibility of restrictions on the movement of both labor and capital are very high. The global markets, with finance capital at their helm, recognize no borders and boundaries.[43]

Unimpeded and unrestrained, global markets are becoming formidable leveraging agents in international politics. Transnational corporations have grown to the level at which their annual incomes have far exceeded the economies of many nation-states. The survival of many nation-states is dependent on transnational activities. Meanwhile, the governance mechanisms of indigenous peoples are puny compared to the instruments of governments. It seems to me that the growing international alliances and networks of indigenous peoples will pave the way to a greater recognition of their political clout.

D. The many peace treaties that were concluded to end direct colonial rules in many countries were brokered by Western countries who were in themselves colonizers of other countries. The settlements and arrangements under which indigenous peoples are currently organized remain to be under the auspices of the (neo) colonial state which are legacies of the colonial past. The havoc and plunder of *colonialism and neocolonialism*, in proportions that are genocidal, continue among indigenous peoples. No apology will repair the dehumanization, marginalization and minoritization suffered by indigenous peoples. The matter of reparation for the enslavement of indigenous peoples, for example, will continue to insert itself in international forums. [44]

---

[42] Richard Falk, Lester Edwin Ruiz and R. B. J. Walker, editors, *Reframing the International: Law, Culture and Politics* (New York and London: Routledge, 2002).

[43] Eleazar Fernandez's critique of the church in a globalized world is astutely covered in his *Burning Center, Porous Borders: the Church in a Globalized World* (Eugene, Oregon: Wipf and Stock, 2011). Here he asserted that "In spite of the hoopla and euphoria of the global village, walls of division and exclusion are rising, hearts are constricting, and moral imagination shrinking" (book's back cover).

[44] In the statement issued by the Ecumenical Caucus at the World Conference Against Racism, Racial Discrimination, Xenophobia and Related Intolerance, racism was asserted as a sin. It called on churches and governments "to acknowledge that they have benefited from the exploitation of African and African descendants and Asian and Asian descendants, and Indigenous Peoples through slavery and colonialism. We further call upon our churches to address

E. The nation-state has become the pimp of *globalization*. While globalization has no regard for traditional notions of national sovereignty, the purveyors of globalization have nonetheless effectively co-opted the nation-state, into full subservience to capital and the market. Globalization has seen to it that economies are integrated into one single market regulated by policies of the World Bank, International Monetary Fund and the World Trade Organization. These are institutions that have been targeted by indigenous peoples for their complicity in the exploitation of indigenous resources – knowledge bases of traditional medicines, indigenous science, and other practices, but also of indigenous governance and conflict resolution.[45]

Pharmaceutical companies have been traveling the high seas and traversing inner roads where leads the rich reserve of indigenous herbal plants. They are now being patented as part of what is called "bio-prospecting." Once patented, the right to the exploitation and development of these herbal medicines belong to the pharmaceutical companies. Even the genetic pool of indigenous peoples is now being patented by the same transnational pharmaceutical companies in search of drugs that they themselves will have the marketing monopoly.

Globalization has meant the capitulation of politics to big business. Many politicians have become willing service agents for and in behalf of global economic lords. Globalization is increasingly homogenizing cultures. The so-called *Mcdonaldization* and the *Cocacolization* of the world are an assault to indigenous peoples' spirituality. In the meantime, indigenous knowledges and practices are incorporated in the global market. Linda Tuhiwai Smith, once more: "There is a direct relationship between the expansion of knowledge, the expansion of trade and the expansion of empire. That relationship continues, although in the reframed discourse of globalization it is referred to as the relationship between the expansion of technology/information, the expansion of opportunities and the expansion of "the market." Although much has been written about the development of trade and the role of traders and trading companies imperialism, including the role of indigenous entrepreneurs in the process, the indigenous world is still coming to grips with the extent to which the "trade" of human beings, artifacts, curios, art works, specimens and other cultural items has scattered our remains across the globe."[46]

F. Mother Earth has been trapped into the *world wide web of markets and financial speculation*. Its wealth is being wantonly extracted to fuel the insatiable greed for gain and profit that globalization fosters. Mother Earth is but a real estate – to be sold and refinanced after five to seven years. No need to take root. No qualms about being uprooted. It is no wonder why it is very hard to convince Western society about how much Indigenous Peoples value land beyond their actual and speculated monetary value.

Sarah Lery Mboeik, an indigenous woman from Indonesia, used the Timorese view of land to explain the value of land: "In the Timorese view, land (nain, pah, or afu) plays an important role in human life. According to the Timorese (the Atoin Meto), land doesn't only embody aspects of the economy and well being for a people, but also is connected to social, political, cultural, psychological and religious issues. The Atoin Meto view land as their life. This is obvious in their expression, "Mansian moin na ko nain," which literally means humanity lives from the land. The interconnectedness of Atoin Meto with the land is so strong it forms their though patterns and behavior towards land."[47]

The issue of development aggression, a term referring to the increased use of land – usually expropriated from traditional owners especially Indigenous Peoples – for corporate projects that undermine

---

the issue of reparations as a way of redressing the wrongs done, and to be clear that the trans-Saharan and transoceanic-Atlantic, Pacific and Indian slave trade and all forms of slavery constitute crimes against humanity." See http://www.ncccusa.org/publicwitness/ecumenicalcaucus.html accessed on 6 January 2013.

[45] Mander and Tauli-Corpuz, *op. cit.*

[46] Tuhiwai-Smith, *op. cit.*

[47] WCC Conference in Chiang Mai, Thailand, *op. cit.*

the sustainability of land itself, needs to be raised anew in light of globalization. It seems to me that the commodification of land continues to alienate us from the Great Sustainer.

G. Religions and religious and theological canons must be reexamined and challenged at their very core. It must be challenged when it contributes to stripping of human dignity and self-worth of peoples. It must be challenged for its contribution in ethnic conflicts, civil strife, and many of the wars in history and the ones we witness today. The struggle of the Dalits of India provides an example.[48]

The Rev. Y. Moses of India described the Dalit struggle this way: "The movement for Dalit liberation from oppression and struggle for justice is not a new phenomenon. It has a history dating as early as the creation of the Dalit problem by the oppressors of the Dalits. Indeed, the many religious revolts both in ancient and modern India leading to the birth of Buddhism, Jainism and Sikkhism were essentially revolts against the social system that perpetuated the Dalit problem … The Dalit struggles today assume different forms. They include the struggle for self-identity, for social justice and human rights, and for political space … And in the context of the attempts to keep the Dalits divided on the basis of religion, the counter efforts to unite all the Dalits assumes special significance."

Theology must boldly challenge today the deification of the market. As in the Christian religion, theology must once more proclaim that our God is a jealous God – that God hates the worship of mammon. Globalization peddles a theology of mammon and of unbridled wealth. In its stead, the theology of Jubilee and shalom must be taught, preached and lived. This is a theology that admonishes us to give the land a deserved rest, which calls us to cancel debts, and to free slaves and release prisoners.

H. Unless and until a standard – in law and practice – addresses with primacy the victim and the marginalized, especially the most vulnerable ones and those most at risk and therefore in most need of protection, standards amount to no relief and lead to no liberation. The Chiang Mai conference, once more: "Indigenous women and children share a greater burden in the marginalization and exploitation of Indigenous Peoples. Their participation in society is doubly subordinated to systems of hierarchy, present in the dominant cultures in which they find themselves, as well as in some of our own indigenous communities."[49]

Whatever venue it is that indigenous peoples participate in, remember that the dominant discourse continues to marginalize and minoritize them. It is important that alternative paradigms be offered by indigenous peoples. Our traditional knowledge base is full of these paradigms. We must develop these paradigms and offer them to the world. We participate in international standard-setting, asserting that our indigenous paradigms have a place in the protection of human rights of all, in safeguarding everyone's human dignity, and in keeping intact the integrity of our humanity's common patrimony – our Mother Earth.

Macli-ing Dulag, an Igorot in the Philippines who was killed by the military forces of the dictator Ferdinand Marcos in the late seventies as he led opposition to the construction of what would have been the Chico Dam, said: "We do not own the land; the land owns us. For how could we own that which far outlives us?"

Our struggle to reclaim our lands is the same struggle to assert our spirituality. In our ancestral lands are our sacred ties and sites. In these lands today lie our survival as indigenous peoples. In them our produce is harvested, our abodes are pitched, and our reverence for God's creation made real. In them, we nourish our indigenous ways of knowing, being and doing. In our lands are the repositories of our traditional knowledge and the locus for our contemporary response to God's revelations and bidding. In these ancestral lands, our children are born, raised and buried.

I was a participant in the Chiang Mai consultation referred to earlier in this paper. The concluding statement of that conference, a collective voice, seems proper and adequate to close:

---

[48] Clarke, *op. cit.*

[49] WCC Conference in Chiang Mai, Thailand, *op. cit.*

Together we would like to affirm

1. That interfaith and interreligious dialogues among indigenous peoples of varied religious traditions and beliefs be continued and coordinated.
2. That in order to respect indigenous religions and beliefs, proselytism and coercive mission should cease.
3. That our spiritualities, indigenous systems and intellectual and traditional knowledge be respected and recognized and that the central place and meaning of the land in the lives of indigenous peoples be honored.
4. That religious and international bodies like the United Nations take measures for indigenous communities who are displaced from their lands.
5. That the aspirations of Indigenous Peoples for self-determination are respected and recognized.
6. That the concept of the nation-state as well as the theory and practice of national sovereignty be rethought, allowing for plurality and diversity in the peoples that make up each nation-state.
7. That Indigenous Peoples be mobilized to participate in international standard setting about themselves and their concerns and those parties to these standards fulfill their pledges and obligations.
8. That research and studies to deepen our indigenous spiritualities be conducted.
9. That efforts of Indigenous Peoples be supported at the United Nations and other intergovernmental bodies, the Commission on Human Rights, Working Group on Indigenous Populations, … [and] the Sub-Commission on Prevention of Discrimination and Protection of Minorities….

Bibliography

Anaya, S. James. *Indigenous Peoples in International Law* (New York and Oxford: Oxford University Press, 1996)

Bautista, Liberato C. and Elizabeth Rifareal, editors, *And She Said No!: Human Rights, Women's Identities and Struggles* (Quezon City: National Council of Churches in the Philippines – Program Unit on Human Rights, 1990)

Cariño, Feliciano V. The Philippine Dialogue: An Interpretative Report", in Feliciano V. Cariño, ed., *Church, State and People: The Philippines in the '80s [Report and Papers of a National Theological Dialogue, Manila, Philippines, November 10-13, 1980]* (Singapore: Christian Conference of Asia – The Commission on theological Concerns, 1981)

CCA and NCCP. *Minoritized and Dehumanized: Report and Reflections on the Condition of Tribal and Moro Peoples in the Philippines* (Hong Kong: Christian Conference of Asia – Urban Rural Mission and Quezon City, Philippines: National Council of Churches in the Philippines – Peoples' Action for Cultural Ties, 1984)

Clarke, Sathianathan. *Dalits and Christianity: Subaltern Religion and Liberation Theology in India* (New Delhi: Oxford University Press, 1998)

Daye, Russell. *Political Forgiveness: Lessons from South Africa.* (Maryknoll, N.Y.: Orbis Books, 2004)

Falk, Richard, Lester Edwin Ruiz and R. B. J. Walker, editors, *Reframing the International: Law, Culture and Politics* (New York and London: Routledge, 2002)

Fassett, Thom White Wolf. *Giving Our Hearts Away: native American Survival* (New York City: Women's Division, General Board of Global Ministries – The United Methodist Church, 2008)

Fernandez, Eleazar S. *Burning Center, Porous Borders: the Church in a Globalized World* (Eugene, Oregon: Wipf and Stock, 2011)

__________. *Reimagining the Human: Theological Anthropology in Response to Systemic Evil* (St. Louis, Missouri: Chalice Press, 2004)

Fiag-oy, Geraldine. Indigenous Women Struggle for Human rights in the Cordilleras", in Liberato C.

Bautista and Elizabeth Rifareal, editors, *And She Said No!: Human Rights, Women's Identities and Struggles* (Quezon City: National Council of Churches in the Philippines – Program Unit on Human Rights, 1990)

Guia, Katrin de. *Kapwa: The Self in the Other: Worldviews and Lifestyles of Filipino Culture-Bearers* (Pasig City: Anvil Publishing, 2005)

Gutierrez, Gustavo. *Las Casas: In Search of the Poor of Jesus Christ* (Maryknoll, New York: Orbis Books, 1993)

Lee, Deborah and Antonio Salas, *UnFaithing U.S. Colonialism* (Berkeley, California: PACTS and Dharma Cloud Publishers, 1999)

Mander, Jerry and Victoria Tauli-Corpuz, editors, *Paradigm Wars: Indigenous Peoples' Resistance to Economic Globalization [A Special Report of the International Forum on Globalization – Committee on Indigenous Peoples]* (San Francisco, California: International Forum on Globalization, 2006)

Mendoza-Strobel, Lenny. Editor, *Babaylan: Filipinos and the Call of the Indigenous* (Davao City: Ateneo de Davao University –Research and Publication Office, 2010)

Miller, Robert J. *Native America, Discovered and Conquered: Thomas Jefferson, Lewis & Clark, and Manifest Destiny* (Lincoln, Nebraska: University of Nebraska Press, 2008)

National Council of Churches in the Philippines. *In the Image of God...We Are Created: Reflections and Perspectives on Human Rights* (Quezon City, Philippines: National council of Churches in the Philippines and European Union, 2012)

__________. *A Public Faith, A Social Witness: Statements and Resolutions of the National Council of Churches in the Philippines.* Volumes I and II, 1995. Volume III, (Quezon City, Philippines: National Council of Churches in the Philippines)

Nono, Grace, *The Shared Voice: Chanted and Spoken Narratives from the Philippines* (Pasig City: Anvil Publishing and Fundacion Santiago, 2008)

Obusan, Teresita and Angelina R. Enriquez, editors, Pamamaraan: Indigenous Knowledge and Evolving Research Paradigms (Quezon City: Asian Center – University of the Philippines, 1994)

Roy, Chandra K., Victoria Tauli-Corpuz and Amanda Romero-Medina, editors, *Beyond the Silencing of the Guns* (Baguio City: Philippines: Tebtebba, 2004)

Ruiz, Lester Edwin J. "Towards Communities of Resistance and Solidarity: Some Political and Philosophical Notes" in TUGON*: An Ecumenical Journal of Discussion and Opinion*, Vol. VII, No. 3 (Quezon City: National Council of Churches in the Philippines, 1987)

Rusling, General James, "Interview with President William McKinley," *The Christian Advocate*, 22 January 1903. [Copy courtesy of United Methodist Archives, Drew University, Madison, New Jersey, USA]

Schirmer, Daniel Boone and Stephen Rosskam Shalom, editors. *The Philippines Reader: A History of Colonialism, Neocolonialism, Dictatorship and Resistance* (Boston: Shalom End Press, 1987)

Tauli-Corpuz, Victoria, Leah Enkwise-Abayao and Raymond de Chavez, editors, *Indigenous People's Self-Determined Development: Towards and Alternative Development Paradigm* (Baguio City, Philippines: Tebtebba, 2010)

Tauli-Corpuz, Victoria and others, editors, *Guide on Climate Change and Indigenous Peoples, Second Edition* (Baguio City, Philippines: Tebtebba, 2009)

Tauli-Corpuz, Victoria and Erlyn Ruth Alcantara, *Engaging the U.N. Special Rapporteur on Indigenous People: Opportunities and Challenges* [The Philippine Mission of the UN special Rapporteur on the Situation of Human rights and Fundamental Freedoms of Indigenous People] (Baguio City, Philippines: Tebtebba and Danish Development Agency, 2004)

United Methodist Publishing House. *The Book of Resolutions of The United Methodist Church 2012* (Nashville, TN: The United Methodist Publishing House, 2012)

World Council of Churches and the Philippine Ecumenical Writing Group. *Moving Heaven and Earth: An Account of Filipinos Struggling to Change Their Lives and Society* (Manila, Philippines: Commission on the Churches' participation in Development – World Council of Churches and the Philippine Ecumenical Writing Group, 1982).

(45) Dalits As an Issue for Asian Ecumenism

Joseph Prabhakar

Though I was raised in a Church that is part of the ecumenical movement, I first heard of the word ecumenism not from the pulpit of the church I was part of, but from the fundamentalist millenarian literature that attempted at discerning the signs of the coming of Christ by locating the presence of the antichrist in various institutions (which had some serious racial overtones) including the ecumenical movement. In such literature the World Council of Churches and the National Councils were seen as paving the way for final manifestation of the Anti-Christ. There are several Christians in India who buy this fundamentalist demonization of the ecumenical movement.

My understanding of ecumenical movement became more meaningful when I began to read some of the publications of WCC and NCCI that radically transformed my way of understanding of the Church and my vocation as a minister of the gospel. It is through these theological reflections that I began to understand God as being on the side of the poor and the vocation of the Church as being a prophetic movement. I found in the ecumenical movement a site for my own theological formation and the pursuit of Christian discipleship. In the call of the ecumenical movement to be one in Christ, in Christ's continued praxis, I found hope for the world since the movement was world directed, seeking to learn from the world and simultaneously serve the world. The ecumenical theology in India that found its expression through the Dalit theological project enabled me to deal with my own selective amnesia of my historic past of my fore-parents by privileging my Christian identity as my preferred identity. In the process it helped me to trace my roots as a Dalit and perceive my engagement in the Dalit movement as being central to my pursuit of Christian discipleship. Ecumenical theology and the ecumenical movement were thus sites of my faith formation and the discernment of my vocation.

However, my closer proximity to ecclesial and ecumenical power in the course of time left within me disillusionment since the Church that claimed itself to be 'one body' of Christ still suffered the marks of the body of *Purusa.* [1] Caste is well and alive in the Indian Church and its institutions. A cursory look at the Christian matrimonial columns would suggest how deeply caste is rooted in our minds. Caste plays its role while appointments are made and leaders are elected. The caste of our minds is yet to be transformed by the gospel that calls us to be one in the re-membered body of Christ.

With these observations I place the following propositions in re-conceiving ecumenism in India.

1. Dalit struggle has always been a quest for inclusion. Therefore, consequently Dalits envisioned that all may be one, one day. Having historically suffered the extreme consequences of exclusion within the caste structure Dalit imaginations of the divine and human have been that the divine is the hospitable one and the destiny of humankind is to become one humanity through its emancipatory project of annihilation of caste. Dalit communities embraced Christianity with a dream that by being included into the body of Christ they may bring the caste to an end.
2. The first affirmation that we make about the Church in our Creedal formulae is that it is One. This oneness of the Church flows from the Biblical understanding of God as the One who is the source, redeemer and the end of creation. As the creator, the sustainer and the redeemer, God seeks out to the world to be one with the world. Christ is the symbol of this Oneness of God with humanity and the rest of creation.

---

[1] The four-fold caste system finds its origin in the Vedic cosmology that finds its expression in the Rig Vedic *Purusa* hymn. It suggests that the four castes came into being through the dismemberment of the body of *Purusa*, thus sanctioning the caste system as being divinely ordained and the purity and pollution of these castes as being ontologically given.

3. Unlike the Vedic cosmology that vis-à-vis the caste system seeks to suggest the caste-fragmented body of humanity as being divinely ordained and ontologically given, the Christian affirmation is that all humanity traces its origin to Adam and Eve, the symbols of the collective human self, which is created in the image of God. The oneness of humanity finds its biblical foundation in the creation narrative where it is affirmed that we are all from one stuff *adamah* and the one Spirit (Gen 2: 4-7).
4. While redeeming the world, God in Christ embraces the world that is otherwise fragmented, by becoming part of creation. In so doing God in Christ takes into Godself the creation. In his suffering and death, God in Christ becomes one with the world by engaging with it in solidarity with its brokenness. In his resurrection, Christ becomes the foretaste of the one that is to come, the new world and the new heaven. By symbolically locating this new heaven and new earth in the body of Christ the Bible affirms the oneness of these two which were thus far polarized symbols. The work of Christ has to be understood as at-one-ment wherein the broken (Dalit) body of Christ, the fragmented human body, is re-membered.
5. In the New Testament understanding of the cross of Christ, the cross is understood to have occasioned the breaking of barriers between the human communities: between the male and female, the Greeks and the Jews and between the circumcised and the uncircumcised. This reconciliation is effected by calling those who crucify to repentance by raising the voice on behalf of the crucified. The message of the early Christian faith community was: You killed Jesus, but God raised him from the dead. In this proclamation, the early Christian community declared God's vindication of the crucified people and called the crucifiers to follow the lead of the crucified people for their own salvation. The invitation to partake in the body of Christ is thus a declaration of the emergence of a new community wherein all are made to be one.
6. The Church as the continued body of Christ witnesses to this eschatological vision by manifesting this oneness as its own provisional character. The Church needs to rid itself of its caste character and purge itself to become alive unto the oneness of all humanity.
7. *Oikoumene* as "the household" seems to have first found its literary expression in the context of empire to refer to the Roman Empire. It is in this context that the Church used the expression "the household of God" to subvert the empire. The affirmation of oneness of the world is affirmed not with the emperor as its center but the Crucified One, and consequently the crucified people as its center. The oneness in Christ is thus not a naïve oneness that overlooks the class, caste, race and gender disparities but affirms its oneness against the empire, caste, racism and patriarchy. It means forging solidarity with and around the broken communities.

Bibliography

Clarke, Sathianathan, *Dalits and Christianity: Subaltern Religion and Liberation Theology in India.* Oxford: Oxfor University Press, 1999.

Devasahayam, V. ed. *Frontiers in Dalit Theology.* Chennai: ISPCK/Gurukul, 1997.

Massey, James & Shimreingam Shimray, eds. *Dalit-Tribal Theological Interface: Current Trends in Subaltern Theologies.* New Delhi: TTC/WSC and CDS, 2007.

Massey, James. *Roots-Concise History of Dalits,* CDA Pamphlet No. 3, New Delhi, 2001.

Massey, James, *Towards Dalit Hermeneutics: Rereading the Text, the History and the Literature.* Delhi: ISPCK, 1994.

Massey, James. *Indigenous People: Dalits – Dalit Issues in Today's Theological Debate.* Delhi: ISPCK, 1994.

Nirmal, A.T, ed. *A Reader in Dalit Theology.* Madras: GLTC & RI, n.d.

Raj, Vinaya, *Re-imaging Dalit Theology.* Thiruvalla: CSS, 2008.

Rugus, Peniel Rajkumar, *Dalit Theology and Dalit Liberation: Problems, Paradigms, and Possibilities.*

London: Ashgate, 2010.
Singaram, Charles. *The Question of Method in Dalit Theology*. Delhi: ISPCK, 2008.
Wilson, K. *The Twice Alienated: Culture of Dalit Christians*. Hydrabad: Booklinks Corporation, 1982.
Wilfred, Felix. *Dalit Empowerment.* New Delhi: ISPCK, 2007.

(46) Common Challenges and Responses on HIV and AIDS in Asia

Erlinda Senturias

Addressing Stigma and Discrimination

Many church leaders and theological educators think that HIV is a medical issue but not a theological issue. In 2002, some theological seminaries in Myanmar expelled a number of students and faculty members after they were diagnosed with HIV. An NGO-based medical team wanted to conduct an HIV awareness seminar in one of the known theological seminaries in Indonesia in 2001. The officials gave permission on condition that they did not talk about condoms, lest the church would stop supporting and sending students to the seminary. These two cases reflect the attitudes of many theological seminaries towards the HIV pandemic.

Wati Longchar, a Naga theologian from India, shared stories from his people. He said that Nagas love talking, sharing, eating and visiting friends. But when they came to know that a person was sick of AIDS, nobody visited and everybody avoided talking even to the family members of the concerned person. A pastor was invited by the family of a young man who was dying from AIDS. With much fear and anxiety, the pastor went to the house but refused to enter the room where the patient was. He prayed at the adjacent room and left the house hurriedly without seeing the patient. The pastor feared he would be infected if he sat near or touched the patient. These stories show how churches have denied pastoral care, love and concern, and even stigmatized AIDS patients and their family members. Thus, the vision of an inclusive, healing, and prophetic community, which upholds the right and dignity of every human being and transforms a world challenged by HIV and AIDS, remains to be a distant dream in Asia.[1]

This story from Nagaland reveals the need for an adequate church response to the HIV and AIDS pandemic. Tuensang, the largest and easternmost district of Nagaland, is second to Manipur in terms of having the most intravenous drug users (IVDU). Thirty-four out of forty-one IVDU in Tuensang were found positive for HIV as of 2007. To address the issue, the National Development Outreach, supported by the Catholic Relief Service (CRS), launched the "Capacity Building on HIV and AIDS" in September 2004. The project aims to enhance the capacity of 1352 Baptist Churches under the Nagaland Baptist Church Council (NBCC) and theological institutions on HIV and AIDS to create awareness among the communities of Nagaland.

Dimapur Church in Nagaland, an influential church in a predominantly Christian state of Nagaland, was reported by Teresa Rehmar in her article, "Nagaland's Houses of Healing" for Tehelka on April 14, 2007 as one of those churches where the pastor preached on safeguarding against HIV and AIDS, and on the need for love and compassionate care for the vulnerable people living with HIV during a Sunday worship service. Meren Jamir, Associate Director of the project, believes that one way to check HIV and AIDS is by "abstaining from adultery and pre-marital sex and building a family life based on trust."

Experiential Learning in Asia Involving People Living with HIV and AIDS

One of the challenges described by a woman from Kuala Lumpur, who is living with HIV, is the lack of confidentiality and the continuing stigma and discrimination. She narrated how she had wanted to join a

---

[1] Wati Longchar, "CCA Journey Towards Building HIV and AIDS Competent Church and Theological Education," in *Building HIV Competent Churches: Called to Prophecy, Reconcile and Heal,* eds. Erlinda N. Senturias and Liza B. Lamis (Chiangmai: CCA, 2010), 186-187.

church retreat but two days before the retreat, her pastor called saying she should not attend the retreat as he had shared with other church members her situation. Unable to take the discrimination and stigma, she tried to commit suicide by jumping off a ship. She was saved by God's grace in the nick of time. She was referred to Positive Living of Pink Triangle and was introduced to Malaysian Care. She participated in their retreats, where she received a lot of positive support, met other empowered women, and became empowered herself.[2]

Malaysian Care was established in 1978 by Christians in Malaysia who envisioned a visible expression of holistic mission of Christ to the poor and needy. Their mission is to "display Christ's love, compassion and justice, and proclaim the Kingdom of God through the whole gospel to the whole person in the whole nation." The stated ethos are: indigenous in entity; evangelical in theology; ecumenical in involvement; holistic in approach; integrated in service; partnership in caring; and equipping for ministry. Pax Tan Chiow Lian, Senior Director for Prison, AIDS and Drugs Unit of Malaysian Care, is a Baptist pastor trained in Lutheran Seminary. He has been ministering to those in prison, drug users, and people living with HIV and AIDS for the past 20 years. Malaysian Care provides training of trainers, training in counselling and other forms of services for the community and for those who want to learn about HIV and AIDS.

Experiential Learning through South-to-South program is a common practice among Asian churches, usually facilitated by the Christian Conference of Asia (CCA). Exposure programs are conducted in places where churches demonstrate good practices of dealing with difficult situations such as stigma and discrimination of people living with HIV and AIDS. The Church of Christ in Thailand AIDS Ministry (CAM) was formally created in 1993 by a group of Christian leaders concerned about the growing AIDS epidemic in Thailand beginning in the mid-80s. The experience of committed pastors in serving people living with HIV and AIDS helped build 27 HIV Competent Churches in Thailand. Fifteen of these churches receive funds from the Global Fund on AIDS, Malaria and Tuberculosis. A number of awareness building and capacity building workshops and seminars organized by CCA since 2001 included exposure program in areas where CAM has presence in the community and in the local church.

One example is the Personnel Exchange Visit between the Church in Xishuangbanna and The Church of Christ in Thailand AIDS Ministry in 2009. Janejinda Pawadee, a CCA staff who earlier coordinated the Mekong Ecumenical Partnership Program (MEPP), shared that sex, HIV and AIDS are not easy subjects to talk openly about in the Mekong countries, including parts of China. But a church in Xishuangbanna, a Tai Lue ethnic minority, started to work on HIV and AIDS with the help of some partners as part of its integral mission. A group of women from Xishuangbanna had visited Thailand to learn about CAM's work. Challenged by these Chinese women, the MEPP initiated a Personnel Exchange Program between the churches in Xishuangbanna and Thailand. The program aimed to provide participants opportunities for mutual learning and experience sharing, and to enhance personal and team development skills on HIV and AIDS work.

ETE-WCC/CCA Journey Towards Building HIV & AIDS Competent Church and Theological Education[3]

CCA was involved in creating awareness among the churches through its Programme Area on Justice, International Affairs, Development and Service (CCA-JID) since the latter part of the 80s. CCA's involvement took a new turn after the creation of a joint consultancy work with the World Council of

[2] A testimony of a woman living with HIV shared in the Pre-Assembly Forum of People Living with HIV and AIDS in April, 2010, Kuala Lumpur – Malaysia.

[3] Wati Longchar, *Returning to Mother Earth: Theology, Christian Witness and Theological Education (*PTCA Series No. 4), (Kolkata: PTCA/SCEPTRE, 2012), 304-310.

Churches (WCC) in 2001 on Ecumenical Theological Education. One of the mandates of ETE at that time was to promote new areas of studies such as overcoming violence, promoting gender justice and inclusive communities for all. The ETE team identified HIV & AIDS as an important area that required urgent theological response and intervention because most of the affected people are poor, marginalized and oppressed. The stigma and discrimination attached to HIV and AIDS was creating a situation where thousands, many among whom are widows and orphans, were facing death amidst deepening poverty. The churches and theological institutions ought to be agents of change, influencing society to meaningfully address the causes of the disease, its impact, its prevention and especially issues related to stigma and discrimination. Thus, the ETE team began to work in collaboration with the Health and Healing Desk of WCC, Global Ministry of Methodist Church, USA and other mission partners to accompany the theological communities in addressing the issue. Initially, the team decided to accompany churches and theological institutions in the following three areas:

1. *Awareness programme.* Creating awareness is the first step towards change. ETE collaborated in sub-regional consultations for theological teachers, church leaders and NGO workers; national seminars for those involved in theological education by extension. ETE facilitated and supported a few colleges interested in offering course(s) on HIV & AIDS. This awareness programme led to the publication of two theological resource books: *HIV & AIDS: A Challenge to Theological Education* (2004, which has been reprinted 2 times) and *Health, Healing and Wholeness: Asian Theological Perspectives on HIV & AIDS* (2005). A total of 197 theological teachers and church leaders participated in the awareness programme. A random survey was made later and it was very satisfying to see the visible change in the attitudes of pastors and church workers. For example, the Pastor from Nagaland who refused to enter the patient's room wrote that he now regularly visits the Samaritan Home and other families without fear. He wrote: "I am ashamed of my ignorance. The seminar opened my eyes. Now I touch, eat and drink together and talk with the AIDS patients." Similarly, pastors in many congregations are now more open and sensitive in their ministry of care for those infected and affected by the pandemic.

As mentioned earlier, certain students and faculty members in Myanmar who were found to be infected with HIV were expelled from the colleges or seminaries. During the national seminar in Myanmar, Anna May Chain, the then Principal of Myanmar Institute of Theology, challenged participants, saying: "The seminary should accept them, should allow them to stay in the dormitory. We are made in God's image. God has given each one of us responsibilities to contribute to making this world a beautiful place. Having HIV & AIDS in no way detracts from anyone their worth and dignity as a human being. If seminaries reject them, the churches will also not use them. The seminaries should rethink our policies." Today, students and teachers are accepted and no longer stigmatized on the campus. Some colleges started offering the course on HIV & AIDS, even before it was made mandatory by the university/association. These are some of the positive contributions made through such awareness programmes.

2. *Curriculum Transformation: Mainstreaming of HIV & AIDS in Theological Education.* The awareness programme paved the way for curriculum transformation. The importance of HIV & AIDS care and prevention through theological education was acknowledged by many leaders. To institutionalize the course, a well structured curriculum approved by the Academic Committee or Senate was needed. Without that it would be difficult to offer a credited course; or, it would only be an elective or optional course. To transform and institutionalize HIV & AIDS in theological education, ETE collaborated in organizing two major workshops on curriculum transformation – one in Manila for member schools of the Association of Theological Education in South East Asia (ATESEA) and the other in Jorhat for the Senate of Serampore College (University) affiliated colleges. The Manila workshop developed four courses and the proceedings were published in the ATESEA Occasional Papers, entitled, *HIV & AIDS: Challenges for Theological Colleges*, including seven liturgies to be used in the colleges. The Jorhat workshop developed two courses for the Senate of Serampore (University) affiliated colleges. Then, through the accreditation and affiliation

mechanism, the colleges were encouraged to offer the course on HIV & AIDS as core course for all ministerial candidates. It is quite satisfying to see that a course on HIV & AIDS is now being taught in all the colleges under the ATESEA and the Senate of Serampore College (University).

We also realized that developing a course alone is not sufficient to bring about perspectival change in theological orientation. It was felt that the issue should be integrated in other disciplines as well. Thus, the workshops also reviewed the existing theological curricula and suggested areas where integration of HIV & AIDS could be done. In addition, we found that gender inequality is a major factor associated with the spread of HIV. In this connection, a workshop was organized in collaboration with the Foundation for Theological Education in South East Asia (FTESEA) and the Women Commission of ATESEA in 2006 which brought 47 women theological educators from all over Asia in Yangon. The theme, "Women, Peace-building and HIV & AIDS Concern" uncovered the nexus between patriarchy and HIV & AIDS. Some of the papers were published in *CTC Bulletin* (CCA) and *Ministerial Formation* (WCC).

3. *Teacher's Pedagogy Seminar on HIV & AIDS.* Again, developing a course alone will not mainstream HIV & AIDS in theological education if the teachers are not trained on how to handle the course. Therefore, as part of the awareness programme and to provide teaching orientation from HIV perspective, ETE decided to accompany theological associations in training teachers. Teacher's pedagogy training was organized in Jakarta, Yangon, Bangalore and Fiji. A total of 164 teachers benefitted from this programme.

It is very encouraging to see that apart from institutionalizing HIV & AIDS in theological colleges, a good number of students have undertaken research on HIV & AIDS at B.D/M.Div, M.Th and Doctoral levels. The HIV and AIDS topic is integrated into several other required courses like biblical studies, theology and ethics, Christian ministry, etc. Most colleges observed December 1st World AIDS Day with special liturgy and programme. Most of the seminaries/colleges provide the opportunity of Internship in HIV & AIDS ministry setting especially in interfaith context. Concurrent field work provides opportunity to students to associate with NGOs working with HIV & AIDS every week.

Continuing Challenges for Ministerial Program

The Church is one institution whose influence affects members' lives as shown in religious beliefs and convictions that affect their decisions in responding to daily problems, difficulties and concerns. The church indeed plays a critical role in shaping and re-shaping people's perceptions, attitudes, values and behaviours in social, economic and political spheres of human existence. Indeed, the Church and religious-based organizations can be significant agents of social change.

Theology does not stop the spread of the HIV virus. But it does spread negative and judgmental attitudes among people. Our narrow theological formations lead people to believe that HIV is the result of immoral and sinful activities, and therefore, as sin, it merits punishment from God. Negative attitudes stigmatize, exclude and discriminate against people with HIV, and create feeling of guilt among many people. This is as serious as, or perhaps even more serious than the virus itself. This causes people to remain silent due to fear of discrimination. It also perpetuates the myth that the infection only happens among drug addicts, sex workers, and people of different sexual orientation.

We also have the wrong notion that people living with HIV will die soon. They have no hope and no future. Actually nobody knows whether one's life will be long or short. What is important is that we make each day count. Some people may live more than 90 years, full of complaints and grumbling, that life seems more like a burden to them. What is important in life is not the years of a person's life but the way we experience life, in its joys and sorrows, and in how we share our life with others meaningfully.

We also have a negative understanding of human sexuality. Sex is still seen as a taboo topic and sinful. Thus, many of our pastors only speak on moral values, never on family planning or sexual abuse – which touch on the topic of sex and sexuality.

In spite of many positive developments, not many institutions concerned with theological education, training and formation of ministers stress this role of the Church and religious-based groups in educating and informing their members about HIV and AIDS, and inculcating values that will affect their behavior and make them less vulnerable to the disease. Theological education needs to equip our students in understanding HIV and AIDS theologically so that they would know how to effectively minister to people who are afflicted by this disease and enable their respective congregations to be competent to deal with the issue.

Various approaches can be used to incorporate HIV and AIDS issue into a theological curriculum. One strategy is to revise the entire course offering to ensure that AIDS is related to every subject being offered. Thus Bible or theology or preaching courses highlight HIV and AIDS along with the central discipline being taught. Realistically, however, this approach is usually not adopted, since it requires every course in the curriculum to be changed and there are many valid reasons why this is not so viable. Another strategy is to create a special degree program within a particular department that focuses on AIDS. This might happen in the area of practical theology, ethics, pastoral care, or some other program. Not all seminaries, however, have the necessary resources, size, or faculty to achieve such an objective. A third strategy is to introduce a single course or series of courses appropriate to the context and resources of the theological institution or college. Such an approach draws upon the interest and experience of persons available in a particular setting. The faculty member could be from any discipline of academic studies or be someone with expertise in the field of HIV and AIDS.

Wati Longchar reported on the following positive outcome on awareness building on HIV and AIDS in theological schools and churches[4]:

- More theology students are undertaking research on HIV and AIDS at various levels;
- Incorporation of HIV and AIDS in Biblical Studies, Theology and Ethics;
- Observance of World AIDS Day with special liturgy and programme;
- Seminaries provide opportunities of Internship in HIV and AIDS ministry in an interfaith setting;
- Field work provides opportunity to associate with non-governmental organizations working on HIV and AIDS;
- Adoption of Policy on HIV and AIDS leading to reduction in stigma and discrimination;
- Churches are prioritizing HIV and AIDS in their ministry and mission;
- Possibilities for developing a professional Diploma Course on HIV and AIDS Care and Prevention.

Developing Policies on HIV and AIDS

The National Council of Churches in India (NCCI) was the first ecumenical group in Asia to develop a policy on HIV and AIDS. NCCI engaged the different constituencies and partners "to break the silence of Churches on HIV and AIDS." A series of Round Table meetings of church leaders, experts and representatives from Church-based organizations were organized in Delhi, Bangalore, Kolkata and Nagpur. To consolidate the result of the round table meetings, a National Consultation was held at the Ecumenical Christian Centre in Bangalore from March 26-28, 2008 to develop a policy on HIV and AIDS. The outcome of the consultation was a proposed "NCCI policy on HIV and AIDS: A Guide to Churches in India" presented in the XXVIth Quadrennial Assembly at Shillong in May 2008. The policy reflects the voices of 30 member churches, 17 regional Christian Councils, 17 All India Christian Organizations, 7 related agencies and 3 autonomous bodies of NCCI across India. NCCI is available for assistance in developing, mentoring, implementing and reviewing the policy from the theological, mission engagement, gender, sexuality, general education and church life perspectives.

---

[4] Wati Longchar "CCA Journey", 192.

The second ecumenical country group that developed the HIV and AIDS policy is the Communion of Churches in Indonesia. It took six years before the policy could be approved in February 2011.

CCA took some time to develop the HIV and AIDS Policy. Awareness building seminars, capacity building workshops and national consultations were held before a draft policy on HIV and AIDS could be presented to the CCA General Committee (GC) in September 2008. When it was first presented, the GC members decided to table it in order for the committee to own the document. The draft was approved on October 1, 2009 after changing a sentence from respecting different forms of sexual orientation to "We need to be aware that there are different forms of relationship." Further studies were recommended to make a study on human sexuality that is rooted in the Asian context.

A Way Forward

Confronting AIDS and reaching out to people living with AIDS calls us to be in relationship with people in our communities, nation and world who live somewhat "on the edges." These are the very people to whom Jesus would minister and with whom he would associate, if his incarnation had happened in these modern times. He was always reaching out to those on the fringes of society – whether to the leper, the prostitute or the tax collector, scorned by their societies and religious institutions. In the 20th century, "doing AIDS work" is doing "God's work."

As we have noted, we have achieved many things and there is no doubt about visible impacts on the life of the Church and Theological Institutions. But we are yet to create an HIV-free world. We continue to strive towards creating an HIV-Free Church and Society. We need further research on the following:

1. Theological resources on HIV prevention which will involve re-reading of the Bible.
2. Research on the interconnection between HIV and people with disabilities, people with different sexual orientations and gender related issues.
3. Develop skill oriented training courses for grassroots workers in collaboration with hospitals and faith-based NGOs (there are lot of potential if the Universities can develop a Diploma Course on HIV Care and Prevention).
4. Strategize interfaith collaboration in the local context.
5. Empowerment of local congregation for HIV Care and Prevention.[5]

Suggested Resources

Aguilan, R. Victor, ed. *HIV and AIDS: Challenges for Theological Colleges in Asia.* Manila: ATESEA, 2006.

Facing AIDS: The Challenge, the Churches' Response. Geneva: WCC, 2001 (reprint)

Longchar, Wati. *Health, Healing and Wholeness: Asian Theological Perspectives on HIV & AIDS.* Jorhat: ETE-WCC/CCA, 2005.

Longchar, Wati. *Returning to Mother Earth: Theology, Christian Witness and Theological Education* (PTCA Series No. 4), (Kolkata: PTCA/SCEPTRE, 2012), 304-310.

Senturias, Erlinda N. and Liza B. Lamis, eds. *Building HIV Competent Churches: Called to Prophesy, Reconcile and Heal.* Chiangmai: CCA, 2010.

[5] Wati Longchar, *Returning to Mother Earth,* 314-315.

(47) Persons with Disabilities in Society and Church in Asia

Wati Longchar / Arulampalam Stephen

Introduction

Theological reflection from the perspective of persons with disabilities[1] is almost silent in all our theological discourse. Persons with disabilities whose voices were never heard in the church, and whose experiences were never considered in doing theology, are raising new theological questions: Are we not created in the `Image of God'? Is our disability a curse from God? Is our physical impairment result of our parent's sin? Or our personal sin? Are we sinners? Why are we excluded from the church which is for all? Why do people look upon as inferior? How do we contribute our gifts to the life of the church and society? Christian theology and ministry of our church will remain incomplete without addressing those issues and concerns. It demands a new way of reading the Bible, doing theology and ministerial practice.

Persons with Disabilities in Society

It is said that 10% of the human population has some deformity or other, yet they seldom receive any attention. In many societies persons with disabilities are treated as second-class people, object-of-charity or even abandoned. They are subjected to prejudicial attitudes and discriminatory acts by the able-bodies majority. Persons with disabilities are the most marginalized social group. They do not exercised and enjoyed the same basic rights as their non-disable counterparts. In the context of economic competition, the persons with disabilities experience discrimination in employment opportunity because employers in both public and private sectors regard persons with disabilities as weak, helpless and incompetent to perform work. The International Workshop on "Disability Discourse for Theological Colleges" in Bangalore made an observation that

> Globalization is further making the situation of the disabled very vulnerable. The economic growth oriented approach to development, privatization, competition, and emphasis on standardization of labour will further marginalize disabled persons. The preference given to smartness, efficiency, swiftness, beauty, etc. will do greater damage to the life and work of persons with disabilities.[2]

Therefore, persons with disabilities are usually the first to be discharged and the last to be hired in any form of employment.

There is also a close linkage between the poverty and disability – disability causes poverty and poverty causes disability. Persons with disabilities constitute the disproportionate number of the poor in the developing countries. 97% of children with disabilities who live in the developing world do not have any form of rehabilitation and 98% do not receive any education.

In many families persons with disabilities are not be given due respect. Even if the person is the eldest if he/she has disability then he/she will not be allowed to involve in decision making processes of the family. This is linked to the belief that people with disabilities are inadvertently mentally disabled and therefore

---

[1] Disability is a condition that hampers, impedes or prevents a person from performing normal activities which include caring for onself, doing manual tasks, walking, seeing, standing, hearing, speaking, learning and working.

[2] Wati Longchar, ed. "Group Report" in *Disability Discourse for Theological Institution* (Jorhat: ETE-WCC/CCA, 2006), p. 55.

unable to make right decisions. What this does is creates a division in the family and is an outright violation of a basic human right of the persons with disabilities. It undermines the persons' intelligence as well. Some of common discriminations experiences by persons with disabilities in society are:

1. *Inheritance:* Disable person cannot inherit properties of their parents. A disabled would not be considered when family gives a share of land to the children especially the male.
2. *Stigmatization:* Disability connected to superstitions culminates into stigma. They are looked upon as inferior, sinner or impure/imperfect beings.
3. *Infanticide:* In some societies children with disabilities are being killed on the ground evil or sin connection or to protect family's prestige/status.
4. *Abandonment:* In some cases children with disabilities are abandoned simply on grounds of keeping away `the curse', or stigma.
5. *Confinement:* Often as a means of hiding what is perceived to be a disgraceful aspect in the family, a disabled child is kept in seclusion from those who visit that home never to share that there is a disable child.
6. *Illiteracy:* Persons with disabilities are not given equal treatment in accessing the right to education.
7. *Disease:* Due to lack or denial of adequate treatment many people with disabilities are left to die from disease as a means of getting rid of the handicap in the family.
8. *Denial:* They are denied of political, economic and education rights. Some church even denied ordination of the disabled on the ground that a disabled minister may distract others whom he/she is supposed to serve.

Cultural Beliefs and Disability

Among many societies, there is a strong belief that nothing just happens. It is believed that bad things or unfortunate events are considered to be caused by the evil spirit and good things are the result of the blessings from the good spirit. If something happens in one's life e.g. serious suffering, death, accident, disability, even death of animal and poor harvest people always considered as a consequence of bad action, e.g. the killing animals while one's wife is pregnant, giving false witness on land matters, killing of innocent person, telling lies, violation of religious observance, violation of restricted days, taboos, etc. Some societies see disability are a result of children conceived out of incest or wedlock, an expectant woman doing certain practices that are taboo (e.g. eating certain first or eating the meat of cat, tiger, etc), having sex outside marriage; killing animals, and laughing at the person with disability. Other consider like failure to respect and appease ancestors result in disability. `Blindness', `cripple', `still born', `mental imbalance', `demon's possess', etc. are associated with those evil practices. If such person is given a place in the community, the whole village community is affected. Thus, society does not give any opportunity to disabled people even though they are able to do it. Even today persons with disabilities are not taken seriously in political matters or not allowed to be involved in religious matters. In some context, they are not allowed to speak in public.

In many societies, having a disabled born in a family is seen as bad omen. The birth of a child with impairment or impaired later in life is viewed with suspicion, as they may be associated with the wrongs committed by parents or grandparents against God, the gods or ancestral spirits. Efforts to trace the wrong doer often lead to blame on one spouse, usually the woman. In some societies, the presence of disability at birth was often considered to be reflective of a broken relationship between the family and God. Often "the child was killed and sent back to God so that He might send another child without disability. Such children were killed with the full approval of the community and the question of infanticide never arose."[3]

---

[3] Samuel Kabue, "Introduction of EDAN & Disability Discourse in Theological Education" a paper presented at

Such understanding still dominates many societies. Culture colludes with scripture, the living condition of people with disabilities suffer many forms discrimination and isolation in society. We shall further examine Christian understanding of the interconnection between our construction of God, sin, suffering and disability and see its implication in the life of society.

Christian Theology and Disability

God – whose construct?

Theology is God-talk, discourse on God. God is Spirit but we construct images of God metaphorically. Our theological discourse is shaped by our culture and metaphors constructed in a given context. Hebrew and Greek thought provided foundations and philosophical resources for construction of Christian theology. Influenced by patriarchal culture, life is perceived in hierarchical-dualistic way. God is also perceived hierarchically and dualistically as is the God-world-human relationship. Other dualism includes abled-disabled, holy-unholy, soul-body, permanent-temporal, man-woman, human-nonhuman, spirit-matter, living-nonliving beings etc. In this view of life the latter is always seen as inferior and associated with evil, unclean and damnation. The former is superior, holier and more valuable, and the former has the ultimate right over the later. This perception of life has a wide range of implications to those people living a healthy life with disability.

Influenced by this view of life, abled people construct a God who is impassable – beyond change. God is incomprehensible being, omnipotent, omniscient, or omnipresent. This all powerful, all-knowing God is present everywhere, the holy of holies is above all. Gnostics believed that such a God cannot be related to the material world. The visible world cannot be the creation of the Holy Almighty God. God is pure transcendental and spiritual being. The world is created out of matter; it is sinful world and destined to destruction. The Holy God does not come into contact with the sinful material world, but separated from it.

Within this framework, able-people formulate a patriarchal, success, beauty and perfect-oriented images of God like the Ruler, Lord, King, Almighty, Father, Master and Warrior. These are all military and success-oriented images of God. Though God is merciful, loving, comforter, sufferer, compassionate and liberator, we tend to over-emphasis on the trimphalistic images of God. K.C. Abraham says that "all these images are constructs of abled people for the abled people."[4] These images have made Christianity a religion of, and for rulers, elite and the upper-class. The theological concepts or images of God which we uphold today are in deep crisis because they are not capable of liberating poor and marginalized people such as those with disability and those living with HIV. This consciously or unconsciously promote the following views of Christian life:

1. Prosperity, good health, healing, success are seen as blessings from God to be celebrated. Physical disabilities, sickness like HIV and cancer, poverty and failure in life are seen as punishment and curses from God. Any theology that measure life in terms of blessings, money, perfection and success can be called prosperity theology. This is not the teaching of the Bible, but domestication of God. It is equal to worship of mammon.
2. We tend to promote a transcendental, holy nature of God who does not come in contact with the world. God accepts only the perfect, unblemished ones. Persons with disabilities are distorted images of God, imperfect, unclean, unholy and sinners who therefore, should not be allowed in the temple service; their presence defiles the holy place. In the name of maintaining holiness and sacredness, we exclude, discriminate and deny opportunities to persons with disabilities, women and

---

"Disability Studies Resource Material Writer's Workshop" from 24-28 June 2008 at Mombasa, Kenya, p. 4.

[4] K.C. Abraham, "Theological Reflections on the Experience of the Disabled" in *Doing Theology from Disability Perspective,* eds. Wati Longchar & Cordon Cowans (Manila: ATESEA, reprint, 2011), p.169.

persons infected by disease like leprosy (and today HIV). Such discriminatory attitude and practice is sin. We suspect that this kind of Christian teaching is a construct of the abled-bodied rich and powerful people to protect their selfish interest, privilege and position. God's name is used to exploit people who are vulnerable. Many people with disabilities have been denied for employment in Christian ministry and ordination or even deny admission to theological colleges. Even though colleges want to give admission, the infra-structures are sometimes not disabled friendly. The worst, abled people have full of negative and prejudicial attitudes toward persons with disabilities. Narrow interpretations of the 'holiness of God' continue to implacably exclude people with disabilities from living a healthy life in the church and society.

3. We conceive God as an all-powerful 'super-magician'. Everything is possible, if we have faith in God. God has the power to heal even the terminal disease like cancer and to raise people from death. Yes, God is all powerful and there is nothing impossible for him. We need to pray for each other for God's mercy and healing. But the danger is that those who are not healed are considered faithless, and branded as sinners. We often think that persons with disabilities are sick; we want to heal them of their disabilities. But did Jesus heal all the sick people during his ministry? Did he raise all the death during his ministry? No, Jesus did not. It was not the intention of Jesus. Jesus himself suffered pain and died on the cross. Suffering and death is part of God's creation. No human person can escape from death and suffering. Even the innocent suffers, e.g. Job. `Super-magic' expectation of healing, or our prayers are not answered due to lack of faith bring more pain, anxiety and psychological crisis to people who experience pain and suffering in life. People die, suffer not because of sin, or punishment from God; it is the will of God. If we narrowly interpret healing-faith in terms of miraculous **'**CURE' alone, then we are mis-reading the biblical teaching. Such one-sided interpretation of God's work will reinforce denial and stigmatization to people with disabilities.
4. This view of God and reality of life looks down the body. The soul of human beings is more important than body which does not matter. The soul is the highest aspect of a human person which finds its true destiny by escaping from this perishable body and world. So, why should we care for the body? Why should we care for people with disabilities or people living with HIV? We do not have to worry for the body if it is temporal and perishable.

Such constructs of God contradict the true message of the Scripture. The Bible affirms that God became flesh; became Immanuel. Jesus is the incarnation of God and gave his life for the downtrodden people. He touched, cared, loved and worked for the liberation of people who have been excluded and stigmatized in the society.

We need to move consciously away from the hierarchical-dualistic and success/beauty-oriented construct of theology. We need to redefine our theology in the context of persons with disability and with other marginalized communities. We should seek theological metaphors that counter and de-legitimize male abled-rulers and oppressors. A God without compassionate hand is not the God of the Bible. Any language of God that fails to answer the cry of the marginalized people such as persons with disabilities, wounded woman, tribals, dalits, people living with HIV, for total freedom and right to fullness of life is not holistic. God-talk should be free from the institutionalized-patriarchal-hierarchical-dualistic views of life; instead be a living reality for people. We need a new theological paradigm in which God is perceived as fellow sufferer, companion, and great comforter as a divine power that is not dominating or controlling. Rather than dialectical power in weakness, this is a liberating and transforming power that is effective in compassionate love, care and service.[5] This nature and power of God is powerfully revealed in the life and ministry of Jesus Christ.

---

[5] *Ibid.*, p. 172.

Sin and disability

An important biblical insight that has influenced the life and church is the doctrine of sin and creation of humanity. The presence of persons with physical impairment in society created much debate in Christian church especially on the question of perfect God, imperfection creation and the consequence of sin, etc. Two positions of the church may be cited here to show the interconnection between disability and sin.

A) Disability as Consequence of Sin: A Source of Exclusion

The concept of sin is differently used in the Christian circle. Some theologians speak of `missing the mark', the other speak of `dethroning God and enthroning self at the centre of one's life' etc. But the most crucial issue is: how does the Christian understanding of sin affect the lives of persons with disabilities?

A dominant view of physical impairment is that it is the consequence of sin. Even today majority of Christians would say that it is the consequence of sin, punishment from God and a curse to the family. This belief is further re-imposed by the doctrine of rebirth (*karma samsara*) in Hinduism[6] and Primal religious belief on evil spirit[7]. This wrong interpretation of disability linking with sin has caused much damage to persons who live as healthy persons with disabilities. It has become a source of exclusion in society. Classical theologians regarded the "original sin" as the universal and hereditary sinfulness of human since the fall of human. It is accepted that since all human beings are the descendants of the first couples: Adam and Eve, they all inherited the sin of their parents and then all become sinners. Augustine taught that the original sin is transmitted through sexual act. The original sin has distorted God's perfect order of creation and the consequence of which is imperfect order of creation. Since imperfect creation is the result of sin, they do not come under the scheme of God's grace. It is direct consequence of sin and the work of demons, that it is a curse and punishment from God. Though the offence the persons with disabilities commit is relatively insignificant and most often they are not even conscious of their so-called misdeed, many people take it for granted till today that their disability is manifestation of their own personal or parents' sin in the past; it could be during this present life or in the past life. Unfortunately, the church takes more seriously like smoking, drinking, or going to movies on Sunday as sin. But neglect the sinful acts the society commits to disable people by way of discrimination, prejudice and exclusion that have serious consequences on their lives. This social sin is more serious. There are sufficient proofs that Christian theology of (the original) sin is the root of the denial and exclusion of persons with disabilities in society and church. It gives justification to escape from institutionalized form of social evil. Physical impairment as the work of demon and consequence of sin has deprived persons with disabilities in church and public life. This wrong notion of the traditional view of sin have not only neglected people's real life situation, but also affirms oppressive context and do not give direction for transformation of life. This wrong understanding has contributed to exclusion of persons with disabilities from active involvement in spiritual, social and developmental life of the church.

B) Sin and Image of God

Throughout the centuries, the churches have never acknowledged that persons with disabilities are created in the image of God. Some theologians exclude them by interpreting `the image of God' in terms of `perfection' – perfection was understood in terms of physical and mental endowment. There is no beauty in the disabled. Any form of disability makes a person less than human – they are not created in the image of God. Some understood in terms of `rationality'. Persons who cannot articulate do not represent God's image. Some interpretations focus on the exercise of power. God created humans to exercise power and

[6] The doctrine of rebirth teaches that the cyclic process of life. The condition of present life is determined by the past deeds. Disability is product of past misdeeds and we can do nothing for it.

[7] The traditional primal religion strongly advocates that "bad things are caused by the evil spirits and good things are the result of the blessing of benevolent spirit".

have dominion over the rest of creation, a capacity into which God invites humans to participate. Persons with disabilities are not capable of exercising power and so they do not reflect God's image. The others interpreted in relation to human capacity for creativity and freedom. Since persons with disabilities cannot exercise creativity and freedom fully, they cannot be counted as full `being'[8]. These are all able people's interpretations and they do not respect life especially those who live a healthy life with physical impairments. Disagreeing with the dominant Christian interpretations, Gordon Cowans, writes:

> None of the above formulations takes sufficiently into account the experience of disability, particularly the experiences of persons born with impairments. Many persons are born with impairments which inhibit their capacity to engage and interact with their environment in the same way as others.[9]

The dominant interpretations of sin and the image of God justified extermination of people born with physical impairments. Killing, apart from "imperfect beings" like persons with disabilities, of any person is considered as sin because human person is precious, created by God in his own image. The Reformers who held deliberate discharge of semen as crime were negative towards persons with disabilities. *Onan* deserved to die, (Gen. 38:8-10) taught Calvin, for the crime of the unproductive discharge of semen. Deliberate spilling of semen outside of intercourse between a man and a woman was considered crime worth of death.[10] But in the case of persons with disabilities, Luther and Calvin held them in contempt and justified their removal from society by death as "an act well-pleasing to God". A person with disabilities represents a distorted image of God and so they are sub-human. A person does not commit crime by killing disabled person.

Discrimination, denial, exclusion at homes, churches and society is rooted on this understanding of God's structure of creation. It perpetuates people to treat disable people as inferior not only with respect to their specific physical limitations, but also "total being". They are treated like a second-class people, object-of-charity or even abandoned. Some parents do not give them adequate food, medical treatment and some of them never take them out of their homes. Their presence is considered as a burden, but not as a precious gift. Society makes them absolutely dependent by denying privileges and opportunities in all sectors, including in the church. This is sin and it contradicts the Kingdom's value.

Suffering and disability

Broadly we may categorize the source of suffering into two. First, the suffering perpetuated by unjust system. For examples, globalization and patriarchy. Globalization is a new form of colonialism. The global market turns human beings and their cultural activities and earth's resources into commodities for profit. The weak, namely the migrant workers, farmers, consumers, small entrepreneurs and the whole eco-system are the victims of globalization. The unjust financial system, ever increasing ideology of consumerism, materialism, individualism, competition and greed erode life-affirming values, fragments communities and increase poverty; the value system which are driven by the powerful financial co-operations. The patriarchy perpetuates injustice to women. Women are being denied of equal opportunity in religious and public life. They are institutionalized form of violence. It is demonic. It causes suffering to a large majority of people on the basis of sex, colour, caste, religion and economic status. These are human made suffering. They are contrary to Kingdom's value. Human made sufferings can be transformed by reordering our

---

[8] Gordon Cowans, "Towards a Liberatory Theology of Disability; Humanity in Creation, Disability and the Image of God" in *Disabled God Amidst Broken People: Doing Theology from Disability Perspective*, ed. by Wati Longchar and Gordon Cowans, (Manila: ATESEA, 2007), pp.47-48.

[9] *Ibid*., p. 48.

[10] Cited by Adrian Thatcher, "The Virus and the Bible-How Living with HIV helps the Church to read it" a paper presented at workshop on "Ethics on HIV & AIDS Prevention" at on 8th January, 2008 at Johannesburg, p. 5.

lifestyle, attitudes and structures of human relations in community informed by Kingdom's values. It demands sharing and just relationship. K.C. Abraham upheld justice as the key for liberation. He wrote,

> Prophets bring to our awareness the concept of compassionate love as integral to justice. For them a just relationship is possible only if all are included and cared for. Therefore the test of justice is how society treats the most vulnerable sections. They are not asking for charity, but they demand, in their own way, justice and participation. Justice that includes compassion is a necessary correction.[11]

Persons with disabilities who are not able to organize themselves and fight for their rights, K.C. Abraham further said that "The disabled are denied their basic human rights and they are excluded from society. To restore their dignity is to struggle for it.... But in the case of mentally challenged, they are not capable of organizing themselves. In solidarity with them, care givers and others should create an awareness of their hurts and struggle for their rights."[12]

Second, the suffering such as unexpected illness, the death of a loved one, accident, lost of job etc. When the tragic disease and death happen to us, we ask why Lord? When a child is born with physical impairment, we ask why Lord? We often think that it is the result of some mistake we committed. It is a punishment from God. Job strongly rejected the idea that suffering is God's punishment and that our suffering is caused by our own personal sins. Jesus also refuted the idea.

We often explain the innocent suffering or physical impairment in terms of "virtuous suffering". Nancy L. Eiesland criticized the position that physical impairments were a sign of divine election by which the righteous were purified and perfected through painful trails. Such idea gives a notion that "disability as a temporary affliction that must be endured to gain heavenly rewards."[13] She further wrote:

> The biblical support of virtuous suffering has been a subtle, but particularly dangerous theology for persons with disabilities. Used to promote adjustment to unjust social situations and to sanction acceptance of isolation among persons with disabilities, it has encouraged our passivity and resignation and has institutionalized depression as an appropriate response to `divine testing'. Viewing suffering as means of purification and of gaining spiritual merit not only promotes the link between sin and disability but also implies that those who never experience a "cure" continue to harbor sin in their lives. Similar to the practice of emphasizing self-sacrifice to women, the theology of virtuous suffering has encouraged persons with disabilities to acquiesce to social barriers as a sign of obedience to God and to internalize second-class status inside and outside the church.[14]

The idea of virtuous suffering encourages passivity that whatever happens is the will of God and compromise with unjust system. The idea of virtuous suffering blinds our eyes to see injustice and ignore people to struggle for change. The experience of suffering should lead us to fight for justice and dignity.

Jesus and Disability

Jesus brought people with disability, the poor and rejected one by the society into the centre of God's Kingdom. All human beings are precious, valuable and they must be respected. Jesus challenged the discriminatory practice and attitude of abled rich people. Those who were discriminated, excluded,

---

[11] K.C. Abraham, "Theological Education and Disability" in *Disability Discourse for Theological Institution* ed by Wati Longchar (Jorhat: ETE-WCC/CCA, 2006), p. 14.
[12] *Ibid.* p. 14.
[13] Nancy L. Eiesland, *The Disabled God: Towards a Liberatory Theology of Disability* (Nashville: Abingdon Press, 1994), p. 72.
[14] *Ibid.* p. 72-73.

ostracized, rejected on the basis of disease and disability were challenged by Jesus. A few examples may be cited here:

1. The healing of lepers (Mt. 8:1-4; Mk 1:40-45; Lk 5:12-16; 17:11-19) is an extraordinary act of Jesus. Leprosy was considered not only a serious disease, but also unclean – they must be quarantined and must live outside of human habitation (Lev 13:46, Num 5:2-3). Since they were considered unholy, unclean, they were required to shout "Unclean, Unclean, Unclean" when they come near human habitat (Lev. 13:45-46). Anything that comes into contact with the lepers is considered unclean and therefore, such things must be burned and discarded (Lev. 13:52-57; 14:40-45). Such disease requires cleansing. Until a leper is declared clean by the priest, he/she cannot go back to lead a normal life. Jesus broke the cultural and religious norms of his time when he touched and healed the lepers (MT. 8:3; Mk 1:41; Lk 5:13). Jesus set love and compassion above any religious norms and rituals that dehumanized certain people. Jesus demonstrated that no disease can be branded as a disease of/for the sinners.[15] Jesus reached out and touched the leper. That was a radical step demonstrated by Jesus. Jesus need not have touched him – but he did – to break ritual taboos that kept people apart. Social barriers need to be broken down if true healing is to take place. Jesus demonstrated to the disciples that they must come out of attitudes that bind the people in seclusion. Jesus commissioned his disciples to go and do the same act of healing even to the leper (MT. 10; 8).[16] Then, are we willing to break the religious taboos and extend a compassionate hand to the people with disability?
2. Another powerful compassionate hand of God is the story of woman with the haemorrhage (Mk 5:25-34, Mt. 9:20-22; Lk 8:41048). The woman was sick twelve long years. Defiling the Jewish norm, she went and touched Jesus. Haemorrhage was considered as unclean and they must be separated from people. The Jews considered even normal menstruation was considered unclean. Even the bed where she rests and everything on which she sits were considered unclean (Lev. 15:26). Anyone touches such things were thus considered unclean (Lev. 15:27). The person could be cleaned only when the priest makes a cleansing offering (Lev. 15:29-30). When the woman touched, Jesus turned and asked "Who touched my clothes?" In front of all his followers, Jesus then declared her healed and cleansed. Jesus broke the social stigma. The social stigma associated to her due to her disease nullified by declaring "Go in peace" (Mk 5:34).[17]
3. Jesus act of healing of shriveled man on Sabbath (Mark 3:1-12) is another to challenge to Jewish leaders. They did not want the shriveled man to be healed in the Synagogue on the Sabbath because for them Sabbath observance was more important than saving life. They were afraid that this man would enter the synagogue with the ailment which would defile the holy place. Religious rituals, laws and finding fault were more important than saving life. But for Jesus, life was more important. Against their ritualism, Jesus said, "The Sabbath was made for humankind and not humankind for the Sabbath". The Pharisees were watching whether the withered hand would be healed by Jesus. Jesus healed that person in spite of all the religious restrictions. Care and healing is of prime importance than religious practices.[18] Jesus broke the religious rituals.

Jesus liberative work for the sinners, unclean and socially rejected people led him to the cross. The cross stands for suffering in its most cruel form. Jesus' identification with the victims of suffering and stigma

---

[15] V.J. John, "Biblical Approach to Understanding HIV/IDS: Some Insights from the Life of Jesus in the Gospels" in *Health, Healing and Wholeness,* ed. Wati Longchar (ETE-WCC/CCA, 2005), pp. 86-87.

[16] Razouselie Laseto, "Jesus and Disease: A Search for a Place for HIV & AIDS in Jesus' Approach to Human Disease" in *Health and Life: Theological Reflections on HIV & AIDS,* ed. Razouselie Lasetso (Jorhat: ETC Programme Coordination, 2007), pp. 39-40.

[17] *Ibid.*, 41.

[18] *Ibid.,* p. 37, see also V.J. John, *op. cit.,* p. 90.

was the significance of the cross. Having done no wrong, Jesus suffered, hence identified with all who suffer ignominy and injustice, rejection and discrimination in their life. The cross was the symbol of the suffering of the innocent and hence a symbol of solidarity with all who suffer, especially with the socially ostracized sufferer, and this is the essence of the meaning of the cross.[19] Jesus stood for the cause of the sick and disabled. He defended them against the prevailing attitude that suffering and physical impairment is due to sin. Jesus rather reached out and touched them to bring healing to the sick and disabled. He not only healed them of their physical infirmities but also restored them to their rightful place in the society. Because of his compassionate love for the disabled and sick, Jesus did not hesitate to break the Sabbath law (Mk 3:1-6). Jesus' whole motive behind his healing ministry was not to present himself as a kind of healer or super-magician but his aim was to start a movement of hope from the hopeless; a movement from nobody to somebody. On encountering Jesus, the sick and disabled experience the worth and dignity of life. In the Kingdom of God there is nothing such as unclean or sinner that cannot be made clean again.[20]

We can imagine what Jesus would do for persons with disability today in our church and society. Jesus will not take the road of denial, discrimination, ostracization and isolation.[21] He would be there with them to bring healing and hope. Jesus would certainly condemn the Pharisaic attitude of abled people. Therefore, it is not our duty to pass judgment and undermine them, but accept those with disability the way they are and minister to them with compassion, open-hearted acceptance, love and care. Allow them to grow and contribute their gifts for the church and society. The stigmatization of people with disability calls the Church to ask itself what it means, in our time, to be the inclusive community that Jesus proclaimed. As a community of disciples of Jesus Christ, the Church should be a sanctuary, a safe place, a refuge, a shelter for the stigmatized and the excluded. The disciples of Jesus are thus called to work for a church of all and for all.

Celebration of God's Gifts

Ecumenical Disability Advocates Network (EDAN) has drawn the attention that without inclusion of the gifts of persons with disabilities, we cannot talk about the unity of the church. There is no unity of the churches without acknowledging the gifts of persons with disability. All people with or without disabilities are created in the image of God and called to an inclusive community in which they are empowered to use their gifts.

The world will be poorer without the contribution of persons with disabilities. Jesus protected, forgave, loved and cared for them. Jesus strongly disputed the connection between sin and blindness, saying "It was not that this man sin or his parents, but that the works of God might be made manifest in him" (John 9:3). Jesus challenged the Jewish's understanding that God punishes sinners by blinding them or their animals (Ex. 4:11). In Jewish society, a person with a defect in the body was not allowed to come near the Lord's offering (Lev. 21:18-21). The blind and the lame were not allowed to come into the house of the Lord (2 Sam 5:9).

We need to affirm that diversity is an integral part of Creation. Society – from its most basic unit (the family) to its broader forms (the church and the community) – has to be a place where everyone, regardless of gifts and abilities, is genuinely welcomed, given every opportunity to participate meaningfully, and nurtured toward fulfillment. Churches will remain a disabled community without the inclusion of persons with disabilities. We need to work together more rigorously so that our common vision for the establishment of an inclusive, affirming and empowering global society may be realized. Let us strife to create a society and church where everyone, regardless of gifts and ability, is genuinely welcomed, given every opportunity to participate meaningfully, and nurtured towards fulfillment.

---

[19] *Ibid.,* p. 88.
[20] *Ibid.,* p. 40.
[21] Razouselie Lasetso, *op. cit.,* p. 44.

(48) Ethnic Minority Identities in Muslim Contexts in Asia

Joseph Kumar

Dominant cultural groups have through the ages have always exerted authority on minority groups very often detrimental to their well being. At times there has been warfare, conflict and pain unprecedented in nature like in Sri Lanka between the Tamils in the north and the majority Sinhala community. The conflict in South Thailand between the Pattani Malays and the Thai where increasingly death is becoming more common, the Rohingya and the Burmese because the later feels that they are Bangladeshi immigrants and so should not be in the country. In Malaysia it is between the Malays and the rest mainly Chinese and Indians where the Malays assert as masters of the land in relation to the minorities who are crying out for equal citizenship rights. The indigenous (aborigines) people in Australia and marginalization; The Moro in the Philippines and the struggle for self rule; The Han People ideology who make up 90%, assert assimilative policies on minorities like the Uighur and Tibetans in China. Wealthy Chinese descent Indonesians who are mainly Christians desiring to live in harmony in the largest Muslim nation. As vast is Asia so is her diversity. Homogeneity is a quest in many nations where in the last century the demographic landscape in Asia began to change with migration. Once powerful, ethnic, religious or national communities fearing an erosion of dominance and in the light of minorities who have become bold to voice and challenge dominant rule has given rise to conflict.

In some parts of Asia religion exacerbates conflict. In Malaysia the dominant Muslims mainly in the ruling Malay political party to maintain her hegemony on society have created a rumour that Christians who make only 9% of the population are going to take over the country and make this a Christian nation. A siege mentality is created and therefore anything Christian in this country has to be curbed for they have sinister plans. Hence the controversy over the use of the Arabic word 'Allah' is a copyright of Muslims in the country and others are forbidden to use. In Indonesia attempts are being made to ban churches on streets that carry Islamic names. While there is no law of this nature in this country however Islamic fundamentals are enforcing it in some areas. Hindu Fundamentals in India and their continual battle against Muslim and Christian minorities in India openly stating that these are alien religions in Hindu India. The cry of the minorities is real in Asia and our Lord hears and desires the same of the church, i.e. to be sensitive to the cries of the ethnic and religious minorities. What has the church to offer to these communities broken, oppressed and powerless?

Today's new migrant workers are adding to minority discrimination. DDD jobs – dirty, demeaning and dangerous are what new migrant workers do. Domestic workers verbally and sexually abused. Factory workers work long hours with very poor housing and health benefits and very often exploited by agents both by sending and receiving nations. Asia sends out the most migrant workers and is also recipient of the most. Nations like Nepal, Indonesia, Bangladesh, Philippines, Vietnam, Sri Lanka and many other poorer nations send out their citizens to work in Singapore, Malaysia, Hong Kong and other richer nations in Asia. To some of these migrant workers they themselves are exploited and abused by minorities in the receiving nation. As long as unequal development takes place in Asia these new migrant workers concerns would continue to be a reality.

Who is the Majority?

A dominant community usually is presenting the single largest national, ethnic or religious group in relation to smaller communities (minorities) living within a given geographical area. In the Asian context population numbers are important unlike the South African scenario where wealth and power gave the

Anglo Saxons the upper hand in relation to Africans even though they were smaller in number. The majority due to their numbers dominate politics, religion and culture and enjoy greater privileges. A CCA-URM publication on *No Place in the Inn* states that this group use different mechanisms like educational, police, military, judicial and political institutions to maintain hegemony and ensure the continued subjugation of minorities.[1]

Who is the Minority?

The CCA-URM report on *Identity and Justice,* a study on Race and Minority issues, says a minority is "a group of people who, because of their physical or cultural characteristics, are singled out from others in the society in which they live for differential and unequal treatment, and who therefore regard themselves as objects of collective discrimination"[2] Nationalistic origins can also be singled out for discrimination.

For example Malaysia

Malaysia situated just above the equator has natural resources of value and free from natural disasters. The early colonial rulers fully aware of the potential for trade worked at exploiting her resources. Migrant settlers were encouraged from India and China to help develop the rubber and tin industries. China and India were nations experiencing poverty and hence many sailed to Malaya then to work as labourers and as civil servants to mainly serve British capitalistic and administrative needs. The lead up to independence in 1957 brought to the fore a thorny concern and that is ethnicity or racism[3]. The majority Malays who were dominant in this region before the coming of colonial rulers wanted to ensure their rightful place in the nation is ensured by the British when they granted independence. The trade off is that the migrants would be granted citizenship but Malay hegemony would be upheld. As the preservation and dominance of the Malays took prominence the minority Chinese and Indians also began to lobby from an ethnic perspective for their right to stay in Malaya. Political parties were established along ethnic lines with the pure interest of only serving the well interest of a particular community. Hence the journey of the Malaysian people began to view almost all aspects of her well being from the ethnic perspective. Politics, economics, education, social mobility all took on an ethnic perspective. The ethnic divide became entrenched in Malaya. Every segment of Malaysian society has been deeply affected by this ethnic divide. No day passes by without some form of mention in the media for the need to be sensitive to the different ethnic groups in this nation.

Malaysia is a nation of 28 million comprising of 50% Malays, 24% Chinese, 7% Indians and 11% indigenous are the main ethnic groups in the country. The majority community of the Malay time and again reminds the other minority communities especially the Chinese and Indians that they are only in this country at their pleasure. Chinese and Indians are reminded that if they cannot toe the line to fit in the Malay agenda then they should return to their ancestor homes of China and India. This is their land 'Tanah Melayu' (land of the Malays). Chinese and Indian immigrants who came to this nation about hundred years ago are being treated as second class citizens. The minorities believe that there is institutionalized racism. The Malays as rulers enacted laws that enshrined that they were the privileged people of the nation. A quota system was created to ensure that Malays were given priority for education especially in universities

---

[1] CCA – URM *No Place in the Inn: Voices of Minority Peoples in Asia.* Urban Rural Mission – Christian Conference of Asia Tokyo 1979:2-4

[2] CCA – URM *Identity and Justice: Report of an Ad Hoc Meeting on Race and Minority Issues in Asia.* Urban Rural Mission – Christian Conference of Asia, Hong Kong 1977:1-2

[3] Racism and not ethnocentrism is commonly used in the Malaysia to explain differences of the Malaysian people. The author believes that the divide is not biological but cultural accentuated with religion and therefore uses ethnicity. However this paper uses both interchangeably with the same meaning.

(Malay over meritocracy), in the job market where more than 90% of all government staff are Malays; the awarding of all government contracts to Malays; purchase of houses are discounted, business license priority; company employment must be at least 30% Malay even though they may not be qualified. The list is endless.

Systemic discrimination became the norm where the citizens are not treated equally. Ethnic issues are over political power and the material benefits that flow from it. Harold Crouch a political analyst says "The ethnic group that wins political power is likely to use it in the interests of its own constituents. Ethnic leaders will use political power to ensure that their group gets privileged access to bureaucratic appointments, commercial opportunities and higher education" He goes on to even state that projects carried out in the constituency would be disproportionate[4]. Marginalized groups would actually have to go up against the system that is discriminatory. A communally divided society has to struggle with cultural distinctiveness. Crouch says cultural perceptions are far less susceptible to bargaining and compromise[5]. What brand of bread should I buy? Which petrol or diesel is good for my car? What is my choice – Coca Cola or Pepsi? Which bank should I save my money? Simple choices have turned ugly where tribalism rules. Chinese and Indians are encouraged not to patronize products belonging to Malays and likewise the Malays under the guise of religion (halal) want to ensure that they do not buy non Malay products.

Creation of cultural islands is the outcome of the Malaysian reality. Segregation is the norm. Schooling, play, employment, housing and even worship carry a strong ethnic flavor. Modern Malaya is plagued with communalism. New parties are created jostling among the already many to champion the cause of an ethnic group. The preservation and survival of an ethnic group rests within. The ethnic divide has affected the psyche of the Malaysian people that everything is monochrome.

Reaction of communities to the Malay agenda has tremendous implication to the Malaysian people. Indians who feel greatly affected by discriminative policies of the Malays has seen their wealth equity in the nation reduced to 1.5%. Dialogue was no more affective and disillusioned with the political party serving their interests took their grouses to the streets of Kuala Lumpur. In 2008 more than 30,000 Indians rallied against the government in regards discriminative policies favouring the Malays. The Indians feel marginalized. This marginalization has resulted in many of the young engaged in crime. However the Chinese continue to engage in dialogue to preserve their interests. All efforts by the government to reverse discriminative policies are not bearing fruits.

Theological Framework

(a) Human dignity

Dignity is a central theme for communities who are marginalized or oppressed. Equality disparities in society are an issue of dignity and compounded further amongst minorities. Juergen Moltmann in his work *On Human Dignity* says that dignity is given by the Creator when God made humans in His image, and for this dignity to be fully realized there is a need to exercise human rights. He says,

> Human dignity…requires human rights for its embodiment, protection, and full flowering. Human rights are the concrete, indefeasible claim of human dignity. Without human rights, human dignity cannot be historically realized in action.[6]

[4] Harold Crouch *Government and Society in Malaysia* London Cornell University Press 1996:155
[5] Crouch 1996:156
[6] Jurgen Moltmann *On Human Dignity* London SCM Press 1984:x-ix

If human rights are founded on men and women made in the image of God then the missiological task of the church is to stand for the right of all people for in that process there is a declaration that all are one, that all humanity is an expression of the one almighty God. Kayle Haselden states adds that each person must be accorded respect and dignity and equal status not because he is an image bearer but the fact God made all humans. Every aspect of goodness in all humanity is invariably tied up to the creator. "Man's dignity is conferred upon him; his worth is bestowed"[7]. All humans are special, unique and sacred because of God the creator. He goes on to state that if we deny the worth in one person this is to deny worth to all. Even the worst in a person does not negate the worth God the Father grants to a person. Therefore he says that

> …the sacredness, the infinite worth, of individual personality has nothing to do with culture or intellect or colour or race or morality or faith; but it has to with God, with the God who in His will and wisdom created all men in His image and destined them for His likeness[8].

If every person recognizes this worth then the capacity for love, respect, dignity and the equality which is so needed amongst humans would be a reality. Forrester states that today's generation "want to be respected and recognized for what they are, in their difference and distinctiveness…They do not want to set aside as of no importance their religious beliefs, their personal and family history, their 'embeddedness' in a particular time, and place, and culture and community shaped by a particular story"[9]. Charles Taylor on his politics of equal dignity says

> "Non-recognition or misrecognition…can be a form of oppression, imprisoning someone in a false, distorted, reduced mode of being. Beyond simple lack of respect, it can inflict a grievous wound, saddling people with crippling self-hatred. Due recognition is not just a courtesy but a vital human need."[10]

All of us are created in God's image having Adam as the progenitor of humans. There is an ontological bond with every person irrespective of human constructs of race, ethnicity, or nationalism. This reality established in Christ needs to be celebrated, not tribalism or nationalism which very often is the case now.

(b) Christian identity

Humans are fallen creatures; they need to be restored, renewed? Without Christ there is no hope for any change. Jesus Christ is the image of God (Col 1:15). He personifies God's image – par excellence. Jesus is the revelation of all what God is. He mirrors in its fullness who and what the Father is. In Christ we begin the process of change of being sanctified. In Christ we begin to see the common descent of all humanity, the capacity to love the different other because he/she is a reflection of the image of God though distorted. More so as Christ gave his life for all humanity we take on his likeness in living for others. We use our God given endowments for the well being of humanity. The glory of the Father once again begins to reflect through humanity. This is the identity that all must cherish. This is Christian Identity that, which comes from outside of us (humankind) as was bestowed in the beginning, now is being restored through the second Adam – Jesus Christ.

---

[7] Kyle Haselden *The Racial Problem in Christian Perspective* Harper Torchbooks New York Harper and Row Publisher 1964:170

[8] Ibid 172

[9] Duncan B. Forrester *On Human Worth: A Christian Vindication of Equality* London SCM Press 2001:40-41

[10] Ibid 42

> Human identity…is essentially constituted by its relationship to God as the creature, reconciled sinner and glorified child of God. Who we are is determined in and through this relationship, and on this basis of this identity we are called to relate to others…. [11]

Where Christian identity needs to be at the fore Miroslav Volf, a Croatian theologian, states that "tribal identity is today asserting as a powerful force, especially in cases where cultural heterogeneity is combined with extreme imbalances of power and wealth"[12]. People are more interested in expressing tribal affiliations than even national affiliations, while the only truth is that all are made in the image of God. He says tribal identity today is the only remedy left in a world where the dehumanizing of people is a growing reality. People feel secure in their culture-in-group. Segregation becomes the chosen way; cultural islands in urbanized centers present the human way to cope with imbalances of society especially for those who lack advocacy and economic power. Where the Christian faith has not been able to break boundaries erected by communities there is need of a critical assessment of the Christian faith if inroads are to be made in changing communities.

Volf's assessment is that tribalism would be a permanent feature of human relationship; therefore in his seminal work *Exclusion and Embrace* he does share about the possibilities of reducing tribal conflicts. His work on creating the right social agents against social arrangements comes about because there are not enough social agents to sustain social arrangements. He says that there is a dire need "of social agents capable of envisioning and creating just, truthful, and peaceful societies, and on shaping a cultural climate in which such agents will thrive."[13] These statements indicate the sad state of the empirical church. The church is the place where people come and have the dark recesses of life addressed and not covered. The concept of "Christ above culture" uses culture as a vehicle to bring the Good News. In reality we see culture deified and Christ taking only a functional role. Globalization has accelerated the need of cultural groups to preserve their human heritage. The danger is that in so doing we are slowly pushing the transcendent God of all culture to the periphery. Volf has raised a crucial concern with regard to Christians faith. There can be no social agents when belief does not transmute into changed realities. This arises partly from a truncated understanding of the doctrine of humanity.

(c) The welcoming of strangers

In Exodus 12:40-49 the Passover is celebrated to commemorate the liberation of the people of God from Egypt. Two Hebrew words are used to indicate the presence of outsiders within the Israelite community. The Hebrew word *Gerim* is translated as sojourners or foreigners who have accepted Yahweh, meaning that they must now have been circumcised. They were being assimilated into the Hebrew way of life. The Hebrew word *Nokrim* are also termed as foreigners but refers to those who have not assimilated into the Hebrew way, meaning that they were yet to be circumcised. All those in the *gerim* category are accorded equal status with the Israelites[14]. Frank Cruesemann says that *gerim* are people who neither had family or land and vulnerable and therefore God enacted laws that sought the well being of these people[15]. Exodus 23:9 says, "You know the heart of the stranger, for you were strangers in the land of Egypt." Exodus 22:20

---

[11] J. Daniel Hays *From Every People and Nation: A Biblical Theology of Race. New Studies in Biblical Theology Series* Illinois Inter Varsity Press

[12] Miroslav Volf *Exclusion and Embrace: A Theological Exploration of Identity, Otherness, and Reconciliation* New York Abingdon Press 1997:20

[13] Ibid 21

[14] R. Marin-Achard *Gur* in E. Jeeni and C. Westermann eds. Theological Lexicon of the Old Testament Peabody, Mass. Hendrickson1995:307-309

[15] Dietmar Mieth and Lisa Sowle Cahill Ed *Migrants and Refugees* London SCM Press 1984:102

"You shall not wrong a stranger or oppress him, for you were (yourselves) strangers in the land of Egypt." "You shall have one law for the stranger and for the native; for I am Yahweh, your God" (Lev 24:22 NIV).

The underlying theological presupposition is that God is compassionate and gracious (Ex 22:27). The Israelites know what it means to be refugees, landless and dependent on the well being of others. Scripture is telling us that we should not forget who we were, and as a recipient of God's heavenly grace, be also gracious to those in need especially the landless, and displaced. Strangers who came into contact with the Israelite community were given respect, dignity and privileges normally accorded to the Hebrews. Strangers were definitely warmed to these laws that embraced and also included them into the larger community. No one was discriminated because of ethnicity, colour or nationalism. These were laws that were winsome. Israel by her character was different from the other nations around her. God through Israel as a community was reaching out to all especially to those who came into contact with the Israelite community.

Attractiveness

How attractive is the Church as the agent of hope and new life to a nation fragmented? The Church is the paradigmatic community of what it means that Jesus came to give humanity fullness of life.[16] The Church as a community reflecting the attributes of God is imperative if she wants to engage meaningfully in the brokenness of humanity. Two models for the mission of the church are espoused. The centripetal model is the church that attracts. Often this is stated to be the Old Testament model. Israel is the light to the nations. She struggled to understand mission as going out as seen in the Jonah narrative. Rather she was very open to people from all tribes and nations joining this community subject to fulfilling all her religious regulations. In contrast the New Testament model for mission is centrifugal which means to go. Often the Church is made to understand that she must go and that is credible Christian witness whilst whether she is an image bearer of Christ is overshadowed by the later. However both these models need be incorporated in the mission of the Church. The image of the Church and her acts of compassion must be complimentary. The centripetal model of the church must always be kept in tension in relation to the church going out into the world. The Church as a community consisting of those who are followers of the Lord Jesus is imbued with Godly nature and therefore is called upon to exemplify this as she relates with all of His creation. Peace and security must be imbibed within the people of God for the Church to bring hope and new life to all. It is the church that is learning to deal with her own diversity becomes the model for community to respond appropriately. This is her evangelistic task.

However the sad reality often is that the church has also been deeply affected by the anomalies of the nation. Dominant cultures tend to exert their rights over minorities. Duncan Forrester in his work on the church as the egalitarian community says that "the church has been deeply penetrated and corrupted by the inequalities and divisions of the world. It has absorbed much of this into its own structures and ways of working. It reflects and reinforces divisions and inequalities....".[17] What Forrester says in a way explains why the church is slow to respond to brokenness in community because within her borders there is pain. Within the structure of the church ethnocentrism thrives.

Critical Investigation

There is a great need by individuals and ecclesial communities to search their hearts for sin especially in regards the different other. "Search me, God and know my heart; test me and know my anxious thoughts.

[16] John 10:30a

[17] Duncan B. Forrester *On Human Worth: A Christian Vindication of Equality*. SCM Press London 2001 198

See if there is any offensive way in me and lead me in the way everlasting." (Psalm 139:23-24, NIV). A deep critical investigation would help in the processes for change to allow the Holy Spirit to reveal anomalies in how we relate with others. There is also the need for boldness to acknowledge these mistakes and to make open confession and a cry for repentance. Unless the Christian community is engaged in these processes then healing and reconciliation is a reality hoped for. Theo Tschuy states in Ethnic Conflict and Religion that there are 'dark recesses' in Christian belief. He states that churches have a 'pious declaration' but are not moved or have the capacity (theological framework) to engage in the brokenness and hurts of humans. He says that if Christianity wishes to shake off its ambivalence and become a truly prophetic instrument in God's hand, it must engage in a credible self-examination which acknowledges its disobedience and spells out its multiple forms of complicity.[18] Chris P. Price interviewed by *Christianity Today* says that our theology should interrogate our lives.

> The theology that undergirds community is opening our lives up to be interrogated by the Sermon on the Mount. That defines what it means to be a church that follows Jesus Christ faithfully. Allowing ourselves to study Scripture without justifying the way our lives already exist and allowing ourselves to go on a journey whereby we will be interrupted. And to be listening together in friendship with others for those interruptions. [19]

The church must acknowledge that apathy and failure to respond to injustices is tantamount to sin.

Dissent

'The accepted norm or spiritual authority is not to be challenged and if there was difficulty just let it be.' Most evangelical and charismatic churches espouse this perceived ideal. This is generally the theological stance of many churches in Asia. Fear is instilled on proponents of the faith that any dissent would be judged and the dissenter may come under a curse. Church polity, leadership and governance are therefore not challenged which results in the church becoming complacent. Power abuse is the result. Dissenting voices must be encouraged, allowed and seen in a positive perspective. Checks and balances must be in place within the body of Christ for it to mature and grow into Christ likeness which in turn empowers her ministry to the world. Jesus Christ is the dissenting voice that challenged the norms or spirituality established by the Scribes, Sadducees and more so the Pharisees. He created the new order of hope and new life that is a reality for all generations.

The Church because of her uniqueness is to become a model that represents and portrays the liberating acts of God, i.e. a God who unites all people irrespective of race/ethnicity, creed or class. Peace and security should be an experienced reality in the Church for all ethnic and minority groups. The church embodies and personifies that hope and lives in hope for that new reality where all would be granted dignity and treated justly. No one person is slighted, where the egalitarian status of the church is not only confessed but lived. The peoples of each nation come to table knowing that they are respected as coequal, that all communities be included and embraced. Then the Church becomes a living symbol where tribal, national or religious identities are not erased, but appreciated respected and enjoyed. In the cross of Christ they are a non entity. The Church as community which is learning to deal and appreciate her diversity is the unspoken witness to communities that have been deeply divided because of the different other.

---

[18] Theo Tschuy, *Ethnic Conflict and Religion: Challenge to the Churches*. WCC Publications Geneva 1997. 140
[19] Christ P. Price Theology Should Interrogate Our Lives www.christianitytoday.com/ct/2002/147/ 12-4-2002

Dialogue

Minority concerns have to come to the table within the church as well as in society. They have to be talked about positively with the view to aid. The concerns of minorities must not be feared but boldly addressed. Boldly means not only to face and address unjust realities but also their implication for the very understanding of the Gospel which is equally challenging. Minority concerns thus move from the periphery to the center in the life of the church. Discrimination prejudices and stereotyping has to end within the local church. It needs the voice and hands of the total Christian fraternity in the nation. The dominant culture within the Christian community must become cognizant of the imbalances in society especially in respect of minorities. The dominant culture within the church has to confront challenges from minority groups within her fold. Weaker cultural communities need the assistance of all especially from larger and stronger cultural groups. The ecclesial community should be committed to assist minorities in their struggle for justice.

Dominant cultures within the community need to be sensitive to limitations and struggles of minorities. Their voice must be heard and they must be granted opportunities for leadership. The onus is on the dominant culture to ensure that minorities are included in all conversations. Minorities fear that their identity, expressions would be usurped by the dominant culture. Minorities already perceive a slow erosion of their identities when language and cultural expression are curbed. Therefore dominant cultures within the church need to be assuring that the distinctiveness of minorities will always be preserved, respected and embraced. 'Just follow the majority' is the easier dictum, but the Christian response to minority issues is the greater the more it becomes engaged for the weaker parts in society. Christians stand in solidarity with communities which have experiences being hurt not only within her Christian fold but also with those outside. The nurturing community learns to address imbalances within her fold and through these experiences she is equipped to take on larger challenges of community.

A democratic system poses challenges to minorities. It is easier for dominant groups because of their numbers they tend to rule. All decisions because of the democratic process can work in their favor and legally right. However is there justice? It is therefore important that dominant communities work under an inclusive agenda. The fundamental rights of equality, justice and expression should also be accorded to minorities. Minorities must be a part of general society and not apart.

Intermarriages

Cross Cultural marriages blurs ethnicity and nationalism. This exogamic reality is not to kill diversity but is about remapping the borders and understanding of cultural identity. It broadens the concept of diversity and tribalism. Miscegenation definitely helps to reduce the ethnic divide. Intermarriages and the children from such family unions normally have a better cross-cultural ethos. They are normally accepted in both cultural settings. While the church cannot be a broker for cross cultural marriages however she can be a bridge for culturally different people to meet in positive settings. She must present same faith intermarriages positively and be an intermediary in adverse situations. The church has to develop positive structures for people to meet.

Coming together for worship

Worship is a spiritual exercise and instills within us a deeper sense of purpose in coming together. When worship is devoid of community then that worship is truncated. Most of the worship today in the church divorces itself from realities of the people especially with regard to integration. When there is a sense of clear purpose then this intent is realized in combined worship gatherings. In a spiritual atmosphere the gathering community learn and see the different other in the light of the cross. Worshipping together is a powerful means to integrate communities. As in the Book of Revelation when from all tribes and people groups gather at the feet of the Lamb and worship Him, today's worshipping community must mirror that reality. It is a foretaste of all things which the people of God will experience in its fullness. In the ensuing interaction, inhibitions, stereotyping or any negative perception of the different other is better understood. It becomes a spiritual exercise to repent and remove all social constructs of the different other that are detrimental for harmonious relationship.

Conclusion

The empirical church must put its house in order addressing its truncated constructs of theology, church polity and piety and only then does her mission becomes a force to be reckoned with. Egalitarianism by itself is not enough, for the church to be a force, she needs to address aspects of injustice and to work towards reconciliation and these virtuous acts of piety are winsome. Racism and ethno-centrism must be purged first from the life of the church for it is sin and denies our identity as children of God. Our faith in God transmutes into change in living social realities and it is not the social gospel but the gospel as God in his son Jesus Christ fully intended. Forrester says if the church is to be in any real sense an exemplary community, a community which demonstrates the possibilities and the blessings of loving fellowship, it must take very seriously in its own life the message and the principles it offers to the world.[20] The Church needs to keep this reality in the centre as it is not pious statements or creeds that are going to make her but her acts. The church is a body that enlivens the gospel and that is her ultimate witness.

Bibliography

CCA – URM, *No Place in the Inn: Voices of Minority Peoples in Asia.* Urban Rural Mission – Christian Conference of Asia Tokyo 1979

CCA – URM, *Identity and Justice: Report of an Ad Hoc Meeting on Race and Minority Issues in Asia.* Urban Rural Mission – Christian Conference of Asia, Hong Kong 1977

Harold Crouch, *Government and Society in Malaysia* London Cornell University Press 1996

Duncan B. Forrester, *On Human Worth: A Christian Vindication of Equality* London SCM Press 2001

J. Daniel Hays, *From Every People and Nation: A Biblical Theology of Race. New Studies in Biblical Theology Series* Illinois Inter Varsity Press

Kyle Haselden, *The Racial Problem in Christian Perspective* Harper Torchbooks New York Harper and Row Publisher 1964

R. Marin-Achard, Art. *Ger* in E. Jeeni and C. Westermann eds. Theological Lexicon of the Old Testament Peabody, Mass. Hendrickson1995

Dietmar Mieth and Lisa Sowle Cahill Ed, *Migrants and Refugees* London SCM Press 1984

Juergen Moltmann, *On Human Dignity.* London SCM Press 1984

Theo Tschuy, *Ethnic Conflict and Religion: Challenge to the Churches.* WCC Publications Geneva 1997

Miroslav Volf, *Exclusion and Embrace: A Theological Exploration of Identity, Otherness, and Reconciliation* New York Abingdon Press 1997

[20] Duncan Forrester *On Human Worth: A Christian Vindication of Equality*, London: SCM Press 2001:199

(49) Migration and Migrants as an Ecumenical Challenge in Asia

Chung Sook-Ja

As a Korean feminist theologian who was born and raised in Japan and has been living in Korea for 50 years, migration is not only personally related but also socially and economically imbedded in my whole life. This paper, originally based on my almost 16 years of experience at the Namyangju Women's Center for Migrant Workers in Korea, has been broadened to include migration concerns in Asia.

Labor Migration in an Era of Globalization

International labor migration is an intrinsic feature of globalization. All countries are affected whether as sending, transit, or receiving countries, or a combination of any of these. Two basic reasons for labor migration are relief from domestic unemployment and the interest to earn foreign exchange. In the Philippines, for example, overseas migration has become a pair of crutches, easing unemployment and generating foreign income to fuel the faltering economy. Indeed, it has become a safety valve for domestic unemployment and the aspirations of educated workers for higher wages.[1]

Migration results from poverty and the wide economic gap between developed and undeveloped countries. This gap also produces relational discrimination between the powerful rich and the weak poor. Although migrants may appear to be the least, weak, poor, oppressed, marginalized and discriminated against, they are the real life givers to both the receiving and sending countries. It is through them that the sending and receiving countries prosper and develop.

Piyasiri Wickramasekera, a former senior migration specialist at the International Migration Program of the International Labor Organization, suggested a way to avoid discriminatory language when talking about labor migration and migrants. He suggested using "sending and receiving labor countries" instead of "sending and receiving countries", "regular and irregular migration" instead of "legal and illegal migration" or "documented and undocumented migration", and "female domestic workers" instead of "house maids", etc.[2] Sometimes, however, I use the terminology used in the Korean translation.

In terms of migration trends, some traditional labor-sending countries have continued to be mainly labor-sending, e.g. the Philippines and Sri Lanka. But as a result of fast growth, a few countries have moved from being labor-sending to labor-receiving. For example, Korea moved from labor-sending in the early 1980s to labor-receiving by the end of the same decade. Thailand became a net receiver of labor since the early 1990s even as it also sends migrants abroad. International labor migration is insignificant for India and China in relation to their population or labor force. Yet states such as Kerala in India have relied on overseas labor migration for a considerable time. The feminization of migration has also been a noticeable trend, with an increasing number of female migrant workers settling for low-paid domestic work compared to construction work. Hong Kong and Singapore represent the major destinations for Asian women domestic workers while Japan represents the major destination for Asian women entertainers. Women migrants are among the most vulnerable groups in all countries.[3]

---

[1] Piyasiri Wickramasekara, "Asian Labour Migration: Issues and Challenges in an Era of Globalization," accessed on 20 October 2012 at http://www.ilo.org/public/english/protection/migrant/download/imp/imp57e.pdf.
[2] *Ibid.*
[3] *Ibid.*

United Nations Convention on Migrants' Rights

On 1 July 2003, the International Convention on the Protection of the Rights of All Migrant Workers and Members of their Families entered into force, following the signing by 20 ratifying states.[4] It is a comprehensive international treaty for the protection of migrant workers' rights and their families, emphasizing the connection between migration and human rights. The Convention is based on the principle of equal rights and human rights of all human beings. Migrants have their basic human rights not only as workers but also as human beings. These include freedom from inhumane living and working conditions, physical and sexual abuse, and degrading treatment; freedom of thought, expression and religion; access to information on their rights; right to legal equality; access to educational and social services; and right to participate in trade unions.[5]

However, in the system of capitalism and globalization, labor is treated as a form of capital for the benefit of the company or country. To increase their benefits, companies and countries often ignore migrants' human rights; instead, they abuse the workers verbally and physically to control them. As the population of migrants has enormously increased, so have issues of human rights violations. In fact, many labor receiving countries did not ratify the Convention.

Some Experiences of Labor Migration

From the Korean experience, migrants can be grouped into three. One group is the regular migrants under the Employment Permit System (EPS) of the Korean Labor Law, with regular employment visa. Although regular migrants are legally free to go anywhere in Korea, they often do not have the right to find, select, or decide on their work places. Under the EPS, only the employer has the right to select and decide on migrant workers. Very often, the migrants' work experiences, education and special skills are often ignored.[6] There is no way for them to leave the factories without the owners' permission. Moreover, they can't do much unless they know the Korean language and the places in Korea.

Another group consists of the migrant women who come to Korea to marry Korean men under the international marriage program. Many of them are recruited from the Philippines, Vietnam, China, Indonesia, etc. by international marriage-making brokers and through the Korean religion of Unification. Recruited in groups, they are made to undergo a mass wedding ceremony in Korea. Unfortunately, many of them end up living miserable lives because of several reasons: they hardly know their husbands; usually their husbands are much older and too poor to support their families back home; and they cannot easily get a permanent visa. Often, these migrant women's lives are worse than the workers under the EPS. Many of them may have come to Korea with dreams, only to find themselves in a life of slavery. They usually have no opportunity of redress because of language barriers, lack of money or lack of a place to go and to ask for help. Many of these women have suffered from many kinds of violation at the hands of their husbands and other family members such as brothers-in law.

Still another group is the group of irregular (or undocumented) migrant workers with no legal visa. Many of them come to Korea through the trainee system[7], the EPS, or as tourists, and remain in Korea after their visas expire. They include those who are over-stayers on tourist visa and are engaged in work,

---

[4] United Nations Educational, Scientific and Cultural Organization, *United Nations Convention on Migrants' Rights* (Paris: UNESCO, 2005) accessed on 20 October 2012 at http://unesdoc.unesco.org/images/0014/001435/143557e.pdf

[5] *Ibid.*

[6] Namyangju Women's Center for Migrant Workers is located near furniture manufacturing companies (more than 300 companies in the area). Those hired in the stone-bed making company have to move the stones with their whole body. This is a really dangerous and difficult work for the migrants.

[7] The trainee system became a way of getting cheap labor and exploiting them. Trainees worked just as much as Korean regular workers, for just one-third of the salary.

students engaged in employment, or trainees overstaying their visas. Regular migrants who continue beyond their contract period or are running away from their designated employers and persons trafficked into the sex industry may end up as irregular migrant workers. Although they came to Korea with a legal status, some might become victims of deceit by factory owners who do not honor the contract (e.g. on working time, monthly salary and overtime pay and holidays). This is why many migrant workers under the trainee system have given up their visa status and became irregular workers: they would rather work in other factories which would give higher salary and provide better working conditions even if their own security is at stake. Since some of them have stayed in Korea for over 20 years, they are usually welcomed by furniture manufacturing factories because they can communicate in Korean and have better skills. Also, because of their irregular status, factories do not have to be responsible for the '4 great insurances' (employment, industrial disaster, pension, and medical).

Related to migration is the trafficking of persons, which is the recruitment, transportation, harboring or receipt of persons by means of threat, force, or other forms of coercion or deception for purposes of exploitation. Traffickers are those who transport migrants and profit economically or otherwise from their relocation. Trafficking of human beings has been recognized as a gross human rights violation.

Migration and Ecumenism in the Korean Context

Almost all migrants who come to Korea speak of their desire to help their parents, brothers, sisters and children back in their home countries. Even though they come from countries of different cultures and religions, they try to learn Korean language, adjust to Korean weather, taste Korean food and accept Korean culture, because they want to live and work in Korea. They dare to overcome all kinds of barriers so that they can stay in Korea because they want to support their families and enable their children to study in college to overcome poverty in the future. Thus, migrants have learned and lived the way of crossing barriers of nationalism and cultural and religious differences.

The majority of the migrant workers in the Namyangju area are Filipinos and Bangladeshis. Almost all Filipino migrant workers are Catholic and they regard infant baptism to be very important. Many Filipino couples have asked for their babies born in Korea to be baptized even though the Women's Center for Migrant Workers is not related to the Catholic Church. Then they take their babies to be reared by the family of either father or mother in the Philippines while they continue working in Korea. So while in Korea, they often become members of the Women's Center and the Migrant Women Church.[8]

The Bangladeshi migrant workers around the area also come to the Center and become members as they avail of the center's services, e.g. counseling and advice especially for some of their issues such as unpaid salaries and retirement fees, and the night school where they learn Korean language, computer, music and the Bible.[9] Being Muslims, they do not attend the worship at the center but they have their own worship times in their rooms. This is where wider ecumenism is at work: while the Filipino and Bangladeshi migrant workers cannot come together on religious matters, they help each other overcome the issues they face in their work and life in Korea. Migrants and migrant workers are surely members of the Household of God even though they may follow different religions. They have the heart to rise above the suffering, to be responsible toward their extended families and to produce life through their own bodies. They know how to forgive, to share, to take care of each other, to love their neighbors, and to build an egalitarian society in this world.

---

[8] Namyangju Women's Center for Migrant Workers was founded by the writer, a Presbyterian pastor, and her partner, a pastor of the United Church of Canada in 1997; the Migrant Women Church was established in the Center in 2005.

[9] The night school, starting from 8:00 pm, was started by the Center in 2002 to protect women migrant workers from crimes, which often occurred in Filipino communities.

If it is true that "Ecumenism is the promotion of unity or cooperation between distinct religious groups or denominations of Christianity[10],"it might equally be true that 'ecumenism is the action of learning and accepting other cultures and creating peace with other people for life.' If so, these migrant workers are living ecumenically every day.

Migration and Theology

The Bible uses "Kingdom of God" for the new community. But I would like to use "Household of God", as suggested by feminist theologian Letty M. Russell who said:

> I want to argue that it is possible to begin with the biblical understanding of God's oikonomia, or householding of the whole earth, and thus be able to describe the exercise of authority in both the private and the public realms as a participation in God's householding and partnering activity. [11]

The "Household of God" as the new community is the community of the oppressed, the poor, and the discriminated against, such as the migrant women/workers. Indeed, migrants are important members in God's oikonomia, the household of God. This is why migration is an ecumenical challenge in Asia.

The Bible has many stories of migration which happened for the main reason of survival, including marriage, escaping from a brother's anger or jealousy, famine, etc. One such story is of Jacob and Esau (Genesis 27). According to the Jewish law, Jacob as the younger son had no birthright to receive his father's blessing. In order to get his father's blessing he made a deal with his brother and deceived his father. As a result, he had to migrate to his uncle's house to escape from his elder brother's anger. There he had to work for his uncle Laban for 14 years to marry two wives, Leah and Rachel, and two concubines. Then he had 12 sons.

According to the Old Testament understanding of blessing, Jacob was the most blessed man in the Bible. His blessing was the result of his life of migration. These issues are similar to the reality of today's migrant workers – i.e. the quest for security in life, better life in another country through labor migration, and the possibility to raise children. Through international marriage migration, Korea can also increase its population.

More migration issues are found in the story of Joseph, the 11th son of Jacob (Genesis 37:1-50:26). Due to his older brothers' jealousy, Joseph was sold to someone from Egypt. However, after interpreting the Pharaoh's dream, he was made governor over the land of Egypt and, through him, all Jacob's family could move to Egypt and survive the famine. The Bible tells the story as if God prepared the survival of Israelites in Egypt. The book of Exodus (chapters 1-15) tells about the growth of the migrants in Egypt, and also the increase in their oppression because of their large population.

The stories in Genesis and Exodus give us many insights into migration. First, migration is a way for people's survival. Second, migrants are often used as tools for the prosperity of the receiving countries. Third, migrants are expelled after finishing their duty. Fourth, if migrants continue to stay in the receiving countries, they should become servants or slaves for the masters of the receiving countries. Fifth, there is no negotiation between migrants and the masters without fighting. Sixth, the living God who created heaven and earth always stands on the side of the oppressed, in this case, the migrants.

Jesus also became a migrant, escaping from Herod's anger right after he was born (Matthew 2:13-23). Abraham was a migrant who obeyed God by faith (Hebrews 11:8~12). Today, migrants are among the most oppressed and the least in the world. Yet, it is God who lives in the lives of the oppressed and the least, loving strangers such as migrants (Deuteronomy 10: 17~19).

---

[10] Ecumenism – Wikipedia, the free encyclopedia. http://wikipedia.org/wiki/Ecumenism.
[11] Letty M. Russell, *Household of Freedom: Authority in Feminist Theology* (Philadelphia: Westminster, 1987), 82-85.

Conclusion

Migration is important for the poor as it gives them an opportunity to start their new lives in new places. Migration is needed for the oppressed to be free and for a new community to be created. Migration can help to bring understanding between nations. Migration can lead to acceptance of different cultures, different religions and different languages. Migration can mix colors and blood. Migration can help us to actualize wider ecumenism in this world.

However, migration also creates separation of families, classism between haves and have-nots, nationalism and racism, etc. Under these conditions, migrants suffer from discrimination, injustice, loss of their rights and dignity. In such a situation, migrants dream of a better world where there is peace, justice and equality. This dream has been put into a song which is now sung by migrant workers who attend the Namyangju Women's Center for Migrant Workers:

> Although we are migrant workers now, our dream is to create an equal society,
> Where all the people have their daily food, all the children study as their talents,
> Society of working, sharing, and creating together,
> Society without nationalism, classism, and sexism,
> Society with love and justice,
> Our dream is to create such an equal society.[12]

Bibliography

Russell, Letty M. *Household of Freedom: Authority in Feminist Theology.* Philadelphia: Westminster, 1987.

United Nations Educational, Scientific and Cultural Organization, *United Nations Convention on Migrants' Rights* (Paris: UNESCO, 2005) accessed on 20 October 2012 at http://unesdoc.unesco.org/images/0014/001435/143557e.pdf

Wickramasekara, Piyasiri. "Asian Labour Migration: Issues and Challenges in an Era of Globalization," accessed on 20 October 2012 at http://www.ilo.org/public/english/protection/migrant/download/imp/imp57e.pdf

---

[12] Words by Chung Sook Ja, director of the Namyangju Women's Center for Migrant Workers, while music was added by Kim Kyung Eui, her daughter who is also a co-worker of the Center. This song has been sung in Korean by migrant workers especially when there are demonstrations about migrants' human rights.

PART V

CHURCHES TOGETHER IN GOD'S MISSION – MAPPING ASIAN ECUMENISM

(50) Churches Together in God's Mission – Aotearoa New Zealand

Michael Wallace

Since the 19th century Christians in Aotearoa have worked together on various projects. Aotearoa was one of the first countries in the world to form a National Council of Churches,[1] then close it and form a new style of ecumenical body which subsequently closed. The seeming failure of conciliar ecumenism in Aotearoa coexists with profound ecumenical co-operation.

1. Early Days of Ecumenism

Since Christianity arrived in Aotearoa, there has been a mixture of co-operation and suspicion between Christians of different traditions. Anglican missionaries arrived in 1814[2] followed by Methodists in 1822[3] and Roman Catholics in 1838.[4] While Methodists and Anglicans sometimes collaborated, at other times there was competition and ill-will. Relationships between the French Roman Catholics and British Anglicans and Methodists were complicated by the colonial ambitions of their respective countries.

Following the signing of the Treaty of Waitangi in 1840 by Maori chiefs and the British crown, immigration caused the non-Maori population to increase rapidly, quickly overtaking the Maori population.

Presbyterians arrived as a settler church in 1840; other denominations were established from the 1850s onward. With the settlers came the denominational divisions and tensions of Europe. Relationships between Roman Catholics and Protestants were difficult for many decades, in part influenced by conflict between the British government and the people of Ireland.

Over the 19th century, Christianity became the dominant faith in Aotearoa, with Anglicans in the majority in most places,[5] Presbyterians as the second largest group nationally, followed by Roman Catholics and Methodists.[6]

2. Early Ecumenical Projects

Ecumenical collaboration in the later 19th century included social service[7] and moral campaigns.[8] In 1877 education of children became free, secular and compulsory. As a result, Protestant churches co-operated to provide religious instruction in state schools.[9]

---

[1] The Federal Council of Churches of Christ in the US formed in 1908 was the first.

[2] Rev. Samuel Marsden (1765 – 1838) of the Church Missionary Society is believed to have preached the first sermon in Aotearoa at Oihi Bay, Bay of Islands on Christmas Day 1814.

[3] Rev. Samuel Leigh established the first Wesleyan mission station in Whangaroa, Northland in 1823.

[4] The French Marist Bishop Baptiste François Pompallier (1802 – 1871) arrived in the Hokianga in January 1838.

[5] Except in the south of the South Island where Scottish Presbyterians were the majority and some areas were Roman Catholics were in the majority.

[6] This pattern held until the 1996 Census when Romans Catholics overtook Presbyterians as the second largest denimination.

[7] 'Female refuges (homes for reforming prostitutes rather than sheltering battered women) were established on an interdenominational basis from the mid-1860s', *The Anglican Care Network Information Kit*, Anglican Care, no date.

[8] Such as keeping the Sabbath holy.

[9] The Churches' Education Commission (and its predecessor organisations) has provided Christian religious education in state schools for over 100 years. The Commission is currently made up of 16 denominations; the Roman Catholic Church has observer status.

In the 19th and 20th centuries parts of the Protestant churches worked together on prohibition of alcohol. The Christian Women's Temperance Union was a powerful ecumenical organisation which arose as a leader of the prohibition movement and in the movement for women's suffrage. In 1893, New Zealand became the first country in the world where women could vote, in large part due to the collaboration of women from different Christian traditions.

3. Expressions of Ecumenism

(a) Youth movements

Young people's movements were crucial for introducing New Zealanders to ecumenical co-operation. The first YMCA branch in Aotearoa was started in 1855 and the first YWCA branch in 1878. The Student Christian Movement was established in New Zealand in 1896 by John R.Mott. These youth movements, especially the SCM were to be important places for ecumenical learning and incubators for ecumenical leaders.

(b) Church union scheme

Following the successful union of two Presbyterian denominations in 1901, a wider union of churches was proposed. Presbyterians, Congregationalists and Methodists conversed for several decades until the three denominations established a Joint Standing Committee in 1951 to pursue unity talks.

A draft basis for union was drawn up by the three churches and the Associated Churches of Christ in 1962. The draft was superceded in 1964 when the Anglicans joined the negotiations. However the Anglican General Synod rejected the Plan for Union in 1976 and the other churches did not pursue the previous draft basis for union.

In spite of the rejection of the Plan, joint parishes involving the five churches which had been part of unity talks continued to be established. In 1984 the five negotiating churches[10] reaffirmed their commitment to unity and formed the Negotiating Churches Unity Council. The Forum of Co-operative Ventures was formed as the co-ordinating body for joint parishes, this body is now known as Uniting Congregations of Aotearoa New Zealand.

(c) National Council of Churches

The National Council of Churches was formed in 1941 by the Anglican, Associated Churches of Christ, Baptist, Congregationalist, Methodist and Presbyterian churches.[11]

The NCC played an important role in promoting Christian unity and in connecting Aotearoa with the international ecumenical movement.[12] It was instrumental in establishing ecumenical chaplaincies in hospitals, prisons and workplaces. The NCC created a platform from which the churches together could witness to the nation. One of its first actions was to initiate the Campaign for Christian Order, which was concerned to encourage Christian involvement in the shaping of society. The NCC provided national

[10] Anglican, Associated Churches of Christ, Congregational Union, Methodist and Presbyterian.

[11] Subsequently the Salvation Army, the Religious Society of Friends, the Greek Orthodox Church, the Liberal Catholic Church and the Cook Islands Christian Church joined.

[12] Aotearoa churches have been involved with WCC, EACC and later CCA since their inception. The NCC promoted New Zealand participation in these bodies. Several New Zealanders have provided leadership on governing bodies of international ecumenical organisations and several NCC staff (notably H.W. Newell, Alan Brash and Ron O'Grady) became staff of the international ecumenical organisations.

leadership on social justice, international affairs, refugees, immigration and aid and development.[13] From the 1940s the NCC was involved in work against racism. NCC programmes addressing racism in Aotearoa and overseas, including protesting sporting links with apartheid South Africa and work on the Treaty of Waitangi were central to the national dialogue on racism.

Following Vatican II there was a new era in Roman Catholic ecumenical engagement in Aotearoa.[14] In 1969 the Joint Working Committee of the NCC and the Roman Catholic Church was formed; the Roman Catholic Church did not become a member of the NCC, but collaborated with the NCC.

In 1987 the NCC was closed to allow a new ecumenical body to emerge.

(d) Conference of Churches in Aotearoa New Zealand

The Conference of Churches in Aotearoa New Zealand commenced in 1988; it attempted to fill the space the NCC had created and operate in a more inclusive way, specifically to include the Roman Catholic Church.

The founding vision was for an inclusive movement grounded in local realities. The leadership structure was radically different from the NCC; women, young people and lay people were fully involved. The goals were: unity, mission, bicultural partnership, justice and peace, theological action, inclusiveness, women, links with churches, international perspective, communication and dialogue and prophetic courage.

CCANZ continued some functions and programmes of the NCC (notably the Programme on Racism) and developed its own programmes. CCANZ's structure, systems and content as well as the changed ecclesial and ecumenical landscapes, meant it did not enjoy the same ownership and support of the churches that the NCC had enjoyed. CCANZ closed in 2005.

(e) Te Runanga Whakawhanaunga i nga Haahi

Until the 1840s churches in Aotearoa were primarily Maori. Large-scale immigration resulted in Maori becoming marginalised within the churches. In the 20th century Maori organised to claim space in the churches.[15]

The Maori section of the National Council of Churches was formed in 1947 with membership of the Maori sections of the Anglican, Methodist and Presbyterian churches, later Baptist and Roman Catholics joined. The Section advocated for the Maori language and tackled injustices affecting Maori. It undertook important work on Maori enculturation of theology and liturgy. The Section reflected the deep sense of unity felt amongst Maori Christians and Maori impatience at divisions in the church.

In 1982, the member churches of the Maori Section formed their own, autonomous council of churches - Te Runanga Whakawhanaunga i nga Haahi o Aotearoa, which has outlasted both NCC and CCANZ.

---

[13] In 1944 the NCC and the Red Cross set up the aid agency CORSO. Christian World Service was formed in 1945 as the aid and development arm of the NCC, it continues as an ecumenical organisation with the support of the churches.

[14] Examples of the new ecumenical spirit: 1. A joint Board for Theological Studies including Roman Catholics was set up in 1968. The national Roman Catholic and Presbyterian seminaries collaborated in the Faculty of Theology at the University of Otago in Dunedin (1971-1996). This arrangement ceased due to the university restructuring theological teaching. In 1973 Methodist and Anglican national seminaries entered partnership to offer theological education in Auckland. The University of Auckland Consortium for Theological Education (1988- 2002) included Anglican, Baptist, Methodist and Roman Catholic seminaries. The consortium was succeeded in 2003 by the Auckland University School of Theology. 2. Since the 1960s the Anglican, Baptist, Methodist, Presbyterian, Roman Catholic and Salvation Army denominations have been working together in social services; these churches constitute the New Zealand Council for Christian Social Services.

[15] 1928 Anglican assistant bishop for Maori, 1954 Presbyterian Maori Synod, 1973 Methodist Maori Division, 1978 National Catholic Maori Council, 1978 Anglican Bishopric of Aotearoa.

4. Challenges to Ecumenism

(a) Changes in youth movements

In Aotearoa the YWCA and YMCA struggle to retain a meaningful relationship with their Christian heritage and have been effectively absent from the ecumenical movement in Aotearoa for decades.

Since the 1970s SCM in Aotearoa has sometimes struggled for its existence. However SCM has continued to gather students in universities from different Christian traditions, bringing them into the wider ecumenical movement and forming new ecumenical leaders.

(b) Rejection of church union scheme

The rejection of the Plan for Union in 1976 was a crisis for the ecumenical movement in Aotearoa, disappointing many. When the Plan was abandoned, joint parishes (which had been set up with the idea that they would join a unified church) were left in a precarious position.

Some in the uniting parishes movement are impatient with the churches' lack of commitment to unity. There is some concern that the uniting parishes are becoming de facto a new denomination.

(c) Perceived radicalism of ecumenical movement

From the 1940s until today perceived radicalism and political activism alienated some church members from the ecumenical movement.[16] The NCC's Programme on Racism and the WCC's Programme to Combat Racism gave some the perception that the ecumenical movement was promoting extreme political positions and funding terrorism. Even though the churches not the NCC were members of the WCC; the NCC was targeted by those critical of the WCC and the ecumenical movement.

On political and other issues the churches were unsure if they wanted the national ecumenical body 'to be a leader taking ecumenical initiatives or their servant co-ordinating shared concerns'.[17]

CCANZ's progressive stance on women, biculturalism and social issues fed the idea for some that the ecumenical movement was primarily about social justice and not Christian unity.

(d) Closure of CCANZ

The Baptists chose not to join CCANZ, the Lutheran and Roman Catholic churches which initially joined CCANZ later left.

Critics would say that CCANZ's vision and structure was drawn up by ecumenical enthusiasts rather than church leaders and doomed to failure.[18] CCANZ's emphasis on shared leadership (consensus decision making, participation of women and young people), no particular place for church leaders in the structure and the method for selecting leaders were all problematic to church hierarchies. Leadership by strong women and those who had little loyalty to denominations was challenging to the churches.

At times CCANZ took stances that did not reflect the majority opinion in the churches, this along with its strong commitment to the Treaty of Waitangi, its low visibility and the lack of a strong church unity agenda made CCANZ controversial. All of this combined with the churches' ambivalence as to whether they wanted a prophetic or servant organisation reduced CCANZ's appeal to its own members.

---

[16] 'Such criticism (of the NCC) as there was centred on the amount of the financial commitment requested and the allegedly radical character of the (1941) Campaign for Christian Order'. P 24 *Forty Years On*

[17] Davidson, A., *Christianity in Aotearoa* (Wellington, New Zealand Education for Ministry Board, 1997) p 123

[18] Lineham, P., 'Why the Conference of Churches in Aotearoa New Zealand failed: The birth, life and death of an ecumenical experiment in New Zealand' in *Where the Road runs out: Research essays on the ecumenical journey* Cant, G. (ed.) (Christchurch, CCANZ, 2005)

In 1988 after his denomination had voted not to enter CCANZ and because he was concerned about Baptist isolation, the General Secretary of the Baptist Union established the Church Leaders' Forum.[19] An ecumenically wide group of leaders started to meet regularly and to form relationships outside CCANZ. Tensions arose between this group and CCANZ about which grouping could make statements on behalf of the churches.[20]

In its latter years CCANZ did not have the full support of the churches; therefore when church budgets were shrinking its funding was not prioritised and the organisation was closed.

(e) Changes in churches

The churches in Aotearoa have changed considerably in the last 50 years, the membership in mainline churches has declined markedly, as has their income. Budgets for ecumenical activity have shrunk considerably in the past decades.

As church membership has declined, denominations have been tempted to look inward instead of looking to the wider ecumenical family. The new denominationalism has meant that for many people, their theological sources, perspectives and formative experiences are denominational rather than ecumenical. In general, the churches have become less ecumenically literate; some have actively cut ecumenical links, while others have let them wither through neglect.

Some churches have experienced a growing theological division between evangelical-conservative and ecumenical-liberal viewpoints. The charismatic movement of the 1960s and '70s, which had an important impact on many churches tended to be theologically conservative and disinterested in the ecumenical movement. In some churches leadership of the denomination has passed from those representing the ecumenical-liberal stream to those representing the evangelical-conservative stream.

From the 1980s there has been a national organisation for evangelicals: the Evangelical Fellowship, then Vision New Zealand, then Vision Network and in 2011 the NZ Christian Network. In the 1990s, some churches acknowleged that the ecclesial landscape had changed and questioned whether the ecumenical organisation, the evangelical organisation or both should have their support. Change in leadership from ecumenical to evangelical has radically changed ecumenical perception and participation of some churches.

In other churches ecumenical energy has moved from multilateral bodies to bi-lateral dialogues. In 2011 several bi-lateral dialogues are underway in Aotearoa.[21] Bi-lateral relationships may be preferable for churches as they are easier to manage and less expensive than a council or conference of churches. A recent fruit of bi-lateral dialogue was the signing of the Anglican-Methodist covenant in 2009. At the signing, Bishop John Bluck referred to the failed Plan for Union when he said, 'The covenant we are about to sign picks up the broken hopes of 1976'.[22]

5. The Future

(a) The current model

One future for Ecumenism in Aotearoa is to continue with the current model. This model includes ecumenical organisations and arrangements which function without a national body to focus or co-ordinate ecumenical activity.

---

19 *Ibid* p 55

20 *Ibid* p 59

21 Including: Roman Catholic- Presbyterian, Roman Catholic- Anglican, Roman Catholic-Methodist, Anglican-Methodist.

22 From Bishop John Bluck's sermon at the Anglican-Methodist Covenant Service in Auckland, May 24 2009.

The danger with this model is that lack of co-ordination, lack of collective memory and lack of communication between ecumenical endeavours, means ecumenical organisations, bi-lateral dialogues and churches risk becoming detached from the rich ecumenical experience of the last 100 years and at risk of constantly re-inventing the ecumenical wheel.

Emphasis on bi-lateral dialogues means that some churches are excluded from ecumenical conversations.

The absence of a national ecumenical body means that the space the NCC created for a national Christian voice has disappeared. The national organisation of evangelicals and the church leaders have tried to claim that space; however the church leaders have made few statements and the evangelicals have a more conservative agenda than many of the churches.

Global and regional expressions of ecumenism are also sidelined in the existing model. Churches are largely ignorant of wider ecumenism; New Zealanders are not being reminded about or inspired by the wider ecumenical family and not being enabled to contribute to the international ecumenical movement. In the current model, ecumenical organisations in Aotearoa can feel abandoned by the churches which set them up, supported them or commissioned them to minister on their behalf.

(b) National dialogue for Christian unity

Another future is one in which there is a national ecumenical council. In 2007 the Methodist National Conference mandated their president to convene a dialogue of church leaders on ecumenism in Aotearoa. After meetings in 2008 and 2009 it was agreed to explore establishing an ecumenical body and that 'the focus must be on an ecumenism that seeks the visible unity of the church and serves the mission of the church. Further the new entity must include church leaders or their nominees, and it must be open and inclusive'.[23]

The new entity is seeking to avoid the perceived weaknesses of CCANZ - lack of emphasis on unity of the church, detachment from the churches, lack of church leader involvement, whilst embracing CCANZ's strength - namely inclusivity.

In 2011 the churches which have participated in the National Dialogue are: Anglican, Assemblies of God, Baptist, Christian Churches (formerly Associated Churches of Christ), Congregational Union, Methodist, Presbyterian, Religious Society of Friends, Roman Catholic, Salvation Army and Wesleyan Methodist. Both the evangelical New Zealand Christian Network and the Uniting Congregations of Aotearoa New Zealand have participating observer status. Initial discussions have focussed on Christian unity and terms of reference for the proposed Churches' Commission for Christian Unity. The terms of reference are being taken to the churches that have participated in the national dialogue. Members of the national dialogue will meet again in March 2012 to consider the responses and what next steps can be taken.[24]

Conclusion

Aotearoa has a long and rich ecumenical history. Much has been achieved together and there is still much to do. From the 1990s some parts of the ecumenical movement were in decline and many wondered if the 'ecumenical winter' in Aotearoa was permanent. However ecumenical activity has never ceased and in 2011 there are signs of renewal.

Reflecting on the National Dialogue for Christian Unity, the Mission and Ecumenical Secretary of the Methodist church John Roberts says:

---

[23] Roberts, J., 'An ecumenical thaw', (Christchurch, *Touchstone* Magazine of the Methodist Church, 2009)

[24] Roberts, J., 'What became of the good ship Oikoumene?', (Christchurch, *Touchstone* Magazine of the Methodist Church, 2011)

All of this suggests that the churches in the dialogue are ready to move out of the ecumenical winter. An ecumenical thaw is beginning to take place. It may not yet be an ecumenical spring, but there are real signs of promise.[25]

Bibliography

Bluck, J. (ed.), *Ecumovement: Towards a new Ecumenical Body in Aotearoa*, (Christchurch, Steering committee of the new ecumenical body, 1986)

Brown, C., *Forty Years On: A history of the National Council of Churches in New Zealand 1941-1981,* (Christchurch, NCC, 1981).

Davidson, A., *Christianity in Aotearoa* (Wellington, New Zealand Education for Ministry Board, 1997)

Cant, G. (ed.), *Where the Road runs out: Research essays on the ecumenical journey* (Christchurch, CCANZ, 2005)

Roberts, J., 3 articles written for *Touchstone* Magazine of the Methodist Church of New Zealand

'An ecumenical thaw' 2009, 'NZ churches edge towards Christian unity' 2010, 'What's become of the good ship Oikoumene?' 2011

[25] Roberts, J., 'An ecumenical thaw'.

(51) CHURCHES TOGETHER IN GOD'S MISSION – AUSTRALIA: ECUMENISM IN TRANSIT

David Gill

In a forgotten corner of Sydney stands a marker commemorating the continent's first act of Christian worship. On 3rd February 1788, in the presence of the British governor and his entourage, some 700 convicts assembled under the muskets of their marine guards to be treated to a sermon by the new colony's chaplain. With that improbable congregation began the Christian history of Australia.

In the years following, the Anglo-Celtic churches arrived accompanying their people. Anglicans became the most numerous, followed by Roman Catholics, then Methodists, Presbyterians and smaller Protestant groups. Almost everyone wore a Christian label, denominational identity mattered and the Catholic/Protestant divide yawned wide. Other faiths remained effectively invisible.

Things now look very different. Census figures tell the story. The continent that Portuguese map makers four centuries ago labelled *Terra Australis del Espiritu Santu* – "The South Land of the Holy Spirit" – has been changing its religious complexion, fast.

Australia now has more Buddhists than Baptists, more Muslims than Lutherans, twice as many Hindus as members of the Salvation Army. The latest census is likely to show over a third of the population either has abandoned religion altogether or refuses to answer the religion question, with the historic Protestant churches the biggest losers. The exodus is most marked among those of European ancestry – and among the young, so expect it to continue, probably increase.

Church statistics confirm this. Pentecostal churches may be holding steady, even growing, but in most denominations membership stats trend downwards. Worshippers are aging, congregations shrinking, parishes merging, budgets tightening. Less visibly, the morale of those who remain in the pews – and in the pulpits – is suffering too.

At the same time there have been gains that do not show up in census results and church statistics. The old Protestant/Catholic sectarianism has gone forever. Australia can no longer pretend to be an Anglo-Celtic enclave – the whole world has taken up residence. Ecclesiastical institutions may be struggling, but the religious life of the nation is not only more diverse but probably richer than ever before.

Ecumenism in this country, as a result, faces big changes. The prospect should surprise nobody. After all, we are talking about an ecumenical *movement*. And that movement's record, from its inception in modern form just over a century ago, has been one of constant change.

Recall for a Moment that History

Australia's ecumenical story parallels the experience of churches elsewhere, though with an unusually diverse set of players. Following earlier less structured initiatives, especially among students, the 1940s saw a decision by most Protestant churches to form a council of churches. In the 1970s and 80s, a number of Eastern and Oriental Orthodox churches joined and eventually outnumbered them. Membership expanded further when, in 1994, the National Council of Churches in Australia became one of the few national ecumenical bodies in Asia to include the Roman Catholic Church.

More important was the transformation that could not be seen. Within and beyond such structures, Christians from different backgrounds were learning to read their bibles together, to pray together, to discern together their common calling. Friendships were forming. Trust was growing. Across the barriers of centuries people were changing and, albeit slowly, their churches were starting to change too.

But Now a New Game is Shaping

First, **interfaith relationships** have fresh urgency – not only because of what has been happening in the wider world, but due to changes in the nation, even in the next street.

Seeking the visible unity of Christians is one thing. Building bridges of understanding, trust and cooperation with people of other faiths is, of course, quite another. That distinction is important, although at the present time, alas, it tends rather easily to get lost. But though each exercise has a different goal, the lessons learned as Australians of different churches have reached out to each other should be borne in mind as, now, different religious communities set about doing the same.

Specifically, here are ten such tips for togetherness which bear remembering.

- Remember that before we are Jews, Christians, Muslims or anything else, we are human beings. We share our mortality, our hopes and dreams, our follies and foibles, our need for divine mercy.
- Treat other religions the way we would like other people to treat ours. It is too temptingly easy to compare my religion at its best with someone else's at its worst. Better, and fairer, to look at both in terms of what at their best they aspire to be.
- Remind ourselves regularly that none of our religions has captured God. "God, the eternal Presence, does not permit himself to be held," warned the Jewish philosopher Martin Buber. "Woe to the man so possessed that he thinks he possesses God". Woe even more to the religion that makes the same mistake.
- Recognize the common challenge facing all faith communities, stemming from the shallow secularism of contemporary Australia. How to help people rediscover the treasure we seem to have hidden from their eyes is a challenge we share.
- Be alert to opportunities that may arise for the different faith communities to stand together. Our leaders have done so when churches, mosques or synagogues were under attack, or when hysteria was being whipped up against one group or another by populist politicians or irresponsible media.
- Some in each of our religious communities carry bad memories, from other times and places, of treatment meted out to them by people of other religions. The scars are real, but don't let them limit what we attempt in Australia today. This is a new time, a new context.
- Prepare yourself for a paradigm shift. For centuries our religious communities have defined themselves *over against* each other. We are now being invited to think in a new way and define ourselves *in relationship* with each other. Expect some lively debate, not least with nervous co-religionists who take fright at the prospect.
- Seize every opportunity to build mutual understanding and confidence. More things are wrought by friendship and good neighbourliness than this world dreams of.
- Do not lose sight of any of Australia's faith communities. It is right, now, to focus on relationships between Jews, Christians and Muslims, but don't give the impression that we think monotheistic religions are the only ones that matter. Jews and Muslims in this country have squirmed often enough in the face of Christian arrogance. Take care not to replace that with a sort of "children of Abraham" arrogance towards Buddhists, Hindus and others.
- Keep your sense of humour. Religious people who take themselves too seriously are a danger to traffic. "He who sits in the heavens laughs," says Psalm 2, and we should too – focusing, of course, on our own follies and foibles, before those of others.

Second, **interchurch relationships** are in need of a fresh impetus. True, enormous progress has been made. Cooperation now happens on many fronts, ranging from theological education to striving for the more humane treatment of asylum seekers. Dialogues, bilateral as well as multilateral, have cleared many obstacles from the road to unity. A covenanting process has encouraged particular churches to engage with each other in translating theological advances into specific cooperative efforts.

At four points, however, new emphases are required.

We need *a more receptive ecumenism* – in the sense that churches should engage with each other not primarily in terms of what "we" have that "you" should accept, but trying to discern the gifts and graces your church has that mine should try to receive.

We need *a more self-critical ecumenism*. What is it about my church that makes it difficult for others to understand, to deal with or even to take seriously? Instead of what do we have that we believe you should accept, let us come clean about what we have that we fervently hope you won't ever want!

We need *a more empathetic ecumenism*. Much progress has been made at the cerebral level on matters of doctrine and church order. For that we thank God. However, the challenge is not just to understand what another church believes, but to enter as far as we are able into what it feels like to believe that way: how the people of that tradition live their beliefs, pray in the light of their doctrines, cope with their form of the magisterium and survive under their particular ecclesial roof.

We need *a more confident ecumenism*. Too many eyes have been fixated on the problems, too much time spent lamenting the frustrations, too many voices speaking of an alleged ecumenical winter. Of course there is some reality in all that. But Pope John XXIII was able to look at the tough realities of his time and proclaim, joyfully "This is the springtime of the Church". In like spirit, we should be claiming this for what it is: the springtime of the ecumenical movement. We have journeyed so far. There is nothing to suggest God is about to bring our journeying to a screeching halt.

Third, ecumenism's **mode of operating** will need to change. Churches are discovering that they must trim denominational staff and decision-making machinery at national and diocesan or state levels. The ecclesiastical bureaucracy to which they have become accustomed, a curious late 20th century phenomenon, is no longer sustainable. No surprise then that some of the country's ecumenical bodies, already operating on a shoestring, are now at a point where their viability is in question too.

This, it must be emphasized, is not the end of the ecumenical movement per se, just the passing of a phase in the way we organize it. There will be losses to grieve over, but also some gains to rejoice in. Anyone who has witnessed an ecumenical body wasting precious time and energy on budgets and staff appointments, when it was meant to be a means enabling the churches to grow towards their common calling, will see some appeal in the prospect of a de-bureaucratized ecumenism.

After Cardinal Caraffa became Pope Paul IV in 1555, Saint Ignatius Loyola was asked what he would do if the new pontiff were to act against the Society of Jesus, to which Loyola had devoted so much of his life. "Even if the Society were to melt away like salt in water," he replied, "I believe that a quarter of an hour's recollection in God would be sufficient to console me and to reestablish peace within me".

Australia's churches will need to become equally relaxed about their inherited ecumenical structures and ways of work. And equally confident that, in the good purposes of God, whatever is of enduring value in their movement will go forward.

(52) CHURCHES TOGETHER IN GOD'S MISSION – BANGLADESH

David A. Das

Introduction

From the very beginning, the people of Bangladesh have been overcoming many life threatening challenges in their life struggle. Christians are an inseparable part of peoples' life. There are many negative factors which have been contributing to the marginalized people's struggle, but there are also positive factors which break through stagnancy and accelerate the inner force of people to overcome circumstances and this is God's gracious gift to our people. This is the secret of people's strength and hope for the future. Christians are an integral part of this land and at times as an organized group and at other times as individuals, they have played a significant role in the people's struggle for justice during the history of their two hundred years of Nationhood.

1. Facets of Daily Challenges for Life in Bangladesh

Bomb blast at Romna Botomul

On 14th April, 2001 under a vast Tree in the Cultural park near the University of Dhaka, a huge group of a Cultural Team comprising popular Artists had gathered to perform traditional cultural songs in front of a mass gathering of many who have come to Celebrate Bengoli New Years Day. In middle stage of the Program several bombs blasted among the Artists and Viewers. Within a minute 24 people died and hundreds were injured badly. Among them some were also Christian. With this deadly injustice act the normal peace of the whole nation had been broken down. During reports covered by national media it was stated that one local extreme religious communal group had done this atrocity in collaboration with international religious terrorist links.

Hilsha fising

Each year in the largest river Padma hundreds of fisherman struggle to catch the Hilsha fish, the national fish of Bangladesh, against the strong stream of wave. With their combined strategic technique they tightly band each other boats and nets to overcome the wave. At the same time, as they go out to extremely remote areas in the river and in distance from their villages, many pirates attacked them by looting and snatching their fish and belongings. However they were strongly united and bound together with courageous will-power, thereby surviving in their livelihood in the midst of high risk but strengthened by their strong unity and courage.

From very beginning people of Bangladesh had to overcome many furious challenges in their life struggles. And Christians always have been an inseparable part of peoples' life. Christians are born in Bangladesh and have become inseparable with the soil of this country. Christians are an organic part of the people's struggle during the history of the two hundred years of this Nation. Christians once they join together ecumenical spirit have achieved an even more prominent role in this journey.

2. Brief History of the Ecumenical Movement in Bangladesh

The age of Christianity as a whole in this land is more than five hundred years, while the age of Protestant Christianity is for almost two hundred years. Though it was born in the western missionary womb, the patterns and mindsets of Christians in this country has been remarkably contextualized during its last one hundred years journey. The first organized group with a traditional ecumenical spirit was started with the formation of the National Council of Churches in Bangladesh in the middle of 20th Century which was build up by Protestant national leaders. The general forms of ecumenical movement in Bangladesh were developed in a way, which was different than in some other parts of the world due to the specific conditions and distinct marks of the local situation.

The need for Christian efforts for unity and Christian promotion of social change through religious practice began mainly due to the western evangelical zeal, which was brought about the mission projects implanted by William Carey and his two friends Joshua Marshman and William Ward in India, when they founded the Serampore College in 1818, the highest possible level of progressive and modern way of thinking based on educational institutions at that time. Dr. Carey came to India in 1793 and moved into Serampore in 1800. He spent these valuable years by preaching and teaching languages and translating the Bible into many languages. He converted many people to Christ and founded many Churches and School (almost a hundred) to educate Indian children. Education was carried out in vernacular. This was very beneficial but limited. Gradually Dr. Carey and his friends came to realize that Indians would not have the full benefit of education if subjects of higher and more comprehensive nature were not taught to the Indian youth. This was the reason for establishing the Serampore College, which became known as a main centre of higher education and also for campaigns and efforts towards social reformation and justice as it was through this College that a movement started not only in education, but also in united social reformative efforts, which we may be regarded as the first ecumenical movement facing contemporary challenges of that time.

It is important to remember that many of our Christian leaders in Bangladesh, who have been identified as ecumenical initiators have studied in Serampore and after having finished their studies made remarkable efforts to organize the ecumenical movement in our united Bengal, especially the land of present Bangladesh.

Beginnings of the missionary movement in Bangladesh

After western missionary organizations gradually flourished many of them contributed to a remarkable impact by forming a solid base of modern Ecumenical Movement, as it is by the Student Christian Movement (SCM), the Young Men Christian Association (YMCA) and Young Women Christian Association (YWCA) that the ecumenical movement was built up in early stages. The National Council of Churches in Bangladesh (NCCB) belongs to this renewal movement inspired by young Christian leaders. These movements inspired indigenous zeal and evangelistic spirit although due to western mission influence many good elements of contextualization and transformational processes have weakened or faded out later gradually.

3. Contemporary Challenges for Ecumenism in Bangladesh – The Issue of Human Rights Violations

The challenge of political violence

Bangladesh is a parliamentary democracy, with broad powers exercised by the present Prime Minister Shekh Hasina, the leader of the Bangladesh Awami League with a 14 party alliance currently in power. The leader of the Opposition is Khaleda Zia of the Bangladesh Nationalist Party (BNP) which is a 4 party alliance of pro-Islamic communal forces. Both of them dominate the political scene. Political competition between them is vigorous, and violence is a pervasive feature of current politics in Bangladesh.

On February 19, 2009, the Government passed the Anti-Terrorism Bill by the Parliament keeping a provision for capital punishment (death penalty) as the maximum without due considerations or feedback from the people. The given definitions of 'terrorism' and 'terrorist activities' are so wide and unclear that it leaves scope for all possibilities of misuse and violation of human rights, especially against people from the opposition, while peaceful meetings and processions should be the democratic and political rights of everyone, guaranteed in Article 37, 38 and 39 of the Constitution.

The Government's human rights record remained poor and it continues to commit numerous serious abuses. Security forces are often committing extrajudicial killings and police forces are often employing excessive, sometimes lethal force in dealing with opposition demonstrators, also routinely employing physical and psychological torture during arrests and interrogations. Prison conditions are extremely poor and were a contributing factor in some deaths in custody. Police corruption remains a big problem. Nearly all abuses went unpunished, and the climate of impunity remained a serious obstacle to ending abuse and killings.

The Rapid Action Battalion (RAB) is a special police force, created to combat criminal gang activity. But since its inception in 2004, RAB has been implicated in the unlawful killing of at least 700 people up to March 2012. Due to the weak criminal justice system, the tendency of taking the law into one's own hands is increasing, as people are losing their confidence in the police and judiciary. By expressing their high concern Amnesty International has called on the authorities to set up an independent and impartial body to thoroughly investigate the allegations on HR violation.

The challenge of freedom of speech and media

While the Constitution provides for freedom of speech and of the press the Government did not respect these rights in practice. Individuals cannot criticize the Government publicly without fear of reprisal. As in past years, journalists pressed for repeal of the Official Secrets Act of 1923. According to the Act, a citizen must prove why he or she needs information before the Government will provide it. The Act protected corrupt government officials from public scrutiny and hindered transparency and accountability of the Government at all levels. There is no doubt that a large number of journalist's killings have taken place with the help of political support by using multi-faceted crime syndicates. Journalists fall prey to terrorists and criminals, while writing about these syndicates.

The challenge of discrimination of weak religious groups

The Constitution establishes Islam as the state religion and also in principle stipulates the right – subject to law, public order, and morality – to practice the religion of one's choice, and the Government generally respected this right in practice. Although the Government is secular according to the law, religion exerts a powerful influence on politics. The Government was sensitive to the Muslim consciousness of the majority (approximately 88 percent) of the population in Bangladesh while failing to protect the rights of minority groups. Discrimination against members of the religious minorities existed at both the governmental and societal level. Violence particularly happened, before and after any national election, specially against Hindus and Christians.

Recently the government has refused to recognize the existence of 'Indigenousness' of Adivasi people by arguing that they are simply ethnic minorities. This wrong designation removes the groups from protections and rights of their ancestral land afforded by the UN Declaration on the HR of Indigenous Peoples and ILO Convention 169, both of which Bangladesh has ratified. The Government made a Peace Accord in 1998 with the predominant rebel group 'Jano Sanghati Samity' who had done a decade long armed struggle for their rights. But although the ruling party had pledged in its election manifesto to improve their situation the lands of "Adivasi" people were encroached, their temples and houses were vandalized and people were prevented from visiting the temple. In this way Bengolis, mainly the Muslims, are increasingly trying to eliminate "indigenous" people from their ancestral land.

The challenge of injustice to women and children

In 2010, the High Court ruled illegal all Fatwas (expert opinions on Islamic law) in order to end the extrajudicial enforcement of penalties by religious leaders. The Court stated that only those muftis (religious scholars) who have expertise in Islamic law are authorized to declare a fatwa. However, in practice village religious leaders often made declarations on their own, calling them 'fatwa'. Fatwa are commonly dealing with marriage and divorce issues, or are imposing punishments for perceived moral transgressions against women. Victims are punished by whipping, are lashed or shunned by their neighbors. As a consequence many have committed suicide.

The rate of usual injustices afflicted on women like discrimination, sexual violence, assaults, torture or acid throwing have increased during the last years, which is a growing human rights concern. Incidents of gang rape are frequently reported in the media, but victims rarely go to the police for fear of reprisal.

Although the government undertook programs in the areas of primary education, health, and nutrition, as ratified in the UN Convention on the Rights of Child, but many of these efforts were supplemented by local and foreign NGOs. These joint efforts allowed the country to make significant progress in improving health, nutrition, and education. However, more than one-half of all children are still chronically malnourished and profoundly affected by macro and micronutrient deficiencies. Every year, 30,000 children become blind due to Vitamin A deficiency. According to human rights groups, 575 children were abducted, nearly 1,300 suffered unnatural deaths, and over 3,100 children fell victim to serious abuses such as rape, sexual harassment, torture, and acid attack during the last year.

There still is extensive trafficking of children primarily to India, Pakistan, Middle East countries, largely for the purpose of prostitution and forced labor. UNICEF estimated that there were 29,000 child prostitutes working in the country.

The challenge of injustice to workers

Millions of Bangladeshi Garment Workers took to the streets of Dhaka recently to protect their rights as workers only to find their basic human rights violated again. Chilling images illustrate systemic violence and corruption, as workers went on strike to demand a better wage. Currently, the legal minimum wage for a garment worker in Bangladesh is 11½ Bangladesh Taka / hour (an estimated $25/ month). The workers are asking for a 35 ½ Bangladesh Taka / hour minimum wage, as the living costs increased 100-200% since 2006, when the current wage was set, which is below the poverty line. Insulted garment workers, predominantly women, have taken to the streets again–attacking factories, burning cars and blocking highways. Labor rights group the International Trade Union Confederation has said garment workers in Bangladesh are paid the least in the world. Meanwhile, business is booming for Bangladesh's garment industry. The garment industry however is earning $12 billion in a year by exporting their products and generates 80 percent of the country's export income.

The challenge of migrant workers from Bangladesh

Bangladeshi Workers in different countries is a growing concern for Bangladesh. According to a Govt. estimate every year Bangladesh is sending about 400,000 workers abroad and at present 7.0 million Bangladeshis are working in different countries, mainly in the Gulf. Most of the time these Bangladeshi workers are treated as slaves. They are not only losing their jobs, but most of them are living like in jails or under sub standard conditions and in very inhuman situations. Nobody is taking care of them, not even served by the Bangladeshi Consulate in those countries. Only recently the Bangladesh cabinet approved the proposal of ratifying the UN Convention on Protecting the Rights of Migrant Workers and their Family Members.

The challenge of climate refugees

The issues of climate justice and climate refugees in becoming ever more urgent: In Dhaka City there is Abdul Majid (65) who has been forced 22 times to move as a victim of the annual floods that ravage Bangladesh. There are millions like Majid in Bangladesh who has been displaced subsequently during many years. In future there could be many millions of climate refuges more if scientists' predictions of rising seas and more intense droughts and storms are becoming true.

Bangladesh is already facing consequences of a sea level rise, including salinity and unusual height of tidal water. Government officials and NGOs estimate about 10 million people are already threatened by annual floods and storms continue to damaging riverine and coastal islands.

Because of this increasing Climate Injustice the additional threat of global warming, the country's future is under pressure from a rising population and shrinking farmland. Concerned International bodies and NGOs are fighting hard to find options to accommodate Environmental Refugees. They have covered 3,5 million people in Bangladesh's coastal areas and islands, but many more are still left. The environmental refugee situation will turn into a dangerous problem in the future and the Bangladeshi government may find it difficult to face the challenge.

4. Ecumenical Responses to Counter Current Challenges in Bangladesh

Churches proposals to the government of Bangladesh

Leaders of almost all Ecumenical Associations and Christian organizations have forwarded some *key recommendations*, which the Government should take seriously to improve the human rights situation in the country.

1. There is a controlled and dependent Human Rights Commission, which usually acts like an organ of the government. Instead the government should establish an independent, neutral, credible, transparent and effective National Human Rights Commission.
2. The Government should stop immediately extrajudicial killings as per its commitment in its election manifesto. All involved in the acts of extrajudicial killings must be brought to justice through proper and independent investigation.
3. The Judiciary must be strengthened and its neutrality be strengthened to bring back people's confidence in it.
4. The Government must take effective action to stop all forms of criminalization in the name of politics.
5. All repressive laws including the Anti Terrorism Act 2009 should be repealed and replaced by other acts.
6. Incidents of attacks on journalists, legislators and Judges must be properly investigated and perpetrators of such acts and the killers of all journalists killings to be brought to justice.
7. The Government should accept the demands put forward by the workers of the garments, state-owned industries and other factories.
8. The Government should take appropriate measures to stop violence against women and Children, and the offenders must be brought under the purview of the law to ensure that justice is served.

Churches proposals at the regional level

Churches are becoming more engaged with two developments at the regional level which involve Bangladesh:

One of the most pertinent developments in South Asia since the end of Britain's Colonial rule is the emergence of the *South Asian Association for Regional Cooperation* (SAARC). On December 8th, 1985, the SAARC charter was signed by the governments of Bangladesh, Bhutan, India, Maldives, Nepal, Pakistan and Sri Lanka. The stated as goals of the SAARC Charter that the countries will work together, in a spirit of friendship, trust and understanding, to improve the people's quality of life; to accelerate economic growth, social programs, and cultural development; to strengthen self-reliance among South Asian States; and to promote collaboration in economic, social, cultural, technical, and scientific fields.

Of great importance for more church related witness and lobbying is also the South Asian Forum for Human Rights (SAFHR)**:** Many HR organizations in individual SAARC countries are struggling hard to improve the living situation of their respective peoples. An attempt to foster cooperation between these groups, organized by jurists, educators and representatives of NGOs gathered in December 1990 at the Third World Congress on Human Rights in New Delhi. This was perhaps the first occasion where non-governmental Representatives of SAARC countries from over fifty NGOs created the *South Asian Forum for Human Rights* (SAFHR). The establishment of SAFHR has fulfilled the long-cherished dream of creating a focal point for discussion of trans-border human rights issues to establish Justice in the region. The SAFHR provides hope for millions of destitute persons in South Asia who are denied their basic rights and fundamental freedoms.

5. The Forms of Organized Ecumenical Working in Bangladesh

Ecumenical working processes in Bangladesh have taken at least four different forms which each in his own way is contributing to struggling against the challenges which the country is facing. One can distinguish (a) Inter-denominationally based Ecumenical Organizations; (b) Inter-denominationally based Para-Church Ecumenical Organizations; (c) Denominationally based Ecumenical Groups and (d) Denominationally based Ecumenical Development Organizations.

The National Council of Churches in Bangladesh

Initiated as the East Pakistan Christian Council (EPCC) in the year 1949 the 1st Annual Assembly of EPCC was held in 1957. After the emergence of sovereign Bangladesh in 1971, the Christian leaders of EPCC renamed the organization as the National Council of Churches-Bangladesh (NCCB) in 1974.

NCCB is the Ecumenical Fellowship of Churches in Bangladesh and works for the greater unity in diversity in order to promote Faith, Witness and Service towards a just, humanitarian and peaceful world. Today NCCB brings together 13 protestant denominational churches and 7 Christian organizations with more than One Lac twenty thousand (one hundred twenty thousand) Christians all over the Country, including a close functional relationship with Roman Catholics and other bodies.

The birth of an ecumenical body in a backward and superstitious multi-faith-setting like Bangladesh was a challenge, but it can look back to an effective journey of 60 years upholding the spirit of greater unity and reconciliation. We need encouragement for future generations to get involved with NCC-Bangladesh today, in order to encounter all the challenges today.

In the NCC Bangladesh, the Christian leaders (from Churches & development organizations) have committed to work together for fruitful interfaith dialogue between the different faiths communities in Bangladesh, particularly also between Christian and Muslims at every level of the society. Sharing of experiences, expertise and joint bible study have worked as fuel for re-capturing our spirituality as

Christian networks to take the lead in organizing productive interfaith dialogues for better tolerance between different faiths.

In recent years NCCB has been more competent in ecumenical outlook by dealing with issues of other faith communities. The essence of this present trend of ecumenical movement is unity and reconciliation while diversity of people's lifestyle is affirmed. NCCB is now committed to identify itself in solidarity with the suffering people in the greater society in all its ministries and witness.

The Bangladesh Student Christian Movement

The SCM movement was initiated in the student hostel at Barisal, a city 250 km south from Dhaka City, in 1957. Ms. Labonnya Prova Halder, a student of that Hostel while visiting Kolkata to participate in a student conference met some friends there and brought the spirit to form a 'student movement' back to her land in Bangladesh. Many of her friends welcomed the idea and the movement started with a small but strong enthusiastic group. Very soon the impulse of that light spread out in the Capital City of East Pakistan, Dhaka and gradually many other cities were reached. In the following year the SCM of East Pakistan was linked with the SCM of West Pakistan and they jointly formed the all Pakistan SCM and became recognized in 1976 as affiliated member of the World Student Christian Federation (WSCF).

Being a part of the tiny Christian minority community the active spirit and courageous commitment of SCM has been vibrant and inspired the community and the society as whole. Because of its uncompromising protesting attitudes SCM has been trying to be an effective 'critical arm of the Church' in Bangladesh. But due to this stance SCM also has been tortured within and outside the society as well. But never was her movement spirit been given up.

The YMCA

The Young Men's Christian Association is a membership based, Christ centered, international, voluntary, ecumenical youth movement. Being the witness of Christ, it works for a humanitarian society to attain justice and peace in Bangladesh. The YMCA in Bangladesh was first formed in Dhaka in the year 1965. As response to the need of that time the YMCAs naturally involved itself mostly in the relief and rehabilitation activities to mitigate the human sufferings of the country in the initial stage. Presently the National Council of YMCAs of Bangladesh has affiliated ten local YMCAs throughout the country.

Programs to alleviate poverty and eradicate illiteracy became the primary thrust of the YMCAs of Bangladesh during its early days. Education was seen as a prerequisite to fight poverty. Most of the local YMCAs have a number of free children's schools, adult literacy programs to eradicate illiteracy and vocational training centers offering training in different trades with a view to create skilled hands to obtain employment for the youth.

The National Movement of YMCAs in Bangladesh has been involved in the process of the empowering people since 1989. Empowerment of the people has become imperative to sustain the development efforts in our country. The YMCA movement in Bangladesh re-affirms to work for the extension of the Kingdom of God in order to restore the distorted image of humanity through building People's Organizations. The thrust of the Community Organizing Program is to empower its beneficiaries in three major areas, in economic empowerment, in social empowerment and in political empowerment.

The YWCA of Bangladesh

Based on the motto "By Love Serve One Another", the YWCA has been working in Bangladesh since 1961. The YWCA of Bangladesh was founded just after the Independence of the Country in 1972 by an organized prayer group of few self empowered Christian women. As a Christian women's movement, this very organization works in Bangladesh where Christianity is a microscopic minority and women are the most deprived group in the society. It is always striving to empower women for a society where equality, justice, peace and care for environment are prevailed. YWCA is more an ecumenical organization than a development organization, as it serves the community and people, particularly women and children, irrespective of caste, creed and religion with love. Right now, the YWCA of Bangladesh has reached about more than 80,000 women, man and children in the community through its different activities and services in 13 local branches.

The Catholic Bishop Conference in Bangladesh

The Episcopal Commission for Christian Unity and Inter-Religious Dialogue (EC-CUID) is one of the 13 Episcopal Commissions of the Catholic Bishops' Conference of Bangladesh. The main objectives of the Commission are to promote dialogue among the people of different religions and Christian unity among the churches and ecclesial communities in Bangladesh.

To address Ecumenical challenges and to promote Christian Unity CBCB is actively engaged in the following activities:

1. The four days National Training Course on Ecumenism Course which is catholic in participation only. Objectives of this training course are to disseminate the Church's teaching on ecumenism and to promote Christian Unity among the Christians of various denominations.
2. The Christian Unity Octave Preparation, including the publication and circulation of a booklet for Christian Unity Octave every year in cooperation with other Churches;
3. Seminars on present issues like Climate Change, Church Problem and concerns.
4. Other Ecumenical Activities like bi-lateral dialogues with the different Churches, ecumenical prayers organized jointly with other Churches and denominations; common prayers at major Christian feasts; Publication of "Oikkotan," a quarterly bulletin of the Commission.

The ecumenical Asia-Pacific Student and Youth Network (EASYNET)

Since its inception in 2001 EASYNET Bangladesh network brought together the Alliance of YMCAs, Bangladesh Student Christian Movement (SCM), Youth Department of the National Council of Churches in Bangladesh (NCCB), Alliance of YWCAs & International Young Christian Students (IYCS) and Bangladesh Catholic Student Movement (BCSM). Easynet maintains a close network to diminish hindrances between the denominations and organizations for better cooperation and common brotherhood to promote ecumenism. EASYNET Bangladesh facilitates different interfaith dialogue sessions and inter-denominational discussion and gatherings.

6. Towards Greater Ecumenical Collaboration in Mission in Bangladesh Today

The United Forum of Churches in Bangladesh (UFCB)

There has been a process towards a larger and united national forum which is called 'United Forum of Churches in Bangladesh (UFCB), comprising the Catholic Bishop Conference in Bangladesh (CBCB-catholic), the National Council of Churches in Bangladesh (NCCB-ecumenical) and the National Christian Fellowship of Bangladesh (NCFB-evangelical) which is another landmark of the greater ecumenical journey. In the decade of the early seventies this cooperation was started and continued up to last year (2011) in order to allow in a situation of emergency common actions to be made by these three national groups together. In July 2011 it was formed as a structural forum by signing a MOU among all participating associations, however the structure, rules of operation and comity remained rather loose and informal in nature.

Their main objectives of UFCB were to share internal, national and global concerns of the Christian Community in Bangladesh, to voice officially the opinion of the Christian Community in Bangladesh on different national issues and to present the concerns of the Christian Community to the Government of Bangladesh.

On 13 April, 2012 UFCB organized a seminar study and analyze two theological papers on the theme "Church and Witness", namely the paper "Church and Mission: Biblical-Theological View Point" and the paper "Christian Witness in a Multi-Religious World : Recommendations for Conduct" from WCC, WEA and RCC. The main objectives of this seminar were to reflect on the common identity as Church and Mission of Bangladesh, to reflect the common Christian Witness in this multi-religious society and to experience fellowship among the Christian denominations in Bangladesh.

The Ecumenical Theology Education Fund of Bangladesh

Since it's inception the National Council of Churches in Bangladesh is sincerely concerned about theological education in the country. To promote greater ecumenical cooperation for fostering ecumenical theological education in the country the National Council of Churches in Bangladesh formed the 'Ecumenical Theology Fund of Bangladesh' in 2008 through a patronizing role of WCC. Since it's inception ETEFB has successfully done some programs to ensure Ecumenical Cooperation, building the Spiritual life and broader theological understandings of its Member Church believers.

The Theological Association of Bangladesh

In 2008 almost all theological institutions have organized the "Theological Association of Bangladesh" to ensure greater cooperation among them to promote ecumenical initiatives of theological education and to serve their common interests. Their main programmatic objectives are: a. to arrange a theological/spiritual seminar at least once in a year for theological students. b. to organize the same at least once in a year for theological teaching staff; c. to publish a Theological Magazine at least once in a year for Faculties, Students and Others; d. to provide assistance and support whenever any member institution needs it.

The cooperation of individual theological institutions

Beside the 'Theological Association of Bangladesh' many individual theological Institutions are concerned to extend their cooperation to each other. Holy Spirit Major Seminary arranges seminars and issue based meetings with other theological institutions. St. Andrews College is involved in interfaith Dialogue with the Department of World Religions of University of Dhaka and with the Interfaith Dialogue Commission of Catholic Church. This opened a door to meet with other faith people and to have better understanding.

The Christian Association of Bangladesh

As an inter-denominational organization the 'Christian Association of Bangladesh (BCA)' is a forum of Christian lay people formed in 1972 (initiated already in 1968). It has been always pro-active in protesting and resisting any injustice, attack and violence against Christians and the church. At the same time, BCA has been always trying to uphold the demands of the community welfare. It also fights for important rights of Christians in Bangladesh articulated by a central Executive Committee of 51 persons representing most of the mainline churches which are running the BCA. There are 53 local units and four associate units in the country. At present BCA is engaging itself for having at least one Minister in the Cabinet of Government to be taken from Christians; to allow Christians to have a place in the various policy making bodies in the Government; to reinstate the national Constitution must to the former position of 1972 in order to uphold the Religious Neutrality, Parliamentary Democracy, Social-justice and Communal Harmony in the society.

The Christian Religious Welfare Trust

The Christian Religious Welfare Trust is a body which was created under the Christian Religious Welfare Trust Ordinance 1983, working under Religious Affairs Ministry, People's Republic of Bangladesh. It came into existence on 5th of November 2009 by a gazette notification. It has a seven member Board of Trustee to execute the purposes and objectives of the Trust which are to provide for the religious welfare of the Christian Community, to provide financial assistance for the maintenance and administration of places of Christian religious worship and to adopt measures for the maintenance of sanctity of places of Christian religious worship.

7. Conclusion

To strengthen the future Ecumenical Movement we need to consider some points, which might be identified as factors, because they are playing very important role in organizing and making possible the Movement success or failure. For successfully encountering of the present challenges of ecumenical movement, we must have to consider those factors effectively and strategically, which are negative as well as positive in their nature, background and effectiveness. From our experience, we have noticed that from its very beginning our ecumenical movement we have two-fold negative factors, these are internal and external, and two-fold positive factors, these are also internal and external as well.

- Overcoming internal negative factors such as weak ecumenical conviction, pessimistic attitudes of leaders/organizers and weak zeal for the movement etc. The leaders need to be more pro-active and dedicated to ecumenical spirit and need to re-module and re-structure the awareness building and sensitizing programs on ecumenism.
- To overcome internal negative factors such as financial constrain and resources problem etc. the leaders have to take creative and risk taking measures to encourage and strengthen the utilization process of local resources to enhance the financial position.
- Regarding internal negative factors such as over confidence, wrong decision, weak and wrong strategy, lack of organized efforts etc. the leaders need to do self-critical study and analyze process of all past programs, incidents, events and even some of the previous decisions.
- For external factors less cooperation and non-cooperation of churches and organizations; negative attitudes of Churches and concerned organizations; superstitions etc. the organizers have to take some measures to improve the self understanding level of leaders, increase effective communication and relationship with them.
- Commitment, zeal and sacrifice for movement, pro-active, and cross-bearing lifestyle become essential for leaders. Prophetic stand, team spirit and cooperation as among leaders should be inculcated and proper strategic plan of action should be done in all activities.
- Articulating and prophetic stand against the massive negative forces such as effects of globalizations, misuse of internet/website, cell-phone culture, climate disasters and climate injustice, hardship of life etc. the ecumenical leaders have to take measures to sensitize and increase the awareness of those negative as well as positive impacts; we need to plan how to develop `a fit-into strategic plan of action and adaptation' in those area of concerns.

Bibliography

Araujo, Alex. *Globalization and the Chuch.* London, Routledge, 1995.
David Bosch. *TransformingMission : paradigm shifts in the theology of mission* (Maryknoll, Orbis 1991)
Pratap Chandra, Gine Edt, *A Journey Of Faith In Action,* Council of Serampore College, Serampore, 2011.

Pratap Chandra Gine & Tapan Kumar Banerjee Edt., *AJourney from Carey to Tagore : Socio-Cultural Transformation,* Council of Serampore College, Serampore, Kolkata, 2011.

George Mathew Nalunnakkal, *Green Liberation: Towards an Integral Ecothelogy*, ISPCK/NCCI, Delhi,1999.

Norman Goodall, *The Ecumenical Movement*, Oxford University Press, London, 1964

Kim, Young-bock. *Confession of Guilt and New Responsibilities.* CTC Bulletin 3 1982. (1): 8-14.

Niles, Preman D. *World Mission Today.* The Council of World Mission, London, 1995.

Several National Daly Newspapers (Bangla & English) published in Dhaka during last several months.

Speicher, Sara. *The economics of evangelism : an ecumenical challenges in Bangladesh.* WCC News, 2009.

Susanto Sarker, Parbota Dr. William Carey : Jibon-O-Sadhona, Parbota Printers, Dhaka, 1993.

Ecumenism in Thought and Deed, Dept. of Communication and Publication, NCC – Bangladesh, Dhaka, January 1998.

Jean Stromberg, *Mission and evangelism : an ecumenical affirmation,* WCC, Geneva, 1983.

Verstraelen, F. J. et al. Eds. *Missiology : An Ecumenical Introduction*. Grand Rapids: William B. Eerdmans Publishing Co. 1995.

Wickeri, Philip L. Edt. *The people of God Among All God's people: Frontiers in Christian Mission.* Hong Kong: CCA and the Council of World Mission, 2000.

(53) Churches Together in God's Mission – Bhutan

Wangchuk Lhatru

People of Bhutan

The word 'Bhutan' is derived from the Sanskrit root word 'Bhootan' meaning 'end of Tibet' or 'Bhu-utan' meaning `high land.' Bhutan is located between two giant nations with a total area of 47,000 squares kilometers. Bhutan is a land-locked country not much known to the world. Bhutanese people are composed of 15 tribes.[1] The total population of Bhutan is 6, 34,982. Each tribe has its own distinct language and dialects. One tribe cannot communicate easily to another tribal group because of this and other barriers. Although the two languages Dzongkha and Nepali have their own scripts, Dzongkha is the only language officially recognized by the Government. Out of 15 tribes, Tsanglha peoples are a majority and are believed to be the first settlers of Bhutan. The Tsanglhas originated from the Tibeto-Burman racial group that penetrated to Bhutan from the East. As a result, they are also found in Arunachal Pradesh, India, and in the Tawang and Yunnan provinces of China.[2]

In 1971, Bhutan became a member of United Nations Organization (UNO) which paved the way to introduce the country to the outside world as one of the sovereign independent countries in the world. His Majesty King Jigme Khesar Namgyel Wangchuck is the head of the state and the symbol of unity of the kingdom and of the people of Bhutan. His monarchial government is democratically constituted in nature. The constitution is the supreme law of the state. Bhutanese people are given freedom of thought, conscience and religion by this farsighted leader, His Majesty, the King of Bhutan. Under his leadership the people of Bhutan are truly blessed and happy.[3]

The present government under the leadership of Druk Phuentsum Tsogpa, the 2008 elected Prime Minister Jigme and he is admired by the people of Bhutan and he is also known as an ` intellectual giant' in Bhutan. Prior to his election as Prime Minister, he worked in different capacities and he has rich experiences in different fields of education, diplomatic and internal affairs. He has represented the country in different forums and his presentations were highly appreciated by the people. He is also an advocate of Gross National Happiness.

Traditionally, Bhutanese people practice primal faith. Jetsen Jamyang was the most respected god of wisdom in Bhutanese society and his name is chanted by every individual to gain wisdom and enlightenment. In all schools in Bhutan, the morning prayers are offered to Lord *Jetsen Jamyang* for wisdom and knowledge till today. Buddhism was introduced to Bhutan by the person called Zhabdrung Ngawang Namgyel in 1616. This man was believed to be from Tibet, one of the reincarnations of Lord Buddha, and history says that he was the one who unified the divided country and became the first Buddhist theocratic king of Bhutan.

---

[1] The following tribes are recognized by the government: Tsanglha, Nglong, Khengpa, Lepcha, Chalipa, Trongsarpa, Bumthangpa, Kurtutpa, Layapa, Brokpa, Zhala, Brahmi, Bothpa, Doyas, Lhotsampa

[2] Ibid.

[3] Ibid.

Arrival of Christianity in Bhutan

After the declension of the Nestorian Church in AD1300, the Roman Catholics sent a number of missionaries to China and other parts of Central Asia. Missionaries started to proceed towards Tibet, in most cases they had to take a route via the Himalayan Kingdom to reach Tibet.

On one occasion two Portuguese missionaries, Fr. Stephen Cacelo and Fr. Joas Cabral happened to pass through the land of Bhutan on 25th March, 1627.[4] They met the Bhutanese Monarch (Shabdrung Ngwang Namgyel) who received them warmly and invited them to stay in Bhutan. They were even asked by the King to preach the gospel freely in Bhutan and establish a church. He also presented two monks of 12 and 19 years of age to learn the life and teaching of Jesus Christ.

In spite of all these good gestures from the Monarch of Bhutan, the two missionaries ignored the king's request and left for Tibet leaving Bhutan untouched by the Gospel. After a long gap of more than three centuries, Silesian Fathers were invited to Bhutan later to start educational institutions in the early '60's. The most prominent person who came to Bhutan was Fr. William Mackey from Canada. During his stay in Bhutan, he introduced western education to Bhutan. In recognition of his great contribution in the field of education, the 4th King of Bhutan gave him the title "**The Heart Son of Bhutan.**"

Mission Movement in Bhutan

Several mission organizations came and started their mission activities in the 1960s and some of the major denominations were:

a) **Pentecostal mission**: Pentecostalism was introduced by missionaries from Kalimpong and Darjeeling of India in the later part of the 1960s. They came under the umbrella "Thimphu Christian Fellowship" under the leadership of Pastor Pema Bhutia.

b) Elshadia: This is a mission movement still operating underground for security reasons.

c) **Baptist Mission:** The first Baptist mission came to Bhutan in the year 1990 sponsored by the Nagaland Missionary Movement (NMM). The first missionary was Pastor Joseph Reddy (from Andhra Pradesh, sponsored by NNM) and he introduced the gospel to brother Lhatru Wangchuk of Jamung village from Trashigang district and this man accepted the Lord Jesus as his personal Savior and Lord. This man is currently working as the General Secretary of National Christian Council of Bhutan.[5]

The Formation of different Councils in Bhutan

Bhutan Council of Churches' Fellowship (BCCF): The arrival of different denominations and missionary activities led to the formation of the first ever council in year 2004. The Bhutan Council of Churches' Fellowship was formed comprising all the Protestant denominations and independent fellowships in Bhutan. In this council a majority of the Christian organizations had joined and initially the council was very successful, but later it failed to maintain the membership due to several factors. The first President was Pastor Jigme Norbu and now Mr. H.B. Chetri is the president. Negotiations are going on to revitalize the fellowship.

Bhutan Evangelical Alliance (BEA): Between 2006 and 2007, the Bhutan Evangelical Alliance was formed under the leadership of Pastor Timothy Tsewang Dorji .The Alliance is now a member of the Asian Evangelical Alliance in 2007 and is looking for membership with the World Evangelical Alliance.

National Christian Council of Bhutan: On 30th January, 2008, a meeting was called by the Bhutan Council of Churches' Fellowship to discuss the problems and challenges in Bhutan at Thimphu. All the

---

[4] Ibid.p.150.

[5] *Rev. Lhatru Wangchuk is founder Principal of Bhutan Bible Institute and present General Secretary of NCC Bhutan.*

former members of the Bhutan Council of Churches' Fellowship as well as other churches were invited. The members unanimously agreed to re-activate the council and changed the nomenclature to "The National Christian Council of Bhutan" (NCCB). In this meeting Rev. Vinod participated as an international observer and supervisor of the meeting. He has been working in the past with some of Lhotsampa speaking groups, especially with brother Dhanraj and friends. To look after the Council, Rev. Lhatru Wangchuk was elected as the General Secretary of NCCB. Currently, there are five denominations with the NCC Bhutan and about 1000 individual members.

The word `ecumenical' was a foreign concept for Bhutanese churches. After the formation of the National Christian Council of Bhutan, people have understood the importance of witnessing to Christ in unity. The Bhutan Council of Christian Fellowship, (BCCF) Bhutan Evangelical Alliance, (BEA) and Druk Yeshupai Tsogpa (DYT) are now in the process of coming together to be part of the NCC Bhutan. To strengthen the ecumenical movement, NCC Bhutan needs more resources – both human and financial support and ecumenical formation and education programs for the churches and councils. The birth of NCC Bhutan is also the birth of the Ecumenical movement in this context. Now the challenge ahead of the NCC Bhutan is to initiate more ecumenical initiatives where all the Christian communities, irrespective of denominations, come together for service, witness and mission.

Ecumenical Initiatives

The NCCB and other churches have initiated some of the following projects:

Dzongkha Bible Translation Project: Dzongkhag Bible Translation Project was started in the year 1994 by Mr. Wangchuk Drukpa from Trongsarpa tribe. Due to his hard labor, the New Testament in Dzongkha was published in 2000. This is one of the first major Christian literatures ever produced in the National language, Dzongkha, in Bhutan. Although the Word of God is available for Dzongkha speaking people, the converts are very few and many are yet to hear the Word of God.

Tsanglha Bible Translation Project: The Tsanglha tribe is one of the major tribes in Bhutan, but nothing much has been done among this tribe. Although the Norwegian Santal Mission has started translation work for the Tsanglha people in year 1989 by Jigme Norbu from Tsanglha tribe assisted by Mr. Erick, the work could not progress much due to misunderstanding between natives and non-natives over the language issue. Just recently, after a 20- year gap, the Tsanglha New Testament was printed in 2009 and free distribution of the Bible is taking place among the Tsanglha tribe.

Bhutan Bible Institute: This institute was established in 2007 with ten students, two girls and eight boys. BBI is run as an independent body under supervision of the General Secretary of NCCB. Now it has grown up to 200 students. The graduates are working in different parts of Bhutan as Pastors and Evangelists among the Buddhists in Bhutan. BBI is the hope of the Bhutanese Christian community. On 20th of October, 2012 a further development was started: During a meeting at Dr. Tshewang's residence Dr. Tshewang himself, Rev. Lhatru Wangchuk, and Dr. Chimi Dorji discussed very seriously the immediate need for a Theological Seminary in Bhutan and for the Himalayan Region in general. During this discussion, the name "Himalayan Theological Seminary" was proposed by Rev. Wangchuk and this name was approved and accepted among the founders and it was then that HTS was born and conceptualized in the hearts and minds of its founders. There is a distinct course programme, a board of management and a group of international advisors in the meantime. Detailed information are available on the leaflet and project outline of the Himalayan Theological Seminary (HTS) since end of 2012.

The Prospect of Bhutanese Theology

As stated earlier, the Catholic Mission came to Bhutan in the early 1960s on the request of the Government of Bhutan and they had been asked to establish educational institutions in Bhutan. Along with the Catholic Mission in Bhutan, the Pentecostal group came and they preached the gospel purely in terms of Pentecostalism so much so that the worship patterns are 'pentecostalized' even today. The major tribes have remained untouched by the gospel of Christ till today. We need a theology and a missiology relevant to Buddhist society: a Gospel that touches not only spiritual realms, but also a gospel that empowers people to participate in the pains and sufferings of the Bhutanese people. This means Bhutanese theology and missiology must answer the problems of the people.

The present Bhutanese Philosophy "Gross National Happiness" (GNH) is developed by the fourth king of Bhutan. His ultimate and absolute vision is to make his subjects happier by the year 2029 by implementing the philosophy of Gross National Happiness to the people of Bhutan.

This philosophy, if we can interpret in the light of the Word of God will be one of the best Bhutanese Christian theologies and missiologies. Another driving theology and missiology could be nurturing Christianity in the womb of Buddhism. These are some of the future prospects of Bhutanese theology and missiology.

Bibliography

DargyeYonten. *History of the Drukpa kagyud School in Bhutan*: 12th to 17th Century, Delhi: Omega Traders, 2001, p.212.

Thumra. Jonathan H, "*The Naga Primal Religion and Christianity: A theological reflection*", in V.K Nuh (ed.), In Search of Praxis Theology for the Nagas, Delhi: Regency Publications 2003, p59.

______Rev. Lhatru Wangchuk . *A comparative Study on the Teaching of Buddhism and Christianity in the Aspects of God, Man and Salvation from Bhutanese Perspectives,* M.A Thesis MRC, p.97

_____Rev. Lhatru Wangchuk *is founder Principal of Bhutan Bible Institute and present General Secretary of NCC Bhutan.2009.*

(54) Churches Together in God's Mission – Cambodia I: A Brief Survey from the Kampuchea Christian Council

Van Arun Rasmey

1. Introduction

For many Cambodian Christians, very little is known about the history of the ecumenical movement in the country. Without the traditional expressions of the ecumenical movement, however, the spirit of ecumenism through solidarity has been felt by Cambodian people. This was done, for example, through the work of a number of staff and personnel related to the World Council of Churches and the Christian Conference of Asia, who accompanied, gave advice and motivated the Christians in Cambodia. This accompaniment later led to the formation of the Kampuchea Christian Council (KCC). Through such an accompaniment, at least 1000 persons became aware of the ecumenical movement, 200 youth were trained as leaders, and 300 men and women were able to get vocational training to improve their living conditions and became Christian.

The Kampuchea Christian Council (KCC) is very young and quite different from other national councils in other countries of Asia. KCC's experience of ecumenism is very short and new compared to that of other members of CCA. By being a member of CCA, KCC got an opportunity to participate in the journey of CCA, learn the value of the ecumenical movement and the need to build unity among Christians and with other religions.

The information in this paper was collected through non-formal interviews and discussions with certain people who have some memory of the history of KCC but because we do not have a written history of all this, we do not have formal references or bibliography.

2. Brief Christian History

Cambodia is a country located in Southeast Asia, in the southwestern part of the Indochina peninsula. Cambodia was colonized by France for almost 90 years. In the middle of the 16th century, the three countries of Cambodia, Vietnam and Laos were considered parts of Indochina. Roman Catholic mission reached Indochina four centuries before the Protestant mission. In the early 20th century, the Protestant missions came to Cambodia and various missions continue to come to this day.

About 95 per cent of the people are followers of Buddhism, which is the state religion of Cambodia. Christian followers constitute a tiny minority. In 1923, the Christian Missionary Alliance (CMA) was the first protestant mission to open an office in the capital city of Phnom Penh. Later, CMA established a Bible School at Battambong province in 1925. In 1929, CMA translated the New Testament into Khmer and in 1954 completed the translation of the whole Bible. In 1949, CMA moved the Bible School to Takhmoa area, south of Phnom Penh in Kandal province. At that time, Christians were not allowed to do evangelism. Nevertheless, church leaders tried their best to preach the good news of Jesus to the people there.

In 1970 Cambodia was caught in a civil war which forced many people to move from the provinces to the city, and some to live in camps. While the country faced political and economic problems, Christian mission grew as Christian missionaries brought food and the gospel to many people who were hungry and hopeless. The solidarity of Christian missionaries helped to assure the people who did not have enough food to eat and who then came to see some hope through God's love. In April 1972, Stanley Mooneyham conducted an evangelistic rally in the capital city of Phnom Penh with result that some 2000 persons responded to the gospel. Through that event, the number of Christians increased. A series of discipleship and leadership training activities followed. Unfortunately, the political situation in the country changed when Cambodia came under the Khmer Rouge led by Pol Pot. This period lasted from April 13, 1975 to January 7, 1979.

During the period from 1975 to December 1978, all religious activities were stopped. People were moved from their homes, and forced to work very hard. Many suffered from starvation and diseases. Followers of all kinds of religion were killed or sent to prison.

The period from 1979 to 1989 was much better situation as very committed Christians could form again into small groups, secretly worshipping at home. Sometimes people in the home churches were arrested by the government. The government did not allow us to study English and communicate with foreigners. Christians had no freedom to express their belief because the government considered Christians to be linked to the CIA (Central Intelligence Authority of the United States of America).

In early 1980-85, Christians in Cambodia were one body in Christ. There was no denomination as such. As Khmer Christians, we simply helped and supported each other. We had no denominational labels, except that we were Khmer Christians.

During the period of 1985-89, mission groups from different denominations and Christian organizations came to Cambodia to start their mission work. These included CMA, New Apostolic Mission, Overseas Missionary Fellowship, World Vision, and the World Council of Churches. Their mission work helped in the social development of the country.

In 1989 the government of Cambodia allowed Christians to gather as home churches as long as they did not involve in political activities. Also, they could not reclaim the property of church denominations that had been taken over by the government. Still, the churches grew and increased in number day by day.

Later, however, problems arose as a result of the different denominations that missionaries brought with them. The denominational differences and the differences in theological teachings brought by foreigners and Khmer missions from abroad confused many of our people. Conflicts arose as some of our Khmer church leaders received training from certain missionaries who claimed that their group was better or holier than others. Soon many denominations got established in Cambodia. However, the relationships of many Khmer church leaders also got broken as they ended up following the different denominations of the missionaries they aligned with.

3. Kampuchea Christian Council History

In 1992 -93, the World Council of Churches invited some church leaders, men and women, to join the journey of the ecumenical movement through Bible study and prayer together in their office at Boeung KengKong.

In 1994, when the WCC project was being phased out in Cambodia, Mathews George Chunakara, representing CCA and WCC, facilitated the coming together of home churches' leaders and some leaders of church denominations to join the Christian Ecumenical Center (CEC). Also in 1994, the Cambodian Christian Women's Association (CCWA) was organized and entrusted a wooden house (8m x 12m) and land (20m x 30) to support its livelihood projects (sewing and weaving) and training courses of women, youth, and pastors.

The CCWA also began networking with other groups – including the CCA-Women's Desk and the Asian Women's Resource Center for Culture and Theology (AWRC). Through such networking, a series of theological workshops were conducted for the women members of CCWA in Cambodia over the years.

Through engagements between CEC and WCC and CCA from 1995-98, we received scholarships and opportunities for some of our members to study in theological schools, universities and seminaries, or attend seminars and trainings in leadership, management and development, and human rights conducted by

CCA or WCC in different countries in Asia. We received resource persons from CCA who came to build the capacity of our church leaders, women, and youth members of CEC.

In 1998 the CEC committee invited church members to discuss how to continue the ecumenical movement because they believe that the movement for unity is very important for Cambodians. They decided to organize a new group which was named Cambodia Unity Center (CUC). Later, the CUC was renamed Kampuchea Christian Council (KCC), which remains to this day. KCC is an ecumenical organization of mostly home churches and independent churches, rather than denominational churches.

The WCC and CCA have continued to support some of the ecumenical and development programs through theological trainings and scholarships. In June 2000, KCC became a full-fledged member of CCA at its 11th General Assembly in Tomohon, Indonesia.

4. Issues and Challenges

The KCC as a young ecumenical organization in Cambodia faces a lot of issues and challenges not only from the society at large but also internally. Because many of the church leaders are not formally trained in theology or have gone only for short trainings with various mission groups that come to Cambodia, they cannot understand or appreciate the idea and vision of wider ecumenism. Many of them are so used to their own style of leading churches, and they often do not understand their role as members of KCC or as officers in the Executive Committee. Sometimes their traditional theology keeps them from recognizing the need to work with other religious groups in Cambodia. This then leads to misunderstanding and conflicts, also lack of accountability and responsibility which are needed to strengthen or lead KCC to realize the ecumenical vision.

Despite the internal challenges, KCC continues to strive to be an expression of the ecumenical movement in Cambodia. KCC has forged partnerships and networking with other CCA member churches and councils (like the Presbyterian Church in Korea (PCK), the Presbyterian Church of the Republic of Korea (PROK) and the Presbyterian Church in Taiwan (PCT), as well as other Christian organizations such as the Lutheran World Federation (LWF), Church World Service (CWS), Asian Church Women's Conference (ACWC) and International Committee of the Fellowship of the Least Coin (ICFLC). Through such relationships, KCC has been enabled to have more capacity building activities for its members – many of whom live in very remote areas and provinces.

Programs conducted by CCA in Cambodia include Ecumenical Enablers' Training and workshops on agriculture, climate change, and building HIV-competent churches. CCA has also given places for participants from Cambodia to attend its programs for youth, women and men held in different countries. One of these programs is the Asian Ecumenical Course, a 14-day program wherein younger people learn more about the ecumenical movement in Asia. The program on building HIV-competent churches included participants from other faith groups – e.g. Buddhists and Muslims.

While KCC is struggling to promote the wider unity which is the ecumenical vision that we share with other members of CCA, we continue to face the challenges brought by certain missionaries from abroad who have financial power and promote teachings that are anti-ecumenical. This then creates suspicion among our church leaders and can even lead to conflicts and division. Because our local church leaders lack formal theological training, they can easily be swayed by teachings from these other groups. It can also be this lack in education and lack in confidence that keep the KCC Christian leaders from having dialogue with other Christians and especially with other faith groups. Because of these issues and challenges, the ecumenical movement is moving very slowly in Cambodia.

I hope that God's glory will be revealed when relationships everywhere will be healed – there will be no more discrimination; instead, there will be love, faith, hope, forgiveness, helping each other and working together in this journey of the ecumenical movement. Leaders do not have the same talents or skills but the most important thing is their faithfulness in leadership, gentleness, courage, and steadfastness to resist temptation. I hope that partners in the ecumenical movement, such as CCA and its members will continue to provide training to those of us who are still young and poor in ecumenical leadership, accompanying us as we strive to be transformed and to grow in the vision of unity.

Churches Together in God's Mission – Cambodia II: Detailed Account of Christianity and Ecumenism

Mathews George Chunakara

Introduction

Today's Cambodia, an ancient kingdom (Khmer) in Southeast Asia also called Kampuchea or *Kambuja* in Sanskrit, used to be known as a land of the "enigmatic smile". It was on 17 April 1975 that Cambodia fell under the control of the Khmer Rouge, led by Pol Pot. The takeover of Cambodia by the Khmer Rouge also led to the destruction of the Christian church in Cambodia. Pol Pot's "*Ankga Leou*", "the Organization on High" turned Cambodia into a nationwide prison and death camp where millions of Cambodians were starved to death or killed. The country was under Khmer Rouge control until 1January, 1979. '*Toul Sleng'* , a high school located in the capital Phnom Penh and converted by the Khmer Rouge into a prison where thousands of people were tortured to death, is a genocide museum now. Among the pictures hanging on the walls of the museum some are of Christian leaders, pastors and ordinary members who lost their lives because of their faith. The stories written and photos exhibited on the walls of '*Toul Sleng'* are only a part of much wider stories of the traumatic experiences and dark memories of Cambodian history during the Pol Pot era. The Killing Field located outside Phnom Penh also tells stories about how hundreds of thousands of people were brutally murdered, many for their faith and beliefs.

The Khmer people are the biggest ethnic group in the country and the majority of them are followers of Theravada Buddhism. But for long time, they mixed Hindu religious rituals and primal religious practices together in their religious and cultural practices. Although it is commonly understood that Cambodians are generally Theravada Buddhist followers, a strong influence of animism was an integral part of their worship and belief for centuries. For example, the belief in the re-birth and incarnation of the soul existed among Cambodian people even before Hindu or Buddhist religious practices influenced them. It was easy for the early Khmers to adopt the Hindu or Buddhist way and rituals as they did not conflict with their centuries-old practices, rooted in animistic rituals. At the same time, Christian missions and their evangelization efforts did not make any inroads into Khmer religions. However, one cannot negate the rich cultural tradition and historical religious context of the country.

Once an epic centre of a great culture and tradition in South East Asia, Buddhism is practiced by over 90 per cent of Cambodia's 14 million population. Buddhism arrived in Cambodia during the first centuries A.D. The basic force which shapes social and moral development in Cambodia has been the Buddhist religion. People's lives traditionally revolved around the *Wat (Buddhist Temple)*, which was a prominent feature of each community, especially in rural areas until the Khmer Rouge takeover. During the Khmer Rouge era (1975-1979), most of Cambodia's Buddhist monks were murdered and most Buddhist temples (*Wats*) were destroyed. From the 7th to 15th centuries, the Angkor priest-kings built up the country, built great temples and controlled much of South-East Asia. Then followed 500 years of regional and global conflicts with Thai, Vietnamese, French, Japanese and US invasions or occupations, before the Vietnam War spilled over to Cambodia in 1970-75.

The people of the 181,035-square-km country did not begin their own war. The Cambodian War was a consequence of stronger external powers and was not ignited by a civil war. After the Geneva Agreements in 1954, Cambodia became independent and King Norodom Sihanouk gave up his throne in 1955 to become head of the State. Until 1965, he attempted to keep Cambodia as a neutralist state based on the harmony of all social classes. However, informal agreements in 1965 allowed Cambodia's ports to be used to transport military weapons and goods to the Democratic Government of North Vietnam (DRVN) and the Provisional Revolutionary Government (PRG) organized in the South by the opposition. In 1963, The US ended its AID programme for Cambodia, resulting in the Peasant Revolt of Nattambang in 1967. The Government of National Salvation was established in 1967 after the revolt, with Lon Nol as Defence Minister and, since 1955, Sihanouk as the Prime Minister. After the military coup and removal of Sihanouk in 1970, the military organized the National United Front of Kampuchea (FUNK) in Cambodia, and Prince Sihanouk formed the Royal Government of National Union (GRUNK) with his base in China. The Khmer Rouge elements and leaders were divided into two organizations, but fighting for the same cause against the Lon Nol government. The new government pressured the DRVN and PRG to withdraw their troops from Cambodian soil and to stop transferring material through Cambodia. During the early 1970s, Cambodia became a battleground of fighting factions and armies. There were not only loyalists of different groups or leaders in Cambodia, but international forces too - FARK (Sihanoukists), FANK (Lon Nol Republic), Khmer Rouge, Khmer Vietminh, US Armed Forces, North Vietnamese, Viet Cong and the South Vietnamese.

The USA, which was spearheading the Vietnam war, assisted Lon Nol to improve his army, the *Forces Armees Nationales du Kampuches* (FANK). A diversity of forces was involved in the territory of Cambodia. US-backed South Vietnam forces entered Cambodia to hunt down the National Liberation Front and North Vietnam DRVN forces that were using the infiltration routes for men and supplies. Khmer liberation forces, some being anti- and some pro-Sihanouk, and others which were pro-and anti-DRVN, multiplied while the war intensified between the US-backed Lon Nol anti-communist government and liberation forces. The dissatisfaction and political bickering among various groups within the country and from outside opened the way for the Khmer Rouge to intensify their efforts against Lon Nol. On 17 April, 1975, Lon Nol's regime collapsed when the Khmer Rouge entered Phnom Penh. Pol Pot's regime took an agrarian socialist approach by forcibly relocating people from the cities to the countryside to solve shortages of food and supplies. The Khmer Rouge successfully isolated Cambodia from all overseas contacts and influence.

The Khmer people suffered immensely under the Pol Pot regime. Besides relocation and forced labour, purges were conducted against the educated, wealthy, Buddhist monks, other religious leaders or active members of churches, former soldiers, doctors, lawyers and former government officials. Any suspected dissidents to Pol Pot were killed. The restructuring of Cambodian society meant the elimination of several sectors of society and exclusion from the international community. Embassies were closed down. Foreign economic and/or medical assistance was refused. Radios and means of transportation such as bikes were confiscated. The use of money was prohibited. Businesses were shut down. Religion was forbidden. The health care system was eliminated and education stopped. The people had no chance of leading a normal and liberated life. Christian missionaries from overseas working in the country were expelled. No liberation movements were in motion since even people suspected of disloyalty were killed. Cambodia was sealed off from the outside world. No emergency aid or relief assistance was made available to the Khmer people.

The liberation of the Khmer people from the Pol Pot regime came on 7 January 1979, when the Vietnamese army launched an invasion seeking to end Khmer Rouge border attacks. The Vietnamese army ousted the Khmer Rouge in 1979, but civil war between four contending armies with support from superpowers under the leadership of the US and the Soviet Union raged for years. The peace process negotiations finally gained momentum after the collapse of the Soviet Union and changing international political alliances. Finally, the Paris peace accord culminated the peace process in a UN-supervised election in 1993, which gave way to a new political situation in which the religious situation also became a dominant reality. It was in this context that Cambodian Christianity in the post-Pol Pot era experienced a new resurrection. Missionary activities started flourishing in Cambodia with the aim of planting more churches, or evangelizing and converting more Cambodians to Christianity. The new wave of mission and evangelism activities by overseas missionaries as well as Cambodian Christians who returned to the country from refugee camps gave new impetus to church growth. This led to a new era of Christian mission and witness in Cambodia after such a long time-gap of political disorder, social chaos and civil wars.

Christianity in Cambodia

Christian mission to Cambodia was always a herculean task for missionaries due to severe persecutions or restrictions. The first attempt to introduce Christianity into Cambodia was in 1517, but it did not take off well. It is generally believed that Christianity was introduced to the Khmer people during the 16th century, but a Nestorian mission in Cambodia in the early part of the century is also hypothesized. The Nestorian Church was a first-century Assyrian church from Odessa (now Tblisi) in the Ukraine. It got its name from John Nestorius in the fifth century. By the middle of the sixth century (500 AD +), the Nestorian Church had spread into Egypt, Syria, Arabia, Mesopotamia, Persia, India, Ceylon, China and Mongolia. Some scholars believe that 'Indochina' (the colonial terminology used to indicate Vietnam, Laos and Cambodia as a geographical sub-region under the French) was penetrated by Nestorian Christians as well during early centuries.

Paul Ellison, whose missionary parents were pioneers among Protestant missionaries in Cambodia sent by the Christian and Missionary Alliance (C&MA), and who later served himself in Cambodia as a C&MA missionary, states that "church history records evidence in Vietnamese and Cambodian culture that points to early Christian missionary activity in Indochina. In Damascus, Syria, there was a Nestorian Church Conference which was attended by Indo-China representatives in 450 AD. In order to send a representative to this conference, the region had to have 70,000 adherents to the faith."[1] Ellison believes that this fact alone strongly suggests that missionaries from Syria were active in Indochina in early church times. He cites examples like creation accounts, fall accounts, and flood epics among the certain minority groups. "Even today you can see the use of the cross in the countryside to ward off evil spirits – a practice in use for many centuries now although Cambodians don't know the background nor explain the meaning behind the crosses they paint on their house." Ellison's research has found that the Cham people, originally from Central Vietnam, had ancient terms for the Father, Son and the Holy Spirit.

Ellison further suggests that "In this, we see what might have been the positive effects of early church missionary endeavours, which shows in part the extent and effects of Nestorian Missions. But on the negative side, there seemed to be no lasting presence as the Syrian church failed to translate scriptures because there was no written language for the peoples in the Indochina area at that time, and they also apparently failed to train indigenous leaders."[2]

---

[1] Alliance Biblique Fancaise (Paris), Handout on the Translation of the Bible into the Khmer Language shared at the CCS
conference in Santa Cruz in 1991 . Cited in' Cry of the Gecko: Introduction', Cambodian Christian.com, January 20, 2010

[2] *ibid*

But it is commonly accepted that it was not until the 16th century that Christianity could make an entry in Cambodia. Tome Piers, a Portuguese apothecary who wrote the *Suma Oriental que trata do Mar Roxo até aos Chins* (Summa of the East from the Red Sea up to the Chinese), had written extensively about all aspects of life in Cambodia between 1512 and1515. But he had not mentioned anything about Christians or Christianity. This indicates that he could not trace any Christian presence existing in Cambodia during his visit to the country in the 16th century.

Roman Catholic missions had started their activities in the countries of the Indochina region – Vietnam, Laos and Cambodia – only in the 16th century. The first Roman Catholic missionary, a Portuguese Dominican, Gasper da Cruz, visited Cambodia in 1555. He left the country a year later because he was disappointed in his mission, especially the superstition of the natives and their loyalty to Buddhist monks. He observed that the native people "dare make nothing of themselves nor accept anything new without leave of the king, which is why Christians cannot be made without the king's approval"[3]. During the same period, other Portuguese Dominicans and Franciscans also came from Malacca. Jesuit missionaries and priests from Goa, India also laboured in the area, and in 1570's, the Christian presence was established in Cambodia through the efforts of Portuguese and Spanish Catholic missionaries who arrived from Malacca and the Philippines. However, they had to face strong resistance from the locals. Silvestro de Azevedo, OP, was put to death in 1576; Father Bastide was slain in 1588. When a missionary of the Paris Foreign Mission (MEP) arrived in the country in 1665, he found the Portuguese ecclesiastical governor Paul da Acosta at Colompe (Phnom Penh), where he was taking care of about 400 Portuguese who were driven out from Makassar (in Indonesia) by the Dutch, who controlled the area. However, it was very difficult for the MEP to evangelize the local people, as they did not welcome a new religion introduced by foreign missionaries. Bishop Louis Laneau, the first apostolic vicar of Siam (then part of the Khmer kingdom) from the Paris Foreign Mission, and the general administration of Mission in Indochina sent MEP missionaries to Cambodia in 1680 and 1682. But all these missions were faced with numerous challenges and failed in their endeavours. Among all the Roman Catholic missions, French Catholics had the most success, especially after Cambodia became a French colony in 1863. The Vicariate of Cambodia gained its administrative jurisdiction over eight provinces of Cochin China (now this area belongs to Vietnam) ruled by the French, and those areas had about 5,000 Roman Catholic Church followers. The history of the centuries-old missions of the Roman Catholic Church in Indochina, which includes Cambodia, proved that Christian gospel was not easily acceptable to the Khmer, although the Khmer people had earlier accepted religions from India, Thailand, Ceylon and Burma.

Christianity, introduced into Cambodia in the 16th century, made little headway, at least among the Buddhists. In 1850, the Holy See established the Apostolic Vicariate of Phnom Penh, covering all the regions of the Kingdom of Cambodia. The Vatican estimated in 1953 that Cambodian Christians numbered around 120,000 making it, at the time, the second-largest religion in the country. In April 1970, just before repatriation of Vietnamese back to Vietnam, it was estimated that about as many as 62,000 Christians lived in Cambodia and that 50,000 of them were possibly Vietnamese. In 1972, there were probably about 20,000 Christians in Cambodia, most of them Roman Catholics.[4]

The much anticipated destruction of the church finally started with the takeover of Phnom Penh by the Khmer Rouge. According to Fr. Francoise Ponchaud, on the very first day that the Khmer Rouge entered Phnom Penh, the Sisters of Providence and the Benedictine monks, both French and natives, were rounded up at the Providence convent: "In the early hours of the morning of April 17, the Khmer Rouge presented themselves at the Providence convent and gave orders to evacuate the premises. The sisters and monks obeyed without a word. Each one, carrying a bundle of belongings, entered the pitiful human flood which

---

[3] David P. Chandler, A History of Cambodia, Silkworm Books, Thailand, 1993, p.82.

[4] http://www.country-studies.com/cambodia/christianity.html

ran unrelentingly outside the city".[5] That was the beginning of the subsequent turmoil faced by Christianity in Cambodia. During the four years of the Pol Pot regime, Christianity was totally wiped out. All the Cambodian priests and religious, except the handful of sisters who happened to be outside the country, and a great number of Khmer Catholics, lost their lives during the years of the genocide. All but three churches were completely destroyed. At the end of the Khmer Rouge period, in 1979 and in the early eighties, there were only a small number of Catholics among the several hundred thousand who lived in the refugee settlements along the Thai border. With the return of the refugees to Cambodia in the early nineties, Catholic communities in the northwest slowly began to gather and worship together. Refugee members maintained their faith, since they had received intense formation during their exile in Thailand. Although property rights were lost during the years of turbulence and exile, the Catholic Church was able to buy back certain property and buildings; for example, the buildings which were formerly the hospital of the Providence Sisters in Battambang. This place was converted quickly into a pastoral centre for nurturing the small communities back to full life.

In 1990, the Catholic communities were given permission to worship freely in Cambodia, and 'Caritas Cambodia' re-established its work after 15 years. Bishop Yves Ramousse, who was expelled during the first days of Khmer Rouge takeover and had been responsible for the pastoral care of Cambodian communities dispersed around the world since 1983, officially returned to Cambodia in 1992. Several Roman Catholic priests from other countries then also started assisting the Catholic faithful in Cambodia. A Cambodian priest, Tonlop Sophal, was ordained only in 1995, and later became the Vicar General of Battambang.

In the history of Cambodia's Roman Catholic Church, except at one time, all bishops were from the MEP France. They all served as Vicar Apostolate or Coadjutor. In Roman Catholic tradition, an Apostolic Vicariate is a form of territorial jurisdiction of the Roman Catholic Church established in missionary regions and countries where a diocese has not yet been established. It is essentially provisional, though it may last for a century or more in several contexts with the hope that the region might generate sufficient numbers of Catholics for the Church to create a diocese. In Cambodia, it has always been considered as a missionary region under the leadership of a Vicar Apostolate or Coadjutor. The first Catholic Bishop in the country was Bishop Dominique Lefèbvre, MEP., who was Vicar Apostolic of Cambodia from 1872 to 1882 prior to his other assignment as Coadjutor Vicar Apostolic of Western Cochin, Vietnam (1872-1873). Subsequently, several other bishops from France from the same MEP mission society served in positions as Apostolic Administrator or Coadjutor Vicar Apostolic. Bishop Marie-Laurent-François-Xavier Cordier, MEP (1882-1895), Bishop Jean-Baptiste Grosgeorge, MEP. (1896-1902), Bishop Jean-Claude Bouchut, MEP (1902-1928), Bishop Valentin Herrgott, MEP (1928-1936), Bishop Jean-Baptiste-Maximilien Chabalier, M.E.P. (1937-1955), Bishop Gustave-André-Ferdinand Raballand, MEP. (1956-1962), Bishop Yves-Georges-René Ramousse, MEP. (1962-1976), Bishop Joseph Chhmar Salas (1976-1977), Bishop Yves-Georges-René Ramousse, MEP. (1992-2001), Bishop Emile Destombes, MEP. (2001--2010), Bishop Olivier Schmitthaeusler, MEP. (2010.10.01 – ...) served at different times. Bishop Yves Ramousse served twice and served the longest as head of the Cambodia's Roman Catholic Church. When the Khmer Rouge took control on 17 April 1975, Bishop Ramousse was the Bishop in Phnom Penh. In less than two weeks, on 30 April, he was expelled from the country together with many other foreign priests. Most Cambodian priests remained in the country, but very few would survive. These native priests also were forced to work in rice fields and many of them were executed.

When on 1 January 1975, the Khmer Rouge launched rocket and shell attacks on the capital Phnom Penh, this signalled what would happen in the coming days. Foreigners and well-to-do Khmers started leaving the country. The central council of the Foreign Missions of the Catholic Church had a meeting and

[5] Francois Ponchaud, The Cathedral of the Rice Paddy', Le Sarment, Fayard, 1990, p.142

also warned missionaries about the situation and asked them to leave the country at the earliest. During a meeting of the priests convened by Bishop Ramousse, it was decided to call back Fr. Joseph Chhmar Salas who was on a sabbatical year in France. He returned to Cambodia immediately and subsequently, on 7 April an official papal Bull named Fr. Joseph Chhmar Salas as Bishop. He was ordained on 13 April 1975, and on 14 April he was appointed Bishop and Coadjutor of the Apostolic Vicar of Phnom Penh. Salas was born in Phnom Penh on 21 October 1937. For his formation as a priest, he was sent to Paris and was ordained in 1964. His first assignment was in the Apostolic Prefecture of Battambang. Subsequently, he was sent to France for more studies. When Bishop Ramousse was expelled from the country by Khmer Rouge on 30 April 1975, Salas was asked to head the church, but he was sent by the Khmer Rouge Regime to a rice field in Kompong Thom. He died of exhaustion in September 1977 in the Traing Kork Pagoda.

Since his reappointment in Cambodia by the Vatican in 1992, Bishop Ramousse served as Bishop of Phnom Penh until his retirement in 2001. He was subsequently succeeded by Bishop Emiles Destombes. Emiles Destombes first arrived in Cambodia as a missionary in 1964, but he was also expelled from the country in 1975. He returned to Cambodia in 1979 and was appointed Vicar General of Phnom Penh in 1992; in October 1997, he was appointed Coadjutor Bishop of Phnom Penh to assist Bishop Ramousse. During the ordination ceremony of the new bishop, the aged mother of the late Khmer Bishop Joseph Chhmar Salas was assisted to the altar to present Bishop Destombes with his Episcopal cross. The cross had been given by Bishop Ramousse to the 35-year-old Khmer priest Salas when he ordained him bishop, just before all foreign missioners were expelled in 1975.[6] In 1995, Father Pierre Sophal Tonlop became the first Khmer priest ordained in years. In December 2001, four other young Khmer men were also ordained priests. Both occasions became great events for the Catholic community of Cambodia. Instead of foreign priests serving in Khmer parishes, the Cambodian Catholic community had Khmer priests leading their communities at least in some areas. Due to the shortage of Cambodian priests, the Catholic Church in Cambodia had to get priests from Canada, England, France, Ireland, Italy, Thailand and the United States.

Although the Catholic Church in Cambodia has been actively engaged in mission for two decades now since an organized structure was re-established, the Catholic Church has not been expanding, unlike the Protestant churches in Cambodia. But the growth and mission of the Catholic Church is steady and it does not seem to be over-enthusiastic about converting more Buddhists to Catholicism. Today, Cambodia's Roman Catholic Church is administratively divided into one Apostolic Vicariate (Phnom Penh) and two Apostolic Prefectures (Battambang and Kompong Cham) with about 25,000 members in about 60 parishes served by about 35 priests; two Apostolic Prefects and one Bishop as Vicar Apostolic.

In a culture of personality-based Christian Protestant groups and where organizational and denominational competition in mission and evangelism prevail, even the government finds it difficult to understand who is who in the Cambodian churches. On the contrary, the Catholic Church is an exception to this culture as it has a unified structure and vision for its future mission in Cambodia. When the government finds it difficult to understand the multiplicity of denominations and mushrooming growth of Christian organizations, the Catholic Church and its leaders are widely respected by the government. Bishop Schmitthaeusler, Vicar Apostolic of Phnom Penh says "the attitude of the government to the Catholic Church is very positive and they are happy with us because we have a clear structure". In most cases, today's Protestant Churches in Cambodia face a lack of a clear structure !.

Protestant Christian Missions

Protestant missionaries arrived in Cambodia almost four centuries after the arrival of the Roman Catholic missionaries. Although several attempts were made to gain entry, Protestant missionaries had been rigidly

---

[6] "Cambodia Coadjutor Bishop's ordination shows church is alive in Cambodia", UCAN News, October9, 1997.

excluded for centuries.[7] The Christian and Missionary Alliance (C&MA) was the first Protestant mission to arrive in Cambodia in 1923 under the leadership of Arthur Hammond and David Ellison. They were allowed to open a station in Phnom Penh in February 1923. The second station was opened in Batambang in September of the same year. The early years were very difficult for them as well as for other missionaries who followed them in subsequent years. They met discouraging experiences not only with the Khmer people, but also with the French authorities. While the French governor gave his verbal consent to preach the gospel, he declared that "it was useless to try to convert these bigoted Buddhists".[8] However, they continued in their mission of propagating the gospel with greater commitment, translated and printed the first Cambodian Bible and other literature, established a Bible School and brought several to Christ.

The French government which was more lenient towards the Roman Catholic mission restricted the Alliance's missionary activities to a limited area and in 1933, all evangelistic activities were stopped. This was followed by a royal edict which restricted missionary efforts to those areas in which work had been established prior to December 1932. This policy of restriction affected the expansion of C&MA mission activities until in 1946, when the country was abrogated by a new constitution that granted religious liberty. By that time, the church had survived the Second World War as well as the Japanese occupation. However, a nationalist movement, the *Issarak* , which demanded complete independence from France, became active in many areas of the country, which restricted the visit of the missionaries to isolated groups of believers. Meanwhile, C&MA had been successful in establishing missions in nine of the total seventeen provinces. The church started to grow through its 18 congregations and also established self-supporting churches among Khmer, Vietnamese and ethnic Chinese communities in the capital.

A monumental result of the work of the first missionaries was the translation and printing of the entire Bible in the Khmer language. In 1929, the New Testament was translated into Khmer and in 1954, the entire Bible. The British and Foreign Bible Society assisted in this effort and opened a Bible House in Phnom Penh. Hundreds of thousands of pages of gospel literature were printed annually for distribution across the country. At the same time, a new project started in collaboration with Far East Broadcasting Company in Manila, preparing radio programmes in Khmer.

In 1925, the C&MA established a Bible School in Batambang; it was shifted to a more centrally located area, Ta Khamau, near Phnom Penh in 1949. The faculty of the Bible School was led by a resident missionary couple. Cambodians as well as foreign missionaries based in Phnom Penh were part of the faculty. Short-term Bible courses were conducted for several years in Battambang province, and a large number of students graduated from the central Bible School in Ta Khamau. C&MA used to organize annual national-level conferences, and these were attended by representatives from different parts of the country. Annual youth conferences for two weeks were also organized, and a Cambodian National Youth Fellowship was subsequently formed. The evangelism work of the Alliance in which Cambodians were also taking a leading role was spreading to different provinces of the country. In 1965, the government's anti-American crusade forced the missionaries to withdraw from their mission fields. After working very hard for 43 years since the arrival of the first Protestant missionaries in 1923, the Protestant church had grown to as many as 12,000 members in 1965 and the missionary activities were left with the locally named Khmer Evangelical Church established by the C&MA. As the mission activities were expanded, in 1974 the Overseas Missionary Fellowship (OMF) was invited by the C&MA, mainly to help its mission among the new converts. Don Cormack, in his book "Killing Fields Living Fields" states:

> During the first twenty-five years of church planting in Cambodia, the Bible was completely translated. The seminary was established and proven as a training ground for the pastors and lay leaders of those early scattered

[7] Missionary Atlas, A Manual of The Foreign Work of the Christian and Missionary Alliance, Christian Publications, Inc, Harrisburg, Pa, 1964, p.66

[8] *ibid*

> village house churches; and a harvest was brought in which, though small, was hardy and enduring. The secret being that each new believer learned the true nature of Christian discipleship.[9]

The mission of C&MA also had been difficult in Cambodia from the very beginning. In 1962, the C&MA reported that:

> When missionary work was initiated in Cambodia, the third largest Alliance mission filed, failure was freely predicted. But Cambodians have been converted, and their lives are testimonies to the fact that the gospel is the power of God unto salvation. Yet considering the total population, the response has been disappointing. Buddhism binds the people and makes the preaching of the gospel difficult.[10]

While expressing their frustration about the slow process of evangelization, the Alliance observed in 1962 in the same report that Cambodia's 6.2 million people were largely unreached. The report summarizes the new plans of the Alliance as follows:

> And now political conditions in Asia and within the country indicate that time is running out. To share in the responsibility, an effort is being made to facilitate occupancy of a part of Cambodia by the Far Eastern Gospel Crusade. Their first missionaries arrived in 1961 to work in Svai Reing and Prey Veng provinces and those areas of Kompong Cham and Kandal provinces situated east of the Mekong River. This area has a population of approximately one million. The Alliance is continuing working the remaining fifteen provinces and those areas of the above provinces which lie west of the Mekong.[11]

The Protestant missions worked among some of the hill tribes and among the Champ. Other missionary activities were also held in Cambodia subsequently. In 1953, an American Unitarian mission maintained a teacher-training school in Phnom Penh, and Baptist missions functioned in Batambang and Siemreap provinces. The work of the Christian missions and missionaries continued to be difficult; at the same time, new Christian converts among the Cambodians also faced problems within their own local situations. This is how Cormack describes the situation: "To be a Christian in Cambodian society was to be a social pariah, misunderstood and ill-treated, a convenient scapegoat for blame and abuse."[12] Cormack testifies that the early believers or converts to Christianity were "mainly rice farmers, unsophisticated country folk". He believes that "God chose the 'foolish' and the 'unwise' of Cambodian society to be the foundation stones of his church. It was they who were least inclined to flee to the West, and best able to endure the rigours of the rural-based communist system in the late 1970s and 1980's"[13] However, a large number of those Christians were persecuted or perished during the Pol Pot era. Several of the Christian pastors and lay leaders were killed.

I had opportunities in the 1990's to spend time on several occasions with two pastors who survived the Pol Pot cruelties – Pastor Seang Ang of Ta Khamau church on the outskirts of Phnom Penh, and Pastor Ngor Von from Kompong Thom. They told me stories of the early Cambodian churches and their work until Pol Pot's era begun. Pastor Seang Ang was working underground in the early 1980s, and he used to travel to different places in Cambodia to share the gospel and visit some secret prayer groups. This was a time when practicing Christianity was restricted for Cambodians. Lim Saroeuin, who is a son-in-law of Pastor Seang Ang, now serves as the pastor of the Ta Khamau church and director of spiritual formation of the Agape International Missions in Cambodia. He shared with me the experiences of his father-in-law.

---

[9] Don Cor Mack, Killing Fields, Living Fields, OMF International, MARC: Crowborough, U.K, 1997, p.64.
[10] Missionary Atlas, *op.cited,* p 69
[11] *ibid*
[12] *ibid*
[13] *ibid*

Pastor Seang Ang had visited the Thai border area and met with some pre-1975 believers who survived the genocide, but he opted to stay in Kao I Dang refugee camp, Thailand and started preaching. He also took time out to meet with some of his old colleagues. While he was living in the camp, Pastor Ang was selected to resettle in a third country, but he decided not to go. He wanted to return to Cambodia and build up the church. In 1984, he returned to Phnom Penh, but he was imprisoned for three months. He was warned and released on condition that he would not be involved in any Christian activity.

Many Cambodians started leaving their country during the period of the Khmer Rouge as well as due to civil war and conflicts after the Khmer Rouge period. According to Cormack, "the first Cambodian refugees were to be found in groups of hundreds encamped in the forests near streams and pools, sheltering under branches and the blankets they had brought with them. Eventually they were rounded up by the Thai Army and contained in small camps, or in the environs of isolated Buddhist temples".[14] In 1979, many Cambodians fled the country for their lives, seeking stability and peace. The refugee camps in Thailand became their home for many years to come. Along with the UNHCR, some Christian NGOs and missionaries were servicing refugees and their many and various needs. Cormack, who was part of the missionaries' effort in rendering support to Cambodian refugees from the very beginning recollects:

> From the very beginning, Christian missionaries were in the vanguard of those providing food, clothing and shelter. But we were also to provide far more. Speaking both Cambodian and Thai, we could also offer friendship, comfort, counsel and spiritual succour. From single copies of Cambodian Christian books and tracts snatched from Phnom Penh as we fled, large quantities of Christian literature were printed in Bangkok for distribution. There was also in Thailand a good stock of Gideon Cambodian New Testaments which the Gideon kindly allowed us to distribute.[15]

Several of those Cambodian refugees became Christians during their stay in the camps. In each camp, Christian believers were born. The number of Cambodians attending worship services on Sundays increased and churches were taking root. Some people who were already part of churches in Phnom Penh in earlier days took the lead in some of those church groups in the camps: they visited, distributed literature, conducted Bible courses and liaised with missionaries who came in regularly from nearby towns. These church groups among the refugees became an integral part of the camps, and the numbers of Khmer believers in camps increased. In 1980, there were more registered Khmer Christians among the refugees in camps in Thailand than in all of Cambodia before 1970. But a large number of them were repatriated to Western countries, mainly to the United States, Canada, Australia, France, and New Zealand.

There were various statistics from time to time about the early churches and Christian missions in Cambodia. It was recorded that in 1972, there were about 20,000 Christians in Cambodia, most of whom were Roman Catholics. Before the repatriation of the Vietnamese in 1970 and 1971, it was estimated that possibly as many as 62,000 Christians lived in Cambodia. According to Vatican statistics, members of the Roman Catholic Church in Cambodia numbered 120,000 in 1953, which at the time made Christianity the second largest religion in the country after Buddhism. In 1968, the Apostolic Vicariate of Phnom Penh was divided into three: Phnom Penh, Kompong Cham and Battambang. In April 1970, just before repatriation, it was estimated that there were about 50,000 Vietnamese Catholics in Cambodia. Many of the Catholics remaining in Cambodia in 1972 were Europeans — mainly French.

American Protestant missionary activity increased in Cambodia, especially among some of the hill tribes and among the Cham, after the establishment of the Khmer Republic. Steinberg reported that in 1953, an American Unitarian mission maintained a teacher-training school in Phnom Penh, and Baptist missions functioned in Batambang and Siemreap provinces. The 1962 census, which reported 2,000

[14] ibid

[15] ibid

Protestants in Cambodia, remained the most recent statistic for some years. In 1982, French geographer Jean Delvert reported that three Christian villages had existed in Cambodia, but he gave no indication of the size, location, or type of any of them. Observers reported that in 1980, there were more registered Khmer Christians among the refugees in camps in Thailand than in all of Cambodia before 1970. After the Paris Peace Agreement in 1991, large numbers of people, among those many Christians, started returning from refugee camps in Thailand to Cambodia;. The Protestant Christians who were in Cambodia in the early 1990's were mostly people who were once in refugee camps; the Roman Catholics were mostly people of Vietnamese ethnic origin who migrated to Cambodia after 1979.

Cambodian Christianity in a New Era Under New Communist Rule

The Pol Pot era witnessed a situation in which all religions were banned or forbidden. Church building and church-related institutions were totally destroyed or transformed into warehouses or military barracks. The Christianity and its institutional frameworks in Cambodia which was destroyed completely during the Pol Pot era started resurrecting in the post-Pol Pot era. The struggles of Christians and Christian missions in Cambodia have a rich history to record. Quite often, I think about what Don Cormack, who spent 20 years of his life in Cambodia as a missionary, reported on the fruitless toil, joyous spiritual awakening, persecution and indescribable devastation of the Cambodian church over the two decades - an experience that resembles that of the terrible invasion of Judah by locusts in about 400 B.C. described in apocalyptic imagery by the Prophet Joel and quoted by Don Cormack from the book of Joel: "What the cutting locust left, the swarming locust has eaten. What the swarming locust has left, the hopping locust has eaten, and what the hopping locust has left, the destroying locust has eaten." (Joel 1:4)

In January 1979, Vietnamese military forces invaded Cambodia and deposed Pol Pot. From 1979 to 1989, Cambodia was ruled by the Vietnamese-supported government of the People's Republic of Kampuchea, under the leadership of Heng Semarin. After Pol Pot was deposed and the situation started slowly improving, tens of thousands of Cambodians returned to Phnom Penh from the border camps. Among the returnees were many Christians. With the help of some remaining Christians who survived the Pol Pot era, some of them initiated fellowship groups in and around Phnom Penh in places such as Bung Yipun, Duey Mec, and the Old market, at Tumnup Tik, Praek Talong and Takmau. All together, there were only about hundred Christians in those different fellowship groups scattered around Phnom Penh. Four pastors of the Khmer Evangelical Church, an offshoot of the C&MA work in the country, were still alive and survived the killing field era of Pol Pot - Pastor Siang Ang, Pastor Ngor Von, Pastor Hom and Pastor Reach Yeah. They were the spiritual sources of leadership of the emerging church groups in the new era of Cambodia in the early 1980s. However, they were unable to come together for their worship or spiritual gathering for very long, as the new Heng Semarin government was suspicious of Christians and their foreign connections. The church meetings were forcibly closed in several areas. Pastors like Reach Yeah were branded as agents of the CIA. During the Indochina war and communist takeover in Laos and South Vietnam, several pastors and Christians were accused of CIA connections, and to a certain extent, it was also proven that CIA agents had infiltrated churches and operated through Christian pastors. The new government in Cambodia, which was again a communist government, was wary about CIA infiltration in the country through Christian churches. Moreover, the new Cambodian government was very much under the influence of the Vietnamese government and the Vietnamese Communist Party. A large number of Vietnamese soldiers and intelligence staff were also working in Cambodia. All these factors influenced the decisions of the Cambodian authorities from time to time to think and act on the assumption that CIA agents were possibly operational in Cambodia through Christians or churches.

Although Pol Pot was ousted, Cambodia was another communist state supported by Vietnam and the Soviet Union. In the area of religious freedom, the practice of Theravada Buddhism was allowed, but not

Christianity. This was mainly because Christianity was viewed as a Western religion. Although, it was risky, some Christians who survived the Pol Pot cruelties took the initiative to organize worship services in houses, but they were arrested and imprisoned. The Christian leaders who initiated house churches were branded as agents of the American CIA.. In addition to Pastor Seang Ang, Christian leaders like Ban Sam Ol, Timothy, Muth Bunthy, Ngeth Marene, Barnabas Mam and Sar Paulerk were very active in underground Christian mission in the early eighties. Barnabas Mam explained to me in early 1990s about his involvement in 1980's in initiating an underground English teaching school and his efforts to compose and record Khmer Christian hymns. He composed and recorded several Christian songs and they were secretly transported to the camps on the Thailand- Cambodia border. Barnabas Mam's song "*Ey lou nis knhom dang hoeille tha,* .... (Now I know by God's own grace…) was added to Sound the Bamboo, CCA Hymnal 2000.[16] This was the first time that a native Christian Khmer hymn was popularized in Asia through the regional ecumenical organization, the CCA. Like Barnabas, his activities were closely watched by the government's secret services and he was under surveillance, but later he escaped to Thailand.

Freedom of Worship in the New Era

By the end of 1980s, the country had been witnessing signs of changes in the political realm especially through international mediation for a negotiated political settlement. In 1989, a group of local church leaders approached the government with a request for permission to organize worships in their homes. Finally on 9 April 1990, the government gave permission for the churches to function openly. This was also the period that witnessed intensive negotiations for a peace settlement through international mediation, and several people started returning to Cambodia from Thai refugee camps, among them several Christians. Some Khmer people who became Christians while living in the camps started taking initiatives to organize worship services.

During the period in which several overseas mission agencies started sending their representatives to Cambodia. Brian Maher, who became a missionary to Cambodia later, writes about his 1990 visit to Cambodia :

> This was my first visit to the Land between the Tiger and Crocodile with Rev. Kong Chhon and the Rev. Sithan Lee. There were about 9 house churches existing in and around Phnom Penh at that time. Church leaders I met were Yorng Soth (C&MA), Sar Paulerk (Toul Tompong), Eang Chhun (Tonle Basaac), Im Chhrorn (Psa Tmei 1), Khieu Vanlorn (CCC), Taing Nary (CCC), Lav Hourn, Muth Bunthy (Santho Mok). Some other Church leaders I met were Bin David, Ngin Sacrovar, Pen Chin (Kompong Chhnang) and Ung Sophal. Chhon and Sithan Lee organized a meeting in one of the performing arts centres with about 700 people in attendance near Psa Dam Kor. A gospel message was preached and maybe 30 people came forward. During this trip I taught the youth (ages 16-30 single) while Chhon and Sithan taught pastors and elders. We met up with Bruce Carlton of CSI, Alice Compain of OMF, Steve Westergren of C& MA and a staff of World Relief who were just getting their work off the ground in 1990. Westerners and relief worker were followed and thought to be spies.[17]

This was the time that more and more overseas missionaries started visiting Cambodia in search of new avenues for establishing their denominations or para-church groups. In order to meet the growing needs of trained pastors and evangelists, the Phnom Penh Bible School (PPBS) was started in 1992. The PPBS was legally recognized by the State of Cambodia on March 1992. In order to meet the growing needs of pastors and Christian educators to work among the new Christian converts, the various denominations of the world Christian community and Christian organizations joined together to support the opening of the PPBS with

---

[16] Sound the Bamboo: CCA Hymnal 2000, Hymn No. 289, Christian Conference of Asia, Hong Kong, 2000

[17] Cry of the Gecko, op.ctied, Cambodian Christian .com

Khmer as the main language and English as the second one. The PPBS remained as an interdenominational Christian institution.[18]

Cambodians have been in hope and rejoicing since the negotiations for a political settlement of Cambodia reached its final stages in early 1991. Finally, agreements on a "Comprehensive political settlement of the Cambodia conflict" was signed in Paris, France on 23 October 1991. The "Principles for a new constitution for Cambodia"[19] were also agreed upon by all parties to the conflict. The principles agreed as part of the political settlement covered provisions in the new constitution to assure protection of human rights, and stipulated that "the constitution will contain a declaration of fundamental rights, including the rights to life, personal liberty, security freedom of movement, freedom of assembly, assembly and association…".

Arrival of New Missionaries

Since the news spread about the possibility of a new political climate in the country, and refugees were returning from camps back to Cambodia, a new era for evangelization also started in the country. Several Christian missionary organizations and denominations from Western countries including the Khmer Diaspora church representatives and churches and mission groups from Asian countries such as South Korea, Singapore, Malaysia, Hong Kong and the Philippines started arriving for missionary activities. Most of them started their work in the country's capital, and several started their missions in the provinces. Some of these mission organizations started English teaching centres for local students. Other denominations and their diaconal divisions started orphanages, old-age homes and other social service missions.

Some mission bodies that had earlier worked in Cambodia before 1975 came back in the new era, for example the OMF, formerly known as the Overseas Missionary Fellowship, and the China Inland mission, first involved in Cambodia in 1973. An OMF team came to Phnom Penh in 1973 to work with the Evangelical Church of Cambodia, alongside the C&MA missionaries. OMF was involved in the Ta Khamau Bible School and youth centre near the Olympic market in Phnom Penh. Alice Compain, a prominent missionary who was instrumental in composing many Khmer hymns and who worked in Cambodia prior to 1975, returned in 1990.

Certain other para-church groups started their missionary activities among minority ethnic groups such as Kuay, Mnong, Krug-Brout, and Jarari. Stieng, Poar, Kavet, Mel, Kaco, Cham, Rahe, Lun, Tampuan, Samre, Karol and Thmon in the Ratanakiri provinces of Northeast Cambodia and other border areas close to Thailand and Vietnam. As the number of overseas mission agencies and para-church groups started growing in different parts of Cambodia, the country became a missionary battlefield. Some of the Asian churches, especially from South Korea, started sending large numbers of missionaries to work in Cambodia. Most of them were sent by individual congregations and not by the central mission departments of the mainline denominations. The competition in missionary activities confused the new converts who had never heard of denominational affiliations. Similarly, the para-church groups from Western countries that became active in Cambodia in church planning ministry as well as in social service sectors added more confusion for local Khmer Christians.

The Assemblies of God started a fairly large mission whose thrust was "evangelism and discipleship working together to establish the church of Jesus Christ". Similarly, the Baptist missions as well as several other para-church organizations from the West also started mission activities with components of social

---

[18] Setan Lee, PPBS Director, in a note written on August 16, 1993 which was published CCS news, Issue No.3, year 1, 1993

[19] 'Agreements on A Comprehensive Political Settlement of the Cambodia Conflict', Paris, 23 October 1991, United Nations,
Department of Public Information, January 1992, p.39

services at various levels. The Baptist church launched a programme to train church leaders. The Rural Leaders Training programme initiated at the Russey Keo Khmer Baptist Church aimed at equipping new generation church leaders especially for ministry in new congregations in rural provinces. The Baptist Church announced that the Rural Leaders' Training was not a denominational programme, but was "evolved out of a concern to follow up on the many congregations which were appearing throughout Cambodia" during that period.[20] The module designed for the rural leaders training were designed to last for two weeks and to take place once every three months. Different groups were participating in different sessions of the training programmes. This system had been developed in such a way as to accommodate rural leaders who were not able to give up their farming or other subsistence income sources. This programme was also designed to allow rural leaders to maintain their regular source of income while at the same time providing a quality training programme which would equip them to carry out their ministry.[21] The training classes were conducted by local Khmer staff as well as trainers from various other Christian groups such as Campus Crusade for Christ, C&MA, OMF, Phnom Penh Bible School and Baptist church leaders.

Several other training programmes were also conducted in the country by various other groups in the 1990s in which ethnic Khmer expatriates played significant roles. These Khmer expatriates were mostly individuals who had emigrated from refugee camps to other countries through refugee resettlement packages, and were sent back to Cambodia through the sponsorships of Khmer congregations in the Western countries to work for various missions. On the one hand, it was assumed that these expatriate Khmer Christian leaders possessed more cultural sensitivities to engage in evangelization with local people. However, it was also noted in various contexts that they brought their Western evangelical and charismatic values and ultra-conservative theological views with them, which was not suitable in a predominantly Buddhist setting. They could not fine-tune their Western conservative theological and biblical interpretations with cultural sensitivity and contextualization.

Gospel and Mission Without Cultural Sensitivities

The hidden dangers of lack of cultural sensitivity became very evident during the first few years of the massive evangelization process initiated by certain Western funded groups. The training programmes they organised for the new converts often did not take into consideration the cultural and religious values of local people. Church planting mission through aggressive missionary evangelism became a common pattern in several areas, which created more tensions among communities. For example, the "God Bless Cambodia Crusade" under the leadership of American evangelist Mike Evans, held in November 1994 at the Olympic Stadium in Phnom Penh, ended up as a fiasco. This incident generated a furore over the missionary activities that had sprung up in Cambodia within such a short period of time when the new Constitution allowed freedom of religion. Christian pastors and followers from the provinces told us about their bitter experiences and the after-effects of the 'Evans Crusade' at Phnom Penh's Olympic stadium. The organizers of the 'Mike Evans Ministries' (MEM) crusade promised a miracle of healing as an outcome of his 'God Bless Cambodia Crusade'. The Crusade advertisements promised that "the blind would see and the lame would walk". But when no healings occurred during the event, desperate audience waiting there for several days rioted and finally Mike Evans was forced to flee the country. This event severely harmed Cambodia's minority Christian community at the time they were attempting to build up the church and faith for the first time in the post-Pol Pot era, especially when they had finally obtained official freedom for worship and propagation of the gospel. The minority Christians experienced

---

[20] . Bruce Carlton, "Rural Leaders' Training program", CCS News, Issue No.5, Year, 2 , June/July, 1994.
[21] *ibid*

intimidation by gangs on motorbikes, stones being thrown at churches, insults and persecution of pastors and believers, and were even branded as being responsible for magic for having converted Buddhists to Christianity. Cambodian Christians were insulted by their fellow Cambodians for believing in the "Western God, Jesus". Referring to the Mike Evans crusade and the Olympic Stadium riot, Minister/Secretary of State for Religious Affairs Mr Hien Vanniroth on a visit to the CCA headquarters in Hong Kong expressed his government's concern over missionary activities in Cambodia which portrayed "Buddhists as evil people as they worship an idol God".

The Minister also complained about how difficult it was to get Christians to work together although they are a small community. The power of money, overseas influence and material assistance to people to convert from other religions to Christianity with the support of certain missionaries were pin-pointed as real problems hindering communal harmony in Cambodia. In an interview with the *Phnom Penh Post*, Hien Vanniroth said that "some foreign-supported churches are giving money to people if they join their churches". He also said that "it is very difficult to get Christians to work together".[22] Buddhist monks and Buddhists believers have also been struggling to understand the wave of Christian missionary evangelism.

Immediately after the Mike Evans episode, the Foreign Correspondence Club of (FCC) in Phnom Penh organized a debate entitled "Does Cambodia Need Christianity?" The panellists selected to speak on this occasion were one of the four Supreme Patriarchs of Cambodian Buddhism Venerable Maha Goshananda, Ahmad Yahya, a member of Parliament from the Muslim ethnic Cham who was then also the Chairman of the Cambodian Islamic Committee, and a Roman Catholic Maryknoll priest Rev. Jim Noonan on behalf of Christianity. Ahmed Yahya, with whom I had many encounters and who later became a good friend, told me in a private conversation later about this panel discussion in which he had expressed his opinion that Christianity should be an integral part of the new Cambodian society. He had appreciated the position taken by the Ven. Maha Goshananda, who had emphasized religious tolerance, appreciating the role of Christianity in Cambodia. However, Yahya mentioned that he was surprised to note that some Western journalists who came from a Christian background had raised questions in such a way to the panellists, as if Christianity could become problematic to Cambodia in the future. The only English newspaper of Cambodia at that time, the Phnom Penh Post published several stories about Mike Evan's Crusade and also other problems created by certain Christian sects which created communal disharmony. Local Khmer language newspapers also reported on stories of communal hatred being precipitated in villages due to Christian missionary activities.

While this missionary competition continued to spread, local Christians also shifted their loyalties from one denomination or organization to another. A question raised in many quarters was: "What is the unique contribution of Christianity or the Christian message to Cambodia?" In other words, the new Christianity brought by foreigners in the new era had not been helping the Cambodians to grow with much-needed spiritual nourishment, but lured them to organizational and hierarchical values. Brian M. Maher of the International Technical Assistance programme in Cambodia observed in this regard:

> I often wondered why some "old-timers" were often so cynical and seemed to treat the Khmers a little on what I thought was the harsh side. What I have learned since is that we Westerners think being patient, long-suffering, easy-going, laid back and forgiving is the most Christ-like, and that is how we should be here. Sooner or later we will realize that much of our understanding of those qualities is culturally influenced. If we don't adjust our manner to each person and situation, we'll get burned unnecessarily and we won't help the Khmers at all. For example, the Western Christian way is to be overly forgiving and extremely patient. Doing this does not teach responsibility and accountability. It often gives the people we are trying to help limitless boundaries to what they want to do and not what they should be doing.

---

[22] "The stones being thrown at Christians", Mang Channo, Phnom Penh Post, March 10-23, 1995, p.17

> A majority of Asian Christian Missionary Groups are doomed to rough roads ahead as they copy the colonial missionary mind-set that the Western missions are so eager to put behind them. The danger of building big buildings, offering higher salaries, buying motor bikes further confuses the integrity of the Khmer church. With Cambodia being a patronage society as it is, such church planting methodologies only serve to facilitate further dependency on entities other than God.[23]

Ecumenical Accompaniment in Cambodia

The ecumenical movement has a long history of involvement and accompaniment in Cambodia, especially in nurturing and shaping ecumenism and the ecumenical movement in the local context. However, ecumenical accompaniment in Cambodia since 1979 was mainly in the area of humanitarian assistance and development-related projects. Intensive ecumenical involvement in these areas in Cambodia began immediately after Vietnamese invasion and ouster of the Pol Pot regime in 1979. The country was swamped with emergency assistance and thereafter development assistance through the efforts of the ecumenical family only after the overthrow of the Pol Pot regime. In fact, Kampuchean refugees in Vietnam were assisted with food supplies because of the widespread flooding in Vietnam in 1978. The WCC's Fund for Reconciliation and Reconstruction in Indochina was not requested by the Pol Pot regime, and therefore no projects were undertaken inside Cambodia. However, after the collapse of the regime, the ecumenical family did not waste much time in sending relief and finding ways to help rehabilitate the Khmer people who had suffered. The ecumenical family quickly mobilized and organized to send emergency supplies. This was possible mainly because of the WCC's direct involvement in Vietnam for several years, and also thanks to the reputation gained due to the selfless work and development assistance provided to Vietnamese people in their war torn context through official arrangements with the Vietnamese government.

As Cambodia was totally isolated from the rest of the world, WCC or CCA could not make any contacts with the people or government in Cambodia during the Pol Pot era, although both WCC and CCA were involved in relief work in Vietnam and Laos during the American war in Indochina and in the post war period of reconstruction of these two war torn countries. On 17 May 1979, Frans Tumiwa of CCA and Brian Turner of Christian World Service New Zealand met in Hanoi, Vietnam with Mr. Chea Soth, Ambassador for the national United Front for the Salvation of Kampuchea (FUNSK) to express the concern of Christians throughout the world for the suffering of the Khmer people. As a result of this meeting, the WCC and the CCA received an invitation to send a delegation as soon as circumstances allowed the authorities in Phnom Penh to be the host. Finally, the delegation was able to enter Kampuchea only on 14 August 1979. Members of a four member team representing WCC and CCA were the first foreign nationals allowed to visit Cambodia by the new government. Mr. Frans Tumiwa, CCA executive secretary for Indochina programme and development and service received Visa No 1 stamped on his passport from the authorities in Phnom Penh on their arrival.

Following the discussions at the WCC Central Committee meeting in January 1979,[24] the Commission on Inter-Church Aid, Refugee and World Service (CICARWS) together with CCA sent a three member team to Cambodia in early October and based on their reports WCC launched an appeal to the churches on 16 October 1979 for US$ 2.5 million for relief work in Cambodia.

Suffering was an understatement to describe the conditions of the Cambodian people, but the ultimate concern of ecumenical family members were the gross human rights violations, genocide, starvation and

[23] Bian M.Maher, "Tyranny of the urgent", CCS News & Views, April/May 1996, p.5

[24] Minutes of the Thirty First meeting, central Committee, World Council of Chruches, Kingston, Jamaica, 1979, p.p46.47; 72

disease the people faced during the Pol Pot regime. When 1.5 million people fled to Thailand (600,000) and to Vietnam (900,000), the plight of the Cambodians in the refugee camps became a concern for several ecumenical agencies related to the WCC. The movement of Kampuchean refugees into Thailand consequently displaced 200,000 Thai villagers. Kampuchean refugees in Vietnam had largely returned, but the refugees in Thailand had swelled immensely, creating a big headache for the government of Thailand. The WCC's CICARWS enabled the Church of Christ in Thailand to initiate relief to Kampuchean refugees and internally displaced Thais on the Cambodian-Thailand border. Housing assistance was given to displaced Thais and supplementary feeding for Kampuchean refugees. While the Church of Christ in Thailand (CCT) continued to take charge of assisting the refugees on the border of Thailand, starting from 1979, the WCC/CCA took responsibilities for the operations in and around Phnom Penh.

After the Pol Pot regime, additional thousands of new refugees left Cambodia in 1979; they were considered "illegal immigrant" by the Thai authorities. They too were seeking a safer and better haven for themselves and their families. Although they were considered illegal immigrants by the Thai authorities, they had the same reasons to leave Kampuchea; thus assistance to them did not differ from that given to those refugees who were already there. The WCC coordinated with ICRC, UNHCR, UNICEF and OXFAM on supplies in order to avoid overlapping of materials and efficient food distribution. The increasing number of refugees from Kampuchea to the Thai border posed a problem to the Thai government. It was their priority to give aid to the Kampucheans on their side of the border. It also threatened their political neutrality if any aid was given to Kampuchea from Thailand or if they extended assistance to other relief organizations. They recommended that the WCC avoids involving Thailand until Kampuchea would have had found a political solution and the withdrawal of Vietnamese forces. Though the Thai authorities wanted full authority in the delivery of supplies, the WCC was in constant and arduous negotiations with the Thai authorities to send aid to Kampuchea. Until their stipulations were honoured, they didn't advocate help to Phnom Penh, but on occasions granted permission for airlifts to deliver food and medical supplies from Geneva to Kampuchea with no refuelling and reloading in Bangkok.

The churches involvement in Kampuchea's relief work began with airlifts of medical and relief supplies from Europe. Two of the WCC Inter-Church Aid, Refugee and World Service (CICARWS)-related agencies participated in the effort - HEKS of Switzerland and CIMADE of France. Since the first airlift, the WCC/CCA operation partnered with one air shipment, which was responsible for two chartered flights. The flights took medicines, medical equipment and dried and canned fish into the country. 5,500 tons of food and other supplies were shipped by sea from Singapore into both Kompong Som and Phnom Penh. A major part of relief was directed to two public hospitals and one orphanage in Phnom Penh and another hospital and orphanage in Kampong Speu. During the Pol Pot regime, pharmaceutical production machines were deliberately damaged. WCC/CCA took the responsibility of rehabilitating the two pharmaceutical production laboratories. The ecumenical family stepped up the pharmaceutical industry and hospital supplies in the country. Catering to hospitals and the pharmaceutical industry showed WCC's emphasis on the rejuvenation of the health sector. It was observed that the Ministry of Health was the weakest governmental department and WCC/CCA helped the ministry to re-establish their health care system. Even school supplies and notebooks were distributed to children. Means of transportation were greatly needed in order to assist the distribution of relief supplies, much of which was concentrated in one area. In 1986, the WCC signed a cooperative agreement with the Ministry of Agriculture with the commitment to cooperate in the development of 6000 hectares of rice lands, including the rehabilitation of an irrigation canal network. The WCC donated topographical equipment, storage facilities for seed, fertilizers, and plant protection chemicals for agricultural development.

When WCC started its relief and development assistance to Cambodia, it was on the basis of humanitarian principles. There was no religious motive behind such support. Although there were Protestant churches in different parts of the country, the WCC did not have any member churches in

Cambodia even before the takeover by Pol Pot. The WCC representative who was sent to Cambodia for coordinating the humanitarian assistance was a French pastor, Jean Clavaud, who served in the Evangelical Church of Cambodia between 1960-1975. He was based in Phnom Pen as the WCC/CCA representative from 1979-1982. He set up an office so that distribution of supplies to the people could be monitored. His knowledge of the Khmer language and his intimate knowledge of the country was a constructive advantage for the WCC/CCA to operate effectively. Pastor Clavaud's main responsibility was to oversee the reception, supervision and distribution of food equipment, liaise with the government authorities and coordinate WCC/Christian Conference of Asia (CCA) efforts with other relief organizations in Phnom Penh.[25] Meanwhile, Clavaud also took initiatives to organize ecumenical worship services in Phnom Penh which expatriate aid workers stationed there as well as some local Khmer Christians also attended. The worship services organized by Clavaud created anger and misunderstandings on the part of government authorities. As a result of this, he was expelled from the country by force in 1982.[26] Clavaud's expulsion marked the beginning of a three-year suspension of WCC activities in Cambodia. Activities continued after intense negotiations with Kampuchean authorities in 1985, and resumed projects begun before the WCC's suspension in 1982 and started with other development projects. The WCC also supported the Ministry of Industry dispensary, which primarily served factory workers in the southern suburbs of the country, and regularly supplied laboratory instruments, basic chemical agents and new dentist cabinets. The WCC Kampuchean Programme office acted as a purchase agent and monitored the application of the imported articles and instruments.

A Shift in Ecumenical Accompaniment Foci

The Ecumenical Forum on Vietnam, Laos and Cambodia (VLC Forum) with members mainly from the ecumenical development agencies in Europe and North America, which was coordinated by the WCC Asia Desk, extended all kinds of support to the Cambodia development programmes. In addition to the WCC, other members of the ecumenical family who were involved in humanitarian aid and development assistance such as HEKS, Lutheran World Service and Church World Service, USA also continued their field operations. Country representatives of all these organizations were based in Phnom Penh. In 1992, the WCC decided to close down its field operations, and this was the time that a joint programme with the CCA was initiated. It was decided to accompany the newly formed churches and the ecumenical initiatives of small Christian communities. It was in this context that the VLC Forum supported the WCC idea of focusing its involvement on support to local Christian communities in their faith journey and ecumenical journey. With such an aim, the WCC and CCA jointly appointed a Liaison Secretary for the WCC/CCA Indochina programme. One of the main responsibilities assigned to the Liaison Secretary was to assist the closure of the WCC office in Phnom Penh and arrange a smooth transition of WCC's on-going programmes with various government ministries to local organizations or through other ecumenical development agencies working in Cambodia. By mid-1993, Mathews George Chunakara was appointed as Liaison Secretary / Ecumenical Enabler of the VLC programmes to develop programmes in relation to local churches in all three Indochina countries as well as advocacy on various issues such as reconciliation and peace in war torn Cambodia, human rights, landmines; advocacy on lifting the economic embargo against Vietnam, impacts of *Agent Orange defolio* in Vietnam; unexploded ordnance clearance in Laos as well as the issue of religious freedom and to assist the clocal churches in developing good church-state relations. However, most of the work of the Liaison Secretary was focussed on Cambodia as it had already

---

[25] Ecumenical Peace Service, World Council of Churches, 18 October, 1979

[26] Park Kyung Seo, "On-going Ecumenical Involvement and Future Direction", in Ecumenical Response to Indochina, Mathews
George Chunakara, (Ed.), Christian Conference of Asia, Hong Kong 1995, p.32

become an open society whereas Vietnam and Laos still remained closed-door societies. Socially and politically, both Vietnam and Laos, were controlled and religious freedom, especially involvement from overseas Christian bodies, was limited or restricted in these countries.

A meeting of the VLC Forum met in Bangkok in October 1993 and decided to find new ways to develop ecumenical initiatives for Cambodia and explored the possibility of constructing an Ecumenical Centre for the Churches in Cambodia. In February 1994, a four-member team composed of CCA General Secretary Bishop John V. Samuel, WCC Asia Secretary Park Kyung Seo, and Church of Christ in Thailand General Secretary Sint Kimachandra and Mathews George Chunakara visited Phnom Penh and had discussions with the local church leaders. The members of the team reviewed the on-going ecumenical involvement in Cambodia. As the VLC Forum meeting in Bangkok in the previous year had budgeted US$ 120,000 for the proposed Ecumenical Centre, the VLC Forum Core Group meeting held in New York on June 1994 again discussed this possibility, but a major question discussed concerning the fact that "in Cambodia, church leaders are still disunited and have no plans and vision. Who is going to be the owner of the Ecumenical Centre?" Although this idea of an Ecumenical Centre was encouraging and had good intentions of developing ecumenism in the local contexts in Cambodia, "the property and the building might further divide the churches in Cambodia and in that context, it is better to wait some more time to crystallise the idea in a proper way". In this context, the Core Group meeting authorized the Liaison Secretary to continue to discuss the idea with the Cambodian churches.

Cambodian Christian Women's Association

A women's fellowship used to meet at the former WCC office for a weekly prayer meeting. Now that the WCC office was closed down and the idea of an Ecumenical Centre was not taking shape, it was decided to rent a smaller building for conducting programmes and as a meeting place of the local churches. As this new place was meant for enabling local ecumenical activities, it was named the 'Cambodia Ecumenical Centre' (CEC). One staff person from the former WCC field office, Ms Keo S. Vuthy, was retained as office manager, and two other staff, a driver and caretaker, were also retained to work for the new office. A visiting pastor from the CCT, Rev. Rung, who was sent by the CCT to assist the local churches, was also asked to be based in this Ecumenical Centre whenever he was in Cambodia. CEC became the base for all CCA and WCC related international contacts, visits, and programmes in Cambodia. The Liaison Secretary also retained an office at the CEC during his frequent visits.

During the visit of the ecumenical delegation in February 1994, the members of the delegation discussed with the local women's fellowship leaders the possibility of registering a Christian Women's NGO. The Liaison Secretary followed this discussion up with the local women's group. He met with the then Deputy Foreign Affairs minister Ms Pok Marina, and sought her assistance to get the women's fellowship registered as a local NGO. Pok Marina helped the process of registering the women's group with the social welfare ministry as a local NGO under the name the 'Cambodia Christian Women's Association' (CCWA). The members of the women's fellowship met and elected their own office bearers with Ms Yos Em Sithan as president. While the process for registration was going on, the Liaison Secretary discussed the idea of naming the organization the Cambodia Ecumenical Women's Association (CEWA), but Mrs Sithan was not in favour of using the term "Ecumenical". This was mainly due to the fact that certain international evangelical organizations from the USA based in Phnom Penh were exerting some influence on the leaders of the women's fellowship and trying to attract the women's group to their orbits. For a while there was confusion in the CCWA leadership and in their programme thrusts as well. CWS country director Ms Linda Hartke was requested to assist in advising the CCWA, but the CCWA leaders were not very keen to seek her help and this was also mainly due to the influence of certain para-church groups. CWS arranged with its intern Amy Spradling from the United Methodist Church, USA, to teach the members of the

CCWA English. Later, another intern, Ms Emma Leslie from Australia, was also brought to Cambodia to teach CCWA members English with the assistance of the Frontier Internship Mission (FIM) in Geneva.

The CCWA also started three projects with financial support through WCC/CCA VLC Forum – training in weaving and tailoring; and a microcredit programme to assist the rural women. CCWA planned training in weaving and tailoring for twelve young women at a time and two batches every year. Each time, CCWA recruited young women from the provinces with the help of local church groups, and they were housed during the training period. While the new rented building was expected to be a centre for local ecumenical activities, most of the building was occupied by the CCWA for accommodating the trainees of the tailoring programme, weekly Bible study, weaving and tailoring machines, etc. As this became inconvenient for other programmes to be conducted at the Ecumenical Centre, the CCWA project was shifted to another rented building. The space rented for the CCWA project was still not sufficient, and this was brought to the attention of the Liaison Secretary by the CCWA president. Finally, the Liaison Secretary made a proposal to buy a small building outside Phnom Penh in the name of the CCWA, which was officially registered with the government as a local NGO. While the Liaison Secretary took the initiative of raising special funds for purchasing a building for the CCWA project, the CCWA officers under the leadership of Ms Yves Em Sithan and CEC office manager Ms K.S.Vuthy identified a property on the outskirts of Phnom Penh. The price paid for the property, a small piece of land and an old building in a dilapidated condition, was US$ 6,800, but in the end, a total of about $13,000 was spent for various other expenses such as constructing an additional two-storied wooden building for meetings, training and office space, a compound wall on four sides, electricity connections, digging a well and fixing a water pump and also for the land registration expenses. The funds required for this were raised by the Liaison Secretary from different sources. A Norwegian mission organization known as Christian Mission to Buddhists - CMB (subsequently the name of this organization was changed to *Aeropagus*) contributed a major part of the amount required. The Liaison Secretary had earlier arranged a familiarization visit for Rev. Ernest Harbakk, who was Asia Secretary of the CMB, to Cambodia, Vietnam and Laos and they travelled together to all three countries. As Rev. Harbakk understood the need for local churches in Cambodia, he responded favourably to the request and convinced his Board back in Norway to allocate some funds for purchasing a property for CCWA. The new project centre for the CCWA was inaugurated in May 1996 by the-then CCA General Secretary Feliciano V. Carino. The inaugural function was attended by participants of an international consultation organized by CCA on internally displaced people. Several Asian church leaders who participated at the CCA consultation also attended the inauguration of the CCWA project centre. Soitua Nababan of Indonesia, Henrietta Hutabarat, then CCA Associate General Secretary, S.M Chowdhury, Bangladesh, Ipe Joseph, General Secretary, NCC India, Subodh Adhikari, General Secretary of NCC Bangladesh, Samuel Gill, General Secretary, NCC Pakistan, Joseph Pattiasina, General Secretary of PGI, Indonesia, etc., were some of the Asian church leaders who were present at that function. A WCC staff member, Helen Musa also was present.

CCWA became the first Christian organisation or institution in the country that could own its own property at that time.

The CCWA has been expanding its activities and it gave many young women the opportunity to get technical skills in weaving and tailoring which helped them to get jobs in garment factories or to be self-employed on completion of their training. The training also had an inbuilt component of spiritual development and Christian and ecumenical formation as it was a six-months residence programme. Some of those young women became active in their local areas in organizing prayer meetings and conducting Sunday prayer fellowships. Unfortunately, problems cropped up at the leadership level of CCWA, and this affected CCWA's smooth functioning as in the earlier days. Later, CCWA became the Women's Desk of the Kampuchea Christian Council.

Early Initiatives for Ecumenical Formation: Cambodia Ecumenical Centre

Towards the end of 1994, the earlier plan of initiating a Cambodia Ecumenical Centre was re-evoked. A meeting of Cambodian church leaders was convened by the Liaison Secretary on behalf of CCA , WCC and the VLC Ecumenical Forum in July 1994 in Phnom Penh, in which representatives of different churches and congregations from different provinces attended. A bylaw for the smooth functioning of the new ecumenical structure was also adopted. A seven-member management board was elected. The Ministry of Religious Affairs officially recognized the CEC in November 1994. The CEC became a centre for all ecumenical activities in Phnom Penh. Rev. Rung, the visiting pastor from CCT Thailand, facilitated Bible classes for local groups. A youth conference was organized under the auspices of the CEC, in which the Liaison Secretary promoted the idea of forming a Cambodian Christian Youth Association as a body similar to the CCWA. Many young people welcomed the idea, and subsequently a new youth organization was formed under the name of CCYA. The CCYA started mobilizing young Cambodian youths, mostly students who were studying in high school and colleges. English training courses and computer training were also arranged for young people through CEC and CCYA. A music group was also formed. Through the CCYA, several young people were identified to go for theological training. Smak Sothy Sithara, Eang Chhun, Yi Narith, Chim Pich, Dara Cheat, Uy Dy etc., were selected and sent to theological schools and seminaries in Hong Kong, Malaysia, Sri Lanka and India. Scholarships were arranged by CCA and WCC for their studies in Hong Kong Lutheran Theological Seminary, the Malaysia Theology Seminary, the Gurukul Theological Seminary, the Mar Thoma Episcopal Jubilee Institute in Tiruvalla, Kerala, India and the Cathedral Institute in Colombo, Sri Lanka.

Various ecumenical formation trainings also were organized by the CEC jointly with various CCA programme units – youth, women, theology, Christian education, Indochina Desk, etc. Several church leaders from other Asian countries facilitated the ecumenical training programmes. At certain times, training programmes were organized at provincial levels in Kompong Thom, Kompong Cham provinces. Through CEC, several local church leaders, and pastors were selected to visit different Asian countries as part of a people-to-people visit programme developed as part of the CCA/WCC Indochina programme. While CEC became the organizing and facilitating body of ecumenical activities in Cambodia under the overall supervision and guidance of the Liaison Secretary, several local leaders got opportunities to understand the need for united activities rather than independent operations of local churches. In the Cambodian church context, it was very difficult for the local churches to come together and to be engaged in any ecumenical activity. The programmes organized by CCA and the opportunities gained through visits to other countries and participation at international ecumenical programmes in other Asian countries gave opportunities for many Cambodian Christians to understand the ecumenical spirit. Those involvements slowly helped them to welcome the idea of a proper ecumenical structure in Cambodia.

First Attempt for an Ecumenical Council in Cambodia

In fact, there was an earlier effort by Cambodian Christian leaders themselves to form a national ecumenical council as early as 1992 and early 1993. When the number of Christian believers started slowly growing at that time, the number of denominations also started growing very fast, which resulted in a disproportionate level of denominationalism among a handful of Cambodian Christians (a maximum of two or three thousand Protestant Christians in the early 1990s). As the multiplicity of denominations increased factionalism among the small number of Cambodian Christians, the WCC field office in Phnom Penh gave support to a group of Cambodian church leaders to form an ecumenical platform. Several church leaders representing various Protestant denominations met together in early 1993 at the WCC office in Phnom Penh, and they decided to establish an ecumenical organizational structure under the name of the General Council of Churches in Cambodia (GCCC).

The GCCC claimed it had a membership of 11 denominations – CMA, Baptist, Nazarene, Church of Christ, Methodist, Seventh-Day Adventist, Assembly of God, Chinese Church, Vietnamese Church, Presbyterian and Independent – and a total of 89 congregations with about 3,000 members. They elected four officers: Sar Paulark (President), Ng Sam (Vice President), Eang Chhun (General Secretary) and Yes Em Sithan (Treasurer). But the GCCC did not last long, due to disagreements at the leadership level, and very soon, when the CCA/WCC Liaison Secretary took charge in September 1993, it was already a defunct organization. He tried to bring the disunited group together again after his first visit to Cambodia in September 1993. In August 1994, he again contacted all of them and visited all officers of the GCCC individually at their residences or work places. During those meetings, he made a proposal to organize a one-day retreat for church leaders. Each leader agreed to the proposal, and they also agreed to select five local church leaders from each group to participate in the retreat. As an outcome of this discussion, a retreat was organized on 24 September at the CEC in which 27 local church leaders attended. The need to revive the local ecumenical structure was also discussed at that stage. All officers of the defunct GCCC were invited to participate in various CCA programmes.

Subsequently, GCCC Secretary Eang Chhun attended a three-week training in Thailand on – Healing Ministry; the Vice-president Nng Saom attended the Asian Ecumenical Course for three weeks in Hong Kong; the President Sar Paulark took part in an Indochinese Church leaders' team visit to Malaysia, Sri Lanka and India; and Treasurer Ms Sithan attended a workshop on Integrating Faith with Shalom in Myanmar. These attempts were made to provide opportunities for Cambodian church leaders to understand the ecumenical movement better as they were denied such opportunities in the past due to the political situation and the fact that the country had remained closed for many years. Although, the GCCC is still defunct, all these leaders were relating with CEC and participating in various activities of CEC on individual basis. Among them, Sithan and Eang Chhun worked very closely through CEC. The various activities organized by the CEC in the past years gave impetus to discussion of the need for an ecumenical council in Cambodia to bring together the growing Christian churches from various denominational backgrounds which until then were totally disunited and functioning independently without relating to one another.

Founding of National Ecumenical Council: Kampuchea Christian Council (KCC)

Through the work of the CCA Indochina programme, a new initiative was taken to bring together various denominations and church groups in a common platform to form a national ecumenical council. Much groundwork was already done for ecumenical formation since 1993. In addition to that, special efforts were made to discuss this idea with several church leaders. Finally, a wider representative meeting, a special convention of church leaders from different parts of Cambodia, was held in Phnom Penh on 6-7 August 1998. The delegates decided to form the Kampuchea Christian Council (KCC). The Convention adopted a Constitution for the KCC[27] and also elected office bearers with Tun Kakada as President (Baptist Church), Pen Sorithy, as First Vice President, Eang Chhun as second Vice president, Eang Suhay as Treasurer. Smak Sothy Sithara who was sent to Hong Kong Lutheran Theological Seminary after four years of studies returned to Cambodia in 1999 and he was appointed General Secretary of KCC.

The founding of the KCC roused new hopes and enthusiasm among several churches and their leaders. The decision to form the KCC was communicated to the Cambodian government Ministry of Religious

[27] . The first draft of the Constitution of the KCC was drafted by Mathews George Chunakara, taking examples of HKCC Constitution which provides scope for individual congregations are eligible to become members of KCC. In a context like in Cambodia where large numbers of congregations are not affiliated to any denominations, but remain independent. This is the main reason for adopting the pattern of membership in KCC with three different segments: independent congregations, denominations and Christian/ ecumenical organisations.

Affairs and the KCC was officially recognized by the Ministry as a coordinating body of various churches at the national level. The news about the formation of a new national Christian council in Cambodia was well received by many churches in Asian countries, especially those who had been receiving Cambodian church leaders in their countries as well as those who had opportunities to visit Cambodia on various occasions to take part in different programmes or exchange visits since 1993. The churches in Hong Kong, especially the Hong Kong Christian Council (HKCC) and the CCA, assisted the Cambodian churches in their efforts to form the KCC. The HKCC and its member churches in Hong Kong sponsored the visit of 18 Cambodian church leaders to Hong Kong in May 1998 while they were in deep discussion on the formation of a national ecumenical council, seeking new ideas and gaining experience to inform their efforts in this direction, and discussing the draft of a constitution for the new body.

In a report after the founding of the KCC, the Executive Secretary of CCA, who is also the Liaison Secretary of the CCA/WCC programme, wrote:

> The formation of the KCC was a breakthrough in Cambodian church and ecumenical history, although we cannot expect any miracle from this united effort of some churches. The fact is that at least some churches and related bodies are part of this symbolic action of church unity. The KCC membership comprises of the Baptist Church, Cambodia Independent Churches, the Presbyterian Church in Cambodia, Swiss Methodist Church in Cambodia, Church of Christ in Cambodia, Church of Christ in Cambodia (USA), Cambodian Christian Youth Association and Cambodia Pastors' Fellowship. The SCM of Cambodia has been formed recently and the SCM also will be a member of KCC.[28]

The CCA general committee at its meeting in November 1998 decided to accept the application of KCC as a full member of the CCA at the next General Assembly in 2000. Finally, KCC was accepted as new member of the CCA at the general Assembly held in Tomohon, Indonesia in June 2000.

During the period of 2002-2003, internal leadership problems affected the KCC as well as the CCWA (Cambodia Christian Women's Association). By the time CCA and WCC had intervened and made arrangements for reorganization of the KCC and its programme structures, CCWA became the women's desk of KCC, the property purchased initially for CCWA was transferred to KCC. The headquarters of the KCC was shifted from central Phnom Penh to the new city area where the CCWA office was located. The building was renovated and an additional room added for the KCC office. CCYA became the youth desk of KCC, and a youth secretary was appointed. A new KCC leadership was elected at the General Assembly in 2008 for a five-year term. Now that there were organisational problems and leadership changes in certain positions, this has affected the full participation of several of its member bodies as well as the on-going work of the Council. A solidarity team visited Cambodia from 27 to 31 October 2012 met with several leaders of KCC and had extensive discussions of future of the ecumenical movement in Cambodia, especially on ways and means to revitalize the KCC.

New Version of Khmer Bible: Model for Ecumenical Collaboration

The initiative developed for translation of a new version of Khmer Bible became the best model for Cambodia's ecumenical collaboration. Efforts were made for some time to translate the Bible into Khmer. The Bible Society of Cambodia officially started to function or begun its existence as an ecumenical body in the country on 17 April 1993, but efforts for the translation of new version of the Khmer Bible started much earlier with interdenominational collaboration. On 10 October 1993, an historic event took place at the main Roman Catholic Church in Phnom Penh, where Christians from different denominations gathered to witness the celebration of the release of the new translation of the New Testament in Khmer language.

[28] Report by Mathews George, CCA Executive Secretary to CCA Indochina Committee, October 1998.

The two main translators of the Khmer version of the New Testament were Arun Sok Nhep and Francois Ponchaud, a French Roman Catholic priest. Ponchaud had worked many years in Cambodia prior to the Khmer Rouge takeover, and he was one of the last foreigners who left Phnom Penh when the Khmer Rouge took over the country. Two days before the launching of the new version of the New Testament Bible, the Steering Committee of the Bible Society met with Jen-Li Tsai, the Regional Secretary of the United Bible Society, and a new Committee of the Cambodian Bible Society was officially elected. The committee had 14 members and four officers: the President (Sar Paulerk), Vice president (Sang Khum Salay), Secretary (Barnabas Mam) and Treasurer (Pracat You). The meeting also decided that the Cambodian Bible Society should join with the United Bible Society and officially apply for membership in this worldwide body. The formation of a Bible Society in Cambodia with several denominations including the Roman Catholic Church as members became a landmark in the history of Cambodian Christianity. The translation of the whole Bible was finally completed in 1997. A team of church leaders who were part of the process visited King Norodom Sihanouk and presented him a copy of the Khmer Bible. The members of the delegation were Father Ponchaud, Arun Sok Nhep, Mok Wai Mung, Sar Paulerk, Barnabas Mam, Yos Em Sithan and Yorng Soth.

Growing Church

About 20 years ago, when I first visited Cambodia at the beginning of my special assignment to work with the people and churches in Vietnam, Laos and Cambodia on behalf of the global ecumenical family, one of my first questions to people whom I met was "How many Christians are there now in Cambodia ?" Almost all responded that there were about 3,000 Protestant Christians and between 5000-7000 Roman Catholic Christians. But this was not the case in subsequent years. There was rapid growth of Christian believers in some areas, but more visible was the missionary competition due to the wide spread of denominations and evangelical para-church groups. The rush of missionaries from overseas to Cambodia with an agenda of church-planting and evangelism introduced more confusion among the local Khmer people who were just starting their new faith journey.

Despite the fact that Cambodian Christianity and the churches in Cambodia have been undergoing persecution and restrictions over decades, Christians in Cambodia have increased in comparatively large numbers during the past two decades. Thousands of people have been converted to Christianity since the early 1990s. During my meeting on 30 October 2012 with the Minister of Religious Affairs Mr Min Khin and officials of the Christians Affairs Department of the Ministry, the minister told me that Christians including Protestants and Roman Catholics now make up around 1.5 to 2 per cent of the total population of Cambodia. It is also a fact that during the past years, Cambodia has become a missionary battlefield. What we witness today is a trend in a country where Buddhism has been the main religion for more than 800 years, that Christianity is gaining a foothold. According to Ministry of Religion and Cult statistics, there are 700 registered churches in Cambodia today and at least 200 church buildings in different parts of the country. About 500 of them are meeting in houses or organize worship services at the residences of pastors or lay leaders who organize prayer meetings or local congregations. Still, many congregations or house churches are not registered.

Pastor Vibol Uong, Chairman of the National Christian Churches Network Cambodia and advisor for Christianity to the president of the National Assembly and to the Ministry of Religion shared details with me more about the current situation of the Protestant churches in Cambodia. According to Vibol, Protestant Churches or congregations or prayer groups are functional in about 4000 villages of the total 14,693 villages in Cambodia today. If we accept the government's estimation that between 1.5 to 2 per cent of Cambodia's total population of 14 million people are Christians, then we may conclude that the total number of Christians in Cambodia is around 250,000. Most Christians in Cambodia belong to various protestant Churches or para-church groups.

The Ministry of Religion and Cult has recognised 14 denominations, confederations or councils or denominations of various Christian churches, para-churches and organizations in Cambodia. Some congregations or independent churches hold membership simultaneously in different federations or Councils. In certain councils or national bodies, individual congregations as well as denominations or national denominational associations are members. But some others have members including international and local Christian NGOs. Among these groups registered with the Ministry of Religious Affairs, the most prominent and active ones are the Evangelical Fellowship of Cambodia (EFC), the Cambodian Christian Federation (CCF), the Cambodian Christian Evangelical Alliance (CCEA), the National Christian Churches Network-Cambodia (NCCN-C), the Kampuchea Christian Council (KCC), etc. Other recognized bodies are denominational bodies such as the Methodist Mission in Cambodia, the Presbyterian churches council, different Baptist denominations or groups, etc.

Since the country was opened for religious activities, several different Methodist churches and missionaries also started work in Cambodia. Among those, the Korean Methodist Church, the Methodist Mission of Singapore, the World Federation of Chinese Methodist Churches, the United Methodist mission unit of France and Switzerland, and the United Methodist General Board of Global Ministries are prominent. In addition to these, several Korean Methodist missionaries sponsored by individual congregations in Korea are also working in Cambodia. In 2002, through the work of the United Methodist Church Global Ministry, different Methodist churches and mission agencies were brought together and a common platform, the Methodist Mission in Cambodia (MMC), was formed. In September 2005, bishops from five mission partner agencies of Methodist churches from overseas went to Cambodia and ordained three Cambodian elders, appointing them as superintendents of three of the seven projected districts. At that time, the United Methodist Church in Cambodia estimated a total of 163 Cambodian pastors plus missionaries, several of whom were serving as "missionary superintendents". According to the Global Ministries of the United Methodist Church Cambodia Initiative programme, in 2012 “the MMC has more than 180 congregations in different parts of Cambodia and all partners of MCC are now working together to continue to develop it to become an autonomous Methodist Church by 2016”.

The Cambodia Baptist Union (CBU) is the other denomination widely spread in different provinces with proper organizational structures. CBU is a federation of 304 local Baptist Churches scattered in the rural areas of Cambodia. Most of those small congregations were started as an outcome of the church-planting mission of the Southern Baptist Church over the past 20 years or so. In addition to this, there is a Bible Baptist Church, Independent Baptist Churches, the Presbyterian Council of Churches, Mormons, Jehovah’s Witness, Seventh-Day Adventists, and the New Apostolic Church, etc., which are also active with official government recognition. In addition to these registered groups or organizations, there are many other church-planting ministries and para-church organizations involved in mission and evangelism working in Cambodia. More than 80 international para-church groups and international Christian NGOs are also operational in Cambodia with different organizational structures and registrations with other government departments. For example, following the earlier practice during the Communist government, one particular group, the Christian Protestant Community, has registration with the Ministry of the Interior. There are other para-church groups working even without any registration. An African ministry under the name of the Christian Redemption Church, Nigeria has been trying to establish its mission in Cambodia for some time now, but has not availed the required registration.

The number of Cambodian Christians has grown from 200 in 1989 to an estimated 200,000 or more within the past two decades. Steven Westergren of the Christian and Missionary Alliance once described this kind of growth trend of in Cambodian Christianity as “typical of countries that have come out of a communist situation, out of a deprived situation. The isolation and violence created a vacuum, an enormous vacuum. When the doors opened in 1990-91, Cambodians were like sponges ready to soak up anything - both good and bad." Westgren's analysis is valid as we understand more and more of the situation and the traumatic experiences of the Cambodians over the decades. During my frequent visits to Cambodia in the 1990s, I used to attend church services in different places: in Phnom Penh and beyond, in cities and rural areas. I worshiped with simple, innocent Khmer folk who were struggling to understand the Christian faith introduced to them by fellow Cambodians or overseas missionaries working in Cambodia. They were struggling to understand differences between denominations and doctrines which were totally alien to them. But they had one thing in common in their faith and prayer: their prayers for both the persecuted and the persecutors. They prayed for God's grace to transform both.

Christian Witness in Buddhist Cambodia

More than 90 per cent of Cambodia's 14 million people are Buddhists. The number of Christians has been estimated by the Ministry of Religion and Cult of the Royal Government of Cambodia as from 1.5 to 2 per cent of the total population of 14 million. However, the number of denominations, churches and para-church groups, national and international Christian organizations, missionaries from overseas and the number of Bible schools or teaching centres that are formally and informally operational etc., is proportionately higher when compared with the number of Christians in the country. This opens another question of Christian witness in a majority Buddhist country like Cambodia. In July 2007, the Ministry of Religion and Cult declared that "Christians in Buddhist-dominated Cambodia are officially banned from evangelizing because they 'disrupt society". It was also stated that "Christians are prohibited from visiting people's houses by knocking on the door and waiting to say 'the Lord has arrived.". In addition, the directive said that "Christians are restricted to only distributing religious literatures in churches". The Ministry of Religion also directed that proper authorization and permission is necessary before the construction of a church. Similar directives or proclamations were issued in 1999 and 2003 by the government with a warning that violating the regulations by persons and groups faces possible prosecution.

International and local media reported at that time and the officials noted that although the new order applied to all non-Buddhist groups, its primary purpose was to curb Christian evangelism, amid reports of children being tricked into converting. Local media reported that Christian missionaries were accused of offering cakes and other sweets to children in exchange for their conversion to Christianity. Furthermore, church groups offer food, clothing and free English lessons as a means of introducing people to Christianity. In response, the directive banned using money or other means to persuade people to convert. The Ministry of religion then categorically stated that the groups' tactics "disturb the daily lives of people and can cause other insecurities in society".

Despite the allegations, Christians and Buddhists live together in peace in most parts of Cambodia. However, there have been instances of sectarian violence and tensions and this has become an increasing phenomenon in some areas. When I was in Phnom Penh in May 2006, reports were published on increasing attacks against churches and Christians in Kandal, Kompong Chhang and Prey Veng, Svay Rieng provinces at various times in previous years. Those conflicts were the outcome of Buddhists' anger, mostly against tactics used by some churches to find new converts, ranging from aggressive evangelizing to bribing church goers. Many Buddhists think that erosion of the Buddhist tradition could tear the nation apart again, and that if people start to convert through aggressive missionary evangelism, there will be more conflicts in Cambodia in the name of religion in the future. Religious persecution in Cambodia is not a matter of concern for many church leaders in the country. But Christianity and churches are seen as foreign, and that is the general perception of most Cambodians, especially in rural areas where chances are higher for precipitating conflicts.

It is in this context that the churches in Cambodia need to think about their witness and mission in a predominantly Buddhist society. The question before the Cambodian Christians is what they can offer to their fellow Cambodians that is unique when they are engaged in a Christian mission and witness. Can they propagate the gospel of love and grace in a local cultural context instead of following the western Christian missionary approach?. Fr Gerald Vogin of the *Missions étrangères de Paris* (MEP) who has been a missionary in Cambodia since 1992 sees the attraction of Christianity and the meaning of mission in a Buddhist country. In response to a question on what was the most effective aspect of Christianity in his mission in Cambodia, Fr Vogin once said: "People see how Christians live and are surprised by the ways they help each other. Today's Cambodia is deeply scarred by the violence of the past. The current hopelessness and poverty are rooted in it. Circumstances are such that they encourage people to only look out for themselves."

In this situation, it is very important to reflect on the mission and witness in Cambodia in an inter-religious context. The Roman Catholic Church in Cambodia has been trying to teach its members there to reflect on their lives as Catholics from a faith perspective rather than from a legalistic view that stresses what is forbidden and what is permitted. Most Cambodian Christians live in Buddhist environments and they have Buddhist members in their own families. This offers a context in which to address the inter-religious situation as a practical aspect in their day-to-day lives. This is what Father Francoise Ponchaud, who understood the Khmer culture well and spent most of his life in Cambodia, once said; "We want people to share faith and culture problems not so much from a theoretical point of view but from their concrete experience in their daily lives".[29] Even the Catholic Church discusses with its members how to deal with certain sensitive matters like: "Why and how to respect a Buddhist monk?; What to do in front of a Buddhist statue? What is it that they want to express when they burn incense sticks, offer food to their ancestors, or participate in Buddhist rites such as a ceremony for the dead or marriage?."[30] On the contrary, the old missionary attitude and approach of the Protestant churches in Cambodia are eliciting more negative attitudes to Buddhism. Often the statements and preaching become more polemic and they create more communal tensions.

It was with great interest that I once read news about a former Khmer Rouge solider who became a follower of Jesus. During his several years of playing an active role with the notorious Khmer Rouge, the former soldier, Ung Khorn, planted landmines, set booby traps and led 200 soldiers into battle, killing innumerable numbers of people. But a few years ago, together with several other ex-Khmer Rouge members, he sought forgiveness and decided to follow Jesus Christ. This is the other side of the story of real conversion that happened through the work of Holy Spirit. Nobody can say that such conversions happen in Cambodia because of money or material assistance.

"Building Again on Old Foundations"

While presenting the report of activities of the CCA-WCC Indochina Programme at the Biennial meeting (1993-1995) of the Vietnam, Laos and Cambodia Ecumenical Forum in November 1995, I made several observations and analyses of the church situation in Cambodia. As a person who was working then as the Liaison Secretary of the CCA–WCC Indochina Programme, I asked the members of the Ecumenical Forum, who represented various ecumenical organizations and churches from different parts of the world including church leaders from Indochina: "How do we rebuild and strengthen the people and churches in a divided community in Indochina which experienced long years of war, isolation, poverty, suffering, lack of freedom, trauma and marginalization?". This question was mainly in the context of the situation in

[29] "Cambodia National Catholic Synod Discusses Interreligious Relationships",»,UCA News, February 23-25, 1998.
[30] *ibid*

Cambodia. Then I concluded my report with the following verse from the book of the Prophet Isaiah (58:12):

> Your people will rebuild what has long been in ruins, Building again on the old foundations. You will be known as the people who rebuilt the walls, who restored the ruined houses.

I look back to those times of our ecumenical journey with the people and churches in Vietnam, Laos and Cambodia. Dramatic changes have been taking place in various areas in these countries over the past two decades, especially in Cambodia. There have been significant changes in the political, social, economic and even cultural fields in Cambodia. The landscape of Christianity has changed over the years, and the most visible changes in ecclesial and ecumenical realms are more evident in Cambodian today.

(55) CHURCHES TOGETHER IN GOD'S MISSION – CHINA

Cao Shengjie

The Protestant churches in China are growing unprecedentedly fast. According to the Blue Paper (Statistics from 31 provinces and municipalities sample survey) made in 2010 by the Institute of World Religions of China Social Science Academy, the number of Chinese Protestant Christians is 23.05 million, more than 30 fold of the statistics in 1949 (700,000).

One of the features of the Chinese church is that it has come into a "post-denominational stage" with three characteristics:

1. No denominational organizations exist in China any more. Grass-root churches have come together to worship in the form of Union Worship since 1958.
2. Three-Self Patriotic Movement Committee (TSPM, organized in 1954) and China Christian Council (CCC, organized in 1980) are the two legal national Christian organizations in China. CCC is an umbrella organization for churches in China. It is "to unite all churches throughout China with Christ as our Head in developing together our role in building up the Body of Christ, so as to bear excellent witness to the Gospel of Christ."[1] As a uniting church in the process of formation, CCC was accepted as a full member of WCC in its Seventh Assembly in Canberra in 1991.
3. Following the principle of mutual respect, churches have the freedom of choice in ritual and theological emphases. CCC, working together with TSPM, communicates with Christians through local CC/TSPM, serving church ministry (printing Bibles, opening theological seminaries, providing devotional materials, etc) and takes its responsibility of guidance and supervision.

As I have worked for CCC since its founding, I would like to share with you some of my experiences.

Historical Review

Like many churches in Asian countries, Christianity was brought in by foreign missionaries at the time of colonial aggression, and directly under the protection of unequal treaties of their governments in China. One distinctive result was that churches in China belonged to different mission boards of different denominations in different countries. According to a general survey of Christian mission agencies in China in the year 1920, there were 4726 churches run by 54 mission boards from seven large denominations in China.[2] This phenomenon aggravated the notion that Christianity was labelled unfriendly by Chinese people as a 'foreign religion". Far-sighted Chinese Christian leaders long expected to build up a real Chinese church rooted in Chinese soil.

In the latter part of 19th century, a Chinese scholar Chen Mengnan became Christian. He said "The truth of God is from heaven, when it comes to certain foreign countries, it is theirs; yet when it comes to our country, it is ours. We should propagate the truth by ourselves." He started to open a church run by Chinese, instead of foreigners.

After the Boxer Uprising in1900, Chinese people were more humiliated by heavy indemnity to the Eight Power Military Forces. As Chinese Christians were misled to side with foreign forces in the war, the image of Christianity viewed by people was unfavourable for the development of the church. In 1906, a Presbyterian pastor Yu Guozhen in Shanghai established The Independent Church of Jesus. Claiming honour for both the nation and the church, they would not accept any foreign domination both in the fields

[1] Constitution of the China Christian Council

[2] Christian Occupation of China, published by the Special Committee on Survey and Occupation, China Continuation Committee, published in 1922, Shanghai

of finance and personnel. This Independent Church Movement had a wide- ranging impact in China. One striking feature was that this independent church movement was not denominational.

In the 1920s of the 20th century, facing the New Cultural Movement and the Anti-Christianity Drive in China, Christian intellectuals further realized that the Chinese Church must get rid of the foreign religion. They advocated the "Indigenization of Christianity" in China. Zhao Zichen (T.C. Chao) and Liu Tingfang (Timothy Liu) were prominent leaders .They did not think that the Chinese church should sever the ties with mission boards, but the Chinese church must be run by Chinese leaders and Chinese theology must be integrated within Chinese culture. Through the influence of Edinburgh Mission Conference in1910, the National Council of Chinese Churches was established in 1922. Initially, it was only a union of main-line churches of various mission boards, yet Chinese Christian leaders used this forum to declare their visions. In the article "Making the Christian Church in China Indigenous" written by Liu, said, "There is strong sentiment against denominationalism. The Chinese Christians put forward denominational differences as one of the serious obstacles to making the church indigenous." "The rising generation, however, unless indoctrinated again by missionaries, will stand together against denominationalism in any acute form."[3]

In 1927, a united church, under the banner of "church unity in the spirit of self-ruling, self-supporting and self-propagating", composed mainly by Presbyterians and Congregationalists, called `The Church of Christ in China' was formed. Though it could not cover all churches in China, and ultimately became a new large denomination, it expressed the fervent desire of unity from Chinese Christians. When the WCC was founded in 1948, four Chinese churches, namely, The Church of Christ of China, Chung Hua Sheng Kung Hui (Anglican), Congregational church (China south) and Baptists (Shanghai and Zhejiang Synod) were founding members, and T. C. Chao was elected as one of the six WCC presidents.

Reviewing the history, one finds that the Chinese Christians supported independence, and yet their earnest desire was to be free from denominationalism which resulted in a visible unity among them. However, when China was a semi-colonial country, churches were mostly ruled by foreign missions,and that basic picture could not be changed easily

The founding of New China in 1949 created a new situation for the church. In 1950, Chinese Christians led by Wu Yaotsung (Y. T. Wu) and other 40 leaders launched the Three-Self Patriotic Movement (Three-self stands for self-administration, self–support, and self-propagation of the Gospel). The Three-self Manifesto[4] signed by hundreds of thousand of Christians expressed their positive attitudes towards supporting New China and renewing our church to be a real independent one. When missionaries withdrew and financial ties with them were cut off, the Chinese churches worked closely together under the Three-self Movement and survived. In the process of cooperation, Christians of different denominations enhanced their mutual understanding and friendship gradually. In the year 1958, churches began to worship together. Then comes the calamity of the so-called 'Cultural Revolution', (1966-1976) when all the churches and church bodies were closed down. But when the government re-implemented the right policy of religious freedom, churches reopened in 1979, Christians were so grateful and excited that they all rushed into a few churches to worship in tears not caring about which denomination the churches originally belonged to. Union Worship has been carried on,a big step forward on the way to the unity of Chinese Churches.

Reflections on Union Worship

Many people will ask if the Union Worship, a product of our context, was an expedient measure, whether it can be sustained, and why the Chinese church has come into the post-denominational stage.

---

[3] The Chinese Recorder, May 1922, No.5. (Vol. LIII, p.300)

[4] The original name of that document is "The path to be energetically pursued by Christianity in China, within the effort of a New China's national reconstruction" .Chinese edition published in *People's Daily*, Beijing, Sep 23, 1950.

As an immediate cause, the social situation of Great Leap Forward (hasten the speed to build up our socialist society) in 1958 has direct influence on pushing churches to worship together. At that time Chinese people worked day and night, without weekend rest, the number of church-goers dwindled greatly, and it naturally affected the normal church life. Union Worship was the suggestion and the best choice from grass root churches.[5] After the reopening of churches in 1979, there were some external reasons why most of Chinese Christians still stayed with it. Churches reopened gradually in a period when there were not enough church buildings for worshippers, nor even to have separate denominational settings. National denominational organizations were all damaged during the Cultural Revolution, and many denominational leaders passed away. Most importantly, Christians have been quite accustomed to attending such worship, especially those new Christians, who hardly have any knowledge about denominational differences. Besides all these conditions, there are, I think, some other factors inherent in the Chinese situation which have been playing a subtle role too. They are described below.

Historically, denominationalism is something foreign. In the past it was quite absurd to see Chinese Christians located in the north of China to call themselves Southern Baptist or Southern Presbyterians, following the terminology of the American Civil War. Chinese Christians joined certain denominational churches only by chance, not knowing much about differences among them. I heard the late Jiang Wenhan, a Lutheran scholar, head of the student department of the National YMCA, once say, he knew the name of Martin Luther until he went to study in USA.

Culturally, Confucianism is the most influential traditional idea among Chinese people, which advocated the philosophy of "mean" and "harmony in diversity". Confucius persuaded people that when different perspectives were encountered, the best way was not confrontation, but toleration. During the prosperous historical stage, like Tang Dynasty, different religions came to China peacefully and were all tolerated such as Buddhism from India which came through a Chinese monk's hard pilgrimage to get the scroll, and then spread it widely in China. The Nestorianism (Christian) was brought in by Syrian missionaries along the Silk Road, and was quite flourishing in 635-845A.D. Islam came to China in the 7th century, and became the national religion of some ethnic groups. In our cultural cultivation, extremism was not the mainline ideology. There was never a religious war in our history.

Socially, since 1949, China has held high the banner of "unity". In the Constitution of The People's Republic of China, the basic task of the nation is to concentrate its efforts on socialist modernization. With this common goal, people of different ethnic groups, different religious believers are all 'the forces that can be united'.[6] Though the leading party, the Chinese Communist Party embraces atheism, they take the difference in faith as a minor one, under the gigantic task of unity.[7] In recent years, religious people are encouraged to play a positive role in building up a harmonious society.[8] Therefore, unity is an important witness of the Chinese church. It could be a huge disgrace if the church discarded unity.

Ecclesiastically, when churches were divided into various denominations in China, they always condemned each other, holding that only my views and traditions were right and yours were wrong. Besides, they tried to proselyte Christians in other denomination by saying "you will not be saved unless you join our church." This phenomenon in China was called the "stealing of sheep" which caused great resentment among the Chinese people. They used to ask, "How many gods do you believe in?" Since the Three-self Movement started, it has been stressing upon "seeking the common ground while keeping the differences". We are fully aware that we believe in the only Triune God who loves all creatures; we

---

[5] Tien Feng, the magazine of TSPM committee, Shanghai, 1958,No.9-11

[6] Preamble of the Constitution of People's Republic of China.

[7] The Basic Viewpoint and Policy on the Religious Questions during Our Country's Socialist Period issued by CPC Central Committee, 1992 (Chinese edition in the Selected Documents on Religious Work in the New Period, Beijing, 1995)

[8] Religious Harmonization: New Boundary of Religious Work (in Chinese) *Peoples' Daily*, Jan 13,2010

remember the farewell prayer of Jesus for his disciples that "they may be one"; we acknowledge that God's abundance is so great that no denomination can monopolize it. We should love each other and respect each other, instead of excluding each other. It is true that different denominations have different theological perspectives which can hardly be mixed with others', therefore, we start from cooperation of activities rather than debate on theological issues, and this seems to be an easier way for reaching unity.

CCC's Efforts for Promoting Unity

CCC always remembers the words of Paul, that we "making every effort to maintain the unity of the Spirit in the bond of peace" (Col 4:3), and thus have several projects to promote our internal unity in recent 30 years.

1. Common Catechism

In 1981, then general secretary Bp. Zheng Jianye convened a team in Nanjing Union Theological Seminary to work out a catechism without denominational background. The draft was sent to many former denominational leaders to assure that it included the basic tenet of Christian truth which each Chinese Christian should believe. Millions of copies of this pamphlet have been published for new believers' as a guidebook, and it has been also translated into English and German to help Chinese Christians abroad to understand the basic faith of Chinese Christians.

2. The New Hymnal

In the past, different denominations used different hymnbooks. Though many hymns were the same, the Chinese translations were different. An editorial committee and staff were set up in Shanghai in 1981 to work for a New Hymnal with two principles: One was the principle of comprehensiveness and mutual respect, by which we selected hymns from historical treasuries, different nationalities, and different denominational origins according to our needs. The other was promoting indigenization of sacred music, by gathering hymns of Chinese Christian writers or composers, or melody adapted from Chinese music. This hymn book included 400 hymns (102 by Chinese writers) and it was published in1983 (staff book in 1985, bi-lingual edition in 1989). It has been widely accepted by churches all over country, selling more than 15 million copies. In 2010, a Supplement to it was published adding 200 hymns (61 by Chinese writers and composers).

3. The Church Order

As the church orders of different denominations had been out of use, CCC stipulated a new one from 1991. It was based on four elements, i.e. Biblical teaching, historical traditions of the church, experiences of churches worldwide, and the situation of China. Like the new Catechism and the New Hymnal, it reflected that CCC would keep the heritage of the church historically and ecumenically. Seven main sections were included, i.e. general principals, faith, church, sacraments, church members, holy order, and church organization. In a sense, it is preliminary and simple, far from enough to meet the needs in all areas, but a basic mechanism has been formed. It is not obligatory, but an advisory sample for the churches to adopt as they wish. It is encouraging to see that both the provincial and municipal CC have accepted it.

4. The reconstruction of theological thinking

This appeal was made by Bp Ding Guangxun (K.H. Ting, Honorary President of CCC) in 1988, asking theological teachers and preachers to rethink our theology, which mostly originated from the West of the last century and to make it more adaptable to the situation of the Chinese church today. Some discussions on theological issues have been underway. e.g. as Christians are a minority in our society, what is the right attitude of Christians toward truth, goodness and beauty outside the church? In terms of "sanctification", what is the proper relationship between Christians and people of other faiths? In recent years, more discussions on reconciliation, harmony and peace in family, church, community and nation are taking place. Young theologians continue to make their creative contributions.

5. Ecumenical learning through international church exchanges and participation in WCC activities

CCC has wide communication with churches outside, which helps greatly to improve mutual understanding, sharing and mutual learning. For example, women make up more than 70% of the Chinese congregation, and women's ordination has been quite popular in China since 1981 due to urgent needs, yet Feminist Theology was not known by many female pastors then. When our society opened up to the outside world, church people have had more opportunities to study abroad. In 1992, I went to study in the Ecumenical Institute at Bossey. The subject of that graduate school was 'Toward an Inclusive Community.' It really opened my eyes. Though the usage of inclusive language was not imported, the essence of Feminist Theology was helpful for raising gender awareness. Then two visiting groups from the Asian Christian Women's Conference brought us much light on how to understand the Bible from a women's perspective. In 1995, a Women's Ministry sub-committee was set up under CCC/TSPM, and Chinese church women reflected our presence in the NGO Forum before World Women's Congress in Beijing. Today, Chinese women are more conscientious in representing our church and society.

Such initiatives have helped Christians in China to widen our horizon, to increase our common understanding of the church universal, and to strengthen our unity both nationally and internationally.

Current Challenges

Though most Christians in China are satisfied with Union Worship and the church is developing smoothly, yet some negative elements are emerging as well.

1. Under the influence of Cultural Pluralism in the world, denominationalism can also develop on the pretence of preserving distinction. Our Union Worship does not require uniformity in church life, yet there are some Christians in China who are reluctant to give up denominational biases. They are enthusiastic to revive denominational duifferences. Things are more serious when they are encouraged by their counterparts outside China to split the Chinese church.

2. The core of church unity in China is the three-self movement. We want to build up the church along the three-self principle, that is to love our country and our church at the same time. We observe law and accept the registration of the church with the government. Nowadays in China there are some separated Christian groups or sects, claiming that they will "hear God, not man", and decline to abide by the Regulations on Religious Affairs issued by the government. Supported by foreign anti-China forces, some of them even attack Christians working for the Union Worship as "treacherous", not loyal to the Christian faith. Though CCC/TSPM has tried to unite them, much needs to be done yet.

3. As the government is better implementing the policy of religious freedom, most preachers are zealous in doing evangelization, interested and satisfied with increasing the number of Christians, with less consideration of how to build up a healthy church in our society. China is such a vast country with a huge population and divided regions. As CCC is not a united church yet, churches in most areas organized themselves loosely under the local CC/TSPM. It is hardly possible for local churches to think and act fully as CCC requires. CCC/TSPM has accumulated rich experiences in our church formation, yet we have not summarized and systematized them theologically, which means a lack of ecclesiology is undermining our theological thinking. We have not developed a systematic theory and practice that can be accepted by all churches. Thus, the key problem , according to my observation,is the absence of an intensive study and popular education of Chinese ecclesiology, including ecumenism. Only when theological guidelines are clear, can unity be strengthened and developed.

(56) CHURCHES TOGETHER IN GOD'S MISSION – HONG KONG

Lo Lung-Kwong

Ecumenism at The Cross Roads

The establishment of The Union Church by James Legge in 1844 may symbolize the earliest effort of ecumenism in Hong Kong as it was organized as a church to include westerners with different denominational backgrounds (mainly non-conformists) and also the Chinese.

James Legge (1815-1897) was among the earliest group of missionaries to arrive and continued to serve in Hong Kong (1843-73) instead of taking Hong Kong as a stepping stone to go to China. He followed the footstep of Robert Morrison (1782-1834), the first Protestant missionary sent to China in 1807. Both of them were missionaries of the London Missionary Society (LMS, founded in 1795 mainly by Congregationalist and Presbyterian churches in Britain, reorganized as Council for World Missions, CWM, in 1977). In 1807, Robert Morrison arrived in Macau. It is an island 64 km away from Hong Kong and had been under Portuguese control as permitted by the Chinese government with a strong presence of Catholics since the16th Century.

While all foreigners were allowed by the Chinese government, to stay in Macau but not to enter China, Robert Morrison had spent much of his time in Macau and also established a mission station at Malacca, Malaysia, for preparing mission works to go to China.[1]

The first Chinese Bible was translated and published by Morrison at Macau and Malacca. He could finish such an important task within just 16 years (1807-1823). Most of his manuscripts of the New Testament were based on an earlier version prepared by Fr. J. Basset (1662-1707) who was sent by the Foreign Missions of Paris to China in1689.

In Macau, missionaries of different traditions had to work closely together to face difficulties imposed by the Chinese government for foreigners were not even allowed to learn Chinese. Co-operation between missionaries of different backgrounds happened always because they faced common threats and had practical needs.

From 1842, within ten years, missionaries of the Baptist Church, London Missionary Society, the Anglican Church Missionary Society, the Basel, Rhenish, and Berlin Missionary Societies, the American Congregational Church, and the British Methodist Church arrived in Hong Kong.[2] In those days, missionaries supported one another, and built their churches in the same area, Western District, and along the same roads, Hollywood Road and then Cain Road as well as Bonham Road.

A Chinese congregation also gathered in the Union Church. The first Chinese pastor, Rev. Ho Fuk-tong, was ordained in 1846; elders and deacons were elected in 1847. The congregation adopted a constitution of "The Independent Chinese Church of Hong Kong" in 1875 and moved out to a new building in 1888 and established an independent church named "To Tsai Church" (means "Reached by Word" in English). However, the influence of the Union Church was long lasting; the church was named Hop Yat Church (Chinese translation of Union Church) in 1926 after a newly built church building was erected at Bonham Road until today.

---

[1] See Harrison, Brian, *Waiting for China: The Anglo-Chinese College at Malacca, 181-1843, an Early Nineteen-Century Missions* (Hong Kong: HKU Press, 1979).

[2] See Carl T. Smith, *Chinese Christians Elites, Middlemen, and the Church in Hong Kong* (Hong Kong: OUP, 1985) 2-6.

In the 19th century, most of the churches in Hong Kong experienced good relationship and co-operation, among themselves. There were three characteristics: (1) many missionaries used Hong Kong as a stepping stone for entering China to do missionary work, (2) Chinese pastors and lay leaders become core members and leaders in many churches, (3) missionaries supported churches to run schools and provide medical services. With this background, the churches in Hong Kong have had a long tradition of educational and social ministry as well as maintaining a close relationship with the churches in China.

In 1949, the history of Hong Kong turned to a new page for the Communists took over mainland China and the population of Hong Kong grew from 600,000 after the Sino-Japanese War (Second World War) in 1945 to more than 1.6 million in 1949. After most of the missionaries were expelled from mainland China in 1950, almost all denominations which worked in mainland China moved to Hong Kong. From then on, Hong Kong became a super market of churches.[3]

According to the 2009 annual report of the Hong Kong government, among the populations of 7,026 400, the Christian community — comprising mainly Protestants and Roman Catholics — numbered about 670,000 followers. There are around 50 Protestant denominations and hundreds of independent churches. According to a census conducted by Hong Kong Church Renewal Movement (HKCRM), there were around 1,250 Chinese Protestant congregations in 2009. The Protestant, Roman Catholic and Orthodox (started in 1997) churches maintained a spirit of fellowship with the Hong Kong Christian Council (HKCC).[4] Since 80's, during the Week of Prayer for Christian Unity promoted by WCC, a Joint Ecumenical Communion Service followed by a breakfast gathering has been held with participants from member denominations of HKCC and the Roman Catholic Diocese every year. The number of attendants, mostly pastors, has been growing in the last decade from around a 100 to more than 200, including some pastors of non HKCC member churches.

The earliest ecumenical institution of Hong Kong is the Hong Kong Chinese Christian Church Union (HKCCCU) founded in 1915.[5] The Union was established with the support of missionaries, especially the Bishop of the Anglican Church in Hong Kong which is part of the state church of England. The Union was established to serve the common concern of Chinese churches, especially the need of a Chinese Christian cemetery. Just as the western Christians had been granted a cemetery at Happy Valley in 1845, which was put under a joint management of different denominations and mission bodies, Chinese Christians too had the same need. The cemetery became an important instrument for Chinese Christians and Churches with different backgrounds to join hands. Up to now, the Union is one of the most active Christian organizations in Hong Kong which has a current membership of 350 congregations of various denominations and independent churches. These 350 congregations represent the most historical congregations of mainline denominations, and around half of the Protestants in Hong Kong. While membership of the Union is based on congregations who serve the common and practical needs of Christians, the Union is conservative in theological orientation and on social issues. Nevertheless, while the income from the cemetery is constant and large, the Union runs two Old People's homes, a Christian weekly newspaper, a secondary school and also an occasional city-wide evangelistic rally, such as the Billy Graham Crusade.

The Hong Kong Christian Council (HKCC) founded in 1954, six years after the establishment of the World Council of Churches, which represents the world ecumenical movement, continued in Hong Kong. Her membership is based on denominations, such as the Anglican Church (in Chinese, Sheng Kung Hui), and the Church of Christ in China (which was formed in 1927 in mainland China by merging most of the Presbyterian churches, United Brethren churches, the Lutheran Church, Methodist Church, Salvation Army and ecumenical organizations, such as Hong Kong Bible Society, YMCA and YWCA and some

---

[3] For a general introduction of Christianity in Hong Kong, see Lo, Lung-kwong, "Taiwan, Hong Kong, Macau" in *Christianities in Asia*, ed. Peter C. Phan (Oxford: Wiley-Blackwell, 2011) pp. 173-196.
[4] See information of HKCC online: http://www.hkcc.org.hk
[5] See information of HKCCCU online: http://www.hkcccu.org.hk

congregational churches to become an indigenized denomination as a product of the ecumenical movement after the 1911 Edinburgh Mission Conference).[6] The Orthodox Metropolitanate of Hong Kong and Southeast Asia started their work in 1997 and joined HKCC.

While the above mentioned HKCCCU represents individual congregations and aims to fulfill the practical needs of Christians with a conservative ethos, the HKCC represents mainline denominations and organizations which favoured the ecumenical theological orientation and mission concerned. There are three main tasks of HKCC: (1) to promote an ecumenical spirit and movement among local churches to participate in mission, (2) to represent the interests of Hong Kong churches to negotiate and liaise with the Hong Kong government on social issues and public policies, (3) to support the re-building of the relationship between Hong Kong and Chinese churches. Under HKCC, there is the largest Christian social service agency, Hong Kong Christian Service which employed more than 1,200 full time workers. She had also served as a platform to get the various denominations to participate in the founding of United Christian Medical Service which runs the United Christian Hospital with more than 1,170 beds. She has also been active in managing the Christian Family Service Centre and is the first hospital to provide western medicine, the Alice Ho Miu Ling Nethersole Hospital, which was founded by missionaries in 1887. In 1959, the Christian Industrial Committee (CIC) was founded. However, it was active only after 1967 when the riots by industrial workers occurred. Since then, CIC has been actively concerned about the welfare of labour workers, and was famous for her pioneer role in labour and social issues as well as promoting social movements and organizing trade unions since her beginning until the end of the 20th century. Her historical mission was completed after the number of labourers dropped dramatically from more than 1 million in the 70's to less than 100,000 at the end of 90's. Most, if not all, factories moved to mainland China at the end of 20th century. The reunion of Hong Kong to China in 1997 and the political reform which started in 1991 changed the political ecology of Hong Kong for political interest groups and parties as well as newly formed trade unions had replaced the role of CIC. An ecumenical seminary, Chung Chi Theological Seminary, was formed in 1963 and sponsored by Church of Christ in China, Hong Kong Council, United Methodist Church, British Methodist Church, American Baptist Mission and Anglican Church; all are members of HKCC at that time. This seminary was further supported by the Basil Mission (locally named as Tsung Tsin Mission which worked among the Hakka people) by the merger of their seminary into it in 1966. Eventually, in 1968, this ecumenical seminary become an integral part of Chung Chi College, a Christian college sponsored by the United Board for Christian Higher Education in Asia and mainline denominations, which is one of the three founding colleges of The Chinese University of Hong Kong (CUHK), a comprehensive public university for research sponsored by the Hong Kong Government. However, the theological school had to be privately funded by the College and the sponsoring denominations. The theological school was renamed as the Divinity School of Chung Chi College (DSCCC), CUHK, in 2004. The Pentecostal Holiness Church joined as a sponsoring denomination in 2008 and made the School more ecumenical in nature. The ground breaking ceremony of the new chapel of the Divinity School in 2007 was attended by officials not only of the representatives of the sponsoring denominations, but also the Cardinal of the Catholic Church and the Patriarch of the Orthodox Church. This is the only theological education institute formed as an integral part of a government sponsored university in Hong Kong and probably in Asia. There are 15 member schools in the Hong Kong Theological Education Association (HKTEA), DSCCC being the only one oriented to ecumenical theology.

HKCC has also played a role in promoting ecumenical efforts in religious broadcasting. The Religious Broadcasting and Television Advisory Committee (RBTAC) traces its origins back to before World War II when the Hong Kong Government and the mainline Christian Churches of Hong Kong worked out a means

---

[6] See Merwin, W., A*dventure in Unity: The Church of Christ in China* (Grand Rapids: Eerdmans, 1974).

for religious broadcasting to be well-organized and well -produced. The Committee began as a broadly ecumenical group and has continued as such to this day. Two members are appointed by the Roman Catholic Church and four by the HKCC. Two of the HKCC representatives are from the Anglican tradition, while the other two represent Protestant denominations. An Executive Secretary of HKCC serves as the producer. In the 1960s, Hong Kong Radio (a government- funded Radio) invited 5 church bodies - the Catholic Diocese, the Anglican Church, the Methodist Church, the Hong Kong Council of the Church of Christ in China, and the Baptist Convention of Hong Kong - to form the "Radio and Television of Hong Kong (RTHK) Chinese Religious Broadcasting Advisory Committee", producing broadcast programmes with Christian content. HKCC serves as the co-ordinator of the committee and provides producers for the programmes.

Since 1970, HKCC has organized a mission conference for every decade, which has tried to draw leaders of different Christian traditions together to discuss the common mission of the Church in Hong Kong. In 1976, the HKCC created the "Five Loaves & Two Fish" resources sharing programme to raise funds for supporting relief works in other countries or areas. In recent years, a lot of resources have been used in mainland China. The HKCC serves also as the secretariat for the Colloquium of Six Religious Leaders formed in 1978 which is supported by the Hong Kong Buddhist Association, the Diocese of Hong Kong Catholic Church, the Confucian Academy, the Chinese Muslim Cultural and Fraternal Association, the Hong Kong Taoist Association and the HKCC. This Colloquium organizes inter-religious seminars, mutual visits and Chinese New Year Gathering every year in which all participate. Moreover, an independent organization, The Christian Study Centre for Chinese Culture and Religions, established in 1957 with strong support from the church leaders closely related to the HKCC, has actively devoted itself, from its very beginning, to organizing various activities related to inter-religious dialogue, including the publication of an English academic journal, *Ching Feng*.

At the end of the 1970s, most of the missionaries withdrew from Hong Kong. The discussion of integrating different denominations into one indigenized denomination was initiated among the Church of Christ in China, the Hong Kong Council, and the Methodist Churches with British and American background, and the Anglican Church. However, only the Methodist Churches with British and American background respectively had successfully integrated into The Methodist Church, Hong Kong, in 1975.

The rapid growth of the economy of Hong Kong in the 70's had enabled most of the mainline churches to become financially independent of their western mother churches. Young Christians from different denominations who were born or grown up in Hong Kong after 1949 become more and more active in carrying out church ministries with local concern. These include social issues, in particular those related to the livelihood of low-income people, such as the strike for the rights of the blind workers, campaign against corruption and against the expansion of the gambling enterprise and the flooding of pornography in media. Various Christian groups were organized after several social movements to advocate Christian social concern, such as the Social Policy Committee of HKCC, Justice and Peace Commission of the Hong Kong Catholic Diocese and Christians for Hong Kong Society. A coalition against the bus fare increase was formed at the end of the Mission Conference organized by the HKCC in November of 1980 along with leaders of mainline churches as well as conservative churches. It was the first time a city-wide social movement led by Christians was joined by non-Christian organizations as well such as the left wing trade unions. A campaign for building a hospital in the Hong Kong Island East in 1982 was led by priests and members of the local Catholic, Methodist, and Baptist churches as well as by evangelical and independent churches.

During the Sino-British negotiations on the future of Hong Kong to return to China from 1981-84, three public documents explaining the Protestant's view on the future of Hong Kong were released in 1984.[7] For

[7] All three documents (in Chinese; English translation is available) were released in 1984, just before the conclusion of the Sino-British negotiation on the future of Hong Kong in September of 1984. They are: "A Manifesto of the

Catholics, Cardinal John Wu issued a Pastoral Letter "March into the Bright Decade: On the Pastoral Commitment of the Catholic Diocese of Hong Kong", in 1989, to encourage the political commitment of Catholics.

However, the political challenges caused by the reunion of Hong Kong into China in 1997 forced the church leaders to make their political stance toward China explicit. They divided along the line on whether Christians in Hong Kong should be more critical of the Chinese communist government or not? The split become obvious when the Beijing government appointed some church leaders to be members of the Consultative Committee for Basic Law of Hong Kong in 1984. In 1986, the Committee on Social Policies of the HKCC was asked by the Executive Committee not to publicize critical opinions toward Hong Kong and China governments. The Chairperson resigned to protest the decision, and the General Secretary, Kwok Nai Wang, tendered his resignation in 1988 and organized the Hong Kong Christian Institute by inviting individual Christian leaders to become members of this new ecumenical institute to promote a critical stance on the Hong Kong and China governments.

At the time of the student demonstration for democracy at Tiananmen Square, Beijing, in the spring of 1989, Protestants and Catholics organized coalitions respectively to support the development of democracy in Hong Kong and China. It was a critical moment when the previously divided church leaders became united upholding the same political stance. However, after the crack down of the student movement on June 4, the division became even bigger.

The historical background of the churches in Hong Kong helped to continue the formal and informal relationship between Christians in Hong Kong and those in China. In 1980, when the official "three-self" churches[8] in China were allowed to have public activities after the Cultural Revolution, a delegation of church leaders organized by the HKCC visited the Chinese Christian leaders and churches in Shanghai and Hangzhou. In return, a delegation led by Bishop K. H. Ting visited Hong Kong in 1981. These events symbolized the re-establishment of institutional relationship between churches in Hong Kong and in China, i.e. the China Christian Council (CCC) and Three-self Patriotic Movement Committee (TSPMC). Unfortunately, the complicated relationship between churches in Hong Kong as well as the institutional and non-institutional churches in China, i.e. churches not registered with CCC and TSPMC, further divided the churches in Hong Kong.

Prospects of Ecumenism in Hong Kong

Hong Kong has become the Special Administration Region of the PRC since 1997; this change has great impact on the churches in Hong Kong. The political stance towards Hong Kong and China governments as well as the issues related to the relationship between churches in Hong Kong and institutional/non-institutional churches in China have divided the church leaders as well as different denominations in Hong Kong. This has made the position and the role of HKCC as an ecumenical agent more difficult. However, the role of HKCC in soliciting ecumenical effort in social concern, church unity, broadcasting, inter-religious dialogue, and promoting support of ministries in mainland China continued. The conservative

---

Protestant Churches on the Religious Freedom," "The Conviction Held by Christians in Hong Kong in the Midst of Contemporary Social and Political Change," and "A Position Paper on the Future of Hong Kong by the Delegation of Christian Leaders Visiting Beijing." For a brief analysis of the issues related to the future of Hong Kong Church in 1997, see Lo, Lung-kwong, "The Future of the Church in Hong Kong" in *Word & World: Theology for Christian Ministry* Vol. XVII, No. 2, Spring, 1997, pp. 203-211

[8] "Three-self" means the "three-self principles" - self-government, self-support and self-propagation – under which the Christian church, including Protestant and Catholic, is allowed to organize openly with the supervision of the Religious Affairs Bureau of the State Government.

HKCCCU became very active to build relatively good relationships with Hong Kong and China governments as well as with institutional churches in China.

How to further promote the ecumenical spirit among Hong Kong churches? The practical needs among Christians and churches now seemed inadequate in contrast to the past. Theological traditions also seem to have not much influence in such circumstances. The divided ideological and political stance of church leaders and denominations has brought ecumenism in Hong Kong to the crossroads.

Furthermore, the social, economic and political situation of Hong Kong kept changing rapidly. The joint effort between HKCC and HKCCCU to cope with the issues of poverty has developed into a Hong Kong Christian Network for Serving the Poor which is joined also by some evangelical organizations, such as the Hong Kong Church Renewal Movement (HKCRM), and the Industrial Evangelical Fellowship. This provides a new chance for ecumenical co-operation. The controversial policy on moral and national education imposed by the government on all schools has aroused the opposition of many school-sponsoring bodies, including Catholics and Protestants, ecumenical and evangelicals. These new challenges may be a good chance for different groups of Christians to find ways of jointly witnessing to our common faith in this age of crisis.

Further Reading

Harrison, Brian, *Waiting for China: The Anglo-Chinese College at Malacca, 181-1843, an Early Nineteenth-Century Missions*. Hong Kong: HKU Press, 1979.

Carl T. Smith, *Chinese Christian Elites, Middlemen, and the Church in Hong Kong*. Hong Kong: OUP, 1985

Merwin, W., A*dventure in Unity: The Church of Christ in China*. Grand Rapids: Eerdmans, 1974.

(57) CHURCHES TOGETHER IN GOD'S MISSION – INDIA

Roger Gaikwad

In surveying the ecumenical situation in India, we shall be focussing on the history of the National Council of Churches in India (which represents about 14 million Christians drawn from Reformation and Orthodox Church Traditions, consisting of 30 Member Churches,[1] 7 Related Agencies,[2] 17 Regional Christian Councils,[3] 17 All India Organisations,[4] and 3 Autonomous Bodies[5]) and the contemporary challenges and opportunities which the NCCI faces today.

The Formation of the National Missionary Council

It was mainly the Protestant mission bodies working in India that first realized the importance of ecumenical cooperations and relationships. Province-wise inter-denominational private meetings of missionaries from 1855 onwards led to the first *National General Missionary Conference* in Allahabad in 1872, and the venture was repeated every ten years.[6]

The initiative for official ecumenical cooperation came with the formation of the *South India Missionary Association*[7] in 1897. Ecumenical organizations also started taking shape at the beginning of

---

[1] Andhra Evangelical Lutheran Church; 2. Arcot Lutheran Church ; 3. Baptist Church of Mizoram; 4. Bengal-Orissa-Bihar Baptist Convention; 5. Chaldean Syrian Church of the East; 6. Church of North India; 7. Church of South India; 8. Convention of Baptist Churches of the Northern Circars; 9. Council of Baptist Churches in North East India; 10. Council of Baptist Churches in Northern India; 11. Evangelical Lutheran Church in Madhya Pradesh; 12. Good Samaritan Evangelical Lutheran Church; 13. Gossner Evangelical Lutheran Church in Chotanagpur;14. Hindustani Covenant Church;15. India Evangelical Lutheran Church;16. Jeypore Evangelical Lutheran Church;17. Malabar Independent Syrian Church; 18. Malabar Jacobite Syrian Orthodox Church; 19. Malankara Orthodox Syrian Church. 20. Mar Thoma Syrian Church; 21. Mennonite Brethren Church; 22. Mennonite Church In India; 23. Methodist Church in India; 24. Northern Evangelical Lutheran Church; 25. Presbyterian Church of India; 26. Salvation Army; 27. Samavesan of Telugu Baptist Churches; South Andhra Lutheran Church; 29. Tamil Evangelical Lutheran Church; and 30. The National Organization of the New Apostolic Church.

[2] All India Sunday School Association; 2. Christian Institute for the Study of Religion and Society; 3. Christian Literature Society; 4. Christian Medical Association of India; 5. Church's Auxiliary for Social Action; 6. Ecumenical Church Loan Fund – India; and 7. Henry Martyn Institute, International Centre for Research, Interfaith Relations and Reconciliation.

[3] Andhra Pradesh Council of Churches; 2. Bengal Christian Council; 3. Bihar Council of Churches; 4. Chhattisgarh Christian Council; 5. Gujarat Council of Churches; 6. Jharkhand Council of Churches; 7. Karnataka Christian Council; 8. Kerala Council of Churches; 9. Madhya Pradesh Christian Council; 10. Maharashtra Council of Churhes; 11. North East India Christian Council; 12. North West Frontier Christian Council; 13. North West India Council of Churches; 14. Santalia Council of Churches; 15. Tamilnadu Christian Council; 16. Utkal Christian Council; and 17. Uttar Pradesh Council of Churches.

[4] All India Association for Higher Christian Education; 2. Association of Theologically Trained Women of India; 3. Bible Society of India; 4. Board of Theological Association of Senate of Serampore College; 5. Christian Association for Radio and Audio Visual Services; 6. Christian Endeavour in India; 7. Christian Union of India; 8.Ecumenical Council for Drought Action and Water Management; 9. Indian Society for Promoting Christian Knowledge; 10. Inter-Church Service Association; 11. The Leprosy Mission; 12. Lott Carey Baptist Mission in India; 13. National Council of YMCAs of India; 14. National Missionary Society of India;15. Student Christian Movement of India; 16. United Evangelical Lutheran Church in India; and 17. Young Women's Christian Association of India

[5] All India Council of Christian Women; 2. Urban Rural Mission; and 3. India Peace Centre.

[6] K. Baago, *A History of the National Christian Council of India 1914-1964* (Nagpur: The National Christian Council, 1965), pp. 4-5.

[7] Ibid, p.5.

the 20th century such as the *National Missionary Society* in 1905, the *United Theological College* in 1910, the *Student Christian Movement in India* in 1912, and the *National Missionary Council* (NMC) in 1914.

One of the significant achievements of the NMC was the Statement on Comity which "laid down specific rules for arbitration and conciliation, territorial arrangements, transfer of mission workers, etc. But above all, it emphasized that Comity basically consisted in cooperative efforts for the common purpose, the evangelization of India."[8] However, as the name suggests, it was a council of missions and not of churches.

From National Missionary Council to National Christian Council

The nationalist movement for independence "forced the National Council to reconsider the entire character of the relationship between churches and missions."[9] J.H. Oldham, in a booklet entitled, *The World and the Gospel* (published in 1916) had said, "The aim of the foreign missionary work is to plant *the Church* of Christ in every part of the non-Christian world as a means to its evangelisation."[10] It was during his visit to India that at the meeting of the NMC in January 1923 at Ranchi that the name was changed to "National Christian Council of India, Burma and Ceylon."

The NCC was established on the basis 'that the only bodies entitled to determine the policy of the Churches and Missions are the Churches and Missions themselves'. Regarding its membership, it was made a constitutional rule that half the members in both the National and the Provincial Councils should be nationals.[11]

The Role and Identity of the National Christian Council till the 1940s

1. NCC and the national movement

The National Christian Council got formed during the time when the national movement for independence was gaining considerable momentum. The Council was in a dilemma as to the kind of response it should make to the freedom struggle. In general it neither identified itself with nor disassociated itself from the movement for political independence.

2. NCC and evangelism and mission

As regards to evangelism, the Church went through different phases. During the 1920s the evangelistic drive faced opposition not only from Hindus, but also from some missionaries and Indian Church leaders.[12] In a society burdened by great economic and social problems and ridden by communalism, the NCC engaged in Rural Reconstruction and Industrial Mission programmes.[13] During the 1930s emphasis was given to Higher education in a changing India, particularly the Christian character of Christian Colleges[14] and the study of Christian Mass Movements in India.[15] The Mass Movement Study signified the shifting emphasis from school work to unequivocal evangelism. The NCCI started publishing "Tracts for the Times", an aid to churches with reports and practical suggestions for evangelistic campaigns.

---

[8] Ibid, p.20.
[9] Ibid, p. 31.
[10] Ibid, p. 33.
[11] Ibid.
[12] For details cf. Ibid, pp. 40-42.
[13] For details cf. Ibid, pp. 45-48.
[14] Cf. Ibid, pp. 51-52.
[15] Ibid, p. 53.

3. Church-centered direction in the council

In the 1930s it was stressed several times that the Church's nature is mission or evangelism. So also it was said that evangelism must be Church-centred.[16] This Church-centred approach led to amendments in the Constitution of the Council in 1936. Among a few new 'Objects of the Council', was added the statement, "The objects of the Council shall be to take all possible steps to give effect to the principle that in the Christian enterprise the Church is central and permanent." In the article on membership, organized Church bodies (and no longer only missions and Provincial Councils) were admitted to direct representation on the Council in proportion to the number of their communicant members.[17]

The Emergence of the 'National' Character of the Council from the 1940s

K. Baago notes three important changes that took place in the identity and role of the Council at the beginning of the 1940s.[18] First, it became what it had never really been before – a *Nationa*l Council. The deliberations both in Commission discussions and the Council debates, the administrative leadership and the Secretariat became predominantly Indian.[19]

Second, the attitude of the Council to the Nationalist Movement had so far been rather ambiguous; now it came out unequivocally in support of the Congress and its demand for Indian Independence. When India became independent, the Council became the representative of the non-Roman Catholic churches. It expressed the views of the churches it represented on matters such as the drafting of the Constitution of India.[20]

Third, on the issue of integration of Church and Mission, the Council in 1944 stated, "The time has now come when missions from the West should carry on their activities in and through the organizations of the Church, wherever they have been developed, and cease to function through Mission councils or other organizations which are not an integral part of the life and work of the indigenous Church."[21] So also the Council advocated the handing over of mission property to the Church. The period of transition from mission to church which started in 1923 thus came to its completion.

Critique of the National Council in the 1970s

Between 1965 and 1977, the Council made serious attempts to reorganize itself. However, the question was often being asked: Was the Council playing an effective role in the life of the churches and the Indian society? Therefore the Council appointed an Evaluation Commission in the mid-seventies drawn from its own constituent members.

This commission[22] pointed out several reasons for the struggles of the Council, one of them being that while the NCCI wisely devolved its administrative responsibility for many ecumenical agencies like Christian Medical Association of India (CMAI), Christian Institute for Study of Religion and Society (CISRS), Board of Theological Education (BTE), Christian Association for Radio and Audio Visual Services (CARAVS) and Churches' Axillary for Social Action (CASA), the NCCI's inability to keep a structural relation with them which emphasizes the NCCI's spiritual concern for the total Christian

---

[16] Ibid, p. 58.
[17] Ibid, p. 59.
[18] Ibid, p. 61.
[19] Ibid, p. 63.
[20] For details cf. Ibid, p. 62.
[21] Ibid, p.74.
[22] Cf. *Report of the Evaluation Commission of the National Christian Council of India* (Nagpur: National Christian Council of India, 1978)

enterprise in India had made the NCCI one among many ecumenical agencies rather than the spiritual focus of all.[23]

In discussing the nature of the Council, the Commission proposed that the Council should be seen as a covenant relation among the Churches of India engaged together in a common mission and moving towards a goal. In defining the "Churches in India" the Commission proposed that (1) the new National Council of Churches should give a decisive central place to the Churches as officially organised according to their own conceptions of polity; (2) that at the same time, the Council should open itself to those movements and organizations which promote the Church's mission and ecumenism in India at various levels and which are prepared to give in their own structural expression to their decision to work "in association with the Council" and be oriented to the Churches e.g., Regional Christian Councils, autonomous ecumenical agencies engaged in special fields, and frontier movements.

As a follow-up to the Evaluation Commission's report, the NCCI was re-organized as the National Council of Churches in India in 1979.

The NCCI in Recent Times

The situation in India has become quite complex since the last 30 years. Fundamentalism and communalism have been on the rise, thereby causing much tensions and even violence in the India pluralistic society. Globalization has been impacting the economy causing an ever increasing divide between "Shining India" and "Suffering Bharat". Dalits, Indigenous Peoples (tribals and adivasi), Maoists, and the like are all engaged in struggles for justice. Ecological exploitation of the natural resources of the country is proving to be hazardous.

The NCCI with its limited resources continues to minister to the Church and Society through its Commissions (Unity, Mission and Evangelism; Justice, Peace and Creation; Policy, Governance and Public Witness; Dalits; Tribals/Adivasis; Communication; and Youth) and through its autonomous bodies (All India Council of Christian Women; Urban Rural Mission; and India Peace Centre). However, the Church in India has been faced with the rise of charismatic movements, new church groups, mushrooming Bible schools and theological colleges, as well as the emphasis on confessionalism rather than ecumenism. This emphasis on confessionalism leads Churches to give priority to their own programmes, and therefore NCCI is sometimes seen as a competitor rather than as a facilitator. Naturally, member churches are less inclined to own the NCCI. At the same time newer bodies like the All India Christian Council, Global Council of Indian Christians, etc. have been staking their claim to be the forum of Christians and Churches in India and for championing their causes. While we do have a body like the National United Christian Forum (having the CBCI, NCCI and EFI), it has yet to prove to be effective at all levels – national, sub-regional and local. It is the midst of such challenges that the NCCI has to discover its significance and relevance.

Further Readings

Baago, K. *A History of the National Christian Council of India 1914-1964*. Nagpur: The National Christian Council, 1965.

Massey, James and Wati Longchar, *Edinburgh 2010: Witnessing to Christ Today in India.* Kolkata: BTESSC/SATHRI/SCEPTRE, 2010.

[23] The Evaluation Commission does not make explicit reference to divisions in the Church with the rise of the Evangelical Movement from the 1950s. The evangelical movement criticized the ecumenical movement as being less Bible-centred and more social-centred, neglecting the concerns of individual salvation and evangelism, etc. This movement gave rise to the establishment of the Evangelical fellowship of India, and other related evangelical bodies and programmes. This development also affected the credibility and work of the NCCI.

Massey, James. Ed. *Ecumenism in India Today.* Bangalore: BTESSC/SATHRI, 2008.
Mathai Zakariah, ed. *Ecumenism in India.* Delhi: ISPCK, 1980
Philip, T.V. *Exumenism in Asia.* Delhi: ISPCK & CSS, 1994.
Rongpi, Solomon and Wati Longchar, Jesus Christ – The Light of the World: Revisiting New Delhi 1961 WCC Assembly on Mission and Ecumenism. Kolkata: NCCI/SCEPTRE, 2011.
Rajaiah D. Paul, *Ecumenism in Action.* Madras: CLS, 1972.
Sahu, D.K. *United and Uniting: A History of the Church of North India.* Delhi: ISPCK, 2001.
Snaitang, O.L. *A History of Ecumenical Movement: An Introduction.* Bangalore: BTESSC/SATHRI, 2004.
Victor, Vinod, et al., *Ecumenism: Prospect and Challenges.* New Delhi: ISPCK, 2001.

(58) Churches Together in God's Mission - Indonesia

Zakaria J. Ngelow

The ecumenical movement in Indonesia, prior to the 1930s, was a movement among Western missionaries. Toward the Second World War, congregations in the mission fields began to organize into Indonesia churches, and consequently the ecumenical movement was taken over by the Indonesian church leaders. This paper is a short description of the ecumenical movement in Indonesia among Protestant churches which was institutionalized in the Council (now Communion) of Churches in Indonesia.

Historical Background

Modern Christianity entered Indonesian history in the 16th century. Indonesia has been at the main international trade route, long before the Christian era. But there is no evidence of the notion that Nestorian Christianity arrived in this archipelago since the 7th century. Modern Christianity was introduced first by the Roman Catholic priests who accompanied the Portuguese trade vessels in the North Moluccas, the Spice Islands. The first baptism was reported among Mamuya tribal headmen in 1534. In the following decades, the Jesuit priests successfully planted the Gospel among the people of Halmahera Island. But assassination of a local ruler, Sultan Hairun of Ternate, in 1570 by a Portuguese admiral brought disaster to the Christians. Revenge was taken against the Portuguese and their local Christian allies. Christians were killed or forced to convert to Islam.[1] For a long time no Christian mission activity was allowed in that region. But later in 1865 Dutch Protestant missionaries arrived in Halmahera Island to introduce Protestant Christianity. Eventually a church was founded in 1947, the Evangelical Christian Church of Halmahera.[2]

In early 17th century the Dutch fleet took over power after defeating the Portuguese, which forced the latter to leave the archipelago. The Dutch power developed a new policy of moving to the south. Instead of concentrating her trade in the North Moluccas with its Islamic sultanate powers, the Dutch East-Indies Company developed Ambon and Lease islands in the less Islamized region of the South Moluccan islands. In the long run the Dutch policy of moving to the South opened opportunity for the Ambonese to receive western education and therefore to play significant roles in the colonial services and Christian mission history. The change in colonial power from the Portuguese also affected religious life: Roman Catholic congregations were forcibly converted to Protestantism and put under the ministry of the Dutch Calvinist Church. The congregations were mainly in the Eastern region but also in some big cities scattered in different islands of the country. Some Roman Catholic congregations were left untouched in Flores Island.

In the 19th century all Protestant congregations in Indonesia were united by the Dutch government into an institution called Protestant Church in Netherlands-Indies (Indies Church) and put under Dutch colonial administrative supervision. The spirit of religious freedom after the French revolution (1789-1799), on the other hand, was applied by the Dutch in the colony: various mission boards were given opportunity to work in the country. Missionaries, mainly from the Netherlands (Calvinist denomination) and Germany (mixed Lutheran), arrived to promote the Gospel of Christ among Indonesian people. So did Roman Catholic missionaries. Basic education, medical service, and other social activities were employed as vehicles for the Gospel propagation. But the Dutch colonial policy was to allow mission works only among the non-

---

[1] John Villiers, "Las Yslas de Esperar en Dios: The Jesuit Mission in Moro 1546-1571" in *Modern Asian Studies*, Vol. 22, No. 3, Special Issue: Asian Studies in Honour of Professor Charles Boxer (1988), pp. 593-606. Online version at: http://www.asienundeuropa.uzh.ch/aboutus/persons/assistenzprofessuren/trakulhun/classes/teaching/Villiers1988.pdf.

[2] See James Haire, *The character and theological struggle of the church in Halmahera, Indonesia, 1941-1979.* Frankfurt am Main – Bern: Verlag Peter D. Lang, 1981. Indonesian translation available.

Muslim communities. Missionaries then worked among tribal communities, mostly in the Eastern Indonesia, Kalimantan and Sumatra islands. Java, with a mostly Muslim population (and later also Bali with a mostly Hindu population), was closed to missions. But the Gospel found its own way into the heart of Javanese and Balinese people and eventually churches were planted among them.

The colonial church of Indies Church and missionary churches were the main background of the Protestant churches in Indonesia. The Indies Church was reorganized into ethnic church of the Minahassans (1934), Moluccans (1935) and Timorese (1947).[3] Churches from mission works background were also organized in line with ethnic/tribal communities. Other Christian denominations, mostly of American background, were introduced in the 20th century.[4]

Christian Council of Eastern Indonesia

The Eastern part of Indonesian archipelago was different from the rest of the country. Geographically it consists of more islands (Molluccas, for example, is nicknamed the province of a thousand islands), and its population consists of small but numerous ethnic and sub-ethnic groups with their own different cultures and languages. And because churches were organized along the line of ethnic communities, many churches were found in this region. While denominationally or dogmatically there are no principal differences, different ethnic or sub-ethnic groups, and different mission boards, led to separate church institutions.

But since the early 20th century there emerged an ecumenical consciousness among the missionaries of different mission boards. They worked for the possibility of founding one institution for the Protestant church in the country. The ideal was formulated in the objective of the Indonesian Council of Churches in 1950, to form the United Church in Indonesia.[5]

In the Japanese prison camp some leaders of the missionaries spent their time planning for organizing an ecumenical institution for different missions and churches after the Second World War. Before the war, leaders of different mission boards and churches in Eastern Indonesia engaged in a work to develop ecumenical consciousness through a local mission council. This council was founded in 1930 in Makassar as a response to ecumenical spirit promoted by the second International Mission Conference in Jerusalem (1928). The mission council gathered mission leaders from different mission groups who worked in different parts of the region, and formed denominations like Salvation Army, and Church and Mission Alliance. During the Japanese military occupation, the regime forced a Christian unity of all Christians of different organizations, which was indeed helpful to mutually introduce the different denominations.

After the war, a national missionaries' conference was held in August 1946 in Jakarta, where some Indonesian church leaders were also invited. The conference discussed a draft of an Indonesian Christian Council, presented by the Mission consul, M. de Niet. The conference agreed that the different mission and church institutions will continue to share issues concerning dogma, church polity and liturgy; and work together in the field of theological education and other Christian education, mission, medical works, communication and information, and youth ministry. It was in this conference that the formulation of "one united church" was first introduced as the objective of the ecumenical movement in Indonesia.

---

[3] After Indonesian independence, the Dutch name, Indische Kerk, was replaced by Indonesian name, Gereja Protestan Indonesia (GPI). Reorganization resulted in four churches of Minahasa, Maluku, Timor, and the rest in the Protestant Church of Western Indonesia (GPIB), but GPI herself was not dissolved and become a synod of churches, not of congregations.

[4] For a broad outline of Indonesian church history, see Jan Sihar Aritonang and Karel Steenbrink (eds), *A History of Christianity in Indonesia* (Leiden - Boston: E.J. Brill, 2008).

[5] "Membentuk Gereja Kristen yang Esa di Indonesia," Gereja Kristen yang Esa can also be translated to Universal Christian Church.

Indonesian church leaders from Eastern Indonesia, e.g. W.J. Rumambi (Minahasa Church), E. Durkstra (Timor Church) and F.H. de Fretes (Moluccan Church), straightaway gathered participants from Eastern Indonesia to plan for an immediate regional conference. Rumambi was appointed secretary for the conference preparation committee. He was a strongly ecumenical proponent. He stressed that unity of the church was God's will, and it is a serious sin to disobey God's will on church unity. He also believed that the mission of the church after the world war was to reconcile the broken world, a big task that could not be done by a broken church. Another important leader from Eastern Indonesia was H. Bergema, a missionary and theologian who said that the right time (*kairos*) for the churches to be united has come. He related the unity and mission task of the church with Jesus' intercessory prayer (Jn 21:17). Bergema mentioned common theological education as a strategic way for the ecumenical movement. He was appointed by the 1946 Jakarta conference to prepare a theological school for the Eastern Indonesian region, the second after the Bogor (now Jakarta) Theological School (founded in 1934).

Rumambi and Bergema worked hard for the preparation for a Conference of Churches and Missions that took place on 15-25 March 1947 in Malino – some 70 km. to the mountain area eastward of Makassar. A total of 40 representatives from churches, mission boards and Christian organizations attended the conference. They came from different parts of Sulawesi, Maluku, Papua, Sumba and Timor. There were four observers and ten organizers in the conference. On 17 March 1947 the conference agreed to set up an ecumenical council, the Council for Common Work of Christian Churches, with a central office in Makasar. It was known as the Christian Council (Indonesia: Madjelis Keristen). The conference also underlined that the council was just a branch of a national council to be founded in the near future. It also accepted a constitutional draft for the future national council. The spirit then was ecumenical and nationalistic. The objectives of the Christian Council were formulated in three points:

1. To support anything to help strengthen convictions on Christian unity among churches and Christian institutions.
2. To be an information center and representing churches, Christian institutions and Missions.
3. To do research and promotion toward the creation of one Christian Church in Indonesia.[6]

The Malino Christian conference also agreed to set up a common theological education in Makassar, and a lecture ministry. The theological school was opened on 18 September 1948 in Soe, Timor, where it was hosted for a few years before it moved to Makassar. This theological school is the only institution from the early ecumenical movement in this region.[7]

Makassar became a center for ecumenical movement in Eastern Indonesia after the war, because it was the main gate (of sea and air traffic) to the region; and at that time it became a political center as capital for the newly created Eastern Indonesian State.[8] Ecumenically minded church leaders in Eastern Indonesia were also strongly Indonesian nationalistic followers. Their vision for church unity, therefore, was a church for the whole Indonesia. Rumambi moved to Jakarta and together with other Indonesian church leaders worked to realization of the vision for an Indonesian church council promoting unity of churches in the country.

---

[6] So far the history of this council is only available in Indonesian. See P.N. Holtrop, *Selaku Perintis Jalan Keesaan Gerejani di Indonesia. Sejarah Madjelis Keristen Indonesia bahagian Timur, 1947-1956*. Ujungpandang: ISGIT, 1982.

[7] See for the first decade of this theological school, P.N. Holtrop, *Dari Malino Ke Makassar. Dasawarsa Pertama STT INTIM Ujung Pandang 1947-1957*. Ujungpandang: ISGIT, 1982.

[8] The State of East Indonesia (Negara Indonesia Timur in Indonesian) was a post-World War II establishment of a government over the former Dutch territory of the eastern Netherlands East Indies. It was established on 24 December 1946 and dissolved on 17 August 1950, in the process of the establishment of modern Indonesia. Indonesian nationalists saw the state as a colonial project of the Dutch government to reclaim power over the country. See Ide Anak Agug Gde Agung (translated to English by Linda Owens), *From the Formation of the State of East Indonesia Towards the Establishment of the United States of Indonesia*. Jakarta: Yayasan Obor Indonesia, 1996.

In Yogyakarta, 21-22 May 1946, leaders of Javanese, Chinese, and other churches in Java were gathered in an ecumenical conference. Other Protestant churches were also invited.[9] They were established an ecumenical council in Yogyakarta[10], under leadership of B. Probowinoto as Chairperson. This council was also nationalistic in character, and looked for a unity of all Indonesian churches. But this council did not promote unification of the churches. In its statutes, objective was to work for the common interests of churches, in both direct church and religious matters, and other matters related to them. Membership was opened to all Protestant synods in Indonesia. This council was established in the turbulence years of Indonesia independence revolution, and therefore did not function properly. But its significant contribution to ecumenical movement was its declaration to reject western mission in Indonesia, because mission should be conceived as Indonesia churches responsibility. Missionaries from the west will be accepted as assistance to and will be under Indonesian church supervision. The declaration caused tension with the "mother churches" from the Netherlands. Reconciliation was achieved in a conference of representatives of both sides in Kwitang church in Jakarta, 19-24 May 1947. The conference released a document, *Kwitang Accord*, that mission in Indonesia was responsibility of Indonesia churches, but they did need assistance from churches abroad. This agreement was applied by established a Council of Churches Representatives, where membership should be three fourth Indonesian. This structure was known as *Kwitang Structure*.[11]

Among the family of Indies Church, serious concern to ecumenical movement was expressed in an invitation to become member of the family. Reorganization of the colonial church was resulted in a citrus fruit model of unity: different members adopted the same church order, liturgy and the creed. Churches was invited to join, but the churches rejected while accused it as an abortive action to the plan of establishing a church council.

Communion of Churches in Indonesia

A preparation committee to establish a national church council was appointed in Jakarta. T.S. G. Mulia as Chairperson and W.J. Rumambi as Secretary. A meeting of 19 persons represented 29 churches, and 28 observer on 7-13 November 1949 accepted a statute of the national council, named Council of Churches in Indonesia. They planned that an official formation will be in a conference the next year. And it was on 22-28 May 1950 at the campus of Jakarta Theological Seminary. On Pentecostal Sunday of 25 May 1950 representatives of 29 Indonesian churches founded the Council of Churches in Indonesia.[12] At this conference the membership position of mission body was also became a point of contention. Rumambi supported by some delegations to accept mission as associate members of the council, but Probowinoto – with the Kwitang Accord spirit – supported by others, rejected. These two faction came to a solution that there will be a mission department in the national council.[13]

The main motivation in the formation of the Council of Churches in Indonesia was to establish a united church(es) in Indonesia. But after two decades the leaders of the ecumenical movement realized that it is

---

[9] They were Mardjo Sir and Moedjodiharjo (Java Christian Church); Kartosoegondo and Daniel (North Central Java); Widjotohardjotaroeno, Poerbowijogo (South Central Java); Abednego (Pasundan); Tan King Hien and The Tjiauw Bian (Central Java Chinese Church).

[10] Dewan Permoesjawaratan Geredja-geredja di Indonesia (in short Dewan Geredja or DPG).

[11] See Zakaria J. Ngelow, *Kekristenan dan Nasionalisme. Perjumpaan Umat Kristen Protestan dengan Pergerakan Nasional Indonesia, 1900-1950*. Jakarta: BPK Gunung Mulia, 1994, pp. 252 ff.

[12] Some 60 years later the member churches of the Council (since 1984, Communion) increased to almost three times. There is no support to integrate all the churches into one superchurch, but to bring into reality the unity of the church in terms of unity in vision and in commitment, and mutual support in actions and mutual support.

[13] In the world ecumenical movement, churches and mission were different organizations. IMC was integrated into WCC later in 1961.

impossible to form a single Christian church in Indonesia. In the past, the Dutch colonial government created a single Protestant church, the Indies Church, but it denied the basic character of the church as a free and voluntary fellowship of the believers.[14] Theological study also supported that from the beginning unity of the church in the New Testament was unity in diversity. The Council task, therefore, was not to become a kind of committee to form a united church, but a forum where churches can meet and work, pray and celebrate, but also struggle together on how to develop a common vision, to deepen their common commitment, and to share their joy and sorrow as one body of Christ. Just after the establishment of the Council churches in Indonesia exposed to the young nation problems. Christians in Moluccan region troubled by pro Dutch colonial rebellion; and in Sulawesi and West Java and other places suffered severely under pro-Islamic ideology rebellions.

In the 1950s, the national council compared the member churches doctrines, polity and liturgy to proof that there is no principal different among the churches. The main idea was to look for possibility of uniting the churches. But at the same time more churches emerged in the mission field, and struggle for her own identity and autonomy. Ecumenical movement in Indonesia, therefore, rowing between two reefs of unity and autonomy of the churches.

Towards the sixth General Assembly of 1967 in Makassar, a committee prepared drafts of churches unity in a synodical synod order and a draft of Common Understanding of Faith.[15] The drafts were rejected by the assembly to find another possible form, but adopted the drafter's idea of executive board, consist of all synod moderators. Meanwhile Indonesian churches entered the period of New Order regime with concentration on economical development. Churches were mobilized to participate in the national development. Implication for the ecumenical movement was unity conceived more and more in activities: common actions rather than structural organic integration. It was a shift from structural-organization to functional-organism unity. A combination of both approaches to unity – of institutional integration and of common vision and mission – was presented to the tenth General Assembly 1984 in Ambon in a draft of "the Five Unity Documents". The documents were (1) Common Understanding of Christian Faith; (2) Charter of Mutual Acceptance and Recognition; (3) the Main Common Tasks and Mission; (4) Towards Self-support in Theology, Human Resources and Finance; and (5) Statutes of Communion of Churches in Indonesia. As mentioned in the last document, the name of the ecumenical institution was changed from Council to Communion, which was signified the deeper character of ecumenical unity. The unity of the churches, hopefully, will be witnessed through application of these documents. These documents were renewed at every five years at general council. A document of Churches Unity Charter was added later.

The Communion of Churches in Indonesia is not work *to create* the united church in Indonesia, as in the past, but *to bring into reality* the united church in Indonesia. Theological understanding behind this new formulation was that the unity was already given; it is a will and gift of God. The churches in the ecumenical movement have to work for the realization of the church unity. The ecumenical institution coordinates common tasks of the churches, as the third document was designated to be a reference for member churches. Concern to issues of poverty, of human rights (notably of women, children, marginalized or disabled), injustice, corruption, or violence, become common concern of the churches. In a national conference recently the Communion of Churches in Indonesia expressed her concerns on phenomena in the life of the church and the nation. Internal conflicts among the churches disgrace the Christian witness; ethnic and religious primordialism threatened national integration; and neo-capitalism greediness exploitation of our natural resources resulted in ecological crisis. The Communion, therefore,

---

[14] S ee H. Kraemer, *From Missionfield to Independent Church: Report on a Decisive Decade in the Growth of Indigenous Churches*. The Hague: Boekencentrum, 1958.

[15] Tata Sinode Oikoumene Gereja-gereja di Indonesia, known in short as Tata Sinogi, and Pemahaman Iman Bersama (PIB).

appeals for churches and the nation to work for reconciliation, for national harmony, and for ecological protection.

But the Communion of Churches in Indonesia is not the only ecumenical body among Protestant churches. While they are member of the Communion, the Pentecostal churches and Evangelical churches have their own respective national communion. At the grass roots, tension between congregation of different denomination became phenomena, mainly because evangelistic tends to proselyte members of other churches. In some other cases, congregations were cleavage between ecumenical and evangelical wings.

Regional Communion of Churches

While there were no serious dogmatic, political or theological problems among the churches, sociological aspects became problems. Some churches are denominational; others are ethnic or regional. A church split into two or more churches following the ethnic or sub-ethnic lines. Tension emerged between churches – members of national churches council – as an ethnic church follows her members to set up congregations in another region dominated by another church.[16] To address this kind of problems, but also to promote local unity, regional council or communion was needed. The importance of regional and local ecumenism was revived when true ecumenicity was actualized by the churches in their common concerns and actions in the same place. Thus, the national council of churches motivated churches to set up regional councils.

Regional councils of churches (Indonesia: Dewan Gereja-gereja Wilayah, DGW) were founded by the local churches. Churches in Jakarta, North Sumatra, North Sulawesi, Maluku, and other regions founded their respective councils. Council of Churches in North and Central Sulawesi was and is one of the most enthusiastic. In 198x the member churches of the council "upgraded" the council into a "General Synod" (Indonesia: Sinode Am).

In Makassar, a regional council was newly founded in early 1963, but it was seen as a continuation of the Christian Council.[17] While the Christian Council in the past covered the Eastern Indonesia area, the newly founded regional council, the Indonesian Council (now Communion) of Churches in South, West and Southeast Sulawesi (will be shortly called Regional Communion) covered only South, West and Southeast part of Sulawesi Island.

Churches in the three provinces of South, West and Southeast Sulawesi came from different backgrounds. There was a congregation of Indies Church in Makassar (dated 17 October 1852) but since late 17th century there was a Protestant community in this city. In some other places like Bonthain (now Bantaeng), Bulukumba, and Selayar, Parepare and Palopo there were Protestant congregations since early 20th century, mainly among civil servants and military. While most of the southern part of the Sulawesi peninsula was occupied by the Muslims of Bugis and Makassar, and the western part by the Muslims Mandar, the northern part was Christianized by Protestant Dutch missionaries since the early decade of the 20th century. Some churches, like the Toraja Church, the Toraja Mamasa Church emerged from their works.[18] In the southeast the Protestant Church of Southeast Sulawesi emerged out from Muslim

---

[16] Tension among churches was also caused by charismatic or new Pentecostal movements. The charismatic proponent began to trouble the churches in South Sulawesi in the 1980s. They introduced a more lively liturgy compared to the rather boring church service of the traditional church. They also taught baptism by the Spirit and therefore re-baptized church members. And of course these took the people away from their original congregations. Some churches tried to accommodate some features of the movement to keep their members in the church.

[17] In 1963 a Council of Regional Churches (Indonesia: Dewan Gereja-gereja Wilayah) for South and Southeast Sulawesi was formed.

[18] From Toraja Church split the Indonesia Protestant Church of Luwu (1966); and from Toraja Mamasa Church emerged the Western Sulawesi Christian Church (1977).

population; so was the South Sulawesi Christian Church among the Bugis and Makassar. In most of the regencies capital Christians have their congregation(s) among the vast Muslim majority. Christians in the three provinces are about 10% (of ca. 12 millions people).

The Regional Communion recently has seven synods in its membership, five classes of churches, and some ecumenical congregations called "Ecumenical Communion of Christian Community".[19] The Regional Communion membership is open to any churches or congregation in the region; it is closely related but organizationally not part of the national communion. Church membership also covers non-members of the national communion. Its main character is local or regional coordinator of ecumenical movement to promote church unity. In a document of this institution, church unity was put in a common ministry of the churches, which also pay attention to advocacy ministry for the people:

> Church unity was understood as realization of common ministry, fellowship and witness. Common ministry, therefore, being done from the churches, by the churches and for the churches, the nation and the people in South, West, and Southwest Sulawesi, to support our witness of Jesus Christ as the Lord and Savior of the world. We are conscious that churches are part of plurality and complexity of Indonesia, and therefore have to work hard with the rest of the people to develop new and prosperous Indonesia, with high regard for the supremacy of the law, human rights and democracy.[20]

The Ecumenical Communion of Christian Community (may be called Ecumenical Community) was the solution to the modern phenomena of industrial or sub-urban population mobility. Christians from different churches found themselves in the same residential area attached to an industrial area or to a new housing resident. And rather than have their own congregations, they were organized into a congregation of mixed church backgrounds. In some places around Makassar these mixed congregations were attached to a local church, while others in industrial residential area were put under the ministry of Regional Communion. The Regional Communion appointed a pastor from a related church. In most of the cases the members are treated as double membership, as member of local Ecumenical Community congregation, but at the same time also regarded as member of her/his original church. This treatment should be revised as it is not fair from an ecclesiological perspective.

Churches in South, West and Southeast Sulawesi have recently been exposed to social, economic, and political problems. This region is known as one of the centers for radical Islamic movement. Rebellious Islamic movement disturbed the Christian congregations in the 1950s to 60s. And the new generation is the proponent of Islamic shari'a law. Mobilization of the people in this region is high due to economic situation. Agro-industry (notably palm oil and cacao plantations) and mineral mining have caused marginalization of people and ecological crises. Internally churches suffer from crises of human and financial resources, and also of leadership conflicts. The Regional Communion agenda, therefore, are concentrated on empowerment and advocacy programs.

Indonesia Christian Church (Gereja Kristen Indonesia, GKI)

Among churches in Java with Indonesian Christians of Chinese background since 1920s gathered in a church council. Eventually they were organized into three synods of Indonesia Christian Church in Eastern Java, Central Java and Western Java. There was along process to unite the three synods into General Synod

[19] In Indonesian it is called Persekutuan Oikumene Umat Kristen (POUK). The member churches are Christian Church of West Sulawesi, Indonesian Protestant Church of Luwu, Indonesian Christian Church of South Sulawesi, Protestant Church of Southeast Sulawesi, South Sulawesi Christian Church, Toraja Church, and Toraja Mamasa Church.

[20] From the document "Pokok-pokok Tugas Panggilan & Panggilan PGIW Sulselbara Periode 2010-2015". [The Main Common Tasks of the Indonesian Communion of Churches Region South, West and Southwest Sulawesi.]

of Christian Church in Indonesia. In the long ecumenical history of ecumenical movement in Indonesia the unification of these churches is the only case.[21]

In the process of founding Chinese church(es) during 1926-1928 the Indonesian Chinese congregations in Java founded their own first ecclesial organization to unite themselves.

> Its official name, significantly expressed in two languages, Chinese and Malay, was Tiong Hoa Kie Tok Kauw Tjong Hwee (THKTKTH) and Bond Kristen Tionghoa (BKT), the Chinese Christian Union. This was an expression of their Chinese roots which had been modified by the process of indigenization into the local cultures of the Indies.[22]

These Chinese congregations deliberately organized as Chinese church(es) rather than join denominational churches.

> Their wish to remain Chinese, while becoming Christian, was expressed in several ways. BKT was founded for the Chinese Christian only, as Christians from other ethnic groups in the Archipelago each had had their own church organization. BKT's principal "enemy" was what they called "denominationalism" which was qualified as a Western product that caused schisms and therefore confused the Chinese to come to believe in the One Lord Jesus Christ. The Gospel accepted from the Dutch was felt as "not yet Chinese" and they wanted to transform Christianity into a Chinese religion just as Buddhism. This line of sentiment was arrested and modified in the next two phases of the GKI's history by its Malay or Indonesianness strand, as this strand was becoming more and more focal within the identity of the GKI.[23]

The Indonesian Chinese congregations in Java eventually organized into three different churches of East Java on 22 February 1934, West Java on 24 Maret 1940, and Central Java on 8 Agustus 1945. In 1949 they established Dewan Geredja-geredja Kristen Tionghoa di Indonesia (DGKTI, the Council of the Christian Chinese Churches in Indonesia), with new orientation to be Indonesian churches. In 1955 Chinese name of the churches were replaced to Indonesian, Gereja Kristen Indonesia (Christian Church of Indonesia). The process to unification was revived when on 27 Maret 1962 the three churches declared commitment to integration. It took 26 years to be accomplished. On 26 August 1988 the three churches united in the General Synod of Christian Church in Indonesia.

Closing Remarks

The Ecumenical movement among Protestant churches in Indonesia was pioneered by missionaries before the war, and eventually in 1950 institutionalized in the Indonesian Council of Churches (later in 1984 renamed Indonesian Communion of Churches). One important movement behind this was the formation of the Christian Council for Eastern Indonesia in 1947 in Malino, Makassar. The ecumenical and nationalistic spirit of Malino conference later revived in the regional council of churches in South, West and Southeast Sulawesi. While in its early history the ecumenical movement occupied with an internal ideal of uniting the churches, recent development exposed the churches to external common concerns of poverty, injustice,

---

[21] For a short information in English of the General Synod of Christian Church of Indonesia, see "Sejarah Sinode GKI" at http://www.gki.or.id/content/index.php?id=4. [Access on 10 June 2010.] The Communion of Churches in Indonesia Region North, Central Sulawesi and Gorontalo renamed the communion to General Synod, but its character is just churches council, not churches unification. Some church leaders from this region repeatedly suggested to proclaim the establishment of the Gereja Kristen Yang Esa di Indonesia (the United Christian Church in Indonesia) but without significant conceptual substance.

[22] "Sejarah Sinode GKI" at http://www.gki.or.id/content/index.php?id=4.

[23] "Sejarah Sinode GKI" at http://www.gki.or.id/content/index.php?id=4.

human rights, women's rights, communal conflicts and ecological crises. Good leadership, relevant theological insight, and committed members are some topics to be addressed to be able to engage in that ecumenical movement direction.

Bibliography

Ide Anak Agug Gde Agung (translated to English by Linda Owens), *From the Formation of the State of East Indonesia Towards the Establishment of the United States of Indonesia*. Jakarta: Yayasan Obor Indonesia, 1996.

Jan Sihar Aritonang and Karel Steenbrink (eds), *A History of Christianity in Indonesia*. Leiden - Boston: E.J. Brill, 2008.

James Haire, *The character and theological struggle of the church in Halmahera, Indonesia, 1941-1979.* Frankfurt am Main – Bern: Verlag Peter D. Lang, 1981.

P.N. Holtrop, *Dari Malino Ke Makassar. Dasawarsa Pertama STT INTIM Ujung Pandang 1947-1957.* Ujungpandang: ISGIT, 1982.

P.N. Holtrop, *Selaku Perintis Jalan Keesaan Gerejani di Indonesia. Sejarah Madjelis Keristen Indonesia bahagian Timur, 1947-1956*. Ujungpandang: ISGIT, 1982.

H. Kraemer, *From Missionfield to Independent Church: Report on a Decisive Decade in the Growth of Indigenous Churches*. The Hague: Boekencentrum,1958.

John Villiers, "Las Yslas de Esperar en Dios: The Jesuit Mission in Moro 1546-1571" in *Modern Asian Studies*, Vol. 22, No. 3, Special Issue: Asian Studies in Honour of Professor Charles Boxer (1988), pp. 593-606

(59) CHURCHES TOGETHER IN GOD'S MISSION – IRAN

Sebouh Sarkissian

1. Historical Background

On the eve of His Ascension Jesus Christ delegated his disciples to "go into the whole world and preach the goodness", also to "make all nations my disciples". This was Jesus' last command to his disciples while He was on earth. The disciples, faithful to their Lord's, order began their mission by preaching the "Good News" to all humanity.

The Bible tells us that on the day of Pentecost Jesus' followers and disciples, while they were all together, were filled with the Holy Spirit. Among them were "Parthians, Medes, Elamites, inhabitants of Mesopotamia, of Judea and of Capadocia, of Pontus and Asia......" (Act 2:9).

Another incident of early history is the visit of the magis from the East to the new born King. According to William Barclay, a famous New Testament scholar, the East in this context is thought to be Iran. Church tradition says that the Apostles Bartholomew and Thomas both preached in Persia and later went in Armenia and India.

Historical evidence tell us that Iran had known Christianity from the earliest times of apostolic preaching, when Christianity was first preached in this part of the world, namely in the eastern regions of Asia minor and north-eastern regions of Mesopotamia and Syria. The apostles and their immediate successors did not know any boundary between east Syria, Mesopotamia, Armenia and Persia.

Thus beginning in the first century, Christianity had been preached outside of Palestine in various areas including Edessa, the capital of the kingdom of Osrohene at the time from where it penetrated Armenia and Persia. The famous Syrian Orthodox patriarch of 13th century says: "From Osrohene the faith undoubtedly had shown forth quite early to the East".

Since its very beginnings, the Christian era of ecclesiastical disputes, including personal rivalries among church leaders, theological controversies, conflicting political allegiances and nationalistic tendencies, undoubtedly brought dissensions among the Christians not only, during the Roman and, later Byzantine empire, but also the Sassanid empire. Nevertheless, the sense of unity and belonging to the same body that is the Church was not completely lost among the Christians, who for centuries struggled to maintain their faith and Christian identity

It is a historical fact that there were times when Christianity, as a new religion, which was different from the established and traditionally institutionalized religion in the century-old country, suffered persecution in Iran. This happened in other parts of the world as well, as in the Roman empire. There were also times when Christianity was not merely tolerated but also favoured, as under the Sassanian kings.

The occupation of Persia by Muslims, in the middle of the 7th century, first benefitted Christians, not only in Persia but also in Egypt and Syria, as they became protected minorities under Islam. But later on, from the 10thcentury onwards religious tensions led to persecution. The invasions by European Christians put Asian Christians in danger. For a short period during the Mongol rule there was relief for Persian Christians until the Mongols officially adopted Islam in 1305.

The Christians, despite the hard times they experienced, continued their Christian witness in Persia. For centuries without interruption Christianity in Iran, having passed through days of growth and days of tribulation, never ceased to exist and bear witness, though in relatively small numbers:

During the 18th and 19th centuries evangelical churches of the West, such as the Catholic church, began missionary activities in Iran. This movement on the one hand helped local Christians indirectly by improving education in church-related activities but on the other hand these missionary activities from the West also weakened the existing traditional churches through proselytism.

2. The Present Situation

Since the middle of the last century the Middle East has been going through political turmoil. Political unrest and the socio-economic crisis on the one hand, and the nationalistic ideologies on the other hand, have put the whole Middle East in a status of uncertainty and insecurity. A new phenomenon then began to emerge, the immigration movement, which led middle eastern people to think about moving to another place in search of much more secure and peaceful place. Thus moving has become a widespread phenomenon.

In Iran, following the Iranian Revolution, especially in the first years of the revolution, a certain degree of uncertainty and insecurity as a result of persecution and discrimination led many Iranian Christians and Muslims to leave the country. History tells us that all revolutions, regardless to their nature in their first days, bring a kind of uncertainty, insecurity and also persecution, but after that storm new life begins to emerge.

In Iran many were affected in the first period of revolution and many emigrated due to the socio-economic situation. At this point and for the benefit of future historians one has to admit that the immigration process started very vivaciously as a result of the activity of Hebrew Immigrant Aid Society (HIAS): HIAS, according to their sources[1], is assisting Iranian religious minorities in their applications to the US government for refugee status.

Nowadays a number of Christian denominations exist in Iran:. The Armenian Orthodox and Apostolic Church, for one, with her ethnic and distinctive culture and language counts some around 100.000 hundred thousand believers. Others include:

- The Assyrian Church of the East with some 7000 adherents
- The Chaldean Catholic Church with some 7000 adherents

There are also various other denominations of Evangelical background:

- Presbyterians, including the Armenian and Assyrian Evangelical Churches.
- Pentecostals. including Armenian and Assyrian Pentecostal Churches.
- The Assembly of God.
- The Anglican Church.

Having mentioned all these denominations let me add that there are also Armenian Catholics and Evangelicals. However, regardless of their dogmatic differences, all Armenians belong to the same culture and use the same language. On the other hand, Christians in Iran, in spite of a few difficulties, also enjoyed certain advantages such as financial help and maintenance of their historical churches and monuments.

In the time of worldwide ecumenical movements and activities the churches are called upon to cooperate and act together. This is the burden put on the shoulders of the churches. However, at the same time as we speak about inter-religious dialogue and cooperation, we should commit ourselves to a better understanding of our mission and deepen our knowledge for the sake of our Christian identity:

Iran is a Muslim country with its own constitution and laws. Christians in Iran, regardless to their ethnic and denominational belonging, have to respect the law, as the constitution contains two articles related to religious minorities and guarantees the rights of recognized Christian minorities, including representation in the parliament and special family law.

In recent years Iran, through the Centre for Interreligous Dialogue in Iran (CID), is having a dialogue with several Christian institutions, traditional churches, with the Holy Sea, the WCC, the Russian church,

---

[1] http://www.hias.org/

the Armenian Catholicosate of Cilicia and many Evangelical churches. The government, however, is very suspicious of churches or Christian groups which are involved in missionary activities in Iran.

If we believe in the importance and relevance of inter-religious dialogue and cooperation, let us engage in better understanding and enriching ourselves through mutual respect, acceptance, while remaining always committed to our Christian identity and cultural specifities.

I conclude with the following two remarks;

1. What is peculiar to Iran, I suppose is the very, fact that religious faith, regardless of its essence, has been deeply incorporated into the very ethos of society through a process of indigenization. The Armenians and I believe to some extent the Shiite Iranians and other Christians as well, have nationalized their faith in order to safeguard their ethnic identity, but of course one has to be careful. It is necessary priority should be given to identifying with the Word of God and never with the word of man.
2. The Christians being a minority in Iran can no longer afford to live in isolation from each other. They must deepen their ecumenical partnership with the churches inside Iran as well as with the churches outside the region.

Loyalty to our distinct identity in Christ and realistic openness to our Muslim neighbors and compatriots have to be the starting points and driving force of life and togetherness. This also is the will of God our Creator to whom we all belong.

(60) CHURCHES TOGETHER IN GOD'S MISSION – JAPAN LEARNING ECUMENISM TOGETHER: JAPANESE CHRISTIANS AND THE ECUMENICAL MOVEMENT IN JAPAN

Toshimasa Yamamoto

Introduction

A compounded triple disaster of great earthquake, tsunami, and nuclear power plant accident occurred in East Japan on March 11, 2011. Many people (more than 2,500) are still missing. The nuclear power plant accident in Fukushima is also still ongoing, with no sign of it being put under control. The ecumenical movement in Japan today cannot be discussed without referring to this triple disaster.

Naoya Kawakami, General Secretary of the Sendai Christian Alliance Disaster Relief Network (Touhoku HELP) shared voices of people in Fukushima in his paper for the CCA Consultation on Ecology, Economy and Accountability which was held in Indonesia on November, 2012. The paper says, "Mothers with children were first very confused by the information from the government which said that "radiation does not have any immediate bad effects". Those who really worried about the health of their children badly wanted to escape from Fukushima but had difficulties in trying to convince their husbands and relatives to leave because they believed the government assurance that everyone was safe. But mothers are still worried what to feed to their children, whether it is safe to hang clothes outside or not, and if it is necessary to wear face masks."

This kind of pain and disaster is part of what the ecumenical movement will need to respond to during this day and age. Churches in Japan that had not worked together before are working together now and responding to the threat of radiation as well as meeting the needs of the survivors. We cannot respond alone but with the help of working ecumenically and with other faiths within Japan as well as worldwide.

Bearing in mind this earthquake disaster and the nuclear power plant accident and ongoing concern on the radiation in Japan, the ecumenical community locally and globally has sustained us. In looking at how ecumenism began in Japan, we need to go back to the history how Christianity first entered Japan.

History of Persecution and Martyrdom

The Portuguese traders were the first Europeans to make contact with Japan in 1543. Francis Xavier, one of the original founders of the Society of Jesus, arrived in Kagoshima (in southern Japan) from Portugal with two Jesuit assistants to begin missionary work on August 15, 1549. The country at that time was divided by conflict among the *daimyo* (local feudal lords). Although Xavier and his colleagues spoke no Japanese and knew nothing about Japanese culture and religion, their missionary work was surprisingly successful. According to one report, Xavier baptized 150 people during his ten months in Kagoshima and by the year 1580, it was estimated that 150,000 Japanese had become Christians.

Xavier's method of proselytizing in Japan was to first gain the support of the country's leaders which would result in conversion of the masses they controlled. Many *daimyo* welcomed the missionaries as representatives of Portugal, hoping to attract Portuguese trade and military aid. But in 1587, the shogun Toyotomi Hideyoshi, suddenly issued an edict calling for the expulsion of all missionaries. Hideyoshi had become aware of the association between missionaries and European soldiers in colonial outposts such as Manila. As a result, persecution began with some Christians being killed and churches and seminaries burned. This persecution ceased temporarily upon the death of Hideyoshi in 1598. However, in spite of the persecution, the number of Christians in Japan had grown to more than 300,000 by the end of the sixteenth century. Tokugawa Ieyasu came to power as the new ruler of Japan in 1600. He was relatively tolerant of Christianity for a time, but local persecution still took place. 132 recorded martyrdoms took place between 1600 and 1612 and thousands more Japanese Christians were stripped of their property and banished. After the death of Ieyasu in 1616, much more brutal persecutions were carried out under the successive Tokugawa shoguns. Cruel torture was inflected before putting the Christian to death. As a result of this persecution, Christianity in Japan became an underground movement.

Christians were subjected to the practice of *fumie*, or "picture trampling." Suspected Christian was asked to step on a holy picture or bronze medal picture of Jesus as proof that they were not Christians. Many Christians chose not to step on the picture but to die in their faith. Many Japanese at that time had a strong sense of filial piety to their Feudal Lords, even a willingness to die for them. Therefore, the Tokugawa government used the *"fumie"* to weed out the Christians who could not step on the *"fumie"* because of their strong filial piety to Christ the Lord.

In the best-selling novel, "Silence" by a Catholic writer, Shusaku Endo, he tells the story of the last missionary priest in Japan who painfully lays his foot on the tablet picture of Jesus. The priest hears these words spoken by the Christ in bronze picture; '"Trample, trample, I, more than anyone, know of the pain in your foot. Trample, for it was to be trampled on by men (sic) that I was born into this world. It was to share people's pain that I carried my cross."

Forced Ecumenism, Nationalism and Confession

During World War II, Japanese Christians were watched and prosecuted once again. The Japanese government was very suspicious of Christians and oppressed them in various ways. Even before the Kyodan (the United Church of Christ in Japan) was formed, there were a number of church leaders who accepted that the state religion of Shinto was a "super-religion" and revered the Emperor, but there were also some church leaders who did not support this belief and were subsequently arrested. Japanese pastors who were interrogated by the Japanese military/police were often asked this question: "Who is greater? Jesus Christ or the Emperor?" If the pastor answered, "Jesus", they would be taken to prison and tortured, but if they answered, "the Emperor" then they would be mocked for not answering as a Christian pastor should. Questions were also asked in devious ways such as, "If Jesus and the Emperor were both drowning in a river at the same time, who would you save first?" (One clever pastor answered, "Whoever is closest to me.")

To the later shame of many Christians, some church leaders even urged the Christians in Korea and Taiwan (both countries were Japanese colonies at that time), to accept shrine worship. This brought much suffering to Christians in those countries. All Protestant denominations were forced to join together as one group, called the Kyodan. This was not done in the spirit of ecumenism but because it made it easier for the Japanese government to control and watch the church if they were under one church body. This newly formed Kyodan attempted to rationalize Japan's atrocities by sending a letter to the Asian churches which interpreted Japan's military expansion as "historical progress" and "God's will." It is regrettable that the Kyodan at the time succumbed to pressure to write such a shameful letter.

It was not until much later, in 1967, that the Kyodan, which is now the largest Protestant denomination in Japan and also a member church of the NCC-J, issued a "Confession of Responsibility during World War II" which stated that "In the name of the Kyodan, we issued a statement at home and abroad in which we approved of and supported the war and encouraged prayers for victory. Indeed, even as our country committed sin, so we too, as a church, fell into the same sin… Now, with deep pain in our hearts, we confess our sin and ask the Lord for forgiveness. We also seek the forgiveness of the peoples of all nations, particularly in Asia, and of the churches therein." Since then, many member churches and organizations of

NCC-J have repented, confessed their sins, and asked for forgiveness from God and our neighbors in Asia. Churches in Japan have a mandate and desire to live the gospel of reconciliation with their Asian sisters and brothers.

Postwar Ecumenical Movement in Japan

The ecumenical movement was formative both domestically within Japan and internationally with the birth of World Council of Churches (WCC) in Geneva and when the present NCC-J was established in 1948.

In the 1950s the NCC-J, in cooperation with the Kyodan, invited Lawrence Lacour to Japan and organized an evangelistic crusade that was remembered as one of the epoch making "Lacour Crusades." The NCC-J was involved in the early stages of the Faith and Order movement and latter published a Japanese translation of the Lima Liturgy and BEM (Baptism, Eucharist and Ministry) in the 1980s. However, in general, the ecumenical movement in Japan was, from the beginning, a more "life and work " oriented, praxis-based movement than the Faith and Order centred theoretical unity-seeking movement. Since the end of the War, it was the NCC-J that spearheaded the movement and has served as the center of numerous ecumenical activities.

During the 1960s and 70s, division occurred between social action oriented groups and evangelical groups within Protestant churches like the Kyodan over the U.S - Japan Security Treaty. There was a campus struggle at the Tokyo Union Theological Seminary which polarized students and faculty members. The division had profound repercussions for the ecumenical movement in Japan. However, in spite of the polarization of Japanese churches in the 1960's and 70's, the ecumenical movement was strengthened and energized through involvement with the struggle of Korean residents in Japan, the Buraku liberation movement and the democratization process in South Korea.

The Alien Registration Law in 1952 required the fingerprinting of all foreign residents in Japan. Oh SooHae, a member of the Korean Christian Church in Japan and a Commissioner in the WCC Programme to Combat Racism (PCR) shared her personal insight: "The Japanese government does not want to recognize the existence of minorities in Japan." The ecumenical movement in Japan took this issue very seriously and dedicated itself to work for the realization of human rights for all Korean residents who suffered discrimination in Japan. It supported the all-out struggle against the alien registration system, which applies to all foreign residents in Japan.

The Buraku people, although Japanese, have been systematically discriminated against since the Tokugawa Shogunate (1603-1868). At that time, Japanese were divided into four occupation-related social strata: samurai, farmers, artisans and merchants. Person not included was the Emperor, who was at the top, and the "non-persons" on the bottom, who were later called "Buraku." The Buraku people were assigned specific jobs, such as the slaughter of animals, that tanning of animal hides, and the burial of the dead, that were considered to be unclean according to Shinto and Buddhism social concepts.

The Japanese family register system was a major factor in the perpetuation of discrimination. Every Japanese is registered at birth in their family's permanent register at their local city hall, which makes it possible to trace any individual's birthplace or permanent address. This is one way that perspective employers and families of marriage partners can trace whether a candidate is from a certain background, such as Buraku. The Kyodan established a Special Committee on Buraku Liberation Issues in 1975 and the Kyodan Buraku Liberation Center was set up in 1981. The NCC-J also formed a committee on Buraku discrimination issues in 1976. In 1981, the Doshuren, a national assembly of about seventy religious organizations, including Christian, Shinto and Buddhist organizations, was founded to address discrimination within religious communities and teachings.

As stated earlier, Christian churches and organizations in Japan have confessed and repented before God that we were part of the past war efforts and have begged for forgiveness from our neighboring countries.

By remembering our past and taking what history has taught us seriously, we have been trying to walk a new path with the determination that we will never again commit the same sin. These have been our strongest collective memories and reminders of the ecumenical movement in Japan. As part of our efforts in building solidarity, the ecumenical movement in Japan, through its life and ministry, had the privilege of working together with Christians and other people during Korea's democratization process in the 1970's. We also provided symbolic ecumenical spaces such as the "Tozanso Process" for the encounter of Christians in the DPRK and South Korea in 1984. We have been involved with humanitarian aid to the DPRK since 1996. We need to continue our efforts to build communities of peace for all based on our ecumenical memories and biblical reminders.

The ecumenical movement in Japan, though small in number, has played a significant role in advocating justice in the area of human rights, women's rights, education and the peace movement together with NGOs and citizen's groups both within Japan and around the world. The ecumenical networks, to which Japanese churches and the NCC-J in particular relate, including the CCA and the WCC, have been enabling Christians in Japan to stand in solidarity with people and partner churches throughout Asia and other parts of the world. Post-war ecumenical memories are the basis of our common commitment to peace and justice for all. They are positive seeds of hope for the ongoing ecumenical movement in Japan.

Main Tasks and Mission

The followings are itemized ongoing tasks and the possible mission of the ecumenical movement in Japan.

1. Further collaborations with the World Council of Churches (WCC) and Christian Conference of Asia (CCA)

Getting involved more in the ecumenical process toward a peaceful unification of the Korean Peninsula, and sharing concerns continuously on such issues as peace, economic justice, minority rights, women, education, the youth, and the environment.

2. The Peace Constitution and Article 9 Conference

Article 9 of the Japanese Constitution is considered by people in Asia as evidence of a pledge that it would never cause military aggression again. For people in Asia, the Peace Constitution is like a "life insurance" on Japan in preventing it from becoming a war-making country. There have been three inter-religious conferences on Article 9, the first in Tokyo (2007), the second in Seoul, Korea (2009) and the third in Okinawa (2011)

3. Unity of churches and expansion of their dialogue

NCC-J has been promoting unity of churches as their basic priority, in response to Jesus' prayer "that all may be one." (John 17:21). The prayer meetings for the unity and annual dialogue meeting with the Catholic Bishop Conference in Japan have been organized.

4. Ecumenical Disaster Response

NCC - Japan Ecumenical Disaster Response Office (NCC-JEDRO) was established as a response to the triple disaster following the massive earthquake of March 11, 2011. JEDRO was established with the strong encouragement and support of the ecumenical movement, especially the Churches Forum in North East Asia of the Christian Conference of Asia. JEDRO collaborates with ACT Alliance and the worldwide ecumenical movement.

5. Financial and organizational review

Many churches and Christian organizations are facing severe financial crisis due to the decline of their membership and the staff reductions. The financial scale, the organizational structure and tasks of the ecumenical movement in Japan need to be reviewed accordingly. Creating new visions and dream will revitalize the ecumenical movement.

Bibliography

Reischauer, Edwin O., Japan: *The Story of a Nation*, Tokyo Charles E. Tuttle Company.

Francis, Carolyn Bowen and Nakajima, John Masaki: *Christians in Japan*, Friendship Press Inc, New York, 1991.

Endo, Shusaku: *Silence,* Shincho Press, 1966,Park West Publications (English)

The Kyodan Executive Committee: *Confession of Responsibility During World War II*, Feb. 20, 1967

Iglehart, Charles W.: *A Century of Protestant Christianity in Japan*, Tokyo, Charles E. Tuttle Company, 1959.

Policies for the NCCJ's Activities for the 36th General Assembly Term, NCC Japan, 2006, NCCJ 36th General Assembly Materials.

Report Document: The 3rd Asia Inter-Religious Conference on Article 9 of the Japanese Peace Constitution, NCC Japan, 2012

NCC -JEDRO E-mail: relief311@gmail.com; URL. http://jedro.jp/jp

(61) Churches Together in God's Mission – Korea
Ecumenism in (South) Korea:
The Cooperation of the Churches Hosting the 10th Assembly of WCC

Park Kyung-seo

Pre-History

The ecumenical movement in Korea began in tandem with the invasion of the Korean peninsula by Western imperial powers and Japanese colonial intrusion from the late 19th century onwards.

The Christian Jesus was introduced to the Korean people through the history of martyrdom experienced by the Roman Catholics at the hands of the Joseon dynasty that continued throughout the years since its introduction to Korea through China and Macao. It is also worth noting that before the arrival of western missionaries from the U.S. the gospel was translated into the Korean language in Shenyang, China and Japan in 1882 and 1884, respectively. As a result, in 1887 a Permanent Committee for the Translation of the Bible was formed jointly by the Methodist and Presbyterian missions in 1887, and the entire New Testament was translated with the help of the Korean, Suh, Sang-yoon. This can be referred to as the first united project and genesis of the ecumenical movement in Korea.[1]

The missionary enterprise in Korea began with the translation and dissemination of the Korean Bible from Manchuria and Japan during the late 1870s and early 1880s. On the basis of such accommodation of the gospel by the Korean people and active evangelism the denominational missionary activities of western churches began after 1884[2] when the first two missionaries to Korea, Rev. Underwood and Rev. Appenzeller,[3] from the Presbyterian and Methodist churches respectively in the U.S.A. landed together in Korea in 1885. This missionary experience also brought together the two experiences of denominational division and ecumenical cooperation.

The translation and dissemination of the Bible by the indigenous people before the arrival of foreign missionaries was unique to Korea in the history of world Christianity.[4]

The arrival of denominational missions in Korea beginning with the Northern Presbyterians and Northern Methodists from the U.S.A. was followed by the Anglicans in 1890, the Australian Presbyterians in 1891, the Southern Presbyterians from the U.S.A. in 1892, the Southern Methodists from the U.S.A. in 1896, Canadian Presbyterians in 1898 and the Salvation Army in 1908. As this list of denominations clearly shows, in the short span of 20 years or so these missionaries who arrived in Korea sought to expand their denominational territories, and as a consequence the Korean churches still bear the marks of their efforts. Although such denominationally oriented mission activities contributed to the escalation of denominational divisions, Christian missions also had the beneficial effect of accelerating the transition of Korea from a feudal society to a contemporary one. While denominationalism made the growth of ecumenism in Korea difficult, at the same time it contributed to the growth of Christianity in Korea.

---

[1] Ncc Korea;70th anniversary committee "United Church and World" 1994 page 14

[2] Lee, Deok-Ju, "The Historical Developments of Union Movement in the Korean Church" in *Gidoggyo Sasang* (*Christian Thought*), 1996. pp10-11.

[3] See also: http://www.newworldencyclopedia.org/entry/Henry_G._Appenzeller

[4] Lee, Young-Hoon, "Evangelism and Church Growth in the Korean Church" in *Sinhak Sasang* (*Theological Thought*), 1998. pp.221-2. See also contribution No 7 from *Min Young Jin* on Bible translation in Korea and Asia in part II of this volume.

Many Korean church historians agree that the meeting of missionaries that took place in 1905 at the home of D.A. Bunker, a Methodist missionary, was the beginning of ecumenism in Korea. It was at this meeting that the missionaries from different denominational backgrounds met and agreed to form a Church of Christ in Korea and to cooperate on united activities. I also would agree that this meeting has the significance of being the genesis of the Korean ecumenical movement. While the earliest history of the Korean church reveals the strengths of unity, Korea soon experienced the aggression of Japanese imperialism as Korea was colonized by the Japanese in 1910. However, this aggression and intrusion also led to strengthening the united efforts of the Korean churches for freedom from colonial oppression. During this period the Korean churches also engaged in a great revival movement during 1903 and 1907. Each of the denominations divided their areas of responsibility and conducted a joint evangelism movement called, the Million Souls Movement which became the seedbed for the national liberation movement. Along with the many missionaries who encouraged these movements Korean preachers, such as GIL, Sun-Joo, KIM, Ik-Doo, LEE, Yong-Do and JOO, Ki-Cheol, were also instrumental in promoting the Christian faith. Additionally, the Korean churches formed a united Christian newspaper in 1906 and established many Christian schools, colleges and hospitals. They also published a united hymnal that was used by all the denominations.

The clutches of Japanese colonial powers became stronger as the years passed and the Japanese forced the Korean people to adopt Japanese names and sought to erase the Korean language and culture. They also severely persecuted any intellectuals or individuals who sought to encourage the Korean struggles for independence by imprisoning and torturing them. As a result on 1 March, 1919 the Korean people organized a nationwide independence movement against the Japanese colonialists. The Korean Christians were key figures in this movement and led the March First Independence Movement with leaders from other faiths.

As well as their involvement and leadership in the March First Independence Movement the Korean Christians were also instrumental in leading the Korean people's struggles for justice throughout the 36 years of Japanese colonial rule. Christians, irrespective of their denominational differences, were instrumental in the Gwangju Students' Independence Movement of 1929 as well as the trial of the 105 Independence Fighters. Their involvement was motivated by the Christian teachings of liberty and the universal rights of all human beings created in God's image. Christians had been involved in the struggle for independence from Japanese colonial rule from a very early stage through their involvement in societies, such as the Independence Society which was formed in 1896 and the Hwangseong Christian Youth Society that was formed in 1903. In all of these movements for independence the Christians participated irrespective of their denominational affiliation. Prayer meetings for independence that were organized by Christians were attended by thousands of Christians from all denominations and were also attended by non-Christians as well. A good example would be the week of prayer organized by the Sangdong Church in November of 1905.

Through the various efforts of Christians in struggling for independence and the united participation of Christians, Korea finally gained its independence when the Second World War ended with the victory of the allied forces. However, before this moment in history, the efforts of the Korean churches' union efforts bore fruit in the formation of the Joseon Christian United Council that was attended by 53 representatives from the different churches (19 Presbyterian, 11 Northern Methodist, 6 Southern Methodist, 8 North Presbyterian missionaries, 5 South Presbyterian missionaries, 6 Canadian Presbyterian missionaries and 2 missionaries from the Australian Presbyterian mission). This became the forerunner of the present day National Council of Churches in Korea.

Historically, this year, 2012, marks the 88th anniversary of the founding of the National Council of Churches which has continued to function as the central point for the Korean ecumenical movement. For seven years, from 1938 to 1945, the Japanese colonial authorities disbanded the Council and it could no longer function. However, with independence the disbanded Council and other ecumenical institutions once again began their work and in September 1946 they formed the current NCCK with 13 organisations during the first Assembly of Korean Christian United Organizations that was held at the Joongang Church in Insadong, Seoul.

With the independence of Korea after 36 years of colonial oppression in August 15 1945 the Korean people were ecstatic and hoped for a united country that would be founded on the principles of liberty and democracy. However, contrary to their wishes Korea was divided along the 38th parallel, leading to the division of the 75 million Korean people, the pain and suffering and injustice of which continues to this date.

More specifically, the suffering and hunger of the people in North Korea who are groaning under the oppressive authoritarian regime has given a new task for the ecumenical movement in Korea.

The following is part of a policy paper that was written by the NCCCUSA in 1991 as they were preparing to send a delegation to North Korea. Although 20 years have passed, little has changed on the Korean peninsula. I also participated in this meeting, and so I quote from part of this document below.

Korea, the Last but One Nation Divided Since 1945 (the Pain of 75 Million People)

Throughout our long history, Korea has been blessed with cultural, linguistic and ethnic unity, and a beautiful land, rich in resources and in productive agricultural areas which for millennia have been sufficient to support its population. The land is small, roughly the size of Great Britain.

An estimated seventy million persons live there, one-third north, two-thirds south of the Demarcation Line. Korea has never posed a threat to its powerful neighbors: China, Russia, or Japan but its key strategic position bridging Asia and the Pacific made these oft-aggressive powers anxious to dominate the peninsula. Japan's main islands are located a scant 120 miles to the southeast. About the same distance to the west lies China's Shantung Peninsula.

Korea shares its northern border for about 150 miles with China, and for eleven miles in the northeast with the Russia. Seventy-five miles further north is Vladivostok, one of Russia's principal naval bases, and a vital outlet to the Pacific. Korea has for ages been a focus of contention among North East Asian powers eager to shore up their strategic defenses or to have a base from which to launch attacks against others. It is not surprising therefore that when the United States pursued its "Manifest Destiny" into Asia and the Pacific in the late nineteenth century, it also viewed Korea as a pawn to be conquered, controlled, neutralized, or traded in order to attain or preserve control over other territories. In the 1905 Taft-Katsura Agreement, for example, the U.S. accepted Japan's ambitions regarding Korea on condition that the U.S. would have a free hand in the Philippines.

For centuries, Korea has been a barometer of the political climate of its region. Since 1945 it has become an indicator of the state of peace and security in the world. It was over control of this land that the Cold War produced its first hot regional war which claimed about four million casualties. Since then the "Korean conflict" has time and again reverberated beyond the borders of the peninsula and of the region.

Across the demilitarized zone today are faced off, at the ready, two of the world's largest standing armies, each backed by superpower military forces which in case of any major contingency would almost certainly get involved directly or indirectly. The South armed forces plus 28.500 U.S Troops are under direct U.S. command in the R.O.K.-U.S. Combined Forces Command, and are equipped with sophisticated weaponry, including nuclear arms. The U.S. Pacific Fleet and U.S. bases in Japan, as well as logistic support from Japan's Self Defense Forces, add to South military reserve. Current U.S. Policy is to exert strong pressure on Japan to extend the scope of its regional military role. The North armed forces, of the size comparable to the South's despite its smaller population, are neighbored by Chinese and Russia allies with nuclear weapons based nearby in the eastern part of Russia. Frequent military incidents along the

Demarcation Line between tense military forces on both sides threaten to explode into broader warfare. A build up of tension has the potential to provoke a global nuclear war.

The Korean Peninsula: A Focus of Tension, Conflict and Division

Such conflict is not new for Koreans. Throughout its 3.000 years of recorded history, this land has been trampled by armies pursuing conquest, subjugated by foreign powers, forced into undesired alliances, occupied and humiliated. But it is a fact that for thirteen centuries before 1945, neither the land nor the people of Korea were ever divided. Therein lies both the tragedy of division and the hope that it can be overcome. People so bound together over millennia do not easily forget their common ancestry, history, tradition, language and culture, nor readily accept the division of their nation and land.

Recently the tension between North and South Korea has been escalated unfortunately due to Nuclear tests by North Korea and the military conflict between the two Koreas. The Ecumenical Movement by South Korea still tries hard to sustain the communication connection with NCC North Korea (Christian Federation DPRK.) providing Humanitarian Aid to the churches in North Korea. Preparing for the 10th General Assembly of WCC, the NCC of Korea has had a series of meeting with churches in North Korea for the common implementation of a Peace Train march from Berlin to Pusan via Pyong Yang of North capital city and Seoul South capital city and also about inviting delegates of North Korean Churches to the Busan Assembly etc. Koreans sincerely hope that a powerful statement on Peace settlement on the Peninsula will be issued to whole world from the 10th Assembly of WCC.

The Churches in North Korea

Christianity in North Korea was more visible and active in compared to the South until the Korean War (1950-1953). During this Korean War the Communists with the support of the Soviet Union Troops killed and tortured many Christians and many Christians had to escape to the South.

Those who couldn't flee to the South have however survived until the time Christianity was allowed by the Communist Government with provision of registration in detail in the early 1980's. In 1983, the Korean version of the Old and New Testaments were printed in China just as the Hymnal book in North Korea. From 1984 onwards the House Churches of the North are using these Bibles and Hymnals.

When the WCC has convened for the first time for a North and South Dialogue 1984 in Tosanso, Japan, after the WCC staff had visited North Korea negotiating with the Government for permission to send a Church Delegation to this historical meeting in August 1984, for some unknown reason, instead of sending delegates of the North, the Christian Federation North Korea sent their congratulatory telegram to this meeting.

Two years later, the Commission of International Affairs (CCIA) of WCC in cooperation with the WCC Asia Task Force, in 1986, 2nd -5th September, had convened with careful preparation in advance, the so-called Glion I consultation in Geneva, where 6 delegates of NCC South and 5 delegates of North Federation had fully participated along with 60 other Churches representatives from USA, Soviet Union, West & East Germany, Canada, U.K, Japan and other countries .

This historical meeting between South and North was the first since Korea's division in 1945. Afterward the Glion meeting encounters had been convened every two years by the World Council of Churches (in 1988, 1990, and in 1992 in Kyoto) allowing North and South Korea to have direct contact and a window through which they can communicate with each other, which continues up to today. Since the churches of the two Koreas meet in Seoul or Busan, the Christians are always grateful to the World Council of Churches for this initiative and facilitation.

With regard to Christians, one can count approximately more than 10.000 Christians in North Korea. Through financial contributions from WCC and South Korea, two churches have been constructed in Pyong Yang, in 1996 and 1988 and since 1989 Pyong Yang Theological College has been active training in young pastors for a three years' course, theological books from South having been sent by the WCC Asia Desk. Since 1998 the Churches in the South have been providing a substantial amount of humanitarian Food Aid to the Korean federation in the North, and this type of cooperation has been continued up to the present.

This cooperation is a clear demonstration by the Churches in the South of Christian love, solidarity and reconciliation. So far the North has indicated to the South that the Christian Federation Church representatives will participate in the Bussan 10th Assembly.

In fact North Korea has participated in the Assembly in Canberra, Harare and Port Allegre. Therefore we hope very much, that they will also come to Busan and celebrate with the World Christian Family.

•

Current Issues of the Ecumenical Movement in South Korea

It has been announced by the National Statistics Bureau, that of the Protestant population of 43 million population of South Korea, 25% are Christian and 40% Buddhist . But a new tendency in this figure is that the Roman Catholic Church members are steadily increasing, while Protestants are decreasing. This means that many protestant families have become Catholic. The reason behind this conversion is the fact that many protestant churches are interested only in the church growth and in financial gains or progress rather than in spiritual reflections and social services. For example, only 5% of Protestant members in South Korea are youth which is an alarming sign for the future. The Preparation Committee PROK has informed that around 300 youth will be recruited as local stewards for the Bussan Assembly. The PCK and the Anglican Church are thinking of the same arrangement.

With regard to the Evangelical Churches in Korea both Ecumenical and non- Ecumenical churches are equally strong and influential. Both coexist in peace, therefore it is imperative that non-ecumenical churches be well represented at the Busan Assembly as well. It has been informed that representatives of evangelical churches are also serving the local preparatory process.

Hankichong (CCK; Christian Council of Korea; Evangelical) which was established in 1998 represents all non- ecumenical churches in Korea with 22 Churches as members of this council including PCK and Methodist, who are also member churches in NCC Korea. This organization has been facing an existential crisis because of corruption scandals in its election, which led to splitting into two factions both bringing their strong arguments to the secular court, which has made many Christians sad and tired. As of today this council is not functioning, while both factions are criticizing each other. Many Christian groups are insisting that this council should be dissolved immediately. This dispute has made many Christians uninterested and also indifferent. This means, only a small number of church leaders are still interested in this, and this means mainly in hegemony, the power for decision making in the Council, ultimately for leadership positions.

As mentioned at the beginning, denominationalism had been introduced by missionaries when they brought the Christian Faith to Korea in the early stages, proud of their mother churches in western countries, as USA, Canada, Scotland, UK, Australia etc. However, an important fact to mention is that since more than 10 years, a united worship of the resurrection at 5:00 AM ,with the CCK and NCCK participating, has been conducted. We therefore pray that some day in the near future one united church in Korea will be born.

Programs of NCC Korea During Last Seven Years for Social Issues (Justice and Peace Committee NCC Korea)

In the year 2006, USA had announced that their Korea - based troops will be eventually coordinated with strategic flexibility by sending them to disputed areas in Asia and other regions. This announcement has raised concerns to the Korean people, whether this will create feelings of enmity from those countries and could lead to avoiding Koreans. The NCC Korea has convened an urgent meeting to express the Ecumenical position warning against this potential development.

Further, the churches campaigned to raise funds for the victims of the Indonesian Tsunami and handed it over to provide aid to the churches in Indonesia. In the same year, a special task force for an USA-Korea Free Trade Agreement has started its mission for an in-depth study group.

In Korea, there are around half million undocumented migrant workers, working illegally, and occasionally the Ministry of Justice checks and arrests those workers and after some interrogation in a custody camp it expels them. This custody camp in Yoesoo has been burnt with fire and 13 illegal workers were killed. The NCC Korea in 2007 has organized a fact finding team and called a big press conference and requested the Government to compensate them and the Korean parliament was asked to create laws for these undocumented workers.

Christmas worship had been specially organized with people who had lost their homes and land due to a relocation project of the US Military camp in Seoul, to Pyongtaek area. A massive campaign for the Abolition of the Death Penalty had been organized with other religions, initiated by PCK and NCC Korea originally in the early 80's. The other religions were Buddhism, Chondoism and Catholicism etc.

When Utoro village, with an intensive Korean population near Osaka Japan, , was informed by the District Government of Japan that soon it would be demolished due to a rehabilitation project, the Koreans there protested for proper compensation, The NCC Korea has called for an international solidarity consultation with NCC Japan.

Since 6 years, the government has been trying to have a naval base in Cheju Island, The NGOs, but also other civil movement groups for environmental protection are against the construction of this military base. The NCC Korea has joined this collective campaign, and confrontations between Government and Protest groups are ongoing. Every day protest actions are registered and this struggle has continued for the last 6 years. No hopeful negotiation signs have appeared to date.

For the period 2008-2010 it can be reported, that ecumenical input to the presidential election for the issue of peace and reconciliation programs is a continuing endeavor too. In Korea there are around 1,5 million migrant workers living with Koreans, already many of them married to Koreans and as of today more than 300.000 multicultural families are registered. One third of these 1.5 million migrant workers are undocumented and there is a campaign to stop Human Rights violation of these migrant workers' rights. Ecumenical solidarity campaign groups have been working for them since the '90s and fortunately Human Rights violations are now decreasing. Nevertheless there are still some bad cases filed and NCC Korea is taking up those cases.

200 Pastors have signed in solidarity for the INDEPENDENCE Principle of National Human Rights Commission of Korea under the New Government and submitted it to the Government. Independence of NHRC Korea according to UN Paris Principle should be kept always regardless of regime changes. FTA USA and Korea should be cautiously dealt with by the parliament, so that workers, farmers and other marginalized groups are not further ignored and their right to a happy life should be further promoted.

Dismissal of seasonal workers in E-Land Super market has been tackled by the ecumenical solidarity group and some measures of negotiation between workers and owners have been reached. However, the issue of non regular workers in this country is still unsolved. Globalization has brought polarization, as well as the problem of non- regular workers with the justification of maximizing the profit of business circles in Korea as in other countries.

The NCC Korea also has issued a statement protesting the presence of Israeli troops in the Gaza area of Israel and requesting to stop this inhuman action and attack. A one church consultation on Human Security and building peace community in North East Asia region was organized where church representatives from Japan, Taiwan and Korea have participated. A major fund-raising activity by churches of Korea has been coordinated by NCC Korea for relief work to the victims of Hukushima Tsunami and the tragedy of the Nuclear Power station, Later, for more effective coordination, a meeting had been convened by Korea where churches in Taiwan and Japan have participated. So too for Haiti earth quake victims, a fund has been raised and handed over to the churches in Haiti.

During the presidential election campaign, the current president Lee, Myung-Bak had announced that a multi-million dollars project for the rehabilitation of four big rivers costing would be undertaken providing many new jobs for unemployed youth and workers. Civil groups for environmental protection and groups for Ecological sustainability have demonstrated against this project. NCC Korea has joined this campaign. Yet the government project has been implemented and so far there has been a no winner as such. Time alone will tell who was correct and which party is incorrect.

Korea had joined the USA's Vietnam War in 1975. Many young Korean soldiers had fought against Vietnamese troops and many Koreans were killed. In Korea, there were more than 15.000 retired soldiers from the Vietnam War who have suffered by the after effects of this war from toxic defoliant, and many affected soldiers had also passed away. As a result of appealing by Churches and NGOs to the Government during the last 20 years, very recently the Government has announced these affected retired soldiers as persons of national merit and they will receive a monthly compensation from the Government. This was a result of the long lasting campaign by churches and NGOs and NCC Korea.

For nearly 2000 years, there has been a movement between Japan and Korea, to campaign with a very concrete program for the common ownership of Japanese Constitution Article No. 9 concerning peace. This campaign had originated in the midst of the Japanese conservative party's plan for expansion of their self defense forces. NCC Japan and NCC Korea have held meetings every year, rotating the venue between Japan and Korea. After the Fukushima incident, a new program has been initiated for a 'nuclear -free zone' campaign on the Korean Peninsula. There are still opposing views regarding this among the people, but NCC Korea is trying to find an alternative energy and agitating against the nuclear station. Korea has 22 nuclear power stations and the government is planning more stations. There are still many ongoing programs are with the NCC Justice/Peace commission, such as relief work for the victims in Fukushima, and there are follow-up programs after FTA with USA and European Union and other countries and the follow-up programs regarding the four big river's rehabilitation project being implemented.

A Survey on Ecumenical Institutions in Korea

In this final short survey we can give only a few examples out of many ecumenical organizations which serve in the South Korean context:

Korea Environment Movement: Solidarity for Integrity of Creation

In the year 1981 the Green Church membership movement, Green healing concert, Environmental Sunday worship movement were established regarding the issue of Air Pollution in Korea. In this there was close cooperation between Protestant and Catholic Churches. In June one Sunday has been designated as Ecological Sunday. Other programmes also have been instituted such as the Life Daily Bread movement and plantation campaign in Mongolia to protect Yellow Dust effect from Gobi and Chinese Deserts.(Desert

Reclamation Project), Clean Project for 4 major Rivers in Korea, and the Anti-Naval base construction in Cheju Island.[5]

Korea Church Women United

With Ecumenical vision, almost all church women got together for the healing programs caused by National Division, social injustice, and programs for church renewal and international cooperation. As major programs; The Fellowship of the Least Coin, Gender Equality, De-mining Campaign and the Nuclear- Free- Zone Movement etc.[6]

Human Rights Center of NCC Korea

This organization was started in the late 70's, when the nation had suffered with a Military Dictator. They claimed that the Human Rights Movement is the clear expression of the Social Gospel out of Christian Witness. More programs were created for the Demolishment of National Security Law, Non Regular Worker's Rights and Annual Human Rights Award etc.[7]

Christian Home and Family Life Association in Korea

In 1954, immediately after the Korean War ended, this organization has started to publish a monthly magazine called " New Family" one of oldest Christian Monthlies in Korea, which has been circulated to Military bases, Hospitals and Prisons and other detention camps and contributed enormously for Christian Witnesses.[8]

Korea Christian Service

Eight denominations of Korean protestant Churches and NCC Korea had started their services in 1963. This is a well represented organization on behalf of Churches in Korea for Social Services in the area of Humanitarian Aid for both Korea and other areas as relief work for the victims of natural calamities in almost the whole world, such as Vietnam, Chile, Haiti, China, Japan etc. Also some Programs and Aid for the eradication of extreme poverty in Africa and in other continents.[9]

Korea Students Christian Federation (KSCF)

Christian Students of almost many Universities of Korea were the member of this organization established in 1968 and were actively engaged and involved for the Anti Dictatorial Movements and Democratization Movement in Korea during the '70's and '80's. During the '70s the struggle for true democracy had been the priority of this students' movement.

Nowadays the situation has changed, as democratization has been reached to a certain degree of satisfaction. But still this organization is active for spiritual discipline, Human Resource Development Programs and Campaign for a Free Nuclear World. etc.

Many programs of KSCF are well organized in close cooperation with WSCF in Geneva, Switzerland, in solidarity and for follow-up work.[10]

---

[5] http//www.greenchrist.org/
[6] http://www.kcwu.org/
[7] http://www.ncchr.or.kr
[8] http://www.godpeople.com
[9] http://www. charity. or, kr
[10] http://www.kscf.or.kr/

Ecumenical Youth Council in Korea (EYCK)

Youth and students of six member churches of the NCC Korea are the main members of this Ecumenical Youth Council who are very busy and engaged for the preparation of the forthcoming WCC 10th Assembly in Busan.

Interdenominational training programs are being convened and conducted for the preparation of the 10th Assembly. Recently they have jointly organized with Japanese EYC a training program in the Fukushima area. Visiting the victims are the main priority during the Assembly in Busan.[11]

Beside the above mentioned organizations, there are; Korean Association of Women Theologians (http://kawt.co.kr)

Christian Institute for the Study of Justice and Development; (http://www.jpic.org) who are very active in the implementation of their programs. Do visit their homepages.

Bibliography

NCC Korea on her 70th Anniversary 1998 Seoul "United Church and World"

Lee, Deok-ju 1996 Christian Thought Magazine "The Historical Developement of Union Movement in Korean Churches"

Lee, Young-hoon 1998 Teological Thought Magazine "Evangelism & Church Growth in the Korean Churches"

Ninan Koshy 2005 WSCF "A History of the Ecumenical Movement in Asia

Park, Kyung-seo 1998 CCA Hong Kong "Reconciliation & Reunification;Ecumenical Approach to Korean Peninsula"

Park, Kyung-seo 2007 Ewha University Publishing Co. " Promoting peace and Human Rights on Korean Peninsula"

[11] http://www.eyck.or.kr/

(62) Churches Together in God's Mission – Korea
A Case Study on Reconciliation with North Korea

Victor W.C. Hsu

Context

At the end of World War II in 1945, Korea was arbitrarily divided along the 38th parallel by mutual agreement between the USA and the USSR, bringing an end to Japan's 35-year occupation of the peninsula. In 1948, the Government of the Republic of Korea (ROK) was formed in the South under the leadership of Syngman Rhee, followed shortly by the proclamation of the Democratic People's Republic of Korea (DPRK) in the North under Kim Il Sung. The outbreak of the Korean War (1950-1953) left an estimated ten million families separated across Panmunjom. The cease fire remain effective today in the 1953 Armistice Agreement.

Initial hopes and intentions of Korean independence and reunification succumbed to Cold War tensions. The South developed under the dominant influence of the USA, while the North strengthened its relationships with the Communist world. Both sides developed in a militarist mode, increasing tensions and solidifying the division, which became a primary symbol of Cold War confrontation. North Korea became one of the world's most closed and rigidly structured societies and the divided Korea is the most militarised and dangerous peninsula in the post Cold War era.

As regards inter-Korean relations, the most dramatic were the summits between the late Chairman Kim Jong Il with Presidents Kim Dae Jung (2000) and Roh Moo Hyun (2007)[1]. The far-reaching "Joint Declaration" issued on June 15, 2000 encouraged several governments to normalize diplomatic relations with the DPRK and contributed to an increasing rapprochement with South Korea, which included new agreements on family reunions, tourism and economic cooperation. However, a series of natural disasters in the North in the mid-1990s led the DPRK to appeal to the international community for massive economic and material assistance to cope with devastating floods and consequent famines. Many observers have noted that these significant developments might have precipitated new openings in North Korean society.

Religion in North Korea

Korea has a long history of repression of religion, especially of religious beliefs of foreign origin. Christianity was especially resisted after it arrived on the peninsula in the late 18th century, and was systematically attacked under the Japanese imperial domination from 1910 to 1945. Japanese rulers severely persecuted all religious believers as they sought to impose Shintoism as the national religion. In 1945 the North Korean leadership adopted an aggressive Stalinist Communism form of atheism of with systematic repression of religious ideas and organizations, especially between 1946 and 1958[2]. A large

---

[1] There have been several inter-Korean agreements since 1953. The first was a 1972 communiqué outlining important principles for unification. The second was a Joint Declaration on the Denuclearization of the Korean peninsula in December 1991. The most comprehensive was signed in January 1992, known as Agreement on Reconciliation, on-aggression and Exchanges and cooperation.

[2] "North Korea," Dwain C. Epps, The Encyclopedia of Christianity, Volume 3 (J-O), Erwin Fahlbusch, Jan Milic Lochman, John Samuel Mbiti, Jaroslav Pelikan, Lukas Vischer (English language edition of the Evangelisches Kirchenlexikon, Eerdmans-Brill, Grand Rapids, Michigan, 2003)

number of churches and other places of worship were destroyed[3]. Confucianism, Buddhism and Shamanism all had deep historical roots in Korea and continued to be widespread in North Korea after 1945, though Buddhists were those who were repressed with particular harshness.

Concomitantly, in 1947-1949, the Communist leadership created organizations to manage and control the activities and religious practices of religious groups[4]. In 1983, Kim Il Sung declared limited religious freedom, allowing these organizations a degree of latitude in contacting and organizing members.

Until very recently widespread doubts in South Korea and elsewhere prevail about the existence of churches in North Korea. Less is known about religion in North Korea than in almost any closed society. Hard facts on the conditions of religious believers after 1945 are still hard to come by, making assessments necessarily approximate. As more international observers have been granted access to the DPRK in recent years, more information is gradually coming to light. Some general estimates of numbers of followers of religions have been made and are given here.

Roman Catholic Church

Though persecuted badly and having suffered martyrdom, Roman Catholic Church's believers were estimated to number some 18,000 in 1884. In 1945 North Korea had two suffrage dioceses of Seoul and a third related to the church in China. Half of Roman Catholic Christians and all their priests and administrators are said to have fled to the South after 1945, leaving an estimated 25,000 in the North. From the late 1980s there have been visits to Catholic Christian communities by both ecumenical delegations and Roman Catholic Church hierarchs. The *Changchun* "cathedral" was erected in 1988 in Pyongyang, at the same time as the Protestant Bongsu Church. Though still without ordained clergy, Korean-speaking priests and bishops from Japan, and Vatican officials regularly visit and conduct the sacraments.

Protestant Churches[5]

The earliest Protestant missions in North Korea were the Presbyterian and Methodist ones, the former by far more numerous in 1945. About 65% of the total number of Protestant Christians in Korea prior to 1945 were in the northern part. For the Presbyterian Church, the figure was even higher, at 75%. These percentages are based on statistics given for Korean Christianity in the years 1941-1942 by the Institute for Korean Church History[6].

Christian minorities belonged to the Holiness and Seventh-day Adventist churches and the Salvation Army. Many members fled to the South when the Communist government came into power in 1945, and many more joined the mass emigration during the Korean War. The Korean Christians Federation (KCF) estimates its membership at 100,000 persons, worshiping together in some 10,000 house churches around the country[7]. In the mid-1980s it re-established its theological seminary and gained permission to build two churches, *Bongsu*[8] and *Chilgol*[9], in Pyongyang. They had a seating capacity of 400 and 150 members,

---

[3] In-chul Kang in "A Recognition of Modern Religious History in North Korea", claims that about 120,000-170,000 Christians evacuated to the South. Heung-soo Kim, Ed. 1992, 172-173.

[4] North Korea created the Korean Christians Federation (KCF) in 1946, grouping together all Protestant Christians without reference to their former denominations. Similar associations were also created for the indigenous religion, Buddhism and the Roman Catholic Church.

[5] A Russian Orthodox Church was opened in 2005 for the diplomatic corps

[6] *Hankuk Kidokyo eui Yoksa* (A History of Christianity in Korea), vol. 2, Seoul, Kyomunsa, 1990, 261. It records that 223,339 of 351,222 Protestant Christians in Korea were in the North.

[7] Ibid. Encyclopedia.

[8] Built in 1988 and renovated and reopened in 2010.

respectively. They remain the only parishes today permitted the privilege of public worship. Humanitarian workers and diplomats based in Pyongyang regularly attend the Sunday worship services.[10]

Well-informed visitors to the DPRK put the present numbers of practicing Christians in North Korea at a much lower levels than those used by the KCF, suggesting a total of some 13,000, grouped together in some 675 house churches, mostly along the west coast, served by some 40 trained pastors and 20 ordained lay leaders.[11] Much of the first information about the KCF and its structure came directly from its former General Secretary, Rev. Koh Gi-jun, and has been recorded in official reports of the ecumenical delegations including those in the Canadian Council of Churches, the National Council of Churches of Christ in the USA and the WCC.[12]

Reestablishment of Ecumenical Contact

Despite reports to the contrary from a few church-related individuals who visited North Korea between 1981 and 1985, there are widespread and serious doubts about the existence of a living Christian community in that country. In an attempt to reach out beyond their borders, the KCF wrote to the World Council of Churches (WCC) in 1974 to inquire about possible membership, but there was no reliable means to maintain subsequent communication. The KCF did join the Christian Peace Conference in 1976, however, and sent representatives to some of its meetings in Eastern Europe. In November 1984, the WCC organized a world consultation on "Peace and Justice in North-East Asia: Prospects for Peaceful Resolution of Conflicts" in Tozanso, Japan. The main agenda item was the threat posed by the continuing division of the Korean Peninsula. The KCF was invited, but could not attend. It did, however, send a message welcoming the ecumenical initiative and wishing it success.

In early 1985, the National Council of the Churches of Christ in the USA (NCCCUSA) visited[13] North Korea for the first time in more than 40 years. They met with senior state officials and representatives of the KCF and worshiped with house church congregations in Pyongyang and Kaesong. Later that year, two senior staff members[14] of the WCC made a visit there and proposed to the KCF that they consider joining in a face-to-face meeting with leaders of the National Council of Churches in Korea (NCCK).

In September, 1986 the WCC convened a "Seminar on the Biblical and Theological Foundations of Christian Concern for Peace" in Glion, Switzerland in which four representatives of the KCF and six from the NCCK participated, providing the first opportunity for Christians from North and South to meet one another since Korea's division in 1945. This historic gathering was followed by two further similar WCC-sponsored North-South Christian encounters[15] in Glion, Switzerland – where the KCF and NCCK developed a common prayer for peaceful reunification in North and South, a tradition that continues to this day. Similar conferences were held in Kyoto, Japan in 1995 and in Macao in 1996. This has since become known as the "Tozanso Process." It is so significant that the WCC marked both the 20th and the 25th anniversaries with ecumenical consultations attended by both the KCF and the NCCK.

---

[9] Opened in 1990

[10] The author has been welcomed at the church by the pastor and the choir on a week day.

[11] Ibid. Encyclopedia

[12] When the KCF started to meet with the WCC in mid-1980's it had five pastors who were ordained prior to 1945. Today only one of them is till living.

[13] Led by Dwain Epps

[14] Ninan Koshy and Erich Weingartner of the Commission of the Churches on International Affairs

[15] 1988 and 1990

The Tozanso Process of Peace and Reconciliation

1. Genesis

During the 1970s prominent leaders in South Korea were imprisoned for expressing their desire for unification. The most prominent among them is Moon Ik-Hwan who was received by President Kim Il Sung. For any individual or institution expressing a desire for unification violated the National Security Law. Those arrested were denied visitor privileges. In fact, these cases posed a special problem for the churches in South Korea because the NSL prohibited any public discourse on reunification. Advocacy, educational and campaign activities regarding reunification became out of bounds for the South Korean churches although active representation was made on their behalf in Europe, in Japan and in North America.

In early 1980's, the NCCK set reunification as its priority for that decade. In the wake of the Kwangju massacres those were dark days in the history of a proud nation. It recognised that democratization of Korea must be accompanied by efforts for unification for, as long as the division of Korea persisted, martial law and the NSL were always going to be invoked to harass, persecute and imprison human rights activists or anyone who dared to promote unification. In such a highly explosive context with South Korea under a brutal military dictatorship, the NCCK requested the WCC to support its desire to make contact with the Christian community in the North so they could take up the unification agenda together. Indeed, under the leadership of the NCCK, the churches in Korea manifested the vision to be a beacon of hope as prominent leaders exhorted the ecumenical movement to express their solidarity with the Korean people's struggle for justice, human dignity, peace and the reunification of Korea.

2. The Tozanso findings

This was then the context of the ecumenical consultation held in Tozanso, Japan, in 1984 on "Peace and Justice in Northeast Asia." Despite the division and walls of separation that were both physical and spiritual, Tozanso threaded a complex web of barriers and initiated lines of communication between Christians of North and South Korea. That historic consultation proposed that the churches need to take initiatives with regard to:

- humanitarian concerns for separated families
- public involvement in discussions on unification
- overcoming enemy images
- increasing participation of women and youth in the struggles for peace and justice
- stemming the arms peace.

3. The Glion encounters

The Tozanso consultation launched *a series of first-time events* that included face-to-face meetings of Korean ecumenical delegations from both sides of the DMZ. In fact these encounters became known by the name of the beautiful Swiss village, Glion. The most notable were Glion I, II and III held in two-year intervals beginning with 1986. These precious encounters gradually expanded into visits by churches and ecumenical agencies to both parts of Korea as well as visits by delegations of the KCF to churches in Asia, North America, Europe and other parts of the world. Collectively these programs and events became known as the Tozanso process widely regarded as precursor of rapprochement on the Korean Peninsula. In fact, if one were to compare the policies of the South Korean and the United States governments towards North Korea, the ecumenical movement may rightfully claim credit for those components related to exchanges and cooperation, confidence building measures and other steps aimed at the reduction of tension. As a result of the close coordination and collaboration among ecumenical partners, the recommendations made by church bodies were remarkably similar to the major policy statements on the Korean Peninsula by the NCCCUSA in 1986, the NCCK consultation in 1988 and the WCC in 1990.

4. WCC strategy for Glion I in 1986

In the case of the Tozanso consultation the strategies employed by the WCC had to be based on quiet diplomacy necessitated by the highly sensitive agenda. That responsibility fell on the Commission of the Churches on International Affairs (CCIA) to facilitate the participation of church leaders from South Korea so that they could help shape the ecumenical framework for contacts with the North Korea Christian community. Unlike in human rights advocacy in which CCIA only played a supportive role, here, due to the NSL, CCIA played an active role while keeping in close touch with the NCCK, especially its General Secretary, Rev. Kim Kwan Suk and CCIA Commissioner from South Korea, Mr. Kang Moon Kyu.

The *preparation* began with several strategy consultations in discrete settings held in Germany, Japan and the USA without any publicity. Both Philip Potter and Emilio Castro, the two former General Secretaries who served as Directors of the Commission on World Mission and Evangelism were extremely supportive of these meetings. Participants were knowledgeable church leaders that included Koreans from within Korea and Koreans in the Diaspora. Mr. Oh Jaeshik who was with the Christian Conference of Asia when the process began and later became the Deputy General Secretary of the NCCK, and the Rev. Park Sang Jung as the General Secretary of the Christian Conference of Asia (CCA) were among the Koreans who were closely involved both in giving counsel and facilitating activities. These closed-door sessions were designed to build consensus about the basic ecumenical framework that spelled out the roles and the responsibilities of the ecumenical agencies and the churches in Korea.

The *absolute confidentiality* of these "informal consultations" was essential for three main reasons: the intelligence and security networks were effective and almost ubiquitous, the agenda had yet to be defined and the participation of South Korean leaders had to be protected.

One key decision from this series of ecumenical consultations concerned the topic of the Tozanso meeting. Given the NSL, it was clear that the agenda could not be open about the peace and reunification of Korea. It was decided to have a broad topic: peace and justice in North East Asia. While this camouflage formulation necessitated looking at the Korean peninsula in a regional and global geopolitical context, this approach actually sharpened the analysis and provided a solid foundation for appreciating the division of Korea as a tripwire on the ideological fault line which could set off a major worldwide conflagration.

Once *consensus* was achieved about the objectives of the Tozanso consultation, CCIA had the challenging task of persuading the member churches in Korea to participate, given the tense aftermath of the Kwangju Massacres which found the Chun Doo-Hwan regime on the defensive, even as the forces of democratization were reassessing their strategy. Such a situation turned out to be advantageous to the CCIA staff who, in their task of persuasion, pointed to the 1979 assassination of President Park Chung-Hee by his own security chief, the student uprisings and the subsequent massacres in Kwangju as the rationale and context to address peace with justice. They urged the church leaders to seize the moment to work with the WCC to help bring about peace with justice on the Korean peninsula. The CCIA staff assured the church leaders that permission would be obtained from the government for them to participate in Tozanso.

5. WCC South Korea Strategy

The next major step was to convince the *South Korean government* that it was in its interest to allow the church leaders to travel to Tozanso. In addition to the geopolitical analysis used with the church leaders, CCIA staff informed the government that blocking South Korean church leaders' participation would create serious negative consequences. They showed the government a list of prominent international church personalities who would be among the participants: two Presidents and the General Secretary of the WCC, General Secretaries and moderators of churches and NCC's from Australia, France, UK, Germany,

USA, the USSR and Cuba, in addition to those from several of Korea's neighbouring countries, Japan, Taiwan, Hong Kong and the Philippines. The South Korean government officials understood that the CCIA staff argument about a potential negative publicity was not a bluff. In the media all across the globe they had been stung by the negative publicity generated by the CCIA's 1979 publication on human rights in their country. The WCC and the ecumenical family had demonstrated a *consistency and effectiveness* in their advocacy regarding the Korean situation. The government knew that the WCC network was well organized and was at the same time poised to mount any publicity that would be viewed as detrimental to the regime. The tough negotiations in 1984 with the Korean government took place secretly with a very powerful official who requested anonymity. At the end of this negotiating session, he told the CCIA staff that "this meeting with you never happened."

6. WCC DPRK Strategy

With the DPRK, the task was slightly less complicated by the fact that the WCC had no member church in the DPRK. The contacts made by the CCIA staff were limited to the KCF and the DPRK Permanent Mission to the United Nations in Geneva. The KCF participated actively in Christian Peace Conference (CPC) which held peace-related meetings regularly in such places as Prague, Geneva, Helsinki and Vienna. The CCIA as a member of the Conference of NGOs in Consultative Status with the UN (CONGO) was frequently invited by the CPC to its meetings. As a result of these contacts, which were augmented by occasional visits of DPRK diplomats in Geneva to the WCC, the KCF began to have some appreciation of WCC's work. It was especially interested in the WCC position on peace and disarmament which it found to be compatible with its own concerns about the arms race. But it was the agenda of the Tozanso consultation that attracted the attention and interest of the KCF and the DPRK authorities. They were impressed that an international organization, despite the tense and complex geopolitical relations in N. E. Asia, was willing to tackle the issues in this region as threats to world peace. For them, the proposed meeting in Japan was the first international conference on such a topic.[16]

During the preparation phase, information about the various CCIA contacts with the KCF and the DPRK authorities were deliberately withheld from the South Korean church agencies and church leaders. They judged that, given the NSL, it was unwise to burden them with the information. But they took great pains to assure them that contacts were being pursued with the KCF to ensure that the latter was fully aware of the proposed Tozanso consultation. They ruled out inviting the KCF as such an encounter would be problematic on two counts. The first was that it would violate the NSL causing all South Korean leaders to be arrested upon their return. The second was that for such a historic encounter involving North and South Christian communities, extreme care was necessary in preparing the agenda. To bring the two sides together without careful preparation and prior discussion between the two parties would have been counterproductive, especially when the WCC itself was not yet clear about the agenda that it might want to propose in such an encounter.

The painstaking process of keeping the KCF informed about the Tozanso consultation turned out to be key as subsequent events demonstrated. The KCF sent a congratulatory message wishing the Tozanso consultation every success, giving the first hint of their interest in pursuing the ecumenical agenda of forging contacts between the two sides.

The confidence built in the "Tozanso Process," enabled representatives of the KCF to travel four times to the USA between 1989 and 1997 for official meetings with US church counterparts. All these visits outside the DPRK, and several more to Germany, Canada, Australia, Brazil, Harare and elsewhere

---

[16] In preparation for the consultation, the CCIA wrote to the two Korean governments, China, the USA and the USSR asking about their policy for Korea unification. Only the DPRK responded with information about its position. The USA said it had no position on the issue. China and the Soviet Union did not reply.

provided unprecedented opportunities for encounter and planning for joint initiatives to promote reunification between representatives of the KCF and the NCCK. Toward the end of the decade of the 1990's, some representatives of the NCCK, because of the "Sunshine Policy" of President Kim Dae Jung, were able for the first time to travel to the DPRK for meetings with their Northern counterparts on the Korean Peninsula itself and these visits have continued and become more frequent since.

These ecumenical efforts opened the way for the DPRK officials to request the WCC international humanitarian assistance for flood victims. Action by Churches Together (ACT) and several churches were among the first to provide help.[17] The fact that this was given through the KCF significantly broadened the State's recognition of the role of this Christian body in society. Built with international church assistance, the KCF noodle factory and bakery produced noodles and bread for broad public distribution. It also distributed clothing, medical supplies and other essentials donated by its ecumenical partners abroad.

WCC's involvement in Korea is certainly a unique ecumenical story that deserves to be documented. It owes its success to clarity of vision among the leaders of that time who were willing to take calculated risks to implement a complex strategy straddling a seemingly ideological divide. Important aspects of this effort which can serve as lessons for ecumenical methodology include:

1. Unity among actors within and without Korea.
2. Clear objectives around which the actors coalesced and supported.
3. Well-defined strategy and ecumenical discipline in implementation.
4. Clearly identified roles and responsibilities for the network of actors.
5. Excellent coordination in the implementation of the strategy.

As this article goes to press, North/South relations between the NCCK and the KCF had been stymied during the five-year term of President Lee Myung Bak who reversed the engagement policy of his two predecessors. No official contacts were allowed unless sanctioned by the administration. Moreover, the negotiations on the nuclear issue in the DPRK in the six-party talks are at a stalemate. The peninsula remains extremely volatile politically and there is a constant risk for a major military conflagration either by accident or design. A glimmer of hope for change may be gleaned from the official platforms of the three Presidential candidates. Each promised to change the current South Korea policy towards North Korea should he or she be elected on December 19 this year.

The Tozanso process placed the WCC in the front and centre of the unfolding drama still being played out on the peninsula. It can play a most influential and critical role which perhaps no other institution can. Not only has it been for three decades a pioneer in promoting peace and justice in North East Asia and in working on the peace and unification of Korea; it has also developed a unique access to the political authorities on both sides. It has an international network of concerned actors eager to play a supportive role. The situation calls for a renewed commitment of leadership, resources and expertise and the reactivation of a worldwide ecumenical network to rededicate itself to the worthwhile agenda of peace with justice in Korea.

Bibliography

"North Korea," Dwain C. Epps, The Encyclopedia of Christianity, Volume 3 (J-O), Erwin Fahlbusch, Jan Milic Lochman, John Samuel Mbiti, Jaroslav Pelikan, Lukas Vischer (English language edition of the Evangelisches Kirchenlexikon, *Eerdmans-Brill, Grand Rapids, Michigan, 2003)*

Peace and Justice in North East Asia: Prospects for Peaceful Resolution of Conflicts (CCIA Background Information 1985/1, World Council of Churches), Ed. Erich Weingartner

S. Masahiko, "Christianity in North Korea after the Liberation, 1945-1950", in Heung-soo Kim ed., *Haebang hu Bukhan Kyohoe Sa*, (Seoul, Dasan Kulbang, 1992), 36-40

[17] Most of the aid was coordinated by the Asia Secretary of the WCC, Park Kyung Seo.

Reunification: Peace and Justice in the 1980s, (Christian Conference of Asia, 1988)

Park Kyung Seo, *Reconciliation-Reunification: The Ecumenical Approach to Korean Peninsula* (Christian Conference of Asia, 1998).

"Report of the International Christian Consultation on Justice and Peace in Korea", 1988. National Council of Churches in Korea

Allen D. Clark, *A History of the Church in Korea* (The Christian Literature Society of Korea, 1971)

Bruce Cumings, *Korea's Place in the Sun: A Modern History* (W.W. Norton & Company, 1997)

David B. Barrett, editor, *World Christian Encyclopedia* (Oxford University Press, 1982)

Don Oberdorfer, *The Two Koreas: A Contemporary History* (Addison-Wesley, 1997)

Sun-Kyung Yi, *Inside the Hermit Kingdom: A Memoir* (Key Porter Books, 1997)

Kang Chol-Hwan, *Aquariums of Pyongyang: Ten Years in the North Korean Gulag* (Basic Books, 2001, translation from the French original)

(63) CHURCHES TOGETHER IN GOD'S MISSION – LAOS ECUMENISM AND THE ARRIVAL AND SURVIVAL OF PROTESTANTISM

David Andrianoff

From its earliest beginnings ecumenism has characterized the Protestant church in Laos. Various mission groups and individuals—both missionaries and nationals—established the Protestant church in Laos. The "Liberation" of Laos and the establishment of the Lao People's Democratic Republic inaugurated the post-mission era of the Protestant church, with the Lao Evangelical Church surviving and then beginning to thrive after the departure of foreign missionaries.

Ecumenism and the Arrival of Protestantism in Laos

The Lao Evangelical Church was woven together like a tapestry from various missionary strands, including American Presbyterians, Swiss Brethren Assemblies, the Christian and Missionary Alliance, the United Bible Society, Overseas Missionary Fellowship, Baptists, and others. Today these interlaced strands form a largely united church tapestry.

Ecumenism characterizes the history of Protestantism in Laos. A Christian and Missionary Alliance (C&MA) publication brought the need of missionary work in Indochina to the attention of a Swiss Brethren student in England. As a result, the Swiss Brethren Assemblies began a mission in southern Laos. As the Swiss were not able to expand their mission into northern Laos, both the Swiss Brethren and the American Presbyterians, who had earlier pioneered Protestant mission work in northern Laos, asked the C&MA to expand into northern Laos. To further augment the C&MA program, the Swiss Brethren sent them two Lao church leaders. The Overseas Missionary Fellowship (OMF) joined the Swiss Brethren program in southern Laos; they also provided a missionary to help the C&MA with Hmong Bible translation. After the change in government and the departure of the missionaries in 1975, the church in the south united with the church in the north forming the Lao Evangelical Church.

Five overlapping epochs define the advent of the Protestant church in Laos: From 1872 to 1934 American Presbyterian missionaries based in northern Thailand worked around Luang Prabang in northern Laos. From 1902 to 1975 Swiss Brethren missionaries worked in Song Khone and southern Laos. From 1929 to 1975 Christian and Missionary Alliance missionaries worked in Luang Prabang and northern Laos. From 1950-1975 the C&MA worked in Xieng Khouang Province primarily among Hmong and Khmu. From 1975 to the present national leadership has united the Lao Evangelical Church for all of Laos.

With each wave of missionary activity the Good News found initial receptivity among marginalized peoples. For the American Presbyterians the Khmu ethnic minority, who provided slave labor to the royal family and dignitaries of Luang Prabang, came to faith. For the Swiss Brethren the Phi Bop—people accused of being demon-possessed and thrown out of their villages—came to faith. The first convert of the C&MA in northern Laos, was an Annamese (Vietnamese). In 1950 members of the Hmong ethnic minority began coming to faith.

Individual missionaries dominated each epoch: American Presbyterian missionary Daniel McGilvary established Protestant work in northern Laos in 1898. Gabriel Contesse with Maurice Willy began Swiss mission work in Song Khone in southern Laos in 1902. Ed Roffe established the C&MA work in northern Laos in 1929. Ted Andrianoff provided the initial contact with the gospel for the Hmong in Xieng Khouang in 1950.

Local leaders implemented the establishment and growth of the church with the missionaries. Nan Tit, the first Protestant believer in Laos, and Khmu believers in his and surrounding villages kept their faith in the absence of regular missionary presence. Saly Kounthapanya, youngest son of Tit Koun, one of the first baptized believers for the Swiss Brethren in southern Laos, provided initial leadership to the C&MA—established Gospel Church of Laos (GCL) in northern Laos. Pastor Bee Thao, a Hmong graduate of the Vientiane Bible school provided leadership to the Lao Evangelical Church after the missionaries and church leaders had fled the country. Khamphone Khounthapanya, nephew of Saly Khounthapanya replaced Bee Thao when he moved to the U.S.

1. Daniel McGilvary and the American Presbyterian Mission (1872-1934)

American Presbyterian missionary Daniel McGilvary made five visits to northern Laos from his base in Chiang Mai, Thailand, between 1872 and 1898. His exploratory visit with Vroom in 1872 took him to Luang Prabang where the Lao king resided. Returning to Laos in 1893 with Robert Irwin he reached Muang Sing in the far north. Again in 1893 with Katherine Andrews Denman, McGilvary visited Muang Pong, the southernmost town of the Sipsong Panna region, which encompassed northern Laos and southern China. Returning from visiting Luang Prabang in 1897, people from the group of McGilvary and Denman came upon a camp of 30 Khmu. McGilvary gave a tract to Nan Tit, who became the first person in Laos to come to faith in Jesus Christ.

On his last visit to northern Laos in 1898, Dr. McGilvary was accompanied by Thai evangelists.. When they stopped at the Khmu village previously visited they found a ready response to the gospel. The local district chief embraced the Jesus-religion:

> He was a venerable man near seventy, and though for years hoplessly crippled by paralysis of the lower limbs, his bright mind and business talents had raised him to his present position, and given him a commanding influence. I shall never forget our first interview. He had heard the rumour that our religion would overcome the spirits and save from sin. Crawling painfully on his hands to meet us, he welcomed us to his village and his people. He had heard of the Jesus-religion, and wished to embrace it (McGilvary 2003:403-4).

Every family in the village made the decision to follow Christ. McGilvary notes (2002:404) that "It was a great day, just the like of which I had never seen. It settled the decision of hundreds, possibly of thousands of people." Thus began the first Protestant church in Laos. McGilvary spent ten days teaching hymns and basic literacy to the young people. Thai Christian workers remained behind another five months, further teaching the new believers in the faith. At the end of December the Thai missionaries returned to Chiang Mai filled with joy, reporting that 87 people from three villages were waiting to be baptized. Most of them had memorized a 90-question catechism in Thai (their third language).

The American Presbyterian mission gave responsibility for the work in Laos to the Thai church—the first missionary work of the Thai Protestant church. In 1900 Chi Ma baptized 41 adults in this village. With the French in firm control of Laos, in 1903 American Presbyterian missionaries Campbell and McKay were refused entry to Luang Prabang. A year later they did successfully visit Luang Prabang. Hugh Taylor, stationed in Nan in northern Thailand, then assumed responsibility for the work in northern Laos, making periodic visits until 1934.

2. Gabriel Contesse and the Swiss Brethren (1902-1975)

At the end of the nineteenth century Gabriel Contesse, a young Swiss studying at Bible college in the U.K., received a tract from the Christian and Missionary Alliance appealing for missionaries for Annam (currently part of Vietnam). He contacted the C&MA to inquire about serving in Annam. As the C&MA work in Vietnam would not begin for another ten years, Contesse requested that his own church body—the Swiss Brethren Assemblies—send him. Needing a companion, he convinced Fritz Audetat, but Audetat would not be ready for a few years. Maurice Willy, a frequent traveler to French colonies, agreed to accompany Contesse. In September 1902 Contesse and Willy found themselves in Song Khone in southern Laos.

Contesse and Willy used the Thai New Testament to share the gospel. In March 1903 two Buddhist monks offered to teach them the Lao language. After taking off his yellow robes, one monk translated the Gospel of John from Thai into Lao. On Easter Sunday, 1905, Contesse and Willy baptized Tit Peng. A year after arriving in Laos, Maurice Willy married Henriette, who had studied tropical medicine in Thailand. But the following year they returned to Switzerland, exhausted. In 1906 Gabriel Contesse married Margaruerite in Switzerland and they returned to Laos, joined by his brother Charles and his wife Ethel. In 1908 Gabriel and Margaruerite Contesse, shortly followed by Charles and Ethel Contesse, all died of cholera. This severe blow to mission work stimulated Maurice Willy to expedite his return to Laos with Fritz Audetat accompanying him. The following year Henriette Willy died of dysentery; as a result Maurice returned to Switzerland. For the next three-and-one-half years Fritz Audetat found himself alone in southern Laos. In addition to holding 12 evangelistic meetings a week he immersed himself in translating the Bible into Lao. In 1926 the Lao New Testament was published. The C&MA press in Hanoi published the entire Lao Bible in 1932.

The Swiss missionaries also made occasional trips to northern Laos. On one such trip in 1927 Fritz Audetat met American Presbyterian missionary Hugh Taylor who begged the Swiss mission to include northern Laos in their program. Since the Swiss did not have sufficient personnel, Taylor and Audetat contacted the Christian and Missionary Alliance in Vietnam, requesting them to expand into northern Laos.

3. Ed Roffe and the C&MA (1929-1975)

In 1929 Ed Roffe, escorted by D.I. Jeffrey, chairman of the C&MA Indochina field, arrived in Luang Prabang to begin the C&MA's work in Laos. Luang Prabang served as the royal capital of Laos. Jeffrey stayed two nights before heading back to mission headquarters in Tourane (present day Danang). Roffe was on his own, 19 ½ days' travel away from his nearest C&MA neighbor. Eight months after arriving in Laos, Roffe went to Hong Kong to marry his fiancé Thelma Mole. A year after applying for official authorization to conduct missionary work in Laos, the Lao king authorized Roffe to evangelize within the Kingdom of Luang Prabang. Roffe then requested help from the Swiss Mission in the south. They sent Thao Cita, a veteran leader, and Saly Khounthapanya, a teen-aged second-generation believer.

In mid-December 1931 Hugh Taylor and his wife, of the American Presbyterian mission in Thailand, visited the Christian Khmu village earlier established by McGilvary to turn over the Presbyterian work to the C&MA. During the visit Taylor's wife contracted typhoid and died. Hugh Taylor buried her on the banks of the Mekong River, not far from Luang Prabang, where they had hoped to retire.

In 1932 an Annamese man and his Lao wife, neighbors of the Roffes, converted to Christianity. This man had earned his wealth buying the annual opium crop and selling it to the French government. One year, after he had spent all he had purchasing that year's crop, the French government stopped purchasing opium. He tried to sell it in China, but it was confiscated, and he was left penniless. At that point he met the Roffes and the Lord. Years later his grandson graduated from seminary in the Philippines. He moved to France, where he ministers to both Lao and Vietnamese.

In 1936 C&MA and Swiss missionaries formally divided up Laos with the C&MA working in the northern three-sevenths of the country, and the Swiss Brethren working in the four-sevenths of southern Laos.

The Japanese invasion of Laos disrupted foreign mission work. After the end of the war C&MA missionaries and new recruits returned to Laos. In 1956 the C&MA ordained Saly Khounthapanya to the ministry. The following year the Gospel Church of Laos was formally organized with its own constitution and Rev. Saly as president. Two years later Moon Duangmala—a Khmu whose Christian heritage went back to the first church established by McGilvary, was ordained.

4. Ted Andrianoff and C&MA Work with the Hmong (1950-1975)

In 1947 Ted and Ruth Andrianoff, newcomers to Indochina, studied the French language in Dalat, Vietnam. At the 1948 Indochina missionary conference, Ed Roffe, Laos Field Chairman, asked where they would like to work. Ted answered, "We have no preference. We will take the will of this conference to be the will of God for us" (Andrianoff 2001:29). Since none of the other missionaries had volunteered to go to Xieng Khouang in the mountainous area north of Vientiane, the field assigned the Andrianoffs there.

In 1950 the C&MA sent Khmu worker Nai Keng from Luang Prabang to Xieng Khouang to help the Andrianoffs. Keng rented a house belonging to Bua Yia, the personal shaman of Touby Lyfong, the most powerful chief of the Hmong ethnic group in northern Laos. As Keng and his wife moved into the house, neighbors told them, "You won't stay here long. That house is haunted by evil spirits." Keng responded, "Our God is more powerful than any evil spirits." Watching Keng live in his haunted house Bua Yia asked Keng about this powerful God. Andrianoff joined Keng at Bua Yia's house and they explained the biblical story. After Bua Yia expressed faith in this power, they destroyed his spirit paraphernalia and prayed together—Andrianoff in English, Keng in Lao and Bua Yia in Hmong. Two days later, thrilled with the first converts in Xieng Khouang and the first Hmong converts, the Andrianoffs left for the C&MA annual field conference in Vietnam. When the Andrianoffs returned to Xieng Khouang two months later they were met by Keng and Bua Yia who presented them with a notebook containing the names of nearly 1,000 people who had come to faith in Christ while the missionaries were away.

Shortly after the Andrianoffs had left for their conference Bua Yia asked Nai Keng to accompany him as he visited Hmong villages surrounding the town of Xieng Khouang, telling them about the power of God. As news of Bua Yia's conversion spread, invitations came to visit villages farther and farther away from Xieng Khouang. Most of the villages came to faith in Jesus Christ as entire villages.

By the time the Andrianoffs left for furlough three years later, over 5,000 people had come to faith in Christ. In the meantime the Bible school moved to Xieng Khouang, and the Linwood Barneys began translating the Bible into the Hmong language. The mission also sent Saly Khounthapanya to help the work in Xieng Khouang.

In 1967 the United Bible Societies arranged with the C&MA and the OMF for Doris Whitelock of the OMF to continue the translation of the New Testament into the Hmong language. The process involved the cooperation of the C&MA, OMF, the Lao national church and the Bible Societies. Whitelock, who had developed the Hmong script in Thailand, transferred to Laos in June 1968.

5. The Lao Evangelical Church (1975-present)

With the "Liberation" of Laos and the political establishment of the Lao People's Democratic Republic in 1975, the church changed dramatically. During the warfare between the communist Pathet Lao and the rightist Royal Lao Government, most of the Hmong-dominated church sided with the rightist government. Most of the missionaries in the north were from the U.S. which supported the rightist government. With the Pathet Lao victory in 1975 all the missionaries left the country and virtually all the Hmong church leaders and the majority of Hmong Christians fled to Thailand. The church in the north was left as "sheep without a shepherd." The church in the south, with a congregational church government, planted by missionaries from neutralist Switzerland fared much better. While the Swiss missionaries did eventually leave the country, Lao leaders in the south did not feel pressure to leave. Eventually the new government recognized the church leadership in the north, with the Lao Evangelical Church representing the Protestant church for both the north and the south. Although the Protestant church in the south did not change their church government style, they joined the Lao Evangelical Church.

Summary of Ecumenical foundations of Protestantism in Laos

Early missionaries to Laos worked together to create the ecumenical tapestry of the Lao Evangelical Church: The first Protestant church was planted in northern Laos among the Khmu by American Presbyterian missionary Daniel McGilvary. At the time of McGilvary's last visit to Laos, Swiss Gabriel Contesse read a brochure printed by the Christian and Missionary Alliance appealing for missionaries to Indochina. Gabrielle Contesse and Maurice Willy responded to this appeal and began Swiss Brethren missionary work in southern Laos. With insufficient resources to expand into northern Laos, the Swiss Brethren and Presbyterians invited the C&MA to work in northern Laos. The Swiss Brethren then sent some of their key workers to provide assistance to the C&MA in the north. After the breakthrough among the Hmong in northern Laos, the OMF sent a missionary to work with the C&MA to translate the Bible into the Hmong language. Each group perceived the importance of combining and sharing resources to reach the kingdom of Laos.

Although the early days of Protestant work in Laos were not easy for the missionaries, with sicknesses and deaths, God prevailed and the church of Jesus Christ exists today—a tribute to these servants of Christ and to their spirit of ecumenism in accomplishing their task.

Ecumenism and the Survival of Protestantism in the Lao People's Democratic Republic (1975-1992)

Since the "Liberation" of Laos in 1975 the Lao Evangelical Church progressively adjusted its response to the authoritarian Lao People's Democratic Republic, and gradually increased its contacts with the church outside of Laos. The first three years after "Liberation" as the society adjusted to independence, the Church responded in fear by keeping quiet and fleeing. From 1979 through 1983, as Lao society tried to construct socialism, the church cautiously compromised with the newly-established socialist structure, and began reconnecting with the broader church. From 1983 to 1988 as the government consolidated its position, in some regions the church boldly confronted the social restrictions. It also expanded its contacts outside the country. From 1989 to 1992, the government promoted democratization, and the church responded by engaging the government. It also engaged the worldwide Body of Christ. This historical analysis of the survival of the Protestant church in Laos ends with the death of Kaysone Phomvihane (November 21, 1992) penultimate leader of Laos and founder of the Lao Communist Party.

1. Independence and flight (1975-1978)

The Lao People's Revolutionary Party united Laos under Marxist-Leninist socialism in 1975. Although Laos officially proclaimed independence from France in 1953, Laos recognizes December 2, 1975, as its day of liberation and independence. Immediately following independence the government began implementing new socio-political policies. Even though intricately intertwined with the Vietnam War, the Lao revolution did not follow the course of either Vietnam or Cambodia. Compared to these neighboring countries, the revolution leading to the liberation of Laos was relatively uneventful.

When it came to power the Lao People's Democratic Republic (LPDR) took advantage of its considerable popularity among the population. By the end of 1976, though, it had lost much popular support as the hoped for new prosperity did not occur. The Lao People's Revolutionary Party (LPRP—the communist party) imposed a puritanical code on society, discouraging men from wearing wide trousers or long hair and women from wearing cosmetics, tight skirts, or pants. The enforcement of these new standards caused further dissatisfaction, and many fled to Thailand. The flight of most of the professional middle class seriously undermined the government's administrative capabilities. In September 1976, the government taxed the agricultural sector—its only available source of local revenue. The farmers, who had never experienced taxation, reacted negatively. In response to the ensuing economic crisis, in early 1978 the government tried to collectivize agriculture, attempting to create a socialist society. The peasants responded with even more resistance, including destroying their crops, and many peasants fled to Thailand.

The new government publicly proclaimed religious freedom, with the state the protector of religion. While it tolerated some Buddhist activities, it curbed the independence of the Sangha. The LPRP tried to use the Sangha to propagate socialism, and monks who did not teach political materials were sent to re-education camps (i.e. confinement). As a result, the supreme patriarch fled to Thailand in March 1979, with other monks following him. The Party discouraged people from attending religious functions, even forbidding people from offering food to monks and requiring monks to find other means of livelihood. The government eventually reversed this decision.

With strong anti-American sentiment and demonstrations in the larger cities of Laos during April and May 1975, all North American missionaries left Laos. Some Swiss missionaries in the south remained until the end of August when local believers convinced them that they would be better off if the missionaries left the country. This ended the continuous presence of Swiss missionaries in Laos since 1902. The Mennonite Central Committee (MCC) began working in Laos in early 1975, and remained, providing a consistent source of encouragement to the church.

The new regime tried to close the church by seizing church properties, destroying Christian literature, and sending church leaders to re-education camps. The Catholics lost six of their seven church buildings in Vientiane to the government. When local party officials appropriated the Protestant Nasai church in Vientiane for meetings, and took over the Vientiane Bible School for a military barracks, the Protestant church began holding services in its two smaller church buildings on alternate Sundays to retain use of both buildings. The Savannakhet Bible School property became a nurses training school. The Luang Prabang city church housed the city police station. The literature stocks stored in the Vientiane Bible School as well as the volumes in the library were systematically burnt. Fear and uncertainty spread widely among the believers. Many church leaders responded by fleeing to Thailand. The beginning of December 1975 the government arrested the President of the LEC, later charging him with operating the Bible School without authorization and holding unregistered meetings. He spent three years in a re-education camp.

During the early years of the new regime the church had little contact with the outside world, nor did it seek any connections. Hunkered down for self-protection, the church found itself in a state of fear. And it had good reason for fear—virtually all the trained church leaders in the north had fled the country. The president of the church, who had chosen not to flee, was arrested and sent to re-education camp. Would the church survive these forces at work against it? Although outsiders were somewhat fearful, they established some contact. Service Missionaire Evangelique (SME--Swiss Brethren) missionaries visited the country annually. The Mennonite Central Committee maintained some contact with the church. And the Christian Conference of Asia (CCA) of the World Council of Churches established some contact with the church. But for the most part, the first years after "Liberation" were not ecumenical. Even contacts between churches within Laos were very limited.

2. Construction and compromise (1979-1982)

In an effort to construct socialism within Lao society the new regime created the Lao Front for National Construction (LFNC) in February 1979. The government reshuffled top-level personnel and expanded the Council of Ministers. The Lao People's Revolutionary Party (LPRP) provided the direction for

Lao society, the government (LPDR) provided the administration, and the mass organizations (LFNC) provided the organization and mobilization.

In mid-July 1979, the LPRP suspended the collectivization program—a victory for economic pragmatism over ideology. In 1980, for the first time in its history, Laos achieved self-sufficiency in rice production. With its inadequate road system, however, Laos still had to import rice.

Pursuing a more liberal policy towards Buddhism, the government recognized Buddhism as integral to Lao cultural identity, although it still curbed the independence of the Sangha. Intending to down-grade the influence of Buddhism, the government proclaimed all religions equal. The Lao Front for National Construction stated that the purpose of religion was to make people good. The Party perceived religion as a psychological crutch which people would no longer require once they knew more.

The church approached the increased freedoms with cautious compromise. Still feeling considerable paranoia, the church did not accept the invitation of the LFNC to register at that time. Yet it established good cooperation with the Department of Religious Affairs of the Front. The president of the LEC was released from re-education camp and re-integrated into the church. Believers generally worshiped freely and shared their faith on an individual private basis.

The church began to open up to other churches and church bodies. It started to increase its contacts with some of the more accessible churches within Laos. It also made some contacts with outside churches and organizations. The MCC and SME maintained their contact with the church, and supported a few programs. Other Protestant para-church organizations such as Church World Service, World Vision, the Southern Baptists, and World Concern, made periodic visits to Laos and attempted to initiate programs—all tightly controlled by the government.

3. Consolidation and confrontation (1983-1988)

Beginning with the standing and central committees of the LFNC meeting together in an enlarged session in March 1983, the LPDR further consolidated its position and planned its future. These meetings were preoccupied with ideology, political education and planning. The leadership of Laos tried to maintain friendly relations with all nations.

Religious restrictions eased up considerably throughout Laos. By 1985, Party members entered the monkhood for brief periods. Some members of the Politburo and their families regularly attended Buddhist festivals. The degree of religious freedom, however, varied according to locality. Two provinces--Vientiane Savannakhet--experienced general freedom of religion. Some localities, on the other hand, had virtually no religious freedom.

In September 1983 the church held a province-wide conference for church leaders in Vientiane—the first occasion for church leaders to meet together since liberation. The church followed this up by holding three seminars each year to teach village elders from Vientiane Province. The LEC took advantage of the social situation to increase its connections with the outside world. Young people, including Christian young people, went to the Soviet Union and other Eastern European countries for education, where many of them met other followers of Christ, and others came to faith in Christ.

Provincial authorities exerted considerable autonomy in determining relations with the church; in some regions the church boldly responded with confrontation. When the president of the Savannakhet Province LPRP committee resisted the church's registration process, church leaders confronted the committee, referring to the directive from the central government. The LPRP then acquiesced. Provincial authorities in other areas of the country, however, perceived the church as an adversary, and closed churches and arrested church leaders. Party leadership in Luang Prabang was particularly antagonistic towards the church, arresting pastors in 1984, 1985, and 1986. During this same time Vientiane Party officials publicly praised Christians as model citizens.

Inter-church contacts and relations increased throughout Laos. The Lao Evangelical Church experienced a transition when the president of the church left for Australia, and a Hmong pastor assumed leadership of the LEC. In addition to non-governmental organizations visiting Laos on an increasingly frequent basis, the church had contact with churches outside Laos, primarily within the Soviet-bloc nations. Thus it experienced some new elements of ecumenism.

4. Democratization and engagement (1988-1992)

District, provincial and national elections were held in 1988 as Laos moved toward democratization. The LPRP's greatest challenge was transforming desperately poor traditional Lao society into an integrated socialist society. Their efforts to make new socialist men and women of the Lao people, with Marxism-Leninism dominating the political and spiritual life of this multi-ethnic society, came against many deep-seated Lao beliefs. The LPRP found a tremendous challenge trying to effect the transition from the gentle, complacent, Theravada Buddhist Lao to a disciplined, atheistic, socialist person.

The Party recognized the continuing value of Buddhism in defining Lao national identity. It espoused the policy of keeping good traditions while rejecting bad traditions. Good traditions contributed to the goals of the Party; bad traditions caused anti-social behavior. Even though district authorities had to approve anyone joining the Buddhist monkhood, many young men put on the yellow robes in order to receive an education.

The Lao Marxist-Leninist society remained anti-Christian, so the church had to learn to engage the society. As the LPRP struggled to create new Lao socialist men and women, the church provided the opportunity for truly new men and women in Christ. The church also initiated new programs, including leadership training.

The LEC further expanded its horizons and engaged the wider community of believers. The LEC sent delegates to attend a conference of evangelical churches from socialist countries in East Germany in September 1988. In July 1989 Lao church leaders attended the Lausanne Congress on World Evangelization II in Manila.

When the president of the LEC left Laos for the U.S. he was replaced by a dynamic and gifted leader for the church who expanded the church's local and international exposure. The ecumenical aspect of the LEC expanded considerably. The church increased its contacts with the Lausanne Congress on World Evangelization, the World Council of Churches and the World Evangelical Fellowship. Denominations and Christian non-governmental organizations began taking up residence in Laos, providing on-going contact with the church. The increasing numbers of Christian organizations and vastly expanding numbers of expatriate followers of Christ has presented new opportunities as well as significant challenges to ecumenism for the LEC. The direction of the church is clearly ecumenical. The church has survived the hard times and is engaging the worldwide Body of Christ.

Summary of the Lao Evangelical Church in the Lao PDR

The church has come a long way from its response of fear and church leaders fleeing the country in the early days after the "Liberation" of Laos. When the government tried to construct a new society the church responded with compromise. The government consolidated its position, and the church confronted the government. As the government proceeded toward democratization, the church sought ways to constructively engage the government. Persecutions of Christian believers in Laos have not ceased. Still, the Lao Evangelical Church is finding its way forward to serve the Kingdom of God within the context of the Lao People's Democratic Republic. The LEC is also increasingly reaching out to and interacting with church bodies outside of Laos.

Conclusion

For nearly 100 years, from the 1880s to the mid 1970s, missionaries from a variety of denominational backgrounds laid the foundation for the Lao Evangelical Church—the Protestant church in Laos. Since 1975 local Lao church leaders have ably assumed responsibility for guiding the Lao Evangelical Church, comprised of several denominational strands, and connecting the LEC with the worldwide Body of Christ.

Bibliography

Andrianoff, Jean, *Chosen for a Special Joy: The Story of Ted and Ruth Andrianoff.* Camp Hill, PA: Christian Publications, 2001

Decorvet, Jeanne and Georges Rochat, *L'Appel du Laos.* Yverdon, Switzerland: Henri Cornaz, 1946

McGilvary, Daniel, *A Half Century Among the Siamese and the Lao: An Autobiography.* Bangkok: White Lotus, 2002

Roffe, George Edward, *"Roffe & Church" History.* Unpublished manuscript, 1997

(64) CHURCHES TOGETHER IN GOD'S MISSION – MALAYSIA A PROFILE OF THE MALAYSIAN CHURCHES IN ECUMENISM

Thu En Yu

1. Introduction

The coming of Christianity into the Malay Peninsula is closely related to the conquests of western imperial forces. The mission of the mainline churches was once shrouded in colonialism.

In 1511, the Portuguese conquered Melaka and simultaneously introduced the Roman Catholic Church to that city. The Portuguese regime was cruel and its government corrupt, hence it alienated the general populace. The Portuguese suppressed Muslims and thus caused the Malays to hate the church. Except for a small number of women and children, the mission of the church then was a total failure.[1] When the British East India Company occupied Penang in 1786, the Anglican Church followed suit.[2]

In 1885, William Oldham founded the Methodist Church in Malaya and Singapore. Oldham recruited William G. Shellabear, an Anglican, to work in the ministry of the Methodist Church. Shellabear became the first foreign missionary to initiate evangelism among the Malays in Singapore and Malaya. He also led in the translation of the Bible into the Malay language.[3] In 1885, the Presbyterian Church also landed in Johore. An Englishman, John Chapman established the Brethren Church in Malaya in 1860. In the twentieth century, the churches that successively entered Malaya were the Evangelical Lutheran Church in 1907, the Mar Thoma Church in 1927, the Assemblies of God in 1934, the Baptist Church in 1938 and the Lutheran Church in 1950.[4]

Since 1511, Christianity has been present in the Malaysian Peninsular for about five hundred years. Now Christians constitute only about eight per cent of the Malaysian Peninsular's population, and of these, about half are Catholics.

Since the inception of the rule of James Brooke over Sarawak, a plan was made to pave the way for the entry of the Anglican Church with the formation of the Borneo Church Mission in 1846. However, its first missionaries, led by Francis McDougall, arrived only on 29 June 1848. McDougall was consecrated bishop in 1855 for the Diocese of Labuan, which also included Sarawak.[5] The Roman Catholic Church began physically only with the arrival of Don Carlos Cuarteron in Labuan on 8 May 1857.[6]

The churches began to penetrate mainland Sabah only after the British North Borneo Chartered Company formally exerted its rule. In 1881, the Mill Hill missionaries of the Roman Catholic Church extended their evangelism to Papar. In 1882, the Basel Christian Church was established by the southward overseas migration of the Basel Mission Hakkas from China. The Anglican Church expanded to Sabah

[1] Refer to Jim Baker, *Crossroad: A Popular History of Malaysia and Singapore,* (Singapore: Times Books International, 1999), p. 58-59.

[2] Robert Hunt, Lee Kam Hing and John Roxborogh, eds., *Christianity in Malaysia: A Denominational History,* (Petaling Jaya: Pelanduk Publications, 1992),

[3] Robert Hunt, "The Legacy of William Shellabear," in *International Bulletin of Missionary Research,* Volume 26, No. 1, (2002), pp. 28-31.

[4] Robert Hunt, eds., *Christianity in Malaysia,* pp. 199-258.

[5] Refer to Brian Taylor, "S. P. G. and North Borneo," in Khoo Kay Keng, ed., *Diocese of Sabah Silver Jubilee 1962-1987,* p. 16.

[6] Cuarteron received his formal appointment to spearhead the Borneo mission in 1855. Refer to John Rooney, *Khabar Gembira: A History of the Catholic Church in East Malaysia and Brunei 1880-1976,* (London: Burns & Oates, 1981), p. 20-21.

only in 1888 by building its first church in Sandakan. In 1952, with the collaboration of the Basel Christian Church, the Basel Mission sent its first missionary, Henrich Honeggar, to the Rungus, a Kadazandusun tribe, hence the inception of the Protestant Church in Sabah.[7] The churches established in the twentieth century include Grace Chapel, the Baptist Church, Sidang Injil Borneo, the Pentecostal Church and the Assemblies of God . Further, the Methodist Church in Sarawak also extended its wing to Sabah.

2. British Colonial Era

Apart from the Roman Catholic Church, the other mainline churches and most of the evangelical denominations were established during the British colonial era. In almost two hundred years between 1786-1957, the churches in Malaysia were no different from their mother mission back in their respective countries of origin because most of them came alongside the extension of colonialism.[8]

The trademarks of Christians in Malaysian history are magnificent church premises, academically high-quality mission schools and a middle-class intellectual community. These stately church buildings stand out prominently in urban centres as renowned landmarks of their respective townships. They were not found in rural areas. This is obvious evidence that they were targeting the middle and high classes in their mission. This is especially so with the English speaking churches, which were the centres of foreign worshippers and thus had, more or less, links with the colonial government. They were perceived, in essence and in spirit, as official churches.[9]

Colonial churches adopted the policy of racial segregation. Their worshippers were identified by race and economic status. The Chinese and Indian speaking churches fared no better, their spheres of activities were confined to their respective communities. The members of Chinese and Indian churches were predominantly immigrant labourers from China and India who had come to Malaysia in pursuit of a better livelihood, working in tin mines and rubber estates. Their hard work contributed to their economic prosperity and therefore they could afford to gradually build their churches in various centres. Their churches had the advantage of uplifting the members in a colonial setting and were therefore not only a symbol of status and identity for the members, but also a vehicle to politics and consequently power for the relevant communities.

The above mentioned three different communities with their respective identity and power relation were active in the churches, and they represented three distinct societies, namely, English speaking society, Chinese speaking society and Indian speaking society. There were objective factors that totally segregated the churches from the Malays as well as the mountain tribes or Orang Asli.

The British colonial administration deliberately alienated the Malays from the other ethnic communities, a political tactic of divide and rule. The administration had an explicit accord with the Malay rulers, giving the rulers sovereignty over the religion and customs of the Malays. Moreover, Malays were not integrated into colonial economic development. They were the forgotten lot; economically, educationally and culturally, they lagged far behind.

The immigrant Chinese and Indian communities on the hand were accorded due attention by the colonial administration. Owing to their Christian adherence, they were then identified more with colonial interests. Hence, the Malays distrusted and disliked the non-Malay communities. After independence, the Malays vented their sentiment in various forms of retaliation.[10]

---

[7] See Thu En Yu, *Muhibbah: The Church's Ministry of Reconciliation in the Pluralistic Society of Malaysia, unpublished Ph.D dissertation,* p. 41-42.
[8] Thu En Yu, *Muhibbah: The Church's Ministry of Reconciliation in the Pluralistic Society of Malaysia,* pp. 42-43.
[9] See Lawrence Brown, *Christianity and the Malays,* (London: SPCK, 1921), p. 77.
[10] See Thu En Yu, *Muhibbah: The Church's Ministry of Reconciliation in the Pluralistic Society of Malaysia,* pp. 43-44.

During the colonial era, the churches were developed along communal lines. As a result, they lacked the sensitivity to deal with the issues of a pluralistic society. They were perceived to demonstrate no effort in the shaping of a pluralistic society. The Malays were left outside the churches, a logical course because the colonial administration discouraged the intervention of the churches in the religious affairs of the Malays. The poor and impoverished grassroots of the Chinese and Indian communities, and the indigenous tribes, were also outside the field of vision of the churches.[11]

It is evident from the above historical sketch that, during the colonial era, the churches conspicuously exhibited the following three shortcomings:

1. Lack of indigenization

The churches reflected religion in a western cultural cloak which was alien to local culture, thinking, and social structure.

2. Lack of universal outlook

The churches confined themselves to the middle and upper classes, avoiding the grassroots level of society, and therefore they did not identify with the masses.

3. Lack of multiracial sensitivity

The churches did not address social injustices, racial animosity, or economic imbalances, and hence contributed to perpetuating communal hostility and economic exploitation.[12]

On the positive aspect, the churches had made excellent contribution to education and moral uplifting. The Catholic Church, the Methodist Church, the Anglican Church, the Basel Christian Church, and the Seventh Day Adventist have a good network of schools, offering good quality education, from the kindergartens up to tertiary institutions. Apart from evangelism, the next greatest dedication of resources was educational work. This had a profound impact on the society socially, culturally and morally.[13]

Education had facilitated a change in the thinking of the people, and led to progress in the society. During the colonial era, the mission schools gave birth to a competent community of leaders and professionals. It thus laid an excellent foundation for the independence of Malaysia.

3. Post-Independence Era

During the colonial era, the churches had a unique position in the society. Church leaders were treated as equals by the colonial administration officials. The Anglican bishop was next to the governor in civil standing. Upon independence, there was a reshuffling of relationships. Malay Muslims evolved from being the ruled to being the rulers with exalted status. Such a change reversed the respective roles between the master and the servant. The Malays could not immediately forget the wound of their past history, feeling that the shadow of their past oppression was still cast over them. They were on the lookout for opportunity to even a score with the former oppressors. The Chinese and the Indians, especially the Christians, had thus another mentality. With the abrupt and dramatic change in identity and power relations, all of them quickly adjusted to tackle the challenges ahead.

The Council of Churches of Malaya[14] participated in the deliberations on the formulation of the national constitution. The issues that preoccupied the churches at that time were primarily human rights and religious freedom. The Council of Churches of Malaya even recommended to the Reid Constitution

---

[11] See Lawrence Brown, *Christianity and the Malays,* p. 77.

[12] See Thu En Yu, *Muhibbah: The Church's Ministry of Reconciliation in the Pluralistic Society of Malaysia,* pp. 45.

[13] See Michael S. Northcott, "Christian-Muslim Relations in West Malaysia," in *The Muslim World,* Volume LXXXI, No. 1, (Edinburg: University of Edinburg, 1991), p. 52.

[14] The Council of Churches of Malaya was founded in 1946 and was renamed as the Council of Churches of Malaysia in 1974.

Committee and the Malay rulers the establishment of a secular state, while at the same time safeguarding religious freedom and racial harmony.[15]

Regrettably, the relevant recommendation was not accepted *in toto*. Islam was eventually made the official religion. Article 11 of the Federal Constitution affirmed the right of all people to profess, practice and propagate their religion, albeit there was an express prohibition to the propagation of non-Muslim religions among the Muslims.[16] The constitution adversely affected Christian education in the various mission schools by giving a favourable position to Islam in the required religious education in these mission schools. This constitutional provision deprived the churches of the means to evangelize through education. The church leaders registered their protest over such pro-Islam provision but to no avail. In August 1957, the constitution became *fait accompli*; the same constitution was later made the constitution of Malaysia. Helplessness and disillusion befell the churches. They were left to wait and see what would happen, and to rest their hopes on the ruling executives, hoping they would not deviate from their former fair practice of religious freedom.

In the initial post-independence era, the churches could not cope with the various drastic changes. The worst mistake had been that they had not formulated appropriate strategies toward the development of indigenization over time. Furthermore, the churches had in the past been identifying themselves with the colonial government and thus adored the English language at the expense of the Malay language. After independence, Malay emerged to be the national language and the medium of instruction, a turn of fortune that was hard to accept for the churches and which threw them off course. The churches lost their identity and power relations overnight. The churches and the Muslim society were poles apart, and the resulting climate was full of suspicion and misunderstanding. In the first place, the churches ought to be aware themselves and reflect critically on the root cause. The dilemma they were in then was a result of their past deeds. When the Malays were oppressed during the colonial era, had the churches ever shown any concern?

As early as 1891, William Shellabear had been prophetic in emphasising Malay; he learnt the language for more than a decade, while at the same time embarking on the translation of the Bible, in order to facilitate the mission to the Malays. He also appealed to the churches to discard the intentional oversight of the Malays.However,his colleagues and other missionaries did not recognize his attempt. If the churches in the colonial era had had the vision and mind of William Shellabear, the history of post-independence churches would have been different.

The polarization of race and religion eventually led to the May 13, 1969 racial riot, notoriously known as the May 13 incident.[17] After the incident, the churches assumed a proactive role and participated in the programs of national reconciliation. In addition to dispensing aid in money and in kind, multitudes of Christian voluntary workers helped in rehabilitating affected areas, the assistance to Muslim victims being remarkable.[18]

In order to promote national unity and integration, the government instituted the National Consultative Council which polled the opinions of all quarters and formulated long-term schemes of national reconciliation. The churches readily participated in the council providing their input.

The relevant council soon formulated The New Economic Policy (NEP), which was to decide the national economic development of the country for the next twenty years. The NEP aimed to redress the economic imbalances between the Malays and the non-Malays. It also mapped affirmative action plans to endow the Malays with privileges in the economy, education and administration of the country. It aspired to build a balanced society economically and educationally within a period of twenty years.

---

[15] Robin Woods, *An Autobiography,* (London: SCM Press, 1986), p. 117.

[16] Article 11(4) of the Federal Constitution of Malaysia.

[17] Gordon P. Means, *Malaysian Politics: The Second Generation,* (Singapore: Oxford University Press, 1991,), p. 1-8.

[18] Thu En Yu, *Muhibbah: The Church's Ministry of Reconciliation in the Pluralistic Society of Malaysia,* p. 48.

The NEP was essentially a communalist approach to economic development. The development schemes inevitably had an adverse impact on the interests of the non-Malay communities, because it was re-apportioning a large chunk from the existing economic cake to the aspiring Malay entrepreneurial community. Both the Chinese and Indian communities, including the Christians were dissatisfied. Tan Chee Khoon, an opposition statesmen, was highly critical of the said policy. His utterances reflected the opinions of the silent majority of the Christian community. The outcome was a foregone conclusion. The other communities and the churches were then left to their own devices in search of solutions; in fact, they were struggling for survival amidst adversity.

The national Islamic authority set up the Islamic Dakwah Foundation of Malaysia, a missionary arm that carries out evangelism as well as proselytization throughout the country. The Department of Islamic Development, with the endorsement of the Malay political leadership, implements Islamization of the government machinery. The wave of perpetuation of Islamic activities provoked religious sensitivities, and communal polarization further deepened. In view of this turn of events, the Council of Churches of Malaysia was proactive in initiating inter-religious interaction and mutual understanding and consequently a non-Muslim inter-religious forum was formed in 1983. This body, named the Malaysian Consultative Council of Buddhism, Christianity, Hinduism and Sikhism (MCCBCHS), held its first conference in 1984.[19] The conference was declared open by Tunku Abdul Rahman, the first Prime Minister of Malaysia. Invitations were sent to Muslims; it was regrettable no other Malay attended.

The aims of the council were:

1. to promote understanding, mutual respect and co-operation between people of different religions.
2. To study and resolve problems affecting all inter-religious relationships.
3. To make representations to the Government, when necessary, regarding religious matters.[20]

In this inaugural conference, MCCBCHS focused on deliberations concerning religious freedom and Islamization. The Christians raised three main issues, namely, the ban on Malay Bibles, the ban on Christian education among mission schools, and the ban on the public use of Christian symbols. These issues were among the memorandum the consultative council presented to the government subsequently. Since then, MCCBCHS has served to become a vehicle for inter-religious consultation and mutual understanding. It has also become an organized channel that informs the government authorities about public opinions on religious affairs.

Only when minorities confront common challenges, can the other religions realize the importance of mutual understanding and co-operation. In fact, many incidents arising out of prejudice and misunderstanding have since been amicably settled. This author has been a leader of the Council of Churches of Malaysia, and was privileged to participate and witness the encouraging process of inter-religious interaction. In retrospect and prospect, Christianity was certainly guilty of self-glorification, especially the sentiment of holier-than-thou.We should, in humility, learn together with the others and gain maturity together

Prior to independence, Christianity had adopted a posture of apathy towards other religions. Even among the various denominations within the Christian family, the lack of interaction was accompanied with occasional skirmishes. Christianity is represented by the Roman Catholic Church, the Council of Churches of Malaysia for the mainline churches, and the National Evangelical Christian fellowship for the evangelical, Brethren and charismatic confessions. At the initiative of the Council of Churches of Malaysia, these Christian bodies combined in 1986 to form a Christian umbrella organization, the Christian Federation of Malaysia (CFM). Undesirable social changes had instead galvanized the churches, a classic

---

[19] Paul Tan Chee Ing and Theresa Ee, "Introduction," in Tunku Abdul Tahman Putra and others, *Contemporary Issues on Malaysian Religions,* (Petaling Jaya: Pelanduk, 1984), p. 13.

[20] Paul Tan Chee Ing and Theresa Ee, "Introduction," in *Contemporary Issues on Malaysian Religions,* p. 13.

case of everything worked for the good. The federation, apart from promoting inter-denominational co-operation and mutual concern, also served as a common mouthpiece to express its position vis-à-vis the government and other religions. The federation and MCCBCHS often respond to the government on religious freedom and human rights. The formation of MCCBCHS and CFM has far-reaching significance for the ties among the non-Muslim religions as well as the Christian denominations, and for exchange between the religious communities and the government. The role as bridges of these organizations has been accorded recognition; they serve as effective channels for consultation and exchange to stem the tide of misunderstanding and dissatisfaction.

Bibliography

Baker, Jim. *Crossroad: A Popular History of Malaysia and Singapore,* Singapore: Times Books International, 1999

Hunt, Robert, Lee Kam Hing and John Roxborogh, eds., *Christianity in Malaysia: A Denominational History,* Petaling Jaya: Pelanduk Publications, 1992.

Rooney, John. *Khabar Gembira: A History of the Catholic Church in East Malaysia and Brunei 1880-1976,* London: Burns & Oates, 1981

Sinn, Elizabeth, ed. *The Last Half Century of Chinese Overseas.* Hong Kong: Hong Kong University Press, 1998.

Wong, Tze-ken Danny, *The Transformation of an Immigrant Society: A Study of the Chinese in Sabah.* London: Asean Academic Press, 1998.

(65) THE CHURCHES TOGETHER IN GOD'S MISSION –MONGOLIA[1]

Hugh P. Kemp and Bayarjargal Garamtseren

At the height of their power in the thirteenth century, the Mongols ruled the world's largest ever land empire. Since the time of their demise in 1368, the Mongols have struggled to keep their identity, bearing the weight of Chinese overlords, feudal poverty, and Tibetan-Buddhist theocracy. In 1990, Mongolia emerged from seven decades of communism to become a multi-party democratic republic. Concurrently, the Christian church in Mongolia has become established. There were three known Mongolian Christians in the late 1980s: in the 2010 census, there were 41,117 Christians, representing 2% of the population of the republic.[2]

While this growth is remarkable, it is important to recognize the social and historical context. With the collapse of communism in 1990, memorials to Chinggis Khan (1162-1227) proliferated. Chinggis has been re-invented and re-venerated as the founder of the Mongol nation.[3] His *yasa*, a legal framework built on case-law, allows for freedom of religious expression. While essentially Shamanists – they worshipped *Tenger*, a personified heaven – the khans were indifferent to other religions. Religious tolerance was conditional, however, on obedience to the khan. The *yasa* still has influence: the Law of the Relationship of Church and State (1993) allows for three official state religions: Shamanism, Tibetan-Buddhism and Islam. As in the *yasa*, one's religion is seen to be inconsequential to the welfare of the state, so long as citizens are obedient to the law.[4] Indeed, since 1990 many new religions have come to Mongolia. One journalist writes of an 'explosion' of Faiths in Mongolia.[5]

However, Shamanism is at the heart of a Mongol, even if it is overlaid by Tibetan-Buddhism, introduced explicitly and officially by Kublai Khạn (r. 1260-1294). Outwardly, Tibetan-Buddhism appears to be the dominant partner. Tourists today will notice Gandan Tibetan-Buddhist temple dominating the western sector of Ulaanbaatar. Monasteries are being reopened, temples are being built, and novices trained. On the surface, it seems that Tibetan-Buddhism is the main filter through which Mongols interpret their world.

To add to this religious dynamic, communism heavily suppressed all religion with purges in the 1930s. Approximately 700 Tibetan-Buddhist monasteries were demolished or turned into museums. Monks were killed or secularized while the nomads were organized into production units. Communism led to a

---

[1] This article was originally written for this Handbook under the title: *Emerging identity and vision: challenges for the church in Mongolia*

[2] A census only records self-perception. Additionally, this census only recorded those 'over 15 years of age'. Mongolian Government, *Хүн Ам, Орон Сууцны 2010 Оны Улсын Тооллогын Үр Дүн (Mongolian Population and Residency Census)* (Government of Mongolia, 2010 [cited 1st May 2012]); available from http://www.toollogo2010.mn/doc/Main%20results_20110615_to%20EZBH_for%20print.pdf.

[3] Chinggis Khan is more widely known in English as 'Genghis Khan'. However, the spelling 'Chinggis' is coming into wider use to recognise that 'Genghis' represents an older spelling derived from an original French spelling, and secondly, that 'Chinggis' is closer to how the word is said in Mongolian, and is the choice of Mongolian writers themselves.

[4] This does not mean, of course, that Christianity in particular, or more widely the shear number of new religions in Mongolia has not been critiqued, particularly in the media. Two articles serve to illustrate this, both translations from Mongolian newspapers. Loosely translated, one is "Christ and Rats are Gnawing at Mongolia" (No author is named for this article, but it appears in *Ulaanbaatar*, April 9, 1996.) The other is "The Religion of the Cross has been Amalgamated with the Buddhist Religion" (authored by A. Nerbish, and appearing in *Il Tovchoo*, No. 18, May 1998).

[5] Worldwide Religious News, *Dalai Lama's Visit Shines Spotlight on Mongolia's Explosion of Faiths* (Associated Press, 25th August, 2006 [cited 1st December 2012]); available from http://wwrn.org/articles/22521/

pragmatic atheism. It bred a class of civil servant who is neither Shamanist or Tibetan-Buddhist. These civil servants were disillusioned that the ideals of the communist state to which they had given their lives collapsed overnight in 1990. It also bred a generation of young people who knew nothing of either ancient Shamanism or Tibetan-Buddhism.

Changing economic fortunes since 1990 have also brought new challenges to the Mongolians: new television programmes, easier access to the internet, freedom to travel. Market reform and profit-driven consumerism motivate a new kind of entrepreneur. New foreign relationships have been fostered with China, Japan and Korea. Nevertheless, with the collapse of the state welfare system, together with inflation and brutal market reforms, thousands have been left poorer, indebted, abused, and marginalized.

Birth of the Modern Mongolian Church

These changes were not as sudden as may first appear. During the late 1980s reform had been in the air. Internal restlessness grew as news of upheavals in other communist lands, culminating in the fall of the Berlin wall by 1990, motivated many. It is perhaps only by the grace of God and the constraint and wisdom of the nation's leaders that Ulaanbaatar did not have a Tiananmen Square like incident in 1990.[6]

Some Christians had visited the Mongolian People's Republic during the 1980s, on tourist visas, praying for the day when it would become more accessible. When Mongolia opened in 1990, two key resources were available in the first three years that resourced the young church. The United Bible Societies (UBS) released a newly translated New Testament called *Shin Geree,* and Campus Crusade for Christ International (CCCI) had their film *Jesus* (1979) translated and widely distributed. Both were used extensively. Mongolian evangelists showed the *Jesus* film outdoors or in a local cinema, then preached and sold copies of *Shin Geree,* and gave an appeal for conversion. Such endeavors often birthed a house group or a church. The effect of the dual use of the *Jesus* film and the New Testament *Shin Geree* cannot be underestimated: they have been instrumental in hundreds of Mongolians becoming Christians.

In sum, from the perspective of Christian missions, Mongolia was an open book in 1990. Prior to 1990, the country had had no recent history of missions, no Western colonial history, no established church, few recognizable Christians, and no colloquial Bible. It is significant that the two key missional tools in the early days, the UBS New Testament *Shin Geree* and the CCCI's *Jesus* film, were non-sectarian and inter-denominational. Wary of Mongolia's neighbours' harsh treatment of religion, both expatriate and Mongolian Christians were keen to evangelize Mongolia as quickly as possible. It was no surprise that the period from 1990 to 1993 was frantic with evangelistic activity and church planting.

However, in December 1993, local papers published the text of a new law: the "Law on the Relationship of Church and State."[7] The young Christian community reacted immediately, claiming that it discriminated against Christianity. The Law declared Tibetan-Buddhism to be the predominant religion that would receive state patronage. The implication was that to be a genuine Mongol, one was naturally a Tibetan-Buddhist.

The formulation of the law was inevitable. Naming Tibetan-Buddhism as the state religion was merely describing what already was. The two other official religions did the same: Shamanism was simply recognizing Mongolian history; Islam recognized Muslim Kazaks in the four western provinces. The fact that Christian numbers had been growing quickly – estimates suggest around 2,000 by 1993 – looked

[6] In June 1989, thousands of Chinese youth gathered in Beijing's Tiananmen Square to demonstrate in favour of political reform. The Chinese army suppressed and killed thousands of the demonstrators on June 4th, 1989; this was the so-called Tiananmen Square Incident. A similar demonstration by Mongolians occurred in January 1990 in Ulaanbaatar's Sukhbaatar Square. The demonstrations were allowed to continue and were not suppressed by the army.
[7] For an English version see D. N. Collins, "Mongolian Law on Church State Relations: A Translation from the Russian Text," (Ulaanbaatar: 1993).

suspiciously like a factor in the formulation of the law. This new law was successfully challenged on constitutional grounds by a consortium that included Christian Mongolian leaders, and some parts were repealed.

Article 4.2 of the law puts a high place on the unity of the Mongol people, their historical and cultural traditions and civilization. The challenge then was to present Christ to the Mongolian people in Mongolian ways: the church had to take on a Mongolian face as quickly as possible. Foreign missionaries had to take a background role. Eventually, Christians settled down to wait and see the outcome. Singapore and Hong Kong had similar laws, and Christian churches there seemed to do fine.

The threat had been felt greatest amongst new churches planted by Protestant missionaries. Meanwhile the Roman Catholic church adopted a strategy that was unaffected by this law. Mongolia had been assigned by the Holy See to the *Congregatio Immaculati Cordis Mariae* (The Congregation of the Immaculate Heart of Mary, that is, the CICM), and arrived as both a mission endeavour and as a Vatican embassy, in 1992, when Archbishop John Bulaitis presented his papers to Mongolian President P. Ochirbat, thus becoming the first Nuncio to the republic of Mongolia.[8] Mission to Mongolia was not new to the CICM, having had experience in Inner Mongolia since 1865. Having a clear and visible presence, with a secure legal status has allowed the Catholic church to grow at a slow but steady pace.

In a similar fashion, the Russian Orthodox church has had a different status to the Protestants. Because the Russians have had a presence in Mongolia since 1872, Christianity had been perceived by the Mongolians to be *Christos shashin*, that is, the religion of the Russians who worshipped *Christos*. The Orthodox kept mainly to themselves – as Russians – having only one church building in Ulaanbaatar. From 2007, the church has found a stronger public presence in its re-built Holy Trinity Church. Both Catholic and Orthodox presence has been less overtly evangelistic than Protestants. Nevertheless, across the whole of Christian presence in Mongolia, we suggest four factors that contributed to the initial success of the Christian church, from 1990.

Firstly, the New Testament in colloquial Khalka-Mongolian was available for all Christians, of any denomination. Moreover, literacy was high and most could read it. Here was something new, well presented and well distributed. Curiosity drew many to read it. The New Testament had a context; it was usually coupled with the *Jesus* film and preaching. When the Roman Catholic mission was established from 1992, it too was resourced by this New Testament. Nevertheless, there has been some debate as to its efficacy, and a number of other translations have been undertaken. Widely used now is another full Bible, published by the Mongolian United Bible Society (MUBS),[9] simply called *Ariun Bible*. A revised edition became available in April, 2012.

Secondly, although it was tempting for foreign Christians to act independently in Mongolia, most realized the benefits of working together. There was wide cooperation, vision sharing, and praying together. Coming out of InterDev meetings in the early 1990s, partnerships gave rise to various aid and development projects, an international church and an international school, the Union Bible Theological College (UBTC), and the Mongolian Center for Theological Education by Extension (MCTEE). Joint planning also resulted in an annual ministry consultation, city-wide evangelistic campaigns, a united "March for Jesus" in Ulaanbaatar, music-writing workshops, combined worship services, joint Easter and Christmas celebrations, and, as already mentioned, united legal challenge to the 1993 Law on the Relationship of Church and State. When CICM fathers arrived in 1993, they were warmly welcomed and personal relationships were quickly cultivated.

---

[8] Emil P. Tscherrig, "Mongolia and Christianity: History and Quest of New Direction," in *Christianity and Mongolia*, ed. Gaby Bamana (Ulaanbaatar: Antoon Mostaert Mongolian Study Center, 2006). 9.

[9] MUBS is the renamed former Mongolian Bible Translation Committee (MBTC), which was founded in mid 1990s mainly to provide an alternative translation to *Shin Geree,* which continues to be available from the Bible Society of Mongolia.

Thirdly, while there has been much cooperation regarding aid and development, there has also been a lot of church planting particularly by the Protestant churches. With a Mongolian population of only 2.5 million, some saw the potential of evangelizing the whole nation. The Mongolians themselves kept up the momentum. And who better to do it? Some churches systematically prayed, evangelized and established house groups in stairwells, then buildings, housing estates, suburbs and so to whole towns.

One Mongolian church planted 19 daughter churches before its own sixth anniversary. Mongolian evangelistic teams went to Buryatia (in Russia) and Hohhot (in Inner Mongolia) by 1996. Within Mongolia itself, Mongols began to evangelize the Kazaks, the Chinese and the residual Russian population. More recently there have been intentional church plants amongst Mongolian emigrants: there are, for example, at least forty Mongolian congregations in South Korea, ten in the United States, and three in the United Kingdom in 2012.

Fourthly, the training of leaders, and leadership transition, remains a high priority, right across all churches. Individual churches have trained their own people as Sunday school teachers and home group leaders. The inter-church and inter-agency Union Bible Theological College was set up to provide high quality, in-country leadership training. The Mongolian Centre for Theological Education by Extension was started in 1995, providing distance-learning courses to pastors who couldn't come into Ulaanbaatar for training. A number of Mongolian leaders have won scholarships to seminaries and Bible Colleges in South Korea, America, Singapore, Australia, New Zealand and Europe.

The Mongolian Evangelical Alliance

Much of the growth has been in the Protestant churches. The Roman Catholic and Russian Orthodox church each have a single presence and together comprise less than 5% of the Christians. They cooperate with Protestant churches for Bible translation through the Mongolian United Bible Society (MUBS), where they and a number of NGOs have seats on the board.[10] In contrast, the diversity of Protestant presence in Mongolia is extremely wide: on the whole, unity and cooperation amongst Protestants is expressed in the Mongolian Evangelical Alliance (MEA).

MEA was formed in 1997, registered as an NGO in 1999, and is the biggest entity representing the Christian church. In 2012 MEA claimed a membership of 396 churches and 47 Christian agencies, representing 80% of all Christians.[11] MEA is a member of World Evangelical Alliance (WEA) and Asia Evangelical Alliance (AEA). The General Secretary in 2012, Batbold Munkhzul, serves on the Executive Council of AEA. Additionally, that the Asia Lausanne meeting took place in June 2011 in Ulaanbaatar – with 260 participants from 18 countries – was a global recognition of Mongolia's Christian profile, and particularly the work of the MEA.[12]

Under the motto of "One Lord, One Faith, One Spirit", the mission of MEA is to promote unity and cooperation among all Christian churches and organizations. MEA has a presence in every province of

---

[10] The abbreviation 'NGO' is widely recognised as short hand for Non-Governmental Organization. It includes non-profit organisations, both Christian and non-Christian. In the case of the MUBS, the NGOs involved are Christian.

[11] Mongolian Evangelical Alliance, *Монголын Эвангелийн Эвслийн Товч Түүх (History of the Mongolian Evangelical Alliance)* (Mongolian Evangelical Alliance, [cited 2nd December 2012]); available from http://www.mea.mn/?page_id=66. It is wise to note here that 'Protestant' is not a word widely used in Mongolia. 'Evangelical' means those churches founded on traditional evangelical values, like the centrality of the preached word of God, evangelism and personal conversion and a response to the Gospel. These types of churches were the first to be established in Mongolia between 1991 and 1993. There are other so-called Christian churches in Mongolia which would be regarded as marginal by mainstream Evangelical, Catholic and Orthodox traditions: these would include the Latter Day Saints (Mormons), Jehovah's Witnesses, and Witness Less, to name only three.

[12] The Lausanne movement is a global network of Evangelical theology and practice, taking its name from Lausanne, Switzerland where its first conference was held in 1974.

Mongolia: it has ministries to children, youth, and women, with active social involvement, and think-tanks in theology, mission, and legislation, with workshops on praise and prayer. One of the strengths of the MEA is that of the strong relationships of the Mongolian leaders. Together, there is a commitment continually to explore what it means to grow a uniquely 'Mongolian' church with a common goal.

To this end, personal relationship building is woven into the fabric of programmes like Asian Access' three year leadership development programme. These relationships continue after graduation. When church leaders know each other personally, their congregations are more likely to understand theological differences and to co-operate on any one project. This relational way of operating is a cultural trait: Mongolians are community-oriented people. Moreover, these Christian leaders are young, mainly under the age of 40. Considering that many were part of the first generation of Christians in the 1990s, they have been together for twenty or so years. This youthfulness of leadership has meant an open, energetic and enthusiastic approach to new ideas, big challenges and visions.

In addition, these leaders are not only connected by personal relationship within Mongolia, but in other countries as well. Through its participation in AEA, MEA maintains connections with Asian churches, particularly South Korean. Koreans have a similar historical, cultural and linguistic heritage to the Mongolians. The South Korean church, broadly within the Evangelical and Pentecostal stream of Christianity, has had a strong mission focus, and is the biggest single-ethnic missions community in Mongolia. The majority of Protestant congregations in Mongolia have been influenced by Korean partners. The leadership of MEA itself includes a Korean who is seconded to it. Where Protestant churches find themselves more and more referencing themselves to Korean churches, the CICM order of the Catholic church relates to leadership structures in Beijing, the Philippines, and its headquarters in Brussels. The Orthodox church references itself naturally to its Russian leadership in Moscow, but new energy for mission from partners in America and elsewhere suggest that the Orthodox church is able to move beyond its own Russian cultural heritage in the context of Mongolia.[13]

By the late 1990s, leadership of many churches had transitioned to Mongolians. Today, Mongolian Christians lead at least 50% of all churches and some of the large mission agencies. For example, Campus Crusade for Christ,[14] Youth With A Mission, Evangelism Explosion, and Union Bible Theological College are all led by Mongolians with local staff. In addition, Mongolians themselves have started various new ministries, unaffiliated with out-of-country-interests in evangelism, church planting, rehabilitation for alcohol and other addictions, prison ministries, hospice, and sport outreaches. Finding common ground amongst Mongolian leaders has been less troublesome than attempting to bring together missionaries who come from many different denominations, languages, and cultures with a variety of personal and institutional agendas.

One particular poignant illustration of this has been the recent history of Bible translation.[15] While the New Testament *Shin Geree* certainly was significant in the early 1990s, terminology has been reassessed by Mongolian Christians, particularly the word used for 'God'. While some expatriate missionaries have excessively and detrimentally argued over the term, the overwhelming majority of Mongolians themselves

---

[13] See for example the emerging relationship with the Orthodox Church of America (OCA) and new partners offering themselves for mission service in Mongolia: http://oca.org/news/oca-news/mission-mongolia-oca-parishioner-kurt-bringerud-prepares-for-unusual-career (accessed 11th December, 2012). The Orthodox church has commenced similar endeavours to other churches in Mongolia – translation, children and youth programmes and the likes – and the website noted above claims 40 baptisms (by March, 2012), presumably all Mongolian.

[14] Campus Crusade for Christ International (CCCI), has been attempting to change its name to a less pejorative one from 2011. The word 'Crusade' has been a problem.

[15] For an overview of Bible translation in Mongolian see Bayarjargal Garamtseren, "A History of Bible Translation in Mongolian," *Bible Translator* 60, no. 4 (2009).

have re-adopted and become content with a different – and arguably more traditional – word. [16] More than 95% of Mongolian churches now use the vocabulary in the MUBS version. Indeed, in the diaspora congregations, it is the only version used. For example, in February 2012, a conference was convened hosted by the United Kingdom Mongolian Christian Fellowship (UKMCF) in London. This drew Mongolian Christians from nine European churches representing more than 200 Mongolian Christians. A casual poll was taken to reveal that all, without exception, use the MUBS' version of the Bible, *Ariun Bible*.

Rising to choose, argue for, and defend an indigenous Christian vocabulary is evidence for a developing sense of 'Mongolian' Christianity. Because of the Mongols' heightened sense of history from the days of Chinggis Khan, Christians too have sourced an indigenous identity from their own historical narrative.[17] This history spans from the 7th century to the early 1900s, and has involved the Assyrian Christians,[18] the Franciscan Order, the CICM Order, and a rich array of Protestant agencies right across the Mongolian steppe: Kalmykia, Buryatia, Inner Mongolia, and Mongolia proper.[19] Thus there is a shared memory that informs identity.[20] To develop this unique Mongolian identity, not only is an indigenous Christian vocabulary emerging, but songs written in Mongolian melody with Mongolian lyrics for Mongolian instruments also better express the heart and affection of the Mongolians, and are clearly appreciated over imported – and inevitably translated – worship songs. And these worship songs have permeated all denominational expressions of Christian faith and worship. The term 'Mongolian Christian Church' has become the key phrase in the strategy and cooperation in the Church, and represents in a seminal way a theoretical category for ecumenism.

Following David Bosch's category of inculturation,[21] new agents of mission are the Mongolians themselves, in a local situation, yet concurrently referent to regional bodies. In this, the 'Mongolian

---

[16] The issues in Mongolia are not unique and occur in many places where there is a first generation of Bible. The UBS version of the New Testament – *Shin Geree* – uses a short phrase translated as *Lord of the Universe* (Yurtontseen Ezen - _jmfywnay Tpty), whereas the MUBS version, simply 'Holy Bible' – *Ariun Bible* – uses the word Burhan (Dejhgy). It is the UBS version that is innovative in this case, as all previous translations of scripture portions amongst the Mongols since the 18th century, including a full Bible translation done in Buryatia (southern Siberia), by 1846, use Burhan. The debate is to do with which term is more indigenous or generic, and which might compromise Christian nuance due to alleged association with Buddhism. For the debate see Hugh Kemp, *Steppe by Step: Mongolia's Christians - from Ancient Roots to Vibrant Young Church* (London: Monarch, 2000)., also, Bayarjargal Garamtseren, "A History of Bible Translation in Mongolian", *Bible Translator,* 60, no.4, (1990), and Philip Elder, "The Controversy Surrounding Translating 'God' into Mongolian in the 1990s" (MA thesis, Trinity College, Bristol, United Kingdom, 1999). A third term – *Tenger* – still remains a possibility for the generic word for 'God'. This is a term for heaven or sky, inherited from the days of Chinggis Khan. The word *tenger* is used casually and in an ad hoc way for 'God' by some Christians today. However, like all translation, *tenger* is also problematic. David Stern demonstrates that *burhan* and *tenger*, have Shamanistic roots. See David Stern, "Masters of Ecstasy," *National Geographic*, December 2012.

[17] For a brief outline of Mongolian Christian history see Hugh Kemp, "Mongolia," in *A Dictionary of Asian Christianity*, ed. Scott W. Sundquist (Grand Rapids: Eerdmans, 2001).

[18] By "Assyrian Christianity" we mean the eastward movement of the Christian church along the Silk Road by Christians also known as 'Nestorians'. The arrival of this so-called 'Church of the East' in 635 AD in Changan (Tang dynasty capital) is announced on the Hsian Fu stele, now housed in the Museum of the Forest of Steles in Xian, China. Nestorian Christianity grew to have significant presence throughout China, and in particular many Mongol princes and bureaucrats during the 13th century were Nestorians. The term 'Assyrian Christian' is now preferred as it is acknowledged that 'Nestorian' came to mean 'heretic', that is, non-Catholic, by Franciscan monks who later travelled to Mongol heartland and China, and discovered the Nestorians had already been in the East for quite some many years already.

[19] For a fuller treatment of this long and varied history see Kemp, *Steppe by Step: Mongolia's Christians - from Ancient Roots to Vibrant Young Church*

[20] Robert Pinsky, "Poetry and American Memory," *The Atlantic Monthly* 1999.

[21] David J. Bosch, *Transforming Mission: Paradigm Shifts in Theology of Mission*, vol. 16, *American Society of*

Christian Church' is an emerging Asian church, rooted plainly in a rich (though erratic) Christian heritage. Signs of incarnation are evident: leadership training, song writing, Bible terminology and translation, relationship building, political involvement – these are all initiated and executed by Mongolian Christians. A 'double movement' of listening to each other (including Protestants to and with Catholic and Orthodox), to history and to the culture, motivates many to think in christological categories: where the word for 'God' has been self-chosen, this also invites new Mongolian categories for christology. While there is a desire to 'win the nation for Christ', this is not merely to 'Christianize Mongolia', but, to use the words of Bosch, to engage Gospel with culture that is 'inclusive, [so that …] this experience [will] be a force animating and renewing the culture itself'.[22]

This 'Mongolian Christian Church' is indeed the common vision and goal in itself, for it is about continuing emerging identity. While embodied in the MEA, it is not limited to it. From 2004, the target of 10% of the population as disciples of Christ by the year 2020 had emerged and today this goal of '20/10' mobilizes and energizes much of the work of MEA and its member churches. The goal is translated as 300,000 disciples and 3,800 churches. To reach this goal, MEA calls for all churches and organizations to plan together and cooperate, right across the full Christian spectrum.

Thus Mongolian Christians have much to celebrate for what has been accomplished in unity and cooperation through MEA in Mongolia. As the body of Christ grows numerically, obviously there will be many new challenges. Fellowship and personal relationship among the national leaders will always need to be maintained at local and national level.

Future Challenges

An area that still needs much original thinking and development is church planting among nomadic people. In the main, western urban church models have been trans-planted into Mongolia's urban population, but Mongolians themselves will have to create and fashion an appropriate model for Mongolian rural people. This is consistent with the need to reconceptualize mission particularly for nomadic peoples, explicitly articulated from the late 1990s.[23]

In addition, although the national leadership has emerged rapidly, the Church is still young and has much room for growth. The wisdom, experience and support of missionaries will continue to be valued. National leaders will benefit from critical self-reflection and deeper biblical grounding, with a wise ear to history and experience. The Catholic church has much to offer in this regard: the CICM has had a long history amongst the peoples of Ordos region in Inner Mongolia. In addition, there is a history of Bible translation that gives a bigger context to current debates. Hence the 'quality' growth of the goal '20/10' needs to be emphasized and understood in terms of practical plans at local church and personal discipleship level, informing these with a deep sense of history, place, and identity.

Compared to the current 8% annual church growth worldwide,[24] the Mongolian church needs to grow at 23% per annum in order to reach this '20/10' goal.[25] This will require focused strategic thinking, planning and cooperative implementation in the areas of training of leaders, discipling of Christians, reaching the teenage and youth and imagining church planting models appropriate for different contexts in Mongolia.

Missiology Serious (Maryknoll, NY: Orbis Books, 1991), 453-57.

[22] Ibid., 455.

[23] Malcolm J Hunter, "Think Nomadic," *International Journal of Frontier Missions* 17, no. 2 (2000).

[24] Jason Mandryk, *Operation World: The Definite Prayer Guide to Every Nation*, 7th ed. (Nottingham: IVP Books, 2010).

[25] At the current population growth of 1.4%, it is estimated that the population of Mongolia will be 3,135,000 in the year 2020. National Statistics Office, *Үндэсний Статистикийн Хороо (Mongolian National Statistics Office)* (National Statistics Department, 2012 [cited 2nd December 2012]); available from http://www.nso.mn/v3/.

Purevdorj Jamsran, principal of the Union Biblical Theological College, reminds us that Christians have been at the forefront of many social and educational changes and have gained a good reputation in Mongolian society.[26] To fulfill the '20/10' vision, Christians will need to continue to be so.

Indeed, it is imperative that Christians must play a strategic part in nation building. In the late 1990's Mongolia began "opening the books" on 70 years of communism. Atrocities, missing persons, purges and mismanagement began to be addressed. There is now a great opportunity for Mongolian Christians to preach, demonstrate, and lead the nation in acts of reconciliation, and this to be demonstrated by an actual ecumenism where all Christians demonstrate a unity that brings honour to Christ. With the legal precedent for toleration set down by Chinggis Khan in the *yasa*, the Mongolian church has every right to be in the forefront of political and social change. It is a church born at a time when the nation is at a critical turning point. In God's timing, and in God's grace, Mongolia's modern Christian church will continue to bear a solid witness to Christ in the nation and graciously continue to live out the power and truth of the Gospel.

Bibliography

Bosch, David J. *Transforming Mission: Paradigm Shifts in Theology of Mission*. Vol. 16, *American Society of Missiology Serious*. Maryknoll, NY: Orbis Books, 1991.

Collins, D. N. "Mongolian Law on Church State Relations: A Translation from the Russian Text." Ulaanbaatar, 1993.

Elder, Philip. "The Controversy Surrounding Translating 'God' into Mongolian in the 1990s." MA thesis, Trinity College, Bristol, United Kingdom, 1999.

Garamtseren, Bayarjargal. "A History of Bible Translation in Mongolian." *Bible Translator* 60, no. 4 (2009): 215-23.

Hunter, Malcolm J. "Think Nomadic." *International Journal of Frontier Missions* 17, no. 2 (2000): 9-13.

Jamsran, Purevdorj. *Монгол Чуулган Өнгөрсөн 20 Жилд (Mongolian Church in the Last 20 Years)* Mongolian Evangelical Alliance, 2012 [cited 26 October 2012]. Available from http://www.mea.mn/?p=276.

Kemp, Hugh. "Mongolia." In *A Dictionary of Asian Christianity*, edited by Scott W. Sundquist. Grand Rapids: Eerdmans, 2001.

———. *Steppe by Step: Mongolia's Christians - from Ancient Roots to Vibrant Young Church* London: Monarch, 2000.

Mandryk, Jason. *Operation World: The Definite Prayer Guide to Every Nation*. 7th ed. Nottingham: IVP Books, 2010.

Mongolian Evangelical Alliance. *Монголын Эвангелийн Эвслийн Товч Түүх (History of the Mongolian Evangelical Alliance)* Mongolian Evangelical Alliance, [cited 2nd December 2012]. Available from http://www.mea.mn/?page_id=66.

Mongolian Government. *Хүн Ам, Орон Сууцны 2010 Оны Улсын Тооллогын Үр Дүн (Mongolian Population and Residency Census)* Government of Mongolia, 2010 [cited 1st May 2012]. Available from http://www.toollogo2010.mn/doc/Main%20results_20110615_to%20EZBH_for%20print.pdf.

National Statistics Office. *Үндэсний Статистикийн Хороо (Mongolian National Statistics Office)* National Statistics Department, 2012 [cited 2nd December 2012]. Available from http://www.nso.mn/v3/.

Pinsky, Robert. "Poetry and American Memory." *The Atlantic Monthly* 1999, 60.

Stern, David. "Masters of Ecstasy." *National Geographic*, December 2012, 110-31.

[26] Purevdorj Jamsran, *Монгол Чуулган Өнгөрсөн 20 Жилд (Mongolian Church in the Last 20 Years)* (Mongolian Evangelical Alliance, 2012 [cited 26 October 2012]); available from http://www.mea.mn/?p=276.

Tscherrig, Emil P. "Mongolia and Christianity: History and Quest of New Direction." In *Christianity and Mongolia*, edited by Gaby Bamana, 6-10. Ulaanbaatar: Antoon Mostaert Mongolian Study Center, 2006.

Worldwide Religious News. *Dalai Lama's Visit Shines Spotlight on Mongolia's Explosion of Faiths* Associated Press, 25th August, 2006 [cited 1st December 2012]. Available from http://wwrn.org/articles/22521/

(66) CHURCHES TOGETHER IN GOD'S MISSION – MYANMAR

Smith N. Za Thawng

1. The Beginnings

The history of ecumenism in Myanmar could be attributed to three main streams, viz., first, the International Ecumenical Youth and Student Movements; second, the indigenous patriotic Christian youth movement; and third, the impact of the 1910 Edinburgh World Missionary Conference.

2. Historical Movements

(a) The twin bodies, Young Men's Christian Association (YMCA) in 1894 and the Young Women's Christian Association (YWCA) in 1900 arrived and stayed rooted on Myanmar soil. The National Council of YMCAs of Myanmar was established in 1951 and there are now 15 member local YMCAs and thirteen associates. The main concerns and program priorities of the YMCAs are such: youth empowerment, HRD, vocational skills trainings, early childhood development and pre-school education, micro-finance and community development. The National YWCA was established also in 1951 and there are now ten local YWCAs, the main concerns and program priorities of the YWCAs being micro-finance, vocational skills training, reproductive health education and street childrens programs.

(b) The Student Christian Movement (SCM) of Myanmar began with the establishment of the Student Christian Association of India, Burma and Ceylon (SCAIBAC) in 1912. At the time the Province of British India covered the present India (including Pakistan and Bangladesh), Burma (now Myanmar) and Ceylon (now Sri Lanka). The SCM of Burma became a movement of its own after the nation's political independence in January 1948. The SCM existed and functioned as an autonomous ecumenical body. The political change through a military coup in 1962 (parliamentary democracy was abolished and a one party Socialist rule was imposed) compelled the Burma SCM to take refuge under the umbrella of the Burma Christian Council in the name of the University Christian Work Department. However, the SCM could continue to uphold its original aims and purposes. The SCM always strived to maintain solidarity among students, university teachers and senior friends. The SCM is proud of its legacy in nurturing successive national ecumenical leaders in the country both for the churches and for the society at large. Myanmar SCM had always been an active member of the WSCF at both Asia-Pacific regional and inter-regional levels. Amidst continued political uncertainties, the SCM continues to exist and operate not only regular programs such as prayer meetings, Bible studies, leadership seminars, annual program planning, etc. but some special programs were also conducted, such as student volunteer work camps, frontier mission activities and womens' empowerment.

(c) The local indigenous ecumenical youth movement *"Thaingthar Luhlin"* (meaning patriotic youth) was an outcome of the patriotic spirit for political freedom coupled with an ecumenical spirit for Christian unity as pioneered by some zealous Christian youth leaders in 1946 amidst the struggle for national independence. A year later they renamed themselves as *BA-KHA-LA (*Myanmar abbreviation of) "All Burma Christian Youth League". Their striking slogan ran like this:

> Lest we fail to be united for our denomination's sake, where is Christ?
> Lest we fail to be united for racism's sake, where is Christ?
> Lest we fail to show our Christian spirit to others, where is Christ?

They changed their name again in 1951 into Burma Christian Youth Council (BCYC), and renamed it as United Christian Youth of Burma (UCYB) in 1955, and changed again to Burma Church Youth Fellowship (BCYF) in 1967. The Ecumenical Youth Movement was an independent body until it decided for structural amalgamation with the Burma Council of Churches and became its Youth Department in 1979. The Ecumenical Youth Movement put high priorities on Ecumenical Youth Leadership Training, Education for Ecumenism, Gospel and Culture, Rural Youth programs, etc. The Youth Department maintained a working relationship with the youth concern desks of CCA and WCC.

(d) In January 1913, John R. Mott visited Yangon and conducted a conference in the name of the Continuation Committee (of the 1910 Edinburgh World Missionary Conference) which was attended by representatives of the foreign missions and others. The Burma Representative Council of Missions (BRCM) was formed in 1914 with the representatives of five Missions and four organizations, viz., American Baptist Mission, Society for Propagation of the Gospel (Anglican) Mission, the Methodist Episcopal Mission (USA), English Wesleyan Mission, Leipzig Lutheran Mission, British and Foreign Bible Society, YMCA, YWCA, Women's Christian Temperance Union, etc. The BRCM was reconstituted as the Christian Council in Burma in 1923. After independence in January 1948, the Burma Christian Council (BCC) existed as an autonomous National Christian Council. With the military regime taking over in March 1962 and with the compulsion of all foreign missionaries to leave the country by mid 1966, the ecumenical tasks together with the entire Church leadership fell upon the shoulders of the National Christian leaders. In 1972, the Church leaders decided to reconstitute the Council as Burma Council of Churches (renamed Myanmar Council of Churches since 1990 as the then military government changed the country's name to Myanmar from Burma).

MCC was a founding member of the National Christian Council of the East Asia Christian Conference (EACC in 1957), now the Christian Conference of Asia (CCA since 1973) and maintained active membership and cooperation with it to date. MCC also maintained an active working relationship with the World Council of Churches (WCC) since its formation in 1948.

Today, MCC is comprised of 14 mainline national denominational churches, half of which are members of CCA and four of which are members of WCC. A dozen national ecumenical organizations are affiliated to MCC, such as YMCA, YWCA, Bible Society, Christian Literature Society, Association for Theological Education in Myanmar (ATEM), etc. There are more than twenty active local councils of churches in the regions corresponding with MCC. Priorities of MCC programs include: towards a visible church unity, integrated and sustainable development, relief and service to human needs, human resource development, ecology, gender equity, holistic mission, ecumenical education, HIV and AIDS, disability, women and youth.

3. Relationships with the Roman Catholic Church and Evangelical/Pentecostal Churches

(a) A National Ecumenical Joint Commission was formed between the MCC and the Catholic Bishops' Conference of Myanmar (CBCM) after Vatican II in 1968. Its main responsibility was to translate, reproduce and distribute the documents of the *World Octave of Prayer for Christian Unity* produced by the Joint Working Group of WCC and Vatican, and to encourage the observance of Prayer Services at local churches throughout the country every year during January 18th-25th. The Joint Commission conducted the very first National Study Seminar in 1990. After a lapse of a dozen years, the Joint Commission was able to organize another National Ecumenical Study Seminar in 2002 with the theme "That They All May Be One" reflecting on the Papal Encyclical of Pope John Paul II, i.e. *"Ut Unum Sint"*. Since then National Ecumenical Study Seminars were conducted in consecutive years. Since 1999 every year, MCC and CBCM jointly sponsored Christmas Worship and Fellowship Dinner to which State authorities were invited and where Christmas messages were delivered by Church leaders and Christmas greetings were given by the authorities. These occasions facilitated open dialogue and conversation between Church leaders and State authorities.

(b) There are two main groups among the Evangelical & Pentecostal Churches in Myanmar, viz., The Myanmar Evangelical Christian Fellowship (MECF) and the Myanmar Christ's Mission Co-operation Board (MCMCB) formed in 1981 and 1990 respectively. They are operating with voluntary services as there are no full-time staff working in the offices. Since around 2000 MCC extended invitations to them to attend our Biennial General Meetings (as fraternal delegates) and to participate at our study and training seminars and conferences. They responded positively. Our relationships improved steadily with better and greater understanding, mutual friendship and fellowship. Further mutual coordination and cooperation is anticipated in the future.

4. Some Pioneering Ecumenical Initiatives

(a) Association for Theological Education in Myanmar (ATEM)

ATEM was established in 1986 by the MCC with the purpose of promoting higher ecumenical theological formation and education for the churches in Myanmar. As of now there are 32 member theological schools accredited to ATEM. ATEM is functioning as an ecumenical network of coordination and facilitation for faculty development, library promotion, common curriculum, production of reference books and teachers' handbooks, common study on contextual theological issues and concerns. Ecumenics is a regular course of study in all ATEM member schools. ATEM is working in close collaboration with MCC-MEI, ATESEA, CCA, WOCATI, WCC-ETE.

(b) Myanmar Ecumenical Institute (MEI)

MEI is the Myanmar version of the Ecumenical Institute Bossey of the WCC. It started in 1987 as a Comprehensive Leadership Promotion Program (CLPP) of the MCC. Its main purpose is to facilitate research, study and training programs to supplement as well as to initiate new programs which are not available or insufficient at theological institutions for new generations of Christian leadership in Myanmar. The historic inaugural one-month intensive program called *Ecumenical Leadership Course (ELC)* was launched in 1992 at the Prof. Dr. Hla Bu Memorial Building (before the Myanmar Ecumenical Sharing Centre MESC was constructed) in Yangon with a very simple and humble beginning. The 30th course was conducted in August 2011. The major subjects studied are: History of the Ecumenical Movement, Education for Ecumenism, Christian Leadership and Management, Mission in Context, Church and Society, Holistic Development, World Religions and Confessional Distinctives. Special topics studied among others are: Globalization, Civil Society, Ecology, Gender, Justice and Peace and Disability.

MEI in coordination and collaboration with ATEM was able to facilitate special training seminars on "Teaching Ecumenics" which was attended by more than 180 teachers from various ATEM member schools. A common syllabus on Ecumenics course is being prepared for use beginning from the academic year 2012-13. Another focus of the MEI is on Research Programs on the History of the Church in Myanmar (from an ecumenical perspective).

(c) Week of Prayer for Peace and Reconciliation

In 2002, the leaders of MCC and CBCM decided to launch a Week of Prayer for Peace and Reconciliation specifically for Myanmar. This prayer program focused on National Unity, Peace and Reconciliation, and was conducted every year during September 28th – October 4th at the local churches in major cities and towns throughout the country.

(d) Judson Research Center (JRC)

The JRC was initiated by the Myanmar Institute of Theology (MIT) in 2003. (The name was given in commemoration of the first American Baptist missionary Adoniram Judson). The main purpose of the Center is to promote good relationships between different religious and ethnic communities in Myanmar through mutual dialogue, seminars and conferences. Several seminars and sharing sessions have been conducted. Issues of common concerns, such as, globalization, ecology, culture, ethnicity and gender have been deliberated upon and discussed.

(e) Peace Studies Center (PSC)

The Center program was launched in 2006 by MIT with the hope of becoming a Resource Center for institutions, organizations, groups and churches interested in peace building and conflict transformation. Several study workshops and seminars had been conducted not only at the Center in Yangon but also at various places in the regions and states. A plan is underway to launch a Masters Program in Peace Studies at the MIT in the near future.

(f) National Inter-Church Prayer Committee

In recent years, a new joint activity emerged somehow in the spirit of the Global Christian Forum. As Christian leaders from various churches met together, they came agreed on forming a prayer committee where all Christians may join hands and hearts in prayer. The National Inter-Church Prayer Committee was formed in 2006 with select leaders from the MCC, CBCM, MECF and MCMCB. The Committee's main purpose is to uplift the prayer life and spirituality of each individual Christian to motivate and strengthen the renewal of the churches to become evangelizing congregations and witnessing communities as the ''light of the world and salt of the earth''. The last National Prayer Conference was held in Yangon, September between 21st-23rd, 2011.

5. Challenges and Opportunities

Among endless lists, the following can be regarded as most crucial for the promotion of Ecumenism in Myanmar:

- Christian Unity – an imperative that the world may believe
- National Unity – through ethnic/racial unity and inter-religious harmony
- Poverty eradication, integrated and sustainable development
- Integrity of Creation – ecological and environmental concerns
- Education for Peaceful and Democratic Culture and Practices (Lifestyle)

Bibliography

MCC Historical Records (1914-1989) (in Myanmar) published by MCC on the occasion of its Diamond Jubilee in 1989, Yangon.

Burma SCM Diamond Jubilee (1912-1987) (in English and Myanmar) published by MCC University Christian Work department, 1987, Yangon.

"Hlaing Lae Gyar Ga Hlae Nge Lay" (in Myanmar) published by MCC Youth Department on the occasion of MCC Diamond Jubilee Celebration, 1989, Yangon

Fifty Years Witness: Student Christian Movement (in English) published by Burma SCM, 1963, Yangon.

Most of the contemporary historical accounts are based on the personal experience of the author, Revd Smith N. Za Thawng (National Secretary of Burma SCM, 1979-83; Coordinator of MCC Comprehensive Leadership Promotion Program, 1987-96; MCC Asso. General Secretary, 1996-2001; MCC General Secretary, 2001-2005)

(67) Churches Together in God's Mission – Nepal
Ecumenical Situation and Interdenominational Church Cooperation

K.B. Rokaya, Narayan Maharjan and Ganesh Tamang

Beginning of Christianity

There were scanty traces of the presence of Christians from the mid 18th century in Nepal. According to Makhan Jha, the Capuchin missionaries driven out of Peking and Lhasa were the first Christians to settle in 1745 at Patan in Nepal. Before they could make some progress in conversion, the Gorkhas entered Kathmandu valley and expelled them.[1] King Prithvi Narayan Shah equated Christian missionaries with the British and was opposed any missionary activities. He was afraid of the growing power of the British in India,[2] that he even suspected indigenous Nepali Christians as traitors, secretly working for the British. Christians were persecuted and driven away from their own homeland.

After the expulsion of Christians, the entire nineteenth century was silent about Christian activities in Nepal. Nearly two hundred years later, the Indian Christian Mission came to Nepal in 1951 to run some schools and hospitals. After they were allowed to stay in Nepal, they began making converts from the lower section of society, and according to 1981 census, their number had reached to 3,891.[3] After the democratic changes in 1950, Nepal allowed foreign missionaries to come in and provide health, education and architectural/engineering services, but they were strictly forbidden to convert people to Christianity. Though there were no earlier missionary enterprises, the first such foreign mission known as the International Nepal Fellowship entered Nepal in 1952. The United Mission to Nepal followed in 1954; but these mission organizations were mostly involved in social welfare programs like hospitals, clinics, and schools.

An agreement between His Majesty's Government of Nepal and the United Mission to Nepal (25 May 1975) was made which states: "The UMN agrees to conduct its activities in the fields of Education, Health Services, Agricultural, Technical and Development Services and other fields subject to separate agreements concluded with the concerned Ministries and Department of HMGN".[4] Until today, UMN and other missions continue their services as social workers or international non-governmental organizations.[5] It is safe to say that these Christian mission agencies were not meant for propagating the Gospel; they had written agreement with the government where they promised to abstain from any involvement in evangelism and Christian religious activities in Nepal. However, to some extent, a meager number of Nepalese became Christian due to these missions' influence with whatever the motivations were there. In such a context, it is understandable that well-defined theology and proper biblical foundations were not so important for those missionaries and their converts but conformity to missionary's life-style and culture took precedence over Biblical and theological understanding of Christian faith.

Hardly any churches were established by the mission agencies. Missionaries never came to Nepal as the preachers or religious clergy. With one or two exceptions, there are no expatriate pastors in Nepali congregations. The majority of churches in the initial stages began as the Nepali believers gathered for

---

[1] Makhan Jha, *The sacred complex of Kathmandu, Nepal: Religion of the Himalayan Kingdom* (New Delhi: Gyan Publishing House, 1995), 8f.

[2] Bandana Rai, *Gorkhas: the Warrior Race* (Delhi: Kalpaz Publications, 2009), 169.

[3] Makhan Jha, *op.cit.*, 8ff.

[4] Jonathan Lindell, *Nepal and the Gospel of God* (Kathmandu: The United Mission to Nepal, 1997), 270.

[5] See also website: http://www.umn.org.np/new/index.php

prayer and fellowship. The credit also goes to the Nepalese diasporas in Darjeeling and Kalimpong, India and the Nepali migrant workers in different parts of the world, in particular the Gurkhas who were instrumental in introducing the Gospel in Nepal although they did not serve the Lord with theological labels or denominational badges.

Another factor for the spread of Christianity is through education and military services. As there were no opportunities for higher education in Nepal, many young people went abroad for higher education. While abroad, some of them came into contact with Christianity and embraced Christianity. They came back to Nepal, shared their faith with their family members and others and established Churches. Some Nepalese came into contact with Christianity through military service in British and Indian army.

Despite the significant presence of small number of denominations such as Assemblies of God (which was and is exclusive), the pre-1990 church in Nepal do not project the understanding of the western or Indian denominationalism. Moreover, Christians in minority were struggling for their survival till 1990 rather than identifying themselves with their own theologies and denominations. It is also true that those denominationally defined Christians were not clear about their theological convictions. There was a time of toleration among Christians that their naiveté about one's theological conviction would not hinder the inter-church relation and unity was somewhat maintained. Majority of Christians in Nepal have come to Christ without missionary effort and they do not belong to any particular theological affiliation. These Christians make the church in Nepal as unique in terms of self-supporting, self-governing and self-propagating. Until 1990, to some extent, Nepali churches were bearing striking resemblances to the first century church where churches were actively involved in bearing witnesses, healing and performing miracles in the name of Jesus Christ without any theological prejudices. The household concept of God, *oikoumene*, which was clearly seen in the first century, was beautifully reflected in the churches of Nepal. In essence, even today, Nepali churches in the grassroots level (local Christians) are evangelical by nature even though the church leadership has often betrayed them.

After 1990, the Christian faith and practices were no more illegal in Nepal and the history of Christianity enters into a different phase of its development. Along with freedom, many denominations were imported from the West and other Asian countries, not because they had been pioneer churches, but because the local Nepali church leaders embraced the foreign denominations in order to enhance the material assistance and monetary gain. Unfortunately, as the result, the formerly practiced values, doctrines and styles were compromised; following the denominations' statements of faiths, they either become extremely charismatic or legalistic and they failed to formulate their own statements of faith and worshipping style. Alien practices brought division among churches and between believers for minor issues.

Nepal is no longer a Hindu nation. On 18th May 2006 the government of Nepal declared the nation, a "secular state." All citizens, regardless of religion, would have equal rights. The exact number of Christians in the population is exaggerated in almost all the reports produced by the different Christian organizations so as to meet their vested interests. I am personally most convinced by the survey of DAWN Nepal done in 2005, which shows that there are 2,799 churches and 2,74,462 Christians in the nation.[6]

The Nature of the Church

The Nepalese church is nearly sixty years old. There are positive signs of its gradual growth in quality and quantity. Personal evangelism is actively carried out in Nepal with local initiatives. The worship service takes place on Saturday, not because of doctrinal reasons, but because Saturday is the public holiday. The worship style is charismatic, yet certain denominations have muted the voices of worshippers in these days

[6] DAWN Nepal, *National Church Survey of Nepal* (Kathmandu: Nepal Research and Resource Network, 2007), 6.

due to pressure from their foreign donors. The architectural designs of the church buildings are not particular; a rented room or a spacious room works out. A recent fashion has been a cheaply erected worship cottage with corrugated tin and bamboos on an open rented plot of land. Healing from sicknesses is the most effective way to lead people to Christ, especially the practice of exorcising the demon which is commonly practiced here. Leading these believers to the conviction of their sins and assurance of salvation through Christ alone is the second most important step to prevent them from becoming just a crowd around Jesus following him for the bread alone (John 6, 25).

The growth of the church is phenomenal in Nepal but it must also be critically analyzed. In Nepal's context, however, it is literally imbalanced and lop-sided; the number of churches have increased, not because of pioneering new churches but because of splitting – anybody can begin a church and become the pastor without recognition by dividing the existing local church. There are numerous churches/congregations with a handful of members; nevertheless they add to the number of churches. Therefore, the church in Nepal is going through a critical stage; at the grassroots level it is still very close to the New Testament church but some current trends among its leaders, which are due to their lack of qualification or ethics, tend to destroy its New Testament characteristics by bringing in all types of unhealthy practices and teachings.

Though Christianity made some positive contributions in the Nepalese society such as breaking down the barriers of caste system, reducing the economic burden on the people and the health and education services provided by mission agencies; liberating the people of Nepal from the endless cycle of rituals and superstitions and giving them new hope, the Church in Nepal had the following shortcomings:

- Emphasis only on evangelization and indifference to socio- political, economical and other issues faced by the society and nation;
- Failure in preserving and promoting our meaningful traditions, cultures and social norms and values that determine our national and cultural identity.
- Negative attitudes of Christians towards people of other faiths and lack of initiatives to develop harmonious relationship with them and working together on common issues.
- Lack of involvement and contribution to issues of peace, justice and human rights.
- Absence of a representative Christian body to represent the Christians in Nepal at national and international level.
- Negative attitude and wrong perception of the society towards Christians.

The Formation of NCCN and Programmes

Several attempts were made to bring the churches under one umbrella in Nepal to initiate inter-denominational activities for common good and mutual enrichment. Firstly, Nepal Christian Fellowship (NCF) was formed in 1960 to fight against human rights violation in Nepal. After the introduction of `party-less' form of government by the King of Nepal in 1960, Christian suffered persecution and discrimination in many fronts. The country became more autocratic/dictatorial. Christians who raise their voices for democratic right and freedom were arrested. They were even prohibited to worship and fellowship in a particular place. During this time, the NCF took care of the prisoners and their families. In 1990, the NCF was registered with the government and initiated social, education and development works. Except Catholic, majority of the Protestant denominations came under this umbrella. However, the organization became weakened after the dawn of multi-party system in 1991. The denominational churches began to seek their separate identities to be link with their respective international bodies. For example, the Assembly of God in Nepal (AGN), the Baptist Church Council Nepal (BCCN), and later the United Methodists and Methodists Church and the Anglican Church Nepal (ACN) got link with their respective international organizations. Charismatic, Pentecostal also got separated in 1980 and formed an organization known as *Guru Sangati* (Masters Fellowship of Inter-church group). Secondly, a major Christian conference was organized in 1990 and decided form themselves as Nepal Christian Society (NCS). However, the Nepal Christian Society could not fulfill as expected mainly due to leadership and other organizational issues. The organization got defund within a few years without much initiatives. The situation of cooperation among the different church groups remained very much divided.

To address the above challenges and to bring together all the churches under one umbrella for common witness, the National Council of Churches in Nepal (NCCN)[7] was established in 1999 under the initiative and leadership of K. B. Rokaya with the support and cooperation of Churches in Nepal. Though NCCN was founded in 1999, it became fully operational only from June 2003. K.B. Rokaya assumed the responsibility as its first General Secretary and mandated to devote time for NCCN's institutional development. NCCN was formally registered with the government of Nepal in May 2004 under the name Nepal Rastriya Mandali Parisad with the following objectives:

- To unite the Christians in Nepal and encourage them to be actively involved in social and national development;
- To work for peace in society by promoting the spirit of tolerance, cooperation and understanding among the various religious communities in Nepal;
- To contribute to the development, preservation and promotion of the positive aspects of the religions and cultures of Nepal by conducting various studies and research;
- To support the efforts and activities of any religious group, organization and institution for the promotion of human rights, peace, justice and reconciliation;
- To contribute to the elimination of poverty, illiteracy, ignorance, and backwardness prevalent in the Nepali society;
- To develop and strengthen networking with all groups, organizations and institutions with similar objectives at the national and international level.

NCCN is an ecumenical body open to any individual or church or organization which subscribes to the objectives of the NCCN. It strives to unite the Christian community in Nepal, equip them spiritually; encourage them to be involved in social issues and work for the betterment of society. The NCCN envisions a better society with peace, justice, equality, religious harmony, faith in God and fullness of life for all.

The launching of the South Asia Ecumenical Partnership Programme (SAEPP) from July 2003 as a joint programme of the five NCCs of Nepal, India, Pakistan, Sri Lanka and Bangladesh and ecumenical partners from the North have played an important role in the institutional capacity building of NCCN in the initial period.

Since its inception, NCCN has been focusing its activities mainly in the four programme areas: Leadership Capacity Building, Peace and Reconciliation, Inter-faith Cooperation and HIV and AIDS. Other priority areas include institutional capacity building of NCCN, policy advocacy and networking of the churches at national, regional and global level.

Under leadership Capacity Building programme, NCCN has organized series of leadership capacity building trainings for pastors and church leaders all over the country. So far 27 capacity building programmes and church leaders conferences have been organized and around 6500 pastors and church leaders have benefitted through these training programmes.

---

[7] See the following website: http://nccnepal.org/

Formation of the United Christian Alliance of Nepal (UCAN)

Nepal is now in a new political context. The result of the people's war, the monarchy in Nepal is abolished for forever. The country is declared a democratic secular state. Christian community, as a minority group, has a key role to play in secular state: How to ensure freedom of religion? How and whose group should represent the Christian community in Nepal? On the other hand, some of the majority religious group raises their fundamentalists tune challenging the freedom of religion in the new Constitution. Since majority of the Christians come from dalit and tribal background, many of them are poor and socially discriminated. How do we ensure social justice to all sections of the society? All these challenges demanded united Christian voices for common good. To ensure religious freedom and liberty, and social justice to minority, a committee was formed to make appropriate recommendations to the new Constitution of the country. After several meetings of the representatives from all the churches - denominational and nondenominational evangelical churches including the Catholic Church, agreed to sign a MOU to form the United Christian Alliance of Nepal (UCAN) on the 4th of June 2010 with the following objectives: a) To address Christian community's needs and problems, b) To address ethical and moral issues in Nepal including corruption, c) To articulate common Christian opinions and present the issue to the government and diplomatic sectors relevant to common national issues. In the founding document from UCAN from June 2010, it is stated that

> As the world is going through national, social and moral crisis, the Gospel of Jesus Christ is the only hope for national integrity, unity, peace and development. This alliance will not interfere in the internal affairs of its members as regard to their faith statement, worship practice, styles of management and theological issues. Church groups and Christian communities founded on basic Christian principles and beliefs which are nationally and globally accepted and recognized, may become members of this alliance.

UCAN had a couple of press conferences during the year 2010. UCAN has made representation to the law making constituent assembly subcommittee for the amendments of the draft criminal and panel laws. UCAN also organized number of inter-religious peace initiatives. UCAN is also in dialogue with AGAPE and the Baptist Church Council of Nepal to join the forum.

Conclusion

The history of Christianity is about 60 years only. People of Nepal are now experiencing the democratic right, freedom of religion and liberty. Along with the political change, many Christian denominations have established churches, even up to the extent of sheep stealing. Competition among various denominations is visible. Simple believers are in great confusion. In God's World - Called to be One" is a divine imperative, but not an option. Every person is called to strive to be one with one another not because it is expedient but because God has called into existence of one people. It is God's will that God's people to be one and together – to be united and diverse at the same time. We are called to be one not because we are same, but because we are different; not because all are good or all lead to the same goal. But because we are called to be one because we are all created by God in his own image. Therefore, this `called to be one" is not just a desire for closeness, or a model for coexistence. This is a unity in diversity. This is not a matter of compromising or harmonizing the differences, but it is a prophetic movement compelled by the power of the Holy Spirit to live and work together.

(68) Churches and Ecumenical Relations – Pakistan

Maqsood Kamil

The history of the Church in Indo-Pak precedes the creation of modern Pakistan in 1947. St. Thomas whose rationalistic and empiricist mind first elicited the bedrock of Church's confession (John 20:28) after his encounter with the risen Lord is said to have brought the gospel to Taxila, adjacent to the capital of Pakistan[1]. It is in this city where he is said to have established the first Church[2]. But the present Church and numerous denominational churches in Pakistan are the fruit of the modern missionary efforts from Europe and America in the 19th and 20th centuries. Pakistan is an ideological Islamic state which is predominantly Muslim 96% and Christians are roughly 2.5%. This very tiny minority is, unfortunately, divided into almost all the Christian or so called Christian denominations. Although Pakistan is predominantly a Muslim country, yet sectarianism is very strong because enmity between the different sects of Islam in Pakistan is also obvious and deadly. How do the churches belonging to different denominations relate to each other? To what extent do churches reflect the dominant religio-political environment of Pakistani society? What are the challenges facing churches? What is the history of ecumenical relations among churches in Pakistan? What should be the nature of ecumenical cooperation among the churches in Pakistan? What is the future of ecumenical relations in Pakistan?

Light from the Past

To find answers to some of our questions, we need to look into the past. The roots of the ecumenical cooperation in North-western India can be traced in the history of cooperation among the mission agencies, way before the beginning of the modern ecumenical movement which has its roots in Edinburgh 1910[3]. American Presbyterians might be called pioneers in initiating ecumenical relations. The first missionary to enter Punjab was Walter Lowrie, an American Presbyterian, who arrived in Ludhiana in 183[4]. Jalandhar was the next mission station where Golaknath, [a Brahmin convert of the renowned Scottish missionary Alexander Duff, adopted by the American Presbyterians], started the work. In 1949 at the request of some British officials, much the revered American Presbyterian missionaries John Newton and C.W. Forman arrived in Lahore. They were the first to establish a mission centre in Lahore[5], and they in turn invited the CMS missionaries to come to Punjab and work alongside them[6]. The first concrete example of ecumenicity among the CMS and Presbyterian missionaries may be seen in their close cooperation in theological education. H. M. Clark wrote about the opening of St. John's Divinity College in Lahore that,

---

[1] Rooney, John 1984. *Shadows in the dark: A history of Christianity in Pakistan up to the 10th Century*. Rawalpindi: Christian Study Centre. Young, W. G 1969, 1999. *Handbook of Source Material for Students of Church History*. Delhi: ISPCK.

[2] Neill, Stephen. 1984. *A History of Christianity in India: The Beginning to AD 1707*. Cambridge: Cambridge University Press. pp 26-30.

[3] FitzGerald, Thomas E. 2004, *The Ecumenical Movement: An Introductory History*. Westport, CT: Praeger Publishers. P2.

[4] Powell, AvrilAnn, 1995. *Contested Gods and Prophets: Discourse Among Minorities in Late Nineteenth-Century Punjab,* in Malington, Mark I and Heywood, Colin M eds. *Renaissance and Modern Studies*. Vol. 38. Nottingham: The University of Nottingham. P39.
Heyward, Victor E.W 1966, *The Church as Christian Community*, London: Lutterworth Press. p149.

[5] Ibid.

[6] Clark, Robert. 1904. *The Missions of the Church Missionary Society and the Church of England Zenana Missionary Society in the Punjab and Sindh*. London: Church Missionary Society. P130.

The Presbyterian missionaries' attended in full force, and the happy catholicity of the institution was further evidenced by the noteworthy fact that the agents of the American Presbyterian Mission and those of the Church of Scotland were sent to it for training together with the members of the missions of the church of England. The elder generation of the Punjabi clergy of various communions look back today to the time when they sat together as brother students at the feet of Mr. French and Mr. Clark in Lahore[7].

The next important institution established as an ecumenical venture was the Punjab Auxiliary in 1863 which is now known as *The Pakistan Bible Society.* The Bible Society was an ecumenical venture from the very beginning and it continues to be so even today. Its board member is made up of the Church of Pakistan, The Presbyterian Church of Pakistan, Associated Reformed Presbyterian Church, and The Full Gospel Assemblies of Pakistan. These two examples of ecumenical cooperation during pre-partition from India show the desire of the missionaries of different traditions to work together as closely as possible. Isaac Devadoss, has shown in his essay *An Historical Survey of Ecumenism in India* that,

Historically, the Modern Missionary Movement came in the form of a number of foreign missions from Europe and America. Each propagated its own type of teaching and its own system of organization and discipline, with the inevitable result, a number of separate Christian communities came into existence, as Anglican, Methodist, and Presbyterian and so on. Though they maintained their denominational positions, they formed the habit of consulting together on common problems. A measure of co-operation in evangelistic methods, in running institutions and in matters of discipline, became necessary and developed an unwritten convention of Comity. There was more brotherly *(sic)* feeling and co-operation between the denominations in India than there was at that time in the West[8].

This spirit of working together for the common problems faced by the different mission agencies for finding common solutions, and brotherly and sisterly love and cooperation might be called the seeds of ecumenism, which later grew and bore fruit under the strenuous efforts of the national Church leaders in India and Pakistan.

After the Creation of Pakistan

After the partition of India in 1947, the first tangible example of ecumenical cooperation can be seen in the formation of the *West-Pakistan Christian Council* in 1948, which later became the National Council of Churches in Pakistan in 1975. However, the most significant ecumenical cooperation among the major protestant churches could be seen in theological education. Gujranwala Theological Seminary was originally established by the missionaries of the United Presbyterian Church of North America in 1877. But when Pakistan came into being church leaders of all major protestant denominations were keen to have a united theological institution. Consultations to this end were held from 1946 to 1953 which resulted in establishing of the united board of directors of the Gujranwala Theological Seminary in 1954[9]. Since then, GTS has become an ecumenical theological institution. Although there has been a mushrooming of many Bible schools, Bible colleges and Seminaries, GTS continues to be the only ecumenical theological institution. The Christian Study Centre in Rawalpindi is another important institution established as an ecumenical venture. This important institution has been playing a very important role in strengthening Muslim -Christian relations. One of the most exciting ecumenical achievements in the recent years is the establishment of Forman Christian College/University in Lahore. Forman Christian College was originally established by the Presbyterians and named after its missionary founder Charles W. Forman who arrived in Lahore in 1847. Forman Christian College became one of the most celebrated colleges of India and its graduates continued to occupy high positions in the governments of both India and Pakistan until recently.

[7] Clark, H.M. 1907. *Robert Clark of the Punjab*, London: Andrew Melrose. P284.
[8] Devadoss, Isaac D. 2010. *An Historical Survey of Ecumenism in India*. Edinburgh 2010.org.
[9] This information is taken from the Gujranwala Theological Seminary's website: www.gtspk.org

It suffered a deadly blow when the government of Pakistan nationalized all Church related educational institutions in 1972. After more than 30 years of long battle the Presbyterian Church succeeded in reclaiming its educational institutions and reconstituted F.C College/A charted university board in 2003. Although the property belongs to the Presbyterian Church there is a wonderful spirit of ecumenical cooperation among the Presbyterians, Episcopalians (Church of Pakistan) Roman Catholics and other Churches.

Efforts for Church Union

Christian denominationalism in the former colonies of the western powers has its historical roots in the western churches and their missionary movements. Most of the churches established by the missionaries became extension of their home churches and were governed by the rules and policies of their home churches. R.E. Frykenberg has demonstrated, especially in the case of the Anglican Church, that missionary efforts were largely geared towards the enlargement of their church dominion[10]. Comity[11] agreements whether unwritten or written reinforced this concept of ecclesiastical dominion. Even native ministers, lay leaders and congregations seem to have nourished a fair amount of prejudice, pride and parochialism over against the denominations other than their own. As D.T. Niles has rightly observed in his article, "Church Union in North India, Pakistan and Ceylon" that "how difficult it was for the uniting churches to recognise each other's theologies and traditions, as equally legitimate and authoritative expressions of the one indivisible yet divided church"[12]. Perhaps, the most important and humbling factor that brought the uniting churches together was to recognise that the broken and divided church was not the will of the Lord and all churches in their brokenness fall short of the one true Church.

Consultations on church union in Pakistan began in the second half of the 20th century. Leaders of the United Presbyterian Church are said to be the initiators of discussions on church unity. Gujranwala Theological Seminary, an ecumenical institution, played an important role in hosting the dialogue. In the Presbyterian Church, lay leaders, elders and head of the Presbyterian institutions appeared to have enjoyed a much greater influence than those in the Episcopal traditions. Lay leaders felt threatened as they envisioned their subjugation to the future bishops, if the church had to join the union church. So they opposed the church union under Episcopacy and thus the leaders of the U.P church pulled out of the negotiations for the church union. Yet in 1970 four other churches which were part of the dialogue succeeded in creating a new united church known as "The Church of Pakistan". It is a union of the Anglicans, Lutherans, Methodists and Scottish Presbyterians. This union has been a difficult journey and the effort to retain unity has been threatened many times. But the "united" church of Pakistan has survived the forces of division and destruction, and continues to provide inspiration and hope for further church unions.

The Second example is union within two Presbyterian churches, i.e., the United Presbyterian Church (U.P. Church) and the Lahore Church Council (LCC). Both these Presbyterian churches were established by the Presbyterian missionaries from USA. The Founding missionaries of LCC were C.W. Forman and John Newton whom I have already mentioned. The Founding missionary of the U.P. Church was Andrew

---

[10] Frykenberg, R.E. 2008. *Christianity in India: From beginning to the present.* Oxford: Oxford University Press.p243.

[11] Comity is a principle, in which each Mission was recognized as occupying certain territories and it was agreed that other Mission should abstain from entering and working in those territories. C. B. Firth, *An Introduction to Indian Church History,* Delhi: ISPCK, 1976, p. 234.

[12] D.T. Niles article, "Church Union in North India, Pakistan and Ceylon" was first published in "The Ecumenical Review Volume 14, Issue 3, pages 305–322, April 1962, and was Article first published online: 16 APR 2010. I have used this online article.

Gordon who arrived in Sialkot in 1855.[13] It was he who baptized Ditt, a convert from *Chuhras*[14]. Ditt became father of the mass conversion movement of Chuhras' to Christianity[15]. Although, two different Presbyterian Churches that sent those missionaries had merged in USA in 1858[16], U.P and LCC continued to function separately in Pakistan. Finally, leaders of U.P and LCC realized that they need to be united and negotiations for church union began in 1992. Since there were no serious issues of theology or polity, discussions were more focussed on the administrative issues and the new constitution. In November 1993, Pastors and elders of both churches came together and held their first united assembly in Naulakha Church Lahore under the new constitution and name "The Presbyterian Church of Pakistan". This union too has faced many problems and yet it continues to survive.

Challenges and Future of Ecumenism in Pakistan

At this point it is important to ask: what is the future prospect of ecumenism in Pakistan? What are some of the challenges that need to be overcome? Are any signs that might help promote further Church unity? We shall begin with the challenges which may be divided into internal and external challenges.

Internal challenges

As discussed above there have been two efforts for church union made in the history of the church in Pakistan. Internal tensions between the united churches are an open secret. The factors behind the continuing tension within the united churches need in-depth study and critical analysis for meaningful and effective union. Let us look at the internal challenges.

1. *Parochialism.* It appears that churches in Pakistan, generally, suffer from parochialism. Webster's dictionary defines "parochialism" as the quality or state of being parochial; especially selfish pettiness or narrowness (as of interests, opinions and views). This definition describes quite correctly the present state of the Pakistani Churches. Denominational/diocesan and congregational interests are given priority over the larger church of Christ. Churches seem to have a very narrow or even no understanding of the theological meaning of the body of Christ (1 Cor. 10:16-17; 12:27, Eph. 4), which is the Church. The concept of healthy interdependence of different organs of the body which is ultimately created and support by Christ himself does not seem to have taken root in the thinking of the church leaders. Their theology and ecclesiology appears to be very restricted along with their opinions, views, interests and their vision of the church. Although ecclesiology as part of the doctrinal theology is taught as a doctrine, it seems that the problem for such thinking might be due to the absence of ecumenical studies in the theological schools. Hence a curriculum on ecumenism is imperative.
2. *Denominational pride and prejudice.* Closely related with parochialism, are denominational pride and prejudice. This attitude is tied up with the issues of identity and certain pride that denominational- minded people take in the historical roots and service of their denominations. This issue is still alive in the Church of Pakistan even after forty years of union. Anglican priests and bishops consider themselves better and above the priests of Methodists, Lutherans and Presbyterian

---

[13] Stock, Frederick and Margaret. 1975. *People Movements in the Punjab: with special reference to the United Presbyterian Church.* South Pasadena, Calif: William Carey Library. P17.

[14] *Chuhras* were an outcaste group of people in Punjab. They were menial workers who ate carrion and removed the dead animals. Some of them dealt in hides and skins. They are considered as unclean.

[15] Webster, John C.B. 2010. *Large-Scale Conversion to Christianity in Late Nineteenth Century Punjab as an early Dalit Movement*, in Chetan Singh (Ed) 2010. *Social Transformation in North-Western India during the Twentieth Century.* Chandigarh: Manohar.p 343-44.

[16] Stock 1975:17.

origin. The bishop of the Diocese of Lahore still holds the title of "The Lord Bishop", even though he is neither a member of "The House of the Lords[17]", nor are other bishops of the church of Pakistan under his authority. Presbyterians, Pentecostals, Roman Catholics and other denominations too seem to have fallen prey to such attitudes. Considering one's church to be superior, holier and more important than the others, closes the doors for larger cooperation.

3. *Internal politics.* Pakistan in its short history of 65 years has been a weak and unstable country. Church politics pretty much reflects the political life of the Pakistani nation. At the time of the Church union in 1970 (Church of Pakistan) and 1993 (Presbyterian Church of Pakistan), there were certain dissident groups that opposed the unions and refused to join the united Churches. A splinter group of the Methodist Church established a separate Methodist conference and continued to fight battles in the court for a long time. A group of LCC did the same thing and challenged the unity between U.P. and LCC. The same examples are also found in the Full Gospel Assemblies and other denominations. These groups have caused considerable loss to the united efforts of churches, and have contributed to their instability. A small group of LCC churches defected from the Presbyterian Church of Pakistan in 2005. There are a number of other former Presbyterian churches which continue to exist separately even today. This internal politics and instability makes churches short-sighted and a real challenge for the development of ecumenism.
4. *Lack of visionary leadership.* There is a tremendous dearth of leadership, especially visionary leadership, in the Church in Pakistan. This problem will become more visible when we will reflect on the external challenges. At this point it is important to note that after 1993 when U.P and LCC were united, there have been no further talks for church unity in any forum. The obvious reason seems to be that the church leaders do not have the vision or even a desire for church unity. A Bishop of the Church of Pakistan was addressing a group of Church leaders at NCCP and said that it is not possible to have church unity. I pondered on his assertion and questioned in my mind: why did Jesus pray for the unity of His Church if it was simply impossible? Was Jesus wrong? Were the leaders of the ecumenical movement who obviously base their vision on Jesus's prayer in John 17, wrong? My conviction is that the problem lies neither with Jesus prayer for unity nor with the vision of the leaders of the ecumenical movement, but with the leaders of small churches who obviously fear that they will lose their leadership and position of influence if they were to unite with the larger churches and on the other hand, leaders of the larger churches are afraid to deal with the problems that unions bring with them. At the heart of the problem lies lack of vision that can alleviate fears and courage for the greater unity of the Church of Christ. Proverbs 29:18 must serve as a constant reminder for the visionless church leaders.
5. *Entrepreneurial and personal ministries.* During the last two three decades, there have been a mushrooming of private ministries of an entrepreneurial nature. Some pastors and lay-leaders of Pentecostal and charismatic churches have set up their personal congregations and ministries. This trend is also very strong within the larger denominations. Educated pastors and lay leaders find that this is an easier way to become richer and gain personal glory. The Internet has made it very convenient for people to search and connect with the churches in the west, especial large congregations of charismatic nature and missionary activities. This trend is dividing the churches and acts as a counter movement to the ecumenical spirit. As these rich and powerful individuals are becoming more visible they are providing inspiration for other individuals to follow suit.

---

[17] Certain bishops of the Church of England are also members of the House of Lords. There is no House of the Lords in Pakistan.

External challenges

Churches in Pakistan are facing considerable external challenges which are deeply disturbing not only for ecumenism, but even for the very existence of the church. We may consider few of them here.

1. *Disunity and separatist movements.* As I have already mentioned, Pakistan has been a weak and unstable country from its very inception, but the situation seems to be getting worst after 1971, when East Pakistan broke away and became Bangladesh. There are strong separatist movements in Baluchistan and Sindh provinces and a host of militant and extremist religious organizations there are flexing their muscles to grab power. The coalition government of Pakistan seems to be up against the powerful state institutions, especially the Military and Judiciary[18]. Political parties seem to have no vision and no direction. In this situation, which does not seem to improve in the near future, the state -owned institutions are being destroyed and the entire nation appears to be confused. Economic, social and security problems are threatening the unity of the nation. In this kind of environment where unity seems to be falling apart, churches are also experiencing the same situation. Sadly, the negative mind-set of the nation is also reflected in the churches.
2. *The Rising tide of Persecution.* The persecution of Christians has been gradually rising since the late 70s, when general Zia ul-Haq took over the country via a coup. He tried to 'Islamise' Pakistan through implementing certain *Sharia Laws*. He also introduced discriminatory separate electorate for minorities, whereby minorities could only vote for minority candidates for the designated seats in the provincial and federal assemblies. Since then *Sharia laws* have been misused to persecute minorities. There is an ever growing number of criminal cases registered against Christians on the charges of blasphemy and desecration of the *Quran*. Apart from that there has been whole scale destruction of Christian villages and colonies, worship places and a number of Christians have been killed by the Muslim mobs. It is just recently that the international community has started taking notice of the serious situation of the Pakistani Christians.
3. *Insensitivity of the Overseas Churches.* Western churches, consciously or unconsciously, are still playing a divisive role that may be a serious challenge for e ecumenism. Churches are generally weak and many of them still receive support for their programmes from overseas churches. This monitory and personnel support comes with a certain agenda from the supporting churches. Most often than not, overseas churches are insensitive to the local churches' contexts. The receiving churches also, in their bid to please donors, seem to behave like obedient servants and tend to become insensitive to the national challenges to which churches must respond. New missionary churches coming from the west and even from Korea are further dividing the existing churches. New churches are being established, "sheep stealing" or dividing the existing churches tends to be more inward- looking and parochial.

The Future of Ecumenism in Pakistan

Historical records and the present situation of the Pakistani churches, as described above, do not present us with a very bright picture. Two examples of church unions that we have cited did not inspire other churches to follow their footsteps. It appears, on the one hand that these unions might have discouraged other churches from pursuing similar goals. I can recall that in one of the General Assembly meetings of the Presbyterian Church of Pakistan the possibility of union with the Church of Pakistan was discussed.

[18] Both military and Judiciary (Supreme Court of Pakistan) have tried to destroy the PPP led coalition government. Military tried to muster support from the Arab state for another coop. Supreme Court convicted former Prime Minister for contempt of court and disqualified him to hold public office. A retired justice of the Supreme Court of India has severely criticised the decision of the Supreme Pakistan. (See Pakistani newspapers on June 19, 2012 and July 3, 2012).

The house severely criticised the ineffective of union of the COP citing the problems in various dioceses[19]. For example, Multan Diocese was without a bishop for years and the repeated elections brought more problems. Karachi diocese had two bishops consecrated by two different groups of bishops of the divided synod, and a fierce battle for the control of the diocese is going on. I have also heard that the most senior leaders of the PCP who come from U.P. background repeatedly said that they regretted the union with LCC.

But having said this we must not take the past as the ultimate determent of the future of the churches in Pakistan. In my opinion, the future of ecumenism will be determined by the present and future leaders of the churches and how they respond to the changing scenario in Pakistan. It is my conviction that denominationalism is a luxury and evil which is unaffordable in Pakistan. I do hope, as the time passes, the other leaders and scholars will also arrive at the same conclusion. As long as the prayer of our Lord Jesus for the oneness of the Church on earth remains unanswered and St. Paul's beautiful images of body and bride of Christ for the church remain in the Bible, they will continue to judge, challenge and condemn the divided nature and disunity of the Church. But these images will also continue to inspire the broken and divided churches to strive for greater unity in the power and presence of the Holy Spirit who is the bond of unity between the Father and the Son.

As the persecution of the Christians is growing in Pakistan as well as all over the Muslim world, it is hoped that churches will realize the seriousness of the situation and the need for the greater unity among churches. In the meantime, it seems important as well as urgent for us to make deliberate efforts to educate the churches, especially church leaders about the theological, social, economic and political importance of the unity of the churches in the context of a dominant and extremely aggressive Islam. The seminaries and bible colleges must include courses on ecumenism in their curricula. Resources must be made available for the training of the serving pastors and lay leaders for overcoming parochialism and denominationalism. As faith, love and hope are eternal (1Cor 13:13); we must have faith in the love of God and remain hopeful for greater unity among the churches in future amidst all the odds.

Conclusion

In this short reflection on the churches and ecumenical relations in Pakistan, I have tried to demonstrate that the roots of ecumenism in the North Western India (present Pakistan) are found in the missionary enterprise from the West. The history of the missions in Pakistan can give us good understanding that missionaries were not only a cause of the problem (for implanting denominational Christianity), but they were also, paradoxically, also the pioneers of ecumenical relations. The Churches in Pakistan need to return to the original spirit of missionary cooperation and grow toward full unity. Since persecution of Christians is growing, and the persecutors do not distinguish between Roman Catholics and Protestants or Pentecostals and Presbyterians, this experience must bring churches closer to the visible and tangible unity. I have witnessed that crises have forced Christians from all denominations to sit together and work together. At the times of tragedies and crises, we forget denominationalism. This should encourage churches to keep on pressing for greater cooperation and unity for the peace and security of the Christians in Pakistan. Being a sheer minority should also convince churches to consider uniting. The old axiom "union is strength" should give guidance. There is every reason to be hopeful that the greater church unity will become a reality. But to realize that vision conscious efforts must be made. Ecumenism must be taught not only in the theological schools but also in Sunday school. The pulpit is still the strongest means of communication among the churches in Pakistan. Pulpits must be used to preach the unity of the Church of

[19]Iqbal Nisar (d.1990) used to describe the union of the COP as "Orange Union". He meant by this epithet that it was a superficial union, not a union of heart and soul.

Christ in and though Christ. Parochialism and denominational arrogance have no place in the church. Church leaders, pastors and teachers must make efforts to educate congregations regarding what it really means to be the church of Christ: essentially an indivisible body. The present brokenness of the churches must be overcome, especially in countries like Pakistan for the glory of God and His Son, Jesus the Christ, creator, redeemer and sustainer of the Church.

Bibliography

Clark, H.M. 1907. *Robert Clark of the Punjab*, London: Andrew Melrose.

Clark, Robert. 1904. *The Missions of the Church Missionary Society and the Church of England Zenana Missionary Society in the Punjab and Sindh*. London: Church Missionary Society.

Devadoss, Isaac D. 2010. *An Historical Survey of Ecumenism in India*. Edinburgh 2010.org.

Firth, C.B. 1976. *An Introduction to Indian Church History,* Delhi: ISPCK.

FitzGerald, Thomas E. 2004, *The Ecumenical Movement: An Introductory History.* Westport, CT: Praeger Publishers.

Frykenberg, R.E. 2008. *Christianity in India: From beginning to the present.* Oxford: Oxford University Press.

Heyward, Victor E.W 1966, *The Church as Christian Community*, London: Lutterworth Press.

Marian-Webster Online Dictionary 2012. Excessed on 01/07.2012: http://www.merriam-webster.com/

Neill, Stephen. 1984. *A History of Christianity in India: The Beginning to AD 1707.* Cambridge: Cambridge University Press.

Niles, D. T. (1962), *CHURCH UNION IN NORTH INDIA, PAKISTAN AND CEYLON.* The Ecumenical Review, 14: 305–322. doi: 10.1111/j.1758-6623.

Powell, AvrilAnn, 1995. *Contested Gods and Prophets: Discourse Among Minorities in Late Nineteenth-Century Punjab,* in Malington, Mark I and Heywood, Colin M eds. *Renaissance and Modern Studies.* Vol. 38. Nottingham: The University of Nottingham.

Rooney, John 1984. *Shadows in the dark: A history of Christianity in Pakistan up to the 10th Century.* Rawalpindi: Christian Study Centre.

Stock, Frederick and Margaret. 1975. *People Movements in the Punjab: with special reference to the United Presbyterian Church.* South Pasadena, Calif: William Carey Library.

Webster, John C.B. 2010. *Large-Scale Conversion to Christianity in Late Nineteenth Century Punjab as an early Dalit Movement*, in Chetan Singh (Ed) 2010. *Social Transformation in North-Western India during the Twentieth Century.* Chandigarh: Manohar.

Young, W. G 1969, 1999. *Handbook of Source Material for Students of Church History*. Delhi: ISPCK.

(69) Churches Together in God's Mission – Philippines

Rex R.B. Reyes, Jr.

Ecumenism in the Philippines is understood as the proclamation of the Word that became flesh and dwelt among us (John 1.14). At once it is a call to evangelism as it is a call for the churches to be in solidarity with the poor.

It is encouraging that J. Matthey recalls the search for unity and the search for peace as "classical ecumenical priorities in mission" especially in citing the importance of mission and creation in the ecumenical discourse.[1] Indeed, the search for just and lasting peace is the hallmark of ecumenical work in the Philippines, especially as it relates to genuine agrarian reform and the defense of patrimony. The lack of genuine agrarian reform is one of the roots of insurgency in this country. Going further back, it was one of the reasons that sparked sporadic revolts during Spanish colonial period, leading toward the revolution for independence towards the closing decades of the 1800s. The defense of patrimony likewise dates to the same period when the United States took over as the colonial master of the Philippines following the end of the Spanish-American war. The intervention of the US in the Philippine revolution against Spain was not accidental. US foreign policy was already in place.[2] The colonial ruler even saw divine inspiration for such a policy that would leave its mark in the Philippines to the present day.[3]

Ecumenism in the Philippines had its early stages when denominational groups in the United Sates started trooping to the Philippines by the 1900's. Backed by their missionary boards or societies in the U.S., these denominations adopted a comity agreement to prevent overlapping. They came together occasionally for fellowship and produced tracts and publications. This fellowship of churches was mainly for the propagation of the so-called Protestant Christianity in the Philippines. Not until 1963 did this fellowship finally emerge as the National Council of Churches in the Philippines (NCCP). A major ecumenical paradigm shift for the NCCP took shape soon after its founding and well into the next decade. The resurgence of nationalist movements in the 60's was also inspired by the anti-Vietnam war movement and the clear domination of the US in many parts of Asia as part of the Cold War. The proclamation of Martial Law in 1972 would provide the ecumenical perspective in the Philippines. It is maintained that such a perspective affirms the WCC definition of ecumenism. The General Secretary of the NCCP at that time, Bishop La Verne Mercado, would

---

[1] Matthey, Jacques in the Editorial of the *International Review of Mission*. 100.2 (393) WCC Publications, November, 2011. P. 146

[2] In his study "A Contribution to the Study of Feudalism and Capitalism in the Philippines" (1982) Merlin Magallona cited US Senator Beveridge, who in 1896 said that as the US needed more markets and the need to expand capital and increase investment "Think of the Americans who would invade the mine and field and forest in the Philippines".

[3] In what is now known as "Manifest Destiny", US President McKinley told a group of Methodist leaders in 1903: "When next I realized that the Philippines had dropped into our laps I confess I did not know what to do with them. I sought counsel from all sides – Democrats as well as Republicans – but got little help. I thought first that we would take only Manila; then Luzon; then the other islands, perhaps also. I walked the floor of the White House night after night until midnight; and I am not ashamed to tell you gentlemen, that I went down on my knees and prayed to Almighty God for light and guidance more than one night. And one night late it came to me this way – I do not know how but it came: 1) that we could not give them back to Spain – that would be cowardly and dishonorable; 2) that we could not turn them over to France or Germany, our commercial rivals in the Orient – that would be bad business and discreditable; 3) that we could not leave them to themselves – they are unfit for self-government, and they would soon have anarchy and misrule over there worse than Spain's was; and 4) that there was nothing left for us to do but to take them all, and to educate the Filipinos, and uplift and civilize and Christianize them, and by God's grace do the very best we could for them as our fellowmen for whom Christ also died. . . . and the next morning I sent for the Chief Engineer of the War Department and told him to put the Philippines on the map of the United States". Cf. H de la Costa. *Readings in Philippine History*, p. 219.

later on state what NCCP was all about. In his valedictory report to the General Convention, he said: "The NCCP has constantly sought to make its programs and services relevant and responsive to the needs and challenges of our church and society. The Council operates on the belief that the Gospel is directed to the ministry of advocacy, a prophetic role, by announcing the Good News of Jesus Christ and at the same time denouncing that which is not in line with the Christian Gospel. It is the being of Jesus Christ which defines our ministry in the NCCP. . . The activities and actions of the Council are motivated by the demands of the Christian faith and centered in Christ, the Head of the Church and the Lord of us all".[4]

Ecumenism in the Philippines is a fellowship of churches. As a fellowship, it seeks to be a visible sign of unity by weaving a common interpretation of the World Council of Churches' definition of ecumenism as it bears upon the issues and concerns of the people in the Philippines. This fellowship furthermore seeks cooperation in witness and service as it implies unity and common action forged by the realities of oppression, increasing poverty and the violation of human rights that has plagued this country from the beginning and made worse by the three-fold assault of economic globalization, i.e. privatization, economic liberalization and deregulation. This fellowship is not limited to its member-churches and associate members alone. Living out this fellowship also means cooperating with other government and non-government organizations in the pursuit of peace and justice. While it is thus a fellowship of its members, it is equally a fellowship of churches bound by a common calling to be churches in solidarity with the people.

Ecumenism is a people's movement. This self-understanding is profoundly eschatological, the end of which is peace and justice that is made available in the present. Aside from calling the churches to be solidarity in the struggle of the people for genuine freedom, it is also a constant challenge for church renewal. The mission statement following the summit organized by the NCCP puts in sharp focus what this means: "Mission is accompanying people in their journey, as exemplified in the account of the walk to Emmaus. The church facilitates and creates the space for the faith movement to surge forward – a spirituality emerging from the vulnerable in the margins. . . It is working for justice and peace as stewards of creation, and joining in the creative process of building as opposed to unjustly regarding migrant works as commodities to profit from. Mission, finally is sharing; it thrives when resources are shared – not based on charity, but as a Christian value – for it is what makes us Christian. Sharing liberates both the receiver and the giver." This is particularly true in the Philippines and in the rest of the global south where the earth's resources are controlled by the few.

The same mission statement has characterized the Philippines as a country haunted by poverty, injustice and ecological damage, which pose a serious threat to future generations. "This is more clearly seen in the go-signal given to the mining sector to open areas for exploitation by transnational corporations employing destructive methods of extraction." Most of these areas are home to farmers and indigenous peoples.

As such, the church "must reflect the ecumenical vision of unity and oneness . . . with those victimized by the economies of greed that ignore that needs of men, women and children." Casting our nets, we "can we will find those sent away because they cannot make the grade. There we will find those who sell their bodies just to be able to live. There we will find those who are exploited in the name of money, causing separated families, broken homes, narcotized youth and cynical adults".

Finally, ecumenism in the Philippines understands mission "as listening to people's stories about what happens to them as a result of uninformed decisions and misguided esteem for conquest and domination. . . Siding with the poor is not an option then for churches, but a mandate, an imperative even as we churches need to be evangelized and need space for self-conversion to sustain the fire of spirituality".[5]

---

[4] Bishop La Verne Mercado was himself thrown into prison by President Marcos, a few months after he assumed the position of General Secretary of NCCP in 1973.

[5] The quotations in the final portion of this paper were all taken from the "Incarnation of Faith: Voices from the East, Voices of the Oppressed". This is the Mission Statement following the Philippine Mission Summit organized by the National Council of Churches in the Philippines last February 21-22, 2012.

(70) CHURCHES TOGETHER IN GOD'S MISSION – SINGAPORE INITIATIVES FOR ECUMENISM IN SINGAPORE

Michael Poon

Modern ecumenical movement from its beginnings grew out of two considerations: a missiological concern for "joint action for mission" in the local situation; and an ecclesiological concern for the development of independent churches in what have been "mission fields" of parent churches and mission agencies in the West. Singapore arguably offers an important case study of how these two theological concerns find expressions in the complex intraregional matrices in Asia in post 1945 times.

Harvey Perkins' explanation of the twofold strategy of ecumenical engagement in Asia provides a convenient starting point for exploring Singapore's ecumenical experiences. For him, the Christian Conference of Asia (CCA) and its predecessor East Asia Christian Conference (EACC) from the start sought:

1. Through consultations and conference to create groups of people who share common ideas out of a common vision, and influenced by them, penetrate the normal work of the churches with them; and
2. To build up in the life of the churches and countries a group of people who are willing to probe the frontiers of the Christian enterprise, to encourage and nurture them and relate them in solidarity to each other.[1]

In other words, ecumenism is a movement from 'the fringe to the fringe.' Those who "share common ideas out of a common vision" do not necessarily belong to the church establishment – and usually they do not. They see their task in terms of probing "the frontiers of the Christian enterprise." My aim in this survey is to chart the strategic role Singapore has played in working out this ideal, and how the island republic in fact radically challenges this model of engagement.

Clearly, journeys in ecumenism are never isolated experiences. Therefore, ecumenical situations in different countries – as defined by national boundaries – necessarily overlap with one another. Churches need to discover their own identities by connecting their own experiences with those of others. This is especially true for Singapore. Geographically, Singapore is connected to Malaya and Borneo. Culturally and linguistically, it is informed by India and China. In its mission history, it was a logistic centre of Western missionary outreach (through South Asia) to the island worlds of Southeast Asia. More important, it served as a bridgehead for mission to China – in the pre Opium War years in the 19th century, and after the Western missionary withdrawal from China at the wake of the Communist victory in China in 1949.

Singapore's unique role in inter-church cooperation in fact arises from its economic and cultural geography. Singapore's success lies in its traditional entrepôt role. It offers a secure and stable haven in times of political and social unrest in neighbouring countries. It is also a 'free-port' in the sense that peoples of different ethnic and religious traditions can thrive on the strength of their own merits, free from caste and ethnic discrimination that has plagued many Asian countries.[2]

Singapore, therefore, is a communication and economic centre. This strategic role has shaped the character of ecumenical initiatives in the island. Formally speaking, the founding of the National Christian Council of Malaya (Malayan Christian Council, MCC) in Orchard Road Presbyterian Church on 9 January 1948 signalled the start of modern ecumenical movement in the island.[3] The objects of the Council were

---

[1] Harvey Perkins, "A Time of Vision and a Time for Vision," in *Minutes of the General Committee Meetings, April, 1982, Kuala Lumpur*, ed. Christian Conference of Asia (Singapore: CCA, 1982), 145.

[2] Cf. Norton Ginsburg, *The Pattern of Asia* (Englewood, N.J.: Prentice-Hall, 1958). 384-385, footnote 8.

[3] John Fleming, "Some Notes on the History and Development of the Malayan Christian Council," Papers of John Robb Fleming, Box 4, Folder 1, Centre for the Study of World Christianity, New College, Edinburgh University.

"to bring together the Christian forces of Malaya for consultation on all matters concerning the Christian good of its peoples, and for common action when such action is desired, and to promote in every comity and co-operation amongst the Christian bodies of the country." MCC's formation grew out of the adverse situations during the Japanese occupation. The Anglican bishop Leonard Wilson organised a "Federation of Christian Churches" shortly after Singapore fell to Japan in 1941. The Federation aimed to hold united worship services and deal with charitable work among the poor and needy. It was suspended by the Japanese authorities in 1943. The concentration camp experiences drew church leaders to make plans for future co-operation. Trinity College, a union seminary, was founded in 1948 as a direct result of these wartime discussions.[4]

MCC commanded formal support from mainline churches in Singapore and Malaya. The founding members were the Methodists, Anglicans, Presbyterians, YMCA and the Bible Societies. By 1964, MCC members had expanded to include the Mar Thoma Syrian Church, the Salvation Army in Malaya, the Orthodox Syrian Church in Malaya, the Orthodox Church in Malaya, the Evangelical Lutheran Church of Malaya, and the Student Christian Movement.[5]

MCC's work in Singapore (and Malaya) was impressive. Its Christian Education Commission was responsible for the teaching of Christianity in government and grant-aided schools; a Literature Commission was set up to promote the distribution of Christian literature in Singapore and Malaya, and produce books for use in the churches. MCC also set up a Student Christian Centre to provide chaplaincy to the University of Malaya. These initiatives clearly grew out of perceived Communist threat in Singapore and Malaya. The Emergency Act in 1948 resulted in the birth of 'New Villages,' which in fact were resettlements of ethnic Chinese populations to remote areas, to deprive Communist 'rebels' from local support.[6] The authorities saw in the churches a reliable ally to stem the spread of Communism, especially among the young people. The government welcomed the churches to work in the 'New Villages.' The churches as well saw this to present an opportunity for service and evangelism, and so were willing partners to these government-sponsored initiatives in the 1950s. From 1952, MCC set up the New Villages Co-ordinating Committee for ministry in the resettlement camps.

Admittedly, MCC was not pro-government in all matters in the turbulent years of transition from British rule to the eventual founding of the Federation of Malaysia and the Singapore's Republic by the mid 1960s. It has taken action on public questions such as public lotteries, legalised gambling, and especially on the right to evangelise the Malay population.

However, ecumenical initiatives in the 1950s were largely foreign-driven: John Fleming, MCC's general secretary from 1952 to 1958, was a Scot missionary from China; his successor Chung Chi-An came from Taiwan. Key projects were also dependent on financial support from the West. Local contribution was minimal. This pattern in fact persisted in many post 1945 region-wide ecumenical undertakings.[7]

Nevertheless, Singapore's strategic location has clearly made it a centre of such ecumenical undertakings in Asia. Briefly:

---

[4] *At the Crossroads: The History of Trinity Theological College 1948-2005* (Singapore: Trinity Theological College, 2006), 39-40.

[5] See Malayan Christian Council, *The Churches Working Together 1964. Reports Presented to the General Council February 1965* (n.p.: Malayan Christian Council, 1965).

[6] John Fleming, *A Survey of the New Villages in Malaya* (Singapore: Malayan Christian Council, 1958); *A Survey of the New Villages in Malaya*, revised ed. (Singapore, Malayan Christian Council, 1959).

[7] See Michael Poon, "The Association for Theological Education in South East Asia, 1959-2002: a Pilgrimage in Theological Education," in *Supporting Asian Christianity's Transition from Mission to Church,* ed. Samuel Pearson (Grand Rapids: Eerdmans, 2010), 363-402, 417-432; "On Volatile Grounds: A History of Church Partnership in Asia," in *Church Partnerships in Asia: A Singapore Conversation*, ed. Michael Poon (Singapore: Genesis Books, 2011). 21-50. See also Yap, *From Prapat to Colombo* (Hong Kong: Christian Conference of Asia, 1995).

- In 1952, C. S. Smith and S. R. Anderson in their Southeast Asian tour identified Singapore to be a strategic location for training of Chinese for Christian ministry in Southeast Asia;
- In 1957, the provisional constitution of the Association of Theological Schools (ATSSEA) in South East Asia was drafted in Singapore;
- From 1957 to 1963, the first five ATSSEA (Summer) Theological Study Institutes were held in Singapore;
- In 1959, the first meeting of ATSSEA was held in Trinity Theological College;
- From 1959 to 1982, the first South East Asian theological journal *South East Asia Journal of Theology*, was published in Singapore;
- From 1959 to1974, and 1981 to 1998, Singapore was the ATSSEA headquarters, and later that of the Association for Theological Education in South East Asia (ATESEA).
- In 1963, EACC held a "Situation Conference" in Singapore, which resulted in the "Joint Action in Inter-Church Aid" initiatives in the 1960s;[8]
- In 1974, Christian Conference of Asia established its first permanent headquarters in Singapore; CCA adopted Trinity Theological College's informal logo for its own use.
- Singapore continued to be CCA headquarters until its expulsion by the authorities in 1987. The Singapore years, especially during Yap Kim Hao's tenure as CCA's general secretary from 1973 to 1985, was a time of remarkable growth, when CCA was instrumental in reconnecting Asian churches with churches in Indochina and China.[9]

To make sense of Singapore's ecumenical situation, we need to look back to the years before the Pacific War. Remarkably, we find in the 1920s and 1930s instances of local and church-based participation in inter-church co-operation. Political events in China prompted these earlier efforts. At the turn of the 20th century, ethnic Chinese communities in Singapore had become a revolutionary base for political reform in China. The heightened political and social awareness led to the forming of Christian-led social reform movements in Singapore. The founding of the Anti-Opium Society in Singapore in 1906 was a case in point. The raised national awareness also led Chinese-speaking churches to form the Singapore Chinese Christian Inter-Church Union on 10 October (National Day of China's Republic!) in 1931. It was this Inter-Church Union that invited the controversial Chinese revivalist John Sung to conduct the historic evangelistic campaigns in Singapore from 1935 to 1940. A main aim was to effect spiritual revival in the territory. After all, the Chinese speaking churches need the numbers to justify their claim for their own independent synod and annual conferences. The John Sung revivals met these local expectations. The revivals became a common platform for all Chinese speaking churches in Singapore. An inter-denominational evangelistic organisation (Singapore Christian Evangelistic League) was founded in 1935, and the first 'union' seminary (Chin Lien Seminary) two years later in 1937. These initiatives galvanised the local Christian population to face the hardship during the Japanese occupation. More far-reaching, these successes emboldened the local Chinese Christians. In 1936, the Chinese-speaking Methodist churches could set up their own 'Malaysia Chinese Mission Conference. In 1948, a Chinese YMCA came into being to advance the interests of the ethnic Chinese community, to which the foreign-led YMCA (founded in 1902) was less able to attend.

This detour to the pre 1945 years helps us to be alert to the undercurrents in the development of MCC/CCA-led ecumenical movements in the post-war years. Fleming recognised that MCC could not garner support from the Chinese-speaking churches. He identified as well the influence of Carl McIntire and the International Council of Christian Churches at work among Singaporean Chinese speaking

---

[8] *One People: One Mission. The Situation Conferences of EACC*, ed. John Fleming (Singapore: Tien Wah Press, 1963).

[9] Yap Kim Hao, *A Bishop Remembers* (Singapore: Gospel Works, 2006), 96-115. See also Yap, *From Prapat to Colombo* (Hong Kong: Christian Conference of Asia, 1995).

churches.[10] The theological liberal/conservative divide however cannot fully explain the Chinese churches' lukewarm reception towards MCC. What Fleming perhaps did not fully appreciate was the anti-colonial sentiments in the post-war world. For the local populations, British leadership were thoroughly discredited in the Fall of Singapore to Japan, and therefore no longer had the moral standing to dictate affairs in Singapore and Malaya. MCC-, CCA-, and WCC-connected top-down and foreign driven ecumenical initiatives worked, therefore, so long as they are financed by outside sources.

Ironically, new forms of American Christianity began to assert their influences in Singapore. Conservative and evangelical Christian groups in America were the first to exploit globalisation for furthering their interests. The increasingly affordable air travel and long-haul flights became a main instrument of worldwide coordination and partnership. Carl McIntire used this to huge advantage to counter WCC's influence in Asia, from his first visit to Singapore in December 1949 to the end of the 1950s.[11]

American Christianity indeed provided an alternative reference point for Singapore Christians to locate their identity. It supplanted the earlier form of Christianity that was based on trans-Atlantic demarcation. The Pacific exchange becomes increasingly important for post 1945 ecumenical movements. Singapore is clearly the Asian hub. For instance, the National Association of Evangelicals (in America) was instrumental in helping the Singapore Chinese Christian Inter-church Union to set up the Singapore Theological Seminary (later renamed Singapore Bible College) in 1952. In 1970, the World Evangelical Fellowship convened a Theological Assistance Program Consultation in Asia in Singapore (to counter the influence of WCC-sympathetic Theological Education Fund), which led to the founding of the Asia Theological Association. In other words, Singapore's central location makes it a centre of region-wide ecumenical projects, as well as a contested ground for competing interest groups from the West. Singapore becomes a theatre where different camps in post-liberal Western Christianity to globalise their local quarrels. Singapore churches, in an island republic that strictly-speaking has little tradition to build on, would at the same time exploit these social networks to locate their own spiritual identities. As a case in point, the birth of English-language based charismatic renewals among young people in 1972 owed its rise to American Pentecostalism.[12]

CCA-related ecumenical movement came to an abrupt end in Singapore in December 1987. The Singapore government closed the CCA office and deported its staff. The Singaporean authorities alleged, among others, that CCA "has been using Singapore as a base to support 'liberation movements' in other Asian countries."[13] The National Council of Churches of Singapore and the Methodist Church soon after ended their CCA membership. Singaporean churches have not restored their membership to CCA and WCC to the present-day.

The banishment from Singapore prompted CCA to undergo intense soul-searching in the General Committee Meeting in 1988. Heavy on its mind was how CCA should continue in the changed political situations in Asia. Ron O'Grady and Ninan Koshy were most critical of the Singaporean government and

---

[10] Fleming, "Some Notes on the History and Development of the Malayan Christian Council."

[11] Carl McIntire, *The Battle of Bangkok* (Collingswood: Christian Beacon Press, 1950); *ICCC-WCC: What's the Difference* (n.p.: n.p.; n.d.).

[12] Michael Poon, "The Clock Story: An Inconvenient Truth, An Inexpressible Gift," in *The Clock Tower Story: The Beginnings of Charismatic Renewals in Singapore*, ed. Michael Poon and Malcolm Tan (Singapore: Trinity Theological College, 2011), 9-23. See also James Wong, Wong, *God's Fellow Worker: A Testimony of the Lord's Call, Empowerment, and Sustenance in His Harvest Field* (Singapore: James Wong, 2008).

[13] See the discussions on the Singapore incident in *The CCA General Committee Meeting, Hong Kong April 1988* (Osaka: CCA, 1989), 38-51; Ron O'Grady, *Banished: The Expulsion of the Christian Conference of Asia from Singapore and Its Implications* (Hong Kong: International Conference of Asia, International Affairs Committee, 1990); Yap Kim Hao, *From Prapat to Columbo*, 134-145; Ninan Koshy, *A History of the Ecumenical Movement in Asia*, v. 1 (Hong Kong: CCA, 2004), 263-273.

churches. For them, Singapore misunderstood the role of the church in society and the way in which church and state relate to each other. O'Grady was especially dismissive of the fundamentalist positions of Anglicans in Singapore.[14] Koshy further insisted CCA to be "The Guardian of the Ecumenical Vision in Asia."[15] Regardless of the merits of these criticisms, perhaps CCA then did not subject their "from the fringe to the fringe" model to closer scrutiny. Such model does not invite ownership from the local churches. More important, such WCC-, CCA-, and mainline denomination-led ecumenical initiatives were too aloof to engage rival carriers of Christianity in the globalising age." The growing transnational networks, independent churches, and mega-churches would in time become their main detractors, and assert their claims to be 'guardians of the ecumenical vision' as well.

To keep Singapore secular, the government introduced the Maintenance of Religious Harmony Act in 1990. Under the Act, the Presidential Council on Religious Harmony was formed to advise the government on matters affecting the maintenance of religious harmony. In response to the 9-11 attacks in New York and Washington, in 2003, the Declaration of Religious Harmony was issued by the national bodies of all mainstream religious groups to affirm the importance of and commitment towards religious harmony. The Inter-religious Harmony Circle was formed to promote inter-religious harmony. In fact, from the 1990s the National Council of Churches in Singapore has become a main platform for Singapore churches to express Christian views on various government initiatives.

Ecumenism, however, is far from being domesticated in Singapore. 1973 onwards, charismatic Christianity has exercised an increasing role in uniting Singaporean Christians and churches for common witness in the island and in mission abroad. Ironically, charismatic Christianity is conceptually socially disruptive. But it succeeds to repackage itself to become socially respectable and politically correct in Singapore. The Love Singapore Movement (established 1995, which repackaged Peter Wagner's Spiritual Warfare Network Movement),[16] the Go4th National Mission Conference (founded 2002), and the Celebrate Christmas in Singapore (founded 2004)[17] are cases in point. These nation-wide and inter-church initiatives offer Singaporean churches to probe acceptable limits with the authorities: making Christianity publicly visible in the nation on the one hand, and Singaporean churches to be bases (!) for aggressive evangelism outside its national boundaries on the other. The recent decades also witness the rise of China and the growing geopolitical relations between Asia and Africa. Singaporean churches have capitalised in these changed landscape to assume a bridge role in connecting China with Southeast Asian churches and with churches in Africa.[18]

To end, Singapore's ecumenical situation affords sobering lessons for partnership in the third millennium when Western churches can no longer hold the sway.

Bibliography

Fleming, John. "Some Notes on the History and Development of the Malayan Christian Council." In *Papers of John Robb Fleming*. Edinburgh: Centre for the Study of World Christianity, New College, Edinburgh University.

---

[14] O'Grady, 35.

[15] Koshy, 263.

[16] See Tan-Chow MayLing. *Pentecostal Theology for the Twenty-First Century: Engaging with Multi-Faith Singapore* (Aldershot: Ashgate, 2007).

[17] Go4th National Mission Conference, http://go4th.org.sg/; Celebrate Christmas in Singapore, http://www.celebratechristmasinsingapore.org/.

[18] See Michael Poon, *Pilgrims and Citizens: Christian Social Engagement in East Asia* Today (Adelaide: ATF, 2006); *Church Partnerships in Asia*, xiii-xxv. Note also the strategic role of Singapore Anglicans in the global South church partnerships. http://www.globalsouthanglican.org/.

-----. *A Survey of the New Villages in Malaya*. Singapore: Malayan Christian Council, 1958.
-----. *A Survey of the New Villages in Malaya*. Revised ed. Singapore: Malayan Christian Council, 1959.
Ginsburg, Norton Sydney. *The Pattern of Asia*. Englewood Cliffs, N.J.,: Prentice-Hall, 1958.
Koshy, Ninan. *A History of the Ecumenical Movement in Asia*. 2 vols. Hong Kong: Christian Conference of Asia, 2004.
Malayan Christian Council. *The Churches Working Together 1964. Reports Presented to the General Council February 1965*. n.p.: Malayan Christian Council, 1965.
O'Grady, Ron. *Banished: The Expulsion of the Christian Conference of Asia from Singapore and Its Implications*. Hong Kong: Christian Conference of Asia, 1990.
Perkins, Harvey. "A Time of Vision and a Time for Vision." In *Minutes of the General Committee Meetings, April, 1982, Kuala Lumpur*, edited by Christian Conference of Asia, 141-51. Singapore: CCA, 1982.
Poon, Michael Nai-Chiu. "The Association for Theological Education in South East Asia, 1959-2002: A Pilgrimage in Theological Education." In *Supporting Asian Christianity's Transition from Mission to Church : A History of the Foundation for Theological Education in South East Asia*, edited by Samuel Campbell Pearson, 363-402, 17-32. Grand Rapids: Eerdmans, 2010.
-----. *Church Partnerships in Asia: A Singapore Conversation*, CSCA Christianity in Southeast Asia Series. Singapore: Genesis Books, 2011.
-----. *Pilgrims and Citizens: Christian Social Engagement in East Asia Today*, Series on Christianity in Asia. Adelaide: ATF Press, 2006.
Poon, Michael Nai-Chiu, and Malcolm Tan. *The Clock Tower Story: The Beginnings of the Charismatic Renewals in Singapore*, CSCA Occasional Papers Series. Singapore: Trinity Theological College, 2011.
Tan-Chow, MayLing. *Pentecostal Theology for the Twenty-First Century: Engaging with Multi-Faith Singapore*. Aldershot: Ashgate, 2007.
Trinity Theological College. *At the Crossroads: The History of Trinity Theological College, 1948-2005*. Singapore: Trinity Theological College, 2006.
Yap, Kim Hao. *A Bishop Remembers*. Singapore: Gospel Works, 2006.
-----. *From Prapat to Colombo : History of the Christian Conference of Asia (1957-1995)*. Hong Kong: Christian Conference of Asia, 1995.

(71) CHURCHES TOGETHER IN GOD'S MISSION – SRI LANKA

Stephen Arulampalam

Introduction

"*Oikoumene*" is derived from the Greek word *oikein*, which means "to inhabit". With the meaning of "inhabited earth" or "the whole world", the term has been used since Herodotos (5th century). The Church and The World, Spiritual and missionary contain social dimensions that belong together in a comprehensive understanding of *oikoumene*. *Oikoumene* is a relational, dynamic concept which extends beyond the fellowship of Christians and churches to the human community within the whole creation. The transformation of the *oikoumene* as the "inhabited earth" into the living household (*oikos*) of God- remains the calling of the ecumenical movement. The ecumenical movement represents the manifestation of Christian concern for a world community in Justice and Peace. In the light of this, churches in Sri Lanka are being called by God to go beyond their barriers to promote wider ecumenism. I would like to make some suggestions to promote wider ecumenism among the church denominations and other living Religions.[1]

A Brief History of the Ecumenical Movement in Sri Lanka

Pietism, evangelical awakening, modern missionary movements and nationalism opened the way for churches in Sri Lanka to think about church unity.

It is recorded that Harward, a missionary in Sri Lanka, had "no small satisfaction that, when the first English clergymen landed here, our house was the first into which they entered on their arrival in Colombo, and our pulpit was the first from which they began their missionary career." This was the testimony of the pioneer Wesleyan missionary writing in 1818.

In the early period of missions a good relationship prevailed and the cordiality between the Church of England missionaries and the Methodists is a marked contrast to the bitterness that arose later on. The influence of the Oxford movement which laid special emphasis on the authority of the Bishop had its repercussions in Ceylon too. The leaders of the movement recalled the Anglicans to their Catholic traditions. Methodism, they said, was outside the Catholic Church, and its ministry and its sacraments were not valid. Hence the influence of the Oxford movement was felt in Church relations in Ceylon shortly after 1838.

The Baptist and the Wesleyan Missionaries shared one another's chapels and frequently spoke on the same platforms at public meetings. However, there was not much fellowship with the Roman Catholics and the Protestant denominations during the early years. In the North there was a definite attempt on the part of the missionaries to cooperate and the records state that there was a monthly meeting to which the Wesleyan and both the C.M.S and American missionaries came together for fellowship and prayer. At the first meeting in August 1819, the topic was "Brotherly Love"[2] The Wesleyan missionaries had as their motto John Wesley's words, "Friends of all and enemies of none", and comity began with a partition of the field. The American missionaries confined themselves to a purely Tamil area amongst the people in the Jaffna peninsula. Similarly when the missionaries of the Church Missionary Society arrived in the North, a

---

[1] Virginia Fabella, M.M, R.S. Sugirtharajah, Dictionary of Third World Theologies, Orbis Books: Maryknoll, 2000, p.82.

[2] "A Century in Ceylon" 1816-1916. Helen I. Root

distinct territory was assigned to them. All this was done by common consent, thereby avoiding the waste caused by overlapping and needless rivalry. In those early years the denomination of a convert was commonly determined by topography rather than Theology.

In 1902 the different churches had their own programme of activity and there was hardly any idea of comity and co – operation. There was however an organization known as the "Christian Alliance," with J. A. Spear as its first president. This group met for fellowship and prayer and exchange of views. The Jaffna Christian Union was founded in November 1907 and also in 1922 the first united Christian Women's Teacher Training was begun at Vembadi, in the Northern part of Sri Lanka. The World Missionary Conference held in Edinburgh in 1910 was the great occasion which gave impetus to the reunion of churches. There was a greater interest among the laity too to work towards a more effective unifying of the separate churches. The visit of John R. Mott to Colombo in 1912 not only brought zest and enthusiasm for closer cooperation among the churches but also led to the formation of the National Christian Council of Ceylon. In 1939 the Christian Seva Ashram was started ecumenically at Maruthanarmadam in the Northern part of Sri Lanka for inviting Christians to come together for worship and common life. D. T. Niles (Methodist), Bishop Kulendran (CSI), Sevak. Selvaretnam (Periyannan) were instrumental in building this Ashram.

In 1934 there was convened the first conference of Church leaders in Ceylon to discuss the problems relating to Church Union. The conference met at Trinity College, Kandy, from August 17th to 21st . As a result of this conference, there was formed society in Ceylon of the 'Friends of Reunion.' The earliest impetus towards Church Union in Ceylon came, however, through the participation of the Congregational, Methodist, and Anglican Churches in Ceylon in the South India negotiations. The Congregational Church (the Jaffna Council of the South India United Church) was part of the negotiating Churches in South India, while the Methodist and Anglican Churches in Ceylon sent observers. In the final stages, the South India Scheme of union was referred to the various dioceses of the Church of India, Burma and Ceylon, and as such was discussed also and voted upon by the Diocesan council of the Church Ceylon. The vote was in favour of the South India Dioceses going into the proposed Union. This contact with the progress of the South India negotiations was invaluable as were also the services of intercession, the observance of Christian Unity Week, and the Church Union conferences arranged both by the 'Friends of Reunion' and the National Christian Council of Ceylon. This paved the way for the opening of formal Church Union conversations.

The invitation to the Churches in Ceylon to explore the possibility of opening negotiations for Church Union was issued by the Ceylon Provincial Synod of the Methodist Church in February 1940 and, with the acceptance of the invitation by the Churches, there was set up in November 1940 the Joint Committee on Church Union. The Churches represented were the Church of Ceylon (Anglican), the Methodist Church, the Churches in the Presbytery of Ceylon, the Baptist Church and the Jaffna Council of the South India United Church (Congregationalist). These five Churches were the five Constituent Churches of the National Christian Council of Ceylon. The Dutch Reformed Church, however, which was one of the Churches in the Presbytery of Ceylon, withdrew from the Negotiating Committee in 1952. In 1955 a new the church union scheme was introduced and accepted by churches. In 1971, all churches had voted in favour of the Church union scheme.[3]

In 1963 the Theological College of Lanka was founded at Pilimatalawa, where the joint training of Anglicans, Methodists and Baptists is undertaken. The attempt here is to build together a fellowship that will continue when these candidates go out to take up their work as ministers of the Gospel. It was at this stage that 3 members of the Church of Ceylon challenged in a court of law the vote on Church Union taken at the 86th Annual sessions of the Diocesan Council of the Diocese of Colombo on the 27th, 28th and 29th

[3] Scheme of Church Union in Ceylon, The Christian Literature Society, 1963

October 1971. The voting was as follows 55 voting for the resolution, 11 against, and 3 abstaining out of 69 members of the clergy who were present. It was pointed out that there were averments in the plaint that took up the position that the voting did not reflect the consent of two thirds of the entire order of the clergy which had been obtained for the acceptance and approval of this Resolution The Judgment was given on June 20, 1974, and the 89th session of the Diocesan council has passed by but Church Union is still not a reality. The sin of division still persists and "may all be one" is still the prayer of the Christian community in Sri Lanka.

On 30th of November 2008, the NCC Churches agreed to go through the experience of confederation. This particular event opens the gates to the churches to not only exchanging the pulpit and altars but also sharing resources among the churches.

The Role of the Ecumenical Movements in the Context of Anti-Conversion Bill and War in Sri Lanka

St. James College, a state school, where I gained my primary education is nearly 140 years old. The Old Boys associations of that school celebrated its centenary celebration in 2009. In the recent past, some of the former students formed a Hindu Old Boys Association of the school. They have dual membership. Hindu old boys have membership on the Old Boys Association as well as their own association. These former students who were responsible for the formation of the Old Boys Hindu front felt that the leading people in the Old Boys Association are Christians and that they dominate. Religious tensions entered the schools as well; from what I hear there are tensions among different religious groups in many other schools as well. All these are because of the history of Christianity in our country. The people of other faiths have grievances against Christians.

When we think about the mission under the colonial period, European super powers had reached the entire world during the 19th and 20th centuries; we can see that colonizers and missionaries sailed in the same boats. According to the understanding of colonialists they have civilized the inhabited world. Nevertheless it is very clear that Christianization and colonization are two sides of the same coin. Especially in Sri Lanka colonial powers (Portuguese 1505 to 1658, Dutch 1659 to 1796 and British 1796 to 1948) had ruled for over 450 hundred years (1505 – 1948 C.E.) and during that period they had introduced Christianity in different ways to Sri Lankan society.[4] In 1796, the Church Missionary Society (CMS) and the Wesleyan Missionary in 1814, the Baptist 1812, and the American Board of Ceylon Foreign Mission 1818 came to Sri Lanka to present an image of Christ which was loaded with western triumphalism and exclusivist and dividing attitudes. Their main focus was converting people from Hinduism to Christianity.

'Bitter experiences of past missionary movements still remain in the hearts of people; there were various misappropriated approaches implemented by those colonial powers.[5] The aspects of religion and nationality are closely integrated with each other. Also, the other major allegation against the Christians is cultural pollution like mixed marriages, destroying temples, killing of some religious leaders as well as Buddhist monks and building churches in villages initiated by them since the colonial period.

Majority of Hindus clearly expressed that Christian churches are the representatives of western nationalism and to be a Christian is to be less a Sri-Lankan. They assumed that they are using Christianity as an instrument to create the division among the Tamils as in the beginning Aryans and Brahmins used caste as an instrument to separate Tamils. In the light of this, religious persecution started in Jaffna in the Northern part of Sri Lanka.

---

[4] Lorez F. B., *History of Colombo* (Colombo:Diocese of Colombo,1946)p.102.

[5] B. Bastiampillai, *Religion- Conversion or Conviction*, Daily News, 2004, March 12th, p.10.

Since 1985, as a minority religion, Christianity faced many violent attacks by the Buddhist movements in Sri Lanka. Most attacks were instigated by the movement known as the Buddhist fundamentalists and Hindu fundamentalists in Sri Lanka. One such example is an attack on 2nd December 2004 in the village of Kammalawa, Kuliyapitiya, in western Sri Lanka. On that day more than one hundred people arrived at the Believer's Church threatening to kill the pastor if he did not close down the church. That same night they attacked the church with rocks damaging roof tiles, a door and several windows. Following this three people were taken into custody by the police.[6]

A political party grew out of the organization known as "*Sinhala Urumaya*"[7] whose founder was Thilak Karunaratne. "*Jathika Hela Urumaya"* is a party led by Buddhist monks and on May 31st 2004, this party consisted of *11 Monks* and *42-laity* totalling fifty-three members, and their election manifesto emphasized the need to establish a 'Dharma Rajjya" (Righteous Kingdom).[8]

> Various factions of Buddhist extremists are calling on the government to pass a law to ban conversions. Clerics in several districts have vowed to take collective action against Christians, particularly those working amongst the poverty-stricken rural areas. Buddhist leaders and organisations are also exerting pressure on the prime minister and the government to rescind visas for Christian missionaries.[9]

Accusations of unethical conversion have led to an outpouring of public support for legislation to outlaw such activity. In response, the Jathika Hela Urumaya (JHU) drafted a bill entitled the "Prohibition of Forcible Conversion of Religion"[10] and introduced this in parliament in July 2004. Not to be outdone, the Sri Lankan government, led by the Minister of Buddhist Affairs, prepared its own bill which received the approval of the Cabinet and is currently being redrafted for submission in parliament.[11] Because of the various arguments, debates and the Supreme Court decision these bills were not passed. Even the Roman Catholic Church and the NCC churches came to the court with their arguments. And also the main concerns[12] regarding the bill were highlighted and an Inter religious Council[13] was proposed as an alternative to mediate in matters of religious disputes. The closing to the letter captures the gist of the argument of the Church Ecumenical leaders. While we may have made some errors in the past, we believe Jesus Christ is leading us on a journey from privilege to responsible servant-hood. In the recent past, we have strived to transform into a more open, understanding and inclusive Church rooted in and appreciative of our ancient heritage and culture. This incident indicates how Christian churches responded ecumenically and inter religiously to the new crisis.

I would like to focus your attention to another incident now, since as a country, we are going through the process of reconciliation. Siva, a student who studies in Grade 5, has gone through much internal displacement. In fact he was born in the midst of displacement and floods. He is very clever and intelligent. His purpose was to get good results in the Grade: 5 scholarship examination this year. On August 11th, due to the shelling from Mugamalai area[14], Siva and others also were forcibly displaced from Pallai. Siva was

---

[6]http://www.globalengage.org/media/article.aspx?id=3094,(27.05.2008).

[7]A group of people who worked for the Sinhalese Nationality.

[8] http://www.Amarasara.Net/jhu/jhu/ - samuluwa l. htm p.

[9] http://jmm.aaa.net.au/articles/10371.htm (12.05.2008)

[10] See: http://www.persecution.net/srilankalaw.htm; http://wwrn.org/articles/7531/; http://www.cpalanka.org/the-prohibition-of-forcible-conversion-of-religion-bill/; http://www.nceasl.org/NCEASL/rlc/statements/Bill_for_the_Prohibition_of_Forcible_Conversion_of_Religion.php

[11] http://www.christianitytoday.com/ct/2004/september/2.23.html

[12] http://www.christiantoday.com/article/second.anticonversion.law.in.sri.lankan.parliament/2657.htm

[13] http://religionsforpeace.org/news/press/press-release.html; http://www.rfp-europe.eu/index.cfm?id=202658

[14] Mugamalai area - heavy fighting between LTTE and Government's military is taking place.

not able to sit for the Grade 5 scholarship exam which was supposed to be held on 12th of August, 2006. He is living with regret and tears due to his frustration.

"Samartha says that building community is like building a good city, takes time, effort and planning. One needs to lay pipelines to bring in fresh water as well as gutters to drain off the waste. A city needs places to do serious work as well as parks and playgrounds and meeting places.[15] In light of this statement building a community is a necessary mission of the church in the context of the anti-conversion bill and the post-war situation. The most burning issue in Sri Lanka now has been the problem of the Tamil and Singhalas. The damage caused to the Tamil and Singhala communities before and after the arms struggle of the Tamil militants is immeasurable. Similarly, the right of the Muslim minority in Sri Lanka, especially in the North and East, should be taken into account with serious concerns to find a just solution. These are problems of human dignity and equal rights of the minorities, along with millions of poor and the marginalized in Sri Lanka. Therefore reconciliation among the political victims should be the necessary concern of the church. Bosch indicates that mission means serving, healing and reconciling: these are interdependent.[16] This kind of thinking assists the church to widen the necessity of coming together for serving and healing the wounds of the people. Therefore, we should be ready to go beyond our identity in order to see the otherness of others.

On the 21st of March in 2009, a Conference was organized by the Roman Catholic Church in the Northern part of Sri Lanka in Kilinochi. Widows and Children from the Northern part of Sri Lanka (Tamils), Southern part of Sri Lanka (Sinhalese) who were affected by the war were invited for this conference. Four hundred and fifty (450) people participated at the conference and they started sharing their experiences and memories. While they were sharing their stories; a fifteen year- old Tamil boy started sharing his memories. He had lost his parents due to the war and was living with his two younger brothers at present. While he was sharing, he gave up mid-way as he could not continue his story due to shock and frustration. While he was still crying, a widow from the South (a sinhala) who lost her husband due to the battle in the north, presently living with three children suddenly got up and said "My dear son don't cry, from today onwards you will be my son." This particular historical and moving statement forced churches and other living religions to work together for peace and reconciliation among the war victims ecumenically and inter-religiously. Therefore, we are called by God to promote ecumenism in the context of the anti-conversion bill and war.

Suggestions and Conclusion

1. Introducing inclusive language is very appropriate in the context of religious pluralistic community. In John 4: 24, Jesus introduced God as a spirit and this concept brought Samarians and Jews together. In the same way, churches should be ready to use inclusive language in their life and worship to bring people together.
2. Let us take steps to correct the selective fundamentalist reading of scripture. This means developing ourselves through study of the Bible, for instance helping people to re-read texts like John 14: 6 with help found within John's Gospel itself.
3. We need to develop an inclusive Christology and help people to identify God revealed in Jesus at work within other religions without claiming that the Gospel or the Bible is the source of inspiration. God's Spirit is a spirit of freedom.

---

[15] S. Wesley Ariarajah, *Not Without my Neighbour: Issues in Interfaith Relations* (Geneva: WCC Publications,1999) P. 24

[16] David Bosch, *Transforming Mission: Paradigm shift in Theology of Mission* (Maryknoll: Orbis Books,2006)P.494

4. We need to identify people of other faiths who show remarkable transcendence from both fundamentalist and communalist attitudes and work together closely with them, encouraging them in their witness within their own communities and enabling Christians to overcome their communal prejudices by accepting such people as real close friends without always wanting to convert them.
5. Education in our schools should have co-curricular courses which enable better understanding of each other's faith.

Bibliography

S. Wesley Ariarajah, *Not Without my Neighbour: Issues in Interfaith Relations* (Geneva: WCC Publications, 1999)

Bastiampillai. B, *Religion- Conversion or Conviction*, Daily News, 12th of March 2004,

David Bosch, *Transforming Mission: Paradigm shift in Theology of* Mission (Maryknoll: Orbis Books, 2006),

W. Carr (Ed), *The New Dictionary of Pastoral Studies* (Michigan: Grand Rapids, 2002)

Virginia Fabella, M.M, R.S. Sugirtharajah, Dictionary of Third World Theologies, (Maryknoll:Orbis Books, 2000)

Lorez F. B, *History of Colombo* (Colombo: Diocese of Colombo, 1946),

Norman E. Thomas (Ed), "Messianic Mission:" Classic *Texts in Mission and World Christianity,* (New York: Orbis Books, 1995)

Scheme of Church Union in Ceylon, The Christian Literature Society, 1963

A group of people who worked for the Sinhalese Nationality, http://www.globalengage.org/media/article.aspx?id=3094, accessed on (27.05.2011)

JHU, http://www. Amarasara. Net/jhu/jhu/ - samuluwa l. htm p.1, accessed on (10.02.2010)

(72) Churches Together in God's Mission – Taiwan

Chiu Shu-pin

Development of Christian Mission in Taiwan

As Yap Kim Hao points out, the Ecumenical Movement in Asia emerged from the western missionary movement.

Taiwan first encountered Christianity in the 17th century during the period of the Dutch occupation. At that time, "Vereenigde Oost-Indische Compagnie (VOC)" was the chartered company to run the affairs of Dutch colonies and missionaries were also sent by the company to spread Catholic Christianity in Northern Taiwan. The Dutch missionary movement lasted for only 38 years (1624-1662) until its defeat by a Ming Dynasty General, Koxinga (國姓□), from Mainland China.

It was two hundred years later that Christianity was accompanied by the footprints of missionaries to reach the land of Taiwan again. Christian mission in Taiwan can be described as a branch of missionary movements of the church in Europe and North America in 19th century. Catholic priests were first to arrive in 1859. During this period, the first protestant missionary to Taiwan was Dr. James L. Maxwell sent by the Presbyterian Church of England (now the United Reformed Church), who started his task with his assistants in southern Taiwan in 1865. Meanwhile, the beginning of the history of missionary evangelization in northern Taiwan was marked by Rev. George Leslie Mackay's (from the Presbyterian Church in Canada) landing at Tamsui in 1872.

The third wave of development for the Christian Church was the result from the Chinese Nationalist Party's loss of their sovereignty to the Communists in Mainland China in 1949. Following the arrival of more than 150,000 refugees from China, the Mandarin Churches was affiliated to the western missions, such as the Lutheran Church, the Baptist Church, the Methodist Church, and the Anglican Church. All of them strived for evangelizing those new comers. Local self-established Churches, such as Christian Assembly Church, Church of God, Bread of Life Christian Church, and Mandarin-speaking Church, were also established after this time.

A Historical Sketch of Inter-denominational Competition and Discord

Since the second coming of Christianity in Taiwan was brought about by the Catholic Church and Presbyterian Churches, consequently, competition and tension arouse from denominational division. Apart from the historical factor of dogmatic differences, the conflicts also took place because of the zeal to increase church membership. Such conflicts, criticizing each other were reflected in their documents

During the early period of Japanese colonization (1895-1945), Japanese government was in amity with Christianity, and it basically did not interfere with the church's evangelization activities. Church attendance rose because churches were seen as shelters from the riot of transition period. The Japanese Church showed its consideration for evangelizing the Japanese residents and therefore started to establish Japanese churches in Taiwan. However, after the breakout of the World War II (1939-45), Japan was in opposition to almost all the Western missionaries' mother nations, its policy regarding religion turned from drafting management into tight monitoring. Western missionaries were not only advised to leave their mission field by their home countries, but were also expelled from Taiwan by Japanese colonial government. The tension and competition between Taiwanese Churches became alleviated.

After the War, a large number of Chinese Christians - following the withdrawal of the Chinese Nationalist Party - arrived and reestablished churches in Taiwan. Most of these churches, affiliated to traditional protestant denominations, hold pretty close theological stances to the Presbyterian Church, nevertheless, some of the newly founded churches, such as Christian Assembly Church and True Jesus Church which were introduced into Taiwan in the mid 20's of 20th century, were much more critical of the others. Their church frames and teachings were distinctly different from those forenamed Churches, therefore, they criticized their forerunners fiercely, and that made a grêat impact on church relations. Besides, the competition for increasing church membership, especially among aboriginals, rose again by the termination of Japanese colonization. Since then, it was not only the Catholic Church and Presbyterian Church that once again enthusiastically plunged into striving for converting non-believers and establishing new churches, but those newly introduced and founded Churches also joined the competition. The competition caused hostility and misunderstanding among those denominations and Churches, and even split aboriginal groups living in the same villages.

Another reason for discord among Churches and denominations were differences of church history and perspectives on political concerns. The Presbyterian Church in Taiwan (PCT) has been the oldest and biggest denomination, and it has identified with the people, the land and the history of Taiwan. Its concerns for political reformation, human rights, sovereignty of Taiwan and the future of Taiwan became more unequivocal in 1970's. It even made a solemn political declaration that Taiwan must be "a new and independent country." (A Declaration on Human Rights, August 16, 1977) Its political articulation gave rise to a great pressure from the Nationalist Government. On the other hand, since most of the other denominations and churches were transplanted to Taiwan from China, they were pro-government. They either blamed PCT for intervening in politics, or broke off relations with the PCT. The inter-denominational dialogue and ecumenical participation were therefore suspended because of pressure from the government. PCT has been taking an active part in international church organizations, but most of the other Churches were opposed to ecumenism at the instigation of the government. For instance, World Council of Churches (WCC) was wrongly accused of being fraternal to the Communists, as a result of which the PCT was once forced to renounce WCC. After the 70's, the disparity extended to theological positions due to PCT's concern for the socio-political contexts in Taiwan and its openness to various emerging theological trends like contextual theology, liberation theology, and feminist theology.

Expressions of Ecumenism in Taiwan

Similar to other parts of the world, the Ecumenical Movement in Taiwan was called forth by protestant churches, such as the Presbyterian Church, one of the oldest and the biggest Christian denominations in Taiwan. The Presbyterian churches in southern Taiwan first set up the southern presbytery in 1896, which was known as Tainan Synod of the Presbyterian Church at that time; Taipei Synod also summoned its first meeting in Tamsui in 1904. Taking the similarities of their origin, belief and system into consideration, representatives from both sides gathered to discuss the issues of unification in 1912. During the period of preparation, cooperation was put into effect by using the same hymnal book, publications, and church systems. In 1952, the two Synods approved the motion of unification respectively and convened the first general assembly of the PCT. Soon after its coming into existence, the PCT joined international church organizations like World Council of Churches (WCC), World Presbyterian Alliance, World Alliance of Reformed Churches (WARC), and the Christian Conference of Asia (CCA).

As for promoting partnership within Taiwanese Churches, several local interdenominational organizations have made efforts in furthering coöperation including:

(1) Churches Union of the Republic of China. This had originated with the Chinese National government in 1954, was loosely structured, has been serving the political interests of the government, but does not substantially function as an ecumenical organization.

(2) National Council of Churches of Taiwan (NCCT). Founded in 1991,it is the forerunner of the Ecumenical Cooperative Committee of Taiwan (formed in 1966), which replaced the Ecumenical Consultative Committee of Taiwan (created in 1963, the Catholic Church acceded in 1967). The Mission statement of NCCT is "The purpose of the Council is to attain unity in Christ, through strengthening the relationship of churches, promoting cooperation in various services, undertaking social welfare, charitable works, and educational matters, proclaiming the Christian message, and participating in the common mission of the church to the world."

(3) Chinese Christian Evangelistic Association (CCEA). This started with an inter-church evangelization movement, "Year 2000 Gospel Movement" in 1987. It registered with the government in the name of Chinese Christian Evangelistic Association and aimed to increase church membership to 2,000,000, congregations to 10,000, and missionaries to 200. Although the movement did not fulfill its goal, the association was transformed into a permanent organization focused on promoting church growth and cooperation, business as mission, family and community development and world mission. For these organizations, ecumenism has been expressed in engaging in the tasks of churches of evangelism, missions, prayers, social welfare, and emergency rescue care.

There are also some "non-organizational" instances of co-operation among Taiwanese Churches. Exchange of faculty among Protestant seminaries, and among Protestant and Catholic seminaries are acceptable, even encouraged. Although Churches maintain diverse perspectives on political and social concerns because of theological stances and political factors, many examples of cooperation in issues of improving social welfares, human rights, and Bible translation have been set. Since Churches recognize the importance of living and working together, the tensions and conflicts, especially among the aboriginal churches, are eased off through joint activities of celebrating Christmas, Easter, and evangelistic services. Dialogues about gospel and culture, contextualization, and other shared interests take place on the base of mutual respect and hence bring about reconciliation. With regard to inter-religious dialogue little can be noted possibly because of difficulties in finding a common ground in traditional belief of truth, and lacking practical benefits resulting from dialogue.

Conclusion

To sum up, ecumenism in Taiwan is still being processed, since differences of historical experiences, living contexts, doctrines, and practices contributing to the divisions of Churches have not been easily settled. In addition to the above, there arise divergent issues and opinions out of the changing society and it will take time for Churches to clarify how to deal with these emerging challenges together. Nevertheless, ecumenism does not mean to live and work in uniformity, but to respect the differences of one another. The "Catholic" Church we foresee is the one that is unified and tolerates plurality and diversity.

References

Yap Kim Hao, "Ecumenical Movement," A Dictionary of Asian Christianity, 258.

Cheng Yang'en, "A General Survey of the Development of Protestant Christianity in Taiwan." http://taiwanpedia.culture.tw/en/content?ID=368

Ku Weiying, "A General Survey of the Development of Catholic Church in Taiwan." http://taiwanpedia.culture.tw/en/content?ID=369&Keyword=catholic

Yap Kim Hao. "Ecumenical Movement." A Dictionary of Asian Christianity, 258-65.

中華基督教福音協進會。http://www.ccea.org.tw
《台灣基督長老教會百年史》。台北：台灣基督長老教會，1965。
王昭文。〈教派合作的虛與實〉。《新使者》90 (2005, 10): 11-14。
天主教會台灣地區主教團。http://www.catholic.org.tw
房志榮。〈地方教會與合一運動〉。《神學論集》28 (1976): 221-29。
----------〈大公運動〉。《神學論集》92 (1992):193-201。
臺灣聖經公會。http://www.biblesociety-taiwan.org
蔡維民。〈宣教主義下的宗教對話〉。《世界宗教學刊》1(2003):101-28。

(73) CHURCHES TOGETHER IN GOD'S MISSION – THAILAND

Pradit Takerngrangsarit and Kenneth Dobson

Protestant Christianity came to Thailand concurrently, but by no means coincidentally, with the industrialization and modernization of the component states that now comprise Thailand. The missionaries were key players in modernization. It was the technical expertise of the missionaries in the 1830s and 1840s that the kings (Rama III, IV and later Rama V) found valuable, particularly the models of education and scientific-based medicine the missionaries brought. Throughout the 19th century the main, and practically the only, missionary agency working in Siam (central and southern Thailand) and in Lanna and Lao regions (northern Thailand and parts of Laos and south China) was the American Presbyterian Mission of the Presbyterian Church in the USA. The Presbyterians were full participants with other Protestant missionary endeavors of that time in the effort not to overlap, duplicate and compete with each other. So the Presbyterians worked in Thailand, the Methodists in Malaya, the Baptists in Ava (Burma) and everybody worked in their own part of China while nobody worked in most of Laos.

By the time the Presbyterians were celebrating the centennial of their mission in Siam in 1928 the vision of the times had become the vision of the mission: a united church. By the time Siam became a thoroughly modern constitutional monarchy called Thailand in 1932, and the united Church of Christ in Thailand was organized in 1934, the door was left open for all Protestants to join, and it was hoped and expected that they would, for the trends favored the ecumenical vision. Those joining at the time included mostly Presbyterian congregations along with a few American Baptists (including the first Protestant Christian Church in Siam, Maitreejit Church in Bangkok) and churches of the British Churches of Christ and Lutherans of the German Marburger Mission. The ecumenical movement, born at the Worldwide Missionary Conference in Edinburgh in 1910 was leading toward the World Council of Churches in 1948 with the still glowing hope of uniting and more uniting. Unity and cooperation were in the wind and the wind was equated with the Holy Spirit. The Church of Christ in Thailand was one of the founding members of the World Council of Churches.

But the same impetus which prompted the World Council of Churches, namely the compelling need for a united response to the horror and suffering that World War II brought, also opened the country of Thailand to other Protestant missionary enterprises. Another thing which encouraged other Protestant groups to come to Thailand at the end of World War II was the fact that such a large percentage of the population (99%) was still not Christian. The field looked white to the harvest and the Church of Christ in Thailand was missing from whole areas of the country. The main agencies undertaking new post-war efforts were the Christian and Missionary Alliance, the Seventh Day Adventists, the Southern Baptists and the China Inland Mission (re-named the Overseas Missionary Fellowship). It can be said that the one thing these diverse groups had in common was an unwillingness to cooperate in an ecumenical church effort. As elsewhere, these groups were also protective of theological positions which they were not willing to compromise. So the period of 1950 to 1980 was one of rapid expansion of missionary agents and operations and a disintegration of the vision of there ever being just one church for Thailand. The Thai government insisted on the right, in principle, to monitor and control all Christian enterprises, as it did Buddhism and Islamic religious work. But in practice religions are left alone as long as they do nothing to undermine the three basic national institutions — the Royal institution of the King, the national state, and the institution of religion (actually meaning Buddhism under the leadership of the Supreme Patriarch of the Sangha). The proliferation of missionary groups was addressed by a government decree that all Christian groups must register and report activities annually under one of the five organizations existing at the time: the Roman Catholic Church, the Church of Christ in Thailand, the Southern Baptists, the Mission (i.e. the

Seventh Day Adventists) and the Evangelical Fellowship of Thailand. The Evangelical Fellowship was organized in 1969 expressly for the purpose of forming an organization to register all the diverse groups who would not or could not join any one of the other four. The EFT organization has no role in the work of its members, and the Fellowship is not a Church but a collection of church organizations and mission undertakings of a great variety.

During the 1970s South East Asia was a region of serious unrest and population migration. Communist insurgency movements threatened to bring war to Thailand as it had to Indo-China or revolution as it had in Indonesia. Revolutions rocked Thailand in 1973 and 1976. Civil war, in fact if not in name, spread in Burma, and then there was the disaster of the killing fields in Cambodia. Because of these conflicts, migration into and through Thailand made world headlines and had an impact on the country. Ethnic minority villages began to proliferate in Thailand alongside kinfolks who had been in the country for generations. Through the patient work of H.M. the King of Thailand, however, most of the ethnic minority groups living in Thailand began to think of themselves as Thai, rather than as isolated ethnic groups or as temporary residents from Burma or Laos. This set the stage in the 1980s for large Karen and Lahu Baptist groups to join the Church of Christ in Thailand, which, by some counts, doubled the number of Christians in the CCT.

During the 1980s the rigid divisions between various groups began to soften. Cooperative efforts became possible and then became common. Community radio stations, social outreach, evangelistic campaigns, prayer groups, health and human services and educational efforts including the United Bible Society involved Christians of all labels. Simultaneously, the theological and doctrinal stances of the Protestant groups grew closer together and became less strident than a generation earlier. This is not to say, however, that the ecumenical vision revived. The ecumenical movement as it once was, is no more and never will be again. The churches in Thailand can still jointly claim only something like 1% of the population as members, with about the same number unattached (and uncounted) self-designating Christian believers outside the Church. The religious work of the churches is still mainly parochial, with and for church members and converts. Cooperative efforts are overwhelmingly done as community efforts by individuals with church-related institutions (schools and hospitals) sometimes participating, but not often as official church representatives. On a personal and local level, however, the amount of friendship and openness has never been greater. This could not inconceivably lead to a renewal of an ecumenical vision, but that is still not in view.

The Church of Christ in Thailand remains the largest, and in many ways the only, supporter of ecumenism. But it is an ecumenism that would be unrecognizable by our ancestors.

At the same time, a new generation of missionaries has been arriving in Thailand from Korea. These various Presbyterian missionaries are also variously committed to a united church strategy. Some insist on virtual autonomy, others cooperate in parallel endeavors, and some consider themselves full participants in the missions and ministries of the CCT. This new generation from Korea is augmented by volunteers and others from the USA and Europe, but as a whole the new generation is unmotivated by ecumenism. In fact, the stance of this individualistic generation militates against ecumenism.

As the 21st century gets underway ecumenism has been reinterpreted in Thailand as it has by the World Council of Churches as an agency or aspect of cooperation and mutual ministry. Thailand is a crossroads for South East Asia. To an extent, through the end of the first decade Burma remains all but closed although doors are reopening rapidly. Church work in Laos is handicapped, particularly any that would appear ecumenical. And the groups in southern China ethnically related to Thai people are just beginning to be able to re-establish ties with neighboring Church groups. Thailand's strategic location was one of the reasons that the Christian Conference of Asia (CCA) moved its headquarters to Payap University in north Thailand in 2006. The new era of ecumenism is oriented towards aspects of ministry and mission rather than toward organic unity. There is occasional cooperative participation in city-wide evangelistic campaigns, retreats by pastors, seminary students and women's groups, and a willingness by national church groups to co-sponsor projects with Buddhists. Refugee rights, both for those who have crossed borders into Thailand and those who are internally displaced, and the rights of documented and undocumented workers and stateless people, human trafficking, HIV/AIDS and ethnic cultural preservation are among the top ranking issues being addressed in ecumenical and united ways. In coming decades the thaw in relations could reignite the flame of ecumenism in a new generation.

We live together, but our enclaves are largely separate. There are paths through our hedges and chinks in our fences, but they still keep us apart more than promote togetherness. We work together separately, as it were. We work together on large national efforts, but we do it separately. We work together on short-term local projects more frequently. On the whole we talk and visit and collaborate but we go back to our separate homes and lives. The level of hostility or suspicion may be less, but.... There is still a "but" when we try to think of these others as Christian brothers and sisters. "They are Christian, too, but...."

Bibliography

Church of Christ in Thailand, Archives of the. Payap University, Chiang Mai, Thailand. www.payap.ac.th

Swanson, Herbert. "Khrischak Muang Nua" (the text is in English, an analytical / critical study of Thai Church history). Bangkok: Chuan Press, 1984.

Wells, Kenneth. *History of the Protestant Church in Thailand*. Bangkok: Suriyaban Press (no date, 1950s).

See also Resources for the Study og Thain Church History, http://www.herbswanson.com

(74) Churches Together in God's Mission – Timor Leste

Albino DaCosta

1. Introduction

Timor Leste is the youngest country in Asia and has a young member church in the Christian Conference of Asia. Thus, our experience in the ecumenical movement is relatively new compared to other countries in Asia. We praise God for the experiences that Igreja Protestante iha Timor Lorosa (IPTL) got by joining the WCC and WCRC in 1991 and CCA in 2000. Our journey together in the ecumenical movement through CCA, WCC, WCRC and other bilateral relationships with ecumenical churches has encouraged us through mutual respect and understanding as one body of Jesus Christ in spite of the diversity in life and traditions. Here we are pleased to share our experience and the fruit of the ecumenical movement in our journey, particularly as a member of the regional body, the CCA.

2. IPTL Brief History[1]

First of all, I have to admit that we do not have a complete written history yet. The available documents that we have are fragments of the story of the church, which still need to be compiled to have a full story of the history of IPTL.

To begin with, Roman Catholicism was adopted as the official religion of Timor Leste, being a colony of Portugal, or "*Provincias Ultramarinas*" (Overseas Province). The Igreja Protestante iha Timor Lorosa'e (IPTL, Protestant Church in East Timor) was known as Gereja Kristen di Timor Timur (GKTT), which had a long journey from the colonial period up to date. Beside her long journey, IPTL also had a unique experience – that of having been organized and developed by the people of East Timor itself since the beginning whereas other churches , even the churches in Asia , still have a strong relationship with a particular church in Europe or America as their "mother church", the fruit of the work of missionaries from other continents.

In my conversation with a few people, I gathered that they also recognize that the Protestant Church came together with the colonial expansion. Here I only focus on the period from 1950 up to now. In the 1950's few missionaries (from Holland, America, Angola, Germany) came to Timor Leste in a short period of time. They came as pilgrims and they were able to distribute brochures, booklets and tracts of Christian teaching. But since they did not get permission to stay, they left Timor Leste. From that distribution, some of Timorese were able to read and discuss the content, which differed from the Catholic teaching at that time, especially the teaching on salvation by faith in Jesus Christ and the freedom of lay people to read the Bible. Among those people, two served as team leaders of the small group, namely Vincente de Vasconcelos Ximenes[2] and Marcelo Cireneu who were ordained as pastors in 1985 in Hosana Church in

---

[1] This history was collected through non-formal discussions or interviews with important people who were related directly or indirectly to the IPTL Journey and History. The people include the Rev. Francisco M. de Vaconcelos, Former Moderator (2000 – 2008); Rev. Agustinho de Vasconcelos, Actual Secretary of Synod Department of Justice and Peace, and National Post of CAVR (Commission of Peace, Truth and Reconciliation), Mrs. Filomena de Vasconcelos, Rev. Moises A. da Silva, actual moderator, Evangelist Luis Mendonsa, Evangelist Paul da Silva and others who cannot be mentioned here. The Rev. Albino da Costa has written something on this in his undergraduate paper in the Seminary in Batu-Malang, Indonesia in 1997.

[2] Mr. Vicente de Vasconcelos was captured and jailed from 1945-1947 in Atauro island near the Capital Dili and Mr.

Dili. Both Vicente de Vasconcelos and Marcelo Cireneu started their ministry within their family. They had prayer meetings every evening in their house in Fatumeta, Dili although they were still members of the Catholic Church. In fact, Vasconcelos was a katekista (catechist or teacher) of Catholic teaching. The material they used for discussion was a book entitled **"Imitacao de Jesus Cristo" (The Imitation of Jesus Christ).**

As the group became bigger, it soon disturbed the Roman Catholic Church. To maintain the Catholic Church's teaching and to stop the movement from spreading, a priest of the Roman Catholic Church in Fatumeta decided to take serious action through church discipline, i.e. by not allowing the members of the group to partake of Holy Communion. One day in 1972, Vasconcelos and his family attended mass in a small schoolroom in Mauleuana, Dili. The priest started saying that he (Vasconcelos) and his group were followers of Lucifer and when the Holy Communion time came, the priest did not allow him and his group to take the bread. Thus, in front of the other members in the mass, Vasconcelos declared: "From now on I will leave the Roman Catholic Church". The group bravely continued their study of the book, *Imitacao de Jesus Cristo.* A year later, he bought a Bible to teach his family and his group members.

In 1956, the first baptism was conducted in Fatumeta. The group grew very slowly because they were persecuted under the Portuguese regime of Antonio Salazar but it continued to grow. The other group church was established separately and later become the Assembly of God Church (Igreja Evangelica de Deus) led by late Jose Seabra Gomes. The latter group then made contact with the Assembly of God in Portugal and they sent 2 missionaries, namely Pastor Miguel Francisco Coias and Pastor Virgilio Condeco[3] to help the mission in 1968-1973, which was started by the Timorese people. Both groups worked together until May 1977, but the group split up – one joined the mainstream church (PGI) while the other group joined the Assembly of God in Indonesia. Unfortunately, Pastor Virgilio Condeco had to leave Timor Leste in the middle of 1975 as the political situation made it difficult for him to stay.

3. Occupation as "Blessing In Disguise"[4]

Timor Leste declared her Independence on 28 November 1975 by FRETILIN representing majority of the people in Timor Leste. However, the Indonesian army invaded Timor with full military power through land, navy and air forces on 7 December 1975. The decision to invade Timor Leste was taken one day after U.S. Secretary Henry Kissinger met Soeharto in Jakarta. From the date of annexation by Indonesia, the East Timor Liberation Army, together with the people of Timor Leste, started to resist this occupation. During this war of resistance many Timorese were killed as also many Indonesian troops. The recorded number of Timorese people who were killed during 24 years was approximately 200,000. Many were killed during fighting, some disappeared, and some died of starvation, especially at the end of 1975-1980's.

During the 24-years occupation, Indonesia imposed their Constitution in Timor Leste. Much physical development happened in Timor Leste during the period. As written in Indonesian Constitution (UUD) Article 29, all people have freedom to choose from any of the 5 formal religions: Islam, Catholic Christianity, Protestant Christianity, Buddhism, and Hinduism. Through this constitutional provision, the Protestant Church in Timor Leste got the freedom to grow like other protestant churches in Indonesia. Many people from Indonesia including some military personnel, public employees and business people, who came to Timor Leste, supported or got involved in evangelization.

Through this initiative, the Protestant churches grew significantly in all the districts in Timor Leste. In 1978, an agreement was made between the local church leaders and the Communion of Churches in

---

Marcelo Cireneu from 1972-1973.

[3] Reff. Da Costa, Albino, Partisipasi GKTT Imanuel Dalam Meningkatkan Perekonomian Masyarakat di Desa Foiloro, Lospalos Timor-Timur (Paper), Theological Seminary "I-3", Batu-Malang, Indonesia, 1997, pg 26-29

[4] This was addressed by Mr. Vicente de Vasconcelos Ximenes, first moderator in the first anniversary of GKTT/IPTL

Indonesia (CCI/PGI) and Gereja Masehi Injili Timor (GMIT) Kupang, Indonesia to send Rev. Baria from GMIT as a church worker. Later in the same year, all the leaders decided to establish a united coordination body, known as "Badan Koordinasi Jemaat Kristen Protestan di Timor-Timur (Bakor – JKPTT)". During this period, Mr. Vicente de Vasconcelos and Mr. Marcelo Cereneo had been ordained as pastors and were involved in evangelistic work in different districts, along with some pastors who came from GMIT Kupang, Indonesia and some military chaplains.

In 1981, 'BAKOR-JKPTT' sent some Timorese for formal theological education in Indonesia and they were enrolled in the Graduate program. The Protestant churches in Timore Laste have now more cooperation with other churches in Indonesia through CCI/PGI like GMIM-Manado, GPM-Ambon, GMIH-Halmahera, GKI Papua, GKS Sumba, GKJW, GKI Jawa Tengah, and GKSS South Sulawesi.

During 7th-9th July 1988 all Protestant church leaders from 13 districts came together to form a Synod called, "Gereja Kristen di Timor-Timur", GKTT (The Christian Church in East Timor). It is an ecumenical member church of PGI (Communion Churches in Indonesia, CCI). ***Pastor Vicente de Vasconcelos*** was elected as its First Moderator for a period, 1988-1992. Unfortunately, he passed way on 4 May 1992 before his term.

4. IPTL and Ecumenical Movement

(a) During the Struggle for Independence

The relationships between IPTL and CCA, WCC, and other ecumenical bodies like NCCA-Australia, UCA Australia, PKN-Dutch actually started during the period of East Timor's struggle for independence. In 1979, Dr. Park Kyung Seo, Asia Desk Secretary of WCC, and Rev. Dr. Park Sang Jung, General Secretary of CCA, made a solidarity visit to Timor Leste. In 1991, IPTL (formerly known as GKTT) became a full-fledged member of WCC at its General Assembly in Canberra, Australia in 1991 and then in WARC, which is now WCRC.

In 1994 WCC and CCA jointly organized a Christian Conference to discuss the ecumenical venture in East Timor. In 1995, four years after the Santa Cruz Massacre on November 1991, CCA made a solidarity visit. A Task Force Group for Timor was created by CCA to monitor the situation of East Timor churches.

It is a matter of regret that PGI as an ecumenical umbrella did not give much support and ignored the independent struggle in East Timor. In fact, PGI walked out of the CCA General Assembly in 1985[5], since CCA tabled the East Timor issue on the agenda. When CCA-WCC organized Christian Conference for East Timor in 1991,the PGI issued a statement supporting the Indonesian government's position.

(b) The New Era of IPTL

Through the support of the international communities and ecumenical bodies such as CCA and WCC, the United Nations took Timor Leste issue seriously. In 1999, the UN Security Council decided to give an opportunity for Timorese to participate in a referendum (popular consultation). On 30 August 1999, the referendum was successfully (?done?) despite the pressure from the Indonesian military. More than 70% of the Timorese chose to be free from Indonesia. As a consequence, Timor Leste was thrown into chaos again. Many militant groups supported by the Indonesian military brutally attacked and killed many of their own brothers and sisters, including Catholic priests and sisters. Thousands of people were killed and houses and public facilities were burned to ashes. Many people were forced to evacuate to Atambua and Kupang, NTT-Indonesia, including most of members of GKTT who are now IPTL members. The month of September, 1999 was like a 'black month' and IPTL became helpless because of that situation. The

[5] At this time the IPTL/GKTT Synod was not established yet. There was only a uniting body which was called "BAKOR-JKPTT" (Coordination Body of the Christian Protestant Churches in East Timor.

economy was totally shattered. Many pastors evacuated to Kupang for safety. Only a few pastors remained in the country during this critical period of September – November 1999, e.g. Rev. Francisco M. de Vasconcelos, Rev. Luis Pinto, Rev. Agustinho de Vasconcelos, Ex Rev. Daniel Marcal[6] and some evangelists. Later, between November 1999 – 2003, some of the IPTL pastors and evangelists returned from Kupang and Atambua to strengthen the IPTL ministries. The 3rd Synod General Assembly took place on 4 – 9 July 2000. It was the first Assembly after the political freedom. By a majority vote, the Assembly decided to change the name of Gereja Kristen di Timor-Timur (GKTT) to Igreja Protestante iha Timor Lorosa'e (IPTL).

After independence, IPTL used the opportunity to work with ecumenical partners both at the regional and global levels for different ecumenical initiatives. In 2000, IPTL became a full-fledged member of CCA during its General Assembly in Tomohon, Indonesia. Though IPTL has formally discontinued its membership from PGI (CCI), it is still committed to work together and maintain relationships for the extension of God's kingdom.

IPTL continue to receive support for various ecumenical programme after becoming a full-fledged member of CCA and WCC. Training programmes and seminars on human rights, human dignity, peace and interfaith dialogues, etc. have equipped our leaders on various ecumenical issues. IPTL has many times been invited to involve and share its ideas through many programmes of Peace Reconciliation, Interfaith dialogue at the national and regional levels which are being regularly organized by Asia-Pacific countries every year since 2005.

Through the support and guidance of CCA and WCC, IPTL has established bilateral and stronger relationships with other ecumenical bodies, such as the Uniting Church of Australia, Uniting Church of Christ and Disciples of Christ in USA, United Church of Canada, Presbyterian Church in the Republic of Korea (PROK), Presbyterian Church in Korea (Dongan and ILSIN), Gereja Masehi Injili di Timor (GMIT) Kupang, PGI, and other Christian faith-based organizations such as YMCA and SCM Timor Leste, Child Care International (CCI-Anglican), Child Evangelism Fellowship (CEF from Korea). There are now lots of opportunities to develop relationships with many other ecumenical bodies or Christian faith-based organizations around Asia and in the world.

5. IPTL's Involvement in the Ecumenical Movement

(a) Regional and Global

All programmes that IPTL had taken in part or involved in were through CCA, WCC and WCRC. We are aware of our weaknesses to make our regular contribution as a full-fledged member due to financial constraints. We hope that the ecumenical fraternity will understand our difficulties as a new country and new member just emerging from a situation of war and conflict. We continue to depend on the contribution of our partners for our programmes. Our congregations are still very weak financially to support their ministers.

(b) National Ecumenical Movement

IPTL, as the only ecumenical organization in Timor Leste, has a moral responsibility to lead the ecumenical movement. It had initiated an ecumenical preparation team for the National Council of

[6] Mr. Daniel Marsal was IPTL pastor and General Secretary for period 2000-2004. But later he resigned from his position to work with CWS in Timor Leste from 2003 – 2010s. Then he joined his brother, Arlindo Marsal, in starting a new church named The Presbyterian Evangelical Church Timor Leste which is a split from IPTL in 2009.

Churches in 2001, but it could not be established as the other Evangelical and Pentecostal churches are not ready yet for such a venture. We continue to have dialogue in this direction.

(c) Challenge

During and after independence, many 'Evangelical' missionaries have come and continue to work in Timor Leste. Some of them work independently to re-evangelize the members of the Roman Catholic Church and some work in collaboration with the local church. However, it is sad to note that the churches are split due to a narrow understanding of evangelism and Christian faith. Aggressive evangelism and a 'sheep stealing' approach continue to create confusion, conflict among local communities and believers. Therein lies a great challenge for the ecumenical movement.

(75) CHURCHES TOGETHER IN GOD'S MISSION – VIETNAM

Tu Thien van Truong

It is commonly agreed that present Vietnamese Protestant Christianity came into existence about a century ago under the mission of the Christian and Missionary Alliance (CMA) to Vietnam in 1911.[1] The Evangelical Church of Vietnam[2] (ECVN), the first Protestant church, was officially established in 1927. Other Protestant groups such as the Seventh-day Adventists, Southern Baptists, Pentecostals, Mennonites, the Church of Christ, and the Quakers entered Vietnam in the following decades. Until the Vietnam War ended in 1975, however, the question of ecumenical responsibility and interdenominational fellowship have yet to be seriously addressed by the early Vietnamese churches. Three major causes have contributed to this lack of ecumenical focus: First, the early Protestant churches were in their premature stage of establishment therefore the ecumenical cooperation was not the utmost priority for these young churches. Instead, and rightly so, the early Vietnamese Protestant churches focused solely on evangelical activities seeking to increase membership though there was no doubt that early Vietnamese Protestant Christians did evangelism out of the love for the Lord and for the lost souls.

Second, the CMA's theological orthodoxy regards all indigenous people and their religious organizations in "un-Christian countries" like Vietnam as demonic entities; thus the idea of working together with other religious groups will certainly not be accepted. Biblical texts like 2 Corinthians 6:14-16[3] have often been interpreted by the CMA to claim biblical support for non-collaborative attitude with other non-Christian groups. The early Vietnamese Protestant has also regarded the Vietnamese Catholics in this negative category. This kind of unbiblical and erroneous position of orthodoxy is still being held by many in the ECVN circle.

Third, political turbulence in Vietnam in the first half of twentieth century was another main reason that has prevented ecumenical movement among Vietnamese Protestant churches. Vietnam became a French colony after a series of colonial wars that took place between 1858 and 1883; in these conflicts, the French has inflicted heavy casualties on the country. Sharing the same consequences brought about by the war was the religious affiliations and organizations. Religious activities were suspected of political motives by the governing authorities. For example, upon the outbreak of WWI the French government in Vietnam issued a decree prohibiting any further work among native Protestants, closing all chapels and mission stations with the exception of Tourance (now Da Nang City), and ordering all the missionaries whose names could be traced to a German origin to leave the country. In 1945, Vietnam regained its independence, but then was internally divided in 1954. This led to a civil war which lasted for thirty years. The North was supported mainly by the Soviet Union and China, and the South was supported by the United States and its allies. This war was ended in 1975 when the Communist North took control of the South. It was understandable that ecumenical movement could not be exhorted in the time of war. Instead, churches would try to do their best within their own denominational boundaries.

---

[1] As it was documented, however, that there already existed in the country a French Protestant church along with its Vietnamese members even before the arrival of the CMA's missionaries.

[2] The ECVN was divided into two groups—ECVN (North) and ECVN (South)—due to the division of the country in 1954 for political reason. Since 2010 leaders of the two groups have been working for the reunification and are waiting for the Vietnamese government's approval.

[3] "Do not be yoked together with unbelievers. For what do righteousness and wickedness have in common? Or what fellowship can light have with darkness? What harmony is there between Christ and Belial? Or what does a believer have in common with an unbeliever? What agreement is there between the temple of God and idols?"

After the war ended in 1975, except for the ECVN, the Vietnam Christian Mission,[4] the Seventh-day Adventists, and the Southern Baptists, other Protestant groups stopped their open activities though some of them had underground activities. All the Protestant churches lived under the post-war effect: they were perceived and treated as remnants of the enemies of the state by the new government because of their previous relationship with foreign organizations. Furthermore, adhering to Karl Marx's understanding of religion the Vietnamese Communist government wanted to eradicate religions in order to build a real communist country.[5] As a result, an anti-religion policy was imposed on religious groups. Religious groups were not free to express themselves but had to conform to the government's anti-religion strategic plan. This period was a difficult time for religious groups, especially for groups that had relationship with foreign missionary organizations or churches. Among these were the Protestant churches because they had relationship with American missionary organizations. As a result, the Vietnamese Communist government has considered the Protestant churches as the enemies of the state. The ruling government confiscated and shut-downed many properties and buildings that belongs to the local Vietnamese Protestant churches. Church leaders were jailed or harassed. The government controlled all religious activities and prohibited any evangelical activities be conducted outside of the church walls. However, as traditional Vietnamese people conducted their life in the way of running water: when one way is closed it finds other ways to flow, Vietnamese church leaders and believers could still find ways to live and propagate their faith against the control of the government. Persecution could not eliminate the Protestant churches and other religious groups.

In the late 1980s a number of leaders separated themselves from the ECVN and established the so-called "house churches".[6] In the beginning stage these house churches operated underground like a religious movement rather than organized religious institutions. These house churches grew rapidly even under the government's strict control. In fact, the government could not exercise control over house churches as they did with the ECVN since these churches did not organize and work in traditional ways, i.e., open and in public view. Growth in membership was significant in this period. Some other previously established churches such as the Seventh-day Adventists, Southern Baptists, Pentecostals, Mennonites and Vietnam Christian Mission also resumed their open operations in this period.

There were other causes that might have contributed to this development. Since the early 1990s, Vietnam has been exporting labor overseas, mainly to the Eastern European Bloc. At the end of that decade, the demand for cheap labor shifted to Asian countries such as South Korea and Malaysia. In addition to this exporting of the Vietnamese workers to developed countries, outstanding students supported by the Communist Party also began to go abroad to Russia and Eastern Europe for higher education opportunities. A good number of these young scholars have been converted to Christianity during their time abroad. Many of them went back to their hometowns and shared their new beliefs with families, friends, and neighbors. It is quite amazing that a majority of them came from Northern parts of Vietnam. As a result, they were able to evangelize in areas where the government did not allow strangers to visit and evangelize. Many Vietnamese Christians believed this was a miracle of God.

---

[4] Vietnamese name: Hội Truyền Giáo Cơ Đốc Việt Nam. This church was locally established in 1956 by the CMA missionary G. H. Smith who paid attention to evangelism to Vietnamese people in mountainous areas. The church was officially established in 1956, but the evangelism work among the people in mountainous areas had already begun earlier around 1930.

[5] Marx thought religion was a form of ideological consciousness in the sense that it was delusional, involved false beliefs, and might also involve false or irrational values. For Marx, religion was part of people's psychological adjustment to their class position and social role. Until social conditions were changed so that people's true human needs could be effectively satisfied in communist society, religion would persist.

[6] This term is confusing, however, because today a number of these "house-churches" have legal recognition and have public/official church buildings and facilities.

As the years go by, the number of churches under various denominations increased along with the growth of Protestant Christians in Vietnam. To date, there are nearly one hundred Protestant groups of various denominations operating in Vietnam. Since most of the leaders of the house churches came from the ECVN, these churches had fellowship with one another very naturally. However, Vietnamese Protestant Christianity's ecumenical responsibility and interdenominational fellowship are still in its beginning stage. There are a number of fellowships among Vietnamese Protestant churches. In order to have a closer look at the ecumenical movement in Vietnam, one of the biggest fellowships will be in focus.

In 1994, leaders of three house church groups met for fellowship and prayers. As a result of these meetings, two years later the Vietnamese Evangelical Fellowship (VEF) was established with seven church participants. The purpose of this fellowship was: 1) to have fellowship with one another, 2) to stabilize church staffs (i.e., to prevent members and staffs of churches to move between churches and cause disorder), and 3) to become a representative to work with the government.[7] As of 2012 this fellowship has 29 church participants including some legally recognized churches.[8]

In addition to the fellowship that VEF's members have with one another, VEF's leaders also set up short-term projects for ecumenical work including training seminars for church leaders, women, youth, and children. For evangelism, VEF had organized several mass evangelism events with financial help from foreign organizations. VEF also worked with Christian groups from other countries to do relief or to help poor children in remote villages.

VEF also tried to have fellowship with the ECVN, but did not get positive response from this church. Most of the top leaders of the ECVN tend to think that house churches are not as orthodox in doctrines as they are. To be more precise, top leaders of the ECVN tends to think that they are the only ones who have the correct interpretation and theological understanding of the Scriptures. Therefore, they erroneously believed that if they have fellowship with those who have wrong biblical and theological understandings that could hurt their belief or lead the church—the ECVN—to go astray. With this false conviction, it is not hard to predict that the ECVN will not have any fellowship with any other churches in the near future (though it is ironic that this non-ecumenical attitude will not stop the ECVN's local churches as well as its top leaders from receiving financial assistance from non-ECVN churches in the USA or South Korea). Sadly because of its theological perspective, for this largest Protestant organization in the country, ecumenical responsibility and fellowship with other non-ECVN churches is neither a priority nor a need even after a hundred years of history.

Outside of the ECVN circle, many ecumenical projects completed by other Protestant churches in Vietnam brought good experience for these churches. The desire to have fellowship with one another among many churches is strong as they want to work together in bigger projects in the future. However, weak organization and financial non-transparency have prevented the growth of the VEF and other fellowships. For example, leaders of bigger churches in VEF wanted to have control over this fellowship and usually they discussed things among themselves and set up agendas for other smaller churches to follow. This way discouraged many members of the fellowship.[9] And financial non-transparency seems to be the main reason for discontent among church leaders.[10] Money from foreign organizations has caused

---

[7] Rev. Ho Tan Khoa, interview with the author via Telephone, 5 May 2012. Rev. Khoa is the President of Presbyterian Church of Vietnam. He also currently serves in the Executive Committee of the Vietnamese Christian Fellowship.

[8] Today most of Protestant churches/denominations registered their activities with the government (required by Vietnam's law). As of 2009, eleven Protestant churches/denominations have been given legal status by the government.

[9] Rev. Nguyen Huu Bay, interview with the author via Telephone, 3 May 2012. Rev. Bay is a senior pastor of the Independent Baptist Church of Vietnam.

[10] Rev. Nguyen Quang Duc, interview with the author, Da Nang City, Vietnam, 15 April 2012. Rev. Duc was the Deputy Secretary of the Vietnam Christian Mission.

long-term serious problem for churches in poor countries like Vietnam though in some way it helps churches grow in numbers.

Generally speaking, most Vietnamese Protestant churches are doing well in term of ecumenical fellowship. House church leaders could sit with one another to pray and sing hymns. But in term of ecumenical work, such cooperation among these young churches is very much superficial and has no depth. It can be said that most of the leaders and members of these churches know very well the brother/sisterhood of Christians. They know that as Christians they need to love other people as the Lord has taught them. However, Vietnamese church leaders often cannot stand against the temptation of money, fame and other personal gains. As a result, their cooperation was often driven by selfish motives. Though it is sad but it is true that when church leaders sat together to organize mass evangelism or relief projects, they did so mainly because they got financial support from individuals or organizations outside of the country.

Until today no attempt had been made by Vietnamese Protestant churches for cooperation with other religious groups including Vietnamese Catholic church though the Vietnamese Catholic church has helped some Protestant churches in a number of cases when these churches needed help. Cooperation with other religious groups was never mentioned or even thought of by most Protestant church leaders.

With the above observations in mind, one might suggest that it will take many years for the Vietnamese Protestant churches to mature in ecumenical cooperation so that these churches can truly open up able to work with one another and with other non-Protestant religious groups. To that end, there remain several challenges for Vietnamese Protestant church leaders and members to overcome. These challenges are discussed in the following section of this paper. The following suggestions can serve as guiding principles for successful ecumenical cooperation.

First, mature cooperation requires equality in decision making process. This equality can only happen when the basic rule of mutual respect is observed among participants. That is, teamwork among church leaders in any fellowship or cooperation is a crucial element to the success of the cooperation. Every participant in the fellowship, no matter he/she comes from a big or small church, has the right to access all the information related to any cooperative works or projects of the fellowship. Care must be taken so that the voice of every member can be heard in the discussion and decision making process.

Second, Vietnamese Protestant churches need to learn to be financially independent. Financial independence will help prevent selfish profit driven motives that are harmful to any ecumenical cooperation. As it was mentioned in the preceeding, financial non-transparency was one main reason that has discouraged many members of VEF. To have successful cooperation every church needs to contribute financially. However, this is not to say that all group members have to contribute the same amount of money for an ecumenical project. The amount that each group member contributes should depend on the financial situation of that group. It can be big or small. But when a group wants to get involved in an ecumenical project it should be financially independent, i.e., it should not try to use the cooperative budget for its internal operation, if it wants the cooperation to be successful.

Third, though church growth in numbers is of importance for Protestant churches in Vietnam since they are small in numbers, church leaders should recognize that the church's evangelistic ministries are much larger than the ministry of evangelism, i.e., the ministry to get people from other religious groups to convert. As *missio Dei* is holistic, Christians need to share the Good News in their daily life in words and in deeds for a holistic mission. That is, sharing the Good News will be manifested in sharing the work that God has done in Jesus and also in sharing the bread one has with those who are in need. This means that Christians' involvement in the life of their community is of significant importance. This was stated in the World Conference on Mission and Evangelism in San Antonio, 1989:

> Christian mission is the humble involvement of the one body of Christ in liberating and suffering love, the witness of God's saving acts in Christ, and the practice of God's incarnational love for all humankind. This

mission is expressed through the communion of love and justice which embodies the church's self-giving solidarity with the human family.[11]

The above insight teaches that Vietnamese Protestant churches need to set aside their "grow-in-numbers" agendas in order to work with one another to show God's love for Vietnamese people in particular and for all humanity in general.

Lastly, in Vietnam today a large number of people are still condemned to a life of poverty, injustice, and exploitation. Millions of people suffer indefinitely because of rampant socio-political and economic injustice. Vietnamese Christians have responsibility to address these matters. "The privilege of a Christian life cannot be sought apart from its responsibilities."[12] If a Vietnamese Protestant church chooses to "remain silent in the face of injustice and oppression, both in society at large and in the church itself, it jeopardizes its entire evangelistic ministry."[13] Socio-political involvement is a Christian duty, as it is affirmed in the Lausanne Covenant, "evangelism and socio-political involvement are both part of our Christian duty".[14] In this light, Vietnamese Protestant churches need to think of working with Vietnamese Catholic church and also with other religious groups for the common good of Vietnamese people and Vietnamese society.

Due to the CMA's theological perspective that is also widely accepted in the ECVN and other Vietnamese Protestant churches, it is difficult for these churches to take initiative to work with other religious groups. However, working with other religious groups can help Vietnamese Protestant churches fulfill Jesus Christ's commandment, "Love your neighbor as yourself" (Mark 12:31). Vietnamese Protestant churches believe that all human beings are created by God. As such, working with people in other faith is an indication of that belief. This is also expressed in the wisdom of traditional Vietnamese people who believe that all human being in general or all Vietnamese people in particular have the same origin. They say, "*Đừng nài lương giáo khác dòng, cũng là con Lạc cháu Hồng khi xưa*" ("*Do not mind differences between lương and giáo; For we all are descendants of Lạc and Hồng.*")[15]

In conclusion, it can be said that Vietnamese Protestant churches value Christian fellowship and many churches are working well for it. Indeed, one can be optimistic for the result of the fellowship among Vietnamese Protestant churches though the majority of Vietnamese Protestant churches are still afraid of having fellowship with the Vietnamese Catholic church. But in term of cooperation among Vietnamese Protestant churches or between Vietnamese Protestant churches with other religious groups, Vietnamese Protestant churches need to improve themselves if they want to have successful cooperation. Hopefully mature ecumenical cooperation will soon happen in Vietnam.

---

[11] "Mission in Christ's Way: Your Will Be Done," San Antonio, 1989, *New Directions in Mission & Evangelization 1: Basic Statements 1974-1991*. Ed. James A. Scherer & Stephen Bevans (Maryknoll, NY: Orbis Books, 1992), 75.

[12] Lesslie Newbigin, *Foolishness to the Greek: The Gospel and Western Culture* (Grand Rapids: William B. Eerdmans Publishing Company, 1986), 124.

[13] "Stuttgart Consultation, 1987" in *New Directions in Mission & Evangelization 1: Basic Statements 1974-1991*. Ed. James A. Scherer & Stephen Bevans (Maryknoll, NY: Orbis Books, 1992), 67.

[14] Http://www.lausanne.org/en/documents/lausanne-covenant.html. Under the heading of Christian Social Responsibility. Accessed on 26 May 2012.

[15] *Ca Dao Viet Nam (Vietnamese Folk-Poetry)*. *Lương* signifies Vietnamese people who follow their conscience, *giáo* for people who are Catholic. The phrase, "*Con cháu Lạc Hồng,*" or sometimes "*Con Lạc cháu Hồng*" means that Vietnamese people have the same root.

Bibliography

Interviews with the author

Ho, Tan Khoa, interview with the author via Telephone, 5 May 2012.

Nguyen, Huu Bay, interview with the author via Telephone, 3 May 2012.

Nguyen, Quang Duc, interview with the author, Da Nang City, Vietnam, 15 April 2012.

Articles, books and internet sites

"Mission in Christ's Way: Your Will Be Done," San Antonio, 1989, *New Directions in Mission & Evangelization 1: Basic Statements 1974-1991*. Ed. James A. Scherer & Stephen Bevans. Maryknoll, NY: Orbis Books, 1992.

Newbigin, Lesslie. *Foolishness to the Greek: The Gospel and Western Culture.* Grand Rapids: William B. Eerdmans Publishing Company, 1986.

"Stuttgart Consultation, 1987" in *New Directions in Mission & Evangelization 1: Basic Statements 1974-1991*. Ed. James A. Scherer & Stephen Bevans. Maryknoll, NY: Orbis Books, 1992.

Http://www.lausanne.org/en/documents/lausanne-covenant.html. Accessed on 26 May 2012.

Part VI

Ecumenical Formation in Asian Theological Education

(76) Theological Education and Ecumenical Challenges in Asia

H.S. Wilson

The Nature and the Task

As per David Tracy, "Of all the disciplines, theology is that one where action and thought, academy and church, faith and reason, the community of inquiry and the community of commitment and faith are most explicitly and systematically brought together."[1] Regarding the nature of theological education, Daniel Aleshire states, "Theological education is a socially constructed enterprise, and when times and issues change, the case for theological education needs to be reconsidered, if not reconstructed."[2] Both quotations speak of the dynamic nature and task of theological education. The challenge therefore is: how to pursue theological education as a dynamic endeavor empowering Christian community for Christian witness in the midst of challenges in Asia.

During the hey days of Protestant mission in the 19th century around the globe, the need for theologically well equipped missionaries as well as appropriately trained local personal was urgently felt giving rise a number of theological training programs. The Ecumenical Missionary Conference held in New York City in 1900 has expressed these concerns as follows. "Every foreign missionary, whether preacher, teacher, doctor, translator, or writer of books, is essentially an evangelist, the scope of whose work will be measured by his ability to multiply himself by the native evangelists he finds, trains and guides. In this ability or the lack of it, more than anywhere else, lies the difference between small and great missionaries. . . . .Next in importance to finding the right men for evangelists is the method of their training. Good men easily may be spoiled by faulty training, while by thorough training on right lines those of only moderate gifts may attain a good degree of effectiveness."[3] What is envisaged in this plea is not just imparting training but facilitating the development of a cadre of effective and appropriate leaders.

As in the 19th century, in the beginning decades of the 21st century, we as Asians have to spell out the nature of training and kind of leaders we need. In the contemporary Asia, theological training has to equip the candidates both for ministry and mission within and beyond Christian community. Besides serving designated congregations, theologically trained candidates should to be able to engage with denominations, churches, Christian fellowships other than their own. They should be able to relate to neighboring communities other faiths, and engage in socio-political concerns of larger community as ministry and mission demands it. As in earlier centuries of western mission outreach, religious pluralism poses continuous challenge to Asian Christians even today. Wilbert Buhlmann articulated this reality as follows: "Asian continent is most religious .... At the same time this is a mystery – Asia is the least *Christians of all continents.*"[4] Therefore one can say that theological education in contemporary Asia has the task of preparing candidates for transformation of Christian community for the sake of the transformation of the whole society where it is located.

---

[1] "On Theological Education: A Reflection" in *Theological Literacy for the Twenty-First Century.* Eds. Rodney L. Peterson with Nancy M.Rourke. Grand Rapids, MI: Eerdmans, 2002, p.15

[2] Daniel O. Aleshire, *Earthen Vessels. Hopeful Reflections on the work and future of theological schools.* Grand Rapids, MI: Eerdmans, 2008, p. 3

[3] S.H.Chester, "The Development of Native Workers" in *Ecumenical Missionary Conference, New York, 1900.* Vol. II. New York: American Tract Society, 1900, pages 215 and 257.

[4] Walbert Buhlmann. *The coming of the third Church. An Analysis of the present and the future.* Trs. By R. Woodhall, 1974, p.160-161.

In this article by theological education it is meant formal or non-formal training of individual Christians for ministerial/missional leadership among Protestant churches and beyond. The purpose of theological education is to equip and instill self-realization of one's discipleship, and a lifelong commitment to transformation and liberation not only of oneself, but of all the peoples of God and the whole of creation from the perspective of the gospel of Jesus Christ. Therefore theologically trained candidates should be equipped with spiritual, experimental and cognitive knowledge and strength to minister the community to accomplish the transformation and liberation witnessed in the ministry of Jesus Christ.[5] By ecumenism it is meant visioning solidarity for the task of ministry and mission beyond traditional understanding of cooperation among Protestant denominations especially in organizing and managing the programs and institutions of theological education. In the recent years such cooperation has been seen among churches and Christians of various Protestants denominations, Evangelical, Pentecostal churches and even with some of the Roman Catholic seminaries in Asia. However, in Asia engagement and interaction with the multifaith communities in the theological education, in the spirit of wider ecumenism is crucial for building a better human community in Asia.[6]

Asian Scene

Theological education in Asia dates back to the arrival and establishment of Churches of Oriental Orthodox tradition and multiplied with the successive Christian sojourns to Asia of Roman Catholic, Protestant missions from Europe and North America. From simple beginning as institutes for training native catechists and evangelists, more structured seminaries have emerged in Asia as Christian communities grew in numbers and needed theologically trained leaders. Given the historical circumstance, most of these seminaries were modeled after theological institutions of western countries adopting uncritically the structures, teaching methods and curriculums. Therefore the contents were predominantly shaped by the pastoral and missionary theologies of the west, and that legacy continues even today in much of the theological education programs of Asia. That legacy was partly perpetuated by the training of faculty members of Asia in the west or following curriculums adopted from the west, and/or the close collaboration of Asian theological education with western Christianity. Yet the same time it has to be acknowledged that a lot of innovative programs of theological education and ministerial formation have been taking place in Asia in response to local contexts some of which are carried through ecumenical cooperation and spirit. With these varied legacies, theological education as institutes of professional higher education has been functioning in many of the Asian countries for more than a century with vigor, meeting the demands of the churches, Christian institutions and individuals who are interested in the ministry and mission.

John Roxborogh had estimated the scenario of theological educational institutes in the beginning of 21st century as follows. "It is likely that by 2000 there were more than 500 university departments, theological schools, Bible colleges and other institutions connected with Christian theological education in Asia, and a similar number in Africa. The World Christian Encyclopaedia records 35 university departments teaching theology and 11 theological education associations in Asia. In Africa there were 28 university departments teaching theology and 12 theological education associations. By 2000 there were some 25,000 Roman Catholic seminarians attending 335 seminaries in Asia, and some 20,000 seminarians attending 180 seminaries in Africa. There has been a dramatic increase in the demand for training in the last 50 years, and

[5] Moonjang Lee, "Theological Education as Embodiment of Jesus" in *Understanding World Christianity. The vision and work of Andrew F. Walls.* Eds. William R. Burrows et al. New York: Orbis Books, 2011, p. 79-88.
[6] H.S. Wilson. "Interfaith Challenges and Theological Education in Asia" in *Theology Beyond Neutrality. Essays to Honour Wesley Ariarajah.* Eds. Marshal Fernando and Robert Crusz. Colombo: Ecumenical Institute, 2011.

in the case of Roman Catholic seminarians the increase is over 8 fold since 1950."[7] Hope Antone notes that theological education in contemporary Asia (may be true in other parts of the world) are carried through denominational seminaries (mostly belonging to historic denominations), non-denominational (mostly more conservatives), and the ecumenical seminaries (mostly inter denominations and minority groups).[8] The Roman Catholics maintain their own program of theological training supervised closely by the ecclesial hierarchy. These different patterns of managing theological education allow churches to ensure in preserving their respective historic and theological perspectives. However, through decades of ministering in each others' neighbourhood, these four distinct Christian communities, Roman Catholic, Protestant, Evangelical and Pentecostal have developed certain level of co-operation in theological education through association of theological education/Schools in Asia and/or individual initiatives of seminaries, cluster of seminaries, exhibiting some levels of inter-denomination and ecumenical cooperation and support.

Among the Protestant Christians in Asia there are three associations, Board of Theological Education of the Senate of Serampore College (BTESSC, covering South Asia), Association for Theological Education in South East Asia (ATESEA, covering South east Asia), North East Association of Theological Education (NEAATS, covering North East Asia), and a number of national associations like Association of Theological Education in Myanmar (ATEM), Association of theological schools in Indonesia (PERSETIA), the theological commission of China Christian Council (CCC) with 20 plus seminaries and Bible schools. Besides, all Asia associations like the Asian Theological Association (ATA), Asian Pentecostal Theological Association (APTA) are assisting in theological education in their respective evangelical and Pentecostal churches. In the past two years representatives of these associations have been in consultation to form a fellowship of theological education in Asia—*Asia Forum for Theological Education* (AFTE). In the communiqué that has been issued by the first meeting of AFTE (held from June 9 to 12 at the Trinity Theological College, Singapore), the participants affirmed that "that there is need for greater solidarity between different churches transcending stereotyped views of each other as 'ecumenical', 'evangelicals' or 'charismatic' in witnessing to Christ in today's world." Such solidarity among theological educators are needed for mutual learning for the sake of preparing leaders for the churches in Asia, and to work towards common standards and accreditation for insuring quality theological education. [9]

In the coming decades, a number of theological schools will upgrade themselves as strong academic institutions devoting needed human and financial resources. Some have already reached the goal of theological excellence. However, in their quest for excellence, Asian theological educators should not fail to take into consideration the Asian realities and engaging with them for the sake of transformation as per the vision provided in the gospel. That calls for serious soul searching about the models of theological education that is authentic to Asian ethos. Even the premier western centers of theological excellence in Oxford, Edinburgh, Toronto, and Princeton in the last several years have incorporated changes in their training programs for ministry in response to the changing situation in the western and world Christianity may be more than many of the Asian theological schools have done.

Addressing the Challenges

Changing the old habits and practices are not easy even in the changed circumstances. For example regardless of Christianity having phenomenal growth in the regions of South, as Timothy Tennent has

---

[7] http://roxborogh.com/Projects/theologicaleducation.htm. Even though I do not deal with Roman Catholic Theological education, I inserted the projection by John Roxborogh to give a glimpse to training in the Roman Catholic Church in Asia

[8] Hope Antone, "The state and prospects of Theological Education in Asia" in *Ecumenical Theological Education in Changing Context*, ed. Wati Longchar, Jorhat, Assam: ETE-WCC/CCA, 2005, p.

[9] Asian Forum on Theological Education (AFTE). Communiqué June 12, 2012.

noted that Western world still exercises hegemony over the global church. "The Western world continues to hold up its own theological discourse as normative for the rest of the global church." Such hegemony is also exercised in the area of theological education "The Western church is still the center of gravity for advanced theological education . . .West continues to produce the most theological literature" almost in all areas of theology. One area of hegemony is the dominance and "importance of the English language in the global theological discourse . . . and has become the de facto language of choice for much of the global Christian discourse." [10] Therefore the Asian churches have a double task of rethinking of theological education in relation to Asian realities and also appropriately claiming the space that shifting of the gravity of center of Christianity has provided by transcending from the continued hegemonic power of the western Christianity.

Geevarghese Mor Coorilos has the following observation about the need for claiming theological space. He states that we observe in nature that everything that is living requires space to grow and prosper to be its own. Womb provides such space for a new life to form and grow. Seeds provide space and nourishment for an emergence of a new plant. Everybody is in need of space to grow and blossom.[11] "Theological exercise is also a spatial category. With a colonial legacy in our minds, our thinking of space is conditioned, influenced, by Western colonial logic. One of the first steps we need to take to develop an Asian theology is to reclaim our Asian sense of space. . . Every project of colonization, of imperialism starts with the conquest of space. . . Our space means our lands, our social relationships, our contexts, our resources, everything. Even the Western project of evangelization in Asia had this philosophy behind it: conquest of space."[12] The awareness of Asians needing their space to organize themselves has been long recognized but the effort to follow it through by Christian communities has been often sporadic and disconnected.

In 1970s with visionary mandate of promotion of contextualization of theological education by the Theological Education Fund, the contextual nature of all theological formations was slowly began to be accepted by theologians around the world.[13] That awareness has made many Asian theological communities to give attention to the contextual realities and demands in their task of doing theology. It gave a further impetus to indigenization and inculturation efforts in Asia. The various movements in Asia like peoples, women's, socio-economic, political, cultural, liberational, tribal, ecological were able to articulate their struggles in theological categories giving birth to a number of Asian theologies like Dalit, Minjung, Adivasi, tribal, women's, inter-faith etc. giving voice to living local theologies. With four decades of such contributions, there is awareness for the need for inter-contextual engagements and inter-weaving of the independently emerged contextual theologies for the sake of mutual edification and enrichment, and building Asian theological solidarity.

Four decades back, the Association for Theological Schools in South East Asia (ATESEA) taking seriously the situation in Asia has formulated a set of theological principles called, *The Critical Asian Principals* (CPA). CPA was adopted in 1972 to give direction for its doctoral program to take the contextual realities seriously. CPA has identified several realities that were predominant in most parts of Asia then. Many of those realities continue to show their grip on sections of Asian population even today. They are: plurality and diversity in races, peoples, cultures, social institutions, religions and ideologies; colonial experience of large section of Asia; search for appropriate civil and political orders in national

---

[10] Timothy C. Tennent. "New Paradigm for 21st century mission: Missiological reflections in honor of George K Chavanikamannil" in *Remapping Mission Discourse*. Eds. Simon Samuel and P.V.Joseph. Delhi: NTC/ISPCK, 2008, p.194-195.

[11] Geevarghese Mor Coorilos "Theologizing in Asian Context" in *CTC Bulletin,* June 2011, p. 47-51.

[12] Ibid p.47.

[13] *Ministry in context: the third mandate programme of Theological Education Fund (1970-77).* Written and edited by the TEF staff. Bromley: Theological Education Fund, 1972.

building, modernization; quest for social and economic justice against authoritarian cultures; re-affirmation of self-identity, and cultural integrity.[14] One can identify similar attempts by other Asian associations/fellowship of theological schools. The minority status of Christianity and Christianity's association with West makes existence a bit more complex for Asian Christians especially in the present context of tension between a number of western and Islamic nations.

ATESEA revisited CAP in the first decade of 21st century as situation world over and in Asia have changed bringing new challenges and opportunities. Through a process of consultation, ATESEA worked out "Guidelines for Doing Theologies in Asia—Responses to the Challenges of a New Era". The Guidelines have identified following critical issues in Asia: Religious fundamentalism, gender justice, ecological concern, disease and disasters, globalization and global empire, neo-colonial sweep, spirituality, identity, power struggle, peoples movements, ecumenism, information and technological change and challenges, reclaiming of indigenous and minority rights.[15] What these list of issues project is the need for transformation in almost all aspects of societal life in Asia.

Therefore to respond to Asian realities, theologically trained persons have to be a catalyst of change from the perspective of disciple of Jesus Christ. As I have stated in the beginning of this essay, the purpose of theological education has to be reconsidered as equipping and instilling self realization of one's discipleship along with the academic accomplishments so that such individuals can enable the Christian communities that they are going to minister to develop similar kind of realization of discipleship. It calls for looking afresh to the ministry of Jesus and reassessing the inherited goals of western mission outreach to provide clues for some modest fresh beginnings. In Asia what is most needed is the recapturing vision of Christianity as a fellowship of disciples of Jesus Christ constantly engaging in the world for its transformation.

Relearning From the Ministry of Jesus

Revisiting the ministry of Jesus and what he intended his disciples to accomplish, may throw some light to the challenges faced in Asia.[16] Times have changed and humanity has developed various institutions for education and developed numerous methods of pedagogical skills. However, one aspect that connects the vision of Jesus to the contemporary struggle in Asia is a quest for a new order of life for the sake of holistic living for everyone through reformative and revolutionary changes. Like the time of Jesus the people in the lower strata of society (numerous of them in Asia) are looking for a radical breakthrough in the political and social order for their well-being and the well being of all.

The Jesus movement was inevitably a social movement with spiritual underpinning. People from the Jewish community and beyond responded to call of Jesus movement because in that movement they saw a possibility of socio-political changes that they were anticipating for long. Jesus spoke about the need for changes from the perspective of the eventual unfolding of reign of God of complete social harmony. The question therefore: Are Asian Christians providing such impulses for social change in the societies where they are placed. And if theological education it meant to form such leaders, the question to ask: Is theological training equipping theological trainees in the aspects of social change and providing them a vision that Christianity is a social movement with religious and spiritual principles guiding and shaping them?

The following observation may help in focusing and retrieving the discipleship of Asian Christians. In expounding Matthew 28:19 Donald McGavern who worked for many years in India makes an important

[14] *Association for Theological Education for South East Asia Handbook 2005-2007*, Manila: ATESEA, p.84 ff

[15] *Association for Theological Education for South East Asia Handbook 2007-2008*, p. 85ff

[16] Moonjang Lee, "Theological Education as Embodiment of Jesus" in *Understanding World Christianity. The vision and work of Andrew F. Walls*. Eds. William R. Burrows et al. New York: Orbis Books, 2011, p. 79-88.

observation.[17] His suggestion was that missionaries instead of putting emphasis on discipleship mentioned in the passage as the first requirement, they put emphasis on teaching and baptism. When people were converted to Christianity, the missionaries established *mission stations* for the sake of teaching them about the truth of Christianity. This method isolated local Christians from their communities as well as gave them the false notion about Christianity. McGavern pointed out that *mission station* is a contradictory concept as mission stands for sending forth or reaching out whereas station indicates a stationary status. As a result of the idea of mission station/compound mentality that western missionaries introduced as a stage in Christian nurturing, congregations ended up as teaching centers. Consequently, theological schools were inappropriately perceived as centers for training teachers for congregations. Consequently they became primarily centers of theological enquiry and excellence. There is a tendency on the part of those who were trained in such a mentality to act as 'little' professors/professionals in their congregations. As a result congregations became maintenance and re-fabricating stations at the expense of equipping people as discipleship in the world. What is needed is a shift from maintenance to missional mentality.

Among the realities of Asia the minority status of Christianity is a challenging task for Asian Christians. In some of the countries of Asia Christians belong to double minority status as they predominantly belong to minority ethnic and linguistic communities within a nation state. It can be said with some certainty that large portion of Asia is not going to be Christians in the foreseeable future. So how are Asians going to revise theological education pattern emanated from Europe in the context of majority Christian community, respected and supported by the state, known as Christendom status. Christendom privilege is fast vanishing in it home base, Europe but still lingering in Asia. There is need to transcend from Christendom ethos of training whatever the residues are still lingering. If Christianity has to contribute to alternates for dominant structures and powers in the society as a fringe community, the curricula and total program of theological education has to have that perspective. In Asia concern of the church cannot be limited to the well being of Christians. Since Christians exist in the larger society of people of other faith and cultures, the well being of the larger society also has to be the equal concern of the church. Accordingly in ministerial training in Asia individual formation contributing to congregational formation has be done with the perspective of total transformation of the society in which the Christian community is located. Thus as per the gospel mandate Christian community becomes a catalyst of new humanity rather than a catalyst of segregation.

Self Assessment for the Sake of Renewal

In the opening paragraph I have quoted from Dan Aleshire pointing that "theological education is socially constructed enterprise". If that is so, in order to understand and re-orient theological education there is a need for every seminary and theological education program to arrange for periodic self-assessment for review of its respective social location and theological vision. Such self assessment is needed to evaluate whom it is serving, what purpose it is accomplishing and to what extent it is faithful to its calling as instrument of nurturing disciples of Jesus Christ. Discipleship in the 21st century in Asia mandates that the effort of Christianity as a minority community is best put to use in ecumenical cooperation and support. If a seminary is operating in an isolated, non-ecumenical way, besides the ecclesial and theological justification, the social reasons can also be discernable through the self-assessment survey. In the context some of the mega social, economic, cultural and political concerns that are faced in Asia, Christians need ecumenical solidarity to use their resources in a more effective and productive way. The ecumenical spirit can certainly begin in their training of leaders. Normally, people who are involved in full time in theological education, is relatively small section of the Christian community. Therefore initiating

[17] By citing Donald McGovern I do not subscribe to his homogenous unity theory of mission but I do recognize wisdom in pleading for reinterpretation of the so called great commission, Matt. 28:19 to meet the Asian challenge.

ecumenical connections and experiments may not be that difficult task provided there is strong conviction and commitment.

I will list some areas of investigation to provide an idea of the range of inquiry that is needed for a process of self-assessment. That is why my sub title for the article is 'a checklist for journey forward". Some of this information may be available through the national or regional association offices. In this process self-assessment one has to be a theological archaeologist (to look into the past), sociologist (to assess the present trends) and a visionary (to suggest possible direction for the future).

1. The denominational and church affiliations of candidates currently enrolled and the pattern of candidates enrolled in the past several years.
2. The specific enrolment plans if any to promote the ecumenical ethos of the seminary.
3. The denominational and church affiliations of faculty members.
4. The institutions where the faculty members predominantly undertake their graduate studies.
5. The female and male composition of candidates in training, faculty and leadership of the seminary.
6. The composition of the visiting faculty, from Asia, other regions of South and North. The courses they teach and the administrative and academic roles they play.
7. The interdenominational agreement for training candidates, appointing faculty and providing field/pastoral experience and exposure. The periodic assessment of impact of such agreements on the institution for the sake of better use of resources.
8. The subjects that are taught, the teaching methodology that is followed and the bibliography that is used for core courses.
9. The composition of the governing Board of Council. The process that is followed to their appointment them on the Board. The expectation of the seminary from its Board of governors.
10. The different components of the budget, the local and overseas contributions, alumni and other regular support. The value of endowment and other stipulated funds for faculty support, financial aid for students etc.
11. Overall focus of training? For training pastors, missionaries, persons for specialized ministries etc.

The above information will certainly facilitate the seminary to find its ecclesial and social belonging, constraints and ecumenical possibilities. If a seminary community does not know its potentials and its needs, its ecumenical possibilities are truncated. However ecumenical journey is a daunting and slow process. Since Christians have been living for centuries in self segregated divisions and communities, ecumenical ethos will not be created easily. World Christianity is yet to see an end to self-generated divisions still perpetuated by sections of Christians. Therefore ecumenism is a journey in faithfulness to the vision of unity Jesus spoke transcending the comfort and privilege of segregated Christian self sufficient existences often resulted from arrogances of exclusive truth claims, assumption of superiority of class, color, race, ethnicity, nationality, class etc.

Revisioning to be Relevant in Asia

Reiterating what David Tracy has mentioned (cited on first paragraph of first page) that the discipline of theology is where action and thought are brought together, my wish is that theological education be reshaped with two equally important components. One is a cognitive part of providing knowledge about Christianity with input on Bible, theology, history of Christianity and Pastoral practices, integrated as much as possible. The other equally important component is to equip the ministerial candidates with practical skills to engage with the community, both for the sake of nurturing Christian community/congregation (that one is responsible) and to minister towards building a holistic relationship with community at large for the enrichment of all the members of a given society. It is an old idea of 'parish', including the wellbeing of all in a given place where a Christian community is located. Even though theological training in Asian context has been framed to place equal emphasis on academic studies and pastoral practices, through the years as the theological education programs have been upgraded to graduate level of studies, the emphasis has shifted more to academic study at the expense of training ministerial candidates in pastoral and human skills to get engaged with communities, Christians and others in one's locality of ministry. In the prevailing Asian situation the leaders trained in theological institutions do not have the luxury of limiting their ministerial involvement only to give good biblical-theological counsel without personally engaging in various aspects of community life including interfaith dialogues and engagements. I have resisted making any proposals for models of theological education except highlighting some possible directions as Asian context is quite plural and in constant flux.

Even before Christianity was introduced to people of Asia, religious training for leadership was part of the various religious traditions that were in existence in Asia. Mostly such trainings were in the form of apprenticeship under the senior religious leader or given in the monasteries and religious centers. Such formation is in place even today. This model resonate the early church practices of ministerial formation. Fr. K.M. George indicates that in the Malankara Orthodox Syrian Church in India with its early church tradition and strong ascetic-monastic heritage influences, the method of theological education imparted through its seminary has a strong sense of mentoring through community living.[18] Similar type of ministerial formation is still the prevailing model in the Roman Catholic seminaries in Asia. Even in a number of Protestant theological seminaries such mentoring and community living is in practice but the overall ethos tends to be the promotion of an individual with academic accomplishments than to become a fellow disciple for the sake of common ministry and mission.

The western Protestant missionaries introduced a new pattern of training in Asia that was familiar to them and was functioning well in their context. Glen Miller points out that "After the Elizabethan settlement, the English church soon replaced the standard of monastic education for clergy with a classical university education . . . Elizabeth I envisioned the Anglican pastor as a person of letters, intellectually prepared to take his place next to the squire as a member of the ruling class. . . . Both the Continental and the English traditions of university education have had powerful effect on the United Sates."[19] Eventually in Europe with the enthusiasm of missionary societies, and in the USA because of its socio-political position on church and state separation, the independent seminaries supported on a voluntary basis by the respective denomination or persons belonging to those denominations came into existence, a corporate enterprise. Inevitably with western Christianity both the above models of divinity schools and independent seminaries made inroads to Asia and supported by the western personal and resources, and subsequently western trained Asians. As Asian Christians we need not be restrict ourselves to the Asian religious traditions or western Christian tradition but venture into the models that will address Asian reality. Multiplying innovative attempts and giving publicity to them is a better way forward than the easy compromise of repeating the familiar. Openness to mutual learning from Asian colleagues and others around the globe with similar quest and ecumenical commitment may take Asian theological education in that direction. The search for appropriate theological education in our time is not a special quest of Asians. Asians must be open and certainly benefit from insights coming from different sources as long as they have relevance to their context.[20] In turn they also are obliged to make contribution to the renewal of world Christianity by sharing their own insights and experiences.

---

[18] K. M. George, "Theological Education in the Oriental tradition" in *Handbook of Theological Education in World Christianity*. Eds. Dietrich Werner, David Esterline, Nansoon Kang and Joshva Raja. Oxford: Regnum, 2010, p.624.
[19] Glenn Miller, "Why the Seminary? A Historical Inquiry" in *Multiple Paths to Ministry. New Models for Theological Education.* Lance R. Baker and B. Edmon Martin, Eds. Cleveland, OH: The Pilgrim Press, 2004, p.119.
[20] Robert Banks. *Reenvisioning Theological Education. Exploring a Missional alternative to current models.* Grand Rapids: Wm Eerdmans, 1999.

Bibliography

Aleshire, Daniel O. *Earthen Vessels. Hopeful Reflections on the work and future of theological schools.* Grand Rapids, MI: Eerdmans, 2008.

Baker, Lance R. and B. Edmon Martin, Eds. *Multiple Paths to Ministry. New Models for Theological Education.* Cleveland, OH: The Pilgrim Press, 2004.

Banks, Robert. *Reenvisioning Theological Education. Exploring a Missional alternative to current models.* Grand Rapids, MI: Eerdmans, 1999.

England, J. C., et al. Eds. *Asian Christian Theologies. A Research Guide to Authors, Movements, Sources.* (Three volumes). Maryknoll, NY: Orbis, 2002, 2003, 2004.

Huang, Po Ho. *Mission from the underside: transforming theological education in Asia.* Bangalore: SATHRI, 2010

Lonchar, Wati. Ed. *Ecumenical Theological Education in Changing Context.* Jorhat, Assam: ETE-WCC/CCA, 2005.

Phan, Peter C. Ed. *Christianities in Asia.* Malden, MA: Wiley-Blackwell, 2011.

Scott, Sunquist et al Eds. *A Dictionary of Asian Christianity.* Grand Rapids, MI: Eerdmans, 2001.

Suh, David Kwang-sun et al. Eds. *Charting the future of theology and theological education in Asia.* Delhi: ISPCK, 2004.

Werner, Dietrich, David Esterline, Nansoon Kang and Joshva Raja, Eds. *Handbook of Theological Education in World Christianity.* Eds. Oxford: Regnum, 2010

Werner, Dietrich, Ed. *Training to be ministers in Asia.* Taiwan: PTCA, 2012.

(77) Models of Teaching / Learning Ecumenism in Asia

Hope S. Antone

How do we foster the spirit of ecumenism? Does teaching about the ecumenical movement teach people to become ecumenical in their thinking, outlook, attitude, behavior and lifestyle? In my experience, learning about the history of the ecumenical movement is helpful, but it does not automatically lead to having an ecumenical perspective. One may know the facts about the different expressions of the ecumenical movement and the factors that led to their founding at local, national, regional and global levels. But having such information does not necessarily or automatically lead to one becoming an ecumenical person. This was recently confirmed by an Ecumenics lecturer who shared at a meeting that one student, after finishing the course said, "What we learned in this course is all good, but we still need to know how to make our ordinary church members more ecumenical."

Not all seminaries in Asia have Ecumenics or Ecumenism in their curricula. In the few places where the subject is in the curricula, it is usually offered as an elective course – which means that it is offered only when there are enough students who enroll in it. Another reason why ecumenism is not mainstreamed in Asian seminaries is because of the negative propaganda that the ecumenical movement has been subjected to in some parts of Asia.[1]

A good number of Asian seminary leaders have justified their lack of emphasis on ecumenism as a subject by claiming that their theological institutions are already ecumenical because they have a diverse population of teachers and students – i.e. they come from different denominations, different ethnic groups, or even different nationalities. Does having a diverse population of students and teachers automatically promote ecumenism? Having a plurality of ethnic, linguistic, denominational or national groups in a seminary *may* help promote ecumenism but it does not automatically lead to having an ecumenical perspective or outlook. The institution has to intentionally do something about that gift of plurality so that it can enhance the spirit of ecumenism.

Asian Perspective of Ecumenism

The Asian perspective of ecumenism is affected and shaped by the contextual realities in Asia. Given the reality of plurality in Asia, what is required is wider ecumenism. In the earlier period of the history of the ecumenical movement, ecumenism was simply understood as the movement towards church or Christian unity – e.g. "to enable the whole church to bring the whole gospel to the whole world".[2] Also in the beginning of the ecumenical movement, efforts toward Christian unity meant those by mainstream or classical Protestant denominations. With the reality of many other Christian groups, ideological groups and faith groups that are clearly present in Asia, and with the challenges of ecological devastation in the region,

---

[1] Whenever the author conducted ecumenical trainings during her tenure as Joint Executive Secretary for Faith, Mission and Unity of the Christian Conference of Asia (CCA), she always began by asking what images came to people's minds when they heard the words 'ecumenism', 'ecumenical' or 'ecumenical movement'. In certain countries, there were more negative than positive images which reflected a misperception or lack of understanding of what the movement really represents. Asked how they came to have such images (perceptions or understanding), many participants said they heard them from certain foreign missionaries who came to their countries and who explicitly warned them about the ecumenical movement.

[2] Harvey Cox spoke of the "original purpose" of the ecumenical movement during the 45th anniversary celebration and international symposium of CCA in August 2002. See his paper, "Religious Values of the Ecumenical Movement," in *Living in Oikoumene*, Hope S. Antone, ed. (Hong Kong: CCA, 2003).

Asians have understood afresh the meaning of *Oikoumene*, by going to the root of the word, *oikos* (house/household/family/nation) and all who dwell therein, hence, the whole inhabited earth. In understanding *Oikoumene* afresh, Asians are recovering the Asian sense of household, which is inclusive of all people regardless of bloodline, the animals, and plants. Hence, another understanding of *Oikoumene* is the whole world as the household of God, and Ecumenism as living together in the household of God. This is the wider ecumenical vision – which transcends church or Christian unity and humanity, and embraces the whole of God's creation.

In Asia, teaching ecumenism involves all efforts to equip people with the wider ecumenical vision of living together in the household of God – where all God's children are called to love and serve each other and care for all of God's creation. The Asian understanding of God's children is not limited to those with Christian label only – for all people are God's children regardless of whether they acknowledge God as their parent or not. Living together in the household of God also means being aware of the brokenness in God's creation. God's creation has been broken and violated due to the domination systems of sexism, racism, classism, casteism, ethnocentrism, anthropocentrism and imperialism. Living together in the household of God finally means being committed to recovering the interconnectedness, interrelatedness and interdependence of all that God created.

Whether the opportunities for teaching are formal (i.e. academic) or informal (i.e. non-academic), teaching ecumenism in Asia must be based on this wider ecumenical vision. It is therefore intentional, purposive, and imperative.

During my time with the Christian Conference of Asia, I developed a framework to help describe this wider ecumenical vision through the following shifts[3] in perspective, attitude and behavior:

From competition to cooperation of denominations

While the ecumenical movement began with the need for unity in the mission fields, the denominations that came about reflected the divisions and rivalries of mission bodies. The sense of denominationalism has lingered to this day, shown in the continuing competition and rivalry, if not animosity and mistrust among denominations, and more so in their inward-looking attitudes geared toward self-preservation and self-propagation alone. For churches to be truly ecumenical, they need to move away from the tendency to compete, and instead to work together in cooperation and partnership.

From condemnation to dialogue with other daiths

Asian churches are the minority in Asian countries, except in the Philippines and Timor Leste. Although many Asian churches have inherited a strong missionary zeal to "bring Christ (and salvation) to the nations", some Asian theologians are already calling for recovering the essence of being truly Asian – that of being interreligious, i.e. being open to dialogue, mutual understanding and respect, and mutual critique for mutual transformation. For churches to be truly ecumenical, they need to move away from the tendency to condemn and judge other religious or faith communities, and instead to be open to dialogue with them.

From isolation to collaboration with civil society

While other regions of the world have declared the fall or end of communism, a number of Asian countries are still host to various ideologies – e.g. Communist, Socialist, Maoist, Marxist, etc. – whether as the dominant ideology of the government in power or as the ideology of groups that are clamoring for change. However, Asian churches have inherited the communist-scare resulting from the Cold War between the

---

[3] Hope S. Antone, "Mission and Evangelism with an Ecumenical Vision," in *Windows into Ecumenism* (Hong Kong: Christian Conference of Asia, 2005), 136-8. The author formulated this framework in 2003 for a national youth program in Dharan, Nepal and since then she has been using it as the framework of her ministry as Joint Executive Secretary for Faith, Mission and Unity of the Christian Conference of Asia.

superpowers and also from the pietistic Christian tradition that prioritized spiritual concerns over the concrete needs of people. For churches to be truly ecumenical, they need to move away from the tendency to isolate from civil society and people's movements, especially those working for justice and peace, knowing that social problems affect everyone regardless of faith or creed.

From disintegration to integrity of creation

Many countries in Asia are often hit by natural disasters but the signs of global warming and climate change are also increasingly felt with more intensity and frequency. Disintegration of God's creation is felt when domination systems oppress certain groups because of their gender, race, class, caste, sexuality; and when human beings claim to be more important than the rest of creation. For churches to be truly ecumenical, they need to move away from the tendency to be complicit with disintegration and brokenness, usually through their inaction, and instead actively work to recover the interrelatedness, connectedness, and interdependence of all that God created. This means ecological justice and also justice among peoples regardless of gender, race, class, caste, sexuality, etc.

I believe that the four shifts in the framework are the benchmarks of a wider ecumenical vision. The fact that they are shifts in thinking, perspective, outlook, attitude and behavior implies that ecumenical learning is not only a cognitive process of accumulating facts and information – it calls for real change and commitment to transformation. I will now share how this framework has helped to guide the teaching/learning of ecumenism in formal and non-formal settings.

Model 1: Teaching/Learning Ecumenism through an Ecumenical Ethos

Seminaries with a diversity of faculty and students provide a natural environment for teaching ecumenism. That diversity must be utilized through intentional activities of meaningful interactions and encounters for better understanding of and respect for differences. Such encounters may include but should not be limited to the sharing of cultures and festivals, or recognizing different languages, ethnicities and nationalities present with the diverse population of students, faculty and staff, e.g. during an International Day celebration. An orientation program at the beginning of the semester or school year can include group dynamics and values clarification sessions that would encourage self-awareness and respect for others. To encourage awareness, understanding and respect for others and to foster a sense of solidarity with each other, activities can also be organized for the sharing of situations and problems faced by different groups of people due to their ethnicity or nationality (or lack thereof). Such encounters can also lead to a critical realization of one's tendency to hold prejudices and stereotypes about others and otherness, which prevent one from appreciating, respecting and celebrating differences. Activities that touch the hearts of people – e.g. through a personal self-assessment of their openness and tolerance to others (or lack thereof) – have longer lasting impact on people.

Another way that ecumenism can be taught (or caught) through the ecumenical ethos is by the worship life of the community. Worship life in the seminary or organization can be enriched through using different liturgical traditions and resources represented in the community, instead of using only one denomination's way of worship all the time. A representative committee planning the worship consisting of students and faculty can create ecumenical worship experiences that utilize the resources from people's experiences, traditions and wisdom. These are some useful practices needed in creating an ecumenical ethos in order to foster the ecumenical spirit.

Model 2: Teaching/Learning Ecumenism as an Academic Subject

If the subject of ecumenism (or ecumenics) is offered as a course[4], it should not only focus on cognitive learning of the history and formation of the ecumenical movement. Instead it should begin with where the students are – e.g. a sharing of their own perceptions of ecumenism (negative and positive) and their own faith and ecumenical journeys. It is quite fun to hear students' answers to the following questions: "What do people in your context say about ecumenism?" "What do you say about ecumenism?" Or, "What comes to your mind when you hear the words, *ecumenism*, *ecumenical*, *ecumenist*? Where did you hear about such things?" This exercise has helped me to understand why in some places there seems to be an aversion (or allergy) to ecumenism. This will also set in proper perspective the negative propaganda against ecumenism and the ecumenical movement.

Inputs on the history of the ecumenical movement – especially the different ecumenical expressions at local, national, regional and global levels – will be useful together with a word study of *Oikoumene* and its related words – like *Oikos*, Ecumenism, Economy, Ecology – to revisit the meanings of these words. Biblical and theological foundations of ecumenism should be put side by side with the cultural and sociological foundations. While there are definitely passages in scriptures that speak about living together and striving for unity and reconciliation, it is also important to look into the indigenous ways of living together in harmony and connectedness. It is quite interesting to note early practices of living together and caring for each other and creation, despite the ethnic and religious differences, even long before the formal ecumenical movement began.

The framework on the wider ecumenical vision is an important tool to show Asia's particular take on Ecumenism. This means including intrafaith ecumenism, interfaith ecumenism, faith-ideology dialogue, and interconnectedness with the whole of creation. Students will be very engaged when they do reports on any of these topics or case studies on the state of intrafaith or interfaith ecumenism in their respective countries, using the framework of wider ecumenism. Inputs on the theology of dialogue and trends in intrareligious and interreligious cooperation would be useful. So will be the challenges posed by domination systems of sexism, racism, classism, casteism, ethnocentrism, anthropocentrism, and imperialism which have contributed to the brokenness in the household of God. Again, students will be very engaged when they do reports or case studies on any of these domination systems.

Classes need not be done only within the four walls of the classroom, using books and lectures. Visit to other churches, religious communities, and groups addressing critical issues in the community would facilitate meaningful encounters with the people in their real life situations. Inviting guest speakers or facilitators from other faith communities or ideological groups, or those working on conflict transformation and peacebuilding and the like would definitely enrich the class experience. For their final projects, students need not write formal or academic research papers. Instead, they can do practical projects on how to promote wider ecumenism in their own contexts. This is also a good tool to evaluate how the lessons have impacted the students.

Model 3: Teaching/Learning Ecumenism through Joint Formation Programs

Another model of teaching ecumenism is through non-formal ecumenical courses and training programs. These include the courses and training programs offered by ecumenical organizations like the Christian Conference of Asia (CCA) and the National Council of Churches. Since 1976, the CCA has been organizing the annual regional Asian Ecumenical Course (AEC) to train the next line of ecumenical leaders. AEC has four components: Asian reality, ecumenical vision, community building, and leadership

[4] Examples of activities come from the course syllabi prepared by Hope S. Antone for teaching Ecumenics at McGilvary College of Divinity of Payap University in Chiang Mai, Thailand in 2010 and 2012.

training. Since 2000, the National Council of Churches in the Philippines (NCCP) has been organizing its national Basic Ecumenical Course (BEC) to prepare more ecumenical cadres for its member churches and the ecumenical movement. In 2003 and 2010, respectively, a Philippine BEC was jointly organized by NCCP and CCA, with some participants from other Asian countries. In 2011, the first Indonesian BEC was jointly organized by CCA and the Communion of Churches in Indonesia, with some participants from Malaysia and Timor Leste. While the regional AEC gathers around 20-25 participants from among the 100 or more member churches in Asia, the BEC can gather 30-35 participants from all over the country, with a few international participants from a few neighboring countries.

Barbara Stephens, former CCA Education secretary whose responsibility included organizing the Asian Ecumenical Course, described the purpose of AEC in her Introduction to *Finding the Way Together:*

> It must be recognized that intentional courses such as the Asian Ecumenical Course are not the only ways in which people learn about ecumenism or the only source from which leadership for the ecumenical movement can emerge. However, they provide a valuable opportunity for people to reflect on what the ecumenical task is today, and to think seriously about the way in which this task can be carried out. Such courses can also be the means whereby those who have responsibility in denominational structures can develop an ecumenical perspective.[5]

By holding the AEC in different countries of Asia, participants learn ecumenism through the day to day "classroom" or learning setting in Asia. The setting provides the starting point for analysis of Asian reality, with participants contributing reports on their respective contextual realities. Immersion in selected communities of the host country enriches participants' experience of encountering other people in their own situations and provides a mirror through which they can see problems and challenges that people face. In view of such contextual realities, the history of the ecumenical movement and the wider ecumenical vision are presented. The history of the ecumenical movement does not only focus on the founding of the various expressions of the ecumenical movement especially in the 20th century. Rather, it goes back to the earlier forms of ecumenism even before the coming of Christianity to Asia. John England puts it succinctly in his book:

> To limit the extent of Asian Christian history to the last few centuries, and worse, to categorize this simply as 'history of mission', is to assume not only that genuine Christian faith and practice began in Asia only in the sixteenth century for Roman Catholics, or in the nineteenth century for Protestants, but that the 'One living God' of Christian understanding has been somehow absent from all previous Asian history.[6]

The wider ecumenical vision does not only focus on the quest for unity among Christians and churches but also on the obstacles to the wider unity of human beings and of the whole creation. Hence, the ecumenical vision also highlights the signs of brokenness in the household of God, challenging participants to think of ways to address the brokenness. Community building is promoted through the ethos of living together, building trust through sharing of faith journeys, and enriching experiences through worshipping together, regardless of differences in ethnicity or nationality, denomination, gender, educational or professional background. Leadership training is ensured as participants are grouped into teams and assigned to lead the day's activities, and as they learn to represent their church or ecumenical organizations, e.g. through the sharing of reports on their contextual realities and the ecumenical journeys of their churches or NCCs. A culminating activity of the course is the sharing of Action Plans which each

---

[5] *Finding the Way Together: Education for Ecumenical Understanding and Action* (Singapore: CCA, 1986), ix.
[6] John C. England, *The Hidden History of Christianity in Asia: The Churches of the East Before 1500* (Delhi: ISPCK and Hong Kong: CCA, 1998), 2.

participant prepares – showing how they will take back what they have learned from the course in order to spread the wider ecumenical vision with others.

Model 4: Teaching/Learning Wider Ecumenism through Joint Actions for Peace and Justice

Teaching and learning do not just happen in formal courses or non-formal educational activities. The wider ecumenical vision is also taught or learned (caught) in daily living, especially through practices that promote positive encounters of people from different cultural, political or faith backgrounds. In Asia, many positive encounters happen through joint actions for peace and justice, for health and wholeness, for reconciliation and healing. In fact, many of these address the gruesome brokenness in the household of God. Such joint actions do not dwell on dogmatic or doctrinal teachings, but on commonly shared values such as justice, peace and total wellbeing. Such joint actions include the promotion of ethnic and religious harmony, socio-economic justice, rehabilitation of victims and survivors of natural and human-made disasters, justice for the marginalized groups, and justice for creation.

As a visible sign of the intrafaith ecumenism that Asian Christians have tried to live out and manifest, the CCA and the Federation of Asian Bishops Conferences (Roman Catholic partner of CCA) have on several occasions organized programs such as the seminars for the Asian Movement for Christian Unity (AMCU), the Joint Ecumenical Formation (JEF), and the Asia Conference of Theology Students (ACTS). The programs are planned and implemented by the staff of the two organizations. More recently, invitations to the AMCU and ACTS were extended to the Asian Evangelical Alliance (AEA) and the Asian Pentecostal Society (APS), thereby broadening the circle. Such programs have helped to bring together representatives from the different Christian communities in Asia, giving them a safe space to share their visions and the challenges that they face in their respective contexts. Many of them realize that there are common concerns that they share but that there are also differences that they need to know and understand. In the process of learning about each other, many of them develop a better understanding of themselves and their traditions, while opening their horizon to the plurality of ways of believing and living out their faith in the same Christ Jesus. As participants get to meet more than one time, they become more familiar with each other that they can even ask questions that have to do with doctrines and dogmas, without being condescending, confrontational or adversarial.

Conscious of the need for wider ecumenism, some of these Christian groups try to work together and in cooperation with other religious or civil society groups in response to other urgent issues in Asia. Among their joint actions are those that address issues like HIV and AIDS, global warming and climate change, human rights violations, ecological disasters, and the like. When followed by a sharing of reflections from participants' respective religious or ideological points of view, joint actions are excellent occasions for teaching/learning wider ecumenism.

Model 5: Teaching/Learning Wider Ecumenism Starting with the Young

The task of teaching ecumenism does not only lie with seminaries or ecumenical organizations – it lies with the churches themselves. It is not a subject or issue for adult members only – it is the concern for the whole community. As I recall my own childhood, I remember that my ecumenical formation was already being shaped by family discussions, the Sunday School at my church, and the Daily Vacation Church School (DVCS) that my church conducted with the village communities. Since my father worked for the Radio Station of the National Council of Churches in the Philippines, I grew up visiting the transmitter site in Banilad, Dumaguete City with the large OIKOUMENE symbol in the middle of the fish pond. That symbol provided a good topic for conversation in my family – what language it was and what it meant. My father always enjoyed sharing new ideas from his readings and engagements not only in his work place but also at home.

Growing up as youth, I also remember that our church youth activities included exposure and outreach service to some of the depressed communities in the provinces. Bible studies and prayer meetings challenged us to put our faith in action in service for and with the poor, deprived and oppressed in our communities. I was 15 years old when I answered the call to volunteer as a teacher of the DVCS. I remember how the teacher's material that year had challenged me to broaden my ecumenical understanding.[7] The theme was "Living in Community" and one of the activities was to visit the different religious places in the neighborhood. At that time, there was no mosque yet in my hometown but we still talked about the need to understand and respect people with other religious beliefs. Since there were no other religious places in our community at that time, I simply took my class to visit different churches in the neighborhood. The theme song of that DVCS was "One God," which continues to inspire me to this day:

Millions of stars placed in the sky by one God
Millions of *folk* lift up their eyes to one God
So many children calling to God by many a different name
One *Parent*, loving each the same
Many the ways all of us pray to one God
Many the paths winding their way to one God
Brothers and sisters there are no strangers
After God's work is done
For your God and my God are one.[8]

Conclusion

Whether it is through socialization from young, intentional study as in a formal or non-formal course, through joint actions and reflections, or through an ecumenical ethos of a given community, the teaching and learning of ecumenism, especially wider ecumenism, is a must in Asia. This is our calling and our responsibility.

The theme of the WCC 13th General Assembly, "God of life, lead us to justice and peace," is a prayerful call to an ecumenical commitment for all of us to join in God's effort to bring about peace with justice not only to people but to the whole creation. This is our calling as members of the household of God, the Oikoumene.

Bibliography

Antone, Hope S. "Ecumenical Formation in Theological Education: Asian Perspectives." In *Handbook of Theological Education in World Christianity*. Dietrich Werner, et al., eds. Oxford: Regnum Books, 2010.

____________. "Living Together in the Household of God: Becoming a Household of Love, Faith and Hope." In *CTC Bulletin*. Vol. XXII, No. 2 (August 2006): 52-60.

[7] The Daily Vacation Church School (DVCS) is a yearly summer program for children from kindergarten to older primary. Every year, the National Council of Churches in the Philippines gathers a group of educators and curriculum writers from various member churches to write the DVCS materials on specific themes or foci.

[8] Song composed by Ervin Drake and Jimmy Shirl and sung by Barbara Streisand. Italicized words mean changes introduced by the author to make the language more inclusive (*folk* instead of men and *Parent* instead of Father).

____________. "Mission and Evangelism with an Ecumenical Vision." In *Windows into Ecumenism*. Hong Kong: Christian Conference of Asia, 2005.

Christian Conference of Asia. *Finding the Way Together: Education for Ecumenical Understanding and Action*. Singapore: CCA, 1986.

Cox, Harvey. "Religious Values of the Ecumenical Movement." In *Living in Oikoumene*. Hope S. Antone, ed. Hong Kong: CCA, 2003.

England, John C. *The Hidden History of Christianity in Asia: The Churches of the East Before 1500*. Delhi: ISPCK and Hong Kong: CCA, 1998.

(78) AN ETHOS FOR TEACHING THEOLOGY ECUMENICALLY IN ASIA

David Suh

"Ecumenical Ethos"

To put it simply, an "ecumenical ethos" or "ecumenical" means *openness*. It is an attitude of opening the heart and mind of a Christian to the Christian community of believers in his/her church, to other believers in other churches or denominations, to other churches around one's neighborhood (a Protestant to a Catholic and vice versa), to other religious believers, that is, non-Christian religions, and to the world of politics, economics and secular culture. It is openness of heart and mind to the other, other than oneself and other than one's own world of beliefs and mindset. It is "going beyond oneself." That is, ultimately, to open to God.

As soon as one opens oneself to others in the world, one *responds* ecumenically. This is to mean that a Christian person will *engage* with his/her own "existential questions" and beliefs, looking and examining its contents, meanings and relevance in the light of the Bible and the Christian traditions and culture of Christian life. It is to bring oneself to *dialogue* with other people in other church traditions in order to understand the commonality and differences as well as diversity in faith and community life. It is not only to dialogue with the people in other Christian communities, but to engage with the people in other religions, belief systems and ideologies. More specifically in the case of Asia, "ecumenical" means to open oneself to engage with Asian religions which are existing and thriving in the Christian neighborhood. Finally, an "ecumenical ethos" means an attitude and readiness to respond to and engage with the world, going beyond the self, the church compound and boundaries of faith and religious communities. Once again, ultimately, this is to respond and engage with God whose presence is everywhere in our life and work, and in the midst of human history and the world.

The purpose and the end of ecumenical openness, responsiveness, and engagement with the world is *metanoia, repentance, transformation, change, growth and maturity*. As Paul has said in his letter to the Corinthians (13:12): "For now we see in a mirror dimly, but then we will see face to face. Now I know only in part, then I will know fully, even as I have been known fully." It is turning around to God for the fullness of life. An ecumenical ethos of openness with others will expand and enlarge one's narrow and limited scope and perspective of life, thereby enrich one's own life to its fullness. It will embrace others with caring and sharing with love, hope and faith (I Corinthian 13:13). An ecumenical ethos will create the culture of peaceful unity in diversity, where different faith orientations and religious faith and practice are in conflict with each other. The final end of ecumenical engagement with the world is to establish and enlarge the Reign of God where justice, peace and the fullness of life in the created world of ours will prevail.

"Ecumenical Ethos" in Theological Education: Hurmhut, 1980

It is enlightening to remember the final report of PTE/WCC consultation held in Herrnhut, Germany in 1980 which interprets "ecumenical ethos" putting into action in theological education at large. I would like to highlight Dietrich Werner's understanding of the Herrnhut consultation on "ecumenical ethos" in theological education in Europe:

> We understand ecumenical learning not as a separate part or sub-division of theology.... It is a dimension of all theology and theological education. It is to do with the readiness to experience and take account of other

> confessions of Christian faith, other religious traditions and other social and cultural realities, in order to see things whole. It has to do with local and concrete issues, not parochially but in the awareness of the whole inhabited earth and in the perspective of unity in Christ.[1]

The Herrnhut report articulates very clearly what it means to put ecumenical ethos into action in all aspects and scope of theological education not only in Germany, Europe but also all around the globe in World Christianity. This means that ecumenical education should *not* be done only in a course or two on ecumenical movement or "ecumenical theology" *separately* from the so-called mainline theological courses such as the Bible, Systematic Theology, Church History, and Practical Theology. But ecumenical learning ought to take place in all the theological courses. Ecumenical ethos should be in all parts and aspects of the theological enterprise of learning.

It should be noted that the Herrnhut Report clearly suggests that ecumenical learning should *not* be done *parochially*. This should be translated into historical and theological contexts of the development of theological education in the so-called two-thirds world. Historically, the early development of theological education in Asia, for example, was solely in the hands of missionaries from the West who brought the Christian Gospel with colonial invaders with guns and gunboats. The missionaries' theological education was very much limited to teaching the Christian Bible most of the times in the language of the missionaries and sometimes in the native language which the missionaries had to learn to speak and translate. Furthermore, the missionaries were to convert the natives to Christian faith, by propagating that Christianity is the only true way to salvation, forcing the natives to reject all other native religions as superstition, ignorance and idol worship. It was none other than "Christian parochialism." Thereby, the converted natives were taught to close their minds about the indigenous and traditional religious and cultural behaviors as backward and evils. The Christian exclusivism worked against other native religions but also against other confessions of Christian faith such as Catholic Church and even other Protestant denominations. In most cases in Asia, the Protestant church goers did not give the name "Christian" to the Roman Catholics: "Christian" means "Protestants," and for the Catholics just "Catholics."

Post-missionary and Postcolonial Theological Education

Soon after the end of the Second World War, most of the Asian nations gained national independence from the Western Empires one after another, and delved into the nation building and decolonization process. In the process, mainline Christian denominations in Asian countries organized themselves for indigenous churches and structures of self-governance. As colonial powers were leaving the newly independent Asian nations, missionaries also left the governing power of the church to the native Christian leaders who has come of age. In the meantime, theological education was handed over to the indigenous theologians, most of which had been sent to the West to study theology and to be trained to succeed the missionary institutions.

However, while the colonized nations were struggling against their past to be liberated from the colonial past and decolonize themselves from the Western bureaucracy, political and economic dominations as well as from the Western ideologies, most of the Christian leaders in Asia decided to stay with the old ways of running the denominational organizations and churches as well as theological education for the ministers and church workers. The colonized minds of Asian Christians have remained colonized, strongly holding onto theology of Biblical literary fundamentalism with a blind sense of loyalty to their missionary teachers

---

[1] Quoted from *Theological Education in Europe.* Herrnhut, 1980, PTE/WCC, 13; in Dietrich Werner's article, "Ecumenical Formation in Theological Education: Historical Perspectives," in *Handbook of Theological Education in World Christianity,* edited by Dietrich Werner, David Esterline, Namsoon Kang and Joshua Raja. Oxford: Regnum Books International, 2010. p. 109.

who had taught exclusivism, legalism, and anti-intellectualism. Most of Asian Protestant churches including Korea are holding onto parochial, individual church-centered and denominational power-oriented anti-ecumenical stance. Theological education and ministrial formation are no exception.[2]

Against this strong theological hegemony of dogmatic and legalistic colonized Protestant churches in Korea, for example, new, ecumenically minded younger leaders began struggling to de-colonize their theology in the 1960's, after the end of Korean War (1950-53) and the April 19 Student Revolution against a Pro-American, Christian dictator President Syngman Rhee (1960). The younger theologians were mostly educated in the progressive and ecumenically committed theological schools in Europe and the US to unlearn their missionary theology of fundamentalism by reading Dietrich Bonhoeffer, Jurgen Moltmann, Karl Barth, Paul Tillich and Bultmann and Reinhold Niebuhr, etc. They were excited about the rise of Secular Theology of Harvey Cox, The Death of God debates, and the Black liberation movement of Martin Luther King, Jr. of the United States. Under the harsh military dictatorships in most of Asian countries in the 1960's and 70's, Asian Christian theologians were challenged by the cries of the oppressed and exploited people and the development of Latin American Liberation Theology. They had to become ecumenical, responding to the world and engaging themselves with the struggle of the people for liberation.

Just about the time when Latin American Liberation Theology was known to the rest of the worldwide Christian circles, the term "contextualization" was introduced by Shoki Coe of Taiwan in 1972 when he was leading Theological Education Fund (TEF) of the World Council of Churches. As the Latin American Liberation theologians are taking their social and political context seriously and responding to the realities with the liberating Gospel of Jesus Christ, Christian theologians in the Two-Thirds World followed them by taking their own contexts in doing their own theology.

Sister Virginia Fabella of the Philippines writes under the entry of "contextualization" in *Dictionary of Third World Theologies*[3]:

> It has been claimed that all theologies, because they are born out of social conditions and needs of a particular context, are in a sense "contextual." In the past, however, there was no conscious effort to understand the context. Philosophical abstractions, church doctrines, and biblical texts—rather than concrete situations and experience—were used as the starting point of theology. This was true of Western theology, which was taught as "universal theology," applicable to all times and contexts.

Furthermore, Fabella claims that contextual theology in the form of Third World liberation theologies give not only serious political and social analyses on the given context and the plight of the people, "but also seek the transformation of unjust and oppressive structures and practices therein." *(ibid)* She names such theological movements as Liberation theology in Latin America, black theology in South Africa, *minjung* theology in Korea, *dalit* theology in India, and the theology of struggle in the Philippines, contextual theologies.

Doing Theology Contextually

Suh Nam Dong, a Korean *minjung* theologian who introduced a *story* or *narrative theology* in doing contextual theology, said that it is to confluence two stories: the stories in the Bible (text) and the stories of the people (context). The stories in the Bible would interpret the stories of the people in suffering, that is, the text would interpret the context. But at the same time the context (the social and political realities)

---

[2] In this regard, Namsoon Kang's article, "Envisioning *Postcolonial* Theological Education: Dilemmas and Possibilities" in the *Handbook of Theological Education in World Christianity* (Regnum, 2010, 30-41) is most helpful.

[3] *Dictionary of Third World Theologies*, edited by Virginia Fabella, M.M. and R.S. Sugirtharajah, Orbis, 2000. pp. 58-59, here p. 58

would interpret the text, the stories in the Bible. It is an "ecumenical ethos" and an "ecumenical way of doing theology" to make the text (the Bible) responsible to the social and political realities. On the other hand, when one learns about the social and political realities in the world and involves in the action to change the situation, he/she comes to reflect on his/her learning and action in the light of the Bible. Here, theologizing, or doing theology, is to bring two stories together. And the hermeneutical cycle of action/reflection would be done in the light of the biblical text.[4]

"Asian context" is wide, vast and complex: it cannot be explained only by political and social problems of ideological confusion, dire poverty and under development as well as many languages and cultures. Aloysius Pieris, a Sri Lankan Catholic theologian, addressed in his book, *Asian Theology of Liberation*[5], two basic realities of Asia, namely, poverty and many religions: There are too many poor and diverse religions. Poverty in most parts of Asia is chronic and below sustenance level. In recent years Asian poverty has worsened in spite of the efforts of nation building and push for economic development in the neo-colonial framework of "globalization." The efforts created wider gap between the richer and poorer people not only within a nation, but also between nations in the region.

Pieris sees the rich possibility of doing theology with Asian spiritual resources of "many religions." He sees that Asian theology of liberation has to pull the rich diversity of Asian religions (which is world religions) into an open dialogue and networking with Asian religious communities to address the issue of Asian poverty. The so-called inter-faith dialogue is not for the attempt of mutual conquest, but for the understanding and mutual bonding for the liberation of the Asian people. In this sense, doing Asian liberation ecumenical theology in the unique Asian context of "many religions" goes beyond "adaptation, accommodation, inculturation and indigenization" as Fabella marks the difference.[6]

C.S. Song and Yeow Choo Lak, with other leading Asian theologians, have been challenging Asian theologians to do Christian theology with *Asian resources*. C.S. Song initiated the theological dialogue in PTCA (Program for Theology and Culture of Asia) in the 1970's with Asian theologians in many seminars and workshops. Yeow Choo Lak has made ATESEA (Association of Theological Education in South East Asia) visible with numerous publications to encourage Asian theologians to do Christian theologies from Asian perspective and Asian context with Asian resources. In 1996 some 200 Asian theologians from India to Korea gathered in Korea to found CATS (Congress of Asian Theologians). In 1976, EATWOT (Ecumenical Association of Third World Theologians) was founded to promote "the continuing development of Third World Christian theologies which will serve the church's mission in the world and witness to the new humanity in Christ expressed in the struggle for a just society" (Article 2, EATWOT Constitution). All of these efforts, among others, have created new vibrant "ecumenical ethos" in doing theology in Asia and beyond.

In the discussion of Asian realities, I would like to add two more issues which Asian theologians must face today. One is the legacy of *colonialism* and another one related to this is the issue of *war and peace.* Since the time the Portuguese landed on the Western Indian shores in 1498, only with a few exceptions, all of Asia had been colonized by the West. In the latter part of the 19th century, and the fist half of the 20th century, Asians had to fight for liberation and national independence, not only against the Western colonial powers but also against an Asian imperial power such as Japan. During the Second World War, almost all of Asia was devastated by the Allied forces, invasion of Japanese army and by the national independence armed struggles. For the first time in human history, newly invented atomic bombs were tested on the Asian people living in Hiroshima and Nagasaki, Japan, to end the Pacific War in 1945.

---

[4] See Huang Po Ho's article, "Contextualization and Inter-contextualization in Theological Education: An Asian Perspective" in *Handbook of Theological Education in World Christianity,* 2010. pp. 123f.

[5] Aloysius Pieris , *Asian Theology of Liberation* (Claretian Publications, 1988)

[6] Fabella, *Dictionary of Third World Theologies, ibid.*

The World War II, or the Pacific War was not the last war fought in Asia. Asian nations were forced to line up along with the ideological line of the "Eastern Bloc" or the "Western Bloc." All of Asia was divided up according to the Western ideologies of capitalism, communism or democracy which came from the colonial language which is alien to Asian churches and traditions. Not only has Asia as a whole been divided along the ideological line, but each nation has been divided into two camps to fight it out to overcome its division. China had to fight to unify under one flag and one ideology of communism. Vietnam had to fight against colonial powers for national integrity and unification, while Korea had to fight the Cold War along the ideological line of East and West, and is still divided to maintain the line of Cold War division, suffering from the threat of armed confrontation for the last half century.

As the people around the world celebrated the end of Cold War when Germany was unified, the Soviet Union was imploded, and Soviet Army pulled out from Afghanistan, the US armed forces invaded Iraq to "crusade" the Islamic world in Asia. Colonial wars waged by the Western Empires have never ended in Asia.

Following colonialism and the Cold War, as well as seemingly never ending global armed conflicts, the forced process of *globalization* has been the issue of most Asian countries. EATWOT met in 1996, addressed the issue of globalization:

> Present globalization is based on monopolies sustained by dominant nations. It is the Third World, the ex-colonies, that are made to suffer under monopolies of technology, finance, information, communication, access to natural resources, and weapons of mass destruction.... Globalization undermines identity. It effects the exclusion and marginalization of people and regions of the world as well as feminization of poverty. We see globalization not as a trans-historical reality, nor a historical necessity, but as a matter of social forces, the balance of which can be changed.[7]

Beyond the war and peace among the peoples and nations, the fundamental issue of human and natural world is now at stake. Rampant economic development drive, which has exploited and destroyed the environment and the total ecological world, has become the basic issue of survival of humanity. In this regard, it is prophetic to challenge the world Christian community to deal with the worldwide issue of *life as well as justice and peace* at the forthcoming 10th Assembly of WCC in Korea, with the announced Assembly theme: "God of Life, Lead Us to Justice and Peace." Indeed, the issues of justice, peace and integrity of creation are the pressing agenda of ecumenical theological education in Asia and beyond for the 21st century.

Ecumenical Learning for the Church Renewal: A Paradigm Shift

If we are to bring "ecumenical ethos" thus far created and nurtured among Asian contextual theologians into churches, into congregational life and formal theological education, we should make a radical paradigm change. What Asian ecumenical learning has to do is to incorporate the work and ethos of Asian contextual theologies. Western theologies cannot be at the center of our teaching and curricula from Sunday School to graduate theological education. The Asian way of doing theology should come into the center stage. It is likely to bring a Copernican revolution in Asian theological teaching and learning. The sun is no longer the Western theological figures. Asian religions and poverty, and the struggles of the people of Asia for life, justice and peace will have to be the source of energy for Asian Christian theology.

This new paradigm of theological education demands a new way of teaching and learning the *Hebrew Bible and the Christian Bible.* They have to be approached with Asian hermeneutical suspicion, with the eyes of Asian poor and many religions. With an Asian feminist theologian like Kwok Pui-lan, we must

---

[7] Special Issue of *Voices from the Third World,* December 1999, p. 201

discover the Bible in the non-biblical world which is Asia as she suggests in the title of her book, *Discovering the Bible in the Non-Biblical World.* [8] She says:

> When women study the Bible, we do not read from a written text. Instead, we share our stories, songs, and dramas. We sing, we dramatize, and we wait for the presence of the Holy Spirit. (Prologue, p.ix)

Her approach is to go directly to the stories of the people, in her case, to the stories of women. Asian women bring their stories to the Bible, and interpret the Bible with their stories of suffering and joy. And their reading of the Bible would give directions to their lives in the world. Suh Nam Dong argued that the Bible is only one of the references that the *minjung* would use in nurturing their faith for liberation. It is not *the only* book that is needed for liberation of the oppressed, exploited and alienated people. Stories of the Bible and stories of oppressed people and of Asian religions emerge in Asian way of doing ecumenical theology. The stories of *minjung,* are mythical stories, fairy-tales, novels, perms, folk plays, masked dances, music and performing arts as well as historical narratives in the non-biblical texts of Asian religions.

Instruction of *church history* in Asian theological schools should be organized in a similar way, starting with "hermeneutical suspicion" on the history of Christian missionary expansion and conquest. Asian church historians have traced the eastward missionary movement from Jerusalem to Beijing and beyond. Instead of telling that the early Christians took the westward direction of the missionary movement, Asian church historians should retell the stories of church history or the world Christian history as an eastward movement of an Asian religion. Asian church historians should narrate the story not from the missionary viewpoint of triumphalism, but from the perspective of the way in which our ancestors responded to the liberating message of the Gospel. We must narrate it as our story, Asian story, not as their story. For this we need historical imagination to deconstruct the Western discourse of colonial expansion and to reconstruct it as the contextualization of Asian Christianity.

When we come to the traditional course on *systematic and constructive theology*, Asian schools of theology for a long time have been obligated to teach Western theological giants such as Augustine, Aquinas, Calvin, Luther, Schliermacher, Barth, Bultmann and Tillich dealing with God, Jesus, the Holy Spirit, church and the world. It is about time to make a paradigm change in doing systematic theology, starting with Asian theological pioneers and with Asian realities of poverty, many religions, and war and peace. We should introduce our own theological giants such as C.S. Song, MM Thomas, DT Niles, Takenaka, Suh Nam Dong, Ahn Byung Mu, Jung Yong Lee, Kwok Pui-lan as well as *dalit theology* in India, *minjung theology* of Korea. We will seriously consider requiring our students to read classical literatures of Buddhism, Confucianism, Daoism and Islam to be able to reconstruct ecumenical theology. If the Western theologians constructed their theologies from Western philosophical traditions from Plato, Aristotle and Hegel and Kant, Asian theologians ought to learn how to reconstruct Asian ecumenical theology from Asian philosophical resources as well.

Ecumenical theology is a responsive theology. It is to respond to the Asian realities, the struggles of the poor and oppressed. In this light, I would like to highlight the need of Asian ecumenical education to address the oppressive Asian patriarchy in the churches and in the societies at large. Asian ecumenical education ought to expose the deep-seated patriarchal consciousness among men as well as women. Liberation of women and partnership of women with men should become an important topic in teaching and learning of the Bible and of the Asian traditional religions. We have to learn to expose how Western Christian theology has enforced Asian religions' ways to oppress and alienate Asian women.

---

[8] Kwok Pui-lan, *Discovering the Bible in the Non-Biblical World* (Orbis, 1995)

"Ecumenical ethos" will nurture "*praxis* learning," learning by serving the community and the world. It is to go out into the world to engage with the poor and alienated and with the people in other faith and religious communities. It is to learn by doing service work in hospital wards, orphanages and prison as well as in the church related kindergartens and schools. It is to learn about the poor and alienated by feeding the homeless, engaging with the problems of migrant workers, and with the problems of mentally and physically disabled people. Ecumenical learning will bring the believers of Jesus Christ out into the world by participating in the religious life of other people as in the program of "Buddhist temple stay." An ecumenical ethos and learning will be enlarged by participating in the various national, regional and global ecumenical conferences in various capacities. And various forms of ecumenical exchanges between churches in Asia will enhance ecumenical faith *praxis* learning amongst all people of God.

Bibliography

Dictionary of Third World Theologies, edited by Virginia Fabella, M.M. and R.S. Sugirtharajah, Orbis, 2000.

Aloysius Pieris , *Asian Theology of Liberation* (Claretian Publications, 1988)

Kwok Pui-lan, *Discovering the Bible in the Non-Biblical World* (Orbis, 1995)

Voices from the Third World, Special Issue of December 1999, p. 201

Dietrich Werner, "Ecumenical Formation in Theological Education: Historical Perspectives," in *Handbook of Theological Education in World Christianity,* edited by Dietrich Werner, David Esterline, Namsoon Kang and Joshua Raja. Oxford: Regnum Books International, 2010. p. 109

(79) ASIAN NORTH AMERICAN CHRISTIANITY, THEOLOGY AND THEOLOGICAL EDUCATION

J. Paul Rajashekar

It is necessary to begin this essay with a word of clarification. The term "Asian American" is a socio-political construct, a convenient designation to identify and homogenize Americans of Asian ancestry and heritage who have made a home in North America. There is no singular "pan-Asian American" identity, if anything, the phrase masks a plurality and multiplicity of identities. It lumps together people of diverse Asian backgrounds, nations, cultures, histories, races, ethnicities, tribes, religions, Christian denominations, customs, languages, castes, socio-economic backgrounds, world-views and so forth. "Asian Americans" therefore represent acolorful mosaic of people aggregated as a culturally descriptive label. It originated in the 1960's in the era of Civil Rights movement in the United States as an expression of self-identity and determination and thus repudiating the earlier stereotype characterization of Asians as "Orientals." As a marker of "pan-Asian" identity, it is a "racialized" or "race based" category in the identity politics of America that lumps together diverse and unrelated groups of people into a homogenized or monolithic identity that belies actual realities.

It is a category that reifies and essentializes the non-European "Other," to see Asians in North America as an indistinguishable group in the eyes of the dominant racial group: the "white Americans."In a nation of immigrants, the dominant racial group claims its identity simply as "Americans," without reference to their country of origin, other minority groups are identified in terms of race, color, ethnicity or country of origin: "African/Black American," "Native American," "Hispanic American," "Asian American," and the like. Demographic minority communities as a group are further sub-divided or self-distinguish themselves into sub-categories: "Korean American," "Asian Indian American," "Japanese American," "Chinese American," "Cuban American," "Mexican American," and so on. Such racialized classifications, as in the case of "Asian Americans," unwittingly imply that they are "aliens," "perpetual foreigners," or a "diaspora" who do not really belong in North America, notwithstanding the fact that in the United States people of Asian heritage have been living for over five generations, well assimilated culturally, but not necessarily structurally, into the American fabric![1] Thus the designation, "Asian American" has served as a innocuous handle to define, differentiate, or marginalize diverse and unrelated groups of people into a homogenized whole.

The Demographic Face of Asian Americans

While significant numbers of people from Asia are recent immigrants to North America (since 1965), Asian people arrived in the United States as early as late 16th century (Filipino sailors in the Spanish colonial era) and large scale immigration of Chinese occurred in mid-19th century. The most recent comprehensive demographic data comes from a study released by the Pew Research Center in July 2012, entitled, *The Rise of Asian Americans*.[2] The survey claims that the growth of Asian Americans in recent decades has significantly contributed to the diversity of the U.S. religious landscape. From less than 1% of the total U.S. population in 1965, Asian Americans have increased to 5.8% (or 18.2 million in 2011, according to the U.S. Census). Chinese represent the largest group (23.2%), followed by Filipino (19.7%), Indian (18.4%), Vietnamese (10%), Korean (9.9%) and Japanese (7.5%). A vast majority of Asian

---

[1] Ronald Takaki, *Strangers from a Different Shore: A History of Asian Americans* (Boston: Little, Bown, 1989).

[2] All demographic data cited in this essay comes from the Pew Report on *The Rise of Asian Americans* available on the web: www.pewforum.org/asian-americans

Americans (74.1%) are foreign born with the exception of 73% of Japanese who are American born. It is also worth noting that the growth of US Asian population in recent decades has been largely responsible for the growth of non-Abrahamic faiths in the United States, particularly Buddhism and Hinduism. Counted together, Buddhists and Hindus today account for about the same share of the U.S. public as Jews (roughly 2%). At the same time, most Asian Americans belong to the country's two largest religious groups: Christians and people who say they have no particular religious affiliation.

According to The Pew survey, Christians are the largest religious group among U.S. Asian adults (42%), and the unaffiliated are second (26%). Buddhists are third, accounting for about one-in-seven Asian Americans (14%), followed by Hindus (10%), Muslims (4%) and Sikhs (1%). Followers of other religions make up 2% of U.S. Asians. Not only do Asian Americans, as a whole, present a mosaic of many faiths, but each of the six largest subgroups of this largely immigrant population also displays a different religious complexion. A majority of Filipinos in the U.S. are Catholic, while a majority of Korean Americans are Protestant. About half of Indian Americans are Hindu, while about half of Chinese Americans are unaffiliated. A plurality of Vietnamese Americans is Buddhist, while Japanese Americans are a mix of Christians, Buddhists and the unaffiliated.

The Pew Research Center survey is the most recent comprehensive data on Asian Americans available in the United States.Reactions to this survey have been mixed among Asian Americans. The report, which hailed Asians as the fastest-growing and highest-achieving racial group in the country, drew widespread criticism from Asian American scholars, advocates and lawmakers who raised alarm about the report, and warned against taking it seriously at all. There were widespread criticism that the survey provided a great deal of data, it also caste Asian Americans as economically successful "model minority," without accounting for the economic disparities among Asian communities, especially recent immigrants and refugees from Southeast Asia, and thus provided a stereotypical view of Asian Americans. Nonetheless, the statistical data provides a snapshot of various aspects of Asian American Community.

The reality of Asian American communities in the US is indeed complex and their identity in relation to mainstream America is ambiguous. Asian Americans are in search of their identity and belonging, neither embraced in the Asian continent nor in North America! Unlike European immigrants, Asian Americans have not been able to "blend" or "melt" into the American mainstream because of their physical or distinct racial identity and experience, racial discrimination and exclusion, even those who have "assimilated" into the mainstream American culture.[3] The American born generations of Asians have had to cope with a "hybrid" identity, neither "here nor there" and are challenged to navigate between "American" or "Asian" identity and often straddling between two distinct identities and cultures. According to the Pew Survey, 75.1% of Asians in the US are foreign born and the rest are native born, 14% describe themselves as "American," 62% describe themselves by using the country of origin and only 19% describe themselves as "Asian American." These statistics are indicative of the complexity of defining Asian American identity and experience in the US.

Asian American Christianity

Christians make up the largest single religious group (42%) within the Asian American Community. Only two of the country-of-origin groups, Filipino (89%) and Korean (71%) are overwhelmingly Christian. Among Asian Americans as a whole, 22% are Protestant and 19% are Catholic and 1% belong to other

[3] For a succinct overview of Asian American situation, see Timothy Tseng, et al, "Asian American Religious Leadership Today: A Preliminary Inquiry," *Pulpit & Pew Research Reports*, (Durham, NC: Duke Divinity School, 2005).

Christian groups (Orthodox and Mormon). Most Filipino Americans are Catholic (65%), while most Korean Americans are Protestant (61%). The chart below provides denominational details:[4]

	Chinese	Filipino	Indian	Japanese	Korean	Vietnamese
	%	%	%	%	%	%
Christian	**31**	**89**	**18**	**38**	**71**	**86**
Protestant	22	21	11	33	61	6
Evangelical	13	12	8	13	40	2
Mainline	9	9	3	19	21	4
Catholic	8	65	5	4	10	30
Other	-	3	2	1	-	-

Further breakdown of the above statistics also yields interesting information. Among Asian American Protestants as a whole as a whole, the most common denominational families are Presbyterian (19%) and Baptist (18%). Nondenominational Christians make up 14%. Roughly one-in-ten Asian-American Protestants are Methodist (9%), and 7% belong to Pentecostal churches and denominations. Other denominational families each account for less than 5% of Asian-American Protestants. Looking at all Asian-American Protestants, there is a higher proportion of born-again or evangelical Protestants (58%) than mainline Protestants (42%).

The numeric growth of immigrant Asian Christians to the US has indeed drawn the attention of mainline Protestant denominations. Major denominations have begun to advocate greater representation, creation of staff positions and development of ministry resources for meeting the needs of Asian American Christians. With the gradual decline in membership of mainline denominational churches (some call it the "de-Europeanization" of the church) there is now an added impetus to invite new immigrant communities by introducing ethnic specific ministries both in Protestant and Catholic denominations. Many mainline denominations have begun to pursue the goal of a "multicultural church," therefore established ethnic specific caucuses or Asian American/Pacific Islander associations to foster "Asian American consciousness." Some immigrant churches (for example, the Korean Presbyterian Church in the US or the Association of Church of South India Congregations in the US) have established independent identities and maintain relatively low level of relations with mainline denominations.

Understandably, there are many sociological factors that foster this "separatist" tendencies (experience of racialization, cultural insecurity, need to maintain values and traditions from homelands, linguistic affinities, socialization needs, sense of identity, etc.) but there is also a growing trend to form of "non-denominational" or independent congregations and fellowships with an evangelical, Pentecostal or "fundamentalist" orientations, often led by entrepreneurial lay leaders with little or no theological training. These separatist tendencies among Asian American congregations exhibit an anti-ecumenical stance while distancing themselves from established mainline denominations whose acceptance of people of different sexual orientation into the ministerial vocation being a divisive issue. These developments reinforce denominational divide among immigrant congregations and seldom are they part of the ecumenical initiatives and dialogues of mainline denominations. It is not surprising that new immigrant congregations want to preserve the theological interpretations, values and traditions from their homelands, bequeathed to them in the age of Western missions in Asia. They provide a sense of security in an alien cultural context where immigrants find themselves. The leadership styles, patterns of ministry and congregational expectations of Asian immigrant churches are markedly different in the North American context. In the process Asianized forms of Christianity are introduced which is different from established "white" mainline churches. Successive waves of new Asian immigrants to the US have made the task of developing

[4] Taken from the Pew Survey: Chapter 1, *Religious Affiliation.*

an integrated Asian American congregations all the more challenging. As new immigration continues to fuel congregational growth, generational transitions and inter-generational conflicts are increasingly becoming a cause for concern.[5]

Emergence of Asian American Theologies

Situated in the North American context, Asian American theologians have sought to articulate a contextually relevant theology that addresses issues at the heart of Asian American experience: the interface between faith and culture, race relations, immigration concerns and Asian ministry. Engaging with such issues involves a critical look at inherited theological traditions and constructively reengaging the Christian faith in light of Asian American experience, consciousness and resources. While these theological attempts tend to integrate or straddle between "American" and "Asian" realities and experiences, there is also a clear desire that such articulations need to transcend narrow ethnocentric theologies in a globalized world. The emerging Asian American theologies, unlike the European theologies, make no normative claims of universality. In a true sense they are contextual theologies. It should be noted that there is a greater degree of mutual engagement among Asian American theologians, irrespective of their ethnicity, culture or denominational background, than found among Asian American churches and congregations.

Jonathan Tan's book, *Introducing Asian American Theologies*, provides a succinct overview of the struggles and challenges facing Asian American theologians. Tan notes that the early inspiration for constructing Asian American theologies came from theologies articulated by Black theologians in the late 1960's. Black theology and Black consciousness in the African American community empowered Asian American intellectuals, student activists and church leaders to take up the cause of Asian American communities in the US. The "first generation" of Asian American theologians in the 60's and 70's, belonging to mainline Protestant backgrounds, "struggled from the outside of the theological establishment to challenge the entrenched racism and discrimination of both mainstream US society and theological institutions, focusing primarily on issues of race relations, faith and culture, and social justice that confronted the Japanese American, Korean American and Chinese American communities at that time."[6] The most prominent among the first-generation Asian American theologians included, Roy Isao Sano, Paul M. Nagano, Fumitaka Matsuoka, Jung Young Lee, Sang Hyun Lee, David Ng, and Wesley S. Woo.

There was considerable resistance to the efforts of Asian American theologians and leaders within the established mainline denominations. Any challenge to the status quo where church leadership and theologizing was controlled by the dominant white Christians was met with resistance in the guise of prevailing American ideology of "assimilation" of immigrant communities into the institutional structures of the church. Paternalism and subtle racism also played a part in relegating Asian American Christians to a subordinating role. Roy Sano was one of the first to advocate an "Amerasian Theology of Liberation" in 1973.[7] Jung Young Lee explored the concept of "marginality" and attempted to retrieve and embrace traditional Asian cultural and spiritual perspectives in his theological articulations.[8] Sang Hyun Lee pursued "liminality" as a category for constructing an Asian American theology.[9]

---

[5] Timothy Tseng, et al, *Asian American Leadership Today*, pp. 22-25. See also, *Asian American Christianity Reader*, eds. Viji Nakka-Cammauf and Timonth Tseng (Castro Valley, California: The Institute for the Study of Asian American Christianity, 2009).

[6] Jonathan Y. Tan, *Introducing Asian American Theologies* (Maryknoll, NY: Orbis, 2008), pp. 90-91.

[7] Roy I. Sano, *Amerasian Theology of Liberation: A Reader* (Berkley: Graduate Theological Union, 1973).

[8] Jung Young Lee, *Marginality: The Key to Multicultural Theology* (Minneapolis: Fortress Press, 1995); *The Trinity in Asian Perspective* (Nashville: Abingdon Press, 1996).

[9] Sang Hyun Lee, *From a Liminal Place: An Asian American Theology* (Minneapolis: Fortress Press, 2010)

A wave of second generation of Asian American theologians has pursued the struggles of the pioneering first generation theologians, in a deeper and divergent ways. The second generation which has come into prominence since the 1990's and 2000s, is a much diverse group, culturally, ethnically, denominationally, generationally and includes a significant number of Asian American feminist theologians. They now include theologians from Catholic, Evangelical, Pentecostal backgrounds, beside Protestants, and now include Vietnamese American, Filipino American, Indian (South Asian) American, Thai American, and a new generation of Japanese American, Korean American and Chinese American theologians.The second generation has gained a foothold in theological institutions and seminaries and assuming leadership positions as Deans and Presidents in theological institutions. They are also gaining recognition for their scholarship and the perspectives they bring to theological discourse. They have branched out in new interdisciplinary studies, post-colonial studies, Asian American biblical interpretation, cultural studies, political theology, systematic theology, interreligious studies, arts and spirituality, all in relation to their ethnicity and cultures in order to empower Asian American identity and consciousness. With the growth of "Asian Studies" programs in secular universities, the multidisciplinary focus has gained more prominence. While the first generation theologians were more focused on *external* issues of race and racial discrimination in American society, the new generation is far more self-critical about *internal* issues, especially issued of patriarchy, gender, political involvement and racism within Asian American communities.[10]

Space does not permit me to explore some of the themes addressed by new generation of Asian American theologians, except to mention a few notable names. Chinese American feminist theologian, Kwok Pui-lan, has played a major role in galvanizing and mentoring Asian American women theologians and younger scholars through the network of PANAAWTM (the Pacific, Asian, North American Asian Women in Theology and Ministry).[11] Other Asian American feminist theologians include Anne Joh,[12] Grace Ji-Sun Kim,[13] Rita Nakashima Brock and Chung Hyun Kim. Among Catholics, Vietnamese American theologian Peter C. Phan is a prominent figure.[14] Other notable names: Tat-siong Benny Liew[15] (a Chinese American Biblical scholar), Eleazar Fernandez[16] (a Filipino American theologian), Andrew Sung Park[17] (a Korean American theologian), Amos Young[18] (a Malaysian American Pentecostal theologian) among others.

The contributions of a new generation of Asian Americans are bound to grow, judging by the number of Asian American students entering theological education in North America. While the new generations of Asian American scholars and theologians are increasingly making a mark in theological discourse in North America, their contributions are diverse and multidisciplinary. It is not evident that Asian American

---

[10] Jonathan Tan, *Introducing Asian American Theologies*, p.101.

[11] Kwok Pui-lan, *Introducing Asian Feminist Theology* (Cleveland: pilgrim Press, 2000); also, see Rita Nakashima Brock, Jung Ha Kim, Kwok Pui-lan, Seung Ai Yang, eds. *Off the Menu, Asian and Asian North American Women's Religion and Theology* (Louisville: Westminster John Knox Press, 2007).

[12] Wonhee Anne Joh, *Heart of the Cross: A Post-Colonial Christology*(Louisville: John Knox Press, 2006).

[13] Grace Ji-Sun Kim, *The Grace of Sophia: a Korean North American Women's Christology* (Cleveland: Pilgrim Press, 2002)

[14] Peter C. Phan, *Christianity with an Asian face, Asian American Theology in the Making* (Maryknoll, NY: Orbis Books, 2003); With Jung Young Lee, eds. *Journeys at the Margin: Toward an Autobiographical Theology in American-Asian Perspective* (Collegeville, MN: Liturgical Press, 1999).

[15] Tat-siong Benny Liew, *What is Asian American Biblical Hermeneutics? Reading the New Testament* (Berkley: Intersections: Asian Pacific American Transcultural Studies, 2008)

[16] Eleazar Fernandez, ed. *New Overtures: Asian American Theology in the 21st Century*(Seattle: Sopher Press, 2012)

[17] Andrew Sung Park, *From Hurt to Healing: A Theology of the Wounded* (Nashville: Abingdon Press, 2004).

[18] Amos Young, Beyond the Impasse: *Toward a Pneumatological Theology of Religions* (Grand Rapids: Baker Books, 2003).

theologians have articulated any explicit theological methodology. The reference points for an Asian American theology are unclear and vary from theologian to theologian. Their explorations have generally been thematic and if there are any discernible themes or foci they are related to Post-colonial studies which have provided a theoretical framework for critiquing the Asian American experience in the US and challenging the Euro-American theological discourse for its colonialist assumptions. Thanks to the pioneering contributions of R. S. Sugirtharajah,[19] a Sri Lankan born-educated in India, post-colonial biblical scholar, a resident in United Kingdom, post-colonial theory and biblical interpretations have been adopted byAsian/Asian American feminists and liberation theologians. Asian American biblical interpreters have begun to challenge the dominant historical-critical hermeneutics of European and North American white biblical scholars who often ignore issues of race, culture as well questions of power and control in the name of scholarly objectivity. Instead of adopting a supposedly objective or neutral reading of scriptures, Asian American Biblical scholars tend to adopt the perspective of a racialized community long subject to exclusion and injustice. In the realm of systematic theology, Asian American scholars draw upon Asian cultural categories of "han," "minjung," "Chi," "dalit," and the like, as hermeneutical keys in their theological explorations. These are promising developments and one hopes that the younger generation of scholars will find legitimacy and greater acceptance of their contributions that may lead to a "pan-Asian" identity in forging an Asian American theology in the future.

Theological Education

The growing emphasis on Asian American identity and consciousness - especially as it relates to leadership and theology - is clearly evident in theological education. Asian American students have earned accolades in secular fields, especially in science, technology, engineering, education and business. But they are also making an impact in theological education. This is corroborated in the statistical data from The Association of Theological schools (ATS) in the US and Canada. In 1977, the first year ATS collected racial/ethnic information, there were 494 Asian/Pacific Islander seminarians in all degree programs, *including* visa students from Asia. By 2011, that number has swelled into 5,243 Asian American seminarians (3788 male, 1455 female), *excluding* visa students from Asia. This is a phenomenal growth! In 2011, the basic ministerial degree (MDiv) had an enrollment of a total of 2,190 Asian American seminarians (1,801 male and 359 female). Those engaged in advanced research (PhD/ThD) in 2011 is also impressive, total 473 (363 male, 110 female) not counting oversees students. The number of Asian American students engaged in advanced degree programs is significantly higher than African American (a total of 342) and Hispanic American (a total of 180) students. This represents a disproportionately higher percentage of Asian American students pursuing advanced research degrees relative to other racial/ethnic populations in North America.[20]

Another indicator of the growing presence of Asian Americans in theological education is the number of faculty from Asian American background in ATS schools. In 2011, there are now 183 (140 male, 53 female) full-time Asian American professors of all ranks in theological education. This number is bound to significantly increase in the coming years as more and more Asian American students currently engaged in advanced degree programs graduate and seek a career in theological education. The need to enhance racial/ethnic diversity in theological education has long been recognized in ATS schools and the growth of Asian American students in advanced theological research will serve to strengthen that cause. However, it must be noted that most Asian American students are deprived of doctoral advisors or mentors while pursuing their advanced research and thus are forced to pursue the interests of their generally white doctoral advisors. Asian American students are often marginalized in theological institutions, especially in

[19] R. s. Sugirtharajah, *Voices from the Margin*, Third and Expanded Edition (Maryknoll, NY: Orbis Books, 2006).
[20] All data cited from *ATS Annual Reports* available on the web: http://www.ats.edu/Resources.

the university related divinity schools. The entrenched European and dominant white North American theological discourse with universal, normative and objective claims to theological knowledge has considerably hindered the development of Asian American theological identity and scholarship. Few Asian American students have Asian American mentors and have to navigate their research in a racialized theological environment in North America; notwithstanding the fact many Asian American scholars have assumed positions of influence as Presidents and Deans in theological institutions. ATS schools have a long way to go in according legitimate recognition to emerging Asian American scholarship, theology and leadership. The relative paucity of funding from major grant giving foundations for Asian American programs in North America is indicative of the inadequate recognition of the transformative potential of Asian American Christianity in North America.

The Henry Luce Foundation, given the founder's relations with Asia, has been supporting Asian American initiatives. The establishment of Asian Theological Summer Institute (ATSI) at the Lutheran Theological Seminary at Philadelphia, with the support of The Henry Luce Foundation, is a noteworthy initiative. This unique program seeks to mentor Asian and Asian American younger scholars engaged in advanced research by well-known Asian American faculty in North America. Established in 2007 as an annual institute, ATSI has encouraged and mentored over 120 Asian American scholars engaged in doctoral research in North America. ATSI and PANAAWTM are the two Asian American initiatives, which together with the formation of the Association of Asian/North American Theological Educators (AANATE) in 2011, are forming promising developments that foster Asian American theology and theological education.

The inclusion of this essay in a handbook on theological education in Asia not only provides a glimpse into Asian North American Christianity, theology and theological education, but also challenges to rethink our understanding of geography, culture and ethnic/racial heritage in a globalized world. Our understanding of "Asia" can no longer be defined purely in geographical terms, restricting it to the continent of Asia. With the migration and dispersion of people of Asian origin and legacy all across the globe, being an Asian can no longer be defined in relation to or confined to aparticular geography. "Asia" today represents a concept, identity, method, consciousness, belonging or a collective culture that defies a singular definition in all its heterogeneous expressions. The contributions of Asian North American Christians therefore will be a significant part of Asian theological reflections in the future.

Bibliography

Asian American Christianity Reader, eds. Viji Nakka-Cammauf and Timonth Tseng (Castro Valley, California: The Institute for the Study of Asian American Christianity, 2009)

Rita Nakashima Brock, Jung Ha Kim, Kwok Pui-lan, Seung Ai Yang, eds. *Off the Menu, Asian and Asian North American Women's Religion and Theology* (Louisville: Westminster John Knox Press, 2007).

Eleazar Fernandez, ed. *New Overtures: Asian American Theology in the 21st Century*(Seattle: Sopher Press, 2012)

Wonhee Anne Joh, *Heart of the Cross: A Post-Colonial Christology*(Louisville: John Knox Press, 2006).

Grace Ji-Sun Kim, *The Grace of Sophia: a Korean North American Women's Christology* (Cleveland: Pilgrim Press, 2002)

Jung Young Lee, *Marginality: The Key to Multicultural Theology* (Minneapolis: Fortress Press, 1995);

Jung Young Lee, *The Trinity in Asian Perspective* (Nashville: Abingdon Press, 1996).

Sang Hyun Lee, *From a Liminal Place: An Asian American Theology* (Minneapolis: Fortress Press, 2010

Tat-siong Benny Liew, *What is Asian American Biblical Hermeneutics? Reading the New Testament* (Berkley: Intersections: Asian Pacific American Transcultural Studies, 2008)

Andrew Sung Park, *From Hurt to Healing: A Theology of the Wounded* (Nashville: Abingdon Press, 2004).

Peter C. Phan, *Christianity with an Asian face, Asian American Theology in the Making* (Maryknoll, NY:

Orbis Books, 2003);
Kwok Pui-lan, *Introducing Asian Feminist Theology* (Cleveland: pilgrim Press, 2000)
Roy I. Sano, *Amerasian Theology of Liberation: A Reader* (Berkley: Graduate Theological Union, 1973).
R. s. Sugirtharajah, *Voices from the Margin*, Third and Expanded Edition (Maryknoll, NY: Orbis Books, 2006)
Ronald Takaki, *Strangers from a Different Shore: A History of Asian Americans* (Boston: Little, Bown, 1989)
Jonathan Y. Tan, *Introducing Asian American Theologies* (Maryknoll, NY: Orbis, 2008), pp. 90-91.
Amos Young, Beyond the Impasse: *Toward a Pneumatological Theology of Religions* (Grand Rapids: Baker Books, 2003).

(80) Perspectives on the Future of Theological Education in Asia[1]

Dietrich Werner

1. Theological Education is a Backbone for Integral Church Development and Authentic Christian Mission in Asian contexts

The WCC global study report on theological education, published as part of the Edinburgh 2010 process, underlined the conviction that

> theological education is the seedbed for the renewal of churches, their ministries and mission and their commitment to church unity in today's world. If theological education systems are neglected or not given their due prominence in church leadership, in theological reflection and in funding, consequences might not be visible immediately, but quite certainly will become manifest after one or two decades in terms of theological competence of church leadership, holistic nature of the churches mission, capacities for ecumenical and interfaith dialogue and for dialogue between churches and society. The transmission of the ecumenical memory and vision to future generations of pastors and church workers is a priority need in many WCC member churches, its continuation is far from being secured at present.[2]

This reflects the hope of the overwhelming majority of churches in Asia. For them, theological education of future pastors, church leaders and theological teachers is far from being secured at present. This requires more attention to well prepared strategies in order to prepare for the needs of these churches in the 21st century.

2. The Growth and Increasing Pluralization of Asian Christianity

While Christianity remains a minority religion in most Asian countries, there has been an impressive overall increase of the Christian population in Asia between 1910 and 2010 (from 2.4to 8.5 percent), This is likely to increase the Christian population in Asia to over 352 million by 2010.

More detailed regional data note a particular increase of Christian populations in southeast Asia (from 10,8% to 21,8%), but also a sharp decrease in western Asia from 22.9 to 5.7 percent. It is predicted that by 2050 Christianity in Asia will grow to reach 595 million or 11.3 percent of Christians.[3] The most significant increases of Christianity are expected in eastern Asia (251 million Christians or 15.8 percent by 2050) and in southeastern Asia (197 million Christians or 25.7 percent by 2050). More specifically, Christianity will grow particularly in countries like China, India, Nepal and Cambodia and the Philippines. Although there still is a lack of concrete figures and exact data available from some of the emerging churches in specific Asian countries, it is clear that in certain regions (like east Asia, the Himalaya region and southeast Asia) the demand for theological education will not be able to be met by existing institutions and programmes.

Attention also needs to be given to the pluralism within Asian Christianity, and its effects on the landscape of theological education. Christian emigration and immigration as well as inner Asian Christian

---

[1] Reprinted with kind permission from PTCA from: Dietrich Werner, Training to be ministers in Asia. Contextualizing Theological Education in Multi-Faith Contexts, PTCA Series No 3, 2012, p. 307-323

[2] Global Study Report on Theological Education, WCC-ETE 2010, p. 32

[2] *Atlas of Global Christianity*, eds. Todd M. Johnson and Kenneth Ross (2009), Edinburgh University Press, Center for the Study of Global Christianity, p. 107

missions continue to play a major role in spreading the gospel. This will change the demands and programmes for theological education and mission training in Asia considerably. For example, between 40,000 and 80,000 Indians work as missionaries and evangelists to other ethnic groups and there are 250 mission organizations within India. South Korean churches send out 15,000 missionaries to other Asian countries.[4]

3. Unequal Allocation of Resources and Unbalanced Accessibility to Theological Education

The 2010 WCC report on theological education pointed to "an emerging global crisis in theological education which is becoming obvious increasingly and will be marking the next decades in the 21st century, having the potential of endangering the very future and integrity of World Christianity."[5]

Several factors were mentioned which contribute to a picture marked both by enormous achievements during the past 100 years as well as ongoing threats:

1. Most of the resources for theological education – both teaching staff, scholarship funds, theological libraries and publications – are still located in the North. In a situation marked by a remarkable shift of the center of gravity of world Christianity, the majority of needs and demands for theological education are now in the southern hemisphere.

The average full costs for one student each year in Princeton Theological Seminary are some 60.000 USD, but the average costs for a BTh student in an institution for theological education in Nepal are just 1000 USD a year. Access to PhD scholarships, to theological library resources and to research visits for theological students from churches in the south to countries in the north, becomes ever more restricted and difficult – not least due to heavy restrictions on visas and increased health insurance costs.

2. According to UNESCO, the 21st century will see an explosion in the number of higher education students in many Asian countries due to demographic and educational changes which also are reflected in those seeking study opportunities in Christian theology and church related service. Higher education enrollment has increased approximately from 72 million in 1999 to 133 million in 2004. Excluding North America and Western Europe, enrollment in the rest of the world more than doubled in these five years, increasing from 41.1 to 99.1 million. China alone increased its share from 6.4 million in 1999 to 19.4 million in 2004; China has the largest higher education enrollment in the world at more than 23 million in 2005.[6] This massive expansion is taking place for at least two reasons: the social demand for higher education is increasing, along with the economic need for more highly educated human resources.

3. The increasing demand for theological education has led to a mushrooming of new colleges and Bible schools in many regions in Asia, many of which are institutionally unstable. While this proliferation reflects a genuine desire for access to theological education, this also has negative side-effects. Quite a few of the new schools offer only light and "fast food" theological education with impressive titles, but no libraries, developed curricula or common educational framework. Many of the new schools also lack experience or connection with the organized ecumenical movement, or to established regional associations of theological schools, which often serve to accredit or qualify schools. In some contexts, these new schools have arisen because established theological institutions have not been accommodating. In several contexts, the fragmentation, lack of unity and common standards, and the disintegration on the landscape of theological education have reached unprecedented levels.

---

[4] Robert, Dana L, *Christian Mission: How Christianity Became a World Religion* (2009) Wiley-Blackwell: Oxford, p. 78

[5] Global Study Report in Theological Education, WCC, p. 54

[6] More information on the UNESCO Report on Higher Education in the world 2007 on the website of «Global Universities Network for Innovation»(GUNI) http://www.guni-rmies.net/info/default.php?id=89 or the website of the publisher Palgrave Macmillan http://www.palgrave.com/pdfs/0230000479.pdf)

4. Dissimilarities and Discrepancies in Theological Education Standards Between Different National Contexts and Regions within Asia

Given the different historical, political and religious profiles and developments of churches in various Asian contexts, there are enormous differences in their institutional capacities and standards of quality. The following distinctions can be made among the types of theological education institutions in Asia:[7]

1. *Smaller Bible colleges and training centers* or institutes are sponsored by one person or family or by a single church. Many of these schools give a strong emphasis to church planting, evangelism and winning souls. Most of such schools are not accredited or affiliated with any wider theological bodies.
2. *Nondenominational theological seminaries* have been started by several evangelistic groups, revival groups or prayer groups. These tend to have a curriculum that reflects a strong concern for church planting and the traditional concepts and practices of mission — that is, to Christianize others. Some of these schools have sought accreditation from regional theological associations.
3. Particular denominations sponsor *denominational theological colleges or seminaries.* A large number of such schools in Asia are denominationally-oriented, with curricular offerings mandated by their denominations. Although such denominational seminaries may be open to admitting students from other denominations, they emphasize a curriculum that reflects their denomination and focuses on mission and church growth of the particular denomination. The majority of these schools are accredited by regional theological associations.
4. There are several *ecumenical seminaries* born out of the ecumenical movement, but overall, these are still in the minority in Asia. Their curriculum includes some ecumenism, comparative study of religions, interfaith dialogue, feminist theology, tribal or dalit theology, eco-theology, and so forth. However, these courses typically are treated as "elective" or "optional."
5. There are also some *public universities in Asian countries with departments for religious studies* and related theological or historical research, although this is an exception in the interfaith milieu of Asian countries.

Further analysis would be needed to ascertain to what extent each of these types actually contributes to the task of assisting the churches to do contextually relevant mission and to respond adequately to fast changing Asian circumstances.

These different types of institutions correspond to different socio-political settings:

1. Theological education institutions in hubs of theological education in well established and resourced centers for theological scholarship and research often have several (sometimes associated) theological colleges within one urban context, and serve a wider region (e.g., in Hong Kong, Singapore, Seoul, Tokyo);
2. Theological education institutions in regions with a sizeable, even majority Christian population and stable political conditions, and thereby are able to support centers for theological education and research either in the context of a university or college (e.g., South Korea, the Philippines, Indonesia, Taiwan, Japan);
3. Theological education institutions in contexts where Christians are in the minority but are well established, politically stable and have common curricula and quality standards, with systems of affiliation or accreditation (e.g., India, Malaysia, Sri Lanka);
4. Theological education institutions in recently emerging Asian churches, with considerable church growth and some political stability; these generally are in settings in which theological education is being (re)constructed and consolidated (e.g., China, Myanmar);

---

[7] Following a typology offered by: Wati Longchar, Ecumenical Theological Education in Asia: Emerging Concerns for Relevant Theological Curricula, 2009

5. Theological education programmes and institutions in emerging Asian churches with comparatively short histories, political instability or threats to religious identity, and a general lack of common coherence, joint planning and centralized structures; here embryonic theological education is occurring under often precarious conditions (e.g., in Mekong countries, Nepal, Bhutan, Pakistan, Bangladesh).

One of the crucial 21st century challenges for theological education in Asia is to explore the most appropriate forms of inner- and inter-regional solidarity between institutions of theological education. What are the different expectations, points of connectivity and potentials for synergies for ministerial formation and theological education? With reduced funding available from outside, creating appropriate and culturally sensitive networks of mutual support and complementarity between the different sectors of Asian Christianity becomes imperative in the 21st century.

Individual theological schools operating in isolation and on separate tracks from each other, even in neighboring situations, is a matter of concern for understanding and practicing what it means to belong to the one body of Christ. The newly created Asian Forum for Theological Education (AFTE), in which all associations of theological schools are invited to cooperate, is an important platform to work out related mechanisms of Asian solidarity in theological education.

5. The Unfinished Work of Contextualizing Theological Education in Asia

Although theological education in Asia has some ancient roots, such as in the Oriental Orthodox churches, it mainly was begun to accompany mission activities initiated by missionaries from the west only a little over a century ago. Generally speaking, the kinds of theological education brought to Asia were copies of theological schools from western countries, with their structures, disciplines and curricula. Over the years, despite many challenges and attempts to change this, there still is a great need to contextualize theological education properly in Asia cultures and realities. Much theological education in Asia is still marked by 19th century western-based mission movements and by theologies influenced by European colonial expansion, the conquest of nature and technology-dependent development.[8]

In the wake of nationalism, many Asian theologians have become critical of western missionary theological education, and concepts, doctrines and symbols of Asian cultures and religious traditions increasingly have been drawn on for interpreting Christian faith. However, past decades of achievements of Asian liberation and inculturation theologies have remained limited to certain theological and intellectual circles, without really touching the realities of most local worshipping communities. The passionate plea in the 1960s and 70s to contextualize theological education, which marked the emergence of Asian liberation theologies and which through TEF and the voices such as Shoki Coe impacted theological education, remains on the whole an unfinished task. For many today, the vocation of theological education is to bring good news to the poor and to struggle for justice against structures of oppression in Asia. However, networks and structures to support an ecumenical and contextualized approach to theological education in Asia have remained fragile and limited in their outreach. There is a fundamental need to continue to develop Christian theology with Asian resources and to deepen the common search for appropriate, contextualized forms of Asian theological education so as to meet contemporary ministerial and societal challenges, as voiced both by theological faculties, students and church leadership in Asia.

---

[8] Wati Longchar, Ecumenical Theological Education in Asia: Emerging Concerns for Relevant Theological Curricula, 2009

6. Theological Education Related to Today's Multi-Religious Realities

It has been stated that "the Asian continent is the most religious .... At the same time....the least *Christians of all continents*".[9] One of the fundamental 21st century questions for theological education in Asia is how Christian theological education will dialogue with those of different or no faith traditions. The task of theological education in contemporary Asia is to prepare candidates for transformation of Christian communities for the sake of the transformation of the whole society where they find themselves.[10] Yet only some theological schools offer substantial courses and programmes on non-Christian religions, on Asian spiritualities and on interfaith dialogue.

For Christianity in Asia to move out of its privatized pockets and small niches in societies, it is vital to underline that the gospel of Christ is for the life of all and for the peace and justice in the whole of creation, not just for the limited goals and institutionalized interests of a specific religious sector in society that the Christian churches represent. The public character of the gospel of reconciliation demands public interaction and common platforms of learning and research in higher education with representatives of all religious traditions who seek the common good in society, peace, justice, dignity and ecological integrity. In some Asian contexts it has become increasingly difficult for Christian churches and theological education to enter into interfaith dialogue or to encourage deliberate cooperation on peace, justice, human rights and ecological concerns with people of other living faiths. This especially applies in contexts where religious extremism, discrimination and political and and legal means of pressures are applied against Christian communities.

The test case for solidarity within Asia and globally lies particularly in contexts where Christian theological education is threatened and faces hostility or worsening political and religious conditions. At the same time, theological education in Asian societies will be recognized and seen as a legitimate and vital by governments and civil society networks in Asia insofar as they are able to contribute important competencies and insights to ongoing ethical challenges in areas such as bioethics, ecology, human rights and anthropology, especially in the face of economic globalization and exploitation.

7. Overcoming the Ecumenical/Evangelical Divide in Theological Education in Asia

The division between ecumenical or so-called "liberal" and evangelical orientations in theological education, which in many Asian contexts still continues to influence the institutional landscapes of theological education, are not necessarily inherent in Asian Christianity but have their roots in the west. The so-called fundamentalist-liberal dispute, and the split between moderate evangelicals and their ultra-fundamentalist counterparts have their origins in a specific ideological context of the United States of America. They were shaped in the political context of the East-West conflict, and then became globalised and exported into Asian churches in the decades after the 1950s.[11] The communist threat seen as looming over the newly independent Asian nations was accompanied by suspicions that some social and political theological movements were hidden means for extending communist influences in these churches, and therefore had to be countered by evangelicals. In the decades after World War II and decolonialization, Asia and other places in the global South became contested ground for influence, both politically and ecclesiastically.

---

[9] Walbert Buhlmann. *The coming of the third Church. An Analysis of the present and the future.* Trs. By R. Woodhall, 1974, p.160-161.

[10] Henry Wilson, Theological education and ecumenical challenges in Asia. A checklist for journey forward.

[11] Some of the following insights are based upon: Michael Nai Poon, The Rise of Asia Pacific Christianity: prospects and challenges for the church universal, 2011

Organizations based in the USA often were the main driving force behind this dominance. Averting communist influences among the younger churches in southeast Asia was a key concern in the 1952 Anderson-Smith Report on theological education in southeast Asia.[12] Carl McIntire set up the International Council of Christian Churches global network to counter the work of John MacKay and the World Council of Churches. To him, the WCC was sympathetic to the communist cause. McIntire and MacKay convened parallel conferences in December 1949 in Bangkok.[13] Evangelicals adopted similar tactics to counter what they saw as liberal influences among Asian churches. The World Evangelical Fellowship convened a theological assistance program consultation in 1970 in Singapore, in the same period when the ecumenical Theological Education Fund (TEF) was launched. Eventually the Asia Theological Association was set up as an alternative to the ecumenical ATESEA body.[14]

The ongoing evangelical/ecumenical divide in theological education, which today is more visible and influential in some Asian contexts than others, absorbs more energies and creates more distortions than necessary in the face of the common missionary tasks Asian Christianity faces in the 21st century. The urgent need for a clear profile of biblically sound, contextually relevant and spiritually nurturing theological education in Asia can be sharpened only if all committed Christian traditions work together rather than wasting money and energies in debates of the past or in maintaining polarized profiles to please donors.

Strikingly, there is a growing convergence between evangelical and ecumenical leaders engaged in Christian mission, interfaith-dialogue and theological education in Asia today, but the institutional landscapes and "camps" of theological schools and colleges remain structurally divided. "Evangelicals"' and "ecumenicals" or "liberals" (none of these terms fit well any more for existing realities) face similar challenges in Asia and often develop similar answers. Evangelicals from the Lausanne movement and evangelicals with deep commitment within the ecumenical movement often affirm shared understandings of mission, evangelism and education. Thus, churches and networks in Asia should move on and not be caught up in past and false stereotypes or define who they are in opposition to each other, rather than to act and learn together as part of the one body of Christ. There will no major progress in the ecumenical contextualization of theological education in Asia unless there are deliberate attempts to bridge the divides between ecumenical and evangelical/Pentecost networks of theological education operating in Asia. The focus today should be on the common objectives and tasks for all major stakeholders in theological education in relation to the common challenges in Asian contexts. Some separate affiliation systems and hermeneutical orientations may be dependent on and perpetuated more by funding relationships with external partners than internal to Asian theological education itself. The matter is not how and why these distinctions emerged historically but whether they still makes sense, and if not, how different Christian networks for theological education can join forces for common mission and to strengthen the unity of the Christian church in Asia for the future.

---

[12] S. R. Anderson and C. Stanley Smith, *The Anderson-Smith Report on Theological Education in Southeast Asia: Especially as It Relates to the Training of Chinese for the Christian Ministry: The Report of a Survey Commission, 1951-1952* (New York: Board of Founders, Nanking Theological Seminary, 1952); Michael Poon, "The Association for Theological Education in South East Asia, 1959-2002: A Pilgrimage in Theological Education," in *Supporting Asian Christianity's Transition from Mission to Church: A History of the Foundation for Theological Education in South East Asia*, ed. Samuel Campbell Pearson (2010) Eerdmans, Grand Rapids, pp. 363-402, 417-431.

[13] Carl McIntire, *The Battle of Bangkok: Second Missionary Journey,* (1950) Christian Beacon Press, Collngwood.

[14] Michael Poon,"The History and Development of Theological Education in South East Asia," pp. 378-279.

8. Seek Common Principles for Ongoing, Reliable Support for Theological Education

In Asia there are neither common regulations nor explicit recommendations from church leaders for ongoing, reliable sustainable church support for institutions of theological education. Only a minority of Asian churches provide regular and reliable financial support to their institutions of theological education. Only a minority have developed long-term master plans for theological education within their national context. Some churches support only the basic theological degree, which they consider sufficient for becoming a pastor, but do not support the higher-level theological work necessary for developing more contextualized Asian theologies and for theological teaching. In other cases, theological colleges cannot rely on regular church support at all and tend to remain dependent either on external support or create heavy financial burdens for students.

As the 2010 WCC report stated:

> We *affirm* that churches, mission organizations and ecumenical partners have a key responsibility for supporting and enabling high quality institutions of theological education while respecting a certain degree of autonomy in their operating and academic research. There are different models by which this sense of ownership for theological education is expressed in the different church settings. But there are also cases in which a genuine lack of support and ownership for institutions of theological education, particularly those who are supported by an interdenominational set of churches, is experienced.
>
> Theological education not only serves the building up the church from the perspective of the reign of God, but it also creates social awareness, political discernment, social involvement, and Christian participation in transformation processes of societies. Investment in theological education is a direct investment into the social and political development and transformation of society and the raising of its educational levels. Ecumenical partners and funding agencies which focus on development projects should review their guidelines so as to give theological education projects a place and higher priority in their agenda where ever possible.
>
> The only proper remedy against religious fundamentalism is investment in education. Lack of education and theological formation often is one of the root causes for ignorance over against other cultures, religious traditions and special social contexts. Churches which take theological education of both laity and ordained seriously and support all its different levels are better equipped to counteract trends towards religious fundamentalism and communal tensions in their own regions and worldwide.

It was also recommended

> that churches and its agencies (development, mission and others) reconsider their priorities in terms of making more regular support available for institutions of theological education. As there does not exist any set pattern on the percentage which might be recommended to be made available for theological education in Christian churches around the world, we recommend to consider an application of the UNO regulation or recommendation, that nation states should make available at least 6% of their annual gross national product for higher education, to the principles applied in church budgeting for theological education.[15]

[15] The Sixth International Conference of Adult Education of UNESCO (CONFINTEA VI) recommended that at least 6% of the GNP of all states should be devoted to education and that e-learning be increased. Scientific United Nations Educational, and Cultural Organization (UNESCO), "Harnessing the Power and Potential of Adult Learning and Education for a Viable Future: Belém Framework for Action: Preliminary Draft," in *The Sixth International Conference of Adult Education of UNESCO (CO NFINTEA VI)* (Belém, Brazil: UNESCO, 2009).

9. Deepened Joint Research and Data Collection on Recent Developments in Theological Education in Asia

Although much has already been done to encourage the development of contextual Asian theologies, comparatively little research has been done on the actual developments in theological education in Asia. Although the future of churches and their mission is conditioned to a large extent by the quality and stability of theological education, there has been little empirical research on recent trends, difficulties, funding streams and orientations of theological education in Asia. The global survey on theological education project[16] and the related "mapping theological education in Asia" project which is supported by FTESEA and PTCA have been important initiatives to bridge this gap.

10. Jointly Developing Master Plans for the Future of Theological Education in National Contexts

Developing joint strategies for theological education in different Asian national contexts has been hindered by how theological education is fragmented, the isolation of different players and interest groups, and the lack of responsibility and ownership by churches. It would be very helpful if all partners in a given region, assisted by international bodies and accrediting agencies, could agree to develop empirically based, theologically responsible master plans for theological education in all Asia countries. Then it would be easier to bring together all relevant partners in that national context, and with the assistance of international ecumenical partners, to explore new kinds of cooperation in that respective context. If different institutions do not come together but instead protect their own institution at the expense of or in opposition to others, the overall situation of theological education in that country will be weakened. The articles in this Handbook provide a beginning basis for planning and dialogue on elements for such master plans.

11. Explore Possibilities for State Recognition, Greater Public Visibility and Criteria for Assuring Quality Theological Education in Asia

In light of the rapid changes in secular education and in socio-political circumstances in Asia, in many countries the quantity and availability of theological education has been upgraded significantly in the past decades. Theological schools first established as centers to train Christian evangelists who had few academic qualifications have now been upgraded to become degree granting institutions, with higher admission standards and accreditation to assure quality. Membership in theological associations such as ATESEA, Senate of Serampore and ATA has grown rapidly. Yet in Asia there still are few places where there is state recognition of their accreditation and public acceptance.

This exclusion from state and public recognition has not only affected the credibility of the churches' mission and witness regarding public issues in the wider society, but it also has restricted their access to potential resources and engagement with other disciplines Although in Asian countries such as Indonesia, Thailand and Taiwan degrees of seminaries and divinity schools can now be registered and recognized in the state education system, in most Asian countries this is restricted to the private realm and does not engage with other academic disciplines. But this is changing, as theological degrees are recognized by state authorities in more places, such as Korea, Japan, Hong Kong and the Philippines. How might Christian theological education become visible in the public arena and in public universities without diminishing the important tasks of ministerial formation?

[16] https://www.research.net/s/globalsurveyontheologicaleducation

12. Strengthen Existing Associations of Theological Schools and Mutual Networking for Common Doctoral Programs and Teacher Exchange among Asian Churches

Thus far there are three regional associations of theological schools in Asia: Board of Theological Education of the Senate of Serampore College (BTESSC, covering south Asia), the Association of Theological education in South East Asia (ATESEA, covering southeast Asia), and the North East Association of Theological Education (NEAATS, covering northeast Asia). In addition there are a number of national associations like Association of Theological education in Myanmar (ATEM), PERSETIA (association of theological schools in Indonesia), KAATS (Korean association of theological schools) and the theological commission of China Christian Council with over 20 seminaries and Bible schools. In addition there are all Asian denominational associations like the Asian Theological Association (ATA) with some 200 member schools, and the Asian Pentecostal Theological Association (APTA). In the past two years, representatives of these associations have come together to form a fellowship of theological education in Asia, the Asian Forum for Theological Education (AFTE).

Several structural and strategic questions need to be considered in order to prepare for new levels of cooperation and solidarity in the 21st century:

1. What is happening with emerging younger Asian churches and theological schools (e.g., in Mekong region, Himalaya region, and in Mongolia, Kirgistan, Tadschikistan, Turkmenistan etc.) in terms of their belonging to regional associations of theological schools? Should they associate with an existing regional association or form a new network on their own in their context in order to receive the assistance and solidarity they require?
2. Will existing associations of theological schools in Asia come to agree on some common standards for quality, lest their standards and integrity be compromised? Could there be something like an Asian credit transfer system (similar to the European ECTS system) to guarantee the transferability and recognition of course credits between different contexts?
3. How can increasingly scarce financial and personnel resources for theological education best be used, such as through teacher exchange programs and common doctoral seminars of students from different institutions?
4. What mechanisms can facilitate better exchange and accessibility of resources for theological research, theological education and teaching resources within Asia and beyond (such as a common digital library for Asian theological education in cooperation with the Global Digital Library for Theology, GlobeTheoLib[17])?
5. How can planning be implemented that focuses on faculty development areas of theological teaching and research that usually are overlooked but are vital for the future of Asian Christianity (e.g., Asian pastoral theology, Asian missiology, Asian ethics and Asian ecumenism?)

14. Continue and Deepen the Movement to do Theology with Asian Resources

Encouraged by the internal conditions of the church mission developments and the external challenges caused by the international power remapping, Asian Christians after the Second World War became more aware of their identity as "Asian" Christians. Theological educators in Asia came together to form associations to encourage personnel exchanges, resources sharing, and to shape solidarity for theological development in Asia. The Association for Theological Education in South East Asia (ATESEA) was formed in 1957, and grew from a membership of 16 to 102. The Asian Theological Association (ATA) was formed in 1970 and has 212 member institutions from 27 nations[18] (accredited members and associated

---

[17] http://www.globethics.net/web/gtl/globetheolib
[18] http://www.ataasia.com/ata-members

members). Both associations are committed to "train Asians in Asia," while ATESEA has stressed a contextual orientation for theological construction.

It was in the midst of this background, that the Programme for Theologies and Cultures (PTCA) began as a theological movement to serve contextual theological formation and theological education in Asia. First formed in 1983, this became a joint program of the Christian Conference of Asia (CCA), Association for Theological Education in Asia (ATESEA), South East Asia Graduate School of Theology (SEAGST), Tao Fong Shan and Kansai Seminar House. The mandate was to contribute to reorienting young theological faculty members in the theological schools in Asia and doctoral candidates of SEAGST in order to promote contextual awareness of doing theologies and theological education in Asian contexts. This was a considerable shift from the earlier emphasis on political and social contextualization to a theological method involving discernment and interaction with Asian cultural and religious resources in the process of doing theology. Moving from the WCC theological emphasis on "Gospel and Cultures" (Vancouver, 1983) to that of "Gospel in Diverse Cultures" (Canberra, 1991) implied significant theological transformation. Cultures in the "non-Christian" world would no longer be considered as independent from or in opposition to the gospel, but instead as a matrix of it. Several years of workshops under the motto "Doing Theology with Asian Resources" (inspired by C.S. Song and subsequent Asian scholars) fruitfully equipped more than a generation of theological scholars in Asia to become relevant to their own Asian cultural and religious backgrounds.

As PTCA has reflected on how to continue this vital heritage[19] it is important to seek ways by which

- the mission and mandate of the movement for Asian theologies in dialogue with Asian cultural traditions might be continued, with new centers and hubs for theological education in Asia;
- emerging small minority churches in Asia who did not have opportunities to participate in this movement might be enabled to formulate appropriate Asian theologies for their own contexts; church support and ownership for this theological movement is increased for the sake of vital interaction between church leadership and the movement to do theology with Asian resources, so that there will not be a split between what is going on in the churches and in the circles doing theology with Asian resources;
- a more stable situation can develop to provide appropriate leadership and networking both within PTCA and between PTCA and the major associations of theological schools in Asia, so that PTCA might develop into a research wing of the Asian Forum on Theological Education, which intends to bring together all major associations of theological schools from the different Christian traditions in Asia.

---

[19] Part of the following considerations are based on joint discussions during a PTCA Reflection Workshop which was held in January 2012 in Sabah Theological Seminary, Malaysia

(81) A Curriculum on *Ministry and Mission for Life* – A Case Study from Korea

Hyunju Bae

The Presbyterian Church of Korea (PCK) decided to launch the "Decade of Fostering Life"(DFL) in the 87th General Assembly in 2002, and it was basically the PCK's follow-up to the initiative of the "Decade of Overcoming Violence"(DOV) of the WCC. Timeliness and urgency of the movement was recognized, which aims at building the communities of full life for the glory of God in each and every corner of the society and earth. Nevertheless, it did not induce a voluntary participation of the nation-wide local churches and many of them remained indifferent. Recognizing the gap between the importance of the DFL and the apathy of the local churches, some of the ecumenically oriented professors of the Busan Presbyterian University (BPU), one of the seven seminaries of the PCK, came to affirm the importance of education which would help the church to transform a prevalent mentality of church-centrism and localism into an ecumenical vision. The faculty at the BPU decided to begin with raising the consciousness among theological students who are the future local church leaders, in order to give momentum to the movement.

The result was a transformation of the curriculum. The BPU decided to develop a field education course titled "Ministry and Mission for Life," which includes field trips, as a one-year requirement course for the second-year M. Div. students. The initial idea was gestated in 2007, and the preparation committee invited 35 professors, activists, and church ministers, and held seminars four times in 2008. The course was open in 2009, and the text book was published in 2011.[1] Before the publication of the text book, a resource book, for which the teachers wrote their first draft, was used temporarily. The published text book is now being introduced to the local church ministers.

The course has been reformatted, but originally consisted of four parts. The first part is 'Introduction.' It conveys a sense of urgency to invite the students to discern the signs of the times from faith stance, especially ecological and economic crises at the global level. The prophetic vocation of the church in the society is emphasized. The background historical information of the course, that is, an explanation of the DFL of the PCK in solidarity with the DOV of the WCC is given.[2]

The second part addresses the "Theology of Life." The theologians, most of them being professors at the BPU, discuss this theme according to their own specialties, such as Biblical Theology, Systematic Theology, Church History, Christian Ethics, Liturgy, Spirituality, and Missiology.[3]

The third part focuses on the "Mission for Life." It is addressed by Christian activists from the diverse sectors of the society, both local and national, and the topics cover the social welfare for the poor and the

---

[1] The Committee of Ministry and Mission for Life of Busan Presbyterian University, *Ministry and Mission for Life*, I & II (Kyeonggido: Olive Tree, 2011).

[2] "The Process of the 'Decade of Fostering Life' in the PCK and its Theological Direction"(Hong Ryeol Whang); "The Crisis of Life and the Crisis of the Church in the 21th Century"(Jong Yoon Lee);
"The Economic Justice in the 21th Century and the Task of Christianity"(Sung Won Park)

[3] "A Biblical Understanding of Life for the Ministry and Mission for Life"(Hyunju Bae); "The Old Testament Perspective on the Reverence of Life"(Kyeong Jin Min); "The Ministry and Mission for Life in Jesus"(Hyung Dong Kim); "Paul and Ministry for Life"(In Sung Wang); "The God of Life"(Man Park); "A Creation Theological Reflection on Ecology"(Byung Suk Cheon); "The History of the Mission for Life in Busan and Kyungsangnamdo"(Ji Il Tark); "An Ethical Reflection on Life"(Jong Gyoon Park); "Worship: An Event of Creation"(Myung Ho Cha); "The Stumbling Blocks to the Ministry for Life: The Ideologies of Church Growth and Success"(Seung Gi Choi); "The Theological Direction and Task of the Mission for Life in the Era of Neo-Liberal Globalization"(Hong Rhyeol Whang).

disabled, the prevention of suicides, ecological movement, immigrants, immigrant women, multicultural family, North Korea refugees, economic autonomous local communities, and peaceful reunification.[4]

And finally, the church ministers critically reflect the diverse aspects of local ministry, both urban and rural, from the perspective of the "Ministry for Life." The point is to challenge the church leaders to overcome the denominationalism and the obsession of numeric growth of the church and to guide them to build the communities of faith for the abundant life for all in an ecumenical horizon in the 21th century. The basic pastoral areas such as spiritual training, preaching, church education, counseling, and the contacts with the locals through cultural events are addressed. The ministers who experiment innovative ministries both in the cities and in the countries are invited to share inspirations to explore new paradigms of church ministries. The leaders of small-size urban church movement with active leadership in the public square and the churches playing a leadership role in the life-giving agriculture movement in the rural grassroots communities are invited.[5]

This course tried to create a space where the students could meet face to face diverse Christian faith practitioners with many differences across denomination, gender, specialties, localities, and perspectives, and network with them. With its limit of circumstances, it fell short of reaching out to the space of wider ecumenism, and didn't afford to include interfaith interaction which would require another set of educational and theological preparation in this specific context.

As the first convener of the preparation committee for the "Ministry and Mission for Life," I have described its birth process and contents. While this is an attempt at an ecumenical formation in a local seminary, the Institute of Mission Training in the National Council of Churches in Korea has been providing an ecumenical theological lecture series, a program for mission field trip, both domestic and overseas, and leadership formation sessions for the seminary students of its member churches beyond the denominational boundaries since 2009.[6] Finally, the Oikos Summer School organized by Oikos Theological Movement in solidarity with a global Oikotree Movement[7] deserves our attention. Fifteen or so theologians in the PCK gathered together to open a summer school annually in order to offer an intensive ecumenical course to the future Christian leadership. The first summer school was held in 2010, and it invited two global speakers from the WCC network in 2011. The Oikos Theological Movement looks forward to recruiting more students from other Asian countries for the Oikos Summer School in the future.

---

[4] "An Approach to the Ministry and Mission for Life in Light of Christian Social Welfare"(Mu Yeol Choi); "The Mission for Life to Prevent Suicides in the Korean Society"(In Sook Lee); "Poverty, The Poor, and the Mission for Life"(In Young Jung); "The Disabled, the Mission for Life, and the Role of the Church"(Kyung Myun Lee); "The Ecological Crisis and the Mission for Life"(Jae Sung Yang); "The Mission for the Immigrants and the Ministry for Life"(Kyung Tae Kim); "The Mission for the Immigrant Women and Multi-cultural Families"(Hye Jeong Joh); "The Settle-Down Process of the Refugees from the North Korea"(Jae Sook Kim); "The Current State and Task of the Economic Autonomy Movement for the Grassroot Communities in the Eastern Ulsan"(Yong Shik Kim); "The Peaceful Reunification Movement and the Mission for Life"(Hye Won Chae); "A Comprehensive Review of the Mission for Life in Busan"(Ha Won Ahn)

[5] "A Spiritual Training of the Ministers for the Ministry for Life"(Young Su Han); "An Experimental Adoption of Traditional Korean Medicine for the Holistic Healing Ministry"(Su Young Kim); "Preaching in the Ministry for Life"(Dae Shik Lim); "A Report on the Visit to Ecological Communities in Cuba"(Won Goo Huh); "Christian Education for Shaping and Vitalizing the Church into the Communities of Life"(Soon Ae Chang); "Counseling for the Ministry for Life"(Myung Wha Park); "The Ministry for Life and Cultural Mission"(Jae Yeop Han); "The New Paradigm of the Ministry for Life and the Movement of the Small-Size Churches"(Won Don Lee); "The Ministry for Life in the Rural Areas: Life-Giving Agriculture and the Church"(Soo Sang Lee); "A Quest of the New Paradigm of a Convivial Relationship between Urban and Rural Churches"(Dong Jak Shin); "An Ecumenical Solidarity of the Local Churches for the Ministry and Mission for Life"(Woon Seong Kim).

[6] Its director is Rev. Geun Bok Lee, and its coordinator is Ms. Kyeong Im Bae.

[7] See: http://www.oikotree.org/about/

(82) THE ECUMENICAL LANDSCAPE OF ASIAN THEOLOGICAL LIBRARY NETWORKS

Tang Sui Tung

I have a dream… (Martin Luther King)

In 1986, I have had a dream: serving my Lord and Mainland China through the library profession. Hence, I was planning to study Master of Library Science (MLS). Surprisingly, when I was searching for the MLS programs in U.S., I found out that there were very few studies on theological libraries. Among many U. S. accredited library schools there was only one school, i.e. the University of Pittsburgh, offering one three credit course on theological librarianship in its 36 credit MLS program (England 2001)[1]. Hence, I went to Pittsburgh to pursue the dream!

I would like to see India free and strong… (Gandhi 1959)[2]

In 1991, Asian theological librarians and theological educators of eight countries met at Chiang Mai, Thailand. They came up with the dream to develop and to expand Asian theological library networking. With the support of the Program for Theology and Cultures in Asia (PTCA) and under the leadership of Rev. Karmito, Rita and John England, the Forum of Asian Theological Librarians (ForATL) was founded in 1997 (ForATL 2012)[3].

1. Dreams and Landscapes of Asian Theological Library Networking

(a) Networking and Collaboration

Since 1991, the dreams of ForATL (www.foratl.org) are basically twofold: Asian theological library networking and Asian theological library education and training were both seen as the crucial objctives. As stated by ForATL the dreams of this forum are:

1. To facilitate the development and exchange of resources of theology in the Asian contexts for the formation of:
   - national theological library associations or networks,
   - national depositories of Christian literature,
   - union listings, directory of Asian theological libraries, guidelines, indexes, bibliographies, etc for publication;
2. To promote cooperation among, and training of, theological librarians;
3. To arrange short-term courses and workshops and
4. To develop an Asia-wide network of theological libraries.[4]

As the Convener of ForATL, Elizabeth Pulanco, had stated: "In real estate, the mantra is location, location, location. In theological libraries, it can be argued that the mantra is collaboration, collaboration,

---

[1] The author is honored to have the chance to write a preface for Rita and John England's out-standing book on Asian theological librarianship, i.e. Ministering Asian Faith and Wisdom: a Manual for Theological Librarians in Asia.
[2] Gandhi 1959. India of My Dream, 14
[3] The author has been involved in ForATL since 1996 and has been elected as the Executive Committee member of ForATL since 2006
[4] ForATL 2012a

collaboration."[5] Theological library collaboration and networking is an important expression of ecumenism in Asian churches and theological education. When we envision the Asian ecumenism, we always see theological education collaboration as being an important expression and impetus for the promotion of ecumenism. And within the collaboration of Asian theological education institutions, theological library networking (especially seminary library networking) is a particular task and landmark. When the seminaries share books and library financial resources concretely (libraries always involve money) and cooperate on a day to day base among their libraries, ecumenism becomes the focus and ecumenism becomes reality. As Matthew 5:21-22 said, "For where your treasure is, there your heart will be also. The eye is the lamp of the body."

Personally, I have been involved to build up a seminary library network, named Ecumenical Information Network (EIN), in Hong Kong since 1995. Right now, the network members include Lutheran, Roman Catholic, Evangelical, Alliance and Free Church seminaries and the network's union catalog[6] is the largest among the Chinese catalogues in the region (more than 360,000 volumes) (www.ein-hk.info) .

In Hong Kong and among the Chinese, the gap between Protestant and Catholic Christians and seminaries and the gap between Liberal and Conservative strands of Christianity is very big. Hence, this successful seminary library network, which has already lasted for 17 years already, is a milestone for church collaboration in Hong Kong and for Chinese ecumenism. As the founder of the EIN, my motto is "more library networking, more seminary cooperation, more church ecumenism". Asian theological library collaboration and networking is ForATL's conviction for furthering ecumenism in Asian churches and theological education.

To pursue this dream and to move on in this direction, ForATL actively promotes theological library networking at the Asian level and national level through direct and indirect facilitation and its achievement are great. By 2012, ForATL has organized six "Workshop & Consultations" in each of which about 40 theological librarians participated.[7] These "Workshop & Consultations" are the golden chance for theological librarians of different Asian countries to meet each other and to share their dreams for the development of Asian theological libraries as a whole. Through the networking at the Asia wide level, ForATL successfully compiled the Web-based Directory of Asian Theological Libraries (www.foratl.org). The network ForATL is also planning to develop databases for Asian theological journals and theses.

At the same time, the joint "Workshop & Consultation" is also an ideal platform to allow theological librarians of one country to build up their national networking. For example, at the 4th ForATL Worskhop & Consultation in Malaysia in 2006, it was the first time for so many Malaysian theological librarians to meet at the same place. As a result of it, the Malaysia Theological Library Association was founded in 2007. In the 5th ForATL Workshop & Consultation in Singapore in 2009, many area representatives[8]

---

[5] Pulanco and Mazuk 2010, 303

[6] According to the author's limited knowledge, except the EIN Hong Kong which was found in 1995, there may be two more theological library union catalogs only in Asia (I have no information for Korea and Japan, as they have not interaction with ForATL so far.). The Union Catalog of Joint Library Committee Bangalore in India was built in 2010. The union catalog has about 250,000 records and has 4 members that includes Protestant and Catholics. (Thanks for Yesan Sellan, Secretary of India Theological Library Association (www.itla.org), to provide the information.) In Taiwan, 8 Protestant theological libraries established an union catalog in 2010.

[7] The author personally participated in the 3rd, 4th and 5th ForATL Workshop & Consultation.

[8] In ForATL, Area Representatives of the following areas are elected or appointed to promote national theological library networking and to raise the areas' needs:

1. Philippines Area,
2. Indonesia Area,
3. Myanmar Area,
4. Cambodia, Laos, Malaysia, Singapore, Thailand and Vietnam Area,
5. China and Hong Kong Area,

expressed their hope that ForATL can help with the training and networking at the national level (ForATL 2012b, 2). Hence, ForATL sponsored partially the training workshop for Indonesian theological librarians under the theme "Professionalism of Indonesia theological librarian" in 2009, which was the first of its kind for theological librarians in Indonesia at national level. Thanks to the Lord, 85 participants from 53 seminaries all over Indonesia joined the training and through this networking, the Forum of Theological Librarian and Library in Indonesia (ForPPTI) (http://forppti.blogspot.hk/) was founded (ForATL 2012c, 1).

Beyond the Malaysian and Indonesian theological library networks that are directly facilitated by the ForATL in their formation, there are also many national and city level theological library networks that are indirectly facilitated by ForATL. The Philippines Theological Library Association (PTLA) is one of the most active theological library associations in Asia. It was founded in 1987 (before ForATL). The recent interaction between PTLA and ForATL shows the organic networking dynamics in Asian theological libraries, especially at the level between national and Asia level. In every ForATL Worshop & Consultation, PTLA members are always the largest number of participants and do get a lot of ecumenical impetus from ForATL for their own national networking. Many recent active promoters of the PTLA such as Elizabeth Pulanco are all closely related with ForATL.[9] At the same time, ForATL sponsorship for PTLA training conferences is also supporting PTLA to respond to the Philippines government licensing requirements for the theological librarians. The common training conferences in turn strongly consolidated the Philippines national networking. In 2012, the PTLA even hosted the 6th ForATL Worshop & Consultation in Dumaguete, Philippines, in which ForATL was served and the PTLA networking was further strengthened.[10]

ForATL's networking dream is not only limited to Asia, but also reaches out beyond Asia. In the 2009 5th the ForATL Worskhop & Consultation in Singapore met under the theme "Asian theological librarians moving on and reaching out: professional development and collaboration in the light of emerging technologies". In this Workshop & Consultation, in addition to the 32 theological librarians from the Philippines, Indonesia, Malaysia, Thailand, Myanmar, Mainland China, Taiwan, Hong Kong and India, the following representatives from various theological library related associations around the world also participated:

1. Dr.Paul F. Stuehrenberg, Yale University Divinity Librarian,
2. American Theologia Library Association (ATLA) representative
3. Rosemary Watts, Trinity Theological College, Perth, Australia and New
4. Zealand Theological Library Association (ANZTLA) representative;
5. Odile Dupont, Head Librarian of Institute Chatolique de Paris, European Theological Libraries/Biblioth_ques Europ_ennes de Th_ologie (BETH) representative;
6. Alan Linfield, London School of Theology, Association of British Theological and Philosophical Libraries (ABTAPL) representative;
7. Martha L. Smalley, Foundation for Theological Education in Southeast Asia (FTESEA) representative;
8. Dr. Michael Poon, Documentation of Christianity in Asia and Documentation, Archives, Bibliography and Oral History Study Group (DABOH) of IAMS.

---

6. Taiwan, Japan and Korea Area,
7. India, Pakistan and Sri Lanka Area
8. Australia, New Zealand and Pacific Area

[9] Elizebath Pulanco has been the ForATL Executive Committee Member since 2003 and she has become the ForATL Convener since 2006.

[10] Similar organic interaction happens between ForATL and India Theological Library Association which was found before ForATL (in 1985) (www.itla.org).

In the age of the ecumenical movement and of accelerated globalization, the "Western" theological libraries are fully aware that networking with the Asian theological libraries is essential. At the same time, ForATL and Asian theological libraries also want to make their networking dreams more ecumenical. This international ecumenical networking does bear several fruits. In the 2009 ForATL Workshop & Consultation, librarians of Yale Divinity Library, Hong Kong Baptist University Library and Lutheran Theological Seminary Library have had the chance to meet face to face and finalized the ecumenical digitalization project on the historical materials of Hong Kong Anglican, Baptist, Lutheran, United churches and the Hong Kong Church Council. Through this project, the historical materials of different churches are digitalized and hence are better preserved and utilized by the different churches. At the same time, the theological libraries in the West and the East also received a digital copy of these precious historical materials and make the Hong Kong church historical materials available to the churches all around the world. This successful networking and digitalization cooperation platform has proven feasible and hence two other digitalization projects on Hong Kong Christian publishers and Chinese Buddhist mission are now in progress.

The fruit of the ecumenical international networking is encouraging. As an Asian theological librarian who has a conviction for theological library networking, I do dream that Asian theological library networking at the city level (e.g. EIN in Hong Kong), national level (e.g. ForPPTI in Indonesia, PTLA in the Philippines) and at the Asian level (e.g. ForATL) can continue to flourish. As the church is one and ecumenical, I do believe that more ecumenical international networking is essential and will be a trend. The recent development of Globethics.net and GlobeTheoLib, the global digital libraries on Ethics and on Theology by WCC (ETE), are pointing to this direction. I do dream that with the efforts of various library networks in different countries, regions and continents, and the support of various ecumenical organizations, ecumenical theological library networking at this level will be continued, materialized and thus the ecumenical church will be better served. I would dare to share the dream that in 2016 when ForATL will hold its 7th Workshop & Consultation to celebrate its 25th anniversary in Chiang Mai, Thailand (where ForATL first started), representatives from theological library associations from North America, Europe, Britain, Australia and New Zealand, Latin America, Africa and Middle East will also join to have an ecumenical conference. I also dare to dream that at one day at each General Assembly of the World Church Councils, this ecumenical theological library conference will be a visible part of these larger gatherings!

2. Training and Education

Theological networking and collaboration are only means. As a Asian seminary librarian, I believe the end of these means is to facilitate the development and exchange of resources of theology in the Asian contexts, in order that Asian theological education and churches will have better information support. In this Information Age, every community in the society (e.g. medical community, education community) needs improved information support. The church as a community within the society needs this as well, otherwise the church will be diminishing and not coping with the demands of the Information Age. For better information support for the Asian churches and theological education, theological library networking is essential. But to restrict efforts just on library networking is not enough. The Asian theological librarians should have a better training and also education for theological librarianship. Hence, one of the ForATL's dreams is also to promote training and education for Asian theological librarians. In fact, this enhancement of training of theological librarianship is both my personal dream as well as the dream of many Asian theological educators, such as Lutheran Theological Seminary (LTS), Hong Kong.

Besides the teaching faculty, the library is the other cornerstone in theological education. Among Asian seminaries in the past 30 years, with the effort of various churches, missions and foundations, there has been a great progress for theological faculty development. In the near future, we hope that while theological education in Asia will continue to progress, we also hope that improved library development and automation will take please and will be added as another strategic step. However, the Asian churches and seminaries still do lack more formal education for theological librarians[11]. In respond to this big need, Lutheran Theological Seminary (Hong Kong), is the only seminary which – despite very limited resources (www.lts.edu) - started a Theological Librarianship Program since 1998. By 2012, over 40 graduates from this Theological Librarianship Program have gone back to their seminary libraries in Hong Kong, China, Myanmar, Vietnam, Malaysia, Indonesia, Philippines, Samoa etc to serve.

In these 15 years of teaching experience, I reflected that a good Asian theological librarianship program should be oriented both in its theological, western and contextual dimensions:

a. Theological

Comparing with general library science which is the only program in the west, Asian theological librarianship programs should provide both library science and theological knowledge. As Asian theological libraries are always with few staff (2-6 staffs), the librarian (especially the librarian in-charge) may need to select appropriate theological books for the library, classify the books and also communicate with faculty members. Hence, he /she should know not only library science, but also theology. He / She then can properly handle theological information in the respective libraries, communicate well with teachers and students, and earn the respect from the seminary administration.

b. Western

As most Asian seminary libraries have some Western language collections (mainly English, and also German, French and Dutch in some countries), the Asian theological librarianship program should provide up-to-date Western librarianship practices and standards such as DDC, AARC2, MARC etc. With this proper education, the librarians can upgrade their operation and handle these collections more efficiently through standardization and copy cataloging. In the training, the Asian theological librarians should be exposed to the Western library philosophy. This will help them to be more aware of the importance of the library in theological education and no longer regard themselves as second-class staff in the seminaries.

c. Contextual

Most important, the programs should emphasize on contextualisation (which will not be emphasized in the US library science program). The Asian theological librarians should be trained to have a mindset of contextualization and not just copy the western model. Hence, they are able to contextualize the international standards and adapt them to their own national situation and to be sensitive to their special context of their national standards. For example, for the Dewey Decimal Classification Scheme there are over 200 pages for the class of Christianity; but for the China Library Classification Scheme (China national standard classification scheme that with strong communist background) there is only 1 page for class for Christianity. How the seminary libraries in China are able to contextualize and to integrate the international and national standards will be essential for them to properly classify their 8,000 to 60,000 volumes in their libraries.

To provide formal and contextual Asian theological librarianship education is a crucial dream for many Asian theological librarians and educators. As early as 1991, ForATL was dreaming in this direction and therefore was proposing a Master Degree program on Asian theological librarianship (PTCA 1992). Due to

[11] In fact in US, formal education for theological librarians is also lacking. In the late 1980's, I could only find one three credit course in the University of Pittsburgh. Even now, I can only find one three credit distant learning course offered by the University of Illinois with the cooperation of the American Theological Library Association (www.alta.com).

many constraints at that time, the proposed program was not materialized and ForATL concentrated on short-term training and library networking. Even though ForATL could not implement its Asian theological librarianship education dream, however, through the Asian theological library networking (which has become a powerful means) ForATL's education dream was taken up by the Lutheran Theological Seminary (Hong Kong).

In 1996, when I started to involve in ForATL's networking, my seminary and myself began to become more aware of the need for a contextual Asian theological librarianship program. Further through our Asian Lutheran networks and different Asian students in my seminary (they are mainly seminary teachers), this vision from Macedonia was more vivid.

The Asian theological library networking dream and Asian theological librarianship education dream have become closely interrelated in the past 20 years. During this period, ForATL, LTS Theological Librarianship Program, Asian theological library networking have interacted with each other actively. Theological library networking stimulates and supports Asian theological librarianship education. And Asian theological librarianship education in turn also facilitates Asian theological library networking and provides support for more library training. This interaction was not planned before hand. But just like many ecumenical achievements, when many church leaders have strong convictions for ecumenism, by God's grace, unexpected and great achievements can be gained. In 1996, when LTS was planning for the Asian theological librarianship program, the ForATL's un-realized program from 1991 provided us with very useful information and suggestions. Finally in 1998, twelve students were enrolled in the new program. In summer 1999, Rita and John England (the founders of ForATL) came to LTS and taught the contextual Asian theological course with strong a ecumenical spirit. After that summer, one Indonesian graduate of our program started networking among the Indonesian theological libraries. In 2003 she became the Executive Committee Member of ForATL and with the efforts of many theological librarians, the Forum of Theological Librarian and Library in Indonesia (ForPPTI) was founded in 2009.

In 2006, myself was personally elected as the ForATL Executive Committee Member and served as the area representatives of Hong Kong and China. With that responsibility and my personal dream for serving Mainland China church through the library profession, I was more active in promoting theological library training and networking in China.[12] In 2007, one Mainland China student joint LTS Program and in 2009 two participants from Mainland China joined the 5th ForATL Workshop and Consultation. In 2011, the China Christian Council organized a short-term theological library training workshop for all seminary libraries. It was the first of its kind for theological librarians in China at the national level and I had the privilege to be one of the trainers.

Among the 22 seminaries in China, 20 seminaries (over 30 seminary library staffs) joined the training. With this national training opportunity and meeting platform, preliminary theological library networking was starting in Mainland China. A Theological Library Service Group was formed during the training and 3 subgroups were established to serve the 22 seminary libraries in China. These subgroups include collection development, library automation and library training. With the efforts of the networking and their mutual help, two seminary libraries started their automation after the training.

[12] Before 2006, with the vision of Lutheran Theological Seminary (Hong Kong), I have involved in Mainland China seminary libraries quite actively. As early as 1997, I have visited Nanjing Union Theological Seminary (one of the largest seminary in Mainland China) and provided consultation to her library automation and classification scheme change. In 2000, I visited Beijing Seminary Library and provided consultation for her library automation and library management. After 2000, I was helping some Mainland China seminary libraries such as Guangdong Union Theological Seminary Library to computerize. However, the service so far was toward individual library. Library networking has not yet come up.

3. Conclusion

Training and education are really important for seminary library networking. In 2012, 5 seminary libraries in Yangon, Myanmar formed a city-level network and are establishing a computerized union catalog. In Yangon, where electricity shortage occurs almost every day and access to Internet services is still very limited, to automate a seminary library is not an easy task, to establish a computerized library union catalog for 5 seminary libraries is an even more difficult task.[13] I am very glad that these seminary librarians are so bold to dream for God! I was especially thankful when I learned that all of them were my students. Thanks to the Lord!

The Asian theological library networking dream and the Asian theological librarianship education dream are always going hand in hand. These ecumenical dreams can only be achieved through the ecumenical conviction of many Asian theological librarians, theological educators and church leaders.[14] By the grace of God, Asian theological library networking and education at the city-level, national-level and Asia-level are flourishing. Personal dreams and institutional dreams are coming together to achieve a part of God's overall dream. Let's dream for God and dare to say, "I have a dream!"

[13] I have visited more than ten seminary libraries in Yangon in 2010. Even in the hotel, I experienced at lease 2 electricity shortage everyday. Using the hotel's Internet services, I cannot access Hotmail and Yahoo Mail, but Gmail only. Most of the World Wide Web pages e.g. Yahoo.com.hk could not be opened and for those web pages that could be opened, the Internet speed was totally unacceptable.

[14] Personally, I am much in debt for Lutheran Theological Seminary (HongKong) presidents and deans who not only provide strong administrative support, but also provide me very good ecumenical examples. I especially need to mention Dr. Andrew Hsiao, Dr.. Tak-ho Lam, Dr.. Simon Chow, Dr. Ted Zimmerman and Dr. Peter Li.

REGNUM EDINBURGH CENTENARY SERIES

David A. Kerr, Kenneth R. Ross (Eds)
Mission Then and Now
2009 / 978-1-870345-73-6 / 343pp (paperback)
2009 / 978-1-870345-76-7 / 343pp (hardback)

No one can hope to fully understand the modern Christian missionary movement without engaging substantially with the World Missionary Conference, held at Edinburgh in 1910. This book is the first to systematically examine the eight Commissions which reported to Edinburgh 1910 and gave the conference much of its substance and enduring value. It will deepen and extend the reflection being stimulated by the upcoming centenary and will kindle the missionary imagination for 2010 and beyond.

Daryl M. Balia, Kirsteen Kim (Eds)
Witnessing to Christ Today
2010 / 978-1-870345-77-4 / 301pp (hardback)

This volume, the second in the Edinburgh 2010 series, includes reports of the nine main study groups working on different themes for the celebration of the centenary of the World Missionary Conference, Edinburgh 1910. Their collaborative work brings together perspectives that are as inclusive as possible of contemporary world Christianity and helps readers to grasp what it means in different contexts to be 'witnessing to Christ today'.

Claudia Währisch-Oblau, Fidon Mwombeki (Eds)
Mission Continues
Global Impulses for the 21st Century
2010 / 978-1-870345-82-8 / 271pp (hardback)

In May 2009, 35 theologians from Asia, Africa and Europe met in Wuppertal, Germany, for a consultation on mission theology organized by the United Evangelical Mission: Communion of 35 Churches in Three Continents. The aim was to participate in the 100th anniversary of the Edinburgh conference through a study process and reflect on the challenges for mission in the 21st century. This book brings together these papers written by experienced practitioners from around the world.

Brian Woolnough and Wonsuk Ma (Eds)
Holistic Mission
God's Plan for God's People
2010 / 978-1-870345-85-9 / 268pp (hardback)

Holistic mission, or integral mission, implies God is concerned with the whole person, the whole community, body, mind and spirit. This book discusses the meaning of the holistic gospel, how it has developed, and implications for the church. It takes a global, eclectic approach, with 19 writers, all of whom have much experience in, and commitment to, holistic mission. It addresses critically and honestly one of the most exciting, and challenging, issues facing the church today. To be part of God's plan for God's people, the church must take holistic mission to the world.

Kirsteen Kim and Andrew Anderson (Eds)
Mission Today and Tomorrow
2010 / 978-1-870345-91-0 / 450pp (hardback)

There are moments in our lives when we come to realise that we are participating in the triune God's mission. If we believe the church to be as sign and symbol of the reign of God in the world, then we are called to witness to Christ today by sharing in God's mission of love through the transforming power of the Holy Spirit. We can all participate in God's transforming and reconciling mission of love to the whole creation.

Tormod Engelsviken, Erling Lundeby and Dagfinn Solheim (Eds)
The Church Going Glocal
Mission and Globalisation
2011 / 978-1-870345-93-4 / 262pp (hardback)

The New Testament church is… universal and local at the same time. The universal, one and holy apostolic church appears in local manifestations. Missiologically speaking… the church can take courage as she faces the increasing impact of globalisation on local communities today. Being universal and concrete, the church is geared for the simultaneous challenges of the glocal and local.

Marina Ngurusangzeli Behera (Ed)
Interfaith Relations after One Hundred Years
Christian Mission among Other Faiths
2011 / 978-1-870345-96-5 / 338pp (hardback)

The essays of this book reflect not only the acceptance and celebration of pluralism within India but also by extension an acceptance as well as a need for unity among Indian Christians of different denominations. The essays were presented and studied at a preparatory consultation on Study Theme II: Christian Mission Among Other Faiths at the United Theological College, India July 2009.

Lalsangkima Pachuau and Knud Jørgensen (Eds)
Witnessing to Christ in a Pluralistic Age
Christian Mission among Other Faiths
2011 / 978-1-870345-95-8 / 277pp (hardback)

In a world where plurality of faiths is increasingly becoming a norm of life, insights on the theology of religious plurality are needed to strengthen our understanding of our own faith and the faith of others. Even though religious diversity is not new, we are seeing an upsurge in interest on the theologies of religion among all Christian confessional traditions. It can be claimed that no other issue in Christian mission is more important and more difficult than the theologies of religions.

Beth Snodderly and A Scott Moreau (Eds)
Evangelical Frontier Mission
Perspectives on the Global Progress of the Gospel
2011 / 978-1-870345-98-9 / 312pp (hardback)

This important volume demonstrates that 100 years after the World Missionary Conference in Edinburgh, Evangelism has become truly global. Twenty-first-century Evangelism continues to focus on frontier mission, but significantly, and in the spirit of Edinburgh 1910, it also has re-engaged social action.

Rolv Olsen (Ed)
Mission and Postmodernities
2011 / 978-1-870345-97-2 / 279pp (hardback)

This volume takes on meaning because its authors honestly struggle with and debate how we should relate to postmodernities. Should our response be accommodation, relativizing or counter-culture? How do we strike a balance between listening and understanding, and at the same time exploring how postmodernities influence the interpretation and application of the Bible as the normative story of God's mission in the world?

Emma Wild-Wood & Peniel Rajkumar (Eds)
Foundations for Mission
2012 / 978-1-908355-12-6 / 303pp (hardback)

This volume provides an important resource for those wishing to gain an overview of significant issues in contemporary missiology whilst understanding how they are applied in particular contexts

Beate Fagerli, Knud Jørgensen, Rolv Olsen, Kari Storstein Haug and Knut Tveitereid (Eds)

A Learning Missional Church

Reflections from Young Missiologists

2012 / 978-1-908355-01-1 / 218pp (hardback)

Cross-cultural mission has always been a primary learning experience for the church. It pulls us out of a mono-cultural understanding and helps us discover a legitimate theological pluralism which opens up for new perspectives in the Gospel. Translating the Gospel into new languages and cultures is a human and divine means of making us learn new 'incarnations' of the Good News.

Cathy Ross (Ed)

Life-Widening Mission

2012 / 978-1-908355-00-3 / 163pp (hardback)

It is clear from the essays collected here that the experience of the 2010 World Mission Conference in Edinburgh was both affirming and frustrating for those taking part - affirming because of its recognition of how the centre of gravity has moved in global Christianity; frustrating because of the relative slowness of so many global Christian bodies to catch up with this and to embody it in the way they do business and in the way they represent themselves. These reflections will - or should - provide plenty of food for thought in the various councils of the Communion in the coming years.

REGNUM STUDIES IN GLOBAL CHRISTIANITY

David Emmanuel Singh (Ed)

Jesus and the Cross

Reflections of Christians from Islamic Contexts

2008 / 978-1-870345-65-1 / 226pp

The Cross reminds us that the sins of the world are not borne through the exercise of power but through Jesus Christ's submission to the will of the Father. The papers in this volume are organised in three parts: scriptural, contextual and theological. The central question being addressed is: how do Christians living in contexts, where Islam is a majority or minority religion, experience, express or think of the Cross?

Sung-wook Hong

Naming God in Korea

The Case of Protestant Christianity

2008 / 978-1-870345-66-8 / 170pp (hardback)

Since Christianity was introduced to Korea more than a century ago, one of the most controversial issues has been the Korean term for the Christian 'God'. This issue is not merely about naming the Christian God in Korean language, but it relates to the question of theological contextualization - the relationship between the gospel and culture - and the question of Korean Christian identity. This book demonstrates the nature of the gospel in relation to cultures, i.e., the universality of the gospel expressed in all human cultures.

Hubert van Beek (Ed)

Revisioning Christian Unity

The Global Christian Forum

2009 / 978-1-870345-74-3 / 288pp (hardback)

This book contains the records of the Global Christian Forum gathering held in Limuru near Nairobi, Kenya, on 6 – 9 November 2007 as well as the papers presented at that historic event. Also included are a summary of the Global Christian Forum process from its inception until the 2007 gathering and the reports of the evaluation of the process that was carried out in 2008.

Dietrich Werner, David Esterline, Namsoon Kang, Joshva Raja (Eds)
The Handbook of Theological Education in World Christianity
Theological Perspectives, Ecumenical Trends, Regional Surveys
2010 / 978-1-870345-80-4 / 800pp

This major reference work is the first ever comprehensive study of Theological Education in Christianity of its kind. With contributions from over 90 international scholars and church leaders, it aims to be easily accessible across denominational, cultural, educational, and geographic boundaries. The Handbook will aid international dialogue and networking among theological educators, institutions, and agencies.

Young-hoon Lee
The Holy Spirit Movement in Korea
Its Historical and Theological Development
2009 / 978-1-870345-67-5 / 174pp (hardback)

This book traces the historical and theological development of the Holy Spirit Movement in Korea through six successive periods (from 1900 to the present time). These periods are characterized by repentance and revival (1900-20), persecution and suffering under Japanese occupation (1920-40), confusion and division (1940-60), explosive revival in which the Pentecostal movement played a major role in the rapid growth of Korean churches (1960-80), the movement reaching out to all denominations (1980-2000), and the new context demanding the Holy Spirit movement to open new horizons in its mission engagement (2000-).

Paul Hang-Sik Cho
Eschatology and Ecology
Experiences of the Korean Church
2010 / 978-1-870345-75-0 / 260pp (hardback)

This book raises the question of why Korean people, and Korean Protestant Christians in particular, pay so little attention to ecological issues. The author argues that there is an important connection (or elective affinity) between this lack of attention and the other-worldly eschatology that is so dominant within Korean Protestant Christianity.

David Emmanuel Singh & Bernard C Farr (Eds)
Christianity and Education
Shaping of Christian Context in Thinking
2010 / 978-1-870345-81-1 / 374pp

Christianity and Education is a collection of papers published in *Transformation: An International Journal of Holistic Mission Studies* over a period of 15 years. The articles represent a spectrum of Christian thinking addressing issues of institutional development for theological education, theological studies in the context of global mission, contextually aware/informed education, and academies which deliver such education, methodologies and personal reflections.

J.Andrew Kirk
Civilisations in Conflict?
Islam, the West and Christian Faith
2011 / 978-1-870345-87-3 / 205pp

Samuel Huntington's thesis, which argues that there appear to be aspects of Islam that could be on a collision course with the politics and values of Western societies, has provoked much controversy. The purpose of this study is to offer a particular response to Huntington's thesis by making a comparison between the origins of Islam and Christianity.

J Kwabena Asamoah-Gyada
Contemporary Pentecostal Christianity
Interpretations from an African Context
2013 / 978-1-908355-07-2 / 238pp

Pentecostalism is the fastest growing stream of Christianity in the world. The real evidence for the significance of Pentecostalism lies in the actual churches they have built and the numbers they attract. This work interprets key theological and missiological themes in African Pentecostalism by using material from the live experiences of the movement itself.

David Emmanuel Singh (Ed)
Jesus and the Incarnation
Reflections of Christians from Islamic Contexts
2011 / 978-1-870345-90-3 / 245pp

In the dialogues of Christians with Muslims nothing is more fundamental than the Cross, the Incarnation and the Resurrection of Jesus. Building on the *Jesus and the Cross*, this book contains voices of Christians living in various 'Islamic contexts' and reflecting on the Incarnation of Jesus. The aim and hope of these reflections is that the papers weaved around the notion of 'the Word' will not only promote dialogue among Christians on the roles of the Person and the Book but, also, create a positive environment for their conversations with Muslim neighbours.

Bal Krishna Sharma
From this World to the Next
Christian Identity and Funerary Rites in Nepal
2013 / 978-1-908355-08-9 / 238pp

This book explores and analyses funerary rite struggles in a nation where Christianity is a comparatively recent phenomenon, and many families have multi-faith, who go through traumatic experiences at the death of their family members. The author has used an applied theological approach to explore and analyse the findings in order to address the issue of funerary rites with which the Nepalese church is struggling.

Ivan M Satyavrata
God Has Not left Himself Without Witness
2011 / 978-1-870345-79-8 / 260pp

Since its earliest inception the Christian Church has had to address the question of what common ground exits between Christian faiths and other religions. This issue is not merely of academic interest but one with critical existential and socio-political consequences. This study presents a case for the revitalization of the fulfillment tradition based on a recovery and assessment of the fulfillment approaches of Indian Christian converts in the pre-independence period.

REGNUM STUDIES IN MISSION

Kwame Bediako
Theology and Identity
The Impact of Culture upon Christian Thought in the Second Century and in Modern Africa
1992 / 978-1870345-10-1 / 507pp

The author examines the question of Christian identity in the context of the Graeco–Roman culture of the early Roman Empire. He then addresses the modern African predicament of quests for identity and integration.

Christopher Sugden
Seeking the Asian Face of Jesus
The Practice and Theology of Christian Social Witness
in Indonesia and India 1974–1996
1997 / 1-870345-26-6 / 496pp

This study focuses on contemporary holistic mission with the poor in India and Indonesia combined with the call to transformation of all life in Christ with micro-credit enterprise schemes. 'The literature on contextual theology now has a new standard to rise to' – Lamin Sanneh (Yale University, USA).

Hwa Yung

Mangoes or Bananas?

The Quest for an Authentic Asian Christian Theology

1997 / 1-870345-25-5 / 274pp

Asian Christian thought remains largely captive to Greek dualism and Enlightenment rationalism because of the overwhelming dominance of Western culture. Authentic contextual Christian theologies will emerge within Asian Christianity with a dual recovery of confidence in culture and the gospel.

Keith E. Eitel

Paradigm Wars

The Southern Baptist International Mission Board Faces the Third Millennium

1999 / 1-870345-12-6 / 140pp

The International Mission Board of the Southern Baptist Convention is the largest denominational mission agency in North America. This volume chronicles the historic and contemporary forces that led to the IMB's recent extensive reorganization, providing the most comprehensive case study to date of a historic mission agency restructuring to continue its mission purpose into the twenty-first century more effectively.

•

Samuel Jayakumar

Dalit Consciousness and Christian Conversion

Historical Resources for a Contemporary Debate

1999 / 81-7214-497-0 / 434pp

(Published jointly with ISPCK)

The main focus of this historical study is social change and transformation among the Dalit Christian communities in India. Historiography tests the evidence in the light of the conclusions of the modern Dalit liberation theologians.

Vinay Samuel and Christopher Sugden (Eds)

Mission as Transformation

A Theology of the Whole Gospel

1999 / 978-18703455-13-2 / 522pp

This book brings together in one volume twenty five years of biblical reflection on mission practice with the poor from around the world. This volume helps anyone understand how evangelicals, struggling to unite evangelism and social action, found their way in the last twenty five years to the biblical view of mission in which God calls all human beings to love God and their neighbour; never creating a separation between the two.

Christopher Sugden

Gospel, Culture and Transformation

2000 / 1-870345-32-0 / 152pp

A Reprint, with a New Introduction,

of Part Two of Seeking the Asian Face of Jesus

Gospel, Culture and Transformation explores the practice of mission especially in relation to transforming cultures and communities. - 'Transformation is to enable God's vision of society to be actualised in all relationships: social, economic and spiritual, so that God's will may be reflected in human society and his love experienced by all communities, especially the poor.'

Bernhard Ott

Beyond Fragmentation: Integrating Mission and Theological Education

A Critical Assessment of some Recent Developments
in Evangelical Theological Education
2001 / 1-870345-14-2 / 382pp

Beyond Fragmentation is an enquiry into the development of Mission Studies in evangelical theological education in Germany and German-speaking Switzerland between 1960 and 1995. The author undertakes a detailed examination of the paradigm shifts which have taken place in recent years in both the theology of mission and the understanding of theological education.

Gideon Githiga

The Church as the Bulwark against Authoritarianism

Development of Church and State Relations in Kenya, with Particular Reference to the Years after Political Independence 1963-1992
2002 / 1-870345-38-x / 218pp

'All who care for love, peace and unity in Kenyan society will want to read this careful history by Bishop Githiga of how Kenyan Christians, drawing on the Bible, have sought to share the love of God, bring his peace and build up the unity of the nation, often in the face of great difficulties and opposition.' Canon Dr Chris Sugden, Oxford Centre for Mission Studies.

Myung Sung-Hoon, Hong Young-Gi (eds.)

Charis and Charisma

David Yonggi Cho and the Growth of Yoido Full Gospel Church
2003 / 978-1870345-45-3 / 218pp

This book discusses the factors responsible for the growth of the world's largest church. It expounds the role of the Holy Spirit, the leadership, prayer, preaching, cell groups and creativity in promoting church growth. It focuses on God's grace (charis) and inspiring leadership (charisma) as the two essential factors and the book's purpose is to present a model for church growth worldwide.

Samuel Jayakumar

Mission Reader

Historical Models for Wholistic Mission in the Indian Context
2003 / 1-870345-42-8 / 250pp
(Published jointly with ISPCK)

This book is written from an evangelical point of view revalidating and reaffirming the Christian commitment to wholistic mission. The roots of the 'wholistic mission' combining 'evangelism and social concerns' are to be located in the history and tradition of Christian evangelism in the past; and the civilizing purpose of evangelism is compatible with modernity as an instrument in nation building.

Bob Robinson

Christians Meeting Hindus

An Analysis and Theological Critique of the Hindu-Christian Encounter in India
2004 / 987-1870345-39-2 / 392pp

This book focuses on the Hindu-Christian encounter, especially the intentional meeting called dialogue, mainly during the last four decades of the twentieth century, and specifically in India itself.

Gene Early

Leadership Expectations

How Executive Expectations are Created and Used in a Non-Profit Setting

2005 / 1-870345-30-4 / 276pp

The author creates an Expectation Enactment Analysis to study the role of the Chancellor of the University of the Nations-Kona, Hawaii. This study is grounded in the field of managerial work, jobs, and behaviour and draws on symbolic interactionism, role theory, role identity theory and enactment theory. The result is a conceptual framework for developing an understanding of managerial roles.

Tharcisse Gatwa

The Churches and Ethnic Ideology in the Rwandan Crises 1900-1994

2005 / 978-1870345-24-8 / 300pp

(Reprinted 2011)

Since the early years of the twentieth century Christianity has become a new factor in Rwandan society. This book investigates the role Christian churches played in the formulation and development of the racial ideology that culminated in the 1994 genocide.

Julie Ma

Mission Possible

Biblical Strategies for Reaching the Lost

2005 / 978-1870345-37-1 / 142pp

This is a missiology book for the church which liberates missiology from the specialists for the benefit of every believer. It also serves as a textbook that is simple and friendly, and yet solid in biblical interpretation. This book links the biblical teaching to the actual and contemporary missiological settings with examples, making the Bible come alive to the reader.

Allan Anderson, Edmond Tang (Eds)

Asian and Pentecostal

The Charismatic Face of Christianity in Asia

2005 / 978-1870345-94-1 / 500pp

(Published jointly with APTS Press)

This book provides a thematic discussion and pioneering case studies on the history and development of Pentecostal and Charismatic churches in the countries of South Asia, South East Asia and East Asia.

I. Mark Beaumont

Christology in Dialogue with Muslims

A Critical Analysis of Christian Presentations of Christ for Muslims from the Ninth and Twentieth Centuries

2005 / 978-1870345-46-0 / 227pp

This book analyses Christian presentations of Christ for Muslims in the most creative periods of Christian-Muslim dialogue, the first half of the ninth century and the second half of the twentieth century. In these two periods, Christians made serious attempts to present their faith in Christ in terms that take into account Muslim perceptions of him, with a view to bridging the gap between Muslim and Christian convictions.

Thomas Czövek,

Three Seasons of Charismatic Leadership

A Literary-Critical and Theological Interpretation of the Narrative of Saul, David and Solomon

2006 / 978-1870345-48-4 / 272pp

This book investigates the charismatic leadership of Saul, David and Solomon. It suggests that charismatic leaders emerge in crisis situations in order to resolve the crisis by the charisma granted by God. Czovek argues that Saul proved himself as a charismatic leader as long as he acted resolutely and independently from his mentor Samuel. In the author's eyes, Saul's failure to establish himself as a charismatic leader is caused by his inability to step out from Samuel's shadow.

Richard Burgess

Nigeria's Christian Revolution

The Civil War Revival and Its Pentecostal Progeny (1967-2006)

2008 / 978-1-870345-63-7 / 347pp

This book describes the revival that occurred among the Igbo people of Eastern Nigeria and the new Pentecostal churches it generated, and documents the changes that have occurred as the movement has responded to global flows and local demands. As such, it explores the nature of revivalist and Pentecostal experience, but does so against the backdrop of local socio-political and economic developments, such as decolonisation and civil war, as well as broader processes, such as modernisation and globalisation.

David Emmanuel Singh & Bernard C Farr (Eds)

Christianity and Cultures

Shaping Christian Thinking in Context

2008 / 978-1-870345-69-9 / 271pp

This volume marks an important milestone, the 25th anniversary of the Oxford Centre for Mission Studies (OCMS). The papers here have been exclusively sourced from Transformation, a quarterly journal of OCMS, and seek to provide a tripartite view of Christianity's engagement with cultures by focusing on the question: how is Christian thinking being formed or reformed through its interaction with the varied contexts it encounters? The subject matters include different strands of theological-missiological thinking, socio-political engagements and forms of family relationships in interaction with the host cultures.

Tormod Engelsviken, Ernst Harbakk, Rolv Olsen, Thor Strandenæs (Eds)

Mission to the World

Communicating the Gospel in the 21st Century:

Essays in Honour of Knud Jørgensen

2008 / 978-1-870345-64-4 / 472pp (hardback)

Knud Jørgensen is Director of Areopagos and Associate Professor of Missiology at MF Norwegian School of Theology. This book reflects on the main areas of Jørgensen's commitment to mission. At the same time it focuses on the main frontier of mission, the world, the content of mission, the Gospel, the fact that the Gospel has to be communicated, and the context of contemporary mission in the 21st century.

Al Tizon

Transformation after Lausanne

Radical Evangelical Mission in Global-Local Perspective

2008 / 978-1-870345-68-2 / 281pp

After Lausanne '74, a worldwide network of radical evangelical mission theologians and practitioners use the notion of "Mission as Transformation" to integrate evangelism and social concern together, thus lifting theological voices from the Two Thirds World to places of prominence. This book documents the definitive gatherings, theological tensions, and social forces within and without evangelicalism that led up to Mission as Transformation. And it does so through a global-local grid that points the way toward greater holistic mission in the 21st century.

Bambang Budijanto

Values and Participation

Development in Rural Indonesia

2009 / 978-1-870345-70-4 / 237pp

Socio-religious values and socio-economic development are inter-dependant, inter-related and are constantly changing in the context of macro political structures, economic policy, religious organizations and globalization; and micro influences such as local affinities, identity, politics, leadership and beliefs. The book argues that the comprehensive approach in understanding the socio-religious values of each of the three local Lopait communities in Central Java is essential to accurately describing their respective identity.

Alan R. Johnson

Leadership in a Slum

A Bangkok Case Study

2009 / 978-1-870345-71-2 / 238pp

This book looks at leadership in the social context of a slum in Bangkok from a different perspective than traditional studies which measure well educated Thais on leadership scales derived in the West. Using both systematic data collection and participant observation, it develops a culturally preferred model as well as a set of models based in Thai concepts that reflect on-the-ground realities. It concludes by looking at the implications of the anthropological approach for those who are involved in leadership training in Thai settings and beyond.

Titre Ande

Leadership and Authority

Bula Matari and Life - Community Ecclesiology in Congo

2010 / 978-1-870345-72-9 / 189pp

Christian theology in Africa can make significant development if a critical understanding of the socio-political context in contemporary Africa is taken seriously, particularly as Africa's post-colonial Christian leadership based its understanding and use of authority on the Bula Matari model. This has caused many problems and Titre proposes a Life-Community ecclesiology for liberating authority, here leadership is a function, not a status, and 'apostolic succession' belongs to all people of God.

Frank Kwesi Adams

Odwira and the Gospel

A Study of the Asante Odwira Festival and its Significance for Christianity in Ghana

2010 /978-1-870345-59-0 / 232pp

The study of the Odwira festival is the key to the understanding of Asante religious and political life in Ghana. The book explores the nature of the Odwira festival longitudinally - in pre-colonial, colonial and post-independence Ghana - and examines the Odwira ideology and its implications for understanding the Asante self-identity. Also discussed is how some elements of faith portrayed in the Odwira festival can provide a framework for Christianity to engage with Asante culture at a greater depth.

Bruce Carlton

Strategy Coordinator

Changing the Course of Southern Baptist Missions

2010 / 978-1-870345-78-1 / 268pp

This is an outstanding, one-of-a-kind work addressing the influence of the non-residential missionary/strategy coordinator's role in Southern Baptist missions. This scholarly text examines the twentieth century global missiological currents that influenced the leadership of the International Mission Board, resulting in a new paradigm to assist in taking the gospel to the nations.

Julie Ma & Wonsuk Ma

Mission in the Spirit:

Towards a Pentecostal/Charismatic Missiology

2010 / 978-1-870345-84-2 / 312pp

The book explores the unique contribution of Pentecostal/Charismatic mission from the beginning of the twentieth century. The first part considers the theological basis of Pentecostal/Charismatic mission thinking and practice. Special attention is paid to the Old Testament, which has been regularly overlooked by the modern Pentecostal/Charismatic movements. The second part discusses major mission topics with contributions and challenges unique to Pentecostal/Charismatic mission. The book concludes with a reflection on the future of this powerful missionary movement. As the authors served as Korean missionaries in Asia, often their missionary experiences in Asia are reflected in their discussions.

S. Hun Kim & Wonsuk Ma (eds.)

Korean Diaspora and Christian Mission

2011-978-1-870345-91-0 / 301pp (hardback)

As a 'divine conspiracy' for Missio Dei, the global phenomenon of people on the move has shown itself to be invaluable. In 2004 two significant documents concerning Diaspora were introduced, one by the Filipino International Network and the other by the Lausanne Committee for World Evangelization. These have created awareness of the importance of people on the move for Christian mission. Since then, Korean Diaspora has conducted similar research among Korean missions, resulting in this book

Jin Huat Tan

Planting an Indigenous Church

The Case of the Borneo Evangelical Mission

2011 / 978-1-870345-99-6 / 363pp

Dr Jin Huat Tan has written a pioneering study of the origins and development of Malaysia's most significant indigenous church. This is an amazing story of revival, renewal and transformation of the entire region chronicling the powerful effect of it evident to date! What can we learn from this extensive and careful study of the Borneo Revival, so the global Christianity will become ever more dynamic?

•

Bill Prevette

Child, Church and Compassion

Towards Child Theology in Romania

2012 / 978-1-908355-03-4 / 377pp

Bill Prevett comments that ¨children are like 'canaries in a mine shaft'; they provide a focal point for discovery and encounter of perilous aspects of our world that are often ignored.¨ True, but miners also carried a lamp to see into the subterranean darkness. This book is such a lamp. It lights up the subterranean world of children and youth in danger of exploitation, and as it does so travels deep into their lives and also into the activities of those who seek to help them.

Samuel Cyuma

Picking up the Pieces

The Church and Conflict Resolution in South Africa and Rwanda

2012 / 978-1-908355-02-7 / 373pp

In the last ten years of the 20th century, the world was twice confronted with unbelievable news from Africa. First, there was the end of Apartheid in South Africa, without bloodshed, due to responsible political and Church leaders. The second was the mass killings in Rwanda, which soon escalated into real genocide. Political and Church leaders had been unable to prevents this crime against humanity. In this book, the question is raised: can we compare the situation in South Africa with that in Rwanda? Can Rwandan leaders draw lessons from the peace process in South Africa?

Peter Rowan

Proclaiming the Peacemaker

The Malaysian Church as an Agent of Reconciliation in a Multicultural Society

2012 / 978-1-908355-05-8 / 268pp

With a history of racial violence and in recent years, low-level ethnic tensions, the themes of peaceful coexistence and social harmony are recurring ones in the discourse of Malaysian society. In such a context, this book looks at the role of the church as a reconciling agent, arguing that a reconciling presence within a divided society necessitates an ethos of peacemaking.

Edward Ontita

Resources and Opportunity

The Architecture of Livelihoods in Rural Kenya

2012 / 978-1-908355-04-1 / 328pp

Poor people in most rural areas of developing countries often improvise resources in unique ways to enable them make a living. Resources and Opportunity takes the view that resources are dynamic and fluid, arguing that villagers co-produce them through redefinition and renaming in everyday practice and use them in diverse ways. The book focuses on ordinary social activities to bring out people's creativity in locating, redesigning and embracing livelihood opportunities in processes.

Kathryn Kraft

Searching for Heaven in the Real World

A Sociological Discussion of Conversion in the Arab World

2012 / 978-1-908355-15-7 / 1428pp

Kathryn Kraft explores the breadth of psychological and social issues faced by Arab Muslims after making a decision to adopt a faith in Christ or Christianity, investigating some of the most surprising and significant challenges new believers face.

Wessley Lukose

Contextual Missiology of the Spirit
Pentecostalism in Rajasthan, India

2013 / 978-1-908355-09-6 / 256pp

This book explores the identity, context and features of Pentecostalism in Rajasthan, India as well as the internal and external issues facing Pentecostals. It aims to suggest 'a contextual missiology of the Spirit,' as a new model of contextual missiology from a Pentecostal perspective. It is presented as a glocal, ecumenical, transformational, and public missiology.

REGNUM RESOURCES FOR MISSION

Knud Jørgensen

Equipping for Service

Christian Leadership in Church and Society

2012 / 978-1-908355-06-5 / 168pp

This book is written out of decades of experience of leading churches and missions in Ethiopia, Geneva, Norway and Hong Kong. Combining the teaching of Scripture with the insights of contemporary management philosophy, Jørgensen writes in a way which is practical and applicable to anyone in Christian service. “The intention has been to challenge towards a leadership relevant for work in church and mission, and in public and civil society, with special attention to leadership in Church and organisation.”

For the up-to-date listing of the Regnum books see www.ocms.ac.uk/regnum

Regnum Books International

Regnum is an Imprint of The Oxford Centre for Mission Studies

St. Philip and St. James Church

Woodstock Road, Oxford, OX2 6HR

Web: www.ocms.ac.uk/regnum